Fodor's 2001

Spain

CONTENTS

MAPS

Circled letters in text correspond to letters on the photographs. For more information on the sights pictured, turn to the indicated page number Ⓐ〉 on each photograph.

DESTINATION SPAIN

The Spanish, wrote V. S. Pritchett, "have preserved personality." It's a heady claim, but once you're here, it's hard not to feel that Spain knows something you don't about enjoying life, expressing moods, keeping everything in perspective. You can see it in the regional cultures, each with its own language, cuisine, and distinct ways of dancing in the streets on Saturday night. You can see it in the landscapes and architecture, which change so completely as you move across the country that the land seems to speak for itself. Most of all, you can see it in the people, whose sophisticated knack for leisure ensures you a rich and rousing experience.

MADRID

Madrid's bright skies and boundless energy make every sight and sound seem larger than life. Though you expect royal palaces to be grand, for instance, Madrid's Ⓒ**Palacio Real** has 2,800 rooms. The Prado, Reina Sofía, and Thyssen-Bornemisza museums pack 9,000 Spanish and other European masterworks into an art-saturated half mile. Sunday's flea market in El Rastro is as thick with overpriced oddities as with human activity. The landmark Ⓓ**Fuente de la Cibeles**—with the goddess Cybele on her chariot—seems to symbolize the vigor and joy with which Madrileños embrace everyday pleasures. Both tapa-tasting and dining, the foremost among these, are fired by animated conversation. The cafés in the Ⓔ**Plaza Mayor,** one of Europe's grandest

squares, are perpetually abuzz, and nightlife stretches into the wee hours near Ⓑ**Plaza Santa Ana.** Indeed, late-night social diversions are the heartbeat of Madrid, distracting locals from sleep even as the rest of the Western world prepares for another day at the grindstone. Short of dancing 'til dawn, the best way to catch the spirit of the place is to walk through its compact center, where modern life swirls around Mudéjar and medieval remnants on streets like Ⓕ**Calle Mayor.** Or pay a visit to Ⓐ**Parque del Retiro,** another venue for the local brand of socializing and, true to its name, a retreat from urban stress.

OLD AND

Despite what you may have heard about the rain in Spain falling mainly on the plain, the country's largest such expanse is an arid reach of windy skies and wide vistas. Cut with rocky gorges and fringed with gaunt mountains, this vast plateau is severe, melancholic, and mysterious—and has inspired more than its share of colorful thoughts. It was here that Don Quixote tilted at windmills, and somber Ⓓ**Ávila,** ringed by its original 11th-century wall, gave rise to the mystical ecstasies of St. Teresa, who spent 30 years in the Convento de la Encarnación. Medieval towns rise from the landscape like mirages. Austere Toledo, sitting calmly on a battlement-topped granite cliff, inspired El Greco's moody canvases; golden Ⓔ**Segovia,** following the crest of a rocky ridge, forms postcard views in every direction. The first sight of Ⓒ**Cuenca** startles: how do 500-year-old houses cling to the sides of a precipice? Ⓐ**Salamanca** overwhelms with Renaissance architecture, including one of Spain's largest and most graceful public squares. Valladolid's National Museum of Sculpture, housed in a 15th-century

NEW CASTILE

friars' college, has the largest and finest collection of polychrome wood pieces in the world. Medieval Burgos has long been a center of both religious and military activity—symbolized, perhaps, in the person of native son El Cid, the Christian Reconquest's legendary hero. Prosperous León hums with student activity but is best known for its cathedral, with a whopping 125 stained-glass windows. Perhaps most enticing are the smallest Castilian towns: in a place like Ⓑ**Sigüenza,** it's entirely possible to feel that you are the first traveler ever to explore these mellow stone streets.

CANTABRIA, THE BASQUE COUNTRY, AND LA RIOJA

Spain takes on a different character up north—it's greener, cloudier, and more stubbornly independent in spirit. After all, part of the land is Basque, a country within a country, with its own language and culture as well as its own coastline on the Bay of Biscay, one of the most enchanting shores. ⒷⒹ**San Sebastián,** near the French border, and the Cantabrian resort Santander, to the west, are seaside showpieces, inviting long, slow walks down elegant promenades, through fashionable lanes, and among restful gardens. Ⓐ**La Rioja,** a mixture of highlands, plains, and vineyards in and around the Ebro River basin, produces Spain's best wines. Ⓒ**Bilbao** has experienced a veritable Renaissance with the addition of Frank Gehry's titanium-skinned Guggenheim Museum. Already endowed with an excellent Museum of Fine Arts, renowned Basque restaurants, and various older treasures, Bilbao has become an artistic destination in its own right and may well be Spain's most talked-about city these days.

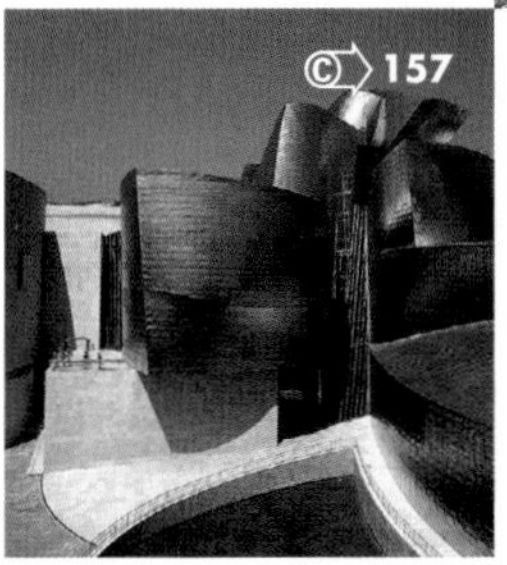

Ⓐ 198

GALICIA AND ASTURIAS

To pay homage to St. James, Christian pilgrims once crossed Europe to a corner of Spain so remote it was called *finis terrae* (end of the earth). Ⓑ**Santiago de Compostela,** their destination, still resonates with mystic importance, especially in and around its magnificent cathedral and on festive St. James Day, July 25. The ancient pilgrimage—the Camino de Santiago—regained popularity as the second millennium drew to a close, but today's pilgrims may or may not hew to the original route. Here in Spain's far northwest, you'll find isolated towns and beaches on the Atlantic Ocean and Bay of Biscay; scattered sets of stilted *horreos* (granaries) like those near charming Ⓐ**Pontevedra**; and the solitary, jagged Ⓒ**Picos de Europa.**

Ⓑ 191

Ⓒ 212

THE PYRENEES

Ⓐ 227

With its own flora, fauna, and alpine ways of life, Spain's natural border with France is a physical force to be reckoned with. As a Christian haven from the Moorish invasion around the turn of the first millennium, the Pyrenees became an unlikely repository of Romanesque art and architecture. Crisscrossed by wide, sunny valleys like Ⓑ**La Cerdanya,** and dotted with such memorable and historic towns as medieval La Seu d'Urgell, Bellver de Cerdanya, Roncesvalles, and Ⓐ**Beget,** the Pyrenees are one of Europe's best-kept secrets.

Ⓑ 229

A 266

BARCELONA AND NORTHERN CATALONIA

B 269

The poet Federico García Lorca called Barcelona's Rambla the only street in the world he wished would never end. A vivid mass of strollers, marketgoers, artists, and vendors, it gets you in the mood for Barcelona's motley and sometimes mesmerizing landmarks. The expansive Ⓐ**Boqueria** market breathes new life into the notion of grocery shopping. Antoni Gaudí's sinuous Ⓑ**Casa Milà** and emphatically unique Sagrada Família church exemplify the early 20th century's Moderniste movement, and the exuberant, Art Nouveau Ⓓ**Palau de la Música** takes aesthetic whimsy that much further. The Gothic Quarter hides the exquisite 14th-century church of Santa Maria del Mar, the small but striking Plaça del Rei, and the cathedral. Linger in the Plaça de la Seu or Ⓒ**Plaça Sant Jaume** and you may catch a celebration of Catalan culture, like *sardana* dancing or *castellers* (human castles). Outside Barcelona are less-explored Catalan towns like medieval Girona, with its Christian-Moorish-Jewish heritage, and the whitewashed village of Ⓔ**Cadaqués** on the Costa Brava, a rocky shore shaded with pines and lapped by a lustrous sea.

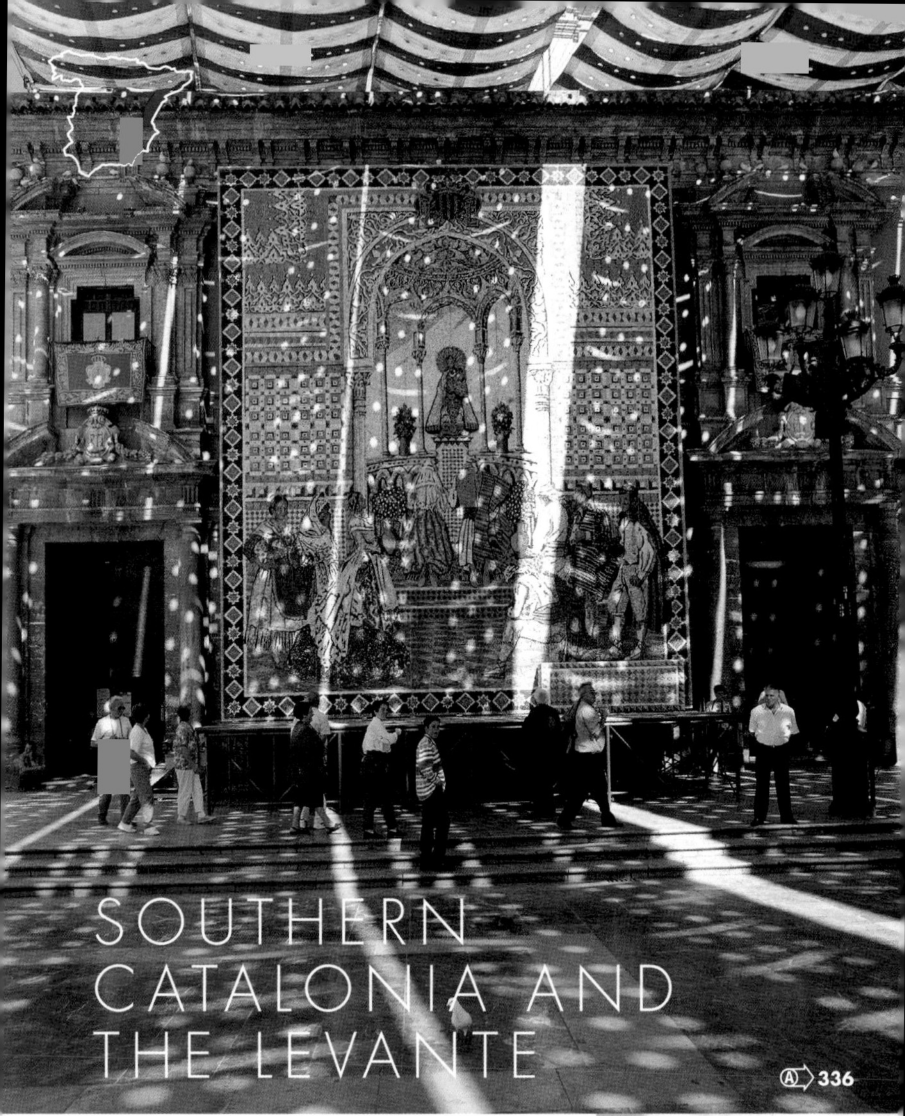

SOUTHERN CATALONIA AND THE LEVANTE

Ⓐ 336

The sun rises (*se levanta*) from the Mediterranean to give the citrus-scented, mountain-backed plain near Ⓐ**Valencia** its name and lend an exotic glow to the city's Christian and Moorish landmarks. The sea yields ingredients for Spain's *paella Valenciana* and makes a dramatic backdrop for the Roman ruins of cosmopolitan Tarragona. Where the sea meets the Ebro River, 200,000 birds enjoy the tranquillity of the Ⓑ**Delta de l'Ebre** Natural Park. Farther inland, castles, fortresses, and the mountains of the Sierra de Beceite lure you far off Spain's beaten path.

Ⓑ 329

Like Don Quixote moving from one picaresque exploit to another across the vast tracts of La Mancha, today's wanderers find plenty of drama in a still-empty landscape that seems to change with every turn of the road. Rice paddies and fragrant orange groves give way to the palm-fringed port city of Alicante, the fertile plains and dry hills of Ⓑ**Murcia,** and the craggy lunar landscapes of Almería. Along the way, ceramics are hand-crafted

SOUTHEAST

from the local white clay in towns like Alicante and rural Ⓐ**Albacete**; and saffron, red peppers, and dates flavor the region's rice-based cuisine. Modern resorts line the Costa Blanca; inland festivities include Alcoy's annual Moros y Cristianos, which features reenactments of the Christians' recapture of Alcoy from the Moors in the 13th century. Still, the scenery steals the show, especially on the crowd-free coast of the Ⓒ**Cabo de Gata,** a haven for rare wildlife and all those in search of an unspoiled beach.

Halfway between France and Africa, these once-remote landfalls off Spain's eastern coast are a playground for northern Europeans, not least because Britain occupied Minorca in the 18th century. ⒸⒹ**Ibiza** blasts to life nightly with the anything-goes heat that has come with 20th-century tourism—but even this disco-mad isle has its quiet coves. Majorca also combines tourist-clogged pockets with undiscovered corners: rugged mountains, abandoned monasteries, and a smattering of Christian and Moorish monuments like the Arab baths in the Balearic capital, Ⓑ**Palma.** On Ⓐ**Minorca** you can explore antique Ciutadella and Mahón between trips to the beach. And Formentera, the most purely pastoral island, retains a wild beauty that no man-made attraction can match.

BALEARIC ISLANDS

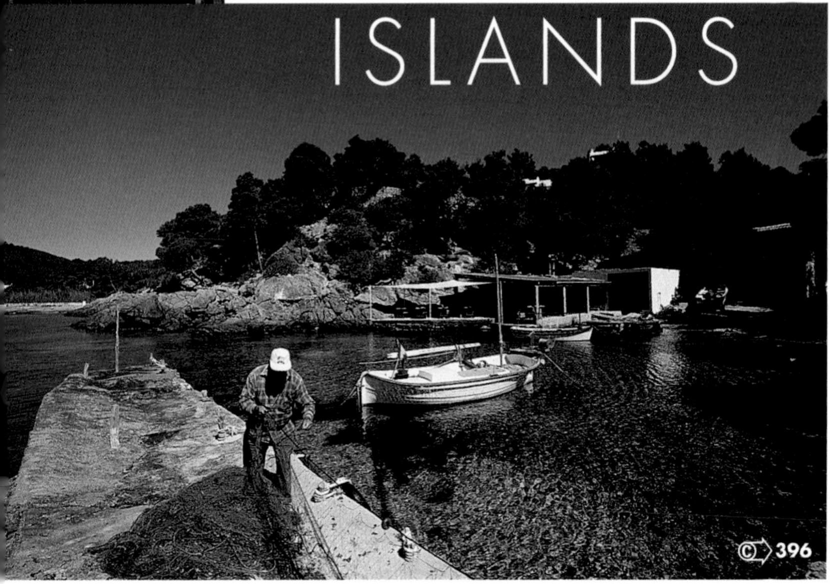

COSTA DEL SOL

Sun-seekers from Europe's bleaker climes, crammed into every cranny of this famous strip, make the whole area feel like a hedonistic carnival. The draws? A whopping 320 days of sunshine a year, and endless beaches on which to bask in it. Although Málaga, the provincial capital, is often bypassed in transit, it has historical and maritime appeal. Ⓐ**Marbella,** a favorite of the rich and famous, adds the seductive charm of a pristinely Andalusian old quarter. For more of the same, head into the mountains, where villages like Ⓒ**Casares** seem wondrously immune to the goings-on along the coast (even as it shimmers below), and the ancient town of Ronda straddles a giant river gorge. East toward Granada, Ⓑ**Nerja** combines a cliff-bound, gray-sand beach with enormous caves full of natural spires.

Ⓐ 467

GRANADA, CÓRDOBA, AND EASTERN ANDALUSIA

Ⓑ 477

The Moors made an important mark on this corner of their caliphate. Granada's Ⓔ**Alhambra** is a marvel of patios, arches, and intricate carvings, with the lush Generalife palace gardens next door. Across a gorge is the Moors' old neighborhood, the Albaicín, an array of ancient white houses tumbling down a hillside. Córdoba's sublime Mezquita—a mosque with a cathedral in the middle—is awesome, its 850 columns topped with red-and-white-striped arches. Near the mosque, the thick-walled homes in Córdoba's medieval Jewish quarter, the Ⓑ**Judería,**

Ⓒ 465

Ⓓ468

all but hide their spectacularly tiled interior courtyards. Around the two cities, Andalusia's olive groves seem to stretch forever in provinces like Ⓓ**Jaén,** interrupted by gems like Ⓕ**Úbeda,** with perfectly preserved Renaissance mansions and churches. The historic mining town of Ⓐ**Guadix** makes a good base for trips to Andalusia's many caves, scooped out of the sandstone mountains and often still inhabited. South of Granada, on the slopes of the Sierra Nevada, lie the villages of the Ⓒ**Alpujarras,** where descendants of transplanted Galicians craft rugs, blankets, baskets, and pottery.

Ⓕ471

Ⓔ455

A legacy of adventure lingers in the Guadalquivir River's sun-baked delta. Columbus, Magellan, and Drake sailed from backwater ports here, and the great harbor of Cádiz has been in use since the 10th century BC. As for Seville, though it's most colorful during its Holy Week festival, Ⓐ**Semana Santa,** it brims with romance all year round. The city's Giralda tower, massive cathedral, and sumptuous Ⓑ**Alcázar** recall Moorish caliphs and Christian kings, and elaborate *azulejo* tiles throughout the city form a cheerful Andalu-

SEVILLE AND WESTERN ANDALUSIA

sian motif. Dusty tapas bars and old palaces look unassuming but enchant *sevillanos* and travelers alike. Farther south, the fishing town of Sanlúcar de Barrameda serves unbeatable giant shrimp, known locally as *langostinos,* and in the vast vineyards around Ⓒ**Jerez de la Frontera,** more than a half million barrels of sherry are maturing at any given time.

EXTREMADURA

A journey through the wooded valleys and ocher farmlands of this western region feels a bit like time travel. The land is hushed and haunting. Even in prosperous Ⓐ**Cáceres,** nothing modern disrupts the Old Quarter, packed with medieval and Renaissance churches and palaces; and in Trujillo, the streets lined with vestigial mansions of Spain's imperial age are nearly deserted. Ancient Ⓑ**Mérida,** founded in 25 BC, is Spain's richest trove of Roman remains. Out in the mountains, the Jerte Valley and the monastery of Our Lady of Guadalupe make dramatic vantage points.

CANARY ISLANDS

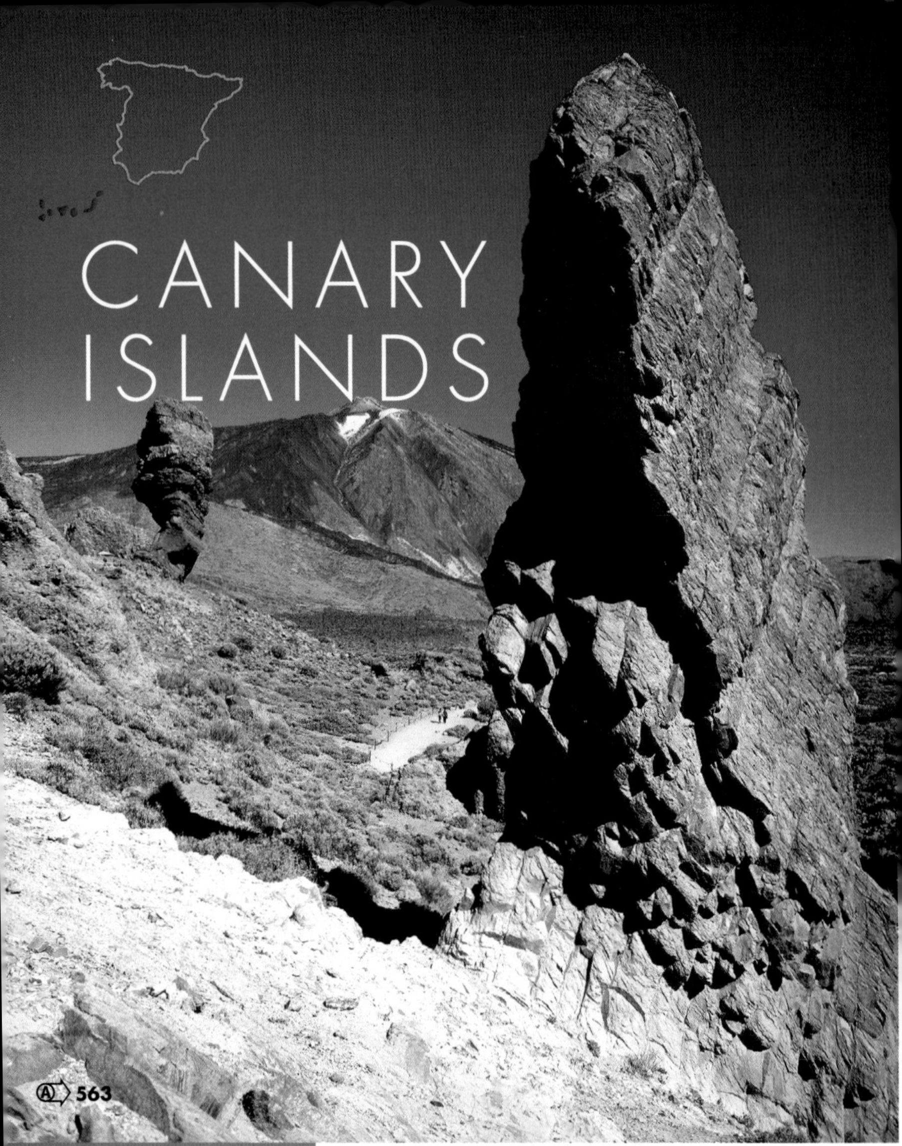
Ⓐ 563

Ⓑ 572

Tempered only by cool Atlantic breezes in summer, the balmy sunshine rarely lets up here, and steady winds and perfect waves attract surfers and windsurfers from all over the world to the coast of Ⓑ**Lanzarote.** Hotels and nightlife abound on Tenerife and Gran Canaria, the largest of the seven islands in this volcanic archipelago. But the islands' natural wonders are unusual among resorts, and Lanzarote's lava-formed water caverns, Ⓒ**Los Jameos del Agua,** as well as Tenerife's volcanic crater, the Ⓐ**Cañadas del Teide,** border on the bizarre.

Ⓒ 573

MOROCCO

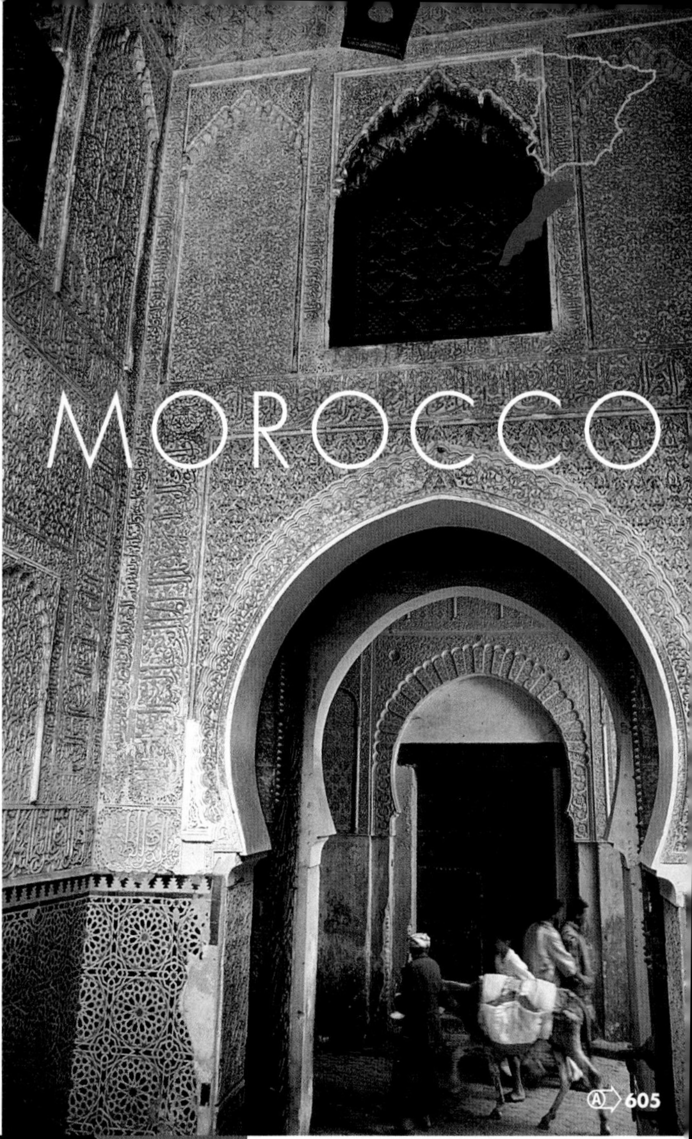

Ⓐ 605

Ⓑ 604

A brief hop across the Straits of Gibraltar, Spain's North African neighbor is a land of brilliant colors and clear skies. Brave the chaos of Tangier to explore the labyrinthine medina in Ⓐ**Fez,** a giant medieval enclave where traffic consists of only people and donkeys. Ⓒ**Marrakesh**—a crush of snake charmers, storytellers, and *souks* (markets)—is backed by the snowcapped Atlas mountains. Essaouira offers seaside respite, and Zagora can launch you right into the Ⓑ**Sahara Desert.** Casablanca and Rabat show Morocco's contemporary face.

Ⓒ 601

GREAT ITINERARIES

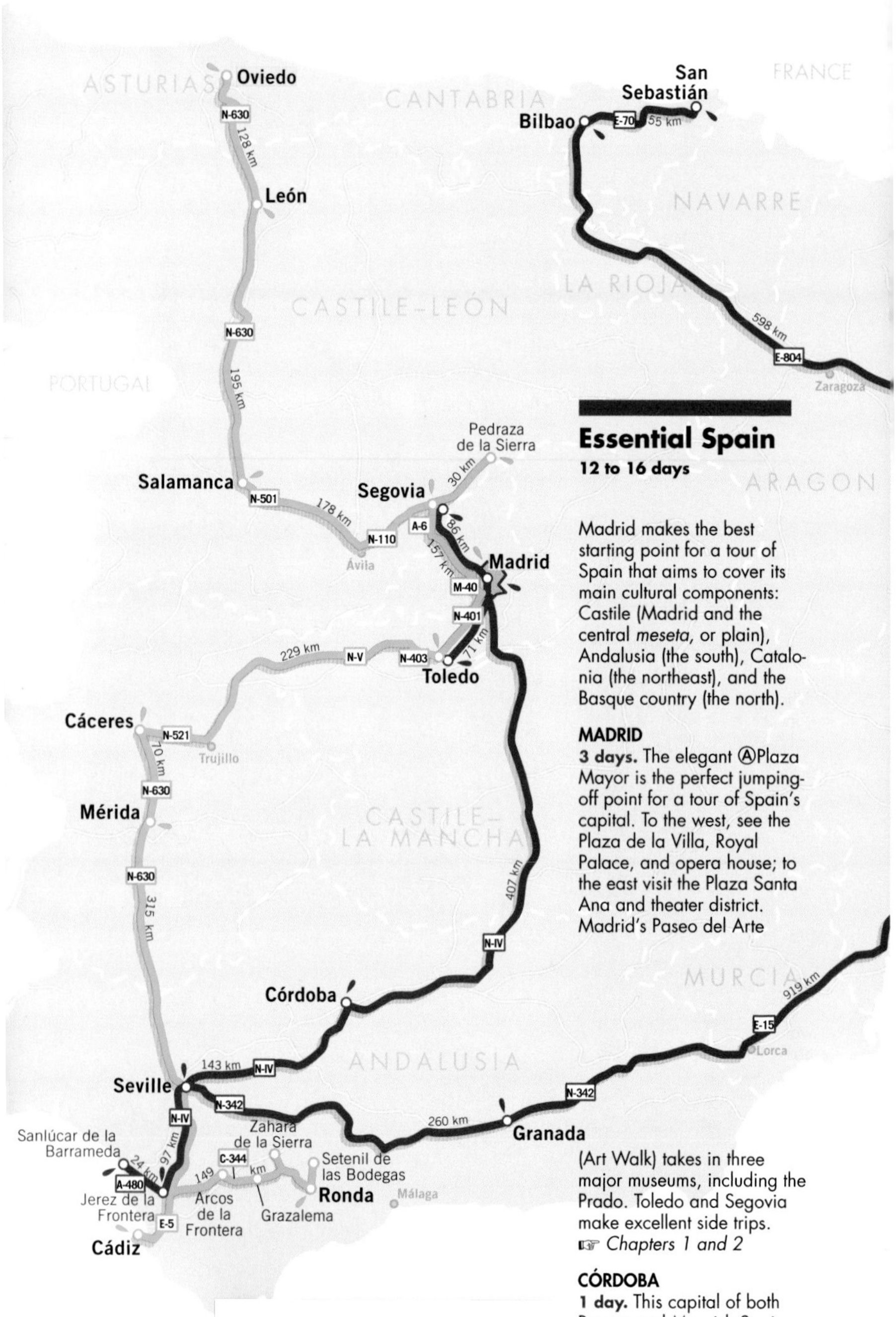

Essential Spain

12 to 16 days

Madrid makes the best starting point for a tour of Spain that aims to cover its main cultural components: Castile (Madrid and the central *meseta*, or plain), Andalusia (the south), Catalonia (the northeast), and the Basque country (the north).

MADRID

3 days. The elegant Ⓐ Plaza Mayor is the perfect jumping-off point for a tour of Spain's capital. To the west, see the Plaza de la Villa, Royal Palace, and opera house; to the east visit the Plaza Santa Ana and theater district. Madrid's Paseo del Arte (Art Walk) takes in three major museums, including the Prado. Toledo and Segovia make excellent side trips. ☞ *Chapters 1 and 2*

CÓRDOBA

1 day. This capital of both Roman and Moorish Spain was a center of Western art and culture in the 8th–11th centuries, to which its stunning mosque bears witness. The medieval Jewish quarter

unfolds in tiny, beckoning alleyways.
☞ *Córdoba in Chapter 11*

SEVILLE
1 day. Seville's Giralda tower, cathedral, bullring, and Barrio de Santa Cruz are visual feasts. Forty minutes south you can sip the world-famous sherries of Jerez de la Frontera, then munch jumbo

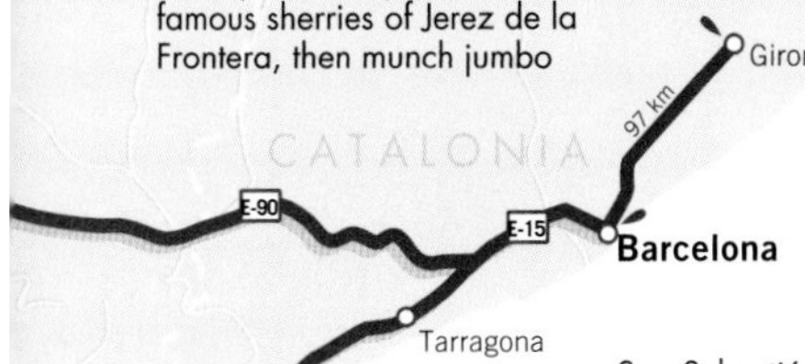

shrimp on the beach at Sanlúcar de Barrameda.
☞ *Seville in Chapter 12*

GRANADA
1 or 2 days. The hilltop Alhambra palace was conceived by the Moorish caliphs as heaven on earth and still strikes many as exactly that. The nearby Generalife palace has lush formal gardens. Down in the city, see the Royal Chapel, with the tombs of Ferdinand and Isabella; the cathedral; and the magnificent Albaicín, the ancient Moorish quarter.
☞ *Granada in Chapter 11*

BARCELONA
3 days. There are three key walks in 2,000-year-old Barcelona: the Gothic Quarter; the Eixample, with Art Nouveau buildings by Gaudí and others; and Gaudí's Güell Park and massive, unfinished Sagrada Família church. A long stroll on the Rambla and a trip to the Boqueria market are other musts, along with the church of Santa Maria del Mar, the Picasso Museum, and the flamboyant Palau de la Música. Day trips might take you to medieval Girona or Roman Tarragona.
☞ *Chapter 6*

BILBAO
1 or 2 days. Bilbao's Guggenheim Museum is worth a trip for the building itself, and the Museum of Fine Arts has an impressive collection of Basque and Spanish paintings. Restaurants and tapas bars abound.
☞ *Bilbao and the Basque Coast from Guernica to Guetaria in Chapter 3*

THE BASQUE COAST
1 or 2 days. The ⒷBasque coast between Bilbao and San Sebastián is lined with beaches, rocky cliffs, and picture-perfect fishing ports.
☞ *Bilbao and the Basque Coast from Guernica to Guetaria in Chapter 3*

SAN SEBASTIÁN
1 or 2 days. San Sebastián is one of Spain's most delicious cities both visually and gastronomically. Belle Epoque buildings nearly encircle the tiny bay, and tapas bars flourish in the old quarter. Duck into a *sidrería* for cider, codfish omelets, and *txuleta de buey* (filet mignon).
☞ *San Sebastián to Fuenterrabía in Chapter 3*

Transportation
Madrid is within 6 hrs of anywhere, but driving times from Andalusia and Catalonia to the Basque country can be twice that. Solution: overnight trains (on some of which you can transport your car) from Málaga to Barcelona or Barcelona to Bilbao. Domestic flights are another option. From Madrid it's a 4-hr drive or a 90-min ride on the high-speed AVE train to Córdoba, then a 45-min AVE ride to Seville. Granada is 3 to 4 hrs from Seville by car, train, or bus. The drive from Granada to Barcelona takes about 9 hrs, the flight 75 min. The overnight train from Andalusia to Barcelona leaves from Málaga. From Barcelona, a 6-hr drive, an overnight train, or a 1-hr flight to Bilbao lands you in the Basque country, where a car is your best mode of transport.

Art and Architecture
10 or 11 days

Most of Spain's finest buildings and artworks are far from the capitals of culture and commerce. This north–south tour avoids the behemoths in favor of smaller settings where quiet monuments can speak.

OVIEDO
1 to 2 days. Asturias is the only section of Spain that the Moors never conquered. Its capital, Oviedo, is full of rare pre-Romanesque churches, mainly from the 9th century. Other high points of Asturias include its 16th-century manor houses, many now inns, and thatch-roof granaries on stilts.
☞ *Oviedo and the Principality of Asturias in Chapter 4*

LEÓN
1 day. Crowned by its 13th-century cathedral, with an abundance of stained-glass windows, prosperous León is rich in history and culture. The marvelously preserved 12th-century frescoes in the Royal Pantheon represent some of the finest Romanesque art in Europe.
☞ *Burgos and León in Chapter 2*

SALAMANCA
1 day. This friendly university city is clothed in golden sandstone. The enormous arcaded Plaza Mayor, plateresque university buildings, and adjacent cathedrals add up to an architectural treasury nonpareil.
☞ *Salamanca and Ciudad Rodrigo in Chapter 2*

SEGOVIA
1 day. After the two-hour trip from Salamanca to Segovia, try to reach the handsomely restored village of Pedraza de la Sierra in time for a lunch of the town specialty, roast lamb, under the wooden arcades bordering the main square. High on the

Castilian *meseta,* medieval Segovia commands stark views, and its charming Plaza Mayor, late-Gothic cathedral, 1st-century Roman aqueduct, and turreted 15th-century ©Alcázar (fortress) make for an exquisite day and a pleasant overnight.
☞ *Segovia and Its Province in Chapter 2*

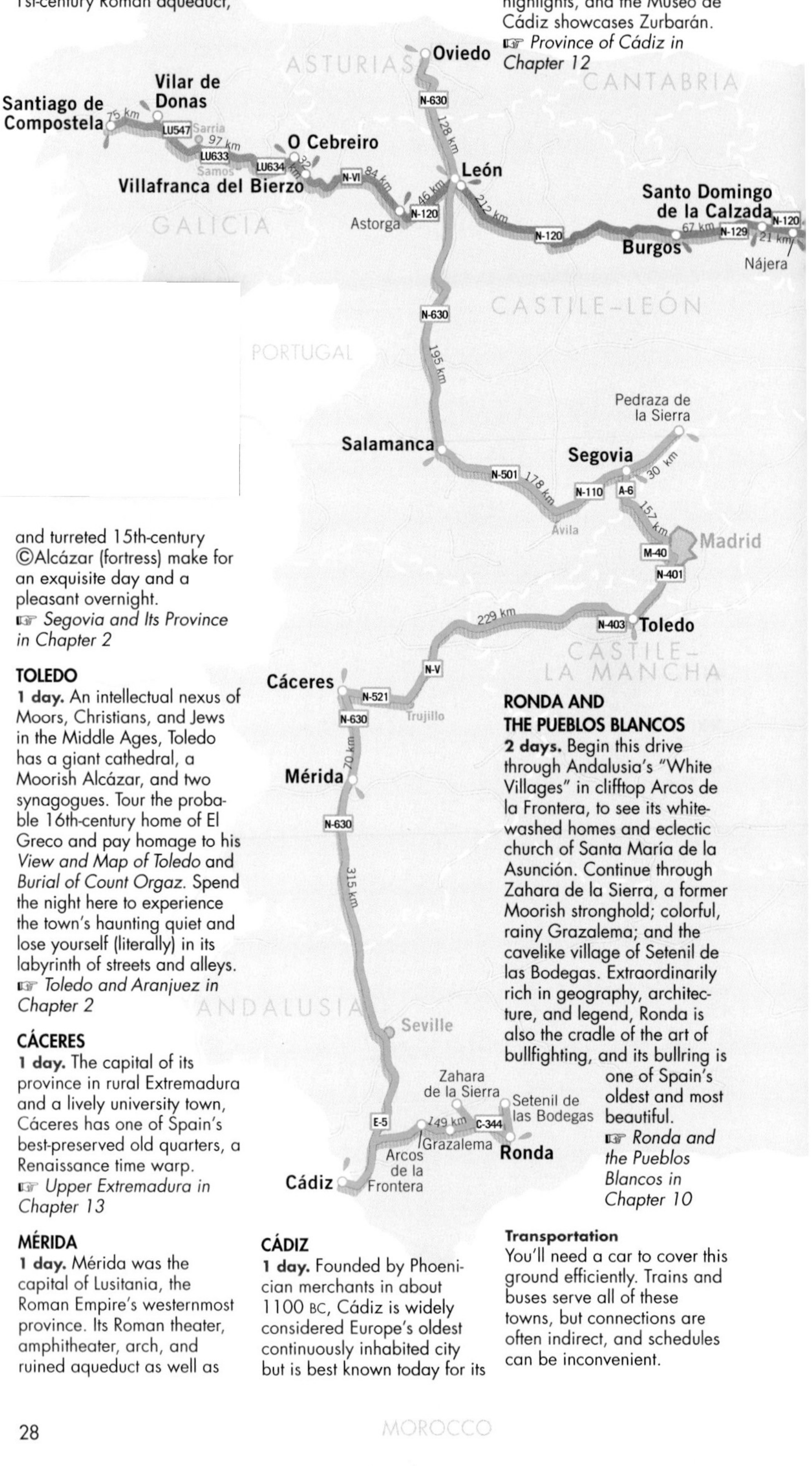

TOLEDO

1 day. An intellectual nexus of Moors, Christians, and Jews in the Middle Ages, Toledo has a giant cathedral, a Moorish Alcázar, and two synagogues. Tour the probable 16th-century home of El Greco and pay homage to his *View and Map of Toledo* and *Burial of Count Orgaz.* Spend the night here to experience the town's haunting quiet and lose yourself (literally) in its labyrinth of streets and alleys.
☞ *Toledo and Aranjuez in Chapter 2*

CÁCERES

1 day. The capital of its province in rural Extremadura and a lively university town, Cáceres has one of Spain's best-preserved old quarters, a Renaissance time warp.
☞ *Upper Extremadura in Chapter 13*

MÉRIDA

1 day. Mérida was the capital of Lusitania, the Roman Empire's westernmost province. Its Roman theater, amphitheater, arch, and ruined aqueduct as well as the bridge over the Guadiana are the leading monuments.
☞ *Lower Extremadura in Chapter 13*

CÁDIZ

1 day. Founded by Phoenician merchants in about 1100 BC, Cádiz is widely considered Europe's oldest continuously inhabited city but is best known today for its rowdy pre-Lenten Carnival. The 18th-century Oratorio de San Felipe Neri and the cathedral are architectural highlights, and the Museo de Cádiz showcases Zurbarán.
☞ *Province of Cádiz in Chapter 12*

RONDA AND THE PUEBLOS BLANCOS

2 days. Begin this drive through Andalusia's "White Villages" in clifftop Arcos de la Frontera, to see its whitewashed homes and eclectic church of Santa María de la Asunción. Continue through Zahara de la Sierra, a former Moorish stronghold; colorful, rainy Grazalema; and the cavelike village of Setenil de las Bodegas. Extraordinarily rich in geography, architecture, and legend, Ronda is also the cradle of the art of bullfighting, and its bullring is one of Spain's oldest and most beautiful.
☞ *Ronda and the Pueblos Blancos in Chapter 10*

Transportation

You'll need a car to cover this ground efficiently. Trains and buses serve all of these towns, but connections are often indirect, and schedules can be inconvenient.

The Camino de Santiago

14 days

The Way of St. James is the most important Christian pilgrimage after those to Jerusalem and Rome. At its peak, in the 12th century, as many as 2 million people walked from all over Europe to the mystical city and cathedral of Santiago de Compostela, in Spain's far northwest. The most popular route, the Camino Francés, crosses the Pyrenees near Roncesvalles and alternates between ancient footpath and modern road. Studded with medieval cathedrals, churches, inns, and hospitals, this drive crosses the Basque Pyrenees, the arid Castilian steppe, and the verdant mountains of Galicia.

RONCESVALLES

1 day. The walk across the Pyrenees to Roncesvalles is one of the Camino's most dramatic sections. It's 8 to 10 hours on foot, or an hour by car over the Valcarlos Pass.
☞ *The Western Pyrenees in Chapter 5*

PAMPLONA

1 day. Pamplona is the first major Spanish city on the Camino Francés. It's famous for July's running of the bulls but has its share of sacred monuments, including a Gothic cathedral and the churches of San Saturnino and San Nicolas.
☞ *Pamplona, Vitoria, and Environs in Chapter 3*

PUENTE LA REINA

1 day. This town's medieval bridge was built for pilgrims in the 11th century. The church of Santiago has a gold sculpture of St. James, and the Church of the Crucifix has a wooden sculpture of Christ on a Y-shaped cross. Just west of Puente la Reina is Estella, a well-placed rest stop with an arcaded square. The Monasterio de Irache dates from the 10th century; next door is a brass faucet that supplies pilgrims with blessed wine.
☞ *Pamplona, Vitoria, and Environs in Chapter 3*

LOGROÑO

1 day. Logroño is the capital of La Rioja, Spain's chief wine-making region. Its church of Santiago el Real has a famous equestrian statue honoring Santiago's legendary role in the Christian Reconquest.
☞ *La Rioja in Chapter 3*

SANTO DOMINGO DE LA CALZADA

1 day. Once the capital of La Rioja and Navarre, Nájera is known for its monastery of Santa María la Real. Santo Domingo ("of the Causeway") devoted his 11th-century life to the construction of amenities for pilgrims, including the hospital he built here, which is now a parador. Santo Domingo's 14th-century ramparts and cathedral are other draws.
☞ *La Rioja in Chapter 3*

BURGOS

2 days. This city's cathedral is one of the greatest in Spain. Of key military significance throughout Spanish history, Burgos has also been a strategic way station on the Camino. In the Monasterio de Las Huelgas Reales is a wooden figure of the saint himself, with a sword said to be used for knighting the princes of Castile into the Order of Santiago.
☞ *Burgos and León in Chapter 2*

LEÓN

2 days. The stained glass on León's cathedral is dazzling. The magnificent 16th-century Hostal de San Marcos was built in the 12th century as a pilgrims' hospital.
☞ *Burgos and León in Chapter 2*

VILLAFRANCA DEL BIERZO

1 day. The Camino routes from France and Portugal merge in Astorga. This town's main attraction is modern: the Palacio Episcopal, designed by Barcelona's Antoni Gaudí in 1889 and now home to the excellent Museo del Camino, dedicated to the pilgrimage itself. The center of medieval Villafranca del Bierzo is the church of Santiago, whose Puerta del Perdón (Door of Pardon) was designed to grant special dispensation to pilgrims unable to complete their journeys.
☞ *The Camino de Santiago in Chapter 2*

O CEBREIRO

1 day. O Cebreiro, at Galicia's eastern edge, has a population of 20, but it also has a 9th-century church, a small inn, modern-day pilgrims' hostels, and several *pallozas*—drystone thatched huts that once housed pilgrims.
☞ *The Camino de Santiago in Chapter 4*

VILAR DE DONAS

1 day. This stop is named for the elegant women (*donas* in Gallego) portrayed in the 15th-century frescoes in the town's Romanesque church. Several Knights of the Order of St. James are entombed here.
☞ *The Camino de Santiago in Chapter 4*

SANTIAGO DE COMPOSTELA

2 days. The end of the road—and nearly the end of Spain—Santiago de Compostela is a feast for the senses after the rigors of the pilgrimage. The Plaza del Obradoiro is an explosion of color and humanity, the Puerta de la Gloria on the famous cathedral is truly glorious, and the Hotel de los Reyes Católicos was a pilgrims' hospital during the 15th century.
☞ *The Camino de Santiago in Chapter 4*

Transportation

Traversing the Camino as a true pilgrim—on foot or bike—takes at least a month and leads you into far smaller hamlets than these. Failing that, connecting the dots above requires a car.

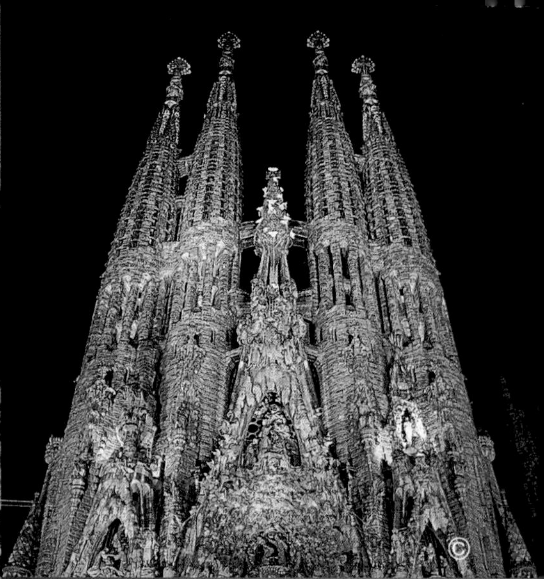

FODOR'S CHOICE

Even with so many special places in Spain, Fodor's writers and editors have their favorites. Here are a few that stand out.

SACRED SITES

Cathedral, Léon. The walls of Léon's soaring Gothic cathedral, begun in 1205, contain more glass than stone. The ethereal feel of the lofty interior is enhanced by a kaleidoscope of colors from 125 stained-glass windows and three giant rose windows. ☞ p. 137

Cathedral, Santiago de Compostela. Destination of Christian pilgrims for almost a millennium, this enormous Galician landmark houses the alleged remains of the apostle St. James, accompanied by Romanesque sculpture, a gold-and-silver high altar, and a dazzling array of decoration and drapery. ☞ p. 192

Ⓘ **Mezquita, Córdoba.** Built between the 8th and 10th centuries, the Mezquita (mosque) is a breathtaking example of Spanish Muslim architecture. Some 850 columns create a forest of onyx, jasper, marble, and granite, all topped with stunning, red-and-white-striped horseshoe arches and surrounded by delicate mosaics and plasterwork. ☞ p. 477

Ⓖ **Monastery of Our Lady of Guadalupe.** Nestled in the Altamira mountains of Extremadura, land of the Conquistadors, this art-filled, 14th-century Gothic and Moorish hybrid is one of the most important spiritual centers in the Spanish-speaking world. Christopher Columbus came here before and after his famous voyage to pay his respects to the Virgin. ☞ p. 541

Ⓒ **Sagrada Família, Barcelona.** Unfinished at the time of Catalan architect Antoni Gaudí's death in 1926, this surreal cathedral has been amended by other architects, who have themselves not shied away from controversy. Take an elevator to one of the spires for a magnificent view of the city. ☞ p. 271

CASTLES AND PALACES

Alarcón, Cuenca. Crossing the narrow bridge into the walled city and castle of Alarcón—a parador with a memorable restaurant—will catapult you back to medieval times. ☞ p. 102

Ⓓ **Alhambra, Granada.** One of Spain's most enduringly popular attractions, this Moorish citadel is an endlessly intricate fantasy of lavishly carved and colored patios, arches, and cupolas. ☞ p. 455

Castle, Sigüenza. At the very top of the beautiful town of Sigüenza, this mighty, crenellated parador has hosted royalty over the centuries, from Ferdinand and Isabella to Juan Carlos. ☞ p. 104

Royal Palace, La Granja. The gardens are the draw here: terraces, lakes, classical statuary, woods, and elaborate fountains encourage aimless ambling. In summer the fountains are turned on one by one, an exciting spectacle. ☞ p. 115

SCENIC HIGHLIGHTS

Pasajes de San Juan. Near the Basque city of San Sebastián, this charming, tiny settlement of 18th- and 19th-century buildings along the *pasajes* (straits) leading into the port of Rentería is famous for its fine restaurants. ☞ p. 169

Ⓑ **Roman ruins.** Mérida has Spain's largest concentration of Roman monuments, including a 64-arch bridge, a fortress, and a Roman amphitheater that once drew crowds of more than 14,000 to grisly duels between gladiators and wild beasts. The enchanting town of Segovia, near Madrid, has a nearly 3,000-ft aqueduct that dates from the 1st century AD. Tarragona, near Barcelona, has a variety of classical remains, most notably an amphitheater overlooking the Mediterranean. ☞ p. 325

Ronda. Dramatically perched on the edge of a giant ravine, the ancient Andalusian town of Ronda has spectacular views, an old Moorish section, and a picturesque bullring with a bullfighting museum. ☞ p. 432

Ⓔ **Salamanca.** Salamanca's medieval university and pair of cathedrals veritably glow with carved sandstone. The center of the university is the Escuelas Mayores, whose ornate eyeful of a frontispiece is surrounded by graceful quadrangles and greens. ☞ p. 121

MUSEUMS

Archbishop's Palace, Astorga. In far-northwestern Castile, a fairy-tale, neo-Gothic building by Antoni Gaudí houses a museum devoted to the Camino de Santiago pilgrimage. ☞ p. 141

Ⓗ **Guggenheim Museum Bilbao.** Frank Gehry's famous titanium pile draws crowds to this shipbuilding city and makes an excellent starting point for travel in the Basque country. ☞ p. 159

Ⓕ **National Museum of Sculpture, Valladolid.** Set in a fanciful 15th-century ecclesiastical building, the superb displays in this unique museum trace Spanish sculpture from the 16th century to the present. ☞ p. 130

Ⓐ **Picasso Museum, Barcelona.** You rather expect to see Juliet leaning over the courtyard balcony of this 15th-century palace, which houses Picasso's childhood sketches and paintings from his Rose and Blue periods. The surrounding cobblestone streets are full of shops and tapas bars. ☞ p. 263

Ⓙ **Prado, Madrid.** One of the greatest museums in the world, the Prado holds masterpieces by various Italian and Flemish painters, but its jewels are the works of Spaniards: Goya, Velázquez, and El Greco. ☞ p. 47

1 MADRID

Madrileños are a vigorous, joyful lot, famous for their ability to defy the need for sleep: they embrace their city's vibrant cultural offerings, and make enthusiastic use of its bars and cafés. Match this energy and you'll take in the museum mile, with more masterpieces per square foot than anywhere else in the world; the palaces and boutiques of regal Madrid; the dark, narrow lanes of medieval Madrid; and the real action, Madrid after midnight.

By Mark Potok and Deborah Luhrman

Updated by Edward Owen

LIFE IN MADRID is lived in crowded streets and noisy cafés, where talking, toasting, and tapa-tasting last long into the night. The capital's endless energy is hard to resist, and its sociable style invites you to jump right in.

Madrid's other main attraction is its unsurpassed collection of art by some of the world's great masters, among them Goya, El Greco, Velázquez, Picasso, and Dalí. Nowhere else will you find such a concentration of masterpieces as in the three museums—the Prado, the Reina Sofía, and the Thyssen-Bornemisza—that make up Madrid's so-called Paseo del Arte (Art Walk).

The first thing you notice here may be the bright blue sky, as immortalized in the paintings of Velázquez. Despite 20th-century pollution, the heavens are still in evidence thanks to breezes that sweep down from the Guadarrama mountains, blowing away urban smog. The skyline has its share of skyscrapers, but these are far outnumbered by more typically *madrileño* towers of red brick crowned by gray slate roofs and spires. Built in the 16th and 17th centuries by the Habsburgs, who made Madrid the capital of the Iberian realm, this architecture gives parts of Madrid a timeless, Old World look. Monumental neoclassical structures, like the Prado Museum, the Royal Palace, and the Puerta de Alcalá arch—the sights most often seen by travelers—make up Madrid's other historic face. Most of these were built in the 18th century, during the reign of Bourbon monarch Charles III; inspired by the enlightened ideas of the age, Charles also created the Parque del Retiro and the broad, leafy boulevard Paseo del Prado.

Modern-day Madrid sprawls northward in block after block of dreary, high-rise brick apartment and office buildings. The population of three million is also moving into surrounding villages and new suburbs, creating traffic problems in and around the city. These new quarters and many of Madrid's crumbling old residential neighborhoods may seem unprepossessing, but don't be put off by first impressions. Much of the city's appeal comes from its vivacious people and the electricity they generate, whether at play in bars and clubs or at work in Spain's finance, advertising, television, and film industries, all headquartered here.

Poised on a plateau 2,120 ft above sea level, Madrid is the highest capital in Europe. It can thus be one of the world's hottest cities in summer, and freezing cold in winter. Spring and summer are the best times to visit, when balmy evenings have everyone in town lingering at outdoor cafés; but each season has its own charms. In winter, steamy café windows and all-night street festivals beckon, and the blue skies are particularly crisp and bright—and that's when Madrid is, according to a local bumper sticker, the next best place to heaven.

The city's sophistication stands in vivid contrast to the ancient ways of the historic towns nearby. Less than an hour from downtown are villages whose farm fields may still be plowed by mules. Like urbanites the world over, Madrileños chill out in the countryside, so getaways to the dozens of Castilian hamlets nearby and to Toledo, El Escorial, and Segovia are cherished by travelers and locals alike.

Pleasures and Pastimes

Art Museums

Madrid's greatest daytime attractions are its three world-class art museums, the Prado, the Reina Sofía, and the Thyssen-Bornemisza, all within 1 km (½ mi) of each other along the leafy Paseo del Prado, sometimes called the Paseo del Arte. The Prado houses Spain's old masters, with the world's foremost collections of Goya, El Greco, and Velázquez topping off hundreds of other 17th-, 18th-, and 19th-century masterpieces. The Reina Sofía focuses on modern art, especially Dalí, Miró, and Picasso, whose famous *Guernica* hangs here; it also shows modern Spanish sculptors, such as Eduardo Chillida, and hosts excellent temporary exhibits. The Thyssen-Bornemisza attempts to trace the entire history of Western art, and has particularly good collections of impressionist and German expressionist works.

Dining

As capital of the realm and home of the king since the 16th century, Madrid has attracted generations of courtiers, diplomats, politicians, and tradesmen, all of whom have brought their own culinary tastes and styles from other parts of Spain and from abroad. Madrid's best restaurants specialize in Basque cooking, Spain's haute cuisine, while numerous seafood houses, as if compulsively craving the distant sea, take full advantage of the abundant fish and shellfish trucked in nightly from both the Atlantic and the Mediterranean coasts. Madrid has long been known as Spain's "first port," the immediate destination of most of the finest produce from Spain's fishing fleet—by far the largest in Europe.

Madrid's own cuisine is based on the roasts and thick soups and stews of Castile, Spain's high central *meseta* (plain). Roast suckling pig and lamb are standard Madrid feasts, as are baby goat and chunks of beef from Ávila. *Cocido madrileño* (garbanzo-bean stew) and *callos a la madrileña* (stewed tripe) are fundamental local specialties. Cocido is a delicious and hearty winter meal consisting of garbanzo beans, vegetables, potatoes, sausages, and pork. The best cocidos are slowly simmered in earthenware crocks over open fires and served as a complete meal in several courses: first the broth, which comes with angel-hair pasta; then the beans and vegetables; and finally the meat. You can order cocido in the most elegant restaurants as well as the humblest holes-in-the-wall, and it's usually offered as a midday selection on Monday or Wednesday. Callos are a much simpler concoction of veal tripe stewed with tomatoes, onions, hot paprika, and garlic. *Jamón serrano* (cured ham)—a specialty from the livestock lands of Teruel, Extremadura, and Andalusia—has become a staple in Madrid; wanderers are likely to come across a *museo del jamón* (literally, ham museum), where endless legs of the dried delicacy dangle in store windows or in bars. Restaurant windows betray a local affinity for pork products in general, particularly hams and baby suckling pigs. As for fast food, busy Madrileños grab a *bocadillo* (sandwich) from a stand for a quick bite.

Although the countryside near the capital produces some wines, these are less than exceptional. The house wine in most basic Madrid restaurants is a sturdy, uncomplicated Valdepeñas from La Mancha. A traditional, anise-flavored liqueur (*anís*) is produced outside the village of Chinchón.

CATEGORY	COST*
$$$$	over 6,000 ptas.
$$$	4,000–6,000 ptas.
$$	1,800–4,000 ptas.
$	under 1,800 ptas.

**per person for three-course meal, excluding drinks, service, and tax*

Lodging

Hotel prices in Madrid are about the same as those in other European capitals. The Ritz, the Palace, and the Villamagna charge upwards of

U.S. $400 a night. If that's too steep, try bargaining: because most hotels cater to business travelers, special weekend rates are widely available. You may be able to save 30% on a Friday, Saturday, or Sunday night, and many hotels throw in extras, like meals or museum admissions. Business travelers on long stays can ask for business discounts, which can be as deep as 40%.

If you're willing to hunt a bit, you can also find *hostales* for 4,000 ptas. or even less. Most of these very cheap rooms are on the upper floors of apartment buildings and share bath facilities. Because they're often full and don't take reservations, we list only a few here—you simply have to go door-to-door and trust your luck. Many such places are concentrated in the old city between the Prado and the Puerta del Sol; start your quest around the Plaza Santa Ana.

CATEGORY	COST*
$$$$	over 25,000 ptas.
$$$	14,000–25,000 ptas.
$$	10,000–14,000 ptas.
$	under 10,000 ptas.

**for a standard double room, excluding tax.*

Tapas Bars

Madrid has some of the best tapas bars in Spain. A *tapa* is a bit of food that usually comes free with a drink; it might be a few olives, a mussel in vinaigrette, a sardine, or spicy potatoes. You can also order a larger plate of this kind of snack, called a *ración,* meant to be shared among friends. Tapas bars are sprinkled throughout the city, but the best place to start a tapa tour is near the Plaza Santa Ana or in the *mésones* built into the wall beneath the Plaza Mayor, along Cava de San Miguel. These are some of the oldest buildings in Madrid, and each bar specializes in a different tapa—for example, potato-and-egg tortillas (a Spanish tortilla is an omelet of sorts, not to be confused with the Mexican tortilla), garlicky mushrooms, or a small wedge of *empanada de atún,* a rich baked pastry stuffed with tuna, egg, and onions.

EXPLORING MADRID

Madrid is a compact city, and most of the sights you probably want to see are concentrated in a downtown area 2½ km (1½ mi) across, stretching between the Royal Palace and the Parque del Retiro. Broad *avenidas,* twisting medieval alleys, grand museums, stately gardens, and tiny, tiled taverns are all jumbled together in an area easily covered on foot. The urban texture is so rich that walking is really the only way to experience those special moments whose images linger—peeking in on a guitar maker at work, or watching a child dip sweet *churros* (deep-fried batter twists, a classic Madrileño snack) into a steamy cup of hot chocolate.

Sadly, muggings are a serious problem in Madrid, and tourists are frequent targets. Be on your guard as you wander, and make an effort to blend in: wear dark clothes, try to keep cameras concealed, and avoid flamboyant map reading. The Japanese Embassy has complained to Madrid authorities that tourists who appear East Asian seem to be at particular risk.

Numbers in the text correspond to numbers in the margin and on the Madrid, Side Trips from Madrid, and El Escorial maps.

Great Itineraries

IF YOU HAVE 2 DAYS

On a brief stay, limit yourself to one or two museums and devote the rest of your time to wandering. See the works of Spain's great masters at the **Museo del Prado** ⑱; then visit the **Palacio Real** ⑤ for a regal display of art, architecture, and history. The palace tour includes admission to the Royal Library and Royal Armory, both sights in their own right. Stroll from Paseo de la Castellana to Paseo del Prado to see the fountains at **Plaza Colón** ㉛: **Fuente de la Cibeles** ㉕ and **Fuente de Neptuno** ⑰. Behold the **Puerta del Sol** ①, then relax at an outdoor café on the **Plaza Mayor** ⑮. Finally, pop into some of the historic tapas bars along **Cava de San Miguel** ㉜.

IF YOU HAVE 4 DAYS

In four days you can uncover historic Madrid, visit more museums, and make an excursion outside the city. Follow the two-day plan above; then visit the **Centro de Arte Reina Sofía** ㉑ and the **Museo Thyssen-Bornemisza** ⑲. Try not to miss the 16th-century **Convento de las Descalzas Reales** ②. Explore the Mudéjar architecture and flamboyant plateresque decoration of medieval Madrid in the **Plaza de la Villa** ⑭ and around the **Plaza de la Paja** ㉛. Venture outside the capital to spend your third night and fourth day in lovely **Toledo** or **Segovia** (☞ Chapter 2).

Central Madrid

Between the Royal Palace and the Puerta del Sol is a stretch of about 1 km (½ mi) that's loaded with historic sites.

A Good Walk

Begin at the **Puerta del Sol** ①, the center of Madrid. If you stand with your back to the clock, Calle Arenal leaves the plaza from the far left: walk down Arenal and turn right into Plaza Celenque. Up on your left at the corner with Calle Misericordia is the **Convento de las Descalzas Reales** ②. Follow Misericordia and turn left into the charming Plaza de San Martín to return to Calle Arenal. Turn right and walk down to Plaza San Isabel II; then, crossing the plaza to your right, walk to the end of the short Calle Arrieta, at which point you'll face the **Convento de la Encarnación** ③. Turn left here into Calle San Quintin and you'll enter the semicircular **Plaza de Oriente** ④. Walk to the right (north) down Calle Bailén.

Here you have a choice of going directly to the magnificent **Palacio Real** ⑤, on your left, or visiting its gardens (1 km/½ mi farther on) and/or taking a cable-car ride. For the latter, cross Calle Bailén and walk to the right: you'll have a lovely view across the formal **Jardines Sabatini** ⑥ over to the Casa de Campo park and the distant Guadarrama Mountains. Walk up Bailén, avoiding the overpass, and turn left down Cuesta de San Vicente, then left into Paseo Virgin del Puerto for the entrance to the palace gardens and the **Campo del Moro** ⑦. If you go straight, crossing the overpass, you'll reach Calle Ferraz; follow the Parque del Oeste on the left and you'll reach the Egyptian **Templo de Debod** ⑧. Farther along Paseo de Pintor Rosales, in the park, is the **Teléferico** ⑨ cable car to the Casa de Campo, which grants panoramic views of Madrid.

Opposite the Royal Palace on the plaza is Madrid's opera house, the **Teatro Real** ⑩. To its right is the Cafe Oriente, a good pit stop. Walking down Bailén with the palace on your right, you can enter its huge courtyard and admire the view from the top of the escarpment. Alongside the palace is the **Catédral de la Almudena** ⑪. Walk past the cathedral and turn right onto Calle Mayor: on your left, in Cuesta de la Vega, are the remains of Madrid's **Arab Wall** ⑫, next to the Parque Emir Mohammed I.

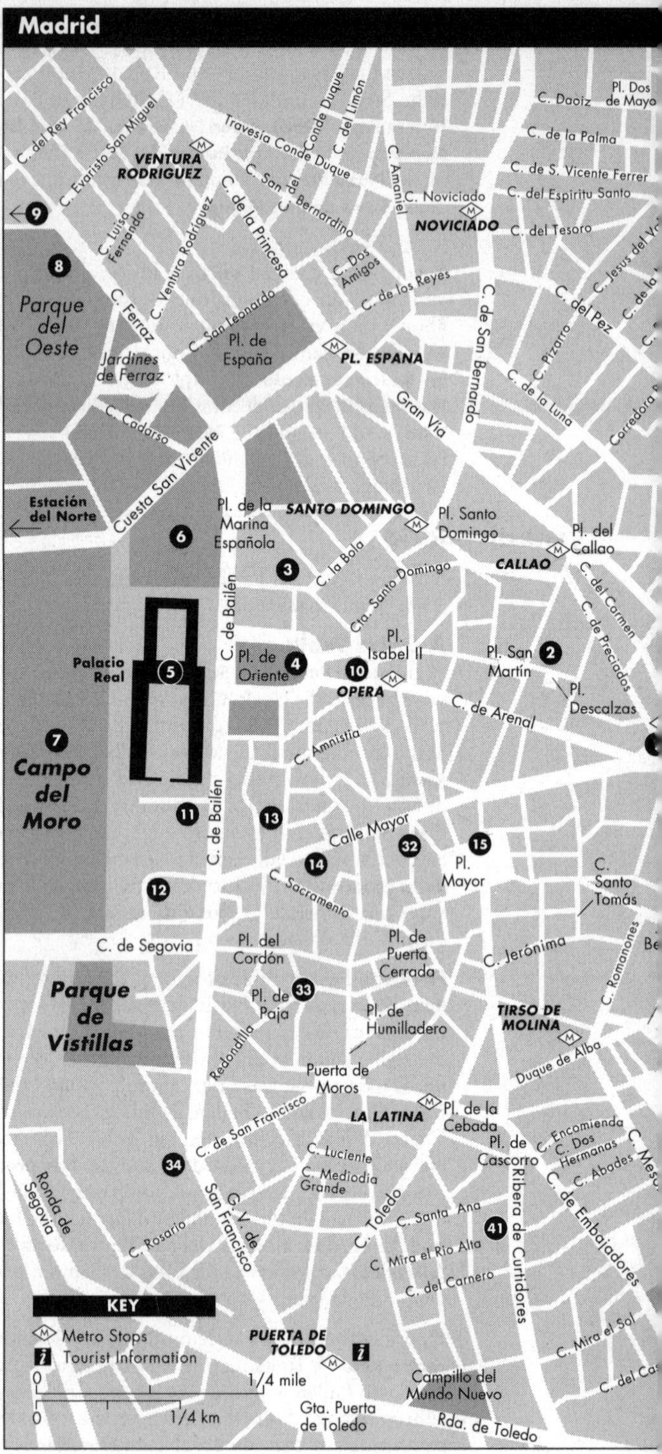

Madrid
C. del Rey Francisco
C. Evaristo San Miguel
VENTURA RODRIGUEZ
Travesia Conde Duque
C. del Conde Duque
C. del Limón
C. Amaniel
C. Daoiz
Pl. Dos de Mayo
C. de la Palma
C. de S. Vicente Ferrer
C. del Espiritu Santo
C. Noviciado
NOVICIADO
C. del Tesoro
C. Luisa Fernanda
C. Ventura Rodriguez
C. de la Princesa
C. San Bernardino
C. del
C. Dos Amigos
C. de los Reyes
C. de San Bernardo
C. del Pez
C. Pizarro
C. de la Luna
Corredora
9
8
Parque del Oeste
C. Ferraz
Jardines de Ferraz
C. San Leonardo
Pl. de España
PL. ESPANA
Gran Via
C. Cadarso
Cuesta San Vicente
Estación del Norte
Pl. de la Marina Española
SANTO DOMINGO
Pl. Santo Domingo
Pl. del Callao
CALLAO
6
3
C. la Bola
Cta. Santo Domingo
C. del Carmen
C. de Preciados
C. de Bailén
Pl. de Oriente
4
Pl. Isabel II
10
OPERA
Pl. San Martín
2
Pl. Descalzas
C. de Arenal
Palacio Real
5
C. Amnistia
7
Campo del Moro
11
13
Calle Mayor
32
15
14
Pl. Mayor
C. Santo Tomás
12
C. Sacramento
C. de Segovia
Pl. del Cordón
Pl. de Puerta Cerrada
C. Jerónima
C. Romanones
Parque de Vistillas
Pl. de Paja
33
Redondilla
Pl. de Humilladero
TIRSO DE MOLINA
Duque de Alba
Puerta de Moros
C. de San Francisco
LA LATINA
Pl. de la Cebada
Pl. de Cascorro
C. Encomienda
C. Dos Hermanas
C. Abades
C. Luciente
C. Mediodia Grande
34
Ronda de Segovia
G. V. de San Francisco
C. Toledo
C. Santa Ana
41
Ribera de Curtidores
C. de Embajadores
C. Rosario
C. Mira el Rio Alta
C. del Carnero
KEY
Metro Stops
Tourist Information
0
1/4 mile
0
1/4 km
PUERTA DE TOLEDO
C. Mira el Sol
Campillo del Mundo Nuevo
Gta. Puerta de Toledo
Rda. de Toledo

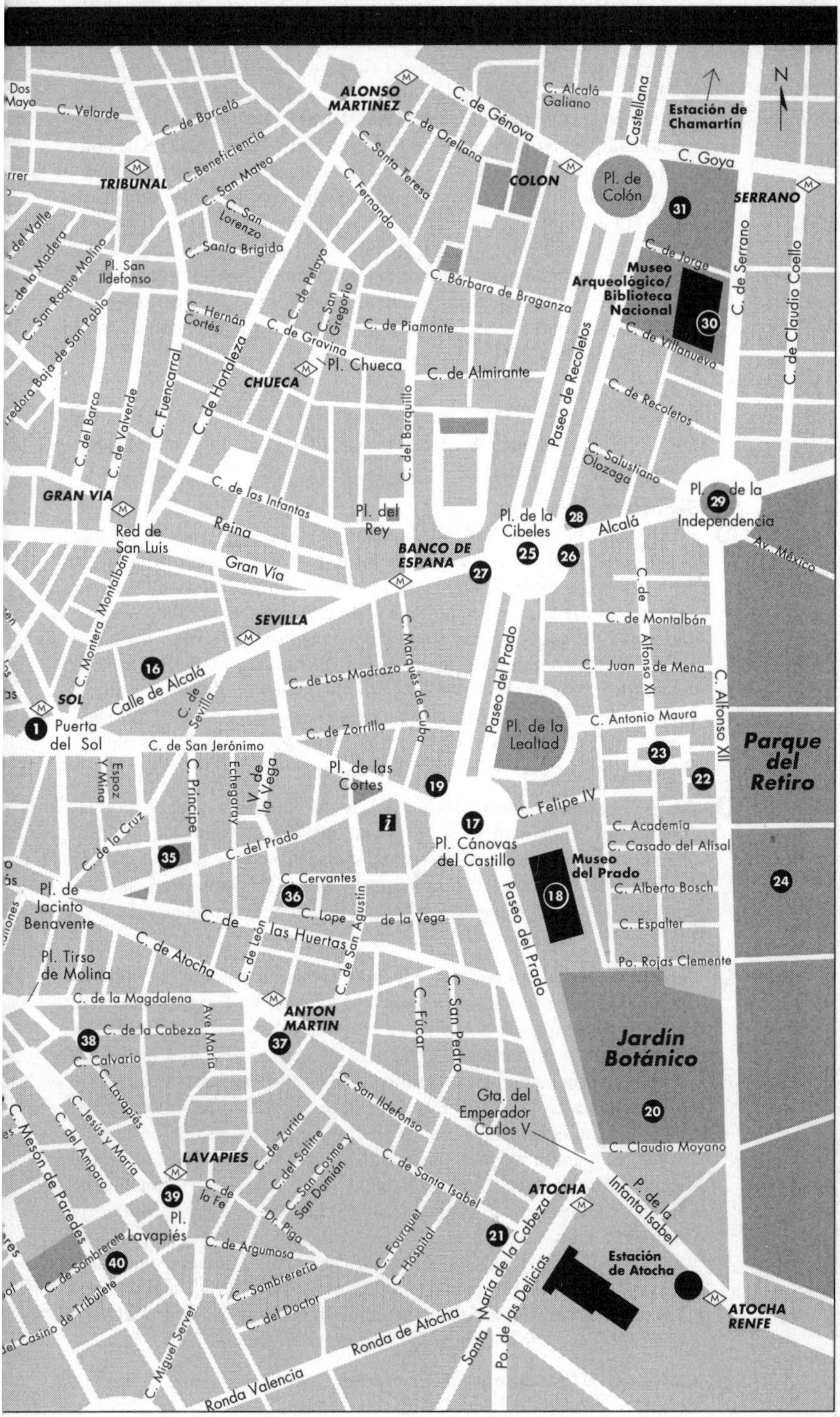
ALONSO MARTINEZ
C. de Génova
C. Alcalá Galiano
Castellana
Estación de Chamartín
N
Dos Mayo
C. Velarde
C. de Barceló
C. de Orellana
C. Santa Teresa
C. Beneficiencia
TRIBUNAL
C. San Mateo
C. Fernando
COLON
Pl. de Colón
C. Goya
SERRANO
31
C. San Lorenzo
C. Santa Brigida
s del Valle
de la Madera
C. San Roque Molino
Pl. San Ildefonso
C. de Pelayo
C. San Gregorio
C. Bárbara de Braganza
C. de Jorge
Museo Arqueológico/ Biblioteca Nacional
30
C. de Serrano
C. de Claudio Coello
C. San Pablo
C. Baja de San Pablo
C. Hernán Cortés
C. de Gravina
C. de Piamonte
C. de Villanueva
Pl. Chueca
C. de Almirante
CHUECA
C. de Hortaleza
C. Fuencarral
Paseo de Recoletos
C. de Recoletos
C. del Barco
C. de Valverde
C. del Barquillo
C. Salustiano Olozaga
GRAN VIA
C. de las Infantas
Pl. del Rey
Pl. de la Cibeles
28
Pl. de la Independencia
29
Red de San Luis
Reina
Alcalá
25
26
Av. México
BANCO DE ESPANA
Gran Vía
27
C. de Alfonso XI
C. de Montalbán
Montera
Montalbán
SEVILLA
C. Marqués de Cuba
Paseo del Prado
C. Juan de Mena
16
C. de Los Madrazo
C. Alfonso XII
SOL
Calle de Alcalá
C. de Sevilla
Pl. de la Lealtad
C. Antonio Maura
Parque del Retiro
1
Puerta del Sol
C. de San Jerónimo
C. de Zorrilla
23
Espoz Y Mina
C. Príncipe
Echegaray
V. de la Vega
Pl. de las Cortes
19
22
C. Felipe IV
17
C. de la Cruz
C. del Prado
Pl. Cánovas del Castillo
C. Academia
C. Casado del Alisal
35
Museo del Prado
C. Cervantes
18
C. Alberto Bosch
24
Pl. de Jacinto Benavente
36
C. Lope de la Vega
C. Espalter
C. de las Huertas
C. de San Agustín
C. de Atocha
C. de León
Po. Rojas Clemente
Pl. Tirso de Molina
C. Fúcar
C. San Pedro
C. de la Magdalena
ANTON MARTIN
Ave María
Jardín Botánico
38
C. de la Cabeza
37
C. Calvario
C. Lavapiés
C. San Ildefonso
Gta. del Emperador Carlos V
C. Mesón de Paredes
C. Jesús y María
C. del Amparo
20
C. Claudio Moyano
LAVAPIES
C. de Zurita
C. del Salitre
C. San Cosme y San Damián
C. de Santa Isabel
ATOCHA
P. de la Infanta Isabel
39
C. de la Fe
Pl. Lavapiés
Dr. Piga
21
C. de Sombrerete
C. de Argumosa
C. Fourquet
C. Hospital
María de la Cabeza
Estación de Atocha
40
C. de Tribulete
C. Sombrerería
C. del Doctor
Po. de las Delicias
ATOCHA RENFE
del Casino
C. Miguel Servet
Ronda de Atocha
Santa
Ronda Valencia

Walk back east up Calle Mayor, crossing Bailén. Turn left into Calle San Nicolás to see the church of **San Nicolás de las Servitas** ⑬. Return to Mayor and press ahead: on your right you'll see the **Plaza de la Villa** ⑭, with Madrid's city hall on the right. Farther up Mayor, bear right in Plaza Morenas and enter the **Plaza Mayor** ⑮ through the arch. The Andalusian Torre de Oro bar on the left displays gory pictures of bullfights, not for the squeamish. On the far side, at No. 33, is the restaurant El Soportal, which gives the plaza's best free tapas with each drink order. (Beware of prices at the other restaurants, especially if you sit outside.) Exit the plaza to the left of El Soportal and head down Calle de Postas and back to the Puerta del Sol. Proceed up the right side of Sol, past the headquarters of the regional government, and perhaps take a tapa in the charming old shop at the restaurant Lhardy, on Carrera de San Jerónimo.

TIMING

Without side trips to the palace gardens or the cable car, you can cover this walk in two hours. Set aside an additional morning or afternoon to visit the Royal Palace.

Sights to See

12 **Arab Wall.** The city of Madrid was founded on Calle Cuesta de la Vega at the ruins of this wall, which protected a fortress built here in the 8th century by Emir Mohammed I. In addition to being an excellent defensive position, the site had plentiful water and was called *Mayrit,* which is Arabic for "water source" and the likely origin of the city's name. All that remains of the *medina*—the old Arab city that formed within the walls of the fortress—is the neighborhood's crazy quilt of streets and plazas, which probably follow the same layout they followed more than 1,100 years ago. The park **Emir Mohammed I,** alongside the wall, hosts concerts and plays in the summer.

7 **Campo del Moro** (Moors' Field). Below the Sabatini Gardens, but accessible only by an entrance on the far side, is the Campo del Moro. Clusters of shady trees, winding paths, and a long lawn leading up to the Royal Palace make for strategically beautiful photographs. Even without considering the riches inside, the palace's immense size (it's twice as large as Buckingham Palace) inspires awe.

11 **Catédral de la Almudena.** The first stone of the cathedral (which adjoins the Royal Palace to the south) was laid in 1883 by King Alfonso XII, and the end result was consecrated by Pope John Paul II in 1993. The building was intended to be Gothic in style, with needles and spires, but as time ran long and money ran short, the design was simplified by Fernando Chueca Goltia into the more austere classical form you see today. The cathedral houses the remains of Madrid's patron saint, San Isidro (St. Isidore), and a wooden statue of Madrid's female patron saint, the Virgin of Almudena, which is said to have been discovered following the Christian reconquest of Madrid in 1085. Legend has it that a divinely inspired woman named María led authorities to a secret spot in the old wall of the Alcázar (which in Arabic can also be called *almudeyna*), where the statue was found framed by two lighted candles inside a grain storage vault. That wall is part of the cathedral's foundation. ✉ *C. &del;Bailén s/n,* ☎ *91/548–9900.* 🎫 *Free.* ⏲ *Daily 10–1:30 and 6–7:45.*

3 **Convento de la Encarnación** (Convent of the Incarnation). Once connected to the Royal Palace by an underground passageway, this Augustinian convent was founded in 1611 by the wife of Felipe III. It holds several artistic treasures, but its biggest attraction is its reliquary, which holds among the sacred bones a vial containing the dried blood of St. Pantaleón, which is said to liquefy every year on July 27. You can enter

Encarnación on the same ticket as the Convent of Descalzas Reales (☞ *below*). ✉ *Plaza de la Encarnación 1,* ☎ *91/547–0510.* 🎫 *400 ptas.* ⏲ *Wed. and Sat. 10:30–2:30 and 4–5:30, Sun. 11–2.*

❷ **Convento de las Descalzas Reales** (Convent of the Royal Barefoot Nuns). This 16th-century building was restricted for 200 years to women of royal blood. Its plain, brick-and-stone facade hides a treasure trove, including paintings by Zurbarán, Titian, and Brueghel the Elder, as well as a hall of sumptuous tapestries crafted from drawings by Peter Paul Rubens. The convent was founded in 1559 by Juana of Austria, whose daughter shut herself up here rather than endure marriage to Felipe II. A handful of nuns (not necessarily royal) still live here, cultivating their own vegetables in the convent's garden. You must visit as part of a guided tour, usually conducted once a day in English and the rest of the day in Spanish. ✉ *Plaza de las Descalzas Reales 3,* ☎ *91/542–0059.* 🎫 *700 ptas.* ⏲ *Tues.–Thurs. and Sat. 10:30–12:45 and 4–5:45, Fri. 10:30–12:45, Sun. 11–1:45.*

❻ **Jardines Sabatini** (Sabatini Gardens). The formal gardens to the north of the Royal Palace are crawling with stray cats, but they're a pleasant place to rest or watch the sun set.

★ ❺ **Palacio Real.** The Royal Palace was commissioned in the early 18th century by the first of Spain's Bourbon rulers, Felipe V, on the same strategic site where Madrid's first Alcázar (Moorish fortress) was built in the 9th.

Before you enter, stroll around the graceful **Patio de Armas** and admire the classical French architecture. King Felipe was obviously inspired by his childhood days at Versailles with his grandfather Louis XIV. Look for the stone statues of Inca prince Atahualpa and Aztec king Montezuma, perhaps the only tributes in Spain to these pre-Columbian American rulers. Notice how the steep bluff drops westward to the Manzanares River—on a clear day, this vantage point also commands a good view of the mountain passes leading into Madrid from Old Castile, and it becomes obvious why the Moors picked this particular spot for a fortress.

Inside, the palace's 2,800 rooms compete with each other for over-the-top opulence. A nearly two-hour guided tour in English winds a mile-long path through the palace. Highlights include the **Salón de Gasparini,** King Carlos III's private apartments—a riot of rococo decoration, with swirling, inlaid floors and curlicued, ceramic wall and ceiling decoration, all glistening in the light of a 2-ton crystal chandelier; the **Salón del Trono,** an exceedingly grand throne room with the royal seats of King Juan Carlos and Queen Sofía; and the **banquet hall,** the palace's largest room, which seats up to 140 people for state dinners. No monarch has lived here since 1931, when Alfonso XIII was hounded out of the country by a populace fed up with centuries of royal oppression. The current king and queen live in the far simpler Zarzuela Palace on the outskirts of Madrid, using this palace only for state functions and official occasions such as the first Middle East peace talks, held here in 1991.

You can also visit the **Biblioteca Real** (Royal Library), which has a first edition of Cervantes's *Don Quixote*; the **Museo de Música** (Music Museum), where five stringed instruments by Stradivarius form the world's largest collection; the **Armería Real** (Royal Armory), with its vast array of historic suits of armor and some frightening medieval torture implements; and the **Real Oficina de Farmacía** (Royal Pharmacy), with an assortment of vials and flasks that were used to mix the king's medicines. ✉ *C. Bailén s/n,* ☎ *91/542–0059.* 🎫 *950 ptas., guided tour*

1,000 ptas. ⏲ Tues.–Sat. 9–6 (Oct.–Mar. 9–5), Sun. 9–3 (Oct.–Mar. 9–2). Closed during official receptions.

4 **Plaza de Oriente.** The stately plaza in front of the Royal Palace is surrounded by massive stone statues of various Spanish monarchs from Ataulfo to Fernando VI. These sculptures were meant to be mounted on the railing on top of the palace (where there are now stone urns), but Queen Isabel of Farnesio, one of the first royals to live in the palace, had them removed because she was afraid their enormous weight would bring the roof down. Well, that's what she *said* . . . according to palace insiders, the queen wanted the statues removed because her own likeness had not been placed front and center.

The statue of **King Felipe IV** in the center of the plaza was the first equestrian bronze ever cast with a rearing horse. The action pose comes from a Velázquez painting of the king with which the monarch was so smitten that in 1641 he commissioned an Italian artist, Pietro de Tacca, to turn it into a sculpture. De Tacca enlisted Galileo's help in configuring the statue's weight such that it wouldn't topple over.

In the minds of most Madrileños, the Plaza de Oriente is forever linked with Francisco Franco. The *generalísimo* liked to speak from the roof of the Royal Palace to his thousands of followers as they crammed into the plaza below. Even now, on the November anniversary of Franco's death, the plaza fills with supporters, most of whom are old-timers, though in a few recent years the occasion has drawn swastika-waving skinheads from other European countries in a chilling fascist tribute.

14 **Plaza de la Villa.** Madrid's town council has met in this medieval-looking complex since the Middle Ages, and it's now the city hall. Just two blocks west of the Plaza Mayor on Calle Mayor, it was once called Plaza de San Salvador for a church that used to stand here. The oldest building is the **Casa de los Lujanes,** on the east side—it's the one with the Mudéjar tower. Built as a private home in the late 15th century, the house carries the Lujanes crest over the main doorway. Also on the plaza's east end is the brick-and-stone **Casa de la Villa,** built in 1629, a classic example of Madrid design with its clean lines and spire-topped corner towers. Connected by an overhead walkway, the **Casa de Cisneros** was commissioned in 1537 by the nephew of Cardinal Cisneros. It's one of Madrid's rare examples of the flamboyant plateresque style, which has been likened to splashing water—a liquid exuberance wrought in stone. ✉ *C. Mayor.* ⏲ *Guided tour in Spanish Mon. at 5.*

15 **Plaza Mayor.** Austere, grand, and often surprisingly quiet compared to the rest of Madrid, this arcaded square has seen it all: autos-da-fé (trials of faith, i.e., public burnings of heretics); the canonization of saints; criminal executions; royal marriages, such as that of Princess María and the King of Hungary in 1629; bullfights (until 1847); masked balls; fireworks; and all manner of events and celebrations. It still hosts fairs, bazaars, and performances.

Measuring 360 ft by 300 ft, Madrid's Plaza Mayor is one of the largest and grandest public squares in Europe. It was designed by Juan de Herrera, the architect to Felipe II and designer of the El Escorial monastery, northwest of Madrid. Construction of the plaza lasted just two years and was finished in 1620 under Felipe III, whose equestrian statue stands in the center. The inauguration ceremonies included the canonization of four Spanish saints: Teresa of Ávila, Ignatius of Loyola, Isidro (Madrid's male patron saint), and Francis Xavier.

This space was once occupied by a city market, and many of the surrounding streets retain the names of the trades and foodstuffs once headquartered there. Nearby are Calle de Cuchilleros (Knifemakers' Street), Calle de Lechuga (Lettuce Street), Calle de Fresa (Strawberry Street), and Calle de Botoneros (Buttonmakers' Street). The plaza's oldest building is the one with the brightly painted murals and the gray spires, called Casa de la Panadería (the Bakery) in honor of the bread shop on top of which it was built. Opposite is the Casa de la Carnicería (the Butcher Shop), now a police station.

The plaza is closed to motorized traffic, making it a pleasant place to sit in the sun or while away a warm summer evening at one of the sidewalk cafés, watching alfresco artists, street musicians, and Madrileños from all walks of life. Sunday morning brings a stamp and coin market. Around Christmas the plaza fills with stalls selling trees, ornaments, and nativity scenes, as well as all types of practical jokes and tricks for December 28, *Día de los Inocentes*—a Spanish version of April Fool's Day.

❶ **Puerta del Sol.** Always crowded with both people and exhaust fumes, Sol is the nerve center of Madrid's traffic. The city's main subway interchange is below, and buses fan out through the city from here. A brass plaque in the sidewalk on the south side of the plaza marks Kilometer 0, the spot from which all distances in Spain are measured. The restored 1756 French-neoclassical building near the marker now houses the offices of the regional government, but during Franco's reign it was the headquarters of his secret police, and it's still known folklorically as the Casa de los Gritos (House of Screams). Across the square is a bronze statue of Madrid's official symbol, a bear with a *madroño* (strawberry tree), and a statue of King-Mayor Carlos III on horseback.

⓭ **San Nicolás de las Servitas** (Church of St. Nicholas of the Servitas). This church tower is one of the oldest buildings in Madrid, and there is some debate over whether it once formed part of an Arab mosque. It was more likely built after the Christian reconquest of Madrid in 1085, but the brickwork and the horseshoe arches are clear evidence that it was crafted by either Moorish workers (Mudéjars) or Spaniards well versed in the style. Inside the church, exhibits detail the Islamic history of early Madrid. ✉ *Near the Plaza de San Nicolás,* ☎ *91/559–4064.* 🎟 *Donation suggested.* ⏲ *Tues.–Sun. 6:30 AM–8:30 PM or by appointment.*

❿ **Teatro Real** (Royal Theater). This neoclassical theater was built in 1850 and was long a cultural center for Madrileño society. Plagued by disasters more recently, including fires, a bombing, and profound structural problems, the house went dark in 1988. Closed for almost a decade for indulgent restoration, it reopened to worldwide fanfare in 1997. Now replete with golden balconies, plush seats, and state-of-the-art stage equipment for operas and ballets, the theater is a modern showpiece with its vintage appeal intact. ✉ *Plaza de Isabel II,* ☎ *91/516–0600.*

❾ **Teleférico** (cable car). Kids love this cable car, which takes you from just above the Rosaleda gardens in the Parque del Oeste to the center of Casa de Campo. Be warned, however, that the walk from where the cable car drops you off to the zoo and the amusement park is at least 2 km (1 mi), and you'll have to ask directions. ✉ *Estación Terminal Teleférico, Jardines Rosaleda (at C. Marques de Urquijo),* ☎ *91/541–7450.* 🎟 *535 ptas.* ⏲ *Apr.–Sept., daily noon–sundown; Oct.–Mar., weekends noon–3 and 4–6.*

❽ **Templo de Debod.** This authentic 4th-century BC Egyptian temple was donated to Spain in gratitude for its technical assistance with the construction of the Aswan Dam. It's near the site of the former Montaña barracks, where Madrileños bloodily crushed the beginnings of a Francoist uprising in 1936. ✉ *Hill in Parque de la Montaña, near Estación del Norte,* ☎ *91/765–1008.* 💴 *300 ptas.; free Wed. and Sun.* ⏲ *Tues.–Fri. 10–1:30 and 4:30–6 (Apr.–Sept. 4:30–7:45), weekends 10–1:30.*

The Art Walk

Madrid's star cultural attractions are its three superlative art museums, all within walking distance of each other via the Paseo del Prado. The Paseo was designed by King-Mayor Carlos III as a leafy nature walk with glorious fountains and a botanical garden for respite in scorching summers. As you walk east down Carrera de San Jerónimo toward the Paseo del Prado, consider that this was the route followed by Ferdinand and Isabella, the Catholic monarchs, over 500 years ago toward the church of **San Jerónimo el Real** (✉ Moreto 4, behind Prado museum, ☎ 91/420–3078). Used by the royal couple as a *retiro,* or place of meditation—hence the name of the nearby park—the church and cloisters were devastated in the Napoleonic Wars. Rebuilt in the late 19th century, the church is now open daily 8–1:30 and 5:30–8:30.

A Good Walk

Exit the **Puerta del Sol** ① into Calle de Alcalá, and you'll find on your left the **Real Academia de Bellas Artes de San Fernando** ⑯. Take the next right, past the elegant bank buildings, into Calle Sevilla and turn left at Plaza Canalejas (where La Violeta, at No. 6, sells violet-flavored sweets) into Carrera de San Jerónimo. (If you cross the plaza into Calle Príncipe, you'll reach the Plaza Santa Ana tapas-bar area.) Walk down San Jerónimo to Plaza de las Cortes. The granite building on the left with the lions is the Congreso, lower house of the Cortes, Spain's parliament.

Carrera de San Jerónimo leads you to the **Fuente de Neptuno** ⑰ in the wide Paseo del Prado. The renowned **Museo del Prado** ⑱ is across the plaza on the right. Immediately on your left is the **Museo Thyssen-Bornemisza** ⑲, and across the plaza on the left is the elegant Ritz Hotel, alongside the obelisk to all those who have died for Spain and, farther on, the Naval Museum. Here you have a choice: tackle one or both of these major museums now, or continue strolling.

Turning right and walking south on Paseo del Prado, you'll see the **Jardín Botánico** ⑳ on the left and eventually the **Atocha** train station, worth a quick visit for its humid indoor park, complete with tropical trees, benches, paths, and a pleasant restaurant. Across the traffic circle, the immense pile of painted tiles and winged statues houses the Ministerio de Agricultura (Agriculture Ministry). The **Centro de Arte Reina Sofía** ㉑, home to Picasso's *Guernica,* is in the building with the exterior glass elevators, best accessed by walking up Calle Atocha from the station and taking the first left.

Retracing your steps to the Fuente de Neptuno, turn right between the Ritz and the Prado. Straight ahead you'll see the **Casón del Buen Retiro** ㉒, on its left the **Museo del Ejército** ㉓, and farther on the vast **Parque del Retiro** ㉔.

Turning left at the Fuente de Neptuno will take you past the **Museo Thyssen-Bornemisza** ⑲ to the **Plaza de la Cibeles** ㉕, surrounded by the **Palacio de Comunicaciones** ㉖, now the post office; the **Banco de España** ㉗; and the **Casa de América** ㉘. Turn right at Cibeles, walk up Calle Alcalá, and you'll see Madrid's unofficial symbol, the **Puerta de Alcalá** ㉙, and, again, the Parque del Retiro. About 100 yards north of Cibeles, on the Paseo de Recoletos, the grand yellow mansion on the right, now a bank headquarters, was once the home of the Marquis of Salamanca, who at the turn of the 20th century built the exclusive shopping and residential neighborhood (northeast of here) that now bears his name. Continue north for the **Museo Arqueológico** ㉚, invaluable if you'll be traveling further in Spain, and the **Plaza Colón** ㉛.

TIMING

Including a visit to the Reina Sofía and a turn in the Parque del Retiro, you can make this walk in two to three hours. Set aside a morning or an afternoon *each* for return visits to the Prado and Thyssen-Bornemisza.

Sights to See

㉗ **Banco de España.** This massive 1884 building, Spain's central bank, takes up an entire block. It is said that the nation's gold reserves are held in great vaults that stretch under the Plaza de Cibeles traffic circle all the way to the fountain. The bank is not open to visitors, but if you can dodge traffic well enough to reach the median strip in front of it, you can take a fine photo of the fountain and the palaces with the Puerta de Alcalá arch in the background.

㉘ **Casa de América.** A cultural center and art gallery focusing on Latin America, the Casa is housed in the allegedly haunted Palacio de Linares, built by a man who made his fortune in the New World and returned to a life of incestuous love and strange deaths. ✉ *Paseo Recoletos 2,* ☎ *91/595–4800.* *Palace tour 450 ptas., gallery free.* ⏲ *Gallery Tues.–Fri. 11–8, Sat. 11–7, Sun. 11–2; palace tours available Tues.–Fri. 9:30–11:30, weekends 10–1:30.*

㉒ **Casón del Buen Retiro.** This Prado annex is just a five-minute walk from the museum and is free with a Prado ticket. The building, once a ballroom, and the formal gardens in the Retiro are all that remain of Madrid's second royal complex, which filled the entire neighborhood until the early 19th century. On display are 19th-century Spanish paintings and sculpture, including works by Sorolla and Rusiñol. At press time the complex was scheduled to reopen in late 2001 after a regal restoration, with brand-new halls devoted to 17th- and 19th-century Spanish art. ✉ *C. Alfonso XII s/n,* ☎ *91/330–2867.* ⏲ *Tues.–Sat. 9–7, Sun. 9–2.*

★ ㉑ **Centro de Arte Reina Sofía** (Queen Sofia Art Center). Madrid's museum of modern art is housed in a converted hospital whose classical granite austerity is somewhat relieved (or ruined, depending on your point of view) by the two glass elevator shafts on the facade.

The collection focuses on Spain's three great modern masters: Pablo Picasso, Salvador Dalí, and Joan Miró. Take the elevator to the second floor to see the permanent collections; the other floors house visiting exhibits.

The first rooms are dedicated to the beginnings of Spain's modern movement and contain paintings from around the turn of the 20th century. The focal point is Picasso's 1901 *Woman in Blue*—hardly beautiful, but strikingly representational compared to his later works.

Moving on to the **Cubist** collection, which includes nine works by Juan Gris, be sure to see Dalí's splintered, blue-gray *Self-Portrait,* in which the artist depicts a few of his favorite things: a morning newspaper and a pack of cigarettes. The other highlight here is Picasso's *Musical Instruments on a Table,* one of many variations on this theme.

The Reina Sofía's showpiece is Picasso's famous ***Guernica,*** which occupies the center hall and is surrounded by dozens of studies for individual figures within it. The huge painting depicts the horror of the Nazi Condor Legion's bombing of the ancient Basque town of Guernica in 1937, a Civil War act that brought Spanish dictator Francisco Franco to power. The work—in many ways a 20th-century version of Goya's *The 3rd of May*—is something of a national shrine, as evidenced by the solemnity of Spaniards viewing it. The painting was not brought into Spain until 1981; Picasso, an ardent antifascist, refused to allow it to enter the country until democracy was restored.

The room in front of *Guernica* contains a collection of **surrealist** works, including six canvases by Miró, known for his childlike graphics. Opposite *Guernica* is a hall dedicated to Salvador Dalí, with paintings bequeathed to the government in the artist's will. Although Dalí is perhaps best known for works of a somewhat whimsical nature, many of these canvases are dark, haunting, and bursting with symbolism. Among the best known are *The Great Masturbator* (1929) and *The Enigma of Hitler* (1939), with its broken, dripping telephone.

The rest of the museum is devoted to more recent art, including the massive, gravity-defying sculpture *Toki Egin*, by Eduardo Chillida, considered Spain's greatest living sculptor, and five textural paintings by Barcelona artist Antoni Tàpies, whose works incorporate such materials as wrinkled sheets and straw. ✉ *Santa Isabel 52,* ☎ *91/467–5062.* 🎫 *400 ptas.; free Sat. after 2:30 and all day Sun.* ⏲ *Mon. and Wed.–Sat. 10–9, Sun. 10–2:30.*

25 **Fuente de la Cibeles** (Fountain of Cybele). A tree-lined walkway runs down the center of Paseo del Prado to the Plaza de la Cibeles, where this famous fountain depicts the nature goddess Cybele driving a chariot drawn by lions. Even more than the officially designated bear and strawberry tree, this monument, beautifully lighted at night, has come to symbolize Madrid—so much so that during the Civil War, patriotic Madrileños risked life and limb to sandbag it as Nationalist aircraft bombed the city.

17 **Fuente de Neptuno** (Neptune's Fountain). Just outside the Palace Hotel and the boutiques-filled Galerias del Prado, on the Plaza Canovas del Castillo, this fountain is at the hub of Madrid's Paseo del Arte, made up chiefly of the redbrick Prado Museum, stretched along the east side of the boulevard; the Thyssen-Bornemisza Museum, across the plaza; and, five blocks to the south, the Reina Sofía art center.

20 **Jardín Botánico** (Botanical Garden). Just south of the Prado Museum, the gardens provide a pleasant place to stroll or sit under the trees. True to the wishes of King Carlos III, they hold an array of plants, flowers, and cacti from around the world. ✉ *Plaza de Murillo 2,* ☎ *91/420–3017.* 🎫 *250 ptas.* ⏲ *Summer, daily 10–9; winter, daily 10–6.*

30 **Museo Arqueológico** (Museum of Archaeology). The museum shares its neoclassical building with the **Biblioteca Nacional** (National Library). The biggest attraction here is a replica of the prehistoric cave paintings in Altamira, Cantabria, located underground in the garden. (Access to the real thing is highly restricted.) Inside the museum, look for the *Dama de Elche,* a bust of a wealthy, 4th-century Iberian woman, and notice that her headgear is a rough precursor to the mantillas and hair combs still associated with traditional Spanish dress. The ancient Visigothic votive crowns are another highlight, discovered in 1859 near Toledo and believed to date back to the 8th century. ✉ *C. Serrano 13,* ☎ *91/577–7912.* 🎫 *500 ptas.; free Sat. after 2:30 and all day Sun.* ⏲ *Museum Tues.–Sat. 9:30–8:30, Sun. 9:30–2:30; reproduction cave paintings, Tues.–Sat. 11–2:30 and 5:30–6:30, Sun. 11–2:30.*

23 **Museo del Ejército** (Army Museum). A real treat for arms-and-armor buffs, this place is right on the museum mile. Among the 27,000 items

on view are a sword that allegedly belonged to the Spanish hero El Cid; suits of armor; bizarre-looking pistols with barrels capable of holding scores of bullets; Moorish tents; and a cross carried by Christopher Columbus. It's an unusually entertaining collection. ✉ *Mendez Nuñez 1,* ☎ *91/522–8977.* *100 ptas.* ⊙ *Tues.–Sun. 10–2.*

★ ⓲ **Museo del Prado** (Prado Museum). When the Prado was commissioned by King-Mayor Carlos III, in 1785, it was meant to be a natural-science museum. The king, popularly remembered as "Madrid's best mayor," wanted the museum, the adjoining botanical gardens, and the elegant Paseo del Prado to serve as a center of scientific enlightenment for his subjects. By the time the building was completed in 1819, its purpose had changed to exhibiting the vast collection of art gathered by Spanish royalty since the time of Ferdinand and Isabella. The museum is now adding a massive new wing, designed by Rafael Moneo, that will resurrect long-hidden works by Zurbarán and Pereda and more than double the number of paintings on display from the permanent collection.

Painting is one of Spain's greatest contributions to world culture, and the Prado's jewels are its works by the nation's three great masters: Francisco Goya, Diego Velázquez, and El Greco. The museum also holds masterpieces by Flemish and Italian artists, collected when their lands were part of the Spanish Empire. The museum benefited greatly from the anticlerical laws of 1836, which forced monasteries, convents, and churches to forfeit many of their artworks for public display.

Enter the Prado via the Goya entrance, with steps opposite the Ritz Hotel, or the less-crowded Murillo door opposite the Jardín Botánico. The layout varies (grab a floor plan), but the first halls on the left, coming from the Goya entrance (7A to 11 on the second floor, or *primera planta*) are usually devoted to **17th-century Flemish painters** including Peter Paul Rubens (1577–1640), Jacob Jordaens (1593–1678), and Antony van Dyck (1599–1641).

Room 12 introduces you to the meticulous brushwork of **Velázquez** (1599–1660) in his numerous portraits of kings and queens. Look for the magnificent *Las Hilanderas* (*The Spinners*), evidence of the artist's talent for painting light. The Prado's most famous canvas, Velázquez's *Las Meninas* (*The Maids of Honor*), combines a self-portrait of the artist at work with a mirror reflection of the king and queen in a revolutionary interplay of space and perspectives. Picasso was obsessed with this work and painted several copies of it in his own abstract style, now on display in the Picasso Museum in Barcelona.

The south ends of the second and top floors (*planta primera* and *planta segunda*) are reserved for **Goya** (1746–1828), whose works span a staggering range of tone, from bucolic to horrific. Among his early masterpieces are portraits of the family of King Carlos IV, for whom he was court painter—one glance at their unflattering and imbecilic expressions, especially in the painting *The Family of Carlos IV,* reveals the loathing Goya developed for these self-indulgent, reactionary rulers. His famous side-by-side canvases, *The Clothed Maja* and *The Nude Maja,* may represent the young duchess of Alba, whom Goya adored and frequently painted. No one knows whether she ever returned his affection. The adjacent rooms house a series of idyllic scenes of Spaniards at play, painted as designs for tapestries.

Goya's paintings took on political purpose starting in 1808, when the population of Madrid rose up against occupying French troops. *The 2nd of May* portrays the insurrection at the Puerta del Sol, and its even more terrifying companion piece, *The 3rd of May,* depicts the nighttime executions of patriots who had rebelled the day before. The garish light effects in this work typify the romantic style, which favors drama over detail, and make it one of the most powerful indictments of violence ever committed to canvas.

Goya's "black paintings" are dark, disturbing works, completed late in his life, that reflect his inner turmoil after losing his hearing and his deep embitterment over the bloody War of Independence. These are copies of the monstrous hallucinatory paintings Goya made with marvelously free brush strokes on the walls of his house by the Río Manzanares, south of Madrid. Having grown terribly ill in his old age, Goya was deaf, lonely, bitter, and despairing; his terrifying *Saturn Devouring One of his Sons* probably represents the cruel, destructive forces of age and time.

Near the Goya entrance, the Prado's ground floor (*planta baja*) is filled with 15th- and 16th-century Flemish paintings, including the bizarre masterpiece *Garden of Earthly Delights,* by Hieronymous Bosch, recently restored. Next come Rooms 60A, 61A, and 62A, filled with the passionately spiritual works of **El Greco** (Doménikos Theotokópoulos, 1541–1614), the Greek-born artist who lived and worked in Toledo. El Greco is known for his mystical, elongated faces. His style was quite shocking to a public accustomed to strictly representational images; because he wanted his art to provoke emotion, El Greco is sometimes called the world's first "modern" painter. Two of his greatest paintings, *The Resurrection* and *The Adoration of the Shepherds,* are on view here. Before you leave, stop in the 14th- to 16th-century Italian rooms to see Titian's *Portrait of Emperor Charles V* and Raphael's exquisite *Portrait of a Cardinal.* ✉ *Paseo del Prado s/n,* ☎ *91/420–3768.* *500 ptas.; free Sat. after 2:30 and all day Sun.* ⏲ *Tues.–Sat. 9–7, Sun. 9–2. www.museoprado.mcu.es*

NEED A BREAK?

La Dolores (✉ Plaza de Jesús 4) is one of Madrid's most atmospheric old tiled bars, the perfect place for a beer or glass of wine and a plate of olives. It's a great alternative to the Prado's basement cafeteria and is just across the Paseo, then one block up on Calle Lope de Vega.

⓲ **Museo Thyssen-Bornemisza.** Madrid's third and newest art center, with lots of space and natural light, occupies the Villahermosa Palace, finished in 1771. This ambitious collection of 800 paintings traces the history of Western art through examples from every important movement, beginning with 13th-century Italy.

The works were gathered from the 1920s on by industrialist Baron Hans Heinrich Thyssen-Bornemisza and his father. At the urging of his Spanish wife (a former Miss Spain), the baron agreed to donate the collection to Spain. Critics have described the collection as the minor works of major artists and the major works of minor artists, but the museum itself is beautiful, and its Impressionist paintings are the only ones on display in the country.

One of the high points here is Hans Holbein's *Portrait of Henry VIII* (purchased from the late Princess Diana's grandfather, who used the money to buy a new Bugatti sports car). American artists are also well represented; look for the Gilbert Stuart portrait of George Washington's cook, and note how closely the composition and rendering resembles the artist's famous painting of the Founding Father himself. Two halls are devoted to the Impressionists and post-Impressionists, including many works by Pissarro and a few each by Renoir, Monet, Degas, Van Gogh, and Cézanne.

Within 20th-century art, the baron shows a proclivity for terror-filled (albeit dynamic and colorful) German expressionism, but there are also some soothing works by Georgia O'Keeffe and Andrew Wyeth. ✉ *Paseo del Prado 8,* ☎ *91/369–0151.* 💵 *700 ptas.* ⏲ *Tues.–Sun. 10–7.*

26 **Palacio de Comunicaciones.** This ornate building on the southeast side of Plaza de Cibeles is Madrid's main post office. ⏲ *Stamps weekdays 9 AM–10 PM, Sat. 9–8, Sun. 10–1; phone, telex, telegrams, and fax weekdays 8 AM–midnight, weekends 8 AM–10 PM.*

★ 24 **Parque del Retiro** (literally, the Retreat). Once the private playground of royalty, Madrid's crowning park is a vast expanse of green encompassing formal gardens, fountains, lakes, exhibition halls, children's play areas, outdoor cafés, and a **Puppet Theater,** featuring free slapstick routines that even non–Spanish speakers will enjoy. Shows take place on Saturday at 1 and on Sunday at 1, 6, and 7. The park is especially lively on weekends, when it fills with street musicians, jugglers, clowns, gypsy fortune-tellers, and sidewalk painters along with hundreds of Spanish families out for a walk. The park hosts a monthlong book fair in May and occasional flamenco concerts in summer.

From the entrance at the Puerta de Alcalá, head straight toward the center and you'll find the **Estanque** (lake), presided over by a grandiose equestrian statue of King Alfonso XII, erected by his mother. Just behind the lake, north of the statue, is one of the best of the park's many cafés. If you're feeling energetic, you can rent a boat and work up an appetite just rowing around the lake.

The 19th-century **Palacio de Cristal** (Crystal Palace), southeast of the Estanque, was built to house a collection of exotic plants from the Philippines, a Spanish possession at the time. This airy marvel of steel and glass sits on a base of decorative tile. Next door is a small lake with ducks and swans. At the south end of the park, along the Paseo del Uruguay, is the **Rosaleda** (rose garden), an English garden bursting with color and heavy with floral scents for most of the summer. West of the Rosaleda, look for a statue called the **Ángel Caído** (Fallen Angel), which Madrileños claim is the only one in the world depicting the prince of darkness before (during, actually) his fall from grace.

31 **Plaza Colón.** This modern plaza is named for Christopher Columbus. A statue of the explorer (identical to one in Barcelona's port) looks west from a high tower in the middle of the square. Beneath the massive plaza is the **Centro Cultural de la Villa** (☎ 91/575–6080), a new performing-arts facility. Behind Plaza Colón is **Calle Serrano,** the city's premier shopping street (think Gucci, Prada, and Loewe). Take a stroll in either direction on Serrano for some window-shopping.

NEED A BREAK?

El Espejo comprises two classy bars near the Plaza Colón—one in an original Belle Epoque setting on a side street, the other in a splendid pavilion of glass and wrought iron in the middle of the Paseo de Recoletos. Pull up a chair on the shady terrace or sit in the air-conditioned, stained-glass bar to rest your feet and sip a cup of coffee or a beer. ✉ *Paseo de Recoletos 31,* ☎ *91/308–2347.* ⏲ *Daily 10 AM–2 AM.*

29 **Puerta de Alcalá.** This triumphal arch was built by Carlos III in 1778 to mark the site of one of the ancient city gates. You can still see the bomb damage inflicted on the arch during the civil war.

16 **Real Academia de Bellas Artes de San Fernando** (St. Ferdinand Academy of Fine Arts). Designed by Churriguera in the waning Baroque years of the early 18th century, this little-visited museum is a showcase of painting and, to a lesser extent, the decorative arts. The same build-

ing houses the **Instituto de Calcografía** (Prints Institute), which sells limited-edition prints from original plates engraved by Spanish artists, including Goya. ✉ *Alcalá 13,* ☎ *91/522–0046.* 🎟 *400 ptas.; free weekends.* ⏲ *Tues.–Fri. 9:30–7, Sat.–Mon. 9:30–2.*

Old Madrid

Plaza Mayor ⑮. Looking up at the erotic mural, exit under the large arch to the far left and walk down Ciudad Rodrigo, then turn left. Across the road is a restored market; down **Cava de San Miguel** ㉜ you'll see tapas bars that go deep into caves under the Plaza Mayor. The entrance to **Las Cuevas de Luis Candelas** (☞ Dining, *below*) is on the left, by the steps up to the Plaza Mayor. Farther down, at Cuchilleros 17, is the historic restaurant Botín. Cross the Plaza de Puerta Cerrada and you'll see an alleyway, Nuncio, on the right: down here on the left is the **Palacio de la Nunciatura.**

Nuncio widens, and on your left at No. 17 is the Taberna de Cien Vinos (☞ Nightlife and the Arts, *below*), a good place to sample Spanish wine. Opposite the tavern is the church of San Pedro el Viejo (St. Peter the Elder), one of Madrid's oldest, with a Mudéjar tower. Bear right and enter Príncipe Anglona to enter **Plaza de la Paja** ㉝. Down on the right is the **Costanilla de San Andrés,** which leads to Calle Segovia and a view of the viaduct above. At the top of Plaza de la Paja is the church of San Andrés; turn right after the church down Carrera San Francisco to visit the **Basílica de San Francisco el Grande** ㉞. Backtrack and turn left after San Andrés down **Cava Baja**—this curving street is packed with bars and restaurants. Casa Lucio, at No. 35, is a favorite of the king; opposite is La Solea, with late-night jazz and, upstairs, flamenco singing. La Chata at No. 24, is a fun Madrid *tasca* (tavern). Continue straight ahead to return to Plaza Mayor.

TIMING

This 90-minute walk requires some short uphill climbs through the winding streets. Allow ample time for stops to absorb the Old World charm—especially in summer, when heat will be a factor.

Sights to See

㉞ **Basílica de San Francisco el Grande.** In 1760, Carlos III built this impressive basilica on the site of a Franciscan convent, allegedly founded by St. Francis of Assisi in 1217. The dome, 108 ft in diameter, is the largest in Spain, even larger than that of St. Paul's in London, where its 19 bells were cast in 1882. The seven main doors were carved of American walnut by Casa Juan Guas. Three chapels adjoin the circular church, the most famous being that of **San Bernardino de Siena,** which contains a Goya masterpiece depicting a preaching San Bernardino. The figure standing on the right, not looking up, is a self-portrait of Goya. The 16th-century Gothic choir stalls came from La Cartuja del Paular, in rural Segovia province. ✉ *Pl. de San Francisco,* ☎ *91/365–3400.* 🎟 *Free.* ⏲ *Tues.–Fri. 11–12:30 and 4–6:30.*

★ ㉜ **Cava de San Miguel.** The narrow, picturesque streets behind the Plaza de la Villa are well worth exploring. From the Plaza Mayor, turn onto the Plaza de San Miguel, with the glass-and-iron San Miguel market on your right. Proceed down Cava de San Miguel past the row of **ancient tapas bars** built right into the retaining wall of the plaza above. Each one specializes in a different food: *Mesón de champiñones* (mushrooms), *Mesón de boquerónes* (anchovies), *Mesón de tortilla* (excellent Spanish omelets), and so on. Madrileños and travelers alike flock here each evening to sample the food and sing along with raucous musicians, who delight in playing non-Spanish tunes for the presumed delight of tourists.

Costanilla de San Andrés. This ramped street leads up from Calle Segovia to the heart of the old city, the Plaza de la Paja. Look down the narrow Calle Príncipe Anglona for a good view of the Mudéjar tower on the church of **San Pedro el Viejo** (St. Peter the Elder), one of the city's oldest. The brick tower is believed to have been built in 1354 following the Christian reconquest of Algeciras, near Gibraltar. Notice the tiny defensive slits, designed to accommodate crossbows.

Las Cuevas de Luis Candelas. The oldest of Madrid's taverns, about halfway down Cava de San Miguel, is named for a 19th-century Madrid version of Robin Hood, famous for his ingenious ways of tricking the rich out of their money and jewels. As Cava de San Miguel becomes Calle Cuchilleros, you'll see **Botín** on the left, Madrid's oldest restaurant and a onetime haunt of Ernest Hemingway (☞ Dining, *below*). The curving Cuchilleros was once a moat just outside the city walls. The plaza with the bright murals at the intersection of Calle Segovia is called the **Puerta Cerrada** (✉ Cava San Miguel and Calle Cuchilleros), or Closed Gate, named for the city gate that once stood here.

Palacio de la Nunciatura (Palace of the Nunciat). Near the Plaza Puerta Cerrada off Calle Segovia, one of Madrid's main medieval streets, this mansion once housed the Pope's ambassadors to Spain. It's not open to the public, but you can peek inside the Renaissance garden. ✉ *Costanilla del Nuncio s/n.*

NEED A BREAK? The **Café del Nuncio** (✉ Costanilla del Nuncio s/n), on the corner of Calle Segovia, is a relaxing Old World place for a coffee or beer against a backdrop of classical music.

33 **Plaza de la Paja.** Located at the top of the hill, on Costanilla San Andrés, the Plaza de la Paja was the most important square in medieval Madrid. Although a few upscale restaurants have moved in, this little square retains its own atmosphere. The plaza's jewel is the **Capilla del Obispo** (Bishop's Chapel), built between 1520 and 1530; this was where peasants deposited their tithes, called *diezmas*—literally, one-tenth of their crop. The stacks of wheat on the chapel's ceramic tiles refer to this tradition. Architecturally, the chapel marks a transition from the blockish Gothic period, which gave the structure its basic shape, to the Renaissance, the source of the decorations. Try to get inside to see the intricately carved polychrome altarpiece by Francisco Giralta, featuring scenes from the life of Christ. Opening hours are erratic; the best time to visit is during mass or on feast days.

The chapel forms part of the complex of the domed church of **San Andrés,** built to house the remains of Madrid's male patron saint, San Isidro Labrador. Isidro was a peasant who worked fields belonging to the Vargas family. The 16th-century **Vargas palace** forms the eastern side of the Plaza de la Paja. According to legend, St. Isidro actually worked little but had the best-tended fields thanks to many hours of prayer. When Señor Vargas came out to investigate the phenomenon, Isidro made a spring of sweet water spurt from the ground to quench his master's thirst. Because St. Isidro's power had to do with water, his remains were paraded through the city in times of drought in the hope that he would bring rain, as recently as the turn of the 20th century.

Castizo Madrid

The Spanish word *castizo* means "authentic," and *los Madrileños castizos* are the Spanish equivalent of London's cockneys. There are few "sights" in the usual sense on this route; instead, you wander through some of Madrid's most traditional and lively neighborhoods. Within these are a growing number of recent immigrants and the attendant employment problems. Muggings are not uncommon, so think twice about this walk if you don't feel reasonably streetwise.

A Good Walk

Begin at the **Plaza Santa Ana** ㉟, the hub of the theater district in the 17th century and now a center of nocturnal activity, not all of it desirable. The dusty plaza is rimmed by a number of notable buildings, including the **Teatro Español** and the tiled **Casa de Guadalajara.** Walk east two blocks on Calle del Prado and turn right on Calle León, named for a lion kept here long ago by a resident Moor. One block on this street brings you to the corner of **Calle Cervantes,** where the author of *Don Quixote* and the "Spanish Shakespeare" lived in what are now called the **Casa de Cervantes** ㊱ and the **Casa de Lope de Vega.**

One block farther on Calle León, turn left on Calle de las Huertas, the premier bar strip in bar-speckled Madrid. One block down Huertas, turn right onto Calle Amor de Dios and walk to its end, at the busy Calle Atocha. Across the street you'll see the church of **San Nicolás.** To the left of the church, walk down **Pasaje Doré** through the Anton Martín morning market, a colorful assortment of market stalls typical of most Madrid neighborhoods.

Turn right on Calle Santa Isabel, by the **Cine Doré** ㊲, and take your first left on Calle de la Rosa—which, after a jog to the right, becomes Calle de la Cabeza. You'll pass the restaurant Casa Lastra (☞ Dining, *below*). On the southwest corner with Calle Lavapiés is the site of the **Cárcel de la Inquisición** ㊳. Turn left here: this is the beginning of the **Barrio Lavapiés,** Madrid's old *Judería* (Jewish Quarter). Lavapiés remains one of Madrid's most castizo working-class neighborhoods, though gentrification is beginning to creep in; the streets have been recobbled, and lighting improved. Explore side streets off Calle Lavapiés, then continue down and south until you reach the heart of the neighborhood, **Plaza Lavapiés** ㊴.

Leave the plaza heading west on Calle Sombrerete. After two blocks you'll reach the intersection of Calle Mesón de Paredes, on which corner you'll see a lovingly preserved example of a popular Madrid architecture, the **Corrala building** ㊵. Life in this type of balconied apartment building is very public, with laundry flapping in the breeze, babies crying, and old women gossiping over the railings. Neighbors once shared common kitchen and bath facilities in the patio.

Work your way west, crossing Calle de Embajadores into the neighborhood known as **El Rastro** ㊶—a shopper's paradise, with streets of small family stores selling furniture, antiques, and a cornucopia of used junk (some of it greatly overpriced). On Sunday, El Rastro becomes a flea market, and Calle de Ribera de Curtidores, the steep main drag, is closed to traffic, jammed with outdoor booths, shoppers, and pickpockets.

TIMING

Allow at least three hours. The point of this walk is really the atmosphere. Any weekday morning is a good time to browse the Anton Martín market; the streets surrounding the Plaza Santa Ana are more interesting after dark, as they're lined with some of Madrid's best tapas bars and nightspots. El Rastro can be saved for a Sunday morning if you decide to brave the crowds at the flea market.

Sights to See

Barrio Lavapiés. The Barrio Lavapiés is the old *Judería.* Like Moors, Jews were forced to live outside the city walls after the Christian reconquest hit Madrid in 1085, and this was one of the suburbs they founded.

38 **Cárcel de la Inquisición** (Inquisition Jail). Unmarked by any historical plaque, the former jail at the southeast corner of Calle Cabeza and Calle Lavapiés is now a large tapas bar, the **Taberna del Avapiés,** named for the old Jewish quarter. Here Jews, Moors, and others designated unrepentant heathens or sinners bent to the inquisitors' whims; the prison later became a Cárcel de la Corona (Crown Prison) for the incarceration of wayward soldiers, priests, and nuns. Ask a bartender if you can see the original, two-story medieval patio out back—it's tiny, but highly evocative.

36 **Casa de Cervantes.** A plaque marks the house where the author of *Don Quixote* lived and died. Miguel de Cervantes' 1605 epic story of the man with the impossible dream is one of the most widely translated and read books in the world. ✉ *C. Cervantes and C. León.*

Casa de Lope de Vega. The home of Lope de Vega, a contemporary of Cervantes', has been turned into a museum that shows how a house of that period was typically furnished. Considered the Shakespeare of Spanish literature, Lope de Vega (1562–1635) wrote some 1,800 plays and enjoyed great success during his lifetime. ✉ *C. Cervantes 11,* ☎ *91/429–9216.* 🎟 *200 ptas.* ⏲ *Sept.–July, weekdays 9:30–2, Sat. 10–2.*

NEED A BREAK?

Taberna de Antonio Sánchez. Drop into Madrid's oldest bar for a glass of wine and some tapas, or just a peek. The dark walls (lined with bullfighting paintings), zinc bar, and pulley system used to lift casks of wine from the cellar look much the same as they did when the place first opened in 1830. Meals are also served in a dining room in the back. Specialties include *rabo de buey* (bull's-tail stew) and *morcillo al horno* (a beef stew). ✉ *Mesón de Paredes 13.*

37 **Cine Doré.** A rare example of Art Nouveau architecture in Madrid, the hip Cine Doré shows movies from the Spanish National Film Archives and eclectic foreign films, usually in the original language. Show times are listed in newspapers under FILMOTECA. The lobby, trimmed with smart pink neon, has a sleek café-bar and a good bookshop. ✉ *C. Santa Isabel 3,* ☎ *91/369–1125.* ⏲ *Tues.–Sun.; hrs vary depending on show times.*

40 **Corrala building.** This structure is not unlike the *corrales* that were used as Madrid's early theaters; there's even a plaque here to remind you that the setting for the famous 19th-century *zarzuela* (light opera) *La Revoltosa* was a *corrala* like this one. City-sponsored musical-theater events are occasionally held here in summer. The ruins across the street were once the **Escalopíos de San Fernando,** one of several churches and parochial schools that fell victim to anti-Catholic sentiments in this neighborhood during the Civil War. ✉ *C. Mesón de Paredes and C. Sombrerete.*

41 **El Rastro.** Filled with tiny shops selling antiques and all manner of used stuff, some of it junk, the Rastro becomes an overcrowded flea market on Sunday morning from 10 to 2. The best time to explore is any other morning, when a little browsing and bargaining are likely to turn up such treasures as old iron grillwork, marble tabletops, or gilt picture frames. The main street of the Rastro is Ribera de Curtidores; the best streets for browsing are the ones to the west (☞ Shopping, *below*).

39 **Plaza Lavapiés.** The heart of the historic Jewish *barrio,* this picturesque plaza remains a neighborhood hub. To the left is the Calle de la Fe (Street of Faith), which was called Calle Sinagoga until the expulsion of the

Jews in 1492. The church of **San Lorenzo** at the end was built on the site of the razed synagogue. Legend has it that Jews and Moors who chose baptism over exile were forced to walk up this street barefoot to the ceremony to demonstrate the sincerity of their new faith. ✉ *Top of C. de la Fe.*

35 **Plaza Santa Ana.** This plaza was the heart of the theater district in the 17th century—the golden age of Spanish literature—and is now the center of Madrid's thumping nightlife. A statue of 15th-century playwright Pedro Calderón de la Barca delivering one of his own lines faces the **Teatro Español.** Inscribed with the names of Spain's greatest playwrights and rebuilt in 1980 following a fire, the theater stands in the same place where plays were performed as early as the 16th century, at that time in a rowdy outdoor setting called a *corrala.* These makeshift theaters were usually installed in a vacant lot between two apartment buildings, and families with balconies overlooking the action rented out seats to wealthy patrons of the arts. Opposite the theater, the **Villa Rosa,** with a facade of ceramic tile, is currently a popular nightspot. The **Hotel Reina Victoria** was not always so upscale but has always been favored by bullfighters, including Manolete. Off to the side of the hotel is the diminutive **Plaza del Ángel,** home to one of Madrid's best jazz clubs, the Café Central. Back on the Plaza Santa Ana is one of Madrid's most famous cafés, the **Cervecería Alemana,** another Hemingway hangout. It still attracts struggling writers, poets, and beer drinkers.

San Nicolás. The predecessor of this plain, modern church was burned in 1936, a story vividly described by writer Arturo Barea in his autobiographical book *The Forge.* Little of the original structure remains. Like many other churches during that turbulent period, the original church of St. Nicholas fell to the wrath of working-class crowds who felt they were the victims of centuries of clerical oppression. ✉ *C. Atocha and Plaza Anton Martín.*

DINING

Madrileños tend to eat their meals even later than other Spaniards, and that's saying something. Restaurants generally open for lunch at 1:30 and fill up by 3. Dinnertime begins at 9, but reservations for 11 are common, and a meal can be a wonderfully lengthy (up to three hours) affair. Restaurants perform equally well at lunchtime, when most places offer a *menú del día* (daily fixed-price special), which includes a main course, wine, dessert, wine, and coffee. If you're not a night owl, make the most of the early-evening tapas hour and try to defy your body clock for at least one night: a late dinner here is the only kind.

Dress in most Madrid restaurants and tapas bars is casual but stylish. Compared to, say, Barcelona, the pricier places are a bit more formal; men often wear jackets and ties, and women often wear skirts.

$$$$ ★ ✕ **Casino de Madrid–La Terraza.** This rooftop terrace just off Puerta del Sol offers two rare opportunities: to see the richly ornamented interior of one of Madrid's oldest and most exclusive clubs (the Casino was a club for gentlemen, not gamblers), and to sample the culinary inventions of Ferrán Adriá, one of the most inventive chefs in Europe. Adriá is not present—he runs his own famous restaurant, El Bulli, near Roses in Catalonia (☞ Chapter 6)—but his exquisite dishes are. His trademarks are the lightest and tastiest of mousses, and ravioli in rare flavors that explode in the mouth. For the gamut of epicurean titillation, splurge on the 11-plate tasting menu, 10,000 ptas. per gastronome. On warm evenings the terrace is stunning. ✉ *Alcalá 15,* ☎

91/532–1275. Reservations essential. AE, DC, MC, V. Closed Sun. and Aug. No lunch Sat.

$$$$ ★ ✕ **Horcher.** Housed in a luxurious mansion at the edge of the Parque del Retiro, this classic restaurant is renowned for hearty but elegant fare served with impeccable style. Specialties include the kinds of game dishes traditionally favored by Spanish aristocracy: wild boar, venison, roast wild duck with almond croquettes. The star appetizer is lobster salad with truffles. Dishes like Stroganoff with mustard, pork chops with sauerkraut, and *baumkuchen* (a chocolate-covered fruit and cake dessert) reflect the restaurant's Germanic roots. (The Horcher family operated a restaurant in Berlin at the turn of the 20th century.) The intimate dining room is decorated with rust-colored brocade and antique Austrian porcelain, and a wide selection of French and German wines rounds out the menu. Jacket and tie are required. ✉ *Alfonso XII 6,* ☎ *91/522–0731. Reservations essential. AE, DC, MC, V. Closed Sun. and Aug. No lunch Sat.*

$$$$ ✕ **Lhardy.** Serving Madrid specialties in the same central location for more than 150 years, Lhardy looks pretty much the same as it must have on day one, with its dark-wood paneling, brass chandeliers, and red-velvet chairs. The menu offers international fare, but most diners come for the traditional cocido a la madrileña and callos a la madrileña. Game, sea bass in champagne sauce, and dessert soufflés are also finely prepared. The dining rooms are upstairs; the ground-floor entry doubles as a delicatessen and stand-up coffee bar that fills on chilly winter mornings with shivering souls sipping steaming-hot *caldo* (chicken broth) from silver urns. ✉ *Carrera de San Jerónimo 8,* ☎ *91/522–2207. AE, DC, MC, V. No dinner Sun.*

$$$$ ✕ **Pedro Larumbe.** This excellent restaurant is literally the pinnacle of the ABC shopping center between Paseo de Castellana and Calle Serrano. Dining quarters include a lovely summer roof terrace, which is glassed in for the winter, and an Andalusian patio. Chef-owner Pedro Larumbe is known for his presentations of such contemporary dishes as *cazuela de cocochas con patatas al pil-pil,* a casserole of tender cheeks of hake, cooked in their own juices combined with oil and garlic, and served with potatoes. There's a salad bar at lunchtime, and the dessert buffet is an art exhibit. Good wine list. ✉ *Castellana 34/Serrano 61,* ☎ *91/575–1112. AE, DC, MC, V. Closed Sun., Easter wk, and 2 wks in Aug. No lunch Sat.*

$$$$ ✕ **Viridiana.** The trendiest of Madrid's top restaurants, Viridiana has a relaxed, somewhat cramped bistro atmosphere and black-and-white decor punctuated by prints from Luis Buñuel's classic anticlerical film (for which the place is named). Iconoclast chef Abraham Garcia says "market-based" is too narrow a description for his creative menu, though the list does change every two weeks depending on what's locally available. You might find red onions stuffed with *morcilla* (black pudding); soft flour tortillas wrapped around marinated fresh tuna; or filet mignon in white truffle sauce. If it's available, try the superb duck pâté drizzled with sherry and served with Tokay wine. The tangy grapefruit sherbet is a marvel. ✉ *Juan de Mena 14,* ☎ *91/531–5222. Reservations essential. AE, DC, MC, V. Closed Sun., Holy Week, and Aug.*

$$$$ ★ ✕ **Zalacaín.** A deep-apricot color scheme, set off by dark wood and gleaming silver, makes this restaurant look like an exclusive villa. Zalacaín introduced nouvelle cuisine to Spain and continues to set the pace 20 years later. Splurge on dishes like prawn salad in avocado vinaigrette, scallops and leeks in Albariño wine, and roast pheasant with truffles; or sample the chef's own choices with a tasting menu. Service is somewhat stuffy, and jackets are required. ✉ *Alvarez de Baena 4,* ☎ *91/561–5935. Reservations essential. AE, DC, V. Closed Sun., Aug., and Holy Week. No lunch Sat.*

$$$ ✕ **Asador Frontón.** This popular, long-established Basque restaurant serves some of the most outstanding meat and fish in Madrid. It has a few satellites now, but the original is more old-fashioned, and still has a jolly waitstaff—unusual in Spain. Appetizers include *anchoa fresca* (fresh grilled anchovies) and *pimientos rellenos con bacalao* (peppers stuffed with cod). The huge, delicious *chuleton* (T-bone steak), seared on a charcoal grill and lightly sprinkled with sea salt, is for two or more; order *cogollo de lechuga* (lettuce hearts) or another vegetable to accompany. The tender *cocochas de merluza* (hake morsels in green parsley sauce) are deliciously light. ✉ *Tirso de Molina 7 (upstairs at back),* ☎ *91/369–1617. Reservations essential. AE, DC, MC, V. Closed Sun.*

$$$ ✕ **Ciao.** Always noisy and packed with happy diners, Ciao is Madrid's best Italian restaurant. Homemade pastas, like tagliatelle with wild mushrooms and *panzarotti* stuffed with spinach and ricotta, are popular as inexpensive main courses; but the kitchen also turns out credible versions of osso buco and veal scallopini, accompanied by a good selection of Italian wines. The decor—mirrored walls and sleek black furniture—convincingly evokes fashionable Milan. A second location (✉ Apodaca 20, ☎ 91/447–0036), run by the owner's sons and daughter, also serves pizza. ✉ *Argensola 7,* ☎ *91/308–2519. Reservations essential. AE, DC, MC, V. Closed Sun. No lunch Sat.*

$$$ ✕ **El Borbollón.** For nearly two decades the friendly Castro family has run this elegant yet comfortable restaurant and bar between Paseo de Recoletos and Calle Serrano, decorated with pink tablecloths, fresh flowers, and paintings of country scenes. Chef Eduardo prepares French-Basque cuisine, with specialties including various crepes, *carré* (a prime cutlet or chop) of lamb, fresh sea bass, turbot, and hake, plus rich game dishes in season. Alfonso Castro, the knowledgeable sommelier, offers good wines and brandies. Dinner reservations are wise; at lunchtime, there's food at the bar. ✉ *Recoletos 7,* ☎ *91/431–4134. AE, DC, MC, V. Closed Sun. and Aug.*

$$$ ★ ✕ **El Cenador del Prado.** The name means "The Prado Dining Room," and the settings are a Baroque salon and a plant-filled conservatory. The Cenador's innovative menu has French and Asian touches, as well as exotic Spanish dishes that rarely appear in restaurants. The house specialty is *patatas a la importancia* (sliced potatoes fried in a sauce of garlic, parsley, and clams); other possibilities include shellfish consommé with ginger ravioli, veal and eggplant in béchamel, and venison with prunes. For dessert try the *bartolillos,* custard-filled pastries. ✉ *C. del Prado 4,* ☎ *91/429–1561. AE, DC, MC, V. Closed Sun. and Aug. 1–15. No lunch Sat.*

$$$ ★ ✕ **El Pescador.** Locals swear that seafood served in Madrid is fresher than in the coastal towns where it was caught. That's probably an exaggeration, but El Pescador, one of Madrid's most respected seafood restaurants, makes it seem plausible. Stop for a drink at the bar and savor the aromas wafting from the kitchen, where skilled chefs dressed in fishermen's smocks prepare shellfish just behind the counter. Among the tapas, the *salpicón de mariscos* (mussels, lobster, shrimp, and onions in vinaigrette) is incredible. The best dish on the dinner menu is *lenguado Evaristo* (grilled sole), named for the restaurant's owner. When it's busy, the place can be cheerful and noisy, with dockside-rustic decor: lobster-pot lamps, red-and-white-check tablecloths, and rough-hewn posts and beams. Unfortunately, the aging waiters can be disagreeably surly. ✉ *José Ortega y Gasset 75,* ☎ *91/402–1290. MC, V. Closed Sun. and Aug.*

$$$ ✕ **Ginza Sushi Bar.** Madrid's first Japanese sushi bar, Ginza opened at the end of 1999, handily located opposite American Express and the Palace Hotel, near the Thyssen and Prado museums. The conveyor belt does a brisk business, with plates priced between 200 and 850 ptas., and there's

a sit-down restaurant upstairs. The staff is cheerful, and Spain's fresh fish is perfect for the tasty morsels. You can reserve seats at the bar. ✉ *Plaza de las Cortes 3,* ☎ *91/429–7619. AE, DC, MC, V. Closed Mon.*

$$$ ✕ **Iroco.** This large, stylish, green-walled establishment is popular with businesspeople at the lunch hour and trendy folk in the evening. In summer, reservations are essential for tables on the garden patio, where Crown Prince Felipe has been spotted. The *nueva cocina* (nouvelle cuisine) is well presented, and the set lunch menu is good value. Classic dishes include prawn rolls, hake in green asparagus sauce, and chocolate mousse. ✉ *Velázquez 18,* ☎ *91/431–7381. Reservations essential. AE, DC, MC, V.*

$$$ ✕ **La Cava Real.** Wine connoisseurs love the intimate atmosphere of this small bar-restaurant, which was Madrid's first true wine bar when it opened in 1983. Still part of Spain's largest wine club (Warning: no beer!), it's also open to the public, smartly decorated in plush reds and dark browns. There are a staggering 350 wines on offer, including 50 by the glass. The charming and experienced maître d', Chema Gómez, can help you choose. Chef Javier Collar designs good-value menus around various wines, and the à la carte selection is plentiful, mainly *nueva cocina* with game in season as well as fancy desserts and cheeses. ✉ *Espronceda 34,* ☎ *91/442–5432. Reservations essential. AE, DC, MC, V. Closed Sun. and Aug.*

$$$ ✕ **La Trainera.** With its nautical decor and maze of little dining rooms, this informal restaurant is all about fresh seafood—the best money can buy. Crab, lobster, shrimp, mussels, and a dozen other types of shellfish are served by weight in *raciones* (large portions). Although many Spanish diners share several plates of these shellfish as their entire meal, the grilled hake, sole, or turbot makes an unbeatable second course. Skip the listless house wine and go for a bottle of Albariño from the cellar. ✉ *Lagasca 60,* ☎ *91/576–8035. AE, MC, V. Closed Sun. and Aug.*

$$$ ✕ **Paradís.** Paradís serves avant-garde Catalan cuisine in a stylish, sophisticated setting that's ideally suited for lunch. (It's brightly lit and touristy at dinnertime.) Magret of duck lacquered with spices, an assortment of sautéed wild mushrooms, and *bacalao de Girona* (cod in the traditional style of this Catalan town) are examples of the rich fare. ✉ *Marqués de Cuba 14,* ☎ *91/429–7303. Reservations essential. AE, DC, V. Closed Sun. No lunch Sat.*

$$ ★ ✕ **Botín.** The *Guinness Book of Records* calls this the world's oldest restaurant (1725), and Hemingway called it the best. The latter claim may be a bit over the top, but the restaurant *is* excellent and extremely charming (and so successful that the owners opened a "branch" in Miami, Florida, in 1998). There are four floors of tiled, wood-beamed dining rooms, and if you're seated upstairs you'll pass ovens dating back several centuries. Musical groups called *tunas* often drop in to meander among the tourist hordes in traditional garb. Essential specialties are *cochinillo asado* (roast suckling pig) and *cordero asado* (roast lamb). It is said that Goya washed dishes here before he made it as a painter. ✉ *Cuchilleros 17, off Plaza Mayor,* ☎ *91/366–4217. AE, DC, MC, V.*

$$ ✕ **Casa Lastra.** Established in 1926, this little Asturian restaurant-bar is popular with locals in the charming Lavapié district. It has a distinctly rustic feel, its half-tiled walls strung with relics from the Asturian countryside, including wooden clogs and cow bells along with sausages and garlic. Specialties include *fabada* (Asturian ham and white-bean stew), *fabas con almejas* (white beans with clams), and *queso de cabrales,* Spain's super-tangy blue cheese, made in the Picos de Europa from a mixture of milk from cows, goats, and sheep. Desserts include baked apples. Great hunks of crisp bread and hard Asturian cider can complement a hearty meal on a 2,200-pta. weekday set menu. ✉ *Olivar 3,* ☎ *91/369–0837. AE, MC, V. Closed Wed. and July. No dinner Sun.*

Asador Frontón	21
Botín	6
Casa Lastra	22
Casa Mingo	1
Casa Paco	7
Casa Vallejo	8
Casino de Madrid–La Terraza	18
Champagnería Gala	25
Ciao	10
Cornucopia en Descalzas	3
El Borbollón	17
El Cenador del Prado	20
El Pescador	15
Ginza Sushi Bar	27
Horcher	30
Iroco	16
La Biotika	24
La Bola	2
La Cacharrería	4
La Cava Real	11
La Gamella	29
La Trainera	14
Las Cuevas de Luis Candelas	5
Lhardy	19
Nabucco	9
Paradís	26
Pedro Larumbe	13
Sanabresa	23
Viridiana	28
Zalacaín	12

Madrid Dining

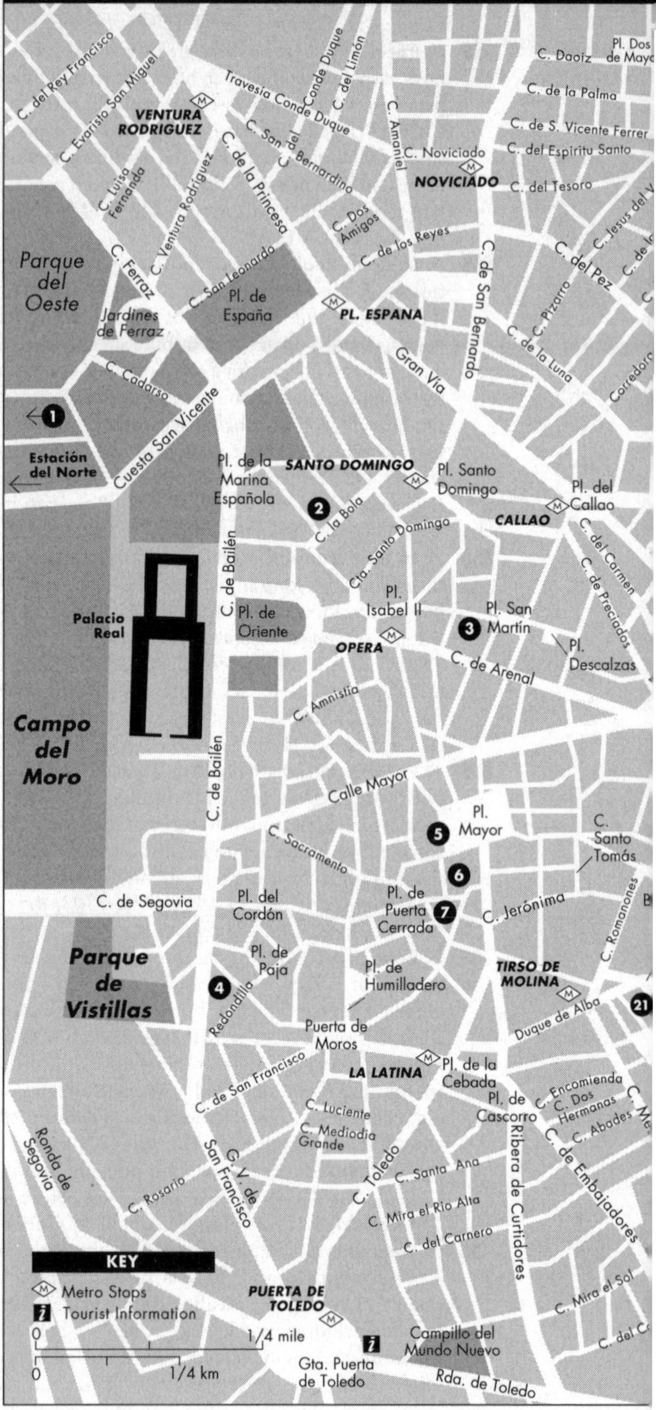

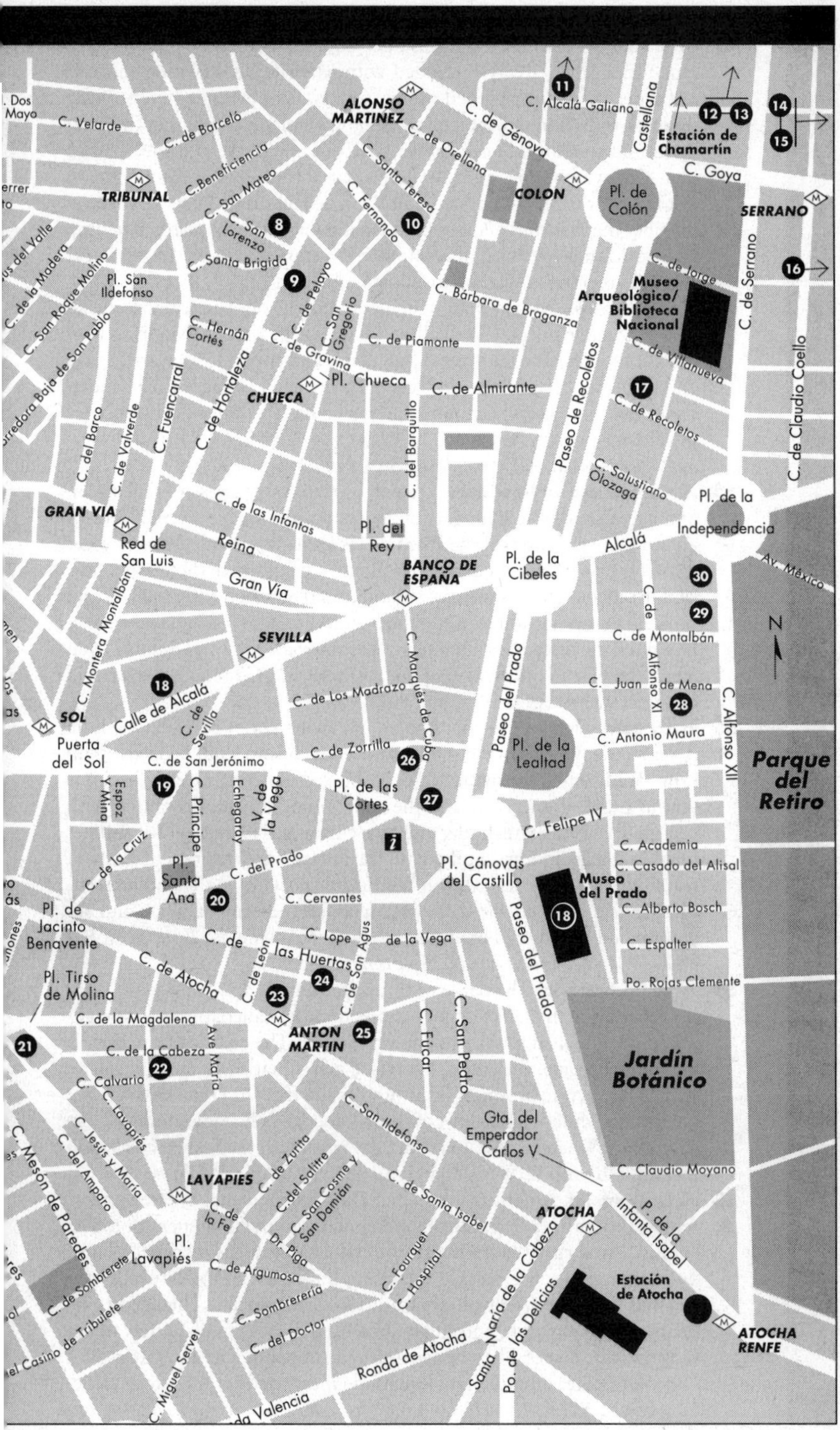
ALONSO MARTINEZ
C. de Génova
C. Alcalá Galiano
Castellana
Estación de Chamartín
C. Velarde
C. de Barceló
C. de Orellana
C. Santa Teresa
TRIBUNAL
C. Beneficiencia
C. San Mateo
C. San Lorenzo
C. Fernando
COLON
Pl. de Colón
C. Goya
SERRANO
C. Santa Brigida
Pl. San Ildefonso
C. de la Madera
C. San Roque
C. San Pablo
C. de Pelayo
C. San Gregorio
C. Bárbara de Braganza
C. de Jorge
Museo Arqueológico/ Biblioteca Nacional
C. de Serrano
C. Hernán Cortés
C. de Gravina
C. de Piamonte
Pl. Chueca
C. de Almirante
C. de Villanueva
C. de Claudio Coello
CHUECA
C. de Hortaleza
C. Fuencarral
C. del Barco
C. de Valverde
C. del Barquillo
Paseo de Recoletos
C. de Recoletos
C. Salustiano Olozaga
Pl. de la Independencia
GRAN VIA
C. de las Infantas
Red de San Luis
Reina
Pl. del Rey
BANCO DE ESPAÑA
Pl. de la Cibeles
Alcalá
Av. México
Gran Vía
C. Montera
Montalbán
C. de Montalbán
SEVILLA
C. Marqués de Cuba
C. de Los Madrazo
Paseo del Prado
C. Juan de Mena
C. Alfonso XI
C. Alfonso XII
SOL
Calle de Alcalá
C. de Sevilla
Puerta del Sol
C. de San Jerónimo
C. de Zorrilla
Pl. de la Lealtad
C. Antonio Maura
Parque del Retiro
Espoz Y Mina
C. Príncipe
Echegaray
V. de la Vega
Pl. de las Cortes
C. Felipe IV
C. de la Cruz
C. del Prado
Pl. Cánovas del Castillo
C. Academia
C. Casado del Alisal
Pl. Santa Ana
Museo del Prado
C. Alberto Bosch
Pl. de Jacinto Benavente
C. Cervantes
C. Lope de la Vega
C. Espalter
C. de las Huertas
C. de San Agus
C. de Atocha
Pl. Tirso de Molina
C. de León
Po. Rojas Clemente
C. de la Magdalena
ANTON MARTIN
C. Fúcar
C. San Pedro
C. de la Cabeza
Ave María
Jardín Botánico
C. Calvario
C. Lavapiés
C. San Ildefonso
Gta. del Emperador Carlos V
C. Mesón de Paredes
C. Jesús y María
C. del Amparo
LAVAPIES
C. de Zurita
C. del Salitre
C. San Cosme y San Damián
C. de Santa Isabel
C. Claudio Moyano
ATOCHA
P. de la Infanta Isabel
C. de la Fe
Dr. Piga
Pl. Lavapiés
C. de Argumosa
C. Fourquet
C. Hospital
Santa María de la Cabeza
Estación de Atocha
C. de Sombrerete
C. Sombrerería
Po. de las Delicias
ATOCHA RENFE
C. de Tribulete
C. del Doctor
Ronda de Atocha
C. Miguel Servet
Ronda de Valencia
N
8
9
10
11
12
13
14
15
16
17
18
19
20
21
22
23
24
25
26
27
28
29
30

$$ ★ ✕ **Casa Paco.** This popular Castilian tavern wouldn't have looked out of place two or three centuries ago. Squeeze your way past the old, zinc-topped bar, always crowded with Madrileños downing shots of red wine, and into the tiled dining rooms. People come here to feast on thick slabs of red meat, served sizzling on plates so hot that the meat continues to cook at your table. The beef is superb, and the Spanish consider overcooking a sin, so be prepared for looks of dismay if you ask for your meat well done (*bien hecho*). You order by weight, so remember that a *medio kilo* is more than a pound. Try the *pisto manchego* (the La Mancha version of ratatouille) to start. ✉ *Puerta Cerrada 11,* ☎ *91/366–3166. DC, V. Closed Sun. and Aug.*

$$ ✕ **Casa Vallejo.** With its homey dining room, friendly staff, creative menu, and reasonable prices, Casa Vallejo is a well-kept secret of Madrid's low-budget foodies. Try the tomato, zucchini, and cheese tart or artichokes and clams to start; follow up with duck breast in prune sauce or meatballs made with lamb, almonds, and pine nuts. The fudge-and-raspberry pie alone is worth the trip. ✉ *San Lorenzo 9,* ☎ *91/308–6158. Reservations essential. MC, V. Closed Sun. No dinner Mon.*

$$ ✕ **Cornucopia en Descalzas.** Owned by two Americans, a Frenchman, and a Spaniard, this young, friendly restaurant on the second floor of an old mansion (just off the Plaza de las Descalzas Reales) serves what it calls Euro-American cuisine. The menu changes with the season; possibilities include grilled entrecote marinated in bourbon and honey, bream on a dill compote, and stewed rabbit with tomatoes, onion, and thyme. In winter, the restaurant becomes a tearoom Saturday and Sunday from 5 to 8. ✉ *Flora 1,* ☎ *91/547–6465. AE, MC, V. Closed Easter wk and last two wks in Aug.*

$$ ★ ✕ **La Bola.** First opened as a *botellería* (wine shop) in 1802, La Bola developed slowly into a tapas bar and eventually into a full-fledged restaurant. Tradition is the main draw; blood-red paneling outside beckons you into the original bar and the cozy dining nooks, decorated with polished wood, Spanish tile, and lace curtains. The restaurant still belongs to the founding family, with the seventh generation currently in training. Dinner is served, but the house specialty is that quintessential Madrid meal *cocido a la madrileña,* served only at lunch and accompanied by crusty bread and a hearty red wine. ✉ *Bola 5,* ☎ *91/547–6930. No credit cards. No dinner Sun.*

$$ ✕ **La Cacharrería.** The name of this restaurant means "junkyard," and it's reflected in the funky decor—a mix of dusty calico, old lace, and gilt mirrors, all tucked into the medieval quarter. The cooking, however, is decidedly upscale, with a market-based menu that changes daily and an excellent selection of wines. Venison stew and fresh tuna steaks with *cava* (sparkling white wine from Catalonia) and leeks have been among the specialties. Whatever else you order, save room for the homemade lemon tart. ✉ *Moreiria 9,* ☎ *91/365–3930. AE, DC, MC, V. Closed Sun.*

$$ ★ ✕ **La Gamella.** American-born chef Dick Stephens has created a new, reasonably priced menu at this perennially popular dinner spot. The sophisticated rust-red dining room, batik tablecloths, oversize plates, and attentive service remain the same, but much of the nouvelle cuisine has been replaced by more traditional fare, such as chicken in garlic, beef bourguignon, and steak tartare à la Jack Daniels. A few of the old signature dishes, like sausage-and-red-pepper quiche and bittersweet chocolate pâté, remain. The lunchtime *menú del día* is a great value. ✉ *Alfonso XII 4,* ☎ *91/532–4509. AE, DC, MC, V. Closed Sun. and Aug. 15–30. No lunch Sat.*

$$ ✕ **Las Cuevas de Luis Candelas.** Hidden just off the southwest corner of the Plaza Mayor, this "cave" is said to be the oldest tavern in Madrid and feels like the medieval cellar of a Spanish mansion. Popular with locals as well as travelers, the tavern is divided into three sec-

tions. You're greeted by a host dressed as the 19th-century bandit himself, and you enter through a long bar where noisy regulars drink and munch tapas. A low stone archway leads to a quieter area where you can sit on low benches, drink from a ceramic jar, and eat *raciones* of such tapas as mushrooms in garlic and cured ham. Farther inside the "cave" are the dining areas, with painted scenes of old Madrid. Barbecued meats are the specialty, and portions are huge and heavy—for a light dinner, stay in the tapas lounge. A guitar player strolls between the ancient rooms, adding to the enchanting, if slightly touristy, atmosphere. ✉ *Cuchilleros 1,* ☎ *91/366–5428. AE, MC, V.*

$$ ✕ **Nabucco.** With pastel-washed walls and subtle lighting from gigantic, wrought-iron candelabras, this pizzeria and trattoria is a trendy but elegant haven in gritty Chueca. Fresh bread sticks and garlic olive oil show up within minutes of your arrival. The spinach, ricotta, and walnut ravioli is heavenly, and this may be the only Italian restaurant in Madrid where you can order (California-style?) barbecued-chicken pizza, although the four-cheese one is good as well. Considering the ambience and quality, the bill is a pleasant surprise. ✉ *Hortaleza 108,* ☎ *91/310–0611. AE, MC, V.*

$ ★ ✕ **Casa Mingo.** Resembling an Asturian cider tavern, Casa Mingo is built into a stone wall beneath the Estación del Norte, across the street from the hermitage of San Antonio de la Florida. It's a bustling place; you share long plank tables with other diners, and the only items on the menu are succulent roast chicken, salad, and sausages, all to be washed down with numerous bottles of *sidra* (hard cider). Small tables are set up on the sidewalk in summer. Get here early (1 for lunch, 8:30 for dinner) if you want to avoid a wait. ✉ *Paseo de la Florida 2,* ☎ *91/547–7918. Reservations not accepted. No credit cards.*

$ ✕ **Champagnería Gala.** Hidden on a back street not far from Calle Atocha and the Reina Sofia museum, this cheerful Mediterranean restaurant is usually packed thanks to its fixed-price three-course menus with wine, which offer a choice of paellas, *fideus* (paellas with noodles instead of rice), risottos, and hearty bean stews. Only *cava,* Catalan sparkling wine, costs extra. The front dining area is a kaleidoscope of painted color, particularly red; the back area incorporates trees and plants in a glassed-in patio. ✉ *Moratín 22,* ☎ *91/429–2562. Reservations essential. No credit cards.*

$ ✕ **La Biotika.** A vegetarian's dream in the heart of the bar district just east of Plaza Santa Ana, this small, cozy restaurant serves macrobiotic vegetarian cuisine seven days a week. Enormous salads, hearty soups, fresh bread, and creative tofu dishes make the meal flavorful as well as healthy. A small shop at the entrance sells macrobiotic groceries. ✉ *Amor de Dios 3,* ☎ *91/429–0780. No credit cards.*

$ ✕ **Sanabresa.** Be prepared for bright lights, plastic plants, spotless white tablecloths, and diners glancing at the TV as they dig into classic, sensibly priced Spanish fare—hearty, wholesome meals like *pechuga villaroy* (breaded and fried chicken breast in béchamel) and, on Thursday, paella. The functional, pink-wall dining room is always crowded, so if you don't arrive early (1:30 for lunch or 8:30 for dinner), you'll probably have to wait. ✉ *Amor de Dios 12,* ☎ *91/429–0338. Reservations not accepted. AE, MC, V. Closed Sun. and Aug.*

LODGING

$$$$ **Ritz.** When Alfonso XIII was preparing for his marriage to Queen Victoria's granddaughter, he realized to his dismay that Madrid did not have a single hotel up to the exacting standards of his royal guests. Thus was born the Ritz, and it was long the most exclusive hotel in Spain. Opened in 1910 by the king himself (who had personally overseen its construction), the Ritz is a monument to the Belle Epoque, its sumptuous public salons furnished with rare antiques, hand-embroidered linens from Robinson & Cleaver, and handwoven carpets. Guest rooms are carpeted, hung with chandeliers, and decorated in pastels, and many have good views of the Prado or the Castellana. Even if you can't stay here, try to visit the garden terrace for a meal: the restaurant, Goya, is justly famous (though very pricey), and Sunday brunch is a lavish affair to the soothing strains of harp music. Weekend tea and supper are accompanied by chamber music from February to May. Alas, because the lobby and lounge are often crowded with conventioneers and partygoers, the Ritz has lost much of its exclusivity. ✉ *Plaza de Lealtad 5, 28014,* ☎ *91/521–2857,* FAX *91/701–6776. 158 rooms. Restaurant, bar, in-room data ports, in-room faxes, in-room VCRs, beauty salon, massage, sauna, health club, parking (fee). AE, DC, MC, V.*

$$$$ ★ **Santo Mauro.** Once the Canadian embassy, this turn-of-the-20th-century mansion is now an intimate luxury hotel, an oasis of calm just a 10-minute cab ride from the city center. The neoclassical architecture is accented by contemporary furniture (such as suede armchairs) in such hues as mustard, teal, and eggplant. The best rooms are in the main building, as is the top-notch restaurant, which has a contemporary menu and, in season, a delightful dining terrace. Rooms in the new annex are duplexes with stereos and VCRs. Views vary; request a room with a terrace overlooking the gardens. ✉ *Zurbano 36, 28010,* ☎ *91/319–6900,* FAX *91/308–5477. 37 rooms. Restaurant, bar, coffee shop, in-room VCRs, pool, sauna, exercise room, meeting rooms, parking (fee). AE, DC, MC, V.*

$$$$ **Villa Magna.** Part of the Park Hyatt group, the Villa Magna is one of Madrid's top luxury hotels, its concrete facade belying an exquisite interior furnished with 18th-century antiques. Prices are somewhat excessive, but it's hard to find such finishing touches as a champagne bar and—in the largest suite in Madrid—a white baby-grand piano. All rooms have large desks as well as VCRs, and all bathrooms have fresh flowers. One restaurant, Le Divellec, has cozy walnut paneling and the feel of an English library, and you can dine on its garden terrace in season. The other restaurant, the Tse-Yang, is Madrid's most exclusive for Chinese food. The hotel has direct access to a branch of El Corte Inglés department store. ✉ *Paseo de la Castellana 22, 28046,* ☎ *91/587–1234,* FAX *91/431–2286 or 91/575–3158. 164 rooms, 18 suites. 2 restaurants, 2 bars, in-room VCRs, barbershop, beauty salon, massage, sauna, health club, baby-sitting, business services, car rental, parking (fee). AE, DC, MC, V.*

$$$$ **Villa Real.** For a luxury hotel that combines elegance, modern amenities, *and* a great location, look no further. The simulated 19th-century facade gives way to lobbies garnished with potted palms. Each room has its own character, albeit with an overall French feel, and many are split-level; some suites have both saunas and whirlpool baths. The hotel faces the Cortés and is convenient to almost everything, and the staff is very friendly. ✉ *Plaza de las Cortés 10, 28014,* ☎ *91/420–3767,* FAX *91/420–2547. 94 rooms, 20 suites. Restaurant, bar, in-room data ports, beauty salon, sauna, meeting rooms, parking (fee). AE, DC, MC, V.*

$$$$ ★ **Westin Palace.** Built in 1912, Madrid's most famous grand hotel is a Belle Epoque creation of Alfonso XIII and has hosted the likes of Dalí, Brando, Hayworth, and Madonna. In 1995 the hotel was acquired by Sheraton, and by 1998 it had undergone its first restoration in 85 years. Guest rooms now meet today's highest standards; banquet halls and lobbies have been lovingly beautified; and the facade has been finely restored. The Palace is more charming and stylish than ever—and while the stained-glass dome over the lounge remains exquisitely original, the windows in the guest rooms are now double glazed. The suites are no less luxurious than the opulent public spaces, and bathrooms are spacious, with double sinks, tubs, separate shower stalls, and other welcome touches such as bathrobes and magnifying mirrors. ✉ *Plaza de las Cortes 7, 28014,* ☎ *91/360–8000,* FAX *91/360–8100. 465 rooms, 45 suites. 2 restaurants, bar, café, in-room data ports, sauna, exercise room, business services, meeting rooms, parking (fee). AE, DC, MC, V. www.palacemadrid.com*

$$$ **El Prado.** Wedged between the classic buildings of *castizo* Madrid, this skinny new hotel is within stumbling distance of the city's best bars and nightclubs and is priced accordingly. Rooms are basic but spacious, and virtually immune to street noise thanks to double-pane windows. Decorative touches include pastel floral prints and gleaming marble baths. ✉ *C. Prado 11, 28014,* ☎ *91/369–0234,* FAX *91/429–2829. 47 rooms. Cafeteria, meeting rooms, parking (fee). AE, DC, MC, V.*

$$$ ★ **Jardín de Recoletos.** This sleek apartment hotel offers great value for the money in a quiet street close to Plaza Colón and upmarket Calle Serrano. The large lobby has marble floors and a stained-glass ceiling, and adjoins a café and restaurant where you can dine or just have drinks beside a pleasant tree-lined patio. The commodious rooms, decorated with light-wood trim, white walls, and beige and yellow furnishings, include sitting and dining areas and discreet, well-equipped kitchens. "Superior" rooms and two-room suites have hydromassage baths and large terraces. Book well in advance. ✉ *Gil de Santivañes 6, 28001,* ☎ *91/781–1640,* FAX *91/781–1641. 36 rooms, 7 suites. Restaurant, café, in-room data ports, in-room VCRs, kitchenettes, parking (fee). AE, DC, MC, V.*

$$$ **Liabeny.** A large, paneled lobby leads to bars, a restaurant, and a café in this 1960s hotel, centrally located near an airy plaza (and several department stores) between Gran Vía and Puerta del Sol. The large, comfortable rooms have floral fabrics and big windows; interior and top-floor rooms are the quietest. ✉ *Salud 3, 28013,* ☎ *91/531–9000,* FAX *91/532–5306. 222 rooms. Restaurant, café, 2 bars, meeting rooms, parking (fee). AE, DC, MC, V.*

$$$ **NH Lagasca.** In the heart of the elegant Salamanca neighborhood, this newish hotel combines large, brightly decorated rooms with an unbeatable location two blocks from Madrid's main shopping street, Calle Serrano. The marble lobbies border on the coldly functional, but they're fine as a meeting place. ✉ *Lagasca 64, 28001,* ☎ *91/575–4606,* FAX *91/575–1694. 100 rooms. Restaurant, bar, in-room VCRs, meeting rooms, parking (fee). AE, DC, MC, V.*

$$$ **Santo Domingo.** An intimate hotel that artfully blends the best of classical and modern design, the Santo Domingo is about 10 minutes' walk from the Puerta del Sol, just off Gran Vía. Rooms are decorated in soft tones of peach and ocher, and those on the fifth floor have excellent views of the Royal Palace. All have voice mail and double-paned windows. An especially friendly and well trained staff gives the place a personal touch. ✉ *Plaza Santo Domingo 13, 28013,* ☎ *91/547–9800,* FAX *91/547–5995. 120 rooms. Restaurant, bar, meeting rooms, parking (fee). AE, DC, MC, V.*

$$$ **Suecia.** The Suecia's chief attraction is its location, right next to the super-chic Círculo de Bellas Artes (an arts society–café–film–theater complex). The large lobby, which includes a café, is often bustling. Guest rooms are trendy, with contemporary art and futuristic light fixtures, but a little worn. ✉ *Marqués de Riera 4, 28014,* ☎ *91/531–6900,* FAX *91/521–7141. 119 rooms, 9 suites. 2 restaurants, bar, baby-sitting, parking (fee). AE, DC, MC, V.*

$$$ **Suite Prado.** Popular with Americans on short stays, this stylish apartment hotel is near the Prado, the Thyssen-Bornemisza, and the Plaza Santa Ana tapas area. The attractive attic studios on the fifth floor have

Atlántico 3
Carlos V 4
El Prado. 8
Hostal Dulcinea. 11
Hostal Villar 7
Inglés. 6
Jardín de Recoletos 16
Liabeny 5
Mora. 14
NH Lagasca 19
Ramón de la Cruz . . . 20
Ritz 15
Santo Domingo. 1
Santo Mauro 21
Suecia 13
Suite Prado. 9
Tryp Ambassador 2
Tryp Fénix 17
Villa Magna 18
Villa Real 10
Westin Palace. 12

Madrid Lodging

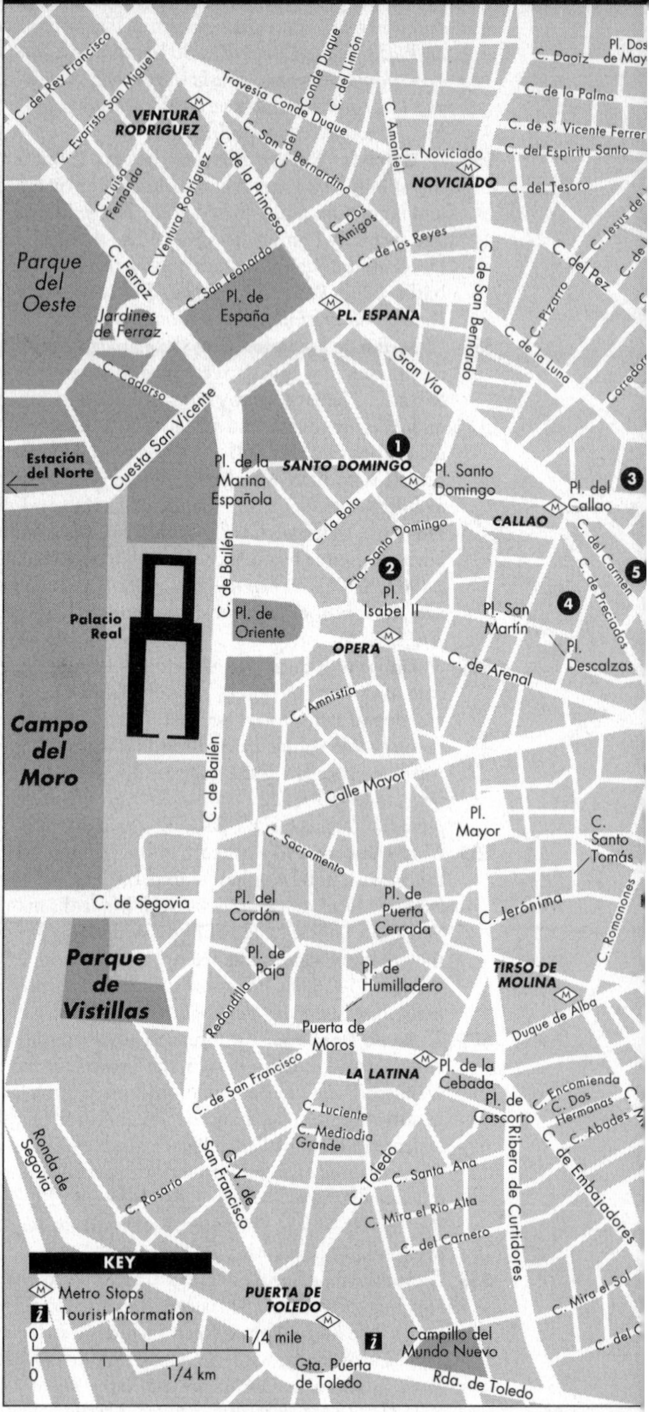

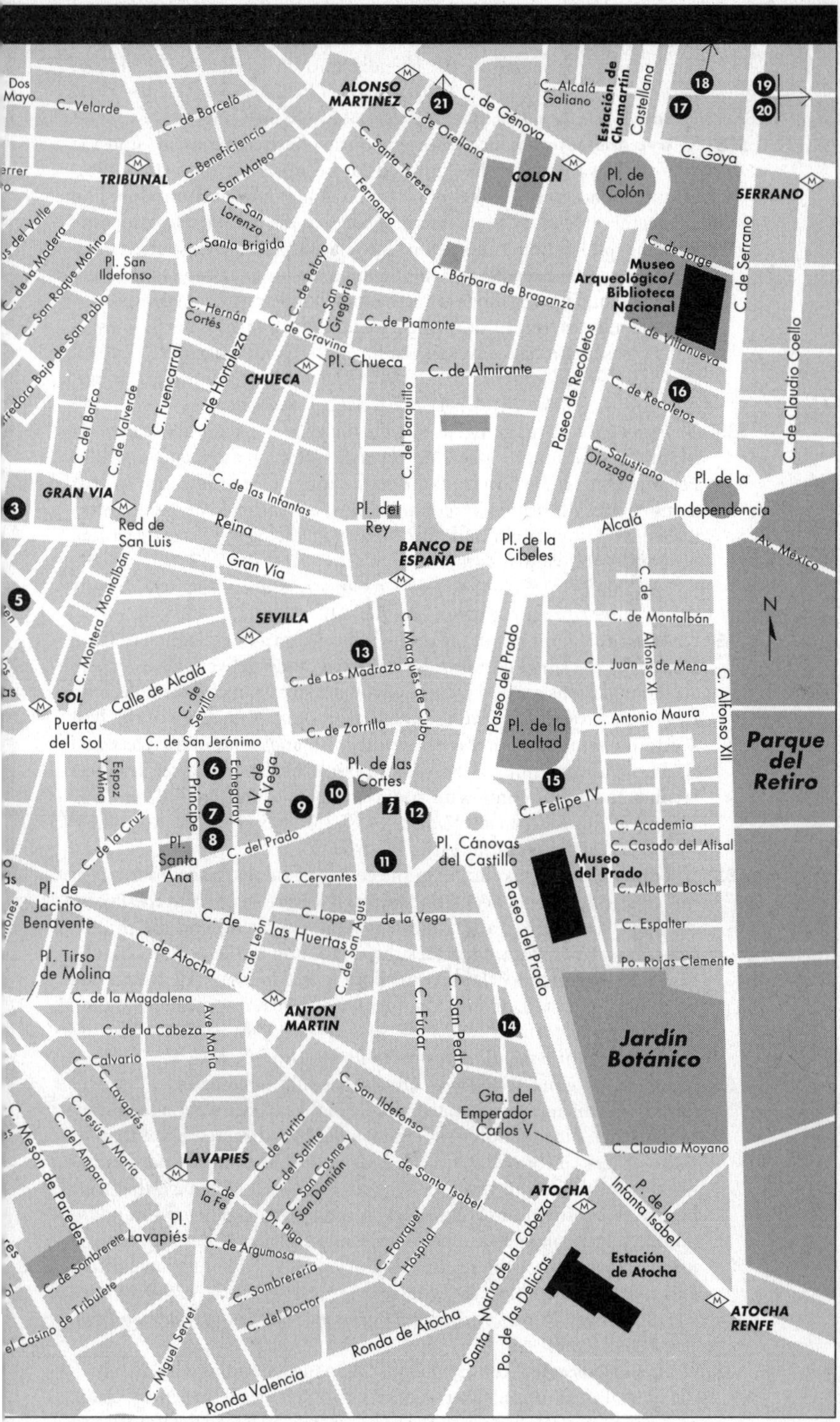
Dos Mayo
C. Velarde
C. de Barceló
C. Beneficiencia
TRIBUNAL
C. San Mateo
C. San Lorenzo
C. Santa Brígida
Pl. San Ildefonso
C. de la Madera
C. San Roque
C. Molino
C. San Pablo
Corredora Baja de San Pablo
C. del Barco
C. de Valverde
C. Fuencarral
C. de Hortaleza
C. Hernán Cortés
C. de Pelayo
C. San Gregorio
C. de Gravina
Pl. Chueca
CHUECA
ALONSO MARTINEZ
C. de Génova
C. de Orellana
C. Santa Teresa
C. Fernando
C. Bárbara de Braganza
C. de Piamonte
C. de Almirante
C. del Barquillo
C. Alcalá Galiano
Estación de Chamartín
Castellana
COLON
Pl. de Colón
C. Goya
SERRANO
C. de Jorge
Museo Arqueológico/ Biblioteca Nacional
C. de Villanueva
C. de Serrano
C. de Claudio Coello
C. de Recoletos
Paseo de Recoletos
C. Salustiano Olozaga
Pl. de la Independencia
GRAN VIA
Red de San Luis
C. de las Infantas
Reina
Gran Vía
Pl. del Rey
BANCO DE ESPAÑA
Pl. de la Cibeles
Alcalá
Av. México
C. de Montalbán
C. de Alfonso XI
C. Juan de Mena
C. Montera
Montalbán
SEVILLA
C. de Los Madrazo
C. Marqués de Cubа
Paseo del Prado
Calle de Alcalá
C. de Sevilla
SOL
Puerta del Sol
C. de San Jerónimo
C. de Zorrilla
Pl. de la Lealtad
C. Antonio Maura
C. Alfonso XII
Parque del Retiro
Espoz Y Mina
C. Príncipe
Echegaray
V. de la Vega
Pl. de las Cortes
C. Felipe IV
Pl. Cánovas del Castillo
C. Academia
C. Casado del Alisal
Museo del Prado
C. de la Cruz
Pl. Santa Ana
C. del Prado
C. Cervantes
C. Alberto Bosch
Pl. de Jacinto Benavente
C. Lope de la Vega
C. de las Huertas
C. Espalter
Po. Rojas Clemente
C. de Atocha
C. de León
C. de San Agus
Pl. Tirso de Molina
C. de la Magdalena
ANTON MARTIN
C. Fúcar
C. San Pedro
Jardín Botánico
C. de la Cabeza
Ave María
C. Calvario
C. Lavapiés
C. San Ildefonso
Gta. del Emperador Carlos V
C. Jesús y María
C. Mesón de Paredes
C. del Amparo
LAVAPIES
C. de Zurita
C. del Salitre
C. San Cosme y San Damián
C. de Santa Isabel
C. Claudio Moyano
ATOCHA
P. de la Infanta Isabel
C. de la Fe
Dr. Piga
Pl. Lavapiés
C. de Sombrerete
C. de Argumosa
C. Fourquet
C. Hospital
C. Sombrerería
C. del Doctor
Santa María de la Cabeza
Po. de las Delicias
Estación de Atocha
ATOCHA RENFE
C. de Tribulete
el Casino
C. Miguel Servet
Ronda de Atocha
Ronda Valencia
N
3
5
6
7
8
9
10
11
12
13
14
15
16
17
18
19
20
21

sloping, beamed ceilings, and there are larger suites downstairs. All apartments are brightly decorated and have marble baths and basic kitchens, but breakfast is served by the friendly staff on weekends. ✉ *Manuel Fernández y González 10, 28014,* ☎ *91/420–2318,* FAX *91/420–0559. 18 suites. Kitchenettes, parking (fee). AE, DC, MC, V.*

$$$ ★ **Tryp Ambassador.** Ideally located on an old street between Gran Vía and the Royal Palace, the Ambassador occupies the renovated 19th-century palace of the Dukes of Granada. A magnificent front door and a graceful three-story staircase are legacies of the building's aristocratic past; the rest has been transformed into elegant, somewhat soulless lodgings favored by executives. Guest rooms are large, complete with sitting areas, and have mahogany furnishings, floral drapes, and bedspreads. The greenhouse restaurant, filled with plants and songbirds, is especially pleasant on cold days. ✉ *Cuesta Santo Domingo 5 and 7, 28013,* ☎ *91/541–6700,* FAX *91/559–1040. 181 rooms. Restaurant, bar, airport shuttle, parking (fee). AE, DC, MC, V. www.tryp.es*

$$$ **Tryp Fénix.** A magnificent marble lobby greets your arrival at this Madrid institution, overlooking Plaza de Colón on the Castellana. The Fenix is also a mere hop from the posh shops of Calle Serrano. Its spacious rooms, decorated in reds and golds, are carpeted and amply furnished, and flowers abound. Ask for a room facing the Plaza de Colón; otherwise, the view is rather dreary. ✉ *Hermosilla 2, 28001,* ☎ *91/431–6700,* FAX *91/576–0661. 213 rooms, 12 suites. Bar, café, beauty salon, baby-sitting, parking (fee). AE, DC, MC, V.*

$$ **Atlántico.** Don't be put off by the location, on a noisy stretch of Gran Vía, or by the small entrance hall: the Atlántico delivers bright, clean accommodations at good prices. Rooms are small but comfortable, with fresh new furnishings. All have tile bathrooms. A member of the Best Western chain, this hotel is a favorite with anglophone travelers and is almost always full, so it's wise to book well in advance. The best layouts and views come with room numbers ending in 3, 4, or 5. ✉ *Gran Vía 38, 28013,* ☎ *91/522–6480,* FAX *91/531–0210. 80 rooms. Snack bar, airport shuttle. AE, DC, MC, V.*

$$ **Carlos V.** If you like to be in the center of things, hang your hat at this classic hotel on a pedestrian street: it's mere steps from the Puerta del Sol, Plaza Mayor, and Descalzas Reales convent, and the price is right. A suit of armor decorates the tiny lobby, while crystal chandeliers add elegance to the second-floor guest lounge. All rooms are bright and carpeted, and the doubles with large terraces are a bargain. ✉ *Maestro Victoria 5, 28013,* ☎ *91/531–4100,* FAX *91/531–3761. 67 rooms, 41 with bath. Bar, airport shuttle. AE, DC, MC, V.*

$$ **Inglés.** Virginia Woolf was among the first luminaries to discover this place, which is smack in the middle of the old city's bar-and-restaurant district. Since Woolf's time, the Inglés has attracted more than its share of less-celebrated artists and writers. Rather drab and deteriorated now, it's best for those looking for location and value rather than luxury. (Run-down suites cost what you'd normally pay for a standard double.) The balconies overlooking Calle Echegaray give you an unusual aerial view of the medieval quarter, all red Mediterranean tiles and ramshackle gables. ✉ *Echegaray 8, 28014,* ☎ *91/429–6551,* FAX *91/420–2423. 58 rooms. Bar, cafeteria, exercise room, parking (fee). AE, DC, MC, V.*

$ **Hostal Dulcinea.** Run by an elderly Spanish couple (who also own the Hostal Corbero, across the street), the Dulcinea is a friendly, clean, and affordable alternative to the pricey hotels on Paseo del Prado. Just off the Plaza Cánovas del Castillo, this upper-floor pension has an arguably ideal location: it's surrounded by the Museo Thyssen-Bornemisza to the north, the Prado to the east, and the vibrant nightlife around the Plaza Santa Ana to the west. Rooms are spare, with wood furniture and minimal trimmings, but comfortable and homey. Calling ahead can get you a great price on one of the three cozy "apartments." ✉ *Cervantes 19, 28014,* ☎ *91/429–9309,* FAX *91/369–2569. 23 rooms, 3 apartments. AE, MC, V.*

$ ★ **Mora.** Across the Paseo del Prado from the Botanical Garden, the Mora welcomes weary travelers with a sparkling, faux-marble lobby and bright, carpeted hallways. Guest rooms are modestly decorated but large and comfortable; those on the street side have great views of the gardens and the Prado, and double-paned windows keep them fairly quiet. For breakfast and lunch, the attached café is excellent, affordable, and popular with locals. ✉ *Paseo del Prado 32, 28014,* ☎ *91/420–1569,* FAX *91/420–0564. 61 rooms. Café. AE, DC, MC, V.*

$ **Ramón de la Cruz.** If you don't mind a 10-minute metro ride (to Manuel Becerra) from the city center, this medium-size hotel is a find. Rooms are large, with modern bathrooms, and the stone-floor lobby is spacious. For Madrid, it's a bargain. ✉ *Don Ramón de la Cruz 94, 28006,* ☎ *91/401–7200,* FAX *91/402–2126. 103 rooms. Cafeteria. MC, V.*

NIGHTLIFE AND THE ARTS

The Arts

As Madrid's reputation as a vibrant, contemporary arts center has grown, artists and performers of all stripes have arrived in droves. The best way to stay abreast of events is to consult the weekly *Guía de Ocio* (published Monday) or daily listings in the leading newspaper, *El País,* both of which are easy to comprehend even if you don't read Spanish. Performance tickets are usually best purchased at the hall itself or, in the case of major pop concerts, at **El Corte Inglés** department stores (☎ 902/400222), **FNAC** (✉ Preciados 28, ☎ 91/595–6100), or **Tele-Entradas** (☎ 902/101212).

The city throws major arts festivals in each of the four seasons. The most comprehensive is the Festival de Otoño (Autumn Festival), from late September to late November, which blankets the entire city with pop concerts, poetry readings, flamenco, and ballet and theater from world-renowned companies. Other annual events include world-class bonanzas of jazz, salsa, African-music, and rock; art exhibits; film festivals; and more, all at very reasonable prices. Many events take place outdoors, in city parks and stadiums.

Concerts/Ballet

The modern **Auditorio Nacional de Música** (✉ Príncipe de Vergara 146, ☎ 91/337–0100) is Madrid's main classical concert hall. The newly reopened **Teatro Real** (✉ Plaza de Isabel II, ☎ 91/516–0600) is the center for ballet and opera. The new, subterranean **Centro Cultural de la Villa** (✉ Plaza de Colón, ☎ 91/575–6080 for information; 91/516–0606 for tickets) has an eclectic program ranging from gospel and blues to flamenco and Celtic dance.

Film

Nearly a dozen theaters regularly show undubbed foreign films, most in English with Spanish subtitles. These are listed in newspapers and in the *Guía de Ocio* under "V.O."—original version. Your best bet for catching an undubbed new release is the **Multicines Ideal** (✉ Doctor Cortezo 6, ☎ 91/369–2518), where half of the nine theaters are usually showing English-language art films. Other leading V.O. theaters include **Alphaville** (✉ Martín de los Heros 14, ☎ 91/584–4524) and **Renoir** (✉ Martín de los Heros 12, ☎ 91/541–4100), both just off the Plaza de España. Excellent, classic V.O. films change daily at the **Filmoteca Cine Doré** (✉ Santa Isabel 3, ☎ 91/369–1125).

Theater

English-language plays are rare. When they do come to town, they're staged at any of a dozen venues; check local newspapers. One theater you won't need Spanish for is the **Teatro de la Zarzuela** (✉ Jovellanos 4, ☎ 91/524–5400), which specializes in the traditional Spanish operetta known as *zarzuela,* a kind of bawdy comedy. The **Teatro Español** (✉ Príncipe 25, ☎ 91/429–6297) keeps 17th-century Spanish classics alive.

Nightlife

Nightlife—or *la marcha,* as the Spanish fondly call it—reaches legendary heights in Spain's capital. It has been said that Madrileños rarely sleep, largely because they spend so much time in bars—not drunk, but socializing in the easy, sophisticated way that's unique to this city. This is true of old as well as young, and it's not uncommon for children to play on the sidewalks past midnight while multigenerational families and friends convene over coffee or cocktails at an outdoor café. The streets best known for their social scenes, however, do tend to attract a younger clientele; these include Huertas, Moratín, Segovia, Victoria, and the areas around the Plaza Santa Ana and the Plaza de Anton Martín. The adventurous may want to explore the scruffier bar district around the Plaza Dos de Mayo, in the Malasaña area, where trendy, smoke-filled hangouts line both sides of Calle San Vicente Ferrer. Equally brave souls can venture a few blocks east to the notorious haunts of neighboring Chueca, popular with gays, where tattoo studios and street-chic boutiques break up the endless alleys of techno discos and after-hours clubs.

Bars

Madrid has countless bars, and while almost all serve food, many are known more for their atmosphere. Some recommendations:

Alhambra. This one-room tavern has been serving excellent wine, beer, and tapas to a gregarious crowd since 1929. Alhambra opens at an eye-popping 9:30 AM; around midnight it fills up, the windows get steamy, and the crowd does pseudo-*sevillana* dance moves to traditional music. When it's packed, they jump right onto the wooden tabletops without missing a beat. ✉ *Victoria 9,* ☎ *91/521–0708.*

Cafe Gijón. Possibly Madrid's most famous café-bar, the Gijón has hosted the city's most highfalutin *tertulias* (discussion groups that meet regularly to hash out the issues of the day) for more than a century. ✉ *Paseo de Recoletos 21,* ☎ *91/521–5425.*

El Clandestino. Run by a French couple who seem to be Spaniards at heart, this bar-café is a hidden, low-key hot spot with a local following: atmosphere without attitude. Impromptu jam sessions are rounded out by two floors alternating mellow jazz with house and ambient music. ✉ *Barquillo 34,* ☎ *91/521–5563.*

Hard Rock Cafe. Wildly popular with young Spaniards, Madrid's version of the U.S. classic opened in 1994, serving up the usual drinks, burgers, and salads with a heavy dose of loud music. ✉ *Paseo Castellana 2,* ☎ *91/436–4340.*

Los Gabrieles. This building is featured in most Madrid tourist literature for its remarkable tiled walls—advertisements from the turn of the 20th century, when this was a high-class brothel. Drinks are unusually pricey. ✉ *Echegaray 17,* ☎ *91/429–6261.*

Oliver. Here are two bars in one: afternoons and evenings, an upstairs lounge and restaurant; late at night, a full-fledged Chueco disco in the brick-lined basement cavern. ✉ *Almirante 12,* ☎ *91/521–7379.*

Palacio de Gaviria. Hidden away on a tawdry commercial street between Puerta del Sol and the Royal Palace, this restored 19th-century palace was allegedly built to house one of Queen Isabel II's lovers. An exotic maze, it now offers drinks in a sophisticated setting, with a disco and frequent late-night jazz in the mirrored ballroom. ✉ *Arenal 9,* ☎ *91/526–6069.*

Soho. Something of a slice of New York in the Salamanca district, Soho has an eclectic menu that includes exotic island drinks as well as Spanish variants of Tex-Mex cuisine. It's filled with rap and reggae fans. ✉ *Jorge Juan 50,* ☎ *91/577–8973. Closed Sun.*

Taberna de Antonio Sanchez. It's reputed to be the oldest bar in Madrid, and the proprietors claim it's been around since 1830. Order wine and tapas at the old zinc bar in front; head to the back for a full meal. ✉ *Mesón de Paredes 13,* ☎ *91/539–7826.*

Viva Madrid. This extremely popular bar has a Brassai motif and a serious personality. Packed with both Spaniards and foreigners, it has become something of a singles scene. There are tables and a small selection of bar food in the rear. ✉ *Manuel Fernández y González 7,* ☎ *91/429–3640.*

Cabaret

Berlin Cabaret (✉ Costanilla de San Pedro 11, ☎ 91/366–2034) professes to provide authentic cabaret as it was performed in Berlin in the '30s. (These days the audience is quite different.) Combining magic, chorus girls, and ribald comedy, it draws an eccentric crowd for vintage café theater. On weekends, the absurd fun lasts until daybreak.

Discos

Madrid's oldest and hippest disco for wild, all-night dancing to an international music mix is **El Sol** (✉ Calle Jardines 3, ☎ 91/532–6490), open 'til 5:30 AM. There's live music around midnight Thursday, Friday, and Saturday. **Joy Eslava** (✉ Arenal 11, ☎ 91/366–3733), a downtown disco in a converted theater, is an old standby. **Pacha** (✉ Barceló 11, ☎ 91/447–0128), one of Spain's infamous chain discos, is always energetic. **Fortuny** (✉ Fortuny 34, ☎ 91/319–0588) attracts a celebrity crowd, especially in summer, when the lush outdoor patio opens for partying under the stars. Put on your best dancing shoes: the door is ultraselective. Salsa has become a fixture in Madrid; check out the most spectacular moves at **Azúcar** (Sugar; ✉ Paseo Reina Cristina 7, ☎ 91/501–6107).

Flamenco

Madrid is not a great city for flamenco, but if you won't be traveling south, here are a few possibilities. Note that prices for dinner and a show tend to be very high; you can save money by dining elsewhere and arriving in time for the show. Drinks are usually extra.

Café de Chinitas. It's expensive, but the flamenco dancing here is the best in Madrid. Try to reserve in advance; shows often sell out. Performances are at 10:30 PM Monday through Saturday. ✉ *Torrija 7,* ☎ *91/559–5135.*

Casa Patas. Along with tapas, this well-known space offers good, if somewhat touristy, flamenco. Prices are more reasonable than elsewhere. Shows are at 10:30 PM Monday–Thursday, midnight Friday–Sunday. ✉ *Canizares 10,* ☎ *91/369–0496.*

Corral de la Morería. Dinner à la carte and well-known visiting flamenco stars accompany the resident dance troupe. Since Morería opened its doors in 1956, celebrities such as Frank Sinatra and Ava Gardner have left their autographed photos for the walls. Shows are daily, from 10:45 PM to 2 AM. ✉ *Morería 17 (on C. Bailén, cross bridge over Calle Segovia and turn right),* ☎ *91/365–8446.*

Nightclubs

Jazz, rock, flamenco, and classical music are all popular in Madrid's many small clubs.

Amadis. Here, telephones on every table encourage people to call each other with invitations to dance. ✉ *Covarrubias 42 (underneath Luchana Cinema),* ☎ *91/446–0036.*

Café Central. Madrid's best-known jazz venue is chic and well run, and the musicians are often internationally known. Performances are usually from 10 PM to midnight. ✉ *Plaza de Ángel 10,* ☎ *91/369–4143.*

Cafe del Foro. This funky, friendly club on the edge of Malasaña has live music every night starting at 11:30 PM. ✉ *San Andrés 38,* ☎ *91/445–3752.*

Café Jazz Populart. Blues, jazz, Brazilian music, reggae, and salsa start at 11 PM. ✉ *Huertas 22,* ☎ *91/429–8407.*

Chocolatería San Ginés. Open from 6 PM to 7 AM, this is traditionally the last stop of the bleary-eyed after a hedonistic night out. Stumble in for great cups of thick *chocolate,* crisp *churros,* and a glass of water. ✉ *Pasadizo de San Ginés (enter by Arenal 11),* ☎ *91/365–6546. Closed Mon.*

Clamores. This famous jazz club serves a wide selection of French and Spanish champagnes. ✉ *Albuquerque 14,* ☎ *91/445–7938.*

Negra Tomasa. Under palm fronds and fishnets, the crowd drinks mojitos (made from sugar, crushed limes, mint, crushed ice, and flavored rum) to horns, maracas, and drums at this Cuban music bar. The house trio draws an international crowd on weekends. ✉ *C. Espoz y Mina and C. Cadiz,* ☎ *91/523–5830.*

Siroco. The music is live until 12:30 AM Thursday to Saturday; then funk and techno reign until 6 AM. ✉ *San Dimas 3,* ☎ *91/593–3070.*

Suristan. This relaxed venue just off the Plaza Santa Ana is a café by day, a college bar by evening, and an avant-garde theater of sorts late at night. It's a hip indie spot for nightly rock and pop concerts, as well as occasional theater and readings. ✉ *La Cruz 7,* ☎ *91/532–3909.*

Torero. A thoroughly modern club despite its name, Torero is for the beautiful people—quite literally: a bouncer allows only those judged *gente guapa* (beautiful people) to enter. It's one of Madrid's most stylin' spots. ✉ *Cruz 26,* ☎ *91/523–1129.*

Tapas Bars

The practice of spending the evening wandering from bar to bar and eating tapas is so popular that the Spanish have a verb to describe it:

tapear. Madrid's selection is endless; the best-known tapas bars are the *cuevas* clustered around Cava de San Miguel (☞ Old Madrid, *above*). A few more suggestions:

Bocaíto. This bar is said by some to serve the best tapas in Madrid—a heady claim. ✉ *Libertad 6,* ☎ *91/532–1219.*

★ **El Abuelo.** A legendary favorite even in the tapa-saturated Plaza Santa Ana area, El Abuelo (The Grandfather) serves only two tapas—and does them better than anyone else: grilled shrimp and shrimp sautéed with garlic. House tradition is to drink the sweet, red homemade house wine while tossing shrimp shells onto the floor. ✉ *Victoria 12,* ☎ *91/521–2319.*

El Rey de Pimiento. This bar serves some 40 different kinds of tapas, including, in keeping with its name (The Pepper King), roasted red pimientos as well as the intermittently hot pimientos *de padrón.* ✉ *Plaza Puerta Cerrada 4,* ☎ *91/365–2473.*

El Ventorrillo. Try to come here between May and October, when tables are set up in the shady park of Las Vistillas overlooking the city's western edge. Specialties include croquettes and mushrooms. This is Madrid's best place to watch the sun go down. ✉ *C. Bailén 14,* ☎ *91/366–3578.*

González. Founded in 1931, González is run by Vicente Carmona, once a professor of Spanish literature in the United States. The smart, trendy deli in front sells (and will ship) the best Spanish wines, olive oils, liqueurs, hams, cheeses, cold cuts, and pastries. The paneled wine bar in back is a great place to sample the wares. ✉ *C. Léon 12,* ☎ *91/429–5618.*

★ **La Chata.** Locals frequent this stylized *castizo* tapas bar, its walls and tree-trunk beams festooned with hams, sausages, chili peppers, and bullfight photos. You get an excellent free tapa with a drink; then choose from an array of snacks on display or some great *revuelto con ajetes* (scrambled eggs with green garlic tops). A slate shows wines available by the glass. ✉ *Cava Baja 24,* ☎ *91/366–1458.*

La Dolores. Crowded and noisy, this wonderful bar is rightly reputed to serve the best draft beer in Madrid. Located just behind the Palace Hotel, it has very few tables in back. ✉ *Plaza de Jesús 4,* ☎ *91/429–2243.*

★ **La Trucha.** Locals praise the exquisite tapas and the medieval-inn decor, hung with hams and garlic. House favorites are the enormous *plato de pescaditos fritos,* an assortment of fried fish, and *plato de ahumados,* an assortment of smoked-fish delicacies on toast. A terrace invites alfresco nibbling in summer. ✉ *Manuel Fernández y González 3,* ☎ *91/429–5833.*

Mesón Gallego. This hole-in-the-wall that serves wonderfully hearty Galician potato soup (a famous cure for those who've drunk too much) called *caldo gallego.* Not for everyone is the *Ribeiro,* the somewhat acidic white wine made with grapes from Galician riverbanks. ✉ *León 4,* ☎ *91/429–8997.*

Museo del Jamón. A small Madrid chain of tapas bars, the Ham Museum has become an institution. Look for the window full of dangling hams with hoofs. The best tapas are, of course, the air-cured hams, which come from all over the country. Don't be daunted by the variety; go for ordinary *serrano* or, if you feel like a splurge, the delicious, acorn-fed *ibérico de bellota.* ✉ *Carrera de San Jerónimo 6,* ☎ *91/458–0163; Mayor 7,* ☎ *91/531–4550; Paseo del Prado 44,* ☎ *91/420–2414.*

Taberna de Cien Vinos. Popular with wine buffs on Madrid's tapas circuit, this wine bar is tucked into a charming old house with wooden shutters and stone columns. You can order a wide selection of Spanish wines by the glass, and the *raciones* border on gourmet. ✉ *Nuncio 17,* ☏ *91/365–4704.*

OUTDOOR ACTIVITIES AND SPORTS

Participant Sports

Golf

Golf Olivar de la Hinojosa (✉ Avda. Dublín s/n, ☏ 91/721–1889), in Campo de las Naciones outside town, is open to the public with two courses (one 18 holes, one 9) and golf lessons.

Horseback Riding

Northeast of Madrid, **Club Hipica Mirasierra** (Carretera de Fuencarral al Pardo, Km 2.2, ☏ 91/747–7627) and the neighboring **Hipica Alameda del Pardo** (Carretera Fuencarral al Pardo, Km 2.3, ☏ 91/372–0958) rent horses and equipment to both children and adults, with lessons and short guided treks.

Jogging

Your best bet is the **Parque del Retiro,** where one path circles the entire park and numerous others weave their way under trees and through formal gardens. The **Casa de Campo** is crisscrossed by numerous, sunnier trails.

Swimming

Madrid has the perfect antidote to the dry, sometimes intense heat of the summer months—a superb system of clean, popular, well-run municipal swimming pools (admission about 350 ptas.). The biggest and best—fitted with a comfortable, tree-shaded restaurant—is in the **Casa de Campo** (take the metro to Lago and walk up the hill a few yards; ☏ 91/463–0050). Another good choice in the city center is the **Piscina Canal Isabel II** (✉ Plaza Juan Zorrila, entrance off Avda. de Filipinas, ☏ no phone), with diving boards and a wading pool for kids.

Tennis

Club de Tenis Chamartín (✉ Federico Salmon 2, ☏ 91/345–2500) is open to the public with 28 courts. There are also public courts in the **Casa de Campo** and on the Avenida de Vírgen del Puerto, behind the Palacio Real. The tourist office has details.

Spectator Sports

Bullfighting

Bullfighting is really a spectacle, not a sport. For those not turned off by the death of six bulls every Sunday afternoon from April to early November, it offers all the excitement of a major stadium event. Nowhere in the world is bullfighting better than at Madrid's **Las Ventas** (✉ C. Alcalá 231, ☏ 91/356–2200; metro: Las Ventas), formally called the Plaza de Toros Monumental. The sophisticated audience, which follows taurine matters closely, is more critical in Madrid than anywhere else, and if you're uninitiated you'll be amazed at how confusing their reactions to the fights can be. Cheers and hoots are difficult at first to distinguish, and it may take years to understand what prompts the wrath of this hard-to-please crowd. For a traveler, the bullfight audience can be the most entertaining part of the experience. Tickets can be purchased at the ring or, for a 20% surcharge, at one of the agencies on Calle Victoria, just off the Puerta del Sol. Most fights start in late afternoon, and the best fights of all—the world's top displays of bullfighting—come during the three weeks of consecutive daily fights that mark the feast of San Isidro, in May. Tickets can be tough to get through normal channels, but they're always available from scalpers in the Calle Victoria and at the stadium. You can bargain, but even Spaniards pay prices of perhaps 10 times the face value—up to 20,000 ptas. or even more.

NEED A BREAK?

El Albero (✉ Pedro Heredia 21, ☎ 91/355–1087) is an atmospheric bullfight bar and restaurant near the bullring. Have a tapa or a meal, perhaps with *rabo de toro,* bull's-tail stew. Enthusiastic owners José and Miguel Martín have entertained *aficionados* since 1991. To find the place, cross Alcalá in front of the ring, walk up and turn left down Maestro Alonso.

Soccer

Spain's number-one sport is known locally as *fútbol.* Madrid has two teams, Real Madrid and Atlético Madrid, both among Europe's best, and two stadiums to match. The enormous **Santiago Bernabeu Stadium** (✉ Paseo de la Castellana 140, ☎ 91/398–4300), which seats 75,000, is home to the more popular Real Madrid, while the **Vicente Calderón Stadium** (✉ Virgen del Puerto 67, ☎ 91/366–4704 or 91/364–0888), on the outskirts of town, is where Atlético Madrid defends. You'll generally have to stand in line at the stadium to get tickets, but tickets for many major games are available at agencies inside Corte Inglés department stores (☞ Shopping, *below*).

SHOPPING

Madrid has more on offer than Lladró porcelain and bullfighting posters; Spain has been recognized in recent years as one of the world's top design centers. You'll have no trouble finding traditional crafts in Madrid, such as ceramics, guitars, and leather goods (albeit not at countryside prices), but don't stop there. The city is now more like Rodeo Drive than the bargain bin that it was just a decade ago. Known for contemporary furniture and decorative items as well as chic clothing, shoes, and jewelry, Spain's capital is stiff competition for Barcelona, a city that now considers itself the fashion capital of Europe. Most shops accept most major credit cards.

Department Stores

El Corte Inglés. Spain's largest department store carries the best selection of everything, from auto parts to groceries to designer fashions. ✉ ☎ *901/122122 for general information,* ☎ *902/400222 for ticket sales.* ✉ *Preciados 3,* ☎ *91/531–9619;* ✉ *Goya 76 and 87,* ☎ *91/432–9300;* ✉ *Princesa 56,* ☎ *91/454–6000;* ✉ *Serrano 47,* ☎ *91/432–5490;* ✉ *Raimundo Fernández Villaverde 79,* ☎ *91/418–8800.*

Marks & Spencer. British chain "Marks & Sparks" is best known for its woolens and underwear, but most shoppers head straight for the gourmet-food shop in the basement. ✉ *Serrano 52,* ☎ *91/520–0000.*

Zara. For those with young tastes and slim pocketbooks (picture hip clothes that you'll throw away in about six months), Zara has the latest looks for men, women, and children. ✉ *Centro Comercial ABC,* ✉ *Serrano 61,* ☎ *91/575–6334;* ✉ *Gran Vía 32,* ☎ *91/522–9727;* ✉ *Princesa 63,* ☎ *91/543–2415;* ✉ *Conde de Peñalver 4,* ☎ *91/435–4135.*

Flea Market

On Sunday, Calle de Ribera de Curtidores is closed to traffic and jammed with outdoor booths selling everything under the sun—its weekly transformation into **El Rastro.** The crowds grow so thick that it takes a while just to advance a few feet amid the hawkers and the gawkers. A word of warning: pickpockets abound here. Hang on to your purse and wallet, and be especially careful if you choose to bring a camera. The flea market sprawls into most of the surrounding streets, with certain areas specializing in particular products. Many of the goods sold here are wildly overpriced.

But what goods! The Rastro has everything from antique furniture to exotic parrots and cuddly puppies; from pirated cassette tapes of flamenco music to key chains emblazoned with symbols of the CNT, Spain's old anarchist trade union. Practice your Spanish by bargaining with the vendors over paintings, colorful Gypsy oxen yokes, heraldic iron gates, new and used clothes, and even hashish pipes. They may not lower their prices, but sometimes they'll throw in a handmade bracelet or a stack of postcards to sweeten the deal.

Off the Ribera are two *galerías,* courtyards where small shops offer higher-quality, higher-priced antiques and other goods. The whole spectacle shuts down around 2 PM.

Shopping Districts

Madrid has two main shopping areas. The first is in the center of town, around the **Puerta del Sol,** and includes the major department stores (El Corte Inglés, the French music-and-book chain FNAC, etc.) and a large number of mid-range shops in the streets nearby. The second area, far more elegant and expensive, is in the northwestern **Salamanca** district, bounded roughly by Serrano, Goya, and Conde de Peñalver. These streets, just off the Plaza de Colón (particularly Calle Serrano), have the widest selection of smart boutiques and designer fashions—think Prada, Armani, and Donna Karan New York, as well as renowned Spanish designers such as Sybilla and Josep Font-Luz Diaz. If you're in the market for clothes, you may find that Spaniards, like Italians, favor brown tones; cool palettes don't prevail, though of course black is readily available.

Galerías del Prado (⊠ Plaza de las Cortes 7) is an attractive mall tucked under the Palace Hotel on the Paseo del Prado. Shop here for fine books, gourmet foods, clothing, leather goods, art, and more. Madrid's newest mall is a four-decker: the **Centro Comercial ABC** (⊠ Paseo de la Castellana 34/Serrano 61), named for the daily newspaper founded on the premises in the 19th century. The building is a beautifully restored landmark with an ornate tile facade; inside, a large café is surrounded by shops of all kinds, including leather stores and hairdressers. The fourth-floor restaurant has a rooftop terrace with scenic urban views. For street-chic shopping closer to medieval Madrid, check out the playful window displays at the **Madrid Fusion Centro de Moda** (⊠ Plaza Tirso de Molina 15, ☎ 91/369–0018), where up-and-coming Spanish design houses fill five floors with faux furs, funky jewelry, and Madrid's most eccentric collection of shoes.

Specialty Stores

Books and Maps—The Outdoors

Established in 1950, **La Tienda Verde** (⊠ Maudes 23 and 38, ☎ 91/535–3810) is a paradise for outdoor enthusiasts planning hikes, mountain-climbing expeditions, spelunking trips, and so forth, with detailed maps and (Spanish-language) guidebooks.

Boutiques and Fashion

Adolfo Domínguez (✉ Serrano 96, ☏ 91/576–7053; ✉ Serrano 18, ☏ 91/577–8280) is one of Spain's best-known designers, with lines for both men and women. One of Spain's premier young designers, **Jesús del Pozo** (✉ Almirante 9, ☏ 91/531–3646) also caters to both sexes. His boutique is an excellent, if pricey, place to pick up some classic Spanish style. **Seseña** (✉ De la Cruz 23, ☏ 91/531–6840) has outfitted Hollywood stars (and Hillary Rodham Clinton) and famous painters since the turn of the century, with capes in wool or velvet, some lined with red satin. **Sybilla** (✉ Jorge Juan 12, ☏ 91/578–1322) is the studio of Spain's best-known female designer. Her fluid dresses and handknit sweaters, which have made her a favorite with supermodel Helena Christensen, come in natural colors and fabrics.

Ceramics

Antigua Casa Talavera (✉ Isabel la Católica 2, ☏ 91/547–3417) is the best of Madrid's numerous ceramics shops. Despite the name, the finest ware sold here is from Manises, near Valencia, but the blue-and-yellow Talavera ceramics are also excellent. **Cerámica El Alfar** (✉ Claudio Coello 112, ☏ 91/411–3587) is laden with pottery from all corners of Spain. **Sagardelos** (✉ Zurbano 46, ☏ 91/310–4830) specializes in distinctive, modern Spanish ceramics from Galicia and has excellent selections of breakfast sets, coffee pots, and objets d'art.

Crafts and Design

Casa Julia (✉ Almirante 1, ☏ 91/522–0270) is an artistic showcase, with two floors of tasteful antiques, paintings by up-and-coming artists, and furniture in experimental designs. It's a great place to hunt for non-traditional souvenirs. **El Arco** (✉ Plaza Mayor 9, ☏ 91/365–2680) has a good selection of contemporary handicrafts from all over Spain, including modern ceramics, handblown glassware, jewelry, and leather items as well as a whimsical collection of pendulum clocks.

Fans

Casa Diego (✉ Puerta del Sol 12, ☏ 91/522–6643), established in 1853, stocks a classic collection of fans, umbrellas, and classic Spanish walking sticks with ornamented silver handles. The British royal family buys autograph fans here—white kid-skin fans for signing on special occasions.

Food and Wine

The Club Gourmet sections in **El Corte Inglés** (☞ Department Stores, *above*) stores present a wide choice of Spanish wines, olive oils, and foodstuffs. Handily located near Plaza Santa Ana and Plaza de les Cortés, **González** (✉ Calle Léon 21, ☏ 91/429–5618) features fine Spanish wines, olive oils, cheeses, hams, dried pulses, and other foods. Sample the offerings at the wine bar at back. **Lavinina** (✉ José Ortega y Gasset 16, ☏ 91/426–0604) claims to be the largest wine store in Europe, and does have a massive selection of bottles, books, and bar accessories. The upscale chain **Mallorca** (✉ Velázquez 59, ☏ 91/431–9909; Serrano 6, ☏ 91/577–1859; Centro Comercial, Goya 6, ☏ 91/577–2123) sells prepared meals, cocktail canapés, chocolates, and wines, and has tapas counters for sampling.

Guitars

José Ramirez (✉ General Margallo 10, ☏ 91/571–8431) has provided Spain and the rest of the world with guitars since 1882. Prices start at 15,000 ptas. The shop includes a museum of antique instruments. **Real Música** (✉ Carlos III 1, ☏ 91/541–3007), around the corner from the Teatro Real, is a music lover's dream, with Madrid's best selection of guitars and other instruments as well as sheet music, CDs, memorabilia, and a savvy staff.

Hats

Century-old **Casa Yustas** (✉ Plaza Mayor 30, ☎ 91/366–5084) carries every type of headgear from the old three-corner, patent-leather hats of the Guardia Civil to the berets worn by the Guardia's frequent enemy, the Basques. These berets are much wider than those worn by the French and make excellent gifts.

Leather Goods

On a street full of bargain shoe stores (*muestrarios*), **Caligae** (✉ Augusto Figueroa 27, ☎ 91/531–5343) is probably the best of the bunch. Posh **Loewe** (✉ Serrano 26 and 34, ☎ 91/577–6056; ✉ Gran Vía 8, ☎ 91/532–7024; ✉ Palace Hotel, ☎ 91/429–8530) features ultra-high quality designer purses, accessories, and clothing made of buttery-soft leather in dyed, jewel-like colors. Prices can hit the stratosphere. **Tenorio** (✉ Plaza de la Provincia 6, ☎ 91/366–4440) is where you'll find those fine old boots of Spanish leather, made to order with workmanship that should last a lifetime and is priced accordingly, starting at 110,000 ptas.

Toys

The charming shop **Gepetto** (✉ Diego de León 47, ☎ 91/563–4507) sells more than just puppets, particularly handcrafted wooden toys in all shapes and sizes. They're on the expensive end, but some of these pieces are works of art and make exquisite gifts for toy lovers of any age.

SIDE TRIPS

El Escorial

42 *50 km (31 mi) northwest of Madrid.*

Felipe II was one of history's most deeply religious and forbidding monarchs—not to mention one of its most powerful—and the great granite monastery that he had constructed in a remarkable 21 years (1563–84) is an enduring testament to his character. Outside Madrid in the foothills of the Sierra de Guadarrama, the **Real Monasterio de San Lorenzo de El Escorial** (Royal Monastery of St. Lawrence of Escorial) is severe, rectilinear, and unforgiving—one of the most gigantic yet simple architectural monuments on the Iberian Peninsula.

Felipe built the monastery in the village of San Lorenzo de El Escorial to commemorate Spain's crushing victory over the French at Saint-Quentin on August 10, 1557, and as a final resting place for his all-powerful father, the Holy Roman Emperor Carlos V. He filled the place with treasures as he ruled the largest empire the world has ever seen, knowing all the while that a marble coffin awaited him in the pantheon deep below. The building's vast rectangle, encompassing 16 courts, is modeled on the red-hot grille upon which St. Lawrence was martyred—appropriate enough, since August 10 was that saint's day. (It's also said that Felipe's troops accidentally destroyed a church dedicated to St. Lawrence during the battle, and he sought to make amends.) Some years ago a Spanish psychohistorian theorized that the building is shaped like a prone woman and is thus an unintended emblem of Felipe's sexual repression. Lo and behold, this thesis provoked several newspaper articles and a rash of other commentary.

El Escorial is easily reached by car, train, bus, or organized tour; simply inquire at a travel agency or the appropriate station. Although the building and its adjuncts—a palace, museum, church, and more—can take hours or even days to tour, you should be able to include a day trip to the Valley of the Fallen, an underground basilica where Gen-

Side Trips from Madrid

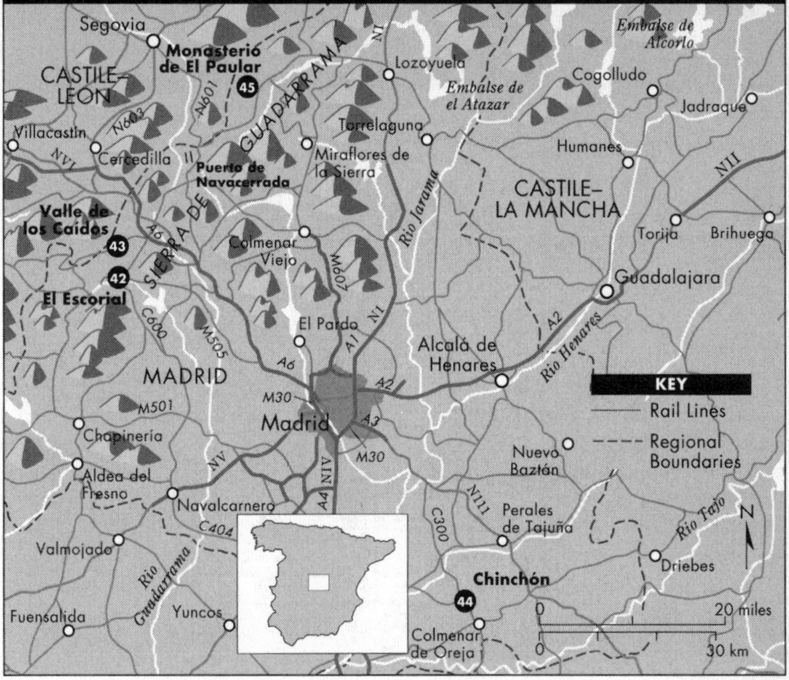

eral Franco is buried. Be prepared for the mobs of tourists who visit El Escorial daily, especially in summer. Midnight mass on Easter Sunday, which includes a candlelight ceremony, also draws a big crowd, so arrive at least half an hour early if you want a seat.

The monastery was begun by Juan Bautista de Toledo but finished in 1584 by Juan de Herrera, who would eventually give his name to a major Spanish architectural school. It was completed just in time for Felipe to die here, gangrenous and tortured by the gout that had plagued him for years, in the tiny, sparsely furnished bedroom that resembled a monk's cell more than the resting place of a great monarch. It is in this bedroom—which looks out, through a private entrance, into the royal chapel—that one most appreciates the man's spartan nature. Spain's later, Bourbon kings, such as Carlos III and Carlos IV, had clearly different tastes, and their apartments, connected to Felipe's by the Hall of Battles, are far more luxurious.

Perhaps the most interesting part of the entire Escorial is the **Panteón de los Reyes** (Royal Pantheon), which contains the body of every king since Carlos I save three—Felipe V (buried at La Granja), Ferdinand VI (in Madrid), and Amadeus of Savoy (in Italy). The body of Alfonso XIII, who died in Rome in 1941, was brought to El Escorial in January 1980. The rulers' bodies lie in 26 sumptuous marble and bronze sarcophagi that line the walls (three of which are empty, awaiting future rulers). Only those queens who bore sons later crowned lie in the same crypt; the others, along with royal sons and daughters who never ruled, lie nearby, in the **Panteón de los Infantes**. Many of the royal children are in a single circular tomb made of Carrara marble.

Another highlight is the monastery's uncharacteristically lavish and beautiful **library**, with 50,000 rare manuscripts, codices, and ancient books, including the diary of St. Teresa of Ávila and the gold-lettered, illu-

- Apartments of Philip II. **14**
- Basilica **4**
- Biblioteca (Library). **9**
- Choir. **3**
- Colegio **11**
- Convent. . . . **10**
- Main Entrance **1**
- Museum. . . . **13**
- Patio de los Evangelistas (Court of the Evangelists) . . **7**
- Patio de los Reyes (Court of the Kings). . . . **2**
- Royal Palace **12**
- Sacristy **6**
- Salas Capitulares (Chapter Houses) **8**
- Stairway to Panteón de los Reyes (Royal Pantheon). . . . **5**
- Tour Entrance . . . **15**

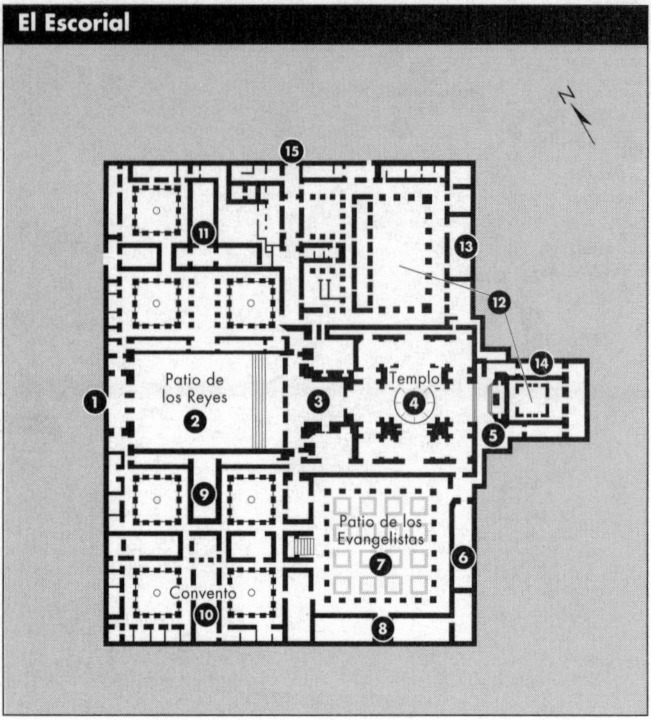

minated *Codex Aureus.* Tapestries, woven from cartoons by Goya, Rubens, and El Greco, cover almost every inch of wall space in huge sections of the building, and extraordinary canvases by Velázquez, El Greco, David, Ribera, Tintoretto, Rubens, and other masters have been collected from around the monastery and are now displayed in the New Museums. In the **basilica,** don't miss the fresco above the choir, depicting heaven, or Titian's fresco *The Martyrdom of St. Lawrence,* which shows the saint being roasted alive. ✉ *San Lorenzo de El Escorial,* ☎ *91/890–5905.* 🎫 *800 ptas.* ⏲ *Apr.–Sept., Tues.–Sun. 10–6; Oct.–Mar., Tues.–Sun. 10–5.*

NEED A BREAK? Many Madrileños find El Escorial the perfect place for an enormous weekend lunch. Topping the list of eating spots is the outdoor terrace at **Charoles** (✉ Floridablanca 24, ☎ 91/890–5975), where imaginative seasonal specialties round out a menu of northern-Spanish favorites, such as *bacalao al pil-pil* (salt cod cooked in oil and garlic at a low temperature) and grilled *chuleta* (steak). Just don't expect picnic prices.

Valle de los Caídos

43 *13 km (8 mi) north of El Escorial on C600.*

The Valley of the Fallen is just a few minutes north of El Escorial. You drive through a pine-studded state park to this massive basilica, which is carved out of a hill of solid granite and commands magnificent views to the east. Topped with a cross nearly 500 ft high (accessible by elevator), the basilica holds the tombs of both General Franco and José Antonio Primo de Rivera, founder of the Spanish Falange. It was built with the forced labor of Republican prisoners after the civil war and dedicated, rather disingenuously, to all who died in the three-year conflict. The inside recalls *The Wizard of Oz* more than anything else, with every footstep resounding loudly off its stone walls. Tapestries of the Apocalypse add to the generally terrifying air. It's an eerie place for the midnight mass held here on Easter Sunday; the granite peak becomes truly awesome when lit by candlelight. ☏ *91/890–5611.* ✉ *Basilica 650 ptas., funicular 350 ptas.* ⏲ *Apr.–Sept., Tues.–Sun. 10–7; Oct.–Mar., Tues.–Sun. 10–6.*

Chinchón

44 *54 km (33 mi) southeast of Madrid, off the N III highway to Valencia on the C300 local road.*

A true Castilian town, the picturesque village of Chinchón seems a good four centuries removed. It makes an ideal day trip, especially if you save time for lunch at one of its many rustic restaurants; the only problem is that swarms of Madrileños have the same idea, so it's often hard to get a table at lunchtime on weekends.

The high point of Chinchón is its charming **Plaza Mayor,** an uneven circle of ancient three- and four-story houses embellished with wooden balconies resting on granite columns. It's something like an open-air Elizabethan theater, but with a Spanish flavor. In fact, the entire plaza is converted to a bullring from time to time, with temporary bleachers erected in the center and seats on the privately owned balconies rented out for splendid views of the festivities. (These fights are rare and tickets hard to come by, as they're snatched up by traveling Spaniards as soon as they go on sale.) The commanding **Iglesia de la Asunción** (Church of the Assumption), overlooking the plaza, is known for its Goya mural, *The Assumption of the Virgin.*

NEED A BREAK?

On winter weekends, city dwellers reserve in droves for the superb cocido at the **Parador de Chinchón** (✉ Avda. Generalísimo 1, ☏ 91/894–0836). Two other popular restaurants on Chinchón's arcaded plaza are **Mesón de la Virreina** (✉ Plaza Mayor 28, ☏ 91/894–0015) and **Café de la Iberia** (✉ Plaza Mayor 17, ☏ 91/894–0998), both of which have balconies for outdoor dining in season, though you may have to call ahead for such a table. The food in both is hearty Castilian fare, such as roast lamb, suckling pig, and thick steaks. Be sure to try the locally made *anís* (anise), a licorice-flavored spirit—Chinchón is so famous for its anís that Spaniards converge here every April for the annual Fiesta del Anís y del Vino (Anise and Wine Festival).

On the way back to Madrid, where C300 joins the main highway, you'll pass through the Jarama Valley. This was the scene of one of the bloodiest battles in which the Abraham Lincoln Brigade (American volunteers fighting with the Republicans against Franco in the Spanish Civil War) played a major role. The fight was immortalized by folk singer Pete Seeger, who sang, "There's a valley in Spain called Jarama . . ." Until just a few years ago, you could find bones and rusty military hardware in the fields here, and there are still a number of clearly discernible trenches.

Monasterio de El Paular and Lozoya Valley

45 *100 km (62 mi) north of Madrid.*

Behind the great *meseta* on which Madrid stands, the Sierra de Guadarrama rises like a dark, jagged shield separating Old and New Castile. Snowcapped for much of the year, the mountains are indeed roughhewn in many spots, particularly on their northern face, but there is a dramatic exception—the Lozoya Valley.

About 100 km (62 mi) north of the capital, this valley of pines, poplars, and babbling brooks is a cool, green retreat from the often searing heat of the plain. Madrileños repair here for a picnic or a simple drive, rarely joined by foreign travelers, to whom the area is virtually unknown.

You'll need a car to make this trip, and the drive is a pleasant one. Take the A6 northwest from Madrid and exit at signs for the Navacerrada Pass on the N601. As you climb toward the 6,100-ft mountain pass, you'll come to a road bearing off to the left toward Cercedilla. (This little village, a popular base for hikes, is also accessible by train.) Just above Cercedilla, an old Roman road leads up to the ridge of the Guadarrama, where an ancient fountain, known as Fuenfría, long provided the spring water that fed the Roman aqueduct of Segovia (☞ Chapter 2). The path traced by this cobble road is very close to the route Hemingway had his hero Robert Jordan take in *For Whom the Bell Tolls,* and eventually takes you near the bridge that Jordan blew up in the novel.

If you continue past the Cercedilla road, you'll come to a ski resort at the highest point of the Navacerrada Pass. Take a right here on C604 and you'll follow the ridge of the mountains for a few miles before descending into the **Lozoya Valley.**

Looming on your left as you approach the valley floor is the **Monasterio de El Paular** (☎ 91/869–1425). Built by King Juan I in 1390, this was the first Carthusian monastery in Castile, but it has been badly neglected since the Disentailment of 1836, when religious organizations gave their artistic treasures to the state. Fewer than a dozen Benedictine monks still live here, eating and praying exactly as their predecessors did centuries ago. One of them gives daily tours every day but Thursday at noon, 1, and 5.

The monastery is attached to the hotel **Santa María de El Paular** (☎ 91/869–1011, FAX 91/869–1006), most of whose rooms were tastefully refurbished in 1996. The hotel is charming but not as grand as similarly priced paradors.

The valley is filled with picnic spots along the Lozoya River, including several campgrounds. To end the excursion, take C604 north a few miles to Rascafria, and then turn right on a smaller road marked for Miraflores de la Sierra. In that town you'll turn right again, following signs for Colmenar Viejo, and then pick up a short expressway back to Madrid.

MADRID A TO Z

Arriving and Departing

By Bus

Madrid has no central bus station; buses are generally less popular than trains (though they can be faster). Most of southern Spain is served by the **Estación del Sur** (✉ Méndez Álvaro s/n, ☎ 91/468–4200), while buses for much of the rest of the peninsula, including Cuenca, Extremadura, Salamanca, and Valencia, depart from the **Auto Res** station (✉ Plaza Conde de Casal 6, ☎ 91/551–7200). There are several smaller stations, however, so inquire at travel agencies for the one serving your destination.

Bus companies of interest include **La Sepulvedana** (✉ Paseo de la Florida 11, near Estación de Norte, ☎ 91/530–4800), serving Segovia, Ávila, and La Granja; **Herranz** (departures from ✉ Fernández de los Ríos s/n, ☎ 91/543–8167; metro: Moncloa), for El Escorial and the Valle de los Caídos; **Continental Auto** (✉ C. Alenza 20, ☎ 91/533–

0400; metro: Ríos Rosas), serving Cantabria and the Basque region; and **La Veloz** (✉ Mediterraneo 49, ☎ 91/409–7602; metro: Conde de Casal), with service to Chinchón.

By Car

Felipe II made Madrid the capital of Spain because it was at the geographic center of his peninsular domains, and indeed many of the nation's highways radiate from Madrid like the spokes of a wheel. Originating at Kilometer 0—marked by a brass plaque on the sidewalk of the Puerta del Sol—these highways include the A6 (Segovia, Salamanca, Galicia); A1 (Burgos and the Basque Country); the N-II (Guadalajara, Barcelona, France); the N-III (Cuenca, Valencia, the Mediterranean coast); the A4 (Aranjuez, La Mancha, Granada, Seville); the N401 (Toledo); and the N-V (Talavera de la Reina, Portugal). The city is surrounded by M30 (the inner ring road) and M40 (the outer ring road), from which most of these highways are easily picked up.

By Plane

Madrid is served by **Barajas Airport,** 12 km (7 mi) east of the city. Europe's longest runway opened for traffic here in 1999. Several major airlines have regular flights from the United States, and others serve London and other European capitals daily. Shopping among Madrid travel agencies will probably get you a lower fare than those available abroad, especially to and from Great Britain. For more information on flying to Madrid, *see* Air Travel *in* Smart Travel Tips. For general information, including details of flight delays, call the airport (☎ 91/305–8343, 91/305–8344, 91/305–8345, or 91/393–6000).

BETWEEN THE AIRPORT AND DOWNTOWN

For a mere 375 ptas. there's a convenient **bus** to the central Plaza Colón, where a taxi can take you to your hotel. Buses leave every 15 minutes between 5:40 AM and 2 AM (slightly less often very early or late in the day). Watch your belongings, as the underground Plaza Colón bus station is a favorite haunt of purse snatchers and con artists. The **metro** is a bargain at 135 ptas. per ticket (or 705 ptas. for a 10-trip ticket that can also be used on city buses), but you have to change trains to get downtown. **Taxis** normally wait outside the airport terminal near the clearly marked bus stop; expect to pay up to 2,000 ptas., more in heavy traffic, plus small holiday, late-night, and/or luggage surcharges. Make sure the driver works on the meter; off-the-meter "deals" almost always cost more. Finally, some hotels offer **shuttle** service in vans; check with yours when you reserve.

By Train

For train schedules and reservations contact **RENFE** (☎ 91/328–9020, www.renfe.es) or go to the information counter in any of the stations below. You can reserve by phone, charge your tickets to a credit card, and even have them delivered to your hotel. Most major travel agencies also sell tickets.

Madrid has three main train stations: *estaciones* Chamartín, Atocha, and Norte. Remember to confirm which station you need when arranging a trip. Generally speaking, **Chamartín** (☎ 91/315–9976), near the northern tip of Paseo Castellana, serves trains bound for points north and west, including Barcelona, San Sebastián, Burgos, León, Oviedo, La Coruña, and Salamanca, as well as France and Portugal. **Atocha** (☎ 91/328–9020), at the southern end of Paseo del Prado, provides AVE (high-speed) train service to Córdoba and Seville and regular service to points mainly south and east, including El Escorial, Segovia, Toledo, Seville, Málaga, Córdoba, Valencia, and Castellón. **Norte** is primarily for local trains serving Madrid's western suburbs.

Getting Around

Madrid's neighborhoods have distinct characters. You'll probably want to start out in the old city, where the main attractions are clustered, but the spirit of adventure will call you to other parts of town.

By Bus

Red city buses run between 6 AM and midnight and cost 130 ptas. per ride. After midnight, buses called *buyos* (night owls) run out to the suburbs from Plaza de Cibeles for the same price. There are signs at every stop listing all stops by street name, but they're hard to comprehend if you don't know the city well. Pick up a free route map from EMT kiosks on the Plaza de Cibeles or the Puerta del Sol, where you can also buy a 10-ride ticket called a Metrobus (705 ptas.) that's equally valid for the metro. If you speak Spanish, call for information (☏ 91/406–8810).

Drivers will generally make change for anything up to a 2,000-pta. note. If you've bought a 10-ride ticket, step just behind the driver and insert it in the ticket-punching machine until the mechanism goes "ding."

By Car

Driving in Madrid is best avoided by all but the bravest souls. Parking is nightmarish, traffic is extremely heavy almost all the time, and the city's daredevil drivers can be frightening. August may be an exception; the streets are then largely emptied by the mass exodus of Madrileños on vacation.

By Metro

The metro is quick, frequent, and, at 135 ptas. no matter how far you travel, cheap. Even cheaper is the 10-ride Metrobus ticket, or *billete de diez,* which costs 705 ptas., is also valid for buses, and is accepted by automatic turnstiles (lines at ticket booths can be long). The system is open from 6 AM to 1:30 AM, though a few entrances close earlier. There are 10 metro lines, and system maps in every station detail their color-coded routes. Note the end station of the line you need, and just follow signs to the correct corridor. Exits are marked SALIDA.

By Motorbike

You can rent motorbikes, scooters, and motorcycles by the day or week at **Moto Alquiler** (✉ Conde Duque 13, ☏ 91/542–0657). If you're *loco* enough to battle Madrid's traffic, this is a fast and pleasant way to see the city. You'll need your passport, your driver's license, and either a cash deposit or a credit card.

By Taxi

Taxis are one of Madrid's few truly good deals. Meters start at 190 ptas. and add 95 ptas. per km (½ mi) thereafter (125 ptas. per km at night, on weekends and holidays, and beyond city limits). Numerous supplemental charges, however, mean that your total cost often bears little resemblance to what you see on the meter. Supplemental charges—over and above your fare—include 150 ptas. on Sundays and holidays and between 11 PM and 6 AM, 150 ptas. to sports stadiums or the bullring, and 400 ptas. (plus 50 ptas. per suitcase) to or from the airport.

Taxi stands are numerous, and taxis are easily hailed in the street—except when it rains, at which point they're exceedingly hard to come by. Available cabs display a LIBRE sign during the day, a green light at night. Generally, a tip of about 25 ptas. is right for shorter rides; you may want to go as high as 10% for a trip to the airport. You can call a cab through **Tele-Taxi** (☏ 91/371–2131), **Radioteléfono Taxi** (☏ 91/547–8200), or **Radio Taxi Gremial** (☏ 91/447–5180).

Madrid Metro

Contacts and Resources

Embassies

Australia (✉ Plaza del Descubridor Diego de Ordás 3, Santa Engracia 120, ☎ 91/441–9300). **Canada** (✉ Nuñez de Balboa 35, ☎ 91/431–4300). **New Zealand** (✉ Plaza de La Lealtad 2, ☎ 91/523–0226). **United Kingdom** (✉ Fernando el Santo 19, ☎ 91/319–0200). **United States** (✉ Serrano 75, ☎ 91/577–4000).

Emergencies

General: (☎ 112). English-speaking **doctors** (✉ Conde de Aranda 7, ☎ 91/435–1823). Major hospitals: **La Paz** (✉ Paseo de la Castellana 261, ☎ 91/358–2600). **Ramon y Cajal** (✉ Carretera de Colmenar, Km 9, ☎ 91/336–8000). **12 de Octubre** (Carretera de Andalucía, Km 5.4, ☎ 91/390–8000).

English-Language Bookstores

Casa del Libro (✉ Maestro Victoria 3, ☎ 91/521–4898), not far from the Puerta del Sol, has an impressive collection of English-language books, including Spanish classics in translation and detailed city guides. It's also a good source for maps, cookbooks, and gifts. **Booksellers** (✉ José Abascal 48, ☎ 91/442–8104) also has a large selection of books in English.

Guided Tours

GROUP TOURS

Your hotel can arrange standard city tours in either English or Spanish; most offer **Madrid Artístico** (including the Royal Palace and the Prado), **Madrid Panorámico** (a half-day tour for first-time visitors), **Madrid de Noche** (combinations include a flamenco or a nightclub show), and **Panorámico y Toros** (on Sunday, a brief city overview followed by a bullfight). The **Municipal Tourist Office** (✉ Plaza Mayor 3, ☎ 91/588–2900) arranges tours of Madrid's old quarters in English every Saturday morning, departing from the tourist office on the Plaza Mayor at 10. The **ayuntamiento** (city hall) has a popular selection of Spanish bus and walking tours under the rubric "Descubre Madrid." The walking tours, which depart most mornings, visit many hidden corners as well as major sights; options include "Madrid's Railroads," "Medicine in Madrid," "Goya's Madrid," and "Commerce and Finance in Madrid." Schedules are listed in the leaflet available from the municipal tourist office. Buy tickets at the Patronato de Turismo (✉ C. Mayor 69, ☎ 91/588–2900). For day trips to sites outside Madrid, such as Toledo, El Escoral, and Segovia, contact **Julià Tours** (Gran Ví 68, ☎ 91/559–9605).

Trapsatur (☎ 91/302–6039) runs the *Madrid Visión* tourist bus, which makes a 1½-hour sightseeing circuit of the city with recorded commentary in English. No advance reservation is needed; just show up at Gran Vía 32. Buses also leave from the front of the Prado Museum every 1½ hours beginning at 12:30 Monday–Saturday, 10:30 on Sunday. A round-trip ticket costs 1,500 ptas.; a day pass, which allows you to get on and off at various attractions, is 2,000 ptas. An identical hop-on, hop-off service on an open-top double decker is operated by **Sol Pentours** (✉ Gran Vía 26, ☎ 902/303903), whose daily tours leave every half hour from Plaza de España, in front of the Crowne Plaza Hotel, between 10 AM and 8 PM. The fare is 1,600 ptas., and the complete ride takes 90 minutes.

PERSONAL GUIDES

Contact the **Asociación Profesional de Informadores** (✉ Ferraz 82, ☎ 91/542–1214 or 91/541–1221) to hire a personal guide.

Late-Night Pharmacies

Emergency pharmacies are required by law to be open 24 hours a day on a rotating basis. Pharmacy windows and all major daily newspapers list the pharmacies open round-the-clock that day.

Travel Agencies

Travel agencies are scattered throughout Madrid and are generally the best way to get deals, tickets, and information without hassles. Some major firms: **American Express,** next door to the Cortés (parliament building) on Génova (✉ Plaza de las Cortés 2, ☎ 91/322–5500); **Carlson Wagons-Lits** (✉ Paseo de la Castellana 96, ☎ 91/563–1202); and **Pullmantur,** across the street from the Royal Palace (✉ Plaza de Oriente 8, ☎ 91/541–1807).

The British-run agency **Madrid & Beyond** (✉ Gran Vía 59-8D, ☎ 91/758–0063, FAX 91/542–4391) can make all your travel and lodging arrangements for you in Madrid, other historic cities, and some rural gems.

Visitor Information

Madrid has four regional tourist offices. The best is on **Duque de Medinaceli 2** (☎ 91/429–4951), near the Palace Hotel, open weekdays 9–7 and Saturday 9–1. The others are at **Barajas Airport** (☎ 91/305–8656), open weekdays 9–7 and Saturday 9:30–1:30; the **Chamartín** train station (☎ 91/315–9976), open weekdays 8–8 and Saturday 9–1; and the remote **Mercado de la Puerta de Toledo** (Glorieta Puerta de Toledo, 3rd floor, ☎ 91/364–1876), open weekdays 9–7 and Saturday 9–1. The **city tourist office** on the Plaza Mayor (☎ 91/366–5477) is good for little save a few pamphlets; it's open weekdays 10–8, Saturday 10–2, and Sunday 10–2.

2 OLD AND NEW CASTILE

Central Spain is a vast, windswept plateau with clear skies, muted colors, and endless vistas. Leaving Madrid, you can savor Segovia, with its outstanding Roman aqueduct and lovely castle and cathedral; Ávila, once home of the mystical St. Teresa and still enclosed by medieval walls; Toledo, long Spain's cultural capital, with legacies from three religions; and Aranjuez, with its French-style Bourbon palace. Farther out, Salamanca beckons with golden sandstone and a university scene, and Burgos and León stand as ancient Castilian capitals with glorious cathedrals.

By Michael Jacobs

Updated by Edward Owen

FOR ALL THE VARIETY in the towns and countryside around Madrid, there is an underlying unity. Castile is essentially an endless *meseta* (plain)—gray, bronze, green, and severe. Over the centuries, poets and others have characterized it as austere and melancholy, most notably Antonio Machado, whose experiences at Soria in the early 20th century inspired his memorable and haunting *Campos de Castilla* (*Fields of Castile*). There is a distinct, chilly beauty in the stark lines, soothing colors, and sharp air of these breezy expanses.

Stone, a dominant element in the Castilian countryside, gives the region much of its character. Gaunt mountain ranges frame the horizons; gorges and rocky outcrops break up flat expanses; and the fields around Ávila and Segovia are littered with giant boulders. Castilian villages are built predominantly of granite, and their solid, formidable look contrasts markedly with the whitewashed walls of most of southern Spain. The presence of so much stone may help to explain the region's rich tradition of sculpture—Castile has one of Europe's most significant stashes of sculptural treasures, many on display in the unrivaled National Museum of Sculpture, in Valladolid.

Castile is more accurately labeled Old and New Castile, the former (Castilla y León) north of Madrid, the latter (Castilla–La Mancha) south—known as "New" because it was captured from the Moors a bit later. Whereas southern Spaniards are traditionally passive and peace-loving, Castilians have been a race of soldiers. The very name of the region (in effect, *la región castilla*, the region of castles) refers to the great east–west line of castles and fortified towns built in the 12th century between Salamanca and Soria. Segovia's Alcázar, Ávila's fully intact city walls, and countless other military installations are among Castile's greatest monuments, and some of them—the castles at Sigüenza and Ciudad Rodrigo, for instance—are also splendid hotels.

Faced with the austerity of the Castilian environment, many have taken refuge in the worlds of the spirit and the imagination. Ávila is closely associated with two of Europe's most renowned mystics, St. Teresa and her disciple St. John of the Cross, and Toledo was the main home of one of the most spiritual of all Western painters, El Greco. Escape into pure fantasy is best illustrated by Cervantes's hero Don Quixote, in whose formidable imagination even the dreary expanse of La Mancha became something magical. Many of the region's architects were similarly fanciful: Castile in the 15th and 16th centuries was the center of the plateresque, an ornamental stone-carving style of extraordinary intricacy, named for its resemblance to silverwork. Developed in Toledo and Valladolid, it reached its exuberant climax in the university town of Salamanca.

Burgos was the 11th-century capital of Castile and the native city of El Cid ("Lord Conqueror"), Spain's legendary hero of the Christian Reconquest. Franco's wartime headquarters were established at Burgos during the Spanish Civil War (1936–39), possibly as much for symbolic as for strategic reasons. Even today the army and the clergy seem to set the tone in this somber city. León is a provincial capital and prestigious university town with a cosmopolitan flavor. Northwest of León, the medieval Camino de Santiago (Way of St. James) leads Christian pilgrims out of Castile and into Galicia as they wend their way toward Santiago de Compostela.

Pleasures and Pastimes

Dining

Castilian food is hearty stuff. The classic Castilian dishes are *cordero* (lamb) and *cochinillo* (suckling pig), the latter roasted in a wood oven. Both are specialties of Segovia, widely regarded as Castile's gastronomic capital thanks largely to such doughty old-style restaurants as Mesón de Cándido and Mesón Duque. In the Segovian village of Pedraza de la Sierra, superb roast lamb is served with hearty red wine.

The mountainous districts of Salamanca, particularly the villages of Guijuelo and Candelario, are renowned for their hams and sausages. Bean dishes are specialties of the villages El Barco (Ávila) and La Granja (Segovia), while *trucha* (trout) and *cangrejos de río* (river crab) are common in Guadalajara. Game is abundant throughout, two prize dishes being *perdiz en escabeche* (the marinated partridge of Soria) and *perdiz estofada a la Toledana* (the stewed partridge of Toledo). Castile's most complex and exotic cuisine is perhaps that of Cuenca; here a Moorish influence appears in such dishes as *gazpacho pastor* (a hot terrine made with a variety of game, topped with grapes).

Among the region's sweets are the *yemas* (sugared egg yolks) of Ávila, *almendras garrapiñadas* (candied almonds) of Alcalá de Henares, *mazapán* (marzipan) of Toledo, and *ponche Segovia* (Segovian egg toddy). *Manchego* cheeses (from La Mancha) are staples throughout Spain, and Aranjuez is known for its strawberries and asparagus.

Much of Spain's cheap wine also comes from La Mancha, home of the largest vineyard in the world. Far better in quality, and indeed among the most superior Spanish wines, are those from the Duero Valley, around Valladolid. Look for the Marqués de Riscal whites from Rueda and the Vega Sicilia reds from Ribera del Duero; Peñafiel is the center of the Ribera region. An excellent, if extremely sweet, Castilian liqueur is Cuenca's *resolí,* made from aquavit, coffee, vanilla, orange peel, and sugar and often sold in bottles in the shape of Cuenca's Casas Colgadas (Hanging Houses). The province of León specializes in *cordero asado* (roast lamb), *afumados* (assorted smoked meats), *morcillas* (varieties of sausages), and *lechón* (suckling pig) and produces a sparkling rosé wine called Bierzo, similar to the acidic Galician Ribeiro.

CATEGORY	COST*
$$$$	over 6,500 ptas.
$$$	4,000–6,500 ptas.
$$	2,500–4,000 ptas.
$	under 2,500 ptas.

**per person for a three-course meal, including wine, excluding tax and tip*

Lodging

Spain's most stylish hotels are usually paradors. Most of the oldest, most attractive Castilian paradors are in quieter towns, such as Almagro, Ávila, Chinchón, Cuenca, León, and Sigüenza; the paradors in Toledo, Segovia, Salamanca, and Soria are modern buildings, albeit with magnificent views and, in the case of Segovia, wonderful indoor and outdoor swimming pools. Of course, there are pleasant alternatives to paradors, such as Ávila's Palacio de Valderrábanos (a 15th-century palace next to the cathedral), Segovia's Infanta Isabel, Salamanca's Rector, and Cuenca's Posada San José, a 16th-century convent.

CATEGORY	COST*
$$$$	over 14,000 ptas.
$$$	8,000–14,000 ptas.
$$	4,000–8,000 ptas.
$	under 4,000 ptas.

**for a standard double room, excluding tax.*

Monasteries

For a sojourn with those masters of the Gregorian chant, the double-platinum monks of *Chant* fame, stop at the Monastery of Santo Domingo de Silos, 58 km (36 mi) southeast of Burgos (☎ 947/390068). Single men can stay here for a maximum of eight days. Guests are expected to be present for breakfast, lunch, and dinner but are otherwise left to their own devices. If the monastery is full, try to drop in for a vespers service. Closer to Burgos (10 km [6 mi]) is the Monastery of San Pedro de Cardeña (☎ 947/290033), which also offers lodging and allows couples and even families—possibly thanks to the monastery's importance in the story of El Cid, the medieval Spanish hero who left his wife and children there when banished into exile.

Exploring Old and New Castile

Castile is a large chunk of Spain, and Old Castile alone could occupy any traveler for weeks. If you're driving, Old Castile, to the north and west of Madrid, can be combined with later ventures to the Basque country or Galicia, while New Castile, south and east of Madrid, can lead you on to Extremadura, Andalusia, or the Mediterranean coast.

Numbers in the text correspond to numbers in the margin and on the Old and New Castile, Segovia, Salamanca, Toledo, and Burgos maps.

Great Itineraries

It's possible, though not ideal, to see Aranjuez, Ávila, Segovia, and Toledo on day trips from Madrid. Salamanca and other major towns can also be day trips from the capital, but you might spend more time traveling than actually being there. Burgos and León are at the northern edge of Castile, en route to elsewhere. If you have a car, spend at least four days in this area, staying in Toledo, Segovia, and Salamanca and passing through Ávila. Both Toledo and Segovia have an extra charm at night, not only because their monuments are beautifully illuminated but also because they're free of the crowds of tourists that congest them by day. To see all of the region's main sights requires at least another four to six days, with overnight stays in Cuenca, Sigüenza, Soria, Zamora, Burgos, and León.

IF YOU HAVE 4 DAYS

Start in **Toledo** ①–⑮, for centuries Spain's intellectual and spiritual capital and the peaceful collective home of Christians, Jews, and Muslims. Spend a full day visiting El Greco's former stomping grounds, then spend the night; move east the next day to **Aranjuez** ⑯, the summer retreat of the Bourbon monarchy. Farther south, check out Don Quixote's windmills at **Consuegra** ⑰ and the medieval town of **Almagro** ⑱, with its unique 16th-century theater. Consider spending a night in Almagro's 17th-century parador; then, after the morning rush hour, head north of Madrid to sublime **Segovia** ㉛–㊶, spending a night there to better enjoy the town's quiet side streets and country vistas as well as its Roman aqueduct and Romanesque churches. On your fourth day, try to catch the fountain display in the gardens of the **Palacio Real de La Granja** ㊷ before returning to Madrid.

IF YOU HAVE 6 DAYS

Spend a full day wandering austere **Toledo** 1–15, once the home of El Greco and full of tiny winding lanes. Spend the night there, then head north to **Segovia** 31–41 for the second day and night. See the medieval **Castillo de Coca** 45 on your way to **Ávila** 46, famous for its intact medieval walls and the legacy of St. Teresa. Continue on to **Salamanca** 50–60 for the third night and spend the next day soaking up the atmosphere and architecture. Head north to **Burgos** 65–70 for the night and the next day. You may want to see the monastery at Santo Domingo de Silos, or the closer San Pedro de Cardeña, and spend the night in one of the two if you can. Finally, dip into the Camino de Santiago pilgrimage route and linger in **León** 77, with its gorgeous cathedral and lively old and new towns.

When to Tour Old and New Castile

The best time to tour central Spain is between May and October, when the weather is sunny. Be warned, however, that July and August can be brutally hot at times, especially south of Madrid. November through February can be cold, especially in the Sierra de Guadarrama, north and west of Madrid.

During the pre-Lenten Carnival, León and nearby La Bañeza are popular party centers. The last week of April, in the cloister at León's San Isidoro, the town councilors and ecclesiastical authorities bow to each other ceremoniously to the delight of all present; this is a reminder of an ancient dispute over the distribution of power between the clergy and the civil authorities.

TOLEDO TO CIUDAD REAL

The contrast between the towns of Toledo and nearby Aranjuez could hardly be more marked. Toledo is a study in austerity, its introverted, gold-toned houses daring you to know them better. Here you can explore the mighty Gothic cathedral and the Tránsito Synagogue; contemplate El Greco's most famous painting, *The Burial of Count Orgaz*; or just roam the winding lanes. Aranjuez, on the other hand, is home to the Palacio Real, a sumptuous French-style palace. Consuegra, quietly featured in any picture of Don Quixote's windmills, is also the saffron capital of La Mancha. Farther south is historic Almagro, a hub during La Mancha's Age of Chivalry.

Toledo

★ *71 km (44 mi) southwest of Madrid.*

Tinged with mysticism and drama, Toledo was long the spiritual and intellectual capital of Spain. If you approach from Madrid, your first glimpse of Toledo will comprise its northern gates and battlements rising up on a massive granite escarpment. The flat countryside comes to an end, and a steep range of ocher-colored hills rises on each side of the town.

The rock on which Toledo stands, bounded on three sides by the Rio Tajo (River Tagus), was inhabited in prehistoric times, and there was already an important Iberian settlement here when the Romans came in 192 BC. The Romans built a fort on the highest point of the rock—where you now see the Alcázar, the dominant building in Toledo's skyline—and this was later remodeled by the Visigoths, who transformed the town into their capital by the middle of the 6th century AD. In the early 8th century, the Moors arrived.

The Moors strengthened Toledo's reputation as a great center of religion and learning. Unusual tolerance was extended to those who continued to practice Christianity (the so-called Mozarabs), as well as to the town's exceptionally large Jewish population. Today the Moorish legacy is evident in Toledo's strong crafts tradition, the mazelike arrangement of the streets, and the predominance of brick rather than stone. For the Moors, beauty was a quality to be savored within rather than displayed on the surface, and it is significant that even Toledo's cathedral—one of the most richly endowed in Spain—is hard to see from the outside, largely obscured by the warren of houses around it. Long after the departure of the Moors, Toledo remained secretive, its lives and treasures hidden behind closed doors and forbidding facades.

Alfonso VI, aided by El Cid, captured Toledo in 1085 and styled himself emperor of Toledo. Under the Christians, the town's strong intellectual life was maintained, and Toledo became famous for its school of translators, who spread to the West a knowledge of Arab medicine, law, culture, and philosophy. Religious tolerance continued, and during the rule of Peter the Cruel (so named because he allegedly had members of his own family murdered to advance himself), a Jewish banker, Samuel Levi, became the royal treasurer and one of the wealthiest and most important men in town. By the early 15th century, however, hostility toward both Jews and Arabs had grown as Toledo developed more and more into a bastion of the Catholic Church.

As Florence had the Medici and Rome the papacy, so Toledo had its long and distinguished line of cardinals, most notably Mendoza, Tavera, and Cisneros. Under these great patrons of the arts, Renaissance Toledo emerged as a center of humanism. Economically and politically, however, Toledo began to decline in the 16th century. The expulsion of the Jews from Spain in 1492, part of the Spanish Inquisition, had particularly serious economic consequences for Toledo; the decision in 1561 to make Madrid the permanent center of the Spanish court led to the town's loss of political importance; and the expulsion from Spain of the converted Arabs (Moriscos) in 1601 resulted in the departure of most of Toledo's celebrated artisan community. The years the painter El Greco spent in Toledo—from 1572 to his death in 1614—were those of the town's decline. Its transformation into a major tourist center began in the late 19th century, when the works of El Greco came to be widely appreciated after years of neglect. Today, Toledo is prosperous and conservative, expensive, silent at night, and closed in atmosphere. Yet Spain has no other town of this size with such a concentration of monuments and works of art.

A Good Walk

The eastern end of the Tagus gorge, along Calle de Circunvalación, has a panoramic view of the town. Here you can park your car (except in the middle of the day, when buses line up) and look down over almost all of historic Toledo. For quicker access to your car after a long day's walk, drive into the city and park by the Alcázar.

A complete tour starts at the **Puente de Alcántara** ①. If you skirt the city walls traveling northwest, a long walk past the Puerta de Bisagra on Calle Cardenal Tavera brings you to the **Hospital de Tavera** ②. If you enter the city wall, walk west and pass the **Museo de la Santa Cruz** ④ to emerge in the **Plaza de Zocodover** ③. Due south of here, on Calle Cuesta de Carlos V, is the **Alcázar** ⑥; a short walk northwest on Calle Nueva brings you to the **Mezquita del Cristo de la Luz** ⑤. From the southwestern corner of the Alcázar, a series of alleys descends to the east end of the **cathedral** ⑦, affording good views of the cathedral tower. Make your way around the southern side of the building, passing the mid-15th-century Puerta de los Leones, with detailed and realistic carvings by artists of northern descent. Emerging into the small square in front of the cathedral's west facade, you'll see the stately *ayuntamiento* (town hall) to your right, begun by the young Juan de Herrera and completed by El Greco's son, Jorge Manuel Theotokópoulos.

Near the Museo de los Concilios, on Calle de San Clemente, take in the richly sculpted portal by Covarrubias on the Convento de San Clemente; across the street is the church of **San Román** ⑧. Almost every wall in this quiet part of town belongs to a convent, and the empty streets make for contemplative walks. This was a district loved by the Romantic poet Gustavo Adolfo Bécquer, author of *Rimas* (*Rhymes*), the most popular collection of Spanish verse before García Lorca's *Romancero Gitano*. Bécquer's favorite corner was the tiny square in front of the 16th-century convent church of **Santo Domingo** ⑨, a few minutes' walk north of San Román, below the Plazuela de Padilla.

Backtrack, following Calle de San Clemente through the Plaza de Valdecaleros to Calle de Santo Tomé, to get to the church of **Santo Tomé** ⑩. Down the hill from Santo Tomé, off Calle de San Juan de Díos, is the **Casa de El Greco** ⑪. (Follow the signs, as this is a tricky labyrinth to navigate.) Next door to the Casa de El Greco is the 14th-century **Sinagoga del Tránsito** ⑫, financed by Samuel Levi, and the accompanying **Museo Sefardi.** Coming out of the synagogue, turn right up Calle de Reyes Católicos. A few steps past the town's other synagogue, **Santa María la Blanca** ⑬, is the late-15th-century church of **San Juan de los Reyes** ⑭. The town's western extremity is the **Puente de San Martín** ⑮. If you're traveling with children who might get weary on this trek, look to Toledo's **Tren Imperial** (☎ 925/142274), a fun little tourist train that chugs past most of the sights above. Tickets are 600 ptas. for adults, 300 ptas. for kids, and the train departs from the Plaza de Zocodover daily at 11 AM, with a night tour added Friday through Sunday.

TIMING

Toledo's endlessly winding streets and steep hills can be exasperating at times, especially when you're looking for a specific sight; but the best way to appreciate this town is to absorb its medieval atmosphere. Plan to spend the whole day.

Sights to See

❻ **Alcázar.** The name means "fortress" in Arabic and alludes to the Moorish citadel that stood here from the 10th century to the Reconquest. The building's south facade, its most severe, is the work of Juan de Herrera, of El Escorial fame. The east facade incorporates a large section of battlements. The finest facade is undoubtedly the northern, one of many Toledan works by Alonso de Covarrubias, who did more than any other architect to introduce the Renaissance style here.

Within the building are a military headquarters and a large military museum—one of Spain's few remaining homages to Francoism, hung with tributes from various right-wing military groups and figures from around the world. The Alcázar's architectural highlight is Covarrubias's harmonious Italianate courtyard, which, like most other parts of the building, was largely rebuilt after the civil war, when the Alcázar was besieged by the Republicans. Though the Nationalists' ranks were depleted, they managed to hold on to the building. Franco later turned the Alcázar into a monument to Nationalist bravery; the office of the Nationalist general who defended the building, General Moscardó, has been left exactly as it was after the war, complete with peeling ceiling paper and mortar holes. The gloomy tour can continue with a visit to the dark cellars, which evoke living conditions at the time of the siege.

Alcázar 6
Casa de El Greco . . . 11
Cathedral. . . . 7
Hospital de Tavera 2
Mezquita del Cristo de la Luz 5
Museo de la Santa Cruz. . . 4
Plaza de Zocodover . . . 3
Puente de Alcántara. . . . 1
Puente de San Martín . . 15
San Juan de los Reyes. 14
San Román. . . 8
Santa María la Blanca 13
Santo Domingo 9
Santo Tomé 10
Sinagoga del Tránsito 12

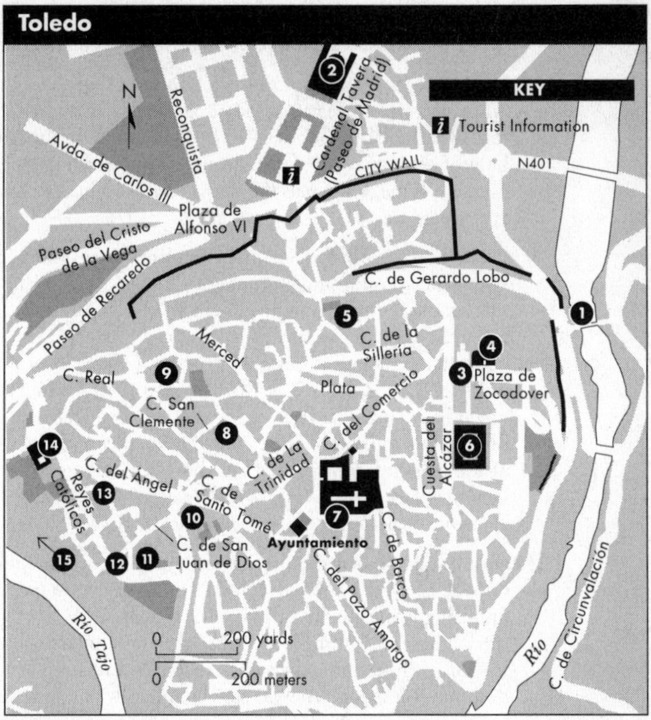

More cheerful is a ground-floor room full of beautifully crafted swords, a Toledan specialty introduced by Moorish silversmiths. At the top of the grand staircase, which apparently made even Charles V "feel like an emperor," are rooms displaying a vast collection of toy soldiers. ✉ *Cuesta Carlos V 2,* ☎ *925/223038.* 🎫 *200 ptas.* ⏲ *Tues.–Sun. 10–2:30 and 4–6 (4–7 in summer).*

11 **Casa de El Greco** (El Greco's House). This tourist magnet is on the property that belonged to Peter the Cruel's Jewish treasurer, Samuel Levi. The artist once lived in a house owned by this man, but it's pure conjecture that he lived in this particular one. The interior, done up in the late 19th century to resemble a "typical" house of El Greco's time, is a pure fake, albeit a pleasant one. The museum next door displays a few of El Greco's paintings, including a large panorama of Toledo with the Hospital of Tavera in the foreground. ✉ *Samuel Levi 3,* ☎ *925/224046.* 🎫 *400 ptas.* ⏲ *Tues.–Sat. 10–2 and 4–6, Sun. 10–2.*

7 **Cathedral.** Jorge Manuel Theotokópoulos was responsible for the cathedral's Mozarabic chapel, the elongated dome of which crowns the right-hand side of the west facade. The rest of this facade is mainly early 15th-century and features a depiction of the Virgin presenting her robe to Toledo's patron saint, the Visigothic Ildefonsus.

Enter the cathedral from the 14th-century cloisters to the left of the west facade. The primarily 13th-century architecture was inspired by the great Gothic cathedrals of France, such as Chartres, but the squat proportions give it a Spanish feel, as do the wealth and weight of the furnishings and the location of the elaborate choir in the center of the nave. Immediately to your right as you enter the building is a beautifully carved plateresque doorway by Covarrubias, marking the entrance to the Treasury. The latter houses a small Crucifixion by the Italian painter Cimabue and an extraordinarily intricate late-15th-century monstrance by Juan del Arfe, a silversmith of German descent; the ceiling is an excellent example of Mudéjar workmanship.

From here, walk around to the ambulatory, off the right side of which is a chapter house featuring a strange and quintessentially Spanish mixture of Italianate frescoes by Juan de Borgoña. In the middle of the ambulatory is a dazzling and famous example of Baroque illusionism by Narciso Tomé, known as the *Transparente*, a blend of painting, stucco, and sculpture.

Finally, off the northern end of the ambulatory, you'll come to the sacristy, where you'll find a number of El Grecos, most notably the work known as *El Espolio* (Christ Being Stripped of his Raiment). One of El Greco's earliest works in Toledo, it offended the Inquisition, which accused the artist of putting Christ on a lower level than some of the onlookers. El Greco was thrown into prison, and there his career might have ended had he not by this time formed friendships with some of Toledo's more moderate clergy. Before leaving the sacristy, look up at the colorful and spirited late-Baroque ceiling painting by the Italian Luca Giordano. ✉ *Arco de Palacio 2,* ☎ *925/222241.* 🎟 *700 ptas.* ⏲ *Mon.–Sat. 10:30–6:30. Sun. 2–6:30.*

❷ **Hospital de Tavera.** You'll find this hospital, Covarrubias's last work, outside the walls beyond Toledo's main northern gate, Covarrubias's imposing Puerta de Bisagra. Unlike the former Hospital of Santa Cruz, this complex is unfinished and slightly dilapidated, but it is nonetheless full of character and has the evocatively ramshackle **Museo de Duque de Lema** in its southern wing, looked after by two exceptionally friendly and eccentric women. The most important work in the museum's miscellaneous collection is a painting by the 17th-century artist José Ribera. The hospital's monumental chapel holds El Greco's *Baptism of Christ* and the exquisitely carved marble tomb of Cardinal Tavera, the last work of Alonso de Berruguete. Descend into the crypt to experience some bizarre acoustical effects. ✉ *Cardenal Tavera 2,* ☎ *925/220451.* 🎟 *500 ptas.* ⏲ *Daily 10–1:30 and 3:30–6.*

❺ **Mezquita del Cristo de la Luz** (Mosque of Christ of the Light). This mosque-chapel sits in a small park above the town's northern ramparts. The gardener will open the gate and show you around; if he's not there, inquire at the house opposite. Originally a tiny Visigothic church, the chapel was transformed into a mosque during the Moorish occupation, and the Islamic arches and vaulting survive—making this the most important relic of Moorish Toledo. The chapel got its name when the horse of Alfonso VI, riding into Toledo in triumph in 1085, fell to its knees out front (a white stone marks the spot); it was then discovered that a candle had burned continuously behind the masonry throughout the time that the so-called Infidels had been in power. The first mass of the Reconquest was said here, and later a Mudéjar apse was added (now shielded by glass). After you've seen the chapel, the gardener will take you across the ramparts to climb to the top of the Puerta del Sol, a 12th-century Mudéjar gatehouse. 🎟 *Tip gardener.* ⏲ *Any reasonable hr.*

❹ **Museo de la Santa Cruz.** One of the joys of this museum is its location in a beautiful Renaissance hospital with a stunning classical-plateresque facade. Unlike Toledo's other sights, the museum is open all day (except Monday) without a break and is wonderfully quiet in the early afternoon. The light and elegant interior has changed little since the 16th century, the main difference being that works of art have replaced the hospital beds; among the displays is El Greco's *Assumption* of 1613, the artist's last known work. A small **Museo de Arqueología** (Museum of Archaeology) has been arranged in and around the hospital's delightful cloister, off which is a beautifully decorated staircase by Alonso de Covarrubias. ✉ *Cervantes 3,* ☎ *925/221036.* 💵 *200 ptas.* ⏲ *Mon. 10–2 and 4–6:30, Tues.–Sat. 10–6:30, Sun. 10–2.*

❸ **Plaza de Zocodover.** Toledo's main square was built in the early 17th century as part of an unsuccessful attempt to impose a rigid geometry on the chaotic Moorish ground plan. Nearby, you'll find **Calle del Comercio,** the town's narrow and lively pedestrian thoroughfare, lined with bars and shops and shaded in the summer months by awnings suspended from the roofs of tall houses.

❶ **Puente de Alcántara.** Here is the town's oldest bridge, Roman in origin. Next to the bridge is a heavily restored castle built after the Christian capture of 1085, and above this a vast and depressingly severe military academy, a typical example of Fascist architecture under Franco. The bridge is off the city's eastern peripheral road, just north of the Puente Nuevo.

⓯ **Puente de San Martín.** A pedestrian bridge on the western edge of the town, the Puente de San Martín dates from 1203 and features splendid horseshoe arches.

⓮ **San Juan de los Reyes.** This convent church in western Toledo was erected by Ferdinand and Isabella to commemorate their victory at the battle of Toro in 1476 and was intended to be their burial place. The building is largely the work of Juan Guas, who considered it his masterpiece and asked to be buried here himself. Guas, one of the greatest exponents of the Isabelline, or Gothic, plateresque, was an architect of prolific imagination and great decorative exuberance. In true plateresque fashion, the white interior is covered with inscriptions and heraldic motifs. ✉ *Reyes Católicos 17,* ☎ *925/223802.* 💵 *200 ptas.* ⏲ *Daily 10–1:45 and 3:30–5:45 (until 6:45 in summer).*

❽ **San Román.** A virtually unspoiled part of Toledo hides this early 13th-century Mudéjar church with extensive remains of frescoes inside. It has been deconsecrated and now serves as the **Museo de los Concilios y de la Cultura Visigótica** (Museum of Visigothic Culture), featuring statuary, manuscript illustrations, and delicate jewelry. ✉ *C. de San Clemente s/n,* ☎ *925/227872.* 💵 *100 ptas.* ⏲ *Tues.–Sat. 10–2 and 4–6:30, Sun. 10–2.*

NEED A BREAK? If the navigational trials of Toledo's maze have you parched, unwind at **Palacio Sancara** (✉ Alfonso X El Sabio 6). Around the corner from the church of San Román, off Plaza Juan de Mariana, this Arabian café-bar has plush couches, low tables, soothing classical music, and colorful tapestries. In the afternoon it's perfect for hot tea and sweets, while at night it draws Toledanos for *copas de noche* (evening cocktails).

⓭ **Santa María la Blanca.** Founded in 1203, Toledo's second synagogue is nearly two centuries older than the more-elaborate Tránsito (☞ *below*). The white interior features a forest of columns supporting capitals of enchanting filigree workmanship. Stormed in the early 15th century by a Christian mob led by St. Vincent Ferrer, the synagogue was later put to a variety of uses—as a carpenter's workshop, a store, a barracks, and a refuge for reformed prostitutes. ✉ *Reyes Católicos 4,* ☎ *925/227257.* 💵 *200 ptas.* ⏲ *Daily 10–2 and 3:30–5:45 (6:45 in summer).*

❾ **Santo Domingo.** A few minutes' walk north of San Román is this 16th-century convent church, where you'll find the earliest of El Greco's Toledo paintings as well as the crypt where the artist is believed to be buried. The friendly nuns at the convent will show you around an odd little museum that includes documents bearing El Greco's signature. ✉ *Plaza Santo Domingo el Antiguo s/n,* ☎ *925/222930.* 🎫 *150 ptas.* ⏲ *Mon.–Sat. 11–1:30 and 4–7, Sun. 4–7 (weekends only in winter).*

10 **Santo Tomé.** Topped with a Mudéjar tower, this chapel was specially built to house El Greco's most famous painting, *The Burial of Count Orgaz,* and remains devoted to that purpose. The painting—the only El Greco to have been consistently admired over the centuries—portrays the benefactor of the church being buried with the posthumous assistance of St. Augustine and St. Stephen, who have miraculously appeared at the funeral to thank him for all the money he gave to religious institutions named after them. Though the count's burial took place in the 14th century, El Greco painted the onlookers in contemporary costumes and included people he knew; the boy in the foreground is one of El Greco's sons, and the sixth figure on the left is said to be the artist himself. In summer, try to come here as soon as the building opens, as you may have to wait in line to get inside later in the day. ✉ *Plaza del Conde 4,* ☎ *925/256098.* 🎫 *200 ptas.* ⏲ *Daily 10–6:45 in summer, 10–5:45 in winter.*

12 **Sinagoga del Tránsito.** Financed by Samuel Levi, this 14th-century rectangular synagogue is plain on the outside, but the inside walls are sumptuously covered with intricate Mudéjar decoration, as well as Hebraic inscriptions glorifying God, Peter the Cruel, and Levi himself. It is said that Levi imported cedars from Lebanon for the building's construction, à la Solomon when he built the First Temple in Jerusalem. Adjoining the main hall is the **Museo Sefardí** (Sephardic Museum), a small museum of Jewish culture in Spain. ✉ *Samuel Levi s/n,* ☎ *925/223665.* 🎫 *400 ptas.; free Sat. afternoon and Sun.* ⏲ *Tues.–Sat. 10–2 and 4–6, Sun. 10–2.*

Dining and Lodging

$$$$ ✕ **Cason López.** No other restaurant in Toledo combines ambience and cuisine so well. A vaulted foyer leads to a patio with marble statues, twittering caged birds, a fountain, and abstract religious paintings; in the dining room, delicately carved wood abounds, and everything gleams with polished details. The market-based menu features fine Castilian and Continental cuisine: starters like garlic-ravioli soup are followed by hearty seconds like braised rabbit with mustard sauce and mashed potatoes, or cod with manchego cheese, onions, and olive oil. Plum-and-cheese mousse with ice cream rounds out a superb meal. The lunchtime *menú del día* is 3,800 ptas. Reservations are wise. ✉ *Sillería 3,* ☎ *925/254774. AE, DC, MC, V.*

$$$ ★ ✕ **Asador Adolfo.** Steps from the cathedral but discreetly hidden away, Adolfo is one of the classiest spots in town. The modern entrance shields an old, intimate interior whose wood-beam ceiling bears painted decoration from the 14th century. The emphasis is on fresh produce and traditional Toledan fare, but there are plenty of innovations. The *tempura de flor de calabacín* (zucchini-blossom tempura in saffron sauce) is a tasty starter; a flavorful entrée is the *solomillo de cerdo* (pork loin with wild mushrooms and black truffles). Finish with a Toledan specialty, *delicias de mazapán* (marzipan delights)—cooked here in a wooden oven, they're the finest and lightest in town. ✉ *Granada 6,* ☎ *925/227321. Reservations essential. AE, DC, MC, V. No dinner Sun.*

$$ ✕ **Hierbabuena.** Here you can dine on an enclosed Moorish patio with plenty of natural light, at tables covered with crocheted tablecloths. The food is just as inviting as the setting, and prices are surprisingly reasonable. The menu changes with the season; possibilities include artichokes stuffed with seafood and steak with blue-cheese sauce. ✉ *Callejón de San José,* ☎ *925/223724. AE, DC, MC, V. Closed Mon. and Aug. No dinner Sun.*

$-$$ ✕ **Restaurant Maravilla.** With a quaint atmosphere and modestly priced menus, Maravilla is a great choice. Specialties include Toledan preparations of partridge or quail and a variety of seafood dishes. ✉ *Plaza Barrio Rey 7, ☎ 925/228582 or 925/228317. AE, DC, MC, V.*

$$-$$$ ★ ✕🏨 **Hostal del Cardenal.** Built in the 18th century as a summer palace for Cardinal Lorenzana, this quiet and beautiful hotel is now owned by the same people who bring you Madrid's famed restaurant Botín. The light-color rooms are decorated with old furniture, and some overlook the hotel's enchanting wooded garden, which lies at the foot of the town's walls. The restaurant, popular with tourists, has a long-standing reputation and a beautiful setting; the dishes are mainly local, and in season you'll find delicious asparagus and strawberries from Aranjuez. ✉ *Paseo Recaredo 24, 45004, ☎ 925/224900, FAX 925/222991. 27 rooms. Restaurant. AE, DC, MC, V.*

$$$$ 🏨 **Hotel Alfonso VI.** Smack in the middle of the historic district, this hotel offers great views of the city from its summer terrace. The rooms are modern, clean, and inviting; the restaurant is decorated in the ubiquitous Mudéjar style and serves delicious food. ✉ *General Moscardó 2, 45001, ☎ 925/222600, FAX 925/214458. 79 rooms. Restaurant. AE, DC, MC, V.*

$$$$ 🏨 **Parador de Toledo.** This modern building on Toledo's outskirts blends well with its rural surroundings and has an unbeatable panorama of the town. The architecture and furnishings nod to the traditional Toledan style, emphasizing brick and wood. ✉ *Cerro del Emperador s/n, 45001, ☎ 925/221850, FAX 925/225166. 77 rooms. Pool. AE, DC, MC, V.*

$$$ 🏨 **Hotel Pintor El Greco.** Next door to the painter's house/museum, this friendly hotel occupies what was once a 17th-century bakery. The modern interior is warm and clean, with tawny colors and antique touches, like exposed brick vaulting. ✉ *Alamillos del Transito 13, 45002, ☎ 925/214250, FAX 925/215819. 33 rooms. AE, DC, MC, V.*

Shopping

The province of Toledo is the most renowned crafts center in Castile, if not all of Spain. The Moors established silverwork, damascene (metalwork inlaid with gold or silver), embroidery, pottery, and marzipan traditions here, and next to Toledo's church of San Juan de los Reyes a turn-of-the-20th-century art school keeps these crafts alive. For cheap pottery, try to stop at the large roadside emporia on the outskirts of town, on the main road to Madrid. Better still, go to Talavera la Reina, 76 km (47 mi) west of Toledo, where most of the pottery is made, and visit the **Museo Ruiz de Luna** (✉ Plaza de San Augustín, ☎ 925/800149). Here the development of Talavera's world-famous ceramics is chronicled with 1,500 tiles, bowls, vases, and plates dating back to the 15th century, and you can watch artisans throw local clay. The museum is open Tuesday through Saturday 10–2 and 4–6:30, Sunday 10–2; admission is 100 ptas. (free on Sunday); and there is, of course, a shop. As for embroidery, the finest in the province comes from **Oropesa** and **Lagartera.**

Aranjuez

16 *47 km (29 mi) south of Madrid, 35 km (22 mi) northwest of Toledo.*

Once the site of a Habsburg hunting lodge on the banks of the Tajo, Aranjuez became a favorite summer residence of the Bourbons in the 18th century—they built a palace and other buildings, designed extensive gardens, and planted woods. In the 19th century, Aranjuez developed into a popular retreat for Madrileños. Today, the spacious and neatly laid-out town that grew up near the palace retains a faded elegance. Children might enjoy the tourist train that trundles around town (☎ 925/142274); tickets are 600 ptas. for adults, 300 ptas. for kids.

Aranjuez's **Palacio Real** (Royal Palace) reflects French grandeur. The high point of the opulent interior is a room covered entirely with porcelain; there are also numerous elaborate clocks and a museum of period costumes. Shaded riverside gardens full of statues and fountains invite pleasant relaxation after the palace tour. ☎ *91/891–1344.* *Palace 500 ptas., gardens free.* *Palace May–Sept., Tues.–Sun. 10–6:15; Oct.–Apr., Tues.–Sun. 10–5:15. Gardens May–Sept., daily 8–6:30; Oct.–Apr., daily 8 AM–8:30 PM.*

The charming **Casa del Labrador** (Farmer's Cottage), a small palace at the eastern end of Aranjuez, was built by Charles IV in 1804 and has a jewel-like interior bursting with color and crowded with delicate objects. Between the Royal Palace and the Casa del Labrador is the **Casa de Marinos** (Sailors' House), where you'll see a gondola that belonged to Philip V and other decorated pleasure boats that once plied the river. *Casa del Labrador 425 ptas., Casa de Marinos 350 ptas.* *May–Sept., Tues.–Sun. 10–6:30; Oct.–Apr., Tues.–Sun. 10–5:30.*

Consuegra

17 *78 km (48 mi) south of Aranjuez, 125 km (78 mi) south of Madrid (Km 119 on N-IV).*

This small but historic town is dominated by a spectacular hilltop castle and eleven white-walled **windmills.** You can drive straight up to the first windmill, **El Bolero** (restored to house the local tourist office), and walk upstairs to see the intricate 16th-century machinery.

Moors and Christians once did battle for the 10th-century **Castillo de Consuegra,** and during the second week in August the town reenacts their medieval conflict twice a day. In the 12th century the castle housed the Knights of St. John of Jerusalem, and here you can readily imagine that most notorious knight of all, Don Quixote, tilting at the windmills. The restored ramparts have classic views of the plains of La Mancha, with the town and saffron fields below. ☎ *925/475731 for tourist office.* *300 ptas.* *Nov.–Mar., weekdays 9–2 and 3:30–6, Sat. 10–2 and 3:30–6, Sun. 10:30–2; Apr.–Oct. weekdays 9–2 and 4:30–7, Sat. 10–2 and 4:30–7, Sun. 10:30–2.*

In October, the fields all around Consuegra are purple with **saffron crocuses** (*Crocus Sativus*). These flowers appear overnight, and the three female stigmas must be hand-picked from each one immediately—each flower produces only once. The stamens are then dried over braziers in private homes to become "red gold" worth 300,000 ptas. per kilogram. The process—which requires 4,000 crocuses to make 2 grams (0.7 oz.) of saffron—has been used for 700 years. Consuegra's **Fiesta de la Rosa del Azafrán** (Saffron Festival), complete with competitions and saffron-based foods, is held here the last week of October. Cooking tips: never buy saffron powder, as it's often adulterated. Crunch up the strands and leave them in some warm water before use to get the full yellow color and subtle flavor.

En Route Return to the N-IV and take the Daimiel exit and bypass to visit **Las Tablas de Damiel,** a wetland wildlife reserve threatened by drought and farm irrigation. In addition to its rare flora and fauna, the park attracts migrating birds in March–April and October–November. The longest of the three marked walks takes an hour, and observation towers aid in viewing; residents include red-crested pochards, broad-billed shoveler ducks, great crested gledes, purple herons, and marsh harriers. *N430 toward Ciudad Real, 12 km (8 mi) west of Daimiel,* ☎ *926/693118.* *Park, daily until dark; visitor center, daily 8:30–6.*

Almagro

⓲ *190 km (118 mi) south of Madrid, 65 km (40 mi) south of Consuegra.*

The perfectly preserved center of this noble town contains the only preserved medieval theater in Europe. The theater stands beside the ancient **Plaza Mayor,** where 85 Roman columns form two facing colonnades supporting green-framed 16th-century buildings. Near the plaza are granite mansions embellished with the heraldic shields of their former owners, knights of yore, and a splendid parador in a restored 17th-century convent.

★ The **Corral de Comedias** theater stands virtually as it was built in the 16th century, with wooden balconies on four sides and the stage at one end of the open central patio. During the golden age of Spanish theater—the time of playwrights Calderón de la Barca, Cervantes, and Lope de Vega—touring actors came to Almagro, which then prospered from mercury mines and lace-making. The Corral hosts a prestigious international theater festival each July. ✉ *Plaza Mayor 18,* ☎ *925/882244.* ⏲ *Tues.–Fri. 10–2 and 4–7 (10–2 and 6–9 July–Aug.); Sat. 10–2 and 4–6 (10–2 and 6–8 July–Aug.); Sun. 11–2 and 4–6 (11–2 and 6–8 July–Aug.). Festival tickets: by credit card, Tele-Entrada,* ☎ *902/101212; with cash, after mid-May, Palacio de los Medrano, San Agustín 7.*

The **Museo Nacional del Teatro** displays models of the Roman amphitheaters in Mérida (Extremadura) and Sagunto (near Valencia), both still in use, as well as costumes, pictures, and documents relating to the history of Spanish theater. ✉ *Callejón del Villar 4,* ☎ *926/882244.* ⏲ *Weekdays 10–2 and 4–7 (6–9 July–Aug.), Sat. 10–2 and 4–6 (6–9 July–Aug.), Sun. 11–2.*

Dining and Lodging

$$$ ★ ✕ **El Corregidor.** Several old houses stuffed with antiques and curios make up this fine restaurant and tapas bar, which serves some of the best food in Castile–La Mancha. The elaborate menu centers on rich local fare, including game in season, fish, and spicy Almagro aubergines, a local delicacy. ✉ *Jerónimo Ceballos 2,* ☎ *926/860648. AE, DC, MC, V. Closed Mon.*

$$$$ ★ ✕🏨 **Parador de Almagro.** Complete with cells, cloisters, and patios, this parador is a finely restored 17th-century Franciscan convent. Some rooms retain the atmosphere of monks' cells, even as they supply all the modern conveniences. The restaurant serves fabulous *pisto manchego,* a sort of La Mancha equivalent of vegetable ratatouille, and *migas,* fried spiced bread crumbs with chopped pork. There's also a bodega-style wine bar. ✉ *Ronda de San Francisco 31, 13270-Almagro,* ☎ *926/860100,* FAX *926/860150. 54 rooms. Restaurant, bar, pool. AE, DC, MC, V.*

Ciudad Real

⓳ *22 km (14 mi) northwest of Almagro, 116 km (72 mi) south of Toledo.*

Alfonso the Wise founded this university town, now the capital of its province, as Villa Real in 1255, and in 1420 Juan II decreed it a bona-fide *ciudad* (city). Since then it has become progressively less regal. Only one of its original gate arches, the **Puerta de Toledo**—built in 1328—remains, and the extensive city wall has disappeared altogether. The cathedral, **Santa María del Prado,** does have a magnificent Baroque altarpiece by Giraldo de Merlo. Ciudad Real's present claim to fame is that it's one of the few stops on Spain's first high-speed train, the AVE, between Madrid and Seville.

SOUTHEAST OF MADRID

Cuenca, Ciudad Encantada, Alarcón

Dramatic landscapes are the draw here: the rocky countryside and magnificent gorges of the rivers Huécar and Júcar make for spectacular views. Cuenca has a museum devoted to abstract art, impressive in both content and setting. Nearby towns like Ciudad Encantada, with its rock formations, and Alarcón, home to a medieval castle, make pleasant excursions.

Cuenca

20 *167 km (104 mi) southeast of Madrid.*

Built into a wild and rocky countryside cut with huge gorges, Cuenca has a haunting atmosphere and outstanding cuisine. The old town rises steeply on the north side of the River Huécar, hugging a spine of rock thrust up between the gorges of the Huécar and Júcar and bordered on two sides by sheer precipices, over which soars the odd hawk or eagle. The lower half of the old town is a maze of tiny streets, any of which will take you up to the Plaza del Carmen. From here the town narrows and a single street, Calle Alfonso VIII, continues the ascent to the Plaza Mayor, which you reach after passing under the arch of the town hall.

Just off Calle San Pedro, clinging to the western edge of Cuenca, is the tiny **Plaza San Nicolás,** a pleasingly dilapidated square. Nearby, the unpaved Ronda del Júcar hovers over the Júcar gorge and commands remarkable views of the mountainous landscape. The best views are from the square in front of the **castle,** at the very top of Cuenca, where the town tapers out to the narrowest of ledges. Here, gorges are on either side of you, while old houses sweep down toward a distant plateau in front. The castle itself, which served as the town prison for many years, is now a hotel.

The **Museo Diocesano de Arte Sacro** (Diocesan Museum of Sacred Art) is housed in what were once the cellars of the Bishop's Palace. The beautifully clear display features a jewel-encrusted, Byzantine diptych of the 13th century; a Crucifixion by the 15th-century Flemish artist Gerard David; and two small El Grecos. From the Plaza Mayor, take Calle Obispo Valero and follow signs toward the Casas Colgadas. ☎ *969/224201.* 🎫 *200 ptas.* ⏲ *Tues.–Fri. 11–2 and 4–6, Sat. 11–2 and 4–8, Sun. 11–2.*

★ Cuenca's most famous buildings, the **Casas Colgadas** (Hanging Houses), form one of Spain's finest and most curious museums, the **Museo de Arte Abstract Español** (Museum of Spanish Abstract Art). Literally projecting over the town's eastern precipice, this joined group of houses originally formed a 15th-century palace; it later served as a town hall before falling into disuse and decay in the 19th century. In 1927, the cantilevered balconies that had once hung over the gorge were rebuilt, and finally, in 1966, the painter Fernando Zóbel decided to create inside the houses the world's first museum devoted exclusively to abstract art. The works he gathered are almost all by the remarkable generation of Spanish artists who grew up in the 1950s and were essentially forced to live abroad during the Franco regime: the major names include Carlos Saura, Eduardo Chillida, Muñoz, Millares, Antoni Tàpies, and Zóbel. Even if you don't think abstract art is your thing, this museum is likely to win you over with its honeycomb of dazzlingly white rooms and its vistas of gorge and sky. 🎫 *300 ptas.* ⏲ *Tues.–Fri. 11–2 and 4–6, Sat. 11–2 and 4–8.*

The **Puente de San Pablo,** an iron footbridge over the Huécar gorge, was built in 1903 for the convenience of the Dominican monks of San Pablo, who live on the other side. If you've no fear of heights, cross the narrow bridge to take in the vertiginous view of the river below and the equally thrilling panorama of the Casas Colgadas. A path from the bridge descends to the bottom of the gorge, landing you by the bridge that you crossed to enter the old town.

Dining and Lodging

$$$ ★ ✕ **El Figón de Pedro.** Owner Pedro Torres Pacheco is one of Spain's most famous restaurateurs and has done much to promote the excellence of Cuenca's cuisine. This pleasantly low-key spot in the lively heart of the modern town serves such local specialties as *gazpacho pastor, ajo arriero* (a paste made with pounded salt cod and served with toasted bread), and *alaju* (a Moorish sweet made with honey, bread crumbs, almonds, and orange water). Wash down your meal with *resolí,* Cuenca's liqueur. ✉ *Cervantes 13,* ☎ *969/226821. AE, DC, MC, V. No dinner Sun.*

$$$ ✕ **Mesón Casas Colgadas.** Run by the same management as El Figón de Pedro (☞ *above*), this place offers much the same fare but in a more pretentious manner. The white, ultramodern dining room is next to the Museum of Abstract Art in the spectacularly situated Casas Colgadas. ✉ *Canónigos 3,* ☎ *969/223509. Reservations essential. AE, DC, MC, V. No dinner Tues.*

$$ ★ ✕ **Las Brasas.** Meats cooked over wood coals and hearty bean concoctions characterize this fairly typical Spanish restaurant. Both the cooking and the fire, visible from the bar, make a meal here comforting and festive. The owners use vegetables from their own garden to make a delicious *pucherete* (white bean soup). The decor is Castilian, with wood floors and dark wood furniture. ✉ *Alfonso VIII 105,* ☎ *969/213821. MC, V. Closed Wed. and July.*

$$$$ **Parador de Cuenca.** One of Spain's newest paradors (1993) occupies an exquisitely restored 16th-century monastery in the gorge beneath the Casas Colgadas. Rooms are furnished in a lighter and more luxurious style than the norm for Castilian houses of this vintage. ✉ *Paseo Hoz de Huécar s/n, 16001,* ☎ *969/232320,* FAX *969/232534. 63 rooms. Restaurant, bar, pool, tennis court. AE, DC, MC, V.*

$$$ **Cueva del Fraile.** This luxurious hotel, 7 km (4½ mi) out of town on the Buenache road, occupies a 16th-century building in dramatic surroundings. The white rooms have reproduction traditional furniture, stone floors, and in some cases wood ceilings. ✉ *Carretera Cuenca–Buenache, 16001,* ☎ *969/211571,* FAX *969/256047. 62 rooms. Pool, tennis court, meeting room. AE, DC, MC, V. Closed Jan.–Feb.*

$$–$$$ ★ **Posada San José.** This is still the only hotel in Cuenca's old town, and it's just as good as—if somewhat more modest than—the nearby parador. Tastefully installed in a 16th-century convent, the *posada* is a hanging house clinging to the top of the Huécar gorge, which most of its rooms overlook. In the spirit of the building, furnishings are traditional, and the atmosphere is friendly and intimate thanks to the owners, Antonio Cortinas and his American wife, Jennifer. Reserve well in advance. ✉ *Julián Romero 4, 16001,* ☎ *969/211300,* FAX *969-230-365. 29 rooms, 21 with bath. Bar, cafeteria. AE, DC, MC, V.*

Ciudad Encantada

21 *35 km (22 mi) north of Cuenca.*

The "Enchanted City" comprises a series of large and fantastic rock formations erupting in a landscape of pines. If you like to explore on foot, this natural phenomenon is well worth a visit; a footpath can guide you through striking outcrops with names like "El Tobagón" (The Toboggan) and "Mar de Piedras" (Sea of Stones).

Alarcón

22 *69 km (43 mi) south of Cuenca.*

This fortified village on the edge of the great plains of La Mancha stands on a high spur of land encircled almost entirely by a bend of the River Júcar. Its **castle** dates to Visigothic times; in the 14th century it came into the hands of the *infante* (child prince) Don Juan Manuel, who wrote a collection of moral tales that rank among the great treasures of medieval Spanish literature. Today the castle is one of Spain's finest paradors. If you're not driving, a bus to Motilla will leave you a short taxi ride away (call 969/331797 for a cab).

Dining and Lodging

$$$$ ✕🏨 **Parador de Alarcón.** As a place to indulge in medieval fantasies, this 8th- and 12th-century gorge-top castle can't be beat. The structure is of Moorish origin, and the interior has a military motif and only 13 rooms, all of them quite small except the turret room. The rooms in the corner towers have as their windows the narrow slots once used to shoot arrows; others have window niches where the women of the household did their needlework. Dinner is served in an arched baronial hall bedecked with shields, armor, and a gigantic fireplace recalling medieval banquets. ✉ *Avda. Amigos de los Castillos 3, 16213,* ☎ *969/330315,* FAX *969/330303. 13 rooms. Restaurant. AE, DC, MC, V.*

NORTHEAST OF MADRID

Alcalá de Henares, Guadalajara, Pastrana, Sigüenza, Medinaceli, Soria, Numancia, El Burgo de Osma

They're off the main tourist tracks, but the provinces of Guadalajara and Soria have a lot to offer and are—for a change—easily accessible by train. The rail from Madrid to Zaragoza passes through every town in this section, allowing a manageable and interesting excursion of two to three days. If you have a car, you can extend this trip by detouring into beautiful, unspoiled countryside.

Alcalá de Henares

23 *30 km (19 mi) east of Madrid.*

Alcalá's past fame was due largely to its university, founded in 1498 by Cardinal Cisneros. In 1836 the university was moved to Madrid, and Alcalá's decline was hastened. The civil war destroyed much of the town's artistic and architectural heritage, and in recent years Alcalá has emerged as a dormer town for Madrid. Nevertheless, enough survives of old Alcalá to suggest what it must have been like during its golden age.

The town's principal monument is its enormous **Universidad Complutense,** built between 1537 and 1553 by the great Rodrigo Gil de Hontañón. (Complutum was Alcalá's Roman name.) Though this is one of Spain's earliest and most important Italian Renaissance buildings, most Italian architects of the time would probably have shrieked in terror at its main facade. The use of the classical order is all wrong; the main block is out of line with the two that flank it; and the whole is crowned by a heavy and elaborate gallery. All of this is typically Spanish, as is the prominence given to the massive crest of Cardinal Cisneros and to the ironwork, both of which form integral parts of the powerful overall design. Inside are three patios, of which the most impressive is the first, comprising three superimposed arcades. A guided tour of the interior takes you to a delightfully decorated room where exams were once held, and to the Chapel of San Ildefonso, with its richly sculpted Renaissance mausoleum of Cardinal Cisneros. ✉ *Plaza San Diego s/n.* 🎫 *100 ptas, guided tour 300 ptas.* ⏲ *Tues.–Fri. 11:30–1:30 and 5–6, weekends 11–2 and 4–7.*

On one side of the university square is the **Convento de San Diego,** where Clarissan nuns make and sell *almendras garrapiñadas* (candy-coated almonds), a town specialty. The other side adjoins the large and arcaded **Plaza de Cervantes,** Alcalá's animated center. Off the plaza runs the arcaded Calle Mayor, which still looks much as it did in the 16th and 17th centuries. Miguel de Cervantes was born in a house on this street in 1547; a charming replica, **Casa de Cervantes,** built in 1955, contains a small **Cervantes museum.** ✉ *Calle Mayor 48,* ☎ *91/889–9654.* 🎫 *Free.* ⏲ *Tues.–Sun. 10:15–1:30 and 4–6:30.*

Dining

$$ ✕ **Hostería del Estudiante.** In one of the first buildings acquired by Spain's parador chain, this restaurant is magnificently set around a 15th-century cloister and features wood-beamed ceilings, a large and splendid fireplace, and glass-and-tin lanterns. Appropriate to the traditional setting is the good and simple Castilian food, which centers on *asados castellanos* (Castilian-style roast meats). The lamb is locally renowned, as is the Postre de Alcalá (an almond puff pastry). ✉ *Los Colegios 3,* ☎ *91/888–0330. AE, DC, MC, V.*

Guadalajara

24 *17 km (10 mi) east of Alcalá, 55 km (34 mi) northeast of Madrid.*

In this quiet, affluent provincial capital, which doubles as a suburb of Madrid, villas with terra-cotta roofs sprawl down the slopes of the Guadalajara hills. The city was severely damaged in the civil war, but its **Palacio del Infantado** (Palace of the Prince's Territory) still stands and is one of the most important Spanish palaces of its period. Built between 1461 and 1492 by Juan Guas, the palace is a bizarre and potent mixture of Gothic, classical, and Mudéjar influences. The main facade is rich; the lower floors are studded with diamond shapes; and the whole is crowned by a complex Gothic gallery supported on a frieze pitted with intricate Moorish cellular work (the honeycomb motif). Inside is a fanciful and exciting courtyard, though little else; the magnificent Renaissance frescoes that once covered the palace's rooms were largely obliterated in the civil war. The ground floor holds a modest provincial art gallery. ✉ *Plaza de los Caídos 1.* 🎫 *200 ptas.* ⏲ *Tues.–Sat. 10:30–2 and 4:15–7, Sun. 10:30–2.*

En Route East of Guadalajara extends the Alcarria, a high plateau crossed by rivers forming verdant valleys. It was made famous in the 1950s by one of the great classics of Spanish travel literature, Camilo José Cela's *Journey to the Alcarria,* in which Cela evoked the backwardness and remoteness of an area barely an hour from Madrid. Even today you can feel far removed from the modern world here.

Pastrana

25 *42 km (26 mi) southeast of Guadalajara.*

High on a hill, Pastrana's narrow lanes merge into the landscape. This is a pretty village of Roman origin, once the capital of a small duchy.

The tiny **museum** attached to Pastrana's Colegiata (collegiate church) displays a glorious series of Gothic tapestries. 125 ptas. *Weekends 1–3 and 4–6.*

Sigüenza

26 *86 km (53 mi) northeast of Guadalajara.*

Sigüenza is one of the most beautiful towns in Castile. Begun around 1150 and not completed until the early 16th century, Sigüenza's remarkable **cathedral** is an anthology of Spanish architecture from the Romanesque period to the Renaissance. The sturdy western front has a forbidding, fortresslike appearance but hides a wealth of ornamental and artistic masterpieces. Go directly to the sacristan (the sacristy is at the north end of the ambulatory) for an informative guided tour. The sacristy is an outstanding Renaissance structure, covered in a barrel vault designed by the great Alonso de Covarrubias; its coffering is studded with hundreds of sculpted heads, which stare at you disarmingly. The tour then takes you into the late-Gothic cloister, off which is a room lined with 17th-century Flemish tapestries. You will also have illuminated for you (in the north transept) the ornate, late-15th-century sepulchre of Dom Fadrique of Portugal, an early example of the classical plateresque. The cathedral's high point is the Chapel of the Doncel (to the right of the sanctuary), in which you'll see Spain's most celebrated funerary monument, the tomb of Don Martín Vázquez de Arca, commissioned by Isabella, to whom Don Martín served as *doncel* (page) before dying young at the gates of Granada in 1486. The reclining Don Martín is lifelike, an open book in his hands and a wistful melancholy in his eyes. More than a memorial to an individual, this tomb, with its surrounding late-Gothic foliage and tiny mourners, is like an epitaph of the Age of Chivalry, a final flowering of the Gothic spirit. *300 ptas. Daily 11–1 and 4–6 (until 7 in summer).*

In a refurbished early 19th-century house next to the cathedral's west facade, the **Museo Diocesano de Arte Sacro** (Diocesan Museum of Sacred Art) contains a prehistoric section and much religious art from the 12th to 18th centuries. *200 ptas. Tues.–Sun. 11–2 and 4:30–6:30 (4:30–7:30 in summer).*

The south side of the cathedral overlooks the arcaded **Plaza Mayor,** a harmonious Renaissance square commissioned by Cardinal Mendoza. The small palaces and cobbled alleys around here mark the virtually intact old quarter. Along Calle Mayor you'll find the palace that belonged to the doncel's family. The enchanting **castle** at the top of the street, overlooking wild, hilly countryside from above Sigüenza, is now a parador. Founded by the Romans but rebuilt at various later periods, most of the structure went up in the 14th century, when it became a residence for the queen of Castile, Doña Blanca de Borbón—banished here by her husband, Peter the Cruel.

Lodging

$$$–$$$$ ★ **Parador de Sigüenza.** Of the many castles in the parador chain, this 12th-century fortress at the very top of town is one of the most impressive and historically significant: the mighty, crenellated structure has hosted royalty for centuries, from Ferdinand and Isabella right up to the present king, Juan Carlos. Some rooms have four-poster beds and balconies overlooking the wild landscape. The excellent dining room makes a leisurely lunch essential, and with roast kid, pheasant, and cod with truffles and cheese, the menu fits the setting. *Plaza del Castillo, 19250, 949/390100, FAX 949/391364. 81 rooms. Restaurant, meeting room, parking (fee). AE, DC, MC, V.*

Medinaceli

27 *32 km (20 mi) northeast of Sigüenza.*

The preserved village of Medinaceli commands an exhilarating position on the top of a long, steep ridge. Dominating the skyline is a Roman triumphal arch from the 2nd or 3rd century AD, the only surviving triple archway of this period in Spain. (The arch's silhouette is now featured on road signs to national monuments throughout the country.) The surrounding village, once the seat of one of Spain's most powerful dukes, was virtually abandoned by its inhabitants by the end of the 19th century, and if you come here during the week you'll find yourself in a near ghost town. Many Madrileños have weekend houses here, and several Americans are also in part-time residence. The place is undeniably beautiful, with extensive views, picturesquely overgrown houses, and unpaved lanes leading directly into wild countryside. The former palace of the dukes of Medinaceli is currently undergoing restoration, and Roman excavations are being carried out in one of the squares.

Soria

28 *74 km (46 mi) north of Medinaceli, 234 km (145 mi) northeast of Madrid.*

This provincial capital prospered for centuries as a center of sheep farming, but it has been marred by modern development and is often beset by cold, biting winds. Still, its situation in the wooded Duero valley is splendid, and it has a number of fascinating Romanesque buildings.

Soria has strong connections with Antonio Machado, Spain's most popular 20th-century poet after Federico García Lorca. The Seville-born poet lived a bohemian life in Paris for many years, but he eventually returned to Spain and taught French in Soria from 1909 to 1911. A large bronze head of Machado is displayed outside the **school** where he taught; and his former classroom (now called the Aula Machado) contains a tiny collection of memorabilia. It was in Soria that Machado fell in love with and married the 16-year-old daughter of his landlady, and when she died only two years later, he felt he could no longer stay in a town so full of her memories. He moved on to Baeza, in his native Andalusia, and then went to Segovia, where he spent his last years in Spain (he died early in the civil war, shortly after escaping to France). His most successful work, the *Campos de Castilla,* was greatly inspired by Soria and by his dead wife, Leonor; both the town and the woman haunted him until his death.

The main roads to Soria converge onto the wide, modern promenade El Espolón, where you'll find the **Museo Numantino** (Museum of Numancia). Founded in 1919, the museum houses local archaeological finds, and few other museums in Spain are laid out quite as well or as spaciously. The collections are rich in prehistoric and Iberian items, and one section on the top floor is dedicated to the important Iberian-Roman settlement at nearby Numancia (☞ *below*). ✉ *Paseo de El Espalón 8,* ☎ *975/221397.* 🎫 *200 ptas.; free weekends.* ⏲ *June–Sept., Tues.–Sat. 9–2 and 5–9, Sun. 9–2; Oct.–May, Tues.–Sat. 9–8:30, Sun. 9–2.*

At the top of Calle Aduana Vieja is the late-12th-century church of **San Domingo,** with its richly carved, Romanesque west facade. The imposing, 16th-century **Palacio de los Condes de Gomara** (Palace of the Counts of Gomara; now a law court) is on Calle Estudios. Dominating the hill just south of the River Dueron is Soria's **parador** (☞ *below*), which shares a park with the ruins of the town's castle. Machado loved the town and valley views from this hill. Calle de Santiago, which leads to the parador, passes the church and cemetery of El Espino, where Machado's wife, Leonor, is buried. Just before the river is the **cathedral,** a late-Gothic hall church attached to a Romanesque cloister.

Across the River Duero from Soria, in a wooded setting overlooking the river, is the deconsecrated church of **San Juan de Duero,** once the property of the Knights Hospitalers. Outside the church are the curious ruins of a Romanesque cloister, featuring a rare Spanish example of interlaced arching. The church itself, now looked after by the Museo Numantino, is a small, didactic museum of Romanesque art and architecture. *100 ptas. Winter, Tues.–Sat. 10–2 and 4–6, Sun. 10–2; summer, Tues.–Sat. 10–2 and 5–9, Sun. 10–2.*

Take an evocative, half-hour walk along the Duero to the **Ermita de San Saturio**; you'll follow a path (accessible by car) lined by poplars. The hermitage was built in the 18th century above a cave where the Anchorite St. Saturio fasted and prayed. You can climb up to the building through the cave. *Free. Winter, daily 10:30–2 and 4–6; summer, daily 10:30–2 and 5–9.*

Dining and Lodging

$$ ✕ **Mesón Castellano.** The most traditional restaurant in town, this cozy establishment has a large, open fire over which succulent *chuletón de ternera* (veal chops) are cooked. Another house specialty is *migas pastoriles* (soaked bread crumbs fried with peppers and bacon), a local dish. ✉ *Plaza Mayor 2,* ☎ *975/213045. AE, DC, MC, V.*

$$$ **Parador de Soria.** The modern parador has a superb hilltop setting, surrounded by trees and parkland, and excellent views of the hilly Duero Valley. Machado came often to this site for inspiration. ✉ *Parque del Castillo, 42005,* ☎ *975/240800,* FAX *975/240803. 34 rooms. Restaurant, bar. AE, DC, MC, V.*

Numancia

29 *7 km (4½ mi) north of Soria.*

The bleak hilltop ruins of Numancia, an important Iberian settlement, are just a few minutes from Soria and accessible only by car. Viciously besieged by the Romans in 135–134 BC, Numancia's inhabitants chose death rather than surrender. Most of the foundations that have been unearthed date from the time of the Roman occupation. *150 ptas. Winter, Tues.–Sat. 10–2 and 4–6, Sun. 10–2; summer, Tues.–Sat. 10–2 and 5–9, Sun. 10–2.*

El Burgo de Osma

30 *56 km (35 mi) west of Soria.*

El Burgo de Osma is an attractive medieval and Renaissance town dominated by a Gothic cathedral and a Baroque bell tower. Many of its historic buildings have been tastefully restored.

Dining and Lodging

$$ ★ ✕ **Virrey Palafox.** The decor inside this modern building is traditional Castilian—white walls, a wood-beam ceiling, and Old World furnishings—and the long dining room has a nonsmoking section, a rarity in Spain. Virrey Palafox is a well-known family enterprise. Produce is fresh and seasonal, vegetables are homegrown, and there is excellent local game year-round. The house specialty is fish, in particular *merluza Virrey* (hake stuffed with eels and salmon). On Saturdays in February and March a pig is slaughtered and a marvelous banquet is held; admission is about 5,000 ptas. and reservations are wise. ✉ *Universidad 7,* ☎ *975/340222. AE, DC, MC, V. Closed Sun. and Dec. 22–Jan. 10.*

$$$ **Virrey II.** A few hundred yards from the restaurant, under the same management, the Virrey II offers pleasant accommodations. Situated on the main square, it adjoins the 16th-century Convent of San Agustín and appears to form part of it. Built in 1990 of traditional materials, the hotel has an Old World look, and the rooms, most of which overlook the plaza, have marble floors, stone walls, and tastefully simple decoration. ✉ *Plaza Mayor 2, 42300,* ☎ *975/341311,* FAX *975/340855. 52 rooms. Dining room, meeting room. AE, DC, MC, V.*

SEGOVIA AND ITS PROVINCE

Segovia, Palacio Real de la Granja, Pedraza de la Sierra, Sepúlveda, Castillo de Coca

The area north of Madrid is dotted with rich and varied history, from the Roman aqueduct in exquisite Segovia to the 16th-century village of Pedraza de la Sierra. Either town makes a pleasant place to spend the night. Other towns worth a visit include Sepúlveda and Castillo de Coca, for their medieval monuments, and La Granja, where the impressive gardens grow even more spectacular when the fountains are turned on, creating an effect to rival that of Versailles.

Segovia

★ *87 km (54 mi) west of Madrid.*

Segovia's breathtaking location—on a ridge in the middle of a gorgeously stark, undulating plain—is only enhanced by its outstanding Roman and medieval monuments, its excellent cuisine, its embroideries and textiles, and its general sense of well-being. An important military town in Roman times, Segovia was later established by the Moors as a major textile center. Captured by the Christians in 1085, it was enriched by a royal residence, and in 1474 the half sister of Henry IV, Isabella the Catholic (married to Ferdinand of Aragón), was crowned queen of Castile here. By that time Segovia was a bustling city of about 60,000 (there are 53,000 today), but its importance soon diminished as a result of its taking the (losing) side of the Comuneros in the popular revolt against the emperor Charles V. Though the construction in the 18th century of a royal palace in nearby La Granja revived the town's fortunes somewhat, it never recovered its former vitality. Early in the 20th century, Segovia's sleepy charm came to be appreciated by artists and writers, among them painter Ignacio Zuloaga and poet Antonio Machado.

Today Segovia swarms with tourists and day-trippers from Madrid, and you may want to avoid it in the summer, especially on weekends or holidays. On weekdays in the winter, you can best appreciate its haunting peace. Note, however, that until sometime in 2001 you'll have to view many of Segovia's historical monuments from a distance, as they're all undergoing a massive restoration to counteract the effects of local pollution. Some of the prettiest plazas are dusty lots at the moment. If you want to see the town as it's meant to be seen, call the Tourist Office of Spain for an update as you're planning your trip.

If you approach Segovia on N603, the first building you see is the cathedral, which seems to rise directly from the fields. Between you and Segovia lies, in fact, a steep and narrow valley, which shields the old town from view. Only when you descend into the valley do you begin to see the old town's spectacular position, rising on top of a narrow rock ledge shaped like a ship. As soon as you reach the modern outskirts, turn

Old and New Castile

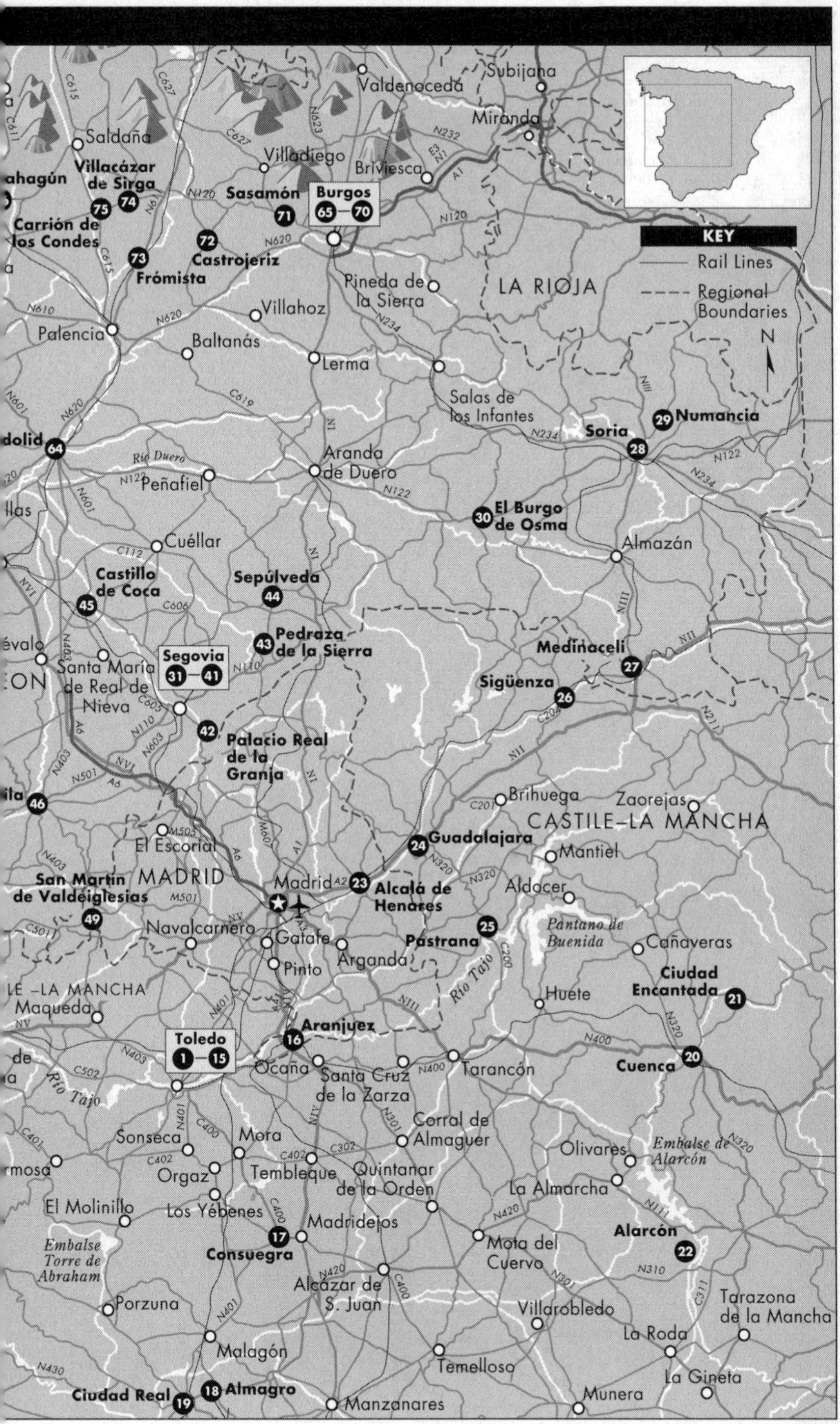
KEY
Rail Lines
Regional Boundaries
N
LA RIOJA
CASTILE–LA MANCHA
MADRID
Valdenoceda
Subijana
Miranda
Saldaña
Villacázar de Sirga 74
ahagún
75 Carrión de los Condes
73 Frómista
72 Castrojeriz
71 Sasamón
Villadiego
Briviesca
Burgos 65–70
Pineda de la Sierra
Villahoz
Palencia
Baltanás
Lerma
Salas de los Infantes
29 Numancia
Soria 28
dolid 64
Río Duero
Peñafiel
Aranda de Duero
30 El Burgo de Osma
Almazán
llas
Cuéllar
Castillo de Coca 45
Sepúlveda 44
43 Pedraza de la Sierra
Medinaceli 27
Sigüenza 26
évalo
Santa María de Real de Nieva
Segovia 31–41
42 Palacio Real de la Granja
ila 46
Brihuega
Zaorejas
El Escorial
24 Guadalajara
Mantiel
San Martín de Valdeiglesias 49
Madrid
23 Alcalá de Henares
Aldocer
Navalcarnero
Getafe
Pinto
Arganda
25 Pastrana
Pantano de Buenida
Cañaveras
Río Tajo
Huete
Ciudad Encantada 21
LE –LA MANCHA
Maqueda
Aranjuez 16
Toledo 1–15
Ocaña
Santa Cruz de la Zarza
Tarancón
Cuenca 20
Río Tajo
Corral de Almaguer
Sonseca
Mora
Olivares
Embalse de Alarcón
rmosa
Orgaz
Tembleque
Quintanar de la Orden
La Almarcha
El Molinillo
Los Yébenes
Madridejos
17 Consuegra
Mota del Cuervo
Alarcón 22
Embalse Torre de Abraham
Alcázar de S. Juan
Porzuna
Villarobledo
Tarazona de la Mancha
La Roda
Malagón
Tomelloso
La Gineta
Ciudad Real 19
18 Almagro
Manzanares
Munera

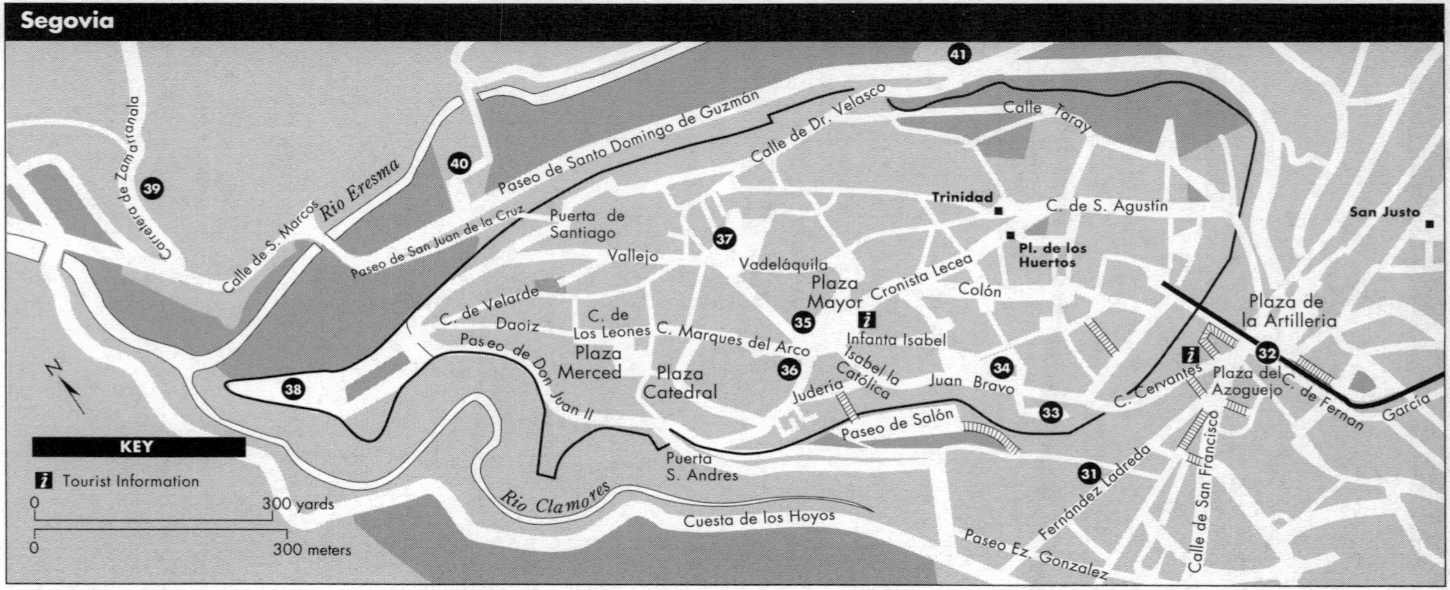

Acueducto Romano **32**
Alcázar. **38**
Ayuntamiento. **35**
Casa de la Moneda **40**
Cathedral **36**
Monasterio de la Santa Cruz **41**
Palacio de Aspiroz/Palacio de los Condes de Alpuente. **33**
San Estéban **37**
San Martín **34**
San Millán **31**
Vera Cruz **39**

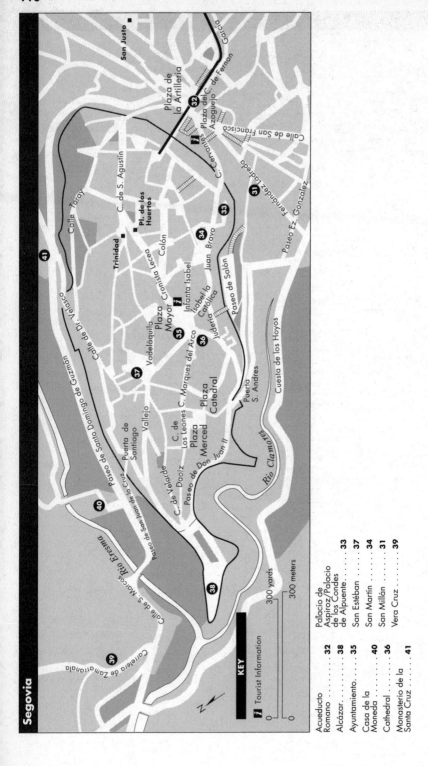

left onto the Paseo E. González and follow the road marked **"Ruta Panorámica"**—you'll soon descend on the narrow and winding Cuesta de los Hoyos, which takes you to the bottom of the wooded valley that dips to the south of the old town. Above, you can see the Romanesque church of San Martín to the right; the cathedral in the middle; and on the far left, where the rock ledge tapers, the turrets, spires, and battlements of Segovia's castle, known as the Alcázar.

A Good Walk

Driving and parking are problems on the narrow streets of old Segovia, so it's best to leave the car behind. In short, start in front of the Roman aqueduct in the Plaza de la Artillería and walk northwest to the Plaza Mayor on Calle Cervantes, ending your excursion at the Alcázar.

Beginning at the church of **San Millán** ㉛, go up Avenida de Fernández Ladreda until you come to the Plaza del Azoguejo, once the town center and marketplace. Directly in front of you are the arches of the grand **Acueducto Romano** ㉜. Turn away from the aqueduct, exit the plaza from the northwest corner, and head up the pedestrian shopping street Calle Cervantes. At the first jog in the street, look to the left: in the distance is the Sierra de Guadarrama. Continue up the same street, now called Calle de Juan Bravo, and veer off to the left onto Herrería for a look at the late-Gothic **Palacio de Aspiroz/Palacio de los Condes de Alpuente** ㉝, covered with Segovian *esgrafiado* plasterwork. Back on Calle Juan Bravo and farther ahead, you'll come to the small, delightful Plaza Martín, on which rises another Romanesque church, **San Martín** ㉞. Just to the west of the church is the town's **Biblioteca y Archivo Historical** (Library and Historical Archive), housed in a forbidding 17th-century stone structure that served as Segovia's jail until 1933. Off to the left of Juan Bravo, across from the Plaza Martín, is the refreshing **Paseo de Salón,** a small promenade at the foot of the town's southern walls. This walk was very popular with Spain's 19th-century queen, Isabel II; it offers good views over the wooded valley to the south and toward the Sierra de Guadarrama.

At the Plaza del Corpus, where Juan Bravo splits into Calle de La Judería Vieja and Isabel la Católica, a right turn leads directly to the Plaza Mayor. A left turn leads up Calle de La Judería Vieja into the former **Jewish quarter,** where Segovia's Jews lived as early as the 13th century. Turn right on Calle de San Frutos, which runs along the east side of the cathedral; from here a short alley leads you to the lively Plaza Mayor, an ideal place for a lunch break or an early evening drink. Facing the arcaded square are the 17th-century **ayuntamiento** ㉟ (town hall) and the eastern corner of the **cathedral** ㊱, its flying buttresses a favorite vantage point for storks. From the plaza, take Calle de Valdeláguila to the church of **San Estéban** ㊲. Calle de Los Leones, lined with tourist shops, slopes gently down from San Estéban toward the western extremity of the old town's ridge. From the partially shaded Plaza del Alcázar, you have excellent views to the north and south. At the western end of the square is the famous **Alcázar** ㊳.

From the Alcázar, you can see the church of **Vera Cruz** ㊴ and the **Casa de la Moneda** (former Mint) ㊵. A walk along the city's peripheral road, Paseo de Santo Domingo de Guzmán, leads to the **Monasterio de la Santa Cruz** ㊶.

TIMING

This walk can be covered in a few hours, depending on how long you stop at each sight.

Sights to See

㉜ **Acueducto Romano.** Segovia's Roman aqueduct ranks with the Pont du Gard in France as one of the greatest surviving examples of Roman engineering. Spanning the dip that stretches from the walls of the old town to the lower slopes of the Sierra de Guadarrama, it's about 2,952 ft long and rises in two tiers—above what is now the Plaza del Azoguejo, whose name means "highest point"—to a height of 115 ft. The raised section of stonework in the center originally carried an inscription, of which only the holes for the bronze letters remain. The massive granite blocks are held together by neither mortar nor clamps, but the aqueduct has been standing since the end of the first century AD. The only damage it has suffered is the demolition of 35 of its arches by the Moors, and these were later replaced on the orders of Ferdinand and Isabella.

Steps at the side of the aqueduct lead up to the walls of the old town, offering at the top an amazing side view of the structure. Modern-day pollution from the freeway that passes through the aqueduct has accomplished what centuries of war and natural disasters could not: the weakening of this structural masterpiece. Thus the road underneath has been closed to traffic and the monument restored. ✉ *Plaza de Azoguejo.*

38 **Alcázar.** Possibly dating from Roman times, this castle was considerably expanded in the 14th century, remodeled in the 15th, altered again toward the end of the 16th, and completely redone after being gutted by a fire in 1862, when it was used as an artillery school. The exterior, especially when seen from the Ruta Panorámica, is certainly imposing, but the castle is little more than a pseudo-medieval sham; and Disney copied its poetic silhouette for use in an even newer context, the Magic Kingdom. The last remnant of the original structure is the keep through which you enter. Crowned by crenellated towers that seem to have been carved out of icing, the keep can be climbed for superb views; the rest of the interior is a bit disappointing. ✉ *Plaza de la Reina Victoria Eugenia,* ☎ *921/460759.* 💳 *400 ptas.* ⏲ *May–Sept., daily 10–7; Oct.–Apr., daily 10–6.*

35 ***Ayuntamiento.*** The 17th-century town hall stands on the active **Plaza Mayor.** It's closed to the public, but it's a great place to sit and watch the world go by. ✉ *Plaza Mayor.*

40 **Casa de la Moneda** (Mint). All Spanish coinage was struck here from 1455 to 1730. The mint is closed for reconstruction, but the exterior is worth a look. ✉ *C. de la Moneda s/n, just south of River Eresma.*

36 **Cathedral.** Begun in 1525 and completed 65 years later, the cathedral was intended to replace an earlier one near the Alcázar, destroyed during the revolt of the Comuneros against Charles V. It's one of the most harmonious in Spain, and one of the country's last great examples of the Gothic style. The designs were drawn up by the leading late-Gothicist Juan Gil de Hontañon but executed by his son Rodrigo, in whose work can be seen a transition from the Gothic to the Renaissance style. The tall proportions and buttressing are pure Gothic, but much of the detailing—on the crossing tower, for instance—is classical. The golden interior, illuminated by 16th-century Flemish windows, is remarkably light and uncluttered, the one distracting detail being the wooden, neoclassical choir. You enter through the north transept, which is marked MUSEO; turn right, and the first chapel on your right has a lamentation group in wood by the Baroque sculptor Gregorio Fernández.

Across from the entrance, on the southern transept, is a door opening into the late-Gothic cloister—this and the elaborate door leading into it were transported from the old cathedral and are the work of Juan Guas, architect of the church of San Juan de Los Reyes, in Toledo. Under the pavement immediately inside the cloisters are the tombs of Juan and Rodrigo Gil de Hontañón; that these two lie in a space designed by Guas is appropriate, for the three men together dominated the last phase of the Gothic style in Spain. Off the cloister, a small museum of religious art, installed partly in the first-floor chapter house, has a white-and-gold 17th-century ceiling, a late and splendid example of Mudéjar *artesonado* work. ✉ *Marqués del Arco 1,* ☎ *921/435325.* 🎫 *Museum 250 ptas.* ⏲ *June–Sept., daily 9–7; Oct.–May, daily 9:30–6.*

41 **Monasterio de la Santa Cruz.** This 13th-century church was established by St. Dominick of Guzmán, founder of the Dominican order, and rebuilt in the 15th century by Ferdinand and Isabella. In 1996 it was turned into a private university, La Universidad Sec. During the academic year, you can see the attractive interior, Gothic with plateresque and Renaissance touches. ✉ *Cardenal Zúñiga s/n,* ☎ *921/471997.*

33 **Palacio de Aspiroz/ Palacio de los Condes de Alpuente** (Palace of the Counts of Alpuente). This late-Gothic palace is covered with a type of plasterwork known as *esgrafiado,* incised with regular patterns; the style was most likely introduced by the Moors and is characteristic of Segovian architecture. The building is now used for city administrative offices and is no longer open to the public. ✉ *Plaza del Platero Oquendo.*

37 **San Estéban.** This porticoed church is the third of Segovia's major Romanesque monuments. Though the interior has a Baroque facing, the exterior has kept some splendid capitals, as well as an exceptionally tall and attractive tower. Due east of the church square is the **Capilla de San Juan de Dios,** next to which is the former pension where the poet Antonio Machado spent his last years in Spain. The family who looked after Machado still owns the building and will show you the poet's room on request, with its paraffin stove, iron bed, and round table. The church is open for mass only. ✉ *Plaza de San Estéban.* ⏲ *Mass daily 8–10 AM and 7–9 PM.*

34 **San Martín.** This Romanesque church stands in an attractive little plaza by the same name. ✉ *Plaza San Martín,* ☎ *921/443402.* ⏲ *Open for mass only.*

31 **San Millán.** This 12th-century church is a perfect example of the Segovian Romanesque and is perhaps the finest church in town apart from the cathedral. The exterior is notable for its arcaded porch, where church meetings were once held. The virtually untouched Romanesque interior is dominated by massive columns, whose capitals carry such carved scenes as the Flight into Egypt and the Adoration of the Magi. The vaulting on the crossing shows the Moorish influence on Spanish medieval architecture. ✉ *Avda. Fernández Ladreda 26, 5-min walk outside town walls.* ⏲ *Open for mass only, daily 8–10 AM and 7–9 PM.*

39 **Vera Cruz.** This isolated Romanesque church, made of the local warm-orange stone, was built in 1208 for the Knights Templar. Like other buildings associated with this order, it has 12 sides, inspired by the Church of the Holy Sepulchre in Jerusalem. Your trip here pays off in full when you climb the bell tower and see all of Segovia profiled against the Sierra de Guadarrama, which is capped with snow in winter. ✉ *Carretera de Zamarramala s/n, on northern outskirts of town, off Cuestra de los Hoyos,* ☎ *921/431475.* 🎫 *150 ptas.* ⏲ *May–Sept., Tues.–Sun. 10:30–1:30 and 3:30–7; Oct.–Apr., Tues.–Sun. 10:30–1:30 and 3:30–6.*

Dining and Lodging

$$$ ✕ **Casa Duque.** Founded by Dionisio Duque in 1895 and still in the family, Casa Duque is the second-most-famous restaurant in town. The intimate interior, with its homey wood-beam decoration and plethora of fascinating *objets,* is similar to that of Cándido (☞ *below*); but Casa Duque is smaller and benefits greatly from its intimate scale and com-

parative lack of tourists. Roasts are the specialty, but the *judiones de La Granja Duque*—enormous white haricot beans from nearby La Granja, served with sausages—are also excellent. The more casual **Café Duque,** next door, serves the restaurant menu's less extravagant items, like rich *crema de congrejo* (cream-of-crab soup). ✉ *Cervantes 12,* ☎ *921/462487. Reservations essential for Casa Duque. AE, DC, MC, V.*

$$$ ★ ✕ **Mesón de Cándido.** More than just a restaurant, Cándido began life as an inn around the 18th century and was declared a national monument in 1941, 10 years after Señor Cándido turned it into a restaurant. Tucked cozily under the aqueduct, it comprises a quaint medley of small, irregular dining rooms covered with memorabilia. With his energy and flair for publicity, Cándido made this the Spanish restaurant best known abroad, and amid the dark-wood beams and Castilian knickknacks hang photos of the celebrities who have dined here, from Hemingway to Princess Grace of Monaco. Cándido passed away several years ago; the place is now run by his son. First-time visitors are virtually obliged to eat the *cochinillo,* the delicacy of which used to be attested to by Cándido's slicing it with the edge of a plate. The trout is also renowned, and the *postre sorpreso* (surprise dessert) is theatrical and delicious. ✉ *Plaza de Azoguejo 5,* ☎ *921/425911. Reservations essential. AE, DC, MC, V.*

$$$ ★ ✕ **Mesón de José María.** In this case, the exceptionally lively bar augurs well for the rest of the establishment. Though relatively new in Segovian terms, the Mesón de José María has already surpassed its formidable rivals culinarily and deserves to be considered one of Spain's finest restaurants. The hospitable and passionately dedicated owner is devoted to maintaining traditional Castilian specialties while concocting innovations of his own. The emphasis is on freshness and quality of produce, and the menu changes constantly. The large, old-style, brightly lit dining room is often packed, and the waiters are uncommonly friendly. Although it's a bit touristy, with a set menu in English, this *mesón* (traditional tavern-restaurant) is equally popular with locals. ✉ *Cronista Lecea 11,* ☎ *921/461111. AE, DC, MC, V.*

$$$$ ✕🏨 **Parador de Segovia.** Architecturally one of the most interesting and handsome of Spain's modern paradors, this low building is spaciously arranged amid greenery on a hillside. The rooms are light, with generous amounts of glass. The panorama of Segovia and its aqueduct is unbeatable, but there are disadvantages in staying so far from the town center. The restaurant serves traditional Segovian and international dishes, such as *lomo de merluza al aroma de estragón* (hake fillet with tarragon and shrimp). ✉ *Carretera de Valladolid (2 km [1 mi] from Segovia), 40003,* ☎ *921/443737,* FAX *921/437362. 113 rooms. Restaurant, indoor and outdoor pools, sauna, meeting room. AE, DC, MC, V.*

$$ ✕🏨 **Las Sirenas.** A few steps from the Plaza Mayor, above Segovia's nicest shops, Las Sirenas has a prime downtown location, a pillared marble lobby, and, from the best rooms, splendid balcony views of the church of San Martín. As the name suggests, the decor is sensuous and classical, with statues of mermaids at the foot of a curving staircase, and Greek vases on antique bedside tables. Drawbacks are the tiny showers and slightly faded furnishings, but all in all it's a hard value to beat. ✉ *C. Juan Bravo 30, 40001,* ☎ *921/462663,* FAX *921/462657. 39 rooms. Bar. AE, DC, MC, V.*

$$$ ★ 🏨 **Infanta Isabel.** This small hotel has a Victorian feel. Perched right on the Plaza Mayor—with an entrance on a charming, if congested, pedestrian shopping street—it has great views of the cathedral. Rooms are light and feminine, with wrought-iron beds and little round tables; and those on the plaza have floor-length shutters and small verandas. ✉ *Plaza Mayor, 40001,* ☎ *921/461300,* FAX *921/462217. 29 rooms. Coffee shop. AE, DC, MC, V.*

Shopping

After Toledo, the province of Segovia is Castile's most important for crafts. Glass and crystal are specialties of La Granja, while ironwork, lace, and embroidery are famous in Segovia itself. For the genuine article, go to **San Martín 4** (✉ Plaza San Martín 4), an excellent antiques shop. **Calle Daiza,** leading to the Alcázar, overflows with touristy ceramic, textile, and gift shops. You can buy good lace from the Gypsies in Segovia's Plaza del Alcázar, but be prepared for some strenuous bargaining, and never offer more than half the opening price.

Palacio Real de la Granja

42 *11 km (7 mi) southeast of Segovia on N601.*

The major attraction in Segovia's immediate vicinity, the Royal Palace of La Granja stands in the town of San Ildefonso de la Granja, on the northern slopes of the Sierra de Guadarrama. (*Granja* means "farm.") Its site was once occupied by a hunting lodge and a shrine to San Ildefonso, administered by Hieronymite monks from the Segovian monastery of El Parral. Commissioned by the Bourbon king Philip V in 1719, the palace has sometimes been described as the first great building of the Spanish Bourbon dynasty. The 19th-century English writer Richard Ford likened it to "a theatrical French château, the antithesis of the proud, gloomy Escorial, on which it turns its back." The architects who brought it to completion in 1739 and gave it such distinction were, in fact, not French but Italian—Juvarra and Sachetti. They were responsible for the imposing garden facade, a late-Baroque masterpiece anchored throughout its length by a giant order of columns. The interior has been badly gutted by fire, and the few undamaged rooms are heavy and monotonous; the highlight of the interior is the collection of 15th- to 18-century tapestries, presented in a special museum. It is the **gardens** that you come to see—here, terraces, ornamental ponds, lakes, classical statuary, woods, and Baroque fountains dot the mountainside. On Wednesday, Saturday, and Sunday evenings in the summer (6–7 PM May–Sept.), the fountains are turned on, one by one, creating one of the most exciting spectacles in Europe. The starting time has been known to change on a whim; call to check the time. ☎ *921/470020.* *Palace 700 ptas., gardens free.* ⏲ *Palace Oct.–May, Tues.–Sat. 10–1:30 and 3–5, Sun. 10–2 (10–6 Apr. and May); June–Sept., Tues.–Sun. 10–6. Garden daily 10–sunset.*

Pedraza de la Sierra

43 *30 km (19 mi) northeast of Segovia.*

Though it's been commercialized and overprettified in recent years, Pedraza is still a striking 16th-century village. Crowning a rocky outcrop and completely encircled by its walls, it is perfectly preserved, with wonderful views of the Guadarrama mountains. Farther up, at the top of the tiny village, is the Renaissance **Castillo Pedraza de la Sierra** (☎ 921/509825), a 14th-century stone castle that the painter Ignacio Zuloaga bought as a private home in the early 20th century. You can visit Wednesday through Sunday 11–2 and 4–6, except when Zuloaga's heirs are in residence; admission is 500 ptas. Two sons of the French king Francis I were held hostage here after the Battle of Pavia, together with their majordomo, the father of the Renaissance poet Pierre de Ronsard. In the center of the village is the attractive, irregularly shaped Plaza Mayor, lined with rustic wooden porticoes and dominated by a Romanesque bell tower.

Dining and Lodging

$$–$$$ ✕ **El Yantar de Pedraza.** This traditional restaurant, with wooden tables and beamed ceilings, is famous for roast meats. Right on the main square, it's the place to come for that most celebrated Pedrazan specialty—*corderito lechal en horno de leña* (baby lamb roasted in a wood oven). ✉ *Plaza Mayor,* ☎ *921/509842. AE, DC, MC, V. Closed Mon. No dinner Aug. 15–Sept. 15.*

$$$ **La Posada de Don Mariano.** This picturesque old building was originally a farmer's home. Each guest room is decorated differently, but all have rustic furniture and antiques. The atmosphere is intimate, though prices are grand. The restaurant, Enebro, serves a good selection of red meat. ✉ *Plaza Mayor 14, 40172,* ☎ FAX *921/509886. 18 rooms. Restaurant, bar. AE, DC, MC, V.*

Sepúlveda

44 *24 km (15 mi) north of Pedraza de la Sierra, 60 km (37 mi) northeast of Segovia.*

A walled village with a commanding position, Sepúlveda has a charming main square, but its main attraction is the 11th-century church of **El Salvador.** The oldest Romanesque church in Segovia's province, it has a crude but amusing example of the porches found in later Segovian buildings: the carvings on its oversize capitals, probably the work of a Moorish convert, are fantastical and have little to do with Christianity.

Castillo de Coca

45 *52 km (32 mi) northwest of Segovia.*

Perhaps the most famous medieval sight near Segovia—worth a detour between Segovia and Ávila or Valladolid—is the Castillo de Coca. Built in the 15th century for Archbishop Alonso de Fonseca I, the castle is a turreted structure of plaster and red brick, surrounded by a deep moat. It looks like a stage set for a fairy tale, and indeed, it was intended not as a defense but as a place for the notoriously pleasure-loving Archbishop Fonseca to hold riotous parties. The interior, now occupied by a forestry school, has been modernized, with only fragments of the original decoration preserved. ☎ *921/586038.* *200 ptas., guided tour 500 ptas.* ⏲ *Oct.–May, Tues.–Fri. 10:30–1:30 and 4:30–6, weekends 11–1 and 4:30–6; June–Sept., Tues.–Fri. 10:30–1:30 and 4:30–8, weekends 11–1 and 4:30–8.*

ÁVILA AND THE SIERRA DE GREDOS

Ávila, Sierra de Gredos, Arenas de San Pedro, San Martín de Valdeiglesias

The mountains of the Sierra de Gredos are a fitting backdrop and counterpoint for Ávila's spectacular medieval walls. In Ávila you can trace the history of the mystic and musical St. Teresa, who lived much of her life here; and in the Gredos mountains you can relax with excellent hiking and skiing. Other sights include the small, attractive villages near Arenas de San Pedro and the ancient stone bulls of San Martín de Valdeiglesias.

Ávila

46 *107 km (66 mi) northwest of Madrid.*

Smack in the middle of a windy plateau littered with giant boulders, Ávila can look wild and sinister. Modern development on the outskirts of town partially obscures Ávila's intact surrounding **walls,** which, restored in parts, look exactly as they did in the Middle Ages. Begun in 1090, shortly after the town was reclaimed from the Moors, the walls were completed in only nine years—a feat accomplished by the daily employment of an estimated 1,900 men. Featuring nine gates and 88 cylindrical towers bunched together, they are unique to Spain in form, unlike the Moorish defense architecture that the Christians adapted elsewhere. They're most striking when viewed from outside the town; for the best view on foot, cross the Adaja River, turn right on the Carretera de Salamanca, and walk uphill about 250 yards to a monument consisting of four pilasters surrounding a cross. And when you ultimately leave Ávila, look back on your way out.

The walls clearly reflect Ávila's importance during the Middle Ages. Populated by Alfonso VI mainly with Christians from Asturias, the town came to be known as Ávila of the Knights, on account of the high proportion of nobles. Decline set in at the beginning of the 15th century, with the gradual departure of the nobility to the court of Charles V in Toledo. Ávila's fame later on was due largely to St. Teresa. Born here in 1515 to a noble family of Jewish origin, Teresa spent much of her life in Ávila, leaving a legacy of various convents and the ubiquitous *yemas* (candied egg yolks), originally distributed free to the poor but now sold for high prices to tourists. Ávila today is well preserved but with a sad, austere, and slightly desolate atmosphere. The quietude is dispelled only for the week beginning October 8, when Ávila celebrates the Fiestas de la Santa Teresa with lighted decorations, parades, and singing in the streets as well as religious observances.

The battlement apse of the **cathedral** forms the most impressive part of the walls. The apse was built mainly in the late 12th century, but the construction of the rest of the cathedral continued until the 18th century. Entering the town gate to the right of the apse, you'll reach the sculpted north portal (originally the west portal, until it was moved in 1455 by the architect Juan Guas) by turning left and walking a few steps. The present west portal, flanked by 18th-century towers, is notable for the crude carvings of hairy male figures on each side; known as "wild men," these figures appear in many Castilian palaces of this period, but their significance is disputed.

The Transitional Gothic interior, with its granite nave, is heavy and severe. The Lisbon earthquake of 1755 deprived the building of its Flemish stained glass, so the main note of color appears in the beautiful mottled stone in the apse, tinted yellow and red. Elaborate, plateresque choir stalls built in 1547 complement the powerful high altar of circa 1504 by painters Juan de Borgoña and Pedro Berruguete. On the wall of the ambulatory, look for the early 16th-century marble sepulchre of Bishop Alonso de Madrigal, a remarkably lifelike representation of the bishop seated at his writing table. Known as "El Tostado" (the Toasted One) for his swarthy complexion, the bishop was a tiny man of enormous intellect, the author of 54 books. When on one occasion Pope Eugenius IV ordered him to stand—mistakenly thinking him to be still on his knees—the bishop indicated the space between his eyebrows and hairline, retorting, "A man's stature is to be measured from here to here!" ✉ *Plaza de la Catedral s/n,* ☎ *920/211641.* 🎟 *250 ptas.* ⏲ *Daily 10–1:30 and 3:30–6:30.*

The 15th-century **Mansión de los Deanes** (Deans' Mansion) houses the cheerful **Museo de Ávila**, a provincial museum full of local archaeology and folklore. It's a few minutes' walk to the east of the cathedral apse. ✉ *Plaza de Nalvillos 3,* ☎ *920/211003.* 🎟 *200 ptas.; free weekends.* ⏲ *Tues.–Sat. 10:30–2 and 5–7:30, Sun. 11–2.*

The **Convento de San José** (or de Las Madres), four blocks east of the cathedral on Calle Duque de Alba, houses the **Museo Teresiano,** which displays musical instruments used by St. Teresa and her nuns at Christmas. Teresa herself specialized in percussion. ✉ *Las Madres 4,* ☎ *920/222127.* 🎟 *100 ptas.* ⏲ *Spring–fall, daily 10–1:30 and 3–6; summer, daily 9:30–1 and 4–7.*

North of Ávila's cathedral, on Plaza de San Vincente, is the much-venerated Romanesque **Basílica de San Vicente** (Basilica of St. Vincent), founded on the supposed site where St. Vincent was martyred in 303 with his sisters Sts. Sabina and Cristeta. The west front, shielded by a narthex, has damaged but expressive Romanesque carvings depicting the death of Lazarus and the parable of the rich man's table. The sarcophagus of St. Vincent, surrounded with delicate carvings from this period, forms the centerpiece of the basilica's Romanesque interior; the extraordinary, Asian-looking canopy above the sarcophagus is a 15th-century addition paid for by the Knights of Ávila. ✉ *Plaza de San Vicente s/n,* ☎ *920/255230.* 🎟 *100 ptas.* ⏲ *Daily 10–2 and 4–7:30.*

On Calle de Lopez Nuñez, the elegant chapel of **Mosen Rubi** (circa 1516) is illuminated by Renaissance stained glass by Nicolás de Holanda. Try to persuade the nuns in the adjoining convent to let you inside.

At the west end of the town walls, situated next to the river in an enchanting farmyard nearly hidden by poplars, is the small, Romanesque **Ermita de San Segundo** (Hermitage of St. Secundus). Founded on the site where the remains of St. Secundus (a follower of St. Peter) were reputedly discovered, the hermitage houses a realistic marble monument to the saint, carved by Juan de Juni. You may have to ask for the key in the adjoining house. ✉ *Avda. de Madrid s/n, toward Salamanca.* 🎟 *Tip caretaker.* ⏲ *Fall–spring, daily 4:30–6; summer, daily 4–6.*

Inside the south wall on Calle Dama, the **Convento de Santa Teresa** was founded in the 17th century on the site of the saint's birthplace. Teresa's famous written account of an ecstatic vision in which an angel pierced her heart would influence many Baroque artists, most famously the Italian sculptor Giovanni Bernini. The convent has a small museum, with relics including one of Teresa's fingers, and you can also see the small and rather gloomy garden where she played as a child. ✉ *Plaza de la Santa s/n,* ☎ *920/211030.* 🎟 *300 ptas.* ⏲ *Daily 10–1 and 3:30–6.*

The **Museo del Convento de la Encarnación** is where St. Teresa first took orders and was then based for more than 30 years. Its museum has an interesting drawing of the crucifixion by her disciple St. John of the Cross, as well as a reconstruction of the cell she used when she was a prioress here. The convent is outside the walls in the north part of town. ✉ *Paseo de la Encarnación s/n,* ☎ *920/211212.* 🎟 *150 ptas.* ⏲ *May–Sept., daily 9:30–1 and 4–7; Oct.–Apr., daily 9:30–1:30 and 3:30–6.*

The most interesting architectural monument on Ávila's outskirts is the **Monasterio de Santo Tomás.** A good 10-minute walk from the walls among blackened housing projects, it's not where you would expect to find one of the most important religious institutions in Castile. The monastery was founded by Ferdinand and Isabella with the financial assistance of the notorious Inquisitor-General Tomás de Torquemada, who is buried in the sacristy. Further funds were provided by the confiscated property of converted Jews who ran afoul of the Inquisition. Three decorated cloisters lead to the church; inside, a masterly high altar (circa 1506) by Pedro Berruguete overlooks a serene marble tomb by the Italian artist Domenico Fancelli. One of the earliest examples of the Italian Renaissance style in Spain, this influential work was built for Prince Juan, the only son of Ferdinand and Isabella, who died at

19 while a student at the University of Salamanca. After Juan's burial here, his heartbroken parents found themselves unable to return to the institution they had founded. In happier times, they had often attended mass here, seated in the upper choir behind a balustrade exquisitely carved with their coats of arms; you can reach the choir from the upper part of the Kings' Cloister. The **Museum of Eastern Art** contains works collected from Dominican missions in Vietnam. ✉ *Plaza de Granada 1,* ☎ *920/220400.* *Cloister 100 ptas., museum 200 ptas.* ⏲ *Cloister daily 10–1 and 4–8, museum Tues.–Sun. 11–1 and 4–6.*

Dining and Lodging

$$ ★ ✕ **El Molino de la Losa.** Few restaurants could have a more distinctive situation than this one. Nearly straddling the serene Adaja River, with one of the best views of the town walls, it occupies a 15th-century mill, the working mechanism of which has been well preserved and provides much distraction for those seated in the animated bar. Lamb is roasted in a medieval wood oven, and trout comes straight from the river; this is also a good place to try the beans from nearby El Barco (*judías de El Barco*). The refreshing garden outside has a small playground for children. ✉ *Bajada de la Losa 12,* ☎ *920/211101 or 920/211102. AE, MC, V. Closed Mon. and Oct. 20–Easter Mon.*

$$ ✕ **Las Canselas.** Locals flock to this little tavern for the 2,000-pta. *menú del día,* packing it full and saving it from a tourist aesthetic. Push your way through the loud tapas bar to the dining room, where wooden tables are covered with paper and heaped with combination platters of roast chicken, french fries, sunny-side-up eggs, and chunks of home-baked bread. The local T-bone steak, *chuletón de Ávila,* is enormous. Don't be intimidated by the no-nonsense waitstaff or the volume of all the Spanish being shouted back and forth; do as the locals do and knock back a *caña* (small shot of beer usually served with a tapa) while soaking up the ambience. ✉ *Cruz Viejo 6,* ☎ *920/212249. AE, DC, MC, V. Closed 2nd half of Jan.*

$$ ✕ **Mesón del Rastro.** This restaurant occupies a wing of the medieval Palacio Abrantes and has an attractive Castilian interior with exposed stone walls and beams, low lighting, and dark-wood furniture. Once again, try the lamb and El Barco beans; also worthwhile is the *caldereta de cabrito* (goat stew). The place suffers somewhat from its popularity with tour buses, and service is sometimes slow and impersonal. ✉ *Plaza Rastro 1,* ☎ *920/211218. AE, DC, MC, V.*

$$$$ ★ **Meliá Palacio de los Velada.** Ávila's top hotel occupies a beautifully restored 16th-century palace. In the heart of the city, right beside the cathedral, it's the perfect place to relax between sightseeing jaunts. Upscale locals gather in the bar and the lovely Mediterranean courtyard, and the restaurant is acclaimed. Rooms are modern and comfortable. More rooms are being added. ✉ *Plaza de la Catedral 10, 05001,* ☎ *920/255100,* FAX *920/254900. 85 rooms. Restaurant, bar, pub, meeting rooms. AE, DC, MC, V.*

$$$ **Parador de Ávila.** A largely rebuilt medieval castle attached to the town walls, Ávila's parador has the advantage of a garden, from which you can sometimes climb up onto the ramparts. Decor is unusually warm and finely executed throughout, mostly in tawny tones, and the public rooms are convivial. Guest rooms have terra-cotta tile floors and leather chairs, and their bathrooms are spacious, gleamingly modern, and fashionably designed. ✉ *Marqués de Canales de Chozas 2, 05001,* ☎ *920/211340,* FAX *920/226166. 61 rooms. Restaurant, bar, café, meeting room. AE, DC, MC, V.*

$$ **Hostal Alcántara.** This small hostel has modest, clean rooms and is just a two-minute walk from the cathedral. ✉ *Estéban Domingo 11, 05001,* ☎ *920/225003 or 920/223804. 9 rooms. AE, DC, MC, V.*

Sierra de Gredos

47 *79 km (49 mi) southwest of Ávila.*

The C502 from Ávila follows a road dating from Roman times, when it was used for the transport of oil and flour from Ávila in exchange for potatoes and wood. In winter, the Sierra de Gredos, Castile's most dramatic mountain range, gives the region a majestic, snowy backdrop. You can enjoy extensive views from the **Puerto del Pico** (4,435 ft), and soon after descending you'll see a perfectly preserved stretch of the Roman road, zigzagging down into the valley and crossing the modern road every now and then. Today it is used by hikers, as well as by shepherds transporting their flocks to lower pastures in early December.

Lodging

$$$ **Parador de Gredos.** Built in 1926 on a site chosen by Alfonso XIII, this was the first parador in Spain. Though modern (it was enlarged in 1941 and again in 1975), the stone architecture has a sturdy, traditional look and blends well with the magnificent surroundings. Rooms are standard parador, with heavy, dark furniture and light walls, and more than half have excellent views of the Sierra. It's an ideal base for a hiking or climbing jaunt. ✉ *Carretera Barraco–Béjar, Km 43, Gredos 05132,* ☎ *920/348048,* FAX *920/348205. 76 rooms. Restaurant, bar, tennis court. AE, DC, MC, V.*

Outdoor Activities and Sports

HIKING AND MOUNTAINEERING

The Sierra de Gredos is Castile's best area for both hiking and mountaineering. You can base yourself at the parador (☞ *above*) or at one of six mountain huts with limited accommodations and facilities. For information on huts and on mountaineering in general, contact the **Federación Española de Montañismo** (Spanish Mountaineering Federation, ☎ 93/426–4267), based in Barcelona.

SKIING

Skiing is popular in both the Sierra de Gredos and the Guadarrama resorts of La Pinilla (Segovia), Navacerrada (Madrid), Valdesqui (Madrid), and Valcotos (Madrid). You can call **ATUDEM** (☎ 91/350–2020) for conditions, but it's better to call the slope you're considering. Call the **Federación Madrileña de Deportes de Invierno** (Madrid Federation of Winter Sports, ☎ 91/547–0101) for general information.

Arenas de San Pedro

48 *143 km (89 mi) west of Madrid.*

This medieval town is surrounded by pretty villages, such as Mombeltrán, Guisando, and Candeleda, where wooden balconies are decorated with flowers. A colorful sight in Candeleda are wicker baskets filled with pimientos for sale. Guisando, incidentally, has nothing to do with the famous stone bulls of that name, 60 km (37 mi) to the east.

San Martín de Valdeiglesias

49 *73 km (45 mi) west of Madrid.*

The **Toros de Guisando** are stone bulls dating from the 6th century BC, thought to have been used as land markers on the frontier of a Celto-Iberian tribe. Just three of many such bulls once scattered around the Castilian countryside (they take their name from the nearby Cerro Guisando, or Guisando Hill), they're now a symbol of the Spanish Tourist Board. To see these taurine effigies, head back east from Arenas on the C501; it's a pleasant drive through countryside bordered to the north by the Gredos range. Just 6 km (4 mi) before San Martín, on the right side of the road, is a stone inscription in front of a hedge; this marks the site where, in 1468, Isabella the Catholic was acknowledged by the assembled Castilian nobility as rightful successor to Henry IV. On the other side of the hedge stand the forlorn stone bulls, whose rustic setting gives them an undeniable pathos and power.

SALAMANCA AND CIUDAD RODRIGO

Salamanca's radiant sandstone buildings, immense Plaza Mayor, and hilltop, riverside perch make it one of the most attractive and beloved cities in Spain. Today, as it did centuries ago, the university predominates, providing an intellectual atmosphere with a stimulating arts scene and nightlife to match. About an hour from here are the preserved medieval walls of Ciudad Rodrigo, an interesting town with fewer tourists.

Salamanca

★ *205 km (127 mi) northwest of Madrid.*

If you approach from Madrid or Ávila, you'll first see Salamanca rising on the northern banks of the wide and winding River Tormes. In the foreground is its sturdy, 15-arch Roman bridge; above this, dominating the view, soars the combined bulk of the old and new cathedrals. Piercing the skyline to the right is the Renaissance monastery and church of San Esteban. Behind San Esteban and the cathedrals, and largely out of sight from the river, extends a stunning series of palaces, convents, and university buildings that culminates in the Plaza Mayor, one of the most elegant squares in all of Spain. Despite considerable damage over the centuries, Salamanca remains one of Spain's greatest cities architecturally, a showpiece of the Spanish Renaissance. It is the warmth of golden sandstone, which seems to glow throughout the city, that you will remember above all things.

Already an important settlement in Iberian times, Salamanca was captured by Hannibal in 217 BC and later flourished as a major Roman station on the road between Mérida and Astorga. Converted to Christianity by at least the end of the 6th century, it later passed back and forth between Christians and Moors and began to experience prolonged stability only after the Reconquest of Toledo in 1085. The town's later importance was due largely to its university, which grew out of a college founded around 1220 by Alfonso IV of León.

Salamanca thrived in the 15th and early 16th centuries, and the number of students at its university rose to almost 10,000. Its greatest royal benefactor was Isabella, who generously financed both the magnificent New Cathedral and the rebuilding of the university. A dual portrait of Isabella and Ferdinand was incorporated into the facade of the main university building to commemorate her patronage.

Nearly all of Salamanca's other outstanding Renaissance buildings bear the five-star crest of the all-powerful and ostentatious Fonseca family. The most famous Fonseca, Alonso de Fonseca I, was the archbishop of Santiago and then of Seville; he was also a notorious womanizer and one of the patrons of the Spanish Renaissance.

Both Salamanca and its university began to decline in the early 17th century, corrupted by ultraclericalism and devastated by a flood in 1626. Some of the town's former glory was recovered in the 18th century, with the construction of the Plaza Mayor by the native Churrigueras, who were among the most influential architects of the Spanish Baroque. The town suffered in the Peninsular War of the early 19th century and

Salamanca

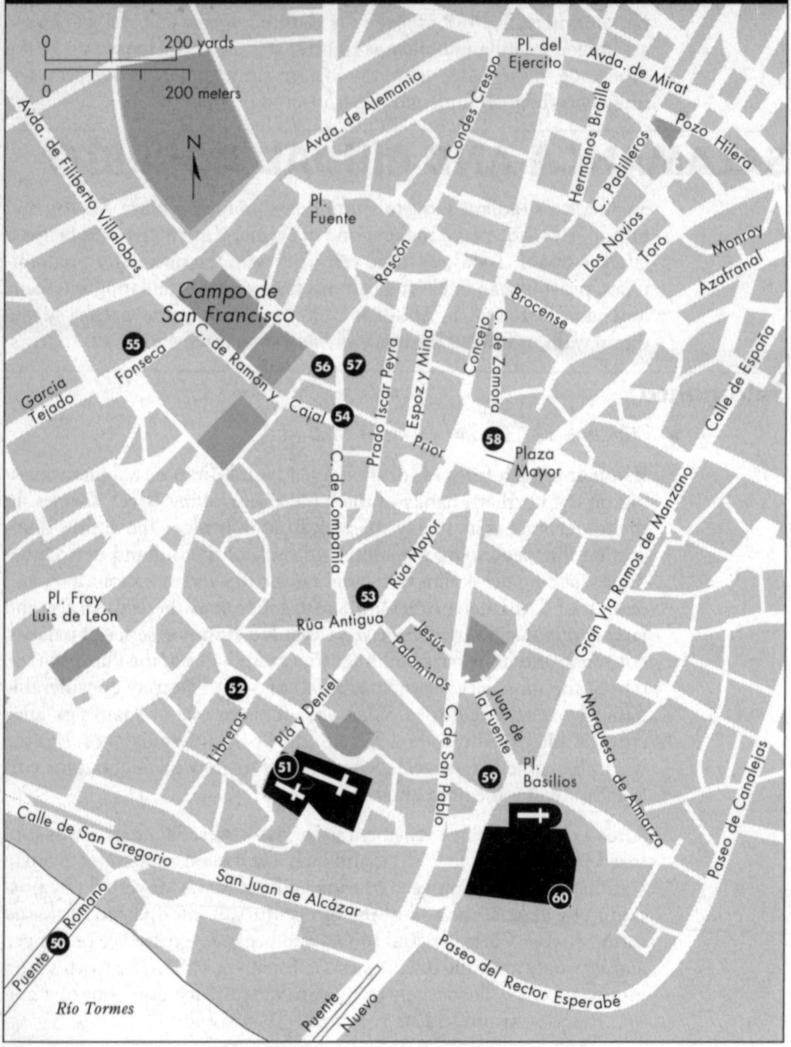

Casa de Las Conchas **53**
Casa de Las Muertes **57**
Cathedrals **51**
Colegio Mayor Arzobispo Fonseca/ Colegio de los Irlandeses **55**
Convento de Las Dueñas **59**
Convento de Las Ursulas **56**
Convento de San Esteban **60**
Palacio de Monterrey **54**
Plaza Mayor **58**
Puente Romano . . . **50**
Universidad **52**

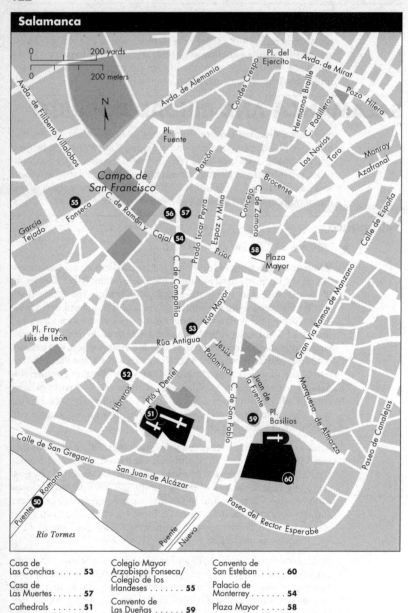

was marred by modern development initiated by Franco after the civil war; but the university has revived in recent years and is again one of the most prestigious in Europe. Try to stay here on a weekend, as the social atmosphere is a sight to behold.

A Good Walk

A good walk in Salamanca starts at the Puente Romano, goes north to the Plaza Mayor, and finishes at the church of San Esteban.

In terms of both chronology and parking space, the well-preserved **Puente Romano** ⑳ makes a good starting point. This is a quiet, evocatively decayed part of town with a strong rural character; in the summer, Gypsies camp here, picnicking and playing music while they exercise their horses. After crossing the bridge, head up the sloping, cobblestone Puerta del Río and make your way up to the old and new **cathedrals** ㊿, built side by side. Across the Plaza Anaya is the neoclassic Colegio de Anaya, which now houses the university's philosophy department. If you face the New Cathedral from the plaza, the back of the main building of the **universidad** (52) is ahead and to your right, facing the cathedral's west facade. Walk between the two down Calle Cardenal Plá y Deniel, turn right on Calle de Calderón de la Barca, then right again on Calle de Los Libreros, and you'll come into the enchanting quadrangle known as the Patio de Las Escuelas. The main university building (Escuelas Mayores) is to your right, while surrounding the square are the Escuelas Menores, built in the early 16th century as a secondary school preparing candidates for the university proper. In the middle of the square is a modern statue of the 16th-century poet and philosopher Fray Luis de León, one of the greatest teachers in the history of the university. On the far side of the Patio is the entrance to the **Museo de Salamanca.**

If you walk north from the Patio de Las Escuelas on Calle de Los Libreros, then bear right onto Rua Antigua, you can't miss the **Casa de Las Conchas** (53). Turn left at Calle de Compañía toward the **Palacio de Monterrey** (54). Off to the left of the palace, follow Calle de Ramón y Cajal to the **Colegio Mayor Arzobispo Fonseca** (55). Walk back east through the Campo de San Francisco. On the corner of Calle Las Ursulas and Calle Bordadores is the **Convento de Las Ursulas** (56). Farther ahead on Calle Bordadores is the bizarre **Casa de Las Muertes** (57).

Walk east along Calle del Prior to the **Plaza Mayor** (58), the center of town. South of the plaza, on Calle de San Pablo, is the Torre del Clavero, a late-15th-century tower topped by fantastic battlements built for the *clavero* (key warden) of the order of Alcántara. Farther down, the Palacio de La Salina is another Fonseca palace designed by Rodrigo Gil de Hontañón. Try to pop inside for a glimpse of the courtyard, where a projecting gallery is supported by wooden consoles carved with expressive nudes and other dynamic forms.

Walking south on Calle de San Pablo and bearing left, you'll circle the Dominican **Convento de las Dueñas** (59). Facing the Dueñas, up a monumental flight of steps, is the **Convento de San Esteban** (60).

TIMING

The length of this walk depends on how much time you spend at each sight, but you'll want to allow at least half a day.

Sights to See

(53) **Casa de Las Conchas** (House of Shells). This house was built around 1500 for Dr. Rodrigo Maldonado de Talavera, a professor of medicine at the university and a doctor at the court of Isabella. The scallop motif was a reference to Talavera's status as chancellor of the Order of St. James (Santiago), whose symbol is the shell. Among the playful

plateresque details are the lions over the main entrance, engaged in a fearful tug-of-war with the Talavera crest. The interior has been converted into a public library. Duck into the charming courtyard, which has an upper balustrade carved with virtuoso intricacy in imitation of basketwork. ✉ *Compañía 2,* ☎ *923/269317.* *Free.* *Weekdays 9–9, weekends 10–2 and 4–7.*

57 **Casa de Las Muertes** (House of the Dead). Built in about 1513 for the majordomo of Alonso de Fonseca II, the house received its name on account of the four tiny skulls that adorn its top two windows. Alonso de Fonseca II commissioned them to commemorate his deceased uncle, the licentious archbishop who lies in the Convento de Las Ursulas (☞ *below*), across the street. For the same reason, the facade also bears the archbishop's portrait. The small square in front of the house was a favorite haunt of the poet, philosopher, and university rector Miguel de Unamuno, whose statue stands here. Unamuno supported the Nationalists under Franco at the outbreak of the civil war, but he later turned against them. Placed under virtual house arrest, Unamuno died in the house next door in 1938. During the Franco period, students often daubed his statue red to suggest that his heart still bled for Spain.

51 **Cathedrals.** For a complete tour of the old and new buildings' exterior (a 10-minute walk), circle the complex counterclockwise. Nearest the river stands the **Catedral Vieja** (Old Cathedral), built in the late 12th century, one of the most interesting examples of the Spanish Romanesque. Because the dome of the crossing tower features strange, plume-like ribbing, it is known as the Torre del Gallo (Rooster's Tower). The much larger **Catedral Nueva** (New Cathedral) dates mainly from the 16th century, though some parts, including the dome over the crossing and the bell tower attached to the west facade, had to be rebuilt after the Lisbon earthquake of 1755. Work began in 1513 under the direction of the distinguished late-Gothic architect Juan Gil de Hontañón, and as at Segovia's cathedral, Juan's son Rodrigo took over the work after his father's death in 1526. Of the many outstanding architects in 16th-century Salamanca, Rodrigo Gil de Hontañón left the greatest mark, as a leading exponent of the classical plateresque. The New Cathedral's north facade (which contains the main entrance) is ornamental enough, but the west facade is dazzling in its sculptural complexity. Try to come here in late afternoon, when the sun shines directly on it.

The interior of the New Cathedral is as light and harmonious as that of Segovia's cathedral, but larger. Here you are treated to a triumphant Baroque effusion designed by the Churrigueras. The wooden choir seems almost alive with anxiously active cherubim and saints. From a door in the south aisle, steps descend into the Old Cathedral, where boldly carved capitals supporting the vaulting feature a range of foliage, strange animals, and touches of pure fantasy. Then comes the dome, which seems to owe much to Byzantine architecture; it's a remarkably light structure raised on two tiers of arcaded openings. Not the least of the Old Cathedral's attractions are its furnishings, including sepulchres from the 12th and 13th centuries and a magnificent, curved high altar comprising 53 colorful and delicate scenes by the mid-15th-century artist Nicolás Florentino. In the apse above, Florentino painted an astonishingly fresh Last Judgment fresco.

From the south transept of the Old Cathedral, a door leads into the cloister, begun in 1177. From about 1230 until the construction of the main university building in the early 15th century, the chapels around the cloister served as classrooms for the university students. In the Chapel of St. Barbara, on the eastern side, theology students answered the grueling questions meted out by their doctoral examiners. The chair in which they sat is still there, in front of a recumbent effigy of Bishop Juan Lucero, on whose head the students would place their feet for inspiration. Also attached to the cloister is a small cathedral museum with a 15th-century triptych of St. Catherine by Salamanca's greatest native artist, Fernando Gallego. ✉ *Plá y Deniel s/n,* ☎ *923/217476.* 💴 *New Cathedral free, Old Cathedral 300 ptas.* ⊙ *New Cathedral daily 10–1 and 4–6, Old Cathedral daily 10–12:30 and 4–5:30.*

55 **Colegio Mayor Arzobispo Fonseca/Colegio de Los Irlandeses** (Irish College). This small college was founded by Alonso de Fonseca II in 1521 to train young Irish priests. It is now a residence hall for guest lecturers at the university. The surroundings are not particularly attractive; this part of town was the most severely damaged during the Peninsular War of the early 19th century and still has a slightly derelict character. The interior, however, is a treat. To the right immediately inside the college is a spacious late-Gothic chapel, and beyond it lies one of the most classical and genuinely Italianate of Salamanca's many courtyards. The architect may have been Diego de Siloe, Spain's answer to Michelangelo. A display of **antique clocks** is open Tuesday–Friday 4–6 and weekends 11–2. ✉ *Fonseca 4,* ☎ *923/294570.* 💴 *100 ptas.* ⊙ *Daily 10–2 and 4–6.*

59 **Convento de Las Dueñas** (Convent of the Dames). Founded in 1419, this convent hides a 16th-century cloister that is the most fantastically decorated in Salamanca, if not in the whole of Spain. The capitals of its two superimposed Salamantine arcades are crowded with a baffling profusion of grotesques that can absorb you for hours. There's another good reason to come here: the nuns make and sell excellent sweets and pastries. ✉ *Plaza Concilio de Trento,* ☎ *923/215442.* 💴 *200 ptas.* ⊙ *Daily 10:30–1 and 4:30–7.*

56 **Convento de Las Ursulas** (Convent of the Ursulines). Archbishop Alonso de Fonseca I lies here, in a splendid marble tomb created by Diego de Siloe during the first half of the 16th century. ✉ *Las Ursulas 2,* ☎ *923/219877.* 💴 *100 ptas.* ⊙ *Daily 10–1 and 4:30–7.*

60 **Convento de San Esteban** (Convent of St. Stephen). The awesome size of this building is a measure of its importance in Salamanca's history: its monks, among the most enlightened teachers at the university, were the first to take Columbus's ideas seriously and helped him gain his introduction to Isabella (hence his statue in the nearby Plaza de Colón, back toward Calle de San Pablo). The complex was designed by one of San Esteban's monks, Juan de Alava. The door to the right of the west facade leads you into a gloomy cloister with Gothic arcading, interrupted by tall, spindly columns adorned with classical motifs. From the cloister, you enter the church at its eastern end. The interior is unified and uncluttered, but also dark and severe. The one note of color is provided by the sumptuously ornate and gilded high altar of 1692, a Baroque masterpiece by José Churriguera. The most exciting feature of San Esteban, though, is the massive west facade, a thrilling plateresque work in which sculpted figures and ornamentation are piled up to a height of more than 98 ft. ✉ *Plaza Concilio de Trento,* ☎ *923/215000.* 💴 *200 ptas.* ⊙ *Daily 9–1 and 4–8 (4–6 in winter).*

Museo Art Nouveau y Art Deco. The setting for this museum is the Casa Lis, a modernist building from the end of the 19th century. On display are 19th-century paintings and glass, as well as French and German china dolls, Viennese bronze statues, furniture, jewelry, enamels, and jars. ✉ *Gibraltar 14,* ☎ *923/121425.* 💴 *300 ptas.* ⊙ *Tues.–Fri. 11–2 and 4–7, weekends 11–8.*

Museo de Salamanca (also Museo de Bellas Artes). Consisting mainly of minor 17th- and 18th-century paintings, this museum is also interesting for its 15th-century building, which belonged to Isabella's physician, Alvárez Abarca. ✉ *Patio de Escuelas Menores 2,* ☎ *923/212235.* 💵 *200 ptas., free weekends.* ⏲ *Mon.–Sat. 10–2 and 4:30–7:30, Sun. 10–2.*

54 **Palacio de Monterrey.** Built after 1538 by Rodrigo Gil de Hontañón, the Monterrey Palace was meant for an illegitimate son of Alonso de Fonseca I. Only one of its four wings was completed, but this one alone makes the palace one of the most imposing in Salamanca. As in Rodrigo's other local palaces, the building is flanked on each side by towers and has an open arcaded gallery running the whole length of the upper level. Such galleries—which in Italy you would expect to see on the ground floor—are common in Spanish Renaissance palaces and were intended as areas where the women of the house could exercise unseen and undisturbed. They also helped to cool the floor below during the summer months. The palace is privately owned and not open to visitors, but you can stroll around the exterior. ✉ *Compañía s/n.*

58 **Plaza Mayor.** Built in the 1730s by Alberto and Nicolás Churriguera, Salamanca's Plaza Mayor is one of the largest squares in Spain, and many find it the most beautiful. Its northern side is dominated by the lavishly elegant, pinkish **ayuntamiento** (city hall). The square and its arcades are popular gathering spots for most of Salamancan society, and the many surrounding cafés make this the perfect spot for a coffee break. At night, the plaza swarms with students meeting "under the clock" on the plaza's north side. *Tunas* (strolling musicians in traditional garb) often meander among the cafés and crowds, playing for smiles and applause rather than tips.

50 **Puente Romano** (Roman Bridge). Next to the bridge is an Iberian stone bull, and opposite the bull is a statue commemorating Lazarillo de Tormes, the young hero of the eponymous (but anonymous) 16th-century work that is one of the masterpieces of Spanish literature.

52 **Universidad.** Parts of the university's walls, like those of the cathedral and other structures in Salamanca, are covered with large, ocher lettering recording the names of famous university graduates. The earliest names are said to have been written in the blood of the bulls killed to celebrate the successful completion of a doctorate.

The **Escuelas Mayores** (Major Schools) dates to 1415, but it was not until more than 100 years later that an unknown architect provided the building with its gloriously elaborate frontispiece, generally acknowledged as one of the finest works of the classical plateresque. Immediately above the main door is the famous double portrait of Isabella and Ferdinand, surrounded by ornamentation that plays on the yoke-and-arrow heraldic motifs of the two monarchs. The double-eagle crest of Charles V, flanked by portraits of the emperor and empress in classical guise, dominates the middle layer of the frontispiece. On the highest layer is a panel recently identified as representing Pope Martin V (one of the university's greatest benefactors), accompanied by cardinals and university rectors. The whole is crowned by a characteristically elaborate plateresque balustrade.

The interior of the Escuelas Mayores, drastically restored in parts, comes as a slight disappointment after the splendor of the facade. But the *aula* (lecture hall) of Fray Luis de León, where Cervantes, Calderón de la Barca, and numerous other luminaries of Spain's golden age once sat, is of particular interest. After five years' imprisonment for having translated the *Song of Solomon* into Spanish, Fray Luis returned to this hall and began his lecture, "As I was saying yesterday . . ."

Your ticket to the Escuelas Mayores also admits you to the nearby Escuelas Menores (Minor Schools), built in the early 16th century as a secondary school preparing candidates for the university proper. Passing through a gate crowned with the double-eagle crest of Charles V, you'll come to a green, on the other side of which is a modern building housing a fascinating ceiling fresco of the zodiac, originally in the library of the Escuelas Mayores. A fragment of a much larger whole, this painting is generally attributed to Fernando Gallego. ☎ *923/294400 ext. 1150.* *300 ptas.* *Weekdays 9:30–1:30 and 4–7:30, Sat. 9:30–1:30 and 4–7, Sun. 10–1:30.*

Dining and Lodging

$$$ ✕ **Chez Victor.** Try this chic restaurant for a break from traditional Castilian food. Chef-owner Victoriano Salvador learned his trade in France and adapts French cuisine to Spanish taste, with whimsical touches all his own. Sample the more traditional *patatas rellenas de bacalao* (potatoes stuffed with salt cod) or the more innovative ravioli *rellenos de marisco* (stuffed with shellfish). Desserts are outstanding, especially the chocolate ones—try the raspberry walnut *tarta de chocolate* with fresh whipped cream. ✉ *Espoz y Mina 26,* ☎ *923/213123. AE, DC, MC, V. Closed Sun. July–Aug.*

$$$ ✕ **El Candil Viejo.** Beloved of locals for its superb, no-nonsense Castilian fare, this cozy tavern is an old-school favorite with professors in pinstripes and students on dates. Aside from a simple salad the menu consists of meat, meat, and more meat, including pork, lamb, kid, sausage, and steak. The homemade sausages are especially good. For tapas, try the *farinato* sausage, made from pork, onion, eggs and bread crumbs, or the *picadillo,* similar but spicier with pepper, garlic, and tomato. ✉ *Ventura Ruiz Aguilera 14–16,* ☎ *923/217239. AE, DC, MC, V.*

$$–$$$ ✕ **Río de la Plata.** This tiny basement restaurant off Calle de San Pablo has been in business since 1958 and retains an old-fashioned character. The gilded yet quiet decor is a pleasant change of scenery, and the fireplace and local crowd provide warmth. The food is simple but carefully prepared, with good-quality fish and meat. ✉ *Plaza Peso 1,* ☎ *923/219005. AE, MC, V. Closed Mon. and July.*

$$$$ **Gran Hotel.** The grande dame of Salamanca's hotels offers stylish Baroque lounges and refurbished yet old-fashioned oversize rooms, just steps from the Plaza Mayor. ✉ *Plaza Poeta Iglesias 5, 37001,* ☎ *923/213500,* FAX *923/213500. 140 rooms. Restaurant, bar. AE, DC, MC, V.*

$$$$ **Palacio del Castellanos.** Housed in an immaculately restored 15th-century palace, this hotel has an exquisite interior patio and an equally beautiful restaurant, as well as a lovely terrace overlooking San Esteban. Rooms are decorated in peach and white, with wooden bed frames, and have modern, white-tile bathrooms. ✉ *San Pablo 58, 37008,* ☎ *923/261818,* FAX *923/261819. 69 rooms. Restaurant. AE, DC, MC, V.*

$$$$ ★ **Rector.** This lovely hotel is a true European experience, from the stately entrance to the high-ceilinged guest rooms. The sitting areas, hallways, and breakfast room are all spotless, spacious, warm, and quiet, and the wonderful owners and staff will devote themselves to your every whim. Take advantage of their willingness to tell you all about Salamanca. You'll feel like you're staying with family—in high places. ✉ *Rector Esperabé 10,* ☎ *923/218482,* FAX *923/214008. 14 rooms. Bar, breakfast room. AE, DC, MC, V.*

$$$ **San Polo.** Built on the foundations of the old Romanesque church by the same name—the ruins of which you can see through windows in the foyer and hall—the relatively new San Polo is near the city center and has a friendly staff. The smallish rooms are decorated in light ocher tones, with white curtains. ✉ *Arroya de Santo Domingo, 37008,*

☎ *923/211177,* FAX *923/211177. 36 rooms, 1 suite. Restaurant, bar, parking. AE, DC, MC, V.*

$$ 🏨 **Hostal Plaza Mayor.** You can't beat the location of this great little *hostal,* just steps from the Plaza Mayor. Rooms are small but modern; the only drawback is the noise level on weekends, when student *tunas* sing guitar ballads at the plaza's crowded cafés until the wee hours. Reservations are advisable, as rooms fill up fast. ✉ *Plaza del Corrillo 20, 37008,* ☎ *923/262020,* FAX *923/217548. 19 rooms. Restaurant. MC, V.*

Nightlife

Salamanca is said to have the second-best nightlife in central Spain. **Mesón Cervantes,** an upstairs tapas bar with an entrance on the southeast corner of the Plaza Mayor, draws crowds to its balcony for a drink and an unparalleled view of the action. Discos are dominated by students, but classy venues abound; for good wine, heaping portions of tapas, and live music ranging from blues to country to Paris swing, try the **Café Principal** (✉ Rua Mayor 9). **Café Moderno** (✉ Gran Vía 75) rocks all night long; this is where after-hours types end the night before tucking into *chocolate con churros* at daybreak.

Shopping

Salamanca has a reputation for fine leatherwork; the most traditional shop in town is **Salón Campero** (✉ Plaza Corrillo 5). For crafts and unusual gifts, including eclectic pottery, ironwork, paintings, and hand-stitched linens, check out **Indiana** (✉ Meléndez 24, ☎ 923/264243).

Ciudad Rodrigo

61 *88 km (54 mi) west of Salamanca.*

Surveying the fertile valley of the River Agueda, the small town of Ciudad Rodrigo has numerous well-preserved palaces and churches and makes an excellent overnight stop on the way from Spain to Portugal.

The **cathedral** combines the Romanesque and Transitional Gothic styles and holds a great deal of fine sculpture. Look closely at the early 16th-century choir stalls, elaborately carved with entertaining grotesques by Rodrigo Alemán. The cloister has carved capitals, and the cypresses in its center lend tranquillity. The cathedral's outer walls are still scarred by cannonballs fired during the Peninsular War. 🎟 *Cathedral free, museum 250 ptas.* ⏲ *Daily 10–1 and 4–6.*

The town's other major monument is its fortified medieval **castle,** part of which has been turned into a parador. From here you can climb onto the town's battlements.

Dining and Lodging

$–$$ ✕ **Mayton.** This restaurant has a most engaging interior, backed with wood beams and bursting with a wonderfully eccentric collection of antiques ranging from mortars and pestles to Portuguese yokes and old typewriters. In contrast to the decor, the cooking is simple; the specialties are fish, seafood, goat, and lamb. ✉ *La Colada 9,* ☎ *923/460720. AE, DC, MC, V.*

$$$–$$$$ 🏨 **Parador de Ciudad Rodrigo.** Occupying part of the magnificent castle built by Enrique II of Trastamara to stand guard over the Agueda Valley, this parador is a series of small, white rooms along the building's sturdy, gently sloping outer walls. At press time the facility was closed for refurbishment, so call before coming to make sure it has reopened. Room 10 has traditionally had original vaulting, and the bathrooms had under-floor heating. Some rooms, as well as the restaurant, overlook a beautiful garden that runs down to the River Agueda; beyond the river, the view surveys fertile plains. ✉ *Plaza Castillo 1,*

37500, ☎ 923/460150, FAX 923/460404. 27 rooms. Restaurant, bar, meeting room. AE, DC, MC, V.

PROVINCE OF ZAMORA AND CITY OF VALLADOLID

Zamora, Toro, Valladolid

Zamora is a densely fertile province divided by the River Duero into two distinct zones: the "land of bread," to the north, and the "land of wine," to the south. The area is most interesting for its Romanesque churches, the finest of which are in Zamora and Toro. The city of Valladolid, in contrast, is less scenic, but it has the National Museum of Sculpture and plenty of interesting history.

Zamora

62 *248 km (154 mi) northwest of Madrid.*

Zamora, on a bluff above the Duero, is not conventionally beautiful, as its many attractive monuments are isolated from one another by ramshackle 19th- and 20th-century development. The town does have lively, old-fashioned character, making it a pleasant place to pause.

In the medieval town center, on the south side of the Plaza Mayor, is the Romanesque church of **San Juan** (open for mass only), remarkable for its elaborate rose window. North of the Plaza Mayor, at the end of Calle Reina, is one of the town's surviving medieval gates, and near here is the Romanesque church of **Santa María.**

Zamora is famous for its Holy Week celebrations. The **Museo de Semana Santa** (Holy Week Museum) houses the sculptures paraded around the streets in processions during that time. Of relatively recent vintage, these works have an appealing provincial quality—for instance, a Crucifixion group filled with what appears to be the contents of a hardware store, including bales of rope, a saw, a spade, and numerous nails. The museum is housed in an unsightly modern building next to the church of Santa María. *300 ptas. Mon.–Sat. 10–2 and 4–7 (4–8 in summer), Sun. 10–2.*

Zamora's **cathedral** is in a hauntingly beautiful square at the highest and westernmost point of the old town. The bulk of the building is Romanesque, but the exterior is most remarkable for its dome, which is flanked by turrets, articulated by spiny ribs, and covered in overlapping stones, like scales. The dark interior is notable for its early-16th-century carved choir stalls. The austere, late-16th-century cloister has a small museum upstairs, with an intricate *custodia* (monstrance, or receptacle for the Host) by Juan de Arce and some badly displayed but intriguing Flemish tapestries from the 15th and 16th centuries. *300 ptas. Mon. 4–6, Tues.–Sat. 11–2 and 4–7 (5–8 in summer), Sun. 11–2.*

Surrounding Zamora's cathedral to the north is an attractive park incorporating the heavily restored **castle,** begun in the 11th century. Now a municipal school, it is open to visitors only when classes are in session. Calle Trascastillo, descending south from the cathedral to the river, affords views of the fertile countryside to the south and the town's old Roman bridge.

Lodging

$$$$ **Parador de Zamora.** This restored 15th-century palace is central yet quiet, with a distinctive patio courtyard adorned with coats of arms and classical medallions of historical and mythological figures. The views

are excellent, and the staff is friendly and resourceful. ✉ *Plaza Viriato 5, 49001, ☎ 980/514497, FAX 980/530063. 52 rooms. Restaurant, bar, pool. AE, DC, MC, V.*

Toro

63 *33 km (20 mi) east of Zamora, 272 km (169 mi) northwest of Madrid.*

Standing above a loop of the River Duero and commanding extensive views over the vast plain to the south, Toro was a provincial capital at one time. In 1833, however, it was absorbed into Zamora's province in a loss of status that worked in some ways to its advantage. Zamora developed into a thriving modern town, but Toro slumbered and preserved its old appearance. The town is crowded with Romanesque churches, of which the most important is the **Colegiata,** begun in 1160. The protected west portal, or Portico de La Gloria, has a colorfully painted, perfectly preserved statuary from the early 13th century. The Serbian-Byzantine dome is also prominent. In the sacristy is an anonymous 15th-century painting of the Virgin, a touching work in the so-called Hispano-Flemish style. It's titled *The Virgin of the Fly* because of the fly painted on the Virgin's robe, a rather unusual detail. *Free. Summer, Tues.–Sun. 11–1:30 and 5–7:30; winter, Tues.–Sun. 11–1 and 6–7; Mon. open for mass only.*

Valladolid

64 *96 km (60 mi) east of Zamora, 193 km (120 mi) northwest of Madrid.*

Modern Valladolid, capital of Castile–León, is a sprawling industrial center in the middle of a flat stretch of Castilian terrain. The surrounding countryside has an agricultural sort of beauty, and the city itself has ★ one outstanding attraction— the **Museo Nacional de Escultura** (National Museum of Sculpture)—and a number of other interesting sights. It's also one of the most important cities in Spain's history. Ferdinand and Isabella were married here, Philip II was born and baptized here, and Philip III made Valladolid the capital of Spain for six years.

Take a taxi—from the bus station, train station, or wherever you park your car—and head for the National Museum of Sculpture, at the northernmost point in the old town. The late-15th-century Colegio de San Gregorio, in which the main museum is housed, is a masterpiece of the so-called Isabelline, or Gothic, plateresque, an ornamental style of exceptional intricacy featuring playful, naturalistic detail. The facade is especially fantastic, with ribs in the form of pollarded trees, sprouting branches, and—to polish off the forest motif—a row of wild men bearing mighty clubs. Across the walkway from the main museum is a Renaissance palace that became a new wing of the museum in 1998, primarily for temporary exhibitions.

The main museum is arranged in rooms off an elaborate, arcaded courtyard. Its collections do for Spanish sculpture what those in the Prado do for Spanish painting—the only difference is that most people have heard of Velázquez, El Greco, Goya, and Murillo, whereas few are familiar with Alonso de Berruguete, Juan de Juni, and Gregorio Fernández, the three great names represented here.

Attendants and directional cues encourage you to tour the museum in chronological order. Begin on the ground floor, with Alonso de Berruguete's remarkable sculptures from the dismantled high altar in Valladolid's church of San Benito (1532). Berruguete, who trained in Italy under Michelangelo, is the most widely appreciated of Spain's postmedieval sculptors. He strove for pathos rather than realism, and his works have an extraordinarily expressive quality. The San Benito altar was the most important commission of his life, and the fragments here allow you to scrutinize his powerfully emotional art. In the museum's elegant chapel (which you normally see at the end of the tour) is a Berruguete retable from 1526, his first known work; on either side kneel gilded bronze figures by the Italian-born Pompeo Leoni, whose polished and highly decorative art is diametrically opposed to that of Berruguete.

Many critics of Spanish sculpture feel that decline set in with the late-16th-century artist Juan de Juni, who used glass for eyes and pearls for tears. Juni's many admirers, however, find his works intensely exciting, and they are in any case the highlights of the museum's upper floor. Many of the 16th-, 17th-, and 18th-century sculptures on this floor were originally paraded around the streets during Valladolid's celebrated Easter processions; should you ever attend one of these thrilling pageants, the power of Spanish Baroque sculpture will be instantly clear.

Dominating Castilian sculpture of the 17th century was the Galician-born Gregorio Fernández, in whose works the dividing line between sculpture and theater becomes tenuous. Respect for Fernández has been diminished by the number of vulgar imitators his work has spawned, even up to the present day, but at Valladolid you can see his art at its best. The enormous, dramatic, and moving sculptural groups assembled in the last series of rooms (on the ground floor near the entrance) form a suitably spectacular climax to this fine collection. ✉ *Cadenas San Gregorio 1,* ☎ *983/250375.* 💳 *400 ptas.; free Sat. 4–6 and Sun.* ⏲ *Tues.–Sat. 10–2 and 4–6, Sun. 10–2.*

The **birthplace of Philip II** is a brick mansion on the Plaza de San Pablo, at the corner of Calle Angustias. The late-15th-century church of **San Pablo** has another overwhelmingly elaborate facade. The city's **cathedral,** however, is disappointing. Though its foundations were laid in late-Gothic times, the building owes much of its appearance to designs executed in the late 16th century by Juan de Herrera, the architect of the Escorial. Further work was carried out by Alberto de Churriguera in the early 18th century, but the building is still only a fraction of its intended size. The Juni altarpiece is the one bit of color and life in an otherwise visually chilly place. ✉ *Plaza de la Universidad 1,* ☎ *983/304362.* 💳 *Cathedral free, museum 250 ptas.* ⏲ *Tues.–Fri. 10–1:30 and 4:30–7, weekends 10–2.*

The main **university** building sits opposite the garden just south of the cathedral. The exuberant and dynamic late-Baroque frontispiece is by Narciso Tomé, creator of the remarkable *Transparente* in Toledo's cathedral. Calle Librería leads south from the main building to the magnificent **Colegio de Santa Cruz,** a large university college begun in 1487 in the Gothic style and completed in 1491 by Lorenzo Vázquez in a tentative, pioneering Renaissance mode. Inside is a harmonious courtyard.

The house where Christopher Columbus died, in 1506, has been extensively rebuilt and is open to visitors; inside, the excellent **Museo de Colón** (Columbus Museum) has a well-arranged collection of objects, models, and explanatory panels illuminating the explorer's life and times. ✉ *Colón s/n,* ☎ *983/291353.* 💳 *Free.* ⏲ *Tues.–Sat. 10–2 and 5–7, Sun. 10:30–2.*

A more interesting remnant of Spain's golden age is the tiny house where the writer Miguel de Cervantes lived from 1603 to 1606. A haven of peace set back from a noisy thoroughfare, **Casa de Cervantes** (Cervantes's House) is best reached by taxi. Furnished in the early 20th century in a pseudo-Renaissance style by the Marquis of Valle-Inclan—the creator of the El Greco Museum in Toledo—it has a cozy atmosphere. ✉ *Rastro s/n,* ☏ *983/308810.* 🎫 *400 ptas.; free Sun.* ⏲ *Tues.–Sat. 10–3:30, Sun. 10–3.*

Dining and Lodging

$$$ ✕ **La Fragua.** In a modern building with a traditional Castilian interior of white walls and wood-beamed ceilings, Valladolid's most famous and stylish restaurant counts members of the Spanish royal family among its guests. Specialties include meat roasted in a wood oven and such imaginative dishes as *rape Castellano Gran Mesón* (breaded monkfish with clams and peppers) and *lengua empiñonada* (tongue coated in pine nuts). ✉ *Paseo Zorrilla 10,* ☏ *983/337102. AE, DC, MC, V. Closed Aug. No dinner Sun.*

$$$$ 🏨 **Valladolid Meliá.** This hotel sits on a modern block in the midst of one of Valladolid's oldest and most attractive districts. The building was erected in the early 1970s and completely redecorated in 1994, with blond-wood furniture and new baths. The first two floors have a pristine, marbled elegance. ✉ *Plaza de San Miguel 10, 47003,* ☏ *983/357200,* FAX *983/336828. 211 rooms. Restaurant, bar, cafeteria, meeting room. AE, DC, MC, V.*

Nightlife

Valladolid is a university town and has nightlife to match. The cafés on the Plaza Mayor are the best places to people-watch as evening falls. For good Catalonian tapas, try **Taberna Pan con Tomate** (✉ Plaza Mayor 18). Tapas are even better in the Zona Santa María la Antigua and on the adjacent Calle Marqués and Calle Paraíso. The modern Zona Paco Suárez is popular with students. More fashionable (and less rowdy) late at night are the Zona Cantarranas (the **Atomium** disco in particular) and the hidden hot spots on and around the Plaza del Salvador.

BURGOS, LEÓN, AND THE CAMINO DE SANTIAGO

Burgos and León are ancient Castilian capitals with lively centers and two of the grandest Gothic cathedrals in Spain. West of Burgos, the N120 to León crosses the ancient Way of St. James, dotted with lovely old churches with exquisite stone carvings, tiny hermitages, ruined monasteries, and medieval villages in gently undulating cereal country. The snowcapped peaks of the Picos de Europa mark the northwestern horizon. West of León, you can actually follow the well-worn Camino as it approaches Galicia and the very last stops on a pilgrimage route that began all the way back in France or Portugal. Wending its way toward the giant cathedral in Santiago de Compostela (☞ Chapter 4), this Castilian leg of the Camino passes through medieval towns and quiet valleys as the terrain gets greener, wetter, and hillier.

Burgos

240 km (149 mi) north of Madrid.

Set on the banks of the Arlanzón River, Burgos is a small city with some of Spain's most outstanding medieval architecture. The first signs of the city, if you approach on the NI from Madrid, are the spiky twin spires of its magnificent cathedral, rising above the main bridge and gate into the old city center. Burgos's second glory is its heritage as the city of El Cid, the part-historical, part-mythical hero of the Christian Reconquest of Spain.

Burgos has been known for centuries as a center of both militarism and religion, and even today you'll see more nuns and military officers on its streets than almost anywhere else in Spain. The city was born as a military camp in 884—a fortress built on the orders of the Christian king Alfonso III, who was having a hard time defending the upper reaches of Old Castile from the constant forays of the Arabs. It quickly became vital in the defense of Christian Spain. The ruins of the castle erected then still overlook Burgos.

The city's identity as an early outpost of Christianity was consolidated with the founding of the Royal Convent of Las Huelgas, in 1187. Burgos also became an important station on the Camino de Santiago, and thus a place of rest and sustenance for Christian pilgrims throughout the Middle Ages.

★ 65 Start your walk at the **cathedral,** the city's high point, which contains such a wealth of art and other treasures that jealous burghers actually lynched their civil governor on the morning of January 25, 1869, for trying to take an inventory. The proud Burgalese apparently feared that the poor man was preparing to remove the treasures.

Most of the outside of the cathedral is sculpted in the Flamboyant Gothic style. The cornerstone was laid in 1221, and the twin 275-ft towers were completed by the middle of the 14th century, though the final chapel was not finished until 1731. There are 13 chapels, the most elaborate of which is the hexagonal Condestable Chapel. You'll find the **tomb of El Cid** (1026–99) and his wife, Ximena, under the transept. El Cid (whose real name was Rodrigo Díaz de Vivar) was a mercenary warrior revered for his victories over the Moors; the medieval *Song of My Cid* transformed him into a Spanish national hero.

At the other end of the cathedral, high above the West Door, is the **Reloj de Papamoscas** (Flycatcher Clock), so named for the sculptured bird that opens its mouth as the mechanism marks each hour. The grilles around the choir feature some of the finest wrought-iron work in central Spain, and the choir itself has 103 delicately carved walnut stalls, no two alike. The 13th-century stained-glass windows that once shed a beautiful, filtered light were destroyed in 1813, one of many cultural casualties of Napoléon's retreating troops. ✉ *Pl. del Rey San Fernando,* ☎ *947/204712.* *Museum and cloister 450 ptas.* *Tues.–Sat. 9:30–1 and 4–7; Sun.–Mon. and holidays 9:30–11:45 and 4–7.*

66 Across the Plaza del Rey San Fernando from the cathedral is the city's main gate, the **Arco de Santa María.** Walk through the gate toward the river and look up above the arch—the 16th-century statues depict the first Castilian judges; El Cid; Spain's patron saint James; and King Charles I.

67 The Arco de Santa María fronts the city's loveliest promenade, the **Espolón.** The walkway follows the riverbank and is shaded with luxuriant black poplars.

68 The **Casa del Cordón,** a 15th-century palace on the Plaza de Calvo Sotelo, is where the Catholic Monarchs received Columbus after his second voyage to the New World. It's now a bank.

69 Three kilometers (2 miles) east of Burgos, at the end of a poplar- and elm-lined drive, is the **Cartuja de Miraflores.** Founded in 1441, this florid Gothic charterhouse has an unusual link to the Americas: its Isabelline church has an altarpiece by Gil de Siloe, said to be gilded with the first gold brought back from the New World. To get there, follow signs from the city's main gate. *Free.* *Church open for mass Mon.–Sat. 9 AM, Sun. 7:30 and 10:15 AM; main building Mon.–Sat. 10:15–3 and 4–6, Sun. 11:20–12:30, 1–3, and 4–6.*

Burgos

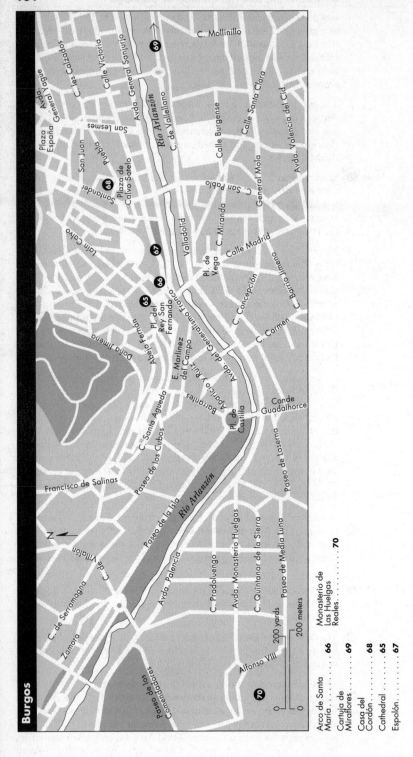

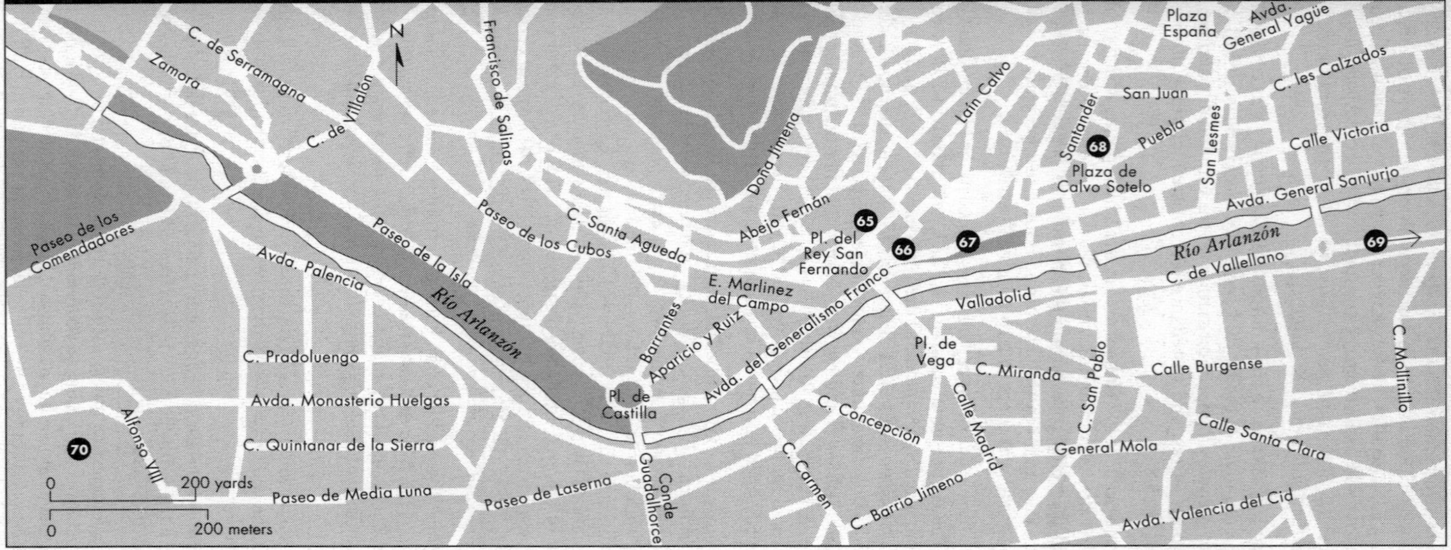
C. de Serramagna
Zamora
C. de Villalón
N
Francisco de Salinas
Doña Jimena
Laín Calvo
Santander
68
San Juan
Plaza España
Avda. General Yagüe
C. les Calzados
Puebla
San Lesmes
Calle Victoria
Plaza de Calvo Sotelo
Avda. General Sanjurjo
Paseo de los Comendadores
Paseo de la Isla
Paseo de los Cubos
C. Santa Agueda
Abejo Fernán
65
Pl. del Rey San Fernando
66
67
Río Arlanzón
69
C. de Vallellano
Avda. Palencia
Río Arlanzón
E. Marlinez del Campo
Avda. del Generalísimo Franco
Valladolid
Barrantes
Aparicio y Ruiz
C. Pradoluengo
Pl. de Vega
C. Miranda
C. San Pablo
Calle Burgense
C. Mollinillo
Avda. Monasterio Huelgas
Pl. de Castilla
C. Concepción
Calle Madrid
Calle Santa Clara
70
Alfonso VIII
C. Quintanar de la Sierra
C. Carmen
General Mola
0
200 yards
Paseo de Media Luna
Paseo de Laserna
Conde Guadalhorce
C. Barrio Jimeno
Avda. Valencia del Cid
0
200 meters

On the western edge of town—a long walk if you're not driving—is
70 the **Monasterio de Las Huelgas Reales,** still run by nuns who live in seclusion behind a double iron grille. Founded in 1187 by King Alfonso VIII and his wife, Eleanor (daughter of England's Henry II), this convent for noble ladies was unprecedented for the powers it gave to the women running it. The present building was originally a summer palace for the kings of Castile; in 1988 it underwent renovations for its 800th anniversary. The convent was conceived in the Romanesque style and housed a royal mausoleum, where its founders still lie. All but one of the royal coffins kept here were desecrated by Napoléon's soldiers, but the one that survived intact contained clothes that form the basis of the convent's medieval textile museum. Don't miss the Chapel of St. James, where Castilian noblemen came to be knighted by the articulated (jointed) statue of Spain's patron saint; the figure lowered its sword arm and dubbed the candidates with a tap on the shoulder. ✉ *1½ km (1 mi) southwest of town, along Paseo de la Isla and left across Malatos Bridge,* ☎ *947/201630.* 🎫 *700 ptas.; free Wed. for EU citizens.* ⏲ *April–Sept., Tues.–Sat. 10:30–1:15 and 3:30–5:45, Sun. 10:30–2:15; Oct.–Mar., Tues.–Sat. 11–1:15 and 4–5:15, Sun. 10:30–2:15.*

Dining and Lodging

$$$ ★ ✕ **Casa Ojeda.** This popular restaurant across from the Casa del Cordón is known for inspired renditions of Burgos classics. How can its roast lamb be so different from any other version of this ubiquitous dish? Try the *morcilla con pimientos rojos* (black sausage with peppers). ✉ *C. Vitoria 5,* ☎ *947/209052. AE, DC, MC, V.*

$$$$ ✕🏨 **Mesón del Cid.** Once a 15th-century printing press, this family-run hotel and restaurant has been hosting travelers and serving up Burgalese food for four generations. Guest rooms, which face the cathedral, are done in traditional Castilian style, and their ample brass beds have porcelain trim. The dining rooms have hand-hewn beams and views of the cathedral from their upper-floor perches. The *pimientos rellenos* (peppers stuffed with meat) are excellent, as is the *sopa de Doña Jimena* (garlic soup with bread and egg). ✉ *Pl. Santa María 8, 48383,* ☎ *947/205971,* FAX *947/269460. 56 rooms, 6 suites. Restaurant, bar, cafeteria, free parking. AE, DC, MC, V.*

Shopping

Burgos is known for its wide variety of cheeses. One of the best is known simply as *queso de Burgos* (Burgos cheese), a fresh, ricotta-like cheese. Pick some up at **Casa Quintanilla** (✉ C. Paloma 17). Another good buy is a few bottles of local Ribera de Duero *tinto* wines, now strong rivals to those of Rioja-Alta.

Sasamón

71 *25 km (16 mi) west of Burgos.*

Turn right off the highway and soon you'll be in the village where the 15th-century hilltop church of **Santa María la Real,** with a magnificent carved portico, stands beside a tree-lined plaza with a tinkling fountain. You can visit on weekdays, 11–2 and 4–6. Pick up keys to the church in the nearby Bar Gloria.

On the north side of the village is the tiny **Ermita de San Isidro Hermitage.** If the hermitage is closed, peer through the small window in the door to see, right in the middle of the aisle, its surreal, 20-ft-tall 16th-century Gothic cross. Carved of stone, it depicts the expulsion of Adam and Eve from paradise through the Tree of Good and Evil with Christ crucified on the top, a naked Adam and Eve below, and a snake entwined around the trunk.

Castrojeriz

72 *20 km (12 mi) west of Sasamón.*

From Sasamón, return to the N120 and cross it to reach Olmillas de Sasamón. After passing a castle on your right, continue south following the CAMINO DE SANTIAGO signs. A few miles after Hontanas, the road passes under an arch of the ruined monastery of **San Anton,** now a farm building. Here you can see the two niches by the road where food was once left out for pilgrims. As you approach Castrojeriz, its ruined hilltop **castle** is clearly visible. To visit the three local **churches,** Romanesque and Gothic, you may have to call the caretaker, Vicente (☎ 947/377034).

$ ✕ **La Taberna.** Antonio and María Jesús have lovingly restored this 18th-century timbered building to run as a bar, a restaurant with good home cooking, and a basic *hostal.* The exotic bird at the bar is, helpfully, able to recognize bank notes. ✉ *General Mola 43,* ☎ *947/377120. MC, V.*

Frómista

73 *54 km (33 mi) west of Castrojeriz.*

Take the small road south from Castrojeriz to Itero de la Vega and Boadillo del Camino to reach Frómista. Just before you arrive, the road crosses the **Canal de Castilla,** begun in 1753 with the dubious idea of linking Salamanca with the port of Santander and never completed. This intersection is known as the crossing of faith and reason.

The town of Frómista has four hospices for present-day pilgrims, and its architectural gem is the 1066 church of **San Martín,** one of the purest Romanesque buildings in all of Spain. Richly sculpted inside, it was part of a monastery in the 11th century, which might explain the geographical breathing room it still enjoys.

Dining

$$ ✕ **Hostería de los Palmeros.** Here in a 17th-century pilgrims' hospital, the kitchen serves good fish, game in season, and baby lamb to diners on an outdoor terrace and a rather formal upstairs dining room with a view of the storks' nests on the church of San Telmo, across the highway. ✉ *Plaza San Telmo 4,* ☎ *979/810067. AE, DC, MC, V*

Villalcázar de Sirga

74 *13 km (8 mi) west of Frómista.*

Driving toward Carrión de los Condes, turn right into the village of Villalcázar. The Templar church of **Santa María la Blanca** features a towering double-arched entrance and the exquisite polychrome 13th-century tombs of Felipe, brother of Alfonso X the Wise, and Leonor, his wife.

Carrión de los Condes

75 *7 km (4½ mi) west of Villalcázar de Sirga.*

Drive through this busy town and cross the River Carrión to reach the **Real Monasterio San Zoilo** on the left. Begun in the 10th century, this former Benedictine monastery has magnificent 16th-century Gothic-Renaissance cloisters and the elaborate tombs of the *condes* (counts) of Carrión. You can visit on weekdays 10:30–2 (plus 4–8 between June and August), and on weekends 10:30–2 and 4–8 year-round.

Lodging

$$ ★ **Hotel Real Monasterio San Zoilo.** This former Benedictine monastery dates back to the 10th century, and its spectacular entrance leads to

hugely impressive public rooms with exposed bricks and timbers. The vast refectory can seat 330. One floor up is the restaurant Las Vigas, which serves good Castilian fare to tables set below a forest of medieval beams (*vigas*). The large rooms are well furnished, and the "Habitación del Conde" suite is especially grand. ✉ *Carrió de los Condes, 34120 Palencia,* ☎ *979/880049,* FAX *979/881090. 33 rooms, 4 suites. Restaurant, bar, meeting rooms, parking. AE, DC, MC, V.*

Sahagún

76 *44 km (27 mi) west of Carrió de los Condes, 63 km (39 mi) east of León.*

The road winds into Sahagún past rolling fields of wheat. The town was allegedly founded by Charlemagne after he conquered the Moors by the nearby River Cea, and Sahagún is in fact a center of Mudéjar craftsmanship, as evidenced in the brick belltowers and trilobed apses of the 12th-century churches of **San Tirso** and **San Lorenzo.**

Nuns in the **Monasterio de Santa Cruz** usually allow visitors to see their treasures, which include a beautifully carved medieval silver casket.

Dining

$$ ✕ **Luis.** Featuring a long bar overlooking the narrow Plaza Mayor, this popular, family-run restaurant cooks local produce with flair. At 1,500 ptas., the *puerros de Sahagún rellenos de mariscos* (Sahagún leeks stuffed with shellfish) are recommended, and there's a good selection of salads. Breakfast, lunch, and dinner are served daily. ✉ *Plaza Mayor 4,* ☎ *987/782058. AE, MC, V.*

En Route To continue west to León and Astorga, follow signs from Sahagún to the fast, new *autopista.*

León

77 *333 km (207 mi) northwest of Madrid, 216 km (134 mi) west of Burgos.*

The ancient capital of the group of provinces known as Castilla y León (Castile and León), sits on the banks of the Bernesga River in the high plains of Old Castile. Historians say that the name of the city, which was founded as a permanent camp for the Roman legions in AD 70, has nothing to do with the proud lion that has been its emblem for centuries but is instead a corruption of the Roman word *legio* (legion).

The capital of Christian Spain was moved to León from Oviedo in 914 as the Reconquest spread southward, launching the city's richest era. Walls went up around the old Roman town, and you can still see parts of the 6-ft-thick ramparts in the middle of the modern city.

Today, León is a wealthy provincial capital and prestigious university town. The wide avenues of western León are lined with boutiques, while the twisting alleys of the half-timbered old town hide the bars, bookstores, and *chocolaterías* most popular with students.

★ León is proudest of its soaring Gothic **cathedral,** on the Plaza de Regla, whose soaring upper reaches are built with more windows than stone. Flanked by two aggressively square towers, the facade has three arched, weatherworn doorways, the middle one adorned with slender statues of the apostles.

Begun in 1205, León's cathedral has 125 long, slender stained-glass windows, dozens of decorative small ones, and three giant, spectacular rose windows. On sunny days, the glass casts bejeweled shafts of light on the beautifully spare, pale-sandstone interior; the windows themselves depict abstract floral patterns as well as various biblical and medieval scenes, all in brilliant colors. A clear glass door to the choir gives an unobstructed view of nave windows and the painted altarpiece, framed with gold leaf. The cathedral also contains the sculpted tomb of King Ordoño II, who moved the capital of Christian Spain to León. The extensive **museum** holds giant medieval hymnals, textiles, sculptures, wood carvings, and paintings, some contemporary. Look for the carved-wood Mudéjar archive, with a letter of the alphabet above each door: it's one of the world's oldest file cabinets. ✉ *Plaza de Regla,* ☎ *987/875770.* 🎫 *Museum 500 ptas.* ⏲ *Cathedral: July–Sept., daily 8:30–1:30 and 4–8; Oct.–June, daily 8:30–1:30 and 4–7. Museum: Oct.–June, weekdays 9:30–1:30 and 4–7, Sat. 9:30–1:30; July–Sept. Mon.–Sat. 9:30–2 and 4–7:30.*

Hidden away just north of the cathedral is the **Fundación Vela Zanetti,** a contemporary, wood-and-windows art museum inside a 15th-century mansion. Zanetti was a 20th-century Castilian artist with a fondness for warm tones and a special interest in human rights. Some of his portraits recall El Greco. Art lovers will find this unknown museum a pleasant surprise. ✉ *C. Pablo Flórez s/n,* ☎ *986/244121.* 🎫 *Free.* ⏲ *Tues.–Fri. 10–1 and 5–8, weekends 11–2 and 6–9.*

Down the street from the cathedral, on Avenida Generalísimo Franco, the **Farmacia Marino,** opened in 1827, offers a glimpse into a Spanish drugstore of yore—only the medicines have changed. The ceiling and walls are richly carved, and the latter include a niche for each apothecary jar.

The arcaded **Plaza Mayor,** in the heart of the old town, is surrounded by simple half-timbered houses. On Wednesday and Saturday, the plaza bustles with farmers selling produce and cheeses. Look at their feet: many still wear wooden shoes called *madreñas,* which are raised on three heels, two in front and one in back. They were designed to walk on mud in this usually wet part of Spain.

Most of León's tapas bars are in the 12th-century **Plaza San Martín.** This area is called the Barrio Húmedo, or Wet Neighborhood, for the large amount of wine spilled here late at night.

Southwest of the Plaza San Martín is the **Plaza de Santa María del Camino,** which, as the plaque here points out, used to be called Plaza del Grano (Grain Square) and host the local corn and bread market. The plaza's rural charm is accentuated by the grass growing between the cobbles, an old timber-frame building beside an arcaded one, and the church of **Santa María del Camino,** where pilgrims stop on their way west to Santiago de Compostela. The curious allegorical fountain in the middle depicts two chubby angels clutching a pillar, symbolizing León's two rivers and the capital.

As you're wandering the old town, look down occasionally and you just might notice small **brass scallop shells** set into the street. The scallop being the symbol of St. James, these were installed by the town government to mark the path for modern-day pilgrims.

★ The sandstone basilica of **San Isidoro el Real,** on Calle Cid, was built into the side of the city wall in 1063 and rebuilt in the 12th century. The **Panteón de los Reyes** (Royal Pantheon), adjoining the basilica, has been called the Sistine Chapel of Romanesque art for the vibrant 12th-century frescoes on its pillars and ceiling. The pantheon was the first building in Spain to be decorated with scenes from the New Testament, and its remarkably well preserved art makes any trip to León worthwhile. Look for the agricultural calendar painted on one archway, showing which farming task should be performed each month. Another panel holds a graphic depiction of the Slaughter of the Innocents. Twenty-three kings and queens were once buried here, but their tombs were destroyed by French troops during the Napoléonic Wars. Treasures in the adjacent **Museo de San Isidoro** include a jewel-encrusted agate chalice, a richly illustrated handwritten Bible, and numerous polychrome wood statues of the Virgin Mary. ✉ *Plaza de San Isidoro 4,* ☎ *987/229608.* *Basilica free, Royal Pantheon and museum 400 ptas.* ⊙ *July–Aug., Mon.–Sat. 9–9, Sun. 9–2; Sept.–June, Mon.–Sat. 10–1:30 and 4–6:30, Sun. 10–1:30.*

Just south of the old town is the **Casa de Botines,** a multigabled, turreted, granite behemoth designed at the end of the 19th century by that controversial Catalan Antoni Gaudí. It now houses a bank.

Fronted by a large, airy pedestrian plaza, the sumptuous **Antiguo Monasterio de San Marcos** is now a luxury hotel, the Parador Hostal San Marcos (☞ *below*). Originally a home for knights of the Order of St. James, who patrolled the Camino de Santiago, and a pit stop for weary pilgrims, the monastery you see today was begun in 1513 by the head of the order, King Ferdinand, who felt that knights deserved something better. Finished at the height of the Renaissance, the plateresque facade is a majestic swath of small sculptures (many depicting knights and lords) and careful ornaments. Inside are an elegant staircase and a cloister full of medieval statues. Have a drink in the bar—its tiny windows are the original defensive slits. The building also houses León's **Museo Arqueológico,** famous for its 11th-century ivory Carrizo crucifix. ✉ *Plaza de San Marcos,* ☎ *987/245061 or 987/236405.* *Museum 220 ptas.* ⊙ *May–Sept., Tues.–Sat. 10–2 and 5–8, Sun. 10–2; Oct.–Apr., Tues.–Sat. 10–2 and 4:30–6:30, Sun. 10–2.*

If you're traveling with children, note that León has a long **park** on the banks of the Bernesga River, with playground equipment every 100 ft or so.

Bars and Cafés

Most of León's liveliest hangouts are clustered in the Plaza Mayor and Plaza San Martín, with the former drawing couples and families and the latter a university crowd. The streets are packed with tapas bars; in the **Plaza Mayor,** you might want to start your crawl at Universal, Mesón de Don Quijote, Casa Benito, or Bar La Plaza Mayor. In the **Plaza San Martín,** the Latino Bar at No. 10 serves a glass of house wine and a choice of one of four generous tapas for just 65 ptas., a gift. Have a *pinchito* (tidbit) at cozy Prada a Tope, which serves the local Bierzo wine out of a big barrel. Other Plaza San Martín haunts are Rancho Chico, Nuevo Racimo de Oro, and La Bicha.

Dining and Lodging

$$ ✕ **Adonias.** Enter the bar and go up one flight to this green, softly lit dining room, furnished with rustic tables and colorful ceramics. The cuisine is based on such regional foodstuffs as cured hams, roast peppers, and chorizo. Try the grilled sea bream or the roast suckling pig, and perhaps the homemade banana pudding with chocolate sauce. ✉ *Santa Nonia 16,* ☎ *987/206768. AE, DC, MC, V.*

$$ ✕ **Casa Pozo.** This longtime favorite is across from City Hall on the historic Plaza de San Marcelo. Past the small bar, the bright dining rooms are furnished with heavy Castilian furniture. Owner Gabriel del Pozo Alvarez—called Pin—supervises the busy kitchen while his son, also called Pin, is maitre d'. Specialties include roast lamb, river crabs with clams, cod with pimiento and olive oil, and deep-fried hake. ✉ *Plaza de San Marcelo 15,* ☎ *987/237103. AE, DC, MC, V. No dinner Sun.*

$$ ✕ **Nuevo Racimo de Oro.** Upstairs in a ramshackle, 12th-century tavern in the heart of the old town, this cozy restaurant specializes in roast lamb cooked in a wood-fired clay oven. The spicy *sopa de ajo leonese* (garlic soup) is a classic, and *solomillo Racimo al Hojaldre* (veal in puff pastry) makes a tasty entrée. *Tarta de San Marcos* is a lemon cake served with whipped cream. ✉ *Plaza San Martín 8,* ☎ *987/214767. AE, DC, MC, V. Closed Wed. No dinner Sun.*

$$$$ ★ ✕▣ **Parador Hostal San Marcos.** This magnificent parador occupies a restored 16th-century monastery built by King Ferdinand to shelter pilgrims walking the Camino de Santiago, and the bridge beside it has helped pilgrims over the River Bernesga for centuries. The plateresque facade is longer than a football field, and the building also houses a church and a museum of archaeology. Hallways and guest rooms have antiques, high-quality reproductions, and some nice contemporary art. One wing is modern; if you want medieval atmosphere, ask for a room in the old section. The bar features a red-striped medieval canopy and high-back leather chairs. The menu in the elegant dining room, overlooking the Bernesga, changes often, but you might find a platter of 10 hot and cold regional appetizers for 1,900 ptas. ✉ *Plaza de San Marcos 7, 24001,* ☎ *987/237300,* FAX *987/233458. 230 rooms. 2 restaurants, bar, pool, beauty salon, parking (fee). AE, DC, MC, V.*

$$ ▣ **Hotel Paris II.** This new hotel is on the modern thoroughfare heading east from Plaza Santo Domingo, halfway between the cathedral and the new town. Guest rooms are entirely comfortable, and the classic basement *mesón* (tavern) snuggles up to the exposed stone of a Roman wall. ✉ *Ancha 18, 24003,* ☎ *987/238600,* FAX *987/271572. 57 rooms. Restaurant, bar, café. AE, DC, MC, V.*

Shopping

ARTS AND CRAFTS

For fine funky gifts, visit **Tricosis** (✉ C. Mulhacín 3, ☎ 987/202953), a gallery opened by art students from the universities of Leon and Gijón, where colorful papier-mâché and experimental media form outstanding lamps, candleholders, vases, and frames.

Lovers of home furnishings will enjoy browsing **Armoan** (Avda. Ramón y Cajal 4, ☎ 987/249203), an exquisitely tasteful European collection. Among the smaller—i.e., more portable—items are clever, soothing prints and artful lamps. In Villar de Mazarife, 22 km (14 mi) west of León toward Astorga, **Monseñor** (✉ Camino de León 21) paints adaptations of Roman archaeological finds and makes tile reproductions of the frescoes in the Royal Pantheon.

FOOD

Tasty regional treats include roasted red peppers, potent brandy-soaked cherries, and candied chestnuts. You can buy these in food shops all over the city, or shop while "doing" tapas at **Prada a Tope** (✉ Plaza San Martín 1), where they're packaged by the house. The gourmet shop **Cuesta Castañón** (✉ Castoñones 2), near Plaza San Martín, has a great range of wines, cured meats, cookies, preserves, and bottled delicacies, not to mention books on related topics. Friendly owner José María González lets you sample the goodies.

En Route Leaving León, follow signs to the N120 and head southwest. Stop to admire the 13th-century Orbigo Bridge, 23 km (14 mi) outside the city, where the knight Quiñones made his stand. Legend has it that Quiñones was the toughest *hombre* on the Camino; in 1434, he staked out his turf on this 24-arch bridge and for a month challenged every other knight who policed the route. You are now on the Way of St. James itself, marked with large scallop signs for drivers and small ones for those who make the journey on foot or bicycle.

Astorga

78 *46 km (29 mi) southwest of León.*

Astorga, where the pilgrimage roads from France and Portugal merge, once boasted 22 **hospitals** to lodge and care for ailing travelers. The only one left today is next to the cathedral. The **cathedral** itself is a huge 15th-century building with Baroque decoration and four statues of St. James. At press time it was being renovated; if it's open now, you can enter daily 9:30–noon and 5–6:30. The cathedral **museum** displays 10th- and 12th-century chests, religious silverware, and paintings and sculptures by various Astorgans.

★ Just opposite the cathedral is the fairy-tale, neo-Gothic **Palacio Episcopal** (Archbishop's Palace), designed for a Catalan cleric by Antoni Gaudí in 1889. Visiting the eccentric palace the last week of August during Astorga's Fiesta de Santa María is a surreal treat for the senses; fireworks explode in the sky casting rainbows of light over Gaudí's ornate, mystical towers. No expense was spared in creating this fanciful building, which now houses the **Museo del Camino** (Museum of the Way). The eclectic collection has folk items, such as the standard pilgrim costume—heavy black cloak, staff hung with gourds, and wide-brimmed hat bedecked with scallop shells—as well as outstanding contemporary Spanish art. ⊠ *Adjacent to cathedral,* ☎ *987/616882.* 400 *ptas.* *Apr.–Sept., daily 10–2 and 4–8; Oct.–Mar., daily 11–2 and 3:30–6:30.*

Dining and Lodging

$$ ✕ **La Peseta.** Family-run since 1865—but now in newer premises near the town hall—La Peseta persists in good home cooking, especially the 4-dish marathon *cocido maragato,* a sort of serial country stew. ⊠ *Plaza de S. Bartolomé 3,* ☎ *987/617275. AE, DC, MC, V. Closed Oct. 15–31. No dinner Sun. except in Aug.*

$$ ✕ **Parillada Serrano.** Popular with locals, and occasionally featuring the likes of game, wild mushrooms, and pork during special gastronomic weeks, this *mesón* serves both contemporary cuisine and traditional roasts of baby lamb. ⊠ *Portería 2,* ☎ *987/617866. AE, MC, V. Closed June. No dinner Thurs.*

$$$ **Astur Plaza.** Centrally located near Astorga's city hall, this gleaming new hotel is well run. Guest rooms, yellow with dark-brown furnishings, get ample light from large windows. The lounge is glassed in; the large bar and Los Hornos restaurant have beamed ceilings and exposed brick walls. ⊠ *Plaza de España 2 and 3, 24700,* ☎ *987/618900,* FAX *987/618949. 32 rooms, 5 suites. Restaurant, bar, parking (fee). AE, MC, V.*

Castillo de los Polvazares

79 *51 km (32 mi) west of León, 5 km (3 mi) northwest of Astorga.*

A short walk or 15-minute drive from Astorga is Castillo de los Polvazares, a 17th-century village built on the site of a fortified Roman settlement. The city's 30-odd residents live in stone houses emblazoned with crests above their green doorways. Walk down the stone streets—there are no sidewalks and no asphalt—and look for storks' nests on top of the village church. Telephone wires are the only evidence of modernity.

Castillo de los Polvazares is in León's Maragatería region, whose people are believed to be a mixture of the ancient Celts and Phoenicians. These doughty traders resisted the Roman invasion of the Iberian Peninsula and reached the height of their prowess as muleteers in the 18th and 19th centuries (hence the wide doorways around town), transporting gold from the Americas to the royal court in Madrid.

Ponferrada

80 *115 km (71 mi) west of León, 64 km (40 mi) west of Astorga on N-VI.*

Nestled in a hilly region with beautiful, fertile valleys, Ponferrada is a mining and industrial center that gets its name from an iron toll bridge built by a local bishop in the 1100s. The tall, slim turrets of the 13th-century **Castillo de los Templarios** (Templars' Castle) on the western edge of town command sweeping views of the countryside and may once have been used by the Knights of the Order of St. James to police the route. Restoration is in progress. ✉ *Florez Osorio 4.* 🎟 *250 ptas.* ⏲ *Apr.–May, Tues.–Sat. 10–2 and 4:30–8, Sun. and holidays 10–2; June–mid-Sept., Tues.–Sun. 10:30–2 and 5–9; mid-Sept.–Mar., Tues.–Sat. 10:30–2 and 4–6, Sun. and holidays 11–2.*

OFF THE BEATEN PATH Leave Ponferrada heading west on the N-VI (toward A Coruña), and take the Las Médulas/Puente de Domingo exit to the N536 toward Carucedo. Turning right here, you can either follow the signs to a viewpoint at Orellán or go to the village of **Las Medulas.** From the latter, you can explore the extraordinary Roman gold mines 21 km (13 mi) west of Ponferrada, where jagged red cliffs rise out of oak and chestnut woods, and great pits lead to deep tunnels, canals, and caves. Bring a flashlight if you dare to explore in depth.

Villafranca del Bierzo

81 *135 km (84 mi) west of León, 20 km (12 mi) west of Ponferrada.*

After crossing León's grape-growing region, where the slightly acidic Bierzo wine is produced, you'll arrive in this medieval village, dominated by a massive and still-inhabited feudal fortress. Villafranca was a destination in itself for some of Santiago's pilgrims: visit the Romanesque church of **Santiago** to see the Puerta del Perdón (Door of Pardon), a sort of spiritual consolation prize for exhausted worshippers who couldn't make it over the mountains. Stroll the streets, look for the crests on the old manor houses, and seek out the onetime home of the infamous Grand Inquisitor Torquemada. On the way out, you can buy some wine at any of three local bodegas.

Dining and Lodging

$–$$ ✕🏨 **Parador de Villafranca del Bierzo.** This modern, two-story hotel sits on a hilltop overlooking the Bierzo valley. Rooms have heavy wood furniture, shuttered windows, and large baths. The brick and wrought-iron dining room serves fresh Bierzo trout, *surtido de verduras naturales* (mixed fresh vegetables), and *tournedo con higos agridulces,* a plump juicy steak wrapped in bacon and served with marinated figs and wild mushrooms. Try the local Bierzo wine, made from the Mencia grape. ✉ *Calvo Sotelo s/n, 24500,* ☎ *987/540175,* FAX *987/540010. 40 rooms. Restaurant, bar. AE, DC, MC, V.*

En Route To follow the Camino into Galicia and on to Santiago de Compostela, *see* Chapter 4.

OLD AND NEW CASTILE A TO Z

Arriving and Departing

By Plane

The only international airport in Castile is Madrid's Barajas. Valladolid Airport has flights to Barcelona. For information on airlines serving Madrid, *see* Madrid A to Z *in* Chapter 1.

Getting Around

By Bus

Bus connections between Madrid and Castile are excellent. Two of the most popular services go to Toledo (1 hr) and Segovia (1½ hrs); buses to Toledo leave every half hour from the **Estación Sur de Autobuses** (⊠ Méndez Alvaro s/n, ☎ 91/527–2961), to Segovia every hour from **La Sepulvedana** (⊠ Paseo de la Florida 11, ☎ 91/304800). Buses to Soria (3 hrs) and Burgo de Osma (2½ hrs) leave from **Continental Auto** (⊠ Intercambiador Autobuses, Avenida de América, ☎ 91/745–6300), while **Auto Res** (⊠ Plaza Conde de Casal 6, ☎ 91/551–7200) serves Cuenca (2 hrs, 50 mins) and Salamanca (3 hrs). **Larrea** (☎ 91/539–0005) sends buses to Burgos and León from the Méndez Alvaro metro stop. Buses from **Burgos** (⊠ C. Miranda 4, ☎ 947/265565) serve both Castile and the Basque country. Buses from **León** (⊠ Cardenal Lorenzana s/n, ☎ 987/211000) serve Castile and Asturias. Services *between* the provincial towns are not as good as those to and from Madrid; if you're traveling between, say, Cuenca and Toledo, you will find it quicker to return to Madrid and make your way from there. Reservations are rarely necessary; if demand arises, additional buses are usually called into service.

By Car

A series of major roads with extensive stretches of divided highway—the NI, II, III, IV, V, and Vl—radiate from Madrid in every direction, making the outlying towns easy to reach. If possible, however, avoid returning to Madrid on these roads at the end of a weekend or a public holiday. Side roads vary in quality, but they give rise to one of the great pleasures of driving around the Castilian countryside—constant encounters with unexpected architectural items and wild and spectacular vistas. Above all, you rarely come across other tourists.

By Train

All the main towns in this chapter are accessible by train from Madrid, and several make feasible day trips: there are commuter trains from Madrid to Segovia (2 hrs), Alcalá de Henares (45 mins), Guadalajara (1 hr), and Toledo (1½ hrs). Train travel in Spain has improved in recent years, but it's still often faster to reach your destination by bus. Trains to Toledo depart from Madrid's **Atocha** station; trains to Salamanca, Burgos, and León depart from **Chamartín**; and both stations serve Ávila, Segovia, El Escorial, and Siguenza, though Chamartín may offer more frequent service to some. The one important town that's accessible only by train is Sigüenza. Check with **RENFE** for details (☎ 902/240202).

Contacts and Resources

Car Rental

Renting a car in Spain is much cheaper if you arrange one before you leave home, through a major international firm (☞ Car Rental *in* Smart Travel Tips). Spain's leading rental agency is **Atesa** (⊠ Infanta Mercedes 90, Madrid, ☎ 91/393–7232). If you do need to rent in Spain, you'll generally find prices more competitive outside Madrid and Toledo. **Alamo, Avis,** and **Hertz** are variously represented in Toledo, Ciudad Real, Segovia, Ávila, Salamanca, Valladolid, Burgos, and León.

Fishing

The most common fish in Castile's rivers are trout, pike, black bass, and blue carp. The main trout rivers are the Eresma, Alto Duero, Júcar, Jarama, Manzanares, Tajo, and Tormes. Madrid's **Consjerí de Medio Ambiente** (⊠ Princesa 3, ☎ 91/580–1653) and **La Asociació Madrileña de Pesca** (☎ 91/320–9054) have more information.

Golf

There are golf courses at Salamanca, Alcalá de Henares, and numerous smaller places around Madrid. Contact the **Real Federación Española de Golf** (✉ Capitán Haya 9, Madrid 28020, ☎ 91/555–2682). The **Club de Golf León** (✉ San Miguel del Camino, ☎ 987/303400) is 15 km (9 mi) outside León.

Guided Tours

Local tourist offices can provide current information on city tours and guides for hire. Be wary of local guides in Ávila and Toledo, however; they can be quite ruthless in trying to impose their services. If you join one, do not buy goods in the shops he takes you to; the prices are probably inflated, and the guide gets a kickback.

For a special art tour of Castile, including Salamanca, contact **Prospect Music & Art Tours Ltd.** (✉ 36 Manchester St., London, W1M 5PE, U.K., ☎ 020/7486–5704, FAX 020/7486–5868). The best of Britain's cultural-tour specialists is **Martin Randall Travel** (✉ 10 Barley Mow Passage, Chiswick, London W4 4PH, U.K., ☎ 020/8742–3355, FAX 020/8742–7766), whose excellent five-day trip includes Madrid and Toledo. **Equiberia** (☎ 920/348338) leads horseback tours ranging from one to 10 days, a unique way to experience the gorges, fields, and forests of the Sierra de Guadarrama. In summer, the tourist offices of Segovia, Toledo, and Aranjuez organize **Trénes Turísticos** (miniature tourist trains) that glide you past all the major sights. Contact the local tourist office for schedules, or call 925/142274 for general information.

Visitor Information

The main regional office is in **Madrid,** near Plaza de las Cortes (✉ Duque de Medinaceli 2, ☎ 91/429–4951). **Salamanca** has another regional office, with information on Castile-León (Casa de las Conchas, Rúa Mor s/n, ☎ 923/268571). Municipal tourist offices have local information and town maps: **Alcalá de Henares** (✉ Callejón de Santa María, ☎ 91/889–2694). **Almagro** (✉ Bernardas 2, ☎ 926/860717). **Aranjuez** (✉ Plaza San Antonio 9, ☎ 91/891–0427). **Astorga** (✉ Glorieta Eduardo de Castro 5, ☎ 689/579191). **Ávila** (✉ Plaza de la Catedral 4, ☎ 920/211387). **Burgos** (✉ Pl. Alonso Martínez 7, ☎ 947/203125). **Ciudad Real** (✉ Avda. Alarcos 31, ☎ 926/212925). **Ciudad Rodrigo** (✉ Puerta de Amayuelas 5, ☎ 923/460561). **Consuegra** (Molino de Viento/Bolero Windmill, ☎ 925/475731). **Cuenca** (✉ Glorieta González Valencia 2, ☎ 969/178800). **Guadalajara** (✉ Plaza de los Caídos 6, ☎ 949/211626). **León** (✉ Plaza de Regla 3, ☎ 987/237082). **Ponferrada** (✉ Gil y Carrasco 4, next to castle, ☎ 987/424236). **Pontevedra** (✉ General Mola 2, ☎ 986/850814). **Salamanca** (✉ Plaza Mayor 14, ☎ 923/218342). **Segovia** (✉ Plaza Mayor 10, ☎ 921/460334). **Sigüenza** (✉ Plaza Mayor 1, ☎ 949/393251). **Soria** (✉ Plaza Ramón y Cajal s/n, ☎ 975/212052). **Toledo** (✉ Puerta de Bisagra s/n, ☎ 925/220843). **Valladolid** (✉ Santiago 19, ☎ 983/351801). **Zamora** (✉ C. Santa Clara 20, ☎ 980/531845).

For a list of campgrounds and recommended outdoor excursions in Old Castile, contact the **Junta de Castilla y León** in Madrid (✉ Espronceda 43, ☎ 91/554–3769).

3 CANTABRIA, THE BASQUE COUNTRY, AND LA RIOJA

The Cantabrian mountains give way to the beach resort of Santander and the lovely medieval town of Santillana del Mar. Endowed with its own moist green hills, rugged coast, and ancient language, the Basque country celebrates gastronomy, sports, and rural culture, and now attracts long-deserved attention thanks to the Guggenheim Museum Bilbao. La Rioja, heading back toward Castile, produces Spain's finest wines.

By George Semler

NORTHERN SPAIN IS A MOIST and misty land of green hills; low, wide russet rooflines; and colorful fishing villages. Santander, once the main seaport for Old Castile on the Bay of Biscay, is a beach resort in a mountainous zone wedged between the Basque country and, to the west, Asturias. The semiautonomous Basque country, with its steady drizzle (poetically called the *sirimiri*), damp verdant landscape, and rugged coastline, is a distinct national and cultural entity within the Spanish state. La Rioja, tucked between the Sierra de la Demanda and the Ebro River, is Spain's premier wine country.

Santander and the Cantabrian region are traditionally a Castilian watering place, with sandy beaches, high sierra (including part of the Picos de Europa), and tiny highland towns.

The Basque region is more a country within a country, or a nation within a state (the semantics are much debated), with a linguistically mysterious, non–Indo-European language of its own: Euskera. In contrast to the traditionally individualistic and passionate Latin peoples who have been their neighbors, the Basques have often been seen as more collective-minded and practical. They are also known to love competition—it has been said that Basques will bet on anything that has numbers on it and moves. Such traditional rural sports as chopping mammoth tree trunks, lifting boulders, and scything grass reflect the Basques' traditional attachment to the land and to farm life as well as an ingrained enthusiasm for feats of strength and endurance. Even poetry and gastronomy become contests in Euskadi, as *bertsolaris* (amateur poets) improvise duels of (often very witty) verse, and male-only gastronomic societies compete in cooking contests to see who can make the best *marmitako,* or tuna stew.

The much-reported Basque independence movement is made up of a small but radical sector of the political spectrum. The underground organization known as ETA, or Euskadi Ta Askatasuna (Basque Homeland and Liberty), has killed more than 700 people in more than 25 years of terrorist activity. Conflict waxes and wanes, but the problem is extremely unlikely to affect travelers.

The Basque country also has longtime connections with both Britain and the United States. In particular, Bilbao and its province, Vizcaya, were the source of most of the iron used by the English during the Industrial Revolution. Primarily an agricultural and fishing region of modest opportunity before industry made it a center of productivity on the peninsula, the Basque country has long sent out waves of immigrants to the New World.

Pleasures and Pastimes

Beaches

Santander has excellent sandy beaches: **La Magdalena,** closest to town; **El Sardinero,** the most elegant and best equipped; and **Matalenas,** near the Bellavista campground. **El Puntal,** west of town, is one of Cantabria's finest beaches. The beach at **Laredo,** halfway between Santander and Bilbao, is one of Spain's best and least-discovered. East of Bilbao, the beach at **Lequeitio** is particularly beautiful. The smaller beaches at **Zumaya** and **Guetaria** are usually quiet and intimate. Zarauz, west of San Sebastián, is another good choice. San Sebastián's best beach, **La Concha,** which curves around the bay along with the city itself, is scenic and clean, but it's packed wall-to-wall in the summer. **Ondarreta,** at the western end of La Concha, is often less crowded, and the relatively new and quiet beach on the northern side of the Urumea River, **Zur-**

riola, is where surfers gather for the breakers. **Hondarribia,** the last stop before the French border, has a vast expanse of fine sand along the Bidasoa estuary.

Dining

The Basque cuisine in and around San Sebastián and Bilbao is widely considered the best food in Spain, combining the fresh fish of the Atlantic with a love of sauces that is rare south of the Pyrenees—a result, no doubt, of Euskadi's proximity to France. The now 20-year-old *nueva cocina vasca* (new Basque cooking) movement has introduced exciting elements. In San Sebastián it's nearly impossible to avoid a great meal. Specialties include *kokotxas* (nuggets of cod jaw), *besugo a la parrilla* (sea bream grilled over coals), *chuleta de buey* (garlicky beefsteak grilled over coals), and the deservedly ubiquitous *bacalao al pil-pil*—cod-flank fillets cooked very slowly in a boiled emulsion of garlic and gelatin from the cod itself, so that the oil makes a popping noise ("pil-pil") and a white sauce is created.

Cantabria is all about mountain cooking—roast kid and lamb or *cocidos* (bean stews)—in the highlands, and fresh seafood on the coast. *Soropotun* is Santander's stew of bonito, potatoes, and vegetables. Navarre is famous for beef, lamb, and vegetable dishes such as *menestra de verduras* (a stew of artichokes, green beans, peas, lettuce, potatoes, onion, and chunks of cured ham). La Rioja is known for meaty stews and roasts in the mountains, vegetable dishes in the Ebro River basin.

The local Basque wine, *txakolí,* is a young, white brew made from tart green grapes, a refreshing accompaniment to both seafood and meats. La Rioja, just south of the Basque country, produces the finest wines in Spain; purists insisting on Basque wine with their Basque cuisine could choose a Rioja Alavesa, from the north side of the Ebro. Navarre also produces some fine vintages, especially rosés and reds—and in such quantity that some churches in Allo, Peralta, and other towns were actually built with a mortar mixed with wine instead of water.

Food is not cheap in the Basque country, but some of Europe's finest cuisine is served here in settings that range from the traditional hewn beams and stone walls of old farmhouses to contemporary international restaurants. Don't miss any chance to go to a *sidrería,* a cider house (in Astigarraga, near San Sebastián, there are no fewer than 17) where *tortilla de bacalao* (cod omelet) and thick *chuletas de buey* provide the traditional ballast for copious draughts of hard apple cider.

CATEGORY	MAJOR CITIES*	OTHER AREAS*
$$$$	over 8,000 ptas.	over 6,000 ptas.
$$$	5,000–8,000 ptas.	4,000–6,000 ptas.
$$	2,500–5,000 ptas.	2,000–4,000 ptas.
$	under 2,500 ptas.	under 2,000 ptas.

**per person for a three-course meal, excluding drinks, service, and tax*

Fiestas

Pamplona's feast of **San Fermín** (July 6–14) was made famous by Ernest Hemingway in *The Sun Also Rises* and remains best known for its running of the bulls. The town's population triples that week, so reserve rooms well in advance. Bilbao's **Semana Grande** (Grand Week), in early August, is bigger than ever: Spain's largest bulls of the season seem to stimulate appetites worthy of Bilbao's fine fleet of restaurants. West of Bilbao, Laredo's **Batalla de los Flores** (Battle of the Flowers) is held the last Friday in August. The coastal town of Lequeitio, east of Bilbao, is famous for its unusual **Fiestas de San Antolín,** in which men dangle (on September 5th) from the necks of dead geese strung on a cable over the inlet. Closer to San Sebastián, in the first week of August, the fishing village of **Guetaria** celebrates Juan Sebastián Elkano's completion of Magellan's voyage around the world. San Sebastián hosts a renowned **international film festival** in late September and celebrates its saint's day on January 19. San Vicente de la Barquera honors its patron saint with a famous maritime procession for **La Folía,** April 21. La Rioja's famous **Batalla del Vino** (Wine Battle), a free-for-all honoring the fruit of the vine, takes place in Haro on June 29. Vitoria's weeklong **Fiesta de la Virgen Blanca** (Festival of the White Virgin) celebrates the city's patron saint with bullfights and general carousing beginning on August 4.

Hiking and Walking

Well-marked footpaths wend from the Cordillera Cantábrica to the Pyrenees and along the Basque coast, connecting towns, scaling mountains, and ambling from one fishing village to another. The air, color, and scenery far exceed anything you'll experience in a car. Try the walks around Zumaya, or the walk over Jaizkibel between San Sebastián and the French border. The GR11 trail crosses the Pyrenees of Navarre, while the Camino de Santiago pilgrimage route crosses Navarre and La Rioja on its way west. Local tourist offices can usually suggest routes of your preferred length and intensity.

Lodging

The largely industrial and well-to-do north is a relatively expensive part of Spain, and this is nowhere more apparent than in room rates. San Sebastián is particularly pricey, especially in the summer, and Pamplona rates double or triple during the San Fermín fiesta in July. Reserve ahead in Bilbao, where the Guggenheim Museum is filling hotels, and nearly everywhere in summer. The quality of hotels, service, and connected restaurants is generally quite high. Another lodging option is a Basque farmhouse from the Agroturismo lodging network; these are economical, authentic, and picturesque. Check with local tourist offices for details and availability.

CATEGORY	MAJOR CITIES*	OTHER AREAS*
$$$$	over 25,000 ptas.	over 15,000 ptas.
$$$	15,000–25,000 ptas.	9,000–15,000 ptas.
$$	10,000–15,000 ptas.	6,000–9,000 ptas.
$	under 10,000 ptas.	under 6,000 ptas.

**All prices are for a standard double room, excluding breakfast and tax.*

Sports and Outdoor Activities

Basques are as passionate about sports as they are about food, and you need not participate to catch the action. If you do want to get up and about, there's excellent skiing, sailing, surfing, windsurfing, and trout or Atlantic-salmon fishing in various parts of this rich terrain.

Pelota is the Basque national sport. Most towns have a local *frontón* (backboard or wall), where games normally start at 4 or 4:30 PM. Other traditional Basque rural sports (*herrikirolak*) include the tug-of-war and log-chopping, ram-butting, and scything competitions. The most idiosyncratic of the local contests is the *harrijasotazailes,* the raising of huge rocks by practiced stone-lifters. *Jai-alai* (a generic term for ball games from handball to *cesta punta,* played with wicker gloves), *trainera* (whale-boat regattas), and horse races round out the ample sports menu. Watch for local postings or ask at the tourist office.

Athletic de Bilbao is the local football giant, with San Sebastián's Real Sociedad just behind. Up-and-down first- and second-division teams also compete in Santander, Pamplona, Logroño, and Vitoria. Ask your hotel or the local tourist office about schedules and tickets.

Exploring Cantabria, the Basque Country, and La Rioja

This chapter covers geographical and cultural phenomena from the Cantabrian Cordillera and the Pyrenees to the Bay of Biscay to the plains of Navarre—part Basque and part Navarrese—to La Rioja, which combines the Ebro River valley, the Sierra de la Demanda, and the edge of Spain's central *meseta* east of Calahorra.

Numbers in the text correspond to numbers in the margin and on the Cantabria, the Basque Country, and La Rioja and Bilbao maps.

Great Itineraries

On the map, this region may not appear to cover much ground, but the most scenic roads are also the slowest. Moreover, each of the main entities—Cantabria, the Basque Country, and Navarre—has enough hills, streams, and villages to spend a lifetime discovering once you've seen the cities of San Sebastián, Bilbao, Santander, Vitoria, and Pamplona.

Ten days to two weeks is a fair frame for this chapter, though you could happily spend most of that time in the tiniest village or fishing port. In six days you can cover the high points and come away with some ideas for future visits. Three days is time enough for a taste.

IF YOU HAVE 3 DAYS

If you're coming from Madrid or Burgos, drive through the Picos de Europa to **Santander** ①. Try to pop over to **Santillana del Mar** ②, one of Spain's loveliest medieval and Renaissance towns, and see the museum on the paintings in the nearby **Altamira Caves.** The next day, follow the Basque coast to **Bilbao** ⑦–⑫ for a morning visit to the Guggenheim Museum; then go on to **San Sebastián** ㉑, stopping for lunch in the fishing port of **Guetaria** ⑳. Drive through **Pamplona** ㉔ and Navarre on your third day, approaching either from the north, if you're continuing across Spain, or from the west (and then north) if you're France-bound.

IF YOU HAVE 6 DAYS

Coming from Madrid or Burgos, drive through the mountains on your way to the coast. Stop at **Santillana del Mar** ② for a look at one of Spain's best-preserved medieval and Renaissance towns. If you've made arrangements eons in advance, see the cave paintings at **Altamira**; if not, visit the accompanying museum. If you have time, detour west to **Comillas** ③ and **San Vicente de la Barquera** ④, one of northern Spain's prettiest fishing villages. In **Santander** ①, check out the beach scene along the Playa de la Magdalena and El Sardinero, and wander around the Plaza Porticada. On day two, explore **Laredo** ⑤ and **Castro-Urdiales** ⑥, both port towns with lovely old quarters. Stop in **Bilbao** ⑦–⑫ to see, among other things, the Guggenheim Museum. Devote your third day to exploring the Basque Coast from Bilbao to San Sebastián, including the fishing ports of **Bermeo** ⑮, **Elanchove** ⑯, **Lequeitio** ⑰, **Ondárroa** ⑱, and **Guetaria** ⑳, each of which outdoes the other in activity, color, and cuisine. Spend day four in sybaritic **San Sebastián** ㉑. **Pasajes de San Juan** ㉒ is a lovely village for lunch. **Hondarribia** ㉓, on the Bidasoa River border with France, is another key visit. Spend your fifth day in **Pamplona** ㉔ and the province of Navarre, from which you can continue through southern Navarre to the Basque capital, **Vitoria** ㉘. On day six, tour La Rioja: drive through **Laguardia** ㉙ and **Haro** ㉛ to the provincial capital, **Logroño** ㉚.

IF YOU HAVE 10 DAYS

Spend one day exploring the mountains between Burgos and Santander. Have a look at the highland town of Reinosa, and drive down N611 along the River Saja past semi-abandoned villages such as Bárcena

Cantabria, the Basque Country, and La Rioja

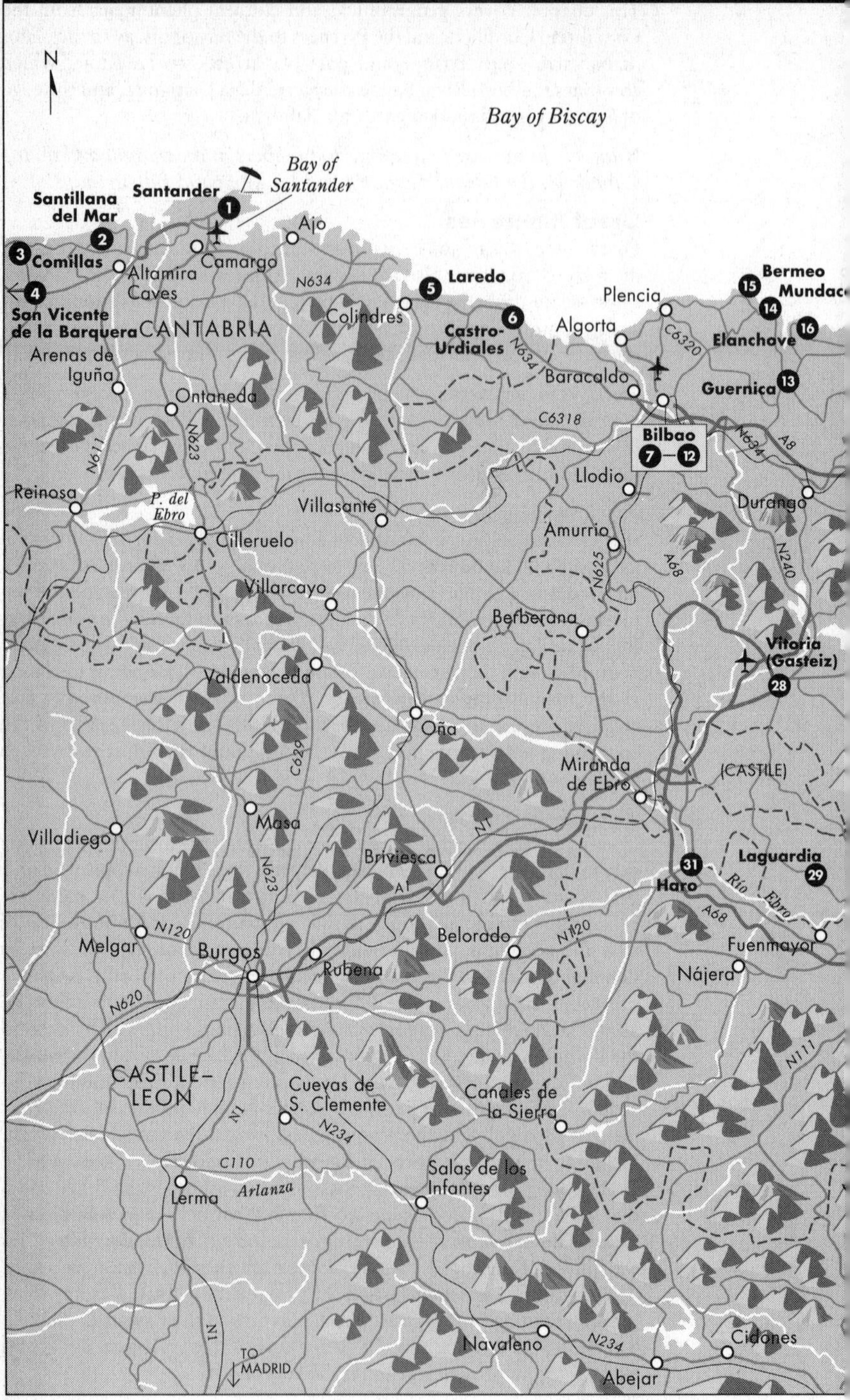

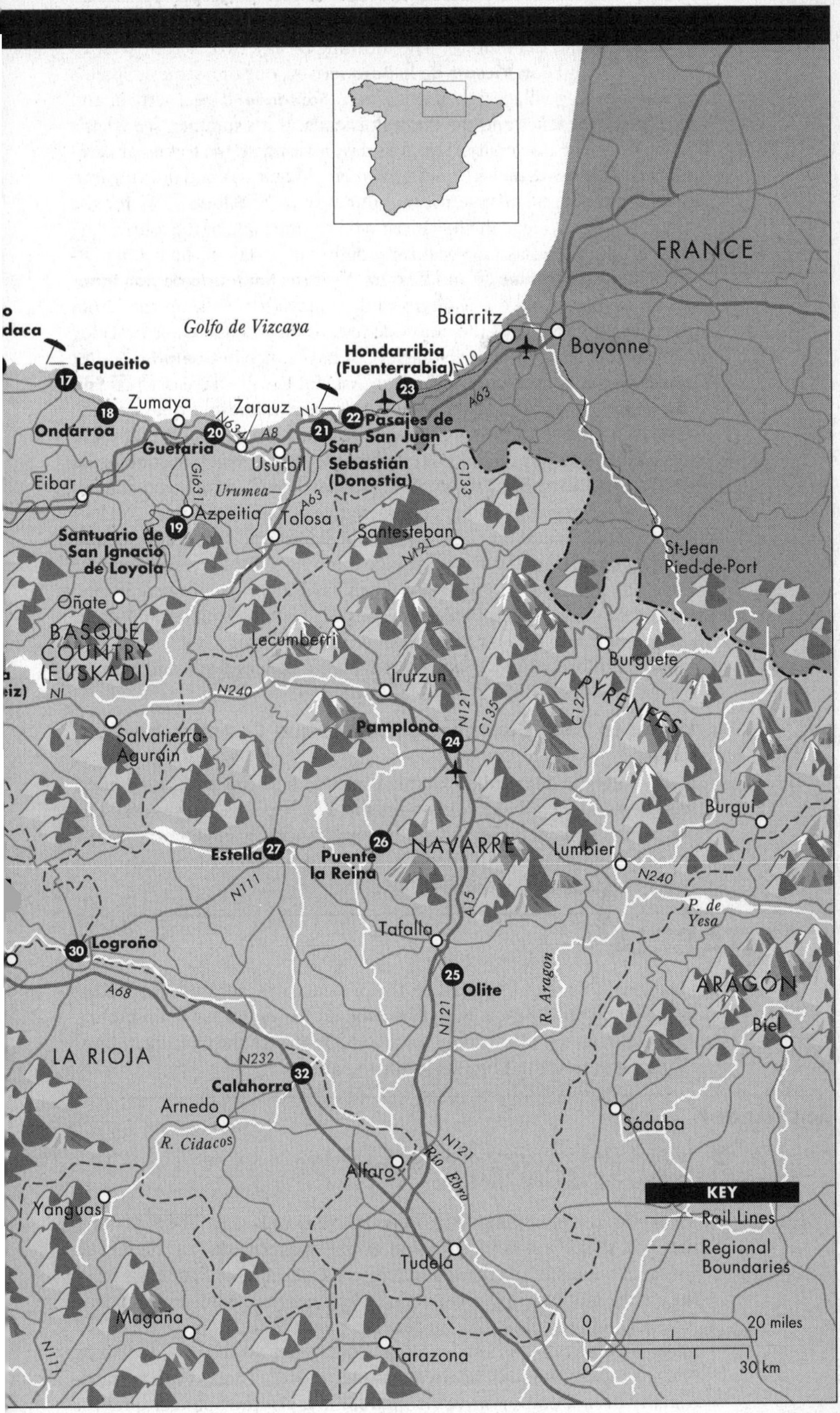
FRANCE
Golfo de Vizcaya
Biarritz
Bayonne
Hondarribia (Fuenterrabia)
Lequeitio
Zumaya
Zarauz
Pasajes de San Juan
Ondárroa
Guetaria
Usurbil
San Sebastián (Donostia)
Eibar
Urumea
Azpeitia
Tolosa
Santesteban
St-Jean Pied-de-Port
Santuario de San Ignacio de Loyola
Oñate
BASQUE COUNTRY (EUSKADI)
Lecumberri
Burguete
PYRENEES
Irurzun
Pamplona
Salvatierra-Aguraín
Burgui
Estella
Puente la Reina
NAVARRE
Lumbier
P. de Yesa
Tafalla
Logroño
Olite
R. Aragon
ARAGÓN
Biel
LA RIOJA
Calahorra
Arnedo
Sádaba
R. Cidacos
Alfaro
Río Ebro
Yanguas
KEY
Rail Lines
Regional Boundaries
Tudela
Magaña
Tarazona
0 20 miles
0 30 km
N10
A63
N1
N634
A8
Gi631
C133
N121
N240
C135
C127
N111
A15
A68
N232
17
18
19
20
21
22
23
24
25
26
27
30
32

Mayor. Spend the night near the **Altamira Caves,** ideally in the parador at **Santillana del Mar** ②. The morning of day two, detour west to **Comillas** ③ and **San Vicente de la Barquera** ④, one of northern Spain's prettiest fishing villages; then drive to **Santander** ①, get settled, and explore the beaches and the Plaza Porticada. If it's summer, see what's going on at the university. The next day, investigate the towns of **Laredo** ⑤ and **Castro-Urdiales** ⑥, walking their old quarters and ducking into one of their excellent taverns, on your way to **Bilbao** ⑦–⑫ for the night. Tour the Guggenheim Museum on the morning of the fourth day; then head up the Basque coast for a night and a day in the fishing villages between **Bermeo** ⑮ and Zarauz. Visit the **Santuario de San Ignacio de Loyola** ⑲; take a walk around Zumaya; or walk up the Urola River estuary to one of the quayside restaurants (Bedua is the best) for a *tortilla de bacalao* (codfish omelet), or have lunch in **Guetaria** ⑳ after walking over from Zumaya through Askizu. Devote day six to **San Sebastián** ㉑, wandering the boardwalk, beach, and old quarter. Day seven is a chance to see tiny **Pasajes de San Juan** ㉒; spend that night in a *caserío* (Basque farmhouse) such as the Artzu, which overlooks the Atlantic Ocean and the town of **Hondarribia** ㉓, which you can explore on day eight. If you're so inspired, take the launch over to Hendaye, France. Spend the night back at the Parador El Emperador before heading up the Bidasoa River into the foothills of the Pyrenees. Explore upper Navarre and **Pamplona** ㉔ on day nine. If you're here during Pamplona's San Fermín blowout, consider trying a smaller and saner version of this legendary fiesta in the village of Lesaka (☞ Chapter 5). Finally, explore **Vitoria** ㉘ and taste wines in **Laguardia** ㉙ and **Haro** ㉛ on the way to La Rioja's capital, **Logroño** ㉚.

When to Tour Cantabria, the Basque Country, and La Rioja

May–June and September–October are the best times to enjoy good weather and avoid the tourist crush, which peaks in August. The Basque country is characteristically rainy, especially in winter; summer is fairly temperate. Extended daylight, an absence of crowds, and sweet temperatures make June ideal.

CANTABRIA

Historically part of Old Castile, the province of Cantabria was called Santander until 1984, when it became an Autonomous Community. Take the slow but memorably scenic N623 through the Cordillera Cantábrica and past the Ebro reservoir to Santander.

Santander

★ ❶ *390 km (242 mi) north of Madrid, 154 km (96 mi) north of Burgos, 116 km (72 mi) west of Bilbao.*

Santander is one of the great ports on the Bay of Biscay. The first thing that will strike you is its situation on the western edge of the Bay of Santander. A major northern beach resort, especially for Spaniards from the south, Santander is surrounded by beaches that, while by no means isolated, happily lack the sardinelike package-tour ambience of so many Mediterranean resorts. A fire destroyed most of the old town in 1941, so the city looks relatively modern; and although it has traditionally been a conservative stronghold loyal to the Spanish state (in contrast to its restless Basque neighbors), Santander is a lively place, especially in summer, when its international university and its music-and-dance festival fill the city with students and performing artists from abroad.

Portus Victoriae, as Santander was then called, was a major port in the 1st-to-4th century Roman Hispania Ulterior (and even earlier under the aboriginal Cántabros). Commercial life accelerated between the 13th and 16th centuries, but the waning of Spain's naval power and a series of plagues during the reign of Felipe II caused Santander's fortunes to plummet in the late 16th century. Its economy revived after 1778, when Seville's monopoly on trade with the Americas was revoked and Santander entered fully into commerce with the New World. In 1910 the Palacio de la Magdalena was built by popular subscription as a gift to Alfonso XIII and his queen, Victoria Eugenia, lending Santander prestige as one of Spain's royal watering spots.

In addition to great beaches, Santander benefits from promenades and gardens, most of them facing the bay. Walk east along the Paseo de Pereda, the main boulevard, to the **Puerto Chico,** a small yacht harbor. Past the Puerto Chico, follow Avenida Reina Victoria and you'll come to the tree-lined park paths above the first of the city's beaches, Playa de la Magdalena. Walk onto the Península de la Magdalena to the **Palacio de la Magdalena,** today the summer seat of the University of Menéndez y Pelayo, which conducts Spanish-language and -culture courses for foreigners. The grounds have dramatic views of the bay.

Beyond the Magdalena Peninsula, wealthy locals have built mansions facing the long stretch of shoreline known as **El Sardinero,** Santander's best beach. The heart of the neighborhood is the Belle Epoque **Gran Casino del Sardinero,** an elegant, twin-tower casino and restaurant worth a quick visit even if gaming tables hold no charms for you. A white building fronted with red awnings and set in a small park among sycamores, the casino lies at the center of the vacationer's Santander, surrounded by expensive hotels and some of the finest restaurants in the area.

In the old city, the center of life is the **Plaza Porticada,** officially called the Plaza Velarde. In August this unassuming little square is the seat of Santander's star event, the International Festival of Music and Dance, a series of outdoor performances in various genres. Across Avenida de Calvo Sotelo from the Plaza Porticada is the blockish **Catedral Buen Pastor** (Good Shepherd Cathedral; ✉ Somorrostro s/n), a building marking the transition between Romanesque and Gothic, though it was largely rebuilt after serious damage in the 1941 fire. The chief attraction here is the tomb of Marcelino Menéndez y Pelayo (1856–1912), Santander's most famous literary figure.

Drop into the **Museo Municipal de Bellas Artes** (Municipal Museum of Fine Arts) for a look at some works by Flemish, Italian, and Spanish artists. Goya's portrait of the absolutist king Fernando VII is worth seeking out; the smirking face of the lion at the king's feet clues you into Goya's feelings toward his patron. The same building holds the Biblioteca Menéndez y Pelayo (☎ 942/234534), a library with some 50,000 volumes, and the writer's study, kept as it was in his day. Admission to the library is free; hours are weekdays 9–2 and 4–9:30, Saturday 9–1:30. ✉ *C. Rubio s/n,* ☎ *942/239485.* 🎟 *Museum free.* ⏲ *Tues.–Fri. 10–1 and 5–8, Sat. 10–1.*

Dining and Lodging

$$ ★ ✕ **Bodega del Riojano.** The paintings on wine-barrel ends that decorate this restaurant have given it the sobriquet Museo Redondo (Round Museum). The building dates back to the 16th century, when it was a wine cellar, and this atmosphere lives on in dark-wood beams and tables. The menu changes daily and seasonally, but the fish of the day is always a sure bet. Desserts are homemade. ✉ *Río de la Pila 5,* ☎ *942/216750. AE, DC, MC, V. No dinner Sun. Oct.–May.*

$$ ✕ **Zacarías.** This popular place is great for local specialties, whether tapas or dinner in full. Owner and chef Zacarías Puente-Herboso is a well-known food writer and an authority on Cantabrian recipes. Try the *maganos encebollados* (calamari and caramelized onion) or the *alubias rojas* (red beans with sausage). ✉ *General Mola 41,* ☎ *942/212333. AE, DC, MC, V.*

$$ ★ **Las Brisas.** Jesús García and his wife, Teresa, run this 75-year-old mansion as an upscale, cottage-style hotel by the sea. Mr. García speaks good English and takes especially good care of his anglophone guests. Each room is different, from dollhouse alcoves to an odd but attractive family duplex. The basement bar and breakfast room are especially cozy. You're a short walk from the beach, and many of the rooms have fine views out to sea. ✉ *C. la Braña 14, 39005,* ☎ *942/270991 or 942/275011,* FAX *942/281173. 13 rooms. AE, DC, MC, V.*

$$ ★ **México.** Don't be put off by the modest exterior. The personal touch still counts in this family-run inn, and the breakfast room is elegant, with Queen Anne chairs, inlaid porcelain rosettes, and oak wainscoting. The rooms are pleasant, with high ceilings and glassed-in balconies. Reserve in advance, as word of this good deal has gotten around. ✉ *Calderón de la Barca 3, 39002,* ☎ *942/212450,* FAX *942/229238. 34 rooms. MC, V.*

Nightlife and the Arts

Santander's big event is its **International Festival of Music and Dance,** which attracts leading artists throughout August. Many festival concerts are staged in the Plaza Porticada; others are held in monasteries, palaces, and churches. Collect information at the tourist office or at seasonal box offices in the Plaza Porticada and the Jardines de Pereda park. The city's **Teatro Coliseum** (✉ Plaza de los Remedios 1, ☎ 942/211460) is normally a movie theater but becomes a theater proper in summer.

Shopping

Santander is known for ceramics. There are several touristy retailers on Calle Arrabal, downtown, but **La Muralla,** at No. 17, is known locally as the best.

Santillana del Mar

★ ❷ *29 km (18 mi) west of Santander.*

This stunning ensemble of 15th- to 17th-century stone houses is one of Spain's greatest troves of medieval and Renaissance architecture. The town is built around the **Colegiata,** Cantabria's finest Romanesque structure, a tour de force with a 17th-century altarpiece, the tomb of local martyr Santa Juliana, and sculpted capitals depicting biblical scenes. The adjoining Regina Coeli convent has a **Museo Diocesano** (☎ 942/598105) with an excellent collection of liturgical art. Both the Colegiata and the museum are open daily from 10 to 1 and 4 to 7 (closed Wednesday, October–May), and admission to each is 400 ptas.

The world-famous **Altamira Caves,** just 3 km (2 mi) southwest of Santillana del Mar, have been called the Sistine Chapel of Prehistoric Art for the beauty of their drawings, believed to be some 20,000 years old. First uncovered in 1875, the caves are a testament not only to early humans' love of beauty but to their technical skill—especially in the use of rock forms to accentuate perspective. Visitors must now apply two or three years in advance to be among the 25 people allowed into the caves each day; if you are a preternaturally early planner, write to the address below with the number and names of the people in your group, and the date you hope to visit. The adjoining **museum,** which shows a film on the paintings, and another cave with interesting rock formations are open to all. ✉ *Centro de Investigación de Altamira, Santillana del Mar 39330, Cantabria,* ☎ *942/818005.*

Dining and Lodging

$$$$ ★ ✕🏨 **Parador de Santillana del Mar.** Built in the 16th century, this lovely parador occupies the erstwhile summer home of the Barreda-Bracho family. The rooms are baronial, with rich drapes and curtains and antique furnishings. The dining hall is elegant, if less than intimate, and the fare is strong in local dishes and traditional recipes. ✉ *Pl. Ramón Pelayo 8, 39330,* ☎ *942/818000,* FAX *942/818391. 56 rooms. Restaurant, bar. AE, DC, MC, V.*

Comillas

❸ *49 km (30 mi) west of Santander.*

This astounding pocket of Catalan Art Nouveau architecture in the green hills of Cantabria will make you rub your eyes in disbelief. Why is it here? The Marquess of Comillas, a Catalan named Antonio López y López (1817–1883)—the wealthiest and most influential shipping magnate of his time—was a fervent patron of the arts who encouraged the great Moderniste architects to use his native village as a laboratory. Antonio Gaudí's 1883–1889 **Capricho** is the main attraction, followed closely by the **Universidad Pontificia** (Joan Martorell and Lluís Domènech i Montaner), or by Domènech i Montaner's **Palacio Sobrellano.** The town cemetery is filled with Art Nouveau markers and monuments, most notably an immense angel by eminent Catalan sculptor Josep Llimona (1864–1934).

Dining

$$$ ✕ **El Capricho de Gaudí.** A chance to dine in a Gaudí creation is all but an obligation, especially if the visual rush is accompanied by fresh turbot with young garlic or roast lamb from the moist Cantabrian hills. ✉ *Barrio de Sobrellano,* ☎ *942/720365. AE, DC, MC, V. Closed Jan. Closed Mon. Oct.–May. No dinner Sun.*

San Vicente de la Barquera

❹ *64 km (40 mi) west of Santander, 15 km (9 mi) west of Comillas.*

Important as a Roman port long before many other larger modern shipping centers, such as Santander, were, San Vicente de la Barquera is one of the oldest and most beautiful maritime settlements in northern Spain. The 28 arches of the ancient **Puente de la Maza,** spanning the *ría* (fjord), and the Romanesque portals of the 15th-century church of **Nuestra Señora de los Angeles** (Our Lady of the Angels) are among San Vicente's most memorable sights, along with the arcaded porticoes of the **Plaza Mayor** and the view over the town from the Unquera road (N634) just inland. San Vicente celebrates La Folía in late April (the name translates roughly as "folly," and the exact date depends not only on Easter but on the high tide) with a magnificent maritime procession: the town's colorful fishing fleet accompanies the figure of La Virgen de la Barquera as she is transported (in part) by boat from her sanctuary just outside town to the village church, where she is honored with folk dances and songs before being returned to her hermitage.

Dining and Lodging

$$ ✕🏨 **Boga-Boga.** This relatively modern building is surrounded by some of San Vicente's most ancient structures in the center of the *casco viejo* (old town). Rooms are comfortable and unpretentious, if not especially charming, but the neighboring context contains all the archaic charm of this venerable seaport village. The restaurant specializes

in seafood such as *merluza al boga-boga* (stewed cod) and *cabracho,* an especially aromatic, dark-meated goat. ✉ *Pl. José Antonio 9, 39540,* ☎ *942/710135,* FAX *942/710151. 18 rooms. AE, DC, MC, V. Restaurant closed Tues. Oct.–May.*

Laredo

❺ *49 km (30 mi) southeast of Santander (N635 southeast, N634 east).*

You would hardly know it today, but Laredo was an early home port of the Spanish Armada, and remained Spain's chief northern harbor until the French sacked it in the 18th century and Santander became the regional capital. This little town was thus visited by the most powerful Spanish royals, including Isabella the Catholic and Charles I, better known as the Holy Roman Emperor Carlos V. When Charles—the most powerful monarch in European history—stopped by in the mid-16th century, he donated two brass choir desks in the shape of eagles. These are now on display in the parish church of **La Asunción** (Church of the Assumption), in the center of the town's tiny *parte antigua* (old quarter). Walk through the old quarter to see ancient mansions with heraldic coats of arms.

Dining and Lodging

$$ ✕🏨 **El Risco.** *Risco* is Spanish for "cliff," an appropriate name for this hotel-restaurant built into the craggy slope overlooking Laredo. The food is an ingenious mixture of classical and contemporary Cantabrian cuisine; try the *pimientos rellenos de cangrejo y de buey de mar* (peppers stuffed with crab and fish). Every room has a spectacular view of the town and cove below. Hotel reservations are essential in summer. ✉ *La Arenosa 2, 39770,* ☎ *942/605030,* FAX *942/605055. 25 rooms. AE, DC, MC, V. Restaurant closed Wed. Sept.–June.*

Castro-Urdiales

❻ *34 km (21 mi) northwest of Bilbao.*

Behind Laredo, the N634 winds up into the hills, with views of the Bay of Santoña over your shoulder. A short drive, parts of it within sight of the coast, takes you into the fishing village of Castro-Urdiales, believed to be the oldest settlement on the Cantabrian coast. Called Flaviobriga by the Romans (*castro* was the Celtiberian word for a fortified village), it became the region's leading whaling port in the 13th and 14th centuries, when it had almost three times today's 13,000 residents. Overlooking the town is the mammoth, rose-color jumble of roofs and buttresses that is the church of **Santa María,** a Gothic work of art; just behind the church is an ancient **castle,** to which a modern lighthouse has been appended. Aside from its arcaded **Plaza del Ayuntamiento** and the narrow streets of its **old quarter** (much of which burned on May 11, 1813), Castro-Urdiales is known mainly for its seafood.

Dining

$$ ★ ✕ **Mesón Marinero.** This pearl of a tavern and restaurant is a gastronomic delight, where local fishermen rub elbows with visiting elites. The array of tapas on the bar will tempt you to forgo the main meal and *tapear* (munch tapas) away your dinner hour; but if you don't succumb, you're in for a treat in the elegant, second-floor dining room overlooking Castro's weathered fishing port. *Besugo* (sea bream) is unbeatable here. ✉ *Correría 23,* ☎ *942/860005. AE, DC, MC, V.*

En Route The 45-minute drive on the N634 from Castro-Urdiales to Bilbao takes you through some of the sprawling industrial development that mars much of Vizcaya, the westernmost of the three Basque provinces.

BILBAO AND THE BASQUE COAST TO GUETARIA

It can be tempting to whip in and out of Bilbao as part of a trip centered elsewhere, but a road trip in the environs has its own rewards. The colorful stretch of coast east of Guernica winds along the edges of the Basque hills, dipping into protected fishing villages.

Bilbao

34 km (21 mi) southeast of Castro-Urdiales, 116 km (72 mi) east of Santander, 397 km (247 mi) north of Madrid.

Time in Bilbao (Bilbo, in Euskera) may soon need to be identified as BG or AG (Before Guggenheim, After Guggenheim). Never has a single monument of art and architecture so radically changed a city—or, for that matter, a nation, and in this case two: Spain and Euskadi. Frank Gehry's stunning museum, Norman Foster's sleek subway system, and the glass Santiago Calatrava footbridge, which allows pedestrians to all but walk on water, have all helped foment a cultural revolution in the commercial capital of the Basque country. Although the inner city was most recently censused at 373,000, greater Bilbao now encompasses almost 1 million inhabitants, nearly half the total population of the Basque country and the fourth-largest urban population in Spain. The region's political and social malaise has been nearly eclipsed by the so-called "Guggenheiming" of Bilbao. The city is now actively leading the Basque country into the next millennium with an optimism and exuberance suggesting that life can indeed imitate art (or at least an art museum).

Founded in 1300 by a Vizcayan noble, Diego López de Haro, Bilbao became an industrial center in the mid-19th century, thanks mainly to the abundance of minerals in the surrounding hills. An affluent industrial class grew up here, as did the working-class suburbs (like Portugalete and Baracaldo) that line the Margen Izquierda (Left Bank) of the Nervión estuary. Many of the wealthy have left in the last 25 years; the fear of kidnapping and the extortion of ETA's so-called revolutionary tax have driven them south to Madrid. The Right Bank suburb of Getxo, for instance, is remarkable for its abandoned mansions.

Bilbao's new attractions get more press, but the city's old treasures still quietly line the banks of the rust-color Nervión River. The *casco viejo* (old quarter)—also known as Siete Calles (Seven Streets)—is a charming jumble of shops, bars, and restaurants on the river's right bank, near the Puente del Arenal bridge. Wide, late-19th-century boulevards, such as Gran Vía (the main shopping artery) and Alameda Mazarredo, are the city's more formal face. Bilbao is also rich in cultural institutions, including a major (BG) museum of fine arts; and epicureans have long ranked the Vizcayan capital one of the top culinary cities in Spain.

7 The **casco viejo** is folded into an elbow of the Nervión River behind Bilbao's grand, elaborately restored **Teatro Arriaga.** Inaugurated in 1890, the Arriaga was a symbol of Bilbao's industrial might and cultural vibrancy by the time it burned nearly to the ground in 1914. Styled after the Paris Opera by architect Joaquín Rucoba (1844–1909), the theater defies easy classification: while its symmetry and formal repetition suggest neoclassicism, its elaborate ornamentation defines the Belle Epoque style. Walk around the building to see the stained glass on its back.

Walled until the 19th century, the old quarter lies around the **Catedral de Santiago** (St. James's Cathedral), open during Mass. This church

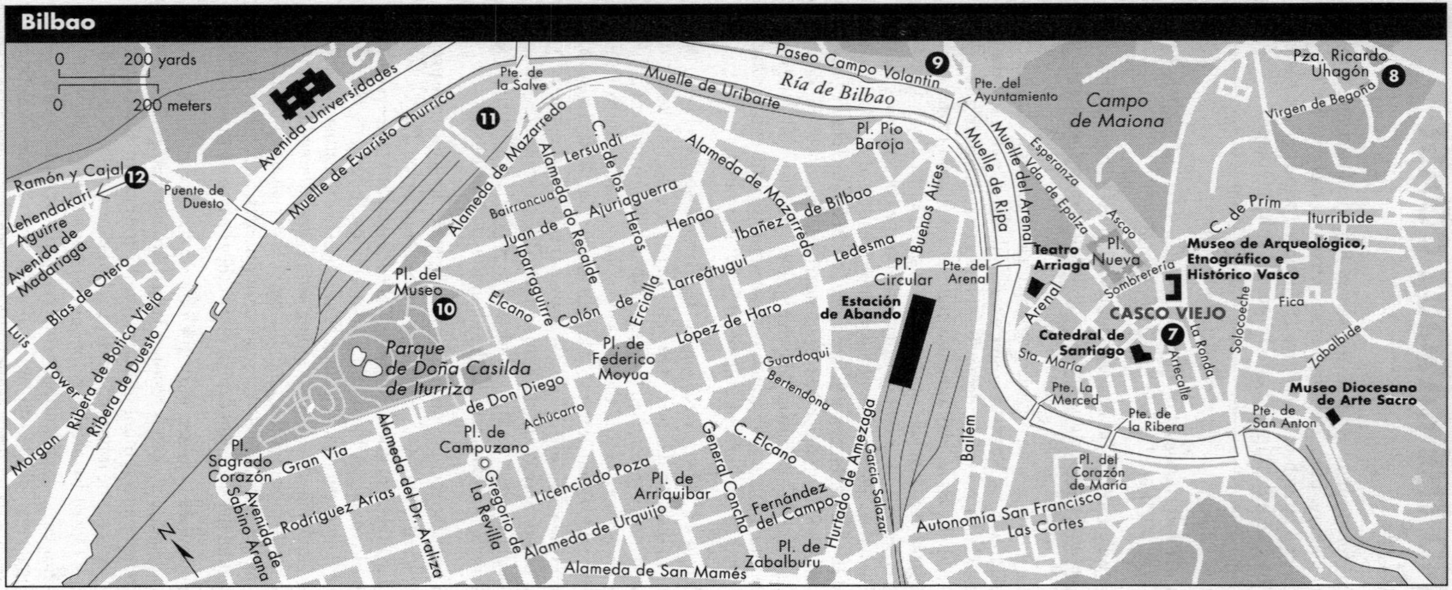

Ayuntamiento 9

Basilica de Begoña 8

Casco viejo 7

Guggenheim Museum Bilbao . . . 11

Museo de Bellas Artes 10

Puente de Vizcaya (Puente Colgante) 12

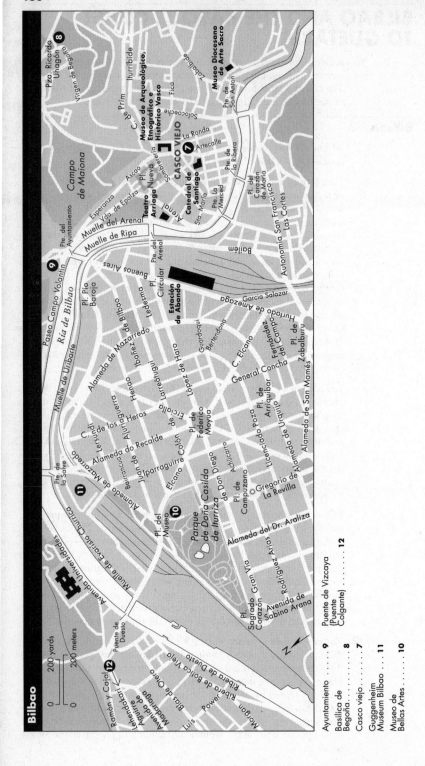

was a pilgrimage stop on one of the routes to Santiago de Compostela. Work on the structure began in 1379, but fire destroyed most of it in 1571; it has a notable outdoor arcade. Throughout the old quarter are ancient mansions and fine ironwork on balconies; the area got a major face-lift after the devastating floods of August 1983 and is now an upscale shopping district replete with bars, restaurants, and happening nightlife. The most interesting square is the 64-arch **Plaza Nueva,** where an outdoor market is pitched every Sunday morning.

The **Museo Arqueológico, Etnográfico e Histórico Vasco** (Museum of Basque Archaeology, Ethnology, and History) is housed in a stunning 16th-century convent. The collection centers on Basque fishing, crafts, and agriculture. ✉ *C. Cruz 4,* ☎ *94/415–5423.* 🎫 *300 ptas. (free Thurs.).* ⏲ *Tues.–Sat. 10:30–1:30 and 4–7, Sun. 10:30–1.*

The **Museo Diocesano de Arte Sacro** (Diocesan Museum of Sacred Art) occupies a carefully restored 16th-century cloister. The inner patio alone, ancient and intimate, is worth the visit. On display are religious silver work, liturgical garments, sculptures, and paintings dating back to the 12th century. ✉ *Pl. de la Encarnación 9,* ☎ *94/432–0125.* 🎫 *Free.* ⏲ *Tues.–Sat. 10:30–1:30 and 4–7, Sun. 10:30–1.*

8 As you head downstream toward the *ayuntamiento* (city hall) stop at Calle Esperanza 6 and take the elevator to the **Basílica de Begoña,** a huge church from which you have a stunning view of Bilbao with the Nervión winding through it. The church's Gothic hulk was begun in 1519 on a spot where the Virgin Mary had supposedly appeared long before.

9 Near the Ayuntamiento Bridge is the riverside ***ayuntamiento*** (city hall), built in 1892.

★ 10 Don't let the Guggenheim eclipse the **Museo de Bellas Artes** (Museum of Fine Arts). Depending on your tastes, you may find the art here more satisfying. The museum's fine collection of Flemish, French, Italian, and Spanish paintings includes works by El Greco, Goya, Velázquez, Zurbarán, Rivera, and Gauguin. One large and excellent section traces developments in 20th-century Spanish and Basque art alongside those of their better-known European contemporaries, such as Léger and Bacon. The building sits on the rim of a pretty swath of green about 30 minutes' walk from the old quarter. ✉ *Doña Casilda Iturriza Park,* ☎ *94/441–0154 or 94/441–9536.* 🎫 *600 ptas. (free on Wed.)* ⏲ *Tues.–Sat. 10–1:30 and 4–7:30, Sun. 10–2.*

NEED A BREAK? Founded in 1926, **Café La Granja** (✉ Pl. Circular 3), near the Puente del Arenal, is a Bilbao classic. It retains its Old World ambience along with good coffee, beer, *tortilla de patata* (potato omelet), and a lunch menu.

★ 11 Covered with a photogenic 30,000 sheets of titanium, the **Guggenheim Museum Bilbao** opened in October 1997 and became Bilbao's main attraction overnight. The enormous atrium, more than 150 ft high, is connected to the 19 galleries by a system of suspended metal walkways and glass elevators. Undulating vertical windows let you peep out at the titanium mounds every so often, and as you walk past them, the various shapes pop in and out of view. With most of its works from New York's Solomon R. Guggenheim Museum, this place is a trip in itself for lovers of contemporary art and architecture. For more on the building and its collection *see* Close-up: The Guggenheim Museum Bilbao, *below.* ☎ *94/435–9080.* 🎫 *1,200 ptas.* ⏲ *Tues.–Wed. 11–8, Thurs.–Sat. 11–8, Sun. 11–8.*

12 Down in the Nervión's estuary, the **Puente de Vizcaya**—commonly called the **Puente Colgante** (Hanging Bridge)—is an 85-year-old symbol of

Close-Up

THE GUGGENHEIM MUSEUM BILBAO

IF PICASSO'S *GUERNICA* WAS THE 20TH CENTURY'S most famous and embattled painting, Bilbao's Guggenheim may be the most celebrated building of all time. Described by Spanish novelist Manuel Vazquez Montalban as a "meteorite," this eruption of light and titanium paradoxically stationed in Bilbao's muscular industrial context has reinvented this city in a dramatic and unprecedented way.

Never seen as one of the most compelling settlements south of the Pyrenees—it's probably the least attractive corner of the quadrangle it forms with Pamplona, San Sebastián, and Vitoria—Bilbao has in one master stroke become one of the hottest destinations in Europe. Perennially chided as the *barrio industrial* (industrial quarter) in contrast to San Sebastián's *barrio jardín* (garden quarter), Bilbao has long been perceived as a polluted steel and shipbuilding center sprawled astride the foul-smelling Nervión estuary. Those who knew that Bilbao was more than this—that Bilbao's "dark, satanic mills" generated a prosperity that supported opera, art, incredible dining, and one of Spain's top football clubs—just shrugged when nonbelievers shied away.

But the Guggenheim has changed all that. Frank Gehry's gleaming brainchild, alternately hailed as "the greatest building of our time" (architect Philip Johnson), "the best building of the 20th century" (Spain's King Juan Carlos), and "a miracle" (Herbert Muschamp, *New York Times*) has sparked a renaissance in the Basque country after more than 60 troubled years. Not all Bilbainos have joined the chorus of praise for this American footprint on their soil, but no one can argue with the figures: in its first year, the Guggenheim attracted 1.4 million visitors, three times the number expected and more than what both Guggenheim museums in New York received together in the same period. Revenue in its first year alone exceeded the original Basque investment. Incredibly, the Guggenheim already holds the Spanish record for single-day visits to a museum (9,300), and the crowds show no sign of diminishing.

The museum itself is as superlative as the hoopla suggests. Gehry's quasi-mechanical tour de force provides an ideal context for the postmodern and futuristic artworks it contains. The smoothly rounded, asymmetrical, ship's-prow–like amalgam of limestone, glass, and titanium ingeniously recalls Bilbao's shipbuilding and steel-manufacturing past while using transparency and reflective materials to create a shimmering, futuristic luminosity. The final section of the Nervión's La Salve bridge is almost part of the structure, rendering the Guggenheim the virtual doorway to Bilbao.

The collection, described by director Thomas Krens as "a daring history of the art of the 20th century," consists of 242 works, 186 from New York's Guggenheim and 50 acquired by the Basque government. The second and third floors exemplify the original Guggenheim collection of abstract expressionist, cubist, surrealist, and geometrical works. Artists whose names are synonymous with the 20th century (Kandinsky, Picasso, Ernst, Braque, Miró, Calder, Malevich) and particularly artists of the '50s and '60s (Pollock, Rothko, De Kooning, Chillida, Tàpies, Iglesias) are joined by contemporary figures (Nauman, Muñoz, Schnabel, Badiola, Barceló, Basquiat). The ground floor is dedicated to large-format and installation work, some of which—like Richard Serra's *Serpent*—was created specifically for the space it occupies. Claes Oldenburg's *Knife Ship*, Robert Morris's walk-in *Labyrinth*, and pieces by Beuys, Boltansky, Long, Holzer, and others round out the heavyweight division in and around what is now the largest gallery in the world.

Bilbao industry. The bridge, a transporter hung from cables, ferries cars and passengers across the Nervión, uniting two distinct worlds: exclusive, quiet Las Arenas, and Portugalete, a much older, working-class town now filled with jobless steelworkers. (Dolores Ibarruri, the famous Republican orator of the Spanish Civil War, known as *La Pasionaria* for her ardor, was born here.) Portugalete is a 15-minute walk from Santurce, where the quayside Hogar del Pescador serves simple and ample fish specialties. *Besugo* (sea bream) is the traditional choice, but the fresh grilled sardines are hard to surpass. To reach the bridge, take the subway to Areeta, or drive across the Puente de Deusto, turn left on Avenida Lehendakari Aguirre, and follow signs for LAS ARENAS.

Dining and Lodging

$$$ ✕ **Bermeo.** Named after the coastal village to the north (☞ *below*), this noted restaurant specializes in fresh market cuisine and traditional Basque interpretations of fish, shellfish, and seafood of all kinds. Try the *rodaballo* (turbot) in vinaigrette sauce. ✉ *C. Ercilla 37,* ☎ *94/470–5700. Reservations essential. AE, DC, MC, V. Closed Aug. 1–15. No lunch Sat.*

$$$ ★ ✕ **Goizeko Kabi.** Here you can choose your own crab or crayfish. The dining rooms are of brick and wood accented by Persian rugs and chairs upholstered with tapestries. Chef Fernando Canales's creations include *láminas de bacalao en ensalada con pimientos rojos asados* (sliced cod in green salad with roasted red peppers) and *hojaldre de verdura a la plancha con manito de cordero* (grilled vegetables in puff pastry with leg of lamb). ✉ *Particular de Estraunza 4 y 6,* ☎ *94/442–1129. Reservations essential. AE, DC, MC, V. Closed Sun.*

$$$ ✕ **Zortziko.** This lovely place combines an ultramodern kitchen with a building that has been declared a historical monument. Try the *langostinos con risotto de perretxicos* (prawns with wild-mushroom risotto) or the *suprema de pintada asada a la salsa de trufas* (guinea hen in truffle sauce). Chef Daniel García is one of the Basque region's culinary stars. ✉ *C. Alameda Mazarredo 17,* ☎ *94/423–9743. Reservations essential. AE, DC, MC, V. Closed Sun. and Aug. 25–Sept. 15.*

$$–$$$ ✕ **Matxinbenta.** Mixing Basque cooking with international cuisine, this cozy spot offers innovative seafood dishes and roasts and prepares the most traditional specialties to perfection. Try the *bacalao Matxinbenta con base vizcaina* (cod prepared on a red-pepper base *al pil-pil*). ✉ *Ledesma 26,* ☎ *94/424–8495. AE, DC, MC, V. Closed Sun.*

$$ ★ ✕ **Gorrotxa.** Carmelo Gorrotxategui's fine eclectic menu mixes Basque, French, and Castilian cuisines. The man can do anything from *foie gras con uvas* (goose liver with grapes) to lobster Thermidor to *chuleta de buey.* The decor is English, with wood paneling and carpets. ✉ *Alameda Urquijo 30,* ☎ *94/422–0535. AE, DC, MC, V. Closed Sun., Holy Week, 1 wk in July, 1 wk in Aug.*

$$ ✕ **Retolaza.** Bilbao has flocked to this traditional Basque restaurant since 1906. Operated by the third generation of its founding family, it has wood beams, low ceilings, and a reasonably intimate and serious feel. The classic Vizcayan fare includes *sopa de aluvias* (red beans and sausage) and *bacalao al pil-pil.* ✉ *Tendería 1,* ☎ *94/415–0643. AE, DC, MC, V. Closed July 24–Aug. 15. No dinner Sun.–Mon.*

$$ ★ ✕ **Victor Montes.** A hot point for the daily *tapeo* (tapas tour), Victor Montes is always crowded with congenial grazers. The well-stocked counter might offer anything from wild mushrooms to *txistorra* (spicy sausages) to *Idiazabal* (Basque smoked cheese) or, for the adventurous, *huevas de merluza* (hake roe), all taken with splashes of Rioja, txakolí, or cider. For a table, reserve as far ahead as possible. ✉ *Pl. Nueva 8,* ☎ *94/415–7067. Closed Sun. evening.*

$$$$ ✕🏨 **Lopez de Haro.** Five minutes from the Guggenheim, Bilbao's only five-star hotel is becoming quite a scene now that the city is a bona-

fide nexus for contemporary art. The converted 19th-century building has an English feel and all the comforts your heart desires. The excellent restaurant, the Club Náutico, serves modern Basque dishes created by Alberto Vélez—a handy alternative on one of Bilbao's many rainy evenings. ✉ *Obispo Orueta 2, 48009,* ☎ *94/423–5500,* FAX *94/423–4500. 49 rooms, 4 suites. Restaurant, bar, cafeteria, exercise room, parking (fee). AE, DC, MC, V.*

$$$ **Ercilla.** This modern hotel fills with the taurine crowd during Bilbao's Semana Grande in early August, partly because it's near the bullring and partly because it has taken over from the Carlton as the place to see and be seen. Impeccable rooms, amenities, and service underscore its reputation. This might not be the place to stay if you're looking for a quiet getaway. ✉ *C. Ercilla 3739, 48009,* ☎ *94/470–5700,* FAX *94/443–9335. 346 rooms. Restaurant, bar, cafeteria, minibars, parking (fee). AE, DC, MC, V.*

$$$ **Carlton.** Luminaries who have trod the halls of this grand dame include Orson Welles, Ava Gardner, Ernest Hemingway, Lauren Bacall, and most of Spain's great bullfighters. During the Spanish Civil War it was the seat of the Republican Basque government; later it housed a number of Nationalist generals. It remains elegant, well attended, and centrally located. ✉ *Pl. Federico Moyúa 2, 48009,* ☎ *94/416–2200,* FAX *94/416–4628. 148 rooms. Restaurant, bar, meeting rooms. AE, DC, MC, V.*

$–$$ **Iturriena Ostatua.** This traditional Basque town house in Bilbao's old quarter has heavy wooden beams, stone floors, and all the trappings of a far more expensive operation. Simple, clean, and anxious to please, it's a great choice for travelers less than eager to part with substantial loot in exchange for sleep and comfort. ✉ *Santa María Kalea 14,* ☎ *94/416–1500,* FAX *94/415–8929. 21 rooms. Breakfast room. AE, DC, MC, V*

Cafés

Bilbao's many coffeehouses and bistros have long provided refuge from the siri-miri and steel mills outside. Along with **Café La Granja** (☞ *above*), you can refuel at the enormous **Café Iruña** (✉ Jardines de Albia), another turn-of-the-century classic, and the **Café Bulevard** (✉ C. Arenal 3), Bilbao's oldest, dating back to 1871. **Café El Tilo** (✉ C. Arenal 1) may be the best of all, with wooden tables and original frescoes by Basque painter Aranoa; it's open weekdays only. **Bar los Fueros** (✉ C. de los Fueros 4), as much a watering hole as a café, is one of Bilbao's most authentic enclaves, perfect for an *aperitivo* or a nightcap. **Café y Té** (✉ Pl. Federico Moyúa 1) has a pleasant marble counter and a combination rural-urban aesthetic.

Nightlife and the Arts

The prized **Teatro Arriaga** (✉ Pl. Arriaga s/n, ☎ 94/416–3244) consistently draws world-class ballet, theater, concerts, opera, and *zarzuela* (comic opera). Opera and *zarzuela* are also performed at the **Teatro Coliseo Alvia** (✉ Alameda Urquijo 13, ☎ 94/415–3954). Bilbao hosts a **music festival** in August; inquire at the tourist office, as venues change.

Bilbao's abundant nightlife breaks neatly down into ages and zones. Students and anyone else who can pass for being thirtyish and under are massively present in and around **Calle Pozas** and the **casco viejo,** where serious *poteo* (tippling) continues late into most nights, especially Thursday to Sunday, and folk dancing sometimes breaks out in the streets. Monday through Wednesday is quieter, barring holidays. Older night owls gather at **Bluesville** and **Flash,** on Calle Telesforo Aranzadi (near the Hotel Carlton), for dinner, dancing, and cocktails. **Whiskey Viejo** and **La Ochoa** on Calle Lersundi are other prime destinations.

Shopping

Basque ***txapelas*** (berets) are famous worldwide and make fine gifts. Best when waterproofed, they'll keep you remarkably warm in rain and mist. Try **Sombreros Gorostiaga** (✉ C. Victor, ☎ 94/416–1276), in the old quarter, for the most famous line of berets, Elosegui.

En Route From Bilbao, pick up the A8 toll road and follow signs to the Guernica exit (Gernika, in Euskera). From there, the Bi635, a good road through Vizcaya's coastal hills, takes you north to Guernica.

Guernica

13 *15 km (9 mi) east of Bilbao.*

On Monday, April 26, 1937—market day—Guernica suffered history's second terror bombing against a civilian population (the first, much less famous, was against neighboring Durango, about a month earlier). The planes of the Nazi Luftwaffe were sent with the blessings of General Franco to experiment with saturation bombing of civilian targets, and decimate the traditional seat of Basque autonomy in the bargain. Since the Middle Ages, Spanish sovereigns had sworn under the ancient **oak tree of Guernica** to respect Basque *fueros* (special local rights—just the kind of local autonomy inimical to the *generalísimo* and his "National Movement" of Madrid-centered Spanish unity). More than a thousand people were killed in the bombing, and today Guernica remains a symbol of independence in the heart of every Basque, known to the world through Picasso's famous painting (now in Madrid's Centro de Arte Reina Sofía).

The city was destroyed—though the oak tree miraculously emerged unscathed—and has been rebuilt as a modern, unattractive place. One point of interest, however, is the stump of the sacred oak, which finally died several decades ago, in the courtyard of the **Casa de Juntas** (a new oak has been planted alongside the old one)—the object of many a pilgrimage. Nearby is the stunning estuary of the **Ría de Guernica,** a stone's throw from some of the area's most colorful fishing towns.

Dining and Lodging

$$ ★ ✕ **Baserri Maitea.** Here's your chance to see the inside of one of the Basque country's traditional *caseríos* (farmhouses): this one is 300 years old. Strings of red peppers and garlic hang from wooden beams in the cathedral-like interior. Entrées include the *pescado del día* (fish of the day) and *cordero de leche asado al horno de leña* (milk-fed lamb roasted in a wood-burning oven). The pastries are homemade. ✉ *Bi635 to Bermeo, Km 2, ☎ 94/625–3408. AE, DC, MC, V. No dinner Sun., except in summer.*

$ ★ 🏨 **Boliña.** Not far from the famous oak in downtown Guernica, the Boliña is pleasant, friendly, and modern, a good base for exploring the Vizcayan coast. Rooms are smallish but comfortable. ✉ *Barrenkale 3, 48300, ☎ FAX 94/625–0300. 16 rooms. Restaurant, bar. AE, DC, MC, V.*

En Route From Guernica follow signs for Bermeo, but before you get there, stop at the Mirador de Portuondo, a roadside lookout with an excellent view of the estuary (at Km 43 on Bi635).

Mundaca

14 *45 km (28 mi) northeast of Bilbao.*

Mundaca (Mundaka, in Euskera) is a tiny town that draws surfers from all over the world, especially in winter, when the waves are some of the world's longest.

Dining and Lodging

$$ ✕ **Casino José Mari.** Built in 1818 as an auction house for the local fishermen's guild, this building, with wonderful views of Mundaca's beach, is now a local eating club. The public is welcome, and it's a prime lunch stop in summer, when you can sit in the glassed-in, upper-floor porch. Very much a local haunt, the club serves excellent fish caught, more often than not, by members. ✉ *Parque Atalaya (in center of town),* ☎ *94/687–6005. Reservations not accepted. AE, MC, V.*

$$ 🏨 **Atalaya.** This 1911 landmark was converted very tastefully from a private house to a hotel. Guest rooms are charming and comfortable, and those upstairs have balconies with marvelous views. Room No. 12 is the best in the house. The breakfast room is cheerful and light. ✉ *Itxaropen Kalea 1, Villa María Luisa Esperanza, 48360,* ☎ *94/687–6888,* FAX *94/687–6899. 15 rooms. Bar. AE, DC, MC, V.*

Bermeo

★ ⓯ *3 km (2 mi) west of Mundaca.*

Bermeo claims the largest fishing fleet in Spain, 62 long-distance boats of more than 150 tons and 121 smaller craft that specialize in hake. Bermeo was long a whaling port; in the 16th century local whalers had to donate the tongue of every whale to help raise money for the church. The town still has one of only two wooden-boat shipyards on the northern coast, and the boats that fill its harbor make a cheerful picture. Drive to the top of the windswept hill, where a cemetery overlooks the crashing waves below. Townspeople tend family tombs at sunset.

Dining

$$ ✕ **Jokin.** You have a good view of the *puerto viejo* (old port) from this cheerful, strategically located restaurant. The fish served comes directly off the boats in the harbor below. Try the *rape Jokin* (angler in a clam and crayfish sauce) or *chipirones en su tinta* (small squid in its own ink) and, for dessert, the *tarta de naranja* (orange cake). ✉ *Eupeme Duna 13,* ☎ *94/688–4089. AE, DC, MC, V. No dinner Sun.*

En Route Head back on the Bi635 past Guernica toward Lequeitio (Lekeitio, in Euskera). For a rewarding side trip, turn left at Muretagana and follow the signs to the road's end in Elanchove (Elantxobe, in Euskera).

Elanchove

⓰ *27 km (17 mi) from Bermeo.*

The tiny fishing village of Elanchove nestles among huge, steep cliffs, with a small breakwater protecting its fleet from the storms of the Bay of Biscay. The view of the port from the upper village is breathtaking. The lower fork in the road leads to the port itself.

The upper village is quite unaccustomed to tourists. Stop into the rustic **Bar Itxasmin,** which has a small restaurant; it's just off the plaza where the road ends.

Dining and Lodging

$ ✕🏨 **Arboliz Jatetxea.** Set on a bluff overlooking the coast, about 2 km (1 mi) outside Elanchove on the road to Lequeitio, this rustic inn is a little far from the appealing harborside bustle, but still pleasant. Rooms are simple, modern, and well kept, and several have balconies. ✉ *Arboliz 12, Ibarranguelua 48311,* ☎ *94/627–6283. 9 rooms, 3 with bath. Restaurant. AE, MC, V.*

Lequeitio

17 *59 km (37 mi) east of Bilbao, 61 km (38 mi) west of San Sebastián.*

This bright little town is similar to Bermeo but has two wide, sandy beaches right by its harbor. Soaring over the Gothic church of Santa María (open for Mass only) is a graceful set of flying buttresses. Lequeitio is famous for its fiestas (September 1–18), which include a gruesome event in which men dangle for as long as they can from the necks of dead geese tied to a cable over the inlet while the cable is whipped in and out of the water by crowds of burly men at either end.

OFF THE BEATEN PATH **SANTIMAMIÑE CAVERNS** – On the Kortezubi road 5 km (3 mi) from Guernica, the Santimamiñe Caverns (✉ Barrio Basondo, Kortezubi, ☎ 94/625–2975) contain some prehistoric cave paintings. Guided visits are offered weekdays at 10:30, noon, 4, and 5:30, except holidays.

Ondárroa

18 *61 km (38 mi) east of Bilbao, 49 km (30 mi) west of San Sebastián.*

Farther east along the coast from Lequeitio, Ondárroa is another gem of a fishing town. Like its neighbors, it has a major fishing fleet painted various combinations of red, green, and white, the colors of the *Ikurriña,* the Basque national flag.

En Route Continuing along the coastal road through Motrico and Deva, you'll approach some of the prettiest fishing ports and culinary centers in the Basque country. Before these, however, as you come into Zumaya, you'll see the turnoff for Azpeitia and the sanctuary of one of Spain's greatest religious figures, St. Ignatius of Loyola, founder of the Jesuits and spiritual architect of the Catholic Reformation (also known as the Counter-Reformation). A half-hour trip up the Gi631 takes you to this colossal structure.

Santuario de San Ignacio de Loyola

★ 19 *Cestona is 34 km (21 mi) southwest of San Sebastián.*

The Sanctuary of St. Ignatius of Loyola was erected in honor of Iñigo Lopez de Oñaz y Loyola (1491–1556) after he was sainted as Ignacio de Loyola in 1622 for his defense of the Catholic Church against the tides of Luther's Reformation. The future founder of the Jesuit Order left his life as a courtier to join the army at the age of 26, but after being badly wounded in an intra-Basque battle he returned to his family's ancestral home, underwent a spiritual conversion, and took up theological studies. Almost two centuries later, Roman architect Carlos Fontana designed the basilica that would memorialize the saint after whom five universities in the United States and Canada and many others worldwide have been named. The structure is Baroque, and an exuberant, Churrigueresque Baroque at that—in contrast to the austere ways of Iñigo himself, who took vows of poverty and chastity after his conversion. The interior is richly endowed with polychrome marble, ornate altarwork, and a huge but delicate dome. The fortresslike tower house contains the room where Iñigo experienced conversion while recovering from his wound. His reputation as a "soldier of Christ" somewhat belies his teachings, which emphasized mystical union with God, imitation of Christ, human initiative, foreign missionary work, and, especially, the education of youth.

Back on the coastal road is **Zumaya,** a cozy little port and summer resort with the fjordlike estuary of the Urola River flowing (back and forth, according to the tide) through town. The **Museo Zuloaga,** on the N634 at the edge of town (☏ 943/862341), has an extraordinary collection of paintings by Goya, El Greco, Zurbarán and others in addition to the Basque impressionist Ignacio Zuloaga himself. It's open Wednesday–Sunday 4–8, and admission is 500 ptas.

Dining and Lodging

$$ ★ ✕ **Bedua.** Locals access this rustic gem by boat in the summer. A specialist in *tortilla de patatas con pimientos verdes de la huerta* (potato omelet with homegrown green peppers), Bedua is also known for *tortilla de bacalao* (codfish omelet), *txuleta de buey* (beefsteak), and fish of all kinds, especially *besugo* (sea bream). ✉ *Cestoa, Barrio Bedua (3 km/2 mi up the Urola from Zumaya),* ☏ *943/860551. MC, V.*

$$ **Arocena.** One of the many spa hotels to which Europeans flocked at the turn of the century, the Arocena has free bus service to the nearby springs, whose medicinal waters are still used to treat liver-related diseases. Rooms facing away from the road have especially fine views of the mountains. The common rooms, including an elegant restaurant and lobby, faithfully retain the hotel's Belle Epoque flavor. ✉ *San Juan 12, Cestona 20740 (10 mins from sanctuary),* ☏ *943/147040,* FAX *943/147978. 109 rooms. Restaurant, bar, pool, tennis court, playground, chapel. AE, DC, MC, V.*

Guetaria

20 *22 km (14 mi) from San Sebastián.*

From Zumaya, the coast road and several good foothpaths lead to Guetaria, known as *la cocina de guipúzcoa,* the kitchen of Guipúzcoa province, for its surfeit of restaurants and taverns. Guetaria was the birthplace of Juan Sebastián Elcano (1460–1526), the first circumnavigator of the globe and Spain's most emblematic naval hero: Elcano took over and completed Magellan's voyage after the latter was killed in the Philippines in 1521. The town's galleonlike **church** has sloping wooden floors that resemble a ship's deck, and the restaurant across the street (☞ *below*) is a great place for *besugo a la parrilla* (sea bream roasted over coals).

Zarauz, the next town, is another beauty, with a wide beach and numerous taverns and cafés.

Dining

$$ ✕ **Iribar.** The Iribar has been grilling fish and beef over coals outside the church for more than half a century (no doubt raising havoc at times with the fasting faithful within). While Kaia and Kai-pe, in the port, are also good places to dine, with views of the harbor's colorful fleet of fishing boats, the Iribar's warm, family atmosphere makes it the best choice. ✉ *Kale Nagusia 38,* ☏ *943/140406. MC, V.*

En Route Heading east toward San Sebastián, you have a choice of the A8 toll road or the coastal N634 highway. The former is a quick and scenic 44 km (27 mi), but the latter will take you through the village of Orio past a few more tempting inns and restaurants, not the least of which is the **Sidrería Ugarte,** in Usurbil.

SAN SEBASTIÁN TO HONDARRIBIA

Graceful, chic San Sebastián invites you to slow down, stroll the beach for a while, and wander the exquisite streets. East of the city, you'll pass through Pasajes, where Lafayette set off to help the colonial forces in the American Revolution. Victor Hugo spent a winter writing here. Just shy of the French border, you'll hit Hondarribia, a quaint and colorful port town.

San Sebastián

★ 21 *100 km (62 mi) east of Bilbao.*

San Sebastián (Donostia, in Euskera) is an unusually sophisticated city arched around one of the finest urban beaches in the world, **La Concha** ("The Shell"), so named for its almost perfect resemblance to the shape of a scallop shell. The best way to see San Sebastián is simply to walk around: the city is full of promenades and pathways, several leading up the hills that surround it, and these are full of the effortlessly fashionable Donostiarras. Built for the enjoyment of both eye and spirit, San Sebastián is now equally treasured for its gifts to the palate.

The first records of San Sebastián date from the 11th century. A backwater for centuries, the city had the good fortune in 1845 to attract Queen Isabella II, who came seeking relief from a skin ailment in the icy Atlantic waters. Isabella was followed by much of the aristocracy of the time, and San Sebastián became a favored summer retreat for Madrid's well-to-do. The city is laid out in a remarkably modern way, with wide streets on a grid pattern, thanks mainly to the 12 different times it has been all but destroyed by fire. The last conflagration came after the French were expelled in 1813; English-Portuguese forces occupied the city, badly abused the population, and proceeded to torch the place. Today, San Sebastián is a seaside resort in a class with Nice and Monte Carlo and becomes one of Spain's most expensive cities in the summer, when French vacationers descend in droves. It is also, like Bilbao, a center of Basque nationalism.

Virtually dead center in the entrance to the bay, the tiny **Isla de Santa Clara** protects the city from Bay of Biscay storms, making La Concha one of the calmest beaches on Spain's entire northern coast. For added drama, a large hill dominates each side of the entrance, and a visit to **Monte Igueldo,** on the western side, is a must. (You can drive up for a toll of 175 ptas. per person or take the *funicular*—cable car—for 200 ptas. round trip; it runs 10–8 in summer, 11–6 in winter, with departures every 15 minutes.) From the top, you get the remarkable panorama for which San Sebastián is famous: gardens, parks, wide, tree-lined boulevards, Belle Epoque buildings, and, of course, the bay itself.

Every corner of Spain claims its culinary identity with pride, but for sheer quality and refinement San Sebastián's cuisine is in a league of its own. Many of the city's restaurants—along with scores of private, all-male eating societies—are in the **parte vieja** (old quarter), on the east end of the bay beyond the elegant **Casa Consistorial** (City Hall) and formal Alderdi Eder gardens. City Hall began life as a casino in 1887; after gambling was outlawed early in the 20th century, the town council moved here from the Plaza de la Constitución, the old quarter's main square. San Sebastián's new concert hall, film society, and convention center, the **Kursaal** (Avda. de la Zurriola, ☎ 943/003000) opened in 1999 to unanimous acclaim. Designed by the world-renowned Spanish architect Rafael Moneo at the mouth of the Urumea River, it is most frequently described as a pair of translucent rocks imbedded in the waterfront. Guided tours, 350 ptas., are given daily at 11:30, 12:30, and 1:30.

Just in from the harbor, in the shadow of Monte Urgull, is the lovely Baroque church of **Santa María,** with a stunning carved facade featuring (who else?) an arrow-riddled Saint Sebastian. The interior is strikingly restful; note the ship above Saint Sebastian high on the altar. Looking straight south from the front of the church, you can see the facade and spires of the **Catedral Buen Pastor** (Cathedral of the Good Shepherd) across town.

NEED A BREAK? Steps from the facade of Santa María, in the heart of the old quarter, the tiny café **Kantoi** (✉ C. Mayor 10) is an attractive place to grab a beverage among newspaper-reading young locals. Have a *chocolate con nata*—thick, dark hot chocolate with real whipped cream.

San Sebastián is divided by the **Urumea River,** which is crossed by three bridges inspired by late-19th-century French architecture. At the mouth of the Urumea, the incoming surf smashes the rocks with such force that white foam erupts to photogenic heights, and the noise is transfixing. Spend some time down here—it's unlike anything else in the world.

Dining and Lodging

$$$$ ✕ **Akelarre.** This restaurant is on the slopes of Monte Igueldo, with spectacular views of both the bay and the city. Chef Pedro Subijana is known for, among other things, his *lubina a la pimienta verde* (sea bass with green pepper) and such Basque classics as *calamares en su tinta* (squid in a sauce of its own ink). ✉ *Barrio de Igueldo,* ☎ *943/212052 or 943/214086. Reservations essential. AE, DC, MC, V. Closed Mon., 1st 2 wks in June, and Dec. No dinner Sun.*

$$$ ★ ✕ **Arzak.** Renowned chef Juan Marí Arzak's intimate cottage on the eastern outskirts of San Sebastián is internationally famous, so reserve well in advance. The entire menu is a wonder, with traditional Basque preparations and contemporary innovations. The pastries are supremely light, and prices are very fair. ✉ *Alto de Miracruz 2,* ☎ *943/285593 or 943/278465. Reservations essential. AE, DC, MC, V. Closed Mon., last 2 wks in June, and 2 wks in Nov. No dinner Sun.*

$$$ ✕ **Panier Fleuri.** One of the most select wine lists in Spain compliments the food here. Both are served in a sober dining room overlooking the crashing surf at the mouth of the Urumea River. Chef Tatus Fombellida is a winner of Spain's national gastronomy prize, no mean feat. Try his *faisán* (pheasant) or the *supremas de lenguado a la florentina* (sole baked with spinach and served with hollandaise sauce) and for dessert the lemon sorbet with champagne. ✉ *Paseo de Salamanca 1,* ☎ *943/424205. Reservations essential. AE, DC, MC, V. Closed Wed., last 2 wks of Dec., 3 wks in June, and Christmas wk. No dinner Sun.*

$$ ✕ **Bar Ganbara.** This happening tapas bar near the Plaza de la Constitución has an ample selection of nibbles ranging from shrimp and asparagus to *jamón ibérico* on croissants to anchovies, sea urchins, and wild mushrooms in season. Proper meals are also served, with an emphasis on meats roasted over coals. ✉ *C. San Jerónimo 21,* ☎ *943/422575. Closed Mon. No dinner Sun.*

$$ ✕ **Sidrería Petritegui.** For hearty dining and a certain amount of splashing around in hard cider, make this short excursion east of San Sebastián. Gigantic wooden barrels line the walls, while tables are piled with *tortilla de bacalao* (codfish omelet), *txuleta de buey* (thick chunks of beef), the smoky local sheepís-milk cheese from the town of Idiazábal, and, for dessert, walnuts and *membrillo* (quince jelly). ✉ *Carretera San Sebastián–Hernani, Km 7, Astigarraga,* ☎ *943/457188. No credit cards. No lunch weekdays.*

$$ ✕ **Urepel.** Both the cuisine and the interior design here balance classic and contemporary elements in a felicitous way. The *chicharro al escama dorada* (a skinned, de-boned mackerel served under a layer of golden-brown sliced potatoes) is a typical Urepel invention. There is no head chef; the kitchen staff works as a team, in prototypically Basque egalitarian fashion. ✉ *Paseo de Salamanca 3,* ☎ *943/424040. AE, DC, MC, V. Closed Sun. and Tues. evening.*

$ ✕ **Casa Vallés.** Just a two-minute walk from the back of San Sebastián's cathedral, this fine little tapas bar and restaurant displays some

30 to 40 different freshly prepared and irresistible creations at midday and again in the early evening. Beloved by locals, it combines excellent food with great value. ✉ *Reyes Católicos 10,* ☎ *943/452210. AE, DC, MC, V. Closed Wed. and June 15–30.*

$$$$ **María Cristina.** The graceful beauty of the Belle Epoque is embodied in San Sebastián's most luxurious hotel, which sits like the queen it's named after on the elegant west bank of the Urumea River. The grandeur continues in salons filled with Oriental rugs, potted palms, and Carrara marble columns, and in bedrooms to match. ✉ *Paseo República Argentina s/n, 20004,* ☎ *943/424900,* FAX *943/423914. 139 rooms. Restaurant, bar, beauty salon, meeting rooms. AE, DC, MC, V.*

$$$ **Londres y de Inglaterra.** This stately hotel has a privileged position on the promenade above La Concha. An Old World aesthetic informs the bright, formal lobby and continues throughout the hotel. The bar and restaurant face the bay, and guest rooms with bay views are the best in town. ✉ *Zubieta 2, 20007,* ☎ *943/426989,* FAX *943/420031. 138 rooms, 7 suites. Restaurant, bar, minibars, casino, meeting rooms, parking (fee). AE, DC, MC, V.*

$$ **Aristondo.** This comfortable farmhouse, just 15 minutes' drive above San Sebastián on Monte Igueldo, is a scenic and economical place to stay. Similar *agroturismo* options nearby include **Izen Eder** (☎ 943/580011) and **Pilotegui** (☎ 943/215348). ✉ *San Martín 54 bis, 20007,* ☎ *943/215558,* FAX *943/463914. 16 rooms. MC, V.*

$$ **Bahía.** A two-minute walk from the beach, this hotel is small but appealing. The welcoming lobby includes a friendly minibar and salon, and the rooms are comfortable and modern. ✉ *San Martín 54 bis, 20007,* ☎ *943/469211,* FAX *943/463914. 60 rooms. Bar. MC, V.*

Nightlife and the Arts

Glitterati arrive in San Sebastián for its **international film festival** in the second half of September. Exact dates vary; ask the tourist office or read the local press for details. The same goes for the late-July **jazz festival,** which draws many of the world's top performers. There are varied programs of theater, dance, and other events year-round at the beautiful **Teatro Victoria Eugenia** (✉ Reina Regente s/n, ☎ 943/481155 or 943/481160), and the new **Kursaal** (Avda. de la Zurriola, ☎ 943/003000).

At night, look for *copas, potes* (both "drinks"), and general cruising in and around the **parte vieja.** The top disco is **Bataplan,** near the western end of La Concha.

Shopping

San Sebastián is nonpareil for stylish home furnishings and clothing. Wander **Calle San Martín** and the surrounding pedestrian-only streets to see what's in the windows. **Ponsol** (✉ C. Narrica 4, ☎ 943/420876) is the best place to buy Basque berets, called *boinas*; the Leclerq family has been hatting Donostiarras for three generations. Stop into **Maitiena** (✉ Avda. Libertad 32, ☎ 943/424721) for a fabulous selection of chocolates.

Pasajes de San Juan

22 *10 km (6 mi) east of San Sebastián.*

General Lafayette set out from Pasajes de San Juan (Pasaia Donibane, in Euskera) to aid the rebels in the American Revolution. There are actually three towns around the commercial port of Rentería: **Pasajes Ancho,** an industrial port; **Pasajes de San Pedro,** a large fishing harbor; and historic **Pasajes de San Juan.** This last is a tiny settlement of 18th- and 19th-century buildings along a single street fronting the bay's outlet to the sea. It's best reached by driving into Pasajes de San Pedro, on the San Sebastián side of the strait, and catching a launch across the mouth of the harbor (about 100 ptas., depending on the time of day). The town is known for its three fine restaurants: Txulotxo, Casa Cámara (☞ *below*), and Artzape.

Dining

$$ ★ ✕ **Casa Cámara.** Four generations ago, Pablo Cámara turned this old fishing wharf on the narrows into a first-class restaurant. The dining room has lovely views and a central tank from which live lobsters and crayfish are hauled up for your inspection. Try *cangrejo del mar* (spider crab with vegetable sauce) or the superb *merluza con salsa verde* (hake in green sauce). ✉ *Pasajes de San Juan,* ☎ *943/523699 or 943/517874. Reservations essential. AE, DC, MC, V. Closed Mon. No dinner Sun.*

Hondarribia

㉓ *12 km (7 mi) east of Pasajes.*

Hondarribia (Fuenterrabia, in Castilian Spanish; this town is more often called by its Basque name) is the last fishing port before the French border. Lined with fishermen's homes and small fishing boats, the harbor is a beautiful but rather touristy spot. If you have a taste for history, follow signs up the hill to the medieval bastion and onetime castle of Carlos V, now a parador.

Dining and Lodging

$$$–$$$$ ✕ **Ramón Roteta.** Set in a beautiful old villa with an informal garden, this restaurant serves excellent food and is an easy choice for anyone staying at the parador. Sample the garlic and shrimp pastries or the rice with vegetables and clams. The pastries are homemade. ✉ *Villa Ainara, C. Irún 2,* ☎ *943/641693. AE, DC, MC, V. Mid-Sept.–mid-June, no dinner Tues.; mid-June–mid-Sept., closed Tues. No dinner Sun.*

$$ ✕ **La Hermandad de Pescadores.** This centrally located "brotherhood" is owned by the local fishermen's guild and serves simple and hearty fare at reasonable prices. Try the *sopa de pescado* (fish soup) or the *almejas a la marinera* (clams in a thick, garlicky sauce). If you come outside peak hours (2–4 and 9–11), you'll find space at the long communal boards. ✉ *C. Zuloaga s/n,* ☎ *943/642738. AE, DC, MC, V. Closed Wed. No dinner Tues.*

$$$$ 🏨 **Parador El Emperador.** Replete with suits of armor and other chivalric bric-a-brac, this parador occupies a superb medieval bastion that dates from the 10th century and housed Carlos V in the 16th century. Many rooms have gorgeous views of the Bidasoa River and estuary, dotted with colorful fishing boats. Reserve ahead and ask for one of the three "special" rooms, with canopied beds and baronial appointments; they're worth the moderate extra expense. ✉ *Pl. Armas de Castillo, 20005,* ☎ *943/645500,* FAX *943/642153. 36 rooms. Bar. AE, DC, MC, V.*

$ 🏨 **Caserío "Artzu."** This family barn and house, with its classic low, wide roofline, has been here in one form or another for some 800 years. Just west of the hermitage of Nuestra Señora de Guadalupe, 5 km (3 mi) above Hondarribia, Artzu offers modernized accommodations in an ancient farmhouse or *caserío* overlooking the junction of the Bidasoa estuary and the Atlantic. ✉ *Barrio Montaña, 20280,* ☎ *943/640530. 6 rooms, 1 with bath. Restaurant. No credit cards.*

En Route The fastest route from San Sebastián to Pamplona is the A15 Autovía de Navarra, which cuts through the Leizarán Valley and gets you there in about 45 minutes. Somewhat prettier, if slower and more tortuous, is the 134-km (83-mi) drive on C133, which starts out near the French border (and Hondarribia) and follows the Bidasoa River (the border with France) up through Vera de Bidasoa. When C133 meets N121 you can turn left up into the lovely Baztán Valley or right through the Velate pass to Pamplona.

PAMPLONA, VITORIA, AND ENVIRONS

Pamplona, the ancient capital of Navarre, draws crowds with its annual feast of San Fermín, but medieval Vitoria, in the Basque province of Alava, is largely undiscovered by tourists. Olite, south of Pamplona, has a storybook castle, and the towns of Puente la Reina and Estella are picturesque stops on the Camino de Santiago.

Pamplona

24 *91 km (56 mi) southeast of San Sebastián.*

Pamplona is known the world over for its running of the bulls, made famous by Ernest Hemingway in his 1926 novel *The Sun Also Rises.* The occasion is the festival of San Fermín, July 6–14, when Pamplona's population triples (along with hotel prices) and rooms must be reserved months in advance. Tickets to the bullfights (*corridas*), as opposed to the running (*encierro,* meaning "enclosing"), to which access is free, can be difficult to obtain. Every morning at 7 sharp a skyrocket is shot off, and the bulls kept overnight in the corrals at the edge of town are run through a series of closed-off streets leading to the bullring, a 902-yard dash. Running before them are Spaniards and foreigners feeling festive enough to risk a goring, most wearing the traditional white shirts and trousers with red neckerchiefs and carrying rolled-up newspapers. If all goes well—no bulls separated from the pack, no mayhem—the bulls arrive in the ring in just 2½ minutes. The degree of peril in the *encierro* is difficult to gauge. Serious injuries occur nearly every day; deaths are rare but always a very real possibility. What's certain is the sense of danger, the mob hysteria, and the exhilaration.

Founded by the Roman emperor Pompey as Pompaelo, or Pameiopolis, Pamplona was successively taken by the Franks, the Goths, and the Moors. The Pamplonicas managed to expel the Arabs temporarily in 750, when they put themselves under the protection of Charlemagne. But the foreign commander took advantage of this trust to destroy the city walls, so that when he was driven out once more by the Moors, the Navarrese took their revenge, ambushing and slaughtering the retreating Frankish army as it fled over the Pyrenees through the mountain pass of Roncesvalles in 778. This is the episode depicted in the 11th-century *Song of Roland,* although the French author chose to cast the aggressors as Moors. For centuries after that, Pamplona remained three argumentative towns until they were forcibly incorporated into one city by Carlos III (the Noble, 1387–1425) of Navarre.

Pamplona's **cathedral,** set near the portion of the ancient walls rebuilt in the 17th century, is one of the most important religious buildings in northern Spain thanks to the fragile grace and gabled Gothic arches of its cloister. Inside are the tombs of Carlos III and his wife, marked by an alabaster sculpture. The **Museo Diocesano** (Diocesan Museum) houses religious art from the Middle Ages and the Renaissance. ✉ C. *Curia s/n.* 💵 *Free.* ⏲ *Cathedral 24 hrs; museum Tues.–Sat. 9–2 and 4–7, Sun. 9–2.*

On Calle Santo Domingo, in a 16th-century building once used as a hospital for pilgrims on their way to Santiago de Compostela, is the ★ **Museo de Navarra** (✉ C. Jaranta s/n, ☎ 948/227831), with a collection of regional archaeological artifacts and historical costumes. The museum is open Tuesday–Saturday 9–2 and 5–7, Sunday 9–2, and admission is 350 ptas. Pamplona's most remarkable civil building is the ornate, 18th-century ***ayuntamiento*** (city hall), on the Plaza Consistorial, which over the years has acquired a blackish color that sets off its gilded balconies. Stop in to see the wood-and-marble interior.

NEED A BREAK? Pamplona's gentry have been flocking to the ornate, French-style **Café Iruña** since 1888. The bar and salons are sumptuously paneled in dark wood. Beyond the stand-up bar is a bingo hall (you must be 18 to play). ✉ *Pl. del Castillo 44.* ⏲ *Daily 5 PM–3 AM.*

One of Pamplona's greatest charms is the warren of small streets near the **Plaza del Castillo** (especially Calle San Nicolás), which are filled with restaurants, taverns, and bars. Pamplonicas are hardy sorts, well known for their eagerness and capacity to eat and drink.

The central **Ciudadela,** an ancient fortress, is a parkland of promenades and pools. Walk through in late afternoon, the time of the *paseo* (traditional stroll), for a taste of everyday life here.

Dining and Lodging

$$$$ ✕ **Josetxo.** This warm, elegant family-run restaurant is one of Pamplona's finest. Specialties include *hojaldre de marisco* (shellfish pastry), an *ensalada de langosta* (lobster salad) appetizer, and *muslo de pichón relleno de trufa y foie*—pigeon stuffed with truffles and foie gras. ✉ *Príncipe de Viana 1,* ☎ *948/222097. AE, DC, MC, V. Closed Sun. except during San Fermín and Aug.*

$$$ ✕ **Hartza.** Archaic and elegant, this rustic place serves some of the most creative cuisine in Pamplona without omitting any of the hearty fare for which Navarre is known. Try the *oca con jugo de trufa y manzana* (goose with apple and truffles). ✉ *Juan de Labrit 19,* ☎ *948/224568. AE, DC, MC, V. Closed Mon.; July 30–Aug. 24; and Dec. 24–Jan. 4. No dinner Sun.*

$$ ★ ✕ **Erburu.** In the heart of the nightlife district, this dark, wood-beamed restaurant is a true find, frequented by Pamplonans in the know. Come here to dine or just to sample tapas at the bar. Standouts are the Basque classic *merluza con salsa verde* (hake in green sauce) and any of a whole range of dishes made with *alcochofas* (artichokes). ✉ *San Lorenzo 19–21,* ☎ *948/225169. AE, DC, MC, V. Closed Mon. and 2nd half of July.*

$ ✕🏨 **Casa Otano.** This friendly, tumultuous hotel and restaurant is simple and well placed, right in the middle of the tapas-and-wine circuit and just a few paces from Pamplona's main square. The restaurant downstairs serves hearty Basque fare. The atmosphere is consistent with the madness that will be raging in the street if you come during San Fermín. ✉ *San Nicolás 5, 31001,* ☎ *948/225095,* FAX *948/212012. 15 rooms. AE, DC, MC, V. Usually closed July 16–31.*

$$$$ 🏨 **Los Tres Reyes.** Named for the three kings of Navarre, Aragón, and Castile—who, it was said, could meet at La Mesa de los Tres Reyes, in the Pyrenees, without stepping out of their respective realms—this modern glass-and-stone refuge operates on the same principle: come to Pamplona and find all the comforts of home. ✉ *C. de la Taconera s/n, 31001,* ☎ *948/226600,* FAX *948/222930. 168 rooms. Restaurant, cafeteria, piano bar, pool, beauty salon, car rental. AE, DC, MC, V.*

$$–$$$$ 🏨 **Yoldi.** This hotel is always teeming with the somewhat snooty foreign *afición*—that is, old-hand bullfight fans. Still, anthropologically they're an interesting lot: knowledgeable-looking Hemingwayoids debating such taurine esoterica as the placement, angle, intent, and aesthetic of the third sword thrust on the second bull in the fifth *corrida* of the fourth *feria* of the last decade. Who could ask for more? ✉ *Avda.*

San Ignacio 11, 31002, ☎ 948/224800, FAX 948/212045. 50 rooms. Bar, cafeteria. AE, DC, MC, V.

$$–$$$ **La Perla.** Hemingway watched his first running of the bulls here, from his balcony over Calle Estafeta. La Perla is the oldest hotel in town, though far from the best. The founder's son was a bullfighter, and the two bulls he killed before retiring preside over the salon. The timeless decor is simple but charming, straight out of *The Sun Also Rises.* Prices shoot up during San Fermín. ✉ *Pl. del Castillo 1, 31001,* ☎ *948/227706,* FAX *948/211566. 67 rooms, 45 with bath. AE, DC, MC, V.*

Nightlife and the Arts

Pamplona has a thumping student life year-round. Summer brings a varied summer program of concerts, ballet, and *zarzuela*; contact the **Teatro Gayarre** (✉ Avda. Carlos III Noble 1, ☎ 948/220139) for information. In August, the **Festivales de Navarra** bring theater and other events.

Shopping

Botas are the wineskins from which Basques typically drink at bullfights or during fiestas. The art lies in drinking a stream of wine from a bota held at arm's length—without spilling a drop, if you want to maintain your honor (not to mention your shirt). You can buy botas in any Basque town, but Pamplona's **Anel** (✉ C. Comedías 7) sells the best brand, Las Tres Zetas—"The Three Z's," written as ZZZ.

The **neckerchiefs** worn for the running of the bulls are sold in various shops, as are *gerrikos,* the wide belts worn by Basque sportsmen during contests of strength, to hold in overstressed organs.

For sweets, try **Salcedo** (✉ C. Estafeta 37), open since 1800, which invented and still sells almond-based *mantecadas* (powder cakes), as well as *coronillas* (delightful almond-and-cream concoctions). **Hijas de C. Lozano** (✉ C. Zapatería 11) sells *café y leche* (coffee and milk) toffees that are prized all over Spain.

Olite

★ 25 *41 km (25 mi) south of Pamplona.*

Much of Olite is ancient and pleasant to walk through. The 11th-century church of **San Pedro** is interesting for its finely worked Romanesque cloisters and portal. The town's parador is part of a **castle** restored by Carlos III in the French style—a fantasy structure of ramparts, crenellated battlements, and watchtowers. You can walk the ramparts in the section not occupied by the parador. *400 ptas.* ⌚ *Daily 10–2 and 4–5.*

Dining and Lodging

$$ ★ ✕ **Parador Príncipe de Viana.** This castle parador is a flight of fancy, named for the grandson of Carlos III, who spent his life here. It's housed in part of Olite's castle complex, and the chivalric atmosphere is well preserved, with grand salons, secret stairways, heraldic tapestries, and the odd suit of armor. ✉ *Pl. de los Teobaldos 2, 31390,* ☎ *948/740000,* FAX *948/740201. 43 rooms. Restaurant, bar. AE, DC, MC, V.*

Puente la Reina

26 *31 km (19 mi) from Olite, 24 km (15 mi) from Pamplona.*

Puente la Reina is an important nexus on the Camino de Santiago: the junction of the two pilgrimage routes from northern Europe, one passing through Somport and Jaca and the other through Roncesvalles and Pamplona. A bronze sculpture of a pilgrim marks the spot. The graceful medieval bridge over the river Arga, one of the most emblematic images on the route, was built for pilgrims by Navarran King Sancho VII el Fuerte (the Strong) in the 11th century. The streets, particularly Calle Mayor, are lined with tiny, ancient houses. The church of **Santiago** (St. James), at the end of Calle Mayor, is known for its gold sculpture of the saint. The **Iglesia del Crucifijo** (Church of the Crucifix) has a notably expressive wooden sculpture of Christ on a Y-shaped cross, gift of a 14th-century pilgrim. Five kilometers (three miles) east of here, the octagonal church of **Santa María de Eunate** was once used as a burial place for pilgrims who didn't make it. Six kilometers (four miles) west of Puente la Reina, the church of **San Román,** in the carefully restored village of Cirauqui, has an extraordinarily beautiful carved portal.

Dining and Lodging

$$ ✕🏨 **Mesón del Peregrino.** A renowned haven for weary pilgrims, this rustic stone house just north of town is hard to pass up. The rooms are small but charming, and the cuisine features roasts, *menestra de verduras* (Navarran vegetable stew), and hearty bean-and-sausage–based soups. ✉ *Ctra. Pamplona–Logrono*, Km 23, 31100, ☎ 948/340075, FAX 948/341190. 15 rooms. AE, DC, MC, V.

Estella

27 *19 km (12 mi) from Puente la Reina, 48 km (30 mi) from Logroño.*

Once the seat of the Royal Court of Navarre, Estella (Lizarra, in Euskera) is an inspiring stop on the Camino de Santiago. Its heart is the arcaded Plaza San Martín, its chief civic monument the 12th-century **Palacio de los Reyes de Navarra** (Palace of the Kings of Navarre). The town is laden with churches. The church of **San Pedro de la Rúa** has a beautiful cloister and a stunning carved portal; across the river Ega, the doorway to the church of **San Miguel** has fantastic relief sculptures of St. Michael the Archangel battling a dragon. The **Iglesia del Santo Sepulcro** (Church of the Holy Sepulchre) has a beautiful fluted portal. **Santa María Jus del Castillo,** converted from a synagogue in 1145, is the only vestige of Estella's medieval Jewish quarter. The nearby **Monasterio de Irache** dates from the 10th century but was later converted by Cistercian monks to a pilgrims' hospital; next door is the famous brass faucet that supplies pilgrims with free-flowing holy wine.

Vitoria

★ 28 *93 km (58 mi) west of Pamplona, 115 km (71 mi) southwest of San Sebastián, 64 km (40 mi) southeast of Bilbao.*

Vitoria's quality of life has been rated the highest in Spain, based on such criteria as square meters of green space per inhabitant (14), sports and cultural facilities, and pedestrian-only zones. Capital of the Basque country and its second-largest city after Bilbao, Vitoria (Gasteiz, in Euskera) is in many ways Euskadi's least Basque city. Neither a maritime nor a mountain enclave, Vitoria occupies the steppelike *meseta de Alava* (Alava plain) and functions as a modern industrial center with a surprisingly medieval *casco antiguo* (old quarter). Founded by Sancho el Sabio (the Wise) in 1181, the city was built largely of gray stone rather than sandstone; so its oldest streets and squares retain a uniquely Vitorian take on the Spanish Middle Ages.

Bordered by noble houses with covered arches and glass galleries, the sloping **Plaza de la Virgen Blanca** occupies the southwest corner of old Vitoria. The monument in the center commemorates the Duke of Wellington's defeat of Napoléon's army in 1813. The **Plaza de España,** just east of here, is an arcaded neoclassical square with the austere elegance of Madrid's Plaza Mayor. The **Plaza del Machete** is named for the sword used by medieval nobility to swear allegiance to the local *fueros,* or special autonomous Basque rights and privileges. A jasper niche in the lateral facade of the Gothic church of **San Miguel,** towering over Plaza del Machete, contains the Virgen Blanca (White Virgin), Vitoria's patron saint.

From the Plaza de la Virgen Blanca, Calle de Herrería follows the egg-shaped outline along the west side of the old city walls. Follow it to the **Palacio de los Alava Esquivel,** at the corner of Calle de la Soledad. Continuing north, you'll see the medieval **Torre de Doña Otxanda** just before Calle de las Carnicerías. Ahead, at the tip of the egg, the ancient brick and wood house at Calle de la Correría 151 is **El Portalón,** a hostelry for 500 years and now an excellent restaurant (☞ *below*). Across the street, the **Museo de la Arqueología** displays paleolithic dolmens, Roman art and artifacts, an ample inventory of medieval objects, and the famous *stele del jinete* (stele of the horseback rider), an early Basque tombstone.

Back toward the town center, the elegant **Torre de los Hurtado de Anda** is across from the exquisitely sculpted Gothic doorway on the western facade of the **Catedral de Santa María.** Halfway down Calle Fray Zacarías Martinez is the 16th-century Renaissance **Palacio de Escoriaza-Esquibel,** with a lovely plateresque patio. Down toward Plaza del Machete, on the corner of Calle Fray Zacarias Martinez (across from San Miguel), is the austere **Palacio Villa Suso,** built in 1538. Through Plaza del Machete to the left, the first street is Calle Cuchillería. **Casa del Cordón,** a 15th-century structure with a 13th-century tower, is identifiable by the *cordón* (rope) decorating one of the pointed arches on the facade. Farther down Calle Cuchillería, past shops featuring antiques and home furnishings, is the 16th-century Palacio de Bendaña and its unique **Museo Fournier de Naipes** (Playing-Card Museum).

Other attractions include the **Museo de Armería** (Arms Museum) displaying everything from prehistoric hatchets to 20th-century pistols and a sand-table reproduction of the 1813 battle between the Duke of Wellington and the French; and the **Museo de Bellas Artes** (Fine Arts Museum), with its Ribera, Zuloaga, and Picasso paintings, both on Paseo Fray Francisco.

Dining and Lodging

$$–$$$ ★ ✕ **El Portalón.** Between the dark, creaky wood floors and the ancient beams, pillars, and coats of arms, this famous 15th-century inn seems too good to be true. The Basque touch with products from the Castilian *meseta* is at its best here. Try the *lomo de cebón asado en su jugo con puré de manzanas* (filet mignon with apple puree) or any of the *merluza* (hake) preparations. Have the Ramonísimo for dessert and you'll smile all the way home. ✉ *C. Correría 151,* ☎ *945/142755. AE, DC, MC, V. Closed Sun., Aug. 10–31, and Dec. 23–Jan. 5.*

$$$ ✕🏨 **Canciller Ayala.** This modern structure is handy for in-town comfort, just two minutes from the old quarter over the lush green Parque de la Florida. The rooms, though unremarkable, are bright and streamlined. ✉ *C. Ramon y Cajal 5, Vitoria 01007,* ☎ *945/130000,* FAX *945/133505. 184 rooms. Restaurant, bar, parking (fee). AE, DC, MC, V.*

$$$ ★ ✕🏨 **Parador de Argómaniz.** Just a 10-minutes drive northeast of Vitoria, this 17th-century palace has panoramic views over the Alava plains and retains a powerful sense of mystery and romance, its long stone hallways punctuated by imposing antiques. Rooms have polished wood floors and huge, terra-cotta-floored bathrooms; some have glass-enclosed sitting areas and/or hot tubs. The vaulted dining room, a converted hayloft, makes breakfast feel like a baronial feast. ✉ *Carretera*

N-I, Km 363, Argómaniz 01192, ☎ 945/293200, FAX 945/293287. 54 rooms. Restaurant, bar, free parking. AE, DC, MC, V.

En Route Between Vitoria and Logroño, on the north bank of the Ebro River, is the wine-growing Rioja Alavesa region. Drive south on A2124 through the Puerto de Herrera pass to the Balcón de La Rioja for a sweeping view of the junction of Alava and the Ebro Valley.

Laguardia

29 *66 km (40 mi) southeast of Vitoria; 17 km (10 mi) west of Logroño.*

Laguardia is a fortified medieval town on a small piece of high ground overlooking the Ebro River and the vineyards of the **Rioja Alavesa**—that portion of wine country that falls in the Basque province of Alava. Walls, towers, and fortified portals are the leitmotifs, along with the many *bodegas* (wine cellars) where wine-tasting is an ongoing process. The 14th-century **Casa de la Primicia** is the town's oldest building. The church of **Santa María de los Reyes** is famous for its unique door, Spain's only polychrome 14th-century Gothic portal, protected by a posterior Renaissance facade.

Dining and Lodging

$$–$$$ ✕🏨 **Posada Mayor de Migueloa.** This 17th-century palace in the quiet pedestrian part of Laguardia has guest rooms built into original beams, walls, and tiles. The innovative cooking ranges from foie gras to *mollejas de cordero* (lamb sweetbreads) to roasts. ✉ *Mayor de Migueloa 20, 01300, ☎ 941/121175, FAX 941/121022. 8 rooms. Restaurant. AE, DC, MC, V. Closed Dec. 20–Jan. 20.*

$$ ✕🏨 **Marixa.** Foodies travel great distances to dine in Marixa's lovely restaurant, known for its excellent roasts, views, and value. The heavy, wooden interior is ancient and intimate, and the cuisine is Vasco-Riojano, combining the best of both worlds. Try the *menestra de riojana verduras* (a mixed-vegetable dish) or the *cordero asado a la parrilla* (lamb roasted over coals). The guest rooms are modern, cheery, and carpeted, with views over the medieval walls of Laguardia to the Ebro Valley beyond. ✉ *C. Sancho Abarca 8, ☎ 941/600165, FAX 941/600202. 10 rooms. AE, DC, MC, V. Closed mid-Dec.–mid-Jan.*

LA RIOJA

Producer of Spain's best wines, this microcosm of highlands, plains, vineyards, and the Ebro River basin is bordered by Navarre and Alava to the north and by Burgos, Soria, and Zaragoza to the south. The area's quarter of a million inhabitants are mainly along the Ebro, in the cities of Logroño, Haro, and Calahorra.

La Rioja's culture and wines both combine Atlantic and Mediterranean influences, as well as Basque tinges and the arid ruggedness of Iberia's central *meseta.* Drained by the Rivers Oja (hence the name *río oja*), Najerilla, Iruegua, Leza and Cidacos, the La Rioja is composed of the Rioja Alta (Upper Rioja), the moist and mountainous western end, and the Rioja Baja (Lower Rioja), the flatter and dryer eastern end, more Mediterranean in climate. Logroño, the capital, lies between the two. Occupied successively by Gascons, Romans, Moors, Navarrans, and Castilians, La Rioja was part of the Cantabrian duchy from 573 to 711. Asturian kings reconquered the region in 1023, and in 1076 Alfonso VI incorporated the region into the Crown of Castile. In the 15th and 18th centuries, La Rioja was part of Castile and Navarre and was later divided between the provinces of Burgos and Soria. La Rioja's original boundaries continued to be ignored throughout the 19th century, while petitions for *fueros* (special rights), such as those enjoyed by the Basques, were rejected. Finally, in 1980, the region regained the name La Rioja, and in 1982 it became a full-fledged Autonomous Community.

Logroño

30 *92 km (57 mi) southwest of Pamplona on N-III.*

La Rioja's capital is a busy city of 130,000 built over and around the Ebro River. A modern industrial center, Logroño has a lovely old quarter between its two bridges, bordered by the Ebro and the medieval walls. Breton de los Herreros and Muro Francisco de la Mata are the quarter's most characteristic streets, and La Rioja's four best religious structures are its dominant landmarks.

The 11th-century church of the **Imperial de Santa María del Palacio** is known as La Aguja (The Needle) for its pyramid-shape, 45-yard Romanesque-Gothic tower. The church of **Santiago el Real** (the Royal St. James), reconstructed in the 16th century, is noted for its equestrian statue of the saint (also known as Santiago Matamoros—St. James the Moorslayer), which presides over the main door.

San Bartolomé is a 13th- to 14th-century French-Gothic church with an 11th-century Mudejar tower and an elaborately sculpted 14th-century Gothic doorway. The **Catedral de La Redonda** is a landmark for its twin Baroque towers.

Many of Logroño's monuments, such as the elegant **Puente de Piedra** (Stone Bridge), were built as part of the Camino de Santiago pilgrimage route. The **Puerta del Revellín,** the **Palacio del Espartero,** and the **medieval walls** are worth tracking down.

Near Logroño, the **Roman bridge** and the ***mirador*** (lookout) at **Viguera** are the main sights in the lower Iregua Valley. The **Castillo de Clavijo,** another panoramic spot, is where Spain's patron saint, Santiago (St. James), mounted on a white stallion, is believed to have helped the Christians defeat the Moors. The **Leza (Cañon) del Río Leza,** not far away, is La Rioja's most dramatic canyon.

Dining and Lodging

Calle Laurel and its neighboring streets, including Travesía del Laurel, Calle de San Juan, and Travesía de San Juan, are collectively known as *el sendero de los elefantes* (the path of the elephants), an allusion to *trompas* (trunks), the Spanish expression for having a snootful. Each bar here is known for a speciality: Bar Soriano for its *"champis"* (*champiñones,* mushrooms); Blanco y Negro for its *sepia* (cuttlefish); Casa Lucio for *migas de pastor* (bread crumbs with garlic and chorizo) and *embuchados* (crisped, sliced lamb tripe); and La Travesía for *tortilla de patatas* (potato omelet). Order a *crianza*—red wine aged at least three years in an oak cask or bottle—and they'll break out the good crystal. A *cosechero* (wine of the year) is served in small shot glasses, while a *reserva* (specially selected grapes aged three years or more in oak cask and bottle) will elicit snifters for the proper swirling, smelling, and tasting.

$$ ✕ **El Cachetero.** Local dishes based on vegetables are the rule here, with roasts of goat and lamb also featured prominently. The cuisine is simple and homespun, and the raw materials are well known for freshness and seasonal relevance. ✉ *C. Laurel 3,* ☎ *941/228463. AE, DC, V. Closed Sun. and first half of Aug. No dinner Wed.*

$$$ ✕🏨 **Herencia Rioja.** This modern hotel near the old quarter has bright, comfortable rooms, a fine restaurant, and a healthy buzz about it. ✉ *Marqués de Murrieta 1, 26005,* ☎ *941/210222,* FAX *941/210206. 81 rooms, 2 suites. Restaurant, bar, cafeteria, exercise room. AE, DC, MC, V.*

La Rioja Alta

The Upper Rioja, the most prosperous part of the wine country, extends from the Ebro River to the Sierra de la Demanda. La Rioja Alta has the most fertile soil, the best vineyards and agriculture, the most impressive castles and monasteries, a ski resort at Ezcaray, and the historical economic advantage of being on the Camino de Santiago.

From Logroño drive 12 km (7 mi) west on route N120 to **Navarrete** to see its noble houses and the Baroque altarpiece in the Asunción church.

Nájera, 15 km (9 mi) west, was the court of the Kings of Navarre and capital of Navarre and La Rioja until 1076, when La Rioja became part of Castile and the residence of the Castilian royal family. The monastery of **Santa María la Real** (☎ 941/363650), "pantheon of kings," is distinguished by its 11th-century Claustro de los Caballeros (Cavaliers' Cloister), a Gothic nobles' cloister with lacy plateresque windows overlooking a grassy patio. The sculpted 12th-century tomb of Doña Blanca de Navarra is the monastery's most famous sarcophagus.

Santo Domingo de la Calzada, 20 km (12 mi) west of Santa María la Real on N120, has always been a key stop on the Camino. Santo Domingo was an 11th-century saint who built roads and bridges for pilgrims and founded the pilgrims' hospital that is now the town's parador. The cathedral is a Romanesque-Gothic pile containing the saint's tomb, choir murals, and an elaborate walnut altarpiece carved by Damià Forment in 1541. The live hen and rooster in a plateresque stone chicken coop commemorate a legendary local miracle in which a pair of roasted fowl came back to life to protest the innocence of a pilgrim hanged for theft. Don't miss a stroll through the town's beautifully preserved medieval quarter.

Enter the **Sierra de la Demanda** by heading south 14 km (9 mi) on LO-810. Your first stop is the town of **Ezcaray,** with its aristocratic houses emblazoned with family crests, of which the **Palacio del Conde de Torremúzquiz** (Palace of the Count of Torremúzquiz) is the most distinguished. Good excursions from here are the Valdezcaray winter-sports center; the source of the River Oja at Llano de la Casa; La Rioja's highest point, at the 7,494-ft Pico de San Lorenzo; and the Romanesque church of Tres Fuentes, at Valgañón.

The town of **San Millán de la Cogolla** is southeast of Santo Domingo de la Calzada. Take LO-809 southeast through Berceo to the Monasterio de Yuso, where a 10th-century manuscript on St. Augustine's *Glosas Emilianenses* is considered the first writing in Castilian Spanish. The nearby Visigothic Monasterio de Suso is where Gonzalo de Berceo, recognized as the first Castilian poet, recited his verse in the 13th century in *román paladino,* the Latin dialect that became the Castilian tongue and ultimately the language of more than 150 million people from the Mediterranean to the South China Sea.

31 **Haro,** 49 km (30 mi) west of Logroño, is the wine capital of La Rioja. Its architectural highlights are the Flamboyant Gothic church of **Santo Tomás,** a single-nave structure from 1564, and the **Basílica de la Vega,** with a figure of the valley's patron saint, La Virgen de Valvanera. Haro's old quarter and ancient taverns are charming, as are the cafés in the Plaza Mayor; local wines flow freely here, at local prices. The wine makers have clustered their *bodegas* in the legendary *barrio de la estación* (train-station district) ever since the railroad first opened in 1863. Guided tours of these hundred-year-old facilities and tasting sessions, some in English, can be arranged at the *bodegas* themselves or at the tourist office (☞ Close-up: Spain's Wine Country, *below*). The June 29 **Batalla del Vino** (Wine Battle) is a wet and epic brawl.

Close-Up

SPAIN'S WINE COUNTRY

THE EBRO RIVER BASIN HAS BEEN IDEAL HABITAT for grapevines since pre-Roman times. Rioja wines were first recognized in official documents in 1102, and exports to Europe flourished over the next several centuries. The phylloxera blight that ruined French vineyards in 1863 brought Spain both the expertise of Bordeaux vintners and an explosion in the demand for Spanish wine.

With its rich and uneroded soil, river microclimates, ocean moisture, and sun, La Rioja is ideally endowed for high-quality grapes. Shielded from the arid cold of the Iberian meseta (plain) by the Sierra de la Demanda and from the bitter Atlantic weather by the Sierra de Cantabria, Spain's prime wine country covers an area 150 km (93 mi) long and 50 km (31 mi) wide along the banks of the Ebro. The lighter limestone soils of the Rioja Alta's (Upper Rioja's) 50,000 acres produce the region's finest wines; the vineyards in the 44,000-acre Rioja Baja (Lower Rioja) are composed of alluvial and flood-plain clay in a warmer climate, ideal for the production of great volume.

The main grape of the Upper Rioja is the Tempranillo—so named for its early (*temprano*) ripening in mid-September—a dark, thick-skinned grape known for power, stability, and fragrance. Other varieties include the Mazuelo, used for longevity and tannin; and the Graciano, which lends aroma and freshness and makes high-quality wine. The Garnacha, the main grape of the Lower Rioja, is an ideal complement to the more acidic Tempranillo. The Viura, the principal white variety, is fresh and fragrant, while Malvasía grapes stabilize wines that will age in oak barrels.

Rioja wines are categorized according to age. Garantía de Origen is the lowest rank, assuring that the wine comes from where it purports to come from and has been aged for at least a year. A Crianza wine has aged at least three years, with at least one spent in oak. A Reserva is a more carefully selected wine also aged three years, at least one in oak. Gran Reserva is the top category, reserved for extraordinary harvests aged for at least two years in oak and three in the bottle.

Rioja wine is distinguished by the fact that most of it ages for a significant length of time in barrels made of old American oak, as opposed to most French wine, aged for less time in barrels made of new French oak. American oak is more porous, causing faster oxidation of the wine, which means more de facto aging in less time. Thus the average Rioja is deeper and smoother, whereas middle-range French wines are sharper and fruitier. The other difference is economic: a Rioja Reserva can cost under $10.

Wine and ritual overlap everywhere in La Rioja. The first wine of the year is offered to and blessed by the Virgin of Valvanera on the riverbank at the Espolón de Logroño. Haro's famous Batalla del Vino (Wine Battle) festival is famous throughout Spain. Everything from the harvest and the trimming of the vines to the digging of fermentation pools and the making of baskets, barrels, and *botas* (wine skins)—even the glassblowing craft employed in bottle manufacture—takes on a magical, almost religious significance here in this hallowed Bacchian haven.

For a tour of vineyards and wine cellars, start with **Haro,** filled with both world-famous *bodegas* (wineries) and stunning noble architecture. Haro's *barrio de la estación* has all of La Rioja's oldest and most famous bodegas. Call the **Carlos Serres** winery (✉ San Agustín s/n, ☎ 941/311308) for a tour of the process. The **Muga** *bodega* (☎ 941/310498) welcomes tasters at just about any hour. Other visits in the Upper Rioja could include **Fuenmayor,** an historic wine-making center with a lovely old quarter; **Cenicero,** with several ancient bodegas; **Briones,** a perfectly preserved Renaissance town; **Ollauri,** home to a lovely cave bodega, "the Sistine chapel of the Rioja"; and **Briñas,** with a wine exhibit.

Dining and Lodging

$$ ✕ **Terete.** A favorite with locals, this rustic place has been roasting lamb in wood ovens since 1877, and serves a delicious *minestra de verduras* (vegetable stew). It also has its own wine cellar, stocked with some of the Rioja's best. ✉ *C. Lucrecia Arana 17,* ☎ *941/310023. AE, DC, V. Closed Mon., July 1–15, and Aug. 15–30.*

$$$ ✕🏨 **Los Agustinos.** Haro's best hotel is built into a 14th-century monastery whose cloister (now a pleasant patio) is considered one of the best in La Rioja. Arches, a great hall, and tapestries complete the medieval look. ✉ *San Agustín 2, 26200,* ☎ *941/311308,* FAX *941/303148. 60 rooms. Restaurant, bar, cafeteria. AE, DC, MC, V.*

La Rioja Baja

La Rioja's eastern area is more Mediterranean than Castilian in climate and vegetation, bordering the plains of Navarre, Soria, and Aragón. Its main river, the Cidacos, joins the Ebro at Calahorra (population 20,000), the region's largest city.

Lower Rioja has a number of key sights, including **Alfaro**'s medieval houses and church of San Miguel; **Arnedo**'s Monasterio de Vico; **Cornago**'s castle, with its four towers (three conical, one rectangular); **Igea**'s Palacio del Marqués de Casa Torre; and **Enciso**'s Parque Jurásico (Jurassic Park), with dinosaur tracks 150 million years old. Ten kilometers (six miles) from Calahorra, there are castle ruins at **Quel. Autol** is the site of rock formations known as *El Picuezo y La Picueza* (roughly, Mr. and Mrs. Rockpile) for their resemblance to man and wife.

Calahorra

32 *46 km (29 mi) southeast of Logroño; 109 km (68 mi) northwest of Zaragoza.*

The birthplace of Roman orator and rhetorician Quintilian (teacher of Tacitus), Calahorra was founded by the Romans 2,000 years ago. You can explore the town's Roman and medieval remains by following the tour posted near Calahorra's ***ayuntamiento*** (town hall)—it covers the Quintilian monument, the Jewish quarter, and the medieval quarter along with the churches of San Andrés, Santiago, and San Celedonio. Ask for a map inside.

Calahorra's most important artistic and architectural riches are in the 12th-century **Catedral de Santa María,** on the site of what has been the regional bishopric since the 5th century. The building was restored in 1485 and completed in the 16th century. The choir is decorated with an intricately ornate screen; the Gothic side chapels and their altarpieces are spectacular; and the chapter room has sculpted alabaster saints as well as a Titian and a Zurbarán. The sacristy has a 15th-century monstrance known as El Ciprés (The Cypress), wrought in gold and silver. The **Museo Diocesano** (Diocesan Museum) displays Calahorra's finest art free of charge after the convent masses, until 1:30 PM; paid visits can be arranged by calling the museum's director, Don Angel Ortega (☎ 941/130098).

Dining and Lodging

$$ ✕ **La Taberna de la Cuarta Esquina.** This simple provincial tavern exemplifies the best of Spain: extraordinarily good and unpretentious food and service. Have a hearty roast or a *menestra de verduras* (vegetable stew). ✉ *Cuatro Esquinas 16,* ☎ *941/310023. AE, DC, V. Closed Tues. (except holidays) and July 12–31.*

$$$ ✕🏨 **Parador de Calahorra.** Calahorra's comfortable parador is the best place to spend a night in La Rioja's second city. The wooden, Castilian-style decor is elegant, and the restaurant serves typical Rioja home

cooking, with a focus on roasts and fresh vegetables. ✉ *Paseo Mercadal, 26500,* ☏ *941/130358,* FAX *941/135139. 60 rooms. Restaurant, bar, cafeteria. AE, DC, MC, V.*

The Sierra–La Rioja Highlands

The rivers forming the seven main valleys of the Ebro basin originate in the Sierra de la Demanda, Sierra de Cameros, and Sierra de Alcarama. These highlands have a character all their own.

The upper **Najerilla Valley** is La Rioja's mountain sanctuary and wildest corner, an excellent hunting and fishing preserve. The Najerilla River is a rich, weed-choked chalk stream and one of Spain's best trout rivers. The **Monasterio de Valvanera,** off C113 near Anguiano, houses the Virgen de la Valvanera, a 12th-century Romanesque-Byzantine wood carving of La Rioja's favorite icon, the Virgin and child. **Anguiano** is renowned for its Danza de los Zancos (Dance of the Stilts), held July 22, when dancers on wooden stilts run downhill into the arms of the crowd in the main square. At the valley's highest point are the Mansilla reservoir and the Romanesque **Ermita de San Cristóbal** (Hermitage of St. Christopher).

The upper **Iregua Valley,** off N111, has the prehistoric **Gruta de la Paz** caves at Ortigosa. The reservoir at **El Rasillo** is La Rioja's center for aquatic sports. **Villoslada del Cameros** is famous for its artisans, who make the region's traditional patchwork quilts, *almazuelas.* Climb to **Pico Cebollera** for a superb view of the valley. Work back toward the Ebro along the River Leza, through Laguna de Cameros and San Román de Cameros (known for its basket weavers), to complete a tour of the Sierra del Cameros.

The upper **Cidacos Valley** leads to the **Parque Jurásico** (Jurassic Park) at Enciso, famous for its dinosaur tracks. The main village in the upper **Alhama Valley** is **Cervera del Rio Alhama,** a center for handmade *alpargatas* (rope-sole shoes). Jews, Moors, and Christians lived here in harmony as long as 400 years after the Reconquest.

CANTABRIA, THE BASQUE COUNTRY, AND LA RIOJA A TO Z

Arriving and Departing

By Boat

Santander is linked year-round to Plymouth, England, by a twice-weekly car ferry. For information, contact **Brittany Ferries** in Santander (✉ Paseo de Pereda 27, Santander 39002, ☏ 942/220000 or 942/214500) or Plymouth (✉ Millbay Docks, Plymouth PL1 3EW, U.K., ☏ 0990/360360), or travel agencies in either country. Book at least six weeks in advance in summer, as the 24-hour passages are often sold out. Another such option is the twice-weekly ferry between Bilbao and Portsmouth; contact **Ferries Golfo de Vizcaya** (✉ Cosme Etxevarrieta 1, Bilbao 48009, ☏ 94/423–4477, FAX 94/423–5496).

By Bus

Daily bus service connects the major cities to Madrid. San Sebastián and Bilbao are especially well served. In Madrid, call the bus company **Continental Auto** for information (☏ 91/533–0400), or go right to the station at Calle Alenza 20.

By Car

Driving is the best way to see this part of Spain, and even the remotest points are an easy one-day drive from Madrid. From the capital, it's

240 km (149 mi) on the N-I or the A1 toll road to Burgos, after which you can take the N623 to complete the 390 km (242 mi) to Santander. The drive from Madrid to Bilbao is 397 km (247 mi); follow the N-I or A1 past Burgos to Miranda del Ebro, where you pick up the A68 into Bilbao. San Sebastián is 497 km (309 mi) from Madrid if you go via Bilbao and take the A8 toll road. Logroño is 333 km (200 mi) from Madrid via Soria, or 114 km (68 mi) east of Burgos on the N120.

By Plane

Sondika Airport (☎ 94/486–9301) is 11 km (7 mi) outside Bilbao. Iberia has regular connections from there to Madrid, Barcelona, France, and England. Smaller airports serve Santander, San Sebastián (at Hondarribia), Vitoria, and Pamplona, with less-frequent (twice-daily) service to Madrid and Barcelona.

By Train

Santander, Bilbao, San Sebastián, Pamplona, Vitoria, and Logroño are well served by direct trains from Madrid's Chamartín Station and, with a change or two, by trains from virtually every major city in Spain. Call **RENFE** in Madrid for information (☎ 91/563–0202).

Getting Around

By Bus

Bus service between the main cities and most smaller towns is comprehensive, but few have central bus stations where you can collect information; most have numerous bus companies leaving from different points in town. Ask at travel agencies, local tourist offices, or the following central bus stations: **San Sebastián** (✉ C. Sancho el Sabio 33, ☎ 943/463974). **Santander** (✉ C. Navas de Tolosa s/n, ☎ 942/211995). **Pamplona** (✉ C. Conde Oliveto 8, ☎ 948/223854). **Logroño** (✉ Avda. España 1, ☎ 941/235983).

By Car

This pocket of Spain is superbly covered by freeways. Because rural landscapes and small towns are some of the main attractions, a car is the ideal mode of transportation.

By Train

Trains are not the ideal way to travel this region, but many cities are connected by rail. The principal train stations: **Bilbao** (✉ Estación del Abando, C. Hurtado de Amezaga, ☎ 94/423–8623 or 94/423–8636). **San Sebastián** (✉ Estación del Norte, Avda. de Francia, ☎ 943/283089 or 943/283599; ✉ RENFE office, C. Camino 1, ☎ 943/426430). **Santander** (✉ C. Rodríguez near center of town, ☎ 942/210211; ✉ RENFE office, Paseo de Pereda 25, ☎ 942/212387 or 942/218567). **Pamplona** (✉ On road to San Sebastián, ☎ 948/130202). **Logroño** (✉ Pl. de Europa, ☎ 941/240202).

In addition, the regional train company **FEVE** (✉ Estación de FEVE, next to Estación de Abando, Bilbao, ☎ 94/423–2266) runs a delightful narrow-gauge train that winds through stunning landscapes. From San Sebastián, lines west to Bilbao and east to Hendaye depart from the Estación de Amara (✉ Pl. Easo 9, ☎ 943/450131 or 943/471852).

Contacts and Resources

Consulates

United Kingdom (✉ C. Alameda Urquijo 2, 8th floor, Bilbao, ☎ 94/415–7600 or 94/415–7722).

Emergencies

Police: ☎ 091.

Guided Tours

Travel agents in the major cities can suggest tours offered by local firms, usually in summer. Pamplona's tourist office keeps a list of private guides and interpreters for hire.

Jai-Alai

The best local *frontón,* from which the finest players depart for Miami and other jai-alai centers in the United States, is **Guernica Jai-Alai.** In Pamplona, try **Euskal Jai Berri** (✉ 6 km/4 mi outside town in Huarte, ☎ 948/331159 or 943/331160) or, in San Sebastián, **Galarreta Jai-Alai** (✉ On highway to Hernani, ☎ 943/551023), both of which host games on Thursdays and weekends.

Visitor Information

General information and pamphlets on all three Basque provinces (Alava, Vizcaya, and Guipúzcoa) are available at the Basque government building in **Vitoria** (✉ Parque de la Florida, ☎ 945/131321) and the tourist office in **San Sebastián** (✉ C. Fueros 1, ☎ 943/426282).

Local tourist offices: **Bilbao**'s main office is near the Teatro Arriaga (✉ Paseo del Arenal 1, ☎ 94/479–5770). There are additional offices outside the Guggenheim (Avda. Abandoibarra 2, ☎ no phone) and at the airport. **Guernica** (✉ Artekale 5, ☎ 94/625–5892). **Haro** (✉ Pl. Monseñor Florentino Rodriguez, ☎ 941/303366). **Logroño** (✉ C. Miguel Villanueva 10, ☎ 941/291260). **Pamplona** (✉ C. Duque de Ahumada 3, ☎ 948/220741). **San Sebastián** (✉ C. Reina Regente s/n, ☎ 943/481166). **Santander** (✉ Estación Marítimo, at ferry landing, ☎ 942/310708). **Vitoria** (✉ Edifício Europa, Avda. Gasteiz, ☎ 945/161598).

4 GALICIA AND ASTURIAS

In Spain's dense, green, misty northwest, Celtic-flavored Galicia and Asturias beckon with medieval villages amid exquisite mountains and quiet beaches. Follow the pilgrimage route of St. James; stand rapt before the cathedral in Santiago de Compostela; stand peacefully on the perilous Atlantic shore at A Coruña; watch silver light dance on a glacier lake beneath the snowcapped Picos de Europa; quaff hard cider in Villaviciosa; and feast on fresh seafood throughout.

By Deborah Luhrman

Updated by Edward Owen and Christine Cipriani

SPAIN'S MOST ATLANTIC region is en route to nowhere, an end in itself. Stretching west from the lonesome Castilian plains to the rocky seacoast, Asturias and Galicia incorporate verdant hills and vineyards, gorgeous *rías* (estuaries), and the country's wildest mountains, the Picos de Europa.

Northwestern Spain is all about green, rainy landscapes, stretching from your feet to the horizon. Ancient granite buildings wear a blanket of moss, and even the stone *horreos* (granaries) are built on stilts above the damp ground. Swirling fog and heavy mist help keep local folk tales of the supernatural alive and kicking. The guitar is replaced by the *gaita* (bagpipe), legacy of the Celts' settlements here in the 5th and 6th centuries BC.

Though Galicia and Asturias are off the beaten track for many foreigners, they are not undiscovered: Spanish families flock to these cool northern beaches and mountains each summer. The city of Santiago de Compostela, whose cathedral is said to house the remains of the apostle St. James, has drawn pilgrims and travelers for more than 900 years—and today's road to Santiago is the same one detailed in the first travel guide ever published, the Codex Calixtinus of 1130. Because so many medieval pilgrims made this journey, northwestern Spain is dotted with churches, shrines, and former hospitals. In the late 20th century the pilgrimage regained popularity among both the faithful and the athletic, with thousands now making the month-long, 700-km (435-mi) trek from the French border every year. Santiago de Compostela welcomed an astonishing 5 million people in 1999, for in addition to being the eve of the third millennium, this was a Holy Year—one in which St. James's Day, July 25, falls on a Sunday.

Asturias, north of the main pilgrim trail, has always maintained a separate identity, isolated by the rocky Picos de Europa. This is the only part of Spain never conquered by the Moors, so Asturian architecture shows little Arab influence. It was from a mountain base at Covadonga that the Christians won their first decisive battle against the Moors and launched the Reconquest of Spain, which, though it took some 700 years, made Spain one of the world's most uniformly Catholic countries.

Note that in the Gallego (Galician) language, the Castilian Spanish *plaza* (town square) is *praza* and the Castilian *playa* (beach) is *praia*. Closely related to Portuguese, Gallego sounds quite distinct from Castilian. Most Castilian road signs in Galicia have been spray-painted to reflect Gallego names.

Pleasures and Pastimes

Beaches

Having allowed unbridled development to tarnish the Costa del Sol, the Spanish government is now promoting the attractions of its northern beaches. The weather in this region is not reliable, but if the sun comes out, you can relax on the sand at Llanes, Ribadesella, Cudillero, Santa Ana (by Cadavedo), Luarca, Tapia de Casariego, Muros, Noya, O Grove, the Islas Cies, Boa, and Testal.

Dining

Galicia and Asturias are famous throughout Spain for their seafood. The quality of the fish is so high that chefs frown on drowning inherent flavors in heavy sauces or pungent seasonings; expect simplicity rather than spice. Fish specialties are *merluza a la gallega,* steamed hake in paprika sauce (Galicia) and *merluza a la sidra,* steamed hake in a tangy Asturian cider sauce (Asturias). Salmon and trout from Asturian rivers are additional treats. The *vieira* (scallop), symbol of the pilgrimage to Santiago, is popular in Galicia, where you can also find bars serving nothing but wine and *pulpo a feira* (boiled and broiled octopus) or *berberechos* (cockles). Ham lovers should try *lacón con grelos,* a baked shoulder of pork served with sautéed turnip tops. Cheeses are delicious all over northwestern Spain: try the tangy *queso Cabrales* (Asturian blue cheese) and the Galician *queso tetilla* (a semisoft cheese in the form of a woman's breast), delicious with *membrillo* (a fruit spread made from quince) for dessert. Valdeón cheese, from the remote Picos de Europa village of the same name, is one of the finest blue cheeses in the world, made from cow's milk and fat, then "perfumed." This damp region is also known for hearty stews—in Asturias try *fabada* (butter beans and sausage), and in Galicia *caldo gallego* (white beans, turnip greens, chickpeas, cabbage, and potatoes). Savory fish or meat pies called *empanadas* are native to Galicia; Asturians enjoy *entrecote con queso Cabrales,* steak topped with a sauce made of the local blue cheese.

The best Galician wine is the smooth, fragrant, white Albariño, perfect with seafood and fast being discovered abroad. The acidic Ribeiro wine is often served in a ceramic bowl rather than a glass. Asturias is known for its *sidra* (hard cider), served either carbonated or still. Brandy buffs should try Galicia's *queimada* (which superstitious locals claim is a witches' brew), made of potent, grappalike *orujo* mixed with lemon peel and sugar in an earthenware bowl, then set aflame and stirred until the desired amount of alcohol is burned off.

CATEGORY	COST*
$$$$	over 6,500 ptas.
$$$	4,500 ptas.–6,500 ptas.
$$	3,000 ptas.–4,500 ptas.
$	under 3,000 ptas.

**per person for a three-course meal, excluding drinks, service, and tax*

Fiestas

The **Festa do Chourizo en Sant Anton de Abedes** (St. Anthony of Abedes Sausage Festival), held January 17 in Verin (Ourense), includes a parade and, well, sausage appreciation in honor of the local patron saint. The **Procesión dos Fachos** (Procession of the Scarecrows, January 20), in Castro Caldelas (Ourense), features a torchlight procession commemorating the village's survival of a cholera outbreak in 1753.

On February 2, a stroll to any plaza may bring you face-to-face with a ritual rooster slaughter. During the **Fiesta del Gallo,** live roosters are publicly killed by young Galician and Asturian women dressed in white to celebrate Candlemas, the day Christ was first presented at the temple. This spectacle is not for vegetarians or the faint of heart—the cock is often buried alive or beaten to death with a club.

The first week of March, the **Fiesta del Queso** (Cheese Festival) in Arzúa, near A Coruña, celebrates food and folklore, including a cheese contest. Viveiro observes **Semana Santa** (Holy Week) with a barefoot procession of flagellants illuminated by hundreds of candles held by spectators and participants alike. Local bands and dance troupes perform at the **Asturian Festival of Music and Dance,** held in Oviedo in late May and early June. The program centers on folk traditions, but it also spotlights contemporary talent, including performance art. Street fairs highlight area crafts and cuisine. On June 14, the feast of **Corpus Christi,** Pontevedra celebrates flowers and the harvest: bearing religious icons on their shoulders, people parade through streets lined with carpets and tapestries. Neighborhood women begin collecting flowers weeks ahead of time, and complete the ritual tapestries the night before the parade.

The **Rapa das Bestas** (Taming of the Beasts—the breaking of wild horses) takes place in Sabuceda, near Pontevedra, the first Saturday in July. July 25 brings a **shepherds' festival** to Cangas de Onís and the Picos de Europa National Park, with bagpipe music and regional dances. **Día de Santiago** (St. James's Day), July 25, is celebrated grandly in Santiago with processions, fireworks, and the appearance of the dramatic *botafumeiro* (incense burner) at mass in the cathedral. The **Albariño Festival de los Vinos** (Wine Festival) enlivens Cambados the first Sunday in August. In Gijón, the last two weeks of August are filled with the **Fiesta de Muestras** (Exposition), which transforms Gijón into a street party complete with bullfights, sports matches, craft fairs, concerts, and all-night parties sponsored by the town council. On August 15, sailors and fishermen in Luarca celebrate the **Fiesta del Rosario** (Feast of the Rosary) by parading their boats through the harbor.

The **Procesión de las Mortajas** (Procession of the Shrouded), in Pobra do Carmiñal (A Coruña), happens the third Sunday in September. Following a tradition that dates from the 15th century, those who have been cured of illness, bad luck, or bad love prepare open coffins, lie in them, and are carried around the village in a procession. At O Grove's **Festa do Marisco** (Seafood Festival), the second Sunday in October, crowds feast on lobster, mussels, clams, *percebes* (black barnacles that look like tiny monster claws and taste something like squid), spiny *néora* crabs, shrimp, and more.

Lodging

The state-run parador chain has cornered the market on charming places to stay northwestern Spain. Galicia alone has nine paradors, three in elegant mansions and two in old fortresses. Other lodgings range from generic high-rises to friendly, family-run inns. Reservations are important between May and October, but not essential the rest of the year. Many rural monasteries provide simple lodgings at very reasonable prices. Contact the nearest Tourist Office of Spain or the parador reservation line for a list.

CATEGORY	COST*
$$$$	over 16,500 ptas.
$$$	12,500 ptas.–16,500 ptas.
$$	8,500 ptas.–12,500 ptas.
$	under 8,500 ptas.

** for a standard double room, excluding tax and breakfast.*

Sports and Outdoor Activities

With so much rugged wilderness, Spain's northwest has become the country's premier outdoor-adventure region. The Picos de Europa and the green hills of Galicia beg to be hiked, trekked, climbed, or just walked; other open-air diversions include horseback riding, canyon rappelling, bungie-jumping, and spelunking.

Ribadesella, Asturias, is the white-water capital of Spain. The season highlight is an international kayak race in August, which starts at Arriondas and finishes in Ribadesella. There are several other navigable waterways for kayakers, rafters, canoers, and jet skiers.

Exploring Galicia and Asturias

If you're driving from Castile–León, follow the end of the Camino de Santiago to Santiago de Compostela. From here, travel west to the beach-blessed historic town of Muros, then south to Pontevedra and the coves and fishing towns of the Rías Baixas. Venture north again to the thriving port of A Coruña before moving east to emerald-green Asturias to experience Oviedo, cider bars, apple orchards, and the jagged Picos de Europa.

No matter how many days you spend here, be prepared to fall in love with this magical region, and to remember it vividly after you leave. In Gallego they call the feeling *morriña,* an indescribable longing for a person or place you've left behind.

Numbers in the text correspond to numbers in the margin and on the Galicia and Asturias and Santiago de Compostela maps.

Great Itineraries

The best way to explore Galicia and Asturias is by car. Five days is enough to get a taste of each; seven days allows more leisurely explorations of the main towns and cities combined with stops in smaller villages. Ten days allows relaxed landloping through scenic countryside and a bit of downtime on the beach.

IF YOU HAVE 5 DAYS

Start in **Santiago de Compostela** ⑤–⑩, where you can easily spend a day and a half on the cathedral and old town. Drive north the second afternoon or evening to **A Coruña** ㉒ and devote day three to admiring the glass galleries on the harbor, exploring the old town, and visiting the Torre de Hercules, the world's oldest functioning lighthouse. On day four, head north for some of Spain's loveliest beaches (and slowest roads), stopping for a stroll around the hilly coastal town of **Viveiro** ㉖. Crossing into Asturias, stop in **Luarca** ㉘, a cozy village in a cove, and the lively coastal city of **Gijón** ㉚. End your tour by driving south to **Oviedo** ㉙, the provincial capital.

IF YOU HAVE 10 DAYS

Spend a day exploring the Camino villages of Samos, Sarria, Portomarín, **Vilar de Donas** ③, and **Leboreiro** ④ en route to **Santiago de Compostela** ⑤–⑩, your base for the next two nights. Over the next two days, visit the cathedral, wander the old town, and perhaps make an excursion to nearby **Pazo de Oca** ⑪, a restored Galician manor house, or **Padrón** ⑫, birthplace of the poet Rosalía de Castro. On day four, drive north to **A Coruña** ㉒, a lively, laid-back port city with a cosmopolitan atmosphere. Head up to the Rías Altas on day five, stopping in picturesque **Betanzos** ㉓ and **Mondoñedo** ㉕. Spend a night on the coast, in hilly **Viveiro** ㉖ or, farther east, **Ribadeo** ㉗, each with exceptional views of its estuary. Day six brings you to the seaside Asturian towns of **Luarca** ㉘, Avilés, and **Gijón** ㉚. On day seven, head inland for a day and night in lively **Oviedo** ㉙. Finally, drive to nearby **Cangas de Onís** ㉝, whence you can visit the famous 8th-century shrine of **Covadonga** ㉞ and spend two days in the spectacular **Picos de Europa National Park.**

When to Tour Galicia and Asturias

Summer is best for swimming and water sports. Spring and fall may be the ideal time to explore, as the weather is reasonable and crowds are few. Winter can be rainy to the point of saturation: not for nothing is this region called Green Spain.

THE CAMINO DE SANTIAGO

Santiago de Compostela, where the apostle St. James is said to be buried, was the third-most-important Christian site in the world during the Middle Ages, after only Jerusalem and Rome. Making the difficult pilgrimage to this remote corner of Spain all but ensured the faithful

Galicia and Asturias

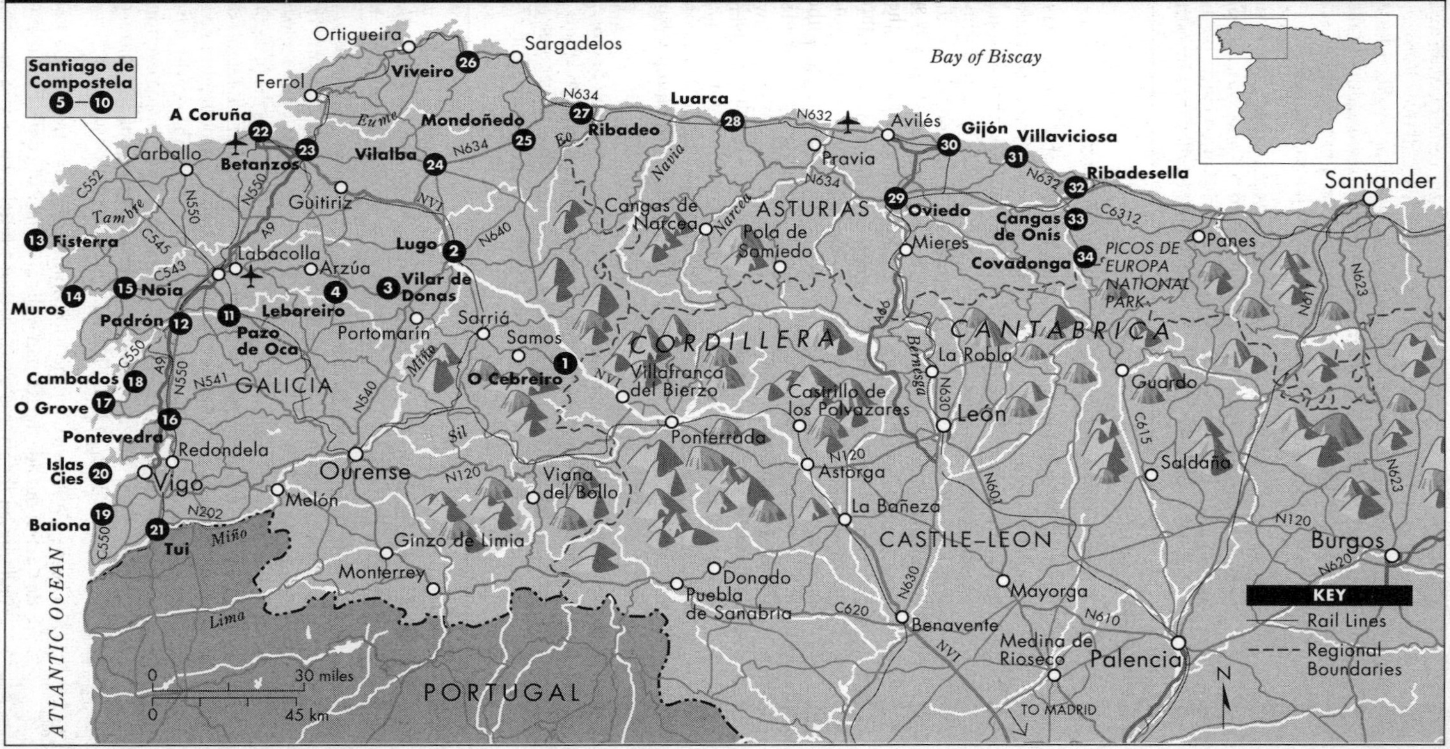

a place in heaven. At peak periods in the 12th century, as many as 2 million people a year traveled to Santiago from all over Europe, and the route was crowded with highway robbers; gallant knights, who swore to protect the pilgrims; and innkeepers, who grew wealthy in the pilgrim trade. There were even souvenir hawkers, providing the scallop shells that pilgrims wore as a symbol of St. James, a fisherman.

The main pilgrimage route, the *camino frances,* crosses the Pyrenees from France and crosses northern Spain, from Roncesvalles to Santiago, marked by scallop-shell signs. If you drive into Galicia on the N-VI from Castile–León, you enter what might be called the homestretch.

O Cebreiro

❶ *32 km (20 mi) northwest of Villafranca del Bierzo.*

From the N-VI at Puerto de Piedrafita, the Way of St. James veers left. Climb the steep, narrow road to O Cebreiro, one of the most unusual hamlets in Spain. Deserted and haunting outside high season (and often fogged-in or snowy to boot), O Cebreiro is a stark settlement built around a 9th-century church. Known for its round, thatched-roof stone huts called ***pallozas,*** the town has been perfectly preserved and is now an open-air museum showing how folks in these windswept mountains lived in the Middle Ages—indeed, lived up until a few decades ago. One hut is now a **museum** of the region's Celtic heritage. Higher up, at 3,648 ft, there's also a rustic 9th-century **sanctuary.**

Dining and Lodging

$ ✕🏨 **Hostal San Giraldo de Aurillac.** Next door to the church, this rural *hostal* offers simple home cooking and a good base for walking the mountains and imbibing the tremendous views. *✉ 27670 O Cebreiro, Lugo, ☎ 982/367125, FAX 982-367015. 15 rooms. Restaurant, bar. No credit cards.*

En Route From O Cebreiro the mountain road takes you through **Samos,** with a Benedictine monastery; **Sarria,** a medieval village with a pilgrims' hospital, La Magdalena; and **Portomarín,** on the Miño River, where the Romanesque church was moved—stone by stone—before a new dam flooded the town.

Lugo

❷ *31 km (19 mi) north of Sarria on C546, 26 km (16 mi) north of Portomarín on LU612*

Just off the A6 freeway, not far from the Camino de Santiago, Galicia's oldest provincial capital is most notable for its 2½-km (1½-mi) **Roman wall.** Built in the year 260, this is the world's last remnant of that particular epoch, and it still completely surrounds the pleasant old town. The walkway on top has good views of the circuit. Lugo's **cathedral** is a mixture of the Romanesque, Gothic, Baroque, and neoclassical styles; it's open daily from 8 AM to 8:30 PM. The nearby Baroque **ayuntamiento** (city hall) has a magnificent rococo facade overlooking the tree-lined Praza Maior. The **Museo Provincial** (✉ Plaza de la Soledad, ☎ 982/242112) has a large collection of sundials.

There's a good view of the Rio Miño valley from the **Parque Rosalía de Castro,** outside the Roman walls near the cathedral. The large white building on the river is a spa (part of a hotel), where you can visit the remains of the **Roman baths.**

Dining and Lodging

$$ ✕ **Mesón de Alberto.** This cozy venue is a classic for excellent Galician fare and professional service. The bar and adjoining *bodega* (win-

ery) serve plenty of *raciónes.* The *surtido de quesos Gallegos* provides generous servings of four local cheeses; ask for some *membrillo* (quince jelly) to go with them and the brown, crusty corn bread. The dining room upstairs offers an inexpensive set menu, but you might elect to splurge on your choice from the huge selection of Gallego gastrology. ✉ *Cruz 4,* ☎ *982/228310. AE, DC, MC, V. Closed Sun.*

$$$$ **Gran Hotel Lugo.** Set in a garden near the Plaza Mayor but outside the city walls, the Gran Hotel is both modern and elegant. The spacious, comfortable rooms, decorated in shades of yellow and brown, look out on either the garden swimming pool or a broad street. ✉ *Avenida Ramón Ferreiro 21, 27002,* ☎ *982/224152,* FAX *982/241660. 156 rooms, 12 suites. Restaurant, pool, parking (fee). AE, DC, MC, V.*

Vilar de Donas

❸ *27 km (17 mi) southwest of Lugo.*

Southwest of Lugo, turn right in Ferradal, pass the picnic ground, and stop at the little **church** in Vilar de Donas to pay tribute to the knights of St. James, whose tombs line the inside walls. The afternoon sun uncannily spotlights carved-stone depictions including the horizontal body of Christ. Portraits of the two medieval noblewomen who built the church are mixed with those of the apostles in the 15th-century frescoes on the apse.

Leboreiro

❹ *38 km (23 mi) west of Vilar de Donas.*

West of Vilar de Donas, the countryside flattens out. Just after the sign for Kilometer 42, turn left for Leboreiro, a farming hamlet with simple medieval stone houses surrounding a **Romanesque church.** On the west side of town, a stretch of the ancient pilgrims' road, paved with granite boulders, and an old bridge are surprisingly intact.

Santiago de Compostela

★ *277 km (172 mi) west of León, 650 km (403 mi) northwest of Madrid.*

Santiago de Compostela was built to impress. Imagine pilgrims walking across Spain for 30 days and finally arriving at the foot of Santiago's great cathedral: the sheer scale of this opulent building is awe-inspiring, its main doors raised two stories above the airy Praza do Obradoiro. The twin graduated towers create a sense of harmony, and a benign St. James, dressed in pilgrim's costume, looks down from his perch. A palpable sense of mystic significance, enhanced by Galicia's misty otherworldliness, and a large, lively university make Santiago one of the most exciting cities in Spain.

One starry night in the year 813, a hermit was directed by a divine light to a field just outside present-day Santiago. He set a dig in motion, and religious leaders unearthed a sarcophagus said to contain the remains of St. James. (The name Compostela probably comes from the Latin *campus stellae,* field of stars.) While James was believed to have preached in Iberia at one point, the means of his posthumous arrival in Galicia remains a mystery; one legend says that after James was beheaded by King Herod, his body floated to Spain in a stone boat, then lay hidden for centuries.

The discovery came at a time when the Moors ruled most of the country, and only a fragment of the Christian army remained. According to those Christian soldiers, it was St. James, armed with a great sword and riding a white charger, who led them to their first victory against the Moors in Clavijo in 844. James thus earned himself the nickname Santiago Matamoros (St. James the Moorslayer) and became the patron saint of Spain. Carrying his banner throughout the Reconquest, the Christians went on to expel the Moors from Spain and conquer much of the Americas.

5 From the **Praza do Obradoiro,** climb the two flights of stairs to the
6 main entrance to Santiago's **cathedral.** The facade is Baroque, yet just inside is one of the finest Romanesque sculptures in the world, the **Pórtico de la Gloria.** Completed in 1188 by Maestro Mateo, this is the cathedral's original entrance, its three arches carved with biblical figures from the Apocalypse, the Last Judgment, and Purgatory. On the left are the prophets; in the center, Jesus is flanked by the four Evangelists (Matthew, Mark, Luke, and John) and, above them, the 24 Elders of the Apocalypse playing celestial instruments. Just below Jesus is a serene St. James, poised on a carved column: look carefully and you'll see five smooth indentations, formed by the millions of pilgrims who have placed their hands here over the centuries. On the back of the pillar, people lean forward to touch foreheads with the likeness of Maestro Mateo in the hope that his genius can be shared.

Dressed in a sumptuous jeweled cloak, St. James presides over the gold and silver **high altar.** Climb the stairs behind the altar to stand at the cathedral's focal point, surrounded by a dazzling array of Baroque decoration, sculpture, and drapery. Here, as the grand finale of their spiritual journey, pilgrims embrace St. James and kiss his cloak. Beneath the altar in the ancient crypt are the alleged remains of St. James and two of his disciples, St. Theodore and St. Athenasius.

A pilgrims' mass is celebrated every day at noon. On special, somewhat unpredictable occasions, a *botafumeiro* (huge incense burner) is attached to the thick ropes hanging from the ceiling and prepared for a famous and fabulous ritual at the end of the pilgrims' mass: as small flames burn inside, eight strong laymen artfully play the ropes to swing the huge vessel in a massive semicircle across the apse. In earlier centuries, this rite served as an air freshener—by the time pilgrims reached Santiago, they smelled, shall we say, ripe. Spanish national television broadcasts this ceremony live on St. James's Day, July 25.

A botafumeiro and other cathedral treasures are on display in the **museums** downstairs and next door—mainly the latter, which explains and partly reconstructs the cathedral's erstwhile Romanesque choir. ✉ *Praza do Obradoiro,* ☎ *981/560527 or 981/583548.* 🎟 *Cathedral free; combined museum ticket 500 ptas.* ⊙ *Cathedral daily 7:30–9; museums July–Oct., Mon.–Sat. 10–1:30 and 4–7:30, Sun. 10–1:30 and 4–7; Nov.–June, Mon.–Sat. 11–1 and 4–6, Sun. 10–1:30.*

On the right (south) side of the nave is the **Porta das Praterías** (Silversmiths' Door), the only purely Romanesque part of the cathedral's facade. The statues on the portal were cobbled together from various parts of the cathedral, giving the result an amusingly motley look. The double doorway opens onto the graceful **Praza das Platerías,** named for the silversmiths' shops that used to line it. The praza's fountain is a popular rest stop in nice weather.

Behind the cathedral, the wide **Praza da Quintana** is the haunt of young travelers and folk musicians in summer. The **Porta Santa** (Holy Door) is open only during those years in which St. James's Day falls on a Sunday (most recently, 1999).

As you pass under the Arco del Arzobispo (Archbishop's Arch) and return to the Praza do Obradoiro, stop into the rich 12th-century
7 **Pazo de Xelmírez** (Palace of Archbishop Xelmírez), an unusual example

Santiago de Compostela

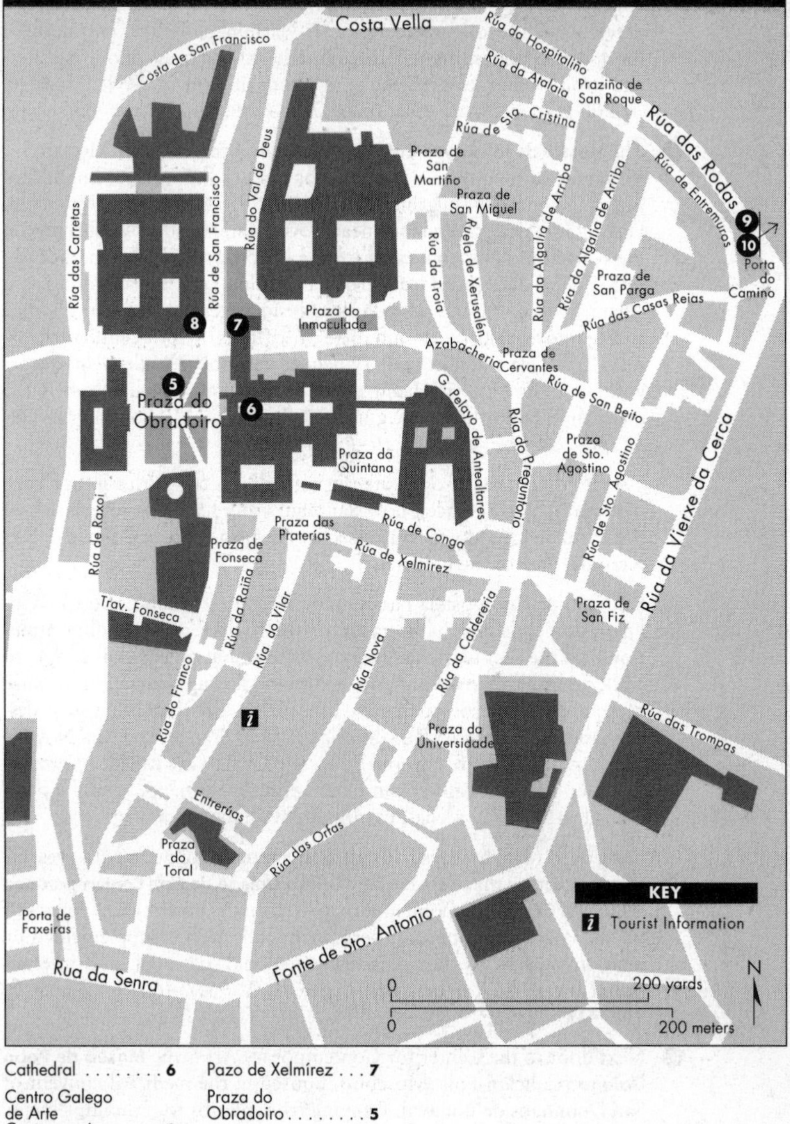

Cathedral 6
Centro Galego de Arte Contemporánea 9
Hostal de los Reyes Católicos 8
Museo de Pobo Galego 10
Pazo de Xelmírez . . . 7
Praza do Obradoiro 5

of Romanesque civic architecture with a wonderfully cool, clean, vaulted dining hall. The little figures carved on the corbels in this graceful, 100-ft-long space are heart-warmingly lifelike, partaking of food, drink, and music with great medieval gusto. Each one is different; stroll around for a tableau of mealtime merriment. ☎ *981/572300.* *200 ptas.* *Easter–Oct. only, Tues.–Sun. 10–1:30 and 4:30–7:30.*

8 The **Hostal de los Reyes Católicos** (Hostel of the Catholic Monarchs), facing the cathedral from the left, was built in 1499 by Ferdinand and Isabella to house the pilgrims who slept on Santiago's streets every night. Having fortified travelers for nearly 500 years, it's the oldest refuge in the world, and was converted from a hospital to a luxury parador in 1953. The plateresque facade bears a Castilian coat of arms along with Adam, Eve, and various saints; inside, the four arcaded patios are adorned with gargoyle rainspouts said to be caricatures of 16th-century townsfolk. There's a small art gallery behind the lobby. Walk-in spectators without room keys risk being asked to leave, but you can tour in the company of an official city guide. ✉ *Praza do Obradoiro 1,* ☎ *981/582200.* *Free.* *Daily 10–1 and 4–6.*

The building directly opposite the cathedral is the 18th-century **Pazo de Raxoi** (Rajoy Palace), now Santiago's city hall. The fourth side of the Praza do Obradoiro is enclosed by the 16th-century **Colexio de San Xerome,** part of the university.

Santiago de Compostela packs many old *pazos* (manor houses), convents, and churches that in most towns would receive headline attention. But the best way to spend your remaining time here is simply to walk around the **casco antiguo** (old town), losing yourself in its maze of stone-paved narrow streets and little plazas. The most beautiful pedestrian thoroughfares are Rúa do Vilar, Rúa do Franco, and Rúa Nova—portions of which are covered by arcaded walkways called *soportales,* designed to keep walkers out of the rain. In Santiago, even the postcards feature rainy scenes, casting the wet stone in a poetic light.

Long open to all byways and cultures, Santiago connects with present-
9 day creativity in the relatively new **Centro Galego de Arte Contemporánea** (Galician Center for Contemporary Art), on the north side of town just off the Porta do Camino. A permanent collection is supplemented by temporary exhibits, both featuring regional, national, and international artists. ✉ *Rúa de Valle Inclán s/n,* ☎ *981/546629.* *Free.* *Tues.–Sun. 11–8..*

10 Next door to the Center for Contemporary Art is the **Museo de Pobo Galego** (Galician Folk Museum), housed in the medieval convent of San Domingos de Bonaval. Ranging from photos to farm implements to models of homes, horreos, and ships, these displays illustrate various aspects of traditional Galician life—the sea, the countryside, crafts, dress, and the arts. The star attraction is a part of the building itself: a 13th-century self-supporting spiral granite staircase that still connects three floors. ✉ *Rúa de Bonaval,* ☎ *981/583620.* *Free.* *Mon.–Sat. 10–1 and 4–7.*

Dining and Lodging

$$$$ ✕ **Don Gaiferos.** Pablo Villar has run Santiago's most distinguished restaurant for almost a decade. Next door to the church of Santa Maria Salomé, the venue is as timeless as its surroundings. If large prawns stuffed with smoked salmon aren't enough to tempt you, know that they're served in a subdued romantic setting with a variety of white Ribeiro wines. The spicy fish stew is enough for two; try to save room for the *leche frita* (fried cream) or delectable bilberry cheesecake. ✉ *Rúa Nova 23,* ☎ *981/583894. Closed Sun. AE, DC, MC, V.*

$$$ ✕ **A Barrola.** Feeling adventurous? The usual tapa here is *oreja con patatas* (ear with potatoes), a Spanish delicacy. With lots of polished wood, a niche with wine and travel books, and a summer terrace, this classy seafood tavern is a favorite with university faculty. If you're not up for pigs' ears, the large house salads, mussels *con santiaguiños* (with the meat of a small crab), *arroz con bogavante* (rice with squid, lobster, and other shellfish), and thick empanadas of tuna and salt cod are equally tasty. ✉ *Rúa do Franco 29,* ☎ *981/577999. AE, MC, V. No dinner Sun.*

$$$ ★ ✕ **Anexo Vilas.** Owner Moncho Vilas likes to mingle with his happy customers and loves to promote Galician cuisine. His cooking has won acclaim from Spanish gourmets; he even prepared a banquet for Pope John Paul II when the pontiff visited Santiago in 1989. Specialties include salmon with clams, *merluza a la gallega* (hake with paprika sauce) or *a la vasca* (in a green sauce), and a tender steak with garlicky potatoes. ✉ *Avda. Villagarcia 21,* ☎ *981/598387. AE, DC, MC, V.*

$$$ ✕ **O Papa Upa.** For traditional Galician food in a lively setting, come here with an appetite: in addition to a decadent assortment of shellfish, the house specialty is the entrecôte Papa Upa, a massive T-bone steak. Chase your meal as the locals do—partake in the "rite of burning firewater" with *queimada,* a potent, flaming drink served with a flourish in a ceramic bowl. ✉ *Rúa da Raiña 18,* ☎ *981/566598. AE, DC, MC, V.*

$$ ✕ **Carretas.** Upbeat yellow walls make a nice casual setting for fresh Galician seafood around the corner from the parador. Fish dishes are plenty, but the house specialty is shellfish: for the full experience, order the labor-intensive *variado de mariscos,* a scrumptious platter of langostinos, king prawns, crab, and barnacles, complete with shell-cracker. *Salpicón de mariscos* presents the same creatures pre-shelled. *Rúa de Carretas 21,* ☎ *981/563111. Closed Sun. AE, DC, MC, V.*

$$$$ ★ ✕🏨 **Hostal de los Reyes Católicos.** If you're drawn to the idea of sleeping in a national monument—on the Praza do Obradoiro, no less—look no further. Behind the parador's 15th-century facade are four two-story courtyard patios, each surrounded upstairs by windowed, carpeted hallways filled with sofas and chairs. Guest rooms are furnished with antiques spanning five centuries, and some have canopy beds. On the down side, rooms are rather dark and are not carefully decorated; remnants of the 1970s diminish the late-medieval splendor of the building. Libredón, the grand, vaulted dining room, serves top-notch regional cuisine and is well worth a trip whether you stay here or not. The tapas bar, Enxebre, is lively and informal. ✉ *Praza do Obradoiro 1, 15705,* ☎ *981/582200,* FAX *981/563094. 136 rooms. 2 restaurants, bar, car rental, parking (fee). AE, DC, MC, V.*

$$$ ★ 🏨 **Pazo Cibrán.** This charmingly restored 18th-century Galician farm mansion is a 20-minute drive from Santiago in rolling countryside. Owner Mayka Iglesias maintains six rooms in the main house and five large rooms in the old stable. The antiques-packed living room overlooks rambling gardens with camellias, magnolias, palms, vines, and a bamboo walk; there's even a library with valuable tomes. Huge breakfasts are served in the *pazo* itself, with lunch and dinner available in the nearby Casa Roberto, another converted house. To get here, take the N525 Ourense road from Santiago and turn right at Kilometer 11, after the gas station. ✉ *San Xulián de Sales, 15885,* ☎ *981/511515. 11 rooms. Breakfast room, library. AE, DC, MC, V.*

$$ ★ 🏨 **Casa-Hotel As Artes.** Steps from the cathedral, this little inn is almost overshadowed by the Hostal de los Reyes Católicos, but in fact offers sunny, old-world quarters for a fraction of the price. Each room has at least one stone wall, recessed windows with beveled wood shutters, polished hardwood floors, and a wrought-iron double bed; and

each is named after a different artiste and decorated accordingly. (The Vivaldi room, for instance, has tasteful music-manuscript curtains.) Robes and slippers are provided, and there's a tiny wooden sauna behind reception. ✉ *Travesía de Dos Puertas 2 (off Rúa San Francisco), 15707,* ☎ *981/572590 or 981/555254,* FAX *981/577823. 7 rooms. Bar, breakfast room, sauna. AE, DC, MC, V. Closed Jan.*

$$ ★ **Hotel-Residencia Costa Vella.** Backed by a perfect little garden, this special inn snuggles right up to Santiago's medieval wall at one of the highest points in the city. The house is classically Galician, but the interior is awash in smooth blond wood and natural light from floor-to-ceiling windows—the better to behold the garden, stone wall, red-tile rooftops, Baroque convent of San Francisco, and green hills beyond. (Ask for a garden view.) The expert decor would look fine in a magazine, from the cheerful yellow wash of the hallways to stylish, mostly red and coral upholsteries to blinding-white bathrooms with primary-color blips. The glass extends to an airy breakfast room and reading area. ✉ *Rúa Porta da Peña 17, 15704,* ☎ *981/569530,* FAX *981/569530. 28 rooms. Bar, breakfast room, lounge. AE, MC, V.*

Nightlife and the Arts

Santiago's nightlife peaks on Thursday night, as many students spend weekends at home with their families. For up-to-date information on concerts, films, and clubs, pick up the student-run magazine *Compostelan* at any newsstand. Bars and seafood-themed tapas joints line the old streets south of the cathedral, particularly **Rúa do Franco, Rúa da Raiña, and Rúa do Vilar.** A great first stop, especially if you haven't eaten dinner, is **Rúa de San Clemente,** off the Praza do Obradoiro, where three bars in a row offer two or three plates of tapas free with each drink, an astonishing value. **O Beiro** (✉ Rúa da Raiña 3, ☎ 981/581370) is a rustic wine bar with a stylish, laid-back professional crowd. **La Trinidad** (✉ San Clemente 6, ☎ 981/583392) is popular with students. The city's most popular dance club is **Casting,** built beneath the glass-bottom pool in the Meliá Araguaney hotel (✉ Alfredo Brañas 5, ☎ 981/595900); you must be dressed well to enter. **Retablo Concerto** (✉ Rúa Nova 13) is a cozy yet cool alternative with live music and less flash. **El Yate** (✉ Sendra 24) is packed around 5 AM for its *chocolate con churros* (thick hot chocolate with strips of fried dough).

The **Auditorio de Galicia** hosts a world-class program of classical music and jazz; the tourist office has details.

The **Hostal de los Reyes Católicos** (☞ *above*) hosts a classical-music course from July 20 to August 10 each summer. Some 150 musicians from several countries participate, and free concerts are held nightly in the hotel's lovely performance hall.

Shopping

ARTS AND CRAFTS

Look for beautifully crafted jewelry with the black stone *azabache* (jet), a dense form of local lignite coal, at **Antonio Uzal Vázquez** (✉ Abril Ares 8). The boutique founded in 1906 and run by **Augusto Otero** (✉ Casa de Cabildo, Praza de Praterías) has fine handcrafted silver. On a tiny lane off Azabachería, **Noroeste** (Ruela de Xerusalén 0, 981/577130) sells contemporary handmade jewelry in gold and silver. Santiago's best leather shop is **Bolchetta,** in the Meliá Araguaney hotel (✉ Alfredo Brañas 5, ☎ 981/595900).

Women in the fishing town of Camariñas fashion exquisite lace collars and scarves as well as table linens. The best place to buy their work, and watch some of it being crafted, is **Bolillos** (✉ Rúa Nova 40, ☎ 981/589776).

Galicia is known throughout Spain for its distinctive blue-and-white ceramics with bold modern designs, made in Sargadelos and O Castro. Peruse a wide selection at **Sargadelos** (✉ Rúa Nueva 16).

Pazo de Oca

⓫ *27 km (17 mi) southeast of Santiago.*

The feudal barons who controlled Galicia's peasant society lived in country manor houses like this one, known as *pazos*. Walk through the gardens to the lily pond and lake, where a stone boat stays miraculously afloat. *☎ 981/587435. 🎫 500 ptas, free Mon. 9–12:30. ⏲ Daily sunrise–sunset.*

Padrón

⓬ *18 km (11 mi) south of Santiago.*

Having grown up beside the Roman port of Iria Flavia, Padrón is where the body of St. James is believed to have washed ashore after its miraculous maritime journey. More recently, Padrón was the birthplace of one of Galicia's heroines, the 19th-century poet Rosalía de Castro. The lovely **Casa-Museo de Rosalía,** where she lived with her husband, an historian, now displays family memorabilia. *✉ Carretera de Herbón, ☎ 981/811204. 🎫 200 ptas. ⏲ Apr.–Sept., Tues.–Sun. 9:30–2 and 4–8; Oct.–Mar., Tues.–Sun. 9:30–1:30 and 4–7.*

The town is just as well known for its delicious *pimientos de Padrón*, tiny green peppers fried and sprinkled with sea salt. The fun in eating these is that one in five or so is spicy-hot. Galicia's biggest **food market** is held here every Sunday, with vendors selling regional fare in tents.

THE COSTA DA MORTE AND THE RÍAS BAIXAS

West of Santiago, scenic C543 leads to the coast. Straight west, the shore is windy, rocky, and treacherous—hence its name, the "Coast of Death." The series of wide, quiet estuaries south of here is called the Rías Baixas (Low Estuaries). The hilly drive takes you through a green countryside dappled with vineyards, tiny farms, and Galicia's trademark horreos, most with a cross at one or both ends.

Fisterra

⓭ *50 km (31 mi) west of Santiago, 75 km (48 mi) southwest of A Coruña.*

There was a time when this lonely, windswept outcrop over raging waters was thought to be the end of the earth—the "*finis terrae.*" (The site's Castilian name is Finisterre.) The known western world sank into the ocean here with a flourish of rocky beaches. All that's left for today's adventurers is a run-down stone *faro* (lighthouse) perched on a cliff; though it's not officially open to the public, you might find the door open. Gazing out at the vast, gray Atlantic from this dilapidated structure can, as George Borrow wrote in the 19th century, "fill the heart with uneasy sensations."

Aside from legends, the only draw in this tiny seaside town is its pleasant (barring storms) main plaza and, just off the plaza's southeast corner, the 12th-century church of **Santa Maria das Areas.** Romanesque, Gothic, and Baroque elements combine in the impressive but rather gloomy facade. *🎫 Free. ⏲ June–Sept., daily 9–2 and 3–6; Oct.–May, daily 10–2 and 4–6.*

Muros

14 *55 km (34 mi) southeast of Fisterra, 65 km (40 mi) southwest of Santiago.*

The cheerful harbor town of Muros is a popular summer resort with lovely, arcaded streets framed by Gothic arches. Nearby Point Louro has good beaches; try Praia de San Francisco or Praia de Area. The bay is dotted with mussel-breeding platforms.

Noia

15 *30 km (19 mi) east of Muros, 36 km (22 mi) west of Santiago.*

The Gothic church of **San Martín** faces resolutely out to sea from this historic town, and gravestones in the medieval **cemetery** bear mysterious Celtic inscriptions. The best places to swim and sun are the Testal and Boa beaches.

Pontevedra

16 *55 km (34 mi) southeast of Noia, 59 km (37 mi) south of Santiago.*

Poised at the head of its *ría,* Pontevedra is the largest city on Spain's west coast after A Coruña. You approach through prefab suburbs, but Pontevedra's old quarter is charming, well preserved, and largely undiscovered. Speckled with bars, it's lively to the point of rowdiness on weekends.

On the western edge of the maze of granite-block streets and plazas is the 16th-century seafarers' church of **Santa María Mayor,** with a plateresque facade, some lovely, sinuous vaulting, and, at the back of the nave, a Romanesque portal.

★ Pontevedra's **Museo Provincial** is a hidden treasure, housed in two 18th-century mansions connected by a stone bridge. Here you're presented with motley facets of Galician history, beginning with a succession of prehistoric and merely ancient objects, including some incredible Celtic jewelry. The second display is a collection of silver from all over the world; moving into the second mansion, you see carved *azabache* (jet) objects, some 17th- and 18th-century etchings and prints of St. James, and several large model ships. Upstairs, the windows in the ceramics room have photogenic views of the neighboring houses and streets. Farther into this floor are drawings and paintings of daily life by 20th-century artists, including caricatures by the Galician nationalist Alfonso Castelao. The original kitchen in this building is intact, complete with stone fireplace; nearby, take the tiny, steep wooden stairs down to the reconstructed captain's chamber on the battleship *Numancia,* which limped back to Spain after the Dos de Mayo battle with Peru in 1866. Completing the loop, upstairs in the first building, are Spanish and Italian paintings and some inlay work. One clever room contains only a 16th-century banquet table and paintings of Spanish food. ✉ *Praza de Leña,* ☏ *986/851455.* 🎫 *200 ptas.* ⏲ *July–Sept., Tues.–Sat. 10–12:15 and 5–8:45, Sun. 11–2; Oct.–June, Tues.–Sat. 10–1:30 and 4:30–8, Sun. 11–2.*

Dining and Lodging

$$ ★ ✕ **Casa Solla.** Owner Pepe Solla makes the most of the bountiful harvest from local coasts and vineyards at his terraced garden restaurant, 2 km (1 mi) outside town toward O Grove. Try the sole in Albariño wine sauce, filet mignon in red wine, and, in summer, fresh figs with Cabrales cheese. ✉ *Avda. Sireiro 7, Km 2, San Salvador de Poio,* ☏ *986/872884. AE, DC, MC, V. Closed Dec. 24–Jan. 2. No dinner Sun.*

$$$ ✕🏨 **Casa del Barón (Parador de Pontevedra).** A 16th-century manor house built on the foundations of an ancient Roman villa in the heart of the old quarter, this relatively dark parador has a baronial stone stairway winding up from the front lobby. Guest rooms have recessed windows with lace curtains and large wooden shutters; some face a small rose garden. The restaurant, which serves tasty seafood and meat dishes, is full of antique mirrors, candelabras, and portraits. ✉ *Barón 19, 36002,* ☎ *986/855800,* FAX *986/852195. 45 rooms. Restaurant, bar, café, library. AE, DC, MC, V.*

En Route Driving west on the C550 you'll pass Albariño vineyards, their vines trained along trellises. It's not uncommon, as you tool through small towns, to see a donkey helping out with cartage.

O Grove

17 *20 km (12 mi) northwest of Pontevedra, 75 km (47 mi) south of Santiago.*

The maritime town of O Grove (El Grove in Castilian) throws an illustrious shellfish festival the second week of October, but you can enjoy the day's catch in taverns and restaurants year-round. From here you can cross a pretty bridge to the island of **A Toxa** (La Toja), famous for its spas. Legend has it that a man abandoned an ailing donkey here and found it up on all fours, fully rejuvenated, upon his return; the waters are still said to have peculiar healing properties. The island's south side has a lovely, fat-palmed, manicured garden anchored on one side by the **Capilla de San Sebastián,** a tiny church covered from head to toe in cockle shells.

Dining

$$$ ✕ **Crisol.** Many and varied sea creatures greet you from an aquarium as you enter this secluded eatery, and sure enough, the menu features lobster, shrimp, spider crabs, scallops, and freshly caught fish. If you can't make up your mind, a house stew (*sopa de pescados mixtos*) combines most of the above. Save room for the regional dessert, *torta dulce de nueces,* a rich, dense almond cake glazed with honey and powdered sugar. ✉ *Hospital 12,* ☎ *986/730029. AE, DC, MC, V. Closed Mon. and Oct.–Easter.*

$$$$ ✕🏨 **Gran Hotel de La Toja.** Extravagant and exorbitant (for the region), this sybaritic Spanish version of Belle Epoque elegance—a classic spa hotel—is beautifully sited on the breezy island just off O Grove, surrounded by pine trees. Guest rooms are simple, their charm slightly faded compared to the grandiose formality of the foyers and salons. The dining areas have expansive sea views. ✉ *36991 Isla de la Toja,* ☎ *986/730025,* FAX *986/730026 or 986/731201. 197 rooms. Restaurant, pool, spa, 9-hole golf course, tennis court, health club, beach, casino, dance club. AE, DC, MC, V.*

Nightlife

Try your luck at **Casino La Toja** (✉ ☎ 986/731000), steps from the Gran Hotel.

Cambados

18 *34 km (21 mi) north of Pontevedra, 53 km (33 mi) south of Santiago.*

This breezy seaside town has a charming, almost entirely residential **old quarter.** The impressive main square, **Praza de Fefiñanes,** is bordered on almost two sides by the imposing 17th-century Pazo de Fefiñanes, now an Albariño bodega.

Dining and Lodging

$$$ ★ ✕ **O' Arco.** Dripping with antiques and charm, the older and smaller of O' Arco's two dining rooms is warmed by a fire on chilly evenings. The list of fish is mouthwatering, and the succulent *lomo de merluza ó Albariño* (fillet of hake in Albariño-wine sauce) fulfills its promise as a Cambados specialty, celebrating the fruit of the local vine. You can also order a shellfish feast for two. Word to the wise: *especial filloas* are light, decadent sugared crepes. Reserve a table in the old room if possible, as there aren't many. ✉ *Rúa Real 14,* ☎ *986/542312. MC, V. No dinner Sun. Nov.–May.*

$$$ ✕🏨 **Parador El Albariño.** Built in 1966 in the style of an old manor house, this airy parador faces the Atlantic from across the promenade. The bar is large and inviting, with natural light and wooden booths. Rooms are warmly furnished with wrought-iron lamps, area rugs, and full-length wood shutters over small-paned windows. The kitchen's *lenguado al vino albariño* (sole in Albariño wine sauce) is simply divine; be sure to order some local Albariño wine in its purest form. ✉ *Paseo de Cervantes s/n, 36630 Cambados,* ☎ *986/542250,* FAX *986/542068. 63 rooms. Restaurant, bar, pool, tennis court. AE, DC, MC, V.*

Nightlife

Bar Laya (✉ Praza de Fefiñanes, ☎ 986/542436) is easy to spot on the Praza de Fefiñanes, as it's filled with a youngish crowd day and night. Stone walls and close quarters keep the bar lively and inviting.

Shopping

Cambados is ground zero for Albariño wines, an elixir hard to find outside Spain. **O Casa do Albariño** (Rúa Principe 3, tel. 986/542236) is a tiny, tasteful emporium of Galician wines and cheeses. One corner of **Bar Laya** (☞ After Dark, *above*) is also given over to a substantial wine shop.

Lots of souvenir shops offer Galician witches and schlock, but **Cucadas** (Praza de Fefiñanes, tel. 986/542511; look for sign "Artesania de Galicia") has a particularly large and amusing selection, some of it quite tasteful, such as baskets, copper items, and Camariñas lace.

Baiona

⑲ *30 km (19 mi) south of Pontevedra, 128 km (80 mi) south of Santiago.*

The A9 expressway takes you from Pontevedra to the industrial center of **Vigo** in about half an hour. Baiona (Bayona in Castilian), a summer haunt of affluent Gallegos, is on the southern bank of the Ría de Vigo. When Columbus's *Pinta* landed here in 1492, Baiona became the first town to receive the news of the discovery of the New World. Once a castle, **Monte Real** is one of Spain's most popular paradors; walk around the battlements for superb views. On your way into or out of town, check out the graceful **Roman bridge.**

Dining and Lodging

$$$$ ★ ✕🏨 **Parador de Baiona.** This baronial-style parador was built inside the walls of a medieval castle, on a hilltop fortified since 200 BC. Rooms are furnished with period reproductions, and some have balconies with ocean views toward the Islas Cies. The commendable restaurant serves regional specialties—order *entremeses variados* (mixed appetizers) for a sampler of typical seafood. The *robalo con navallas,* sea bass with razor clams, is an excellent entrée. ✉ *Carretera de Baiona at Montereal, 36300,* ☎ *986/355000.* FAX *986/355076. 66 rooms. Restaurant, bar, pool, tennis court, health club, beach, playground. AE, DC, MC, V.*

Shopping

The nearby city of Vigo has a branch of the department store **El Corte Inglés** (✉ Avda. Gran Vía 25–27). While in Vigo, peek into the **Universidade Popular de Vigo** (✉ Avda. García Barbón 5), where traditional musical instruments such as the bagpipe are studied, displayed, and sold.

Islas Cies

20 *35 km (21 mi) west of Vigo in Atlantic Ocean.*

The Cies Islands are a **nature reserve,** one of the last unspoiled refuges on the Spanish coast. From July to September, about eight boats a day leave from Vigo's harbor, returning later in the day, for the round-trip fare of 2,000 ptas. The 45-minute ride brings you to fine white-sand beaches. Birds abound, and the only land transportation is your own two feet: it takes about an hour to cross the main island. For camping reservations (required), call **Camping Islas Cies** (☎ 986/438358).

Tui

21 *14 km (9 mi) south of Baiona, 50 km (31 mi) south of Pontevedra, 200 km (124 mi) south of A Coruña.*

If you have ample time, leave Vigo on the scenic coastal route C555, which takes you up the banks of the Miño River along the Portuguese border. If time is short, jump on the inland A55: both routes will deliver you directly into Tui (Túy in Castilian). This site was crucial during the medieval wars between Castile and Portugal, which explains why the 13th-century **cathedral** looks like a fortress. The steep, narrow streets are rich with ancient, crested mansions, evidence of Tui's past life as one of the seven capitals of the Galician kingdom. Today it's an important border town, and you can see the mountains of Portugal from the cathedral.

Dining and Lodging

$$$ **Parador de Tui.** This granite-and-chestnut hotel stands on the bluffs overlooking the Miño, its lobbies decorated by rural antiques and paintings by local artists. Guest rooms are furnished with convincing reproductions. Nice views of the woods surround the dining room, where specialties include river salmon, lamprey eel, and trout. For dessert, try the the *pececitos,* almond-flavored pastries made by local convent nuns. ✉ *Avda. del Portugal s/n, 36700,* ☎ *986/600300,* FAX *986/602163. 30 rooms. Restaurant, bar, pool, tennis courts, parking (fee). AE, DC, MC, V.*

A CORUÑA AND THE RÍAS ALTAS

Galicia's gusty, rainy northern coast has inspired local poets to wax lyrical about raindrops falling continuously on one's head. The sun does shine here, though, suffusing town and country with a golden glow. North of A Coruña, the Rías Altas (High Estuaries) notch the coast as you head east toward the Cantabrian Sea.

A Coruña

22 *57 km (35 mi) north of Santiago.*

One of Spain's busiest ports, A Coruña (La Coruña in Castilian Spanish) prides itself on being the most progressive city in the region. The weather here can be fierce, wet, and windy—hence the glass-enclosed, white-paned galleries on the houses lining the harbor.

To see why sailors once nicknamed A Coruña the Ciudad de Cristal (Crystal City), stroll **Dársena de la Marina,** said to be the longest seaside promenade in Europe. While the congregation of boats is charming, the real sight is across the street: a long, gracefully curved row of houses swathed in **glass galleries.** Built by fishermen in the 18th century, the houses actually face *away* from the sea—at the end of a long day, these men were tired of looking at the water. Nets were hung from the porches to dry, and fish was sold on the street below. When Galicia's first glass factory opened nearby, someone got the idea of enclosing these porches in glass, like ship galleons, to keep wind and rain at bay. Some thought the resulting galleries unsightly, and until the 19th century it was forbidden to cover entire facades with them; you were only allowed the top floor, hence the single row of galleries on the grand Plaza de María Pita—which many of these harbor homes face. Once people discovered the pleasant greenhouse effect, the glass gallery spread across the harbor and eventually throughout Galicia, where it's now an architectural staple.

Plaza de María Pita, focal point of the *ciudad vieja* (old town), is a beauty, and is gorgeously lit at night with a soft, subtle glow. Its north side is given over to the neoclassical **Palacio Municipal,** or city hall, built 1908–12 with three Italianate domes. The **monument** in the center, built in 1998, depicts the heroine herself, Maior (María) Pita, holding her lance. When England's notorious Sir Francis Drake arrived to sack A Coruña in 1589, the locals were only half finished building the defensive Castillo de San Antón (☞ *below*), and a thirteen-day battle ensued. When María Pita's husband died, she took up his lance, slew the Briton who tried to plant the Union Jack here, and revived the exhausted Coruñesos, inspiring women to join the battle as well.

The streets west of Plaza de María Pita are known for their tapas bars, but those to the east hide some lovely, undervisited landmarks. The 12th-century church of **Santiago** (Plaza de la Constitución s/n), the oldest church in A Coruña, was the first stop on the traditional *camino inglés* (English route) toward Santiago de Compostela. Originally Romanesque, it's now a bit of a hodgepodge, with Gothic arches, a Baroque altarpiece, and two 18th-century rose windows. The church smells movingly of age and the sea. The **Colegiata de Santa María** is a Romanesque beauty from the mid-13th century, often called Santa María del Campo (St. Mary of the Field) because it was once outside the city walls. The facade depicts the Adoration of the Magi; the celestial figures include St. Peter, holding the keys to heaven. A quirk of this church is that, due to an architectural miscalculation, the roof is too heavy for its supports, so the columns inside lean outward, and the buttresses outside have been thickened. Couples who want to get married in the old town book this poetic church far in advance.

At the northeastern tip of the old town is the **Castillo de San Antón** (St. Anthony's Castle), a 16th-century fort that stood on an island until its approach was filled. Inside is A Coruña's **Museum of Archaeology,** where you can see remnants of the prehistoric Celtic culture that once thrived in these parts. The collection includes silver artifacts as well as pieces of the Celtic stone forts called *castros.* ☎ *981/205994.* 🎫 *400 ptas.* ⏲ *June–Sept., daily 10–2 and 4–7:30; Oct.–May, daily 10–2 and 4–7:30.*

The **Museo de Bellas Artes** (Museum of Fine Arts), housed in two lovely old mansions on the edge of the old town, features French, Spanish, and Italian paintings and a curious collection of etchings by Goya. ✉ *Plaza del Pintor Sotomayor,* ☎ *981/223723.* 🎫 *450 ptas.* ⏲ *Tues.–Fri. 10–8, Sat. 10–2 and 4–8, Sun. 10–2.*

Across town, on a hill, is the **Casa de las Ciencias** (Science Museum), a hands-on museum where children can learn the principles of physics and technology. *Parque Santa Margarita, 981/274107. Museum 300 ptas., planetarium 200 ptas. Daily 10–7.*

Much of A Coruña sits on a narrow peninsula jutting out to sea, on the tip of which is the **Torre de Hercules**—the oldest still-functioning lighthouse in the world. Originally built during the reign of Trajan, the Roman emperor born in Spain in AD 98, the lighthouse was rebuilt in the 18th century and looks strikingly modern; all that remains from Roman times are inscribed foundation stones. Scale the 245 steps for superb views of the city and coastline—and if you're here in the summer, come back at night, when the tower opens for views of city lights along the Atlantic. Imagine the scene on July 11, 1544, when Spain's Prince Philip set sail with 78 vessels for his wedding to Mary Tudor, the daughter of Henry VIII and Catherine of Aragón. In June 1588, King Philip II assembled another fleet at A Coruña, and the "invincible" Spanish Armada sailed from here to conquer England. It might have succeeded had not a ferocious storm scattered the fleet; the surviving ships limped back into A Coruña a month later. Spain's spirit was badly shaken, and of course Sir Francis Drake paid his visit the following year.

Lining the approach to the lighthouse are some funky sculptures depicting figures from Galician and Celtic legends. At the base of the structure, a small **museum** displays items dug up during the restoration of the lighthouse and surrounding area. *Carretera de la Torre s/n, 981/202759. 400 ptas. Daily 10–6.*

On the other side of town, overlooking the bay, is the slate-covered **Domus/Casa del Hombre** (Museum of Mankind). Designed by Japanese architect Arata Isozaki in the shape of a ship's sail, this extraordinary museum is dedicated to the study of the human being, and particularly the human body. Exhibits, many of which are interactive, range from a close-up film of a human birth to some fascinating panels on language. *Parque de Santa Teresa, 981/217000. Museum 300 ptas. Daily 10–7.*

Dining and Lodging

A favorite for tapas is **El Tequeño** (Plaza de María Pita 21), a casual café-bar specializing in a tangy, cheese-filled pastry called, sure enough, the *tequeño*. Nibble outside on the plaza in nice weather.

$$$ ★ **La Penela.** Set on a corner of the lively Praza María Pita, near the harbor, La Penela is locally famous for its crab and its mussels stuffed with Cabrales cheese, of which you must try at least a tapa-size portion. The smart, contemporary, bottle-green dining room has the perfect atmosphere for feasting on fresh fish and sipping some Albariño. *Praza María Pita 12, 981/209200. AE, DC, MC, V. Closed Sun.*

$$–$$$ **Casa Pardo.** This chic eatery near the port is an elegant study in soft ocher tones, with perfectly matched wood furniture and cool lighting. Try the *merluza a la cazuela* (bay leaf–scented hake and potatoes drizzled with oil and sprinkled with paprika, baked in a clay casserole). For dessert, indulge in almond cake or chocolate mousse. *Novoa Santos 15, 981/287178. AE, DC, MC, V. Closed Sun.*

$$–$$$ **El Coral.** The window is an altar of shellfish, with varieties of mollusks and crustaceans you've probably never seen before. Inside, wood-paneled walls, crystal chandeliers, and 12 white-clad tables provide the setting for an intimate, elegant yet casual meal. Specialties include *turbante de mariscos* (a platter—literally, a "turban"—of steamed and boiled shellfish). *Callejón de la Estacada 9 (at Avda. Marina), 981/200569. Reservations essential. AE, DC, MC, V. Closed Sun. Oct.–May.*

$$ ★ ✕ **Adega O Bebedeiro.** Despite being steps from the Domus, tiny O Bebedeiro is a find, beloved by locals (who pack it full at night) for its authentic cuisine and low prices. It feels like an old farmhouse, with stone walls, floors, and fireplace; pine tables and stools; dusty wine bottles (*adega* means "wine cellar"); and rustic implements everywhere. Bread tumbles out of a basket on the baker's table. The food is top-notch Gallego: appetizers like *setas rellenas de marisco y salsa holandesa* (wild mushrooms stuffed with seafood and served with Hollandaise sauce) are followed by various fruits of the sea at market prices, pulled right off the boat. *Angel Rebollo 34, ☎ 981/210609. Closed Mon. No dinner Sun. DC, MC, V.*

$$$$ **Finisterre.** Superbly located where the old town joins the bay, this grande dame is the oldest of A Coruña's top hotels. Long a favorite with businesspeople and families, it has large, carpeted rooms with modern wood furnishings and bright upholstery. Ask for one overlooking the bay. *✉ Paseo del Parrote 22, 15001, ☎ 981/205400, FAX 981/208462. 127 rooms. Restaurant, bar, 4 pools, beauty salon, sauna, 2 tennis courts, health club, playground. AE, DC, MC, V.*

$$$ **Meliá Confort.** It's not charming, per se—fluorescent lighting abounds, and the decor is ultramodern—but soft blues and nautical prints nod toward Coruña's maritime setting. Convenient to El Corte Inglés and the bus and train stations, this high-rise runs like a well-oiled machine. *✉ Ramón y Cajal 53, 15001, ☎ 981/242711, FAX 981/236728. 181 rooms. Restaurant, bar, sauna, exercise room. AE, DC, MC, V.*

Nightlife

Begin your evening in the **Plaza de María Pita**—bars, cafés, and tapas bars proliferate off the plaza's western corners and farther inland. Try **A Roda 2** (✉ Capitán Troncoso 8, ☎ 981/228671) for excellent tapas—octopus in its own ink, garlic garbanzo beans—and a lively evening atmosphere. **Calles Franja, Riego de Agua, Barrera,** and **Galera** and the **Plaza del Humor** are particularly well stocked with bars, some of which serve Ribeiro wine in bowls. Serious night owls head for the posh and pricey clubs around **Praia del Orzán** (Orzán Beach), particularly along **Calle Juan Canalejo.** For lower-key entertainment, the **old town** has lots of cozy taverns where you can grab a nightcap even as the new day dawns.

Shopping

ARTS AND CRAFTS

Shop for Camariñas lace at **Carmina Touriña** (✉ Panaderas 19, ☎ 981/206290). A wide selection of classic blue-and-white pottery is sold at the factory and museum **Cerámicas del Castro** (✉ Carretera Sada–La Coruña s/n, ☎ 981/60937), outside Coruña in the nearby town of Sada. Glazed terra-cotta ceramics from Buño, 40 km (25 mi) west of A Coruña on C552, are prized by aficionados—stop by **Alfaería y Cerámica de Buño** (✉ C. Barreiros s/n, Buño, ☎ 981/721658) to see vases, plates, and wine jugs based on traditional designs.

CLOTHING

Calle Real is chock-a-block with boutiques selling hot contemporary clothing. Galicia has actually spawned some of Spain's top designers, notably **Adolfo Dominguez** (✉ C. Real 13, ☎ 981/225142). A stroll down **Calle San Andres,** two blocks inland from Calle Real, or **Avda. Juan Flórez,** leading into the new town, may also yield sartorial treasure.

For traditional berets, try **Luis Tomé Pérez Fábrica de Gorras y Boinas** (✉ Linares Rivas 52, ☎ 981/232014), an old-world hat and cap emporium. For hats and Galician folk clothing, stop into **Sastrería Iglesias** (✉ Rego do Auga 14, ☎ 981/221634)—founded 1864—where artisan José Luis Iglesias Rodrígues sells his textiles. Authentic Galician *zapatos* (hand-painted wooden shoes) are still worn in some villages to navigate mud; the cobbler **José López Rama** (✉ Rúa do Muiño 7, ☎ 981/701068) has a workshop fifteen minutes south of A Coruña in the village of Carballo.

Betanzos

★ 23 *65 km (40 mi) northeast of Santiago, 25 km (15 mi) east of A Coruña.*

The charming, slightly ramshackle medieval town of Betanzos is still surrounded by parts of its old city wall. The 12th-century church of **San Francisco** contains the smile-inducing tomb of the nobleman Fernán Perez de Andrade, perched on the backs of a stone bear and boar. A few steps uphill, the 15th-century church of **Santa María de Azougue** was built by the mariners' guild, while the tailors' guild put up the Gothic-style church of **Santiago,** which includes a Door of Glory inspired by the one in Santiago's cathedral.

Shopping

Visit a bagpipe workshop and buy the real thing at **Sellas y Gaitas** (✉ Cerca s/n), open weekdays 10–1 and 5–8.

Vilalba

24 *70 km (43 mi) east of A Coruña.*

This part of Galicia is called *Terra Cha* (Flat Land). Known as the Galician Mesopotamia, it's the source of several rivers, most notably the Miño, which flows down into Portugal. Gentle hills and knolls add texture to the plain.

Dining and Lodging

$$$ ✕🏨 **Parador Condes de Vilalba.** Part of this parador is in a massive 15th-century tower that was once a fortress belonging to the prominent Andrade family. A drawbridge leads to the two-story lobby, which is hung with tapestries. Older guest rooms, including three large octagonal chambers in the tower, have beamed ceilings and wood floors, traditional, hand-carved Spanish furniture, and wooden chandeliers. Some rooms in the new wing are equipped for travelers with disabilities. The restaurant specializes in empanadas (try the empanada *de Rax*, made of beef loin, or the traditional empanada *de atún*, with tuna); for dessert, sample the region's renowned *San Simón*, a cone-shape, birch-smoked cheese served with apples or pears. ✉ *Valeriano Valdesuso s/n, 27800,* ☎ *982/510011,* FAX *982/510090. 48 rooms. Restaurant, bar, sauna, Turkish bath, exercise room. AE, DC, MC, V.*

Mondoñedo

25 *122 km (76 mi) northeast of A Coruña, 52 km (32 mi) northeast of Vilalba.*

Founded in 1156, this dignified town was one of the seven capitals of the kingdom of Galicia from the 16th to early 19th century. The **cathedral,** consecrated in 1248, has a museum, an unusual bishop's tomb with inlaid stone, and medieval murals showing the Slaying of the Innocents and St. Peter. The cathedral dominates the ancient **Plaza Mayor,** where a medieval pageant and market are held the first Sunday in August. The surrounding peaceful streets and squares are filled with old buildings, monasteries, and churches, and include an old Jewish quarter.

The shop **El Rey de las Tortas** (✉ Obispo Sarmiento 2) is known for special dessert pies, or *tortas,* made with pastry, sponge cake, vermicelli, and almonds, and decorated with crystallized cherries and fi-

$ ✕ **A Taberna do Valeco.** Set in a converted mill with exposed stone walls, this tavern on the outskirts of town has been family-run since 1956. Pepe Bouso serves free crispy *empanadas,* sometimes made from wild boar, with each drink; the small restaurant upstairs serves game (in winter), fresh fish, and excellent meat. There's a good wine list. ✉ *Os. Nuiños 6,* ☎ *982/521861. No credit cards. No dinner weekdays.*

En Route Spain's cleanest and least-crowded beaches are north of here. The winding N634 leads to the coast.

Viveiro

★ 26 *184 km (114 mi) northeast of A Coruña, 81 km (50 mi) northeast of Vilalba.*

Situated at the very crux of its own *ría,* this historic town is a popular summer resort. The once-turreted city walls are still partially intact, and seagull cries add invigorating atmosphere to the narrow, hilly lanes. Two festivals are noteworthy here: the Semana Santa processions, in which penitents follow religious processions on their knees, and the Rapa das Bestas, a colorful roundup of wild horses the first Sunday in July (on nearby Mt. Buyo).

Dining and Lodging

$$–$$$ ✕🏨 **Hotel Ego.** The view of the ría from this hilltop hotel just outside Viveiro is unbeatable—tiny islets and all—and every room enjoys it. Rooms are carpeted and contemporary, with enormous mirrors and vanity tables. The glassed-in breakfast room faces the ría and a cascade of trees; on a rainy day, you'd much rather be cooped up here than in town, especially off season. The adjoining restaurant, Nito (another room with a view), and the nearby beach, Area, are both top-notch. ✉ *Playa de Area, off N642, 27850,* ☎ *982/560987,* FAX *982/561762. 29 rooms. Restaurant, bar. AE, MC, V.*

OFF THE BEATEN PATH **CERVO** - Spain's most distinctive blue-, white-, and red-glazed contemporary ceramics are made in the factory, museum, and showroom **Cerámica de Sargadelos** (✉ Carretera Paraño s/n, ☎ 982/557841 or 982/557600), 10 km, or 6 mi, east of Viveiro. Drop in weekdays 8:30–1 and 4:30–6.

Ribadeo

27 *50 km (31 mi) east of Viveiro, 40 km (25 mi) northeast of Mondoñedo.*

Perched on the broad ría of the same name, Ribadeo is the last coastal town before Asturias. From here the views up and across the estuary are marvelous—depending on the wind, the waves appear to roll *across* the ría rather than straight inland. Salmon and trout fishermen congregate upriver. Take the scenic walk or drive north of town to the **Illa de la Pancha** lighthouse (a 5-km/3-mi round trip), connected to the coastal cliffs by a small bridge. The gate to the bridge might be closed, but you can still tramp around the grassy clifftop, savoring the briny air and gorgeous geography.

Dining and Lodging

$$$ ✕🏨 **Parador de Ribadeo.** Most rooms in this modern parador have glassed-in sitting areas with lovely views across the port to Asturias. Decor is unusually warm: parquet floors and cheerful harvest-yellow walls are accented by watercolors and etchings of the surrounding area. Large bathrooms with bold, candy-stripe tile are another happy touch. Fishing, horseback riding, and boating are easily arranged. The ría provides a cornucopia of shellfish for the dining room, much of it swimming around in a decorative holding tank; try the imaginative *sopa de mariscos,* seafood soup with a light pastry top, and do not leave without tasting the chef's fabulous tetilla-flavored ice cream, drizzled with honey. ✉ *Amador Fernández 7, 27700,* ☎ *982/128825,* FAX *982/128346. 47 rooms, 2 suites. Restaurant, bar. AE, DC, MC, V.*

WESTERN ASTURIAS

As you cross into the Principality of Asturias, Galicia's intensely green countryside continues, belying the fact that this is a major mining region. (Ancient Roman conquerors coveted the iron- and gold-rich earth.) You might still hear the mournful notes of the bagpipe. Yet Asturias is more mountainous than Galicia, bordered on the southeast by the imposing, snowcapped Picos de Europa.

Luarca

28 *75 km (47 mi) east of Ribadeo, 92 km (57 mi) northeast of Oviedo*

The N634 wanders through western Asturias toward Oviedo. Along with some beaches, the village of Luarca is tucked into a cove at the end of a final twist of the Río Negro, with a fishing port and, to the west, a sparkling bay. The town is a maze of cobblestone streets, stone stairways, and whitewashed houses; the edge of the harbor is decorated with painted flowerpots. The smells wafting from the port's many bars and restaurants may tempt you to stop for some freshly caught seafood.

Dining and Lodging

$$$$ ★ ✕ **Casa Consuelo.** Opened in 1935 and reputed by proud locals to have the best kitchen anywhere in Asturias *or* Galicia, Casa Consuelo is a sublime experience. The most celebrated dish on the menu is the *merluza* (hake) stuffed with the Spanish delicacy *angulitas* (be warned: these are baby eels that look like thin, white worms) and blue cheese. The relaxed, tavern-style dining room is usually packed with Spaniards enjoying the delicious food and abundant regional wines, so make reservations. ✉ *Carretera N634, Km 317 (6 km/4 mi west of Luarca),* ☎ *985/641696. AE, DC, MC, V. Closed Mon.*

$$ ✕ **El Barómetro.** This small, family-run seafood restaurant in the middle of the harborfront has an inexpensive *menu del día* and a good choice of local fresh fish. For a bit more money, you can dig into *bogavante,* a large-clawed lobster. ✉ *Paseo del Muelle 5,* ☎ *985/470662. MC, V. Closed Sept. 28–Oct. 15. No dinner Wed.*

$$ ✕ **Sport.** Jolly and unpretentious, this restaurant-bar has large windows with river views. The kitchen moves beyond the ubiquitous *fabada* (bean-and-sausage stew) to present locally caught fish and a dish combining *pulpo* (octopus) and boiled potatoes, both sprinkled with olive oil, paprika, and garlic. ✉ *Rivero 8,* ☎ *985/641078. AE, DC, MC, V. Closed Oct. 15–31. No dinner Thurs.*

$$$ 🏨 **Villa La Argentina.** Beautifully restored by the González family, this charming Asturian mansion on the hill above Luarca was built in 1899 by a wealthy *indiano* (Spaniard who made his fortune in South America). Each room is different, but all are beautifully furnished with original paintings and modern bathrooms. There's a small antiques museum on site, as well as a library and a billiards room. The restaurant occupies the old coach house in the garden, surrounded by palm trees and imported shrubs. ✉ *Villar de Luarca s/n, 33700,* ☎ *985/640102,* FAX *985/640973. 12 rooms, 3 suites. Restaurant, bar, pool, tennis court, billiards, library. DC, MC, V.*

Shopping

Aguapaste (✉ Paseo del Muelle 3, ☎ 630/727317) sells the craftwork of 60 Asturian artists. Easily best is the silvery jewelry made with *azabache* (jet).

En Route The coastal road leads to the town of **Cudillero** (35 km/22 mi east of Luarca), which rises up an incline from a tiny port. On a sunny day, the emerald green of the surrounding hills, the bright blue of the sparkling water, the white of the houses, and the smell of the sea might make you want to give it all up and buy a boat here.

Oviedo

29 *92 km (57 mi) southeast of Luarca, 50 km (31 mi) southeast of Cudillero, 30 km (19 mi) south of Gijón.*

Inland, the Asturian countryside starts to look a bit more prosperous. Wooden, thatched-roof horreos strung with golden bundles of drying corn replace the stark granite sheds of Galicia. A drive through the rolling hills and industrialized valleys brings you to the capital city, Oviedo. Though primarily industrial, Oviedo has three of the most famous churches in Spain and a large university, giving it an ancient charm and a youthful zest that most business centers lack.

★ Start your explorations with the two exquisite 9th-century chapels just outside the city, on the slopes of Mt. Naranco. The church of **Santa María del Naranco,** with superb views, and its plainer sister, **San Miguel de Lillo,** 300 yards uphill, are the jewels of an early architectural style called Asturian Pre-Romanesque, which was centuries ahead of its time. The carved hunting scenes and the ceiling vaulting bear designs that didn't show up in the rest of Europe for another 200 years. Commissioned as part of a summer palace by King Ramiro I when Oviedo was the capital of Christian Spain, these masterpieces have survived more than 1,000 years in the same natural setting for which they were intended. From the arched porches of Santa María, the valley of Oviedo spreads out at your feet; on a clear day the mighty, snowcapped Picos de Europa gleam in the distance. ✉ *Carretera de los Monumentos, 2 km (1 mi) north of Oviedo.* ☎ *No phone.* 🎫 *200 ptas.; free Mon.* ⌚ *Apr.–Sept., Mon.–Sat. 10–1 and 3–7, Sun. 10–1; Oct.–Mar., Mon.–Sat. 10–1 and 3–5, Sun. 10–1.*

The tallest building in Oviedo's skyline is the Gothic **cathedral,** built between the 14th and the 16th centuries around Oviedo's most cherished monument, the **Cámara Santa** (Holy Chamber). King Ramiro's predecessor, Alfonso the Chaste (792–842), built this chamber to hide the treasures of Christian Spain during the long struggle with the Moors. Heavily damaged during the Spanish Civil War, it has since been rebuilt. Inside is the gold-leaf **Cross of the Angels,** commissioned by Alfonso the Chaste in 808 and encrusted with pearls and jewels. The cross is inscribed, "May anyone who dares to remove me from the place I have been willingly donated be struck down by a bolt of divine lightning." On the left is the more elegant **Victory Cross,** actually a jeweled sheath crafted in 908 to cover the oak cross used by Pelayo in the battle of Covadonga (☞ Covadonga, *below*). Despite the warning, the crosses and other treasures were stolen from the cathedral in 1977, but were recovered relatively intact as thieves tried to spirit them out of Europe through Portugal. ✉ *Plaza Alfonso II El Casto,* ☎ *985/221033.* 🎫 *400 ptas.* ⌚ *Weekdays 10–1 and 4–6, Sun. for Mass only.*

From the cathedral, look directly across the Plaza Alfonso for the still-inhabited 15th-century **Palacio de la Rúa,** the oldest palace in town. Near the Palacio de la Rúa, on Calle San Francisco, is the beautifully cleaned 16th-century **Antigua Universidad de Oviedo.**

Behind the cathedral, the **Museo Arqueológico,** housed in the splendid Monastery of San Vicente, contains fragments of pre-Romanesque buildings. ✉ *San Vicente 5,* ☎ *985/215405.* 🎫 *Free.* ⏲ *Tues.–Sat. 10–1:30 and 4–6, Sun. 11–1.*

To see some Asturian painting, visit the 9th-century church of **Santullano.** ✉ *Plaza Santullano.* 🎫 *Free.* ⏲ *May–Oct., Tues.–Sun. 11–1 and 4:30–6; Nov.–Apr., Tues.–Sun. noon–1 and 4–5.*

You might want to have a look at the exquisite **Hotel Occidental de la Reconquista** (☞ *below*), a former 18th-century hospice. The Spanish crown prince, who carries the title Prince of Asturias, presents an achievement award each year in the hotel's ornate chapel.

Dining and Lodging

$$$ ★ ✕ **Casa Fermín.** This sophisticated pink-and-granite restaurant has skylights, plants, and an air of modernity that belies its age (it opened in 1924). Founder Luis Gil introduced traditional Asturian cuisine to seminars around the world. Specialties include fabada, wild game in season, hake in cider, and *tortilla de angulas* (omelet with spaghetti-thin baby eels), a pricey delicacy adored by lovers of Spanish haute cuisine. The wine cellar is extensive. ✉ *San Francisco 8,* ☎ *98/21–6452. AE, DC, MC, V. Closed Sun.*

$$$ ★ ✕ **La Boca Mar.** Award-winning *nueva cocina* is presented with flair at this unusual restaurant. Tucked into a vine-covered building in the plaza that houses Oviedo's fish market, La Boca Mar is a jumble of cozy wooden booths. Try fried prawns, filet mignon with sweet mustard, or *angulas* (eels). ✉ *Plaza Trascorrales 14,* ☎ *985/214218. AE, DC, MC, V. Closed Sun.*

$$ ✕ **El Raitan.** Owned by the same family that runs La Boca Mar (☞ *above*), and just across the plaza, El Raitan is perfect for big appetites. The restaurant is styled like an old-fashioned kitchen, with an antique stove in the entrance. There's no lunch menu; at midday everyone is served the same Asturian specialties: seafood soup, crab bisque, vegetable-and-bean stew, fabada, potatoes stuffed with meat, onions filled with tomatoes, rice pudding, crepes, and nut pastries. ✉ *Plaza Trascorrales 6,* ☎ *985/214218. AE, DC, MC, V. No dinner Sun.*

$ ★ ✕ **La Máquina.** For the best fabada in Asturias, head 6 km (4 mi) outside Oviedo toward Avilés, stopping when you see the farmhouse with the miniature locomotive out front. La Máquina's L-shape, whitewashed dining room has attracted diners from all over Spain for 50 years, some of whom think nothing of making a weekend trip solely for the purpose of eating here. The memorable rice pudding is topped with a crisp layer of hot caramel. ✉ *Avda. de Santa Bárbara 59,* ☎ *985/260019. AE, MC, V. No dinner. Closed Sun.*

$$$$ ★ 🏨 **Hotel Occidental de la Reconquista.** Housed in an 18th-century hospice emblazoned with a huge, stone coat of arms, the ultraluxurious Reconquista costs almost twice as much as any other hotel in Asturias. The wide lobby, encircled by a balcony, is decked out with velvet upholstery and 18th-century paintings. A pianist entertains nightly. Guest rooms are large and modern, with comfortable beds and large armchairs. ✉ *Gil de Jaz 16, 33004,* ☎ *985/241100,* FAX *985/241166. 142 rooms, 4 suites, 1 apartment. Restaurant, bar, coffee shop, beauty salon. AE, DC, MC, V.* 🎯

$$ 🏨 **NH Principado.** If you prize friendliness over flash, try the Principado, centrally located between the cathedral and the Plaza de la Escandalera. The NH chain is modern and functional, but this branch feels more distinguished than most. You enter from a pedestrian street; the hotel takes care of luggage collection and parking. ✉ *San Francisco 6, 33003,* ☎ *985/217792,* FAX *985/213946. 70 rooms. Restaurant, bar. AE, DC, MC, V.*

Nightlife and the Arts

A rather rowdy town after dark, Oviedo has plenty in the way of loud live music. The best tapas scene is at the brick tavern **Cabo Peñas** (✉ ✉ Melquiades Alvarez 24), where the cheeses, wines, and stuffed peppers are so tasty that you'll want a *ración* (larger portion). **Sidrería Venicia** is packed with pubs, many of them Irish owing to the region's Celtic heritage. You can get a nightcap at the plant-filled **Sidrería Venicia** (✉ Doctor Casal 13) or take in some loud rock at the brass-and-glass **La Loggia,** across from the cathedral. The old town's main strip of dance clubs is **Calle Canóniga,** shooting away from the cathedral. If you're still awake when the old town goes to sleep, try the new town's **Sir Lawrence** (✉ Eugenio Tamayo 3), whence you might dance out into daylight.

Plays and concerts are presented at the **Teatro Municipal.** Check newspapers for schedules.

Shopping

Shops throughout the city carry azabache jewelry; look for distinctive black azabache pottery at the **Azabacheria** (✉ Galicia 3). For handcrafted leather bags and belts, check out **Escanda** (✉ Jovellanos 5). Antiques aficionados will find a cluster of shops on a few blocks of **Calle de Mon.**

Gourmets who like fabada can take home a do-it-yourself kit—beans and meat conserved in a vacuum pack—from **Casa Veneranda** (✉ Melquiades Alvarez 23).

Gijón

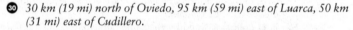

30 *30 km (19 mi) north of Oviedo, 95 km (59 mi) east of Luarca, 50 km (31 mi) east of Cudillero.*

Gijón (pronounced "hee-*hone*") can seem overwhelming at first, presenting you with factories, warehouses, and other accoutrements of heavy industry. Ask most Spaniards for their favorite Asturian city, however, and they're likely to name this one fondly. Full of hidden hot spots and friendly people, Gijón is part fishing port, part summer resort, and part university town, packed with inviting cafés and excellent restaurants.

The promenade along **Praia San Lorenzo** extends from one end of town to the other. Across the narrow peninsula and the Plaza Mayor (on the corner of which is El Centenario, a good-value seafood and cider bar) is the harbor, where the fishing fleet comes in with the day's catch. The steep peninsula that juts out to sea is the old fishermen's quarter, **Cimadevilla,** now the hub of Gijón's nightlife. From the park at the highest point on the headland, beside Basque sculptor Eduardo Chillida's massive sculpture *Elogio del Horizonte* (Homage to the Horizon), there's a panoramic view of the coast and city.

Gijón's **Termas Romanas** (Roman baths), dating back to the time of Augustus, are under the plaza at the end of the beach. ✉ *Campo Valdés,* ☎ *985/345147.* 🎟 *500 ptas.* 🕙 *Tues.–Sat. 10–1 (11–1:30 in summer) and 5–7 (5–9 in summer), Sun. 11–2.*

The **Museo de la Gaita** (Bagpipe Museum), is just across the river on the eastern edge of town, past Parque Isabel la Católica. A collection of bagpipes from all over the world is augmented by workshops where you can see the instruments crafted. ✉ *La Güelga s/n,* ☎ *985/332244.* 🎟 *Free.* 🕙 *Sept.–June, Tues.–Sat. 10–1 and 5–8, Sun. 11–2; July–Aug., Tues.–Sat. 11–1:30 and 5–9, Sun. 11–2.*

Dining and Lodging

$$$$ ✕ **El Puerto.** Set at the end of a quay, with picture windows overlooking the yacht harbor, this classy joint is co-owned by your host, Antonio,

and the chef, Miguel, a slick team who add imaginative touches to fine shellfish, seafood, and meats. A recent entrée: honeyed roast duck with caramelized kiwi. Feast on a four-plate menu or a *parillada de mariscos* (mixed platter of grilled shellfish). Good game is served in season, and the wine list is substantial. ✉ *Claudio Alvargonzález,* ☎ *985/349096. Reservations essential. AE, MC, DC, V. Closed Easter. No dinner Sun.*

$$ ✕ **La Pondala.** Housed in a former chalet, this local favorite east of town is at once friendly, folksy, and romantic. When the weather co-operates, the terrace is a perfect spot for a big afternoon lunch of grilled meat with rice or one of many sweet and savory crepes. The *crepe de pollo y queso Cabrales* (chicken and blue cheese) is wonderful, as are the chocolate and fruit dessert crepes. ✉ *Avda. de Dionisio Cifuentes 27, Somió 0,* ☎ *985/361160. AE, DC, MC, V. Closed Thurs.*

$$$ ✕🏨 **Parador de Gijón.** Housed in an old water mill in a leafy park not far from the San Lorenzo beach, this parador is one of the simplest and friendliest in Spain. Rooms in the new wing are small, with bleached-wood floors and thick pine shutters; but most have wonderful views over the adjacent lake or the park. Locals enjoy the restaurant and garden bar, particularly the *tigres* (spicy stuffed mussels), *pimientos de piquillo rellenos* (green peppers stuffed with squid, mushrooms, and rice), and *oricios* (sea urchins), served raw or steamed with lemon juice or a spicy sauce. For dessert, try fresh figs (in season) with Cabrales cheese. ✉ *Torcuato Fernández Miranda 4, 33203,* ☎ *985/370511,* FAX *985/370233. 40 rooms. Restaurant, cafeteria. AE, DC, MC, V.*

En Route East of Gijón on N632 (until the new *autopista* is finished) is apple-orchard country, the source of Asturias's famous hard cider. Rolling hills, cows, and white chalets create a remarkably Alpine landscape.

Villaviciosa

31 *32 km (20 mi) east of Gijón, 45 km (28 mi) northeast of Oviedo.*

Cider capital Villaviciosa has a big dairy and several bottling plants as well as a picturesque old quarter. Emperor Charles V first set foot in Spain just down the road from here. The town's annual five-day Fiesta de la Manzana (Apple Festival) begins the first Friday after September 8. To taste the regional hard cider, stop into **El Congreso** (✉ Plaza Generalísimo 25), a popular *sidrería* (cider house) that also serves tasty tapas and shellfish straight from the tank. If time allows, check out Villaviciosa's restored 15th-century **castle,** 3 km (2 mi) west of town on the N632. The beautiful sandstone walls, turrets, and archways now enclose a modern hotel and restaurant.

$ 🏨 **Carlos I.** This 16th-century mansion is loaded with character, from the common-area wood floors, antique furniture, potted plants, and oil paintings to the Old World bar-cafetería. Guest rooms, which are spotless and relatively large, have wood furniture of a more recent vintage. ✉ *Plaza Carlos I 4, 33300,* ☎ *985/890121,* FAX *985/890051. 16 rooms. Bar. AE, DC, MC, V.* ❀

Ribadesella

32 *38 km (24 mi) east of Gijón, 48 km (30 mi) northeast of Oviedo.*

The N632 twists around green hills dappled with eucalyptus groves and allows you glimpses of the sea and sandy beaches down plunging valleys. The snow-capped Picos de Europa loom inland. This fishing village and beach resort is famous for the international canoe races held on the Sella River the first Saturday of August; for copious fresh seafood; and for the **Cueva Tito Bustillo.** Discovered in 1968 by Señor

Bustillo, the cave bears 20,000-year-old paintings on a par with those in Lascaux, France, and Altamira (☞ Chapter 3). Giant horses and deer prance about the walls. To protect the paintings, no more than 375 visitors are allowed inside each day; for those turned away, there is a museum of Asturian cave finds. The guided tour is in Spanish. ☎ *985/861118 or 985/861120.* *331 ptas.* ⏲ *Apr.–May, Wed.–Sun. 10–5; June–Sept., Wed.–Sun. 10–5:30.*

OFF THE BEATEN PATH

LLANES – Llanes is a pretty town on the Costa Verde (Green Coast), 40 km (25 mi) east of Ribadesella on the way to Santander. Just 1 km (½ mi) farther east is one of the area's most secluded beaches, the immaculate **Playa Balota,** with private coves for picnicking and the only stretch of nudist sand in Asturias. A highlight in Llanes itself is the daily fish market, where vendors display heaping mounds of freshly caught seafood on ice. Minutes from the market in a narrow passage is **Mirentxu** (✉ Marinero 14, ☎ 985/402236), a Basque-influenced restaurant that serves heaping portions of grilled and fried fish.

Dining and Lodging

$ ✕ **El Repollu.** A block inland from the port and market, this small, homey grill specializes, sure enough, in fish. Try the fresh-grilled turbot, some sweet, grilled *gambas* (shrimp), and perhaps the house Cabrales cheese. ✉ *Santa Marina 2,* ☎ *985/860734. Reservations not accepted. AE, DC, MC, V. Closed Thurs. Oct.–June. No dinner Oct.–June.*

$$ ✕🏨 **Ribadasella Playa.** Passing a peaceful night in this quirky, restored turn-of-the-century mansion on the beach is an unusually pleasant experience. Family-run, it has a timeless, stately charm that puts one in mind of black-and-white European art films. ✉ *Ricardo Cangas 3 33560,* ☎ *985/860715. 17 rooms. Bar. AE, DC, MC, V.*

THE PICOS DE EUROPA

With craggy peaks soaring up to the 8,688-ft Torre Cerredo, the northern skyline of the Picos de Europa has helped seafarers and fishermen navigate the Bay of Biscay since time immemorial. To the south, pilgrims on their way to Santiago enjoy distant but inspiring views of the snowcapped range from the rolling plains of Castile between Burgos and León. Some 300 million years ago, this area was a sea; over a period of 60 million years it collected a layer of calceous deposits more than a mile thick, and a massive shift of the earth's crust threw up the Picos (Peaks). Later, the fractured peaks acquired glaciers, which then left two lakes in their wake. Regular, very heavy rain and snow have created spectacular canyons plunging 3,000 ft, natural arches, caves, and sinkholes, one of them 5,213 ft deep.

The mountains' earliest inhabitants were Neolithic cave dwellers, whose paintings are still on view at Ribadesella. During Visigothic times, the local people were called Ástures, and it was their first king, Pelayo, who defeated the invading Moors in 722 by ambushing them near Covadonga and launching the 700-year Christian Reconquest of Spain.

The Picos de Europa National Park, covering 257 square mi, was established in 1995, with Cangas de Onís its unofficial capital. Only in the 19th century were the mountains first mapped (by a German and a Frenchman); and not until 1904 did a local *marqués,* Pedro Pidal, and a villager from Caín, Gregorio Pérez, become the first to climb El Naranjo de Bulnes, the distinctive bullet of sheer rock that shoots up to 8,283 ft on the northeastern side of the central range. Since then the mountains have become a paradise for climbers, trekkers, and vacationing ramblers, as you could spend more than a week exploring the main trails alone. Opportunities for hiking, climbing, hang-gliding, horseback riding, bicycling, and canoeing abound, and there are two adventure-sport centers in Cangas de Onís, near the "Roman" bridge.

Below the peaks are emerald-green alpine meadows where cattle, goats, and sheep graze in summer. Thick woods of oak, chestnut, lime, and ash slope down to misty gorges where wild cherry and alders twist out of cascading streams. Purple orchids bloom in the woods, and roe deer, chamois, polecats, wild boar, and wolves all make their homes here. Sadly, the Picos' brown bears have been hunted to extinction, though some still exist farther west. The capercaillie, a turkey-like grouse with a raucous mating call, is the Picos' most emblematic bird; other fowl include spy eagles and long-eared owls.

Scenic Routes

The best-known road trip in the Picos—indeed, one of the most eye-popping stretches in Europe—connects Riaño and Cangas de Onís along the twisting Sella Gorge, a route known as the Desfiladero de los Beyos. Another drive takes you up past Covadonga (☞ *below*) to lakes Enol and Ercina. The most spectacular walk is the Ruta de Cares, which starts between Cangas de Onís and Panes. There's another gorge road, Desfiladero de la Hermida, between Panes and Potes.

It takes two hours (longer with side trips) to drive the **Desfiladero de los Beyos** between Riaño and Cangas de Onís. Starting from León, head east on the N601, then turn right for the N625 to Riaño: the N625 skirts a large dam, crosses a bridge to Riaño, then goes left. For a side trip just before the **Puerto de Pontón** (Pontón Pass; 4,232 ft), follow the signs and turn right to the **Puerto de Panderruedas** (4,757 ft) for a panoramic view of the peaks, especially in the early-evening sun.

For the **Ruta de Cares,** drive east on the C6312 from Cangas de Onís toward Panes, stopping just before Arenas de Cabrales: here the road descends a wide valley and reaches a *mirador* (lookout) onto the **Naranjo de Bulnes,** a huge tooth of rock way up in the peaks. The mountain was named for its occasional tendency to glow orange, *naranja,* at sunrise and sunset. Turn right in Arenas de Cabrales to reach Poncebos, and leave the car near here for the four-hour Ruta de Cares walk to Caín through the **Garganta de Cares** gorge. The canyon presents itself fairly soon, so you can turn back without pangs if you don't want to make the full hike. This route is popular, so arrive in Poncebos early in the day to avoid parking problems. You can also access the Ruta at the other end—from **Puerto de Pontón,** a road leads to Puerto de Panderruedas, Posada de Valdeón, and Caín. Groups of friends with two cars sometimes leave them at Poncebos and Caín, then exchange keys when they meet to save the return walk.

NEED A BREAK? Nestled in the gorge, the simple **Hostal Poncebos** (✉ ☎ 985/846447) is good for a quick bar lunch in winter and more substantial dishes like fabada and *cabrito* (kid) in summer. Serious trekkers and mountaineers stay in the 18 rooms upstairs, eight of which have private bath.

If you have another day, leave Cangas and drive via Panes and Potes around the entire park. Consider relocating to the southern side and putting up in the Parador de Fuente De (☞ *below*). Ten kilometers (six miles) south of Potes, turn right at Urdón's hydroelectric power station to **Tresviso** for unforgettable views and a chance to buy some local cheese. Just west of Potes on the C621 is the left turn for the **Monasterio de Santo Toribio,** with a 13th-century Gothic church and 17th-century cloisters. The C621 ends at Fuente Dé; from Potes the N621 continues south to Riaño, a two-hour drive. About halfway there, turn right at Puerta de San Gloria and head up the rough track to the **Monumento al Oso,** where a white stone bear marks another splendid view.

Cangas de Onís

33 *25 km (16 mi) south of Ribadesella, 70 km (43 mi) east of Oviedo.*

Lying partly in the narrow valley carved by the Sella River, Cangas de Onís is the unofficial capital of the Picos de Europa National Park and has the feel of a bracing mountain village. To help plan your rambles, consult the scale model of the park outside the Picos de Europa visitor center in Casa Dago on Avenida Covadonga (☎ 985/848614). The store opposite (at No. 22), El Llagar, sells maps and guidebooks, a few in English.

Cangas has the distinction of having been the first capital of Christian Spain (☞ Covadonga, *below*). A high, humpback **medieval bridge** (also known as the Puente Romano, or Roman Bridge, because of its style) spans the Sella River gorge with a reproduction of Pelayo's Victory, or the Cruz de la Victoria, dangling underneath. Local crafts include basketry and woodwork.

Dining and Lodging

$ ✕ **Sidrería Los Arcos.** This busy tavern with lots of polished wood serves local cider—the waiter pours a dash from a great height, and you *must* drink it immediately to enjoy the effervescent flavor—as well as various wines and scrumptious meals. *Revuelto de morcilla* (scrambled eggs with dark sausage) is served on *totu,* a maize pastry base. Huge, sizzling, fabulous T-bone steaks are also available. ✉ *Plaza del Ayuntamiento (enter on Avda. Covadonga),* ☎ *985/8499277. AE, MC, V.*

$$$ ★ ✕🏨 **Parador de Cangas de Onís.** Superbly located on the banks of the River Sella, just over a mile west of Cangas, this new, friendly parador is part 12th-century Benedictine monastery and part new (matching) wing. The older building, connected to the new one by a glass tunnel, has eleven period-style rooms, some with four-poster beds. The adjacent church, accessible from the hotel's delightful cloistered patio, is still in use; its altar and apses date from the 12th century, the rest from the 17th century. Excellent local dishes, such as *merluza del Cantabrica a la sidra* (hake cooked in cider) garnished with asparagus, are served in the bright dining room. A pool is in the works. ✉ *Monasterio de San Pedro de Villanueva, Carretera N624, 33500 (on N634, take right turn for Villanueva),* ☎ *985/849402,* FAX *985/849520. 64 rooms. Restaurant, bar, meeting rooms. AE, DC, MC, V.*

$$ 🏨 **Aultre Naray.** This 19th-century mansion 15 km (9 mi) east of town is a rare find for outdoor enthusiasts. Overlooking the Escapa mountain range, it's perfectly placed for (and can help organize) hiking, camping, canoeing, and swimming. It's not rustic, though—guest rooms have modern furniture, plenty of light, and, in some cases, pleasant sitting rooms. ✉ *N634, Km 335, Los Campos, Pereyes, Cangas de Onís 33547,* ☎ FAX *985/840808. 10 rooms. Restaurant, bar. AE, DC, MC, V.*

$$ 🏨 **Los Lagos.** Right in the center of town, near the tourist office, this bustling modern hotel has an excellent restaurant and cider bar. Each of the four floors has a different color scheme, ranging from cream to blue. Guest rooms have modern furniture and white-tile bathrooms. ✉ *Jardines del Ayuntamiento 3, 33550,* ☎ *985/849421,* FAX *985/848405. 45 rooms. Restaurant, bar, meeting rooms. AE, MC, V.*

Covadonga

34 *14 km (9 mi) south of Cangas de Onís.*

To experience high alpine meadowland, some rare Spanish lakes, and views over the peaks and out to sea (if ever the mist disperses), take the narrowish road up past Covadonga to **Lake Enol,** stopping for gazing sessions en route. Starting to the right of the lake, a three-hour walk takes in wonderful views from the **Mirador del Rey,** where you'll also find the grave of pioneering climber Pedro Pidal. Farther up the road from Lake Enol are a summer-only tourist office and **Lake Ercina,** where Pope John Paul II enjoyed a picnic during his 1989 tour of Asturias and Galicia.

NEED A BREAK? Near Lake Enol is the **Restaurante el Casín** (✉ ☎ 608/180974, open Mar.–Dec.), with a small terrace bar overlooking the mountains and the lake. The set menu is a mere 1,500 ptas.; à la carte options include restorative fabada, roast *cabrito* (kid), and *cordero* (lamb).

★ Covadonga's **shrine** is considered the birthplace of Spain. Here, in 718, a handful of sturdy Asturian Christians led by Don Pelayo took refuge in the Cave of St. Mary, about halfway up a cliff, where they prayed to the Virgin Mary to give them strength to turn back the Moors. Pelayo and his followers resisted the superior Moorish forces and set up a Christian kingdom that eventually led to the Reconquest. Covadonga itself has a **basilica** in a magnificent mountain setting and a **shrine** in the legendary cave, which includes an 18th-century statue of the Virgin and Don Pelayo's grave. The **museum** displays the treasures donated to the Virgin of the Cave, including a crown studded with more than 1,000 diamonds. ☎ *985/846039.* 🎫 *200 ptas.* ⏲ *Daily 10–2 and 4–7.*

Dining and Lodging

$$$ ✕🏨 **Parador de Fuente Dé.** A hair east of the Cantabrian border, 23 km (14 mi) west of Potes, this modern parador stands in a valley beside a cable car that ascends a soaring rock face to 2,705 ft in about four minutes. Somewhat spartan, it's a fine no-frills base for serious climbers and walkers, and has a good restaurant serving *cocido lebaniego* (a filling local stew) and yummy steaks topped with the local blue cheese. ✉ *Fuente Dé, 39588,* ☎ *942/736651,* FAX *942/736654. 78. Restaurant, bar, meeting room. AE, DC, MC, V. Closed Dec.–Feb..*

$$ ✕🏨 **La Tiendona.** This restored roadhouse is strategically located halfway between the mountains of Cangas de Onís and the beaches of Ribadesella. Rooms are country-style, and the dining room serves regional fare such as smoked salmon, fabada, and cider. ✉ *N634, Km 335, Margolles, Cangas de Onís 33550,* ☎ *985/840474,* FAX *985/841316. 18 rooms. Restaurant, bar. DC, MC, V.*

$$ 🏨 **La Posada de Babel.** In the coastal village of Llanes, this exquisite family-run inn offers roaring fires in the public rooms and plenty of personal attention. One guest room is in a converted granary. ✉ *Los Pasucos y La Pereda, 33509 Llanes,* ☎ *985/402525. 11 rooms. Restaurant, bar, horseback riding, bicycles, library. AE, DC, MC, V. Closed Jan. 5–Feb. 22.*

GALICIA AND ASTURIAS A TO Z

Arriving and Departing

By Bus

ALSA runs daily buses to Galicia and Asturias from Madrid. Several other companies connect the region with major Spanish cities; contact the bus stations in **Santiago** (✉ San Cayetano 12, ☎ 981/587700) and **Oviedo** (✉ Plaza Primo de Rivera 1, ☎ 985/281212) for information.

By Car

The N-VI links northwestern Spain with Madrid. Although it's a four-lane expressway most of the time, the last part of the autopista through the mountains northwest of Villafranca del Bierzo was still under construction at press time. Be warned that this route is heavily traveled by slow-moving trucks, behind which you can really get stuck on the remaining segments of winding two-lane road. Still, although distances are long (609 km/378 mi from Madrid to A Coruña) and traffic slow, driving is the best way to appreciate the countryside in these parts.

By Plane

Galicia is served by an international airport in Labacolla, 12 km (7 mi) east of **Santiago de Compostela** (☎ 981/547500 or 981/547501), with daily Iberia flights to London, Paris, Zurich, Geneva, and Frankfurt and frequent connections to New York. Regular domestic flights connect Santiago with the rest of Spain, including daily service to Madrid and Barcelona. The region's other two domestic airports are in **A Coruña** (✉ ☎ 981/187315) and near San Estéban de Pravia, 47 km (29 mi) north of **Oviedo** (✉ ☎ 985/127500).

Iberia has ticket offices in **Santiago** (✉ Calvo Sotelo 25, ☎ 981/590551), **A Coruña** (✉ Plaza de Galicia 6, ☎ 981/226024), **Oviedo** (✉ Uria 21, ☎ 985/240250), and **Gijón** (✉ Alfredo Truán 8, ☎ 985/351790).

In Santiago, airport buses leave the Iberia office and the bus station. You can catch a bus to the Asturias airport at the Iberia office in Gijón or the Iberia terminal in Oviedo (✉ Marqués de Pidal 20).

By Train

RENFE runs several trains a day from Madrid to Oviedo (7 hrs) and Gijón (8 hrs), while a separate RENFE line serves Santiago (11 hrs). Daytime first-class and second-class cars are available, as is an overnight train with sleeping compartments. RENFE has ticket windows at the stations in **Santiago** (☎ 981/520202), **A Coruña** (☎ 902/240202), **Oviedo** (☎ 985/250202), and **Gijón** (☎ 985/170202).

Getting Around

By Bus

Contact the regional tourist office or bus station (☞ Arriving and Departing, *above,* or Visitor Information, *below*) for information on the numerous local bus routes.

By Car

The divided four-lane highway linking León with Oviedo and Gijón is the fastest way to cross the Cantabrian Mountains. A north–south Galician ("Atlantic") expressway links A Coruña, Santiago, Pontevedra, and Vigo. Elsewhere, roads wind along the coast or climb over hills, always slow and seldom direct; for any trip off the expressway, allow more time than you think it should take.

By Train

Local RENFE trains connect the major cities of Galicia and Asturias with most of the small towns, but prepare for dozens of stops. For principal stations, *see* Arriving and Departing, *above.*

Narrow-gauge **FEVE** trains clatter slowly across northern Spain, connecting Galicia and Asturias with Santander, Bilbao, and Irún, on the French border. Buy tickets at local travel agencies, any FEVE train station, or the FEVE office in Oviedo (✉ C. Monte Gamonal s/n, near FEVE-Asturias train station, ☎ 985/290104) or Madrid (C. General Rodrigo 6, ☎ 91/453–3828).

Contacts and Resources

Car Rentals

If you're coming from the United States, remember that rental rates in Spain are as much as double those you can arrange in advance back home. Plan ahead—reserve a car through Hertz, Budget, or National/Europcar (☞ Car Rental *in* Smart Travel Tips), all of which have offices in León, Santiago de Compostela, Oviedo, A Coruña, Gijón, and/or Vigo. If you can't reserve ahead, try the pricier options below.

Hertz has a main office at Madrid's **Barajas Airport** (☎ 91/305–8457) and branch offices in **Santiago** (✉ Airport, ☎ 981/598893), **A Coruña** (✉ Airport, ☎ 981/663990), **Oviedo** (✉ C. Ventura Rodríguez 4, ☎ 985/270824), **Gijón** (✉ Anselmo Cifuentes 12, ☎ 985/355050) and **Asturias Airport** (✉ Near Oviedo, ☎ 985/548017 or 985/512–7500).

Budget has a main office in **Madrid** (✉ José Abascal 31, ☎ 91/442–0259) and branch offices in **A Coruña** (✉ C. Doctor Fleming 16-bajo, ☎ 981/151112) and **Oviedo** (✉ C. Arquitecto Regueira 5, ☎ 985/244943).

Europcar (Central reservations ☎ 902/105030) has a main office at Madrid's **Barajas Airport** (✉ ☎ 91/393-7235) and branch offices in **Santiago** (✉ Airport, ☎ 981/547740), **A Coruña** (✉ Airport, ☎ 981/187285), **León** (✉ RENFE train station, ☎ 987/230251), **Oviedo** (✉ RENFE train station, ☎ 985/245712), **Gijón** (✉ Avda. de la Constitución 31, ☎ 985/165126), and **Vigo** (✉ Airport, ☎ 986/486878).

Avis has a main office at **Madrid's** Barajas Airport (☎ 91/305–8532 or 91/305–4273) and branch offices in **Santiago** (☎ 981/573908; airport 981/596101); **A Coruña** (✉ Plaza de Vigo 5, ☎ 981/121201; airport 981/666852); and **Oviedo** (☎ 985/562111; airport 985/562111).

Cyber Space

Pilgrims and travelers can send "I made it!" e-mails from **Cyber Rúa Nova** (✉ Rúa Nova 50), which charges 200 ptas. for an hour of computer use. Unfortunately, it can take about that long to connect.

Golf

Asturias has two good golf courses, the **Club de Golf de Castiello** in Gijón (☎ 985/366313) and **La Barganiza** in Siero (☎ 985/742468). Galician courses include **Monte la Zapateira** (✉ C. Zapateira s/n, A Coruña, ☎ 981/285200), 11 km (7 mi) from the city; **Domaio** (✉ Pontevedra province, ☎ 986/330386); **La Toja** (☎ 986/730818); and **Padrón** (☎ 981/598891). Santiago's links are near the airport, at **Campo de Golf del Aero Club Labacolla** (☎ 981/888276). Call the club a day in advance to reserve equipment.

Guided Tours

During peak travel periods, Santiago's **tourist office** (✉ Rúa do Vilar 43, ☎ 981/584081) offers daily two-hour walking tours with multilingual guides. Tours cost 1,000 ptas. per person and leave from the Praza das Praterías, behind the cathedral.

The **Transcantábrico narrow-gauge train tour** offered by FEVE is an eight-day, 1,000-km (600-mi) journey through the Basque country, Galicia, and Asturias, with English-speaking guides and a private bus that takes the group from train stations to artistic and natural attractions. Passengers sleep on the train and dine on local specialties. Trains run from June through September, and the all-inclusive cost is 180,000 ptas. per person. Contact **Transcantábrico** (✉ General Rodrígo 6, 28003 Madrid, ☎ 91/553–7000 or 91/553–0911), **E.C. Tours** (✉ 10153½ Riverside Dr., Toluca Lake, CA 91602, USA, ☎ 818/755–9333 or 800/388–0877), **Conference Travel Int'l.** (✉ 157 Glen Head Rd., Glen Head, NY

11545, USA, ☎ 516/671–5298 or 800/527–4852), or **Marsans** (✉ 66 Whitmore St., London W1H 9LG, U.K., ☎ 0207/224–0504).

Trastur (✉ Muñalen, 33873 Tineo, Asturias, ☎ 985/806036) leads wilderness trips on horseback through the remote valleys of western Asturias. The 5- to 10-day outings are designed for both beginners and experienced cowboys; mountain cabins provide shelter along the trail. Tours begin and end in Oviedo and cost about 18,000 ptas. a day, all-inclusive. In the Ourense area, contact the active folks at **Galiciaventura** (✉ Manuel Pereira 10, 32003, ☎ 988/241810, FAX 988/235374) for guided rafting, spelunking, scuba diving, and trekking excursions. The **Centro Hípico de Turismo Ecuestre y de Aventuras / "Granjo O Castelo"** (✉ Rúa Urzaiz 91–5, Vigo 36201, ☎ 986/425937) conducts horseback rides along the pilgrimage routes to Santiago from O Cebreiro and Braga (Portugal).

Hiking and Climbing

Nortrek (✉ Inés de Castro 7, lower level, Apdo. 626, A Coruña, ☎ 981/151674) is a one-stop source for information and equipment pertaining to hiking, rock climbing, skiing, and bungee-jumping.

The tourist offices in Oviedo and Cangas de Onís can help you organize a trek. The **Picos de Europa visitor center** in Cangas (✉ Casa Dago, Avda. Covadonga 43, ☎ 985/848614) provides route maps, general information, and a useful scale model of the Picos. In summer, another reception center opens between the lakes Enol and Ercina, on the mountain road from Covadonga. For more technical climbing contact **Servicio de Guías de Montaña** (✉ Cangas de Onís, ☎ 985/848916). **El Centro de Aventuro Monteverde** (✉ Sargento Provisional 5, ☎ 985/848079) can organize canoeing, canyon rappelling, bungee jumping, spelunking, horseback riding, and jeep trips. **Turismo y Aventura Viesca** (✉ Avda. Puente Romano 1, ☎ 985/357369 or 600/503000) offers rafting, canoeing, jet skiing, climbing, trekking, bungee jumping, and archery.

Skiing

The region's three small ski areas cater mostly to local families. The largest is **San Isidoro** (☎ 987/731115 or 987/721118), in the Cantabrian Mountains, with one chairlift and 12 slopes. Just east of here is **Valgrande Pajares** (☎ 985/496123), with two chairlifts and eight slopes. West of Ourense, in Galicia, **Mazaneda** (☎ 988/309747) has one chairlift and seven slopes. Valgrande Pajares and Manzaneda also have cross-country skiing.

Water Sports

In Santiago, contact diving experts **Turisnorte** (✉ Rosalía de Castro 72-2-1A, ☎ 981/530009, FAX 981/522810) for information on scuba lessons, equipment rental, guided dives, windsurfing, and parasailing. For courageous and experienced sailors, yachting is a spectacular way to discover the hidden gems of the coast; **Yatesport Coruña** (✉ Avda. del Puerto 28, ☎ 981/611594, FAX 981/624208) rents private yachts and can arrange sailing lessons.

Visitor Information

Tourist offices are usually open 9–2 or 3 and 5–7. For information on all of Galicia, contact the tourist office in **Santiago de Compostela** (✉ Rúa do Vilar 43, ☎ 981/584081). For information on all of Asturias, contact the tourist office in **Oviedo** (✉ Plaza de la Catedral 6, ☎ 985/213385).

Local tourist offices: **Cangas de Onís** (✉ Emilio Laria 2, ☎ 985/848005). **Covadonga** (✉ Avda. de Covadonga s/n, Plaza del Ayuntamiento, ☎ 985/848005). **Gijón** (✉ Marqués de San Estéban 1, ☎ 985/

346046). **A Coruña** (✉ Dársena de la Marina, ☎ 981/221822). **Llanes** (✉ Nemesio Sobrino s/n, ☎ 985/400164). **Luarca** (✉ Plaza de Alfonso X el Sabio, ☎ 985/640083). **Lugo** (✉ Praza Maior 27 (*galerías*, ☎ 982/231361). **O Grove** (✉ Plaza Corgo, ☎ 986/72905). **Oviedo** (✉ Plaza de Alfonso II 6, ☎ 985/213385). **Pontevedra** (✉ General Mola 2, ☎ 986/850814). **Ribadeo** (✉ Plaza de España, ☎ 982/128689). **Ribadesella** (✉ Plaza de la Reina Maria Cristina, ☎ 985/860255). **Tui** (✉ Puente Tripes, ☎ 986/601789). **Vigo** (✉ Jardines de las Avenidas, ☎ 986/430577). **Villaviciosa** (✉ Marques de Villaviciosa 1, ☎ 985/891759).

5 THE PYRENEES

Historically both a barrier and a nexus, the Pyrenees have long been a source of fascination and magic for their many peoples and cultures in both Spain and France. Spanning northeastern Spain, from the Mediterranean to the Atlantic, the Catalan, Aragonese, and Basque Pyrenees are an intoxicating mix of snowcapped mountains, green meadows and valleys, remote glacial ponds and streams, medieval villages, and Romanesque art hidden away in remote chapels, churches, and monasteries.

By George Semler

FOR BETTER OR WORSE, the Pyrenees both join and separate the Iberian Peninsula from the rest of Europe, engendering over the centuries a rich Pyrenean culture distinct from that of Spain or neighboring France. Inhabitants of the prehistoric Pyrenees—originally cave dwellers, later shepherds and farmers—saw their first invaders when the Greeks landed at Empúries, in far-northern Catalonia, in the 6th century BC. The seagoing Carthaginians colonized Spain in the 3rd century BC, and their great general Hannibal surprised Rome by crossing the Oriental (eastern) Pyrenees in 218 BC. After defeating the Carthaginians, the Romans built roads through the mountains: Vía Augusta, from Le Perthus to Barcelona and Tarragona; Strata Ceretana, through the Cerdanya Valley and La Seu d'Urgell to Lleida; Summus Pyrenaecus (or, as the Spanish name Somport reflects, *Summus Portus,* or highest pass), at Somport, to Jaca and Zaragoza; and the Via Lemovicensis from Bordeaux through Roncesvalles to Pamplona, in the Atlantic, or western, Pyrenees.

After the fall of Rome, the Iberian Peninsula was the last of the empire to be overtaken by the Visigoths, who crossed the Pyrenees in AD 409. In the 8th century, the northern tribes then faced Moorish invaders from the south. Although Moorish influence was weaker in the Pyrenees than in southern Spain and only briefly pushed past the mountains into the rest of Europe, this region at the end of the first millennium was a crossroads of Arab, Greek, and European cultures. Toulouse was the melting pot of these influences, the medieval artistic and literary center. Christianity survived the Moors' invasion and occupation largely by fleeing to the hills and thus dotting the Pyrenees with Romanesque art and architecture. When Christian crusaders reconquered Spain, the Pyrenees were divided among three feudal kingdoms: Catalonia, Aragón, and Navarre, proud and independent entities with their respective spiritual "cradles" in the Romanesque mountain monasteries of Ripoll, San Juan de la Peña, and San Salvador de Leyre.

Throughout the centuries, the Pyrenees have remained a strategic factor to be reckoned with. The northbound Moorish empire on the Iberian Peninsula sputtered to a stop here. Charlemagne lost Roland and his rear guard at Roncesvalles in 778, and his heirs lost all of Catalonia in 988. Napoléon never completed his conquest of the Iberian Peninsula largely because the Pyrenees presented insurmountable communication and supply problems. And Hitler was dissuaded by Franco from trying to use post–Civil War Spain as a base camp for his African campaign, a decision that rendered the Pyrenees a path to freedom for Jews and *résistants* fleeing the Nazis.

The Pyrenees stretch 435 km (270 mi) along Spain's border with France. There are three main ranges: the Catalan Pyrenees, the central Pyrenees (in Aragón), and the Basque Pyrenees, which fall gently westward through the Basque country to the Bay of Biscay. The highest peaks are in Aragón—Aneto, in the Maladeta massif; Posets; and Monte Perdido, all of which are about 11,000 ft above sea level. Pica d'Estats (10,372 ft) is Catalonia's highest peak, while Pic D'Orhi (6,656 ft) is the highest in the Basque Pyrenees.

These snowcapped mountains have always been a magical realm, a source of legend and superstition, a breeder of myth and mysticism. Their meadows and valleys have protected the last vestiges of numerous ancient cultures: the Basque village of Zugarramurdi, for example, near the French border, burned Basque witches at the stake in the early 17th century for holding orgiastic ceremonies in local caves, and still commemorates the practice with an annual witches' dinner. Each mountain system is drained by rivers, forming some three dozen valleys between the Mediterranean and the Atlantic; and each valley was all but completely isolated until around the 10th century. Local languages still range from Castilian Spanish to Euskera (Basque), in upper Navarre; to dialects such as Grausín, Belsetán, Chistavíno, Ansotano, Cheso or Patués (Benasqués), in Aragón; to Aranés, a dialect of Gascon French, in the Vall d'Aran; to Catalan, east toward the Mediterranean.

To explore any of these valleys fully—the flora and fauna, the local gastronomy, the peaks and upper meadows, the remote glacial lakes and streams, the Romanesque art hidden in a thousand chapels and hermitages—could take a lifetime. The routes we suggest are introductions to some of Spain's richest and most remote combinations of land and civilization. In a pinch, the cities across the flatlands south of the Pyrenees—Barcelona, Lleida (Lérida, in Castilian Spanish), Huesca, Zaragoza, and Pamplona—make reliable gateways to and from the wilderness; a surprise snowfall in these mountains can bring a hiking trip to an abrupt halt or send motorists scurrying to lower or warmer climes.

Pleasures and Pastimes

Dining

Pyrenean cuisine is characterized by thick soups, stews, roasts, and the use of local ingredients prepared differently in every valley, village, and kitchen from the Mediterranean to the Atlantic. The three main culinary schools are those corresponding to the Pyrenees' three main regional and cultural identities—Catalan, Aragonese, and Basque—but within these are further subdivisions such as La Cerdanya, the Vall d'Aran, Benasque, Roncal, and Baztán. Game is common throughout. Trout (once supplied by anglers, now often raised in lakes and ponds fed by mountain streams), wild goat, deer, boar, partridge, rabbit, duck, and quail are roasted over coals or cooked in aromatic stews called *civets* in Catalonia and *estofadas* in Aragón and Navarre. Fish and meat are often seared on slabs of slate (*a la llosa* in Catalan, *a la piedra* in Castilian Spanish). Wild mushrooms are a local specialty in season, as are wild asparagus, leeks, and herbs such as marjoram, sage, thyme, and rosemary.

CATEGORY	COST*
$$$$	over 6,000 ptas.
$$$	4,000–6,000 ptas.
$$	2,500–4,000 ptas.
$	under 2,500 ptas.

**per person for a three-course meal, excluding drinks, service, and tax*

Fishing

Well populated with trout, Pyrenean streams provide excellent angling from the third Sunday in March to the end of August. Nearly all of the mountains' rivers and streams make fine cold-water fisheries, but the Segre, Aragón, Gállego, Noguera Pallaresa, Arga, and Esca are the most notable. Local ponds and lakes also tend to be rich in trout, providing a good way to combine hiking and angling. Call **Danica** (☏ 608/735376) for horse or helicopter tours with fly-fishing equipment included (for more information, *see* Fishing *in* the Pyrenees A to Z, *below*).

Hiking and Walking

Hiking and mountain climbing are fundamental Pyrenean activities in summer. Local and trans-Pyrenean trails crisscross the region, most with truly unforgettable views. Walking the often grassy crest of the range, with one foot in France and the other in Spain, is an exhilarating experience and well within the reach of the moderately fit. Try walking from Coll de Nuria to Ulldeter over the Sierra Catllar, above Setcases; scaling the Cadí over the Cerdanya; hiking over the Maladeta glacier to Aneto, the Pyrenees' highest peak; or, in autumn, hiking through the Irati beech forest, in upper Navarre. The Iparla Ridge walk, along the Navarre-France border crest, and the Alberes walk from Le Perthus out to the Mediterranean are two more favorite day hikes. Local *excursionista* (outing) clubs, especially the **Centro Excursionista de Catalunya,** in Barcelona (✉ Carrer Paradís 10, ☎ 93/315–2311), can help you get started; local tourist offices may also have brochures and rudimentary trail maps. You can also join equestrian trips, jeep excursions to the upper Pyrenees, and horseback fly-fishing tours of the high streams and lakes from Llívia, in the Cerdanya. Wild-mushroom hunts in piny, hillside meadows are a way of life for many, combining walking, questing, and cooking. (Be 100% certain of any wild mushroom you consume; consult with an expert.)

Lodging

Most hotels in the Pyrenees feel informal and outdoorsy, with a large fireplace in one of the public rooms. Usually built of wood and slate under a steep roof, they blend with the surrounding mountains. Their comfortable, protected atmosphere reflects the tastes of the travelers, who are mostly skiers and hikers. Options include friendly family establishments such as the Güell, in Camprodón, and the Hotel Llívia, in the Spanish enclave of Llívia; grand-luxe places such as Torre del Remei in the Cerdanya Valley; rural accommodations in Basque *caseríos* (farmhouses) like the Iratxeko Berea in Vera de Bidasoa, on the upper reaches of Navarre's Bidasoa River; and town houses such as La Tuca, in Aragón's Canfranc ski station.

CATEGORY	COST*
$$$$	over 15,000 ptas.
$$$	10,000–15,000 ptas.
$$	6,000–10,000 ptas.
$	under 6,000 ptas.

**All prices are for a standard double room, excluding service and tax.*

Romanesque Art and Architecture

The treasury of Romanesque chapels, monasteries, hermitages, and cathedrals in these mountains is rich enough to organize many a trip around. The buildings are in various states of preservation; even a short hike may reveal the picturesque ruins of a 10th-century hermitage. Architectural sites to seek out include the tiny chapel at Beget, above Camprodón; the superb rose window and 50 carved capitals of the cathedral of Santa Maria, in La Seu d'Urgell; the matched set of churches and bell towers in the Noguera de Tor Valley, below the Vall d'Aran; the San Juan de la Peña and Siresa monasteries, west of Jaca; and the village churches of Navarre's Baztán Valley.

Winter Sports

Skiing is the main sport in the Pyrenees, and Baqueira-Beret, in the Vall d'Aran, is the leading resort. Thanks to increasing reliance on artificial-snow machines, there is usually fine skiing from December through March at more than 20 resorts—from Vallter 2000 at Setcases, in the Camprodón Valley, west to Isaba and Burguete, in Navarre. Although weekend skiing can be crowded in the eastern valleys, Catalonia's western Pyrenees, especially Baqueira-Beret, rank among Spain's best winter-sports centers and tend to have more breathing room. Cerler-Benasque, Panticosa, Formigal, Astun, and Candanchú are the major ski areas in Huesca. Numerous resorts offer helicopter skiing and Nordic skiing. Leading Nordic areas include Lles, in the Cerdanya; Salardú and Beret, in the Vall d'Aran; and Panticosa, Benasque, and Candanchú, in Aragón. Jaca, Puigcerdà, and Vielha have public skating sessions, figure-skating classes, and ice-hockey programs. The newspapers *El País, El Periódico de Catalunya,* and *La Vanguardia Española* print complete ski information every Friday in winter (☞ Outdoor Activities and Sports *in* the Pyrenees A to Z, *below*).

Exploring the Pyrenees

Traversing the Pyrenees from the Mediterranean to the Atlantic (or vice versa) is for mountain worshipers a pilgrimage of deep cultural and telluric significance. It's a seven-week hike on foot, but you can make the crossing in 10–14 days by car. The defining valleys are the Camprodón, Cerdanya, Aran, Benasque, Tena, Canfranc, Roncal, and Baztán.

Numbers in the text correspond to numbers in the margin and on the Catalan Pyrenees and the Central and Western Pyrenees maps.

Great Itineraries

Barcelona is the largest pre-Pyrenean base camp. A trip through the Oriental Pyrenees covers an important third of the chain. Five days is enough time to reach the Vall d'Aran and the Noguera de Tor Valley and its Romanesque churches before heading back to Barcelona or farther west or south; such a trip is probably the most cost-effective in terms of time, terrain, art, and architecture. A 10-day trip grants the satisfaction of a sea-to-sea crossing, but you'll spend the bulk of this time in your car.

IF YOU HAVE 3 DAYS

Start from Barcelona, the major urban area with the best communication links. Make your first stop in the mountains 🏨 **Camprodón** ①, then devote the rest of your stay to the Cerdanya Valley: explore 🏨 **Llívia** ⑧ the next day, and on day three drive west down the valley to **La Seu d'Urgell** ⑪. Head back to Barcelona through the Cadí Tunnel.

IF YOU HAVE 5 DAYS

Starting from Barcelona or the Costa Brava, devote your first afternoon and night to 🏨 **Camprodón** ①. Explore the Cerdanya Valley and 🏨 **Llívia** ⑧ the next day, then head to 🏨 **La Seu d'Urgell** ⑪—climbing to **Prat d'Aguiló** ⑩ on the way—for your third day and night. Spend your fourth day and night in the 🏨 **Vall d'Aran** ⑰, and your fifth day absorbing the Noguera de Tor Valley and its Romanesque churches. If you have time, go through **Aigüestortes–Sant Maurici National Park** ⑮. Stop in **Huesca** ㉔ and/or **Zaragoza** ㉕, the capital of Aragón, on your way out of the mountains.

IF YOU HAVE 10 DAYS

With a week and a half, you can contemplate crossing the entire range. From Barcelona or the Costa Brava, the classic crossing begins with a symbolic wade in the Mediterranean at Cap de Creus (☞ Side Trips *in* Chapter 6), peninsular Spain's easternmost point, just north of Cadaqués; from which you cross westward to Fuenterrabía (☞ Chapter 3) to do likewise at the Cabo Higuer lighthouse on the Bay of Biscay. (Of course, you can also travel in the opposite direction, reversing the order of this chapter.) On the westbound trip, a day's drive up through Figueres and Olot (☞ Side Trips *in* Chapter 6) will bring you to 🏨 **Camprodón** ① and the surrounding unspoiled mountain towns, skiing, and wildlife. Stop next in 🏨 **Llívia** ⑧, moving on to the Cerdanya, the widest sunniest valley in the Pyrenees. From there move westward through 🏨 **La Seu D'Urgell** ⑪ to **Aigüestortes–Sant Maurici National**

Park ⑮, the 🏨 **Vall d'Aran** ⑰, and the winter-sports center Baqueira-Beret. Stop in the Noguera de Tor Valley to see its Romanesque churches. Farther west, spend the next few days in 🏨 **Benasque** ㉖, 🏨 **San Juan de Plan** ㉘, **Bielsa** ㉙, the remote valleys of Upper Aragón, 🏨 **Ordesa and Mt. Perdido National Park** ㉚, and 🏨 **Jaca** ㉜, the region's most important town. Finally, move through western Aragón into the Basque Pyrenees to visit the Irati Forest; go through the tunnel under the Velate Pass (or, more spectacularly, over the pass itself) to explore the 🏨 **Baztán Valley** ㊳; and then follow the Bidasoa River down to 🏨 Fuenterrabía (☞ Chapter 3) and the Bay of Biscay.

When to Tour the Pyrenees

If you're a hiker, stick to the summer (June through September, with a definite emphasis on July), when the weather is better and there's less chance of a blizzard or lightning storm at high altitudes. October is an ideal time to enjoy the Pyrenees' still-green valleys and hunt for wild mushrooms. November brings colorful leaves, the last wild mushrooms, and the first frosts. The green springtime thaw, during which you can still ski on the snowcaps, is another spectacular season. For skiing, come between December and April.

THE ORIENTAL PYRENEES

You can reach Catalonia's easternmost Pyrenean valley, the Vall de Camprodón (Camprodón Valley), from Barcelona on N152 through Vic and Ripoll; from the Costa Brava by way of either Figueres or Girona, Besalú, and the new Capsacosta tunnel; or from France through the Col (Pass) d'Ares, which enters the head of the valley at an altitude of 5,280 ft from Prats de Molló. This valley has several exquisite towns and churches; a ski area; and, above all, mountains, such as the Sierra de Catllar, thick with boar, mountain goat, and snow partridge.

Camprodón

❶ *127 km (80 mi) northwest of Barcelona.*

Camprodón, the capital of its *comarca* (county), lies at the junction of the Rivers Ter and Ritort—both excellent trout streams. The rivers flow by, through, and under much of the town, giving it a waterfront character as well as a long history of flooding. The town owes much of its opulence to the summer folks from Barcelona who have built important mansions along the leafy promenade, **Passeig Maristany,** at the town's northern edge. Camprodón's best-known symbol is the elegant **12th-century stone bridge** that broadly spans the River Ter in the center of town; its wide arch descends at a graceful angle from a central peak. The town is also known for its **sausages** of every imaginable size, shape, and consistency and for its two cookie factories, Birbas and Pujol, locked in the embrace of eternal competition. (Birbas is better—look for the image of the bridge on the box.)

Lodging

$$ 🏨 **Güell.** Owned and managed by the charming Güell family, this elegant glass, wood, and stone structure welcomes skiers and general enthusiasts to the Camprodón Valley. Rooms are simple but tasteful, with heavy, Pyrenean wood furniture. ✉ *Plaça d'Espanya 8, 17867,* ☎ *972/740011,* FAX *972/741112. 38 rooms. AE, DC, MC, V.*

Shopping

Don't miss **Cal Xec,** the sausage store at the end of the emblematic Camprodón Bridge. Along with every kind of charcuterie ever conceived, the shop sells Birbas and Pujol cookies.

The Catalan Pyrenees

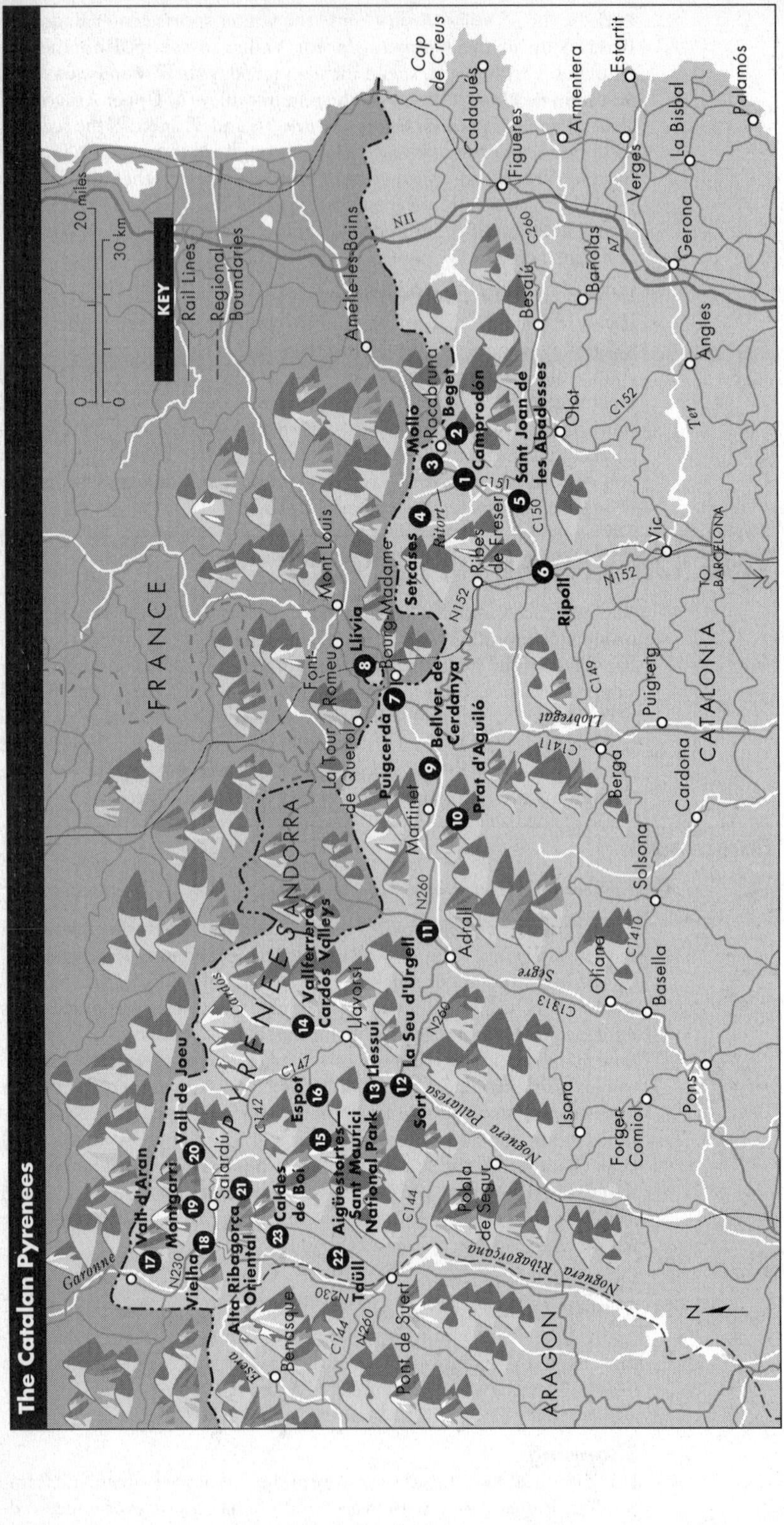

En Route From Camprodón, take C151 north toward the French border at Col d'Ares and turn east toward Rocabruna, a village of crisp, clean Pyrenean stone at the source of the crystalline River Beget.

Beget

❷ *17 km (11 mi) east of Camprodón.*

The village of Beget, considered Catalonia's *més bufó* (cutest), was completely cut off from motorized transportation until the mid-1960s and was only connected to the rest of the world by asphalt roadway in 1980. Beget's 30 houses are eccentric stone structures with heavy wooden doors and an unusual golden tone peculiar to the Camprodón Valley. Graceful stone bridges span the stream in which protected trout feast. The 11th-century Romanesque church of **Sant Cristófol** has a diminutive bell tower and a 6-ft Majestat, a polychrome wood carving of Christ in a head-to-foot tunic, dating from the 12th or 13th century. The church is usually closed, but townsfolk can direct you to the keeper of the key.

Dining

$$ ✕ **Can Po.** Perched over a deep gully, Can Po serves first-rate cuisine in an ancient, ivy-covered, stone-and-mortar farmhouse. Specialties are *entrecot amb crema de ceps* (veal in wild-mushroom sauce) and *anec amb peras* (duck prepared with stewed pears). ✉ *Carretera de Beget s/n, 17867,* ☎ *972/741045. AE, DC, MC, V. Closed Mon.–Thurs. mid-Sept.–mid-July.*

Molló

❸ *25 km (15 mi) northwest of Beget, 24 km (14 mi) from Prats de Molló.*

Molló lies on route C151 on the Ritort stream toward Col d'Ares. Here you'll find the 12th-century Romanesque church of **Santa Cecilia,** a work of exceptional balance and simplicity. The delicate, Romanesque bell tower seems as naturally set into the building and the surrounding countryside as a Pyrenean mushroom.

Lodging

$$ 🏨 **François.** Just 500 yards from the center of town, this charming inn is a good base camp for hiking excursions to Beget and other points in the valley. The owners are patient and friendly, the rooms small but comfortable. ✉ *Carretera Camprodón, 17868,* ☎ *972/130029,* FAX *972/130029. 28 rooms. Restaurant, free parking. AE, DC, MC, V.*

Setcases

❹ *11 km (7 mi) north of Camprodón, 91 km (57 mi) northwest of Girona, 15 km (9 mi) west of Molló.*

This tiny village is nestled at the head of the valley. Although Setcases (literally, "seven houses") is somewhat larger than its name would imply, the town has a distinct mountain spirit and a gravelly roughness, perhaps owing to the torrents flowing through and over its streets en route to the River Ter.

The **Vallter ski area,** above Setcases—built into a glacial cirque reaching a height of 8,216 ft—has a dozen lifts and, on very clear days, views east from the top all the way to the Bay of Roses on the Costa Brava.

On the road back down the valley from Setcases, **Llanars,** just short of Camprodón, has a 12th-century Romanesque church, San Esteban, of an exceptionally rich shade of ocher. The wood-and-iron portal depicts the martyrdom of St. Stephen.

Sant Joan de les Abadesses

5 *21 km (13 mi) southeast of Setcases, 14 km (9 mi) south of Camprodón.*

South of Camprodón, Sant Joan de les Abadesses—named for the 9th-century abbess Emma, daughter of Guifré el Pilós (Wilfred the Hairy), the founder of the Catalonian nation and medieval hero of the Christian Reconquest of Ripoll—is the site of the important 12th-century Romanesque church of **Sant Joan.** The altarpiece is a 13th-century polychrome wood sculpture of the Descent from the Cross, one of the most expressive and human of that epoch. The town's arcaded **Plaça Major** has a medieval look and feel, and the **12th-century bridge** over the Ter is wide and graceful.

Ripoll

6 *105 km (62 mi) north of Barcelona, 65 km (40 mi) southeast of Puigcerdà.*

One of the first Christian strongholds of the Reconquest and a center of religious erudition during the Middle Ages, Ripoll is known as the *bressol* (cradle) of Catalonian nationhood. A dark, mysterious country town built around a **9th-century Benedictine monastery,** it was a focal point of culture throughout the Roussillon (French Catalonia and the Pyrenees) from the monastery's founding, in 888, until the mid-19th century, when Barcelona began to eclipse it for good.

The 12th-century doorway to the church of **Santa Maria** is one of Catalonia's great works of Romanesque art, designed as a triumphal arch. Its sculptures portray the glory of God and of all his creatures from the Creation onward. You can pick up a guide to the figures on the portal (crafted by stone masons and sculptors of the Roussillon school) in the church or at the information kiosk nearby. *Cloister 350 ptas., museum 450 ptas. Tues.–Sun. 10–2 and 3–7.*

North of Ripoll, the **cogwheel train** from Ribes up to Nuria offers one of Catalonia's most unusual excursions. Known as the *cremallera* (zipper), the line was built in 1917 to connect Ribes with the **Santuari de la Mare de Deu de Núria** (Mother of God of Núria). The ride takes 45 minutes and costs 1,500 ptas. round trip. Núria, at an altitude of 6,562 ft at the foot of Puigmal, is a **ski area** and was the site of some of Spain's earliest ice-hockey activity in the 1950s.

The legend of **Núria,** a Marian religious retreat, is based on the story of Sant Gil of Nîmes, who did penance in the Núria Valley during the 7th century. The saint left behind a wooden statue of the Virgin Mary, a bell he used to summon shepherds to prayer, and a cooking pot; 300 years later, a pilgrim found these treasures in this sanctuary. The bell and the pot came to have special importance to barren women, who were believed to be blessed with as many children as they wished by placing their heads in the pot and ringing the bell, each peal of the bell meaning another child. *Free. Open daily except during mass.*

En Route From Ripoll, it's a 65-km (40-mi) drive on the N152 through Ribes de Freser and over the Collada de Toses (Tosses Pass) to Puigcerdà. Above Ribes, the road winds to the top of the pass over a sheer drop down to the Freser stream. Here, even during the driest months, emerald-green pastures remain moist in shaded corners—a sharp contrast to the shale and brown peaks above the timber line. In early spring the climate can range from showers down in Ribes to a blizzard up on the Tosses Pass.

This traditional approach to the Cerdanya has been all but replaced by the road through Manresa, Berga, and the Túnel del Cadí (Cadí Tunnel). Tosses was a barrier for centuries, until the railroad connected Puigcerdà to Barcelona in 1924. The 32 km (20 mi) of switchback curves between Ribes and La Molina kept many would-be travelers in Barcelona until the tunnel cut the driving time from three hours to two and all but eliminated the hazardous-driving factor.

LA CERDANYA

The Pyrenees' widest, sunniest valley—said to be in the shape of the handprint of God—is an Alpine paradise. High pastureland bordered north and south by snow-covered peaks, La Cerdanya starts in France, at Col de la Perche (near Mont Louis), and ends in the Spanish province of Lleida, at Martinet. Split into two countries and subdivided into two more provinces on each side, the valley is nonetheless a geographical and cultural unit with an identity all its own.

As the saying goes, "*Meitat de França, meitat d'Espanya, no hi ha altra terra com la Cerdanya*" ("Half France, half Spain, there's no country like the Cerdanya"): the Cerdanya straddles the border, which meanders through the rich valley floor no more purposefully than the River Segre itself. Residents on both sides of the border speak Catalan, a Romance language derived from early Provençal French, and regard the valley's political border with undisguised hilarity.

Unlike any other valley in the upper Pyrenees, this one runs east–west and thus has a record annual number of hours of sunlight. On the French side, two solar stations collect and store energy near Font Romeu, and a solar oven bakes ceramics in Mont Louis.

Puigcerdà

❼ *170 km (105 mi) north of Barcelona; 65 km (40 mi) northwest of Ripoll.*

Puigcerdà (*puig* means "hill"; *cerdà* derives from "Cerdanya") is the largest town in the valley. From the small piece of high ground upon which it stands, the views down across the meadows and up into the Pyrenees give a dizzying sense of simultaneous height and humility. The **Romanesque bell tower** and the **sunny sidewalk café** beside it are among Puigcerdà's prettiest spots, along with the Gothic church of **Santa Maria** and its long square, the **Plaça del Cuartel.** On Sunday, markets sell clothes, cheeses, fruits, vegetables, and wild mushrooms to shoppers from both sides of the border.

The **Plaça Cabrinetty,** with its porticoes and covered walks, has a sunny northeastern corner where farmers in for the Sunday market gather to discuss their lives and times. The square is protected from the wind and ringed by two- and three-story houses of various pastel colors, some with engraved decorative designs and all with balconies. From the lower end of Plaça Cabrinetty, Carrer Font d'en Llanas winds down to the *font* (spring), where **"Voldria . . . "** ("I wish . . . "), a haunting verse by the Cerdanya's greatest poet, Magdalena Masip (1890–1970), is inscribed on a plaque over the fountain: *. . . and I wish that I could have / my house beneath a fir tree / with all the woods for a garden / and all the sky for a roof. / And flee from the world around me / it overwhelms me and confuses me / and stay quietly just there / drinking the forest in great gulps / with clods of earth for a pillow / and a bed of golden leaves . . .*

A 300-yard walk west from the *font* around the edge of town will bring you to the stairs leading up from the train station to the balcony in front of the town hall. From here, an ample view of the Cerdanya Valley stretches all the way past Bellver de Cerdanya down to the rock walls of the Sierra del Cadí, at the end of the valley.

Le petit train jaune (the little yellow train) leaves daily from Bourg-Madame and from La Tour de Querol, both simple walks into France from Puigcerdà. The border at La Tour, a longer but prettier walk, is marked only by a stone painted with the Spanish and French flags. This *carrilet* (narrow-gauge railway) is the last in the Pyrenees and is used for tours as well as transportation; looking like something out of a Dr. Seuss story, it winds through the Cerdanya to the walled town of Villefranche de Conflent. Popular with adults and children alike, the 63-km (39-mi) tour can take most of the day, especially if you stop to browse in Mont Louis or Villefranche. ✉ *Boarding at SNCF stations at Bourg-Madame or La Tour de Querol.* 🎫 *3,500 ptas. (175 frs.) per person, 2,500 ptas. (125 frs.) per person in groups of 10 or more, payable in French frs. only.* ⏲ *Schedule at Touring travel agency or Turismo office, Puigcerdà; or at RENFE station below Puigcerdà.*

Dining and Lodging

$$–$$$ ✕ **La Tieta.** A 500-year-old town house built into the walls of Puigcerdàs, La Tieta is one of the town's top restaurants. Its garden is an ideal place for a late-night drink in summer. The menu features Cerdanya specialties like *trinxat de Cerdanya* (a rib-sticking puree of cabbage and potatoes with bits of fried salt pork or bacon) as well as roasts cooked over coals. ✉ *C. Alfons I 45,* ☎ *972/880156. AE, DC, MC, V.*

$$ ✕ **Tapanyam.** Longtime restaurateur Pere Compte's new place is thriving. With live music every Saturday in summer, panoramic views of the Pyrenees, excellent mountain cuisine, and fresh seafood, this friendly spot is becoming a Puigcerdà standby. Decor is modern, with bay windows overlooking the valley. ✉ *Plaça d'Alguer 2,* ☎ *972/882360. AE, DC, MC, V.*

$ ✕ **Madrigal.** This popular restaurant-bar near the town hall is the original Compte establishment. The low-ceiling, wood-trim dining room is filled with tables and benches. Selections include tapas and meals of assorted specialties, such as *codorniz* (quail), *caracoles* (snails), *calamares a la romana* (calamari dipped in batter), *albóndigas* (meatballs), *esqueixada* (raw codfish with peppers and onion), and wild mushrooms in season. ✉ *C. Alfons I 1,* ☎ *972/880860. AE, DC, MC, V.*

$$$$ ★ ✕🏨 **La Torre del Remei.** About 3 km (2 mi) west of Puigcerdà is this splendid mansion, built in 1910 and brilliantly restored by José María and Loles Boix of Boix (☞ Martinet, *below*). Everything about La Torre del Remei is superb, from the general Belle Epoque luxury of the manor house to the plush, tasteful rooms, heated bathroom floors, huge bathtubs, and bottle of Moët & Chandon waiting on ice upon your arrival. The restaurant serves top international cuisine with an emphasis on local products such as lamb, trout, and game. Reserve well in advance. ✉ *Camí Reial s/n, Bolvir de Cerdanya, 17463,* ☎ *972/140182,* FAX *972/140449. 10 rooms, 1 suite. Restaurant, pool, 18-hole golf course, putting green. AE, DC, MC, V.*

$$ 🏨 **Hotel del Lago.** This comfortable old favorite near Puigcerdà's emblematic lake is a graceful, tastefully appointed, and renovated series of buildings built around a central garden. A two-minute walk from the bell tower or the town market, it feels bucolic but is virtually in the center of town. ✉ *Avda. Doctor Piguillem 7, 17520,* ☎ *972/881000,* FAX *972/141511. 13 rooms, 3 suites. Breakfast room, pool, free parking. AE, MC, V.*

Nightlife and the Arts

On weekends and holidays, clubs such as **N'Ho Sé, Transit,** and **Gatzara,** in Puigcerdà, and **De Nit,** 5 km (3 mi) from Puigcerdà (near Caixans, on the road to Alp), are filled till dawn with young French and Spanish night owls.

Shopping

Look for local specialties, such as herbs, goat cheese, wild mushrooms, honey, and basketry, in the Sunday markets held in most Cerdanya towns. Puigcerdà's **Sunday market** is as social as it is commercial; the long square in front of the church and former military barracks, known as the Plaça del Cuartel, fills with people and produce. In autumn, it's a great chance to learn about wild mushrooms of all kinds. If it's a horse you're shopping for, come to the annual **equine fair** in early November, a nonpareil opportunity to study both horses and horse traders.

Llívia

❽ *6 km (4 mi) northeast of Puigcerdà.*

A Spanish enclave in French territory, Llívia was marooned by the 1659 Peace of the Pyrenees treaty, which ceded 33 villages to France. Incorporated as a *vila* (town) by royal decree of Carlos V, who spent a night here in 1528 and was impressed by the town's beauty and hospitality, Llívia managed to remain Spanish. The **fortified church** is an acoustic gem; see if anything sonorous is going on. The **ancient pharmacy,** now a museum, was founded in 1415 and is thought to be the oldest in Europe.

Dining and Lodging

$$ ★ ✕ **Can Ventura.** Built into a 17th-century farmhouse, this superb restaurant is the best around Puigcerdà for decor, cuisine, and value. Trout or beef cooked *a la llosa* is a house specialty; the *entretenimientos* (a wide selection of hors d'oeuvres) are delicious. ✉ *Plaça Major 1,* ☎ *972/896178. Reservations essential. MC, V. Closed Mon.–Tues.*

$$ ✕ **La Formatgeria de Llívia.** This unusual restaurant on the east edge of Llívia (en route to Saillagousse, France) is built into a former cheese factory, part of which still functions while you watch. Owners Marta Pous and Juanjo Meya have had great success with their fine local specialties, panoramic views south to Puigmal, and general charm and good cheer. ✉ *Pla de Ro, Gorguja,* ☎ *972/146279. Reservations essential. MC, V. Closed Thurs.*

$$ ✕🏨 **Hotel de Llívia.** Here's an ideal no-frills base of operations for anyone skiing or hiking in France, Andorra, *or* Spain. Hotel Llívia is owned and operated by the warm, generous Pous family, proprietors of Can Ventura (☞ *above*). A spacious place, with large fireplaces and a glass-walled dining room that's nearly as scenic as a picnic in a Pyrenean meadow, the hotel runs spontaneous shuttles to nearby ski resorts and can organize excursions as well as riding, hunting, or trout fishing. ✉ *Avda. de Catalunya s/n, 17527,* ☎ *972/896000,* FAX *972/146000. 68 rooms, 10 apartments. Restaurant, pool, tennis court. DC, MC, V.*

Bellver de Cerdanya

★ ❾ *25 km (16 mi) west of Puigcerdà on N260.*

Bellver de Cerdanya has conserved its slate-roof and fieldstone Pyrenean architecture more successfully than many of the Cerdanya's larger towns. Perched on a promontory over the **River Segre,** which folds neatly around the town, Bellver is a mountain version of a fishing village—trout fishing, of course. The river is the town's main event; how much water is coming down—and whether it's low or high, muddy or clear, warm or cold—supplants the weather as a topic of conversation. Bellver's Gothic church of **Sant Jaume** and the arcaded **Plaça Major,** in the upper part of town, are lovely examples of traditional Pyrenean mountain-village design.

Dining and Lodging

$$ ★ ✕🏨 **Fonda Biayna.** This rustic little mountain retreat seems to have gotten happily stuck in an early Pyrenean time warp, with woodsy decor and a provincial atmosphere. The typical Catalan cuisine includes such gamey dishes as roast rabbit *allioli* (with a beaten sauce of garlic and olive oil), *galtas de porc amb bolets* (pork cheeks with wild mushrooms), and *tiró amb naps i trumfes* (duck with turnips and potatoes). The guest rooms are simple, old-fashioned, and cozy. ✉ *Carrer Sant Roc 11 25720,* ☎ *973/510475,* FAX *973/510853. 16 rooms. AE, DC, MC, V.*

Martinet

10 km (6 mi) west of Bellver de Cerdanya on N260.

The town of Martinet hasn't much to offer except a few cozy watering spots that are hard to pass up in the heat of summer. For a course in trout economy, have a close look over the railing along the river just upstream from the junction of the Llosa and the Segre. Martinet's protected trout are famous in these parts: they dine from 1 to 4, when the sun slants in, cooks off aquatic-insect hatches, and illuminates every speckle and spot on these sleek leviathans.

For a spectacular excursion, drive or walk up the valley of the Riu Llosa into Andorra, or take the short but stunning walk from the village of **Aransa** to Lles: as you pull away from Aransa and onto an alpine meadow, the Cerdanya's palette changes with every twist of the trail. You'll even pass the ruins of a 10th-century hilltop hermitage. (The tourist office in La Seu d'Urgell has simple trail maps.) The village of **Lles** is a famous Nordic-skiing resort with miles of cross-country tracks.

Prat d'Aguiló

★ ⑩ *20 km (12 mi) north of Martinet up a dirt road that is rough but navigable by the average car. Follow signs for "Refugio Prat D'Aguilo."*

The spectacular Prat d'Aguiló, or Eagle's Meadow, is one of the highest points in the Cerdanya that you can access without either a four-wheel-drive vehicle or a hike. The winding, bumpy drive up the mountain takes about an hour and a half (start with ample fuel) and opens onto some excellent vistas of its own. From the meadow, a roughly three-hour climb to the top of the sheer rock wall of the Sierra del Cadí, directly above, reaches an altitude of nearly 8,000 ft. On a clear day you can see Puigcerdà and beyond; the River Segre seems no more than a thin, silver ribbon on the valley floor.

La Seu d'Urgell

★ ⑪ *20 km (12 mi) south of Andorra la Vella, 50 km (30 mi) west of Puigcerdà past Bellver and Martinet along the River Segre.*

La Seu d'Urgell is an ancient town facing the snowy rock wall of the Sierra del Cadí. Its historical importance as the seat of the regional archbishopric since the Middle Ages (6th century) has left it with a rich legacy of art and architecture. The Pyrenean feel of the streets, with dark balconies and porticoes, overhanging galleries, and colonnaded porches—particularly **Carrer dels Canonges**—makes La Seu d'Urgell mysterious and memorable. Look for the medieval **grain measures** at the corner of Carrer Major and Carrer Capdevila. The tiny food shops on the arcaded Carrer Major are intriguing places to assemble lunch for a hike.

★ The 12th-century cathedral of **Santa Maria** is the finest cathedral in the Pyrenees. One of the most moving sights in northern Spain is a show of sunlight casting the rich reds and blues of Santa Maria's southeastern rose window into the deep gloom of the transept. The 13th-century cloister is known for the individually carved, sometimes whimsical capitals on its 50 columns. (They were crafted by the same Roussillon school of masons who carved the doorway on the church of Santa Maria in Ripoll.) Don't miss either the haunting, 11th-century chapel of **Sant Miquel** or the **Diocesan Museum,** which has a striking collection of medieval murals from various Pyrenean churches and a colorfully illuminated 10th-century Mozarabic manuscript of the monk Beatus de Liébana's commentary on the Apocalypse, along with a short film explaining the manuscript. Ask for the attractive and well-organized book detailing every local church on the medieval Vía Románica; it makes a lovely souvenir. *Cathedral, cloister, and museum 450 ptas. Daily 9–1 and 4–8.*

Dining and Lodging

$$ **Cal Pacho.** Sample traditional local specialties at very reasonable prices in this dark, rustic spot, built in the typical Pyrenean style with stone and wood beams. Count on powerful *escudella* (mountain soup of vegetables, pork or veal, and noodles) in winter, and meat cooked over coals or on slate (*a la llosa*) year-round. ✉ *Carrer Lafont 11,* ☎ *973/352719. AE, DC, MC, V.*

$$$$ ★ **El Castell.** This high, wood-and-slate structure just outside Seu is one of the finest places around for both dining and lodging. Rooms on the second floor have balconies overlooking the river; those on the third have slanted ceilings and dormer windows. Suites add a salon. The restaurant specializes in mountain cuisine, such as *civet de jabalí* (wild-boar stew) and *llom de cordet amb trinxat* (lamb cooked over coals and served with puree of potatoes and cabbage). You need a reservation to stay overnight. ✉ *Carretera de Lleida (N260), Km 129, Apdo. 53, 25700,* ☎ *973/350704,* FAX *973/351574. 38 rooms, 4 suites. Restaurant. AE, DC, MC, V.*

$$$ **Parador de la Seu d'Urgell.** For comfortable quarters right in town, don't hesitate to stay at the excellent parador, built into the 12th-century church and convent of Sant Domènec. The interior patio—the cloister of the former convent—is a lush and tranquil hideaway. Rooms are simple but warm-toned, and some look past the edge of town to the mountains. The small pool and the dining room have glass ceilings. ✉ *Carrer Sant Domènec 6, 25700,* ☎ *973/352000,* FAX *973/352309. 77 rooms, 1 suite. Restaurant, indoor pool. AE, DC, MC, V.*

WESTERN CATALAN PYRENEES

The main geographical systems in this section are the valley of the Noguera Pallaresa River, the Vall d'Aran headwaters of the Atlantic-bound Garonne, and the Noguera Ribagorçana River valley, Catalonia's western limit. The space in the middle of the rhombuslike area delimited by the roads C133, N230, and C144 contains two of the Pyrenees' greatest treasures: Aigüestortes–Sant Maurici National Park, and the Noguera de Tor Valley, with its matching set of gemlike Romanesque churches.

Sort

★ 12 *From La Seu d'Urgell, take N260 toward Lleida, head west at Adrall, and drive 53 km (33 mi) over the Cantó Pass to Sort.*

Sort, the capital of the Pallars Sobirà (Upper Pallars Valley), is a center for skiing, fishing, and white-water kayaking. Don't be content with the Sort you see from the main road: one block back, the town is honeycombed with tiny streets and protected corners built against heavy winter weather. Sort is also the origin of the road into the unspoiled

Assua Valley, a hidden pocket of untouched mountain villages, such as Saurí and Olp.

Dining

$ ✕ **Fogony.** If you hit Sort at lunchtime, come straight here for some bracing escudella or some roast lamb or goat before you head up into the high country. ✉ *Av. Generalitat 45,* ☎ *973/621225. MC, V. Closed Mon. except during Christmas wk, Easter wk, and Aug.; closed Jan. 7–22.*

Llessuí

13 *15 km (9 mi) north of Sort.*

At the head of the Upper Pallars Valley, Llessuí's Romanesque church of **Sant Pere** is topped with a typical conical bell tower resembling a pointed witch's hat, characteristic of the Vall d'Aran and its environs. The local **ski area** presides over the valley from the slopes of the Altars peak.

Dining and Lodging

$$ ✕🏨 **Vall d'Assua.** A cozy refuge, this little family-run, family-oriented place is a sure bet for simple Pyrenean home cooking, strong on roasts and thick stews and soups. The guest rooms are small but impeccably clean and comfortable. ✉ *Carretera de Llessuí, 25560 Altrón,* ☎ *973/621738,* FAX *973/621738. 11 rooms. No credit cards. Closed Nov.*

Vallferrera and Cardós Valleys

14 *From Llavorsí—14 km (9 mi) from Sort on C147, at the junction of the Noguera Pallaresa and Cardós rivers—the road up to the Cardós and Vallferrera valleys branches off to the northeast.*

A trip up the Vallferrera Valley is a good way to penetrate some little-known countryside, explore icy trout streams, or browse through the Romanesque and Visigothic (pre-Romanesque) churches and chapels scattered in and around the village of **Alins** under Catalonia's highest mountain, the Pica d'Estats. In the neighboring Cardós Valley, the svelte, Romanesque bell tower of the church of **Santa Maria** rises amid green fields of alfalfa and early wheat and, in May, bright-red splashes of poppies.

Dining and Lodging

$$ ✕🏨 **Cardós.** As a base camp for skiing, hiking, climbing, or fishing excursions up the Cardós Valley, you can't do much better than this handy place in the village of Ribera de Cardos. The hearty fare, centered on sturdy soups, is welcome after you've spent some time at high altitude. The rooms are warm in winter, cool in summer, and always spotless and comfortable. ✉ *Reguera 2, 25570 Ribera de Cardós,* ☎ *973/623100,* FAX *973/623158. 50 rooms. AE, DC, MC, V. Closed Nov.*

Aigüestortes–Sant Maurici National Park

15 *After Escaló, 12 km (7 mi) northwest of Llavorsí, the road to Espot and the Aigüestortes–Sant Maurici National Park veers west.*

This wild domain of meadows and woods in the shadow of the twin peaks of Els Encantats hides more than 150 glacial lakes and lagoons (the beautiful Estany de Sant Maurici among them) as well as streams, waterfalls, and marshes. Forested by pines, firs, beech, and silver birches, it also has ample pastureland inhabited by Pyrenean chamois, capercaillie, golden eagle, and ptarmigan. The park has strict rules: no camping, no fires, no vehicles beyond certain points, no loose pets. Access to the park is free; shelters equipped with bunks and mattresses provide overnight accommodations. For information and reservations contact the park administration (✉ Camp de Mart 35, 25004, Lleida, ☎ 973/246650).

Lodging

The **Ernest Mallafré Refugio** (shelter) is at the foot of Els Encantats near Lake Sant Maurici (☎ 973/624009); the shelter sleeps 36 and is open February–December. The **L'Estany Llong Refugio** (☎ 973/690284), in the Sant Nicolau Valley, sleeps 57 and is open mid-June–mid-October.

Espot

16 *Next to the eastern entrance to Aigüestortes–Sant Maurici; 166 km (100 mi) north of Lleida; 15 km (9 mi) northwest of Llavorsí.*

Espot, which has a **ski area** (Super-Espot), nestles at the valley floor along a clear, aquamarine stream. The **Pont de la Capella** (Chapel Bridge), a perfect, mossy arch over the flow, looks as though it might have grown directly from the Pyrenean slate.

En Route From Esterri d'Aneu, C142 reaches the sanctuary of Mare de Deu de Ares, a hermitage and shelter, at 4,600 ft, and the Bonaigua Pass, at 6,798 ft. The latter offers a dizzying look back at the Pallars Mountains and ahead to the Vall d'Aran and the Maladeta massif beyond, shimmering white in the distance.

Vall d'Aran and Environs

17 *From Esterri d'Aneu, the valley runs 46 km (27 mi) east to Vielha over the Bonaigua Pass.*

The Vall d'Aran is at the western edge of the Catalan Pyrenees and the northwestern corner of Catalonia. North of the main Pyrenean axis, it is the Catalan Pyrenees' only Atlantic valley, opening into the plains of Aquitania and drained by the Garonne, which flows into the Atlantic Ocean north of Bordeaux. The 48-km (30-mi) drive from the Bonaigua Pass to the Pont del Rei border with France follows the riverbed faithfully.

The valley's Atlantic personality shows in its climate—wetter and colder—and its language: the 6,000 inhabitants speak Aranés, a dialect of Gascon French derived from the Occitanian language group. With some difficulty, Aranés can be understood by speakers of Catalan and French. Originally part of the Aquitanian county of Comminges, the Vall d'Aran maintained feudal ties to the Pyrenees of Spanish Aragón and became part of Catalonia-Aragón in the 12th century. In 1389 the valley was assigned to Catalonia.

Neither as wide as the Cerdanya nor as oppressively narrow and vertical as Andorra, the Vall d'Aran has a sense of well-being and order, an architectural consonance unique in Catalonia. The clusters of iron-gray slate roofs, the lush vegetation, the dormer windows (a clear sign of French influence)—all make the Vall d'Aran a distinct geographic and cultural pocket that happens to have washed up on the Spanish side of the border. Hiking and climbing opportunities abound here. Guides are available year-round and can be arranged through the **tourist office** in Vielha (☎ 973/640110).

Vielha

18 *79 km (49 mi) northwest of Sort.*

Vielha (Viella, in Castilian Spanish), the capital of the Vall d'Aran, is a lively crossroads vitally involved in the Aranese movement to defend and reconstruct the valley's architectural, institutional, and linguistic heritage. The octagonal, 14th-century bell tower on the Romanesque parish church of **Sant Miquel** is one of the town's trademarks, as is the 15th-century Gothic altar. The partly damaged 12th-century polychrome wood carving *Cristo de Mig Aran,* displayed under glass, evokes a sense of mortality and humanity with a power unusual in medieval sculpture.

From Vielha you can visit **Salardú,** with an arcaded central *plaça* and an especially tall and graceful bell tower.

The village of **Tredós,** home of the Romanesque church of Santa Maria de Cap d'Aran—symbol of the Aranese independence movement and meeting place of the valley's governing body, the Consell General, until 1827—lies just east of Salardú.

Dining and Lodging

$$$–$$$$ ★ ✕ **Ca la Irene.** In nearby Arties, 6 km (4 mi) east of Vielha, this rustic little haven is known for fine mountain cuisine with a French flair. Three tasting menus and gastronomic gems like poached foie gras in black truffles and roast wild pigeon in nuts and mint make this place a must. ✉ *Mayor 3, Hotel Valartiés,* ☎ *973/644364,* FAX *973/642174. Reservations essential. MC, V. Closed Mon. Nov.–Apr.; closed Oct. 15–Nov. 20.*

$$ ★ ✕ **Era Mola.** Also known as Restaurante Gustavo y María José, this restored stable with wood beams and whitewashed walls serves French-tinged Aranese cuisine. The *confite de pato* (duck stewed with apple) and *magret de pato* (breast of duck served rare with *carradetas,* wild mushrooms from the valley) are favorites. ✉ *Carrer Marrech 14,* ☎ *973/642419. Reservations essential. MC, V. No lunch weekdays Dec.–Apr. except weekends and holidays.*

$$$ ✕🏨 **Parador Don Gaspar de Portolà.** Also known as the Parador de Arties, this modern parador makes liberal use of glass and offers panoramic views of the Pyrenees. Just 7 km (4 mi) from the Baqueira ski slopes, it's big enough to hold a party and small enough for intimacy. ✉ *Carretera Baqueira-Beret s/n, 25599,* ☎ *973/640801,* FAX *973/641001. 54 rooms, 3 suites. Restaurant, pool, exercise room, parking (fee). AE, MC, V.*

$$$ ✕🏨 **Parador Valle de Aran.** This modern granite parador has a semicircular salon with huge windows and spectacular views over the Maladeta peaks. Rooms are furnished with traditional carved-wood furniture and floor-to-ceiling curtains. The restaurant serves preponderantly Catalan cuisine, such as *espinacas a la catalana* (spinach cooked in olive oil with pine nuts, raisins, and garlic). ✉ *Carretera del Túnel s/n, 25530,* ☎ *973/640100,* FAX *973/641100. 135 rooms. Restaurant. AE, MC, V.*

$$ 🏨 **Pirene.** On the left side of the N320 into Vielha, this modern hotel commands some of the best views in town. Rooms are bright and simply furnished. The cozy sitting room and the charming family in charge make a stay here a delight. Book ahead during ski season: you're 15 minutes from the slopes. ✉ *Carretera del Túnel (N230) s/n, 25530,* ☎ *973/640075,* FAX *973/642295. 40 rooms. AE, DC, MC, V.*

Montgarri

⓳ *Salardú is 9 km (6 mi) east of Vielha.*

The sanctuary of **Santa Maria de Montgarri** is 12 km (7 mi) northeast of the town of Baguergue, which is just north of Salardú. This partly ruined 11th-century structure was once an important way station on the route into the Vall d'Aran from France. The beveled, hexagonal bell tower and the rounded stones, which look like they came from a brook bottom, give the structure a stippled appearance not unlike that of a Pyrenean trout. Try to be there for the Romería de Nuestra Señora de Montgarri (Feast of Our Lady of Montgarri), on July 2, a country fair with dancing, game playing, and general carrying-on.

Dining and Lodging

$ ✕ **Casa Rufus.** Nestled in the tiny, gray-stone village of Gessa, between Vielha and Salardú, Casa Rufus is cozily furnished with pine and checked tablecloths. Rufus himself, who also runs the ski school at Baqueira, specializes in local country cooking; try the *conejo relleno de ternera* (rabbit stuffed with veal). ✉ *Sant Jaume 8,* ☎ *973/645246 or 973/645872. MC, V. Closed May–July, Sept., Nov., and Sun.*

$$$$ ★ ✕🏨 **Tryp Royal Tanau.** This luxurious hotel 7 km (4 mi) east of Salardú has lifts directly up to the slopes and every possible comfort and amenity, with prices to match. Undoubtedly the top skiing hotel in the Pyrenees (it's the only five-star establishment in the Vall d'Aran), it's the obvious place to be pampered between assaults on the snowy heights. ✉ *Carretera Baqueira-Beret, Km 7, 25598,* ☎ *973/644446,* FAX *973/644344. 30 rooms, 15 apartments. Restaurant, pool, indoor and outdoor hot tubs, parking (fee). AE, MC, V.*

Outdoor Activities and Sports

Skiing, white-water rafting, hiking, climbing, horseback riding, and fly-fishing are all available throughout the Vall d'Aran. Ask the local tourist office for specifics.

DOGSLEDDING

La Pirena, the Pyrenean version of the Iditarod, rages through the Vall d'Aran in early February. The race runs from Panticosa, above Jaca, to La Molina, near Puigcerdà, February 1–15. For more information contact the tourist office in Jaca (☎ 974/360098).

Vall de Joeu

20 *9 km (6 mi) northwest of Vielha.*

The Joeu Valley, above the town of Les Bordes, grants an intriguing look at Vall d'Aran hydraulics. One of the two main sources of the Garonne, the Joeu River rises (resurfaces, actually) at Artiga de Lin and cascades down the Barrancs waterfalls toward the Garonne. Using colored waters, early 20th-century scientists proved that this "spring" was actually glacier runoff from the Maladeta massif, in the next valley west. The glacier melt cascades into a massive pothole known as the Aigüalluts and reappears 4 km (2½ mi) later at Uelhs deth Joeu (Eyes of Jupiter, in Aranés, for the Roman god's association with rain and agriculture), where it flows north toward the Garonne and, eventually, the Atlantic.

The **Baqueira-Beret Estación de Esquí** (Baqueira-Beret Ski Station), visited annually by King Juan Carlos I and the royal family, offers Catalonia's most varied and reliable skiing. ✉ *25598 Salardú,* ☎ *973/644455,* FAX *973/644488. Barcelona office:* ✉ *Passeig de Gràcia 2,* ☎ *93/318–2776,* FAX *93/412–2942.*

Alta Ribagorça Oriental

21 *From Vall d'Aran take the 6-km (4-mi) Vielha tunnel to the Alta Ribagorça Oriental.*

This valley includes the east bank of the Noguera Ribagorçana River and the Llevata and Noguera de Tor valleys. The latter has the Pyrenees' richest concentration of medieval art and architecture.

From Vielha, route N230 runs south 33 km (20 mi) to the intersection with N260 (sometimes marked C144), which goes west over the

Fadas Pass to Castejón de Sos. Four kilometers (two-and-one-half miles) past this intersection, the road up the Noguera de Tor Valley turns to the northeast, 2 km (1 mi) short of Pont de Suert.

The quality and unity of design apparent in the Romanesque churches along the Noguera de Tor River are the result of the sponsorship—and wives—of the counts of Erill. The Erill knights, away fighting Moors in distant theaters of the Reconquest, left their women behind to supervise the creation of local houses of worship. The women then brought in Europe's leading masters of architecture, masonry, sculpture, and painting to build and decorate the churches. To what extent a single eye and sensibility was responsible for this extraordinarily harmonious and coherent set of churches may never be known, but it's clear that they all share certain distinguishing characteristics: a miniaturistic tightness combined with eccentric or irregular design, and slender rectangular bell towers at once light and forceful, perfectly balanced against the rocky background.

Taüll

22 *58 km (36 mi) south of Vielha.*

A town of narrow streets and tight mountain design—wooden balconies, steep slate roofs—Taüll now has a **ski resort,** Boí Taüll, at the head of the Sant Nicolau Valley.

The three-naved Romanesque church of **Sant Climent,** at the edge of town, was built in 1123 and has a six-story belfry. The proportions, the Pyrenean stone, the changing hues in the light, and the general intimacy of the place create an exceptional balance and harmony. The church's murals, including the famous *Pantocrator,* the work of the "Master of Taüll," were moved to Barcelona's Museu Nacional d'Art de Catalunya (☞ Chapter 6) in 1922; you can see reproductions here. *500 ptas. Daily 9–2 and 4–8.*

Other important **churches** in Taüll include Sant Feliu, at Barruera; Sant Joan Baptista, at Boí; Santa Maria, at Cardet; Santa Maria, at Col; Santa Eulàlia, at Erill-la-vall; La Nativitat de la Mare de Deu and Sant Quirze, at Durro; Sant Llorenç, at Sarais; and Sant Nicolau, in the Sant Nicolau Valley, at the entrance to Aigüestortes–Sant Maurici National Park.

Dining

$$ ✕ **La Cabana.** This rustic place specializes in lamb and goat cooked over coals but also offers a fine *escudella* (sausage, vegetable, and potato stew) and an excellent *crema de carrerres* (cream of meadow mushroom) soup. ✉ *Carretera de Taüll,* ☎ *973/696213. MC, V. Closed Mon. Dec.–Apr., May–June 23, and Oct.–Nov.*

Caldes de Boí

23 *6 km (4 mi) north of Taüll.*

The thermal baths at Caldes de Boí include, between hot and cold sources, 40 springs. The caves inside the bath area are a singular natural phenomenon, with thermal steam seeping through the cracks in the rock. Take advantage of the baths' therapeutic qualities at either Hotel Caldes or Hotel Manantial—services range from a bath, at 1,000–1,500 ptas., to a 3,000-pta. underwater body massage. Arthritic patients are frequent takers. ✉ *Hotel Caldes,* ☎ *973/696230;* ✉ *Hotel Manantial,* ☎ *973/690191. Closed Oct.–June 24.*

Dining and Lodging

$$ ✕▣ **Fondevila.** This solid stone structure 3 km (2 mi) from Taüll is warmly decorated inside with wooden trim and simple country furnishings. The rooms are generously proportioned and cozy. The country cuisine features game in season and various Catalan specialties. ✉ *Carrer Única, 25528 Boí,* ☎ *973/696011,* FAX *973/696011. 46 rooms. AE, DC, MC, V. Closed Oct.–Nov.*

ARAGÓN AND THE CENTRAL PYRENEES

Alto Aragón (Upper Aragón), the northern part of the province of Huesca, contains the Maladeta (11,165 ft), Posets (11,070 ft), and Monte Perdido (11,004 ft) massifs, the highest points in the Pyrenean chain. The north–south valleys were formed by glaciers at their headlands; the still-deeper canyons and gorges were cut by rivers swollen by rainfalls and heavy snow runoff.

Communications here were all but nonexistent until the 19th century. Four-fifths of the region had never seen a motor vehicle of any kind until the early part of the 20th century, and the 150 km (93 mi) of border with France between Portalet de Aneu and Vall d'Aran had never had an international crossing. This combination of high peaks, deep defiles, and lack of communication has produced some of the Iberian Peninsula's most isolated towns and valleys. The residents of much of Upper Aragón speak dialects such as Grausín and Benasqués and have their own variations on the typical Aragonese folk dance, the *jota,* and different kinds of folkloric costumes. The unspoiled setting is habitat for a wide variety of Pyrenean wildlife, including several strains of mountain goat, deer, and—in Ordesa and Mt. Perdido National Park—the recently reintroduced Pyrenean brown bear.

The largely undiscovered cities of Huesca and Zaragoza are at once useful Pyrenean gateways and destinations in themselves. Both retain an authentic provincial character that is refreshingly original in postmodern Spain. Huesca's lovely old quarter and Zaragoza's immense basilica, La Pilarica, are memorable additions to a mountain trip.

Huesca

24 *75 km (46 mi) south of Ainsa, 72 km (45 mi) north of Zaragoza, 123 km (74 mi) northwest of Lleida.*

Capital of Aragón until the royal court moved to Zaragoza in 1118, Huesca was founded by the Romans a millennium earlier. The city became an independent state with a senate and an excellent school system organized by the Roman general Sertorius in 77 BC. Much later, after centuries of Moorish rule, Pedro I of Aragón liberated Huesca in 1096. The town's university was founded in 1354 and now specializes in Aragonese studies.

Huesca's 13th-century Gothic **cathedral** is the most emblematic building in the town's old quarter, its eroded facade topped by an intricately carved gallery. Damián Forment, a disciple of the Italian master sculptor Donatello, is the author of the cathedral's crowning glory, an alabaster altarpiece with scenes from the Crucifixion.

Across the street from the cathedral is the Renaissance ***ayuntamiento*** (town hall). Look for the 19th-century painting of the 12th-century beheading of a group of uncooperative nobles, ordered by Ramiro II. Having called a meeting for the purported pouring of a giant bell that would be audible throughout Aragón, Ramiro proceeded to massacre the leading troublemakers; the expression *como la campana de Huesca* ("like the bell of Huesca") is still sometimes used to describe an event of surprising resonance. The **Museo Arqueológico Provincial,** in the former university buildings, is an octagonal patio surrounded by eight chambers including the **Sala de la Campana** (Hall of the Bell), scene of the infamous beheadings. The museum occupies parts of what was once the royal palace of the Kings of Aragón and holds paintings by Aragonese primitives, including *La Virgen del Rosario,* by Miguel Jiménez, and several works by the 16th-century Maestro de Sigena. ✉ *Plaza de la Universidad,* ☎ *974/220586.* 🎫 *450 ptas.* ⏲ *Tues.–Sun. 10–2.*

The church of **San Pedro el Viejo** has an 11th-century cloister with sculpted capitals. Ramiro II and his father, Alfonso I, the only Aragonese kings not entombed at San Juan de la Peña, rest in a side chapel here.

Huesca's fiestas for patron saint Lorenzo, held August 2–8, are nearly as riotous as Pamplona's San Fermín. *Albahaca* (basil) is Huesca's great crop and symbol; thus, basil and green neckerchiefs are everywhere in Huesca that week.

The **Castillo de Loarre,** 32 km (19 mi) west of Huesca off the N240, is a massively walled fortress nearly indistinguishable from the rock outcroppings that surround it. Inside the walls are a Romanesque chapel and a network of stairways, watch paths, and passages running between the towers.

Lodging

$$ **San Marcos.** The building dates from 1890, and the rooms, though updated for comfort, remain tastefully decorated with traditional touches. Centrally located just outside the 1st-century Roman walls, the hotel is a five-minute walk from Huesca's cathedral. ✉ *San Orencio 10, 22001,* ☎ *974/222931,* FAX *974/222931. 29 rooms. Breakfast room, parking (fee). AE, DC, MC, V.*

Zaragoza

25 *72 km (43 mi) southwest of Huesca, 138 km (86 mi) west of Lleida, 307 km (184 mi) west of Barcelona, 164 km (98 mi) southeast of Pamplona, 322 km (193 mi) northeast of Madrid.*

Despite its hefty size (population 600,000), this sprawling provincial capital remains relatively obscure and is in some ways an oasis of authenticity, a detour from the tourist track. Straddling Spain's greatest river, the mighty Ebro, 2,000-year-old Zaragoza holds an important legacy of everything from Roman ruins to Arab, Romanesque, Gothic-Mudejar, Renaissance, Baroque, neoclassical, and Art Nouveau architecture. Rated one of Spain's most desirable places to live for a variety of reasons (air quality, cost of living, population density), Zaragoza seems to breathe a quiet sense of self-contained well-being.

Hulking on the banks of the Ebro, the **Basílica de Nuestra Señora del Pilar** (Basilica of Our Lady of the Pillar), affectionately known as "La Pilarica," is Zaragoza's symbol and pride. An immense Baroque and eclectic structure with no fewer than 11 tiled cupolas, La Pilarica is the home of the Virgen del Pilar, the patron saint not only of peninsular Spain but of the entire Hispanic world. The fiestas honoring this most Spanish of saints, the week of October 12, are events of extraordinary pomp and fervor, with processions, street concerts, bullfights, and traditional *jota* dancing. The cathedral was built in the 18th century to commemorate the appearance of the Virgin on a pillar (*pilar*), or pedestal, to St. James, Spain's other patron saint, during his legendary incarnation as Santiago Matamoros (St. James the Moorslayer) in the 9th century. La Pilarica herself resides in a side chapel that dates from 1754. The frescoes in the cupolas, attributed to the young Goya, are among the basilica's treasures. The **Museo Pilarista** holds drawings and some of the Virgin's jewelry. *Basilica free; museum, 175 ptas. Basilica daily 5:45 AM–9:30 PM; museum, daily 9–2 and 4–6.*

Zaragoza's cathedral, **La Seo,** across the square from the basilica, is the city's bishopric, or diocesan *seo* (seat). An amalgam of architectures ranging from the Mudéjar brick-and-tile exterior to the Gothic altarpiece to exuberant, Churrigueresque doorways, the Seo nonetheless has an 18th-century Baroque facade that seems to echo those of La Pilarica. The **Museo de Tapices** within features medieval tapestries. *Cathedral free; museum 300 ptas. Cathedral, Mon.–Sat. 10–2 and 4–8, Sun. 5–8; museum, Tues.–Sat. 10–2 and 4–6, Sun. 10–2.*

Not far away, the **Iglesia de la Magdalena** (Church of Mary Magdelene), next to the remains of the Roman forum, has an ancient, brick Mudéjar bell tower. Parts of the **Roman walls** are visible near La Pilarica, as is the medieval **Puente de Piedra** (Stone Bridge) spanning the Ebro. The **Lonja** (stock exchange), the Moorish **Aljafería** (jewel treasury), the **Mercado de Lanuza** (produce market), as well as the various **churches** in the old town—San Pablo, San Miguel, San Gil, Santa Engracia, San Carlos, San Ildefonso, San Felipe, Santa Cruz, and San Fernando—will guide you through this jumble of back streets.

The **Museo del Foro** displays remains of the Roman forum and the Roman sewage system, though the presentation is in Spanish only. Two more Roman sites, the **thermal baths** at Calle de San Juan y San Pedro and the **river port** at Plaza San Bruno, have also just opened to the public. *Plaza de la Seo s/n, 976/399752. 500 ptas. Tues.–Sat. 10–2 and 5–8.*

The **Museo Camón Aznar** (C. Espoz y Mina 23, 976/397328) has a fine collection of Goya's works, particularly engravings. It's open Tuesday to Friday 9–2 and 6–9, weekends 9–2, and admission is 75 ptas. The **Museo Provincial de Bellas Artes** (Provincial Museum of Fine Arts; Plaza de los Sitios 5, 976/222181) is also rich in Goyas; it's open Tuesday to Saturday 9–2 and 4–7, Sunday 9–2, and charges 350 ptas. The **Museo Pablo Gargallo** (Plaza de San Felipe 3, 976/392058) is dedicated to one of Spain's greatest modern sculptors, born near Zaragoza in 1881. Hours are Tuesday to Sunday 9–2 and 4–7, and admission is 350 ptas.

Excursions from Zaragoza include Goya's birthplace at **Fuendetodos,** 44 km (26 mi) to the southeast, and **Belchite,** another 20 km (12 mi) east of Fuendetodos, the site of the deliberately untouched ruins of a town destroyed in one of the fiercest battles of the Spanish Civil War.

OFF THE BEATEN PATH

MONASTERIO DE PIEDRA – An hour's drive south of Zaragoza brings you to the Cistercian Monasterio de Piedra, a lush oasis on the arid Aragonese *meseta* (plain). Founded in 1195 by Alfonso II of Aragón and named for the nearby Río Piedra (Stone River, named in turn for the calcified limestone deposits along its banks), the monastery has a 16th-century Renaissance section that is now a moderately priced private hotel. The 12th-century cloister, wine museum, and caves, waterfalls, and walkways suspended over the riverbed are spectacular. If you can't stay overnight, you can wander the park for 1,000 ptas. *Rte. C202 south of Calatayud, just beyond Nuévalo, 976/849011, FAX 976/849054. 63 rooms. Restaurant, bar. AE, DC, MC, V.*

Dining and Lodging

$$ ★ **El Fuelle.** This old-town favorite is known for fine Aragonese cuisine, a lively ambience, and specialties like *judias blancas* (white beans), *migas*

(a traditional dish of chorizo, peppers, and bread crumbs soaked in olive oil and garlic), and *patatas asadas* (roast potatoes), the most emblematic dish here. ✉ *C. Mayor 58,* ☎ *976/398033. AE, DC, MC, V.*

$$ ★ ✕ **La Matilde.** Conveniently stationed near Zaragoza's spectacular Lanuza market, La Matilde is one of the city's most popular restaurants, justly famed for its *cocina de mercado*—cuisine prepared according to what's freshest and best in the market at the moment. ✉ *C. Predicadores 7,* ☎ *976/441008. AE, DC, MC, V.*

$$ ✕ **La Venta del Cachirulo.** This roadhouse just outside Zaragoza is worth a trip for authentic Aragonese cooking and folklore, including occasional *jota* dancing, singing, and a generally rough-and-tumble approach to delicious food. *Borrajas con almejas* (kale with clams) and *pato con cerezas* (duck with cherries) are among the local dishes served. ✉ *Carretera Logroño (N232), Km 1,* ☎ *976/331674. AE, DC, MC, V. No dinner Sun., except Aug. 1–15.*

$$$–$$$$ ✕🏨 **Tibur.** This small hotel overlooks the cathedral, the basilica, and the stock exchange from its perch less than 100 yards from the Ebro. The setting is discreet and charming, and while the rooms are not spacious, they're nicely decorated. The excellent restaurant, the Foro Romano, serves both international and Aragonese cuisine. ✉ *Plaza de la Seo 2, 50001,* ☎ *976/202000,* FAX *976/202002. 50 rooms. Restaurant, bar, cafeteria. AE, DC, MC, V.*

$$$–$$$$ ★ 🏨 **Goya.** Smack in the city center, the Goya provides a balanced combination of comfort and proximity to the historic sights. A five-minute walk from the Basílica del Pilar and the Ebro River, it offers every convenience along with a sense of being a part of the city's life and times. Rooms are modern and comfortable, if not luxurious. ✉ *Cinco de Marzo, 50004,* ☎ *976/229331,* FAX *976/232154. 148 rooms. Restaurant, bar, café. AE, DC, MC, V.*

Benasque

★ ㉖ *79 km (49 mi) southwest of Vielha.*

Benasque, Aragón's easternmost town, has always been an important link between Catalonia and Aragón. This town of just over 1,500 people packs a number of notable buildings, including the 13th-century Romanesque church of **Santa Maria Mayor** and the ancient, dignified manor houses of the town's old families, such as the **palace of the counts of Ribagorza,** on Calle Mayor, and the **Torre Juste.** Take a walk around and peer into the entryways of these palatial digs; they're left open for this purpose.

Anciles, 2 km (1 mi) south of Benasque, is one of Spain's best-preserved and -restored medieval villages, an excellent collection of farmhouses and *palacetes* (town houses). The summer classical-music series is a superb collision of music and architecture, and the village restaurant, Ansils, combines modern and medieval motifs in both cuisine and design.

The **Cerler ski area** (☎ 974/551012), 6 km (4 mi) from Benasque, covers the slopes of the Cogulla peak, east of town. Built on a shelf over the valley at an altitude of 5,051 ft, Cerler has 26 ski runs, three lifts, and a guided helicopter service to drop you at the highest peaks.

OFF THE BEATEN PATH

Benasque is the traditional base camp for excursions to Aneto, the highest peak in the Pyrenees. You can rent crampons and a *piolet* (ice axe) for the two- to three-hour crossing of the Aneto glacier at any sports store in town or at the Refugio de la Renclusa, a way station for mountaineers; it's an hour's walk above the parking area, which is 17 km (11 mi) north of Benasque. The trek to the summit and back is not difficult, just long—some 20 km (12 mi) round trip, with a 1,500-yard vertical ascent. Allow a full 12 hours.

The Central and Western Pyrenees

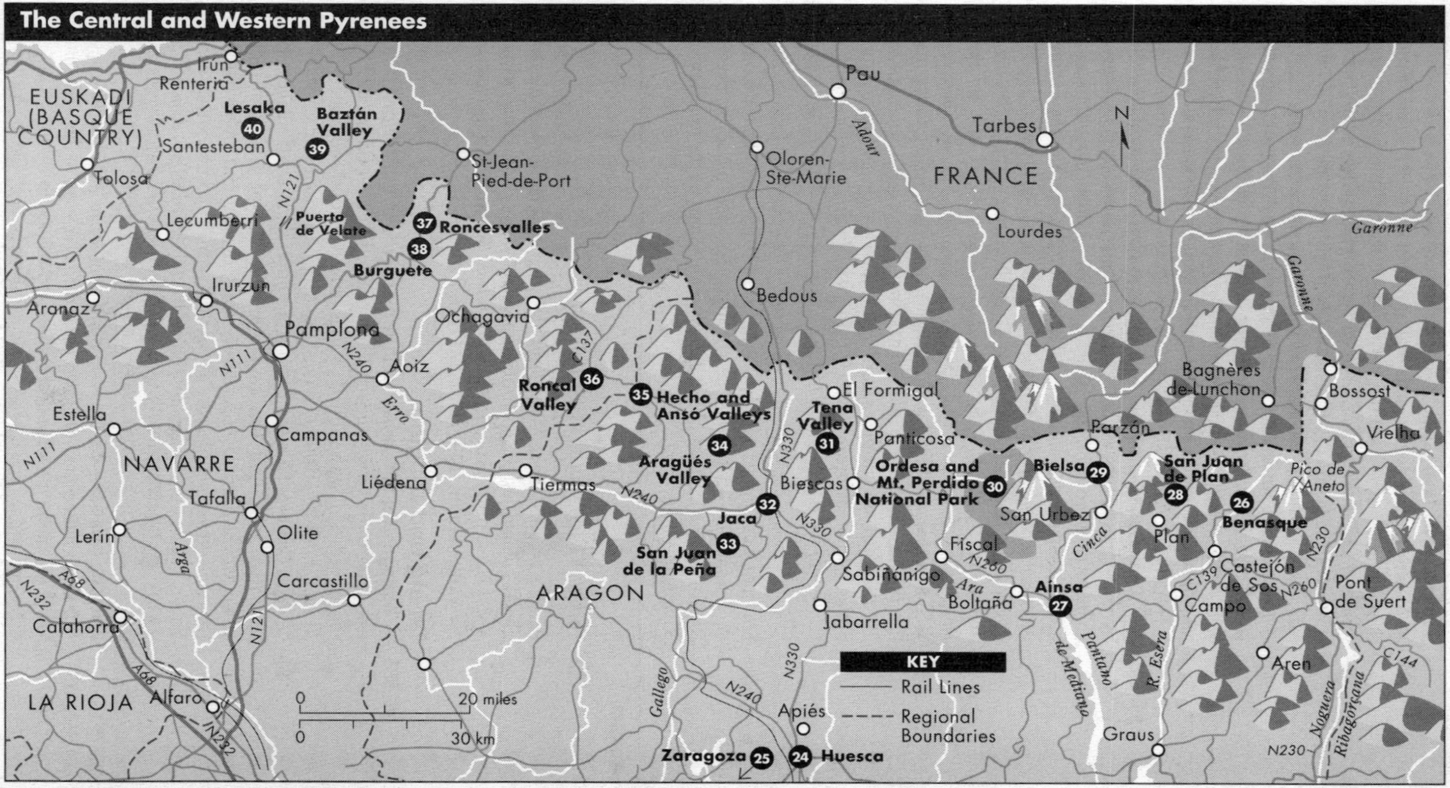

Dining and Lodging

$$ ✕ **Asador Ixarso.** Roast goat or lamb cooked over a raised fireplace in the corner of the dining room make this a fine refuge in chilly weather. The *revuelto de setas* (eggs scrambled with wild mushrooms) is superb, as are the salads. ✉ *San Pedro 9, Benasque,* ☎ *974/552057. MC, V. Closed weekdays Sept. 15–Dec. 8 and Easter–June 29.*

$$ ✕ **Restaurante Ansils.** A rustic place ingeniously redesigned in glass, wood, and stone, Ansils specializes in local Benasqués dishes such as *civet de jabalí* (wild-boar stew) and *recau* (a thick vegetable broth). Holiday meals are served on Christmas and Easter. ✉ *Anciles, Huesca,* ☎ *974/551150. AE, DC, MC, V. Closed weekdays Oct.–June.*

$$–$$$ ✕🏨 **Gran Hotel Benasque.** This spacious new stone hotel is bracketed by the highest crests in the Pyrenees (Aneto and Posets) and serves as an impeccably comfortable base for exploring them. The decor and ambience are modern yet tasteful. The restaurant's mountain cuisine features *sopa Benasquesa* (a hearty highland stew) and *crepas Aneto* (crepes with ham, wild mushroom, and béchamel sauce). ✉ *Carretera de Anciles 3, 22440,* ☎ *974/551011,* FAX *974/551509. 69 rooms. Restaurant, 2 pools, sauna, exercise room. AE, MC, V. Closed Nov.*

$$ ✕🏨 **San Marsial.** Filled with antiques, ancient wooden doors, and artifacts, this comfortable inn also has one of Benasque's best restaurants. Try the lentil soup or the *caldereta de conejo* (rabbit stewed in almonds, olives, and bread crumbs). ✉ *Carretera de Francia (C139) s/n, 22440,* ☎ *974/551616,* FAX *974/551623. 24 rooms. Restaurant, cafeteria. AE, DC, MC, V.*

En Route South of Castejón de Sos, down the Esera Valley through the Congosto de Ventamillo—a sheer slice through the rock made by the Esera River—a turn west on N260 cuts over to Aínsa, at the junction of the Rivers Cinca and Ara.

Aínsa

27 *66 km (41 mi) southwest of Benasque.*

Aínsa's arcaded Plaça Major and old town are classic examples of medieval village design, with heavy stone archways and tiny windows. The 12th-century Romanesque church of **Santa María** has a quadruple-vaulted door. *Free.* ⏲ *Daily 9–2 and 4–8.*

Dining and Lodging

$$–$$$ ✕ **Bodegas del Sobrarbe.** Built into an 11th-century wine cellar, this fine restaurant serves superb lamb roasted in a wood oven. The setting is medieval, with vaulted ceilings of heavy wood and stone. ✉ *Plaza Mayor 2,* ☎ *974/500237. AE, DC, MC, V. Closed Jan. 7–Mar. 1.*

$$ 🏨 **Casa Cambra.** Humming along in a once-abandoned village between Barbastro and Ainsa, this inn is a perfect base for mountain sports of all kinds. The restored 18th-century house of stone and timber has rooms for two to four people, and is part of a tourist complex that includes a restaurant. ✉ *Morillo de Tou, Carretera Barbastro–Ainsa (C138), 22395,* ☎ FAX *974/500793. 17 rooms. No credit cards.*

OFF THE BEATEN PATH **AÑISCLO GORGES** – On the road north from Aínsa, the Añisclo Canyon is 5 km (3 mi) north of the town of Escalona. A road to the west runs 14 km (9 mi) along the edge of the sheer rock divide to Urbez. As you drive into Urbez, you'll see the ancient stone bridge. On the far bank of the river is the cave chapel named for St. Urbez, a hermit monk from Bordeaux who lived there in the 8th century.

San Juan de Plan and the Gistaín Valley

28 *14 km (8½ mi) east of Salinas.*

San Juan de Plan has become a treasury of local folklore. This detour begins with a well-marked road heading east of Salinas, 25 km (15 mi) north of Ainsa. The Cinqueta River drains the Gistaín Valley, flowing by or through the mountain villages of Sin, Señes, Saravillo, Serveta, and Salinas; the town of San Juan de Plan presides at the head of the valley, where an Ethnographic Museum, a weaving workshop, and an early-music and -dance ensemble are the pride of the region. The **Museo Etnográfico** is a fascinating glimpse into the valley's way of life until as recently as 25 years ago. It's open daily 9–2 and 4–8, with an admission of 500 ptas. Don't miss a tour of the weaving industry, restored by Amanda Tyson, the town's resident American.

Dining and Lodging

$$ ✕🏨 **Casa la Plaza.** This charming spot has cozy rooms with original antique furniture, and the restaurant serves excellent cuisine. ✉ *Plaza Mayor s/n, 22367,* ☎ *974/506052,* FAX *974/506052. 13 rooms. AE, DC, MC, V. Closed sporadically Oct.–May; call to confirm.*

Bielsa

29 *34 km (21 mi) northeast of Aínsa.*

Bielsa, at the confluence of the Cinca and Barrosa rivers, is a busy summer resort with some lovely mountain architecture and an ancient, porticoed town hall. Northwest of Bielsa the **Monte Perdido glacier** and the icy **Marboré Lake** drain into the **Pineta Valley** and the Pineta Reservoir. You can take three- or four-hour walks from the parador up to Larri, Munia, or Marboré Lake among remote peaks.

Dining and Lodging

$$–$$$ ✕🏨 **Parador de Bielsa.** This modern structure of glass, steel, and stone overlooks the national park (☞ *below*), the peak of Monte Perdido, and the source of the Cinca River. Rooms are decorated in bright wood, but the best part is your proximity to the park and the views. The restaurant specializes in Aragonese mountain dishes such as *pucherete de Parzán* (a stew with beans, sausage, and an assortment of vegetables). ✉ *22350 Bielsa,* ☎ *974/501011,* FAX *974/501188. 24 rooms. Restaurant. AE, DC, MC, V.*

$$ ✕🏨 **Valle de Pineta.** This corner castle overlooking the river junction is the most spectacular refuge in town. The restaurant is excellent, the views without compare. Try for the top corner room, which looks up and down both valleys. ✉ *Baja s/n, 22350,* ☎ *974/501010,* FAX *974/501191. 26 rooms. AE, DC, MC, V. Closed Nov.*

En Route You can explore the **Valle del Cinca** from the river's source at the head of the valley above Bielsa. From Bielsa, drive back down to Aínsa and turn west on N260 (alternately marked C138) for Broto.

Ordesa and Mt. Perdido National Park

30 *From Aínsa, turn west on N260 for the 53-km (33-mi) drive through Boltaña to Broto and Torla.*

En route to the park, **Broto** is a prototypical Aragonese mountain town with an excellent **16th-century Gothic church.** Nearby villages such as **Oto** have stately manor houses with classic local features: baronial entryways, conical chimneys, and wooden galleries. **Torla** is noteworthy for its mountain architecture and as the park's entry point; it's a popular base camp for hikers.

The Parque Nacional de Ordesa y Monte Perdido is one of Spain's great underrated wonders, a domain many consider comparable to North America's Grand Canyon. The entrance lies under the vertical walls of Monte Mondarruego, source of the Ara River and its tributary, the Arazas, which forms the famous Ordesa Valley. The park was founded by royal decree in 1918 to protect the natural integrity of the Central Pyrenees, and it has expanded from 4,940 to 56,810 acres as provincial and national authorities have added the Perdido massif, the head of the Pineta Valley, and the Escuain and Añisclo canyons. Defined by the Ara and Arazas rivers, the Ordesa Valley is endowed with pine, fir, larch, beech, and poplar forests; lakes, waterfalls, and high mountain meadows; and protected wildlife, including trout, boar, chamois, and the *Capra Pyrenaica* mountain goat.

Hikes through the park (on well-marked and -maintained mountain trails) lead to waterfalls, caves, and spectacular observation points. The standard tour, a full day's hike (8 hours), leads from the parking area up the Arazas River, past the *gradas de Soaso* (Soaso risers; a natural stairway of waterfalls) to the *cola de caballo* (horse's tail), a lovely fan of falling water at the head of the Cirque de Cotatuero, a sort of natural amphitheater. A return walk on the south side of the valley, past the Refugio de los Cazadores (hunters' hut), offers a breathtaking view followed by a two-hour descent back to the parking area. A few spots, while not technically difficult, may seem precarious. Information and guidebooks are available at the booth on your way into the park. The best time to come is from the beginning of May to the middle of November, but check conditions with regional tourist offices before driving into a blizzard in May or missing out on *el veranillo de San Martín* (Indian summer) in the fall.

En Route Follow N260 (sometimes marked C140) west over the Cotefablo Pass from Torla to Biescas.

Tena Valley

31 *40 km (25 mi) west of Ordesa.*

The Valle de Tena, a north–south hexagon of 400 square km (154 square mi), is formed by the Gállego River and its two tributaries, the Aguaslimpias and the Caldares. A glacial valley surrounded by peaks rising to more than 10,000 ft (such as the 10,900-ft Vignemale), Tena is a busy hiking and winter-sports center. Starting from the top, **Sallent de Gállego,** at the head of the valley, has long been a jumping-off point for excursions to **Aguaslimpias, Piedrafita,** and the meadows of the Gállego headwaters at **El Formigal** (a major ski area) and **Portalet.** The Pyrenean *ibon* (glacial lake) of **Respumoso,** accessible by a 2½-hour walk above the old road from Sallent to Formigal, is a peaceful and perfectly horizontal expanse amid all that vertical landscape.

Dining and Lodging

$–$$ ✕🏨 **Morlans.** Rooms here are warm and inviting, and look south over the town to Panticosa's ski area and the mountains beyond. The lower restaurant specializes in roast lamb, goat, and suckling pig; the upper restaurant serves *civets* of deer, boar, and mountain goat, as well as such Upper Aragonese favorites as *pochas* (bean soup with sausage). ✉ *C. de San Miguel, 22066 Barriada de la Cruz,* ☎ *974/487057,* FAX *974/487386. 25 rooms. 2 restaurants. MC, V.*

Jaca

32 *Down the Tena Valley through Biescas, a westward turn at Sabiñánigo onto N330 leaves a 14-km (9-mi) drive to Jaca.*

Jaca, the most important municipal center in Alto Aragón (with a population of more than 15,000), is anything but sleepy. Bursting with ambition and blessed with the natural resources to fuel their relentless drive, Jacetanos are determined to host a Winter Olympics someday.

Jaca hosts or has hosted a Summer University, the Center for Pyrenean Studies, the biannual Pyrenean Folklore Festival, the Winter Games of the Pyrenees, and the World University Winter Games. Either the National or the World Figure Skating Championships are held here nearly every year, and the national ice-hockey King's Cup is often played on Jaca's **Olympic-size ice rink.**

NEED A BREAK? One of Jaca's most emblematic restaurants is **La Campanilla** (✉ Escuelas Pías 8, behind *ayuntamiento*). The baked potatoes with garlic and olive oil are an institution, unchanged for as long as anyone can remember.

Once the capital of the 11th-century kingdom of Jacetania and an important stop on the pilgrimage to Santiago de Compostela, Jaca has an **11th-century cathedral,** one of the oldest in Spain. The **Museo Episcopal** (Bishops' Museum) is filled with excellent Romanesque and Gothic murals. It's open daily 11–1:30 and 4:30–6:30; admission is 450 ptas. The **Ciutadella** (citadel), in town, is a good example of 17th-century military architecture. It's open October–March, daily 11–2 and 4–5, April–September, daily 5–6. Admission is free. The **Rapitán Garrison,** outside town, is also known for its military architecture. It's open July–August, Monday to Saturday 5–8, Sunday 11–1, and admission is free. The door to the *ayuntamiento* is a notable Renaissance design.

The **ski areas** of Candanchú and Astún are 32 km (20 mi) north on the road to Somport and the French border. In summer, a free guided tour covers the valley (the train ticket costs 450 ptas.) and the mammoth (and semi-derelict) belle epoque railroad station at Canfranc, surely the largest and most ornate building in the Pyrenees.

Dining and Lodging

$$ ✕ **La Cocina Aragonesa.** La Cocina's fresh and innovative dishes feature game in season, including venison, wild boar, partridge, and duck. Try the partridge stuffed with foie gras. ✉ *Cervantes 5,* ☎ *974/361050. AE, DC, MC, V. Closed Wed.*

$$–$$$ ✕🏨 **Gran Hotel.** This rambling hotel is central to life and tourism in Jaca. Done up in wood, stone, and glass, it has a garden and a separate dining wing. The comfortable rooms are furnished with rich colors and practical wood furniture. ✉ *Paseo de la Constitución I, 22700,* ☎ *974/360900,* FAX *974/364061. 166 rooms. Restaurant, pool, meeting rooms. AE, DC, MC, V.*

Nightlife and the Arts

Discos such as **Dimensión** and **Oroel** are thronged with skiers and hockey players in season (October–April), but the main nocturnal attractions are the so-called *bares musicales* (music bars), usually less loud and smoky than the discos. Most of these are in the old part of Jaca, around Plaza Ramiro I and along Calle Gil Verges and Calle Bellido.

THE WESTERN PYRENEES

The Hecho and Ansó valleys, in western Aragón, are among the most pristine enclaves in the Pyrenees. Navarre's Irati Forest, the Baztán Valley, and the route down to the Atlantic along the Bidasoa River are rich in natural, human, and historical resources.

San Juan de la Peña

33 *From Jaca, drive 11 km (7 mi) west on N240 toward Pamplona to a left turn clearly signposted for San Juan de la Peña. From there it's another 11 km to the monastery.*

Before starting west through the Aragonese valleys of Hecho and Ansó, loop south to see the **Monasterio de San Juan de la Peña,** a site connected to the legend of the Holy Grail and another "cradle" of Christian resistance during the 700-year Moorish occupation of Spain. The site's origins can be traced to the 9th century, when a hermit monk named Juan settled here on the *peña* (cliff). A monastery was founded on the spot in 920, and in 1071 Sancho Ramirez, son of King Ramiro I, made use of this structure, which was built into the mountain's rock wall, to found the Benedictine Monasterio de San Juan de la Peña. The **cloister,** tucked under the cliff, dates from the 12th century and features intricately carved capitals depicting biblical scenes. ☎ *974/361476.* ✉ *450 ptas.* ⏲ *Oct.–mid-Mar., Tues.–Sun. 11–1:30 and 4–5:30; mid-Mar.–May, Tues.–Sun. 10–1:30 and 4–7; June–Sept., daily 10–noon and 4–8.*

En Route The Aragüés, Hecho, and Ansó are the last three valleys in Aragón. From Jaca, head west on N240 and take a hard right at Puente de la Reina (after turning right to cross the bridge) and continue north along the Aragón-Subordán River. The first right after 15 km (9 mi) leads into the Aragüés Valley along the Osia River to Aisa and then Jasa.

Aragüés Valley

34 *Aragüés del Puerto is 2 km (1 mi) from Jasa.*

Above Aragüés del Puerto is the **Pico de Bisaurín** (Bisaurín Peak), one of the highest in the area (8,638 ft). **Aragüés del Puerto** is a tidy mountain village with stone houses and lovely little corners, doorways, and porticoes. The distinctive folk dance in Aragüés is the *palotiau,* a special variation of the *jota* performed only in this village. At the source of the River Osia, the Lizara **cross-country ski area** is in a flat expanse between the Aragüés and Jasa valleys. Look for 3,000-year-old megalithic dolmens sprinkled across the flat.

Hecho and Ansó Valleys

35 *The Hecho Valley is 49 km (30 mi) west of Jaca. The Ansó Valley is 25 km (15 mi) west of Hecho.*

You can reach the Valle de Hecho by returning to the valley of the Aragón-Subordan and turning north again. The **Monasterio de San Pedro de Hecho,** above the town of Hecho, is the area's most important monument, a 9th-century retreat of which only the 11th-century church remains. *Cheso,* a medieval Aragonese dialect descended directly from the Latin spoken by the Siresa monks, is thought to be the purest—that is, the closest to Latin—of all the Romance languages and dialects. The dialect has been kept alive in the Hecho Valley, especially in the works of the poet Veremundo Mendez Coarasa. The **Selva de Oza** (Oza Forest), at the head of the valley, is above the **Boca del Infierno** (Mouth of Hell), a tight draw where road and river barely squeeze through. Beyond the Oza Forest is a **Roman road** used before the 4th century to reach France through the Puerto del Palo (El Palo Pass)—one of the oldest routes across the border on the pilgrimage to Santiago de Compostela.

The Valle de Ansó is Aragón's western limit. Rich in fauna (mountain goats, wild boar, and even a bear or two), the Ansó Valley follows the Veral River up to Zuriza. Above Zuriza are three **cross-country ski areas,** known as the Pistas de Linza. Near Fago is the sanctuary of the **Vir-**

gen de Puyeta, patron saint of the valley. Towering over the head of the valley is Navarre's highest point, the 7,989-ft **Mesa de los Tres Reyes** (Plateau of the Three Kings), named not for the Magi but for the kings of Aragón, Navarre, and Castile, whose 11th-century kingdoms all came to a corner here—allowing them to meet without leaving their respective realms. Try to be in the town of **Ansó** on the last Sunday in August, when residents dress in their traditional medieval costumes and perform ancestral dances of great grace and dignity. From Ansó, head west to Roncal on the difficult (narrow and winding) but panoramic road through the Sierra de San Miguel.

Dining and Lodging

$$ ✕ **Gaby-Casa Blasquico.** Hecho's top restaurant, this diminutive gem is famous for carefully crafted Aragonese mountain cuisine. It's especially strong on game preparations, from wild boar to venison to partridge or migratory pigeon, but the menu includes a full range of lamb and vegetable dishes. Calling ahead is essential: Gaby will often open for anyone who reserves in advance, even if theoretically closed. ✉ *Plaza Palacio 1,* ☎ *974/375007. MC, V. Closed weekdays Sept.–Holy Week.*

$$ 🏨 **Usón.** For a base to explore the upper Hecho Valley or the Oza Forest, look no further. This friendly little Pyrenean inn will rent you a bike, get you a trout-fishing permit, or send you off in the right direction for a climb or hike. ✉ *Carretera Selva de Oza (HU2131), Km 7, 22720,* ☎ *974/375358. 14 rooms. Restaurant. MC, V. Closed mid-Dec.–mid-Feb.*

En Route The Basque Pyrenees extend west from the Roncal Valley, at the Aragonese border, to Vera de Bidasoa, where the Bidasoa River, the border between France and Spain, flows down through the western Pyrenean foothills to the Bay of Biscay. From the peaks of Anie (8,213 ft) and Orhi (6,616 ft) and the plateau of the Tres Reyes (7,989 ft), the mountains descend west to the Pyrenees' last important height, Larrún (2,952 ft).

Roncal Valley

36 *Take N240 from Jaca west along the Aragón River; a right turn north on NA137 follows the Esca River from the head of the Yesa Reservoir up the Roncal Valley.*

The Roncal Valley, the eastern edge of the Basque Pyrenees, is famous for its sheep's-milk cheese, Ronkari, and as the birthplace of Julián Gayarre (1844–90), the leading tenor of his time. The 34-km (21-mi) drive through the towns of **Burgui** and **Roncal** to **Isaba** winds through green hillsides and Basque *caseríos* housing farmers and their livestock. Burgui's red-tile roofs backed by rolling pastures contrast with the vertical rock and steep slate roofs of the Aragonese and Catalan Pyrenees; Isaba's wide-arched bridge across the Esca is a graceful reminder of Roman aesthetics and engineering techniques. Try to be in the Roncal Valley for El Tributo de las Tres Vacas (the Tribute of the Three Cows), celebrated every July 13 since 1375. The mayors of the valley's villages, dressed in distinctive traditional gowns, gather near the summit of San Martín to receive the symbolic payment of three cows from their French counterparts, in memory of the settlement of ancient border disputes over rights to high pastures and water sources. Feasting and celebrating follow. The road west (NA140) to Ochagavia through the Puerto de Lazar (Lazar Pass) has views of the Anie and Orhi peaks, towering over the French border.

Two kilometers (1 mi) south of Ochagavía, at Escároz, a small secondary roadway winds 22 km (14 mi) over the Abaurrea heights to Aribe, known for its triple-arched medieval bridge and ancient *horreo* (granary). A 15-km (9-mi) detour north through the town of Orbaiceta up to the headwaters of the Irati River, at the Irabia Reservoir, gets you a good look at the **Selva de Irati** (Irati Forest), one of Europe's major beech forests and the source of much of the timber for the fleet Spain commanded during her 15th-century golden age.

Roncesvalles

★ 37 *2½ km (1½ mi) north of Burguete, 48 km (30 mi) north of Pamplona.*

Roncesvalles (Orreaga, in Euskera) is the site of the Colegiata, cloister, hospital, and 12th-century **chapel of Santiago,** the first Navarrese church on the Santiago pilgrimage route. The **Colegiata** (Collegiate Church), built at the orders of King Sancho VII el Fuerte (the Strong), houses the king's tomb, which measures more than 7 ft long. The 3,468-ft Ibañeta Pass, above Roncesvalles, is one of the most beautiful routes into France. A stone **menhir** marks the traditional site of the legendary battle in *The Song of Roland* in which Roland fell after calling for help on his ivory battle horn. The well-marked eight-hour walk to or from St-Jean-Pied-de-Port is one of the most beautiful and dramatic sections of the entire pilgrimage.

Dining and Lodging

$$ ✕🏨 **La Posada.** This 17th-century building with a heavy stone entry is an ancient way station for pilgrims bound for Santiago de Compostela. The accommodations are simple but far more comfortable than the pilgrims' quarters in the neighboring Colegiata. ✉ *Carretera Pamplona–Francia (C135), Km 48, 31650,* ☎ *948/760225,* FAX *948/760225. 18 rooms. Restaurant. AE, DC, MC, V. Closed Nov.*

Burguete

38 *2½ km (1½ mi) south of Roncesvalles, 120 km (75 mi) northwest of Jaca.*

Burguete lies between two mountain streams forming the headwaters of the Urobi River. The town was immortalized when Ernest Hemingway published *The Sun Also Rises,* in 1926, with its evocative description of trout fishing in an ice-cold stream above a moist Navarran village. Travelers to Burguete and Roncesvalles can feel securely bracketed between 11th-century French and 20th-century American literary classics.

Dining and Lodging

$$ ✕🏨 **Hostal Burguete.** This is the inn where Hemingway's character Jake Barnes spent a few days clearing his head in the cool streams of Navarre before plunging back into the psychodrama of the San Fermín festival and his impossible love with Lady Brett Ashley. It still works for this sort of thing, though there don't seem to be as many trout around these days. Good value and simple Navarran cooking make this a good place to stop for a meal or a night. ✉ *C. Única 51, 31540,* ☎ *948/760005. 22 rooms. Restaurant. MC, V. Closed Feb.–Mar.*

En Route To skip Pamplona (☞ Chapter 3) and stay on the trans-Pyrenean route, continue 21 km (13 mi) southwest of Burguete on NA135 until you reach NA138, just before the town of Zubiri. A right turn takes you to Urtasun, where the small NA252 leads left to the town of Iragui and over the pass at Col d'Egozkue (from which there are superb views over the Arga and Ultzana River valleys) to Olagüe, where it connects with NA121 some 20 km (12 mi) north of Pamplona. Turn right onto N121A and climb over the Puerto de Velate (Velate Pass)—or, in bad weather or a hurry, go through the new tunnel—to the turn for Elizondo and the Baztán Valley, N121B.

Baztán Valley

39 *80 km (50 mi) north of Pamplona.*

Tucked neatly over the headwaters of the Bidasoa River and under the peak of the 3,545-ft Garramendi mountain, which looms over the border with France, the rounded green hills of the Valle de Baztán make an ideal halfway stop between the rocky crags of the central Pyrenees and the flat expanse of the Atlantic Ocean, below. Each village in this enchanted Basque valley seems smaller and simpler than the next, with tiny clusters of whitewashed, stone-and-mortar houses with red-tile roofs grouped around a central *frontón* (handball court).

Dining and Lodging

$$ ★ ✕ **Galarza.** This stone town house overlooks the Baztán River in the town of Elizondo. The kitchen serves excellent Basque fare, with a Navarran emphasis on vegetables. Try the *txuritabel* in season (roast lamb with a special stuffing of egg and vegetables) or *txuleta de ternera* (veal raised in the valley). ✉ *C. Santiago 1,* ☎ *948/580101. MC, V.*

$ ★ ✕🏨 **Fonda Etxeberria.** This tiny inn in the Baztán Valley town of Arizcun is an old farmhouse with creaky floorboards and oak doors. The rooms are small but handsome, and although they share baths, the baths are palatial. The restaurant serves simple country dishes, such as bean stew and roast lamb. ✉ *Next to frontón in Arizcun,* ☎ *948/453013. 16 rooms. Restaurant. MC, V.*

Lesaka

40 *71 km (43 mi) northwest of Pamplona.*

If you're around for Pamplona's festival of San Fermín (July 6–14), stop at Lesaka, just 2 km (1 mi) off the N121. Lesaka's patron saint is also San Fermín, and its *sanfermines txikos* (miniature San Fermín fest) may more closely resemble the one described in *The Sun Also Rises* than Pamplona's modern-day international beer brawl does.

OFF THE BEATEN PATH

CABO HIGUER – Follow the Bidasoa River down through Vera de Bidasoa to Irún, Fuenterrabía (☞ Chapter 3), and, for its symbolic value as well as the view out into the Atlantic, Cabo Higuer. This is the end of the road, one of two geographical bookends—Cap Creus, on the Mediterranean, is the other—of a complete trans-Pyrenean trek.

THE PYRENEES A TO Z

Arriving and Departing

By Plane

Barcelona's international airport, **El Prat de Llobregat** is the largest gateway to the Catalan Pyrenees. El Prat is a 15-minute, 2,750-pta. taxi ride from the center of Barcelona, 30 minutes and considerably cheaper (450 ptas.) by train or bus. Airports at Zaragoza, Pamplona, and Fuenterrabía (Hondarribia) also serve the Pyrenees of Aragón, Navarre, and the Basque country.

To travel from Madrid to a Pyrenean jumping-off point, fly to Barcelona on **Iberia**'s shuttle, the Puente Aéreo, or fly Iberia, **Spanair,** or **Air Europa** to Fuenterrabía or Pamplona.

By Train

The overnight train from Madrid's Chamartín Station to either Barcelona or San Sebastián has a distinct advantage: you leave late (9:15 PM–11

PM) and arrive early (7:30 AM–8:30 AM), thus losing no daytime activities at either end.

Getting Around

By Car

The only practical way to tour the Pyrenees, short of hiking, is by car. The most difficult road into the Catalan Pyrenees is over the Collada de Toses (Tosses Pass) to Puigcerdà, but it's free and the scenery is spectacular. Safer, faster, and more expensive but somewhat less scenic (though you will have a great view of the Montserrat massif) is the approach through the Cadí Tunnel. The wide, two-lane roads of the Cerdanya are generally new and well paved; as you move west, roads may be more difficult to navigate, but they are rapidly being improved as the Eje Pirenaico (Pyrenean Axis) N260 nears completion. Generally speaking, Pyrenean roads wind dramatically, so allow extra driving time no matter how well the road is paved. You can rent cars at airports at both ends of the Pyrenees (☞ Chapters 3 and 6).

By Train

There are three railheads in the Pyrenees: Puigcerdà, in the Cerdanya; Pobla de Segur, in the Noguera Pallaresa Valley; and Canfranc, north of Jaca, below the ski resorts of Candanchú and Astún.

Contacts and Resources

Emergencies

Red Cross (☎ 972/200415 Girona; 974/221186 Huesca; 973/267011 Lleida; 948/226404 Navarre). **Police** (☎ 972/201381 Girona; 974/244711 Huesca; 973/245012 Lleida; 948/237000 Navarre).

Fishing

Ramón Cosiallf and **Danica** (☎ 608/735376) can take you fly-fishing anywhere in the world by horse or helicopter, but the Pyrenees are their home turf. For about 15,000 ptas. a day (depending on equipment), you can be whisked to high Pyrenean lakes and ponds, streams, and rivers and armed with equipment and expertise. You can purchase fishing licenses for each autonomous region (Catalonia, Aragón, Navarre) at local rod-and-gun clubs (Asociaciones de Pesca and/or Caza). To avoid being caught without a fishing license over the weekend, pick up a season license (1,600 ptas.) in Barcelona at **ICONA** (✉ C. Sabino de Arana 24, ☎ 93/409–2090), near the Hotel Princesa Sofía, on weekdays between 9 and 2. In Puigcerdà, licenses are available weekdays 9–2 at the office of **Agricultura, Ramaderìa i Pesca** (✉ C. de la Percha 17, ☎ 972/880–515).

Golf

Camprodón has a nine-hole course, **Club de Golf de Camprodón** (☎ 972/130125). The Cerdanya has three golf courses, two near Puigcerdà (**Reial Club de Golf de la Cerdanya,** ☎ 972/141408; **Club de Golf de Fontanals,** ☎ 972/144374) and a nine-hole course at Font Romeu (**Club de Golf de Font Romeu,** ☎ 05/683–1078) in France. Huesca, Jaca, and Benasque also have golf facilities; check with local tourist offices for details. Greens fees are generally between 4,000 and 8,000 ptas.

Guided Tours

The **Touring** travel agency (☎ 972/880602 or 972/881450, FAX 972/881939) in Puigcerdà can help arrange routes, guides, horses, or four-wheel-drive vehicles for treks to upper lakes, peaks, and meadows. Local *excursionista* (outing) clubs, especially the **Centro Excursionista de Catalunya** in Barcelona (✉ Carrer Paradís 10, ☎ 93/315–2311), can advise climbers and hikers.

Outdoor Activities and Sports

Jaca, Puigcerdà, and Vielha have excellent **ice rinks** (Jaca, ☎ 974/361032; Puigcerdà, ☎ 972/880243; Vielha, ☎ 973/642864). Spain's daily newspaper *El País* prints complete ski information every Friday in season; for up-to-the-minute information in Catalan and Spanish, contact the **hotline** in Barcelona (☎ 93/416–0194). For further information, contact the **Federació Catalana Esports d'Hivern** (Catalan Winter Sports Federation; ✉ Carrer Casp 38, Barcelona, ☎ 93/302–7040).

Visitor Information

Regional tourist offices: **Aragón** (✉ Torreon de la Zuda, Glorieta de Pío XII, Zaragoza, ☎ 976/393537). **Barcelona** (✉ Palau Robert, Passeig de Gràcia 107 [at Avda. Diagonal], ☎ 93/238–4000). **Girona** (✉ Rambla de la Llibertat 1, ☎ 972/202679). **Huesca** (✉ Coso Alto 23, ☎ 974/225778). **Lleida** (✉ Plaça de la Paeria 11, ☎ 973/248120). **Navarre** (✉ Duque de Ahumada 3, Pamplona, ☎ 948/211287).

Local tourist offices: **Aínsa** (✉ Avda. Pirenaica 1, ☎ 974/500767). **Benasque** (✉ Plaza Mayor 5, ☎ 974/551289). **Bielsa** (✉ Plaza del Ayuntamiento, ☎ 974/501000). **Camprodón** (✉ Plaça Espanya 1, ☎ 972/740010). **Jaca** (✉ Avda. Rgto. Galicia, ☎ 974/360098). **Puigcerdà** (✉ Carrer Querol 1, ☎ 972/880542). **La Seu d'Urgell** (✉ Avda. Valira s/n, ☎ 973/351511). **Vielha** (✉ Avda. Castiero 15, ☎ 973/640979).

6 BARCELONA AND NORTHERN CATALONIA

Finally recognized as one of the most artistic and dynamic cities in Europe, Barcelona is booming as never before. From the narrow alleys of the Gothic Quarter to the elegant Moderniste Eixample or the action-packed port, this Mediterranean metropolis is creating a buzz heard 'round the world. Picasso, Miró, and Gaudí left indelible marks here, Dalí was never far away, and Catalan culture has flourished since home rule was granted in 1975. The Costa Brava, Girona, Figueres, and the Ampurdan region round out this corner of the Iberian Peninsula.

By George Semler

CAPITAL OF CATALONIA, 2,000-year-old Barcelona has long rivaled and often surpassed Madrid in industrial muscle and business acumen. Though Madrid has revitalized its role as Spain's capital in the last quarter century, Barcelona has relinquished none of its power. After a comprehensive urban refurbishing prior to the 1992 Summer Olympics, Barcelona has come into its own as one of Europe's most attractive contemporary cities. The medieval intimacy of the Gothic Quarter balances the grace and distinction of the wide boulevards in the Moderniste Eixample, just as the Mediterranean Gothic elegance of the church of Santa Maria del Mar provides a perfect counterpoint to Gaudí's riotous Sagrada Família.

Barcelona has long had a frenetically active cultural life. Perhaps most famously, it was the home of architect Antoni Gaudí (1852–1926), whose buildings are the most startling statements of Modernisme—the Spanish, and mainly Catalan, version of Art Nouveau. Other leading Moderniste architects include Lluís Domènech i Muntaner and Josep Puig i Cadafalch. The painters Joan Miró (1893–1983), Salvador Dalí (1904–89), and Antoni Tàpies (born 1923) are also strongly identified with Catalonia. Pablo Picasso spent his formative years in Barcelona, and one of the city's treasures is a museum devoted to his works. Barcelona's opera house, the Liceu—the finest in Spain—has been spectacularly restored after having burned down in 1994; and the city claims native Catalan musicians such as cellist Pablo (Pau, in Catalan) Casals (1876–1973) and opera singers Montserrat Caballé and José (Josep) Carreras. Barcelona's fashion industry is hard on the heels of those of Paris and Milan, and FC (Futbol Club) Barcelona, more a cultural phenomenon than a sports team, is arguably the world's most glamorous soccer club.

In 133 BC the Roman Empire annexed the city built by the Iberian tribe known as the Laietans and founded a colony called Colonia Favencia Julia Augusta Paterna Barcino. In the 5th century, Barcelona became the Visigothic capital; the Moors invaded in the 8th century; and in 801, the Franks under Charlemagne captured the city and made it their buffer zone at the edge of the Moors' Iberian empire. By 988, the autonomous Catalonian counties had gained independence from the Franks. Only in 1137 was Catalonia united through marriage with the House of Aragón. Yet another marriage, that of Ferdinand II of Aragón and Isabella of Castile (who was also queen of León) in 1474, brought Aragón and Catalonia into a united Spain. As the capital of Aragón's Mediterranean empire, Barcelona had grown in importance between the 12th and the 14th centuries, and only began to falter when maritime emphasis shifted to the Atlantic after 1492. Despite the establishment of Madrid as the seat of Spain's Royal Court in 1562, Catalonia enjoyed autonomous rights and privileges until 1714, when, in reprisal for having backed the Austrian Habsburg pretender to the Spanish throne, all institutions and expressions of Catalan identity were suppressed by the triumphant Felip V of the French Bourbon dynasty. Not until the mid-19th century would Barcelona's industrial growth bring about a *Renaixença* (renaissance) of nationalism and a cultural flowering that recalled Catalonia's former opulence.

Catalan nationalism continued to gain strength in the early 20th century. After the abdication of Alfonso XIII and the establishment of the Spanish Republic in 1931, Catalonia enjoyed a high degree of autonomy and cultural freedom. Once again backing a losing cause, Barcelona was a Republican stronghold and a hotbed of anti-fascist sentiment during the Spanish Civil War, with the result that Catalan language and identity were suppressed under Franco by such means as book burning, the renaming of streets and towns, and the banning of the Catalan language in schools and in the media. This repression had little lasting effect, as the Catalans have jealously guarded their language and culture and generally think of themselves as Catalans first, Spaniards second.

Catalonian home rule was granted after Franco's death in 1975, and Catalonia's parliament, the ancient Generalitat, was reinstated in 1980. Catalan is now Barcelona's co-official language, along with Castilian Spanish, and is eagerly promoted through free classes funded by the Generalitat. Street names are signposted in Catalan, and newspapers, radio stations, and a TV channel publish and broadcast in Catalan. The circular Catalan *sardana* is danced regularly all over town. The triumphant culmination of this rebirth was, of course, the staging of the Olympics in 1992—stadiums and pools were renovated, new harborside promenades created, and an entire set of train tracks moved to make way for the Olympic Village. Not content with this onetime project, Barcelona's last two mayors have presided over an urban renewal and the creation of postmodern structures that have made the city a perennial field trip for architecture students.

Today Barcelona is a feast for all the senses, though perhaps mainly the visual one. The pleasures of the palate are not far behind, and music is prospering as never before, with the restored Liceu opera house and new Auditori joining the Palau de la Musica in the city's clutch of gorgeous venues. The air temperature is almost always about right here; more and more streets are pedestrianized; and every now and then, the fragrance of the Mediterranean overcomes urban fumes altogether down at the port, or on the beach at Barceloneta.

Pleasures and Pastimes

Dining

Catalans are great lovers of fish, vegetables, rabbit, duck, lamb, game, and natural ingredients from the Pyrenees or the Mediterranean. The *mar i muntanya* (sea and mountain—that is, surf and turf), a recipe combining seafood with inland or highland products, is a specialty on most menus, in forms such as rabbit and prawns. Dark meat is often served with fruits or sweets, as in duck with pears. The influence of nearby France seems to ensure finesse, while Iberian ebullience discourages pretense. The Mediterranean diet featuring "good" (anticholesterol) virgin olive oil, seafood, fibrous vegetables, onions, garlic, and red wine is nowhere better exemplified than in Catalonia. Spicy sauces are more prevalent here than elsewhere in Spain; you'll find *allioli,* for example—pure garlic and virgin olive oil (nothing else)—beaten to a mayonnaise-like consistency and used to accompany a wide variety of dishes, from rabbit to lamb to potatoes and vegetables. Typical entrées include *habas a la catalana* (a spicy broad-bean stew), *bullabesa* (fish soup-stew similar to the French bouillabaisse), and *espinacas a la catalana* (spinach cooked with oil, garlic, pine nuts, raisins, and bits of bacon). Bread is often doused with olive oil and spread with tomato to make *pa amb tomaquet,* delicious on its own or as a side nibble. Read Colman Andrews' classic *Catalan Cuisine—Europe's Last Culinary Secret,* which lies on nearly every Catalan gourmet's nightstand, for a more detailed rundown of the products and practices of Catalan chefs.

Catalan wines from the nearby Penedès region, especially the local *méthode champenoise* (sparkling white wine known in Catalonia as *cava*), more than adequately accompany all regional cuisine, and new wine makers in the Priorat, Ampurdan, and Costers del Segre regions are producing exciting alternatives.

CATEGORY	COST*
$$$$	over 8,000 ptas.
$$$	5,000–8,000 ptas.
$$	3,000–5,000 ptas.
$	under 3,000 ptas.

**per person for a three-course meal, excluding drinks, service, and tax*

Lodging

Bargains are scarce in Spain these days, but hotels will negotiate room rates if they're not full. Ask about weekend rates, which are often half; faxing for reservations may also get you a good deal. Business travelers may get a 40% break.

CATEGORY	COST*
$$$$	over 25,000 ptas.
$$$	20,000–25,000 ptas.
$$	14,000–20,000 ptas.
$	under 14,000 ptas.

**All prices are for a standard double room, excluding tax.*

Modernisme

More than any other city in the world, Barcelona is filled with buildings and other works of the late-19th-century artistic and architectural movement known as Art Nouveau in France, *Jugendstil* in Germany, *sezessionstil* in Austria, *floreale* in Italy, *modernismo* in the rest of Spain, and modernism in English-speaking countries. This movement was in many ways analogous to the 1960s "greening of America" in that it reflected a disillusionment with the fruits of technology and industry and a return to more natural shapes and aesthetic values. The curved line replaced the straight line; flowers and fruits and wild mushrooms were sculpted into facades. The pragmatic gave way to ornamental excess. Modernisme is everywhere in Barcelona, not only because it tapped into the playfulness of the Catalan artistic impulse (as seen in the works of Gaudí, Picasso, Miró, Dalí, and others) but because it coincided with Barcelona's late-19th-century industrial prosperity and an upsurge of nationalistic sentiment.

Museums

The Museu Picasso is probably Barcelona's best-known museum, but bear in mind that the city has better permanent collections of art, the finest of which is the Romanesque exhibit at the Palau Nacional on Montjuïc. Other lesser-known gems are the Thyssen-Bornemisza Collection at the Monestir de Pedralbes, above Sarrià, and the works of Catalan impressionists at the Museu d'Art Modern in the Ciutadella. The Fundació "la Caixa," at Passeig de Sant Joan 108, frequently offers excellent itinerant shows that have ranged from Kandinsky to William Blake. Gaudí's famous Pedrera (Casa Milà), on the Passeig de Gràcia, has a superb exhibit on the architect's life and work in the Gaudí-designed attic, as well as a model apartment and changing displays in the Sala Gaudí. The new Centre de Cultura Contemporània and Museu d'Art Contemporani, in the Raval area west of the Rambla, have shows and events of all kinds. Other top museums are the Museu d'Història de la Ciutat in the Plaça del Rei, the Museu d'Història de Catalunya in the Port Vell's Palau de Mar, and the Museu de la Ciencia in upper Barcelona.

EXPLORING BARCELONA

Barcelona is made up of two main and contrasting parts. The old city lies between Plaça de Catalunya and the port. Above it is the grid-patterned expansion built after the city's third set of walls was torn down in 1860. Known as the Eixample ("Widening"), this area contains most

Barcelona

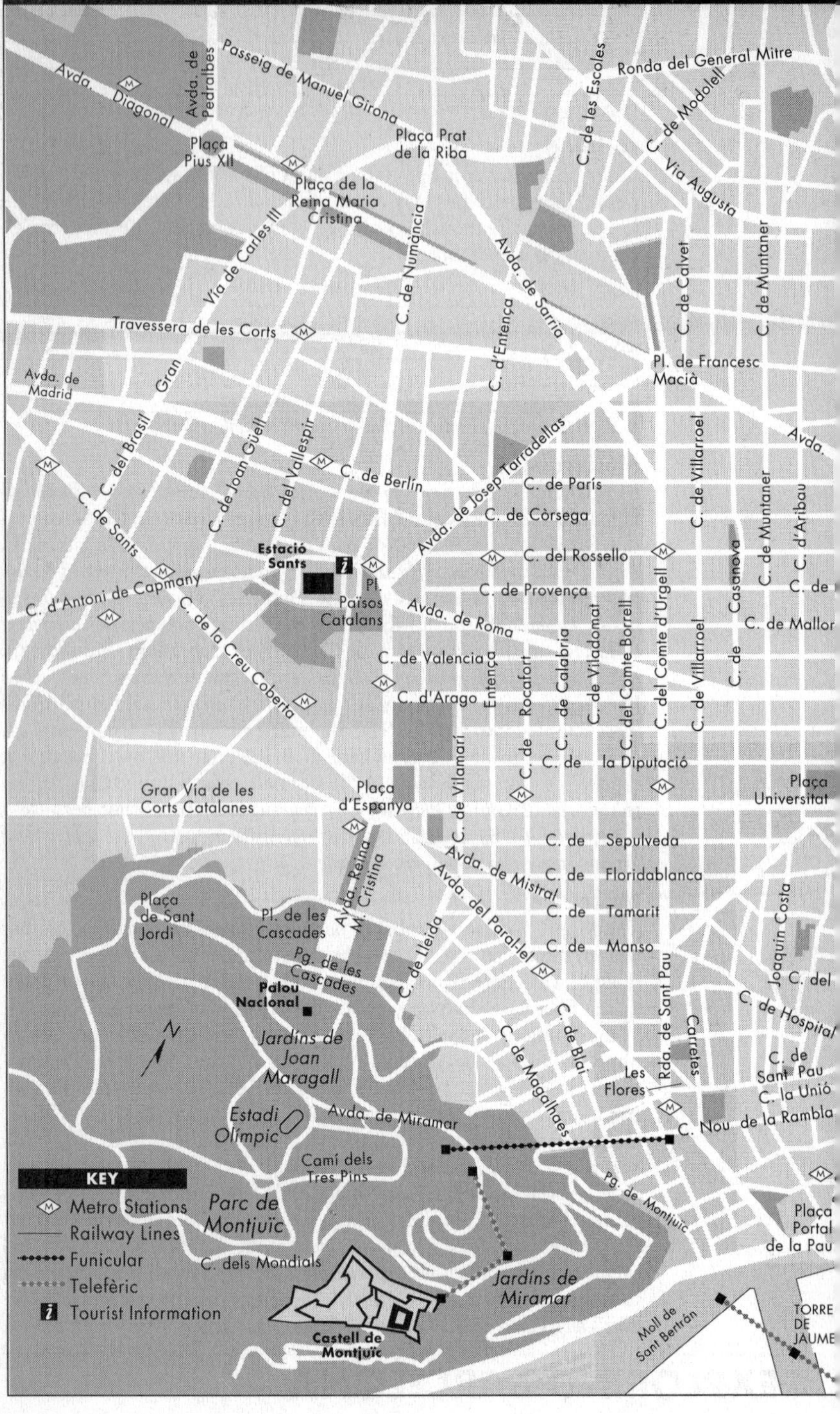
Avda. Diagonal
Avda. de Pedralbes
Passeig de Manuel Girona
Plaça Pius XII
Plaça Prat de la Riba
Plaça de la Reina Maria Cristina
Ronda del General Mitre
C. de les Escoles
C. de Modolell
Via Augusta
Via de Carles III
C. de Numància
Avda. de Sarrià
C. de Calvet
C. de Muntaner
Travessera de les Corts
C. d'Entença
Pl. de Francesc Macià
Avda. de Madrid
Gran
C. del Brasil
C. de Joan Güell
C. del Vallespir
C. de Berlín
Avda. de Josep Tarradellas
C. de París
C. de Còrsega
C. de Villarroel
C. d'Aribau
C. de Sants
Estació Sants
C. del Rossello
C. d'Antoni de Capmany
Pl. Països Catalans
C. de Provença
C. d'Urgell
Casanova
C. de Mallor
Avda. de Roma
C. de la Creu Coberta
C. de Valencia
C. de Calabria
C. de Viladomat
C. del Comte Borrell
C. del Comte d'Urgell
C. d'Arago
Entença
C. de Rocafort
C. de Vilamarí
C. de la Diputació
Gran Vía de les Corts Catalanes
Plaça d'Espanya
Plaça Universitat
C. de Sepulveda
Avda. de Mistral
C. de Floridablanca
Avda. Reina M. Cristina
Avda. del Paral-lel
C. de Tamarit
Plaça de Sant Jordi
Pl. de les Cascades
C. de Lleida
C. de Manso
Joaquín Costa
Pg. de les Cascades
Rda. de Sant Pau
C. del
Palau Nacional
C. de Hospital
Carretes
C. de Blai
C. de Magalhaes
Jardíns de Joan Maragall
Les Flores
C. de Sant Pau
C. la Unió
Estadi Olímpic
Avda. de Miramar
C. Nou de la Rambla
Camí dels Tres Pins
KEY
Metro Stations
Railway Lines
Funicular
Telefèric
Tourist Information
Parc de Montjuïc
Pg. de Montjuïc
Plaça Portal de la Pau
C. dels Mondials
Jardíns de Miramar
Castell de Montjuïc
Moll de Sant Bertrán
TORRE DE JAUME

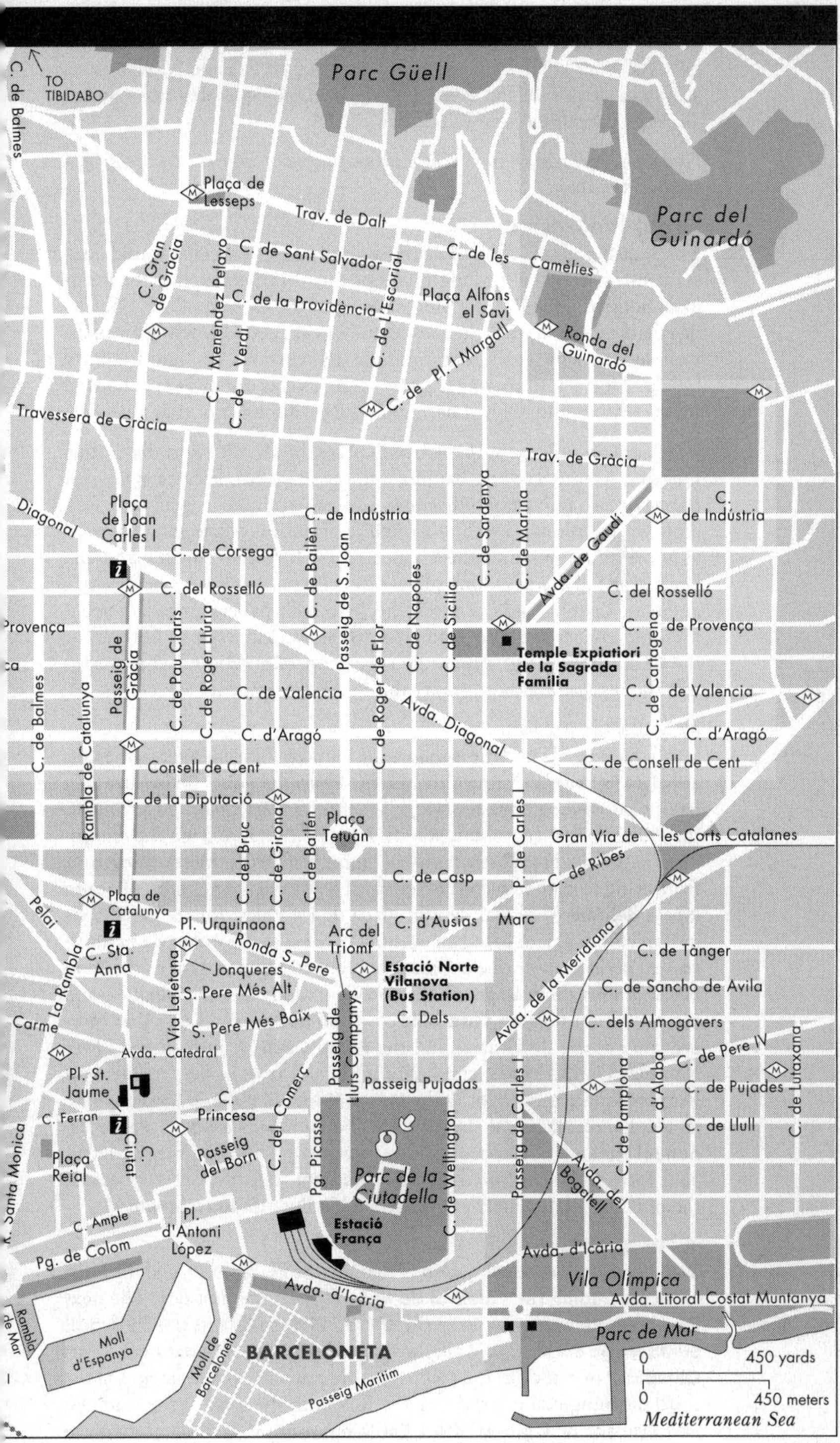
TO TIBIDABO
C. de Balmes
Parc Güell
Plaça de Lesseps
Trav. de Dalt
Parc del Guinardó
C. Gran de Gràcia
C. Menéndez Pelayo
C. de Sant Salvador
C. de l'Escorial
C. de les Camèlies
C. de la Providència
Plaça Alfons el Savi
C. de Verdi
C. de Pl. I Margall
Ronda del Guinardó
Travessera de Gràcia
Trav. de Gràcia
Diagonal
Plaça de Joan Carles I
C. de Indústria
C. de Sardenya
C. de Marina
C. de Indústria
C. de Còrsega
C. de Bailèn
Passeig de S. Joan
C. de Napoles
C. de Sicilia
Avda. de Gaudí
C. del Rosselló
C. del Rosselló
Provença
C. de Pau Claris
C. de Roger Llúria
Passeig de Gràcia
C. de Roger de Flor
C. de Provença
Temple Expiatiori de la Sagrada Família
C. de Cartagena
C. de Balmes
Rambla de Catalunya
C. de Valencia
Avda. Diagonal
C. de Valencia
C. d'Aragó
C. d'Aragó
Consell de Cent
C. de Consell de Cent
C. de la Diputació
Plaça Tetuán
C. del Bruc
C. de Girona
C. de Bailèn
P. de Carles I
Gran Vía de les Corts Catalanes
C. de Casp
C. de Ribes
Plaça de Catalunya
Pelai
C. d'Ausias Marc
Pl. Urquinaona
Ronda S. Pere
Arc del Triomf
C. Sta. Anna
La Rambla
Jonqueres
Estació Norte Vilanova (Bus Station)
C. de Tànger
Via Laietana
S. Pere Més Alt
Avda. de la Meridiana
C. de Sancho de Avila
Carme
S. Pere Més Baix
Passeig de Lluís Companys
C. Dels
C. dels Almogàvers
Avda. Catedral
C. de Pere IV
C. de Lutaxana
Pl. St. Jaume
Passeig Pujadas
C. d'Alaba
C. de Pujades
C. Ferran
C. Princesa
C. del Comerç
C. de Pamplona
C. de Llull
C. Ciutat
Passeig de Carles I
Plaça Reial
Passeig del Born
Pg. Picasso
Parc de la Ciutadella
C. de Wellington
Avda. del Bogatell
Santa Monica
C. Ample
Pl. d'Antoni López
Estació França
Avda. d'Icària
Pg. de Colom
Vila Olímpica
Avda. d'Icària
Avda. Litoral Costat Muntanya
Rambla de Mar
Parc de Mar
Moll d'Espanya
Moll de Barceloneta
BARCELONETA
Passeig Marítim
0 450 yards
0 450 meters
Mediterranean Sea

of Barcelona's Moderniste architecture. Farther out are the former outlying towns of Gràcia and Sarrià, the Pedralbes area, and the Collserola hills. Ask your hotel or the tourist office about the Ruta del Modernisme, a system of guides for seven major Art Nouveau sites (☞ Guided Tours *in* Barcelona A to Z, *below*).

Numbers in the margin correspond to points of interest on the neighborhood maps.

Great Itineraries

The Rambla, the Gothic Quarter, and all of old Barcelona hold constant surprises, even for longtime residents. Markets such as the Rambla's Boqueria, the Raval's Mercat de Sant Antoni, and the Els Encants flea market near Plaça de les Glories are always good browsing grounds, well seeded with cafés, bars, patios, and terraces for mid-itinerary breaks. Don't hesitate to get lost: planned visits are always enhanced by the joys of aimless wandering, and Barcelona is not that vast.

Three days would be sufficient to explore the Rambla and the Gothic Quarter, see the Sagrada Família and the main Moderniste sights, go to one or two important museums, and perhaps take in a concert. Five days would allow a more thorough exploration of the same, as well as more museums and the chance to explore Barceloneta and the Collserola hills. A weeklong stay would give you time to learn the city's authentic rhythms and resources; check the daily papers for gallery openings and concerts; make a side trip to Sitges, Montserrat, Girona, or the Costa Brava; and approach a real understanding of what makes this the biggest and busiest city on the Mediterranean.

IF YOU HAVE 3 DAYS

Stroll the Rambla and the **Boqueria** ⑭ market; then cut over to the **Catedral de la Seu** ①. Detour through the **Plaça del Rei** ③ before heading back to the **Plaça Sant Jaume** ⑦, where the Catalonian government, the Palau de la Generalitat, stands across the square from the *ajuntament* (city hall). From there it's a 10-minute walk to the **Museu Picasso** ⑤, from which another even shorter stroll leads past the church of **Santa Maria del Mar** ⑥ to Cal Pep, in Plaça de les Olles, for the best tapas in Barcelona. Try to catch an evening concert at the **Palau de la Música** ㉛. Day two might be a Gaudí day: spend the morning at the **Temple Expiatori de la Sagrada Família** ㉔, midday at **Parc Güell** ㉖, and the afternoon touring **Casa Milà** ㉓, **Casa Batlló,** and **Casa Lleó Morera,** on Passeig de Gràcia; and the **Palau Güell** ⑪, just off the lower Rambla. On day three, climb Montjuïc and take in the world's best Romanesque art collection at the **Museu Nacional d'Art de Catalunya** ㊸, in the Palau Nacional. Investigate the **Fundació Miró** ㊷, **Poble Espanyol** ㊺, and Olympic facilities, especially Izosaki's superb Palau Sant Jordi and the restored Olympic Stadium. Take the cable car across the port for a late paella at Can Manel la Puda in **Barceloneta** ㊳.

IF YOU HAVE 5 DAYS

Walk the Rambla, the **Boqueria** ⑭ market, the Plaça del Pi, and the Barri Gòtic, including the **Catedral de la Seu** ①, on the first day. The next day, take a few hours to see the **Museu Picasso** ⑤ and the church of **Santa Maria del Mar** ⑥. Walk through **Barceloneta** ㊳ and down to **Port Olímpic** ㊴ or out onto the *rompeolas* (breakwaters) and back. On the third morning you can explore the Raval, to the west of the Rambla, and visit the new **Museu d'Art Contemporani** (MACB) ⑰ and **Centre de Cultura Contemporànea** (CCCB) ⑱ as well as the medieval **Hospital de Sant Pau** ㉕ and Barcelona's oldest church, Sant Pau del Camp. If you have time, have a look at the **Museu Marítim** ⑩, the medieval shipyards, in the Reial Drassanes. In the afternoon you can take a guided tour of the **Palau de la Música** ㉛ and pick up tickets to a concert. Devote your fourth day to Gaudí, the **Temple Expiatori de la Sagrada Família** ㉔ in the morning and **Parc Güell** ㉖ at midday. In the afternoon, walk down the Passeig de Gràcia to see the **Casa Milà, Casa Batlló,** and **Casa Lleó Morera** in the heart of the city's grid-patterned Eixample, and the **Palau Güell** ⑪, just off the Rambla. On day five, explore Montjuïc: visit the **Museu Nacional d'Art de Catalunya** ㊸, in the Palau Nacional; the **Fundació Miró** ㊷; the **Poble Espanyol** ㊺; and the Olympic facilities. In the afternoon, take the cable car across the port and have an outdoor paella at Can Manel la Puda in **Barceloneta** ㊳.

Barri Gòtic

This walk explores Barcelona's Gothic Quarter, a jumble of medieval buildings including the cathedral and the Picasso Museum. Parts of the Barri Gòtic and the Barri Xinès (or Barrio Chino), Barcelona's notorious red-light district, have been much improved over the last decade; you'll happen on squares freshly begotten by the demolition of whole blocks and the planting of palm trees. Bag-snatching is not unheard-of in this part of town, so keep your belongings secure.

A Good Walk

A good walk through the Barri Gòtic could begin at **Catedral de la Seu** ① and move through and around the cathedral to the **Museu Frederic Marès** ② (and its little terrace café, surrounded by Roman walls). Next, pass the patio of the Arxi de la Corona d'Aragó (Archives of the House of Aragón); then turn left again and down into **Plaça del Rei** ③. As you leave Plaça del Rei, the **Museu d'Història de la Ciutat** ④ is on your left. Crossing Via Laietana, pass through the Plaça del Angel and walk down Carrer Princesa; this will take you to Carrer Montcada and a right turn to the **Museu Picasso** ⑤. As you continue down Carrer Montcada you'll pass some of Barcelona's most elegant medieval palaces before emerging into the **Passeig del Born.** Walk back to the church of **Santa Maria del Mar** ⑥, just past the Carrer Montcada end of the Passeig del Born. After spending some time inside, stop into La Vinya del Senyor, an excellent wine bar just opposite the main door. Walk around the church's eastern side through the Fossar de les Moreres. On the west side of Santa Maria del Mar are Carrer Sombrerers, the Gispert spice shop, and the entrance to Carrer Banys Vells, lined with interesting shops and restaurants. Walk to the far end of Banys Vells and go left through Barra de Ferro and Cotoners to Princesa. A walk back across Via Laietana into Carrer Ferran will take you to **Plaça Sant Jaume** ⑦. For a quick tour of Barcelona's *call* (from the Hebrew *qahal,* "meeting"), the medieval Jewish quarter, leave the Plaça Sant Jaume on Carrer del Call, turn right on Sant Domènech del Call, and proceed to the next corner: a synagogue once stood across the intersection on the left, at the corner of Carrer Marlet. Now turn left on Carrer Marlet and proceed to the next corner, Arc de Sant Ramón del Call—high on the right, a stone with Hebrew inscriptions (and a Spanish translation on a plaque) mark all that remains of the Jewish community that prospered here until a 1391 pogrom virtually wiped out Barcelona's Jews a century before the 1492 expulsion. Go left to Carrer del Call and over to Carrer Ferran (via Carrer de la Boqueria and Volta del Remei); then turn right on Carrer Ferran and continue toward the Rambla to reach **Plaça Reial** ⑧, one of Barcelona's few neoclassical squares.

TIMING

This walk covers some 3 km (2 mi) and should take about three hours, depending on stops. Allow another hour for the Picasso Museum.

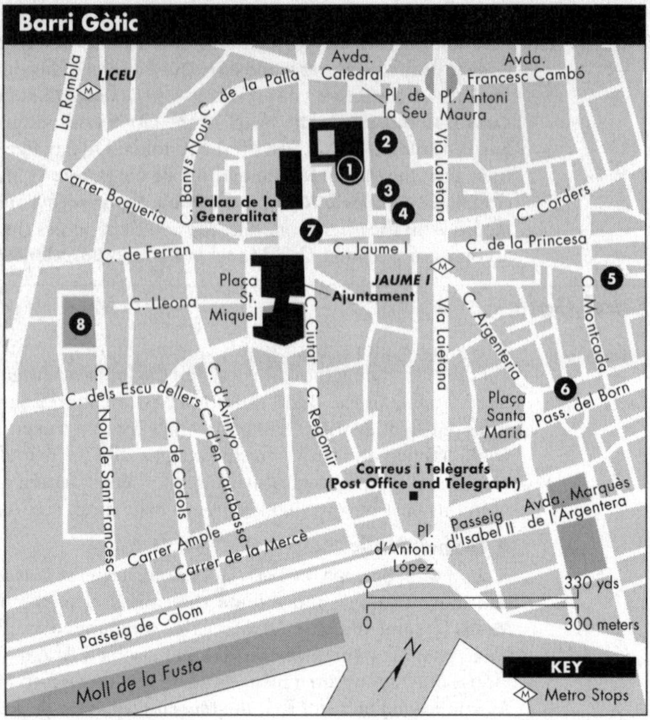

Sights to See

★ 1 **Catedral de la Seu.** On Saturday afternoons, Sunday mornings, and occasional evenings, Barcelona folk gather in the Plaça de la Seu to dance the *sardana,* a somewhat demure circular dance and a great symbol of Catalan identity. The magnificent Gothic cathedral was built between 1298 and 1450, with the spire and neo-Gothic facade added in 1892. Architects of Catalan Gothic churches strove to make the high altar visible to the entire congregation, hence the unusually wide central nave and slender side columns. Highlights are the beautifully carved choir stalls; Santa Eulàlia's tomb, in the crypt; the battle-scarred crucifix (used as a bowsprit in the famous 1571 naval showdown between the Christian and Turkish fleets at Lepanto) in the Lepanto Chapel; the intimate Santa Llúcia chapel, in the front right corner; and the tall cloisters surrounding a tropical garden. The cathedral is floodlit in striking yellows at night; even the stained-glass windows are backlit from inside. ✉ *Plaça de la Seu,* ☎ *93/315–2213.* ⏲ *Daily 7:45–1:30 and 4–7:45.*

Fossar de les Moreres (Cemetery of the Mulberry Trees). This low marble monument stands in the open space on the eastern side of the church of Santa Maria del Mar, honoring those defenders of Barcelona who gave their lives in the 1714 siege that ended the War of the Spanish Succession and established Felipe V on the Spanish throne. The inscription (EN EL FOSSAR DE LES MORERES NO S'HI ENTERRA CAP TRAIDOR, or IN THE CEMETERY OF THE MULBERRY TREES NO TRAITOR LIES) refers to the story of the graveyard keeper who refused to bury those who had fought on the invading side, even when one of them turned out to be his son.

4 **Museu d'Història de la Ciutat** (City History Museum). Just off the Plaça del Rei, this fascinating museum traces the evolution of Barcelona from its first Iberian settlement to its founding by the Carthaginian Hamilcar Barca in about 230 BC to Roman and Visigothic times and

beyond. Antiquity is the focus here: Romans took the city during the Punic Wars, and the striking underground remains of their *Colonia Iulia Faventia Paterna Barcino,* through which you can roam on metal walkways, are the museum's main treasure. Archaeological finds range from parts of walls and fluted columns to recovered busts and vases. Above ground, off the Plaça del Rei (☞ *below*), the **Palau Reial Major,** the splendid **Saló del Tinell,** the chapel of **Santa Àgata,** and the **Torre del Rei Martí,** a lookout tower with views over the Barri Gòtic, complete the self-guided tour. ✉ *Palau Padellàs, Carrer del Veguer 2,* ☎ *93/315–1111.* 🎫 *750 ptas.* ⏲ *Tues.–Sat. 10–2 and 4–8, Sun. 10–2.*

OFF THE BEATEN PATH

MUSEU DEL CALÇAT – Hunt down the tiny Shoe Museum, in a hidden corner of the Gothic Quarter between the cathedral and Carrer Banys Nous. The collection includes a pair of clown's shoes and a pair worn by Pablo Casals. The tiny square, originally a graveyard, is just as interesting as the museum, with its bullet- and shrapnel-pocked walls and quiet fountain. ✉ *Plaça de Sant Felip Neri,* ☎ *93/301–4533.* 🎫 *300 ptas.* ⏲ *Tues.–Sun. 11–2.*

❷ **Museu Frederic Marès** (Frederic Marès Museum). Here, off the left (north) side of the cathedral, you can browse for hours among the miscellany assembled by the early 20th-century sculptor-collector Frederic Marès. Everything from paintings and polychrome wood carvings, such as Juan de Juní's 1537 masterpiece *Pietà* and the Master of Cabestany's late-12th-century *Apparition of Christ to his Disciples at Sea,* to Marès's personal collection of pipes and walking sticks is stuffed into this surprisingly rich potpourri. ✉ *Plaça Sant Iu 5,* ☎ *93/310–5800.* 🎫 *350 ptas.* ⏲ *Tues.–Wed. and Fri.–Sat. 10–7, Thurs. 10–5, Sun. 10–3.*

★ ❺ **Museu Picasso.** The Picasso Museum is across Via Laietana, down Carrer de la Princesa, and right on Carrer Montcada—a street known for Barcelona's most elegant medieval palaces, of which the museum occupies two. Picasso spent several of his formative years in Barcelona (1901–06), and this collection, while not one of the world's best, is particularly strong on his early work. Displays include childhood sketches, pictures from the beautiful Rose and Blue periods, and the famous 1950s Cubist variations on Velázquez's *Las Meninas.* ✉ *Carrer Montcada 15–19,* ☎ *93/319–6310.* 🎫 *750 ptas.; free 1st Sun. of month.* ⏲ *Tues.–Sat. 10–8, Sun. 10–3.*

Passeig del Born. Once the site of medieval jousts, the Passeig is at the end of Carrer Montcada behind the church of Santa Maria del Mar. The narrow, elongated plaza is lined with late-night cocktail bars and miniature restaurants with tiny spiral stairways and intimate corners. Walk down to the Born itself—a great iron hangar, once a major produce market and soon a public library.

❸ **Plaça del Rei.** This plaza is widely considered the oldest and most beautiful space in the Gothic Quarter. Upon Columbus's return from his first voyage to the New World, the Catholic Monarchs received him on the stairs fanning out here and in the Saló del Tinell, a magnificent banquet hall built in 1362. Other ancient buildings around the square are the Palau del Lloctinent (Lieutenant's Palace), the 14th-century chapel of Santa Àgata, and the Palau Padellàs, which now serves as the entrance to the Museu d'Història de la Ciutat (☞ *above*).

❽ **Plaça Reial.** An elegant, symmetrical 19th-century arcaded square, the Plaça Reial is bordered by elegant ocher facades with balconies overlooking the wrought-iron **Fountain of the Three Graces** and some lampposts designed by Gaudí in 1879. Sidewalk cafés line the square, though in recent years the Plaça has earned a reputation for hosting drug push-

Close-Up

COLONIA FAVENCIA JULIA AUGUSTA PATERNA BARCINO

FOR A TOUR OF PROTO-BARCELONA, the 2,000-year-old Roman city of Barcino (pronounced "*Bark*-ino"), start at the freestanding bronze letters spelling BARCINO in Plaça Nova, 50 yards to the right of the cathedral steps. Roman Barcelona was originally enclosed by a 1st-century ritual (decorative) wall built during the Pax Romana, when Roman hegemony in the Mediterranean was uncontested. In the 4th century, with the Visigoths encroaching southward, the city was hurriedly surrounded by a 1,270-yard defensive wall of heavy sandstone blocks cut from Montjuïc.

Eighty-two watch towers, most of them rectangular, guarded this wall, which was 30 ft high and 12 ft thick. In Plaça Nova you can see one of the cylindrical towers used to guard corners. Walk inside the wall up Carrer del Bisbe, turn left on Santa Llúcia, and go into the Arxiu Históric de la Ciutat (Municipal Archive) for a look at the wall from the inside. Returning to the left side of the cathedral steps, pass the 16th-century Casa Pia Almoina (House of Pious Charity) and its unique octagonal tower and walk down Carrer de la Tapineria (named for *tapins,* the medieval wooden shoes once made by cobblers here). To your right, rectangular towers, or parts of them—large stones surrounded by 20th-century brick restoration—are discernible every 50 ft or so.

Noting towers as you go, walk around the left side of the cathedral through Plaça Ramon Berenguer el Gran, down Carrer Tapineria, through Plaça de l'Angel, and across Carrer Jaume I into Carrer Sots-tinent Navarro. A right turn on Carrer Pom d'Or brings you to the Plaça dels Traginers. The cylindrical towers here were placed at the corners of the enclosure to enhance visibility, as this was the sea side of the ramparts. Continue through Carrer Correu Vell and you'll see more sections of Roman wall to your right, in an entryway. Turn right on Carrer Regomir: a few steps up, beyond the tiny chapel of Sant Cristofol, on the right, is Barcino's eastern portal, with pedestrian doors on either side of the central carriage port. The pedestrian door seems low because the city has risen some 11½ ft over the last 2,000 years; the archway visible inside, on the floor, is the former carriageway.

Now cut left through Carrer Comtessa de Sobradiel and turn right on Carrer d'Avinyó. Passing the ornate facade of the Escola de les Arts Aplicades and crossing Carrer Cervantes, look for number 19, the Pakistani restaurant El Gallo Kiriko. Here, one side of the back dining room is a section of the Roman wall with two perfect watch towers—not a bad place for a meal, especially since 2,000 ptas. will more than buy dinner for two. Next door, still at No. 19, the Asociació Excursionista, Expedicionari i Folkloric (AEEF) offers a walk between the 1st-century ritual wall and the 4th-century defensive wall from 7 to 9 PM every weekday except Thursday.

Back out on Carrer d'Avinyó, continue right across Carrer de Ferran and turn right into Carrer del Call, where you'll find, in the back of the textile store at No. 5, another section of perfectly preserved Roman wall. Lean over the rail and you'll discern, at the foot of the wall, a Roman tombstone. More wall is visible in the store at No. 7. Continue up Carrer del Call into Plaça Sant Jaume—once part of the Roman Forum, which was four times the size of the square that now stands between Catalonia's Generalitat (regional government) and Barcelona's *ajuntament* (city hall). To the right of the Generalitat, across Carrer del Bisbe, Carrer Paradis 4 is your last stop: here, at the highest point in the Roman Mons Taber (Barcelona's equivalent of Athens's Acropolis) stood the Temple of Augustus. These massive columns, concealed for hundreds of years by medieval structures, now mark the entrance to the CEC (Centre Excursionista de Catalunya), a mountaineering group. For a walk through the Roman underground, pop into the Museu d'Història de la Ciutat, around the corner off Plaça del Rei.

ers and the homeless, who occupy the benches on sunny days. The place is most colorful on Sunday morning, when crowds gather to sell and trade stamps and coins; at night it's a center of downtown nightlife (☞ Nightlife and the Arts, *below*).

❼ **Plaça Sant Jaume.** This central square behind the cathedral houses both Catalonia's and Barcelona's governments, and was the site of the Roman forum 2,000 years ago. The Plaça was cleared in the 1840s, but the two imposing buildings facing each other across it are much older. The 15th-century ***ajuntament*** (city hall) has an impressive black-and-burnished-gold mural (1928) by Josep Maria Sert and the famous Saló de Cent, from which the Council of One Hundred ruled Barcelona between 1372 and 1714. To visit the interior, which is lavishly endowed with art, you need to make arrangements with the office ahead of time (ask for the *protocolo,* the protocol office). Check listings for free concerts here, the easiest way to get in. The **Palau de la Generalitat,** seat of the Catalan government, is a majestic 15th-century palace—through the front windows you can see the gilded ceiling of the Saló de Sant Jordi (St. George), named for Catalonia's dragon-slaying patron saint. Normally you can visit the Generalitat only on Día de Sant Jordi (St. George's Day), April 23; check with the *protocolo.* The Generalitat hosts carillon concerts on occasional Sundays at noon.

★ ❻ **Santa Maria del Mar.** The most elegant of all Barcelona's churches is on the Carrer Montcada end of Passeig del Born. Simple and spacious, it's something of an oddity in ornate and complex Moderniste Barcelona. The church was built from 1329 to 1383 in fulfillment of a vow made a century earlier by Jaume I to build a church for the Virgin of the Sailors. Its stark beauty is enhanced by a lovely rose window, soaring columns, and unusually wide vaulting. It's a fashionable place for concerts and weddings; if you happen by on a Saturday afternoon, you're bound to see a hopeful couple exchanging vows. ✉ *Plaça de Santa Maria.* ⏲ *Weekdays 9–12:30 and 5–8.*

The Rambla and the Raval

Barcelona's best-known promenade is a constant and colorful flood of humanity past flower stalls, bird vendors, mimes, musicians, newspaper kiosks, and outdoor cafés. Federico García Lorca famously called this street the only one in the world that he wished would never end; traffic plays second fiddle to the endless *paseo* (stroll) of locals and travelers alike. The whole avenue is referred to as Las Ramblas (Les Rambles, in Catalan) or La Rambla, but each section has its own name: Rambla Santa Monica is at the southeastern or port end, Rambla de les Flors in the middle, and Rambla dels Estudis at the top, near Plaça de Catalunya. A complete Rambla hike could begin at the Diagonal and continue down Rambla de Catalunya through the Rambla proper, between Plaça de Catalunya and the Columbus monument; and across the port on the wooden Rambla de Mar boardwalk. El Raval is the area to the west of the Rambla; it was originally a slum outside Barcelona's second set of walls, which ran down the left side of the Rambla.

Alas, Rambla-happy tourists are easy prey for muggers and pickpockets, so be on your guard here: wear dark clothing, read maps discreetly, and keep cameras concealed and wallets secure.

A Good Walk

Start on the Rambla opposite the Plaça Reial and wander down toward the sea, to the **Monument a Colom** ⑨ and the Rambla de Mar. From here you might make a brief probe into the unprepossessingly modern **Port** ⑲, with its shopping center, IMAX theater, and aquarium. As you move back to the Columbus monument, investigate the **Museu Marítim** ⑩ and its medieval **Drassanes Reiales** shipyards. Gaudí's **Palau Güell** ⑪, on Carrer Nou de la Rambla, is the next stop before the **Gran Teatre del Liceu** ⑫. At the Miró mosaic at Pla de la Boqueria, cut right to the Plaça del Pi and the church of **Santa Maria del Pi** ⑬. Back on the Rambla, stroll through the **Boqueria** ⑭ food market and the **Palau de la Virreina** ⑮ exhibition center next door; then cut around to the lovely courtyards of the medieval **Antic Hospital de la Santa Creu** ⑯. Next, visit the new **Museu d'Art Contemporani** (MACB) ⑰ and the **Centre de Cultura Contemporànea** (CCCB) ⑱, on Carrer Montalegre, before hooking back into the Rambla. Finish your walk along Carrer Tallers, ending up in **Plaça de Catalunya** ⑳.

TIMING

This walk covers about 3 km (2 mi). Including stops, allow three hours.

Sights to See

⓰ **Antic Hospital de la Santa Creu.** Surrounded by a cluster of other 15th-century buildings, this medieval hospital is now home to a number of libraries and cultural and educational institutions. You can approach it from the back door of the Boqueria, or from either Carrer del Carme or Carrer Hospital. Particularly impressive and lovely is the courtyard of the Casa de Convalescència, with its Renaissance columns and, in the entryway, the scenes of the life of St. Paul portrayed in *azulejos* (ceramic tiles). ✉ *Carrer Hospital 54 and Carrer del Carme 45.*

Antigua Casa Figueres. This Moderniste grocery and pastry store on the corner of Petxina has a splendid mosaic facade and exquisite Art Nouveau fittings.

Barri Xinès. As you walk south from Plaça Reial toward the sea, Barcelona's notorious red-light district, the Barri Xinès (traditionally called the Barrio Chino in Castilian Spanish), is on your right. China had nothing to do with this; the name is a generic reference to foreigners of all kinds. The area is ill famed for prostitutes, drug pushers, and street thieves, but it's not as dangerous as it looks; in fact, the reinforced police presence here may even make it safer than other parts of the Gothic Quarter.

★ ⓮ **Boqueria.** Barcelona's most spectacular food market, also known as the Mercat de Sant Josep, is an explosion of life and color sprinkled with delicious little bar-restaurants. Marked by a ceramic portrait of the wood-nosed prevaricator himself, **Pinotxo** (stand 66–68), has won international acclaim as a gourmet sanctuary. Don't miss mushroom supplier and expert Petràs and his mad display of wild 'shrooms, herbs, nuts, and berries ("Fruits del Bosc"—Fruits of the Forest) at stand 867–870, at the very back. ✉ *Rambla 91.*

⓲ **Centre de Cultura Contemporànea de Barcelona** (CCCB). This combination museum, lecture hall, concert hall, and exhibition space is worth checking out no matter what's on the schedule. Housed in the restored and renovated Casa de la Caritat, a former medieval convent and hospital, the CCCB now features a reflecting wall, in which you can see over the rooftops to Montjuïc and beyond. ✉ *Montalegre 5,* ☎ *93/412–0781.* 🎫 *750 ptas.* ⏲ *Tues.–Fri. 11–2 and 4–8, Wed. and Sat. 11–8, Sun. 10–3.*

★ ⓬ **Gran Teatre del Liceu.** Barcelona's opera house is one of the most beautiful in Europe. First built in 1848, it has long been a cherished cultural landmark but was gutted in early 1994 by a fire of mysteri-

Antic Hospital de la Santa Creu **16**
Boqueria . . . **14**
Centre de Cultura Contemporània de Barcelona (CCCB). **18**
Gran Teatre del Liceu . . . **12**
Monument a Colom **9**
Museu d'Art Contemporani de Barcelona (MACBA) . . . **17**
Museu Marítim **10**
Palau de la Virreina **15**
Palau Güell. **11**
Plaça de Catalunya . . **20**
Port Vell. . . . **19**
Santa Maria del Pi **13**

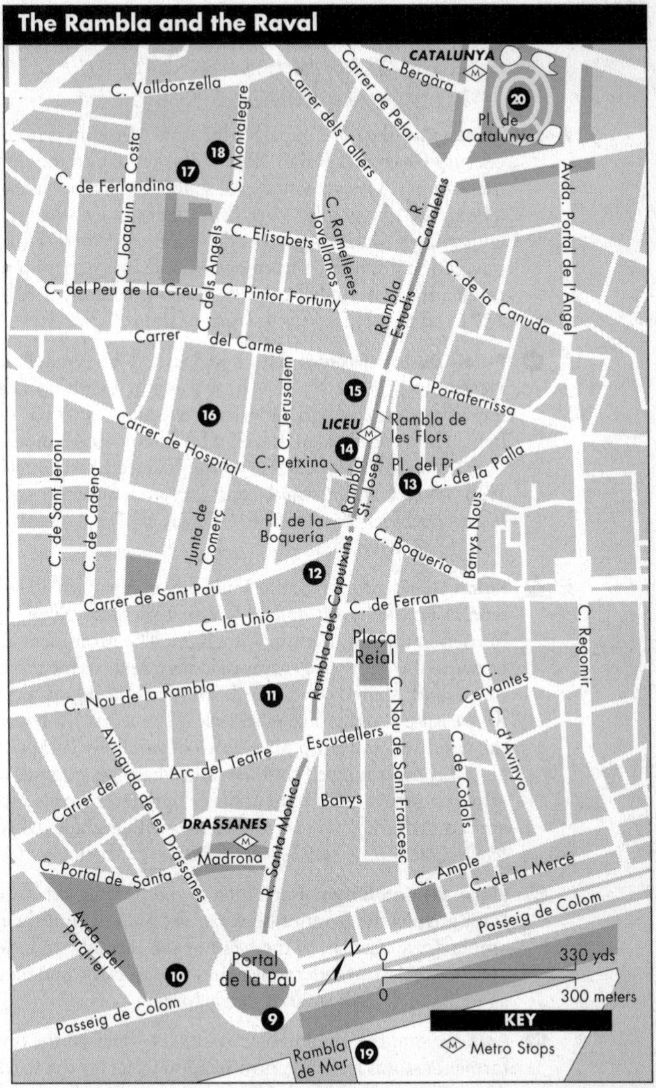

ous origins; soprano Montserrat Caballé stood on the Rambla in tears as the beloved venue was consumed. The restoration has been judged a complete success—indeed, a great improvement. Even if you don't see an opera, inquire about tours of the building; some of the Liceu's oldest and most spectacular halls and rooms were unharmed by the fire, including those of Spain's oldest social club, El Círculo del Liceu. ✉ *La Rambla 51–59,* ☎ *93/485–9900.* 🎟 *Guided tours 800 ptas.* ⏲ *Fri.–Mon. 9:45 AM–10:15 AM.*

9 **Monument a Colom** (Columbus Monument). At the foot of the Rambla, take an elevator to the top of the Monument a Colom for a bird's-eye view over the city. (The entrance is on the harbor side.) ✉ *Portal de la Pau s/n,* ☎ *93/302–5224.* 🎟 *300 ptas.* ⏲ *Weekdays 10–1:30 and 3–6:30, weekends and holidays 10–6:30.*

17 **Museu d'Art Contemporani de Barcelona** (Barcelona Museum of Contemporary Art; MACB). Designed by American architect Richard Meier, this 1992 building houses both a permanent collection and traveling exhibits. Featured 20th-century masters include Calder, Rauschenberg, Oteiza, Chillida, and Tàpies. The optional guided tour is excellent. ✉ *Plaça dels Àngels,* ☎ *93/412–0810.* 🎫 *800 ptas.* ⏲ *Weekdays 11–7, Sat. 10–8, Sun. and holidays 10–3.*

★ ❿ **Museu Marítim.** The superb Maritime Museum is housed in the 13th-century **Drassanes Reials** (Royal Shipyards), to the right at the foot of the Rambla. This vast medieval space seems more like a cathedral than a boatyard and is filled with ships, including a spectacular, life-size reconstructed galley; figureheads; nautical gear of all kinds; and early navigational charts. Headphones and infrared pointers make for a fascinating self-guided tour. ✉ *Plaça Portal de la Pau 1,* ☎ *93/301–1871.* 🎫 *850 ptas.; free 1st Sat. of month after 3 PM.* ⏲ *Daily 10–7.*

⓯ **Palau de la Virreina.** The neoclassical Virreina Palace, built by a viceroy to Peru in 1778, is now a major exhibition center for paintings, photography, and historical items; find out what's on while you're here. The building also houses a bookstore and a municipal tourist office. If you arrive when everything is closed, the consolation prize is a Web-linked computer in the entrance arch (insert credit card). ✉ *Rambla de les Flors 99,* ☎ *93/301–7775.* ⏲ *Tues.–Sat. 10–2 and 4:30–9, Sun. 10–2, Mon. 4:30–9.*

★ ⓫ **Palau Güell.** Antoni Gaudí built this mansion in 1886–89 for his patron, a textile baron named Count Eusebi de Güell, and soon found himself in the international limelight. The prominent Catalan emblem between the parabolic entrance gates attests to the nationalist leanings that Gaudí shared with Güell. The dark facade is a dramatic foil for the treasure house inside, where spear-shape Art Nouveau columns frame the windows and prop up a series of minutely detailed wood ceilings. Gaudí is most himself on the roof, where his playful, polychrome ceramic chimneys seem right at home with later works such as Parc Güell and La Pedrera. You tour the palace with a guide. ✉ *Nou de la Rambla 3–5,* ☎ *93/317–3974.* 🎫 *450 ptas.* ⏲ *Weekdays 10–2 and 4–7:30.*

⓴ **Plaça de Catalunya.** Barcelona's main transport hub, the Plaça de Catalunya is the frontier between the old city and the post-1860 Eixample. Café Zurich, at the head of the Rambla and the mouth of the metro, is a classic rendezvous point. The block behind the Zurich, known as El Triangle, is a strip of megastores.

⓳ **Port.** Beyond the Columbus monument—behind the ornate Duana, or former customs building, now headquarters for the Barcelona Port Authority—is the **Rambla de Mar,** a boardwalk with a drawbridge to allow boats in and out of the inner harbor. The Rambla de Mar extends out to the **Moll d'Espanya,** with its Maremagnum shopping center, IMAX theater, and new aquarium. Next to the Duana, you can board a Golondrina boat for a tour of the port or, from the Moll de Barcelona on the right, take a cable car to Montjüic or Barceloneta. You can also take a boat to the end of the *rompeolas,* 3 km (2 mi) out to sea, and walk back into Barceloneta. Trasmediterránea passenger ferries leave for Italy and the Balearic Islands from the Moll de Barcelona, down to the right. At the end of the quay is Barcelona's new World Trade Center.

⓭ **Santa Maria del Pi** (St. Mary of the Pine). Like Santa Maria del Mar, the church of Santa Maria del Pi is a fine example of Mediterranean Gothic architecture. Its gigantic rose window, which overlooks the diminutive square, is the best in Barcelona. The adjoining squares, **Plaça del Pi** and **Plaça de Sant Josep Oriol,** are two of the liveliest, most appealing spaces in the Gothic Quarter.

The Moderniste Eixample

North of Plaça de Catalunya is the elegant checkerboard known as the Eixample. With the dismantling of the city walls in 1860, Barcelona embarked upon a vast expansion scheme fueled by the return of rich colonials from America, by an influx of provincial aristocrats who had sold their country estates after the debilitating second Carlist War (1847–49), and by the city's growing industrial power. The street grid was the work of urban planner Ildefons Cerdà; much of the building here was done at the height of Modernisme. The Eixample's principal thoroughfares are Rambla de Catalunya and Passeig de Gràcia, where the city's most elegant shops vie for space among its best Art Nouveau buildings.

A Good Tour

Starting in the **Plaça de Catalunya** ⑳, walk up Passeig de Gràcia until you reach the corner of Consell de Cent. You are about to enter the Bermuda Triangle of Moderniste architecture, the **Manzana de la Discordia** ㉑. This is the "city block," or "apple," of discord (the pun only works in Spanish) where the three great figures of Barcelona's late-19th-century Moderniste (Art Nouveau) movement—Domènech i Muntaner, Puig i Cadafalch, and Gaudí—went head to head and toe to toe with three very different buildings: **Casa Lleó Morera, Casa Amatller,** and **Casa Batlló**. The *Fundació Tàpies* ㉒ is just west, around the corner on Carrer Aragó. Gaudí's *Casa Milà* ㉓, known as La Pedrera, is three blocks farther up Passeig de Gràcia. After seeing it, hike or taxi to Gaudí's emblematic **Temple Expiatori de la Sagrada Família** ㉔. Finally, stroll over to Domènech i Muntaner's **Hospital de Sant Pau** ㉕.

TIMING

Depending on how many taxis you take, this is at least a three-hour tour. Add another hour or two to explore the Sagrada Família.

Sights to See

★ ㉓ **Casa Milà.** Gaudí's Casa Milà, usually referred to as **La Pedrera** (The Stone Quarry), has a remarkable, curving stone facade that undulates around the corner of the block. When the building was unveiled, in 1905, local residents were not enthusiastic about the appearance of these cavelike balconies on their most fashionable street. Gaudí's rooftop chimney park is as spectacular as anything in Barcelona, especially in late afternoon, when the sunlight slants over the city into the Mediterranean. The handsome **Espai Gaudí** (Gaudí Space) in the attic has excellent critical displays of Gaudí's works, theories, and techniques, including a spectacular upside-down model of the Sagrada Familia made of hanging beads. The **Pis de la Pedrera,** a restored apartment, gives an interesting glimpse into the life of its resident family in the early 20th century. ✉ *Passeig de Gràcia 92,* ☎ *93/484–5995.* 🎫 *650 ptas. for Espai Gaudí, 650 ptas. for Pis de la Pedrera, 1,100 ptas. for combined ticket.* ⏲ *Daily 10–8; guided tours weekdays 6* PM*, weekends 11* AM*. Jul.–Sept., Espai Gaudí and rooftop also open 9* PM*–midnight.*

㉒ **Casa Montaner i Simó–Fundació Tàpies.** This former publishing house has been beautifully converted to a modern, airy, split-level showcase for the work of contemporary Catalan painter Antoni Tàpies, as well as temporary exhibits. On top of the building is Tàpies' tangle of metal entitled *Núvol i cadira* (*Cloud and Chair*). The bookstore is strong on both Tàpies and Asian art. ✉ *Carrer Aragó 255,* ☎ *93/487–0315.* 🎫 *750 ptas.* ⏲ *Tues.–Sun. 10–8.*

㉕ **Hospital de Sant Pau.** The brick Hospital de Sant Pau is notable for its Mudéjar motifs and wards set among lush gardens. ✉ *Carrer Sant Antoni Maria Claret 167,* ☎ *93/291–9000.* ⏲ *Daily 9–2 and 4–7.*

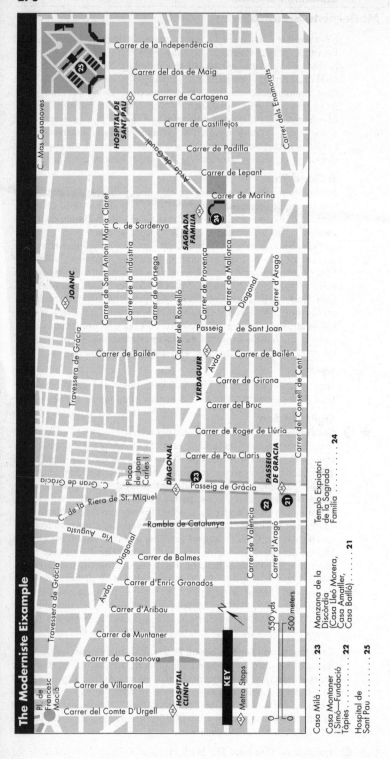

The Moderniste Eixample

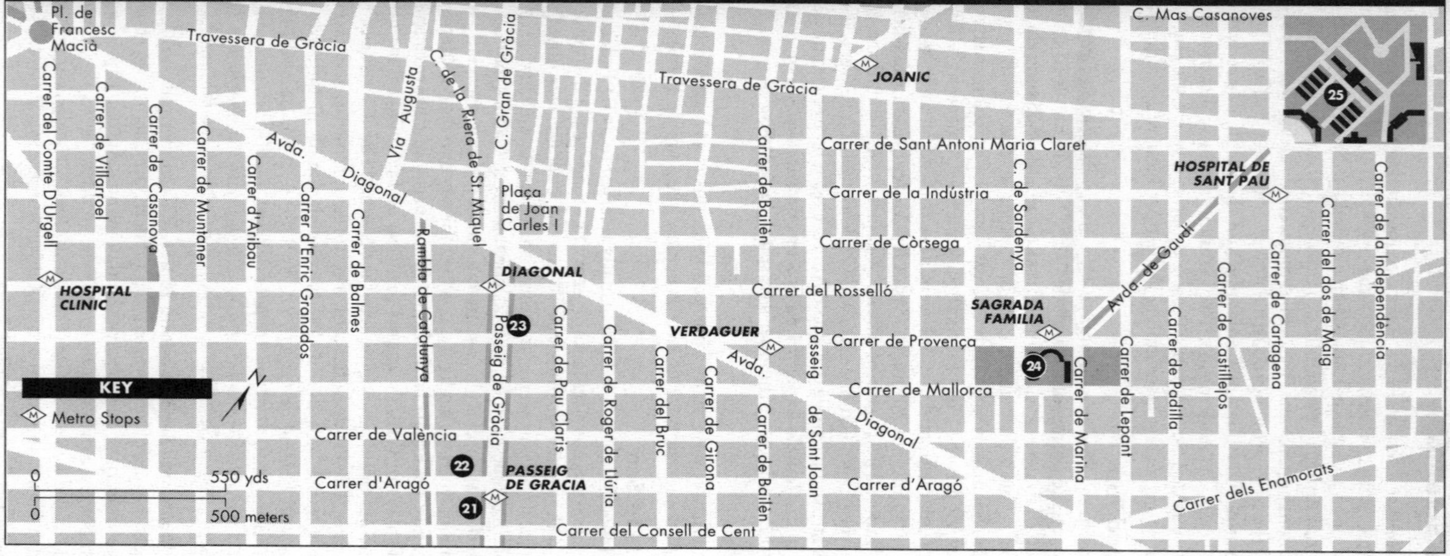

Casa Milà **23**

Casa Montaner i Simó—Fundació Tàpies **22**

Hospital de Sant Pau **25**

Manzana de la Discòrdia (Casa Lleó Morera, Casa Amatller, Casa Batlló) **21**

Templo Expiatori de la Sagrada Familia **24**

㉑ **Manzana de la Discòrdia.** The name is a pun on the word *manzana,* which means both "city block" and "apple," alluding to the architectural counterpoint on this block and to the classical myth of the Apple of Discord. The houses here are spectacular. The ornate **Casa Lleó Morera** (No. 35) was extensively rebuilt (1902–06) by Palau de la Música architect Domènech i Muntaner, and the Eusebi Arnau sculptures on the main floor are excellent. The pseudo-Gothic, pseudo-Flemish **Casa Amatller** (No. 41) is by Puig i Cadafalch. Next door is Gaudí's **Casa Batlló,** with a mottled facade that resembles nearly anything you want it to. Nationalist symbolism is at work here: the scaly roof line represents the dragon of evil impaled on St. George's cross, and the skulls and bones on the balconies are the dragon's victims. ✉ *Passeig de Gràia 35, 41, and 43 (between Consell de Cent and Aragó).*

★ ㉔ **Temple Expiatori de la Sagrada Família** (Expiatory Temple of the Holy Family). Begun in 1882, Barcelona's most emblematic landmark, Antoni Gaudí's Sagrada Família, is still under construction well over a century later. With only one tower completed at Gaudí's death, just short of age 74 (he was run over by a tram and, unrecognized for several days, died in a pauper's ward in 1926), this striking and surreal creation was conceived as a gigantic symbol for the entire history of Christianity. Gaudí's designs called for three facades—Nativity, Passion, and Glory—with four towers each, representing the 12 apostles. These would be joined by four more towers representing the Evangelists: Matthew, Mark, Luke, and John. The 17th tower, dedicated to the Virgin Mary, will be dwarfed by a giant central dome 568 ft high, dedicated to Jesus. At the moment, eight towers are standing; the central nave is slated to be covered by the end of the year 2000, while the Glory facade is not projected to be finished before 2050. You approach toward the southwestern (Passion) facade, sculpted by Josep Maria Subirachs—a powerfully contemporary representation of the last days of Jesus' life. For 200 ptas., you can take an elevator to the top of the bell towers for spectacular views. Walk slowly back down for a closer look at scattered decorative details ranging from broken-bottle designs to colorful fruit by the Japanese sculptor Etsuro Sotoo. Linger on some of the landings, where you can actually touch, among other things, the Subirachs sculpture of Gaudí.

The **museum**—which takes you through the building to the northeastern (Nativity) facade—displays Gaudí's scale models, photographs showing the progress of construction, and photographs of Gaudí's multitudinous funeral. The architect is buried to the left of the altar in the **crypt,** which has its own entrance. ✉ *Plaça de la Sagrada Familia,* ☎ *93/207–3031.* 💰 *900 ptas.* ⏲ *Sept.–Mar., daily 9–6; Apr.–Aug., daily 9–8.*

Upper Barcelona: Sarrià, Pedralbes, Tibidabo, and Parc Güell

A Good Walk

These sights are spread across Barcelona's upper reaches. Because the Monestir de Pedralbes closes at 2, the best way to attack this part of town is to start with Sarrià and Pedralbes, then visit Tibidabo and Parc Güell after lunch. From **Sarrià** ㉘ it's a 20-minute walk or a five-minute cab ride to the **Monestir de Pedralbes** ㉙. **Tibidabo** ㉗ has wonderful vistas on clear days, and the restaurant La Venta is a fine place for lunch in the sun. Gaudí's **Parc Güell** ㉖ is most easily reached by taxi unless you really enjoy walking and don't mind getting lost. Tibidabo and Parc Güell are best seen in mid- to late afternoon, when the sun backs around to the west and dramatically illuminates the views over the city and the Mediterranean.

Sarrià, Pedralbes, Tibidabo, and Parc Güell

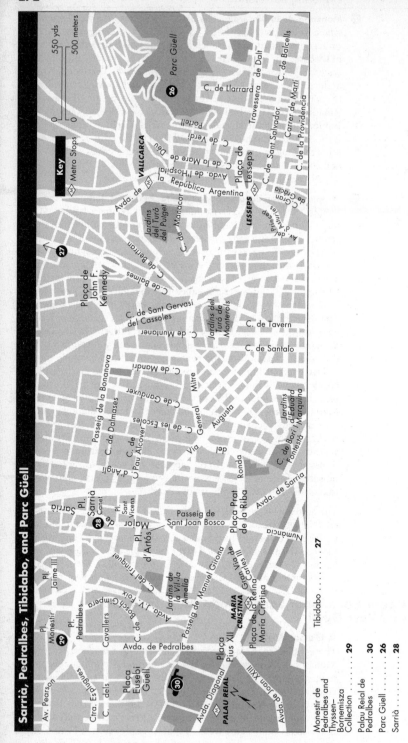

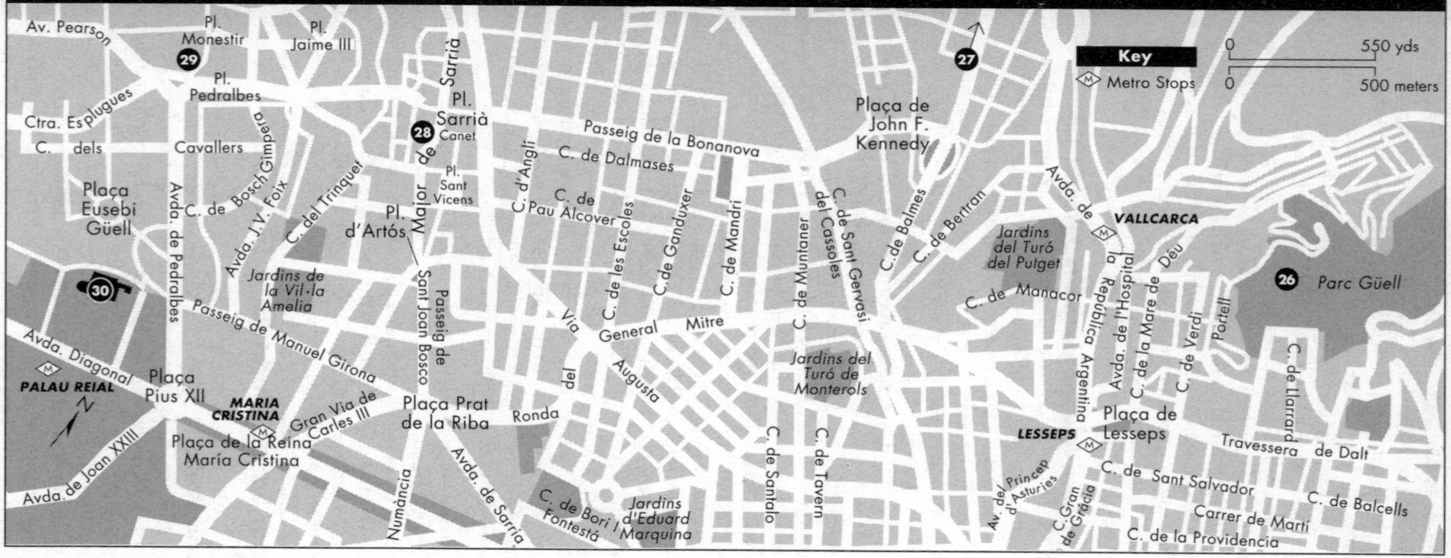

TIMING

If you do it all at once, this is a five-hour outing. Add another two hours if you want to go up to the Collserola Tower.

Sights to See

29 **Monestir de Pedralbes.** Even without its Thyssen-Bornemisza Collection of Italian masters, this is one of Barcelona's hidden treasures. Founded by Reina Elisenda for Clarist nuns in 1326, the convent has an unusual, three-story Gothic cloister, arguably the finest in Barcelona. The chapel has a beautiful stained-glass rose window and famous murals painted in 1346 by Ferrer Bassa, a Catalan much influenced by the Italian Renaissance. You can also visit the medieval living quarters. The monastery alone is a treat, but the **Thyssen-Bornemisza Collection,** installed in 1989 in what was once the dormitory of the nuns of the Order of St. Clare, sends it over the top. Surrounded by 14th-century windows and pointed arches, these canvases by Tiepolo, Canaletto, Tintoretto, Rubens, and Velázquez will restore any weary traveler's soul. ✉ *Baixada Monestir 9,* ☎ *93/203–9282.* 🎫 *Monastery and cloister 400 ptas.; Thyssen-Bornemisza Collection 400 ptas.; combined ticket 700 ptas.; free 1st Sun. of month.* 🕘 *Tues.–Sun. 10–2.*

OFF THE BEATEN PATH

MUSEU DE LA CIÈNCIA – Young scientific minds work overtime in the Science Museum, just below Tibidabo—many of its displays and activities are designed for children ages seven and up. ✉ *Teodor Roviralta 55,* ☎ *93/212–6050.* 🎫 *600 ptas.; children 300 ptas.* 🕘 *Tues.–Sun. 10–8. Metro: Avinguda de Tibidabo and Tramvía Blau halfway.*

30 **Palau Reial de Pedralbes** (Royal Palace of Pedralbes). Built in the 1920s for King Alfonso XII, this palace is now home to a **Ceramics Museum,** which makes a wide sweep of Spanish ceramic art from the 14th to the 18th century. The influence of Moorish design techniques is carefully documented. It's a 20-minute walk downhill from the monastery. ✉ *Av. Diagonal 686,* ☎ *93/280–5024.* 🎫 *550 ptas.; free 1st Sun. of month.* 🕘 *Daily 10–3.*

26 **Parc Güell.** Güell Park is one of Gaudí's, and Barcelona's, greatest resources. Whereas the Sagrada Família can be tiring in its massive energy and complexity, Parc Güell is light and playful, uplifting and restorative. Named after Gaudí's main patron, it was originally intended as a hillside garden suburb on the English model, but only two of the houses were ever built. It's an Art Nouveau extravaganza, with a mosaic pagoda, undulating benches, and large, multicolored lizards guarding a Moderniste grotto. ✉ *Carrer d'Olot 3 (Take metro to Lesseps; then walk 10 mins uphill or catch Bus 24 to park entrance).* 🕘 *Oct.–Mar., daily 10–6; Apr.–June, daily 10–7; July–Sept., daily 10–9.*

The **Gaudí Museum,** within Güell Park, occupies a pink, Alice-in-Wonderland house in which Gaudí lived with his niece from 1906 to 1926. Exhibits include Gaudí-designed furniture, decorations, drawings, and portraits and bust of the architect. ✉ *Parc Güell (up hill to right of main entrance),* ☎ *93/219–3811.* 🎫 *450 ptas.* 🕘 *May–Sept. 10–8, Oct.–Feb. 10–6, Mar.–Apr. 10–7.*

OFF THE BEATEN PATH

"EL BARÇA" – If you're in Barcelona between September and June, go see FC Barcelona play, preferably against Real Madrid (if you can get in). Games are generally played Saturday night or Sunday afternoon at 5, but there may be cup or international games during the week as well, usually on Wednesday. Ask your hotel concierge how to get tickets, or call the club in advance. The massive Camp Nou stadium seats 130,000 and fills almost to capacity. The museum has an impressive array of trophies and a five-screen video showing memorable goals in the history of one of Europe's most colorful soccer clubs. ✉ *Arístides Maillol*, ☎ *93/330–9411*. 💰 *Museum 600 ptas.* ⏲ *Oct.–Mar., Tues.–Fri. 10–1 and 4–6, weekends 10–1 and 3–6; Apr.–Sept., Mon.–Sat. 10–1 and 3–6.*

28 **Sarrià.** This 1,000-year-old village was once a cluster of farms and country houses overlooking Barcelona from the hills. It's now a quiet enclave at the upper edge of the roaring metropolis. Start your exploration at the main square, Plaça Sarrià, which hosts an antiques and crafts market on Tuesday morning, *sardana* dances on Sunday morning, and Christmas fairs in season. The Romanesque church tower, lighted a bright ocher at night, looms overhead. Across Passeig Reina Elisenda from the church, wander through the brick-and-steel **produce market** and the tiny, flower-choked **Plaça Sant Gaietà** behind it. Back in front of the church, cut through the Placeta del Roser to the left and you'll come to the elegant **town hall** in the Plaça de la Vila; note the buxom bronze sculpture of Pomona, goddess of fruit, by famed Sarrià sculptor Josep Clarà (1878–1958). After peeking in to see the massive ceiling beams (and very reasonable set lunch menu) in the restaurant Vell Sarrià, at the corner of Major de Sarrià, go back to the Pomona bronze and turn left into tiny Carrer dels Paletes (with its tiny saint-filled niche on the corner overhead to the right), which leads back to Major de Sarrià. Continue down this pedestrian-only street to the bougainvillea- and honeysuckle-lined **Carrer Canet,** with its diminutive, cottagelike artisans' quarters.

Turn right on Carrer Cornet i Mas and walk two blocks down to Carrer Jaume Piquet. A quick probe to the left will take you to No. 30, Barcelona's most perfect small-format **Moderniste house,** complete with faux-medieval upper windows, wrought-iron grillwork, floral and fruited ornamentation, and organically curved and carved wooden doors. The next stop down Cornet i Mas is Sarrià's prettiest square, **Plaça Sant Vicens,** a leafy space ringed by old Sarrià houses and centered on a statue of the village's patron saint. Note the other renditions of the saint over the square's upper right corner. The café Can Pau is the local hangout, once a haven for such authors as Gabriel García Marquez and Mario Vargas Llosa, who lived in Sarrià in the 1970s, on the cusp of their fame; it's a good place for coffee and a slice of tortilla. To get to the Monestir de Pedralbes from Plaça Sant Vicens, walk back up Mayor de Sarrià and through the market to the corner of Sagrat Cor and Ramon Miquel Planas; then turn left and walk straight west for 15 minutes, past the splendid upper-city mansions of Pedralbes.

Other Sarrià landmarks include the two **Foix** pastry stores, one at Plaça Sarrià 9–10 and the other on Major de Sarrià 57, above Bar Tomás. Both have excellent pastries, artisanal breads, and cold *cava*. The late J. V. Foix, son of the store's founders, was one of the great Catalan poets of the 20th century, a key player in keeping the Catalan language alive during the 40-year Franco regime. ✉ *Plaça Sarrià (take Bus 22 from the bottom of Av. de Tibidabo, or the U-6 train on the FFCC subway to Reina Elisenda).*

NEED A BREAK?

Bar Tomás, on Major de Sarrià on the corner of Jaume Piquet, is a Barcelona institution, home of the finest potatoes in town. Order the famous *doble mixta* of potatoes with *allioli* and hot sauce. Draft beer (ask for a *caña*) is the de rigueur beverage.

27 **Tibidabo.** Tibidabo is one of Barcelona's two promontories, along with Montjuïc, and when the wind blows the smog out to sea, the views

from this hill are legendary. The shapes that distinguish Tibidabo from below turn out to be a commercialized church, a vast radio mast, and the 850-ft communications tower, the Torre de Collserola, designed by Norman Foster. There's not much to see here except the vista, particularly from the tower. Clear days are few and far between in 21st-century Barcelona, but if (and only if) you hit one, this excursion is worth considering. The restaurant **La Venta,** at the base of the funicular, is excellent, and a fine place to sit in the sun in cool weather (the establishment provides straw sun hats). The bar **Mirablau** is a popular hangout for evening drinks overlooking the city lights. ✉ *Take Tibidibo branch off Sarrià subway; Buses 24 and 22 to Plaza Kennedy; or a taxi. At Av. Tibidabo, catch Tramvía Blau, which connects with funicular (☞ Getting Around in Barcelona A to Z, below) to the summit.*

Torre de Collserola. The Collserola Tower, which dwarfs Mt. Tibidabo, is a creation of Norman Foster, erected for the 1992 Olympics amid controversy over defacement of the traditional mountain skyline. The tower has a splendid panorama of the city when conditions allow. Take the funicular up to Tibidabo; from Plaza Tibidabo there is free transport to the tower. ✉ *Av. de Vallvidrera,* ☎ *93/406–9354.* 🎫 *600 ptas.* ⏲ *Wed.–Sun. 11–2:30 and 3:30–8.*

Sant Pere, La Ribera, La Ciutadella, and Barceloneta

Barcelona's old textile neighborhood, around the church of Sant Pere, includes the flagship of the city's Moderniste architecture, the extraordinary Palau de la Música. The Barri de la Ribera, once the waterfront district, surrounds the basilica of Santa Maria del Mar and includes Carrer Montcada, Barcelona's poshest street in the 14th and 15th centuries. Part of the Barri de la Ribera was torn down in 1714 to create fields of fire for the fortress, La Ciutadella. Barceloneta, once the open sea, gradually silted in and became a salt marsh until 1753, when French military engineer Prosper de Verboom designed a housing project for families who had lost their homes. Together, the four areas form a pleasant walk within and around what were once Barcelona's 13th-century walls.

A Good Walk

This neighborhood, or series of neighborhoods, lies generally to the north and east of the Gothic Quarter. From **Plaça de Catalunya** ⑳, it's no more than a 15-minute walk to the **Palau de la Música** ㉛, taking your first left off the Rambla. After inspecting the Palau (guided tours can be arranged on weekdays), continue along Carrer Sant Pere Més Alt to the Plaça Sant Pere on your way past the church of **Sant Pere de les Puelles** and out to the **Arc del Triomf** ㉜, on Passeig de Sant Joan. From there, walk through the Parc de la Ciutadella and the Estació de Françia to the edge of the port, through **Barceloneta** ㊳, and along the beach to the **Port Olímpic** ㊴.

TIMING

Depending on the number of stops, this walk can take a full day. Count on at least four hours of actual walking time.

Sights to See

32 **Arc del Triomf.** This imposing, exposed-redbrick arch was built by Josep Vilaseca as the grand entrance for the 1888 Universal Exhibition.

38 **Barceloneta.** Once Barcelona's pungent fishing port, Barceloneta retains much of its maritime ambience. It's a pretty walk through narrow streets with lines of laundry snapping in the breeze overhead. Stop in Plaça de la Barceloneta and have a close look at the Baroque church

Sant Pere, La Ribera, La Ciutadella, and Barceloneta

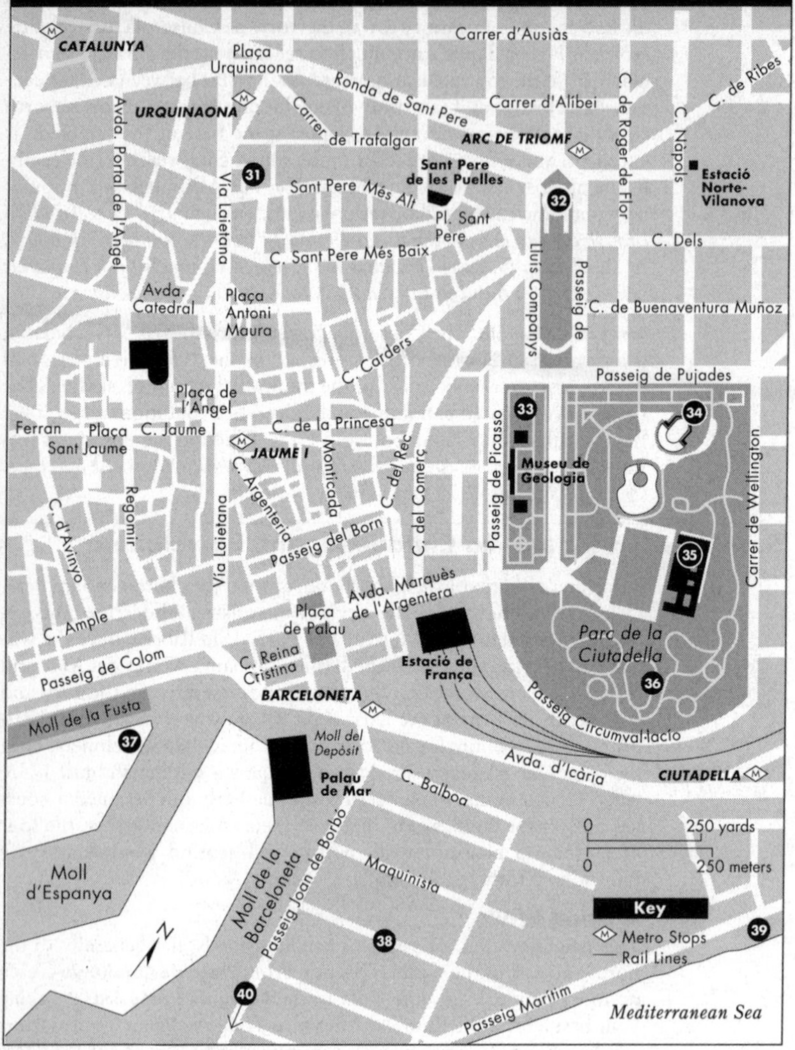

Arc del Triomf. **32**
Barceloneta **38**
Castell dels Tres Dragons **33**
Font de la Senyoreta Paraigua **34**
Palau de la Ciutadella **35**
Palau de la Música **31**
Port Olímpic. **39**
Port Vell. **37**
Telefèric. **40**
Zoo. **36**

of **Sant Miquel del Port,** with its somewhat oversize new sculpture of the winged archangel himself in the alcove on the facade. The tapas bar on the sea side of the square has a robust display of delicacies. Look for the Barceloneta market and the restaurant Can Ramonet (☞ Dining, *below*) on Carrer de la Maquinista.

Barceloneta's **beach,** a little dusty and often crowded in summer, has improved much in recent years and can actually be used for swimming, provided the winds and currents haven't created a backup of some sort. Take a close look at the water before you dive in. In summer the Habana Beach Club, just off the end of Passeig de Joan de Borbó, rages 'til dawn.

NEED A BREAK? Friendly **Can Manel la Puda,** on Passeig de Joan de Borbó, is always good for a tasty, inexpensive feast in the sun. Serving lunch until 4 and starting dinner at 7, it's a handy and popular place for *suquets* (fish stew), paella, and *arroç a banda* (rice with shelled seafood). ✉ *Passeig Joan de Borbó 60–61,* ☎ *93/221–5013. AE, DC, MC, V. Closed Mon.*

33 **Castell dels Tres Dragons** (Castle of the Three Dragons). Built by Domènech i Muntaner as the café for the 1888 Universal Exposition, this arresting building greets you as you enter the Ciutadella from Passeig Lluí Companys. It later became a workshop where Moderniste architects met to experiment with traditional crafts and to exchange ideas. It now holds Barcelona's **Museum of Zoology.** ✉ *Passeig Picasso 5,* ☎ *93/319–6912.* 🎫 *350 ptas.* ⏲ *Tues.–Sun. 10–2.*

Estació de Françia. The elegantly restored Estació de França, Barcelona's main railroad station until about 1980 and still the stopping point for some trains to and from France and points along the Mediterranean, is outside the west gate of the Ciutadella. It's well worth visiting to get a sense of the Old World romance of Europe's traditional railroads. ✉ *Marquè de l'Argentera s/n,* ☎ *93/319–6416.*

NEED A BREAK? You're just a step from the best tapas in Barcelona at **Cal Pep** (✉ Plaça de les Olles 8). Try the *gambitas* (baby shrimp), *pulpo gallego* (octopus), or *garbanzos con espinacas* (garbanzos with spinach), and don't forget to order *pan de coca* (crunchy toast with oil and fresh tomato paste). Don't give up if you have to wait for a while; they'll feed you wine in the meantime.

34 **Font de la Senyoreta del Paraigua** (Fountain of the Lady with the Umbrella). Escape the sights and sounds of the city by this fountain, its lake, and, behind it, the monumental *Cascada,* by Josep Fontserè, designed for the 1888 Universal Exhibition. The waterfall's rocks were the work of a young architecture student named Antoni Gaudí—his first public works, appropriately natural and organic, and certainly a hint of things to come.

Museu de Geologia. The Museum of Geology is next to the Castell dels Tres Dragons, not far from the beautiful Umbracle, the black slats of which help create jungle lighting for the museum's valuable collection of tropical plants. Barcelona's first public museum, it displays rocks, minerals, and fossils along with special exhibits on Catalonia and the rest of Spain. ✉ *Parc de la Ciutadella,* ☎ *93/319–6895.* 🎫 *500 ptas.; free 1st Sun. of month.* ⏲ *Tues.–Sun. 10–2.*

35 **Palau de la Ciutadella** (Citadel Palace). This is the only surviving remnant of Felipe V's fortress, now shared by the Catalan parliament and the Museum of Modern Art. The palace's late-19th- and early 20th-

century Catalan paintings and sculptures, by such artists as Isidro Nonell, Ramon Casas, and Marià Fortuny, form one of Barcelona's artistic treasures. A stroll through this collection makes it very clear that Catalonia's more famous artists—Gaudí, Picasso, Dalí, Miró—emerged not from nowhere but from an exceptionally rich artistic context. ✉ *Plaça d'Armes, Parc de la Ciutadella,* ☎ *93/319–5728.* 🎟 *500 ptas.* ⏲ *Tues.–Sat. 10–7, Sun. 10–2.*

★ ㉛ **Palau de la Música.** The Music Palace, on Carrer Amadeus Vives, is a flamboyant tour de force, designed by Domènech i Muntaner in 1908 and considered the flagship of Barcelona's Moderniste architecture. Wagnerian cavalry explodes from the right side of the stage while flowery maidens languish on the left; an inverted stained-glass cupola overhead seems to offer the manna of music straight from heaven; painted rosettes and giant peacock feathers explode from the tops of the walls; and even the stage is dominated by the busts of muselike Art Nouveau instrumentalists. The visuals alone make music sound different in here, and at any important concert the excitement is palpably thick (☞ Nightlife and the Arts, *below*). If you can't attend one, take a tour of the hall, offered daily at 10:30, 2, and 3 (in English) for 700 ptas. ✉ *Ticket office: Sant Francesc de Paula 2 (just off Via Laietana, around a corner from the hall itself),* ☎ *93/268–1000.*

Parc de la Ciutadella (Citadel Park). Once a fortress designed to consolidate Madrid's military occupation of Barcelona, the Ciutadella is now the city's main downtown park. The clearing dates from shortly after the War of the Spanish Succession, when Felipe V demolished some 2,000 houses in what was then the Barri de la Ribera (waterfront neighborhood) to build a fortress and barracks for his soldiers and fields of fire for his artillery. The fortress walls were pulled down in 1868 and replaced by gardens laid out by Josep Fontserè. Within the park are a cluster of museums, the Catalan parliament, and the city zoo.

㊴ **Port Olímpic.** Choked with yachts, restaurants, and tapas bars of all kinds, the Olympic Port is 2 km (1 mi) up the beach, marked by the mammoth Frank Gehry goldfish sculpture in front of Barcelona's first real skyscraper, the Hotel Arts. The port rages on Friday and Saturday nights, especially in summer, with hundreds of young people of all nationalities circling and grazing until daybreak.

㊲ **Port Vell.** From Pla del Palau, cross to the edge of the port, where the Moll d'Espanya, the Moll de la Fusta, and the Moll de Barceloneta meet. Just beyond the colorful Lichtenstein sculpture in front of the post office, the modern Port Vell complex—the IMAX theater, aquarium, and Maremagnum shopping mall—looms seaward on the Moll d'Espanya. The Palau de Mar, with its five (somewhat pricey and impersonal) quayside terrace restaurants, stretches down along the Moll de Barceloneta. (Try Llevataps or, on the far corner, the Merendero de la Mari.) Stroll through the Museu de Historia de Catalunya (MHC) in the Palau de Mar for a lesson in Catalan history. Along the Passeig Joan de Borbó are a dozen more traditional Barceloneta paella and seafood specialists.

Sant Pere de les Puelles (St. Peter of the Novices). One of the oldest medieval churches in Barcelona, this one has been destroyed and restored so many times that there is little left to see except the beautiful stained-glass window, which illuminates the stark interior. The word *Puelles* is from the Latin *puella* (girl)—the convent here was known for the beauty and nobility of its young women and was the setting for some of medieval Barcelona's most tragic stories of impossible love. ✉ *Lluís El Piadós 1,* ☎ *93/268–0742.* ⏲ *Open for mass only.*

40 **Telefèric** (cable car). The cable car leaving from the tower at the end of Passeig Joan de Borbócan connects the Torre de San Sebastián on the Moll de Barceloneta, the tower of Jaime I in the boat terminal, and the Torre de Miramar on Montjuïc. ☎ *93/225–2718.* *1,300 ptas. round trip, 1,100 one way.* ⏲ *Oct.–June 21, weekends 10:30–5:30; June 22–Sept., daily 10:30–8:30.*

36 **Zoo.** Barcelona's first-rate zoo—home of Snowflake, the world's only captive albino gorilla—occupies the whole bottom section of the Parc de la Ciutadella. There's a great reptile house and a full complement of African animals. ✉ *Parc de la Ciutadella,* ☎ *93/225–6780.* *Adults 1,600 ptas.; children under 13, 1,000 ptas.* ⏲ *Oct.–Apr., daily 10–6; May–Sept., daily 9:30–7:30.*

Montjuïc

This hill to the south of town is thought to have been named for the Jewish cemetery once located on its slopes, though an alternate explanation has it named for the Roman deity Jove, or Jupiter. The most dramatic approach is by way of the cross-harbor cable car from Barceloneta or from the mid-station in the port; but Montjuïc is normally accessed by taxi or Bus 61 (or on foot) from Plaça Espanya, or by the funicular that operates from the Paral.lel (Paral.lel metro stop on the green line).

A Good Walk

Walking from sight to sight on Montjuïc is possible but not recommended. You'll want fresh feet and backs to appreciate the sights here, especially the Romanesque art collection in the Palau Nacional and the Miró Foundation.

The *telefèric* drops you at the Jardins de Miramar, a 10-minute walk from the Plaça de Dante. From here, another small cable car takes you up to the **Castell de Montjuïc** (41). From the bottom station, the **Fundació Miró** (42) is just a few minutes' walk, and beyond it is the **Estadi Olímpic** (Olympic Stadium). From the stadium, walk straight down to the Palau Nacional and its **Museu Nacional d'Art de Catalunya** (43). From here, a wide stairway leads down toward Plaça de Espanya.

TIMING

With unhurried visits to the Miró Foundation and the Romanesque exhibit in the Palau Nacional, this is a four- to five-hour excursion. Have lunch afterward in the Poble Espanyol.

Sights to See

41 **Castell de Montjuïc.** Built in 1640 by rebels against Felipe IV, the castle has been stormed several times, most famously in 1705 by Lord Peterborough for Archduke Carlos of Austria. In 1808, during the Peninsular War, it was seized by the French under General Dufresne. Later, during an 1842 civil disturbance, Barcelona was bombed from its heights by a Spanish artillery battery. The moat contains attractive gardens, with one side given over to an archery range, and the various terraces have panoramic views over the city and out to sea. The castle now functions as a **military museum** housing the weapons collection of early-20th-century sculptor Frederic Marès. ✉ *Carretera de Montjuïc 66,* ☎ *93/329–8613.* *250 ptas.* ⏲ *Oct.–Mar., Tues.–Sat. 10–2 and 4–7, Sun. 10–2; Apr.–Sept., Tues.–Sat. 10–2 and 4–7, Sun. 10–8.*

Estadi Olímpic. The Olympic Stadium was originally built for the Great Exhibition of 1929, with the idea that Barcelona would then host the 1936 Olympics (ultimately staged in Hitler's Berlin). After failing twice to win the nomination, Barcelona celebrated the attainment of its

Montjuïc

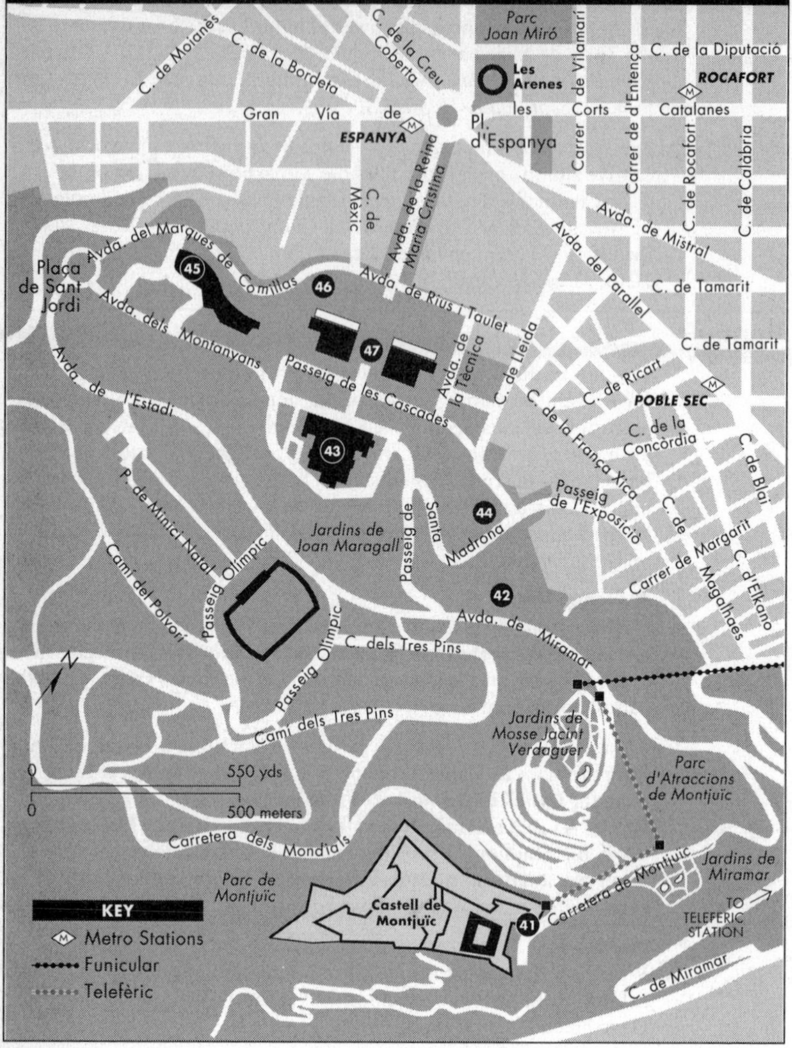

Castell de Montjuïc **41**

Fundació Miró **42**

Mies van der Rohe Pavilion **46**

Museu Arqueològic **44**

Museu Nacional d'Art de Catalunya **43**

Plaça de les Cascades **47**

Poble Espanyol. . . . **45**

long-cherished goal by renovating the semiderelict stadium in time for 1992, providing seating for 70,000. Next door and just downhill stands the futuristic Palau Sant Jordi Sports Palace, designed by the Japanese architect Arata Isozaki. The structure has no pillars or beams to obstruct the view, and was built from the roof down—the roof was built first, then hydraulically lifted into place. ✉ *Passeig Olímpic 17–19,* ☎ *93/426–2089.* ⏲ *Weekdays 10–2 and 4–7, weekends 10–6.*

★ 42 **Fundació Miró.** The Miró Foundation was a gift from the artist Joan Miró to his native city and is one of Barcelona's most exciting showcases of contemporary art. The airy, white building was designed by Josep Lluís Sert and opened in 1975; an extension was added by Sert's pupil Jaume Freixa in 1988. Miró's unmistakably playful and colorful style, filled with Mediterranean light and humor, seems a perfect match for its surroundings, and the exhibits and retrospectives that open here tend to be progressive and provocative, from Moore to Mapplethorpe. Look for Alexander Calder's mercury fountain. Miró himself rests in the cemetery on Montjuïc's southern slopes. During the Franco regime, which he strongly opposed, Miró first lived in self-imposed exile in Paris, then moved to Majorca in 1956. When he died in 1983, the Catalans gave him a send-off amounting to a state funeral. ✉ *Av. Miramar 71,* ☎ *93/329–1908.* 🎫 *850 ptas.* ⏲ *Tues.–Wed. and Fri.–Sat. 10–7, Thurs. 10–9:30, Sun. 10–2:30.*

46 **Mies van der Rohe Pavilion.** The reconstructed Mies van der Rohe Pavilion—the German contribution to the 1929 Universal Exhibition, reassembled between 1983 and 1986—is a stunning "less is more" study in interlocking planes of white marble, green onyx, and glass: Barcelona's esthetic antonym for the Moderniste Palau de la Música. ✉ *Av. Marquès de Comillas s/n,* ☎ *93/423–4016.* 🎫 *450 ptas.* ⏲ *Daily 10–8.*

44 **Museu Arqueològic.** Just downhill to the right of the Palau Nacional, the Museum of Archaeology holds important finds from the Greek ruins at Empúries, on the Costa Brava. These are shown alongside fascinating objects from, and explanations of, Megalithic Spain. ✉ *Passeig Santa Madrona 39–41,* ☎ *93/423–2149.* 🎫 *450 ptas.* ⏲ *Tues.–Sat. 9:30–1 and 4–7, Sun. 9:30–1.*

★ 43 **Museu Nacional d'Art de Catalunya** (Catalonian National Museum of Art). Housed in the imposing **Palau Nacional,** this museum was built in 1929 and recently renovated by Gae Aulenti, architect of the Musée d'Orsay, in Paris. Comprising the world's finest collection of Romanesque and Gothic frescoes, altarpieces, and wood carvings, most of the art exhibited here was removed from small churches and chapels in the Pyrenees during the 1920s to save them from deterioration, theft, and art dealers. Most of the works, such as the famous *Pantocrator* fresco (a copy of which is now back in the church of Sant Climent de Taüll; ☞ Chapter 5) have been reproduced and replaced in their original homes. The museum also contains works by El Greco, Velázquez, and Zurbarán. ✉ *Mirador del Palau 6,* ☎ *93/423–7199.* 🎫 *950 ptas.; 550 ptas. for temporary exhibits only.* ⏲ *Tues.–Wed. and Fri.–Sat. 10–7, Thurs. 10–9, Sun. 10–2:30.*

47 **Plaça de les Cascades.** Upon leaving the Mies van der Rohe Pavilion, you'll see the (at night) multicolor fountain in the Plaça de les Cascades. Stroll down the wide esplanade past the exhibition halls, used for Barcelona fairs and conventions, to the large and frenetic **Plaça d'Espanya.** Across the square is Les Arenes bullring, now used for theater and political rallies rather than bullfights. From here, you can take the metro or Bus 38 back to the Plaça de Catalunya.

45 **Poble Espanyol.** The Spanish Village was created for the 1929 Universal Exhibition. A sort of artificial Spain-in-a-bottle, with faithful reproductions of Spain's various architectural styles, it takes you from the walls of Ávila to the wine cellars of Jerez de la Frontera amid shops, houses, and craft workshops en route. The liveliest time to come is at night, and a reservation at one of the half dozen restaurants gets you in for free, as does the purchase of a ticket for the two discos or the Tablao del Carmen flamenco club. ✉ *Av. Marquès de Comillas s/n,* ☎ *93/325–7866.* *1,000 ptas.* ⏲ *Mon. 9–8, Tues.–Thurs. 9–2, weekends 9–4.*

BEACHES

Barcelona's beaches have improved and proliferated. At the city's south end is the Platja (beach) de Sant Sebastià, recently declared a nudist enclave, followed northward by the *platjas* Barceloneta, Passeig Marítim, Port Olímpic, Nova Icaria, Bogatell, and Mar Bella. Topless bathing is common.

North of the City

North of Barcelona, the first beaches are Montgat, Ocata, Vilasar de Mar, Arenys de Mar, Canet and Sant Pol de Mar, all accessible by train from the RENFE station in Plaça Catalunya. **Sant Pol** is our pick, with clean sand, a lovely old town, and the **Sant Pau** (popularly called La Ruscalleda after its chef, Carme Ruscalleda), one of the best restaurants in Catalonia. The farther north you go, toward the Costa Brava, the better the beaches.

South of the City

Ten kilometers (6 miles) south is the popular day resort **Castelldefels,** with a long, sandy beach and a series of handy and happening bars and restaurants. A 15-minute train ride from Plaça Catalunya's RENFE station to Gavà or Castelldefels deposits you on a 10-km (6-mi) beach for a superlative winter walk: From November to March the sun sets into the Mediterranean, thanks to the westward slant of the coastline here. There are several good places for lamb chops, *calçots* (spring onions), and paella; the best, **Can Patricio,** serves lunch until 4:30. **Sitges,** another 25 minutes south, has better sand and clearer water.

BARS AND CAFÉS

Barcelona may have more bars and cafés per capita—and a uniquely wide variety of same—than any other place in the world. Hangouts range from colorful tapas emporiums and sunny outdoor cafés to tearooms and chocolaterias to a uniquely wide range of bars: *coctelerías* (cocktail bars), *whiskerias* (often singles bars filled with professional escorts), *xampanyerias* (champagne—actually *cava,* Catalan sparkling wine—bars), and beer halls. Most stay open until about 2:30 AM; for after-hours options, *see* Nightlife and the Arts, *below*.

Cafés

Café de l'Opera. Opposite the Liceu opera house, this high-ceiling Art Nouveau space has welcomed operagoers and performers for over a hundred years. For locals, it's a central point on the Rambla traffic pattern; if you're looking for someone, they're bound to pass through here. ✉ *Rambla 74,* ☎ *93/317–7585.*

Cafe Paris. This popular café is always a lively place to kill some time. Everyone from Prince Felipe, heir to the Spanish throne, to poet and pundit James Townsend Pi Sunyer can be spotted here in season. The tapas are excellent, the beer is cold, and the place is open 365 days a year from dawn to dawn. ✉ *C. Aribau 184, at Carrer Paris,* ☎ *93/209–8530.*

Cafe Viena. The rectangular perimeter of this inside bar is always packed with local and international travelers in a party mood. The pianist upstairs lends a cabaret touch. ✉ *Rambla dels Estudis 115,* ☎ *93/349–9800.*

Cafe Zurich. Ever of key importance to Barcelona society, this classic meeting point at the top of the Rambla is the city's prime meeting place. The outdoor tables offer peerless people-watching; the interior is high-ceilinged and elegant. ✉ *Plaça Catalunya 1,* ☎ *93/317–9153.*

Els Quatre Gats. Picasso staged his first exhibition here, in 1899, and Gaudí and the Catalan impressionist painters Ramón Casas and Santiago Russinyol held meetings of their Centre Artistic de Sant Lluc in the early 20th century. The restaurant is undistinguished, but the café is a good place to read the paper and watch the crowd mill in and out. ✉ *Montsió 3,* ☎ *93/302–4140.*

Espai Barroc. Filled with Baroque decor and music, this unusual "space" (*espai*) is in Carrer Montcada's most beautiful patio, the 15th-century Palau Dalmases, one of the many houses built by powerful Barcelona families between the 13th and 18th centuries. The stairway, decorated with a bas-relief of the rape of Europa and Neptune's chariot, leads up to the Omnium Cultural, an institution for the study and exhibition of Catalonian history and culture. The patio merits a look even if you find the café ambience too lugubrious. ✉ *Carrer Montcada 20,* ☎ *93/310–0673. Closed Mon.*

La Bodegueta. If you can find this dive (literally: it's a short drop below the level of the sidewalk), you'll also find a cozy and cluttered space with a dozen small tables, a few places at the marble counter, and lots of happy couples having coffee or beer, and maybe some ham or *tortilla española de patatas* (a typically Spanish, omelet-like potato-and-onion delicacy). ✉ *Rambla de Catalunya 100,* ☎ *93/215–4894.*

Schilling. Near Plaça Reial, Schilling is always packed to the point where you'll have difficulty getting a table. It's a good place for coffee by day, drinks and tapas by night. ✉ *Ferran 23,* ☎ *93/317–6787.*

Coctelerías

Almirall. This Moderniste bar in the Raval is quiet, dimly lit, and dominated by an Art Nouveau mirror and frame behind the marble bar. It's an evocative spot, romantic and mischievous. ✉ *Joaquím Costa 33,* ☎ *93/302–4126.* ⏲ *Daily noon–2 AM.*

Boadas. A small, rather formal saloon near the top of the Rambla, Boadas is emblematic of the Barcelona *coctelería* concept, which usually entails a mixture of decorum and expensive mixed drinks amid wood and leather surroundings. ✉ *Tallers 1,* ☎ *93/318–9592. Closed Sun.*

Dry Martini Bar. The eponymous specialty is the best bet here, if only to partake of the ritual. This seems to be a popular hangout for mature romantics, husbands, and wives, though not necessarily each other's; it exudes a kind of genteel wickedness. ✉ *Aribau 162,* ☎ *93/217–5072.*

El Born. This former codfish emporium is now an intimate haven for drinks, raclettes, and fondues. The marble cod basins in the entry and the spiral staircase to the second floor are the quirkiest details, but everything seems designed to charm and fascinate you in one way or another. ✉ *Passeig del Born 26,* ☎ *93/319–5333.*

El Copetín. Right on Barcelona's best-known cocktail avenue, this bar has good cocktails and Irish coffee. Dimly lit, it's romantically decorated with a South Seas motif. ✉ *Passeig del Born 19,* ☎ *93/317–7585.*

El Paraigua. Behind the *ajuntament,* this rather pricey bar serves cocktails in a stylish setting with classical music. ✉ *Plaça Sant Miquel,* ☎ *93/217–3028.*

Miramelindo. The bar has a large selection of herbal liquors, fruit cocktails, pâtés, cheeses, and music, usually jazz. ✉ *Passeig del Born 15,* ☎ *93/319–5376.*

Tapas Bars

Cal Pep. This lively hangout two minutes' walk east of Santa Maria del Mar (toward the Estació de França) has Barcelona's best and freshest selection of tapas, served piping-hot in a booming and boisterous ambience. It's open Tuesday to Saturday from 1 to 4 and 8 to midnight, Monday from 8 to midnight only. ✉ *Plaça de les Olles 8,* ☎ *93/319–6183.*

El Irati. This boisterous Basque bar between Plaça del Pi and the Rambla has only one drawback: it's narrow and hard to squeeze into. Try coming at 1 PM or 7:30 PM. The excellent tapas should be washed down with *txakolí,* a white Basque wine. ✉ *Cardenal Casañas 17,* ☎ *93/302–3084. Closed Mon.*

Euskal Etxea. Euskal Etxea is the best of the three Basque bars in or near the Gothic Quarter. Try a *txakolí*; the tapas and canapés will speak for themselves. A restaurant and a Basque cultural circle round out this social oasis. ✉ *Placeta de Montcada 13,* ☎ *93/310–2185. Closed Sun.–Mon.*

La Estrella de Plata. On its way to becoming a gourmet haven, this highly respected tapas bar is just across the Plaça de les Olles from Cal Pep—a good alternative if the mob there is too daunting. ✉ *Pla del Palau 6,* ☎ *93/319–7851.*

Sagardi. This attractive, wood-and-stone cider house comes close to re-creating its Basque prototype. Cider shoots from mammoth barrels; hefty, piping-hot tapas make the rounds; and the restaurant prepares *txuletas de buey* (beefsteaks) over coals. ✉ *Carrer Argenteria 62,* ☎ *93/319–9993.*

Xampanyerias & Wine Bars

El Xampanyet. Just down the street from the Picasso Museum, hanging *botas* (leather wineskins) announce one of Barcelona's liveliest *xampanyerias,* stuffed to the gills most of the time. The house *cava,* cider, and *pan con tomate* (bread with tomato and olive oil) are served on marble-top tables surrounded by barrels and walls decorated with *azulejos* (glazed tiles) and fading yellow paint. ✉ *Montcada 22,* ☎ *93/319–7003. Closed Mon.*

La Cava del Palau. Very handy for the Palau de la Música, this champagne bar serves a wide selection of *cavas,* wines, and cocktails, along with cheeses, pâtés, smoked fish, and caviar, on a series of stepped balconies adorned with shiny *azulejos.* ✉ *Verdaguer i Callis 10,* ☎ *93/310–0938. Closed Sun.*

La Vinya del Senyor. Ambitiously named "The Lord's Vineyard," this excellent wine bar directly across from the entrance to the lovely church of Santa Maria del Mar changes its list of international wines every fortnight. ✉ *Plaça de Santa Maria 5,* ☎ *93/310–3379. Closed Mon.*

Xampú Xampany. This cava-tasting emporium on Gran Via is hot—always packed and booming—and a good way to try different kinds of Catalan sparkling wine. ✉ *Gran Via 702,* ☎ *93/265–0483. Closed Sun.*

DINING

Barcelona restaurants are so many and so exciting that keeping up with them is a lifetime project. Stick with local produce and local cuisine: Castilian specialties like roast suckling pig, for example, are bound to taste better in Castile, where the best and freshest piglets prevail. *Menús del día* (menus of the day) are good values, though they vary in quality and are generally served only at lunchtime. Restaurants usually serve lunch 1–4 and dinner 9–11; only a few places, notably Botafumeiro, Los Caracoles, and Set Portes, serve continuously from 1 PM to 1 AM.

$$$$ ✕ **Beltxenea.** Long one of Barcelona's top restaurants, Beltxenea retains an intimate atmosphere in its elegant dining rooms. In summer you can dine outdoors in the formal garden. Chef Miguel Ezcurra's Basque cuisine is exquisite; a specialty is *merluza con kokotxas y almejas,* hake simmered in stock with clams and barbels. The house wines are excellent. ✉ *Mallorca 275,* ☎ *93/215–3024. Reservations essential. AE, DC, MC, V. Closed Sun. and Aug. No lunch Sat.*

$$$$ ★ ✕ **Botafumeiro.** Barcelona's finest Galician restaurant is on Gràcia's main thoroughfare. The mood is maritime, with white tablecloths and pale varnished-wood paneling, and the fleet of waiters will impress you with their soldierly white outfits and lightning-fast service. The main attraction is the *mariscos Botafumeiro,* a succession of myriad plates of shellfish. Costs can mount quickly. Try the half-rations at the bar, where *pulpo a feira* (squid on potato), *jamón bellota de Guijuelo* (acorn-fed ham from a town near Salamanca), and *pan con tomate* (toasted bread with olive oil and tomato) make peerless late-night snacks. People- watching is tops, and the waiters are stand-up comics. ✉ *Gran de Gràcia 81,* ☎ *93/218–4230. AE, DC, MC, V. Closed Mon. No dinner Sun.*

$$$$ ★ ✕ **Drolma.** Chef Fermin Puig has finally taken his well-deserved place among Europe's gourmet elite. Named (in Sanskrit) for Buddha's female side, this intimate perch in the elegant Hotel Majestic, over the corner of Passeig de Gràcia and Carrer Valencia, catapulted to the top of Barcelona's gastronomical charts the minute it opened. Order the taster's menu and you might get pheasant canelloni in foie-gras sauce smothered in fresh black truffles, or giant prawn tails in *trompettes de la mort* (black wild mushrooms) with *sôt-l'y-laisse* (free-range chicken nuggets). Fermin's *foie gras a la ceniza con ceps* (foie gras over wood coals with wild mushrooms)—a recipe rescued from a boyhood farmhouse feast—represents the blend of tradition and inspiration that is making this restaurant famous. ✉ *Passeig de Gràcia 70,* ☎ *93/496–7710. Reservations essential. AE, DC, MC, V. Closed Sun. and Aug.*

$$$$ ★ ✕ **El Racó de Can Fabes.** Santi Santamaria's master class in Mediterranean cuisine is well worth the 45-minute train ride (or 30-minute drive) north of Barcelona to Sant Celoni. Consistently ranked one of the three best restaurants in Spain (along with El Bullí in Roses and Arzak in San Sebastián), this sumptuous display of good taste and even better tastes is a must for anyone interested in fine dining. Catch any train bound for France from the RENFE station on Passeig de Gràcia. ✉ *Sant Joan 6,* ☎ *93/867–2851. AE, DC, MC, V. Closed Mon., Feb. 1–15, and June 21–July 4. No dinner Sun.*

$$$$ ✕ **Jean Luc Figueras.** Charmingly installed in the Gràcia town house that was once Cristóbal Balenciaga's studio, this exceptional place makes everyone's short list of the city's best restaurants. The berry-pink walls,

Acontraluz 3
Agut 23
Beltxenea 13
Botafumeiro 9
Café del'Acadèmia 24
Can Gaig. 10
Can Isidre 17
Can Majó 28
Can Manel la Puda 26
Can Ramonet 27
Casa Calvet 30
Casa Leopoldo 18
Drolma 14
El Asador de Aranda 6
El Convent 19
El Racò d'en Freixa . . . 5
El Tragaluz. 12
Jaume de Provença . . . 7
Jean Luc Figueras . . . 11
La Bona Cuina 21
La Taxidermista 20
La Tramoia 15
L'Olivé. 8
Los Caracoles 22
Neichel 1
Reial Club Marítim 25
Talaia Mar 29
Tram-Tram 2
Via Veneto 4

Barcelona Dining

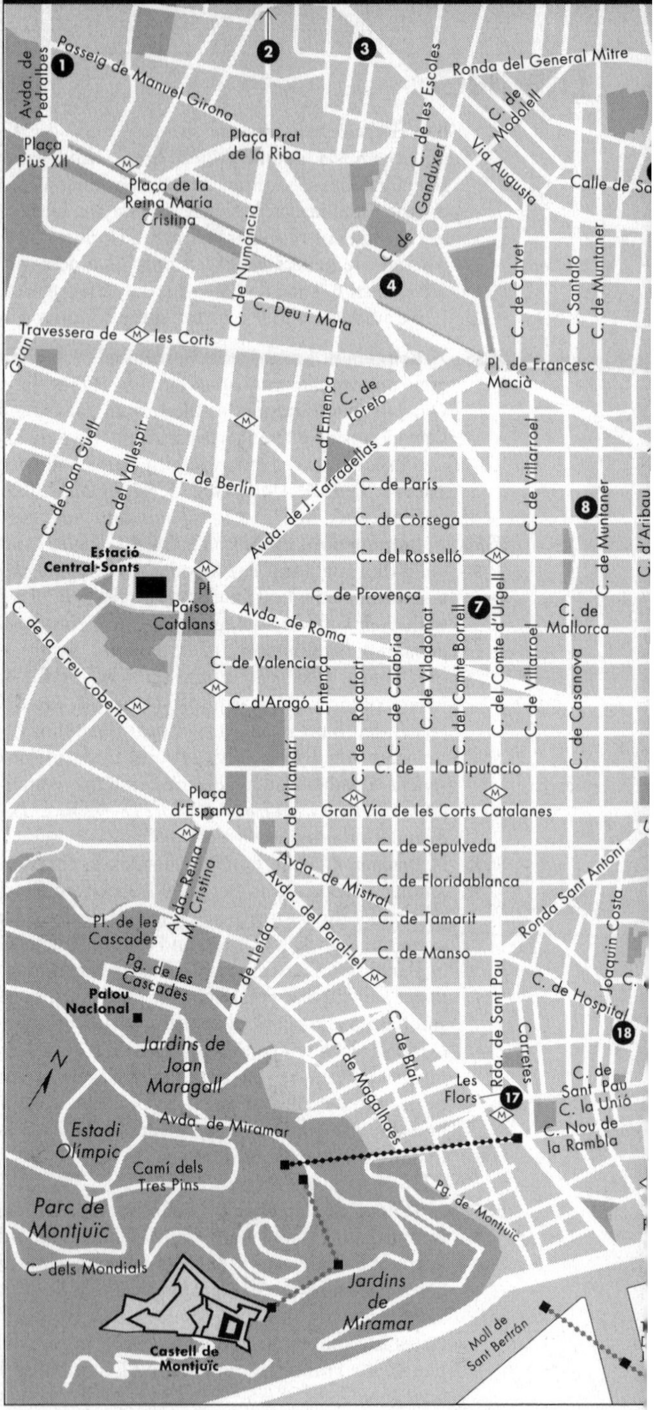

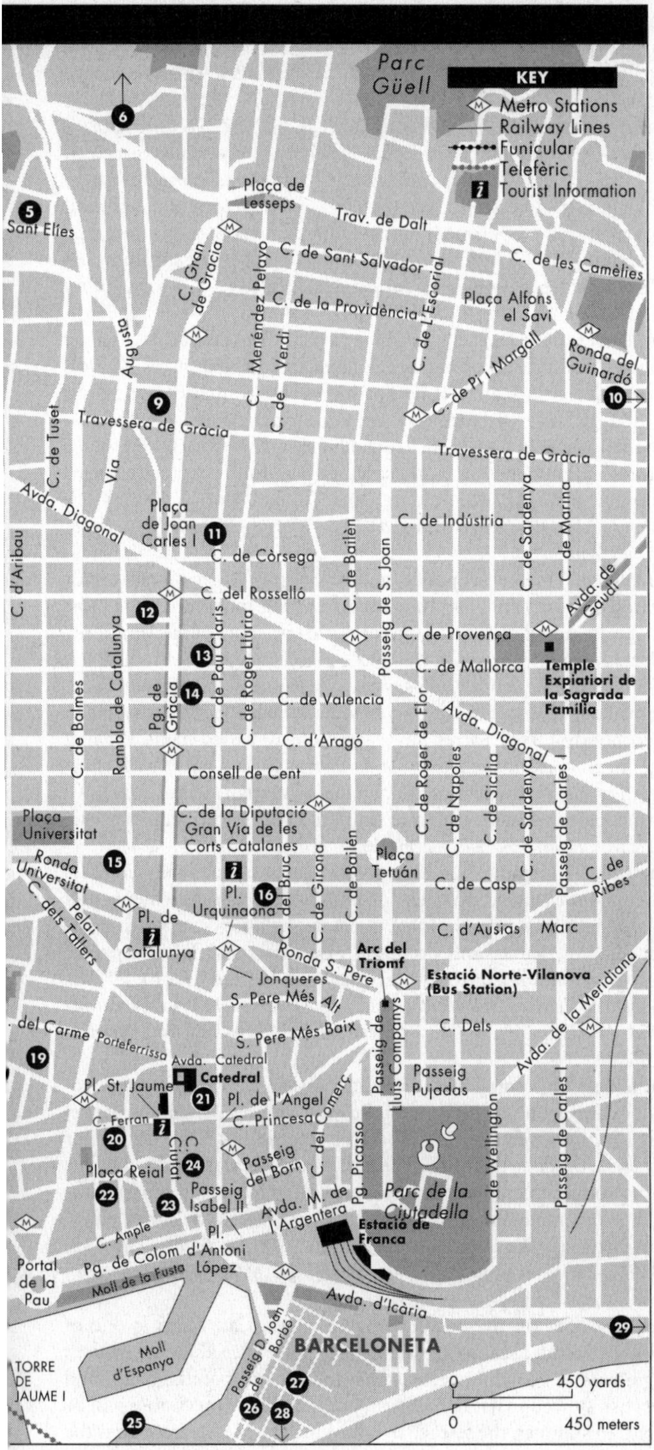
KEY
Metro Stations
Railway Lines
Funicular
Telefèric
Tourist Information
Parc Güell
Plaça de Lesseps
Trav. de Dalt
Sant Elíes
C. de Sant Salvador
C. de les Camèlies
C. Gran de Gràcia
C. Menéndez Pelayo
C. de la Providència
Plaça Alfons el Savi
C. de l'Escorial
Ronda del Guinardó
C. de Pi i Margall
Augusta
C. de Verdi
Travessera de Gràcia
C. de Tuset
Via
Avda. Diagonal
Plaça de Joan Carles I
C. de Indústria
C. de Sardenya
C. de Marina
C. d'Aribau
C. de Còrsega
C. del Rosselló
C. de Bailèn
Passeig de S. Joan
Avda. de Gaudí
C. de Provença
C. de Mallorca
Temple Expiatiori de la Sagrada Familia
C. de Pau Claris
C. de Roger Llúria
C. de Balmes
Rambla de Catalunya
Pg. de Gràcia
C. de Valencia
C. d'Aragó
C. de Roger de Flor
Consell de Cent
C. de Napoles
C. de Sicilia
Passeig de Carles I
Plaça Universitat
C. de la Diputació
Gran Vía de les Corts Catalanes
Plaça Tetuán
C. de Ribes
Ronda Universitat
Pl. Urquinaona
C. del Bruc
C. de Girona
C. de Casp
Pelai
C. dels Tallers
Pl. de Catalunya
C. d'Ausias
Marc
Ronda S. Pere
Arc del Triomf
Estació Norte-Vilanova (Bus Station)
Jonqueres
S. Pere Més Alt
Avda. de la Meridiana
del Carme
Portefferissa
S. Pere Més Baix
C. Dels
Avda. Catedral
Catedral
Passeig de Lluís Companys
Passeig Pujadas
Pl. St. Jaume
Pl. de l'Angel
C. Princesa
C. del Comerç
C. Ferran
C. Ciutat
Pg. Picasso
C. de Wellington
Plaça Reial
Passeig del Born
Passeig Isabel II
Avda. M. de l'Argentera
Parc de la Ciutadella
Estació de Franca
C. Ample
Pl. d'Antoni López
Portal de la Pau
Pg. de Colom
Moll de la Fusta
Avda. d'Icària
BARCELONETA
Passeig D. Joan de Borbó
Moll d'Espanya
TORRE DE JAUME I
0
450 yards
0
450 meters
5
6
9
10
11
12
13
14
15
16
19
20
21
22
23
24
25
26
27
28
29

polished dark-wood floors, and brass sconces make a rich and soothing setting for unforgettable Catalan cuisine with a French accent. Given the small extra cost, the luscious *menú de degustaciò* (taster's menu) is all but your only choice. ✉ *C. Santa Teresa 10,* ☎ *93/415–2877. Reservations essential. AE, DC, MC, V. Closed Sun. No lunch Sat.*

$$$$ ✕ **Neichel.** Alsatian chef Jean-Louis Neichel is universally respected for such French delicacies as *ensalada de gambas al sésamo con puerros* (shrimp in sesame-seed sauce with leeks). The setting is the ground floor of a Pedralbes apartment block—mundane modernity compared to the cooking. ✉ *C. Bertran i Rozpide 16 bis (off Av. Pedralbes),* ☎ *93/203–8408. Reservations essential. AE, DC, MC, V. Closed Sun., Jan. 1–6, Holy Week, and Aug. No lunch Sat.*

$$$$ ★ ✕ **Sant Pau.** Carme Ruscalleda's place in Sant Pol de Mar is a scenic 40-minute train ride along the beach from Plaça Catalunya's RENFE station (look for the Calella train north), and the train drops you right at her door. It's one of Barcelona's best gourmet excursions. Increasingly hailed as one of Catalonia's top culinary artists, Ruscalleda whips up a taster's menu that you won't soon forget—follow her suggestions and those of her husband, Toni. ✉ *Nou 10, Sant Pol de Mar,* ☎ *93/760–0662. AE, DC, MC, V. Closed Mon., Mar. 8–24, and Nov. 1–18. No dinner Sun.*

$$$$ ✕ **Via Veneto.** This Belle Epoque standby may look excessively senior and serious, but it's still very much worth trying for some of the most inventive and carefully prepared international fare south of the Tour d'Argent. Dress up a little or you'll feel out of place. ✉ *Ganduxer 10,* ☎ *93/200–7244. AE, DC, MC, V. Closed Sun. and Aug. 1–20. No lunch Sat.*

$$$ ✕ **Acontraluz.** This stylish covered terrace in the leafy upper-Barcelona neighborhood of Tres Torres has a strenuously varied menu ranging from game in season, such as *rable de liebre* (stewed hare) with chutney, to the more northern *pochas con almejas* (beans with clams). All dishes are prepared with care and flair, and the lunch menu is a bargain. ✉ *Milanesat 19,* ☎ *93/203–0658. AE, DC, MC, V.*

$$$ ★ ✕ **Can Gaig.** This traditional Barcelona venue is close to perfect in design, decor, *and* cuisine. Known for its market-fresh ingredients and traditional yet innovative cooking, the menu balances seafood and upland specialties, game, and domestic raw materials. Try the *perdiz asada con jamón ibérico* (roast partridge with Iberian bacon). ✉ *Passeig de Maragall 402,* ☎ *93/429–1017,* FAX *93/429–7002. Reservations essential. AE, DC, MC, V. Closed Mon., Holy Week, and Aug. No dinner holidays.*

$$$ ✕ **Can Isidre.** This small restaurant just inside the Raval from Avinguda del Paral.lel has a longtime following among Barcelona's artistic elite. Pictures and engravings, some original, by Dalí and other prominent artists line the walls. The traditional Catalan cooking draws on fresh produce from the nearby Boqueria and has a slight French accent. The homemade foie gras is superb. Come and go by cab at night; the area between Can Isidre and the Rambla is risky. ✉ *Les Flors 12,* ☎ *93/441–1139. Reservations essential. AE, MC, V. Closed Sun., Holy Week, and mid-July–mid-Aug.*

$$$ ★ ✕ **Can Majó.** Set on the beach in Barceloneta, Can Majó is one of Barcelona's premier seafood restaurants. House specialties are *caldera de bogavante* (a cross between paella and lobster bouillabaisse) and *suquet* (fish stewed in its own juices), but whatever you choose will be excellent. In summer, the terrace overlooking the Mediterranean is the closest you can now come to the *chiringuitos* (shanty restaurants) that used to line the beach here. ✉ *Almirall Aixada 23,* ☎ *93/221–5455. AE, DC, MC, V. Closed Sun.–Mon. No dinner holidays.*

$$$ ✕ **Casa Calvet.** This Art Nouveau space in Antoni Gaudí's 1898–1900 Casa Calvet just a block down from the Ritz is Barcelona's only opportunity to break bread in one of the great modernist's creations. The dining room is a graceful and spectacular design display while the cuisine is light and Mediterranean with more contemporary than traditional fare. ✉ *Casp 48,* ☎ *93/412–4012. AE, DC, MC, V. Closed Sun., holidays, Aug. 15–31.*

$$$ ★ ✕ **Casa Leopoldo.** Hidden away in the dark Raval (literally, "slum"), Casa Leopoldo serves some of the finest seafood and Catalan fare in Barcelona. Since it's hard to find, the restaurant will have you picked up at any hotel within city limits and driven to the door. Owner Rosa Gil speaks half a dozen languages and takes good care of foreign guests. Try the *revuelto de ajos tiernos y gambas* (eggs scrambled with young garlic and shrimp) or the famous Catalan dish *cap-i-pota,* a stew of morsels of head and hoof of pork. ✉ *Sant Rafael 24,* ☎ *93/441–3014. AE, DC, MC, V. Closed Mon. No dinner Sun.*

$$$ ✕ **El Asador de Aranda.** Designed by Art Nouveau architect Rubió i Bellver, this immense palace 500 meters (1,640 ft) above the Avenida Tibidabo metro station is a hike, but worth remembering if you're in upper Barcelona. The acclaimed kitchen specializes in *cordero lechal* (roast lamb); try *pimientos de piquillo* (hot, spicy peppers) on the side. The ample dining room has a terra-cotta floor and traditional Castilian furnishings. ✉ *Av. del Tibidabo 31,* ☎ *93/417–0115. AE, DC, MC, V. Closed Holy Week. No dinner Sun.*

$$$ ✕ **El Racò d'en Freixa.** Chef Ramó Freixa, one of Barcelona's new culinary lights, is taking founding father José María's work to another level. His clever reinterpretations of traditional recipes, all made with high-quality raw ingredients, have qualified the younger Freixa's work as *cuina d'autor* (designer cuisine). One specialty is *peus de porc en escabetx de guatlle,* pig's feet with quail in a garlic-and-parsley gratin. ✉ *Sant Elíes 22,* ☎ *93/209–7559. AE, DC, MC, V. Closed Mon., Holy Week, and Aug. No dinner Sun.*

$$$ ✕ **El Tragaluz.** *Tragaluz* means skylight—literally, "light-swallower"—and is an excellent choice if you're still on a design high from Vinçón, bd (Barcelona design; ☞ Shopping, *below*), or Gaudí's Pedrera. El Tragaluz is a sensory feast, with a glass roof that opens to the stars and slides back in good weather. The chairs, lamps, and fittings, designed by Javier Mariscal (creator of 1992 Olympic mascot Cobi), all reflect Barcelona's passion for playful shapes and concepts. The Mediterranean cuisine is light and innovative. ✉ *Passatge de la Concepció 5,* ☎ *93/487–0196. AE, DC, MC, V. Closed Jan. 5. No lunch Mon.*

$$$ ✕ **Jaume de Provença.** Locals come here because they've heard about the chef, Jaume Bargués. Dip into his haute-cuisine repertoire for *lenguado relleno de setas* (sole stuffed with mushrooms) or *lubina* (sea bass) soufflé. Located in the Hospital Clinic part of the Eixample, the restaurant is done up in modern black and bottle green. ✉ *Provença 88,* ☎ *93/430–0029. Reservations essential. AE, DC, MC, V. Closed Mon., Aug., and Easter Week. No dinner Sun.*

$$$ ✕ **La Bona Cuina.** When the Madolell family converted their antiques business into a restaurant in the late 1960s, it soon gained respect for its neo-Baroque elegance, intimacy, and nouvelle Catalan cuisine. Fresh fish is the house specialty; try the *bacalao à la Cuineta* (cod with spinach, raisins, pine nuts, and white sauce). The location, overlooking the apse of the cathedral, is memorable. ✉ *Pietat 12,* ☎ *93/268–2394. AE, DC, MC, V.*

$$$ ✕ **Los Caracoles.** Just below the Plaça Reial, a wall of roasting chickens announces one of Barcelona's perennial favorites (especially with travelers), a colorful space with excellent dining and a cosmopolitan atmosphere. A walk through the kitchen into the restaurant can inspire a feeding frenzy. The walls are thick with photos of bullfighters and visiting celebrities, and at night you're likely to be serenaded at your

table. Specialties are Castilian roasts, fresh Mediterranean fish dishes, and, of course, *caracoles* (snails). ✉ *Escudellers 14,* ☎ *93/302–3185. AE, DC, MC, V.*

$$$ ✕ **Reial Club Marítim.** For sunset or harbor views, excellent maritime fare, and a sense of remove from the city, try Barcelona's yacht club, El Marítim, just around the harbor through Barceloneta. Highlights are *paella marinera* (seafood paella), *rodaballo* (turbot), *lubina* (sea bass), and *dorado* (sea bream). Ask for the freshest fish they have and you won't be disappointed. ✉ *Moll d'Espanya,* ☎ *93/221–7143. AE, DC, MC, V. Closed Mon.*

$$$ ✕ **Talaia Mar.** Generally understood as the finest restaurant in the Olympic Port, this bright spot has wonderful Mediterranean views and fresh sea produce as well. The taster's menu is a bargain, a good way to sample the chef's best work for little more than a regular meal would cost. ✉ *Marina 16,* ☎ *93/221–9090. AE, MC, V.*

$$$ ★ ✕ **Tram-Tram.** At the end of the old tram line just uphill from the village of Sarrià, Isidre Soler and his wife, Reyes, have put together one of Barcelona's finest and most original culinary opportunities. Try the *menú de degustaciò* (taster's menu) and you might be lucky enough to get marinated tuna salad, cod medallions, and venison filet mignons, among other tasty creations. Perfectly sized portions and a graceful setting—especially in or near the garden out back—make this a memorable meal. Reservations are a good idea, but Reyes can almost always invent a table. ✉ *Major de Sarrià 121,* ☎ *93/204–8518. AE, DC, MC, V. Closed Sun. and Dec. 24–Jan. 6. No lunch Sat.*

$$–$$$ ✕ **Café de l'Acadèmia.** With wicker chairs, stone walls, and background classical music, this place is sophisticated-rustic, and the excellent Catalan cuisine makes it more than a mere café. It's frequented by politicians from the nearby Generalitat. Be sure to reserve at lunch time. ✉ *Lledó 1,* ☎ *93/319–8253. AE, DC, MC, V.*

$$–$$$ ✕ **Can Ramonet.** The oldest tavern in the port, founded in 1763, this singular flower-festooned house next to the Barceloneta market has barrel-top tables for tapas and regular tables for meals. Paella and seafood are strong suits; try the *arroz negro*—paella colored and flavored in cuttlefish ink. ✉ *C. Maquinista 17,* ☎ *93/319–3064. AE, DC, MC, V. Closed Sun.–Mon. No dinner holidays.*

$$–$$$ ✕ **La Taxidermista.** Don't worry: no road kill is served here. Once a natural-science museum and taxidermy shop, this stylish place is the only commendable restaurant in the sunny Plaça Reial. Interior decorator Beth Gali skillfully designed the interior around original beams and steel columns. Delicacies such as *bonito con escalivada y queso de cabra* (white tuna with braised aubergines and peppers and goat cheese) emerge from a kitchen run by Miquel Plazaola, trained by Juan Marí Arzak (☞ San Sebastian *in* Chapter 3). ✉ *Plaça Reial 8,* ☎ *93/412–4536. AE, DC, MC, V. Closed Mon.*

$$–$$$ ✕ **L'Olivé.** Specializing in Catalan home cooking, this busy and attractive Eixample spot is always filled to the brim with clued-in diners having a great time. You soon see why: excellent food, hearty fare, smart service, and some of the best *pa amb tomaquet* (toasted bread with olive oil and squeezed tomato) in town. ✉ *Muntaner 171,* ☎ *93/430–9027. AE, DC, MC, V. No dinner Sun.*

$–$$ ✕ **Can Manel la Puda.** First choice for a paella in the sun, year-round, is Can Manel, near the end of the main road out to the Barceloneta beach. Any time before 4 will do; it then reopens at 7. Arroz *a la banda* (with peeled shellfish) and paella *marinera* (with seafood) or *fideuà* (with noodles instead of rice) are all delicious. ✉ *Passeig Joan de Borbó 60,* ☎ *93/221–5013. AE, DC, MC, V. Closed Mon.*

$ ★ ✕ **Agut.** Wood paneling surmounted by white walls, on which hang 1950s canvases, forms the setting for the mostly Catalan crowd in this homey restaurant in the lower reaches of the Gothic Quarter. Agut was founded in 1924, and its popularity has never waned—not least because the hearty Catalan fare offers fantastic value. In season (September–May), try the *pato silvestre agridulce,* sweet-and-sour wild duck. There's a good selection of wine, but no frills such as coffee or liqueur. ✉ *Gignàs 16,* ☎ *93/315–1709. AE, MC, V. Closed Mon. and July. No dinner Sun.*

$ ✕ **El Convent.** Hidden away behind the Boqueria market, El Convent offers good value in a traditional setting. The Catalan home cooking, featuring such favorites as *faves a la catalana* (broad beans stewed with sausage), comes straight from the Boqueria. The intimate balconies and dining rooms have marble-top tables and can accommodate groups of two or 20. A bargain *menú del día* makes lunch the best time to come. ✉ *Jerusalem 3,* ☎ *93/317–1052. AE, DC, MC, V.*

$ ✕ **La Tramoia.** This casual restaurant at the corner of Rambla de Catalunya and Gran Via gives marvelous tastes at low prices in a lively atmosphere. Try the onion soup or the *gambas al ajillo* (shrimp cooked in garlic and olive oil) and the allioli. *Tramoia* is Catalan for "backstage" as well as "swindle," or the intrigue behind a deal, and here you're in the middle of both concepts: the place looks like backstage, and you can see the chef behind glass. ✉ *Rambla de Catalunya 15,* ☎ *93/412–3634. AE, DC, MC, V.*

LODGING

Generally speaking, hotels in the Gothic Quarter and on the Rambla are convenient for sightseeing and have plenty of Old World charm but, with notable exceptions, are weaker on creature comforts. Those in the Eixample are generally set in late-19th- or early 20th-century town houses, often Moderniste in design. Downtown hotels like the Ritz, the Claris, the Majestic, the Condes de Barcelona, and the Colón probably best combine style and luxury with a sense of where you are, while the sybaritic new palaces, like the Arts, the Rey Juan Carlos I, the Hilton, and the Princesa Sofía, cater more to business travelers seeking familiarity, convenience, and comfort. Smaller hotels like the San Agustín are less than half as expensive and more a part of city life, though noisier and less plush.

$$$$ 🏨 **Avenida Palace.** At the bottom of the Eixample, between the Rambla de Catalunya and Passeig de Gràcia, this hotel conveys elegance and antiquated style despite dating from only 1952. The lobby is wonderfully ornate, with curving staircases leading off in many directions. Everything is patterned, from the carpets to the plasterwork, a style largely echoed in the bedrooms, though some have been modernized and the wallpaper tamed. If you want contemporary minimalism, stay elsewhere. ✉ *Gran Via 605–607, 08007,* ☎ *93/301–9600,* FAX *93/318–1234. 160 rooms, 14 suites. Restaurant, bar, baby-sitting, business services, meeting rooms. AE, DC, MC, V.*

$$$$ 🏨 **Claris.** Widely considered Barcelona's best hotel, the Claris is a fascinating mélange of design and tradition. The rooms come in 60 different modern layouts, some with restored 18th-century English furniture and some with contemporary furnishings from Barcelona's endlessly playful legion of lamp and chair designers. Lavishly endowed with wood and marble, the hotel also has a Japanese water garden, a rooftop pool, and two first-rate restaurants, one Catalan and the other, La Beluga, devoted to caviar. ✉ *Carrer Pau Claris 150, 08009,* ☎ *93/487–6262,* FAX *93/215–7970. 106 rooms, 18 suites. 2 restaurants, bar, pool, sauna, exercise room, meeting rooms. AE, DC, MC, V.*

Alexandra 6
Avenida Palace. 12
Calderón 11
Citadines 20
Claris. 10
Colón 24
Condes de Barcelona 7
Continental. 16
Fira Palace. 27
Gallery 4
Gran Derby 3
Gran Vía 13
Hotel Arts. 29
Jardí 23
Le Meridien 22
Majestic. 9
Marina Folch 28
Mercure Barcelona Rambla 19
Mesón Castilla 4
Nouvel. 18
Paseo de Gràcia. 5
Princesa Sofía. 1
Regente 8
Rey Juan Carlos I–Conrad International. 2
Rialto. 25
Ritz 14
Rivoli Ramblas 17
San Agustín 21
Suizo. 26

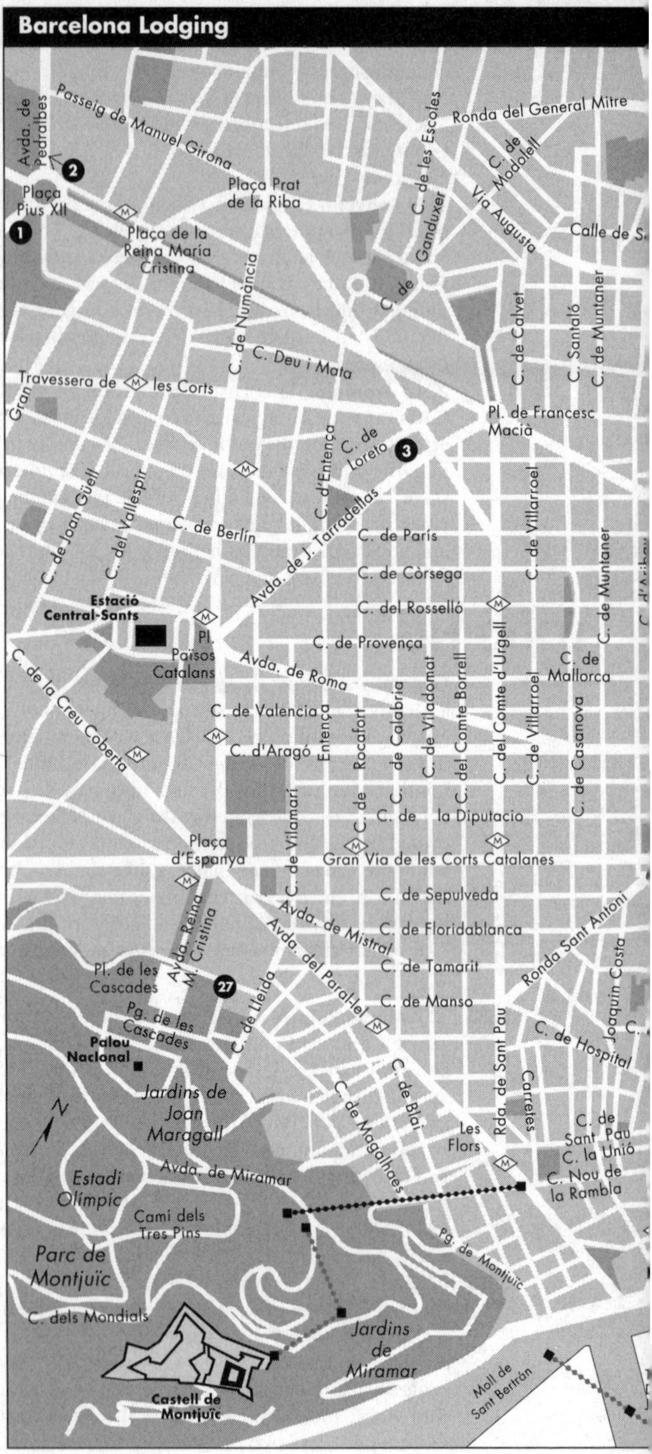

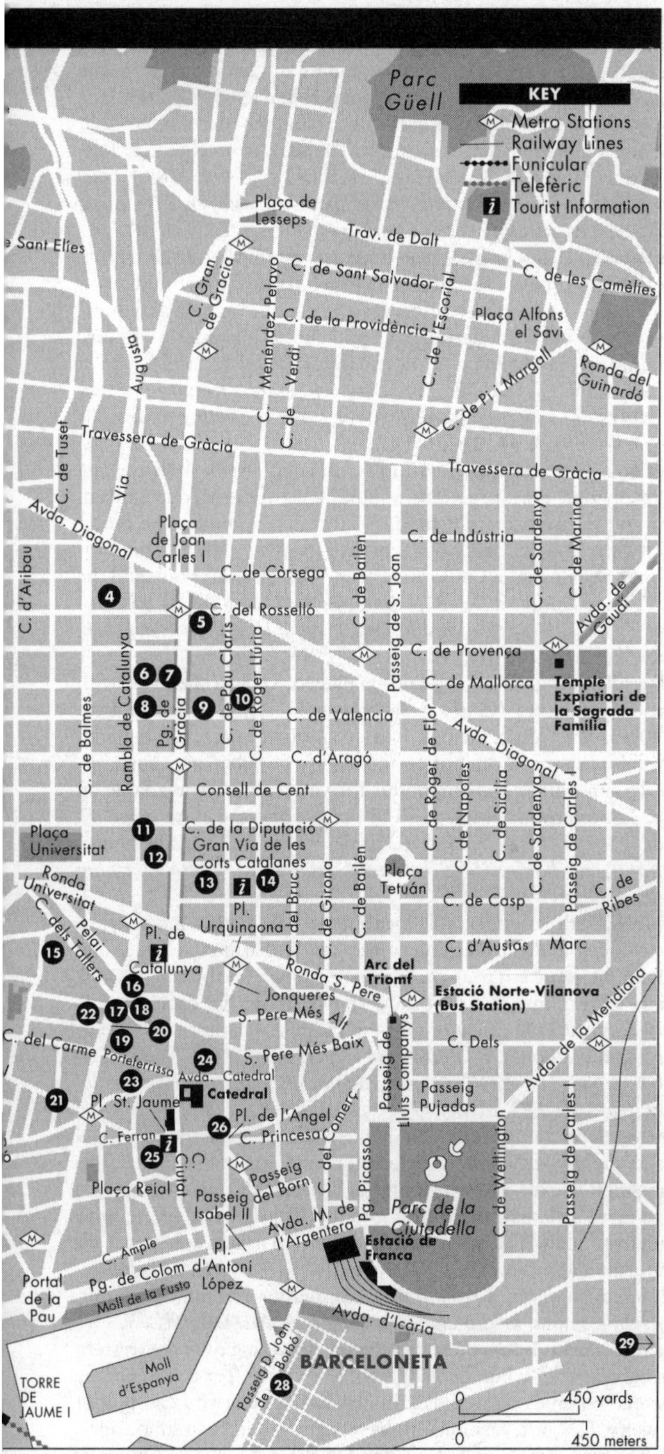
KEY
Metro Stations
Railway Lines
Funicular
Telefèric
Tourist Information
Parc Güell
Plaça de Lesseps
Trav. de Dalt
Sant Elíes
C. Gran de Gràcia
C. de Sant Salvador
C. de les Camèlies
C. Menéndez Pelayo
C. de Verdi
C. de la Providència
C. de L'Escorial
Plaça Alfons el Savi
Ronda del Guinardó
Augusta
C. de Pi i Margall
Travessera de Gràcia
C. de Tuset
Via
Avda. Diagonal
Plaça de Joan Carles I
C. de Indústria
C. de Sardenya
C. de Marina
C. d'Aribau
C. de Còrsega
C. de Bailèn
Passeig de S. Joan
Avda. de Gaudí
C. del Rosselló
C. de Provença
C. de Mallorca
Temple Expiatiori de la Sagrada Família
Rambla de Catalunya
C. de Balmes
Pg. de Gràcia
C. de Pau Claris
C. de Roger Llúria
C. de Valencia
C. d'Aragó
C. de Roger de Flor
C. de Napoles
C. de Sicilia
Passeig de Carles I
Consell de Cent
C. de la Diputació
Gran Via de les Corts Catalanes
Plaça Universitat
Ronda Universitat
Plaça Tetuán
C. de Casp
C. de Ribes
Pelai
C. dels Tallers
Pl. de Catalunya
Pl. Urquinaona
C. del Bruc
C. de Girona
C. d'Ausias Marc
Ronda S. Pere
Arc del Triomf
Estació Norte-Vilanova (Bus Station)
Jonqueres
S. Pere Més Alt
S. Pere Més Baix
C. Dels
Avda. de la Meridiana
C. del Carme
Portaferrissa
Avda. Catedral
Catedral
Pl. St. Jaume
Pl. de l'Angel
C. Princesa
C. del Comerç
Passeig de Lluís Companys
Passeig Pujadas
C. de Wellington
C. Ferran
C. Ciutat
Passeig del Born
Pg. Picasso
Plaça Reial
Passeig Isabel II
Avda. M. de l'Argentera
Parc de la Ciutadella
Estació de França
C. Ample
Pl. d'Antoni López
Pg. de Colom
Portal de la Pau
Moll de la Fusta
Avda. d'Icària
Moll d'Espanya
Passeig D. Joan de Borbó
BARCELONETA
TORRE DE JAUME I
0 450 yards
0 450 meters
1 2 3 4 5 6 7 8 9 10 11 12 13 14 15 16 17 18 19 20 21 22 23 24 25 26 28 29

$$$$ ★ **Condes de Barcelona.** Reserve well in advance—this is one of Barcelona's most popular hotels. The stunning, pentagonal lobby features a marble floor and the original columns and courtyard from the 1891 building. The newest rooms have hot tubs and terraces overlooking interior gardens. An affiliated fitness club around the corner offers golf, squash, and swimming. The restaurant, Thalassa, is excellent. ✉ *Passeig de Gràcia 75, 08008,* ☎ *93/488–1152,* FAX *93/467–4785. 183 rooms. Restaurant, piano bar, indoor and outdoor pools, hot tub, exercise room, business services, meeting rooms, parking (fee). AE, DC, MC, V.*

$$$$ **Fira Palace.** This relatively new hotel has established itself among Barcelona's finest business and convention havens. Close to the Convention Palace, the hotel also offers easy access to Montjuïc and its attractions. Impeccably modern, it's a solid choice for generic creature comfort rather than local color. ✉ *Av. Rius i Taulet 1, 08004,* ☎ *93/426–2223,* FAX *93/424–8679. 220 rooms, 40 suites. Restaurant, bar, pool, barbershop, massage, exercise room, squash, meeting rooms, car rental, parking (fee). AE, DC, MC, V.*

$$$$ **Hotel Arts.** This luxurious Ritz-Carlton monolith overlooks Barcelona from the Olympic Port, providing unique views of the Mediterranean, the city, and the mountains behind. A short taxi ride from the center of the city, the hotel is virtually a world of its own, with three restaurants (one specializing in California cuisine), an outdoor pool, and the beach. ✉ *C. de la Marina 19–21, 08005,* ☎ *93/221–1000,* FAX *93/221–1070. 399 rooms, 56 suites. 3 restaurants, bar, pool, beauty salon, beach, parking (fee). AE, DC, MC, V.*

$$$$ **Le Meridien.** English-owned and -managed, Le Meridien vies with the Rivoli Ramblas (☞ *below*) as the premier hotel in the Rambla area. Guest rooms are light, spacious, and decorated in pastels. The hotel has hosted its share of celebrities and is very popular with businesspeople. Fax machines and computers for your room are available on request. A room overlooking the Rambla is worth the extra noise. ✉ *Rambla 111, 08002,* ☎ *93/318–6200,* FAX *93/301–7776. 206 rooms. Restaurant, bar, baby-sitting, business services, car rental, parking (fee). AE, DC, MC, V.*

$$$$ ★ **Majestic.** With an unbeatable location on Barcelona's most stylish boulevard, surrounded by fashion emporiums like Armani, Chanel, and Verino, the Majestic is a near-perfect place to stay. The building is part Eixample town house and part modern extension, but each room is stylishly decorated. The new restaurant, Drolma, is a destination in itself (☞ Dining, *above*). ✉ *Passeig de Gràcia 70, 08008,* ☎ *93/488–1717,* FAX *93/488–1880. 310 rooms. 2 restaurants, bar, pool, health club, parking (fee). AE, DC, MC, V.*

$$$$ **Princesa Sofía.** Long considered Barcelona's foremost modern hotel despite its slightly out-of-the-way location on Avinguda Diagonal, this towering high-rise offers a wide range of facilities and everything from shops to three different restaurants and the 19th-floor Top City, with breathtaking views. The guest rooms, decorated in soft colors, are ultracomfortable. ✉ *Plaça Pius XII 4, 08028,* ☎ *93/330–7111,* FAX *93/411–2106. 505 rooms. 3 restaurants, bar, indoor and outdoor pools, beauty salon, sauna, health club, parking (fee). AE, DC, MC, V.*

$$$$ **Rey Juan Carlos I–Conrad International.** Towering over the western end of Barcelona's Avinguda Diagonal, this skyscraper is an exciting commercial complex as well as a luxury hotel. Here you can buy or rent jewelry, furs, art, fashions, flowers, caviar, and even limousines. The lush garden, which includes a pond with swans, has an Olympic-size swimming pool, and the green expanses of Barcelona's finest in-town country club, El Polo, spread luxuriantly out beyond. There are two restaurants: Chez Vous serves French cuisine, and Café Polo has a sumptuous buffet as well as an American bar. ✉ *Av. Diagonal 661–*

671, 08028, ☎ 93/364–4040, FAX 93/364–4264. 375 rooms, 37 suites. 2 restaurants (3 in summer), 2 bars, pool, beauty salon, spa, tennis courts, health club, paddle tennis, meeting rooms. AE, DC, MC, V.

$$$$ ★ **Ritz.** Founded in 1919 by Caesar Ritz, this grande dame of Barcelona hotels was restored to its former splendor in the mid-1990s. The imperial lobby is at once loose and elegant; guest rooms contain Regency furniture, and some have Roman baths and mosaics. Service is generally excellent. As for the price, it's almost double that of the nearest competitor. ✉ *Gran Via 668, 08010, ☎ 93/318–5200, FAX 93/318–0148. 122 rooms. Restaurant, bar, coffee shop, sauna, exercise room, babysitting, business services, meeting rooms. AE, DC, MC, V.*

$$$ **Alexandra.** Behind a reconstructed Eixample facade, everything here is slick and contemporary. The rooms are spacious and attractively furnished with dark-wood chairs, and those that face inward have thatch screens on the balconies for privacy. From the airy, marble hall on up, the Alexandra is perfectly suited to modern martini sippers. ✉ *Mallorca 251, 08008, ☎ 93/487–0505, FAX 93/488–0258. 81 rooms. Restaurant, bar, parking (fee). AE, DC, MC, V.*

$$$ **Calderón.** Ideally placed on the chic and leafy Rambla de Catalunya, this modern high-rise has a range of facilities normally found only in hotels farther out of town. Public rooms are huge, with cool, white-marble floors, and the bedrooms follow suit. Aim for one of the higher rooms, from which the views from sea to mountains and over the city are stunning. ✉ *Rambla de Catalunya 26, 08007, ☎ 93/301–0000. 264 rooms. Restaurant, piano bar, indoor and outdoor pools, health club, squash, free parking. AE, DC, MC, V.*

$$$ **Citadines.** This new Rambla hotel is impeccably bright and modern, air-conditioned, soundproofed, and well equipped. Lodgings range from apartments with sitting rooms to one-room studios. All have kitchenettes and small dining areas. The rooftop solarium offers panoramic views of Montjuïc and the Mediterranean. ✉ *Rambla 122, 08002, ☎ 93/270–1111, FAX 93/412–7421. 115 studios, 16 apartments. Breakfast room, kitchenettes, meeting rooms. AE, DC, MC, V.*

$$$ ★ **Colón.** There's something clubby about this elegant Barcelona standby, a surprising charm and intimacy for its size. The location is ideal—directly across the plaza from the cathedral, overlooking weekend *sardana* dancing, Thursday antiques markets, and, of course, the floodlit cathedral by night. Rooms are comfortable and tastefully furnished; try to get one with a view of the cathedral. The Colón was a favorite of Joan Miró, and for a combination of comfort, ambience, and location it may be the best hotel in Barcelona. ✉ *Av. Catedral 7, 08002, ☎ 93/301–1404, FAX 93/317–2915. 147 rooms. Restaurant, bar, breakfast room, massage, babysitting, meeting rooms, travel services, car rental. AE, DC, MC, V.*

$$$ **Gallery.** This modern hotel in the upper part of the Eixample, just below the Diagonal, offers impeccable comfort and service and a central location for middle and upper Barcelona. (In the other direction, you're only half an hour's walk from the waterfront.) It's named for its proximity to the city's prime art-gallery district, a few blocks away on Rambla de Catalunya and Consell de Cent. ✉ *Roselló 249, 08008, ☎ 93/415–9911, FAX 93/415–9184. 110 rooms, 5 suites. Bar, cafeteria. AE, DC, MC, V.*

$$$ **Gran Derby.** This modern Eixample hotel is ideal for families, composed entirely of suites, junior suites, and duplexes with sitting rooms. Decor reflects the local passion for design and innovation: it's entirely contemporary, sleek and slick. Only the location is less than ideal; for sightseeing purposes, it's a bit out of the way, just below Plaça Francesc Macià, but a 20-minute march down the Diagonal puts you on Passeig de Gràcia. ✉ *Loreto 28, 08029, ☎ 93/322–2062, FAX 93/419–6820. 40 suites. Bar, café, parking (fee). AE, DC, MC, V.*

$$$ **Mercure Barcelona Rambla.** The ornate, illuminated entrance takes you from the Rambla through an enticing marble hall; upstairs, you enter a sumptuous reception room with a dark-wood Art Nouveau ceiling. Guest rooms are modern, bright, and functional, and many overlook the Rambla. ✉ *Rambla 124, 08002,* ☎ *93/412–0404,* FAX *93/318–7323. 76 rooms. Bar, cafeteria, parking (fee). AE, DC, MC, V.*

$$$ **Nouvel.** Centrally located just below Plaça de Catalunya, this hotel blends white marble, etched glass, elaborate plasterwork, and carved, dark woodwork in its handsome Art Nouveau interior. The rooms have marble floors, firm beds, and smart bathrooms. The narrow street is pedestrian-only and therefore quiet, but views are nonexistent. ✉ *Santa Anna 18–20, 08002,* ☎ *93/301–8274,* FAX *93/301–8370. 69 rooms. Breakfast room. AE, DC, MC, V.*

$$$ **Regente.** Moderniste decor and copious stained glass lend style and charm to this smallish hotel. The public rooms are carpeted in a variety of patterns; guest rooms, fortunately, are elegantly restrained. The verdant roof terrace (with a pool) and the prime position on the Rambla de Catalunya seal the positive verdict. ✉ *Rambla de Catalunya 76, 08008,* ☎ *93/487–5989,* FAX *93/487–3227. 79 rooms. Restaurant, bar, pool. AE, DC, MC, V.*

$$$ **Rialto.** This hotel seems to have taken a leaf from the paradors' book, with subdued pine floors, white walls, and walnut doors. The rooms (ask for an interior one if street noise bothers you) echo this look, with heavy furniture set against light walls. There's a vaulted bar in the basement and a modern, mirrored *salón* off the lobby. ✉ *Ferran 42, 08002,* ☎ *93/318–5212,* FAX *93/318–5312. 180 rooms. Bar, cafeteria. AE, DC, MC, V.*

$$$ **Rivoli Ramblas.** Behind this upper-Rambla facade lie imaginative, state-of-the-art decor and marble floors. The rooms are pastel in hue, contemporary in design, and possessed of the full range of up-to-date gadgetry. The roof-terrace bar has panoramic views. ✉ *Rambla 128, 08002,* ☎ *93/302–6643,* FAX *93/317–5053. 87 rooms. Restaurant, sauna, health club. AE, DC, MC, V.*

$$$ **Suizo.** The Suizo's public rooms have elegant, modern seating and good views over the noisy square just east of Plaça del Rei. The guest rooms have bright walls and wood or tile floors. ✉ *Plaça del Àngel 12, 08002,* ☎ *93/315–0461,* FAX *93/310–4081. 50 rooms. Restaurant, bar, cafeteria. AE, DC, MC, V.*

$$ **Gran Via.** This 19th-century town house is a Moderniste enclave, with an original chapel, a hall-of-mirrors breakfast room, an ornate Moderniste staircase, and Belle Epoque phone booths. (To stay in character, go around the block to Gaudí's Casa Calvet, at No. 48 Carrer de Casp, for lunch or dinner.) Guest rooms have plain alcoved walls, bottle-green carpets, and Regency-style furniture; those overlooking Gran Via itself have better views but are quite noisy. ✉ *Gran Via 642, 08007,* ☎ *93/318–1900,* FAX *93/318–9997. 53 rooms. Breakfast room, parking (fee). AE, DC, MC, V.*

$$ **Mesón Castilla.** A few steps up Carrer Tallers from the top of the Rambla, this little hotel is well positioned for exploring medieval Barcelona and the Moderniste Eixample. Just around the corner from Richard Meier's MACB (Museu d'Art Contemporani de Barcelona) and the rest of the Raval, rooms here are quiet, comfortable and generally flawless, especially considering the price. ✉ *Valdoncella 5, 08001,* ☎ *93/318–2182,* FAX *93/412–4020. 56 rooms. Bar, cafeteria. AE, DC, MC, V.*

$$ ★ **San Agustín.** Just off the Rambla in the leafy square of the same name, the San Agustín has long been popular with musicians performing at the Liceu opera house. Rooms are small but pleasantly modern, with plenty of fresh wood and clean lines. ✉ *Plaça de San Agustí 3, 08001,* ☎ *93/318–1708,* FAX *93/317–2928. 77 rooms. Bar, cafeteria. AE, DC, MC, V.*

$ ⊞ **Continental.** This modest hotel stands at the top of the Rambla, just below Plaça de Catalunya. Space is tight, but the rooms manage to accommodate large, firm beds. It's high enough over the Rambla to escape street noise, so ask for a room overlooking Barcelona's most emblematic street. This is a good place to read *Homage to Catalonia,* as George Orwell stayed here with his wife in 1937 after recovering from a bullet wound. ✉ *Rambla 138, 08002,* ☎ *93/301–2508,* FAX *93/302–7360. 35 rooms. Breakfast room. AE, DC, MC, V.*

$ ⊞ **Jardí.** Perched over the traffic-free and charming Plaça del Pi and Plaça Sant Josep Oriol, exterior rooms at this lovely budget hotel have pretty views of the Gothic church of Santa Maria del Pi from their own little balconies. They're enjoyable but can be noisy, especially in summer, when you'll want to leave the windows open. All rooms have modern pine furniture and small but new bathrooms. The in-house breakfast is excellent, and the alfresco tables at the Bar del Pi, downstairs, are ideal in summer. There are five floors—the higher, the quieter—and a new elevator. It's not the Ritz, but all in all the Jardí is a great value. ✉ *Plaça Sant Josep Oriol 1, 08002,* ☎ *93/301–5900,* FAX *93/318–3664. 40 rooms. Breakfast room. AE, DC, MC, V.*

$ ⊞ **Marina Folch.** This little hideaway in Barceloneta is entirely new and has views over the port, an excellent restaurant downstairs, and a generous and caring family at the helm. Five minutes from the beach, it's a budget winner. ✉ *Carrer Mar 16 pral., 08003,* ☎ *93/310–3709,* FAX *93/310–5327. 7 rooms. Restaurant. AE, DC, MC, V.*

$ ⊞ **Paseo de Gràcia.** Formerly a hostel, the Paseo de Gràcia has soft-color bedrooms with plain, good-quality carpets and sturdy wooden furniture. Add the location, on the handsomest Eixample boulevard, and you have a good uptown budget option. Some rooms, though not necessarily the newest, have balconies with views west over the city and the Collserola hills beyond. ✉ *Passeig de Gràcia 102, 08008,* ☎ *93/215–5828,* FAX *93/215–3724. 33 rooms. Bar, breakfast room. AE, DC, MC, V.*

NIGHTLIFE AND THE ARTS

Barcelona's arts and nightlife scenes start early and never quite stop. To find out what's on, look in newspapers or the weekly *Guía Del Ocio,* available at newsstands all over town. *Activitats* is a monthly list of cultural events, published by the *ajuntament* and available from its information office in Palau de la Virreina (✉ Rambla 99).

The Arts

Concerts

Catalans are great music lovers. Barcelona's main concert hall is the **Palau de la Música** (✉ Sant Francesc de Paula 2, ☎ 93/268–1000), whose ticket office is open weekdays 11–1 and 5–8, Saturday 5–8 only. Performances run September–June, with Sunday morning concerts at 11 a popular tradition. Tickets range from 1,000 to 15,000 ptas. and are best purchased well in advance. Check the listings in *El País,* Spain's daily newspaper, for concerts around town. The restored **Liceu** opera house is in full swing, though seats are expensive and hard to get, so reserve well in advance (☞ Opera, *below*). The **Auditori de Barcelona** (✉ Lepant 150, near Plaça de les Glòries, ☎ 93/317–1096) schedules a full program of mostly classical music, with occasional jazz and pop. Watch especially for the *Solistas del OBC,* a series of free performances occasionally held in the town hall's opulent **Saló de Cent**—this is world-class chamber music in an incomparable setting. Barcelona's annual summer music festival brings a long series of concerts in June and July. In late September, the **International Music Festival** forms part of the feast of Nostra Senyora de la Mercè (Our Lady of Mercy), Barcelona's patron saint. Pop concerts are held in the Palau Sant Jordi on Montjuïc. The basilica of Santa Maria del Mar, the church of Santa Maria del Pi, the Monestir de Pedralbes, Reial Drassanes, and the Saló del Tinell, among other intimate and ancient spaces, also hold concerts.

Dance

L'Espai de Dansa i Música de la Generalitat de Catalunya—generally listed as L'Espai, or "The Space" (✉ Travessera de Gràcia 63, ☎ 93/414–3133)—is the prime venue for ballet and modern dance, as well as some musical offerings. **El Mercat de les Flors** (✉ Lleida 59, ☎ 93/426–1875), near the Plaça de Espanya, is the more traditional setting for modern dance and theater.

Film

Though some foreign films are dubbed, Barcelona has a full complement of original-language cinema; look for listings marked *v. o.* (*versión original*). The **Icaria Yelmo** (✉ Salvador Espriu 61, near Carles I metro stop) cinema complex in the Olympic Port now has the city's largest selection of films in English. The **Filmoteca** (✉ Av. Sarrià 33, ☎ 93/430–5007) shows three films daily in *v. o.,* often English. Recent releases are shown in *v. o.* at the **Verdi** (✉ Verdi 32, Gràcia), **Arkadin** (✉ Travessera de Gràcia 103, near Gràcia train stop), **Alex** (✉ Rambla de Catalunya 90), **Rex** (✉ Gran Via 463), **Casablanca** (✉ Passeig de Gràcia 115), and **Renoir Les Corts** (✉ Eugeni d'Ors 12).

Flamenco

Barcelona is not richly endowed with flamenco haunts, as Catalans consider flamenco—like bullfighting—a foreign import from Andalusia. **El Patio Andaluz** (✉ Aribau 242, ☎ 93/209–3378) has flamenco shows twice nightly (10 and midnight) and audience participation in the karaoke section upstairs. **El Cordobés** (✉ Rambla 35, ☎ 93/317–6653) is the most popular club with tour groups. Other options include **El Tablao de Carmen** (✉ Poble Espanyol, ☎ 93/325–6895) and **Los Tarantos** (✉ Plaça Reial 17, ☎ 93/318–3067).

Opera

Restored to its rightful opulence, Barcelona's **Gran Teatre del Liceu** is in full swing once again (✉ Box office: Rambla de Capuchinos 63, ☎ 93/317–4142). The season runs September–mid-June.

Theater

Most plays are performed in Catalan, though some are performed in Spanish. Barcelona is well known for avant-garde theater and for troupes that specialize in mime, large-scale performance art, and special effects (La Fura dels Baus, Els Joglars, Els Comediants). The city also hosts a **Festival de Títeres** (Puppet Festival) in April.

The best-known theaters are the **Teatre Lliure** (✉ Montseny 47, Gràcia, ☎ 93/218–9251), **Mercat de les Flors** (✉ Lleida 59, ☎ 93/318–8599), **Teatre Romea** (✉ Hospital 51, ☎ 93/317–7189), **Teatre Tívoli** (✉ Casp 10, ☎ 93/412–2063), and **Teatre Poliorama** (✉ Rambla Estudios 115, ☎ 93/317–7599). All stage a dynamic variety of classical, contemporary, and experimental theater.

Many of the older theaters specializing in big musicals are along the Paral.lel. These include **Apolo** (✉ Paral.lel 56, ☎ 93/241–9007), **Teatre Arnau** (✉ Paral.lel 60, ☎ 93/441–4881), and **Victòria** (✉ Paral.lel 6769, ☎ 93/441–3979). The **Teatre Tívoli** (✉ Casp 8, ☎ 93/412–2063) also produces large-scale musicals. In July and August, an open-air summer theater festival brings plays, music, and dance to the **Teatre Grec**

(Greek Theater) on Montjuïc (✉ Rambla 99, ☎ 93/316–2700), as well as to Plaça del Rei, Mercat de les Flors, and other sites.

Nightlife

Cabaret

Near the bottom of the Rambla, the minuscule **Bar Pastis** (✉ Santa Mònica 4, ☎ 93/318–7980) has both live performances and LPs of every Edith Piaf song ever recorded. **Arnau** (✉ Paral.lel 60, ☎ 93/242–2804) is an old-time music hall that's still going strong.

Casino

The **Gran Casino de Barcelona** (✉ Carrer de la Marina, ☎ 93/225–7878), under the Hotel Arts, is open daily from 1 PM to 5 AM with everything from slot machines to roulette, a disco, and floor shows.

Jazz and Blues

Try **La Cova del Drac** (✉ Vallmajor 33, ☎ 93/200–7032) or the Gothic Quarter's **Harlem Jazz Club** (✉ Comtessa Sobradiel 8, ☎ 93/310–0755), which is small but puts on atmospheric bands. **Jamboree-Jazz & Dance-Club** (✉ Plaça Reial 17, ☎ 93/301–7564) is a center for jazz, rock, and flamenco. **La Boîte** (✉ Av. Diagonal 477, ☎ 93/419–5950) has an eclectic musical menu, as do **Luz de Gas** (✉ Muntaner 246, ☎ 93/209–7711) and **Luna Mora** (✉ Next to the Hotel Arts, in the Olympic Port, ☎ 93/221–6161), offering everything from country blues to soul. The Palau de la Música holds an **international jazz festival** in November, and nearby Terrassa has its own jazz festival in March. The bustling **Blue Note** (☎ 93/225–8003), in the Port Vell's Maremagnum shopping complex, draws a mixture of young and not-so-young nocturnals to musical events and Wednesday night buffets. Food and drinks are served until dawn, and credit cards are accepted.

Late-Night Bars

Bar musical is Spanish for any bar with music loud enough to drown out conversation. The pick of these are **Universal** (✉ Marià Cubí 182–184, ☎ 93/200–7470), **Mas i Mas** (✉ Marià Cubí 199, ☎ 93/209–4502), and **Nick Havanna** (✉ Rosselló 208, ☎ 93/215–6591). **L'Ovella Negra** (✉ Sitjàs 5, ☎ 93/317–1087) is the top student tavern. **Glaciar** (✉ Plaça Reial 13, ☎ 93/302–1163) is *the* spot for young out-of-towners. The **Port Olímpic** is one solid *bar musical,* especially in summer and on weekends, as is **Port Vell**'s Maremagnum area.

For a more laid-back scene, with high ceilings, billiards, tapas, and hundreds of students, visit the popular **Velodrom** (✉ Muntaner 211–213, ☎ 93/230–6022), just below the Diagonal. Two blocks away is the intriguing *barmuseo* (bar-cum-museum) **La Fira** (✉ Provença 171, ☎ 93/323–7271). Downtown, deep in the Barrio Chino, try the **London Bar** (✉ Nou de la Rambla 34, ☎ 93/302–3102), an Art Nouveau circus haunt with a trapeze suspended above the bar. Other character bars include **Bar Almirall** (✉ Joaquin Costa 33, ☎ 93/412–1535), **Bar Muy Buenas** (✉ Carme 63, ☎ 93/442–5053), and, over by the Sagrada Familia, the **Michael Collins Irish Pub** (✉ Plaza Sagrada Familia 4, ☎ 93/459–1964).

Nightclubs and Discos

Most clubs have a discretionary cover charge and like to inflict it on foreigners, so dress up and be prepared to talk your way past the bouncer. Any story can work; for example, you own a chain of nightclubs and are on a world tour. Don't expect much to happen until 1:30 or 2.

Tops for some time now is the prisonesque **Otto Zutz** (✉ Lincoln 15, ☎ 93/238–0722), just off Via Augusta. **Woman Caballero** (✉ Marqués de l'Argentera s/n, left side of Estació de Francia, ☎ 93/319–5356), in the Estació de França, is a new hot spot, as is **El Foro** (✉ Princesa 53, ☎ 93/310–1020). The nearly classic **Up and Down** (✉ Numancia 179, ☎ 93/280–2922), pronounced "Pen-*dow*," is another hot choice. **Bikini** (✉ Deu i Mata 105, at Entença, ☎ 93/322–0005) will present you with a queue on festive Saturday nights. **Oliver y Hardy** (✉ Av. Diagonal 593, ☎ 93/419–3181), next to the Barcelona Hilton, is more popular with the older set (i.e., you won't stand out if you're over 35); **La Tierra** (✉ Aribau 230, ☎ 93/200–7346) and **El Otro** (✉ Valencia 166, ☎ 93/323–6759) also accept postgraduates with open arms. **Zeleste** (✉ Almogavers 122, ☎ 93/309–1204) is another standard hangout, particularly popular with jazz and rock buffs. **La Boîte Mas i Mas** (✉ Av. Diagonal 477, ☎ 93/419–5950) has live music and a nice balance of civilization and insanity.

For an old-fashioned *sala de baile* (dance hall) with a big band playing tangos, head to **La Paloma** (✉ Tigre 27, ☎ 93/301–6897); the kitschy 1950s decor creates a peculiar atmosphere that's great fun.

OUTDOOR ACTIVITIES AND SPORTS

Golf

Barcelona is 15–90 minutes away from many fine golf courses. Call ahead to reserve tee times.

Around Barcelona

Reial Club de Golf El Prat (✉ El Prat de Llobregat, 08820, ☎ 93/379–0278), 36 holes. Note: the greens fee at El Prat is 12,380 ptas. on weekdays and exactly twice that on weekends and holidays. **Club de Golf de Sant Cugat** (✉ Sant Cugat del Vallès 08190, ☎ 93/674–3958), 18 holes. **Club de Golf Vallromanes** (✉ Vallromanes 08188, ☎ 93/568–0362), 18 holes. **Club de Golf Terramar** (✉ Sitges, 08870, ☎ 93/894–0580), 18 holes.

Health Clubs

For specifics, look in the *Páginas Amarillas/Pàgines Grogues* (*Yellow Pages*) under "Gimnasios/Gimnasis." We can recommend the **DiR** network of fitness centers, with addresses all over Barcelona (☎ 901/304030 for general information); the main branch is DiR Diagonal (✉ Ganduxer 25–27, ☎ 93/202–2202). A day membership costs 1,900 ptas. and includes aerobics classes and the use of a sauna, a steam room, a swimming pool, squash courts, and MTV. **Crack,** just off Passeig de Gràcia near the Hotel Condes de Barcelona, is another winner, with a gym, a sauna, pool (summer only), squash courts, and paddle tennis; day membership here costs 2,000 ptas., with a small supplement for courts (✉ Pasaje Domingo 7, ☎ 93/215–2755).

Hiking

The **Collserola** hills behind the city offer well-marked trails, fresh air, and lovely views. Take the San Cugat, Sabadell, or Terrassa FFCC train from Plaça de Catalunya and get off at Baixador de Vallvidrera; the information center, 10 minutes uphill next to **Vil.la Joana** (now the Jacint Verdaguer Museum), has maps of this mountain woodland just 20 minutes from downtown. The walk back into town can take from two to five hours depending on your speed and the trails you choose. For information on hiking farther afield, including the Pyrenees, contact the **Club Excursionista de Catalunya** (✉ Paradis 10, ☎ 93/315–2311) or the **Associació Excursionista, Etnográfica i Folklorica** (✉ Avinyó 19, ☎ 93/302–2730).

Swimming

Piscines Bernat Picornell (✉ Av. del Estadi 30–40, ☎ 93/423–4041), on Montjuïc, is open from 7 AM to midnight, and the fee includes use of a sauna, gymnasium, and fitness equipment in addition to indoor and outdoor pools. Overlooking the beach from Barceloneta, the indoor pool at the **Club Natació de Barceloneta** (✉ Passeig Joan de Borbó, ☎ 93/221–0010)—also known as Complex Esportiu Municipal Banys Sant Sebastiá—is open from 7 AM to 11 PM. Uphill from Parc Güell is the **Parc de la Creueta del Coll** (✉ Castellterçol, ☎ 93/416–2625), which has a huge outdoor pool. In upper Barcelona **Parc Piscines i Esports** (✉ Ganduxer 25–27, ☎ 93/201–9321) has both indoor and outdoor pools. All fees are around 1,000 ptas.

Tennis

The Olympic tennis facilities at **Vall d'Hebron** (✉ Pg. Vall d'Hebron 178–196, ☎ 93/427–6500) are open from 8 AM until 11 PM; clay costs 2,500 ptas. per hour, hard courts 1,800 ptas. **Complejo Deportivo Can Caralleu** (Can Caralleu Sports Complex), above Pedralbes, a 30-minute walk uphill from the Reina Elisenda subway stop (FFCC de la Generalitat), offers hard courts and clean air (☎ 93/203–7874). It's open daily 8 AM–11 PM and costs 1,250 ptas. per hour by day, 1,600 ptas. by night. The upscale **Club Vall Parc** (✉ Carretera de la Rabassada 79, ☎ 93/212–6789) is open daily 8 AM–midnight and charges 2,500 ptas. per hour by day, 3,100 ptas. by night.

SHOPPING

Shopping Districts

Barcelona's prime shopping districts are the Passeig de Gràcia, Rambla de Catalunya, the Plaça Catalunya, Porta de l'Àngel, and Avinguda Diagonal up to Carrer Ganduxer. Farther out on the Diagonal is shopping colossus **L'Illa,** which includes **FNAC, Marks & Spencer,** and plenty of other consumer temptations. The **Maremagnum** mall, in Port Vell, is another option. **Carrer Tuset,** north of the Diagonal, has lots of small boutiques. For affordable, old-fashioned, typically Spanish shops, prowl along **Carrer Ferran** in the Barri Gòtic. The area surrounding the **Plaça del Pi,** from the Boqueria to Carrer Portaferrissa and Carrer de la Canuda, has fashionable boutiques and jewelry and gift shops. The **Barri de la Ribera** around Santa Maria del Mar is increasingly filled with shops of all kinds. Check along Carrer Banys Vells and, one street north of Carrer Montcada along Carrer Flassaders for design stores, jewelry and knickknacks of all kinds. Most stores are open Monday–Saturday 9–1:30 and 5–8, but some close in the afternoon. Virtually all close on Sunday.

Specialty Stores

Antiques

Carrer de la Palla and **Carrer Banys Nous,** in the Gothic Quarter, are lined with antiques shops full of maps, books, paintings, and furniture. An **antiques market** is held every Thursday from 10 to 8, in front of the cathedral. The **Centre d'Antiquaris** (✉ Passeig de Gràcia 57) contains 75 antiques stores. Try **Gothsland** (✉ Consell de Cent 331) for Moderniste design. **Sarrià** is becoming an antiquer's destination, with shops along Cornet i Mas, Pedró de la Creu, and Major de Sarrià.

Art

There is a cluster of art galleries on Carrer Consell de Cent between Passeig de Gràcia and Carrer Balmes, and around the corner on Rambla de Catalunya, including **Galeria Joan Prats** (✉ Rambla de Catalunya 54), **Sala Dalmau** (✉ Consell de Cent 347), and **Sala Rovira** (✉ Rambla de Catalunya 62). The nearby **Joan Gaspart Gallery** (✉ Plaça Letamendi 1) is another player. Carrer Petritxol, which leads down into Plaça del Pi, is also lined with galleries, most notably the dean of them all, **Sala Parès** (✉ Petritxol 5), and **Trama** (✉ Petritxol 8). The Born and Santa Maria del Mar quarter is another art destination. Carrer Montcada has **Galeria Maeght** and others; Carrer Bany Vells, just one street south, has the lovely new **3 ART BCN** (✉ Bany Vells 1). **Galeria Rosa Ventosa** is next to the church of Santa Maria del Mar (✉ Sombrerers 1). **Galeria Verena Hofer** is at Plaça Comercial, across from the Born; and the ticking **Metrònom** is on nearby Carrer Fussina. Near Plaça del Pi, galleries line Carrer de la Palla, particularly **Sala d'Art Artur Ramón** (✉ Carrer de la Palla 23) and **Galeria Segovia-Isaacs** (✉ Carrer de la Palla 8). Other important spaces include **Fundació Caixa de Catalunya–La Pedrera** (✉ Provença 261–265), **Fundació La Caixa–Centre Cultural** (✉ Passeig Sant Joan 108), **Fundació La Caixa–Sala Montcada** (✉ Carrer Montcada 14), and **Sala El Vienès-Casa Fuster** (✉ Passeig de Gràcia 132).

Boutiques and Fashion

Barcelona makes most of the headlines on Spain's booming fashion front. **Chanel** (✉ Passeig de Gràcia 70), **Giorgio Armani** (✉ Av. Diagonal 620), **Loewe** (✉ Passeig de Gràcia 35), and the other big names have shops along Passeig de Gràcia and Avinguda Diagonal. **El Bulevard Rosa** (✉ Passeig de Gràcia 53–55) is a collection of boutiques with the very latest outfits; others are on the Diagonal between Passeig de Gràcia and Carrer Ganduxer. **Adolfo Domínguez,** one of Spain's top designers, is at Passeig de Gràcia 35 and Avinguda Diagonal 570; Toni Miró's two **Groc** shops, with the latest looks for men, women, and children, are at Muntaner 385 and Rambla de Catalunya 100. **David Valls,** at Valencia 235, represents new and young Barcelona fashion design, and **May Day** carries clothing, footwear, and accessories from the cutting edge. **Joaquim Berao,** a top jewelry designer, is at Roselló 277.

Ceramics

Art Escudellers (✉ Carrer Escudellers 5), across the street from the restaurant Los Caracoles, has ceramics from all over Spain, with more than 140 different artisans represented and maps showing where the work is from. While you're there, check out the wine-tasting cellar downstairs. **Itaca** (✉ Ferrán 26) has ceramic plates, bowls, and inspired objects of all kinds, including pottery from Talavera de la Reina and La Bisbal. The big department stores are also worth checking. For Lladró, try **Pla de l'Os** (✉ Boqueria 3), just off the Rambla.

Department Stores

The ubiquitous **El Corte Inglés** has four locations: Plaça de Catalunya 14, Porta de l'Angel 19–21, Avinguda Francesc Maciá 58, and Avinguda Diagonal 617 (Metro: Maria Cristina). **Marks & Spencer** is at the top of the Rambla on Plaça Catalunya and in the shopping mall **L'Illa,** west of Plaça Francesc Macià at Avinguda Diagonal 545, along with a full array of stores from Benetton to Zara. **Plaça Catalunya** now includes **FNAC** and **Habitat,** among other emporiums.

Design and Interiors

Some 50 years old, design giant **Vinçon,** at Passeig de Gràcia 96, has steadily expanded its chic premises through a rambling Moderniste house that was once the home of Moderniste poet-artist Santiago Rusiñol and the studio of his colleague, the painter Ramón Casas. It stocks everything from Filofaxes to handsome kitchenware. A few doors up, at Passeig de Gràcia 102, is the upscale **Gimeno,** with elegant displays ranging from unusual suitcases to the latest in furniture design. **bd** (Barcelona design), at Carrer Mallorca 291–293, is a spare, cutting-edge home-furnishing store in another Moderniste gem, Doménech i Muntaner's Casa Thomas. **Habitat** has stores on Tuset at the Diagonal and in the new Plaça Catalunya Triangle complex behind Bar Zurich.

The area around the church of Santa Maria del Mar, an artisans' quarter since medieval times, is filling with cheerful design stores and art galleries. One of the best, **Testart Design,** at Argenteria 78, is owned and run by Matias Testart and Washington, D.C., native Natasha Chand. Other browse-worthy shops include **Ici et Là,** across the square (⊠ Plaça Santa Maria del Mar 2), **Fem** (⊠ Palau 6, behind the *ajuntament*), **Papers Coma** (⊠ Montcada 20), and **Estudi Pam2** (⊠ Sabateret 1–3).

Food and Flea Markets

The **Boqueria,** on the Rambla between Carrer del Carme and Carrer de Hospital, is Barcelona's most colorful and bustling food market and the oldest of its kind in Europe. Open Monday–Saturday, it's most active before 3 PM. Other spectacular food markets include the two in Gràcia—**Mercat de la Llibertat** (near Plaça Gal.la Placidia) and the **Mercat de la Revolució** (on Travessera de Gràcia)—and the **Mercat de Sarrià** (near Plaça de Sarrià and the Reina Elisenda train stop). Barcelona's biggest flea market, **Els Encants,** is held Monday, Wednesday, Friday, and Saturday 8–7 at the end of Dos de Maig, on the Plaça de les Glòries (Metro: Glòries). The **Mercat Gótic** fills the Plaça de la Seu, in front of the cathedral, on Thursday. **Sarrià**'s main square holds an antiques market on Tuesday. The **Sant Antoni** market, at the end of Ronda Sant Antoni, is an old-fashioned food and clothing spread that's best on Sunday. On Thursday, a produce market (honeys, cheeses) fills **Plaça del Pi** with interesting tastes and aromas. A stamp and coin market fills **Plaça Reial** on Sunday mornings, along with another general craft and flea market near the Columbus monument at the port end of the Rambla.

Gourmet Foods

Casa Gispert (⊠ Sombrerers 23), on the inland side of Santa Maria del Mar, is one of the most aromatic and picturesque shops in Barcelona, bursting with spices, saffron, chocolates, and nuts. Other charming and fragrant saffron and spice shops include **Jobal** (⊠ Princesa 38) and **La Barcelonesa** (⊠ Comerç 27). Near Santa Maria del Mar, **Vila Viniteca** (⊠ Agullers 7) is one of the best wine stores in Barcelona, and the produce store across the way at Agullers 9 sells some of the prettiest cheeses around. **El Magnífico** (⊠ Argenteria 64) is famous for its coffees. **Tot Formatge** (⊠ Passeig del Born 13) has cheeses from all over Spain and the rest of the world.

Miscellany

Lovers of fine stationery will linger in the Gothic Quarter's **Papirum** (⊠ Baixada de la Llibreteria 2), a tiny, medieval-tone shop with exquisite hand-printed papers, marbleized blank books, and writing implements. Lovely **La Manual Alpargartera** (⊠ Avinyó 7), just off Carrer Ferran, specializes in handmade rope-sole sandals and espadrilles. **Solé** (⊠ Carrer Ample 7) sells handmade shoes from all over the world. While in the area don't miss **La Lionesa,** just up the street at Ample 21, a picturesque old-time grocery store.

SIDE TRIPS

Numbers in the margin correspond to points of interest on the Side Trips from Barcelona map.

Montserrat

48 *50 km (30 mi) west of Barcelona.*

A nearly obligatory side trip from Barcelona is the shrine of La Moreneta, the Black Virgin of Montserrat, high in the mountains of the Serra de Montserrat. These weird, saw-tooth peaks have given rise to countless legends: here St. Peter left a statue of the Virgin Mary carved by St. Luke, Parsifal found the Holy Grail, and Wagner sought inspiration for his opera. A monastery has stood on this site since the early Middle Ages, though the present 19th-century building replaced the rubble left by Napoléon's troops in 1812. Montserrat is a world-famous shrine and one of Catalonia's spiritual sanctuaries: honeymooning couples flock here by the thousands seeking La Moreneta's blessing on their marriages, and twice a year, on April 27 and September 8, the diminutive statue of Montserrat's Black Virgin becomes the object of one of Spain's greatest pilgrimages.

To get here, follow the A2/A7 *autopista* on the new upper ring road (Ronda de Dalt), or from the western end of the Diagonal as far as Salida (Exit) 25 to Martorell. Bypass this industrial center and follow signs to Montserrat. You can also take a train from the Plaça Espanya metro station, or a guided tour with Pullmantur or Julià.

Only the basilica and museum are regularly open to the public. The **basilica** is dark and ornate, its blackness pierced by the glow of hundreds of votive lamps. Above the high altar stands the famous polychrome statue of the Virgin and Child, to which the faithful can pay their respects by way of a separate door. ☎ *93/877–7777.* ⏲ *Daily 6–10:30 and noon–6:30.*

The monastery's **museum** has two sections: the Secció Antiga (open Tuesday–Saturday 10:30–2) contains old masters, among them paintings by El Greco, Correggio, and Caravaggio, and the amassed gifts to the Virgin; the Secció Moderna (open Tuesday–Saturday 3–6) concentrates on recent Catalan painters.

Montserrat is as memorable for its setting as for its religious treasures, so be sure to explore these strange, pink hills. The vast monastic complex is dwarfed by the grandeur of the jagged peaks, and the crests are dotted with hermitages. The hermitage of **Sant Joan** can be reached by funicular. The views over the mountains to the Mediterranean and, on a clear day, to the Pyrenees are breathtaking, and the rugged, boulder-strewn setting makes for dramatic walks and hikes.

Sitges, Santes Creus, and Poblet

This trio of attractions south and west of Barcelona can be seen comfortably in a day. Sitges is the prettiest and most popular resort in Barcelona's immediate environs, flaunting an excellent beach, a picturesque old quarter, and some interesting Moderniste bits. It's also one of Europe's premier gay resorts. The Cistercian monasteries west of here, at Santes Creus and Poblet, are characterized by monolithic Romanesque architecture and beautiful cloisters.

By car, head southwest along Gran Via or Passeig Colom to the freeway that passes the airport on its way to Castelldefels. From here, the

Side Trips from Barcelona

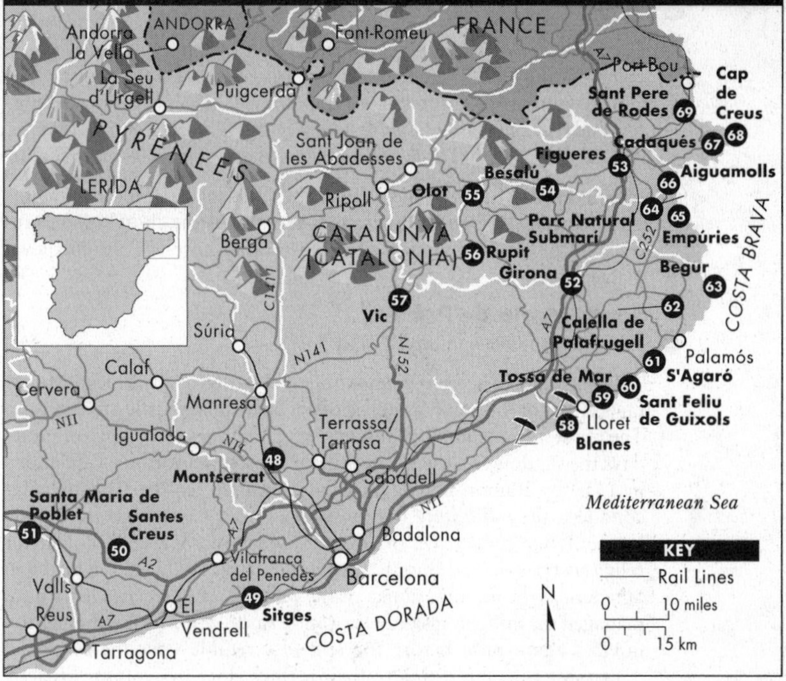

new freeway and tunnels will get you to Sitges in 20–30 minutes. From Sitges, drive inland toward Vilafranca del Penedès and the A7 freeway. The A2 (Lleida) leads to the monasteries.

Regular trains leave Sants and Passeig de Gràcia for Sitges; the ride takes half an hour. To get to Santes Creus or Poblet from Sitges, take a Lleida-line train to L'Espluga de Francolí, 4 km (2½ mi) from Poblet. For Poblet, you can also stay with the train to Tarragona and catch a bus to the monastery (✉ Autotransports Perelada, ☎ 973/202058).

Sitges

49 *43 km (27 mi) south of Barcelona.*

The most interesting museum here is the **Cau-Ferrat,** founded by the artist Santiago Russinyol (1861–1931) and containing some of his own paintings together with two El Grecos. Connoisseurs of wrought iron will love the beautiful collection of *cruces terminales,* crosses that once marked town boundaries. ✉ *Fonollar s/n,* ☎ *93/894–0364.* 🎫 *400 ptas.; free Sun.* ⏲ *Tues.–Sat. 9:30–2 and 4–6, Sun. 9:30–2.*

NEED A BREAK? Linger over excellent seafood in a nonpareil sea-view setting at **Vivero.** ✉ *Passeig Balmins s/n,* ☎ *93/894–2149. Closed Tues. Dec.–May.*

En Route Upon leaving Sitges, make straight for the A2 *autopista* by way of Vilafranca del Penedès. Wine buffs may want to stop here to taste some excellent Penedès wines; you can tour and sip at the **Bodega Miguel Torres** (✉ Comercio 22, ☎ 93/890–0100). There's an interesting **Museu del Vi** (Wine Museum) in the Royal Palace, with descriptions of wine-making history. 🎫 *500 ptas.* ⏲ *Tues.–Sun. 10–2 and 4–7.*

Santes Creus

50 *95 km (59 mi) west of Barcelona.*

Founded in 1157, **Santes Creus** is the first of the monasteries you'll come upon as A2 branches west toward Lleida. Three austere aisles and an unusual 14th-century apse combine with the newly restored cloisters and the courtyard of the royal palace. ☎ *977/638329.* *500 ptas.* *Oct.–Mar., daily 10–1 and 3–6; Apr.–Sept., daily 10–1 and 3–7.*

Montblanc is off A2 at Salida (Exit) 9, its ancient gates too narrow for cars. A walk through its tiny streets reveals Gothic churches with intricate stained-glass windows, a 16th-century hospital, and medieval mansions.

Santa Maria de Poblet

51 *8 km (5 mi) west of Santes Creus.*

This splendid Cistercian foundation at the foot of the Prades Mountains is one of the great masterpieces of Spanish monastic architecture. The cloister is a stunning combination of lightness and size; on sunny days the shadows on the yellow sandstone are extraordinary. Founded in 1150 by Ramón Berenguer IV in gratitude for the Christian Reconquest, the monastery first housed a dozen Cistercians from Narbonne. Later, the Crown of Aragón used Santa Maria de Poblet for religious retreats and burials. The building was damaged in an 1836 anticlerical revolt, and monks of the reformed Cistercian Order have managed the difficult task of restoration since 1940. Today, monks and novices again pray before the splendid retable over the tombs of Aragonese rulers, restored to their former glory by sculptor Frederic Marés; sleep in the cold, barren dormitory; and eat frugal meals in the stark refectory. You can join them if you'd like—18 very comfortable rooms are available (for men only). Call Padre Benito (☎ 977/870089) to arrange a stay of up to 15 days within the stones and silence of one of Catalonia's gems. *600 ptas.* *Guided tour daily 10–12:30 and 3–6 (until 5:30 Oct.–Mar.).*

Girona and Northern Catalonia

The ancient city of Girona, often ignored by visitors who bolt from its airport to the resorts of the Costa Brava, is an easy and worthwhile day trip from Barcelona. Much of the city's charm comes from its narrow medieval streets—with frequent stairways, as required by the steep terrain. Historic buildings here include the cathedral, which dominates the city from the top of 90 steps; Arab baths; and an antique and charming Jewish quarter.

Northern Catalonia boasts the soft, green rolling hills of the Ampurdan farm country, the Alberes mountain range at the eastern tip of the Pyrenees, and the rugged Costa Brava. Sprinkled across the landscape are charming *masías* (farmhouses) with austere, grayish or pinkish staggered-stone rooftops and ubiquitous square towers that make them look like fortresses. Even the tiniest village has its church, arcaded square, and *rambla,* where villagers take their evening *paseo.*

Girona

52 *97 km (60 mi) northeast of Barcelona.*

If you drive here, park in the free lot next to the River Onyar, under the train trestle. Walk along the river to Plaça de la Independencia, admiring Girona's best-known view as you go: the town's pastel yellow, pink, and orange waterfront facades, their windows draped with a colorful array of drying laundry reflected in the shimmering Onyar. Cross the bridge from under the arcades in the corner of the Plaça and find your way to the tourist office, to the right at Rambla Llibertat 1. Then work your way up through the labyrinth of steep streets, using the cathedral's huge Baroque facade as a guide.

At the base of the cathedral's 90 steps, go left through the Sobreportes gate to the **Banys Arabs,** or Arab Baths. Built by Morisco craftsmen in the late-12th century, long after Girona's Islamic occupation (795–1015) had ended, the baths are both Romanesque and Moorish in design. *250 ptas. May–Sept., Tues.–Sat. 10–2 and 4–7, Sun. 10–2; Oct.–Apr., Tues.–Sun. 10–1.*

Across the River Galligants is the church of **Sant Pere** (Holy Father), finished in 1131 and notable for its octagonal Romanesque belfry and the finely detailed capitals atop the columns in the cloister. Next door is the **Museu Arqueològic,** which documents the region's archaeological history since Paleolithic times. *350 ptas. Church and museum daily 10–1 and 4:30–7.*

The stepped **Passeig Arquaeològic** runs below the walls of the Old City. From there, climb through the Jardins de la Francesa to the highest ramparts for a view of the 11th-century Romanesque **Torre de Carlomagno** (Charlemagne Tower), the oldest part of the cathedral.

A five-minute walk uphill behind the cathedral leads to the **Torre de Gironella,** the highest point in the Jewish quarter. It was here that Girona's Jewish community took refuge in early August of 1391, emerging 17 weeks later to find their houses in ruins. Even though Spain's official expulsion decree did not go into effect until 1492, this attack effectively ended the Girona Jewish community. On December 20, 1998, the first Hanukkah celebration in 607 years took place in the gardens here, with representatives of the Jewish communities of Spain, France, Portugal, Germany, and the United States in attendance and Jerusalem's chief Sephardic rabbi, Rishon Letzion, presiding. It was an historic and moving event.

To see the inside of Girona's **cathedral,** designed by Guillem Bofill in 1416, complete the loop around it. The cathedral is known for its immense, uncluttered Gothic nave, which at 75 ft is the widest in the world and the epitome of the spatial ideal of Catalan Gothic architects. The **museum** contains the famous *Tapis de la Creació* (*Tapestry of the Creation*) and a 10th-century copy of Beatus's manuscript *Commentary on the Apocalypse. 375 ptas. Oct.–June, daily 9:30–1:15 and 3:30–7; July–Sept., daily 9:30–7.*

Next door to the cathedral is **Palau Episcopal** (Bishop's Palace), which houses the **Museu d'Art,** a good mix of Romanesque, Catalan Gothic, and modern art. *200 ptas.; free with ticket for Arab Baths (☞ above). Tues.–Sat. 10–7, Sun. 10–1.*

Upon leaving Plaça dels Apòstols along Carrer Claveria, turn right down Carrer Lluis Batlle i Prats. Plunge right into the tiny Carrer Sant Llorenç, formerly the cramped and squalid center of the 13th-century *Call,* or Jewish quarter. Halfway down on the left are the small **Bonastruc Çaporta,** a museum of Jewish history, open Tuesday–Saturday 10–2 and 4–7 and Sunday 10–2, and the **Pati dels Rabís** (Rabbis' Courtyard).

DINING AND LODGING

$$$$ ✕ **Albereda.** Excellent Ampurdan cuisine is served in a bright, if somewhat subdued, setting. Try the *galleta con langostinos glaceada,* a zucchini bisque with prawns. ✉ *C. Albereda 7 bis,* ☎ *972/226002. AE, DC, MC. Closed Sun.*

$$–$$$ ★ ✕ **Cal Ros.** Tucked under the arcades just behind the north end of Plaça de la Llibertat, this historic place combines ancient stone arches with a crisp, contemporary decor and cheerful lighting. The cuisine is gamey and delicious: hot goat-cheese salad with pine nuts and *garum* (black-olive-and-anchovy paste dating back to Roman times), *oca amb naps* (goose with turnips), and a blackberry sorbet not to miss. ✉ *C. Cort Reial 9,* ☎ *972/217379. MC, V. Closed Mon. No dinner Sun.*

$$–$$$ ✕ **Penyora.** Here you'll find both good local fare and, if you order from the prix-fixe menu, a bargain. ✉ *C. Nou del Teatre 3,* ☎ *972/218948. AE, DC, MC. Closed Tues.*

$$–$$$ 🏨 **Ultonia.** This central hotel has plenty of attractive wooden tables, paneling, and cupboards. ✉ *Gran Via Jaume I 22, 17001,* ☎ *972/203850,* FAX *972/203334. 45 rooms. Coffee shop. AE, DC, MC, V.*

$ 🏨 **Bellmirall.** A charming little hostel across the Onyar in the Jewish quarter, Belmirall offers top value in the heart of Girona's historic section. ✉ *Carrer Bellmirall 3, 17001,* ☎ *972/204009. 7 rooms. AE, DC, MC, V. Closed Jan.*

Figueres

53 *37 km (23 mi) north of Girona on the A7.*

This bustling country town is the capital of the Alt Empordà (Upper Ampurdan). Walk along the Figueres Rambla, scene of the *passeig* (*paseo* in Castilian; the constitutional midday or evening stroll), and visit the **Museu Dalí,** a spectacular homage to a unique artist. The museum is installed in a former theater next to the bizarre, ocher-color Torre Galatea, where Dalí lived until his death in 1989. The remarkable Dalí collection includes a vintage Cadillac with ivy-cloaked passengers whom you can water for 25 ptas. Dalí himself is entombed beneath the museum. ✉ *Plaça Gala-Salvador Dalí 5,* ☎ *972/511800.* 🎫 *1,000 ptas.* ⏲ *Oct.–May, Tues.–Sun. 10:30–5:15; June–Sept., Tues.–Sun. 9–7:15.*

DINING AND LODGING

$$–$$$ ★ ✕🏨 **Ampurdan.** Hailed as the birthplace of modern Catalan cuisine, this hotel and restaurant 1½ km (1 mi) north of Figueres on the N-II is better known for its cooking than for its lodging. The restaurant serves hearty portions of superb French, Catalan, and Spanish cooking in a simple setting. Try one of the fish mousses. ✉ *Carretera NII, 17600,* ☎ *972/500562,* FAX *972/509358. 39 rooms. AE, DC, MC, V.*

$$ ✕🏨 **Hotel Duran.** Once a stagecoach relay station, the Duran is now a well-known hotel and restaurant open every day of the year. Salvador Dalí had his own private dining room here, and you can still take a meal with the great surrealist, or at least with pictures of him. Try the *mandonguilles amb sepia al estil Anna* (meatballs and cuttlefish), a *mar i muntanya* (surf-and-turf) specialty of the house. ✉ *C. Lasauca 5, 17600,* ☎ *972/501250,* FAX *972/502609. 70 rooms. AE, MC, V.*

OFF THE BEATEN PATH

AMPURDAN UPLANDS – To explore the Alt Emporda (Upper Ampurdan), take the N-II 10 km (6 mi) north of Figueres and turn west on Gi502. Work your way 13 km (8 mi) west to the village of Maçanet de Cabrenys. Continue to the Santuari de les Salines, where you'll find a chapel and a tiny restaurant open in summer. Above Salines is one of the greatest beech forests in the Pyrenees. Follow signs from Le Perthus to Puig Neulós, at 4,148 ft the highest point in the Alberes range and the easternmost major Pyrenean peak. One of the greatest walks in the Pyrenees is the six-hour hike from Puig Neulós to Banyuls-sur-Mer, on the Mediterranean: the grassy border crest has views south over the Ampurdan and north over the yellow curving strand of the Côte Vermeille.

Besalú

54 *34 km (21 mi) north of Girona.*

Once the capital of a feudal county as part of Charlemagne's 8th- and 9th-century Spanish March, Besalu is 25 km (15 mi) west of Figueres on C260. This ancient town's most emblematic feature is its **fortified bridge,** with crenellated battlements. Other sights are its two churches, **Sant Vicenç** and **Sant Pere,** and the ruins of the convent of **Santa Maria** on the hill above town. The tourist office in the arcaded Plaça de la Llibertat can provide current opening hours for Sant Pere as well as keys to the *migwe,* the rare **Jewish baths** discovered in the 1960s.

The town of **Castellfollit de la Roca** perches on its prowlike basalt cliff over the Fluvià River 16 km (10 mi) west of Besalu.

Olot

55 *21 km (13 mi) west of Besalu, 55 km (34 mi) northwest of Girona.*

Capital of the Garrotxa area, Olot is famous for its 19th-century school of landscape painters and has several excellent Art Nouveau buildings, including one with a facade by Domènech i Muntaner. The **Museu Comarcal de la Garrotxa** (County Museum of La Garrotxa) holds an important assemblage of Moderniste art and design as well as sculptures by Miquel Blai, creator of the long-tressed maidens who support the balconies along Olot's main boulevard. ✉ *Carrer Hospici 8,* ☎ *972/279130.* 🎫 *450 ptas.* ⏲ *Mon. and Wed.–Sat. 10–1 and 4–7, Sun. 10–1:30.*

The villages of **Vall d'En Bas** lie south of Olot off Route A153. A new freeway cuts across this countryside to Vic, but you'll miss a lot by taking it. The twisting old road leads you through rich farmland past farmhouses whose dark wooden balconies are bedecked with bright flowers. Turn off for **Sant Privat d'En Bas** and **Els Hostalets d'En Bas.**

DINING AND LODGING

$$$ ✕ **Restaurante Ramón.** Ramón is so exclusive that he adamantly refuses to be in this book, so please don't let him see it. His restaurant, Olot's gourmet alcove par excellence, is the opposite of rustic: sleek, modern, refined, and international. Samples of the *cuina de la terra* (home cooking of regional specialties) include *patata de Olot* (potato stuffed with veal) and *cassoleta de judias amb xoriç* (white haricot beans with sausage). ✉ *Plaça Clarà 10,* ☎ *972/261001. Reservations essential. AE, DC, MC, V. Closed Thurs.*

$$$ 🏨 **Parador de Vic.** This quietly charming parador, also known as the Parador del Bac de Sau, is 14 km (9 mi) northeast of town off the Roda de Ter road past the village of Tavernoles. The views take in a stunning mountain and nearly lunar landscape over the Sau Reservoir. ✉ *Carretera Vic Roda de Ter, 08500,* ☎ *93/8887311. 36 rooms. Coffee shop, pool, tennis court. MC, V.*

$ 🏨 **La Perla.** Known for its friendly family ambience, this hotel is always Olot's first to fill up. On the edge of town toward the Vic Road, it's walking distance from two parks. ✉ *Av. Santa Coloma 97, 17800,* ☎ *972/262326,* FAX *972/270774. 30 rooms, 30 apartments. Restaurant, bar. MC, V.*

Rupit

56 *33 km (20 mi) south of Olot, 97 km (60 mi) north of Barcelona.*

Rupit is a spectacular stop for its medieval houses and its cuisine, the highlight of which is beef-stuffed potatoes. Built into a rocky promontory over a stream in the rugged Collsacabra region (about halfway from Olot to Vic), the town has some of the most aesthetically perfect **stone houses** in Catalonia, some of which were reproduced for Barcelona's Poble Espanyol.

DINING

$$ ✕ **El Repòs.** Hanging over the river that runs through Rupit, this restaurant serves the best meat-stuffed potatoes around. Ordering a meal is easy: just learn the word *patata.* Other specialties include duck and lamb. ✉ *C. Barbacana 1,* ☎ *93/856–5000. MC, V.*

Vic

57 *66 km (41 mi) north of Barcelona.*

Known for its conservatism and Catalan nationalism, Vic rests on a 1,600-ft plateau at the confluence of two rivers and serves as the area's commercial, industrial, and agricultural hub. The wide **Plaça Major,** surrounded by Gothic arcades and well supplied with bars and cafés, perfectly expresses the city's personality. Vic's religiosity is demonstrated by its 35 churches, of which the largely neoclassical **cathedral** is the foremost. The 11th-century Romanesque tower, El Cloquer, built by the Abbot Oliva, and the powerful modern murals painted twice by Josep Maria Sert (first in 1930 and again after fire damage in 1945) are the cathedral's high points. Next door, the **Museu Episcopal** (Bishop's Museum) houses a fine collection of religious art and relics. *450 ptas.* ⏲ *Mon.–Sat. 10–1 and 4–7, Sun. 10–1:30.*

DINING

$$ ✕ **Ca l'U.** Translated as "The One," Ca l'U is in fact *the* place in Vic for hearty local cuisine with a minimum of pretense and expense. Try the *llangostinos i llenguado* (prawns and sole) or the regional standard, *botifarra i mongetas* (sausage and beans). ✉ *Plaça Santa Teresa 4–5,* ☎ *93/886–3504. MC, V. Closed Mon. No dinner Sun.*

Girona and Northern Catalonia Essentials

ARRIVING AND DEPARTING

By Bus: Sarfa (✉ Estació Norte–Vilanova C. Alí Bei 80, ☎ 93/265–1158) has buses every 1½ hours to Girona, Figueres, and Cadaqués. For Vic contact **Segalés** (Metro: Fabra i Puig, ☎ 93/231–2756), and for Ripoll call **Teisa** (✉ Pau Claris 118, ☎ 93/488–2837).

By Car: Barcelona is completely surrounded by a new network of *rondas,* or ring roads, with quick access from every corner of the city. Look for signs for these rondas; then follow signs to France (Francia), Girona, and the A7 *autopista,* which goes all the way to France. For Girona, roughly a one-hour drive from Barcelona, leave the autopista at Salida (exit) 7.

By Train: Trains leave **Sants** and **Passeig de Gràcia** every 1½ hours for Girona, Figueres, and Port Bou (France). Some trains for northern Catalonia and France also leave from the França Station. For Vic and Ripoll, catch a Puigcerdà train (every hour or two) from Sants or Plaça de Catalunya.

GUIDED TOURS

Trenes Turísticos de RENFE (☎ 902/24–0202) operates guided tours to Girona by train May through September, leaving Sants at 10 AM and returning at 7:30 PM. The company also runs train tours to Vic and Ripoll, leaving Sants at 9 AM and returning at 8:40 PM. The cost for each is 1,500 ptas. Call RENFE to confirm.

The Costa Brava

The Costa Brava (Wild Coast) is a rocky stretch of shoreline that begins at Blanes and continues north through 135 km (84 mi) of coves and beaches to the French border at Port Bou. This tour concentrates on selected pockets—Tossa, Cap de Begur, Cadaqués—where the rocky terrain has discouraged the worst excesses of real-estate speculation.

Here, on a good day, the luminous blue of the sea still contrasts with red-brown headlands and cliffs; the distant lights of fishing boats reflect on wine-color waters at dusk; and umbrella pines escort you to the fringes of secluded *calas* (coves) and sandy white beaches.

Exploring the Costa Brava

58 The beaches closest to Barcelona are at **Blanes,** where launches (✉ Crucetours, ☎ 972/314969) can take you to Cala de Sant Francesc or the double beach at Santa Cristina between May and October.

59 The next stop north from Blanes on the coast road is **Tossa de Mar,** christened "Blue Paradise" by painter Marc Chagall, who summered here in 1934. The only Chagall painting in Spain is in Tossa's **Museu Municipal** (Municipal Museum, ☎ 972/340709), open Tuesday–Sunday 10–1 and 5–8. Admission is 350 ptas. Tossa's walled **medieval town** and pristine beaches are among Catalonia's best.

60 **Sant Feliu de Guixols** follows Tossa de Mar, after 23 km (15 mi) of hairpin curves over hidden inlets. Tiny turnouts or parking spots on this route nearly always lead to intimate coves with stone stairways winding down from the road. Visit Sant Feliu's two fine beaches, **church and monastery,** Sunday market, and lovely **Passeig del Mar.**

61 **S'Agaró,** one of the Costa Brava's most elegant clusters of villas and seaside mansions, is just 3 km (2 mi) north of Sant Feliu. The 30-minute walk along the **sea wall** from Hostal de La Gavina to Sa Conca beach is a delight.

Up the coast from S'Agaró, a road leads east to **Llafranc,** a small port
62 with quiet waterfront hotels and restaurants, and forks right to **Calella de Palafrugell,** a pretty fishing village known for its July Habaneras (Catalan-Cuban sea chanties inspired by the Spanish-American War) festival. Just south is the panoramic promontory **Cap Roig,** with views of the barren Formigues (Ants) Isles and a fine botanical garden that you can tour with a guide March–December, daily 9–9, for 450 ptas. The left fork drops down to **Tamariu,** one of the Costa's prettiest inlet towns. A climb over the bluff leads down to the parador at **Aiguablava,** a modern eyesore overlooking magnificent cliffs and crags.

63 From **Begur,** north of Aiguablava, you can go east through the *calas* or take the inland route past the rose-color stone houses and ramparts of the restored medieval town of **Pals.** Nearby **Peratallada** is another medieval town with fortress, castle, tower, palace, and well-preserved walls. North of Pals there are signs for **Ullastret,** an Iberian village dating from the 5th century BC. **L'Estartit** is the jumping-off point for the
64 spectacular **Parc Natural Submarí** (Underwater Natural Park) by the Medes Isles, famous for diving and for underwater photography.

65 The Greco-Roman ruins at **Empúries** are Catalonia's most important archaeological site. This port, complete with breakwater, is one of the most monumental ancient engineering feats on the Iberian Peninsula. As the Greeks' original point of arrival in Spain, Empúries was also where the Olympic Flame entered Spain for Barcelona's 1992 Olympic Games.

66 The **Aiguamolls** (Marshlands), an important nature reserve filled with migratory waterfowl from all over Europe, lies mainly around **Castelló d'Empúries,** but the main information center is at El Cortalet, on the road in from Sant Pere Pescador. Follow the road from Empúries, crossing the Fluvià River at Sant Pere Pescador, and proceed north through the wetlands to Castelló. From Castelló d'Empúries, a series of roadways and footpaths traverses the marshes, the latter well marked on the information center's maps.

67 **Cadaqués,** Spain's easternmost town, still has the whitewashed charm that made this fishing village into an international artists' haunt in the early 20th century. The Marítim is the central hangout both day and night; after dark, you might also enjoy the Jardí, across the square. Salvador Dalí's house, now a museum, still stands at Portlligat, a 30-minute walk north of town.

The **Museu Perrot-Moore,** in the old town, has an important collection of graphic arts dating from the 15th to the 20th century, including works by Dalí. *500 ptas. June 15–Oct. 15, daily 5–9.*

The **Casa Museu Salvador Dalí,** Dalí's summer house and a site long associated with the artist's notorious frolics with everyone from poets such as Federico García Lorca and Paul Eluard (whose wife, Gala, became Dalí's muse and spouse) to filmmaker Luis Buñuel. Filled with bits and pieces of the surrealist's daily life, it's an important point in the "Dalí triangle," completed by the castle at Púbol and the Museu Dalí, in Figueres. ✉ *Cala de Portlligat (3-km/2-mi walk from town center, along beach,* ☎ *972/251015. 750 ptas. Oct.–June, Tues.–Sun. 10:30–5:30; July–Sept., Tues.–Sun. 10:30–7:30.*

The **Castillo Pubol,** Dalí's former castle-home, is now the resting place of Gala, his perennial model and mate. It's a chance to wander through yet more Dalí-esque landscape: lush gardens, fountains decorated with masks of Wagner (the couple's favorite composer), and distinctive elephants with giraffe's legs and clawed feet. Two lions and a giraffe stand guard near Gala's tomb. ✉ *Rte. 255 toward La Bisbal, 15 km (9 mi) east of A7,* ☎ *972/258063 or 972/511800. 750 ptas. Mid-Mar.–June, daily 10:30–5:30; July–Sept., daily 10:30–7:30.*

68 **Cap de Creus,** just north of Cadaqués, Spain's easternmost point, is a fundamental pilgrimage, if only for the symbolic geographical rush. The hike out to the lighthouse—through rosemary, thyme, and the salt air of the Mediterranean—is unforgettable. The Pyrenees officially end (or rise) here. New Year's Day finds mobs of revelers awaiting the first emergence of the "new" sun from the Mediterranean.

69 The monastery of **Sant Pere de Rodes,** 7 km (4½ mi) by car (plus a 20-minute walk) above the pretty fishing village El Port de la Selva, is the last and one of the most spectacular sites on the Costa Brava. Built in the 10th and early 11th centuries by Benedictine monks—and sacked and plundered repeatedly since—this Romanesque monolith, now being restored, commands a breathtaking panorama of the Pyrenees, the Empordà plain, the sweeping curve of the Bay of Roses, and Cap de Creus. (Topping off the grand trek across the Pyrenees, Cap de Creus is a spectacular six-hour walk from here on the well-marked GR11 trail.)

Dining

$$$$ ★ ✕ **El Bullí.** The word "innovative" falls far short of describing what goes on here. El Bullí is one of the top restaurants in Spain, and the chef, Ferran Adrià, makes your palate his playground with a 12-course taster's menu that includes concepts like *espuma de humo* (foam of smoke)—no joke. It's near Roses in Cala Montjoi, 7 km (4½ mi) from Cadaqués by boat or footpath and 22 km (14 mi) by car. ✉ *Cala Montjoi, Roses, Girona,* ☎ *972/150457. AE, DC, MC, V. Closed Mon.–Tues.*

$$ ✕ **Can Pelayo.** This tiny, family-run restaurant serves the best fish in Cadaqués. It's hidden behind Plaça Port Alguer, a few minutes' walk south of the town center. ✉ *Carrer Nou 11,* ☎ *972/258356. MC, V. Closed weekdays Oct.–May.*

$$ ✕ **Cypsele.** The local fare at this Calella de Palafrugell restaurant includes *es niu,* an explosive combination of game fowl, fish tripe, pork

meatballs, and cuttlefish, stewed in a rich sauce. ✉ *C. Ancha 22,* ☎ *972/300192. MC, V.*

$$ ✕ **Royal.** This sunny, beachside spot in Tamariu serves fisherman-style creations of superb freshness and quality. The *suquet* (fish cooked slowly to create its own juice, or *suc*) is especially commendable. ✉ *Passeig de Mar 9,* ☎ *972/620041. MC, V.*

Dining and Lodging

$$$$ ✕🏨 **El Hostal de la Gavina.** At the eastern corner of Sant Pol beach in S'Agaró, La Gavina is a superb display of design and cuisine founded in 1932 by Josep Ensesa, who invented S'Agaró itself. Complete comfort and superb dining are augmented by tennis, golf, and horseback riding. ✉ *Plaça de la Rosaleda s/n, 17248,* ☎ *972/321100,* FAX *972/321573. 57 rooms, 17 suites. Restaurant. AE, DC, MC, V.*

$$–$$$ ✕🏨 **Rocamar.** Rocamar has modern rooms with splendid views over Cadaqués or out to sea. Service is excellent, and the cuisine is first-rate. ✉ *C. Doctor Bartomeus s/n, 17488 Cadaqués, Girona,* ☎ *972/258150,* FAX *972/258650. 70 rooms. Restaurant, bar, indoor pool, tennis court. AE, DC, MC, V.*

$$ ✕🏨 **Bar Cap de Creus.** Right next to the Cap de Creus lighthouse, this restaurant commands spectacular views. The cuisine is simple and good, and the proprietor rents three apartments (four beds each) upstairs. ✉ *17488 Cadaqués, Girona,* ☎ *972/199005. MC, V. Closed Mon.–Thurs. Oct.–June.*

$$ ✕🏨 **La Riera.** Built into a medieval house, this rustic hotel-restaurant is a quiet and comfortable hideaway in the lovely town of Peretallada, near Begur. The dining room is set up in the former wine cellar and the rooms have ceiling beams over painted ceramic tiles. The fine cuisine includes local specialties such as *anec amb naps* (duck with turnips) and *peu de porc amb cargols* (pig's feet with snails). ✉ *Plaça de les Voltes 3,* ☎ *972/634142,* FAX *972/635040. 6 rooms AE, DC, MC, V.*

Lodging

$$–$$$ 🏨 **Mar Menuda.** This modern Costa Brava hideaway offers as much peace and quiet—*and* as many varieties of water sports—as you can possibly handle. Equipment and instruction are available for windsurfing, sailing, swimming, and scuba diving. The hotel terrace overlooks the coast and the town of Tossa de Mar, with a medieval castle and an old quarter full of cobbled streets. ✉ *Playa Mar Menuda s/n, 17320 Tossa de Mar, Girona,* ☎ *972/341000,* FAX *972/340087. 48 rooms, 10 suites. Restaurant, pool, tennis court. AE, DC, MC, V. Closed Nov. 1–Dec. 27.*

$$ 🏨 **LlanéPetit.** This intimate little Cadaqués inn is just below Hotel Rocamar, at beach level. Charming and slightly less expensive, it has a very Mediterranean air. ✉ *C. Doctor Bartomeus 37, 17488 Cadaqués, Girona,* ☎ *972/258050,* FAX *972/258778. 37 rooms. Bar, breakfast room. AE, DC, MC, V.*

$$ 🏨 **Parador de Aiguablava.** This modern parador stands on a promontory overlooking sheer cliffs and surging seas. The service is impeccable. ✉ *17255 Begur, Girona,* ☎ *972/622162,* FAX *972/622166. 87 rooms. Restaurant, minibars, pool, sauna, exercise room. AE, DC, MC, V.*

Costa Brava Essentials

ARRIVING AND DEPARTING

By Bus: Buses to Blanes, Lloret, Sant Feliu de Guixols, Platja d'Aro, Palamos, Begur, Roses, and Cadaqués are operated by **Sarfa** (✉ Estació Norte–Vilanova C. Alí Bei 80, ☎ 93/265–1158; metro: Arc de Triomf).

By Car: For the fastest trip from Barcelona, start up the A7 *autopista* as if to Girona and take Salida (Exit) 10 for Blanes. Coastal traffic can be slow and frustrating, and the roads tortuous.

By Train: The local train to the Costa Brava pokes along the coast to Blanes every 30 minutes, departing Sants at 13 and 43 minutes after every hour and Plaça Catalunya 5 minutes later.

GUIDED TOURS

From June to September, coach and cruise tours from Barcelona to Empúries, L'Estartit, the Medes Isles underwater park, and the medieval town of Pals are run by **Julià Tours** (✉ Ronda Universitat 5, ☎ 93/317–6454) and **Pullmantur** (✉ Gran Via 635, ☎ 93/318–5195). The Medes Isles stop includes lunch, swimming, and underwater exploration. Buses leave Barcelona at 9 and return at 6. The price per person is 10,500 ptas. with lunch, 8,250 ptas. without.

GOLF

Club de Golf Costa Brava (✉ La Masía, 17246 Santa Cristina d'Aro, ☎ 972/837150), 18 holes. **Club de Golf Pals** (✉ Platja de Pals, 17256 Pals, ☎ 972/637009), 18 holes.

BARCELONA A TO Z

Arriving and Departing

By Bus

Barcelona has no central bus station, but most buses to Spanish destinations operate from the **Estació Norte-Vilanova** (✉ End of Av. Vilanova, a few blocks east of Arc de Triomf, ☎ 93/245–2528). Most international buses use the **Estació Autobuses de Sants** (✉ Carrer Viriato, next to Sants train station, ☎ 93/490–4000). Scores of independent companies operate from depots throughout town (☞ Excursions *in* Guided Tours, *below*).

By Car

Don't be intimidated by driving or parking here. You can often find a legal and safe parking place on the street, and underground public parking is increasingly plentiful, easy, and inexpensive.

By Plane

All international and domestic flights arrive at the spectacular glass, steel, and marble **El Prat de Llobregat** airport, 14 km (9 mi) south of Barcelona, just off the main highway to Castelldefels and Sitges. For information on arrival and departure times, call **Iberia** (☎ 93/401–3131; 93/401–3535; 93/301–3993; 93/302–7656 for international reservations and confirmations). Most flights from the United States connect in Madrid; only Continental, Delta, Iberia, and TWA fly nonstop to Barcelona.

Check first to see if your hotel provides airport-shuttle service; otherwise, you can high-tail it into town via train, bus, taxi, or rental car.

BETWEEN THE AIRPORT AND DOWNTOWN

By Bus. The Aerobus leaves the airport for Plaça de Catalunya every 15 minutes (6 AM–11 PM) on weekdays and every 30 minutes (6:30 AM–10:30 PM) on weekends. From Plaça de Catalunya, it leaves for the airport every 15 minutes (5:30 AM–10:00 PM) on weekdays and every 30 minutes (6:30 AM–10:30 PM) on weekends. The fare is 500 ptas.

By Car. Follow signs to the Centre Ciutat and you'll enter the city along Gran Via. For the port area, follow signs for the Ronda Litoral. The journey to the center of town can take anywhere from 15 to 45 minutes depending on traffic. Peak rush hours are between 7:30 and 9:30 in the morning, 1:30–2:30 in the afternoon, and 7–9 in the evening.

By Taxi. Cab fare from the airport into town is 2,500 ptas.–3,000 ptas.

By Train. The train's only drawback is that it's a 10- or 15-minute walk (with moving walkway) from your gate through the terminal and over the bridge. The train leaves the airport every 30 minutes between 6:12 AM and 10:13 PM, stopping first at the Sants-Estació, then at the Plaça de Catalunya, later at the Arc de Triomf, and finally at Clot. Trains going to the airport begin at 6 AM from the Clot station, stopping at the Arc de Triomf at 6:05 AM, Plaça de Catalunya at 6:08 AM, and Sants at 6:13 AM. The fare is 500 ptas. on weekdays, 550 ptas. on weekends and holidays.

By Train

Almost all long-distance and international trains arrive and depart from the **Sants-Estació** (✉ Plaça dels Països Catalans s/n). En route to or from Sants, some trains stop at another station on **Passeig de Gràcia** at Carrer Aragó; this can be a good way to avoid the long lines that form at Sants during holidays. The **Estació de França** (✉ Av. Marques Argentera s/n), near the port, handles certain long-distance trains within Spain and some international trains. For schedules and fares, call **RENFE** (☎ 902/240202).

Getting Around

Modern Barcelona, above the Plaça de Catalunya, is built on a grid system. The old town, from the Plaça de Catalunya to the port, however, is a labyrinth of narrow streets, and you'll need a good street map to get around it. Most sightseeing can be done on foot—you won't have any choice in the Barri Gòtic—but you'll have to use the metro, buses, or taxis to link sightseeing areas. The Dia T1 pass is valid for one day of unlimited travel on all subway, bus, and FFCC lines. Maps showing bus and metro routes are available free from booths in the Plaça de Catalunya; for general information on public transport, call 93/412–0000.

Turisme de Barcelona (Barcelona Tourism; ✉ Plaça de Catalunya 17 bis, ☎ 906/301282) sells 24-, 48-, and 72-hour versions of the very worthwhile Barcelona Card. For 2,750, 3,250, or 3,750 ptas., you get unlimited travel on all public transport as well as discounts at 27 museums, 10 restaurants, 14 leisure spots, and 20 stores. Other services include walking tours of the Gothic Quarter, an airport shuttle, a bus to Tibidabo, and the Tombbus, which connects key shopping areas.

By Boat

Golondrina harbor boats make short pleasure trips from the Portal de la Pau, near the Columbus Monument. The fare is 750 ptas. for a 30-minute ride. Departures are spring and summer (Holy Week through September), daily 11–7; fall and winter, weekends and holidays only, 11–5. It's closed December 16–January 2. For information call ☎ 93/442–3106.

By Bus

City buses run daily from 5:30 AM to 11:30 PM. The fare is 145 ptas. (155 ptas. Sunday and holidays); for multiple journeys purchase a Targeta T1, which buys you 10 rides for 875 ptas. Route maps are displayed at bus stops. Note that those with a red band always stop at a central square—Catalunya, Universitat, or Urquinaona—and blue indicates a night bus. From June 12 to October 12 the Bus Turistic (9:30–7:30 every 30 minutes) runs on a circuit that passes all the important sights. A day's ticket, which you can buy on the bus, costs 1,400 ptas. (925 ptas. half day) and also covers the fare for the Tramvía Blau, funicular, and Montjuïc cable car across the port. The ride starts at the Plaça de Catalunya.

By Cable Car and Funicular

The Montjuïc Funicular is a cog railroad that runs from the junction of Avinguda Paral.lel and Nou de la Rambla to the Miramar station on Montjuïc (metro: Paral.lel). It operates weekends and holidays 11 AM–8 PM in winter, and daily 11 AM–9:30 PM in summer; the fare is 200 ptas. A *telefèric* then takes you from the amusement park up to Montjuïc Castle. In winter the telefèric runs weekends and holidays 11–2:45 and 4–7:30; in summer, daily 11:30–9. The fare is 450 ptas.

A Transbordador Aeri Harbor Cable Car runs between Miramar and Montjuïc across the harbor to Torre de Jaume I, on Barcelona's *moll* (quay), and on to Torre de Sant Sebastià, at the end of Passeig Joan de Borbó in Barceloneta. You can board at either stage. The fare is 850 ptas. (1,000 ptas. round trip), and the car runs October–June, weekdays noon–5:45, weekends noon–6:15, and July–September, daily 11–9.

To reach the summit of Tibidabo, take the metro to Avinguda de Tibidabo, then the Tramvía Blau (350 ptas. one-way) to Peu del Funicular, and finally the Tibidabo Funicular (450 ptas. one-way) from there to the Tibidabo fairground. It runs every 30 minutes, 7:05 AM–9:35 PM ascending, 7:25 AM–9:55 PM descending.

By Metro

The subway is the fastest, cheapest, and easiest way to get around Barcelona. You pay a flat fare of 150 ptas. no matter how far you travel, but it's more economical to buy a Targeta T1 (valid for metro and FFCC Generalitat trains, Tramvía Blau [blue tram], and the Montjuïc Funicular), which costs 875 ptas. for 10 rides. The system runs 5 AM–11 PM (until 1 AM on weekends and holidays).

By Taxi

Taxis are black and yellow and show a green light when available for hire. The meter starts at 395 ptas. (which lasts for six minutes), and there are supplements for luggage, night travel, Sundays and holidays, rides from a station or to the airport, and for trips to or from the bullring or a football match. There are cab stands all over town, and you can also hail cabs on the street. To call a cab, try 93/387–1000, 93/490–2222, or 93/357–7755, 24 hours a day.

Guided Tours

Turisme de Barcelona (Barcelona Tourism; ✉ Plaça de Catalunya 17 bis, ☎ 906/301282) offers weekend walking tours of the Gothic Quarter (at 10 AM) for 1,000 ptas. Tours depart from the office.

Other urban tours are run by **Julià Tours** (✉ Ronda Universitat 5, ☎ 93/317–6454) and **Pullmantur** (✉ Gran Via 635, ☎ 93/318–5195). Tours leave from these offices, but you may be able to arrange a pickup at your hotel. Prices are 4 ,985 ptas. for half a day and 12,750 ptas. for a full day, including lunch.

Julià Tours and Pullmantur also run day and half-day excursions outside the city. The most popular trips are those to Montserrat and the Costa Brava resorts, the latter including a cruise to the Medes Isles.

Personal Guides

Contact **City Guides Barcelona** (☎ 93/412–0674), the **Barcelona Guide Bureau** (☎ 93/268–2422), or the **Asociación Profesional de Informadores Turísticos** (☎ 93/319–8416) for a list of English-speaking guides.

Special-Interest Tours

La Ruta del Modernisme (the Modernism Route), created by Barcelona's *ajuntament* (city hall), connects seven key Art Nouveau sites: Palau Güell,

Barcelona Metro

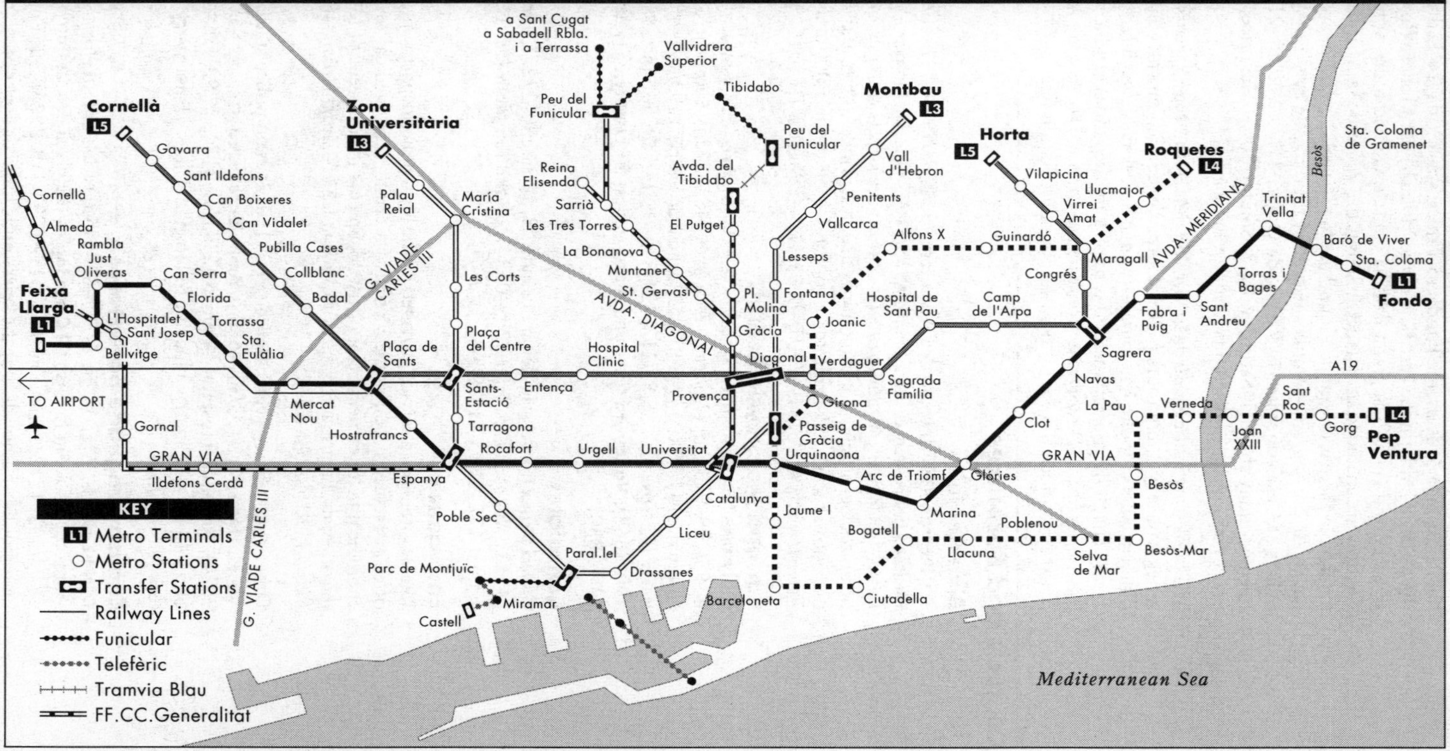

the Palau de la Música, the Fundació Tàpies, Casa Milà (La Pedrera), the Museu Gaudí (in the Parc Güell), the Museu d'Art Modern (in Ciutadella), and Gaudí's Sagrada Família church. Guided tours, some in English, are included at Palau Güell and the Palau de la Música. At Casa Milá there is one guided tour daily (6 PM weekdays, 11 AM weekends). At the Sagrada Família the guided tour costs extra. Buy your tickets at **Casa Amatller** (✉ Passeig de Gràcia 41, ☎ 93/488–0139), open Monday through Saturday 10–7, Sunday 10–2. The price, 600 ptas., gets you 50% discounts at all seven locations.

The bookstore in the **Palau de la Virreina** (✉ La Rambla 99) rents cassettes whose walking tours follow footprints painted on sidewalks—different colors for different tours—through Barcelona's most interesting areas. The do-it-yourself method is to pick up the guides produced by the tourist office, *Discovering Romanesque Art* and *Discovering Modernist Art,* which have art itineraries for all of Catalonia.

Contacts and Resources

Bike Rental

Try **Bicitram** (✉ Marquès de l'Argentera 15, ☎ 93/792–2841) and **Los Filicletos** (✉ Passeig de Picasso 38, ☎ 93/319–7811). **Un Menys**—"One Less," in Catalan, meaning one less car on the streets of Barcelona—organizes increasingly popular outings that tack drinks, dinner, and dancing onto a gentle bike ride for a total price of about 5,000 ptas. ✉ *Esparteria 3,* ☎ *93/268–2105,* FAX *93/319–4298. AE, DC, MC, V.*

Car and Motorcycle Rental

Call **Atesa** (✉ Muntaner 45, ☎ 93/323–0266); **Avis** (✉ Casanova 209, ☎ 93/209–9533) or (✉ Aragó 235, ☎ 93/487–8754); **Europcar**(✉ Viladomat 214, ☎ 93/439–8403; ✉ Estació de Sants, ☎ 93/491–4822); **Hertz** (✉ Tuset 10, ☎ 93/217–3248) or (✉ Estació de Sants, ☎ 93/490–8662); **Vanguard** (cars and motorcycles; ✉ Londres 31, ☎ 93/439–3880).

Consulates

United States (✉ Passeig Reina Elisenda 23, ☎ 93/280–2227), **Canada** (✉ Via Augusta 125, ☎ 93/209–0634), **United Kingdom** (✉ Av. Diagonal 477, ☎ 93/419–9044).

Emergencies

Tourist Attention, a service provided by the local police department, will offer assistance if you're the victim of a crime, seek medical or psychological help, or need temporary documents in the event of loss of the originals. English interpreters are on hand. ✉ *Guardia Urbana, Ramblas 43,* ☎ *93/290–3440.*

Other emergency services: **Police** (☎ 091; 092; main police station ✉ Via Laietana 43, ☎ 93/301–6666). **Ambulance** (Creu Roja, ☎ 93/300–2020). **Hospital** (Hospital Clinic: ✉ Villarroel 170, ☎ 93/454–6000 or 93/454–7000; metro: blue line to Hospital Clinic). **Emergency doctors** (☎ 061).

English-Language Bookstores

BCN Books (✉ Aragó 277, ☎ 93/487–3455) is one of Barcelona's top stores for books in English. **El Corte Inglés** (✉ Plaça de Catalunya 14, ☎ 93/302–1212; ✉ Av. Diagonal 617, ☎ 93/419–2828) sells English guidebooks and novels, but the selection is limited. For more variety, try the **English Bookshop** (✉ Entença 63, ☎ 93/425–4466), **Jaimes Bookshop** (✉ Passeig de Gràcia 64, ☎ 93/215–3626), **Laie** (✉ Pau Claris 85, ☎ 93/318–1357), **Libreria Francesa** (✉ Passeig de Gràcia 91, ☎ 93/215–1417), **Come In** (✉ Provença 203, ☎ 93/253–1204), or **Llibreria**

Bosch (✉ Ronda Universitat 11, ☎ 93/317–5308; ✉ Roselló 24, ☎ 93/321–3341). The bookstore in the **Palau de la Virreina** (✉ La Rambla 99, ☎ 93/301–7775) has good books on art, design, and Barcelona in general.

Late-Night Pharmacies

Look on the door of any pharmacy or in any local newspaper under "Farmacias de Guardia" for the addresses of those open late at night or 24 hours. Alternately, dial 010.

Travel Agencies

American Express (✉ Roselló 257, at Passeig de Gràcia, ☎ 93/217–0070). **Iberia** (✉ Diputació 258, at Passeig de Gràcia, ☎ 93/401–3381; ✉ Plaça de Espanya, ☎ 93/325–7358). **WagonsLits Cook** (✉ Passeig de Gràcia 8, ☎ 93/317–5500). **Bestours** (✉ Diputación 241, ☎ 93/487–8580).

Visitor Information

The **Centre d'Informació Turistic de Barcelona** has two locations (✉ Plaça de Catalunya 17 bis, ☎ 93/304–3421; ✉ Plaça Sant Jaume 1, ☎ 93/304–3421), both open Monday through Saturday 9–9 and Sunday 10–2. There are smaller tourist facilities at the **Sants** train station, open daily 8–8; the **Palau de la Virreina** (✉ Rambla 99), open Monday–Saturday 9–9 and Sunday 10–2; and the **Palau de Congressos** (✉ Av. María Cristina s/n), open daily 10–8 during trade fairs and conventions only. For general information in English, dial **010** between 8 AM and 10 PM any day but Sunday.

Offices with information on Catalonia and the rest of Spain are at **El Prat Airport** (☎ 93/478–4704), open Monday–Saturday 9:30–8 and Sunday 9:30–3, and the **Centre d'Informació Turística** (✉ Palau Robert, Passeig de Gràcia 107, at the Diagonal, ☎ 93/238–4000), open Monday–Saturday 10–7.

From June to mid-September, **tourist information aides** patrol the Gothic Quarter and Ramblas area 9 AM–9 PM. They travel in pairs and are recognizable by their uniforms of red shirts, white trousers or skirts, and badges.

7 SOUTHERN CATALONIA AND THE LEVANTE

Tarragona bursts with Roman antiquities, and Valencia, Spain's third-largest city, is rich in art and architecture. Down the coast between the two—an area known as the Levante because the sun rises (*se levanta*) from the Mediterranean here—a landscape of grayish, arid mountains backs a ribbon of soft, sandy, palm-lined beaches, many marred by modern development. Inland, the rugged ground is dotted with small, fortified towns, strategically important in medieval times.

By Philip Eade

Updated by Katherine Semler

THIS REGION STRADDLES CATALONIA (Catalunya) and Valencia, allowing you to sample the differences and similarities between these two feuding Mediterranean cousins. Valencia was part of the House of Aragon, Catalonia's medieval Mediterranean empire, after Jaume I conquered it in the 13th century, and staunch Valencian nationalists still regard Catalonia and the Catalan language much as Catalonia regards Madrid and central Spain. Valencia was incorporated, along with Catalonia, into a united Spanish state in the 15th century, but the most energetic cultivators of Valencia's separate cultural and linguistic identity still resent their centuries of Catalan domination. The Catalan language prevails in Tarragona, a city and province of Catalonia, but Valenciano, widely considered (though generally not by Valencianos themselves) a dialect of Catalan, is spoken and written on street signs in the Valencian provinces. You may notice the subtle difference in dialect as you move south.

The *huerta* (fertile, irrigated coastal plain) is devoted mainly to citrus and vegetable farming, which lend color to the landscape and fragrance to the air. Grayish, arid mountains form a stark backdrop to the lush coast. These shores have entertained Phoenician, Greek, Carthaginian, and Roman visitors—the Romans stayed several centuries and left archaeological reminders all the way down the coast, particularly in Tarragona, the capital of Rome's Spanish empire by 218 BC. Rome's dominion did not go uncontested, however; the most serious challenge came from the Carthaginians of North Africa. The three Punic Wars, fought over this territory between 264 BC and 146 BC, led to the immortalization of the Carthaginian general Hannibal.

The same coastal farmland and beaches that attracted the ancients call to modern-day tourists, and unfortunately a chain of ugly developments has marred much of this shore. Venture inland, though, and you'll find a completely different world, where local culture has survived intact. This rugged and often strikingly beautiful territory is dotted with small, fortified towns, several of which bear the name of Spain's 11th-century national hero, El Cid, as proof of the battles he fought here against the Moors 900 years ago. Each town has its porticoed Plaza Mayor, whitewashed houses, and countless coats of arms as further reminders of its strategic importance in medieval times.

Founded by the Greeks, the city of Valencia was in Moorish hands from 712 to 1238, apart from a brief interlude from 1094 to 1102, when El Cid reconquered it. Colorful *azulejos* (glazed, patterned tiles) and bright-blue cupolas on churches reflect Moorish traditions here. Spain's golden age left striking souvenirs of the 15th century as well: the Gothic Lonja (Silk Exchange) and mansions, and the Primitive paintings of Jacomart and Juan Reixach in the Museum of Fine Arts. The flamboyant, 18th-century Palacio de las Dos Aguas embodies the vitality of Churriguerismo, the early Spanish Baroque.

Pleasures and Pastimes

Beaches

If you've just come from the Costa Brava, you'll find the beaches in this area quite different, with endless strands of fine-grain sand. Salou has the best beaches at the northern end, along with a lively, palm-lined promenade. More tranquil are the beaches of the Ebro Delta, the best of which is the Playa de los Eucaliptos, reached by a pretty road from Amposta via Montells. Peñíscola's beach seems to go on forever; the sand is soft, and the old city rises up out of the sea at one end as a scenic bonus. Alcocéber has a series of small, uncrowded, sandy crescents, and just to its north is the sophisticated new marina at Las Fuentes. Benicàssim's long, crescent-shaped beach has the most dramatic setting of all, with mountains rising steeply in the background. Valencia itself has a long beach that's wonderful for sunning and has numerous seaside restaurants, but it's not the best place for swimming; for cleaner water, head south to El Saler.

Dining

Romesco (a spicy blend of almonds, peppers, and olive oil), from Tarragona, is used as a sauce for fish and seafood, especially in the *calçotada* (spring onion) feasts of February. If you're here for September's Santa Tecla festival, you can try the *espineta amb cargolins* (tuna with snails), perhaps accompanied by some excellent wine from the nearby Penedés or Priorato vineyards. The Ebro Delta is renowned for its fresh fish and eels, as well as specialties like *rossejat* (fried rice in a fish broth, dressed with garlic sauce). *Jamones* (hams), *cecinas* (smoked meats), and *carnes a la brasa* (meats cooked over coals) all feature in Maestrazgan (mountain) cooking, together with good *trucha* (trout) and *conejo* (rabbit). You should also try the *trufas* (truffles) that grow here. In Valencia and all along the Mediterranean coast you're in the land of *paella valenciana* (a rice dish flavored with saffron and embellished with seafood, poultry, meat, peas, and peppers), Spain's most famous dish. Prepared to order in a *caldero* (shallow pan), paella takes a good 20 minutes to cook, so it's not for travelers in a hurry. Good paella is fabulous, but it's often overpriced due to tourist demand and should never be chosen from a *menú del día,* where it's usually tasteless and disappointing. A variant is *arroz a la banda,* in which the fish and rice are cooked separately; the fish is fried in garlic, onion, and tomato, and the rice is boiled in the resulting stock.

CATEGORY	COST*
$$$$	over 6,000 ptas.
$$$	4,000 ptas.–6,000 ptas.
$$	2,000 ptas.–4,000 ptas.
$	under 2,000 ptas.

**per person for a three-course meal, excluding drinks, service, and tax*

Fiestas

In Valencia, **Las Fallas** fill an entire week in March, reaching their climax on March 19, El Día de San José (St. Joseph's Day), when families throughout Spain celebrate Father's Day. The time-honored feast of Las Fallas grew from the fact that St. Joseph is the patron saint of carpenters; in medieval times, carpenters' guilds celebrated his feast day by making huge bonfires with their wood shavings. Today Valencia explodes into a weeklong celebration of fireworks, flower-strewn floats, carnival processions, top bullfights, and uncontrolled merrymaking to which Spaniards and tourists both flock. On March 19, huge and often grotesque satirical effigies of popular and not-so-popular figures are ceremoniously burned, creating a surprising sense of nostalgia and the ephemerality of life itself. If you're allergic to firecrackers or large crowds, stay away from this one. Tarragona's most important fiestas are those of **St. Magí** (August 19) and **St. Tecla** (September 23), both characterized by colorful processions.

Lodging

Tarragona is worth an overnight stay and has a nice range of standard hotels. Antique, one-of-a-kind lodgings are in gratifying abundance on the Ebro Delta and in the Maestrazgo mountains. On the shore, lodgings are more mundane, with modern high-rises predominating. Just north and south of Valencia, the towns of Puzol and El Saler have some famous luxury hotels, while the city itself offers a reasonable range of historic and modern hotels. If you plan to be in Valencia for Las Fallas, in mid-March, book your room months in advance; prices are sure to rise as the festivities approach.

CATEGORY	COST*
$$$$	over 16,500 ptas.
$$$	9,500 ptas.–16,500 ptas.
$$	6,000 ptas.–9,500 ptas.
$	under 6,000 ptas.

**All prices are for a standard double room, excluding tax.*

Exploring Tarragona to Valencia

Numbers in the text correspond to numbers in the margin and on the Southern Catalonia and the Levante and Valencia maps.

Great Itineraries

Mountain villages; wetlands; sweeping beaches; cities filled with art, architecture, and archaeology—there's plenty to see between Tarragona and Valencia. Tarragona is distinguished by its extraordinarily well-preserved Roman remains and its peaceful, sophisticated atmosphere. Next comes the fertile Delta de l'Ebre (Ebro Delta), rich in fauna and flora, followed by the ancient town of Tortosa, where you can enjoy a splendid night in the hilltop parador. A rewarding loop inland explores the wild Beceite and Maestrazgo mountains, including the ancient, contoured town of Morella. The Costa del Azahar (Orange Blossom Coast) down to Valencia is characterized by orange groves against a backdrop of dry hills. Peñíscola, a cluster of white houses on a promontory, is highly picturesque, though, sadly, tourist development is beginning to surround it. Farther south, the Roman town of Sagunto is of architectural note, with its hilltop fortress and amphitheater. Finally, you reach Valencia, a trove of art and architecture whose highlights include the Gothic Lonja (Silk Exchange); the striking, Baroque Palacio Marqués de Dos Aguas; and the superb Museum of Fine Arts.

IF YOU HAVE 3 DAYS

If you have three days, spend one of them wandering through the Roman, Visigothic, medieval, and modern wonders of **Tarragona** ①, stopping occasionally to enjoy its sweeping views of the sea. Have lunch in the Serallo fishing quarter, dine within the Roman walls, and spend the night in the heart of the city. Set out the next morning for the **Delta de l'Ebre** ⑤ and explore its world-famous nature preserve before having lunch at the restaurant-museum Estany, near Villafranca del Delta. Head south to **Peñíscola** ⑭ for your second night, and devote your third day to **Valencia** ⑯–㉜.

IF YOU HAVE 5 DAYS

Begin with the ancient wonders of **Tarragona** ①. After a night there, move on to explore the **Delta de l'Ebre** ⑤, taking a late lunch at the restaurant-museum Estany, near Villafranca del Delta. Drive up to **Tortosa** ⑥ for a night in the Parador Castillo de la Zuda. Devote day three to the Sierra de Beceite, with visits to Miravet, **Gandesa** ⑦, Calaceite, Valderrobres, Beceite, and Fredes before an overnight rest stop in **Morella** ⑩. On day four, drive through the Maestrazgo mountains for a look at some of the least-visited valleys and villages on the entire Iberian Peninsula. Take the slow but scenic CS802 up through Iglesuela del Cid and around to Villafranca del Cid before driving through **Ares del Maestre** ⑪, Albocácer, and **San Mateu** ⑫ on your way to **Peñíscola** ⑭, where you can spend the night. Finally, travel down the Costa del Azahar to **Valencia** ⑯–㉜.

Southern Catalonia and the Levante

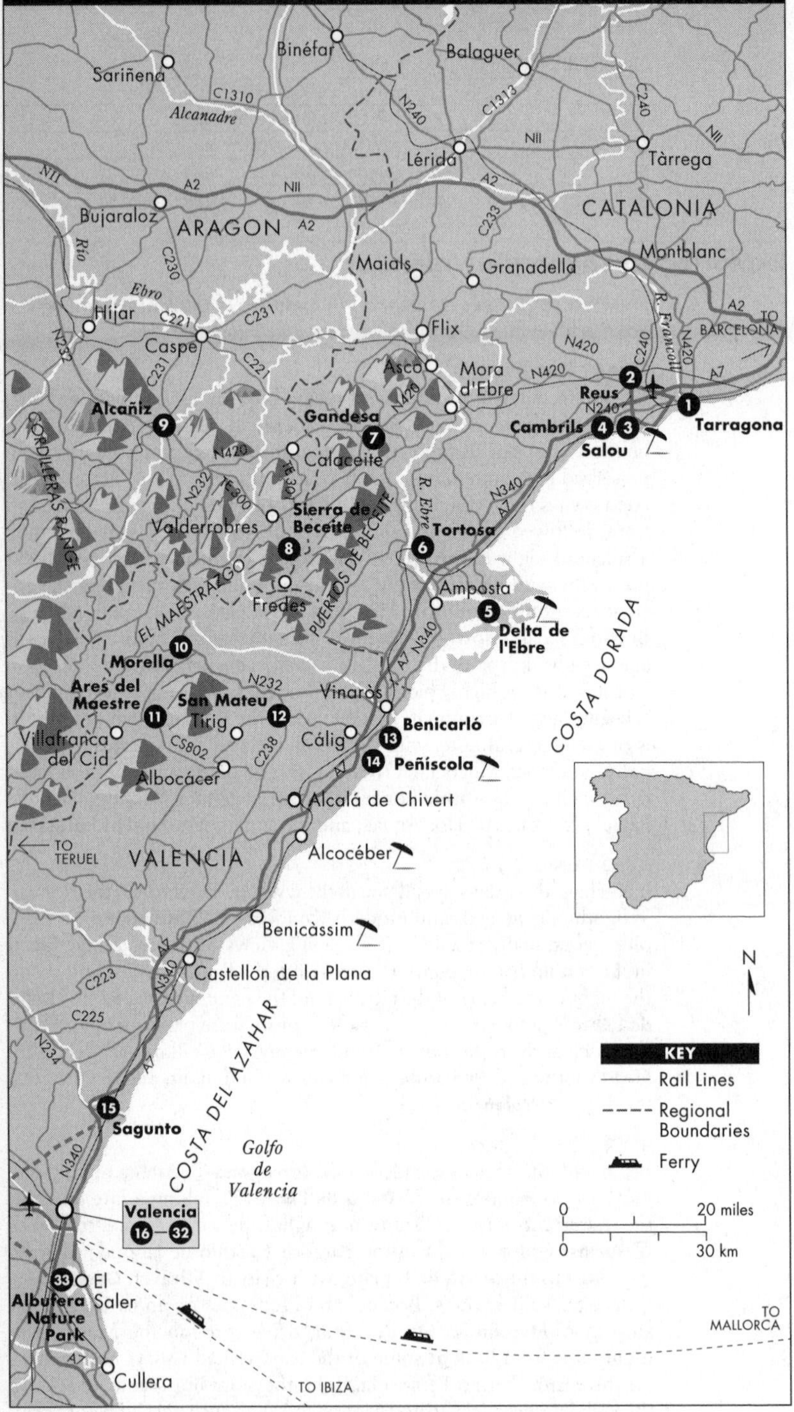

When to Tour Southern Catalonia and the Levante

Try to avoid this region in the summer. The weather is hot and arid, and the beaches are crowded. Fall and spring are probably the best times to visit, but anyone who has seen slanting December light in the delta or the dramatic shadows that a winter sun casts on medieval stone facades might recommend a winter visit just as heartily. Just remember that hours for most sights change with the seasons; many close as early as 5:30 in winter.

TARRAGONA

❶ *98 km (60 mi) southwest of Barcelona, 251 km (155 mi) northeast of Valencia.*

Less than an hour from Barcelona, Tarragona offers a bracing mélange of fresh provincial capital. An ancient outpost of the Roman Empire, it remains a pungent fishing port, busy shipping harbor, and vibrant cultural center.

The name Tarragona promises rich classical remains, and the city does not disappoint. As capital of the Roman province of Tarraconensis (from 218 BC), Tarraco, as it was then called, formed the empire's principal stronghold in Spain, and by the 1st century BC the city was regarded as one of the empire's finest urban creations. Its wine was already famous, and its people were the first in Spain to become Roman citizens. St. Paul preached here in AD 58, and Tarragona became the seat of the Christian Church in Spain until it was superseded by Toledo in the 11th century.

Entering the city from Barcelona, you'll pass the **triumphal arch of Berà,** dating from the 3rd century BC, 19 km (12 mi) north of Tarragona; and from the Lleida (Lérida) road, or *autopista,* you can see the 1st-century **Roman aqueduct** that helped carry fresh water 32 km (19 mi) from the River Gayo. If you approach from the south, past the gasworks, you may think modern Tarragona has forsaken her ancient splendor, but the outstanding monuments are ahead, some having received a valuable face-lift as part of the city's ongoing renovation and rediscovery of its archaeological treasures. Tarragona is divided clearly into old and new by the Rambla Vella; the old town and most of the Roman remains are to the north, while modern Tarragona spreads out to the south.

Start your tour of Tarragona at the acacia-lined Rambla Nova, at the end of which is a balcony overlooking the sea, the **Balcó del Mediterràni.** Walking uphill along the Passeig de les Palmeres, you'll arrive at a striking illustration of the dichotomy between ancient and modern. ★ The remains of Tarragona's **amphitheater** are visible down toward the sea; above stands the modern, semicircular Hotel Imperial Tarraco, artfully echoing the amphitheater's curve. Go down the steps to the amphitheater to see just how well preserved it is—you're free to wander through the access tunnels and along the seating rows. Sitting with your back to the sea, you might understand why Augustus favored Tarragona as a winter resort. In the center of the theater are the remains of two superimposed churches, the earlier of which was a Visigothic basilica built to mark the bloody martyrdom of St. Fructuós and his deacons in AD 259. 🎫 *500-pta. pass valid for all of Tarragona's Roman remains and Casa Castellarnau.* 🕓 *June–Sept., weekdays 9–8, weekends 9–3; Oct.–Mar., weekdays 10–1:30 and 3:30–5:30, weekends 10–2; Apr.–May, weekdays 10–1:30 and 3:30–6:30, weekends 9–3.*

Across the Rambla Vella from the amphitheater, students have excavated the vaults of the 1st-century Roman **Circus Maximus.** The plans just inside the gate show that the vaults now visible formed only a small corner of a vast arena (350 yards long), where 23,000 spectators gathered to watch chariot races. As medieval Tarragona grew, the city gradually swamped the Circus. *500-pta. pass valid for all of Tarragona's Roman remains and Casa Castellarnau. June–Sept., weekdays 9–8, weekends 9–3; Oct.–May, weekdays 10–1:30 and 4–6:30, weekends 10–2.*

Around the corner from the Circus Maximus, up Passeig Sant Antoni, is the former **Praetorium.** This towering building was Augustus's town house and is reputed to be the birthplace of Pontius Pilate. Its Gothic appearance is the result of extensive alterations in the Middle Ages, when it housed the kings of Catalonia and Aragon during their visits to Tarragona. The Praetorium is now the city's **Museu d'Història** (History Museum), with plans showing the evolution of the city. The museum's highlight is the **Hippolytus sarcophagus,** which bears a bas-relief depicting the legend of Hippolytus and Fraeda. *500-pta. pass valid for all of Tarragona's Roman remains and Casa Castellarnau. June–Sept., weekdays 9–8, weekends 9–3; Oct.–May, weekdays 10–1:30 and 4–6:30, weekends 10–2.*

Next door to the History Museum, in a 1960s neoclassical building, ★ is Tarragona's **Museu Arqueològic,** whose collection includes Roman statuary and such domestic fittings as keys, bells, and belt buckles. The beautiful mosaics include the Head of Medusa, famous for its piercing stare. Don't miss the video on Tarragona's history. *350 ptas.; free Tues. June–Sept., Tues.–Sat. 10:30–2 and 4–7, Sun. 10–2; Oct.–May, Tues.–Sat. 10–1:30 and 4–7, Sun. 10–2.*

Follow Passeig de Sant Antoni uphill from the museum (with the city walls on your left) to the ornately sculpted **Portal de Sant Antoni,** and enter the cobbled square. Walk down Carrer d'en Granada—past some lovely arched entryways—to Carrer Sant Bernat, where a right turn will take you into **Plaça del Forum,** once the seat of the provincial Roman authorities. At the far corner of the square you'll see signs for the **cathedral**; walk down Carrer de la Merceria and under the arcade on the right and you'll soon reach the stairway leading up into the **Pla de la Seu,** the cathedral square. The initial rounded placidity of the Romanesque apse, begun in the 12th century, later gave way to the spiky restlessness of the Gothic; the result is confused. If no mass is in progress, enter the cathedral through the cloister. The main attraction here is the altarpiece of St. Tecla, a richly detailed depiction of the life of Tarragona's patron saint. Converted by St. Paul and subsequently persecuted by local pagans, St. Tecla was repeatedly saved from demise through divine intervention. *300 ptas. Daily 10–1 and 4–7 (10–7 in summer).*

As you continue down the steps from the cathedral into Carrer Major, Carrer Cavallers is the second street on the right. Before turning here, continue down to the Plaça del Font for a look at the 19th-century neoclassical ***ajuntament*** (town hall) at the far end.

Back up Carrer Major toward the cathedral, Carrer Cavallers will take you down to the **Casa Castellarnau,** a Gothic *palacete,* or town house, built by Tarragona nobility in the 18th century. Now a museum, it features stunning decor from the 18th and 19th centuries. The last member of the Castellarnau family vacated the house in 1954. *500-pta. pass valid for all Roman remains and Casa Castellarnau. Mon.–Sat. 10–1 and 4–7 (9–8 in summer), Sun. 10–2.*

At the end of Carrer Cavallers is the Plaça Pallol—**Les Voltes,** on the right, a Roman forum with a Gothic upper story added later, is one of the prettiest corners in Tarragona. Through the **Portal del Roser,** to the right, is the entrance to the **Passeig Arqueològic,** a path skirting the 3rd-century BC Ibero-Roman ramparts, built on even earlier walls of giant rocks. The glacis was added by English military engineers in 1707, during the War of the Spanish Succession. Look for the rusted bronze of Romulus and Remus.

Next to the Portal del Roser you can catch Bus 2 to the **Serallo fishing quarter,** where boats form a hive of activity as they unload their catch at the quayside. Sneak a look inside the market, where fish are swiftly auctioned off to fishmongers and restaurateurs. Near the fish market, on the Passeig de la Independencia (also served by Bus 2), is the **Necròpolis i Museu Paleocristià** (Tomb and Paleochristian Museum). Both Christian and pagan tombs have been unearthed here. *Free with ticket to Museu Arqueològic (350 ptas.); free Tues. June–Sept., Tues.–Sat. 10:30–2 and 4–7, Sun. 10–2; Oct.–May, Tues.–Sat. 10–1:30 and 3–5:30, Sun. 10–2.*

Dining and Lodging

$$$ ✕ **Les Coques.** If you have time for only one meal in Tarragona, take it at this elegant little restaurant in the heart of historic Tarragona. The menu is bursting with both mountain and Mediterranean fare. Meat lovers should try the *costillas de cordero* (lamb chops in a dark burgundy sauce); seafood fans should ask for *calamarsets* (baby calamari sauteed in olive oil, garlic, and secret seasonings). Reservations are recommended. ✉ *Bajada Nueva del Patriarca 2 bis,* ☎ *977/228300. AE, DC, MC, V. Closed Sun. and July.*

$$ ✕ **La Puda.** La Puda's quayside location, opposite the fish auction house, guarantees you fresh seafood. The restaurant is popular with locals, but the menu appears in several languages. The simple decor includes a tile floor, salmon-colored walls, and white tablecloths. ✉ *Muelle Pescadores 25,* ☎ *977/211511. AE, DC, MC, V. No dinner Sun. Oct.–Mar.*

$$ ★ ✕ **Les Voltes.** Built into the vaults of the Roman Circus Maximus, this out-of-the-way spot is certain to please hungry travelers lucky enough to discover it. The hearty cuisine includes Tarragona specialties, mainly fish dishes, as well as international recipes, with *calçotada* (spring onions) in winter. ✉ *Carrer Trinquet Vell 12,* ☎ *977/230651. DC, MC, V. Closed July–Aug. No dinner Sun., no lunch Mon.*

$$$ **Imperial Tarraco.** This large, white, half-moon hotel has a superb position overlooking the Mediterranean. The large public rooms have cool marble floors, black-leather furniture, marble-top tables, and Oriental rugs. Guest rooms are plain but comfortable, and each has a private balcony. Insist on a sea view. ✉ *Passeig Palmeres, 43003,* ☎ *977/233040,* FAX *977/216566. 170 rooms. Restaurant, bar, pool, beauty salon, tennis court, meeting rooms. AE, DC, MC, V.*

$$ **Lauria.** This is the most pleasant place to stay in downtown Tarragona. Guest rooms are spacious and comfortable, and their terraces overlook the serene pool and patio area, the Rambla Nova, or the sea. ✉ *Rambla Nova 20, 43004 Tarragona,* ☎ *977/236712,* FAX *977/236700. 72 rooms. Bar, breakfast room. AE, DC, MC, V.*

$ **España.** This modern town house offers comfort at a good price. Guest rooms have white walls, shiny tile floors, and functional 1970s furniture. Each exterior room has a balcony overlooking the Rambla. ✉ *Rambla Nova 49, 43003 Tarragona,* ☎ *977/232712. 40 rooms. Breakfast room. AE, DC, MC, V.*

Nightlife and the Arts

Nightlife in Tarragona takes two forms: older and quieter in the upper city, younger and more raucous down below. There are some lovely, rustic bars in the Casco Viejo, the upper section of old Tarragona. **Poetes** (✉ Sant Llorenç 15), near the cathedral, is a *bar musical* (bar with loud music, usually rock or blues) set in a bodega-like cellar. Quieter talking-and-tippling spots include **El Càndil,** in the Plaza del Forum, and **Museum.** There's another row of dining and dancing establishments down in the new Puerto Deportivo, a newly built pleasure-boat harbor separate from the working port; young people flock here on weekends and summer nights.

The **Teatro Metropol** (✉ Rambla Nova 46, ☎ 977/244795) is Tarragona's center for music, dance, theater, and a variety of cultural events ranging from *castellers* (human-castle formations) to folk dances.

Shopping

You have to haggle for bargains, but **Carrer Major** has some exciting antiques stores. They're worth a thorough rummage, as the gems tend to be hidden away. You can also try the shops just in front of the cathedral and in the Pla de la Seu; **Antigüedades Ciria** (✉ Pla de la Seu 2) has an interesting selection.

SOUTH TO THE MAESTRAZGO

Reus, Salou, Cambrils, Delta de l'Ebre, Tortosa, Gandesa, Alcañiz, Morella, Ares del Maestre, and San Mateu

This chaotic enumeration runs the gamut from the ridiculous, such as the Port Aventura theme park, to the sublime, in the extraordinary natural resources from the Ebro Delta and the Ebro River itself to the Sierra de Beceite and mountain villages such as Morella. This wildly varied route takes you from below sea level (in parts of the delta) to high stone villages in the hills; from wetlands to the arid hinterlands of Tarragona.

Reus

❷ *13 km (8 mi) northwest of Tarragona.*

Reus is an industrial town with the distinction of having been the birthplace of Antoni Gaudí, as well as the longtime home of his fellow Moderniste architect Lluís Domènech i Montaner. If you're into Moderniste architecture, Domènech's **Casa Navàs** is well worth the short detour. Following signs to the center of town, you'll arrive in the Plaça del Mercadal; the Casa Navàs is beside the *ajuntament*. The rich interior decoration includes mosaics, stained glass, tiles with characteristic Moderniste floral motifs, and oddly shaped leather chairs. There are no formal visiting hours, but if you knock on the door at a reasonable time (roughly 9–1 and 4–7), the caretaker will usually let you in. ✉ *San Juan 27,* ☎ *977/345943.* *Free.*

Nightlife and the Arts

The **Teatre Fortuny** (✉ Plaça Prim 4, ☎ 977/318307) is the region's primary theater and opera showcase.

Salou

❸ *11 km (7 mi) south of Reus.*

If you're starting to crave a sunny afternoon at one of the area's finest beaches, you may want to stop in Salou, a modern resort town with a long esplanade of young palms. The town itself is long on glitz and short on culture or aesthetic charm, but history buffs will want to note that the conquerors of Majorca set out from the old port here in 1229.

On the edge of Salou is the macro–theme park **Port Aventura** (✉ Autovéia Salou/Vila-Seca, Km 2, Apartat 90/43480 Vila-Seca, Tarragona, ☎ 902/202220 or 977/779000), which opened in 1995. It boldly offers "the adventure of your life" to anyone brave enough to shell out 6,000 ptas. per person (4,500 per child under 12) for rides, water slides, steam engines, and boat rides through Mexico, China, Polynesia, the American West, and the Mediterranean.

Cambrils

4 *7 km (4½ mi) west of Salou, 18 km (11 mi) southwest of Tarragona.*

Cambrils, another coastal town, is a target for gourmets, who come to dine in Fanny Gatell's restaurant (☞ *below*). Less built-up than Salou, the town also has a pretty marina.

Dining

$$$ ★ ✕ **Casa Gatell.** Fanny Gatell and her sister used to run two renowned restaurants side by side; Fanny now carries on the tradition of exquisite local meals by herself. Try the *fideos negros amb sepionets* (paella in baby-squid ink) or *lubina al horno con cebolla y patata* (roast sea bass with onion and potato). ✉ *Miramar 27,* ☎ *977/360057. AE, DC, MC, V. Closed Mon., Oct., Dec. 20–Jan. 30, and Wed. in winter. No dinner Sun.*

Delta de l'Ebre

5 *77 km (48 mi) southwest of Tarragona, 60 km (37 mi) south of Cambrils.*

The Ebro Delta, a flat piece of wetland à la the Netherlands, juts into and embraces the Mediterranean. The **Parc Natural del Delta de l'Ebre** (Ebro Delta Natural Park) is a major stopping and breeding place for more than 200,000 birds of more than 300 species. An impressive 60% of Europe's bird species can be found here at some time during the year. To get to the park, take N230 and follow signs to Sant Jaume d'Enveja; at Sant Jaume, take a ferry to the town of Deltebre. The Park Information Office (✉ Plaça 20 de Maig, ☎ 977/489679) can tell you how to visit the reserve proper, which occupies the delta's northern, eastern, and southern tips, and give you the required permit.

Dining and Lodging

$ ✕ **L' Estany (Casa de la Fusta).** Smack in the middle of the wetlands and rice paddies, next door to the Casa de la Fusta museum, this restaurant is both a culinary treat and a cultural experience. Chef-owner Luis Garcia is committed to both quality and originality in his food—all based on fish and game caught just off the doorstep—and to the cultural heritage of the area. He lives up to his claim to serve not just meals but "Gastronomy, Culture, and Tradition." ✉ *Partida La Encanyissada s/n (en route from Amposta to Sant Jaume),* ☎ *977/261026. MC, V. Closed Mon. Nov.–Mar.*

$ 🏨 **Molí de Rosquilles.** Once an olive-oil mill, this old stone building is now a charming and cozy hotel. It almost doubles as a monument to the area and its traditions, conserving all of its original architecture and furnishings. A library full of books about the region invites you to delve into the history, geography, and ecology of the Ebro Delta. Food is served for guests only; don't miss the excellent bread, cooked in a wood-burning oven. ✉ *C. Catalunya 6, 43780 Deltebre,* ☎ *977/718052 or 629/358929. 8 rooms. Restaurant, library. MC, V.*

Tortosa

6 *80 km (50 mi) southwest of Tarragona.*

The ancient town of Tortosa, straddling the Ebro River 10 km (6 mi) inland, was successively Roman, Visigothic, Moorish, and Christian. The parador here, set in the ruined hilltop castle of **La Zuda,** is worth visiting even if you don't stay the night; keep to the left bank of the river and follow the signs. Originally a Templar fortress, the castle (and town) passed, around 713, into the hands of the Moors, who kept it until its reconquest by Ramón Berenguer IV, count of Barcelona, in 1153. Moors, Christians, and Jews then lived peacefully together in the town for more than 300 years. From the castle walls, there are sweeping views across the fertile Ebro Valley to the Sierra de Beceite.

Tortosa was the scene of one of the Spanish Civil War's bloodiest battles. The Republicans, loyal to the democratically elected government and already in control of Catalonia, crossed the Ebro here in July 1936 to attack the rebel Nationalists' rear guard. They got no farther than Tortosa, however, and were pinned down in trenches until they were forced to retreat with the loss of 150,000 lives. A conspicuously Nationalist monument rises from the Ebro to commemorate the victory of Franco's forces.

Look for the **cathedral** and follow the warren of streets in its direction. On the way, visit the Renaissance **Colegio Sant Lluís,** which has a pretty arcaded patio, embellished with a frieze depicting the kings of Aragon. The cathedral's main facade is Baroque, but if you enter through the cloister you'll see that the facade hides a purely Gothic design. It was common in 18th-century Spain to tack these exuberant stuccos onto Gothic structures; the style is called Churrigueresque, after its first practitioner, José Churriguera. ⏲ *Cloister daily; cathedral for mass only.*

Dining and Lodging

$$ ✕ **San Carlos.** Joan Ros, chef and proprietor of this small restaurant on the northern edge of the old town, excels in seafood and freshwater fish from the Ebro Delta. *Almejas* (marinated clams) are a specialty. ✉ *Rambla Felip Pedrell 13,* ☎ *977/441048. AE, DC, MC, V.*

$$$ ★ **Parador Castillo de la Zuda.** Few sights around here can equal the superb view from this old Arab castle across the Ebro Valley to the Sierra de Beceite. Dark shades of mahogany and copious tapestries evoke the past. The bedrooms have heavy wood furniture, terra-cotta floors, rugs, and plain walls. ✉ *Parador Castillo de la Zuda, 43500 Tortosa, Tarragona,* ☎ *977/444450,* FAX *977/444458. 72 rooms. Restaurant, bar, pool, playground, meeting rooms, free parking. AE, DC, MC, V.*

Gandesa

7 *86 km (53 mi) northwest of Amposta, 87 km (54 mi) west of Tarragona.*

Renowned for its strong wine (up to 16% alcohol), Gandesa also contains two architectural landmarks. Out on the road to Mora is the extraordinary **Cooperativa Agrícola** (Wine Cooperative), designed by the Moderniste architect Cèsar Martinell in 1919. Its white, Islamic-looking facade does little to prepare you for the remarkable vaulting inside, constructed entirely of small bricks ingeniously arranged to allow for expansion and contraction. This is a working building (it's open weekdays 9–2 and 4–8), and you can buy some local wine here for a sleepy picnic on the way to Alcañiz or Beceite. You can also visit the parish church in the center of town, **L'Assumpció** (open daily), where the geometric patterns on the otherwise Romanesque doorway are attributed to Moorish influence.

Dining and Lodging

$ ✕ **Hostal Piqué.** Though uninviting from the outside, this modern roadhouse has a large, smart dining room with pristine white tablecloths, a tile floor, and highly professional service. The restaurant menu ranges from everyday local options to more expensive rarities. Rooms are inexpensive and comfortable. ✉ *Via Catalunya 68, 43780,* ☎ *977/420068,* FAX *977/420329. 48 rooms. Restaurant. MC, V.*

Sierra de Beceite

❽ *15 km (9 mi) west of Gandesa on N420.*

The mountains of the Sierra de Beceite offer a beautiful excursion as you leave Gandesa, as long as you (and your car) can handle some bumpy roads. Just after you enter the Aragonese province of Teruel, you'll come to **Calaceite** on your right; explore its ancient, labyrinthine streets, which assemble at the arcaded Plaza Porticada. For a closer inspection of the Beceite massif, turn left at the Calaceite crossroads and drive along TE301. Turn right after 18 km (11 mi) at a T junction to reach **Valderrobres,** with a fortified palace and a Renaissance town hall that served as the model for Barcelona's Poble Espanyol. Continue to the town of **Beceite** and follow signs to a *panorama* for a bumpy drive culminating in an impressive vista. Depending on the condition of these forest roads, you can drive all the way to **Fredes,** due south of Beceite. The kings of Catalonia, Aragon, and Valencia are said to have met near here, on the Tossal dels Tres Reis (4,450 ft), to iron out disputes. The best way to explore these hills is either on foot or on horseback; a sign on the way into Beceite points you toward the tourist office, which has trail maps and can arrange horseback rides. From Valderrobres, you can cut back to the Alcañiz road via TE300, which follows the River Matarraña.

Alcañiz

❾ *62 km (38 mi) west of Gandesa, 74 km (46 mi) north of Morella.*

Alcañiz lies on a plain, encircled by the River Guadalope and surrounded by ugly, modern apartment blocks, the result of a recent population explosion following the success of the nearby olive and almond orchards. The highway (N420) enters the town along a street that bustles with new construction. For the old town, turn left at the end of this street to the Plaza Mayor. On the right is the **Lonja** (Exchange), with pointed arches defining its Gothic origin; adjoining it on the corner is the Renaissance **ayuntamiento** (town hall). The galleries and overhanging eaves on both of these buildings mark them as Aragonese. The **Collegiata** church, with its rhythmic Baroque facade, looms over the plaza; its ornate portal is very impressive, but the painted interior is disappointing. Climb to the **hilltop castle,** seat of the Calatrava Knights in the 14th century and now a tiny parador.

Dining and Lodging

$$$ ★ ✕🏨 **Parador de la Concordia.** Installed in the sturdy castle of the Calatrava Knights, this hotel grandly surveys the olive-growing plain and the foothills of the Maestrazgo. Guest rooms have terra-cotta tile floors, patterned rugs, dark furniture, generous beds, and good views framed by shutters. The restaurant serves Aragonese specialties, such as *cordero chilindrón* (lamb in a sauce of tomato, garlic, and pepper). ✉ *Castillo de Calatrava, 44600, Teruel,* ☎ *978/830400,* FAX *978/830366. 12 rooms. Restaurant, bar. AE, DC, MC, V. Closed Dec. 18–Feb. 1.*

Morella

★ ❿ *74 km (46 mi) south of Alcañiz, 64 km (40 mi) northwest of Benicarló.*

The walled town of Morella stands on a towering crag in Castellón, the northernmost Valencian province. It's not immediately evident if you approach from the north, but from the south and east the land drops away sharply, creating a natural fortress—the scene of several bloody battles. Before you reach the town walls, you'll pass a well-preserved 14th-century aqueduct. The **castle,** Morella's most prominent feature, is accessible through the gate on the Plaza de San Francisco, on the uppermost of the town's contoured streets. Just inside the gate is the ruined cloister of an old Franciscan monastery. The walk up to the castle takes a good 15 minutes, and high winds often contribute to its air of impregnability. In 1088 El Cid scaled these walls and wrought havoc among the occupying Moors. During the Carlist Wars of the 16th century, the castle became a stronghold for General Cabrera, who captured Morella in 1838 for Don Carlos, pretender to the Spanish throne. *300 ptas. Oct.–Mar., daily 10:30–6:30; Apr.–Sept., daily 10:30–7:30.*

The blue-tiled dome on the beautiful church of **Santa María la Mayor,** near the castle on Calle Hospital, lends an exotic note to this otherwise Gothic structure. The larger of the church's two doorways, depicting the Apostles, dates from the 14th century. A spiral marble staircase leads to the raised, flat-vaulted choir. The sanctuary got the full Baroque treatment, as did the high altar, which would glisten were it not for the gloomy lighting. The **museum** has a painting by Francisco Ribalta and some 15th-century Gothic panels. *Free. June–Sept., daily 11–2 and 4–7; Oct.–May, daily noon–2 and 4–6.*

Walk down the stepped Calle Cuesta de Prades to the arcaded **Calle Don Blasco de Alagón,** Morella's main thoroughfare. The numerous bars here are packed on weekends. Turn right and you'll soon arrive at the old mansion of **Cardinal Ram,** now a hotel; continuing uphill brings you into the pretty **Plaza de los Estudios,** whose white houses are distinguished by attractive wooden balconies.

Dining and Lodging

$ ★ ✕ **Mesón del Pastor.** Set in a restored 14th-century stone mansion on a side street off Calle Don Blasco de Alagón, this rustic *mesón* combines a family atmosphere with excellent cooking. Chef José Ferrer specializes in Maestrazgan dishes; try the *conejo relleno trufado* (rabbit and truffles enveloped in ham) or the many dishes featuring wild and farmed mushrooms in a variety of sauces. Desserts, too, are homespun; try the *buñuelos con miel* (fried dumplings with honey) or *mousse de acerolas* (mousse with wild fruits). If need be, you can retire directly to a guest room in the attached 12-room inn. ✉ *Cuesta Jovaní 5 and 7,* ☎ *964/160249. MC, V. Closed Wed. No dinner weekdays.*

$$ ★ ✕ **Cardenal Ram.** Installed in one of Morella's most handsome mansions, originally the 14th-century ancestral home of the famous Spanish prelate Cardinal Ram, this hotel oozes history from its bare, stone walls and ubiquitous coats of arms. The tall lobby has a huge tapestry depicting the 1414 visit of Antipope Papa Luna, named Pope Benedict XII during the Great Schism of 1378–1417. (Cardinal Ram was named by the Antipope, whom he then served.) The guest rooms, all different, have pine floors, bare white walls, high beamed ceilings, and magnificent, heavy furniture. The wide beds are covered with Morellan striped bedspreads. ✉ *Cuesta Suñer 1, 12300, Castellón,* ☎ *964/173085,* FAX *964/173218. 19 rooms. Restaurant. MC, V.*

$ **Hostal La Muralla.** This hostelry is nothing special, but it's comfortable and clean, and it sits right on the street that delineates Morella's city walls. A small living and dining area offers relaxation and breakfast. ✉ *Muralla 12, 12300 Morella, Castellón,* ☎ *964/160243. 20 rooms. Cafeteria. MC, V.*

Shopping

The Maestrazgo region produces brightly colored textiles of woven wool. The best buys are the striped *mantas morellanas* (Morellan bedspreads), available in abundance along Morella's Calles Blasco de Alagón and Hospital.

Ares del Maestre

⓫ *50 km (31 mi) southwest of Morella on N232, new road to Villafranca del Cid, and CS802 toward Albocácer.*

Ares del Maestre occupies the most dramatic site of any village in this area. Like Morella, it rests on a crag, but here the drop is more severe and the vistas more rewarding. A very steep climb—windy in winter and scorching in summer—takes you to a ruined **castle.**

OFF THE BEATEN PATH

TERUEL – You may want to make the trip (about 110 km [68 mi]) from Ares del Maestre to Teruel to see the town's famous Mudéjar architecture. Backtrack on CS802 toward Morella. At Villafranca del Cid get on TE811, which will take you to Teruel via the small towns of La Iglesuela, Mosqueruela, Linares de Mora, Rubielos de Mora, and Mora de Rubielos. Once in Teruel, visit the **Mudéjar towers**, built between the 12th and 16th centuries in a style more reminiscent of Muslim minarets than Christian belfries. They were once part of Teruel's city walls. The highlight in the **cathedral** is the coffered ceiling with 13th-century court and hunting scenes, visible from the upper gallery. You can spend the night in one of the spacious rooms of the rustic **Parador de Teruel** (✉ Apdo. 67, ☎ 978/601800) and sample local fare in the parador's restaurant.

San Mateu

⓬ *26 km (16 mi) west of Benicarló; take CS802 southeast from Ares del Maestre to Albocácer, then turn left.*

The small town of San Mateu proudly bears the subtitle Capital del Maestrazgo because it was from here that King Jaume I set out on his decisive reconquering raids in the 13th century, freeing the region finally from Moorish control. Sturdy Gothic mansions near the Plaza Mayor attest to San Mateu's regal past. Visit the Archpriest's Church on the corner of the plaza—its nave is a fine example of the Catalan Gothic style, and the vault covers a wide expanse, dispensing with the need for columns.

The coast beckons once more. From here, the nearest coastal town is Benicarló, via Cervera del Maestre and Cálig.

THE COSTA DEL AZAHAR

Benicarló, Peñíscola, and Sagunto

Named for the orange blossom and its all-pervading fragrance along this sweet coastal plain, the Costa del Azahar was hit hard by the tourist-inspired building boom of the 1960s and '70s. Phoenician (Syrian) trading ships plied these ports some 2,000 years ago, and it is thought that the Phoenicians, patrolling this stretch of coast and gazing uneasily at the menacing backdrop of mountains, gave the country its name—Spagna, or "hidden land." Benicarló and Peñíscola are, with Vinarós, the northernmost towns on the Costa del Azahar (province: Castellón de la Plana), while Sangunto marks the start of the Costa de Valencia.

Benicarló

⓭ *55 km (34 mi) south of Tortosa.*

The village of Benicarló has become an important tourist center. The harbor is a lively confusion of fishing and pleasure craft, and the beaches are well stocked with local and northern European sun-seekers most of the year.

Dining and Lodging

$$–$$$ ✕ **Casa Pocho.** Casa Pocho is named after its owner: Paco Puchal is also known as "El Pocho," or "the Tubby One." Wood paneling and maritime motifs set the scene for the restaurant's famously good seafood. *Langostinos* (prawns) are the best choice. ✉ *San Gregorio 49, Vinaròs,* ☎ *964/451095. AE, DC, MC, V. Closed Mon. No dinner Sun.*

$$$ ✕🏨 **Parador de la Costa del Azahar.** The main attraction of this modern parador, 6½ km (4 mi) north of Peñíscola, is its large, semiformal garden, which runs down to the sea—a perfect place to rest up in peace and quiet, away from the most crowded beaches. The decor doesn't match that of the parador's more atmospheric cousins, but the public rooms are huge, bright, and tasteful, with white-wicker furniture and white walls. Guest rooms have shiny tile floors, white walls, and functional furniture; ask for a sea view. Travelers with disabilities are well accommodated here. ✉ *Avda. Papa Luna 5, 12580, Castellón,* ☎ *964/470100,* FAX *964/470934. 108 rooms. Restaurant, bar, pool, tennis court. AE, DC, MC, V.*

Peñíscola

14 *7 km (4½ mi) south of Benicarló, 60 km (37 mi) northeast of Benicàssim.*

Peñíscola owes its foundation to the Phoenicians. It later became the bridgehead by which the Carthaginian Hamilcar (father of Hannibal) imported his elephants and munitions to wage the first of the three Punic Wars. Carthaginian influence in the peninsula reached its zenith some 20 years later, in 230 BC, but it was eroded by Rome's success in the subsequent campaigns.

★ The **old town** is a cluster of white houses and tiny, narrow streets leading up to the castle, whose setting on a promontory affords perfect surveillance of the coast. You can drive up to the **castle,** but in summer the traffic makes it smarter to leave your car by the town walls and walk. Of chief interest are the chapel and study of the antipope Papa Luna, to whom the 14th-century castle passed in the 15th century. Hardly any of Papa Luna's effects remain, but while you're in his drafty quarters, try to imagine this 90-year-old Frenchman (formerly Pope Benedict XIII) passing the last six years of his life attending mass and composing schismatic bulls, surrounded all the while by hostile Moorish townsfolk. *500 ptas.* ⏲ *Apr.–Sept., daily 10–8:30; Oct.–Mar., daily 10–1 and 3:15–5:30.*

Lodging

$$–$$$ 🏨 **Hostería del Mar.** Officially a "semi-parador," this modern, white hotel next to Peñíscola's long beach meets the paradors' high standards. Most rooms have balconies overlooking the old town. The rustic, beamed public rooms surround a leafy pool terrace; guest rooms have white walls, striped bedspreads, tile floors, and Castilian-style dark wood and leather furniture. ✉ *Avda. Papa Luna 18, 12598 Peñíscola, Castellón,* ☎ *964/480600,* FAX *964/481363. 86 rooms. Restaurant, bar, pool, tennis court. AE, DC, MC, V.*

Between Peñíscola and Sagunto

Alcalá de Chivert is 49 km (30 mi) north of Castellón de la Plana.

The route passes through carob and orange plantations on your way down the Costa del Azahar from Peñíscola to Sagunto. The *autopista* is the fastest road south, but the N340 shares the same scenery and grants easier access to places en route. **Alcalá de Chivert** can claim the tallest belfry in the Valencian provinces. The road here is separated from the sea by the **Sierra de Hirta,** whose rugged outlines contain some ruined castles easily visible from the road. Next down the coast is **Alcocéber,** an expanding but still quiet holiday town with two good beaches. **Benicàssim** (Exit 45 from the *autopista*; coast road from N340) is appealing for the dramatic shapes in its mountainous background, as well as its long, sandy bathing beach and nocturnal action. **Castellón de la Plana,** the provincial capital, has little to warrant the struggle through its suburbs unless you're a fan of the Spanish Baroque painter Zurbarán, 10 of whose works hang in the Convento de las Religiosas Capuchinas on Calle Nuñez de Arce (open for services).

Dining and Lodging

$$ ✕ **Villa del Mar.** This old, country manor house with a verdant dining terrace surrounded by palms and pines makes an elegant and secluded setting. Inside, the decor is modern and the cuisine international as well as regional; try the *arroces valencianos* (Valencian rice dishes). On summer evenings a barbecue is held in the garden. ✉ *Paseo Marítimo Pilar Coloma 24, Benicàssim,* ☎ *964/302852. AE, MC, V. Closed early Nov.–mid-Dec.*

$$$ **Orange.** If it's facilities you're after, look no further: this huge, modern, chalet-style hotel has the widest range in town. It's centrally located, 150 yards from the beach, and surrounded by a garden and trees. Loud patterns in browns and oranges set the tone in the public rooms, and the plain guest rooms are no more than functional. Ask for a sea view; rooms over the pool can be noisy. ✉ *Avda. Gimeno Tomás s/n, 12560 Benicàssim, Castellón,* ☎ *964/394400,* FAX *964/301541. 415 rooms. Restaurant, bar, cafeteria, 2 pools, beauty salon, miniature golf, tennis court, dance club. AE, DC, MC, V. Closed mid-Nov.–mid-Feb.*

$$ **Voramar.** Right on the beach at the north end of Benicàssim, this small, white hotel—the closest thing in town to an old-fashioned resort—is encircled by classical balconies. The decor is rather plain and functional, with tile floors, white walls, and 1970s furniture. Ask for a room overlooking the sea; each has a generous balcony. ✉ *Paseo Pilar Coloma 1, 12560 Benicàssim, Castellón,* ☎ *964/300150,* FAX *964/300526. 55 rooms. Restaurant, tennis court. AE, DC, MC, V. Closed mid-Oct.–Easter.*

Nightlife and the Arts

The top club in Benicàssim is **K'asim,** on Avinguda Gimeno Tomás. Things only really heat up during summer and Holy Week; at other times the atmosphere is decidedly tame.

Sagunto

15 *65 km (40 mi) southwest of Benicàssim, 23 km (14 mi) northeast of Valencia.*

Sagunto will ring a bell if you've read Caesar's history: Saguntum, as the Romans called it, was the sparking point for the Second Punic War. When Hannibal laid siege to the town (at that time a port, from which the sea has since receded), the people heroically held out, faithfully expecting a Roman relief force, and eventually burned the town rather than surrender to the Carthaginians.

Rambling Moorish fortifications dominate the town from the hilltops, and within this citadel earlier **Roman remains** are now being excavated. On the way up, visit the well-restored **amphitheater** (signposted from the town center). More complete than Tarragona's, it went up during the Roman rebuilding five years after Hannibal's siege. Some archaeological finds from this time are displayed in a fascinating museum just opposite the amphitheater. *Amphitheater and museum 400 ptas.* ⏲ *Tues.–Sat. 10–2 and 4–6, Sun. 10–2.*

Nightlife and the Arts

The first two weeks of August bring **Sagunto a Escena,** a festival of classical Mediterranean drama for which Spanish and international theater groups perform a variety of ancient plays in the authentic setting of Sagunto's Roman amphitheater. Contact the tourist office for information (✉ Plaza Cronista Chabret, ☎ 96/266–2213).

VALENCIA

Spain's third-largest city and the capital of the Levante, Valencia is nearly equidistant from Barcelona and Madrid, the nation's two metropolitan giants. Despite its proximity to the Mediterranean, Valencia's history and geography have been defined most significantly by the River Turia and the fertile flood plain, or *huerta,* that surrounds it. The city has been fiercely contested ever since it was founded by the Greeks. El Cid captured Valencia from the Moors in 1094 and won his strangest victory here in 1099: his corpse was strapped to his saddle and so frightened the waiting Moors as to cause a complete rout. In 1102, his widow, Jimena, was forced to return the city to Moorish rule; Jaume I finally drove them out in 1238.

Modern Valencia was most famous for its flooding disasters until the River Turia was diverted to the south in the late 1950s. Since then the city's physical profile has been one of steady transition, with a special eye toward urban beautification. The lovely *puentes* (bridges) that once spanned the Turia look equally graceful spanning a wandering municipal park, and the spectacular new Ciudad de las Artes y de las Sciencias (City of Arts and Sciences), slated for completion in 2001, promises to form an exciting and dynamic architectural link between this river town and the Mediterranean at long last. Valencia is still in a different league from Barcelona and Madrid, lacking coherence and overwhelming charm, but it holds a city's worth of interesting sights and has a character all its own.

Central Valencia

23 km (14 mi) south of Sagunto, 351 km (218 mi) southeast of Madrid, 362 km (224 mi) south of Barcelona.

A Good Walk

Begin your stroll through Valencia's historical center at the **cathedral** ⑯, in the Plaza de la Reina; inside you can visit the museum and climb the Miguelete Tower for good views of the city. Next, cross the **Plaza de la Virgen** ⑰—on the left side of the plaza you'll see the Gothic **Palau de la Generalitat** ⑱, which you have to arrange to visit in advance. Continuing down Calle Caballeros, you'll pass Valencia's oldest church, **San Nicolás** ⑲. After spending some time inside, walk to the Plaza del Mercado and the 15th-century **Lonja de la Seda** ⑳. Opposite are the Iglesia de los Santos Juanes, whose interior was destroyed during the civil war, and the Mercado Central. Travel down Avenida María Cristina to the **Plaza del Ayuntamiento** ㉑, one of the city's liveliest areas and the home of the **ayuntamiento** ㉒ itself. After a five-minute walk down Avenida Marqués de Soto, you'll find the Moderniste **Estación** ㉓. Next to the train station is the **Plaza de Toros** ㉔. Back in the city center, go to Plaza Patriarca and enter the **Real Colegio del Patriarca** ㉕, with a nice Renaissance patio and a museum featuring works by El Greco, among others. Cross Calle Poeta Quirol to the wedding-cake facade of the **Palacio del Marqués de Dos Aguas** ㉖.

Leave Valencia's historical center and cross the riverbed by Puente de la Trinidad to No. 9, Calle San Pio V. Here is the **Museo de Bellas Artes** ㉗, one of Spain's best galleries, with masterpieces of Velázquez, José Ribera, and the Valencia-born Joaquín Sorolla. The **Jardines del Real** ㉘

Ayuntamiento . 22
Casa Museo José Benlliure . 30
Cathedral. . . 16
Estación 23
Jardines del Real. 28
Lonja de la Seda 20
Museo de Bellas Artes 27
Museo de las Sciencias. . . . 32
Palacio del Marqués de Dos Aguas (Ceramics Museum) . . . 26
Palau de la Generalitat . . 18
Palau de la Música. 31
Plaza del Ayuntamiento . 21
Plaza de la Virgen 17
Plaza de Toros 24
Real Colegio del Patriarca . . . 25
San Nicolás 19
Torre de Serranos . . . 29

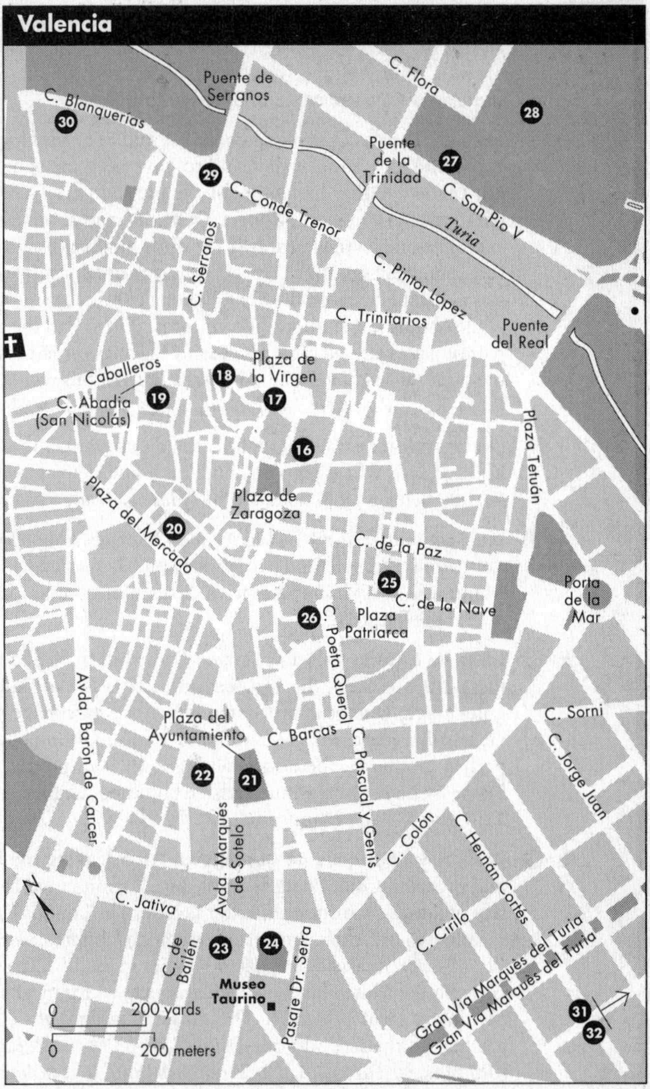

adjoin the museum. Walk up Calle San Pio V to the Puente de Serranos. At the other side of the riverbed is the **Torre de Serranos** ㉙, a gate that once served as the entrance to this Mediterranean city. On the right side is the **Casa Museo José Benlliure** ㉚, where you can admire works of this Valencian painter-sculptor. Finally, end your walk with a stroll south down the riverbed park to the modern **Palau de la Música** ㉛.

TIMING

Depending on how long you linger in museums, this walk should take about five hours.

Sights to See

㉒ **Ayuntamiento.** The municipal tourist office and a museum of the history of Valencia are the main reasons to find the town hall, just a five-minute walk south of the Lonja. *Free.* *Weekdays 9–2.*

⑯ **Cathedral.** Valencia's historic buildings cluster around the 14th-century cathedral in the Plaza de Zaragoza. The cathedral itself has three portals, respectively Romanesque, Gothic, and rococo, the last leading off the Plaza de Zaragoza. Inside, Renaissance and Baroque marble was removed in a successful restoration of the original Gothic style, as is now the trend in Spanish churches.

In a side chapel is a purple agate chalice said to be the Holy Grail (Christ's cup at the Last Supper) and said to have been brought to Spain in the 4th century. Other highlights of the museum are Goya's two famous paintings of St. Francis de Borja, Duke of Gandia, on display in the treasury. The one on the left shows the duke bidding his family farewell before joining St. Ignatius Loyola's newly formed Jesuit Society; the other shows Saint Francis on the right, fighting to save the soul of an impenitent while ghouls linger about like vultures. (Goya had the man naked; the painting was altered after his death.) The blood-red rays shooting from the saint's cross have inspired misreadings of this scene as an exorcism. *Free. Mar.–Oct., daily 10–1 and 4:30–7; Dec.–Feb., daily 10–1.*

Dominating the cathedral to the left of the entrance is the octagonal tower **El Miguelete,** which you can climb for a fine view: it is said that you can see 300 belfries from here. *100 ptas. Daily 10–1 and 4:30–7.*

23 **Estación** (train station). Down Avenida Marqués de Sotelo from the *ayuntamiento* is this splendid Moderniste pile. Designed by Demetrio Ribes Mano in 1917, it is replete with citrus motifs to let passengers know where they've arrived.

★ 20 **Lonja de la Seda** (Silk Exchange). Downhill from San Nicolás, on the Plaza del Mercado, the 15th-century Lonja is a product of Valencia's golden age, when the arts came under the patronage of Ferdinand I. Generally regarded as one of Spain's finest Gothic buildings, it has a perfect Gothic facade dotted with ghoulish gargoyles, complemented inside by high vaulting and twisted columns. *Free. Tues.–Fri. 9–1:30 and 5–9, weekends 9–1:30.*

★ 26 **Palacio del Marqués de Dos Aguas.** After leaving the Plaza Patriarca and crossing Calle Poeta Querol, you'll soon come face-to-face with this building's Baroque alabaster facade. The famous Churrigueresque facade around the corner centers on the figures of the *Dos Aguas* (*Two Waters*), carved by Ignacio Vergara in the 18th century. The palace contains the **Museo Nacional de Cerámica,** with a magnificent collection of mostly local ceramics. The museum's highlight is the Valencian kitchen on the second floor. *96/351–6392. Palace and museum 400 ptas. Tues.–Sat. 10–2 and 4–8, Sun. and holidays 10–2.*

18 **Palau de la Generalitat.** On the left side of the Plaza de la Virgen, fronted by orange trees and box hedges, is the elegant eastern facade of what was the Gothic home of the Valencia Cortes (Parliament), until it was suppressed by Felipe V for supporting the wrong (losing) side during the War of the Spanish Succession in the 18th century. The two *salones* (reception rooms) in the older of the two towers have superb woodwork on the ceilings. Call in advance for permission to enter. *96/386–3461. Weekdays 9–2.*

21 **Plaza del Ayuntamiento.** Down Avenida María Cristina from the market, this plaza is the hub of city life, a fact well conveyed by the massiveness of the Baroque facades. Nearby (opposite the Lonja de la Seda) stands the Iglesia de los Santos Juanes (Church of the Sts. John), whose interior was destroyed during the civil war, and, next door, the Moderniste Mercado Central (Central Market), built entirely of iron and glass.

17 **Plaza de la Virgen.** Leaving the cathedral by the Gothic Apostle Door brings you out into this pedestrian plaza, a lovely place for a refreshing *horchata* (tiger-nut milk) in the late afternoon. Next to its portal,

market gardeners from the *huerta* bring their irrigation disputes before the Water Tribunal, which has met every Thursday at noon since 1350. Verdicts are given on the spot, and sentences range from fines to deprivation of water.

24 **Plaza de Toros.** Adjacent to the train station stands the bullring, one of the oldest in Spain. The best bullfighters are featured on and around July 25 and during the Fallas in March. Just beyond, down Pasaje Dr. Serra, the **Museo Taurino** (Bullfighting Museum) is packed with bullfighting memorabilia, including bulls' heads and matadors' swords from Valencian bullfights. *Free. Weekdays 10:30–1:30.*

25 **Real Colegio del Patriarca** (Royal College of the Patriarch). Toward the center of town, near the university, is the Plaza Patriarca; this *colegio* is on the far side of the square. Founded by San Juan de Ribera in the 16th century, it has a lovely Renaissance patio and an ornate church, and its museum contains works by Juan de Juanes, Francisco Ribalta, and El Greco. The entrance is off Calle de la Nave. *100 ptas. Daily 11–1:30.*

19 **San Nicolás.** Down Calle Caballeros, the main artery of the old part of town (leading out of the Plaza de la Virgen), look for high door knockers—these could be reached without dismounting from one's horse. Turn left, down the tiny Calle Abadía San Nicolás (just after No. 41), to reach a small plaza containing Valencia's oldest church, once the parish of the Borgia Pope Calixtus III. The first portal you come to, with a tacked-on, rococo bas-relief of the Virgin Mary with cherubs, hints well at what's inside: every inch of the originally Gothic church is covered with Churrigueresque embellishments.

Outer Valencia

30 **Casa Museo José Benlliure.** After you cross the Puente de Serranos, turn right down Calle Blanquerías and stop at No. 23. The elegant house of this modern Valencian painter-sculptor contains many of his works. *Free. Tues.–Sat. 9:15–2 and 5:30–9, Sun. 9:30–2.*

28 **Jardines del Real** (Royal Gardens). These gardens, or *viveros* (nurseries), contain a pleasant park with fountains, rose gardens, tree-lined avenues, and a small zoo. *Free. Daily 8–dusk.*

★ 27 **Museo de Bellas Artes** (Museum of Fine Arts). Foremost among the sights outside the city center is Valencia's art museum, one of the best in Spain. To get here, cross the riverbed by Puente de la Trinidad to No. 9, Calle San Pio V. Valencia was a thriving center of artistic activity in the 15th century, and the museum features many of the best works by Jacomart and Juan Reixach—two of several painters known as the Valencian Primitives. Hieronymus Bosch, or El Bosco, as they call him here, is also represented. The first floor contains the murky, 17th-century Tenebrist masterpieces of Francisco Ribalta and his pupil José Ribera, together with a Velázquez self-portrait and a room devoted to Goya. Upstairs, look for Joaquín Sorolla (Gallery 66), the luminous Valencian painter of everyday Spanish life in the 19th century. *Free. Tues.–Sat. 10–2 and 4–6, Sun. 10–2.*

31 **Palau de la Música** (Concert Hall). Stroll south down the riverbed park to this modern hall. For concert schedules, check the *Turia* guide, available at newsstands. *Paseo de la Alameda 30, 96/337–5020.*

29 **Torre de Serranos.** Cross the Puente de Serranos to this 14th-century fortified gate, which guards the entrance to the old city.

32 **Museo de las Sciencias.** The new home of Valencia's **Museo de Paleontología** (Museum of Paleontology), the Science Museum rivals Europe's finest in content, annotation, and architectural design (the building is shaped like a whale). It's a key part of the ambitious new City of Arts and Sciences. ✉ *Arzobispo Mayoral 14-2,* ☎ *96/352–5507.* *500 ptas.*

Dining

$$$$ ✕ **Civera.** Run by the Civera brothers three blocks northwest of the Museum of Fine Arts, this restaurant enjoys local renown for its fresh fish and seafood, cooked *a la plancha* (grilled), *hervidos* (boiled), or *a la sal* (baked in salt). The decor is marine-inspired: white walls, beams, nautical motifs, and sumptuous displays of fish, fruit, and vegetables. ✉ *Lérida 11,* ☎ *96/347–5917. AE, DC, MC, V. Closed Mon., Easter wk, and Aug. No dinner Sun.*

$$$ ★ ✕ **El Timonel.** Decorated as the inside of a yacht, this central restaurant (two blocks east of the bullring) serves outstanding shellfish. The cooking is simple yet benefits from the freshest ingredients; try the *salmonetes* (whitebait) or *pescado de roca* (rockfish). Lunch attracts businesspeople, dinner a fashionable crowd. If you flash your Fodor's guide, the owner might take a special interest in you. ✉ *Félix Pizcueta 13,* ☎ *96/352–6300. AE, DC, MC, V. Closed Mon.*

$$$ ✕ **Eladio.** Some way out of town, this welcoming restaurant is decorated with oak and marble. The many Galician fish dishes are prepared with a mixture of tradition and invention by chef Eladio Rodríguez; try the *mero a la brasa* (charcoal-grilled grouper), and finish up with a mouthwatering Swiss pastry made by Eladio's wife, Violette. ✉ *Chiva 40,* ☎ *96/384–2244. AE, DC, MC, V. Closed Sun. and Aug.*

$$ ✕ **El Plat.** The local press has dubbed this restaurant "El Rey del Arroz" (the King of Paella), because it offers a different variation on Valencia's most celebrated dish every day of the week. The simple decor consists of white, alcoved walls adorned with local ceramics, but the lighting is rather bright. The atmosphere is relaxed, service is attentive, and the location is ideal should you feel like *marcha* (nightlife) after dinner. ✉ *Ciscar 3,* ☎ *96/374–1254. AE, MC, V. Closed Mon. No dinner Sun.*

$$ ★ ✕ **Gargantua.** The scene is a series of apricot-colored rooms crowded with pictures in a 1910 town house. The tone is intimate and chic. The excellent cooking is nouvelle and imaginative, the menu constantly changing. For a regional dish, try the *esgarrat* (grilled cod with green peppers). ✉ *Navarro Reverter 18,* ☎ *96/334–6849. DC, MC, V. Closed Sun., Easter wk, and Aug. No lunch Sat.*

$$ ✕ **La Riuà.** A local secret, this fine restaurant specializes in Valencian cuisine, served in a colorful setting splashed with ceramic tiles. Order a rice dish, fresh fish prepared with *all i pebre* (garlic and pepper), or *pulpitos guisados* (stewed baby octopus). Wash it all down with a cold bottle of *Llanos de Titaguas*, a dry yet snappy white Valencian table wine. ✉ *C. del Mar 27,* ☎ *96/391–4571. AE, DC, MC, V. Closed Mon., Easter wk, and Aug. No dinner Sun.*

$ ✕ **Patos.** Small, cozy, and very popular, this restored 18th-century town house, just north of Calle de la Paz in the old quarter, is a local favorite. Terra-cotta tiles, white tablecloths, wood-panel walls, and overhead beams lend it an earthy look, and you can dine outside in summer. The set menu (a real bargain at 1,500 ptas.) often includes *pato* (duck). Get here by 9:30 PM to be sure of a table. ✉ *C. del Mar 28,* ☎ *96/392–1522. DC, MC, V.*

Lodging

$$$ **Ad Hoc.** This small, beautifully designed 19th-century town house enjoys the finest location in Valencia, with immediate access to the old quarter and the Turia gardens. The hotel's owner, Luis García Alarcón, is an antiquarian, and the hotel reflects his eye for architectural elegance and ancient design. ✉ *Boix 4, 46003,* ☎ *96/391–9140,* FAX *96/391–3667. 28 rooms. Restaurant. AE, DC, MC, V.*

$$$$ ★ **Monte Picayo.** If you enjoy the proximity of a casino and don't mind looking at the sea from a distance, consider the Monte Picayo. Set into a hill and draped in greenery, its modern, tiered structure overlooks the *huerta* and offers a rare degree of luxury. The public areas and guest rooms are spacious and cheerful, and service is impeccable. Each room has a terrace, and nine have private pools. ✉ *Urbanización Monte Picayo, 46530 Valencia,* ☎ *96/142–0100,* FAX *96/142–2168. 83 rooms. Restaurant, 4 bars, 2 pools, beauty salon, miniature golf, 2 tennis courts, casino, dance club, free parking. AE, DC, MC, V.*

$$$$ **Sidi Saler.** This stretch of coastline just south of Valencia suffers from being in mid-development, but Sidi Saler's contemporary khaki facade surrounds an oasis of luxury. The guest rooms are modern, bright, and unremarkable; their achievement is to give you the impression that the beach belongs only to you. ✉ *Playa del Saler, 46012 Valencia,* ☎ *96/161–0411,* FAX *96/161–0838. 276 rooms. Restaurant, 2 bars, indoor and outdoor pools, beauty salon, massage, sauna. AE, DC, MC, V.*

$$$ **Meliá Plaza.** The doors of this beauty open onto the bustling Plaza del Ayuntamiento, in the heart of Valencia. You're a short walk from all major downtown sights and cultural activities. The hotel mixes old-world elegance with all the modern conveniences. ✉ *Plaza del Ayuntamiento 4, 46002,* ☎ *96/352–0612,* FAX *96/352–0426. 101 rooms. Restaurant, bar, sauna, exercise room. AE, DC, MC, V.*

$$$ **Parador de El Saler.** Definitely for golf enthusiasts, this modern parador 18 km (11 mi) south of Valencia has a famous course, with the first tee just outside the front door. The building has an exposed position on the edge of a pine forest, fronted by sand dunes. The bright and spacious reception rooms have cool marble floors, white walls, and baronial furniture; the guest rooms echo this style. Insist on a sea view. ✉ *El Saler, 46012 Valencia,* ☎ *96/161–1186,* FAX *96/162–7016. 58 rooms. Restaurant, bar, pool, sauna, 18-hole golf course, exercise room, soccer. AE, DC, MC, V.*

$$$ ★ **Reina Victoria.** The grande dame of Valencia's hotels is an excellent choice for centrality and time-worn charm. The spacious reception rooms have cool marble floors, with rugs to take the chill off; the smallish guest rooms are clothed in green chintz and deep-pile carpets with a subdued pattern. ✉ *Barcas 4, 46002,* ☎ *96/352–0487,* FAX *96/352–2721. 97 rooms. Restaurant, bar. AE, DC, MC, V.*

$$ ★ **Excelsior.** Set in a centrally located 1930s building, the Excelsior offers the best value in this price category. From the Art Deco restaurant-cum-bar, a spiral marble staircase leads to a dark, wood-paneled salon with a terrace. Guest rooms have olive-green carpets; the beds have brass headboards, and the white walls have old prints. The general vibe is very friendly. ✉ *Barcelonina 5, 46002,* ☎ *96/351–4612,* FAX *96/352–3478. 67 rooms. Restaurant, bar. AE, DC, MC, V.*

$$ **Meliá Confort Inglés.** Once the palace of the dukes of Cardona, this hotel is perfectly located for touring the old town. The rooms are plush and ultramodern; ask for one overlooking the alabaster doorway of the neighboring Marqués de Dos Aguas palace, with the brawny twin atlantes pouring water from two amphorae in illustration of the Marques's name. ✉ *Marqués de Dos Aguas 6, 46002,* ☎ *96/351–6426,* FAX *96/394–0251. 62 rooms. Restaurant, bar. AE, DC, MC, V.*

$ **Continental.** Filling two floors of a town house just off the Plaza del Ayuntamiento, this friendly establishment is an excellent value for the money if all you need is a clean and comfortable room. It has a small lounge and a breakfast room. ✉ *Correos 8, 46002,* ☎ *96/353–5282,* FAX *96/353–1113. 43 rooms. Breakfast room. AE, DC, MC, V.*

Nightlife and the Arts

Castellón and Valencia jointly publish *Que y Donde,* the major listings magazine; *Turia* covers Valencia only, featuring events, prices, and reviews.

The **Feria de Julio** is a month-long festival of theater, film, dance, and classical, jazz, and pop music. Contact the *ayuntamiento* (☎ 96/352–0694). If you're homesick, there's the **Instituto Shakespeare** (✉ Avda. Blasco Ibañez 28, ☎ 96/360–1950), with performances in English and Spanish.

Sleep seems to be anathema here. You can experience the nocturnal way of life at any time except summer, when Valencians disappear on vacation. Plaza Canovas del Castillo and the surrounding streets are the liveliest zone, followed closely by Plaza Xuquer, near the university. For a rougher brand of fun, head to the beach. Calle de Eugenia Viñes is lined with numerous loud clubs and bars; try **Casablanca** (✉ Eugenia Viñes 152, ☎ 96/371–3366) or the aptly named **Vivir Sin Dormir** (Living Without Sleeping) (✉ Paseo Neptuno 42, ☎ 96/372–7777).

For a more sophisticated club, try **Belle Epoque** (✉ Cuba 8, ☎ 96/380–2828) or **Xuquer Palace** (✉ Plaza Xuquer 8, ☎ 96/361–5811); for *sevillanas* (flamenco), try **Albahaca** (✉ Almirante Cadarso 30, ☎ 96/334–1484), **Triana** (✉ Grabador Esteve 11, ☎ 96/374–3001), or **Candela Canovas** (✉ Plaza Canovas del Castillo 6, ☎ 96/373–1882).

Shopping

Try **Salvador Ribes** (✉ Vilaragut 7) for top-quality antiques with correspondingly daunting price tags. For better deals, try the stores on Calle Avellanas near the cathedral. A local crafts market is held daily from 10 to 8 in Plaza Alfonso Magnánimo, at the bottom of Calle de la Paz, and a flea market is held every Sunday morning in the streets around the cathedral.

The town of **Manises,** 9 km (5½ mi) west of Valencia, is another center for Valencian ceramics, known particularly for its *azulejos.*

Side Trip: Albufera Nature Park

33 *10 km (6 mi) south of Valencia*

If you have time to venture out of downtown Valencia (or happen to be staying at the Sidi Soler resort or Parador de El Soler), make your way out to this beautiful wetland 10 km (6 mi) south of the city. A nesting site for more than 250 species of birds, and home to an extraordinary variety of autochthonous fish and marine species, the Parque Natural de la Albufera also has miles of beautiful walking trails. Admission is free. Visit the **Information and Learning Center** (✉ Carretera del Palmar, El Palmar, ☎ 96/162–7345) to learn more about this unusual ecosystem.

Dining

$$$ **La Matandeta.** With its white garden walls, this engaging restaurant appears from a distance to be a shining island in a sea of Valencian rice paddies. Thanks to the huge variety of local bird life—snowy egrets, gray herons—a lunchtime drive to La Matandeta can be almost as eye-opening as the culinary creations of its proprietor, Rafael Galvez. Delicious appetizers include *higado de rape con alcaparras y piñones* (monkfish liver in a caper and pine-nut vinaigrette) and *sardinas marinadas con emulsion de pimientos amarillos* (marinated sardines with a yellow-pepper puree). For the main course, dive into *arroz de conejo, pato, pollo y cara-*

coles—Valencian rice with rabbit, duck, chicken, and escargots. Choose a local white wine, such as the light, dry Cañada Mazan, from the extensive wine list, and don't forget to specify which of the 55 types of olive oil you'd like on your whole-wheat bread or salad. Finish with a slice of *pastelon de la abuela* (grandmother's sin cake) and head for the nearest siesta! ✉ *Carretera Alfafar, Km 4,* ☎ *96/211–2184. V. Closed Mon.*

SOUTHERN CATALONIA AND THE LEVANTE A TO Z

Arriving and Departing

By Boat

Trasmediterránea ferries (✉ Estación Marítima, ☎ 96/367–6512, FAX 96/367–0614) leave Valencia for Majorca and Ibiza Monday through Saturday. They shuttle from Tarragona daily in July and August only (☎ 977/225506).

By Bus

The connection between Barcelona and Tarragona is easy; nine buses leave Barcelona's Estación Vilanova-Norte every day. **Bacoma, S.A.** also dispatches buses from Tarragona (✉ Plaça Imperial Tarraco s/n, ☎ 977/222072). From Valencia, buses continue down the coast and on to Madrid. The **bus depot** (✉ Avda. Menendez Pidal 13, ☎ 96/349–7222) is across the river; take Bus 8 from the Plaza del Ayuntamiento.

By Car

The A7 *autopista* (motorway) provides excellent road access at both ends of this region. A car is extremely valuable, even necessary, if you want to explore the inland Maestrazgo mountains, where much of the driving is smooth, uncrowded, and scenic.

By Plane

The international airport closest to the northern end of this tour is in Barcelona (☞ Barcelona A to Z *in* Chapter 6), 100 km (62 mi) from Tarragona. **Valencia** has an international airport (☎ 96/159–8500) with direct flights to London, Paris, Brussels, Frankfurt, and Milan; it is 8 km (5 mi) west of the city center and is best reached by taxi. For **Iberia** flights, call ☎ 96/351–3739.

By Train

Trains bound for Tarragona (via Zaragoza) leave Barcelona's Passeig de Gràcia and Sants stations every half hour or so (☞ Barcelona A to Z *in* Chapter 6). Tarragona's **RENFE** station (☎ 902/240202) is downhill from the Mediterranean Balcony, south toward the port. Leaving the region from Valencia, you have a choice of train connections to Madrid (via Cuenca) or Alicante (via Játiva). The main station, **Estación del Norte** (☎ 90/352–0202), is on Calle Játiva, next to the bullring; it's very centrally located, only a short walk or cab ride from most hotels.

Getting Around

By Bus

Connections up and down the coast between Tarragona and Valencia are frequent. Transport inland to Morella and Alcañiz can be arranged from Vinaròs, while Castellón and Sagunto have bus lines west to Teruel.

In Valencia, buses are the main mode of public transport; central services start from the Plaza del Ayuntamiento. Services for the beaches and outlying suburbs leave from the Plaza Puerta del Mar. The tourist office can supply details of bus routes.

By Car

Roads in this region are generally very good, but the main N340 can get clogged, and you're often much better off paying extra to use the *autopista*. For car rentals in Tarragona, **Avis** is at Viajes Vibus (✉ Pin Soler 10, Tarragona, ☏ 977/219156). In Valencia you can choose from **Avis** (✉ Isabel la Católica 17, Valencia, ☏ 96/351-0734), **Europcar** (✉ Antiguo Reino de Valencia 7, Valencia, ☏ 96/374-1512; ✉ airport, Valencia, ☏ 96/152-1872), and **Hertz** (✉ Segorbe 7, Valencia, ☏ 96/341-5036; ✉ airport, Valencia, ☏ 96/152-379).

By Train

Within the region, trains run more or less down the coast: Tarragona–Salou/Cambrils–Tortosa–Vinaròs–Peñíscola–Benicàssim–Castellón–Sagunto–Valencia. A line also goes from Valencia to Zaragoza by way of Sagunto and Teruel, and local lines go around Valencia from the station on Cronista Rivelles (90/224-0202).

Contacts and Resources

Consulates

U.S. Consulate (✉ C. de la Paz 6, Valencia, ☏ 96/351-6973), open weekdays 10–1.

Emergencies

Police: ☏ 091.

Ambulance: Castellón (Servicio Médico Urgencias, ☏ 964/211253). Gandesa (Servei d'Ambulancies, ☏ 977/244728). Morella (Cruz Roja, ☏ 964/160380). Tarragona (Creu Roja, ☏ 977/252525). Valencia (Cruz Roja, ☏ 96/367-7375).

Medical assistance: Castellón (Hospital Provincial, ☏ 964/210522). Morella (Ambulatorio, ☏ 964/160962). Tarragona (Hospital Joan XXIII, ☏ 977/295800). Valencia (Hospital Clínico, ☏ 96/386-2600).

Guided Tours

For a guided tour of **Tarragona,** consult the municipal tourist office just below the cathedral (✉ Carrer Major 39, ☏ 977/245203). The tour covers all of the important archaeological sites along with the cathedral.

Servei Turistic Parc (✉ Rambla Nova, 118, ☏ 977/702324), in Amposta, runs guided tours of every kind through the Ebro Delta, Amposta, and Tarragona province in general. Among the options are vineyards, Templar castles, Cistercian monasteries, and gondola-like *perxar* excursions through the canals and lagoons of the delta. Pop in and talk it over with official Tarragona Diputació guide Josep Valldeperas.

You can book guided tours of **Valencia** at the municipal tourist office (✉ Plaza Ayuntamiento 1, ☏ 96/351-0417). Leaving daily at 10 from the *ayuntamiento,* a bilingual guide takes you around the *ayuntamiento* itself, the Lonja, the cathedral, the Ceramics Museum, the bullring, the station, the Museum of Fine Arts, and the Viveros.

In summer, Valencia's regional tourist office (☞ Visitor Information, *below*) organizes tours of the **Albufera,** the marshland south of Valencia, depending on demand. You tour the port area before continuing south to the Albufera (lagoon), where you can visit a traditional *barraca* (thatched farmhouse). You'll end up in the Devesa Gardens, where you can hire boats to explore the canals through the paddies.

Late-Night Pharmacies

Pharmacies (*farmacias de guardia*) stay open late on a rotating basis: one stays open 24 hours in every sizable town or city. To find out whose turn it is, look on the door of any pharmacy or check the local press.

Outdoor Activities and Sports

GOLF

This region is well endowed with golf courses, all of them near or on the coast. Call in advance to reserve tee times. Listed geographically, north to south, courses include the following: **Club de Golf Costa Dorada** (✉ Apdo. 43, Calafells, Tarragona, ☎ 977/168032), 9 holes; **Club de Golf Costa de Azahar** (✉ Carretera Grao–Benicàssim, Grao de Castellón, ☎ 964/280979), 9 holes; **Club de Campo del Mediterráneo** (✉ Urbanización La Coma, Borriol, Castellón, ☎ 964/321227), 18 holes; **Club de Campo El Bosque** (✉ Chiva, 31 km [19 mi] west of Valencia, ☎ 96/326–3800), 18 holes; **Club de Golf Escorpión** (✉ Apdo. 1, Betera, Valencia, ☎ 96/160–1211), 18 holes; **Campo de Golf de Manises** (✉ Apdo. 22029, Valencia, ☎ 96/152–3804), 9 holes; **Campo de Golf El Saler** (✉ Apdo. 9034, Valencia, ☎ 96/161–1186), 18 holes.

SAILING

The safe waters off Spain's eastern coast make for good sailing conditions. Ask local tourist offices about renting boats, or just chance upon rental outfits. Some possibilities are **Club Náutico Tarragona** (✉ Muelle de la Costa, ☎ 977/240360), **Club Náutico Salou** (✉ Espigón del Muelle, ☎ 977/382166), **Club Náutico Castellón** (✉ Port, ☎ 964/280354), and **Club Náutico Valencia** (✉ Camino del Canal 91, ☎ 96/367–9011).

Travel Agencies

Tarragona: **Vibus SA** (✉ Rambla Nova 125, Tarragona, ☎ 977/219278); Valencia: the **Iberia** office (✉ Paz 14, ☎ 96/152–1144), and **Viajes Paz** (✉ Paz 32, ☎ 96/351–8080).

Visitor Information

Three *regional* tourist offices have information on the whole area: **Castellón** (✉ Plaza María Agustina 5, ☎ 964/221000), **Tarragona** (✉ Rambla Nova 118, ☎ 977/238033), and **Valencia** (✉ Paz 48, ☎ 96/398–6422). *Local* tourist offices are as follows: **Benicàssim** (✉ Médico Segarra 4, ☎ 964/303851). **Morella** (✉ Torre San Miguel, ☎ 964/173032). **Peñíscola** (✉ Paseo Marítimo, ☎ 964/481729). **Reus** (✉ San Juan 27, ☎ 977/320349). **Sagunto** (✉ Cronista Chabret, ☎ 96/266–2213). **Tarragona** (✉ Major 39, ☎ 977/245203). **Teruel** (✉ Tomás Nogués 1, ☎ 974/602279). **Tortosa** (✉ Plaza España, ☎ 977/442567). **Valencia** (✉ Plaza Ayuntamiento 1, ☎ 96/351–0417; ✉ Estación RENFE, Játiva 24, ☎ 96/352–0202).

There are **informational phone lines** in Castellón (☎ 964/221000) and Valencia (☎ 96/352–4000); in **Valencia** (✉ Paz 48), a 24-hour machine dispenses information in exchange for 25 pta. coins.

8 THE SOUTHEAST

Spain's fertile Mediterranean plain is a living, breathing quilt of orange groves and rice paddies. Beyond them, mountains give way to the strange, almost lunar desert landscape of Almería. Most travelers come to this region for its beautiful beaches, but the vistas inland are just as pleasing. Both the plains and the coast are dappled with striking white architecture, a legacy of Moorish occupation.

By Philip Eade

Updated by Katherine Semler

SPAIN'S SOUTHEASTERN CORNER is a land of natural contrasts. To the north, the *huerta* (fertile, irrigated coastal plain) generates an orange harvest from late November through April; in spring, fragrant flowers adorn the same trees. The rice paddies stretching south from the Albufera lagoon to Gandía give rise to Valencia's culinary specialty, paella. The farther south you go, the drier and more mountainous the land, until you reach the singular desert-lunar landscape of Almería, backdrop for many a spaghetti-western film in the 1960s. The inland province of Albacete, historically part of Murcia, was the scene of Don Quixote's exploits in the Castilian expanses of La Mancha.

The striking architecture in most southeastern towns attests to the area's long Moorish occupation. Alicante was in Moorish hands from 718 to 1249; Murcia, from 825 to 1243; and Almería, from 712 to 1489, when it was finally reconquered by Ferdinand and Isabella.

Most people come here for the beaches, from the crowded Costa Blanca to the nearly deserted stretches around Cabo de Gata in Almería, renowned for its scuba diving. Mild temperatures in spring and fall allow you to vacation before and after the thickest crowds.

South of Valencia, you can drive along a thin strip between the sea and the Albufera before following the coast around the Cabo de la Nao to the Costa Blanca. Just south of Cullera, head inland through the historic towns of Xátiva and Alcoy en route to Alicante. An exotic and bustling Mediterranean port, Alicante merits a day's exploration before you move inland toward Murcia, past the palm forest at Elche and the ancient town of Orihuela. (Alternately, a trip to Murcia from Madrid takes you through *Don Quixote* country, the province of Albacete.) Murcia, with its superb cathedral, is an important stop before you approach the Africanesque Almería by way of Lorca, Mojácar, and the stunning, crowd-free coast around the Cabo de Gata.

Pleasures and Pastimes

Beaches

Like the region as a whole, the southeastern coastline is abundantly varied, from the long stretches of sand dunes north of Denia and south of Alicante to the rocky coves and sweeping crescents of the Costa Blanca. The benign climate means you can lounge on the beach at almost any time of year. Major beaches have Cruz Roja (Red Cross) stations with helicopters and flags to warn swimmers of conditions: green for safety, red for danger.

Altea, popular with families, is busy and pebbly, but the old town makes a pretty setting. Benidorm's two white, crescent-shaped beaches extend for more than 5 km (3 mi) and are widely considered the best in Spain. Benidorm takes all prizes for après-beach entertainment; just be warned that in summer you'll be sunbathing head-to-toe with your neighbors. Calblanque is on the road between Los Belones and Cabo de Palos, which takes you down a longish, rough track to a succession of nearly deserted beaches frequented by young Murcians. Calpe's beaches have the scenic advantage of the sheer outcrop Peñon de Ifach (Cliff of Ifach), which stands guard over stretches of sand to either side. Denia and Jávea both have family beaches where children paddle in relatively safe waters. Gandía's sandy beach is well kept, and its promenade is lined with bars and restaurants. Although the narrow La Manga del Mar Menor (*Manga* refers to a thin "sleeve" of land), which encloses a huge lagoon, offers some stunning views, it has been ruined by a tasteless sprawl of hotels and condos. Mojácar has a shingly beach backed by bars and good sports facilities, but if you have a car, try some of the deserted beaches to the south. Needless to say, there are no facilities save the odd water tap for campers; and nudity, though illegal, seems generally accepted here, at Calblanque, and just north of Cullera. In Moraira, the best beach is Playa Castillo, just outside the center. Santa Pola and Guardamar del Segura are other good options, with fine, clean sand and pine trees behind the dunes.

Dining

Rice grows better in the Valencian provinces than anywhere else in Spain, which explains why paella originated here. Another rice dish to try is *arroz a la banda* (meat or fish with vegetables and rice, cooked over a wood fire). Remember that paella should be eaten directly after cooking—don't order it from a *menú del día* (menu of the day) unless you can check its freshness. Alicante and Jijona are known for their *turrón,* nougat made with almonds and flavored with honey. In Elche you can savor fresh dates. Murcian cooking uses products of the *huerta* and the sea, with a marked Arab influence in preparation. Traditionally a fisherman's rice dish, *caldero de Mar Menor* is cooked in huge iron pots and has a distinctly oily consistency, flavored by fish cooked in its own juices. Delicious as tapas or a first course are *muchirones* (broad beans in a spicy sauce, similar to the Catalan *habas a la catalana*) and *cocas* (meat pies similar to empanadas). In Almería, the menu features *gazpacho andaluz* (sometimes described as a spicy, liquid salad; characterized here by the addition of croutons) and *pescaditos fritos* (small fried fish), as well as grapes.

CATEGORY	COST*
$$$$	over 6,500 ptas.
$$$	4,500 ptas.–6,500 ptas.
$$	2,000 ptas.–4,500 ptas.
$	under 2,000 ptas.

**per person for a three-course meal, excluding drinks, service, and tax*

Fiestas

Local festivals furnish excellent entertainment. Almería's lively **Festival Internacional de Títeres** (Puppet Theater Festival) is held in January. Denia holds a **mini Fallas** March 16–19 (☞ Fiestas *in* Chapter 7). Alcoy's spectacular **Moros y Cristianos** (Moors and Christians) festival takes place April 21–24 and includes a reenactment of clashes from the Christian Reconquest, the battle to dislodge the Moors at the end of the 15th century. The **Semana Santa** (Holy Week) processions in Murcia are among Spain's most famous; those in Lorca are particularly known for the opulent costumes of both Christian and Roman participants and for the penitents' solemn robes. Altea's **Moros y Cristianos** spectacle, held on the third Sunday in May, is a combination of battle reenactment and pageant, complete with elaborate costumes and the town's youngsters dressed up as knights in shining armor. Alicante's main festival is the **Hogueras de San Juan** (St. John's Day Bonfires), June 21–24. **El Misteri** (the Mystery Play) is performed in Elche in two parts, August 14–15, preceded by a public dress rehearsal (August 13).

Golf

Spain is one of Europe's top golf destinations, and the mild southeastern climate makes this region a fine choice for winter golfing. North to south, golf courses are: Campo de Golf El Saler, 18 holes (☞ Southern Catalonia and the Levante A to Z *in* Chapter 7); Club de Golf Jávea, 9 holes; Club de Golf Don Cayo, Altea, 9 holes; Campo de Golf Villa Martín, Torrevieja, 18 holes; La Manga Club de Golf, Los Belones, three 18-hole courses; and Golf Almerimar, 18 holes. Reserve tee times in advance, and expect to pay about 8,000 ptas. for 18 holes, 4,000 ptas. for 9.

Lodging

Many hotels on the coast are modern high-rises. If you prefer to avoid these, you'll probably have to choose between character and comfort. Spain's paradors have traditionally solved this conundrum, and there are four in this territory: Jávea, Puerto Lumbreras (Lorca), Mojácar, and Albacete. The last of these, though likely to be off most people's itineraries, is the most representative of the rustic parador style. The others are tasteful but modern. Calpe, Alicante, San José, and Almería have older, one-of-a-kind hotels; reserve in advance. Note that some coastal hotels close for the winter.

CATEGORY	COST*
$$$$	over 18,000 ptas.
$$$	11,500 ptas.–18,000 ptas.
$$	7,000 ptas.–11,500 ptas.
$	under 7,000 ptas.

**All prices are for a standard double room, excluding tax.*

Exploring the Southeast

From Valencia's Albufera, inland to Xátiva and Albacete, and down the Costa Blanca through Alicante and on to Murcia, Cartagena, and Almería, this part of Spain is rich in both natural and man-made attractions: beaches, salt lagoons, steppes, mountain villages, and Mediterranean port cities.

Numbers in the text correspond to numbers in the margin and on the Southeast map.

Great Itineraries

Wanderers can choose from three different coastal experiences (the lagoon, the populous beaches of the Costa Blanca, and the deserted strands south of Mojácar), two distinct inland programs (the steppe around Albacete and the mountains near Murcia), and four major cities (Alicante, Albacete, Murcia, and Almería).

In seven days you can see nearly everything—unless, of course, you find the beach or the golf course of your dreams and decide to stay put. Five days will allow a sampling of beaches, inland villages, and the three coastal cities. Three days is enough for a beach or two, an inland village, and at least a look at Alicante, Murcia, and Almería.

IF YOU HAVE 3 DAYS

Start with the Albufera and **El Palmar** ① before continuing through **Cullera** ② and **Denia** ④ to the **Cabo de la Nao** ⑥. Spend the night at the parador in **Jávea** ⑤, or in the village of **Moraira** ⑦. Begin the next day with a visit to the fishing village of **Altea** ⑨ before heading for **Alicante** ⑰ for lunch and continuing on through **Elche** ⑱ and **Orihuela** ⑲ to **Murcia** ㉒ for the night. On your third day, visit **Lorca** ㉕, Aguilas, **Mojácar** ㉖, and the **Cabo de Gata Nature Reserve** ㉗ on the way to **Almería** ㉘ for the night.

IF YOU HAVE 5 DAYS

Explore the Albufera and **El Palmar** ① before continuing through **Cullera** ② and **Denia** ④ to the **Cabo de la Nao** ⑥. Spend the night at the parador in **Jávea** ⑤ or in the village of **Moraira** ⑦. The next day, visit the fishing village of **Altea** ⑨; then hook inland to **Polop** ⑩ and **Alcoy** ⑬ for lunch at the Venta del Pilar. Spend the night in **Alicante** ⑰. On day three, see **Elche** ⑱ and **Orihuela** ⑲ before stopping in **Murcia** ㉒ for the night. On day four, explore **Cartagena** ㉓ and **La Manga del Mar Menor** ㉔ before heading inland to **Lorca** ㉕ for the

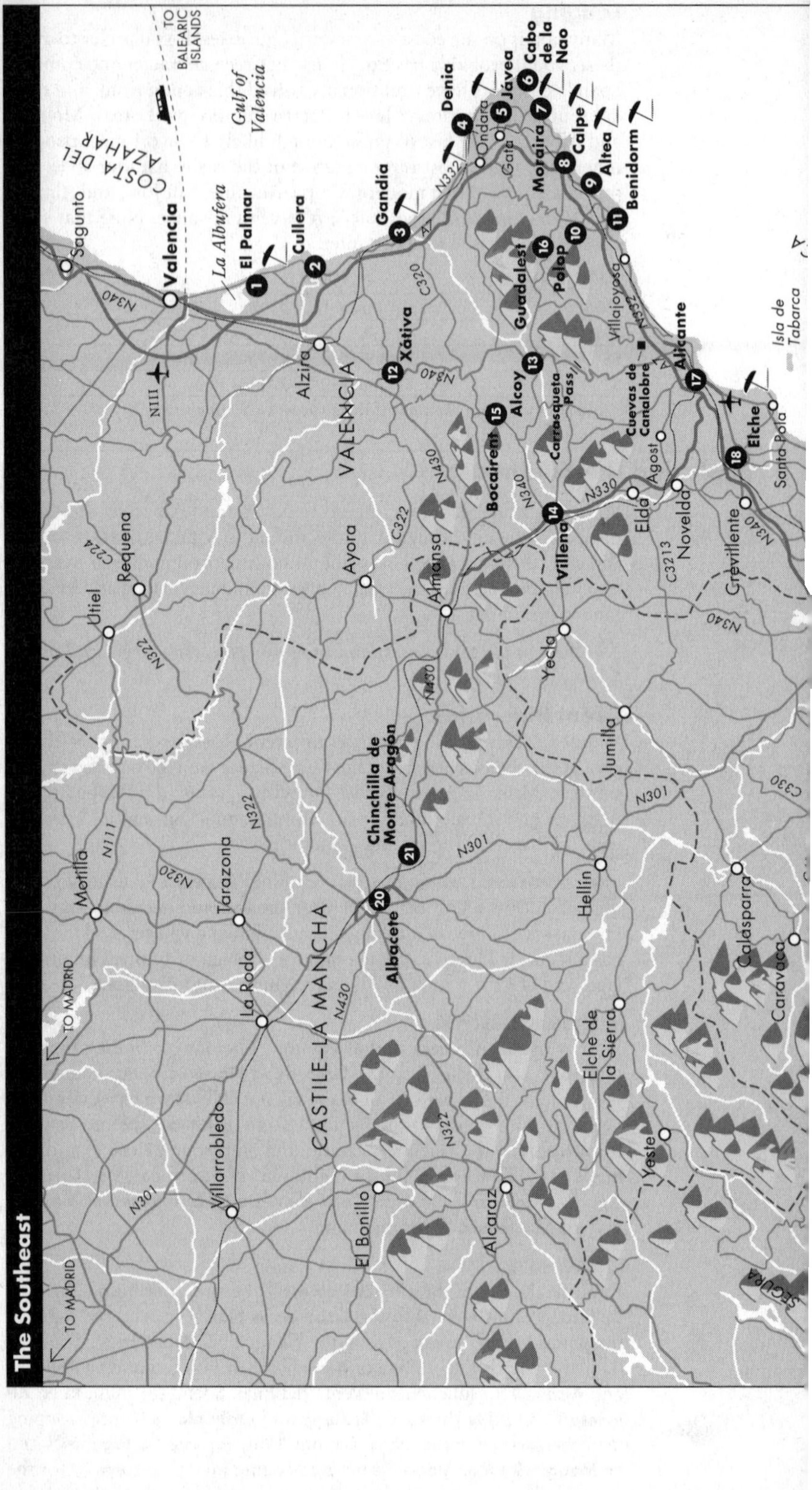
The Southeast
TO MADRID
TO MADRID
TO BALEARIC ISLANDS
COSTA DEL AZAHAR
Gulf of Valencia
Sagunto
Valencia
La Albufera
El Palmar
Cullera
Gandía
Denia
Ondara
Gata
Jávea
Cabo de la Nao
Moraira
Calpe
Altea
Benidorm
Guadalest
Polop
Villajoyosa
Alicante
Isla de Tabarca
Xàtiva
Alzira
VALENCIA
Alcoy
Carrasqueta Pass
Cuevas de Canalobre
Bocairent
Agost
Elche
Santa Pola
Villena
Elda
Novelda
Crevillente
Ayora
Almansa
Yecla
Jumilla
Requena
Utiel
Chinchilla de Monte Aragón
Albacete
Hellín
Calasparra
Caravaca
Motilla
Tarazona
La Roda
CASTILE-LA MANCHA
Elche de la Sierra
Yeste
Villarrobledo
El Bonillo
Alcaraz
SEGURA
N340
N332
A7
C320
N340
N430
N340
N330
C3213
N340
C322
N430
C224
N322
N301
C330
N301
N111
N320
N322
N430
N322
N301
NIII

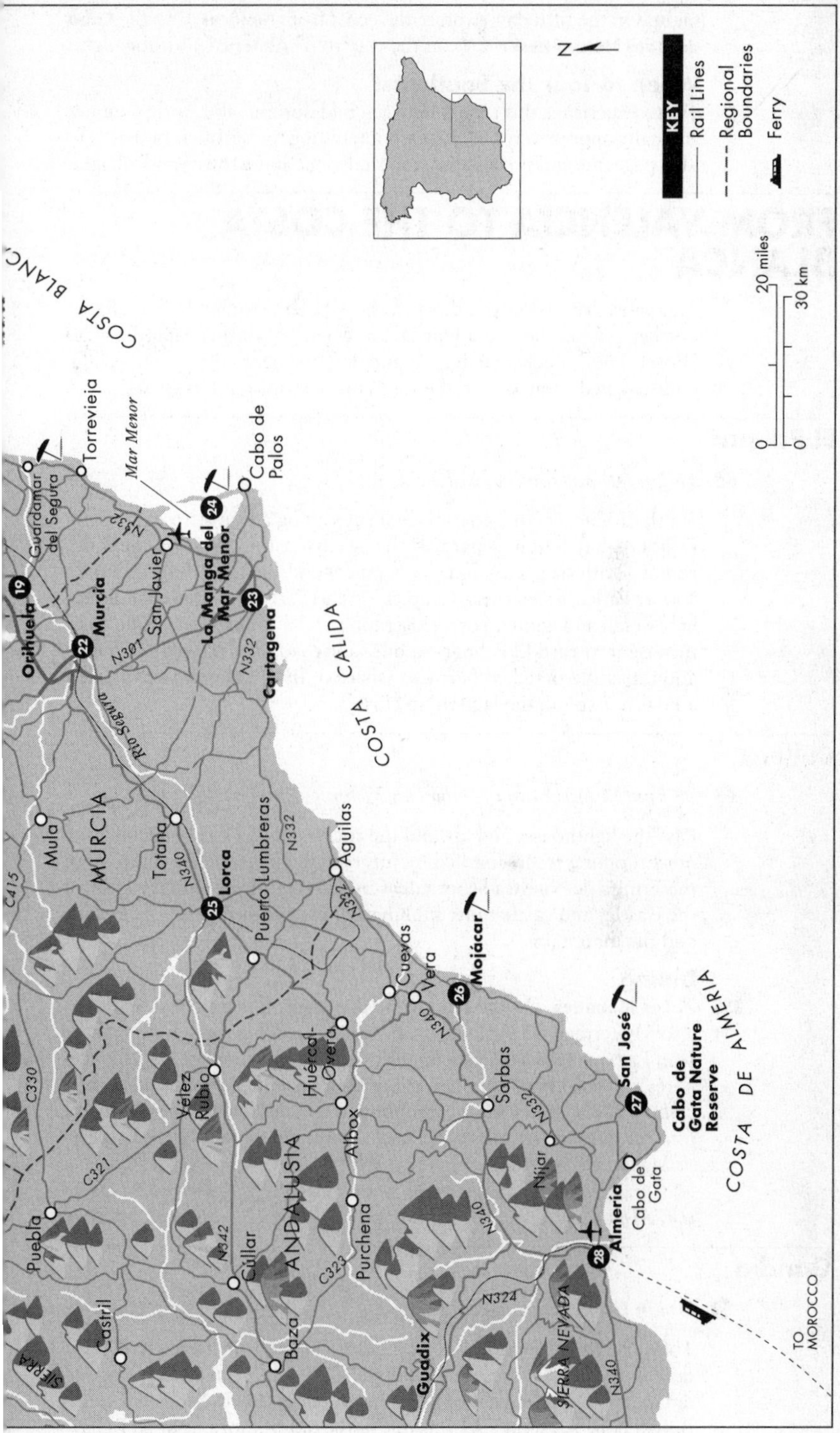
KEY
Rail Lines
Regional Boundaries
Ferry
N
0
20 miles
0
30 km
COSTA BLANCA
Torrevieja
Mar Menor
Guardamar del Segura
Cabo de Palos
La Manga del Mar Menor
San Javier
Orihuela
Murcia
Cartagena
COSTA CALIDA
Mula
MURCIA
Totana
Lorca
Puerto Lumbreras
Aguilas
Cuevas
Vera
Mojácar
Huércal-Overa
Velez Rubio
Albox
Sarbas
San José
Cabo de Gata Nature Reserve
COSTA DE ALMERIA
Nijar
Cabo de Gata
Almería
Purchena
ANDALUSIA
Cúllar
Puebla
Castril
Baza
Guadix
SIERRA NEVADA
SIERRA
TO MOROCCO
Rio Segura
N332
N301
N340
N342
N324
C415
C330
C321
C323
19
22
23
24
25
26
27
28

night. On the fifth day, explore the coast from **Mojácar** ㉖ to the **Cabo de Gata Nature Reserve** ㉗ on the way to **Almería** ㉘ for the night.

When to Tour the Southeast

Try to experience this region between mid-autumn and April; summer is usually oppressively hot. Easter is interesting for the often-bizarre holiday pageants and processions, especially in remote towns and villages.

FROM VALENCIA TO THE COSTA BLANCA

This short drive takes you through the Albuferas wetlands and into the northern end of the Costa Blanca, known as La Marina Alta (the High Shore). These lonely marshlands and deserted beaches are wonderfully undiscovered compared to the sunbathers' strip south of Denia.

El Palmar

❶ *16 km (10 mi) south of Valencia.*

South of Valencia, the coastal road runs along a thin strip of land (La Dehesa) that barely separates the sea from the **Albufera** wetland, rimmed with rice fields and shady pine woods (☞ Side Trip: Albufera Nature Park *after* Valencia, Chapter 7). There are large-scale duck shoots here in fall and winter. For a closer look at the Albufera's unique aura, turn right toward El Palmar—a one-lane road hugs the edge of the lagoon, passing thatched *barracas* (shacks). In El Palmar, you can hire a boat to explore the lagoon up close.

Cullera

❷ *39 km (24 mi) south of Valencia, 27 km (17 mi) north of Gandía.*

Pass the lighthouse, and around the rocky point is modern Cullera, a mushrooming resort marked by futuristic high-rises. The climb up to the **Ermita de Nuestra Señora del Castillo** (Hermitage of Our Lady of the Castle) and **castle ruins** culminates in views of the sea, the *huerta,* and the mountains.

Dining

$$$ ★ ✕ **Les Mouettes.** On the road up to the castle, this tiny restaurant has a lovely terrace with stunning sea views. French owner and manager Jean Lagarce speaks perfect English while chef Jacqueline Lagarce prepares secret recipes from home; try the *lenguado con salsa de nata y champiñones* (sole with mushroom and cream sauce), the *escalope de foie caliente con uvas* (breaded duck liver with grapes), or the *hojaldre de higado de conejo con puerros* (rabbit liver in puff pastry with leeks). ✉ *Carretera Subida al Castillo,* ☎ *96/172–0010. Reservations essential. AE, DC, MC, V. Closed mid-Dec.–mid-Feb. No lunch except Sun.*

Gandía

❸ *30 km (19 mi) northwest of Denia.*

The old town of Gandía lies 4 km (2½ mi) inland from the modern beach development. This became the Borgia (Borja, in Spanish) fief after Ferdinand the Catholic granted the duchy to the family in 1485. The canny Borgia pope Alexander VI was one of the most notorious of all Renaissance prelates, but the family's reputation was later redeemed by the Jesuit St. Francis Borgia (1510–72), born in Gandía and canonized in 1671.

The **Palacio de los Duques** (Ducal Palace), signposted from the city center, was founded by St. Francis in 1546 and still serves as a Jesuit college. Elaborate ceilings and brightly colored *azulejos* (glazed tiles) adorn the 17th-century state rooms. 🎫 *300 ptas.* ⏲ *Guided tours summer, weekdays 11 and 6; winter, Mon.–Sat. 11 and 5.*

Dining

$$ ✕ **Mesón Gallego.** This Galician restaurant is a lucky discovery in the port area. The rough, simple decor is a good setting for hearty Galician dishes such as *pulpo* (octopus), or for fish and meat specialties cooked over coals. Ask for Galician *culcas,* shallow ceramic bowls for drinking the young *ribeiro* wines. ✉ *Levante 37, Grao de Gandía,* ☎ *96/284–1892. AE, DC, MC, V. No dinner Tues.*

En Route As you head south, parchment-colored hills mark the beginning of the province of Alicante. Once past Ondara, which has an unusual stone bullring, you can detour to the **Cueva de las Calaveras** (Skull Cave), near Benidoleig, inhabited by prehistoric humans some 40,000 years ago. ☎ *96/640–4235.* 🎫 *400 ptas.* ⏲ *Daily 9–6 in winter, 9–8 in summer.*

THE COSTA BLANCA

The popular name for the stretch of coast between Cabo de la Nao and Cabo de Palos is the Costa Blanca, or White Coast. Carnations grow in such abundance here that they even faintly perfume the local wine. The Costa Blanca includes the cities of Alicante and Cartagena as well as numerous beach resorts, which have expanded uncontrollably since the 1960s and early '70s. A drive down this shore grants some quiet and picturesque stops, especially off-season; one scenic segment is the road that branches off N332 at Gata de Gorgos (also known as Gata) to the coastal towns of Denia and Jávea.

Denia

❹ *100 km (62 mi) south of Valencia, 8 km (5 mi) north of Jávea and east of Ondara.*

The northernmost beach resort on the Costa Blanca, Denia is a busy tourist town known for its fleet of fishing boats and for its fiestas and celebrations, culminating in the midsummer St. John's Day bonfires (June 23). Backed by the Montgó massif, rising to more than 2,100 ft to the west, Denia's beaches to the north—Les Marines, Les Bovetes, and Les Deveses—are smooth and sandy, while the coast to the south is rocky, forming *calas* (tiny secluded inlets that recall the Costa Brava, north of Barcelona). Denia's most interesting architectural feature is the **Palau del Governador** (Governor's Palace), overlooking the town, with its 12th-century tower and Renaissance bastion. The latter has a Moorish portal with a lovely horseshoe arch. There are also several interesting churches and convents, such as the **Iglesia de la Asunción** (Church of the Assumption). Known as the gastronomical capital of the Costa Blanca, Denia is a good place to sample fresh Mediterranean seafood—try a plate of *picaetes de sepia y calamar* (squid and cuttlefish) or *suquet de rape* (stewed monkfish) at any of the town's fine restaurants. Denia also has the closest ferry connection to the Balearic islands, with two companies, **Balearea** (☎ 96/578–4200) and **Pitra** (☎ 96/642–3120), making the 3½-hour, 80-km (50-mi) crossing to Ibiza and Palma de Mallorca daily (more frequently in summer).

Dining

$$ ✕ **Drassanes.** Built into Denia's original medieval shipyards (for which it's named), Drassanes is a well-known place for fresh, local seafood. The decor is simple and rustic maritime, and both the fare and the people are authentic and good. *Arroz a la banda* (rice cooked with seafood)

is the house specialty. ✉ *C. Puerto 15,* ☎ *96/578–1118. AE, DC, MC, V. Closed Mon. and Nov.*

Jávea

❺ *108 km (67 mi) southeast of Valencia, 92 km (57 mi) northeast of Alicante, 8 km (5 mi) south of Denia.*

A labyrinth of tiny streets and houses with arched portals and Gothic windows, Jávea has an antique aspect contrasted only by its modern church, **Santa María de Loreto.** The church-fortress of **San Bartolomé** is the town's architectural gem; the **Soler Blasco** ethnological and archaeological museum (open mornings only in winter) is another interesting visit. The **Aduanas del Mar** area around the port is well sprinkled with restaurants serving local dishes, such as *arroz a la marinera* (seafood paella).

Lodging

$$$ **Parador de Jávea.** This modern parador is set in a lush palm grove with terrific views of the bay and white-sand beach below. At four stories, it's a low structure, more tasteful than the high-rise hotels elsewhere on the Costa Blanca. Guest rooms are airy and pleasant. ✉ *Avda. del Mediterráneo 7, 03730,* ☎ *96/579–0200,* FAX *96/579–0308. 70 rooms. Restaurant, bar, pool, sauna, exercise room. AE, DC, MC, V.*

Cabo de la Nao

❻ *10 km (6 mi) southeast of Jávea.*

Cabo de la Nao (Cape Nao) is a great spur of land jutting into the Mediterranean toward Ibiza, barely 100 km (62 mi) away. As you round the point, you'll turn from a coast that looks toward Italy to one that mirrors Africa. In the same few miles, you'll pass from an agriculture of oranges and rice to one of olives and palms, from a benign, if variable, climate to one of tawny aridity.

Moraira

❼ *12 km (7 mi) northeast of Calpe, 20 km (12 mi) south of Jávea.*

Moraira has preserved an atmosphere of seclusion in the narrow streets leading down to its harbor. The *casco viejo* (old town) has a good selection of bars and restaurants, while the outskirts have been edified with chalets and private residences. The **castle** and **watch tower** overlooking the port were built to protect Moraira from Mediterranean pirates during the Middle Ages.

Dining and Lodging

$$$$ ★ **El Girasol.** An elegant, ivy-cloaked villa on the Calpe road houses one of the finest restaurants in this region. Owners Joachim and Victoria Koerper preside over a small dining room and terrace. Their cooking is imaginative and outstanding, with an emphasis on French fare; highlights include *ensalada de salmonetes a la vinagretta de naranja* (red mullet salad with orange vinegar) and *solomillo de lechal a la ficele* (veal poached in sherry). ✉ *Carretera Moraira a Calpe,* ☎ *96/574–4373. AE, DC, MC, V. Closed Nov. and Mon. Sept.–June. No lunch Mon.–Sat. July–Aug.*

$$$ **Swiss Moraira.** With a secluded location in a pine forest above Moraira (off the road to Calpe) and well-decorated rooms arranged around a creatively shaped swimming pool, this low-rise luxury hotel is ideal for peace and comfort. During the day, guests leave for the beach and marina, 3 km (2 mi) away. ✉ *C. Haya, 175 Club Moraira, 03724*

Alicante, ☎ 96/574–7104, FAX 96/574–7074. 25 rooms. Bar, pool, tennis court. AE, DC, MC, V.

Calpe

★ 8 *15 km (9 mi) southwest of Jávea, 8 km (5 mi) north of Altea.*

South of Moraira are Calpe and the incredible outcrop known as the **Peñón de Ifach.** Calpe was deserted for nearly 100 years after Barbary pirates killed or enslaved the entire population in the 17th century. The Peñón rises from the sea as a 1,000-ft monolith; the summit is accessible by tunnel. It is said that those who scale these heights at full moon will be hurled to their deaths by goatlike spirits.

Dining and Lodging

$$ ✕ **Al-Zaraq.** Just down the road from the Venta la Chata (☞ *below*), Al-Zaraq offers a tasty break from traditional Spanish fare. The Lebanese menu features lamb and vegetarian delights, such as *cordero en salsa de dátiles* (lamb with date sauce) or *lubina con costra de piñones* (sea bass with a pine-nut crust). ✉ *Carretera de Valencia (N332, Km 172), ☎ 96/573–1615. MC, V. Closed Mon. and Feb.*

$$ 🏨 **Venta la Chata.** This pretty hotel was an 18th-century horse-changing post on the Valencia–Alicante road. The downstairs is rustic, as are the wood furnishings and *azulejo* (glazed-tile) floors in the rooms. The premises include terraced gardens with sea views. Ask for a refurbished room with a balcony or terrace. ✉ *Carretera de Valencia (N332, Km 172), 03710 Alicante, ☎ 96/583–0308. 17 rooms. Bar, tennis court, Ping-Pong. AE, DC, MC, V.*

Altea

9 *10 km (6 mi) south of Calpe, 11 km (7 mi) north of Benidorm.*

Altea is an old fishing village with white houses and blue, ceramic-tiled domes. One of the best-conserved towns on the Costa Blanca, it serves as a foil to the skyscraping tourist towers of Benidorm.

Dining

$$$ ✕ **La Costera.** This restaurant mixes excellent Swiss cooking with bizarre decor and a nightly show. Specialties include the delicious *rostit con carne troceada y champiñon* (chopped meat with mushrooms and potatoes). The place is extremely popular, so reserve in advance if possible. ✉ *Costera del Mestre la Música 8, ☎ 96/584–0230. DC, MC, V. Closed Tues.–Wed., Feb., and Nov.*

Polop

10 *10 km (6 mi) northwest of Altea.*

In the center of Polop is a collection of taps, each donated by a different town or province, that provides the villagers with mountain water.

Benidorm

11 *11 km (7 mi) south of Altea on C3318, 42 km (26 mi) northeast of Alicante.*

Benidorm is a hugely overdeveloped resort with a seemingly bottomless capacity for tourists. Its twin, white crescent-shaped beaches are enhanced by a continual accumulation of sand from other local beaches. For a fantastic view, follow signs to Club Sierra Dorada at the eastern edge of town and climb up to the **Rincón de Loix** (Loix Corner). Hidden among the concrete blocks, the old village still survives.

Dining and Lodging

$$$ ✕ **Tiffany's.** The red and white tones of Tiffany's draw Benidorm's jet set for intimacy and fine international cuisine. Delicacies like *salmón con langostinos* (salmon with shrimp) and *entrecôte al roquefort* (steak with Roquefort cheese) are accompanied by piano music. ✉ *Avda. Mediterráneo, Edifício Coblanca 3, ☎ 96/585–4468. AE, DC, MC, V. Closed Jan. 10–Feb. 10. No lunch.*

$ ✕ **I Fratelli.** The cooking here is Italian, with nouvelle French and international touches. Neapolitan music complements the stylish Moderniste decor: sleek black chairs, white tablecloths, and exotic potted plants. Try the *pescados a la sal* (fish baked in salt) or a pasta dish. ✉ *Dr. Orts Llorca, ☎ 96/585–3979. AE, DC, MC, V. Closed Nov.*

$$$ **Gran Delfín.** The Gran Delfín is the most quietly situated hotel in Benidorm—no mean feat, especially in summer. The salon downstairs is filled with a motley collection of furniture. The bedrooms are Castilian-style, with a smattering of bric-a-brac on the walls. Ask for a room at the front, overlooking the beach. ✉ *Playa de Poniente, 03500, ☎ 96/585–3400, FAX 96/585–7154. 92 rooms, 1 suite. Restaurant, bar, pool, tennis court. AE, DC, MC, V. Closed Nov. 15–Mar. 15.*

Nightlife and the Arts

For a cabaret with Spanish dance and an international musical show, try the **Benidorm Palace** (✉ Carretera de la Diputación, ☎ 96/585–1661). Dinner starts at 8:30, the show at 10 (both one hour later in summer). Alternately, don a crown at the **Nuevo Gran Castillo Conde de Alfaz** (✉ Camino Viejo del Albir, ☎ 96/686–5265) and dine in front of jousting medieval knights. Dinner, drinks, and the show (Friday and Saturday only) cost 3,500 ptas. per person.

Countless bars and discos with names like Jockey's and Harrods (reflecting Benidorm's popularity with Brits and Germans) line Avenida de Europa and the Ensanche de la Playa de Levante.

INLAND: XÁTIVA AND ALCOY

For a break from sea and sand, cut inland to some of the towns and scenes that deepen the light atmosphere of this Mediterranean coast. Xátiva, Alcoy, Villena, and Bocairent have some of the most rustic villages in the Southeast, where people live far more traditional, small-town lives than most of their compatriots.

Xátiva

12 *42 km (26 mi) southwest of Cullera, 50 km (31 mi) north of Alcoy.*

Resting on the dry, vine- and cypress-covered slopes of the Sierra de Alcoy, Xátiva (pronounced "CHA-ti-va"; also spelled and pronounced "Játiva") retains a pink **casco antiguo** (old town) dotted with fountains. Under the Moors, Xátiva was famous for paper production; centuries later it became the birthplace of two of the Borgia popes—Calixtus III and his nephew Alexander VI. The latter issued the famous 1493 Papal Bull granting the Indies to Ferdinand and Isabella, though he's more often remembered for his scandalous private life and role as as the father of Caesar and Lucrezia.

To reach the **castle,** on the slopes of Mt. Bernisa, follow signs up a steep path from the Plaza del Españoleto. Halfway up, the 13th-century **Ermita de San Feliú** (Hermitage of St. Felix) has a beautiful group of Valencian Primitive paintings. Felipe V destroyed the fortress pretty thoroughly as part of his retribution for Xátiva's opposition in the War of the Spanish Succession, but a partial restoration of the castle and a panoramic view reward your efforts. *Free.* *Daily 10–1 and 3–6 (10–1 and 4–7 in summer).*

On the Plaza del Seo stands the enormous **Collegiata** (collegiate church), which houses some Borgia Renaissance marble. Opposite the Collegiata is the 16th-century plateresque facade of the **hospital.** Down Calle Corretgeria, the **Museo Municipal** (Municipal Museum) has a small collection of archaeological finds and paintings by Xátiva's other famous son, José de Ribera. *300 ptas.* *Tues.–Sun. 10–6 (10–7 in summer).*

Alcoy

★ 13 *55 km (34 mi) north of Alicante, 50 km (31 mi) south of Xátiva.*

Alcoy sits at the confluence of three rivers and is famous for the bridges spanning its deep river gorges. The town owes its size (population 67,000) to its textile, paper, and fruit-canning industries. Alcoy's annual **Moros y Cristianos** (Moors and Christians festival), around the time of Sant Jordi (St. George's Day, April 23), is the most spectacular fiesta of its kind in Spain. Colorful processions and mock battles commemorate the Battle of Alcoy, in 1275, when St. George's intervention helped liberate the city from the besieging forces of Al Azraq, ensuring victory for the Christians.

If you miss this event, walk down Calle Sant Miquel, which leads off the Plaza de España, to **Casal de Sant Jordi** (St. George Civic Center), which houses fiesta paraphernalia including costumes worn by the combatants. ✉ *C. Sant Miquel 60,* ☎ *no phone.* *300 ptas.* *Tues.–Fri. 11–1 and 5–7:30.*

Dining and Lodging

$$ ★ ✕ **Venta Saltera.** A few minutes' drive south of Alcoy, this restaurant serves typical local fare, of which the staff is extremely proud. Try the *olleta alcoyana* (Alcoy-style stew, made with white beans and pork). ✉ *Carretera Nacional 340,* ☎ *96/554–4330. AE, DC, MC, V. Closed Wed. and second half of Aug.*

$$ ★ **Reconquista.** There's nothing memorable about this modern high-rise, but it's the most comfortable option for miles around. You can compensate for the plain, dated decor in the bedrooms by requesting a view over the river gorge to old Alcoy. The public rooms have an institutional air, with spotty, gray-tiled floors and functional plastic furniture. ✉ *Puente San Jorge 1, 03803 Alcoy,* ☎ *96/533–0900,* FAX *96/533–0955. 72 rooms. Restaurant, bar. AE, DC, MC, V.*

Villena

14 *40 km (25 mi) west of Alcoy.*

A collection of priceless Bronze Age rings, bracelets, coronets, and bowls of gold was discovered on a dry Villena riverbed in 1963, and is now on display in the archaeology section of Villena's *ayuntamiento* (town hall).

Bocairent

15 *27 km (17 mi) northeast of Villena.*

Heading up the N340 from Villena, find time to stop in Bocairent, where the **Museo Parroquial** (Parish Museum) has paintings by Juan de Juanes, who died here in 1579, along with works by Francisco Ribalta and Joaquín Sorolla.

Guadalest

16 *36 km (22 mi) east of Alcoy.*

Guadalest is an old town. Perched atop a crag within the walls of a ruined castle, it conquers the steep terrain with tiny, stepped streets. Continue as far as Callosa, turn left toward Tarbena, and brave a dip at the foot of the **Cascada de El Algar** (El Algar falls), icy 12 months a year. Nearby **Tarbena,** a village famed for its sausages, introduces you to spectacular rocky-mountain scenery.

ALICANTE, ELCHE, AND ORIHUELA

Luminous Alicante seems to shimmer with the kind of light for which the Mediterranean is famous, while inland Elche's palm forest shades its ancient treasures from the summer heat. Orihuela's twisting back streets tunnel through old Moorish neighborhoods.

Alicante

17 *82 km (51 mi) northeast of Murcia, 183 km (113 mi) south of Valencia by the coast road, 42 km (26 mi) south of Benidorm, 55 km (34 mi) south of Alcoy.*

Alicante, at the convergence of inland and coastal roads, has always been known for its luminous skies. The Greeks called it Akra Leuka (White Summit); the Romans named it Lucentum (City of Light). The city is dominated by the Castillo de Santa Bárbara, set on a rocky peak, but its immediate pride is its grand avenue, the **Explanada,** lined with date palms.

Begin your tour at the tourist office in the arcaded Plaza de Ayuntamiento. It's worth looking inside the Baroque town hall; ask gate officials for permission to explore the ornate halls and rococo chapel on the first floor. Walk through the arched passage through the *ayuntamiento* to the Plaza Santísima Faz, a pedestrian square crowded with sidewalk cafés and restaurants.

From the Plaza Santísima Faz, walk down the busy, pedestrian Calle Mayor and take your first right to reach the cathedral of **San Nicolás de Bari** (open for mass only), built on the site of a former mosque. The cathedral has both an austere Renaissance facade in the style of Herrera (of Escorial fame) and a lavish, Baroque side chapel.

At the far end of Calle Mayor is the **Museo de Arte Siglo XX** (Museum of 20th-Century Art), whose collection of abstract art includes works by Picasso, Miró, Braque, Tàpies, Hockney, and Rauschenberg. *Free. Oct.–Apr., Tues.–Sat. 10–1 and 5–8; May–Sept., Tues.–Sat. 10:30–1:30 and 6–9.*

Across the small plaza from the Museum of 20th-Century Art is the church of **Santa María,** with a rich Baroque facade. From here, it's a short walk down steps, then left along the back of Playa Postiguet to the foot of Mt. Benacantil (700 ft) and the elevator to the castle.

★ Originally built as a Carthaginian fortress around 3 BC, the **Castillo de Santa Bárbara** was extensively modified for numerous wars. From here you have a spectacular bird's-eye view of the city. Within the castle walls, a small museum displays objects associated with the annual St. John's Day bonfires on midsummer's eve. *Castle 400 ptas., museum free. Castle and elevator Sun.–Fri. 10–7 (last elevator ride 6:30); museum, spring–fall, Sun.–Fri. 9–7:30.*

Dining and Lodging

$$$ ✕ **Delfin.** Don't let the fantastic view over the palm-lined Explanada and Alicante's yacht culture distract you from Delfin's imaginative food. Opened in 1961, this restaurant remains on the gastronomic front line and is wholly modern, with bright decor and a breezy terrace. The cooking is divided equally between seafood and rice dishes. Try the *lubina en hojaldre de mousse de langosta y salmón* (sea bass in puff pastry of lobster and salmon mousse) or the *alcachofas rellenas al gratin* (artichoke hearts stuffed with shrimp, béchamel sauce, ham, and cheese). ✉ *Explanada de España 12,* ☎ *96/521–4911. AE, DC, MC, V.*

$$ ✕ **La Tapería.** Located just behind the *ayuntamiento,* this rustic three-room restaurant serves a tasty melange of dishes from all over Spain. The bar specializes in Basque-style tapas (*pinchos*) such as *pastel de pescado* (fish pudding on toast) or the standard olive, anchovy, and pepper combination, while the seated dining room serves local specialties like *dorada a la sal* (sea bream baked in salt) and *olleta alicantina* (greens and legumes Alicante-style). ✉ *Plaza Santísima Faz 3,* ☎ *96/520–6102. MC, V. No dinner Sun.*

$$$ ★ ✕🏨 **Eurhotel Hesperia.** This modern hotel 300 yards from Alicante's port can satisfy all your practical needs. Though the building is insipid, its proximity to the train and bus stations makes it fairly handy. Rates are often reduced by as much as half on weekends. The on-site restaurant, open weekdays, does a thriving business in Mediterranean fish and meat dishes. Try the *merluza con langostinos a la sidra* (hake and crayfish cooked in cider) or the *menestra de verdura a la bilbaína* (Basque-style vegetable soup). ✉ *C. Pintor Lorenzo Casanova 33, 03003 Alicante,* ☎ *96/513–0440,* FAX *96/592–8323. 117 rooms. Restaurant, bar, cafeteria, parking (fee). AE, DC, MC, V.*

$$$–$$$$ 🏨 **Meliá Alicante.** Try the Meliá for both comfort and proximity to the sea. This huge hotel stands on a reclaimed peninsula that juts into the sea right near the city center. The bedrooms are bright and modern, with sweeping views of the beaches and marina. Downstairs, the lobby is a shrine to postmodernism, with cool marble floors and low black tables. ✉ *Playa del Postiguet, 03001 Alicante,* ☎ *96/520–5000,* FAX *96/520–4756. 545 rooms. Restaurant, piano bar, pool, car rental. AE, DC, MC, V.*

$$$ ✕🏨 **Pensión Les Monges.** A family-run pension set in a restored old building, Les Monges has an ideal location in the historical city center, near the port and the beach. Rooms are basic but comfortable. ✉ *C. Les Monges 2, 03002 Alicante,* ☎ *96/521–5046,* FAX *96/514–0120. 14 rooms, 9 with bath. MC, V.*

Nightlife and the Arts

Roughish, lively bars dot the streets behind the *ayuntamiento.* Among the slicker pubs and discos are **Zoo** (✉ Avda. Aguilera 22) and **Paseíto** (✉ C. Jorge Juan 18). In summer, the liveliest places are along the water, on the Ruta del Puerto and Ruta de la Madera.

Shopping

Local **crafts** include basketwork, embroidery, leatherwork, and weaving, each specific to a single town or village. You'll find all these crafts for sale in the major resorts, though their prices may be inflated. The most satisfying places to shop are often local markets, so inquire about market days.

For **ceramics,** go to Agost, a town 20 km (12 mi) inland from Alicante, where potters make jugs and pitchers from the local white clay, whose porosity is ideal for keeping liquids cool. You're bound to see a few potters at work in town, but you can also learn about their craft at the Museo de Alfarería (Pottery Museum; ☎ 96/569–1199). The museum has been closed for refurbishing but plans to reopen in February 2001;

hours are normally Tuesday–Sunday 11–2 and 5–8 (11–2 only in winter), and admission is free.

Elche

18 *24 km (15 mi) southwest of Alicante, 34 km (21 mi) northeast of Orihuela, 58 km (36 mi) northeast of Murcia.*

If Alicante is torrid in summer, Elche is even hotter. Fortunately, this city is surrounded by the largest palm forest in Europe, allowing occasional escape from the worst of the heat. The Moors first planted the palms for dates, Europe's most reliable crop, and the trees still produce these as well as yellow fronds. (Throughout Spain, the fronds are blessed on Palm Sunday and hung on balconies to ward off evil during the coming year.) Colonized by ancient Rome, Elche was later ruled by the Moors for 500 years. The remarkable stone bust known as *La Dama de Elche,* one of the earliest examples of Iberian sculpture (now in Madrid's Museum of Archaeology), was discovered here in 1897. The Misteri (Mystery Play), performed in the Basilica de Santa María on the Feast of the Assumption, August 14 and 15, draws crowds; the performances are spectacular, with a platform bearing the Virgin Mary and guitar-playing angels winched 150 ft up into the dome of the church.

Be sure to visit the **Jardín del Huerto del Cura,** a lush botanical garden and palm grove across from the Hotel Huerto del Cura (☞ *below*), where vibrantly colored flowers grow beneath magnificent palms. *300 ptas.* ⏲ *Apr.–Sept., daily 9–8:30; Oct.–Mar., daily 9–6.*

Dining and Lodging

$$$ ★ **Huerto del Cura.** A subtropical location and a large, private garden in Elche's palm grove make this modern hotel-in-the-spirit-of-a-parador perfect for rest and relaxation. The main building houses the excellent restaurant Els Capellans, which serves regional rice and fish dishes. The bedrooms are in bungalow huts—gloomy, due to their shady location, but tastefully decorated. The palm-ringed swimming pool looks like something you'd hope to find in the Seychelles. ✉ *Porta de la Morera, 03200,* ☎ *96/545–8040,* FAX *96/542–1910. 86 rooms. Restaurant, bar, cafeteria, 2 pools, sauna, putting green, exercise room. AE, DC, MC, V.*

Orihuela

19 *24 km (15 mi) northeast of Murcia, 34 km (21 mi) southwest of Elche, 29 km (18 mi) inland from Guardamar del Segura.*

Palm and orange groves dominate the southeastern countryside as far as Orihuela, on the banks of the Segura—another excuse to linger on the N340 south. The town's air of fading grandeur stems from its past life as the capital of Murcia (until the Reconquest). Stroll through Orihuela's winding streets and visit the Gothic cathedral of **El Salvador** to see its rare, spiral vaulting. The adjoining **museum** has paintings by Velázquez and Ribera.

FROM MADRID TO MURCIA

To get the feel of Don Quixote country, drive to Murcia through Albacete and the flat and arid La Mancha region. This three- to four-hour drive is punctuated by the Parador Nacional Marqués Villena at Alarcón, the Parador de la Mancha at Albacete, the village promontory of Chinchilla de Monte Aragón, and the Roman town of Cieza.

Albacete

20 *172 km (107 mi) northwest of Alicante, 146 km (91 mi) northwest of Murcia, 183 km (114 mi) southwest of Valencia.*

In the Spanish version of Trivial Pursuit, Albacete is the answer to the question "Which town is known as the New York of La Mancha?" Aside from being the largest town in the province, with 160,000 inhabitants, Albacete bears no resemblance whatsoever to the Big Apple and is better characterized as an agricultural center known for its wine and saffron. The **Museo Arqueológico** (Museum of Archaeology), in the Parque Abelardo Sánchez, has Roman mosaics, ivory dolls, and objects dating from the Paleolithic era. ☎ *967/228307.* *300 ptas.* *Tues.–Sat. 10–2 and 4:30–7, Sun. 9–2.*

Dining and Lodging

$$$ ★ **Parador de Albacete.** Set back from the highway, this whitewashed, ranchlike *manchego*-style parador has a rustic, wood-beamed interior and cozy, comfortable bedrooms. The restaurant serves local cuisine; you can never go wrong with the *chuletas de cordero* (lamb chops grilled with garlic). ✉ *Apdo. 384, Carretera N301, 02000 Albacete,* ☎ *967/245321,* FAX *967/243271. 70 rooms. Restaurant, bar, cafeteria, pool, 2 tennis courts. AE, DC, MC, V.*

Chinchilla de Monte Aragón

12 km (7 mi) east of Albacete.

If you detour slightly en route to Alicante, you'll soon see the imposing 15th-century **castle** (21) of Chinchilla de Monte Aragón to your left and, if the day is clear, the distant Sierra de Alcaraz rising to nearly 6,000 ft to the south. Chinchilla is a fine old pottery town.

En Route Back on the N301, most of the 146 km (91 mi) to Murcia runs adjacent to the uplands of La Mancha, where Don Quixote adventured in Cervantes's famous novel. Across the border into Murcia and through the Roman town of Cieza, dominated by its feudal castle, the road drops some 2,700 ft to farmland before reaching the provincial capital.

MURCIA TO ALMERÍA

Soon after Orihuela, you'll enter the province of Murcia, where the N340 follows the course of the Segura, though the foothills of the Sierra de Carrascoy often intervene. This is the driest part of Spain, and the least visited. Tawny hills are punctuated by stretches of fertile *huerta,* moistened by life-giving rivers whose waters irrigate three crops in succession a year. Rich metal deposits supply a busy mining industry. Valenciano gives way to the Andalusian accent.

Murcia

22 *82 km (51 mi) southwest of Alicante, 146 km (91 mi) southeast of Albacete, 219 km (136 mi) northeast of Almería.*

The capital of its province, Murcia was first settled by Romans; later, in the 8th century, the conquering Moors used Roman bricks to build the city proper. It was eventually reconquered and annexed to the crown of Castile in 1243. The Murcian dialect contains many Arabic words, and many Murcians clearly reveal Moorish ancestry. Modern Murcia is a university city with a population of more than 300,000.

★ The **cathedral** is a masterpiece of eclectic architecture. Begun in the 14th century, it received its magnificent facade—considered one of Spain's fullest expressions of the Churrigueresque style—as late as 1737; the 19th-century English traveler Richard Ford described it as "rising in compartments, like a drawn out telescope." The 15th century brought the Gothic **Door of the Apostles** and, inside, the splendid chapel of **Los Vélez,** with a beautiful, star-shaped stone vault. Carvings by the 18th-century Murcian sculptor Francisco Salzillo were added later. Pop into the **museum,** off the north transept, to see Salzillo's polychrome-wood sculpture of the penitent St. Jerome. The monumental 312-ft **bell tower,** built between 1521 and 1792, is presently closed for structural repairs. ☎ *968/216344.* *Museum 200 ptas.* ⊙ *Daily 10–1 and 5–8 (5–7 in winter).*

Wander down Calle Trapería, the pedestrian shopping street. You'll soon reach the 19th-century **Casino,** with the style and aura of a British gentleman's club. The facade is a mixture of classical and modern styles; the inside, inspired by the Alhambra in Granada, features a *patio arabe* (Moorish courtyard) and Mudéjar decor. Despite the name, this has never been a gambling center—Murcians (that is, Murcian men) come to read the newspaper and play billiards.

The **Museo Salzillo,** out by the bus station on Plaza San Agustín, has the main collection of Francisco Salzillo's disturbingly realistic, polychrome *pasos* (carvings), carried in processions every Easter. ☎ *968/291893.* *500 ptas.* ⊙ *Weekdays 9:30–1 and 4–7 (3–6 in winter).*

Dining and Lodging

$$ ✕ **Hispano.** For a typically Spanish brand of rusticity, look no further than the Hispano. A well-known Murcian family of restaurateurs-hoteliers named Abellán created this restaurant some 20 years ago, and it remains extremely popular for Murcian, traditional, and nouvelle cuisine. ✉ *Arquitecto Cerdá 3,* ☎ *968/216152. AE, DC, MC, V.*

$$–$$$ ★ ✕ **Rincón de Pepe.** In the center of the old town, 50 yards from the cathedral's apse, this hotel offers comfort and hospitality. All rooms have modern, bright, simple decor, and the lobby and reception rooms have cool marble floors. The restaurant serves a good selection of *tapeo murciano* (samples of favorite Murcian dishes). Chef Francisco Gonzáles carries on the tradition of using produce from the hotel's own organic farm and the freshest local fish and meat: the fish comes from the nearby Mar Menor, the lamb from Segura. Highlights on the extensive menu include *ensalada de mariscos y trufas* (shellfish and truffle salad) and *cordero segureño asado a la murciana* (local lamb roasted Murcian-style). ✉ *Apóstoles 34, 30002 Murcia,* ☎ *968/212239,* FAX *968/221744. 148 rooms. Cafeteria, parking (fee). AE, DC, MC, V.*

$ **Hispano 1.** Rooms at this centrally located budget hotel are bright and airy, and the public sitting area is large and tasteful. Ask for an exterior room, with a view of the pedestrians-only street. ✉ *Trapería 8 y 10, 30001 Murcia,* ☎ *968/216152,* FAX *968/216859. 45 rooms, 20 with bath, 15 with shower. Breakfast room, parking (fee). AE, DC, MC, V.*

Nightlife and the Arts

Look for the pubs **Latino** and **B12** in the university district.

Cartagena

㉓ *48 km (29 mi) south of Murcia.*

Founded in the 3rd century BC by the Carthaginians, this is Spain's principal naval base. From Cartagena there is easy access to the resort **La Manga del Mar Menor** and the twisty, scenic, 100-km (62-mi) drive along the N332 to the start of the Costa de Almería.

La Manga del Mar Menor

24 *45 km (28 mi) southeast of Murcia.*

La Manga del Mar Menor, which forms Europe's largest saltwater lake (170 square km [105 square mi]), is warmer, saltier, and higher in iodine than the Mediterranean, and is thus well known as a therapeutic health resort for rheumatism patients. The Manga ("sleeve") itself is a 21-km (13-mi) spit of sand averaging some 990 ft wide and enclosing the Mar Menor (smaller sea), a famously flat, calm expanse of shallow water about 20 ft deep. Four canals, called *golas,* connect the Mar Menor with the Mediterranean. The Manga has 42 km (26 mi) of immense, sandy beaches on both the Mediterranean and the Mar Menor sides, allowing bathers to choose more or less exposed locations and warmer or colder water according to season and weather. La Manga Club-Hotel (☞ *below*) claims to be Europe's most complete sports hotel. The principal towns on and near the Mar Menor are Cartagena and San Javier.

Lodging

$$$$ **La Manga Club-Hotel.** Golf pervades this superbly situated luxury clubhouse-hotel, just above the Mar Menor. Most guests are here to wallow in the golfy ambience of what has become all but the home course for Seve Ballesteros. For nongolfers, the resort boasts no fewer than 22 tennis courts and a regulation cricket pitch (which may account for the surfeit of British-registered Range Rovers in the parking lot). You can also rent apartments or villas. ✉ *La Manga Club, Los Belones, 30385 Murcia,* ☎ *968/331234,* FAX *968/331235. 192 rooms. 2 restaurants, 2 bars, 2 pools, hot tub, sauna, 3 golf courses, 22 tennis courts, horseback riding, squash. AE, DC, MC, V.*

Outdoor Activities and Sports

The Mar Menor, notable for the absence of waves of any kind, is a serious sailing destination. Various schools offer windsurfing, waterskiing, catamaran sailing, and other marine diversions.

Lorca

★ 25 *62 km (39 mi) southwest of Murcia, 158 km (98 mi) northeast of Almería, 37 km (23 mi) inland from the Mediterranean at Águilas.*

Leave the main highway for a glimpse of Lorca, an old market town and the scene of some of Spain's most colorful Holy Week celebrations. Your first stop should be the **tourist office** on Lope Gisbert, housed in the beautiful, dilapidated Casa de los Guevara. Head down Alamo to the elegant **Plaza de España,** ringed by a string of rich Baroque buildings, particularly the ***ayuntamiento,*** **law courts,** and **Colegiata** (collegiate church). Follow signs from the plaza up to the **castle.**

Dining

$$ ★ ✕ **Cándido.** On the road into town, this rustic, old-fashioned restaurant has been going strong on its home cooking for more than half a century. The ambience is relaxed, the clientele a happy mix of Lorcans and travelers. The food is locally inspired; try the *trigo con conejo y caracoles* (wheat with rabbit and snails), a typical local dish. ✉ *Santo Domingo 13,* ☎ *968/466907. MC, V. No dinner Sun. in summer.*

Mojácar

26 *93 km (58 mi) northeast of Almería, 73 km (45 mi) southeast of Puerto Lumbreras, 135 km (83 mi) southwest of Murcia.*

A few miles inland, on a hillside overlooking the sea, Mojácar is a cluster of whitewashed cubist houses attesting to the town's Moorish past.

The North African feel and aesthetic have been carefully preserved. In the 1960s, painters and writers gravitated to Mojácar's cliff-dwelling simplicity in search of inspiration, creating a movement that became known as the *Movimiento Indaliano,* named for the *Indalo,* an anthropomorphic protective deity associated with Almería (and especially with Mojácar) since prehistoric times. Mojácar's beaches and reflective charm make it a top destination in this refreshingly undeveloped corner of Spain. The most attractive part of the Almerían coast lies south of here.

Dining and Lodging

$$ ✕ **El Palacio de Mojácar.** Installed in an old, white Mojácar house with exposed beams and fireplace, this restaurant specializes in, well, good food. The friendly chef-owner doesn't cook a large menu, but whatever *is* served tends to be highly inventive, and generally has an international twist. ✉ *Plaza del Cano,* ☎ *950/472846. AE, MC, V. Closed Thurs. and Nov.–Feb.*

$$$ ★ **Parador de Mojácar.** If you prefer to sleep by the sea rather than in the old town, this rambling, white modern parador is the best option in Mojácar. The public rooms are some of the most spacious and tasteful in Spain. Large, open-plan fireplaces add the rustic ingredient. Bedrooms are bright, with Castilian furniture. ✉ *Carretera de Carboneras, 04638,* ☎ *950/478250,* FAX *950/478183. 98 rooms. Restaurant, bar, pool, tennis court. AE, DC, MC, V.*

$$ **El Moresco.** Up in the village itself, El Moresco has a stunning position and tasteful, country decor, but it's often beset by large tour groups. ✉ *Avda. D'encamp 15, 04638 Almería,* ☎ *950/478025,* FAX *950/478262. 147 rooms. Restaurant, pool. AE, DC, MC, V.*

San José and the Cabo de Gata Nature Reserve

27 *40 km (25 mi) east of Almería, 86 km (53 mi) south of Mojácar.*

San José is a small, relaxed village perched over its eponymous bay. As yet out of developers' clutches, it is well placed to take advantage of the all-but-deserted beaches nearby. It has one tiny hotel, a handful of *hostales* (hostels), and a campground. Just to the south is the **Parque Natural Marítimo y Terrestre Cabo de Gata Níjar** (Nature Reserve, ✉ road from Almería to Cabo de Gata, Km 6, ☎ 950/160435). Birds are the main attraction here; the park is home to several species proper to Africa, including the *camachuelo trompetero,* which is not found anywhere else outside Africa. The maritime reserve features special kinds of algae. The **Centro Las Amuladeras** has an exhibit and information on the region. For beach action, follow signs south to the **Playa Los Genoveses** and **Playa Monsul**; a dirt track follows the coast around the spectacular cape, eventually linking up with the N332 to Almería.

Lodging

$$ ★ **San José.** For access to the beautifully rugged coast toward Cabo de Gata, you couldn't choose a happier spot than this tiny hotel in the laid-back village of San José. Superbly positioned on the bay, the medium-size villa has just eight very large guest rooms, all with attractive decor and great sea views, around a large public sitting room with an open fire. It fills quickly, so reserve well in advance. ✉ *C. Correos, 04118,* ☎ *950/380116,* FAX *950/380002. 8 rooms. Restaurant, library. MC, V. Closed Nov.–Mar.*

Almería

28 *219 km (136 mi) southwest of Murcia, 183 km (114 mi) east of Málaga.*

A capital of the grape industry, Almería has tree-lined boulevards and landscaped squares, and its mild climate in spring and fall makes it especially pleasant then. Its core still consists of distinctly Mudéjar, flat-roofed houses forming a maze of narrow, winding alleys. Though now surrounded by modern apartment blocks, the dazzling-white older houses give the city an Andalusian flavor.

Dominating Almería is the **Alcazaba** (fortress), built by Caliph Abd ar-Rahman I and provided with a bell tower by Carlos III. From here you have sweeping views of the port and city. Among the ruins of the fortress, damaged by earthquakes in 1522 and 1560, are landscaped gardens of rock flowers and cacti. *250 ptas. Apr.–Oct., daily 10–2 and 5:30–8; Nov.–Mar., daily 9–1:30 and 3–6.*

Below the Alcazaba stands the **cathedral,** whose buttressed towers make it look like a castle. The defenses were built to fend off frequent raids by Barbary pirates in the 16th century. The overall design is Gothic, with some classical touches around the doors. *Daily 10:30–noon and for masses.*

If you're a film devotee and want to see where spaghetti westerns have long been shot, drive 24 km (15 mi) north on the N340 to **Mini Hollywood,** a film set open to the public when filming is not in progress. *950/365236. 960 ptas. Daily 10–7.*

Dining and Lodging

$$ ✕ **Valentin.** This central spot serves fine regional specialties. *Cazuela de rape* (monkfish baked in a sauce of almonds and pine nuts) is a typical entrée. The decor is Andalusian: white walls, wood, and glass. Valentin is popular, so be on the early side (around 9) to get a table. *Tenor Iribarne 7, 950/264475. AE, MC, V. Closed Mon.*

$$ ✕ **Veracruz.** In Almería's beach barrio, El Zapillo, this popular and excellent seafood restaurant has its own storage tank for oysters, clams, prawns, and lobsters. Its specialty is *parillada de pescado,* a mixed grill of everything that swims in the Mediterranean. *Avda. Cabo de Gata 119, 950/251220. AE, MC, V.*

$ ✕ **Torreluz.** This bustling little eatery in the Torreluz II hotel (*below*) is the best culinary value in town. Famous among locals for its robust portions and brisk lunchtime service, the Torreluz serves an excellent cross-section of southeastern fare. Try the *pollo al ajillo con arroz* (garlic-sauteed chicken with rice) or the *zarzuela de marisco a la marinera* (mixed seafood in a zesty red marinade). *Plaza Flores 1, FAX 950/234399. AE, DC, MC, V.*

$$$ **Gran Hotel Almería.** These rooms have brightly painted walls and chintz coverings to complement their fine views over Almería's harbor. The huge, marbled reception rooms evoke the hotel's golden age, when it hosted film directors who had come to make spaghetti westerns in the desert. *Avda. Reina Regente 8, 04001, 950/238011, FAX 950/270691. 117 rooms. Bar, breakfast room, pool. AE, DC, MC, V.*

$–$$ **Torreluz II.** Value is the overriding attraction of this comfortable and elegant modern hotel. The rooms are slick and bright, with the kind of installations for which you'd expect to pay more. Also worth trying is the restaurant, which serves satisfying Mediterranean fare. *Plaza Flores 1, 04001, FAX 950/234399. 74 rooms. 2 restaurants, cafeteria, bar. AE, DC, MC, V.*

$ **Hostal Sevilla.** If you just want an inexpensive yet comfortable place to stay, this is it. Located within the labyrinth of the old town, Hostal Sevilla gives healthy doses of Andalusian ambience, style, and charm. The whitewashed rooms vary—those on the street side have small terraces, while those on the quieter interior look over the courtyards and rooftops of the old town. All have ceramic-tile floors. *Granada 25, 04001, 950/230009. 37 rooms. MC, V.*

Nightlife and the Arts

There is no shortage of discos and flamenco *tablaos* (floor shows) along the Costa Blanca. Most towns have nightspots; inquire at your hotel.

Outdoor Activities and Sports

TENNIS

Most of the coastal hotels have tennis courts, though most of these are for guests only. Some exceptions are **Hotel Eurotennis** (✉ Villajoyosa, ☎ 96/589–1250), **La Manga Club** (✉ Los Belones, ☎ 968/137234), and **Club de Tenis V. Alegre** (✉ Paraje El Olive, Huercal de Almería, ☎ 950/300390).

Shopping

Among the best buys in antiques, if you can find them at about 1,000 ptas. each, are antique *azulejos*. Look for copper and brass, too, especially Art Deco oil lamps. For quality, more-expensive antiques, visit **Domínguez Cazorla** in Almería (✉ Miguel Segura 3, ☎ 950/231876).

Biar, Chinchilla, and Níjar (north of Almería) are known for ceramics.

THE SOUTHEAST A TO Z

Arriving and Departing

By Boat

From Denia, **Balearea** (✉ Puerto de Denia, ☎ 96/578–4200) sails to Ibiza and Palma de Mallorca at 9 PM daily. From Almería, **Trasmediterránea** (☎ 950/236956) sails to Melilla, a Spanish outpost on the Moroccan coast, at 11 PM Monday–Saturday.

By Bus

Private companies run buses down the coast and from Madrid to Valencia, Benidorm, Alicante, Murcia, Mar Menor, and Almería (☞ Getting Around, *below*).

By Car

The *autopista* A7 from Barcelona runs through Valencia and Alicante as far as Murcia. Tolls, though quite high, are often worth it for the time saved, as well as the safe driving conditions. The other main links with the region are the N111 from Madrid to Valencia and the N301 from Madrid to Murcia via Albacete.

By Plane

The Southeast has four major airports: **Valencia** (☞ Chapter 7); **Alicante** (✉ El Altet, Alicante, 12 km [7 mi] south, ☎ 96/691–9000); **San Javier** (✉ Off N332, ☎ 968/570073), for Mar Menor and Murcia; and **Almería** (✉ 6 km [4 mi] east on Carretera de Níjar, Km 9, or Autovía del Mediterráneo, ☎ 950/213700). **Iberia Airlines** has the most flights (☎ 96/521–4414, 968/285093, or 950/213793).

By Train

For RENFE information, contact the company's offices in **Valencia** (☎ 96/352–0202), **Alicante** (☎ 96/592–0202), **Murcia** (☎ 968/252154), or **Almería** (☎ 950/251135).

Getting Around

By Boat

In summer you can cross from either **Alicante** (☎ 96/521–6396) or **Santa Pola** (☎ 96/541–1113) to the tiny island of Tabarca. Boats leave **Benidorm** hourly for the outcrop Isla de Benidorm; the fare is 750 ptas. round trip.

By Bus

Regular bus service connects the region's towns and cities; the main bus depots are in **Alicante** (✉ Avda. Portugal, ☎ 96/513–0700); **Murcia,** west of town (✉ Plaza San Andrés, ☎ 968/292211); and **Almería** (✉ Plaza Barcelona, ☎ 950/210029).

By Car

Avoid coastal roads in summer; the crowds will slow you down. An exception is the road that hugs the Almerían coast—the views straight down into the water from sheer rocky cliffs, and the varied beach landscapes, are worth taking some time over. You can rent a car in any of the provincial capitals and all major resorts, but it will cost less if you reserve one before you leave home.

By Train

Frequent and comfortable RENFE trains connect the region's chief cities. There's also the locally run FGV line, running along the Costa Blanca from Denia to Alicante.

Alicante has a RENFE station (✉ Avda. Salamanca, Alicante, ☎ 96/522–6840) and a RENFE office (✉ Explanada de España 1, Alicante, ☎ 96/521–1303); the FGV station is at the far end of Playa Postiguet (✉ Avda. Villajoyosa, Alicante, ☎ 96/526–2731), reached by buses C1 and C2 from downtown. **Murcia**'s RENFE station is some way out (✉ Industria, ☎ 968/252154), but there is a RENFE office in town (✉ Barrionuevo, Murcia ☎ 968/212842). **Almería**'s station is on Plaza de la Estación (☎ 950/251135).

Contacts and Resources

Consulates

United Kingdom (✉ Plaza Calvo Sotelo, Alicante, ☎ 96/521–6022), open weekday mornings. **United States** (✉ C. de la Paz 6, 3rd floor, Valencia, ☎ 96/351–6973), open weekdays 10–1.

Emergencies

Police: ☎ 091. **Ambulance:** (☎ 96/511–4676 Alicante; 968/218893 Murcia). **Medical assistance:** Alicante, Hospital del SVS (☎ 96/525–0060); Almería, Torrecárdenas (☎ 950/212100; 950/141188 emergencies); Murcia, Hospital La Arrixaca (☎ 968/841500; 968/222222 emergencies).

Golf

Club de Golf Don Cayo (✉ Conde de Altea 49, Altea, ☎ 96/584–8046), 9 holes; **Campo de Golf Villa Martín** (✉ Apdo. 35, Torrevieja, ☎ 96/676–5160), 18 holes; **La Manga Club** (✉ Los Belones, ☎ 968/137234), two 18-hole courses; and **Golf Almerimar** (☎ 950/497454), 18 holes. Be sure to reserve tee times in advance. Expect to pay around 8,000 ptas. for 18 holes, 4,000 ptas. for 9.

Guided Tours

ORIENTATION TOURS

The ***ayuntamiento*** (town hall; ✉ Plaza del Ayuntamiento, ☎ 96/514–9280) and travel agencies in Alicante organize tours of the city and bus and train tours to Guadalest, the Algar waterfalls, Benidorm, the Peñón de Ifach (Calpe), and Elche. In Benidorm, large hotels arrange similar excursions. The ***ayuntamiento*** in Elche (✉ Plaça de Baix, Elche, ☎ 96/545–1000) organizes tours of the city and environs. From Almería, **Viajes Alborán** (✉ Reina Regente 1, Almería, ☎ 950/237477) runs tours of the city and the Almería region. In Melilla, Morocco, **Viajes Cemo** (✉ Avda. La Gaviota, Urbanización Roquetas de Mar, Melilla, Morocco, ☎ 950/333502) is a good resource. In Murcia, contact **Alquibla** (✉ González Adalid 13, ☎ 968/221219) for tours of the city and region.

SPECIAL-INTEREST TOURS

The *ayuntamiento* in Alicante also runs tours to Jijona, where you can visit one of the famous *turrón* (nougat) factories before seeing the amazing stalactites and stalagmites at the Cuevas de Canalobre (Canalobre Caves). This tour sometimes includes a concert in the cave.

Late-Night Pharmacies

Pharmacies in each town take turns staying open 24 hours. All pharmacies display the address of the *farmacia de guardia,* the one on duty that night.

Travel Agencies

Viajes Barceló (✉ San Telmo 9, Alicante, ☎ 96/521–0011). **Viajes Barceló** (✉ Gerona, Edifício Pinos, Benidorm, ☎ 96/585–4750). **Viajes Hispania** (✉ Urbanización Las Sirenas 3, La Manga del Mar Menor, ☎ 968/564161). **Viajes Internacional Expreso 9** (✉ Jaime I El Conquistador, Murcia, ☎ 968/231662).

Visitor Information

Tourist offices with information on the whole southeastern region are those in **Valencia** (☞ Chapter 7); **Alicante** (✉ Explanada de España 2, ☎ 96/520–0000); **Almería** (✉ Parque Nicolás Salmerón, ☎ 950/274355); and **Murcia** (✉ Alejandro Seiquer 4, ☎ 968/366130).

Local tourist-information offices: **Albacete** (✉ Virrey Morcillo 1, ☎ 967/580522); **Alicante** (✉ Avda. Portugal 17, ☎ 96/592–9802); **Benidorm** (✉ Avda. Martínez Alejos 166, ☎ 96/585–3224); **Calpe** (✉ Avda. Ejércitos Españoles s/n, ☎ 96/583–1350); **Cartagena** (✉ Plaza Castellini 5, ☎ 968/596483; ✉ Ayuntamiento, ☎ 968/506463); **Cullera** (✉ C. del Riu 56, ☎ 96/172–0974); **Denia** (✉ Plaza Oculista Builges 9, ☎ 96/578–0724); **Elche** (✉ Parque Municipal, ☎ 96/545–3831 or 96/545–2747); **Gandía** (✉ Marqués de Campo s/n, ☎ 96/287–7788); **Jávea** (✉ Plaza Almirante Basterreche 24, ☎ 96/646–0605); **Lorca** (✉ López Gisbert, ☎ 968/466157); **Orihuela** (✉ Francisco Díez 25, ☎ 96/530–2747); **Santa Pola** (✉ Plaza Diputación, ☎ 96/541–1100); **Torrevieja** (✉ Costera del Mar s/n, ☎ 96/571–5936); and **Xátiva** (✉ Moncada, ☎ 96/227–3346).

9 THE BALEARIC ISLANDS

There was a time when the Balearics' strategic position—off Spain's eastern coast, halfway between France and Africa—made them an enviable crossroads for trade and a hot point in territorial disputes. They're now envied for different reasons, and great stretches of the coasts of Majorca and Ibiza have been marred by accommodations for package tourists. Still, Menorca and Formentera remain largely unspoiled, and Majorca's northwestern coast is as rough and spectacular as it was when George Sand and Frédéric Chopin spent a winter among its rugged mountains a century and a half ago.

By Sean Hignett

Updated by George Semler

PART OF THE PHOENICIAN, Roman, and Byzantine empires before the Moors invaded them in 902, the Balearic Islands—Majorca (Mallorca), Minorca (Menorca), Ibiza, and Formentera—have long been an important maritime trading and staging post. Lying between 80 and 242 km (50 and 150 mi) from Spain's Mediterranean coast, they are halfway between France and Africa.

The Moors remained until ousted by Jaume I of the House of Aragón between 1229 and 1235. The islands were part of the independent kingdom of Majorca (which included Roussillon and the Cerdanya Valley on the mainland) from 1276 until 1343, when they returned to the Crown of Aragón under Pedro IV. Upon the marriage of Isabella of Castile to Ferdinand of Aragón in 1469, the Balearics became part of a united Spain. During the War of the Spanish Succession, however, Great Britain occupied Minorca in 1704 to secure the superb natural harbor of Mahón as a naval base. The British stayed for almost a century, interrupted only by an invasion in 1756, which gave the French control for 12 years, and a shorter reoccupation by the Spanish 20 years later. Under the Treaty of Amiens, Britain finally returned Minorca to Spain in 1802.

Minorca diverged once more during the Spanish Civil War, remaining loyal to Spain's democratically elected Republican government while Majorca and Ibiza sided with Franco's insurgents. Majorca became a home base for the Italian fleet supporting the fascist cause. This topic is still broached delicately on the islands; they remain fiercely independent of one another in many ways. Even Mahón and Ciutadella, at opposite ends of Minorca—all of 44 km (27 mi) apart—remain locked in bitter opposition over differences dating from the war with Britain.

The tourist boom, which began during Franco's regime (1939–75), turned great stretches of Majorca's and Ibiza's coastlines into unplanned strips of high-rise hotels, fast-food restaurants, and discos. Only recently have ecology-minded residents begun to make headway in lobbying for restrictions on shoreline development.

In 1983 the Balearics became an Autonomous Community. One result has been the general replacement of Castilian Spanish by the Catalan language (banned for official use by Franco) in its Mallorquín, Menorquín, and Ibizencan dialects. This can be confusing, because outside the islands you'll still hear island locations named in Spanish. Within the islands, the problem is compounded by the fact that road signs that have not been officially altered are sometimes obliterated by spray paint. We use Catalan or Spanish according to whichever is used locally. *Avinguda* (avenue), *carrer* (street), and *plaça* (square) are Catalan; *avenida, calle,* and *plaza* are Spanish.

Place names that may cause confusion are (Spanish version first):

Majorca: La Puebla/Sa Pobla; Santa Margarita/Santa Margalida; Colonia San Pedro/Colònia Sant Per; San Juan/Sant Joan.

Minorca: Mahón/Maó; Ciudadela/Ciutadella; San Jaime/Sant Jaume.

Ibiza: Santa Inés/Santa Agnes; San Miguel/Sant Miquel; San Jorge/Sant Jordi; San Antonio Abad/Sant Antoni de Portmany; San José/Sant Josep; San Juan/Sant Joan; Ibiza/Eivissa (Ibiza town is also "Ciutat").

Formentera: San Francisco/Sant Francesc; San Fernando/Sant Ferran.

Pleasures and Pastimes

Beaches

Beaches are a major attraction here, even if some of them are far from peaceful. Note that *cala* is the local word for "cove" or "inlet."

MAJORCA

The closer a beach is to Palma, the more crowded it's likely to be. West of the city, the nice, narrow beach of **Palma Nova/Magalluf** is backed by one of the noisiest resorts on the Mediterranean. **Paguera,** with several small beaches, is the only sizable local resort not overshadowed by high-rises. A little farther along, **Camp de Mar,** with a good beach of fine white sand, is small and relatively undeveloped but is sometimes overrun with day-trippers from other resorts. **Sant Telm,** at the end of this coast, has a pretty little bay and a tree-shaded parking lot.

East of Palma, a 5-km (3-mi) stretch of sand runs along the main coastal road from C'an Pastilla to Arenal, forming an overbuilt package-tour nexus also known collectively as **Playa de Palma.** The beach is nice enough, but again, it's crowded.

The only *real* beach on the northwest coast is at **Port de Sóller,** a scenic bay nearly enclosed by its headlands. **Cala St. Vicenç,** at the top end of this coast, has fine, soft sand in two narrow bays and is only moderately developed. At **Port de Pollença,** on the north coast, the sand is imported, but the resort is attractive and has good water sports. There is frequent water-taxi service from Port de Pollença to **Formentor,** one of the finest beaches on Majorca. The north coast also has the island's longest sand beach; gently shelved, and backed in part by pines, it stretches 8 km (5 mi) from Port de Alcúdia to C'an Picafort and beyond.

On the map, Majorca's Levante, or southeast coast, is peppered with beaches and coves, though few are easily accessed by automobile. **Canyamel,** near the Caves of Artà, is one of the larger undeveloped strands.

A little farther south, **Costa d'es Pins** is an extensive, expensive urbanization, but it has a good sandy stretch backed by a thin line of pines. Tourist buses, decorated to look like train engines, run from here to **Cala Millor,** which has a long, narrow, sloping beach of soft sand. Much of Cala Millor's beach is accessible only on foot, so it's ideal for children, though very crowded in summer. Farther south still, **Cala d'Or** is a pleasant resort, and **Cala Gran,** a short walk away, is even more attractive. **Cala Mondrajó,** a tiny, sandy bay with little development, is also a good bet; it's most easily reached by boat from Portopetre or Cala Figuera.

On the south coast, the dune-backed beach at **Es Trenc,** near Colònia de Sant Jordi, is one of Majorca's few quiet seaside patches. The 10-km (6-mi) walk along the beach from Colonia de Sant Jordi to the Cap Salines lighthouse is one of the island's most secret treasures.

MINORCA

Cala Mesquida, north of Mahón, is popular with the Mahonese; you'll see few tourists here. Another small beach, also development-free, lies on a **headland** beyond one of Menorca's many watchtowers.

Farther west, **Es Grau,** a sandy stretch with dunes behind it, is sometimes a bit littered. Behind **Es Grau** is the S'Albufera nature reserve. Before the lighthouse at the end of Cap Faváritx are the nudist beaches **Cala Presili** and **Playa Tortuga. Arenal d'en Castell,** a sheltered circular bay, and **Arenal de Son Saura** (also known as Son Parc) are the biggest sandy beaches on the north of the island.

At the junction of the Mahón–Fornells and Mercadal–Fornells roads, take the small lane leading west and follow signs to **Binimel.là,** an excellent sandy beach. It's often deserted, and the caves in the tiny coves to the west provide welcome shade in the summer.

The only reasonable and generally accessible beach north of Ciutadella is **Cala Morell.** Minorcans claim that the inlets and beaches at **Cala Algaiarens** are the nicest on the island. **Son Saura, Cala en Turqueta,** and **Macarella,** at the west end of the south coast, are all reached by driving southeast from Ciutadella toward Son Saura. You'll be halted by a gate and a sign prohibiting entry, but no one will bother you if you close the gate behind you. All three are classic Minorcan beaches with trees down to the water's edge, horseshoe coves, and white sand. To the east, **Cala Mitjana, Cala Trebaluger, Cala Fustam,** and **Cala Escorxada** are accessible on land only by foot, but you can rent boats with outboard engines to reach them or Son Saura. You can get to the long, straight, sandy stretches of **Binigaus, Sant Adeodato,** and **Santo Tomas** from Mercadal, and to **Son Bou,** the island's longest beach (with a nudist section), from Alaior.

Cala 'n Porter is a British enclave. The rectangular cove has a sandy beach sheltered by cliffs.

IBIZA

Immediately south of Ibiza town is one of Ibiza's longest stretches of sandy beach, the nearly 3-km (2-mi) **Playa d'En Bossa,** almost entirely developed. Farther on, a left turn at Sant Jordi on the way to the airport leads across the salt pans to **Cavallet** and **Ses Salines,** two of the most natural beaches on the island. Topless bathing is accepted all over Ibiza, but **Es Cavallet** is the official nudist beach. All the remaining beaches on this part of the island are accessible from the Ibiza–Sant Josep–Sant Antoni highway, down side roads that often end in rough tracks.

North of Sant Antoni, there are no easily accessible beaches until you reach **Puerto San Miguel,** an almost rectangular cove with relatively restrained development. Next along the north coast, accessible via San Juan, is Portinaitx, a series of small coves with sandy beaches, of which the first and last, **Cala Xarraca** and **Caló d'Es Porcs,** are the best.

The beaches on the east coast have been developed, but **Santa Eulàlia** remains attractive. The resort has a narrow, sloping beach in front of a pedestrian promenade that, despite being lined by hotels and apartment blocks, is not frenetic, like Sant Antoni.

FORMENTERA

Formentera is best for wild and lonely beaches. The undeveloped Playa de Mitjorn stretches for 7 km (4 mi) along the south of the island. Trucadors, a long, thin spit at the north, has 2 km (1 mi) of sand on each side, and in summer you can wade to Es Palmador, where you'll find more sandy beaches and preponderantly nudist bathers.

Dining

MAJORCA

Seafood forms the basis of many local specialties, such as *espinigada* (a pie topped with tiny eels and spinach) and *panades de peix* (fish pies). Lamb, chicken, pork, and their derivatives are also traditional. *Sobrasada,* the bright-red Majorcan sausage paste, is basically pork and red pepper, and even the fluffy-looking, cloyingly sweet *ensaimada*—a powdery spiral pastry that ranges in size from a breakfast snack to a gift-boxed party special a foot in diameter—is based on *saim* (pork fat). Other specialties are *butifarra* and *llonganissa* sausages, *coques amb verdura* and *trampó* (pizzalike pastries covered with vegetables or finely chopped salad), and *cocarrois* (pastries filled with meat or a mixture of vegetables). *Sopa mallorquina* is a meal of fried vegetables in meat stock, usually served over pieces of thinly sliced bread. *Escaldum* is a stew of chicken legs with potatoes and ground almonds; *tumbet* is a stew of meat or fish with peppers, tomatoes, potatoes, and eggplant.

MINORCA

Until recently, Minorcan restaurant cuisine consisted almost entirely of seafood and was served mainly along the harbors in Mahón, Ciutadella, and the fishing village of Fornells. Fornells is famous for its very expensive *llagosta* (lobster), sold by weight and grilled or served as *caldereta* (soup). Lately, a country cuisine has developed, based on inland and upland products such as rabbit, pork, and slow-baked stews and roasts.

Mayonnaise—which was invented in Minorca during the French occupation and named after Mahón—is usually freshly prepared. Local tapas include *tornellas*—sheep's intestines stuffed with bread crumbs, garlic, and meat, then braided and cooked.

IBIZA AND FORMENTERA

Because much produce comes to Ibiza and Formentera from mainland Spain via Palma, the cost of dining on these islands may seem high, especially in such simple surroundings. Many local products, however, such as potatoes and the native sea bass and bream are prized for their distinctive taste. You can find authentic Balearic specialties inland, off the tourist track; look for *sofrit pagès*—local potatoes and red peppers stewed in olive oil and garlic—and *ratjada eivissenca* (grilled, semi-poached ray).

CATEGORY	COST*
$$$$	over 7,500 ptas.
$$$	5,500–7,500 ptas.
$$	2,000–5,500 ptas.
$	under 2,000 ptas.

**per person for a three-course meal, excluding drinks, service, and tax*

Fiestas

MAJORCA

The first fiesta of the year is that of **Sant Antoni d'Abat,** the traditional blessing of a long procession of animals, on January 17. **Sant Joan Pelós** (literally, "hairy St. John") is celebrated on June 23–24 in Felanitx; a man dresses in sheepskins to represent John the Baptist. The **Romería de Sant Marçal** (Pilgrimage of St. Mark), held June 30 in Sa Cabaneta, involves Majorca's typical *siurells,* primitive ceramic whistles.

MINORCA

Minorca's traditional fiestas are essentially celebrations for the townsfolk and villagers, and have changed little in deference to tourism. Summer begins with Ciutadella's feast of **Sant Joan** (June 23–24), when *caixeres* (townspeople representing all classes) take part in a *jaleo*—they dance on horseback to the sound of a band, attempting to keep the horses up on their hind legs while the crowd gathers beneath. From July on, fiestas follow in quick succession. **Sant Lluís,** at the end of August, has a fiesta spotlighting equestrian activities; Mahón's **Fiestas de Gràcia** (Feast of Our Lady of Grace; September 7–8) are the season's final celebrations.

IBIZA

Ibiza's patron saint—somewhat oddly, given the climate—is **Mare de Déu dels Neus** (Our Lady of the Snows). Her saint's day is actually August 5, but she is honored on August 8 in memory of the conquest of Ibiza, taken from the Moors by Jaume I of the House of Aragón that day in 1235. **Sant Antoni Abat** (January 17) is the annual blessing of the animals, with processions of pets, cavalry, and livestock of all kinds. On February 12 the **Festes de Santa Eulàlia** are a virtual winter carnival. **Sant Josep** (March 19) is known for its folk dancing, which you can also see in the village of Sant Joan every Thursday evening. On June 23–24, witness the island-wide **Festa Major de Sant Joan** (Feast of St. John the Baptist). The **Festa del Mar,** honoring the Mare de Déu del Carme (Our Lady of Carmen), is held July 15–16 in Eivissa, Santa Eulàlia, Sant Antoni, and Sant Josep as well as on Formentera. The August 28th feast of **Sant Agustí** is a tiny upland fiesta with folk dancing and an authentic Ibizencan flavor.

FORMENTERA

On July 15–16 islanders honor the **Virgen del Carmen,** patron saint of sailors, with colorful processions of fishing boats, yachts, and nearly anything else that floats. On July 25, Sant Francesc dances in honor of **Sant Jaume** (St. James), Spain's male patron saint.

Lodging

MAJORCA

Majorca's newer resorts, concentrated mainly on the southern coast, amount to more than 1,500 hotels, many of which serve the package-tour industry. There are plenty of charming, low-cost spots, however, on the northwest coast and in the central countryside.

MINORCA

Apart from a few hotels and hostels in Mahón and Ciutadella, almost all of Minorca's tourist lodgings are in new beach resorts. As on the other islands, many of these are fully reserved by travel operators in the high season, so it's generally most economical to book a package that combines airfare and accommodations.

IBIZA

On Ibiza, hotels are concentrated mainly in coastal Sant Antoni and Playa d'En Bossa. Many of these are excellent, but unless you're eager to be part of a mob, Sant Antoni has little to recommend it. Playa d'En Bossa, newer and close to the town of Ibiza, is less brash, but it lies under the flight path into the airport. To get off the beaten track and into the island's largely pristine interior, look for *agroturismo* lodgings in Els Amunts (The Uplands), in villages such as Santa Gertrudis or Sant Miquel de Balansat.

FORMENTERA

If July and August are the only months you can come here, reserve well in advance, as every bed fills. To get the true feel of this smallest major member of the archipelago, look for the most out-of-the-way *calas* (inlets) and fishing villages.

CATEGORY	COST*
$$$$	over 20,000 ptas.
$$$	10,000–20,000 ptas.
$$	4,000–10,000 ptas.
$	under 4,000 ptas.

**All prices are for a standard double room, excluding tax.*

Exploring the Balearic Islands

Of the four main islands, Majorca and Ibiza are the most heavily developed. Minorca and Formentera remain less populated and wilder. The north coast of Majorca and parts of Ibiza still have as much rocky coastline and diaphanous water as anyone can use at once, but—on balance—go to Formentera for solitude and intimacy; Ibiza for wilderness with heavy concentrations of humanity; Majorca for the mixture of Palma's urban cosmopolitanism with the wild north coast and interior; and Minorca for what may be the best blend of all of the above.

Numbers in the text correspond to numbers in the margin and on the Majorca, Minorca, and Ibiza and Formentera maps.

Great Itineraries

Visiting one island in an archipelago generally means going to a single destination and exploring locally. In the Balearics, however, flights and ferries allow easy excursions to neighboring isles, so that if you stay a week or 10 days you may even have time to sample all four.

A three-day trip to the Balearics does require a choice of just one island. Our choice here would be Majorca, for Palma's superb art and architecture, the villages of the mountainous north coast, and the interior. Five days would still suggest a one-island visit, with time to relax in one place yet explore the island more thoroughly. A ten-day trip might allow an ambitious and curious traveler to see it all, or at least to explore Majorca and Minorca. We suggest sleeping on no more than two islands, with perhaps a day trip to Formentera or Ibiza.

IF YOU HAVE 3 DAYS

Fly to **Palma de Mallorca** ① and spend that day and the next morning exploring the historic city center. The next day, head for the hills—specifically the Sierra de Tramuntana, on the island's north coast—and see the **Raixa palace** ② on your way to the **Jardins d'Alfàbia** ③, **Sóller** ④, **Deià** ⑤, **Son Marroig** ⑥, and Sa Foradada. Spend the night in **Valldemossa** ⑦, where Frédéric Chopin and George Sand spent a winter together. On your third day, finish exploring the Tramuntana mountains: see Sa Granja, and hike down into the Torrent de Pareis ravine and beach if you have time. Visit the monastery at **Lluc** ⑬ before exploring the town and the port of **Pollença** ⑫. Make Alcúdia your last stop before the 40-minute drive back to Palma for your last night.

IF YOU HAVE 5 DAYS

You can either do the Majorca loop from Palma (along the north coast and back through the center), with more time to settle in and explore, *or* devote your trip to Minorca, a good fit for a five-day visit. Spend your first day exploring **Mahón** ⑰. The next day, settle into a secluded beach on the southern coast, and perhaps tour the cave dwellings at **Cales Coves.** Spend the night at **Son Bou** or **Sant Lluís.** On day three, visit the megalithic ruins at Torre d'en Gaumés, Torralba, on your way to Es Mercadal and Minorca's highest point, **Monte Toro.** Have dinner and spend the night in **Fornells.** On day four, take in the beaches at Fornells and Cap de Cavalleria before returning through Es Mercadal and Ferreries to **Cala Santa Galdana.** Dedicate your fifth day to the ruins at Naveta des Tudons, Cala Morell, and **Ciutadella** ⑱.

When to Tour the Balearic Islands

Summer is too hot and crowded here. May and October are probably ideal, with June and September just behind. Winter, from November through March, is quiet, and while the weather is not always warm enough for the beach, it's fine for hiking, golfing, and general exploring.

MAJORCA

More than five times the size of either Minorca or Ibiza, Majorca is shaped roughly like a saddle. The Sierra de Tramuntana, a tough mountain range soaring to nearly 5,000 ft, runs the length of its northwest coast, and a ridge of hills borders the southeast shores; between the two lies a great, flat plain that in early spring becomes a sea of almond blossoms, "the snow of Majorca." Having acquired a reputation as a cheap getaway, especially among Britons and Germans, Majorca gets more than 10 million visitors per year, but the package-tour industry is confined to a narrow coastal strip. Elsewhere, Majorca has relatively undiscovered charms, particularly in the mountains of the northwest and in the interior: caves, bird sanctuaries, abandoned monasteries, tiny museums, and village markets form a good mixture of natural and man-made sights.

Palma de Mallorca

❶ *40-min flight from Barcelona.*

If you look north of the cathedral (La Seu, or the "seat" of the Bishopric, to Majorcans) on a map of the city of Palma, you'll see around the Plaça Santa Eulàlia the jumble of tiny streets that made up the early town. Farther out, a ring of wide boulevards, known as the Avenues, zigzags around—these follow the path of the walls built by the Moors to defend the larger city that had grown up by the 12th century. The zigzags mark the bastions that jutted out at regular intervals. By the end of the 19th century the walls were largely torn down; the only place where you can still see the massive defenses is Ses Voltes, along the seafront west of the cathedral.

A stream bed (*torrent*) used to run through the middle of the old city, dry for most of the year but often a raging flood in the rainy season, causing destruction and drowning. In the 17th century it was diverted to the east, along the moat that ran outside the city walls. The stream's natural course is now followed by La Rambla and the Passeig d'Es Born, two of Palma's main arteries. The traditional evening *paseo* (promenade) takes place on the Born.

If you come to Palma by car, park in the garage beneath the **Parc de la Mar** and stroll along the park. Beside it run the huge bastions guarding the Almudaina Palace; the cathedral, golden and massive, rises beyond. The park has several **ceramic murals** by the late Catalan artist and Majorca resident Joan Miró, as well as various modern **sculptures.**

If you begin early enough, a walk along the ramparts at **Ses Voltes** from the ***mirador*** (lookout) beside the Palma cathedral is spectacular. The first rays of the sun turn the upper pinnacles of **La Seu** bright gold, and begin to work their way down the sandstone walls. From the Parc de la Mar, follow Avinguda Antoni Maura past the steps to the palace. At the Plaça de la Reina, the **Passeig des Born** begins, an avenue with a pedestrian promenade down its center, lined with towering plane trees and fashionable shops. For an even more spectacular and intimate walk up to the Born, retrace your steps to the beginning of Avinguda Antoni Maura and walk left through the **Plaça de la Llotja** (don't miss a chance to visit the Mediterranean's finest civic Gothic building if it's open) then up Carrer de Sant Joan. The stately town house at No. 1 is the well-known nightspot Abaco. Farther up, on Carrer Montenegro at No. 2, is the **Des Puig** house and entryway under an impressive coat of arms. At the corner of Carrer Sant Feliu, have a look at the Renaissance facade of No. 8, the 16th-century Can Salas, and No. 10, next door, known as **Casa de Ses Carasses** for the sculpted masks on the doorway. A right turn on Carrer Sant Feliu takes you back out to the Born just above the Plaça de la Reina.

At the top of the Born, turn right at the Plaça Rei Joan Carles into Carrer de la Unió. A few steps down to the right is the Plaça del Mercat. The 14th-century church of **San Nicolau** and its hexagonal bell tower stand back on the right, with a large tuft of brown grass growing near the top. On the same side of the square, the ornate facades of the pair of buildings at the entrance to Carrer Santacilia, the **Casas Casasayas,**

Majorca

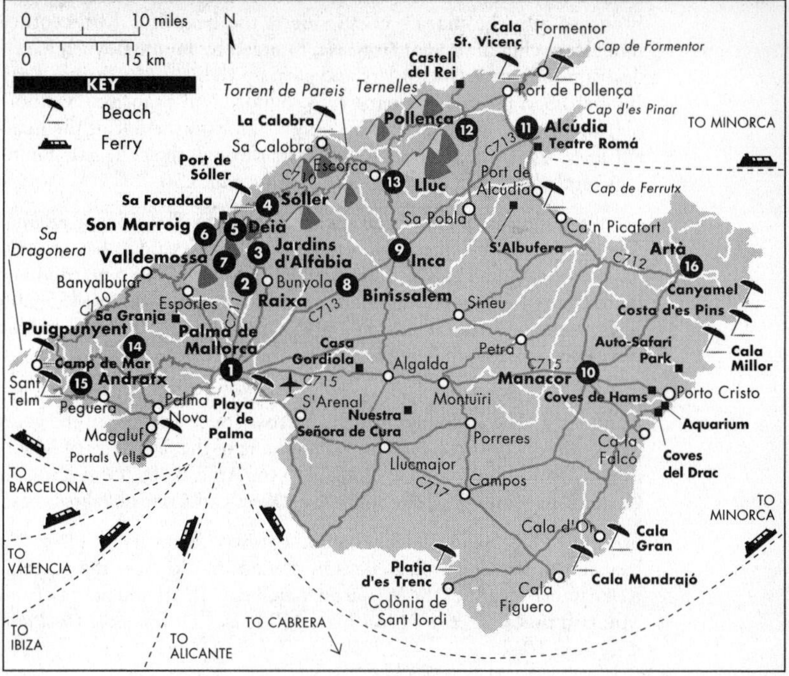

now a bank and a boutique, were designed by Moderniste (Art Nouveau) architect Francesc Roca Simóin 1908. The ornate **Gran Hotel** stands across the way in blinding alabaster splendor, built between 1901 and 1903 by Moderniste master Luís Domènech i Montaner, author of Barcelona's Palau de la Música Catalana. Don't miss the permanent exhibit of the famous Majorcan impressionist Anglada Camarassa.

Past the Palau Berga (on the right at Plaça Weyler 12), near the steps leading up to the right of the Teatro Principal, is the **Forn des Teatre** (Theater Bakery), a unique shop known for its *ensaimadas* and *cocas*. The facade recalls a fairground organ.

The **Teatre Principal** stands in neoclassical symmetry at the top of the Plaça Weyler. From here, stroll up the **Rambla,** around the corner and up to the left. It's a 15-minute walk to the top and back, through flower and book stalls.

From the Forn, climb the steps to the Plaça Marqués Palmer, where an archway on the left leads to the greater expanse of the **Plaça Major.** A crafts market fills this elegant neoclassical square on Monday, Friday, and Saturday mornings between 10 and 2.

Carrer Colom leads away from the Plaça Major past two Art Nouveau buildings worth looking up to admire. The **El Aguila** department store is the first; the second, and more interesting, above a corner bookstore, is **Can Forteza Rei,** designed by its owner, Luis Forteza Rei, in 1909. Farther down Carrer Colom is the Plaça Cort, with the 17th-century ***ajuntament*** (town hall). The olive tree on the right side of the square is one of Majorca's so-called *olivos milenarios*—thousand-year-old oaks—and may be even older. To the west of the ajuntament, the bank **Caja de Baleares Sa Nostra,** on the corner of Carrer Jaume II and the Plaça Cort, occupies a superb Art Nouveau building.

East of the ajuntament, follow Carrer Cadena across the Plaça Santa Eulàlia to Carrer del Convent de Sant Francesc and the Plaça Sant Francesc. On the plaza's north side is the beautiful 13th-century monastery church of **Sant Francesc,** founded by Jaume II when his eldest son took monastic orders and gave up rights to the throne. Fray Junípero Serra, the missionary who founded San Francisco, California, was later educated here; his effigy stands to the left of the main entrance. Enter the church and cloisters through the collegiate buildings on the east side. ⏲ *Mon.–Sat. 9:30–1 and 3:30–7.*

From the church of Sant Francesc, return to the Plaça Santa Eulàlia. The eminent 13th-century scholar Ramón Llull is said to have ridden his horse into the church of **Santa Eulàlia** in pursuit of a married noblewoman of whom he was enamored in his wild youth. In 1435, 200 Jews were converted to Christianity in this church after their rabbis were threatened with being burned at the stake.

Just south of the Plaça Santa Eulàlia, off Carrer d'en Morey, is Carrer Almudaina. The **archway** over the narrow street was one of the gates to the early Moorish citadel and is now one of the few relics of Moorish occupation on Majorca, along with the Arab Baths (☞ *below*). At Carrer d'en Morey 9, peek into the **Can Oleza** patio, one of Palma's best.

From the Plaça Santa Eulàlia, continue down Carrer d'en Morey and bear left down Carrer Portella. On the left, at No. 5, is the graceful Renaissance facade of the **Museu de Majorca,** with art and pottery from Moorish times. ☎ *971/717540.* 🎫 *350 ptas.* ⏲ *Tues.–Sat. 10–2 and 4–7, Sun. 10–2.*

At the bottom of Carrer Portella, turn left onto Carrer Formiguera, a short street that tunnels through the adjoining buildings, then left again up Carrer de Can Serra to the 10th-century **Banys Arabs** (Arab Baths). One of Palma's oldest and most beautiful monuments, the baths are in a quiet lemon grove. ☎ *971/721549.* 🎫 *250 ptas.* ⏲ *Daily 9–6.*

Palma's **cathedral** can be approached from the top of Carrer de Can Serra, where you turn left and follow the meandering streets west to the Plaça Almoina, with a cluster of antiques shops and restorers. An architectural wonder that took almost 400 years to build (1230–1601), the extraordinarily wide (63-ft) expanse of the nave is supported on 14 extraordinarily slender, 70-ft-tall columns, which fan out like palm trees at the top. The nave is dominated by an immense rose window, 40 ft in diameter, from 1370. Look up into the nave: suspended above the Royal Chapel is the curious **asymmetrical canopy** built by Antoni Gaudí, who remodeled the chapel at the beginning of the 20th century. Lights within the canopy come on at regular intervals.

The **bell tower** above the cathedral's Plaça Almoina door holds nine bells, the largest of which is known as N'Eloi, meaning "praise." N'Eloi was cast in 1389, weighs 4 tons, needs 12 men to ring it, and has shattered stained-glass windows with its sound. Continuing around the cathedral, you'll hit the impressive **west facade,** whose blocked windows are the result of alterations following earthquake damage in 1851. ⏲ *Weekdays 10–12:30 and 4–6:30, Sat. 10–1:30.*

Opposite the cathedral is the **Palau de l'Almudaina** (Almudaina Palace), residence of the royal house of Majorca during the Middle Ages and originally an Arab citadel. Now a military headquarters, it can be visited only on guided tours (every half hour). 🎫 *450 ptas.; EU citizens free Wed.* ⏲ *Weekdays 9:30–1:30 and 4–6:30, Sat. 9:30–1:30.*

By this time in your walk, the sun will have crossed the Bay of Palma and the shadows you watched coming down the walls of La Seu in the morning will be working their way back up while you make another tour of Ses Voltes. You might even hear Majorcan *gaitas* (bagpipes) playing as you head back to the Plaça de La Llotja for some refreshment.

The **Llotja** (Exchange), on the seafront a little west of the Born, was built in the 15th century and soon became the most important maritime commodities exchange on the Mediterranean. It's also the Mediterranean's finest example of civic Gothic architecture, a masterpiece of decorative turrets, battlements, and buttresses surrounding tracery-trimmed Gothic windows and perfectly balanced and fluted pillars. ✉ *Plaça de la Llotja.* ⏲ *During exhibits, Tues.–Sat. 11–2 and 5–9, Sun. 11–2.*

If you have some extra time in Palma, consider some other key sights:

The **Castell de Bellver** (Bellver Castle) overlooks the city and the bay from a hillside above the Terreno nightlife area. Built in the 14th century on a circular design, it's a sturdy fortress complete with dry moat and drawbridge. There's a terrific view of Palma and the bay from the ramparts and keep, and within the walls is a fascinating historical **museum.** 🎫 *275 ptas.* ⏲ *Oct.–Mar., Mon.–Sat. 8–6; Apr.–Sept., Mon.–Sat. 8–8.*

The **Museu Fundació Pilar y Joan Miró** (Pilar and Joan Miró Foundation Museum) displays numerous works by the Catalan artist, who spent his last years on Majorca (1979–83). ✉ *Carrer Joan de Saridakis 29,* ☎ *971/701420.* 🎫 *750 ptas.* ⏲ *Tues.–Sat. 10–6, Sun. 10–3.*

The **Poble Espanyol** (Spanish Village), in the western suburbs of Palma, is a reproduction of various Spanish buildings and styles, complete with shops and crafts studios. ✉ *Carrer Capitán Mesquida Veny 39,* ☎ *971/737070.* 🎫 *900 ptas.* ⏲ *Village daily 9–8, crafts shops daily 10–6.*

Dining and Lodging

$$$ ★ ✕ **Koldo Royo.** Crowded with modern art, this chic yellow dining room overlooks the marina through glass walls. Chef-owner Koldo Royo conjures up Basque specialties like lamprey, salt cod, baked hake, tripe, and stuffed quail; try the *pechuguitas de codorniz rellenas de pétalos de rosas* (quail breasts stuffed with rose petals). ✉ *Avda. Gabriel Roca 3,* ☎ *971/732435. AE, MC, V. No lunch weekends Jan. 16–31 or June 16–31.*

$$$ ✕ **Porto Pi.** Dining in this old Majorcan villa in the Terreno area, 1 km (½ mi) west of Plaza Gomila, is like eating in a private home. The elegant central hall–cum–drawing room opens onto several high-ceiling dining rooms with round tables and oil paintings, and you can dine on the terrace in summer. The fine cooking is international, such as *escalopines de foie gras a la parrilla* (barbecued escallops of foie gras). ✉ *Carrer Garita 23 (or Avda. Joan Miró 174),* ☎ *971/400087. MC, V. Closed Sun. No lunch Sat.*

$$ ✕ **Caballito de Mar.** Across from the Llotja at the very center of Palma's port, this handy place focuses on *caldereta de pescado* (thick fish soup) and fish concoctions of all kinds. Try the *rodaballo en vino blanco* (turbot cooked in white wine). The place is much frequented by locals and tourists alike; the only drawback is the nearby traffic. ✉ *Passeig de Sagrera 5,* ☎ *971/721074. AE, DC, MC, V.*

$$ ✕ **Café la Lonja.** Both the sunny terrace in front of the Llotja—a privileged dining spot—and the *Orient Express*–style train wagon inside are excellent places for a drink or meal. Seafood, fish, and paella are the specialties. A good rendezvous point, watering hole, or restaurant. ✉ *Carrer Marina 2,* ☎ *971/722799. AE, DC, MC, V. Closed Sun.*

$$ ✕ **La Bóveda.** This shady place on a back street next to the Llotja is excellent for tapas—light or heavy—and full meals. It's the little brother of the Taberna de la Bóveda, out on the waterfront at Passeig d'en Sagrera 3, and both are good choices, but the sunnier, breezier Taberna suffers from the din of heavy traffic. La Bóveda's menu features fresh seafood

and light dishes ranging from salads to vegetables to mushrooms. ✉ *Carrer de la Botería 3,* ☎ *971/714863. AE, DC, MC, V. Closed Sun. and Feb.*

$$$$ ★ **San Lorenzo.** This tiny place is a gem, if you can get a room. It's built into an aristocratic Majorcan town house, but the rooms are completely modern, and all comforts are impeccable. The design is classic Majorcan: exposed wood beams; watermarked silks in pastel blues, greens, and yellows; and traditional furniture. The suites have terraces and working fireplaces. ✉ *Carrer San Lorenzo 14, 07012,* ☎ *971/728200,* FAX *971/711901. 4 rooms, 2 suites. Bar, café, minibars, pool. AE, DC, MC, V.*

$$$$ **Son Caliu.** The Son Caliu offers grande-dame comfort, service, and style within a sleek, modern exterior. It's particularly popular with golfers, who can choose from among five courses within a half-hour drive. Located on a quiet, private beach 15 km (9 mi) west of Palma, the hotel is ideally placed for touring northwestern Majorca. NASA technology ensures virtually chlorine-free swimming in the two attractive pools. ✉ *Urb. Son Caliu, 07016 Costa de Calvia,* ☎ *971/682200,* FAX *971/683720. 215 rooms, 8 suites. Restaurant, bar, indoor and outdoor pools, beauty salon, tennis court, health club, squash. AE, DC, MC, V.*

$$$$ **Son Vida.** Situated on a hillside outside Palma, this Sheraton contains a 13th-century castle. The antique furniture of the public rooms contrasts with the futuristic, bronze-mirror look of the restaurant El Jardín. Most rooms have panoramic views of Palma Bay, to the south; a few overlook the service area and hillside but, to compensate, are double the size of the others. ✉ *Castillo Son Vida, 07015,* ☎ *971/790000,* FAX *971/790017. 171 rooms. 2 restaurants, 2 bars, 1 indoor and 2 outdoor pools, beauty salon, 4 tennis courts, 18-hole golf course, health club, library, playground. AE, DC, MC, V.*

$$ ★ **Born.** Nicely located on a quiet street just off the busy Plaça Rei Juan Carlos, the Hotel Born occupies the former mansion of a noble Majorcan family. Romanesque arches and a giant palm tree spectacularly cover the central courtyard and reception area. Guest rooms are modest, but their prices are more than reasonable. ✉ *Carrer Sant Jaume 3, 07012,* ☎ *971/712942,* FAX *971/718618. 29 rooms. AE, DC, MC, V.*

Nightlife and the Arts

The City of Palma Symphony Orchestra performs about twice a month in winter at the **Auditorium** (✉ Passeig Marítim 18, ☎ 971/234735), which also offers ballet and drama throughout the year, as does the **Teatre Principal** (✉ Adjacent to Plaça Major, ☎ 971/784735).

With some 200 discos and music bars scattered throughout the city and across the island, Majorca's nightlife is never hard to find. In Palma, the **Plaça de la Llotja** and surrounding streets are the place to go for *copas* (drinking, tapas sampling, and general carousing).

Carrer Apuntadores, on the west side of the Born, is always lively at night. In the cobbled streets of the old town, restaurants and bars jostle each other for room. Try **Abaco** (✉ Carrer de Sant Joan 1) for stately surroundings and Baroque music. The section of the Passeig Marítim known as Avinguda Gabriel Roca is another nucleus of taverns and pubs, the most popular of which are **Pachá, Tito's,** and **Ib's.**

The most incandescent hot spots are concentrated 6 km (4 mi) west of Palma at **Punta Portals,** in Portals Nous, where King Juan Carlos I moors his yacht along with many of Europe's most beautiful people. **Tristan, Flannigan's,** and **Diablito** are the places to dine, ranging in price and flash from Tristan, the best and most expensive, to Diablito, a pizza emporium.

B.C.M., in Magalluf, is the top disco.

Palma's **casino** is on the harbor promenade, at Avinguda Gabriel Roca 4. There's a nominal entry charge, and you'll need your passport (and a collar and tie) to enter. ☎ *971/454012 or 971/450563.* ⏲ *Daily 3 PM–4 AM.*

Outdoor Activities and Sports

GOLF

Majorca is well stocked with courses: **Canyamel** (✉ Carretera de las Cuevas, 60 km/37 mi from Palma, ☎ 971/564457), 18 holes. **Son Vida** (✉ Next to Sheraton Son Vida hotel, 5 km/3 mi from Palma, ☎ 971/791210), 18 holes. **Poniente** (✉ Carretera Cala Figuera, Calvia, ☎ 971/130148), 18 holes. **Santa Ponça I and II** (✉ Calvia, ☎ 971/690211), 18 holes on each course. **Real Golf de Bendinat** (✉ Carretera Palma–Portals Nous, 5 km/3 mi from Palma, ☎ 971/405200), 9 holes. **Pollença** (✉ Carretera Palma–Pollença, Km 49.3, ☎ 971/533216), 9 holes. **Vall d'Or** (✉ Porto Colom–Cala d'Or, Km 7.7, ☎ 971/837068), 18 holes. **Son Servera** (✉ Bahía de Los Pinos, ☎ 971/567802), 9 holes. **Capdepera Golf Club** (✉ Carretera Palma–Cala Ratjada, Km 71, ☎ 971/565875), 18 holes. **Son Antem** (✉ Carretera Lluchmayor–Palma, 3 km/2 mi from Lluchmayor, ☎ 971/180094), 18 holes. **Club de Golf de Pula** (✉ Carretera Son Servera–Capdepera, Km 3, ☎ 971/817034). For more information contact the **Federación Balear de Golf** (Balearic Golf Federation; ✉ Avda. Jaime III 17, Palma, ☎ 971/722753).

HORSEBACK RIDING

The **Escuela de Equitación de Mallorca** (Majorca Riding School; ☎ 971/613157) is at Km 12 on the Palma–Sóller Road.

SAILING

Call the **Federación Balear de Vela** (Balearic Sailing Federation; ✉ Avda. Joan Miró 327, Palma, ☎ 971/402412) or the **Escuela Nacional de Vela de Calanova** (National Sailing School; ✉ Avda. Joan Miró 327, Palma, ☎ 971/402512). The **Club de Mar** (✉ Muelle de Pelaires, south end of Passeig Marítim, Palma, ☎ 971/403611) is famous among yacht sailors. It has its own hotel, bar, disco, and restaurant and can direct you to other clubs on the island.

SCUBA DIVING

Inquire with **Escuba Palma** (✉ C. Jaume I s/n, ☎ 971/694968).

TENNIS

Tennis is very popular here; you'll find courts at many hotels and at private clubs and tennis schools. For information, call the **Federación Balear de Tenis** (Balearic Tennis Federation; ✉ Costa de Sa Pols 6, Local 16, ☎ 971/720956).

WALKING

Majorca is a walker's paradise, particularly in the Sierra de Tramuntana, and you can easily arrange a combination of walking out and taking a boat, bus, or train back. Ask the tourist office for the free booklet "20 Hiking Excursions on the Island of Majorca," which has detailed maps and itineraries. For excellent drawings and maps, track down *12 Classic Hikes Through Majorca,* by the German author Herbert Heinrich, available in the bookstores at key sights. For more information contact the **Grup Excursionista de Mallorca** (Majorcan Hiking Association; ✉ Can Cavalleria 17, ☎ 971/711314).

WATER SPORTS

Water sports of all kinds are abundant here. You can rent windsurfers and dinghies at most beach resorts; both skin and scuba diving are excellent; and the island has a whopping 30 yacht marinas.

Shopping

Majorca's craft specialties are leather shoes and clothing, porcelain, souvenirs carved from olive wood, and artificial pearls. For leather: **Loewe** (✉ Born 2), **Pink** (✉ Plaça Pio XII), **Piza** (✉ Carrer Sant Nicolau 20), and **Don Cocodrilo** (✉ Carrer des Forn del Raco 1). For pearls: **Perlas Majorica** (✉ Avda. Jaume III 11). For antiques: **Persepolis** (✉ Avda. Jaume III 22), **Casa Belmonte** (✉ La Rambla 8), and shops on Plaça Almoina. For pottery: **Las Columnas** (✉ C. Sant Domingo 24, opposite tourist office). For gift-wrapped *ensaimadas*: **Forn Teatro** (✉ Plaça Weyler, at foot of steps leading to the Plaça Major).

Top-name fashion boutiques line **Avinguda Jaume III.** Less-expensive shopping strips are **Carrer Sindicat** and **Carrer Sant Miquel**—both pedestrian streets running north from the Plaça Major—and the small streets south of the Plaça Major. The square itself has an excellent crafts market Monday, Friday, and Saturday mornings from 10 to 2.

Raixa

❷ *13 km (8 mi) north of Palma.*

Heading north from Palma, look to the left to see Raixa, an 18th-century palace set in landscaped gardens. It sits atop a great flight of stairs, with statues and fountains on each side.

Jardins d'Alfàbia

❸ *4 km (2½ mi) north of Raixa on right side.*

At the top of the steps as you approach is a huge, vaulted cistern, built by a Moorish overlord to irrigate the gardens. A path leads around to a café, then winds through a small, thick wood. What's most remarkable about the Alfàbia Gardens is that they're here at all; water is not abundant in this climate. The house is furnished with antiques and lined with painted panels. ✉ *Carretera Palma–Sóller, Km 17,* ☎ *no phone.* 🎫 *500 ptas.* ⏲ *Weekdays 9:30–5:30, Sat. 9:30–1.*

Dining

$$ ✕ **Ses Porxeres.** Former stables at the gardens' edge have been converted into a fine, airy restaurant with a high ceiling and a charming outside garden. The imaginative menu includes Catalan cuisine and Majorcan specialties, such as pheasant stuffed with tiny plums and rabbit prepared with snails. The wine racks lining the walls are well stocked with excellent selections from the Penedès and La Rioja. ✉ *Carretera Palma–Sóller, Km 17,* ☎ *971/613762. MC, V. Closed Aug. and Mon. No dinner Sun.*

Sóller

❹ *17 km (11 mi) north of Raixa, 30 km (19 mi) north of Palma.*

Sóller is a rough but cozy gray-stone town with both a maritime and a mountain feel. Find your way to the Plaça Constitució, dominated by the cathedral; arm yourself with a map at the tourist office, in the ajuntament; and hop a tram down to the Port de Sóller (☞ Getting Around by Train *in* The Balearic Islands A to Z, *below*).

Dining and Lodging

$$ ★ ✕🏨 **El Guía.** Typical of the houses built by Sóller's merchants on the rich rewards of the citrus trade, El Guía is furnished in keeping with that fin-de-siècle style. It's handily located in the center of town, next to the train station. The excellent restaurant serves Majorcan special-

ties. ✉ *Carrer Castanyer 3, 07100,* ☎ *971/630227,* FAX *971/632634. 18 rooms. Restaurant. MC, V. Closed Nov.–Mar.*

$$ ✕🏨 **Hostal Es Port.** This 17th-century manor house is the spectacular ancestral home of the Montis family, who added a modern extension and now run the place as a hotel. Try to get a room in the old section, which has more character. The heavily beamed restaurant is in an old mill, where the olive press makes a striking centerpiece. For a fee, the hotel provides guides who can design and lead walking excursions of varying length and difficulty. ✉ *Carrer Antoni Montis s/n, 07108 Port de Sóller,* ☎ *971/631650,* FAX *971/631662. 156 rooms, 10 cottages. Restaurant, bar, pool, 3 tennis courts, playground. AE, MC, V.*

Deià

❺ *9 km (5½ mi) west of Sóller.*

Deià (Deyá in Castilian Spanish) was made famous by the English poet and writer Robert Graves, who lived here from 1929 until his death in 1985. The village café—up some steps on the left as you enter the village—is still a favorite haunt of writers and artists such as Graves's son, writer Tomás Graves, author of *P'amb oli* (*Bread and Olive Oil*), a guide to Majorcan cooking. On warm afternoons you might find the literati gathered in the beach bar in the rocky cove, a 2-km (1-mi) walk down from the village. Walk up the narrow street, lined with titled stations of the cross, to the village church; the small **cemetery** behind it affords lovely views of mountains terraced with olive trees and of the coves below. It's a fitting spot for Graves's final resting place, which is in a quiet corner beneath a simple slab of stone.

Dining and Lodging

$$$$ ★ ✕🏨 **La Residencia.** A former 16th-century manor house set in olive and citrus groves above the village, La Residencia is superbly furnished with antiques, modern canvases, and four-poster beds. The arched dining room of the restaurant, Es Molí (The Mill), was once an olive mill. Britain's late Princess Diana was a regular guest. ✉ *Finca Son Canals, 07179,* ☎ *971/639011,* FAX *971/639370. 65 rooms. Restaurant, bar, pool, 2 tennis courts. AE, DC, MC, V.*

$ 🏨 **Costa d'Or.** This attractive villa, a little way north of Deià, is set on the terraced cliffside and has a footpath down to the cove. Rooms are small but spare, in clean-lined Balearic white. ✉ *Llucalcari, 07179,* ☎ *971/639025,* FAX *971/639347. 42 rooms. Restaurant, pool. MC, V. Closed Nov.–Apr.*

Son Marroig

❻ *4 km (2½ mi) west of Deià.*

West of Deià is **Son Marroig,** one of the estates of Austrian archduke Luis Salvador (1847–1915), who arrived in Majorca as a young man and fell in love with the place. Speaker of 14 languages and writer of innumerable books on every aspect of Majorcan history, wildlife, and folklore, the archduke acquired estates and built great houses, mostly along the northwest coast, which he then furnished with *miradors* (outlooks) at each spectacular viewpoint. Now a museum, Son Marroig remains much as it was in the time of the archduke and contains his collections of Mediterranean pottery and ceramics, old Majorcan furniture, and paintings. From late July through early October, the Deià International Festival holds classical concerts here. ✉ *Carretera Deià–Valldemossa s/n,* ☎ *971/639158.* 🎫 *350 ptas.* ⏲ *Apr.–Oct., Mon.–Sat. 9:30–2:30 and 4:30–8; Nov.–Mar., Mon.–Sat. 9:30–2:30 and 3–6.*

From the mirador you can see, nearly 1,000 ft below, **Sa Foradada** (as in "perforated"), a spectacular rock peninsula pierced by a huge archway, beneath which the archduke moored his yacht. A pathway, beginning near the café in the parking area, leads down to Sa Foradada (1 hour down, 1½ hours up). Four kilometers (2½ mi) farther, behind the restaurant C'an Costa, on the right, is another of the archduke's miradors, **Ses Pites,** named for the spiky cactus plants that surround it.

En Route Now the road moves slightly inland. After 2 km (1 mi) more, a left turn takes you into Valldemossa.

Valldemossa

❼ *18 km (11 mi) north of Palma.*

The tourist office, in the plaza next to the church, sells a ticket good for the monastery's various attractions. The **Reial Cartuja** (Royal Carthusian Monastery) was founded in 1339, but when the monks were expelled in 1835, it was privatized, and the cells became lodgings for travelers. Later they were leased as summer apartments, which they largely remain today. The most famous lodgers were Frédéric Chopin and the French novelist George Sand, who spent three difficult months here (both the weather and their affair have always been described as tempestuous) in the winter of 1838–39.

The guided tour of the monastery begins in the **church.** Note the frescoes above the nave—the monk who painted them was Goya's brother-in-law. The next stop, in the cloisters, is perhaps the most interesting: a **pharmacy,** equipped by the monks in 1723 and almost completely preserved. Up a long, wide corridor are the apartments occupied by Chopin and Sand, furnished in period style. Only the piano is original, and transporting it here from France was a monumental effort. Nearby, another set of apartments houses the local **museum,** with mementos of Archduke Luis Salvador and a collection of old printing blocks. From here you return to the ornately furnished **King Sancho's palace,** a group of rooms originally built by King Jaume II for his son Sancho. A short piano recital of works by Chopin concludes the optional guided tour, except on Monday and Thursday mornings, when Majorcan folk dancers perform. ☎ *971/612181* 💳 *1,300 ptas.* ⏲ *Nov.–Mar., Mon.–Sat. 9:30–1 and 3–5:30; Apr.–Oct., Mon.–Sat. 9:30–1 and 3–6:30.*

Costa Nord, opened in April 2000 by American actor Michael Douglas, is a cultural center dedicated to Majorca's northwest Sierra de Tramuntana and to Archduke Luis Salvador. A 15-minute film on the natural wonders of the Sierra de Tramuntana (produced and narrated by Douglas) and a life-size reproduction of the interior of the Archduke's yacht make this a fascinating visit. ☎ *971/612425,* FAX *971/612410.* 💳 *1,200 ptas.* ⏲ *Daily 9–7.*

Dining and Lodging

$$$–$$$$ ✕🏨 **Vistamar.** This charming small hotel stands amid 250 acres of olive groves overlooking the sea. The manor house has been faithfully restored to its original, early 19th-century appearance, and the sitting rooms and bedrooms have exposed beams, heavy furniture, and modern art. The restaurant is popular for its excellent Mediterranean cooking. ✉ *Carretera Valldemossa–Andratx, Km 2, 07170,* ☎ *971/612300,* FAX *971/612583. 18 rooms. Restaurant, bar, pool. AE, MC, V. Hotel closed Nov.–Feb. No lunch Mon.* 😎

Sa Granja

21 km (13 mi) northwest of Palma.

Sa Granja (The Farm) was built by a noble family in the 17th century on what had previously been a farm. Once ensconced, they created pools and gardens. The house is now an open-air museum of the Majorcan countryside, including an olive mill and a wide range of ethnographic artifacts. If you come on Wednesday or Friday afternoon, you might catch some folk dancing. The admission fee entitles you to a sampling of local wines, cheeses, and pastries. ☎ *971/610032.* *1,300 ptas.; 1,600 ptas. Wed. and Fri.* *Daily 10–6 (until 7 in June), folk dancing Wed. and Fri. 3:30–5.*

Binissalem

8 *18 km (11 mi) northeast of Palma.*

Drive east along the Passeig Marítim from Palma and take the bypass north. Follow it for about 3 km (2 mi) to the Inca turnoff; this becomes a fast *autopista,* which takes you to the outskirts of Binissalem, the home of Majorca's main **vineyards** and its only D. O. (Denominación de Orígen, i.e., guaranteed-vintage) label.

Lodging

$$$$ **Scott's.** American George Scott and Englishwoman Judy Brabner have converted this 18th-century Majorcan *palacete* (elegant town house) into a graceful and tranquil hideaway that seems light-years removed from the tourist scene. Doubly insulated by Binissalem and the hosts' taste and hospitality, this is an ideal base for forays around the island. The couple serve a memorable breakfast until high noon, and are extraordinarily helpful with suggestions about places to go and things to do. ✉ *Plaza Iglesia 12, 07350,* ☎ *971/870100,* FAX *971/870267. 18 rooms. Breakfast room. MC, V.*

Inca

9 *28 km (17 mi) northeast of Palma.*

Inca is known for its leather factories and its Thursday market, the largest on Majorca.

Dining

$$ ✕ **Celler C'an Amer.** A *celler* is a peculiarly Majorcan combination of wine cellar and restaurant, and Inca has no fewer than six. C'an Amer is widely considered the best, with tables tucked under huge wine vats and heavy oak beams. There's a very pretty garden for warm evenings. Antonia, the dynamic chef-owner, serves some of the best *lechona* (suckling pig) and *tumbet* on the island. ✉ *Carrer Pau 39,* ☎ *971/501261. AE, DC, MC, V. Closed Sun.*

Shopping

Along the old Palma–Inca Road you'll find ***siurells*** (brightly colored ceramic whistles) in Cabaneta, **pottery** in Marratxi, and ***ilengos*** (a traditional peasant fabric) in Santa María, where the amusingly named shop Mas Vieja que mi Abuela ("Older Than My Grandmother") sells **antiques.** Inca has **leather** goods and ***galletas*** (traditional local biscuits). If you don't find what you want in Inca, browse for traditional crafts, leather, and pottery at the enormous emporium just outside town, on the left side of road to Alcúdia.

Manacor

10 *50 km (30 mi) east of Palma.*

Majorca's second-largest town is also an industrial center, thriving on the demand for the island's famous cultured pearls. Known primarily for its pearl-manufacturing process, Manacor is an ideal center from which to storm the island's southeastern holiday coast. The Romans first settled this site, followed by the Moors, who built a handsome mosque where the Gothic parish church of **Nostra Senyora de les Dolores** (Our Lady of Sorrows) now stands.

Dining and Lodging

$$$$ ✕🏨 **La Reserva Rotana.** This luxury hotel occupies a beautifully restored manor house 3 km (2 mi) north of Manacor. Most of the original appointments, including coffered ceilings, ancient woodwork, and Venetian stucco, are still in place. The 500-acre Rotana estate has its own nine-hole golf course, orchards, and kitchen gardens, which supply the excellent restaurant with fresh produce. ✉ *Apdo. de Correos 69, 07500,* ☎ *971/845685,* FAX *971/555258. 21 rooms. Restaurant, pool, 9-hole golf course, putting green, tennis court. AE, DC, MC, V.*

Alcúdia

11 *54 km (34 mi) northeast of Palma.*

Circle the restored remains of Alcúdia's **Moorish city walls**—on Sunday and Tuesday, there's a market outside. Inside, in a maze of narrow streets, are some fine **17th-century houses** and the excellent **Museu Monogràfic de Pollentia,** with Roman and prehistoric items. ✉ *Carrer Sant Jaume 30,* ☎ *971/547004.* 🎫 *400 ptas.* ⏲ *Apr.–Sept., Tues.–Fri. 10:30–1:30 and 5–7, weekends 10:30–1; Oct.–Mar., Tues.–Fri. 10–1:30 and 4–6, weekends 10:30–1.*

Just outside Alcúdia, off the port road, a signposted lane leads to the small, 1st-century BC **Teatre Romá** (Roman Amphitheater), carved directly from the rock of the hillside—facing south, so the audience could enjoy the evening sun. Excavated in the 1950s, the haunting site is always open.

From the Teatre Romá, turn back toward Alcúdia, but at the Inca junction keep right for **Port de Pollença.** This town is less hectic than many of Majorca's coastal resorts, and its waterfront is lined with relaxing cafés and bars.

Outdoor Activities and Sports

BICYCLING

Bicycling is excellent in the flatlands around Port de Pollença; and Alcúdia and C'an Picafort, on the north coast, are ideal. The roads have special bike lanes, and there are rental outlets on every block.

Pollença

12 *5 km (3 mi) inland of the port.*

Climb the **Calvari,** a stone staircase with 365 steps. At the top is a tiny **chapel** with a Gothic wooden crucifix and a fine view that takes in the bays, Alcúdia and Pollença, and Capes Formentor and Pinar. Almost opposite the turnoff to Ternelles is Pollença's **Roman bridge,** the only one on the island.

OFF THE BEATEN PATH **CAP DE FORMENTOR** – If you enjoy twisty, scenic roads to nowhere, pack a picnic and drive to Cap de Formentor, north of Puerto de Pollença.

The road threads its way among huge teeth of rock before reaching a lighthouse at the extreme tip, where the view is spectacular.

Dining and Lodging

$$$$ ✕🏨 **Formentor.** Founded in 1929, this famous hotel is beautifully perched on a cliff at Majorca's northern tip. Terraced gardens descend to an attractive private beach, where a barbecue is fired up at lunchtime. The building is long and white, and the rooms comfortable, if no more than par for the price; despite the remote site, the place lacks intimacy. Former guests include the Duke of Windsor, Winston Churchill, Charlie Chaplin, Aristotle Onassis, and the Spanish royal family. ✉ *Playa de Formentor, 07470,* ☎ *971/899100,* FAX *971/865155. 127 rooms. Restaurant, 3 bars, grill, beauty salon, miniature golf, 5 tennis courts, horseback riding, beach, windsurfing, boating, waterskiing, playground, airport shuttle. AE, DC, MC, V. Closed Oct.–Apr..*

Nightlife and the Arts

Pollença hosts a major international **music festival** in August and early September, during which concerts are performed in the cloisters of the former monastery of Santo Domingo. For schedules and tickets, contact Pollença's *ajuntament* (✉ Calvari 2, ☎ 971/534012 or 971/534016).

Lluc

13 *20 km (12 mi) west of Port de Pollença.*

The **monastery** in the remote mountain village of Lluc is widely considered Majorca's spiritual sanctuary. La Moreneta, also known as La Virgen Negra de Lluc (the Black Virgin of Lluc), resides here, in the 17th-century **church.** The **museum** has an eclectic collection of ceramics, paintings, clothing, folk costumes, and religious items. A boys' choir sings psalms in the chapel every day at 11:15 AM and 7:30 PM (except mid-June–July). The Christmas Eve performance of the pre-Christian Cant de la Sibila (Song of the Sybil) is an annual choral highlight. ☎ *971/517025.* 🎫 *Museum 350 ptas.* ⏲ *Daily 10–5:30.*

Dining and Lodging

$ ★ ✕🏨 **Santuari de Lluc.** The Lluc monastery offers simple, clean, and cheap accommodation, mostly in cells once occupied by priests. Although the vast building has one bar and three Majorcan restaurants, nightlife is restricted, with guests asked to be silent after 11 PM. ✉ *Santuari de Lluc, 07315,* ☎ *971/517029,* FAX *971/517096. 113 rooms, 97 with bath. 3 restaurants, bar, cafeteria. AE, DC, MC, V.*

Torrent de Pareis

2 km (1 mi) east of Sa Calobra.

From Escorca's church of Sant Pere, you can hike down the Torrent de Pareis, a ravine that drops dramatically to the sea. Use proper footwear, don't go alone, and don't attempt the trip if rain is forecast. The *torrent* becomes just that after a downpour and has been known to cause drownings.

En Route It's worth taking the turn to Sa Calobra if you want to see the bottom of the Torrent without climbing down. The road descends in a series of sharp loops to the Mediterranean, where the touristy town and beach at its end are a letdown. For solitude, take the left turn just before Sa Calobra and continue to isolated Cala Tuent, where the only beach development is a fisherman's hut. Beyond the Sa Calobra junction, C710 passes through tunnels and beside reservoirs, with terrific views. If you have time, make a short detour left through Fornalutx and Biniaraix before you reach Sóller.

Fornalutx and Biniaraix

3 km (2 mi) northeast of Sóller.

Both Fornalutx and Biniaraix have been spruced up in recent years by tourist cash, but their cobbled, honey-color plazas and stepped streets are still undeniably charming. Each village has a resident artists' colony.

Banyalbufar

23 km (14 mi) northwest of Palma.

Originally terraced by the Romans, this tiny town overlooks its tiny harbor from high on a cliff. A 1½-km (1-mi) walk southwest leads to the **Mirador Ses Animes** observation point.

Dining and Lodging

$$ ★ ✕▣ **Mar i Vent.** This small, modern, family-run hotel is at the north end of Banyalbufar. Paths lead down to two small, rocky coves for sea bathing. All guest rooms are furnished in traditional style and have mountain and/or ocean views. ✉ *Carrer Major 49, 07191,* ☎ *971/618000,* FAX *971/618201. 23 rooms. Restaurant, bar, pool, 2 tennis courts. MC, V. Hotel closed Dec.–Jan. No lunch Mon.–Sat.*

Puigpunyent

14 *25 km (15 mi) northwest of Palma.*

This village and the little roadways leading to and from it in all directions are a welcome relief from some of Majorca's more heavily traveled routes and routines. Visit the **parish church,** look through the **Son Bru** historical center, and hike up the nearby **Puig de Galatzó** (3,368 ft).

Dining and Lodging

$$$$ ✕▣ **Gran Hotel Son Net.** This stunningly restored mansion, the creation of American David Stein, has quickly established itself as one of Majorca's most luxurious hotels. Sweeping interior spaces of glass and stone overlook the village of Puigpunyent and the surrounding countryside. The restaurant, Sa Tafona, set in an ancient olive press, is an ideal showcase for the wide-ranging culinary skills (French, Majorcan, Mediterranean) of chef Thierry Buffeteau. ✉ *Carrer Castillo de Son Net Puigpunyent, 07194,* ☎ *971/147000,* FAX *971/147001. 24 rooms. Restaurant, bar, grill, pool, sauna, exercise room, tennis courts. AE, DC, MC, V.*

Andratx

15 *23 km (14 mi) southwest of Banyalbufar.*

Andratx is a charming cluster of white and ocher hillside houses, rather like cliff dwellings, watched over by the 3,363-ft Mt. Galatzo. You can take a pleasant walk or drive from here through S'Arracó to the **Castell Sant Elmo** (St. Elmo's Castle) and on to the rocky shore opposite the **Isla Sa Dragonera** (Dragon Cave Isle).

Dining and Lodging

$$$$ ★ ✕▣ **Villa Italia.** This ornate, rose-color villa is one of the island's most sophisticated hideaways. Built in a Florentine style, with marble floors and faux-classical columns, it has splendid views over the port and, to the west, the Mediterranean. ✉ *Camino San Carlos 13, 07157 Port D'Andratx,* ☎ *971/674011,* FAX *971/673350. 16 rooms. Restaurant, bar, pool. AE, DC, MC, V.*

Santa Ponsa

15 km (9 mi) west of Palma.

Santa Ponsa has a sandy beach on its north side and a small fishing port to the south. A spell on the beach and lunch in the port may beckon before you return to Palma by way of the C719 and the *autopista.*

Side Trips

Artà

16 *78 km (48 mi) northeast of Palma.*

The hills of Majorca's northeast, beyond Artà, are nearly roadless, thus keeping Artà somewhat off the beaten path. The north side of town is dominated by its **castle** and the church of **San Salvador.** Just below the church, a sign points (somewhat ambiguously; confirm the direction) to the **Ermita de Betlem** (Bethlehem Hermitage), some 9 km (5 mi) farther on. The road soon degenerates into a rocky track that twists hair-raisingly up between dwarf palms and sea holly and then circles down to the isolated hermitage, the home of a small number of hermetic monks. Behind it, a path leads up the hillside to a fine *mirador.*

Randa

26 km (16 mi) southeast of Palma.

For a quick jaunt from Palma, take C715 east from the city to PM501, turn right, and follow signs to Llucmajor until, after about 3 km (2 mi), a left turn leads to Randa. At the center of this tiny village, turn right and follow a twisting road up the Puig de Randa, which has three separate hermitages. You'll get the best views from the terrace of the Franciscan monastery of **Nuestra Señora de Cura** (known as "El Santuari de Cura"), on the summit. Long a pilgrimage destination for the sick, it was founded in the 13th century by philosopher Ramón Llull (☞ Palma de Mallorca, *above*), and its library contains valuable books that you may be able to see during quiet times. Next to the terrace are a bar and restaurant; the monastery also rents rooms and apartments. ☎ *971/120260,* *350 ptas.* ⏲ *Tues.–Thurs. 10–1 and 4–6, Fri. 10–1.*

MINORCA

Minorca, the northernmost Balearic island, is a knobby, cliff-bound plateau with a single central hill—Monte Toro—from whose 1,100-ft summit you can see the whole island. Prehistoric monuments—*taulas* (huge stone T-shapes), *talayots* (spiral stone cones), and *navetes* (stone structures shaped like overturned boats)—left by the first Neolithic settlers are scattered thickly around the countryside. The British controlled Minorca for much of the 18th century and left their legacy in the forms of Georgian architecture (especially in Mahón); a landscape of small, tidy fields bounded by hedgerows and dry-stone walls and grazed by Holsteins; and language—Minorcan speech is sprinkled with English words. Tourism came late to Minorca, partly because it was traditionally more prosperous than its neighbors, but also because Franco deliberately punished the Republican island by restricting development here. Having sat out the early Balearic boom, Minorca has managed to avoid many of the other islands' teething troubles: there are no high-rise hotels, and the herringbone road system, with a single central highway, means that each resort is small and separate. A lively ecological movement succeeded in having Minorca designated a World Reserve of the Biosphere by UNESCO in 1993.

Mahón (Maó)

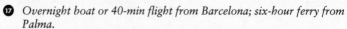

17 *Overnight boat or 40-min flight from Barcelona; six-hour ferry from Palma.*

For a good tour of Mahón (Maó, in Catalan), start at the northwest corner of the Plaça de S'Esplanada and turn right onto Carrer Comte de Cifuentes. At No. 25 is the **Ateneo,** a cultural and literary society with a display of wildlife, seashells, seaweed, minerals, and stuffed birds. On the staircase are ceramics and old tiles; side rooms hold paintings, prints, maps, and mementos of Minorcan writers, poets, and musicians. ☏ *971/360553.* *Free.* *Daily 10–2 and 3–10.*

From the Ateneo, follow Carrer Comte de Cifuentes to Carrer Dr. Orfila, a main shopping street, and turn left; then take the second right through Carrer Bastió onto Carrer Costa d'en Ga. Where the street curves left you'll see the **Teatre Principal** (currently undergoing extensive renovations), built in 1824 as an opera house and now a cinema and theater. If the construction has abated, try to peek inside at the semicircular auditorium, its columns supporting tiers of boxes and a gilded ceiling. ⊠ *C. Costa d'en Ga s/n.*

Continue down Costa d'en Ga into Plaça Reial. From here, Carrer S'Arravaleta, a pedestrian street with more attractive shops, leads to the Plaça del Carme. Up to the right is the church of **La Verge del Carme,** with a fine painted and gilded altarpiece. Adjoining the church are the cloisters, now used, surprisingly, as a **public market.** As you wander through the colorful piles of fruit and vegetables, notice the carvings on the church's west and north walls.

Return up S'Arravaleta and turn right onto Carrer Nou. At the end is the Plaça de la Constitució, dominated by the church of **Santa María,** originally from the 13th century but rebuilt during the British occupation. It was restored after being sacked during the Spanish Civil War. The church's pride is its 3,200-pipe Baroque organ, imported from Austria in 1810.

Behind Santa María is the **Plaça de la Conquesta,** with a statue of Alfons III of Aragón. At the end of the tiny Carrer Alfons III, which leads off the square, is the best view of Mahón's harbor.

Coming up from the port to the Plaça de la Constitució, you'll see the ***ajuntament*** (town hall) on your right. Stroll up Carrer Isabel II, a pleasant street of fine houses. On the corner of Carrer de Rosari, notice the statue of the Virgin up on the wall and the **Palau del Governador** (Governor's Palace) and courtyard on the right.

From the Carrer de Rosari, return to the ajuntament and follow Carrer Port de Sant Roc, immediately opposite. Ahead you'll see the 16th-century gate **Puerta de San Roque,** the only remnant of the city walls built to protect Mahón from the pirate Barbarossa (Redbeard).

Dining and Lodging

$$$ ✕ **La Minerva.** This spectacular quayside restaurant has a floating terrace and a boat, the *Anita,* which serves as an adjoining bar and dining room in summer. Not surprisingly, fish reigns supreme here, but meat roasted over coals doesn't lag far behind. ⊠ *Moll de Llevant 87,* ☏ *971/351995. AE, DC, MC, V.*

$$$ ✕ **Rocamar.** Standing at the extreme end of the twisting, quayside road toward Villa Carlos, Rocamar is an established favorite, serving fresh, simply prepared seafood. You dine four floors up, overlooking the port of Mahón and surrounded by dark-wood paneling and maritime lights. The *pimientos rellenos de langostinos* (peppers stuffed with prawns)

Minorca

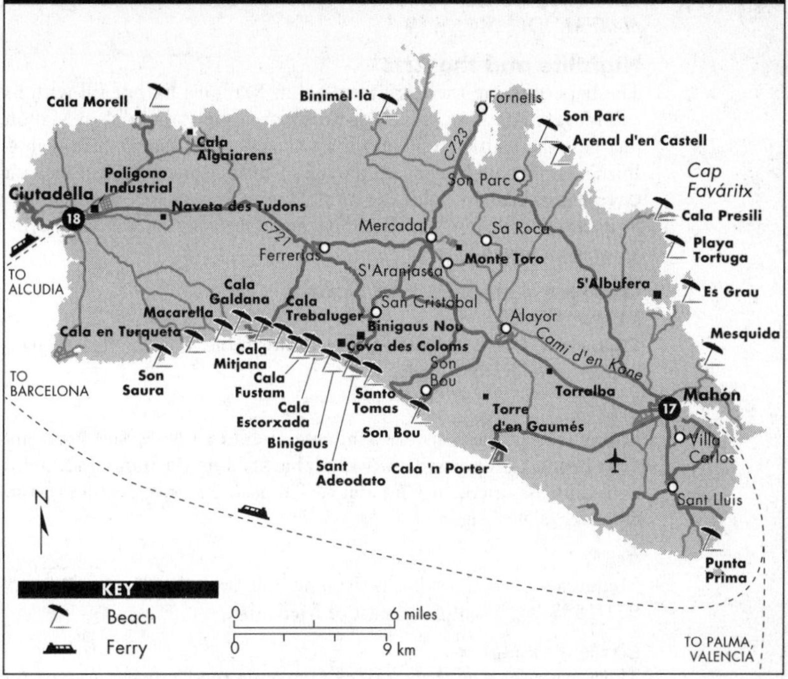

are superb. ✉ *Cala Fonduco 32,* ☎ *971/365601. AE, DC, MC, V. Closed Nov. and Mon. in winter. No dinner Sun.*

$$ ★ ✕ **Gregal.** This waterside restaurant in Mahón's port specializes in fresh fish. *Pescado a la sal* (fish baked in salt) is excellent here. Whether you sit inside or on the airy terrace, you'll have a fine view of the harbor and its yachts, berthed on the seaward side of the palm-fringed esplanade. ✉ *Moll de Llevant 306,* ☎ *971/366606. MC, V.*

$$ ✕ **Jágaro.** With lots of greenery in the recently enlarged garden and huge windows overlooking the harbor, Jágaro feels like a gourmet picnic. Seafood dishes are unusually inventive; try the *carpaccio de mero* (grouper). ✉ *Moll de Llevant 334,* ☎ *971/362390. AE, DC, MC, V. No dinner Sun.–Mon. Nov.–Apr.*

$$$ 🏨 **Port Mahón.** The only high-quality hotel in Mahón is magnificently situated, overlooking the harbor from terraced gardens in a quiet residential district. Steps lead directly down to the fashionable bars and restaurants in the port. ✉ *Avda. Fort de l'Eau 13, 07701,* ☎ *971/362600,* FAX *971/361050. 82 rooms. Restaurant, bar, piano bar, pool, beauty salon. AE, DC, MC, V.*

$$ 🏨 **Hotel del Almirante** (a.k.a. Collingwood House). Halfway between Mahón and Es Castell, the 18th-century residence of Nelson's admiral friend Lord Collingwood has spectacular views of the port. The main Georgian house became a hotel in 1964 but retains its originality *and* Collingwood's ghost, said to favor Room 7. Newer, ghost-free cottages are arranged around the secluded pool. ✉ *Carretera Villacarlos s/n, 07780,* ☎ *971/362700,* FAX *971/362704. 40 rooms. Restaurant, bar, pool, tennis court, recreation room. AE, DC, MC, V. Closed Nov.–Apr.*

$$ 🏨 **Sol Mirador des Port.** As the name suggests, this hotel has superb views over the port. Just five minutes from the docks, it's a convenient base for exploring the eastern end of Minorca. Rooms are adequate to spectacular, depending on the views; decor is modern and chic. The

restaurant serves breakfast and dinner only. ✉ *Dalt Vilanova 1, 07701,* ☎ *971/360016,* FAX *971/367346. 69 rooms. Restaurant, bar, cafeteria, pool. AE, DC, MC, V.*

Nightlife and the Arts

The bars opposite the ferry terminal in Mahón's harbor fill with locals late at night. Discos include **Karai,** in a cave at the edge of Mahón, just past the traffic circle on the Es Castell road; **Pachá,** a branch of Ibiza's famous nightspot, on the left at the entrance to San Luis; and **Cova d'en Xoroi,** in a cliffside pirate's cave high above the sea at Cala 'n Porter. Catch live jazz Tuesdays and Thursdays at the **Casino** bar and restaurant in Sant Climent.

Outdoor Activities and Sports

BIRD-WATCHING

S'Albufera, a wetland nature reserve north of Mahón, attracts many species of migratory birds.

DIVING

Equipment and lessons are available at **Cala En Bosc, Son Parc,** and **Cala Tirant.** Compressed air is available at Club Marítimo, in Mahón, and Club Náutico, in Ciutadella. The island's only decompression chamber is at S'Algar.

GOLF

Menorca's sole golf course is the nine-hole **Urbanización Son Parc** (☎ 971/188875), 9 km (6 mi) east of Mercadal.

HORSEBACK RIDING

There are stables on the left side of the main road between Alayor and Mercadal, just after the Son Bou turn, as well as between Sant Climent and Cala 'n Porter. Elsewhere on the island, look for the sign *picadero* (riding school). Mahón's **Es Fornás** (☎ 971/364422) organizes horseback tours of the island for both beginning and advanced riders, and horse-drawn carriage tours.

WALKING

In the south, each cove is approached by a *barranca* (ravine or gully), often from several miles inland. These make pleasant, reasonably easy excursions. The head of **Barranca Algendar** is down a small unmarked road immediately on the right of the Ferreries–Cala Galdana Road; the barranca ends in the beach resort Cala Galdana.

WINDSURFING AND SAILING

Knowledgeable windsurfers and dinghy sailors head for Fornells Bay. Several miles long and a mile wide, but with a narrow entrance to the sea, it gives the beginner a feeling of security and the expert plenty of excitement. **Windsurfing Fornells** (☎ 971/376400) rents boards and gives excellent lessons in English or Spanish.

A little south of Fornells, at Ses Salines on the same bay, **Minorca Sailing Holidays** (call Tim Morris, 971/376589; in London, ✉ 58 Kew Rd., Richmond, Surrey, U.K., ☎ 0181/948–2100) sells a package that includes airfare and accommodations along with various activities.

Shopping

Minorca is known for gin and shoes, both introduced by the British. The **Xoriguer distillery** (☎ 971/362197), on Mahón's quayside, near the ferry terminal, offers a guided tour, free samples, and, of course, bottles for sale. The island is renowned throughout Spain for its footwear, so many boutiques stock high-quality shoes. Look for leatherwear at **Marks** (✉ S'Arravaleta 18 and Hanover 38), **Patricia** (✉ 31–33 Carrer Dr. Orfila), and **Musupta** (✉ S'Arravaleta 26). Costume jewelry, another local specialty, is best at **Bali** (✉ Corner of Carrer de Lluna and Carrer de Ses Moreres). Up on the Esplanade is a frequent **open-air market** with cheap clothing and souvenirs.

Ciutadella

18 *44 km (27 mi) west of Mahón.*

Ciutadella was the capital of Minorca before the British set up shop in Mahón, and its history and architecture are much richer than Mahón's. As you arrive via the C721 across the island, turn left at the traffic light and circle the old part of the city to the north end of the coniferous **Plaça de s'Explanada.** Turn left here, down Camí de Sant Nicolau. At the end, near an old watchtower and two rather rusty cannons, is a **monument to David Glasgow Farragut,** the first admiral of the U.S. Navy, whose father emigrated from Ciutadella to the United States.

From the Farragut monument, return up Sant Nicolau and park near the Plaça d'es Born. Next to the **ajuntament,** on the west side of the Born, steps lead up to the **Mirador d'es Port,** from which you can survey the whole length of Ciutadella's harbor. The town hall houses an interesting collection of ancient artifacts and pictures. The local **museum,** a repository of anything to do with the city—old street signs, keys, shoes, even a record of land grants made by Alfons III after defeating the Moors—is in an ancient defense tower at the east end of the harbor, the Bastió de Sa Font (Bastion of the Fountain). ☎ *971/380297.* *350 ptas.* ⊙ *Daily 10–1 and 4–6.*

Circle the Born to the north for more views of the narrow port. The monument in the middle of the plaza commemorates the citizens' resistance of a Moorish invasion in 1588. Continue south along the east side of the Born: the whole of this first block is the 19th-century **Palau Torresaura,** built by the Baron of Torresaura, one of the many noble families from Aragón and Catalonia who repopulated Menorca after it was captured from the Moors in the 13th century. It's worth going into one of the tiny shops here just to look at the complex pattern of archways and stairwells.

Turn left onto Carrer Major to enter the old city, where you'll see interesting brass and bronze door fixtures. On the left, at No. 8 (even palaces have street numbers), over the doorway of the Palau Torresaura, is a strange carving of a veiled female face. On the right is the **Palau Salort,** its door knockers carved to resemble entwined serpents. This is the only noble home regularly open to the public. The coats of arms on the ceiling are those of the families Salort (a salt pit and a garden: *sal* and *ort,* or *huerta*) and Martorell (a marten). *400 ptas.* ⊙ *Mon.–Sat. 10–2.*

From the Palau Salort, continue up Carrer Major to the Plaça de la Catedral (Plaça Píus XII). Inside the Gothic **cathedral** is some beautifully carved woodwork, including intricate choir stalls. The side chapel has round Moorish arches with intricate carving, remnants of the mosque that once stood on this site.

From the cathedral, turn south from the Plaça de la Catedral onto Carrer Roser, then left onto Carrer Santíssim, where you'll see **Can Saura** on the right. The ground floor houses one of the best antiques shops in the Balearic Islands. Don't miss the coat of arms dated 1718, the primitive naval paintings at the end of the entrance hall, or the carved ceiling dome.

Turn left onto Carrer del Seminari (Carrer Obispo Vila). On the right is the **Seminari,** the setting for Ciutadella's summer festival of classical music.

Return, keeping north of the cathedral, along Carrer Sant Sebastià. Twisting left and right, you'll reach the steps leading down into the **port.** The waterfront here is lined with seafood restaurants, some of which burrow into caverns far under the Born. Between the restaurants, Carrer Costa del Moll leads left up to the Born again.

Ciutadella is near many of the archaeological curiosities for which Minorca is famous. Returning around the Avenidas, continue straight at the traffic lights, take the next right (Carrer de Pere Martorell), and follow the signs for Cala Morell. Soon you'll be in open countryside, where numerous ***talayots*** (prehistoric stone towers) dot the fields.

Returning to Ciutadella from Cala Morell, take a shortcut through the Polígono Industrial, on the left, to the Ciutadella–Mahón Road. Turn left toward Mahón, and 2 km (1 mi) or so farther on the right are a parking lot and a path leading to the **Naveta des Tudons,** one of the best-preserved of Minorca's mysterious prehistoric remains. The name ("Stone Ship") derives from the monument's shape, that of an upturned boat.

Dining and Lodging

$$ ✕ **Casa Manolo.** This well-established paella and seafood restaurant is at the seaward end of the many restaurants rubbing shoulders on the east side of Ciutadella's narrow port. The white walls and exposed beams of the dining room extend back into the rock face of the steep cliffs rising above. ✉ *Marina 117,* ☎ *971/380003. AE, DC, MC, V. Closed Dec.–Feb.*

$$$ 🏨 **Patricia.** On a quiet boulevard just south of the main plaza, Patricia is close to Ciutadella Creek. The marble hall is light and modern, and the bedrooms have pale carpets, pastel wallpaper, and watercolor paintings. ✉ *Camí Sant Nicolau 90–92, 07760,* ☎ *971/385511,* FAX *971/481120. 44 rooms. Restaurant, bar. AE, DC, MC, V.*

$ 🏨 **Hostal Residencia Ciutadella.** This pleasant modern bar with upstairs guest rooms is in the center of town, a block southwest of the Plaça Alfonso III. The rooms have white walls, shutters, shiny tiled floors, and comfortable beds. ✉ *Carrer Sant Eloi 10, 07760,* ☎ FAX *971/383462. 17 rooms. Bar, cafeteria. MC, V.*

Shopping

Gin, shoes, leather, costume jewelry, and cheese are the main items to shop for here. The central Ses Voltes area is rife with shops of all kinds, as are the Es Rodol zone near Plaça Artrutx and Ses Voltes, and along the Camí de Maó between Plaça Palmeras and Plaça d'es Born. The industrial complex (*polígono industrial*) on the right as you enter Ciutadella has a number of shoe factories, each with shops. Prices may be the same as in stores, but the selections are greater. **Pieme** (✉ Carrer Curniola s/n) specializes in equestrian items. **Azabache** (✉ Carrer del Seminari 36) has designer leatherwear. The town's only ***alferería*** (pottery maker; ✉ Carrer Curniola s/n) has a studio store. One of Minorca's few antiques shops is on the ground floor of the 17th-century **Can Saura** (✉ Carrer de Santíssim).

Side Trips

Monte Toro

24 km (15 mi) northwest of Mahón.

Follow signs in Es Mercadal (the crossroads at the center of the island) to the peak of Monte Toro, Minorca's highest point at all of 1,555 ft. From the monastery on top you can see the whole island and, on a clear day, across the sea to Majorca. Climbing and feasting combine nicely here: stop in the village for a late lunch or early dinner on the way back to Ciutadella.

DINING

$$ ✕ **Ca N' Aguedet.** This rustic spot is open every day of the year, serves a surprisingly good home-grown wine, and presents a wide variety of Menorquín dishes, such as *conejo con higos* (rabbit with figs), *arrò de terra* (rough, whole-grain rice with meat sauce), *sepia con gambas* (cuttlefish with shrimp), and *cranc* (crab). ✉ *Lepanto 30,* ☎ *971/375391. AE, DC, MC, V.*

$$ ✕ **Ca N' Olga.** It's hard to find, but worth it. Off the Camino de Tramuntana, in central Mercadal, Olga's is under an archway to the left (ask for directions if you don't see it). Make for the small patio and try the inventive country cuisine, such as local snails or quail in sherry. ✉ *Pont Na Macarrana s/n,* ☎ *971/375459. AE, DC, MC, V. Closed Mon.–Tues. Jan.–Feb.*

$$ ✕ **Es Pla.** The modest wooden exterior of this waterside restaurant in Fornells' harbor, on the north coast, is misleading. Es Pla is reputedly King Juan Carlos's favorite Minorcan restaurant; the king is said to make regular detours here during Balearic jaunts to revisit his pet dish, Es Pla Caldereta de Langosta (a rich lobster stew). ✉ *Puerto de Fornells,* ☎ *971/375155. MC, V.*

$$ ★ ✕ **Molí d'es Reco.** The Moli is an old mill sitting high above the main Mahón–Ciutadella highway, just outside Mercadal. In winter or on cold evenings, the ground floor offers snug dining, while the rustic, airy terrace is ideal on warm summer days. Rabbit dishes are the specialty, but all of the fish offerings are excellent, too. ✉ *Carrer Major 53,* ☎ *971/375392. MC, V.*

Torralba

14 km (8½ mi) west of Mahón.

Coming from Mahón, turn south immediately upon entering Alaior toward Cala en Porter. Torralba, a megalithic site with a number of stone constructions, is 2 km (1 mi) ahead at a bend in the road, marked by an information kiosk on the left. (As is so often the case in Minorca, you'll be lucky if you find it open.) The massive, T-shaped stone ***taula*** is through an opening to the right. Behind it, from the top of a stone wall, you can see, in a nearby field, the monolith **Fus de Sa Geganta.**

Torre d'en Gaumés

16 km (9½ mi) west of Mahón.

Turn south toward Son Bou on the west side of Alayor. In about 1 km (½ mi), the first fork left will lead you to Torre d'en Gaumés, a far more complex set of **prehistoric ruins** with fortifications, monuments, deep pits of ruined dwellings, huge vertical slabs, and *taulas.*

Cova des Coloms

40 km (24 mi) west of Mahón.

The Cave of Pigeons is the most spectacular cave on Minorca. To reach it, take the Ferreries road at San Cristobal and turn up to the primary school; beyond the school the paved road continues for about 3 km (2 mi) toward Binigaus Nou. You'll see wheel marks and possibly cars at the designated parking area; leave the car. Climb a stile and take the path that follows the right-hand side of the *barranca* (ravine) toward the sea—you'll come to a well-trodden path bearing down into the bottom of the barranca and up the other side. The entrance to the cave is around an elbow, camouflaged by a tree. A flashlight helps.

IBIZA AND FORMENTERA

Ibiza is known far and wide as a hedonistic Mediterranean party site. Yet only on Ibiza and on tiny Formentera, just off Ibiza's southern tip, will you still see women in the fields dressed in the simple country costume of long, black skirt and wide-brimmed straw hat, gathering almonds in their aprons or herding errant goats in the upland reaches of Els Amunts.

Ibiza

⑲ *40-min flight from Barcelona.*

Settled by the Carthaginians in the 5th century BC, Ibiza (Eivissa, in Majorcan and Catalan) remained largely untouched by mass tourism until the 1960s, when it emerged as a wild, anything-goes gathering place for hippies and the international jet set. By the 1990s, its principal resort, Sant Antoni, had become an overdeveloped Balearic version of Torremolinos.

Running along the quay in Ibiza town (Eivissa) is the area known as **Sa Penya** (The Crag, or The Cliff). Once a quiet fisherman's quarter, this neighborhood has been a tourist haunt since the 1960s, springing into life each evening with lively bars, restaurants, and flea markets.

Enter Sa Penya via Carrer Rimbau, which you'll find at the end of Passeig Vara de Rey opposite Hotel Montesol, whose fashionable pavement café is a favorite place for people-watching. **Carrer Rimbau** has some of the exotic boutiques for which Ibiza is renowned, and the alleys off it are crammed with stalls, more boutiques, and restaurants.

Continue on Carrer Major, just east of the church of San Telmo. In this part of Sa Penya none of the streets are quite straight, and the miniature houses appear to have been randomly scattered along the tiny passageways.

From Carrer Major, return to the **Plaça de la Constitució,** just north of San Telmo, where a pretty little building that looks something like a miniature Parthenon houses the local market. Beyond it, a ramp leads up to Las Tablas, the main gate of **Dalt Vila,** the walled upper town. On each side stands a statue, Roman in origin and now headless: Juno on the right, an armless male on the left.

Inside Dalt Vila, the ramp continues to the right between the outer and inner walls and opens into a long, narrow plaza lined with stalls and pavement cafés. Don't worry about losing your way: aim uphill and you'll arrive at the cathedral, downhill and you'll return to the gate. A little way up Sa Carroza, a sign on the left points back toward the **Museu d'Art Contemporani,** housed in the gateway arch. ✉ *Ronda Pintor Narcis Putget s/n,* ☎ *971/302723.* 💰 *500 ptas.* ⏲ *Daily 10:30–1 and 6–8:30.*

Uphill from the Museum of Contemporary Art is a sculpture of a priest sitting on one of the stone seats in the gardens. On the left, the wide **Bastió de Santa Llúcia** (Bastion of St. Lucia) has a panoramic view.

Wind your way up past the 16th-century church of **Sant Domingo,** its roof an irregular landscape of tiled domes, and turn right in front of the *ajuntament* (town hall) housed in the church's former monastery. Then follow any of the streets or steps leading uphill to Carrer Obispo Torres (Carrer Major).

At the top of Carrer Major is the **cathedral,** on the site of religious structures from each of the cultures that have ruled Ibiza since the Phoeni-

Ibiza and Formentera

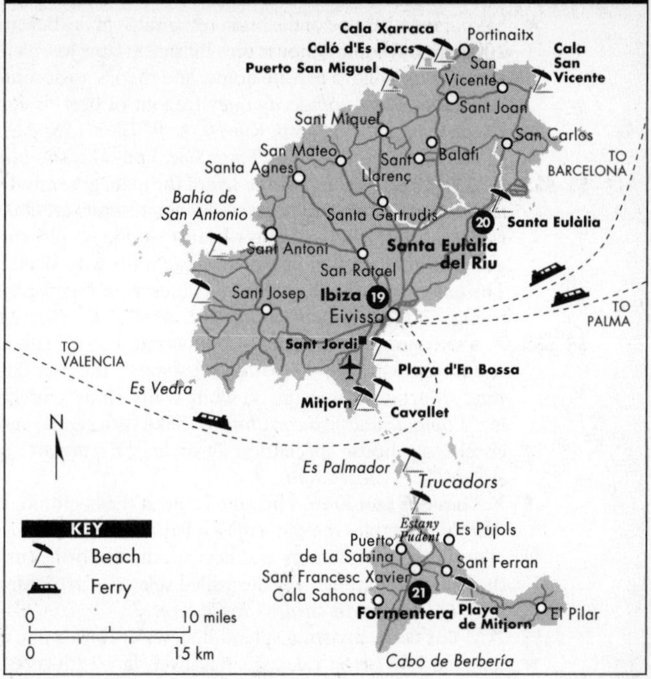

cians. Built in the 13th and 14th centuries and renovated in the 18th century, the cathedral has a Gothic tower and a Baroque nave. The painted panels above the small vault adjoining the sacristy depict souls in purgatory being consumed by flames and tortured by devils while angels ascend to heaven. The **museum,** which you enter through the nave, has an interesting collection of religious art, relics, and ecclesiastical treasures. *Museum 100 ptas.* *Cathedral and museum Sun.–Fri. 10–1 and 4–6:30, Sat. 10–1.*

Across the plaza from the cathedral, the **Museu Arqueològic** has Phoenician, Punic (Carthaginian), and Roman artifacts. ⊠ *Plaça Catedral 3,* ☎ *971/301231.* *300 ptas.* *Mon.–Sat. 10–1 and 4–6.*

A passageway leads from the cathedral to the castle to the **Bastió de Sant Bernardo** (Bastion of St. Bernard). From here there's a panoramic view of the wide bay from Playa d'En Bossa to Figueretas and of the chain of islands that stretches across the sea to Formentera. Steps lead down to a small gate in the bastion, from which you can pick your way along the clifftop to Figueretas and continue along the top of the wall. This trail, by way of the bastions of Sts. John and James, is called the Route of St. John the Baptist, and ends at the steps to the **Portal Nou** (New Gate).

Go down the dark, curving tunnel of the Portal Nou and up the Vía Romana to reach, on the left, the **Puig des Molins** (Hill of Windmills), so called because it was once covered with them. A major Punic necropolis, with more than 3,000 tombs, has been excavated here, and many of the finds are on display in the new **Museu Puig des Molins** (Punic Archaeological Museum) adjacent to it. ⊠ *Vía Romana 31,* ☎ *971/301771.* *400 ptas.* *Mon.–Sat. 10–1.*

Dining and Lodging

$$$ ★ ✕ **Ca Na Joana.** Joana Biarnés, a well-known journalist in a former life, has put together one of the finest restaurants in the Balearics in this small, 200-year-old country house on a hillside in Sant Josep (10 km/6 mi from Ibiza). It feels like a private home, and there's an acclimatized wine cellar below. The *estofado de buey* (ragout of beef) is excellent. ✉ *Carretera Eivissa–Sant Josep, Km 10,* ☎ *971/800158. AE, MC, V. Closed Mon. and Nov.–Dec. No dinner Sun. Jan.–May, no lunch June–Oct.*

$$–$$$ ✕ **El Portalón.** Just inside and left of the main gate into Dalt Vila, a front terrace announces this intimate French restaurant. One dining room is medieval, with exposed heavy beams, antiques, oils, and coats of arms; another, modern, blends dark-orange walls with sleek black furniture. The *pato con salsa de frambuesa* (duck with raspberry sauce) is worth trying. ✉ *Plaza Desamparados 12,* ☎ *971/303901. AE, DC, MC, V.*

$$–$$$ ✕ **S'Oficina.** The entrance is uninviting, but it leads to an attractive restaurant with a small patio and some of the best Basque cuisine on Ibiza. Marine prints hang on white walls, ships' lanterns from the ceiling. *Lomo de merluza con almejas* (hake with clams) and *kokotxas* (cod cheeks) are house specialties. ✉ *Avda. d'Espanya 6,* ☎ *971/300016. AE, MC, V. Closed Sun.*

$ ✕ **Comidas San Juan.** This small café at the beginning of Sa Penya has marble-top tables reminiscent of a Paris bistro. The gloss-painted decor is sterile, but the owners are cheerful, the fish dishes usually good, and the value unbeatable. Try the grilled sole. ✉ *Carrer Montgri 8,* ☎ *971/310766. No credit cards. Closed Sun.*

$$$$ ★ ✕🏨 **Cas Gasí.** Boasting splendid views of Ibiza's one and only mountain, the 1,567-ft Sa Talaiassa, this lovely late-19th-century manor house is surrounded by rolling hills of olive trees, redolent of Tuscany. Airy rooms with wood-beam ceilings and walls in soft orange hues are sparsely and gracefully furnished with brass beds and contemporary designer chairs, in the clean-lined look typical of Ibiza. Open year-round, this quiet upland retreat seems worlds away from downtown Ibiza. Dinner is served on request, breakfast daily on a terrace. ✉ *Camino Viejo de Sant Mateu s/n, 07814 Santa Gertrudis,* ☎ *971/197700,* FAX *971/197899. 10 rooms. Restaurant. AE, DC, MC, V.*

$$$$ ★ ✕🏨 **Hacienda Na Xamena.** Ibiza's most exclusive hotel is also its most isolated: it's on a rocky headland in Sant Miquel, toward the north end of the island. Access to the sea is difficult, involving a long hike down steep steps; but the rooms, arranged around a pretty little patio with a fountain and trees, are sparse and spare—clean-lined, classical Ibizan—and nearly half have hot tubs. Reserve well in advance. ✉ *Apdo. 423, 07000,* ☎ *971/334500,* FAX *971/334514. 56 rooms. Restaurant, bar, 3 pools, tennis court, exercise room. AE, DC, MC, V. Closed Nov.–Apr.*

$$$ ★ ✕🏨 **Cas Pla.** Surrounded by thousand-year-old olive trees and blessed with views over the sea and the fortified church in the village of Sant Miquel, this cozy rural hotel is decorated with superb taste and managed with grace and refinement. A cozy retreat from the Ibiza "scene," it's still just minutes from the beach. ✉ *Apdo. 777, 07800,* ☎ *971/334587,* FAX *971/334604. 16 rooms. Breakfast room, pool, tennis court. AE, DC, MC, V. Closed mid-Nov.–Mar.*

$$$ ★ ✕🏨 **Los Molinos.** This is the best hotel in Ibiza town. It's technically in Figueretes, but it's only a five-minute walk from the center at the end of a relatively quiet street. Guest rooms are standard modern; the more expensive ones have balconies facing the bay. ✉ *Carrer Ramón Muntaner 60, Apdo. 504, 07800 Figueretas,* ☎ *971/302250 or 971/302254,* FAX *971/302504. 154 rooms. Restaurant, bar, pool, beauty salon. AE, DC, MC, V.*

$-$$ **Apartamentos Torre del Canónigo.** Built into a 16th-century tower at the top of the Dalt Vila, 55 yards from the cathedral, these modern apartments have open fireplaces and the flavor of their ancient surroundings. ✉ *Carrer Major 8, Dalt Vila, 07800,* ☎ *971/303884. 7 apartments. Snack bar, kitchenettes. MC, V. Closed Nov.–Mar.*

Nightlife

If the arts are relatively neglected on Ibiza, nightlife certainly is not. Ibiza's discos are famous throughout Europe. In Ibiza town, the trendy place to start the evening is **Keeper** (✉ Passeig Marítim), where you can sip your drink sitting on a carousel horse. There's also a lively, very young scene at **Divino,** another music bar on the Passeig Marítim. The "in" place for older nighthawks is the foyer of the former **Teatre Pereira** (✉ Carrer Comte Roselló). General favorites are **Pachá** (✉ Passeig Marítim s/n), **Amnesia San Rafael** (✉ Sant Antoni road, opposite Km 5 marker), and **Privilege** (✉ Sant Antoni). Hardened discomanes end the night at **Space** (✉ Far end of Playa d'En Bossa), which doesn't even open until 5 AM.

Ibiza's **casino** is in a Cubist building that resembles an Ibizan church, albeit with a pizzeria and piano bar in the side chapels. ✉ *Passeig Marítim s/n,* ☎ *971/313312.* ⏲ *Weekdays 10 PM–4 AM, weekends 10 PM–5 AM.*

Outdoor Activities and Sports

HORSEBACK RIDING

Club Hípico (✉ Carretera de Circunvalación, ☎ 971/345198), in Sant Antoni, has horses and equipment.

SPORTS AND FITNESS COMPLEX

Ahmara (✉ Centro Deportivo, Carretera Sant Josep, Km 2.7, ☎ 971/307762 or 971/307950), on the road to Sant Josep, has tennis courts (and lessons), four squash courts, badminton, indoor football, massage, and a gymnasium, Turkish bath, a sauna, hot tub, pool, restaurant-grill, and bar.

TENNIS

Recommended clubs: **Ibiza Club de Campo** (✉ Carretera Sant Josep, Km 2, ☎ 971/391458). **Aqualandia** (✉ Urb. Punta Martinet, Playa Talamanca, ☎ 971/314060). **Port Sant Miquel** (☎ 971/333019). **Formentera** (✉ Avda. Port Saler, Sant Francesc, ☎ no phone).

WALKING

Landscapes of Ibiza and Formentera (Sunflower Books) outlines 44 walks, none very strenuous, and six bike tours of Formentera.

Shopping

In the late 1960s and '70s, Ibiza built a reputation for extremes of fashion. Little of this phenomenon survives, though the softer designs of Smilja Mihailovich (under the Ad Lib label) still prosper. While Sa Penya still has a few designer boutiques, much of the area is now a "hippie market" (literally—locals call it the Mercat dels Hippies) of overpriced tourist ephemera. You'll still find designer leather clothing at **Azara 5,** in front of the Teatro Pereira. **Pink Fly** (✉ Rimbau 4) and **Modas Olinka** (✉ Pere de Portugal) are well-known boutiques.

In the newer part of town, **Krystal** (✉ Carrers Canarius and Aragón) specializes in designer glassware. **Casa del Café** (✉ Carrers Bisbe Carrasco and Médico Rapuchin) has an amazing range of coffees, teas, and preserves. **Front Line** (✉ Bartolomé Rosello 1) stocks fashions for both adults and children.

Side Trips

Santa Eulàlia des Riu

20 *15 km (9 mi) northeast of Ibiza.*

At the edge of this town, to the right just below the road, a **Roman bridge** crosses what is claimed to be the only permanent river in the Balearics (hence "des Riu," or "of the river"), though the bed is usually only damp. Ahead, on the hilltop, are the cubes and domes of the **church**—to reach it, look for a narrow lane to the left, signed PUIG DE MISSA, itself so named for the hill where Mass was once held. A stoutly arched, cryptlike covered area, clearly of Moorish influence, guards the entrance; inside are a fine gold reredos and blue-tiled stations of the cross.

DINING

$$–$$$ ★ ✕ **Sa Capella.** It's a 20-minute, 15-km (9-mi) drive west of Ibiza, but this enchanting restaurant in the resort of Sant Antoni is well worth seeking out. A former chapel, it was converted with flair and style into an atmospheric restaurant. Try the roast suckling pig—you won't find better. ✉ *Puig d'en Basora, Sant Antoni,* ☎ *971/340057. MC, V. Closed Nov.–Mar.*

$$ ★ ✕ **C'as Pagès.** This old farmhouse, with bare stone walls, wood beams, and columns made of giant olive-press screws, is not for vegetarians. Try the leg of *cordero asado* (roast lamb with baked potato), *pimientos rellenos* (roast peppers), or *sofrit pagès* (lamb and chicken stew), and finish off with *graixonera,* a mixture of sugar, milk, eggs, and cinnamon. ✉ *Carretera de San Carlos, Km 10 (Pont de S'Argentara),* ☎ *no phone. No credit cards. Closed Tues. and Feb.–Mar.*

$$ ✕ **Doña Margarita.** This immaculately whitewashed waterfront restaurant has won several awards for its Ibizan seafood preparations. You dine at pine tables, overlooked by Ibizan landscapes on the alabaster walls. The terrace, next to the crescent beach, is especially pleasant in the evening. ✉ *Passeig Marítim s/n,* ☎ *971/330655. AE, DC, MC, V. Closed Mon. and Nov.*

SHOPPING

Broch, on the Plaça de Espanya, is known for high-quality leatherwear.

Balafi

10 km (6 mi) northwest of Santa Eulàlia.

To reach the fortified village of Balafi, take the Sant Joan road from Ibiza and, passing the left turn to Sant Llorenç, look for a bar on the right next to a ceramics workshop. Turn right onto Sant Carles: almost opposite, on the left, a rough, narrow track leads to Balafi. You'll see some towers in the distance. These have no entrance on the ground floor; in times of peril, residents climbed a ladder to the second floor and pulled the ladder up after them.

Formentera

21 *90 mins (30–40 mins by fast boat) by ferry from Ibiza.*

You can begin this tour from Ibiza, Sant Antoni, or Santa Eulàlia, as all have ferries to La Sabina. Because Formentera consists mainly of beach and countryside, you may be inspired to picnic; buy supplies in Ibiza. It's well worth standing on deck during the short passage, as you'll have excellent views of Ibiza's Dalt Vila and the smaller islands en route. Look for Trucadors, the long stretch of sand that almost links Formentera with Es Palmador.

La Sabina has several car, bicycle, and moped rental agencies, and most people rent bikes to explore this flat little island. From La Sabina, it's only 3 km (2 mi) to Formentera's tiny capital, **Sant Francesc Xavier,** a few yards off the main road. There's an active hippie market in the small plaza before the church. The interior of the whitewashed church is quite simple, its rough, old wooden door encased in iron and studded with nails. Down a short street directly opposite the church, on the left, is a good antiques and junk shop, complete with a small art gallery featuring paintings and olive-wood carvings.

At the main road, turn right toward **Sant Ferran,** 2 km (1 mi) away. Beyond Sant Ferran the road travels for 7 km (4 mi) along a narrow isthmus, keeping slightly closer to the rougher, northern side, where waves come crashing over the rocks when a wind is blowing. Just beyond El Pilar you'll see on the right a windmill, still in good order, with all its sails flying.

The plateau on the island's east side ends at the lighthouse **Faro de la Mola.** Nearby is a **monument to Jules Verne,** who set part of his novel *Journey Through the Solar System* in Formentera. Despite being trampled by thousands of tourists, the bare rock around the lighthouse is carpeted with flowers, purple thyme, and sea holly in spring and fall, while hundreds of swallows soar below. At the edge of the cliff you may see one of the turquoise-viridian lizards endemic to Ibiza and Formentera.

Back on the main road, turn right at Sant Ferran toward Es Pujols. The few hotels here are the closest Formentera comes to beach resorts, even if the beach is not the best. Beyond Es Pujols the road skirts **Estany Pudent,** one of two lagoons that almost enclose La Sabina. Salt was once extracted from Pudent, hence its name, which means "stinking pond," although the pond now smells fine. The other lagoon, **Estany de Peix** (Fish Pond), was once a fish farm.

At the northern tip of Pudent, a road to the right leads to a footpath that runs the length of **Trucadors,** the narrow sand spit that leads to Es Palmador. The beaches here are excellent.

Dining and Lodging

$$$ ✕ **Le Cyrano.** This family-run restaurant on the Es Pujols waterfront is one of the best on Formentera. French cuisine—especially foie gras, snails, and pastries—is the main culinary line, and the universal formula of simple fresh fish is practiced peerlessly here as well. ✉ *Passeig Marítim,* ☎ *971/328386. Closed Nov. 16.–Apr. 1 AE, DC, MC, V.*

$$ ✕ **Sa Palmera.** On the beachfront in Es Pujols, Sa Palmera is known for paella and extremely fresh fish. ✉ *Playa Es Pujols,* ☎ *971/328356. MC, V.*

$$$ ✕🏨 **Cala Saona.** Neither too big nor too small, this friendly hotel is on a charming fisherman's *cala* (inlet) and a sleepy little beach that will prove difficult to leave behind. Rooms are simple, comfortable, and breezy, and the restaurant—serving dinner only—prepares the daily catch with skill and care. ✉ *Apdo. de Correos 88, San Francisco 07860,* ☎ *971/322030,* FAX *971/322509. 116 rooms. Restaurant, bar, tennis court. AE, DC, MC, V. Closed mid-Oct.–Apr.*

$–$$ ✕🏨 **Fonda C'an Rafalet.** This simple inn and restaurant 12 km (7 mi) from La Sabina is known for its fresh seafood and rustic setting, just yards from the water at the tiny fishing port of Es Caló. The sound of inboard engines is the most distressing noise you'll hear, and the thought that they'll return with raw materials for your lunch is bound to make up for any lost sleep. ✉ *Carretera La Mola, Km 12, Apdo. de Correos 225, 07860 Es Caló de Sant Agustí, Sant Francesc Xavier,* ☎ FAX *971/327016. 15 rooms. Restaurant, bar. AE, MC, V. Closed Nov.–mid-Mar.*

$$$ 🏨 **Club La Mola.** This whitewashed waterfront spa at Playa de Migjorn has a certain cliff-dwelling Aztec look and as many comforts as you can possibly consume. The *playa,* while not as wild as it once was, is still one of the least-spoiled beaches on the Mediterranean. ✉ *Apdo. de Correos 23, Playa de Migjorn 07860,* ☎ *971/327069,* FAX *971/ 328069. 326 rooms. Restaurant, bar, miniature golf, tennis court, meeting rooms, car rental. AE, DC, MC, V.*

$–$$ **Sa Volta.** Near the beach in Es Pujols, one of the island's busiest villages, this small and economical option more than fulfills your basic lodging needs. ✉ *Miramar 94, San Francisco 07860,* ☎ *971/328125,* FAX *971/ 328228. 25 rooms. Cafeteria. AE, DC, MC, V. Closed mid-Oct.–Apr.*

Outdoor Activities and Sports

BICYCLING

Cycling is very popular; La Sabina has numerous rental outlets.

BOATING

The graceful sloop ***Princesa de Mar*** circumnavigates Formentera twice daily 9–1 and from 4–8. Xicu Castelló and his merry crew provide plenty of laughs, and the sunset cruise is plenty photogenic. The trip departs from the port in La Sabina and costs 4,000 ptas. per person.

THE BALEARIC ISLANDS A TO Z

Arriving and Departing

By Ferry

BETWEEN THE BALEARICS AND THE MAINLAND

BARCELONA: For travelers with a strong sense of romance, the only way to get to the Balearic Islands is the overnight **Trasmediterránea** ferry from Barcelona (✉ Estació Marítima, ☎ 902/454645). The boat sails at 11, leaving time for a proper dinner before embarking, and the view of the lights of the Mediterranean's greatest city sinking into the horizon lasts for over three hours when visibility is good. The Christopher Columbus statue at the foot of the Rambla points directly at the Trasmediterránea station, and the company's central phone line dispenses information on all of its routes 24 hours a day.

More practical travelers are increasingly using the Barcelona-based car ferry **Buquebus** (✉ Avda. Drassanes 5–6, Edificio Colón, 4a planta, ☎ 93/481–7360), which makes a three-hour trip from Barcelona twice daily, at 7 AM and 3:30 PM, and from Palma twice daily, at 11:15 AM and 7:30 PM. Note that the catamaran design is fast in good weather but unsafe in any other kind, so the Buquebus often cancels crossings.

VALENCIA: Trasmediterránea (✉ Estación Marítima, ☎ 96/367–6512) leaves Valencia for Palma Monday through Saturday at 10:30, arriving 7 AM, with additional and faster service in summer. Ferries return from Palma weekdays at 11:30 AM, Saturday at 10 AM, and Sunday at 11:30 PM. Ferries to Ibiza leave only on Thursday from October to May.

MAJORCA: Trasmediterránea (✉ Estació Marítima 2, Muelle de Peraires, ☎ 971/707377) sails daily (and twice on Sunday) from Palma to Barcelona and daily from Palma to Valencia, weekly (Sunday) from Palma to Mahón and Ibiza. From May to October there is also a daily hydrofoil (Hidrojet) service between Palma and Ibiza; call **Naviera Mallorquina** (☎ 971/710153). From France a service connects Sète and Palma twice a week, June to September.

MINORCA: Trasmediterránea (✉ Nuevo Muelle Comercial, ☎ 971/ 366050) sails from Mahón to Barcelona six days a week in summer (mid-June to mid-September) and every Sunday to Palma and Valencia.

IBIZA: Trasmediterránea (☎ 971/315050) sails at least twice a week to Barcelona and Valencia and once a week (Sunday) to Palma. From May to October there is also daily hydrofoil (Hidrojet) service from Palma and Denia, in the province of Alicante, as well as less frequent service from Valencia and Barcelona. A service operates between Sète (France) and Ibiza twice a week, June to September, calling at Palma on the way.

Between Sant Antoni and Denia, **Flebasa** (✉ Estació Marítim, Ibiza, ☎ 971/310927; ✉ Edificio Faro, Sant Antoni, ☎ 971/342871; ✉ Madrid, ☎ 91/473–2055; ✉ Denia, ☎ 96/784011) runs a car ferry and a fast hydrofoil with bus connections to Madrid and Valencia.

INTERISLAND SERVICE

Flebasa, represented by all travel agencies on Majorca, ferries people and cars daily from Alcúdia (Majorca) to Ciutadella (Minorca) in three to four hours, depending on the weather. A hovercraft makes the journey between Sant Antoni and Benidorm in 2½ hours, daily in the summer months; for information and reservations, contact **Coral Travel** (✉ Carrer Mar 11, Sant Antoni, ☎ 971/343711 or 971/343752; ✉ Carrer Isadora Macabich 14, Santa Eulàlia, ☎ 971/330512 or 971/330561).

Frequent ferry, catamaran, and hydrofoil services between Ibiza and Formentera are run by **Transmapi** (☎ 971/314513; 971/310711; 971/320703 in Formentera), **Marítima de Formentera** (☎ 971/320157), and **Flebasa** (☎ 971/310927).

By Plane

MAJORCA: Iberia, Aviaco, Spanair, and **Air Europa** have direct daily flights between Palma (airport: ☎ 971/262600) and Barcelona, Madrid, Alicante, Valencia, Minorca, and Ibiza, as well as direct flights two or three times a week to Bilbao and Vitoria. Interisland flights should be booked well in advance in the summer. **Iberia** and a large number of charter operators also fly between Palma and major European cities. Bus 17 runs between Palma Airport and the bus station on the Plaça d'Espanya, next to the Inca railway terminus. The last bus from town is at 1:30 AM; the last bus from the airport leaves at 2:10 AM. The fare is 300 ptas., and the journey takes 30 minutes. Taxi fare from Palma Airport to downtown is about 2,750 ptas.

MINORCA: Iberia and its subsidiary **Aviaco** fly direct to Mahón from Barcelona and Palma three or four times daily. Most of the Palma services start and end in Madrid. **Air Europa** and **Spanair** also fly to Mahón, and direct charter flights serve Minorca from many European cities in summer. A metered taxi to Mahón costs about 1,100 ptas.

IBIZA: Iberia and its subsidiary **Aviaco** (☎ 971/395377) have direct daily flights from Barcelona, Madrid, Valencia, and Palma. For airport information, call ☎ 971/157000. An hourly bus service runs between the airport and town from 7 AM to 10:30 PM (on the hour from town, on the half hour from the airport; fare 450 ptas., journey time 15 mins). By taxi, the same route costs about 2,500 ptas.

Getting Around

By Boat

MAJORCA

Boats from Palma, Majorca, to neighboring beach resorts leave from the jetty opposite the Auditorium, on the Passeig Marítim. The tourist office has a timetable.

MINORCA

Excursions to Minorca's remotest beaches—which usually include a paella picnic on the beach—leave daily in summer from the jetty next to the Nuevo Muelle Comercial, in Mahón's harbor.

By Bus

MAJORCA

A good network of bus services fans out from Palma to towns and villages throughout Majorca. Most leave from the city **bus station** (✉ Estació Central, ☎ 971/752224), next to the Inca railway terminus on the Plaça d'Espanya; a few terminate at other points in the city. The tourist office on the Plaça d'Espanya has details and timetables.

MINORCA

Several buses a day run the length of Minorca, between Mahón and Ciutadella, calling at the island's other principal towns (Alayor, Mercadal, and Ferreries) en route. From smaller villages there are daily buses to Mahón and connections, though often indirect, to Ciutadella. A regular bus service from the west end of Ciutadella's Plaça Explanada shuttles travelers between town and the resorts to the south and west.

IBIZA

Buses run every half hour from Ibiza (✉ Avinguda Isadora Macabich) to Sant Antoni and Playa d'En Bossa, and roughly hourly to Santa Eulàlia. Buses from Ibiza to other parts of the island are less frequent, as is the cross-island bus between Sant Antoni and Santa Eulàlia. The timetable is published in newspapers.

FORMENTERA

A very limited bus service connects Formentera's villages, shrinking to one bus each way between San Francisco and Pilar on Saturdays and disappearing altogether on Sundays and holidays. Ibizan newspapers publish details.

By Car

MAJORCA

Majorca's main highways are well surfaced, and a fast, 25-km (15-mi) motorway penetrates deep into the center of the island between Palma and Inca. Palma is ringed by an efficient beltway, the Vía Cintura. For destinations in the north and west, follow the *Andratx* and *Oeste* signs on the beltway; for the south and east, follow the *Este* signs. Driving in the mountains that parallel the northwest coast and descend to a cliffside corniche is a different matter; you'll be slowed not only by winding roads but by tremendous views and tourist traffic. The tunnel through the mountains to Sóller obviates the spectacular but tiring serpentine mountain route, making the island's northwest coast a safe, simple safe 20-minute drive from downtown Palma.

MINORCA

A car is essential if you want to beach-hop here, as few of Minorca's beaches and *calas* (coves) are served by public transport. However, most of the sights are in Mahón or Ciutadella, both of which have reasonable bus service from other parts of the island; and once you're in town, everything is within walking distance. You can easily see the island's archaeological remains in a day's drive, so a reasonable compromise might be to rent a car for just part of your visit. The main roads are good; others can be narrow.

IBIZA

Ibiza is best explored by car or motor scooter, as many of the beaches lie at the end of rough, unpaved roads. The main highways are well surfaced and relatively straight, making for fast driving. Several new roads now cross the island in the north.

By Carriage

MAJORCA

In Palma, you can hire a horse-drawn carriage (with driver) seating four to five passengers at the bottom of the Born; on Avinguda Antonio Maura; in the nearby cathedral square; and on the Plaça d'Espanya, at the side farthest from the railway station. A tour of the city costs about 4,000 ptas.

By Taxi

Taxis in Palma, **Majorca,** charge by the standard taxi meter. For trips beyond the city, charges are posted at the taxi ranks. On **Minorca,** you can pick up taxis at the airport and in Mahón (✉ Explanada, ☎ 971/367111) and Ciutadella (✉ Carrer Josep Antoni, ☎ 971/381896). On **Ibiza,** taxis are available at the airport (☎ 971/305230) and in Ibiza town (✉ Passeig Vara de Rey, ☎ 971/301794, 971/307000, 971/306602), Figueretas (☎ 971/301676), Santa Eulàlia (☎ 971/333033), and Sant Antoni (☎ 971/340074 or 971/341721). On **Formentera,** taxis are in La Sabina (☎ 971/322002 or 971/323016) and Es Pujols (☎ 971/328016).

By Train

MAJORCA

Majorca has two separate railway systems. The **Palma–Inca** line travels to Inca, with stops at about half a dozen villages en route, from the Palma terminus (✉ Ferrocarriles de Majorca, Plaça d'Espanya, ☎ 971/752245). A journey on the privately owned **Palma–Sóller** railway is a must: built by the citrus-fruit magnates of Sóller at the beginning of the century, it still uses the carriages of that era. The line trundles across the plain to Bunyola, then winds through tremendous mountain scenery to emerge high above Sóller. An ancient tram connects the Sóller terminus to Port de Sóller, leaving every hour on the hour, 9–7; the Palma terminal (☎ 971/752051) is near the corner of the Plaça d'Espanya, on Calle Eusebio Estada next to the Inca rail station.

Guided Tours

Most hotels in **Majorca** offer a variety of guided tours; ask your front desk for information. Typical itineraries are the Caves of Artà or Drac, on the east coast, including the nearby Auto Safari Park and an artificial-pearl factory in Manacor; the Chopin museum in the former monastery at Valldemossa, returning through the writers' and artists' village of Deià; the port of Sóller and the Arab gardens at Alfàbia; the Thursday market and leather factories in Inca; Port de Pollença; Cape Formentor; and northern beaches.

Boat Tours

MAJORCA

Nearly every Majorcan resort runs excursions to neighboring beaches and coves—many inaccessible by road—and to the islands of Cabrera and Dragonera. You can also take a morning shopping trip by boat from Magalluf or Palma Nova to Palma; the tourist office has details.

MINORCA

Various sightseeing trips leave Mahón's harbor from the quayside near the Xoriguer gin factory. Several of the boats have glass bottoms for viewing marine life. Fares average around 1,000 ptas.

IBIZA/FORMENTERA

Every resort offers trips to neighboring beaches and to smaller islands off the coast. Trips from Ibiza to Formentera include an escorted bus tour. In Sant Antoni, which has little to offer in the way of beaches, a whole flotilla advertises trips.

Contacts and Resources

Car Rental

Rental agencies at Palma airport include, among others, **Atesa Eurodollar** (☎ 971/789896), **Avis** (☎ 971/789187), **Betacar-Europcar** (☎ 971/789135), and **Hertz** (☎ 971/789670). All four companies have offices on Palma's Passeig Marítim as well.

Agencies at Mahón airport include **Atesa Eurodollar** (☎ 971/789187), **Avis** (☎ 971/361576), **Betacar-Europcar** (☎ 971/366400), and **Hertz** (☎ 971/353967).

Agencies at Ibiza airport include **Atesa Eurodollar** (☎ 971/395393), **Avis** (☎ 971/809176), **Betacar-Europcar** (☎ 971/395384), and **Hertz** (☎ 971/809178). Avis, Betacar, and Hertz also have in-town offices.

Formentera has car, bicycle, scooter, and moped rental agencies in the port of La Sabina: **Autos Formentera** (☎ 971/322156), **Autos Isla Blanca** (☎ 971/322559), **Avis** (☎ 971/322123), **Betacar-Europcar** (☎ 971/395384), **Moto Rent Migjorn** (☎ 971/322306), and **Moto Rent Sabina** (☎ 971/322275).

Consulates

In Palma, Majorca: **United States** (✉ Avda. Jaume III 26, ☎ 971/725051). **United Kingdom** (✉ Plaça Major 3D, ☎ 971/718501). **Ireland** (✉ Sant Miquel, 68A, ☎ 971/719244).

Emergencies

Police: ☎ 091, 092, or 971/381095 in Ciutadella; 971/320210 in Formentera. **Ambulance:** ☎ 061. **Medical assistance:** Clínica Juaneda (✉ Son Espanyolet, ☎ 971/722222). **Fire:** ☎ 080.

Pharmacies

Pharmacies are open late by rotation. Schedules are posted on the door of each pharmacy and in local newspapers.

Travel Agencies

Viajes Barcelos (✉ Avda. Jaume III 2, Palma, Majorca, ☎ 971/5590874; ✉ Avda. Josep María Cuadrado 1, Mahón, Minorca, ☎ 971/360250; ✉ Cami de Maó 5, Ciutadella, Minorca, ☎ 971/380487; ✉ Avda. d'Espanya s/n, Ibiza town, ☎ 971/303250); **Viajes WagonsLits Cook** (✉ Plaça Constitució 9, Mahón, Minorca, ☎ 971/364162; ✉ Passeig Vara de Rey 3, Ibiza town, ☎ 971/301503).

Visitor Information

The regional tourist office for the Balearic Islands is the **Consellaria de Turismo de Balear** in Palma, Majorca (✉ Avda. Jaume III 10, ☎ 971/712216).

MAJORCA

The **Oficina de Turismo de Mallorca** (Majorcan Tourist Board) in Palma's airport (☎ 971/789556) is supplemented by the following local tourist offices: **Alcúdia** (✉ Carretera Port d'Alcúdia Arta s/n, ☎ 971/548615). **Palma** (✉ Carrer Sant Domingo 11, ☎ 971/724090; ✉ kiosk on northeast side of Plaça d'Espanya, facing rail station, ☎ 971/711527). **Pollença** (✉ Carrer Miquel Capllonch, ☎ 971/534666). **Sóller** (✉ Plaça de Sa Constitució 1, ☎ 971/630200; ✉ Carrer Canónigo Oliver, ☎ 971/630101). **Valldemossa** (✉ Ticket office next to monastery, Cartuja de Valldemossa, ☎ 971/612106).

MINORCA

Pick up local tourist information in **Mahón** (✉ Plaça Explanada 40, ☎ 971/363790) and in **Ciutadella** (✉ Plaça de la Catedral 5, ☎ 971/382693). The best all-purpose map is the "Mapa Arqueológico de Menorca," available in bookstores and some hotels.

IBIZA/FORMENTERA

Local tourist offices: **Ibiza** (✉ Passeig Vara de Rey 13, ☎ 971/301900). **Santa Eulàlia** (✉ Carrer Mariano Riquer Wallis s/n, ☎ 971/330728). **Sant Antoni** (✉ Passeig de Ses Fonts s/n, ☎ 971/343363). **La Sabina** (✉ Port de La Sabina, ☎ 971/322057).

10 THE COSTA DEL SOL

Most of the Costa del Sol—the central Andalusian coast—is an overdeveloped package-tour magnet and a retirement haven for Anglo-Saxon sunseekers. Marbella attracts the most glamorous crowd, Torremolinos the wildest; but just a few miles inland from both resorts are breathtaking landscapes and mountain villages, cultural light-years away from the hedonistic carnival raging on the coast. The tiny British colony of Gibraltar retains a curious mixture of English and Andalusian atmosphere.

By Hilary Bunce

Updated by Mark Little

TECHNICALLY, THE STRETCH OF ANDALUSIAN SHORE known as the Costa del Sol runs west from the Costa Tropical, near Granada, to the tip of Tarifa, past Gibraltar. For most of the Europeans who have flocked here over the past 40 years, though, the Sun Coast has been largely restricted to the 70-km (43-mi) sprawl of hotels, holiday villas, golf courses, marinas, and nightclubs between Torremolinos, just west of Málaga, and Estepona, down toward Gibraltar. Since the late 1950s this area has mushroomed from a group of impoverished fishing villages afflicted with malaria and near-starvation into an overdeveloped seaside playground and retirement haven.

In the 1960s and early '70s, hundreds of high-rises shot up in Torremolinos and Fuengirola, and luxury hotels and leafy villas erupted on the shore of Marbella, pushing this former fishing village to the forefront of high-end European resorts. The late 1980s saw a second boom, which brought new golf courses, luxury marinas, villa developments, and yet more world-class hotels.

This might not be the Spain of the independent traveler's dreams, but it does have its attractions. The Costa averages some 320 days of sunshine a year, and balmy days are not unknown even in January or February. Despite the hubbub, you *can* unwind here, basking or strolling on mile after mile of sandy beach and enjoying a full range of land and water sports.

Sunseekers from bleaker climes seem to be crammed into every corner of this region. Choose your base carefully. Málaga and Ronda are the most authentically Spanish cities, particularly Ronda. Torremolinos is a budget destination catering almost exclusively to the mass market; it appeals very much to singles and to those who come purely to soak up the sun and dance the night away. Fuengirola is quieter, and geared more toward family vacations; farther west, the Marbella–San Pedro de Alcántara area is more exclusive and, of course, more expensive.

In some places, mountains roll right down to the Mediterranean; in others, hillsides of olive groves, cork oaks, and terraced vineyards unfold toward vistas of the sea glinting in the distance. The developed coastal strip contrasts vividly with its hinterland. Just a few miles up in the mountains are quiet villages where black-shawled women go about their daily routine much as they did half a century ago, and where donkeys and mules are still used for farm work. Steeped in medieval lore—and the scene of many a Reconquest battle—Andalusia's perched white villages (*pueblos blancos*) are a world apart from the ongoing party on the coast. Gibraltar diverts the Anglophile with its English-style bobbies, pubs, and regal guardsmen.

Pleasures and Pastimes

Beaches

The beaches of the Costa del Sol range from shingle and pebbles at worst (Almuñecar, Nerja, Málaga) to a fine, gray, gritty sand (from Torremolinos westward). Pebbles and pollution can make swimming in the sea unpleasant. Look for beaches flying the blue EU flag, which indicates that the facilities conform to European Union standards. All beaches are packed in July and August, when Spanish families take their annual vacations, and on Sundays from May to October, when they become picnic sites.

All beaches in Spain are free. Changing facilities are usually not available, though you'll find free, cold showers on the major beaches. It's quite acceptable for women to go topless here; if you want to take it *all* off, you'll have to drive to one of the more isolated beaches designated *playa naturista.* The most popular nude beaches are in Maro (near Nerja); between Benalmádena-Costa and Fuengirola; and near Tarifa. Costa Natura, 3 km (2 mi) west of Estepona, is the region's official nudist colony.

The best—and most crowded—beaches are El Bajondillo and La Carihuela, in Torremolinos; the long stretch between Carvajal, Los Boliches, and Fuengirola; and those on both sides of Marbella. You may find the odd secluded beach west of Estepona. For wide beaches of fine sand, you'll have to head west past Gibraltar, around the southern tip of Spain to Tarifa and the Cádiz coast, though strong winds are often a deterrent here.

Dining

Spain's southern coast is known for fresh seafood, breaded with fine flour and exquisitely fried. Sardines roasted on skewers at beachside restaurants are another popular and unforgettable treat. Gazpacho shows up in the Andalusian culinary canon as both complement and antidote. Málaga is best for traditional Spanish cooking, with a wealth of bars and seafood restaurants serving *fritura malagueña,* the city's famous fried fish. Torremolinos's Carihuela district is also a paradise for lovers of Spanish seafood. The resorts serve every conceivable foreign cuisine as well, from Thai to the Scandinavian smorgasbord; Marbella has internationally renowned restaurants. At the other end of the scale, and perhaps even more enjoyable, are the Costa's traditional *chiringuitos,* or *merenderos*; strung out along the beaches, these rough-and-ready, summer-only restaurants serve seafood fresh off the boats.

Because of the international clientele, meals on the coast itself are served earlier than elsewhere in Andalusia, with restaurants opening at 1 or 1:30 for lunch and 7 or 8 for dinner. Reservations are advisable for all Marbella restaurants listed as $$$–$$$$ and for the better restaurants in Málaga; elsewhere, they're rarely necessary. Expect beach restaurants, such as Málaga's Casa Pedro and all those on the Carihuela seafront in Torremolinos, to be packed after 3 PM on Sunday.

CATEGORY	COST*
$$$$	over 6,500 ptas.
$$$	4,000 ptas.–6,500 ptas.
$$	2,500 ptas.–4,000 ptas.
$	under 2,500 ptas.

**per person for a three-course meal, including house wine and coffee and excluding tax*

Fiestas

Málaga holds a colorful parade on January 5, the eve of the **Día de los Tres Reyes** (Feast of the Three Kings, or Epiphany), and the city's **Semana Santa** (Holy Week) processions are among the most dramatic in Andalusia. Nerja and Estepona celebrate **San Isidro** (May 15) with typically Andalusian *ferias.* Midsummer, or the feast of **San Juan** (June 23–24), is marked by midnight bonfires on beaches all along the coast. The **Virgen del Carmen** is the patron saint of fishermen, so fishing communities all along the coast honor her feast day (July 16) with seaborne processions of fishing boats. Málaga and Fuengirola throw popular annual **city festivals,** Málaga's at the beginning of August and Fuengirola's in the fall, October 6–12.

Golf

With nearly 40 golf courses between Rincón de la Victoria (east of Málaga) and Gibraltar, the Costa del Sol has the highest concentration of courses in Europe. Some are quite hilly, making them both spectacular to look at and challenging to play. The best season for golf is October through June; greens fees are lower during the hot summer months.

Certain hotels cater almost exclusively to golfers, and some offer guests reduced greens fees: these include the Parador de Golf, near the Málaga airport; the Byblos, near Fuengirola; Los Monteros, near Marbella; the Hotel Atalaya Park and El Paraíso, between San Pedro and Estepona; and Almenara and The Suites, near San Roque.

Indispensable for anyone trying to make independent golf arrangements is a copy of *Sun Golf*, a free magazine available at hotels and golf clubs. The *Andalucía Golf Guide,* published by Andalusia's regional tourist office, details all the courses on the Costa del Sol; it's available at any Tourist Office of Spain.

Lodging

Most hotels on the more highly developed stretch, between Torremolinos and Fuengirola, offer large, functional rooms near the sea at competitive rates. The area's ongoing popularity as a budget destination means that most such hotels are booked in high season by foreign package-tour operators. Finding a room at Easter, in July and August, or around the October 12 holiday weekend can be difficult if you haven't reserved in advance.

Málaga is poorly endowed with hotels for a city of its size; it has an excellent but small parador that can be hard to book, and few other hotels of note. Marbella, conversely, packs more than its fair share of grand hotels, including some of Spain's most expensive accommodations. Rooms in Gibraltar's handful of hotels are about 50% more expensive than most comparable lodgings in Spain.

CATEGORY	COST*
$$$$	over 20,000 ptas.
$$$	12,000 ptas.–20,000 ptas.
$$	8,000 ptas.–12,000 ptas.
$	under 8,000 ptas.

**for a standard double room, excluding breakfast, tax, and service charge*

Exploring the Costa del Sol

While the coast is generally understood as the area's prime resource, much of it is lined with skyscrapers and crowded with tourists, which may not be what you had in mind when you started planning your getaway. However, the shore is better endowed with hotels and restaurants than the rest of Andalusia, making it an excellent base for exploring the region. Many of Andalusia's most charming secrets lie just inland, and the megasights of Granada, Córdoba, and Seville are only a few hours away.

Numbers in the text correspond to numbers in the margin and on the Costa del Sol and Gibraltar maps.

Great Itineraries

This drive takes in the Costa del Sol from east to west, along the coastal highway N340. It starts in the province of Granada, then heads west along the entire coast of Málaga's province, entering the province of Cádiz briefly at Sotogrande and San Roque, and finishing at the Strait of Gibraltar. (If you arrive at the coast from Cádiz, simply follow the drive in reverse order.) The main towns en route are Nerja, Málaga (the region's capital and only major city), Torremolinos, Fuengirola, Marbella, and Estepona; detours inland bring you to mountain villages and the dramatic scenery of the Chorro gorge. Ronda makes a particularly inspiring excursion, high in the mountains 49 km (30 mi) from the coast.

In a week or 10 days you can see nearly all the major beaches and cities, venture inland, and maybe even hop across to Morocco. Five days is really the minimum if you want to do anything other than drive or lie on the beach. Three days gives you a taste of the major sights and a look at the coast.

IF YOU HAVE 3 DAYS

Explore Granada's Costa Tropical (formerly the Costa del Sol Oriental), the eastern end of Sol. See the villages of **Salobreña** ① and **Almuñecar** ② and the town of **Nerja** ③, with its Balcón de Europa over the sea. Have lunch at one of the sea-view restaurants near the square. Visit the village of **Frigiliana** ④ before proceeding to **Málaga** ⑥ for the night. The next morning, explore Málaga before moving up into the hills for lunch in **Antequera** ⑦. From Antequera, make the 100-km (62-mi) drive over to **Ronda** ⑰ for your second night. Explore Ronda in the early morning and drive to coastal **Marbella** ⑮ for lunch at the beach. From Marbella you can either move west to Sotogrande, **San Roque** ㉔, and **Gibraltar** ㉕–㊲ or head back east to tumultuous **Torremolinos** ⑪ for a night on the town.

IF YOU HAVE 5 DAYS

Follow the itinerary above for your first day, settling down in **Málaga** ⑥ for the night. Devote your second day to exploring Málaga before moving up into the hills for the sunset and a night in the parador in **Antequera** ⑦. On day three, drive from Antequera up to the village of Archidona before working your way back through El Torcal Nature Park, **Alora** ⑧, and the Garganta del Chorro to **Torremolinos** ⑪, where the Carihuela beach district provides a radical change of scenery. On your fourth day, explore the picturesque village of **Mijas** ⑭ before moving on to **Marbella** ⑮ for an afternoon among the glitterati. If this scene is too manicured for your taste, hop up to the village of **Ojén** ⑯ for a complete change of pace. Spend the early evening driving to **Ronda** ⑰ for a look at one of Andalusia's most stunning mountain enclaves. Day five is a chance to see more of Ronda before touring **Olvera** ⑱ and **Setenil de las Bodegas** ⑲, the Roman settlement of Acinipo, **Zahara de la Sierra** ⑳, and the **Sierra de Grazalema** ㉑. Finish this ambitious day with a look at Sotogrande and **San Roque** ㉔ on your way into **Gibraltar** ㉕–㊲.

When to Tour the Costa del Sol

Winter is a good time to be on this coast; the temperatures are moderate, and there are fewer tourists. Fall and spring are also prime opportunities. Avoid July and August; it's too hot and crowded. May and June bring the longest days and the fewest travelers. Holy Week brings memorable ceremonies and processions.

THE COSTA TROPICAL

East of Málaga and west of Almería, the so-called Costa Tropical has escaped the worst excesses of the property developers, and its tourist onslaught has been mild. A flourishing farming center thanks to the year-round mild climate, this area earns its keep not from tourism but from tropical fruit, including avocados, mangoes, papaws, and custard apples. Housing developments are generally inspired by Andalusian village architecture rather than concrete towers. You may find packed beaches and traffic-choked roads at the height of the season, but for most of the year the Costa Tropical is relatively free of tourists, if not devoid of foreign expatriates.

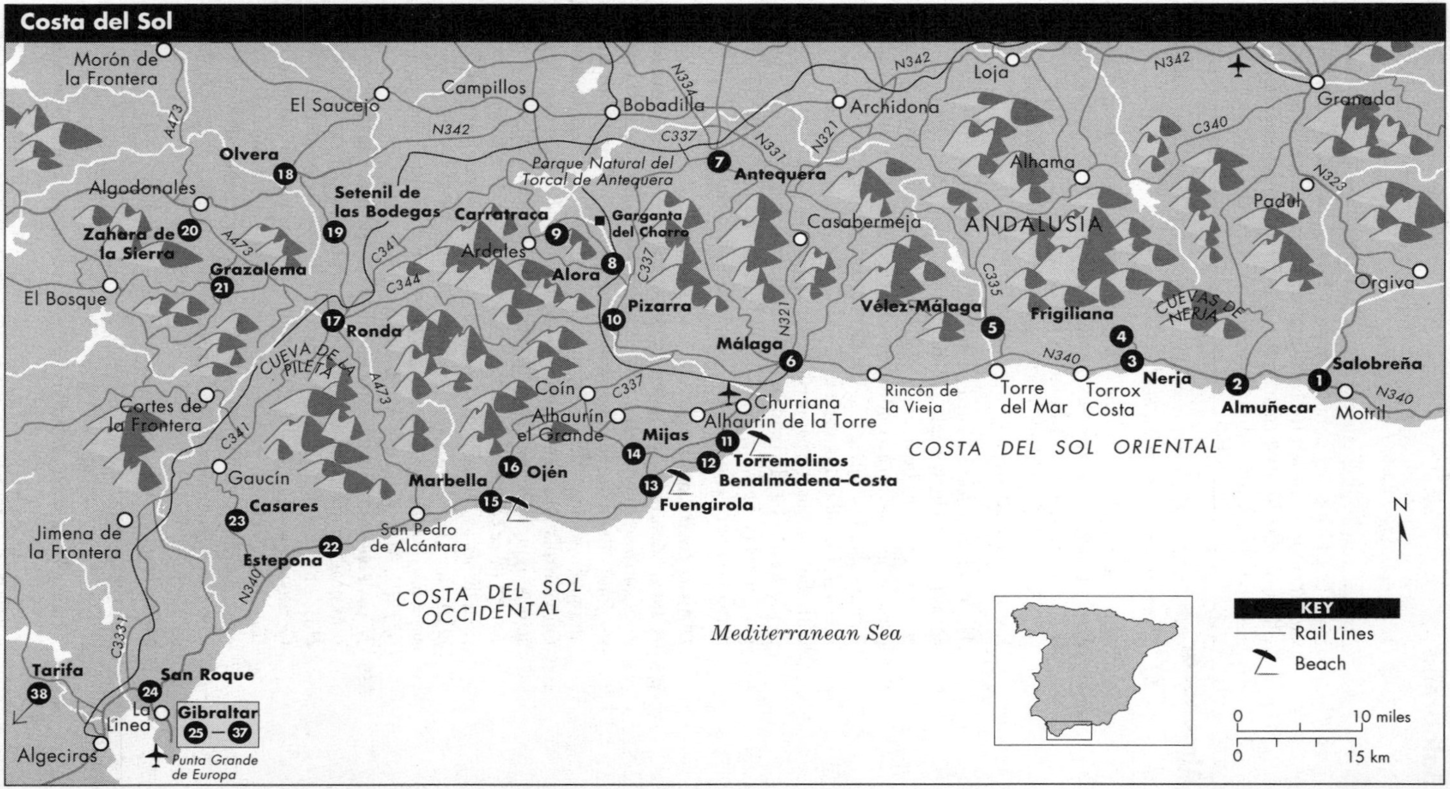
Costa del Sol
Morón de la Frontera
El Saucejo
Campillos
Bobadilla
Archidona
Loja
Granada
Olvera
Algodonales
Setenil de las Bodegas
Zahara de la Sierra
Grazalema
El Bosque
Carratraca
Ardales
Garganta del Chorro
Alora
Parque Natural del Torcal de Antequera
Antequera
Casabermeja
ANDALUSIA
Alhama
Padul
Orgiva
Ronda
Pizarra
Vélez-Málaga
Frigiliana
CUEVAS DE NERJA
Málaga
CUEVA DE LA PILETA
Coín
Alhaurín el Grande
Churriana
Alhaurín de la Torre
Rincón de la Vieja
Torre del Mar
Torrox Costa
Nerja
Almuñecar
Salobreña
Motril
Cortes de la Frontera
Gaucín
Mijas
Torremolinos
Benalmádena-Costa
Ojén
Marbella
Fuengirola
Casares
Jimena de la Frontera
Estepona
San Pedro de Alcántara
COSTA DEL SOL ORIENTAL
COSTA DEL SOL OCCIDENTAL
Mediterranean Sea
Tarifa
San Roque
La Línea
Gibraltar 25 – 37
Algeciras
Punta Grande de Europa
N342
N334
N331
N321
N323
N340
C337
C340
C335
C341
C344
A473
C3331
N
KEY
Rail Lines
Beach
0 10 miles
0 15 km

Salobreña

❶ *102 km (63 mi) east of Málaga.*

You can reach Salobreña either by descending through the mountains from Granada or by continuing west from Almería on the N340. A short detour to the left from the highway brings you to this unspoiled village of near-perpendicular streets and old white houses, slapped onto a steep hill beneath a Moorish fortress. It's a true Andalusian *pueblo.*

Almuñecar

❷ *85 km (53 mi) east of Málaga.*

Almuñecar has been a fishing village since Phoenician times, 3,000 years ago, when it was called Sexi. Later, the Moors built a castle here to house the treasures of Granada's kings. Today Almuñecar is a small-time resort with a shingle beach, popular with Spanish and northern-European vacationers.

The road west from Motril passes through the former empire of the sugar barons who brought prosperity to Málaga's province in the 19th century. The cane fields are now giving way to litchis, limes, mangoes, papaws, and olives; avocado groves line your route as you descend into Almuñecar. The village is actually two, separated by the dramatic rocky headland of Punta de la Mona. To the east is Almuñecar proper, with the ruins of the Moorish castle and a Phoenician burial ground; to the west is **La Herradura,** a quiet fishing community and a perfect place to relax. Between the two is the pretty Marina del Este yacht harbor, a popular diving center along with La Herradura.

Dining and Lodging

$$$ ✕ **Jacqui-Cotobro.** Acclaimed as one of the finest French restaurants on Spain's southern coast, this small establishment sits at the foot of the Punta de la Mona. The dining area is cozy, with bare brick walls and green wicker chairs, and there's a beachfront terrace in summer. On your plate are imaginative combinations of French and Andalusian cooking. The best bet is the *menú de degustación,* with a selection of three courses plus dessert; it changes weekly but might include such dishes as breast of duck in sweet-and-sour sauce followed by *hojaldre de langostinos con puerros* (shrimp pastry with leeks) and *suprema de rodaballo* (turbot). ✉ *Edificio Río, Playa Cotobro,* ☎ *958/631802. MC, V. Closed Mon. and late Nov.–early Dec.*

$$$ 🏨 **Los Fenicios.** This modern Andalusian-style hotel has a good location near the beach in La Herradura, with views of the bay and the cliffs of Punta de Mona to the east and the rocky headland of Cerro Gordo to the west. A gleaming, white entrance with an enormous Moroccan-style ceiling lamp sets the scene. Each room has a terrace and a small sitting area with wicker chairs; ask for a room with a sea view. There's a swimming pool on the roof. ✉ *Paseo de Andrés Segovia, 18697 La Herradura,* ☎ *958/827900,* FAX *958/827910. 42 rooms. Restaurant, cafeteria, pool, meeting rooms. AE, DC, MC, V.*

Nerja

★ ❸ *52 km (32 mi) east of Málaga, 22 km (14 mi) west of Almuñecar.*

The **Cuevas de Nerja** (Nerja Caves) lie between Almuñecar and Nerja on a road surrounded by giant cliffs and dramatic seascapes, the best scenery on this stretch of the coast. Signs point to the cave entrance above the village of Maro, 4 km (2½ mi) east of Nerja. These huge caves were discovered in 1959 by children playing on the hillside; they're now floodlit for better views of the spires and turrets created by millennia of dripping water. One suspended pinnacle, 200 ft long, is in fact the world's largest stalactite. The awesome subterranean chambers make an impressive setting for concerts and ballets during July's Nerja Caves Festival. ☎ *95/252–9520.* *650 ptas.* *Daily 10–2 and 4–6:30 (4–8 in summer).*

Nerja—the name comes from the Moorish word *narixa,* meaning "abundant springs"—is a rapidly developing resort. Happily, much of its growth has been confined to *urbanizaciones* ("village" developments) outside town. The old village of Nerja is clustered on a headland above several small beaches and rocky coves, which offer reasonable bathing despite the gray, gritty sand. In high season, Nerja's beaches are packed with northern Europeans, but the rest of the year it's a pleasure to wander the old town's narrow, whitewashed streets and courtyards. Nerja's highlight is the **Balcón de Europa,** a lookout high above the sea, on a promontory just off the central square.

Dining and Lodging

$$$ ✕ **Casa Luque.** One of Nerja's most authentic Spanish restaurants, Casa Luque occupies a charming old Andalusian house behind the Balcón de Europa church. The menu features dishes from northern Spain, often of Basque or Navarrese origin, with an emphasis on meat and game; good fresh fish is also on offer. The lovely patio is a perfect setting in summer. ✉ *Plaza Cavana 2,* ☎ *95/252–1004. AE, DC, MC, V. Closed Sun.*

$$$ ✕ **Udo Heimer.** Your eponymous host, a genial German, welcomes you warmly to this stylish art deco villa in a new development to the east of Nerja. The visual flair extends to the presentation of the food, which mixes German and Spanish flavors. Favorites include a warm salad of prawns and avocado mousse and an entrée of stuffed quail with Armagnac sauce and sauerkraut. The excellent wine list features rarities from all over Spain. The servers are a bit listless, perhaps overshadowed by their ebullient boss. ✉ *Pueblo Andaluz 27,* ☎ *95/252–0032. MC, V. Closed Wed. No lunch in summer.*

$$$ ✕ **Parador de Nerja.** Surrounded by a leafy garden on the cliff's edge, the rooms in this modern parador have balconies overlooking the garden and, obliquely, the sea; those in the newer, single-story wing open onto their own patios. Some rooms have whirlpool baths. An elevator takes you down to the rocky beach. The restaurant focuses on local cuisine and is known for its fish dishes; the menu changes daily. It might include *pez espada a la naranja* (swordfish in orange sauce) or giant *langostino* (shrimp). ✉ *Almuñecar 8, 29780,* ☎ *95/252–0050,* FAX *95/252–1997. 73 rooms. Restaurant, pool. AE, DC, MC, V.*

$$$ **Paraiso del Mar.** An erstwhile private villa was expanded to form this small hotel, perched on the edge of a cliff overlooking the sea east of the Balcón de Europa. Decor is bright and cheerful, with light-blue and yellow fabrics, lots of potted plants, and sunlight pouring in through picture windows. Some rooms have terraces, four have hot tubs, and most have sea views. ✉ *Prolongación del Carabeo 22, 29780,* ☎ *95/252–1621,* FAX *95/252–2309. 9 rooms, 3 suites. Pool. AE, DC, MC, V. Closed mid-Nov.–mid-Dec.*

Nightlife and the Arts

El Colono (✉ Granada 6, Nerja, ☎ 95/252–1826) is a flamenco club in a typical Andalusian house in the town center. Dinner shows begin at 9 PM on Wednesday in winter, and at 9:30 or 10 PM Wednesday through Friday in summer. You can choose from three prix-fixe menus.

Frigiliana

❹ *58 km (36 mi) east of Málaga.*

The village of Frigiliana sits on a mountain ridge overlooking the sea. One of the last battles between the Christians and the Moors was waged here in 1567. The short drive off the highway rewards you with spectacular views and an old quarter full of cobbled streets and ancient houses. (If you don't have a car, take a bus here from Nerja.)

The Axarquía

❺ *Vélez-Málaga is 36 km (22 mi) east of Málaga.*

The Axarquía region occupies the eastern third of Málaga's province, stretching from Nerja to the city of Málaga. Its coast consists mainly of narrow, pebbly beaches and a string of drab fishing villages on either side of the ugly high-rise resort town Torre del Mar. The great charm of this region lies in its mountainous interior, peppered with picturesque *pueblos,* vineyards, and tiny farms devoted mainly to growing grapes for wine or raisins. The four-lane E-15 highway speeds across the region a few miles in from the coast; traffic on the old coastal road (N340) is slower.

Vélez-Málaga is the capital of the Axarquía. A pleasant agricultural town of white houses, Vélez-Málaga is a center for strawberry fields and vineyards. Worth quick visits are the **Thursday market,** the ruins of a **Moorish castle,** and the church of **Santa María la Mayor,** built in Mudéjar style on the site of a mosque that was destroyed when the town fell to the Christians in 1487.

If you have a car and an up-to-date road map, explore the Axarquía's inland villages. One option is to follow the **Ruta del Vino** (Wine Route) 22 km (14 mi) from the coast, stopping at villages that produce the sweet, earthy local wine, particularly **Competa.** Alternately, you can take the **Ruta de la Pasa** (Raisin Route) through Moclinejo, Almáchar, and El Borge, especially spectacular during the late-summer grape-harvest season or in late autumn, when the leaves of the vines turn gold. History buffs should make a short detour to **Macharaviaya** (7 km/4 mi north of Rincón de la Victoria) and ponder the past glory of this now sleepy village: in 1776 one of its sons, Bernardo de Gálvez, became Spanish governor of Louisiana and later fought in the American Revolution. (His name endures in that of Galveston, Texas.) Macharaviaya prospered under his heirs, and for many years enjoyed a lucrative monopoly on the manufacture of playing cards for South America.

Lodging

$$ 🏨 **Molino de Santillán.** This small, purpose-built country hotel, erected in 1995 in a purely Andalusian style, stands on a farm at the end of a 1-km (½-mi) dirt road just north of the main highway. Rooms have clay-tile floors and are individually furnished with antiques. Those upstairs have balconies and views of the countryside; downstairs rooms have direct access to the garden. The Añoreta golf club and course is a short drive away. ✉ *Carretera de Macharaviaya, Km 3, Rincón de la Victoria,* ☎ *95/211–5780,* FAX *95/211–5782. 9 rooms. Restaurant, pool. AE, DC, MC, V.*

MÁLAGA AND INLAND

The city of Málaga and the towns and villages of the upland hills and valleys to the north create precisely the kind of contrast that makes travel in Spain exciting. The region's Moorish legacy is a unifying visual theme, connecting the tiny streets honeycombing the steamy depths of Málaga, the rocky cliffs and gorges between Alora and Archidona, the layout of the farms, and the crops themselves, including oranges and lemons.

Málaga

6 *175 km (109 mi) southeast of Córdoba.*

With about 550,000 residents, the city of Málaga is technically the capital of the Costa del Sol, though most travelers simply use the airport and bypass the city itself. Approaching the city from the airport, you'll be greeted by an urban sprawl wherein huge 1970s high-rises march determinedly toward Torremolinos. But don't despair: in its center and its eastern suburbs, Málaga is a pleasant port city, with ancient streets and lovely villas amid exotic foliage. Blessed with a subtropical climate, it's covered in lush vegetation and averages some 324 days of sunshine a year.

A word of warning: Málaga has one of the highest unemployment rates in Spain, and poverty and crime are rife (though drug peddling, once fairly common in the streets, has declined). Numerous muggings have been reported; it's best not to carry a purse or any valuables in the streets or on the way up to Gibralfaro (☞ *below*). If you arrive by car, you'll have to contend with pesky *gorrillas,* volunteer parking attendants who demand money to "watch" your car. Stick to areas with parking meters or uniformed parking attendants.

Arriving from Nerja, you'll enter Málaga through the suburbs of El Palo and Pedregalejo, once traditional fishing villages in their own right. Here you can eat wonderfully fresh fish in the numerous crusty *chiringuitos* (fishermen's restaurants) on the beach and stroll Pedregalejos's seafront promenade or the tree-lined streets of El Limonar. At sunset, walk along the **Paseo Marítimo** and watch the lighthouse start its nightly vigil. A few blocks inland from here is Málaga's bullring, **La Malagueta,** built in 1874.

In the city center, the **Plaza de la Marina,** with outdoor cafés and an illuminated fountain overlooking the port, is a pleasant place for a drink. From here, stroll through the shady, palm-lined gardens of the **Paseo del Parque** or browse on **Calle Marqués de Larios,** the main shopping street.

The narrow streets and alleys on each side of Calle Marqués de Larios have charms of their own. Wander the warren of passageways around **Pasaje Chinitas,** off Plaza de la Constitución, and peep into the dark, vaulted *bodegas* where old men down glasses of *seco añejo* or *Málaga Virgen,* local wines made from Málaga's muscatel grapes. Silversmiths and vendors of religious books and statues ply their trades in shops that have changed little since the turn of the century. Across Larios, in the streets leading to Calle Nueva, you'll see shoe-shine boys, lottery-ticket vendors, carnation-sporting Gypsies, beggars, and a wealth of tapas bars dispensing wine from huge barrels. From the Plaza Felix Saenz, at the southern end of Calle Nueva, turn onto Sagasta to reach the **Mercado de Atarazanas,** the most colorful market in all of Andalusia. Stalls sell an amazing assortment of fresh fish, spices, and vegetables. The typical 19th-century iron structure incorporates the original Puerta de Atarazanas, the attractive 14th-century Moorish gate that once connected the city with the port.

NEED A BREAK? The **Antigua Casa de la Guardia** (✉ Alameda 18), around the corner from the Mercado de Atarazanas, is Málaga's oldest bar, founded in 1840. Andalusian wines flow straight from the barrel, and the floor is ankle-deep in discarded shrimp shells.

After exploring the old town, visit the **cathedral,** built between 1528 and 1782 on the site of the former mosque. Mainly Renaissance in style, Málaga's cathedral is not one of the greatest in Spain, having been left unfinished when the funds ran out. (One story holds that the money allocated was donated to the American Revolution instead.) Because it lacks one of its twin towers, the building has been called *La Manquita* (the One-Armed Lady). The lovely enclosed choir, which miraculously survived the burnings of the civil war, is the work of the great 17th-century artist Pedro de Mena, who carved the wood wafer-thin in some places to express the fold of a robe or shape of a finger. The choir also has a pair of massive 18th-century pipe organs, one of which is in good working order and is used for the occasional concert. Adjoining the cathedral is a small **museum** of religious art and artifacts. ✉ *C. de Molina Larios,* ☎ *95/221–5917.* 🎫 *300 ptas.* ⏲ *Mon.–Sat. 9–6:45.*

On one side of the square facing the cathedral's main entrance is the **Palacio Episcopal** (Bishop's Palace), now used for art exhibits (☎ 95/260–2722). Admission is free; it's open Tuesday–Sunday 10–2 and 6–9. From here, walk around the cathedral on Calle Cister and check out its oldest part, the late-Gothic **Puerta del Sagrario** (a side entrance no longer in use).

Turn left and walk up Calle San Agustín past the **Palacio de Buenavista,** home of the future Picasso Museum, due to open in 2001 thanks to the donation of works by Picasso's daughter-in-law Christine and grandson Bernard. Although Picasso's family moved to the north of Spain when he was 10, and he spent the last three decades of his life in exile following the Spanish Civil War, the artist always considered himself first and foremost an Andalusian. Nearly 200 works from different periods of his long career will hang in 13 halls here. Continue up Calle Granada to the **Plaza de la Merced,** where a central obelisk honors José María de Torrijos, a liberal general who was executed in Málaga in 1831 after a failed coup attempt.

No. 15 was the childhood home of Málaga's most famous native son, Pablo Picasso, born here in 1881. It now houses the **Fundación Picasso** and a library for art historians. The interior has been entirely remodeled, with no trace of its original furnishings. The second floor, where Picasso's family lived, now houses a permanent exhibition with engravings and a few pieces of sculpture and ceramics; temporary exhibits of assorted art or memorabilia fill the ground floor. ☎ *95/260–0215.* 🎫 *Free.* ⏲ *Mon.–Sat. 11–2 and 5–8.*

From the Plaza de la Merced, walk down Calle Alcazabilla. On your left are the ruins of a Roman theater, discovered by chance during construction work in the 1950s and now being restored. Just beyond the theater is the Moorish **Alcazaba,** Málaga's greatest monument. This fortress was begun in the 8th century, when Málaga was the principal port of the Moorish kingdom, though most of the present structure dates from the 11th century, when Málaga became a separate kingdom following the splintering of the Córdoba caliphate. The inner palace was built between 1057 and 1063, when the Moorish emirs took up residence; and Ferdinand and Isabella lived here for a while after conquering Málaga in 1487. The ruins are dappled with orange trees and bougainvillea, and their heights afford great views of the park and port. At press time, parts of the fortress were closed for restoration; the whole should be open by 2001. ✉ *Entrance on Alcazabilla.* 🎫 *Free.* ⏲ *Oct.–Mar., Wed.–Mon. 8:30–7; Apr.–Sept., Wed.–Mon. 9:30–8.*

Magnificent views reward a walk up the path from the south wall of the Alcazaba to the summit of **Gibralfaro.** (Thieves have been said to hover here, so avoid going alone, and don't carry valuables.) Alternately, you can drive to Gibralfaro by way of Calle Victoria or take a minibus that leaves 10 times a day between 11 and 7, or roughly every hour, from the bus stop in the park near the Plaza de la Marina. The fortifications were built for Yusuf I in the 14th century; the Moors called them Jebelfaro, from the Arab word for "mount" and the Greek word for "lighthouse," after a beacon that stood here to guide ships into the harbor and warn of invading pirates. The beacon has been succeeded by a small parador (☞ Dining and Lodging, *below*), a delightful place for a meal or drink. *Free. Castle daily 9:30–6.*

On the far side of the city center, beside the river, is the **Museo de Artes Populares** (Arts and Crafts Museum), housed in the old Mesón de la Victoria, a 17th-century inn. On display are horse-drawn carriages and carts, old agricultural implements, folk costumes, a forge, a bakery, an ancient grape press, and Malagueño ceramics and sculptures. ✉ *Pasillo de Santa Isabel 10,* ☎ *95/221–7137. 200 ptas. Weekdays 10–1:30 and 4–7 (5–8 in summer), Sat. 10–1:30.*

Just off the exit road to Granada—too far to walk, but well worth the cab fare from the city center—is the 150-year-old **La Concepción** botanical garden. It was created by the daughter of the British consul, who married a Spanish shipping magnate—the captains of the Spaniard's fleet had standing orders to bring back seedlings and cuttings from every "exotic" country they called at. The garden was abandoned for many years, the tropical plants left to their own devices; but after careful restoration, La Concepción is a luxuriant green jungle, notable for the variety and size of its palm trees. ✉ *Carretera de las Pedrizas, Km 166,* ☎ *95/225–2148. 445 ptas. Tues.–Sun. 10 AM–sundown.*

If you like formal gardens, two others worth visiting are El Retiro and La Cónsula, both on the Churriana road, near the airport. **El Retiro** (☎ 95/262–1600), begun by monks in the 17th century, has an array of exotic birds; it's open 9–7 (9–5 in winter), and admission is 1,250 ptas. **La Cónsula,** surrounding a mansion built by the Prussian consul in 1806, is now the site of the Málaga hotel school's excellent restaurant (☞ Escuela de Hostelería *in* Dining and Lodging, *below*).

Dining and Lodging

$$$ ✕ **Café de París.** The owner of this elegant and intimate Paseo Marítimo restaurant, with a warm, red and mahogany interior, is a former chef at Madrid's Horcher. Sophisticated Spanish diners come from far afield for specialties like *rodaballo del mediterráneo con salsa sin nombre* (turbot with a "nameless" sauce) and *hojaldre de langostinos* (giant shrimp *en croûte*). The *menú de degustación* allows you to try a bit of everything. ✉ *Vélez Málaga 8,* ☎ *95/222–5043. Reservations essential. AE, DC, MC, V. Closed Mon. No dinner Sun.*

$$$ ✕ **Casa Pedro.** It's crowded and noisy, but Malagueños have been flocking to this no-frills fish restaurant for more than 50 years. Out in El Palo, the restaurant has a huge, bare dining room overlooking the ocean. If you're both adventurous and patient, know a little Spanish, and like local color, try joining the families who come for lunch on Sundays. It's quieter the rest of the week. ✉ *Quitapenas 121, El Palo beach (Bus 11),* ☎ *95/229–0013. AE, DC, MC, V. No dinner Mon.*

$$$ ★ ✕ **Escuela de Hostelería.** For a memorable lunch, it's well worth going out of your way to Málaga's hotel and catering school, housed in a 19th-century mansion 8 km (5 mi) outside Málaga on the Churriana road. The dining room itself is a light, airy building of striking modern design, adjoining the La Cónsula mansion and its luxuriant garden. The seasonal dishes are delicious and exquisitely presented. ✉ *Finca La Cónsula, Churriana,* ☎ *95/262–2562. Reservations essential. AE, MC, V. Closed weekends and Aug. No dinner.*

$$–$$$ ✕ **El Chinitas.** At one end of Pasaje Chinitas, the most *típico* of Málaga's streets, this dining spot is decorated with colorful Sevillian tiles. The tapas bar is popular, especially for its cured ham. The second floor has two private dining rooms—groups of 12–20 can and do reserve the Sala Antequera, with a Camelot-style round table—and the third a banquet hall. Try the *sopa viña AB* (a fish soup flavored with sherry and thickened with mayonnaise) or *solomillo al vino de Málaga* (fillet steak in Málaga wine sauce). ✉ *Moreno Monroy 4,* ☎ *95/221–0972. AE, MC, V.*

$–$$ ✕ **Rincón de Mata.** This is one of the best of the many restaurants in the pedestrian shopping area between Calle Marqués de Larios and Calle Nueva. You enter through a small, ground-floor bar; the somewhat cramped dining room is upstairs. The menu is more interesting than most, with such house specialties as *tunedor* (calf in sauce). Not on the menu but often available are *calamares de barca* (fresh squid), prepared grilled. There are tables on the sidewalk in summer. ✉ *Esparteros 8,* ☎ *95/221–3135. AE, DC, MC, V.*

$ ✕ **La Cancela.** In an alley off Calle Granada, at the top of Molina Larios (one block from the Palacio Episcopal), this pretty bistro serves standard Spanish fare, such as *riñones al jerez* (kidneys sautéed with sherry) and *cerdo al vino de Málaga* (pork with Málaga wine sauce), and is ideal for lunch after a morning of shopping. The two dining rooms (one upstairs, one down) are crowded with curious objects: iron grilles, birdcages, potted plants, plastic flowers. In summer, tables appear on the sidewalk for outdoor lunches on what amounts to a sheltered patio. ✉ *Denís Belgrano 5,* ☎ *95/222–3125. AE, DC, MC, V. Closed Wed.*

$$$ ★ ✕🏨 **Parador de Málaga–Gibralfaro.** Surrounded by pine trees on top of Gibralfaro, 3 km (2 mi) above the city, this cozy, gray-stone parador has spectacular views of the city and bay. The attractive rooms—blue curtains and bedspreads, woven rugs on bare tile floors—are the best in Málaga. Reserve well in advance. The restaurant has fabulous views and fine food, including regional specialties as well as an international menu. ✉ *Monte de Gibralfaro, 29016,* ☎ *95/222–1902,* FAX *95/222–1904. 38 rooms. Restaurant, bar, cafeteria, pool, meeting rooms. AE, DC, MC, V.*

$$$ 🏨 **Don Curro.** Just around the corner from the cathedral, this family classic has been overhauled of late, but an old-fashioned air permeates the wood-paneled common rooms, the fireplace lounge, and the somewhat stodgy, wood-floored guest rooms. The best rooms are in the new wing, at the back of the building. ✉ *Sancha de Lara 7, 29015,* ☎ *95/222–7200,* FAX *95/221–5946. 112 rooms, 6 suites. Restaurant. AE, DC, MC, V.*

$$$ 🏨 **Larios.** This elegantly restored 19th-century building is well placed on the central Plaza de la Constitución. Black-and-white tiled floors lend subdued elegance to the second-floor lobby; the rooms are furnished with light wood and cream-colored fabrics and polished off with artsy black-and-white photographs. ✉ *Marqués de Larios 2, 29005,* ☎ *95/222–2200,* FAX *95/222–2407. 34 rooms, 6 suites. Restaurant, meeting room. AE, DC, MC, V.*

$$$ 🏨 **NH Málaga.** Málaga's newest hotel occupies a sleek modern building next to the (usually dry) Guadalmedina River. Well placed near the city center, it caters mainly to business travelers. Guest rooms offer streamlined comfort, with beige curtains and bedspreads and wood floors; and there are nine conference rooms. Special discounts apply on weekends. ✉ *Avenido Río Guadalmedina, 29007,* ☎ *95/207–1323,* FAX *95/239–3862. 129 rooms, 4 suites. Restaurant, meeting rooms. AE, DC, MC, V.*

$$ 🏨 **Las Vegas.** Conveniently located in a pleasant, if somewhat tumultuous, part of Málaga just east of the center, Las Vegas has a dining room overlooking the Paseo Marítimo; a pool; and a large, leafy garden. The rooms in back enjoy good views of the sea, as does the spacious, panoramic dining room. ✉ *Paseo de Sancha 22, 29016,* ☎ *95/221–7712,* FAX *95/222–4889. 107 rooms. Restaurant, bar, pool. AE, DC, MC, V.*

$ **Venecia.** A good budget option, this four-story hotel has a central location on the Alameda Principal, next to the Plaza de la Marina. The rooms are simply furnished but spacious. ✉ *Alameda Principal 9, 29001,* ☎ *95/221–3636.* FAX *95/221–3637. 40 rooms. AE, DC, MC, V.*

Nightlife and the Arts

The region's main theater is the **Teatro Cervantes** (✉ Ramos Marín, ☎ 95/222–4109 or 95/222–0237), whose programs include plays (in Spanish), concerts, and flamenco.

The **Málaga Symphony Orchestra** has a winter season of orchestral concerts and chamber music, with most performances in the Teatro Cervantes. In summer, rock concerts are staged in the bullring.

Málaga's main nightlife districts are Maestranza, between the bullring and the Paseo Marítimo, and the beachfront in the suburb of Pedregalejos. Central Málaga also has a lively bar scene.

Shopping

The **Corte Inglés** department store offers English interpreters, shipping, VAT refunds, and currency exchange. ✉ *Avda. de Andalucía 46,* ☎ *95/230–0000.* ⏲ *Mon.–Sat. 10–9.*

Antequera

❼ *64 km (40 mi) northeast of Málaga, 43 km (27 mi) northwest of Pizarra, 108 km (67 mi) northwest of Ronda (via Pizarra).*

Antequera became one of the great strongholds of the Moors following their defeat at Córdoba and Seville in the 13th century. Its fall to the Christians in 1410 paved the way for the reconquest of Granada—the Moors retreated, leaving a **fortress** on the town heights. Next door is the former church of **Santa María la Mayor,** one of 27 churches, convents, and monasteries in Antequera. Built of standstone in the 16th century, it has a fine ribbed vault and is now a concert hall. Another landmark is the church of **San Sebastián,** whose brick Baroque Mudéjar tower is topped by a winged figure called the Angelote ("big angel"), the symbol of Antequera. The church of **Nuestra Señora del Carmen** (Our Lady of Carmen) has an extraordinary Baroque altarpiece that towers to the ceiling.

Antequera's pride and joy is **Efebo,** a beautiful bronze statue of a boy that dates back to Roman times. Standing almost 5 ft high, it's on display in the **Museo Municipal.** ✉ *Palacio de Nájera, Coso Viejo,* ☎ *95/270–4051.* 🎫 *200 ptas.* ⏲ *Tues.–Fri. 10–1:30 and 4–6, Sat. 10–1:30, Sun. 11–1:30.*

Just outside Antequera, off the Málaga exit road, are the mysterious prehistoric **dolmens,** megalithic burial chambers built some 4,000 years ago out of massive slabs of stone weighing more than 100 tons each. The best-preserved dolmen is La Menga. The site is open Tuesday 3–5:30, Wednesday through Saturday 10–2 and 3:30–5:30 (10–1 and 4–8 in summer), and Sunday 10–2. Admission is free.

Ten kilometers (6 mi) northwest of Antequera, off the A92 highway to Seville, is **Fuentepiedra,** a shallow saltwater lagoon that serves as Europe's major nesting area for the greater flamingo. In February and March, these birds arrive from Africa by the tens of thousands to spend the summer here. The visitor center has information on local wildlife.

From Antequera, you have several options. East of town, along N342, is the dramatic silhouette of the **Peña de los Enamorados** (Lovers' Rock), an Andalusian landmark. Legend has it that a Moorish princess and a Christian shepherd boy eloped here one night and cast themselves to their deaths from the peak the next morning. The rock's outline is often likened to the profile of the Córdoban bullfighter Manolete. Eight kilometers (5 mi) beyond the Peña, the village of **Archidona** winds its way up a steep mountain slope beneath the ruins of a Moorish castle. This picturesque white cluster is worth a detour for its Plaza Ochavada, a magnificent 17th-century square resplendent with contrasting red and ocher stone.

Ten kilometers (6 mi) south of Antequera on C3310, the **Parque Natural del Torcal de Antequera** (El Torcal Nature Park) has well-marked walking trails that guide you among eerie pillars of pink limestone sculpted by eons of wind and rain. Wear sturdy shoes and be careful not to wander from the marked paths, as it's easy to get lost in the maze of rock formations.

Dining and Lodging

$$ ✕ **El Angelote.** Right across the square from the Museo Municipal, these two wood-beamed dining rooms are usually packed. The fare includes some fine local cuisine. Try the *porrilla de setas* (wild mushrooms seasoned with thyme and rosemary) or *perdiz hortelana* (stewed partridge). Antequera's typical dessert is *pío antequerano,* a sponge cake dusted with sugar and cinnamon. ✉ *Plaza Coso Viejo,* ☎ *95/270–3465. MC, V. Closed Mon.*

$–$$ ✕ **Caserío San Benito.** If it weren't for the cell-phone transmission tower looming next to this country restaurant 11 km (7 mi) north of Antequera, you might think you'd stumbled into an 18th-century scene. In fact, this building is of fairly recent vintage: it was built by its current owner, a history buff and collector of old items and documents. The food includes popular local dishes such as *porra antequerana* (a thick version of gazpacho), *migas* (fried bread with bits of sausage), and *conejo con arroz* (rabbit with rice). ✉ *Carretera Málaga-Córdoba, Km 108,* ☎ *95/211–1103. MC, V. Closed Mon. No dinner Wed.–Thurs.*

$$ ✕🏨 **Parador de Antequera.** This modern white parador is set on a hill overlooking the *vega,* Antequera's fertile valley, with the Peña de los Enamorados in the distance. Common rooms are simple but tasteful, with antique carpets on tile floors and taurine prints on the walls. The comfortable guest rooms have twin beds, covered with woven rugs, and spacious tile bathrooms. The spacious dining room, with a lofty wood ceiling, serves good local dishes, such as *pio antequerano* (a salad of orange, cod, and olives) or oxtail in a sauce made with the sweet wine from nearby Mollina. ✉ *García del Olmo, 29200,* ☎ *95/284–0261,* FAX *95/284–1312. 55 rooms. Restaurant, pool. AE, DC, MC, V.*

Alora

★ ❽ *37 km (23 mi) southwest of Antequera, 6 km (4 mi) north of Pizarra.*

Following C337 southwest of Antequera will take you to the turnoff for Alora. From Alora, follow a small road north to the awe-inspiring **Garganta del Chorro** (Gorge of the Stream). Here, in a deep chasm in the limestone cliff, the Guadalhorce River churns and snakes its way some 600 ft below the road. The railroad track that worms in and out of tunnels in the cleft is, amazingly, the main line heading north from Málaga for Bobadilla junction and, eventually, Madrid.

Clinging to the cliffside is the Caminito del Rey (King's Walk), a suspended catwalk built for a visit by King Alfonso XIII at the beginning of the 19th century. Do *not* attempt to walk it: the structure is seriously damaged, and travelers have gotten into a number of accidents here, some of them fatal. North of the gorge, the Guadalhorce has been dammed to form a series of scenic reservoirs surrounded by pine-clad hills. Informal, open-air restaurants overlook the lakes and a number of picnic spots.

Carratraca

9 *17 km (11 mi) northwest of Alora, 54 km (34 mi) northeast of Ronda.*

The old spa town of Carratraca, once a favorite watering hole of both Spanish and foreign aristocracy, has a Moorish-style ***ayuntamiento*** (town hall) and an unusual **polygonal bullring.** Its old hotel, the **Hostal del Príncipe,** once sheltered Empress Eugénie, wife of Napoleon III; Lord Byron also came seeking the cure. The hotel has been closed for many years, but you can still relax in the sulfur baths of Carratraca's splendid marble-and-tile **bathhouse,** open daily July 15–October 15.

En Route From Carratraca, return to Alora, from which C337 takes you back to the coast through citrus and olive groves.

Pizarra

10 *6 km (4 mi) south of Alora, 65 km (40 mi) east of Ronda.*

The highlight of Pizarra is the **Museo Municipal de Pizarra** (formerly known as the Hollander Museum), installed in a renovated farmhouse just south of the village. Over their two decades in Pizarra, American artist Gino Hollander and his wife, Barbara, built up this exceptional collection of paintings and objets d'art, furniture, and archaeological finds. One section houses the archaeological displays, including Moorish and Roman objects; the other is devoted to rustic Andalusian furniture and farm implements. ✉ *Cortijo Casablanca 29, 29560,* ☎ *95/248–3237.* 🎫 *300 ptas.* ⏲ *Tues.–Sun. 10–2 and 4–8 (4–6:30 in winter).*

THE COSTA DEL SOL OCCIDENTAL

After you rejoin N340 11 km (7 mi) west of Málaga, the sprawling outskirts of Torremolinos signal that you're leaving the "real" Spain and entering, well, the "real" Costa del Sol. If you've come for beaches, high-rise hotels, and serious tourist activity, read on; if not, go directly to the next section, "Ronda and the Pueblos Blancos."

Torremolinos

11 *11 km (7 mi) west of Málaga, 16 km (10 mi) northeast of Fuengirola, 43 km (27 mi) east of Marbella.*

Torremolinos is all about fun in the sun. Its wildest days may be over, its atmosphere more subdued than in the roaring '60s and '70s, but swarms of northern Europeans—young and not so young—still throng its streets in season. Scantily attired and fair in hue, they shop for bargains on Calle San Miguel, down sangría in the bars of La Nogalera, and dance the night away in discotheques. By day, the sunseekers flock to the beaches El Bajondillo and La Carihuela, whose sand is a fine, gray grit; in high summer it's hard to find a patch of your own.

Torremolinos has two distinct sections. The first, **Torremolinos** (known to British locals and other expats as "Central T-town"), is built around the Plaza Costa del Sol; Calle San Miguel, the main shopping street; and the brash Nogalera Plaza, full of overpriced bars and international restaurants. The Pueblo Blanco area, off Calle Casablanca, is more pleasant; and the Cuesta del Tajo, at the far end of San Miguel, winds down a steep slope to the Bajondillo beach. Here, crumbling walls, bougainvillea-clad patios, and old cottages hint at the quiet fishing village this once was.

The second, much nicer section is **La Carihuela.** (To find it, head west out of town on Avenida Carlota Alessandri and turn left by the Hotel La Paloma.)

Far more authentically Spanish, the Carihuela retains many old fishermen's cottages and a large number of excellent fish restaurants. The traffic-free esplanade makes for an enjoyable stroll, especially on a summer evening or Sunday at lunchtime, when it's packed with Spanish families.

The **Aquapark,** off the bypass, near the Palacio de Congresos convention center, has water chutes, artificial waves, water mountains, and pools. ☎ *95/238–8888.* *1,975 ptas.* *May–June and Sept., daily 10–6; July–Aug., daily 10–7.*

Dining and Lodging

$$$ ★ ✕ **Juan.** With a sunny outdoor patio facing the sea, this Carihuela hot spot is a good place for seafood in summer. House specialties include the great Costa del Sol standbys—*sopa de mariscos* (shellfish soup), *dorada al horno* (oven-roasted giltheads), and *fritura malagueña.* ✉ *Paseo Marítimo 29, La Carihuela,* ☎ *95/238–5656. AE, DC, MC, V.*

$$ ★ ✕ **Casa Guaquin.** Set on a seaside patio in La Carihuela, Casa Guaquin is widely known as the best seafood restaurant in the area. Ever-changing daily catches are served alongside such menu stalwarts as *coquinas* (wedge-shell clams) and *boquerones fritos* (fried anchovies). ✉ *Paseo Marítimo 63,* ☎ *95/238–4530. AE, MC, V. Closed Mon. and mid-Dec.–mid-Jan.*

$$ ✕ **Europa.** Two blocks inland from the beach, this Carihuela villa is a very Spanish institution—rare for Torremolinos. Alas, much of its garden was sacrificed a few years ago to make way for an expanded dining room with picture windows and potted plants, but the food is still reliable: an international menu that specializes in charcoal-grilled meat along with local fish dishes. ✉ *C. Salvador Allende 34,* ☎ *95/238–8022. AE, DC, MC, V.*

$–$$ ✕ **El Roqueo.** Owned by a former fisherman, El Roqueo is one of the locals' favorite Carihuela fish joints. Ingredients are always fresh, and prices are very reasonable. ✉ *Carmen 35,* ☎ *95/238–4946. AE, DC, MC, V. Closed Tues. and Nov.–mid-Dec.*

$$$ 🏨 **Cervantes.** A busy, cosmopolitan hotel—one of the better lodgings in the heart of Torremolinos—Cervantes is ideal for those who want to be in the middle of things. It's not by the beach, but there's a pool, and the rooms are well furnished and comfortable. Service is good, and the panoramic dining room on the top floor is popular with locals. Drawbacks: package tours often alight here, rooms on the bottom floors can be noisy, and parking can be a problem. ✉ *Las Mercedes, 29620,* ☎ *95/238–4033,* FAX *95/238–4857. 397 rooms. Dining room, 2 pools, beauty salon, sauna, nightclub. AE, DC, MC, V.*

$$$ 🏨 **Sidi Lago Rojo.** In the heart of old Carihuela, this modern, four-story apartment building is just two blocks from the seafront. The rooms are well maintained, and all have balconies; some overlook the pool and small, tree-filled garden. There's no great view, but prices are moderate, and you're close to the town's best bars and restaurants. ✉ *C. Miami 1, 29620,* ☎ *95/238–7666,* FAX *95/238–0891. 144 rooms. Pool. AE, DC, MC, V.*

$$$ 🏨 **Tropicana.** On the beach at the far end of the Carihuela, in one of the most pleasant parts of Torremolinos, is this relaxing resort hotel with its own beach club. The tropical theme is carried throughout, from the leafy gardens and kidney-shaped pool to the common areas, with exotic plants, raffia floor mats, and bamboo furniture, to the rooms, with ceiling fans and marble floors. You're a five-minute walk from a range of good restaurants. ✉ *Trópico 6, 29620,* ☎ *95/238–6600,* FAX *95/238–0568. 84 rooms. Pool, beach. AE, DC, MC, V.*

$ 🏨 **Miami.** Set in an old Andalusian villa in a shady garden west of the Carihuela, Miami is something of a find amid the ocean of concrete towers. Staying here is like visiting a private Spanish home; the rooms are individually furnished, and there's a sitting room with a cozy fireplace. It's very popular, so reserve ahead. ✉ *Aladino 14, at C. Miami, 29620,* ☎ *95/238–5255. 26 rooms. Pool. No credit cards.*

Nightlife

Most nocturnal action is in the center of town and along the Montemar strip heading west from there. Some bars have occasional live music, but Torremolinos is best known for its discos. The trends are in constant flux, but the established hotspots include **Gatsby** (✉ Avda. Montemar 32, ☎ 95/238–5372) and **Paladium** (✉ Avda. Palma de Mallorca 36, ☎ 95/238–4289). Your best bet for flamenco is **Taberna Flamenca Pepe López** (✉ Plaza de la Gamba Alegre, ☎ 95/238–1284).

Benalmádena

⓬ *9 km (5½ mi) west of Torremolinos, 9 km (5½ mi) east of Mijas.*

Benalmádena-Costa is practically an extension of Torremolinos, run almost exclusively by package-tour operators. It has little for the independent traveler, but there's a pleasant-enough marina, which draws Málaga's youth at night. It's also home to the **SeaLife marine center,** where aquariums show varied examples of fish from local waters, including rays, sharks, and sunfish. ✉ *Puerto Marina Benalmádena,* ☎ *95/256–0150.* 🎫 *995 ptas.* ⏲ *Daily 10 AM–midnight in summer, 10–6 in winter.*

Two kilometers (1 mi) inland, at Arroyo de la Miel, you can visit **Tivoli World,** the Costa del Sol's leading amusement park. Don't expect the sleek perfection of Disneyland, but the 4,000-seat, open-air auditorium often showcases international stars alongside cancan, flamenco, or Spanish ballet performances. The park also has roller coasters, a Ferris wheel, illuminated fountains, a Chinese pagoda, Wild West shows, and 40-odd restaurants and snack bars. ☎ *95/244–2848.* 🎫 *600 ptas.* ⏲ *Summer, daily 4 AM–1 AM; winter, weekends 4 AM–midnight.*

Benalmádena-Pueblo, the village proper, is on the mountainside 7 km (4 mi) from the coast and is surprisingly unspoiled, offering a glimpse of the old, pre-tourist Andalusia.

Dining and Lodging

$$$ ✕ **Mar de Alborán.** Right next to the Benalmádena yacht harbor, this seafood mecca has a touch more class than most of its peers and has earned a solid reputation as one of the finest restaurants on the coast. The cheerful dining room is illuminated through picture windows at lunchtime. Dishes such as the Basque-inspired *lomo de merluza con kokotxas y almejas* (hake with cheek morsels and clams) are an imaginative switch from standard Costa fare. Meat is also well represented. ✉ *Avda. de Alay 5,* ☎ *95/244–6427. AE, MC, V. Closed Mon. No dinner Sun.*

$$$ ✕ **Ventorillo de la Perra.** If you've been scouring the coast for something typically Spanish, you may find it in this old inn, which dates from 1785. Outside, there's a leafy patio; inside, a cozy, rustic atmosphere prevails in the dining room and in the bar, whose ceiling is hung with hams. Choose between local malagueño cooking, general Spanish fare, and international favorites. The *ajo blanco* (a cold garlic soup) makes a particularly good appetizer. ✉ *Avda. Constitución 115 (Km 13), Arroyo de la Miel,* ☎ *95/244–1966. AE, DC, MC, V. Closed Mon.*

$$ ✕ **Casa Fidel.** This Benalmádena-Pueblo restaurant is rustic in flavor, with heavy beams and a large fireplace. The menu, however, is based on expertly cooked international dishes. *Entremeses Casa Fidel* is a tasty selection of hors d'oeuvres. Main courses include old favorites like grilled sole; more exotic options, like *perdiz en salsa de vino de Málaga* (partridge in Málaga wine); and a celebrated house specialty, English-style roast lamb. ✉ *Maestra Ayala 1,* ☎ *95/244–9165. AE, DC, MC, V. Closed Tues. and mid-Nov.–mid-Dec. No lunch Wed.*

$–$$ **La Fonda.** This small hotel at the edge of the village grants a true taste of Andalusia only a few miles from the crowded Costa. Rooms have white walls, marble floors, and floral fabrics. Some enjoy peerless views of the coast and the Mediterranean; others look onto the cool interior patio or the village street. The pool is heated in winter. In the same building, under different management, is a restaurant run by Málaga's official hotel school; it's open for lunch on weekdays. ✉ *Santo Domingo 7, 29639,* ☎ FAX *95/256–8273. 26 rooms. Pool. AE, DC, MC, V.*

Nightlife

The **Fortuna Nightclub** in the **Casino Torrequebrada** (✉ Km 220 on N340, Benalmádena Costa, ☎ 95/244–6000) has flamenco and an international dance show with a live orchestra, beginning at 9:30. The gambling casino is open 9 PM–4 AM; passport, jacket, and tie are required.

Fuengirola

13 *16 km (10 mi) west of Torremolinos, 27 km (17 mi) east of Marbella.*

Fuengirola is less frenetic than Torremolinos. Many of its waterfront high-rises are holiday apartments catering to budget-minded sunseekers from northern Europe and, in summer, a large contingent from Córdoba and other parts of Spain. The town is also a haven for British retirees (with plenty of English and Irish pubs to serve them) and a shopping and business center for the rest of the Costa del Sol. Its Tuesday market is the largest on the coast, and a major tourist attraction.

West of the town itself is Fuengirola's most prominent landmark, the hilltop **Castillo de Sohail,** whose partly Arabic name means "Castle of the Star." The original structure dates from the 12th century, but the castle served as a military fortress until the early 19th century, and there were many intervening additions. *200 ptas. Tues.–Sun. 10–2:30 and 4–6.*

Dining and Lodging

$$$ ✕ **Portofino.** This lively restaurant, one of the best in Fuengirola, is camouflaged amid the brassy souvenir shops and fast-food joints on the promenade, just east of the port. The menu is international, with a few nods to the owner's Italian origins. The *carpaccio* (thinly sliced raw fillet steak with cheese) is a popular appetizer; for the main course, try the veal scallops in lemon sauce or the roast lamb. Service is fast, friendly, and professional. ✉ *Paseo Marítimo 29,* ☎ *95/247–0643. AE, DC, MC, V. Closed Mon. No lunch July 1–Sept. 15.*

$$–$$$ ✕ **La Langosta.** Two blocks from the water on a side street in Los Boliches, this tiny restaurant has been a favorite for 40 years. Needless to say, the specialty is *langosta* (lobster), prepared in a variety of ways including langosta *al champán* (lobster in champagne sauce). The *mejillones a la crema de azafrán* (mussels in saffron sauce) are a savory alternative. ✉ *Francisco Cano 1,* ☎ *95/247–5049. AE, MC, V. Closed Sun. No lunch.*

$$ ✕ **El Bote.** This spacious, white beachside restaurant near the eastern end of Fuengirola's Paseo Marítimo is the most popular fish place in town. Indeed, its terrace and proximity to the water make the setting ideal. Start with a selection of shellfish or a mixed fish fry; then—if there are at least two of you—share a fish baked in coarse sea salt. Service tends to be slow in the summer, when crowds appear. ✉ *Paseo Marítimo, Torreblanca del Sol,* ☎ *95/266–0296. AE, MC, V. Closed Tues.*

$$ **Florida.** Almost opposite the port, this simple but comfortable hotel is set back from the sea behind a shady, semitropical garden where you

can sunbathe and sip a drink at the poolside bar. One of Fuengirola's oldest lodgings, it dates back to the years before the land boom and is still managed by its owners. Rooms are on the small side, but are nicely decorated in orange and light-brown tones. ✉ *Paseo Marítimo s/n, 29640,* ☎ *95/247–6100,* FAX *95/258–1529. 116 rooms. Restaurant, bar, pool. AE, DC, MC, V.*

$$ **Villa de Laredo.** Fuengirola's newest hotel has a prime location on the seaside promenade, one block east of the port. Rooms are decorated in cream and navy blue; some have terraces and sea views. The terrace furniture is new, if a bit flimsy. The pool is on the roof. ✉ *Paseo Marítimo 42, 29640,* ☎ *95/247–7689,* FAX *95/247–7950. 50 rooms. Restaurant, pool, parking (fee). AE, MC, V.*

Nightlife and the Arts

Amateur local troupes sometimes stage plays in English at the **Salón de Variétés Theater** (✉ Emancipación 30, ☎ 95/247–4542).

Mijas

★ ⓮ *8 km (5 mi) north of Fuengirola, 18 km (11 mi) west of Torremolinos.*

The picturesque village of Mijas is nestled in the foothills of the sierra just north of the coast. Buses leave Fuengirola every half hour for the 20-minute drive through hills peppered with whitewashed villas. If you have a car and don't mind a mildly hair-raising drive, take the more dramatic approach from Benalmádena-Pueblo, a winding mountain road with some great views. Mijas was discovered long ago by foreign retirees, and the large, touristy square where you arrive may look like an extension of the Costa, yet beyond this are hilly streets of whitewashed houses and a somewhat authentic village atmosphere. Try to come here late in the afternoon, when the tour buses have left and you have the town to yourself.

Park in the Plaza Virgen de la Peña, where you can hire a "*burro taxi*" (guided donkey) to explore the village. Take a quick look at the chapel of Mijas's patron, the **Virgen de la Peña.** Then pop into the **Carromato de Max,** whose collection of miniature curiosities from all over the world includes a rendition of the Last Supper on a grain of rice, Abraham Lincoln painted on a pinhead, and fleas wearing clothes. *500 ptas.* ⏲ *Daily 10–7.*

Wander over to the Plaza Constitución, Mijas's old village square, and walk up the slope beside the Mirlo Blanco restaurant to Mijas's tiny **bullring.** It's one of the few square bullrings in Spain. ☎ *95/248–5248.* *500 ptas.* ⏲ *Daily 10–6.*

Just up the hill from the bullring is the delightful village church of **La Inmaculada Concepción** (the Immaculate Conception). The church is impeccably decorated, especially at Easter, and its terrace and spacious gardens afford a splendid panorama.

Meander through any of the **white streets,** which ultimately head up the hill behind the village—the higher you go, the more authentic the atmosphere. Take a peek inside the tiny church at the bottom of Calle San Sebastián; it's filled with flowers and rococo decorations on gleaming-white walls.

NEED A BREAK? At Calle San Sebastián 4, the **Bar Menguiñez** (or Casa de los Jamones) has a ceiling strung with row after row of hams. Inexpensive meals are served on a handful of tables.

Dining and Lodging

$$$ ✕ **Casa Navarra.** At the bottom of the Mijas-Fuengirola road, this restaurant is a home away from home for transplanted Navarrese, who come south each July to celebrate the feast of San Fermín without the bull runs of their native Pamplona. It serves substantial Basque-Navarrese food, specializing in charcoal-grilled beef chops and such fish dishes as *besugo a la espalda* (sea bream butterflied and roasted over coals). ✉ *Carretera de Mijas-Fuengirola, Km 4,* ☎ *95/258–0439. AE, DC, MC, V. Closed Tues.*

$$$ ✕ **El Padrastro.** Perched on a cliff above the Plaza Virgen de la Peña, "The Stepfather" is accessible by an elevator from the square or, if you're energetic, by stairs. Views over Fuengirola and the coast are the restaurant's main drawing card. The menu features international and Spanish dishes such as *lubina flameada al hinojo* (sea bass flambéed in fennel). A large terrace adds to the alfresco ambience. ✉ *Avda. del Compás,* ☎ *95/248–5000. AE, DC, MC, V.*

$$$ ✕ **Valparaíso.** Halfway up the road from Fuengirola to Mijas, this restaurant is all about setting: the sprawling villa stands in its own garden, complete with swimming pool. In summer, you can dine outdoors on the terrace and dance the night away to live music. Valparaíso is a favorite among local (mainly British) expatriates, who come here in full evening dress to celebrate their birthdays. In winter, logs burn in a cozy fireplace. Try the *pato a la naranja* (duck in orange sauce). ✉ *Carretera de Mijas–Fuengirola, Km 7,* ☎ *95/248–5996. AE, MC, V. Closed Sun. Nov.–May. No lunch.*

$$ ✕ **Mirlo Blanco.** In an old house on the pleasant Plaza de la Constitución, with a terrace for outdoor dining in warm weather, this place is run by the second generation of a Basque family that has been in the Costa del Sol restaurant business for decades. Try Basque specialties on for size, such as *txangurro* (crab) and *merluza a la vasca* (hake with asparagus, eggs, and clam sauce). ✉ *Plaza de la Constitución 13,* ☎ *95/248–5700. AE, MC, V. Closed Jan.*

$$$$ ★ ✕🏨 **Byblos Andaluz.** Standing on the edge of Mijas's golf course (closer to Fuengirola than to Mijas), this luxury hotel is the most expensive on the entire Costa del Sol. Set in a huge garden of palms, cypresses, and fountains, it is first and foremost a spa and is known particularly for its *thalasso* therapy, a skin treatment that uses sea water and seaweed—applied here in a Roman temple of cool, white marble and blue tiles. Both of the outstanding restaurants serve savory regional dishes as well as highly sophisticated international cuisine. ✉ *Urbanización Mijas-Golf, 29640,* ☎ *95/247–3050,* FAX *95/247–6783. 109 rooms, 35 suites. 2 restaurants, indoor and outdoor pools, beauty salon, spa, 18-hole golf course, 3 tennis courts, health club. AE, DC, MC, V.*

$$$ 🏨 **Mijas.** This beautifully situated hotel at the entrance to Mijas has a poolside restaurant and bar; gardens with views of the hillsides stretching down to Fuengirola and the sea; marble floors throughout; wrought-iron window grilles; and Moorish shutters. The lobby is large and airy, and there's a delightful glass-roof terrace. All rooms are well furnished in modern Andalusian style, with wood fittings and marble floors, but only some enjoy the sweeping view of the coast. ✉ *Urbanización Tamisa, 29650,* ☎ *95/248–5800,* FAX *95/248–5825. 99 rooms, 4 suites. Restaurant, pool, spa, tennis court, health club. AE, DC, MC, V.*

Marbella

⓯ *27 km (17 mi) west of Fuengirola, 28 km (17 mi) east of Estepona, 50 km (31 mi) southeast of Ronda.*

Playground of the rich and home of movie stars, rock musicians, and dispossessed royal families, Marbella has attained the top rung on Europe's social ladder. Dip into any Spanish gossip magazine, and chances are the glittering parties that fill its pages are set in Marbella.

Much of this action takes place on the fringes, for grand hotels and luxury restaurants line the waterfront for 20 km (12 mi) on each side of the town center. In the town itself, you may well wonder how Marbella became so famous. The main thoroughfare, Avenida Ricardo Soriano, is distinctly lacking in charm; and the Paseo Marítimo, though pleasant enough, with an array of seafood restaurants and pizzerias overlooking an ordinary beach, is far from spectacular.

Marbella's appeal lies in the heart of the **old village,** which remains miraculously intact. Here, a block or two back from the main highway, narrow alleys of whitewashed houses cluster around the central **Plaza de los Naranjos** (Orange Square), where colorful restaurants vie for space under the orange trees. Climb onto what remains of the old fortifications, and stroll along the quaint Calle Virgen de los Dolores to the Plaza de Santo Cristo. Wander the maze of lanes and enjoy the geranium-speckled windows and splashing fountains.

The **Museo del Grabado Español Contemporáneo** (Museum of Contemporary Spanish Engraving), set in a restored 16th-century building in the old village, has an outstanding collection of modern Spanish etchings. ✉ *Hospital Bazán,* ☎ *95/282–5035.* *300 ptas.* ⏲ *Weekdays 10–2 and 5:30–8:30, Sun. 10:30–2.*

In a modern building just east of the old quarter is the **Museo de Bonsai,** with a collection of miniature trees. ✉ *Parque Arroyo de la Repesa, Avda. Dr. Maiz Viñal,* ☎ *95/286–2926.* *500 ptas.* ⏲ *Daily 10–1:30 and 4–7.*

NEED A BREAK? Stop for a glass of wine and a platter of fried fish at the popular **La Pesquera** (✉ Plaza de la Victoria, ☎ 95/276–5170), at the western entrance to the old town.

The road to **Puerto Banús** has been called the Golden Mile. Here, a mosque, Arab banks, and the onetime residence of Saudi Arabia's King Fahd betray the influence of petro-dollars in this wealthy enclave. Seven kilometers (4½ mi) west of central Marbella (between Km 175 and Km 174), a sign indicates the turnoff leading down to Puerto Banús. Though now hemmed in by a belt of brand-new high-rises, Marbella's plush marina, with 915 berths, is a gem of ostentatious wealth, a kind of Spanish answer to St. Tropez. Huge and flashy yachts, beautiful people, and countless expensive stores and restaurants make up the glittering parade that marches long into the night. The backdrop is an Andalusian *pueblo*—built in the 1980s in imitation of the fishing villages that once lined this coast.

Dining and Lodging

$$$$ ✕ **El Portalón.** This attractive restaurant, with a light, glassed-in dining room, combines two extremes of the culinary spectrum: on the one hand, substantial Castilian roasts; on the other, innovative *cocina de mercado,* based on whatever ingredients are freshest at the market. Unless you're determined to tuck into a roast suckling pig, go for one of a dozen or so *sugerencias del día* (suggestions of the day). The restaurant prides itself on its comprehensive wine list, and wine is sold by the glass in the adjoining *vinoteca* (wine cellar). ✉ *Carretera de Cádiz, Km 178 (across from Marbella Club hotel),* ☎ *95/286–1075. AE, DC, MC, V.*

$$$$ ✕ **La Meridiana.** The local jet set favors La Meridiana, located west of town behind the mosque. Its striking, modern architecture has a Moorish flavor, and the enclosed terrace allows "outdoor" dining year-round. The cuisine is famous for its quality and the freshness of its ingredients, both of which you can taste in the *menú de degustación.* This is a good place to sample *ajo blanco,* a garlicky local version of gazpacho based on almonds instead of tomatoes. ✉ *Camino de la Cruz,* ☎ *95/277–6190. AE, DC, MC, V. Closed Jan. No lunch June–Aug. or Mon.–Tues. Sept.–May.*

$$$–$$$$ ✕ **Santiago.** This busy place facing the seafront promenade has long been considered the best fish restaurant in Marbella. Try the *ensalada de langosta* (lobster salad), followed by *besugo al horno* (baked red bream). Around the corner from the original restaurant (and sharing the same phone number) are Santiago's new tapas bar and a second restaurant specializing in the roasts of the owner's native Castile. ✉ *Paseo Marítimo 5,* ☎ *95/277–0078. AE, DC, MC, V. Closed Nov.*

$$$ ✕ **In Vino.** This classy restaurant is one of the newest additions to Marbella's dining scene, serving top-notch Mediterranean cuisine in a rich, wood-beamed dining room and, in summer, on an Andalusian-style terrace. As the name suggests, it has an extensive selection of wines, kept in a state-of-the-art cellar. ✉ *Carretera de Cádiz, Km 176.5, Río Verde,* ☎ *95/277–1211. AE, DC, MC, V.*

$$$$ ✕🏨 **Los Monteros.** Five kilometers (3 mi) east of Marbella, on the road to Málaga, this exclusive hotel stands surrounded by tropical gardens on the sea side of the highway. The extensive facilities and perks include easy access to an uncrowded beach, special privileges on the adjoining golf course, and gourmet dining in the famous El Corzo Grill. The rooms are formally decorated, and service is impeccable. ✉ *Urbanización Los Monteros, Carretera N340, Km 187, 29600,* ☎ *95/277–1700,* FAX *95/282–5846. 159 rooms, 10 suites. 3 restaurants, 1 indoor and 2 outdoor pools, beauty salon, sauna, 18-hole golf course, 10 tennis courts, exercise room, horseback riding, squash, nightclub, meeting room. AE, DC, MC, V.*

$$$$ ★ ✕🏨 **Marbella Club.** The grande dame of Marbella hotels was a creation of Alfonso von Hohenlohe, the man who "founded" Marbella. The Club has long attracted an international clientele as well as local patricians. The bungalow-style rooms, some with private pools, come in various sizes, and the decor varies from regional to modern. The grounds are exquisite; breakfast is served on a patio where songbirds flit through the lush, subtropical vegetation. ✉ *Carretera de Cádiz, Km 178 (3 km [2 mi] west of Marbella), 29600,* ☎ *95/282–2211,* FAX *95/282–9884. 90 rooms, 36 suites, 10 bungalows. Restaurant, 2 pools, beauty salon, sauna, exercise room, nightclub. AE, DC, MC, V.*

$$$$ ★ ✕🏨 **Puente Romano.** This spectacular, deluxe modern hotel and apartment complex of low, white stucco buildings is west of Marbella, between the Marbella Club (☞ *above*) and Puerto Banús. As the name suggests, there's a genuine Roman bridge on the beautifully landscaped grounds, which run right down to the beach. A nightclub run by legendary nightlife queen Regine and two outstanding restaurants, El Puente and La Plaza, complete the picture. ✉ *Carretera Cádiz, Km 177, 29600,* ☎ *95/282–0900,* FAX *95/277–5766. 149 rooms, 77 suites. 2 restaurants, 2 pools, 10 tennis courts, nightclub, meeting rooms. AE, DC, MC, V.*

$$$ 🏨 **El Fuerte.** The building is vintage 1950s, and the decor is still a bit gloomy for the sunny South, with lots of dark wood; but everything is well maintained. El Fuerte is still the best all-around choice if you want a central hotel near the old town. Most rooms have balconies overlooking the sea. The hotel stands at the end of the Paseo Marítimo, separated from the beach by a pleasant, palm-filled garden with an outdoor pool. ✉ *Avda. El Fuerte, 29600,* ☎ *95/286–1500,* FAX *95/282–4411. 261 rooms, 2 suites. Restaurant, indoor and outdoor pools, 1 tennis court, health club, squash. AE, DC, MC, V.*

$$ 🏨 **Lima.** Here's a good mid-range option in downtown Marbella, two blocks from the beach. Decor is simple, with dark-wood furniture, but all rooms have small balconies. The corner rooms are the largest. ✉ *Avda. Belón 2, 29600,* ☎ *95/277–0500,* FAX *95/286–3091. 64 rooms. Breakfast room. AE, DC, MC, V.*

$ 🏨 **Munich.** Budget accommodation is thin on the ground in swank Marbella, but there are comfortable, basic lodgings in this tumbledown villa, two blocks inland from the lighthouse in a residential part of town. All rooms have a private bath or shower, and five have their own balcony. The beach and the old quarter are a short walk away. ✉ *Virgen del Pilar 5, 29600,* ☎ *95/277–2461. 18 rooms. No credit cards.*

Nightlife and the Arts

Marbella's most famous nightspot is the **Olivia Valere** disco (✉ Carretera de Istán, Km 0.8, ☎ 95/282–8845), an Arab fantasy club near the mosque. In the same area is the trendy **La Notte,** an art deco bar with live music, next to La Meridiana (☞ Dining and Lodging, *above*). Much of the action revolves around the Puerto Banús, in bars such as Sinatra's, Joe's Bar, and La Comedia. The **Casino Nueva Andalucía** (✉ Bajos Hotel Andalucía Plaza, N340, ☎ 95/281–4000) is a chic gambling spot in the Hotel Andalucía Plaza, just east of Puerto Banús; it's open daily 6 PM–5 AM. Jacket and tie are required for men, passports for all. **Ana María** (✉ Plaza de Santo Cristo 5, ☎ 95/277–5646) is a popular flamenco venue in the center of Marbella.

Art exhibits are held in private galleries and several of Marbella's leading hotels, especially the Puente Romano (☞ Dining and Lodging, *above*). The tourist office publishes a free monthly calendar of exhibits and other events.

Ojén

⓰ *10 km (6 mi) north of Marbella.*

For a contrast to the glamour of the coast, drive up to Ojén, in the hills above Marbella. This ancient village is another world. Take a look at the beautiful **pottery** sold here.

Four kilometers (2½ mi) from Ojén is the **Refugio del Juanar** (☞ *below*), a former hunting lodge in the heart of the Sierra Blanca, at the southern edge of the Serranía de Ronda, a mountainous wilderness. Not far from the Refugio, you might spot the herd of **wild ibex** that dwell among the rocky crags; the best times to watch are dawn and dusk, when they descend from their hiding places. A bumpy trail takes you a mile from the Refugio to the **Mirador** (lookout), which has a sweeping view of the Costa del Sol and the coast of northern Africa.

Six kilometers (4 mi) from the turnoff to Juanar, on the A337 road, you reach another Andalusian *pueblo,* **Monda.** The ruins of its hilltop castle are now part of a romantic hotel (☞ *below*).

Dining and Lodging

$$$ ✕🏨 **Castillo de Monda.** Designed to resemble a castle, this parador-like hotel incorporates the ruins of Monda's Moorish fortress, some of which date back to the 8th century. Rooms are decorated with authentic Andalusian tiles and antique fittings. The bar, whose walls are covered with Alhambra-style carvings, and the light-flooded restaurant are on the top floor of this seven-story building, collecting the best views of the surrounding countryside. The building presides over the village from its hilltop location. ✉ *29110 Monda,* ☎ *95/245–7142,* FAX *95/245–7336. 17 rooms, 6 suites. Restaurant, pool. AE, MC, V.*

$$ ✕🏨 **Refugio del Juanar.** This secluded hotel and restaurant was once an aristocratic hunting lodge, counting King Alfonso XIII among the guests. It later became part of the parador chain, and in 1984 it was sold to its staff for the symbolic sum of 1 peseta. The hunting theme prevails, both in the common areas—where a log fire roars in winter—and on the restaurant menu, where game dishes get pride of place. The rooms are simply decorated in a rustic style, and six (including the three suites) have their own fireplace. ✉ *Sierra Blanca, 29610,* ☏ *95/288–1000,* FAX *95/288–1001. 23 rooms, 3 suites. Restaurant, pool, 2 tennis courts. AE, DC, MC, V.*

RONDA AND THE PUEBLOS BLANCOS

Ronda and the whitewashed villages of the mountains behind the Costa del Sol form one of Spain's most scenic and emblematic driving routes. The contrast with Torremolinos could not be more complete. Save time for this region, as it may leave you with some of your most indelible travel memories.

Ronda

★ ⑰ *61 km (38 mi) northwest of Marbella, 108 km (67 mi) southwest of Antequera (via Pizarra).*

Ronda is one of the oldest towns in Spain and is accordingly picturesque and dramatic. To get there, take the winding but well-maintained A473 from San Pedro de Alcántara up through the mountains of the Serranía de Ronda. Secure in its mountain fastness on a rock high over the River Guadalevín, the town is 49 km (30 mi) inland. Once a stronghold for the legendary Andalusian bandits who held court here from the 18th to early 20th centuries, Ronda is now known for its spectacular position and views. The town's most dramatic feature is its ravine (360 ft deep and 210 ft across), known as **El Tajo,** which divides La Ciudad, the old Moorish town, from El Mercadillo, the "new town," which sprang up after the Christian Reconquest of 1485. Tour buses roll in daily with sightseers from the coast, and on weekends affluent Sevillanos flock to their second homes here. Stay overnight midweek to see this noble town's true colors.

The most attractive approach is from the south. Take the first turnoff to Ronda on the road from San Pedro (473), and the town looms before you in all its medieval splendor. Entering the lowest part of Ronda, known as El Barrio, you'll see parts of the old walls, including the 13th-century **Puerta de Almocobar** and the 16th-century **Puerta de Carlos V** gates. The road climbs past the Iglesia del Espíritu Santo (Church of the Holy Spirit) and up into the heart of town. Begin your tour in the Plaza de España, where the tourist office can supply you with a map. Immediately south is Ronda's most famous bridge, the **Puente Nuevo** (New Bridge), an architectural marvel built between 1755 and 1793. The bridge's lantern-lit parapet offers dizzying views of the river far below. Just how many people have met their ends in this gorge nobody knows, but the architect of the Puente Nuevo fell to his death here while inspecting work on the bridge. During the civil war, hundreds of victims on both sides were hurled from it.

Cross the Puente Nuevo into **La Ciudad,** the old Moorish town, and wander through the twisting streets of white houses with birdcage balconies, punctuated by stately Renaissance mansions. Turn left and follow Santo Domingo to the **Casa del Rey Moro.** This so-called House of the Moorish King was actually built in 1709 on the site of an earlier Moorish residence. Despite the name and the *azulejo* (painted tile) plaque depicting a Moor on the facade, it's unlikely that Moorish rulers ever lived here. The garden has a great view of the gorge, and from here a stairway of some 365 steps (known as La Mina) descends to the river. The house is being converted into a luxury hotel and is closed to the public, but you can visit the gardens and La Mina ✉ *Cuesta de Santo Domingo 9,* ☎ *95/218–7200.* 🎫 *600 ptas.* ⏲ *Daily 10–8 in summer, 10–7 in winter.*

Just down the street from the Casa del Rey Moro is the **Palacio del Marqués de Salvatierra,** a Renaissance mansion with wrought-iron balconies and an impressive portal. Note the strange figures carved on the facade. The house is still occupied by descendants of the original family.

Below the Salvatierra palace, a road leads down into the ravine, where two more bridges span the river: the Puente Viejo (Old Bridge), built in 1616 on Roman foundations, and the Puente Arabe (Arab Bridge), a heavily restored Moorish bridge. Beneath the Arab Bridge are the excavated remains of the **Baños Arabes** (Arab Baths), which date from Ronda's tenure as capital of a Moorish *taifa* (kingdom). The star-shaped vents in the roof are an inferior imitation of the ceiling of the beautiful bathhouse in Granada's Alhambra. Gangs of youths have been known to threaten tourists for money here, so be on guard. 🎫 *Free.* ⏲ *Tues.–Sat. 9:30–1:30 and 4–7, Sun. 10:30–1:30.*

Climb back up the hill from the river and make your way to the Plaza Poet Abul Beca. At the end of Marqués de Salvatierra, you'll pass the restored **Minarete Árabe** (Moorish minaret), all that remains of a mosque destroyed after the Reconquest of 1485. Around the corner from the minaret, the collegiate church of **Santa María la Mayor,** which serves as Ronda's cathedral, has roots in Moorish times; originally the Great Mosque of Moorish Ronda, it was rebuilt as a Christian church and dedicated to the Virgen de la Encarnación after the Reconquest. Its flamboyant mixture of styles reflects Ronda's heterogeneous past: the naves are late Gothic, the main altar is heavy with Baroque gold leaf, and the Renaissance belfry incorporates part of the original minaret. ✉ *Plaza Duquesa de Parcent.* 🎫 *200 ptas.* ⏲ *Daily 10–7.*

From the west front of Santa María, the Ronda de Gameros leads to a stone palace with twin Mudéjar towers, known as the **Casa de Mondragón** (Plaza de Mondragón). Appropriated by Ferdinand and Isabella after their victory in 1485, it had probably been the residence of Ronda's Moorish kings. Today you can wander through the patios, with their brick arches and delicate, Mudéjar stucco tracery, and admire the mosaics and *artesonado* (coffered) ceiling. ☎ *95/287–8450.* 🎫 *250 ptas.* ⏲ *Weekdays 10–6 (10–7 in summer), weekends 10–3.*

The Plaza Campillo has good views of the gorge and terraced hillsides. From here, Calle Tenorio leads back up to the Puente Nuevo and into **El Mercadillo,** Ronda's commercial heart—where hotels, restaurants, bars, banks, and stores are clustered. Most of the action lies around the Plaza del Socorro and along the Carrera de Espinel, the main shopping street (better known by its nickname, Calle de la Bola).

NEED A BREAK? For a drink or a snack, try **Don Miguel** (✉ C. Villanueva 4, ☎ 95/287–1090), a restaurant and café with a spectacular terrace view of the gorge and the Puente Nueva.

The main sight in Ronda's commercial center is the **Plaza de Toros,** one of the oldest and most handsome bullrings in Spain. Pedro Romero (1754–1839), the father of modern bullfighting and Ronda's most famous native son, is said to have killed 5,600 bulls here during his long career. In the museum beneath the plaza you can see posters for Ronda's very first fights, held here in 1785. The plaza is owned by the famous, now-retired bullfighter Antonio Ordóñez, on whose nearby ranch Orson

Welles's ashes were scattered (as directed in his will)—indeed, the ring has become a favorite of filmmakers. Every September, the bullring is the scene of Ronda's *corridas goyescas,* named after Goya, whose bullfight sketches (*tauromaquias*) were inspired by the skill and art of Pedro Romero. Seats for these fights cost a small fortune and are booked far in advance; and both the participants and the dignitaries in the audience don the costumes of Goya's time for the occasion. Other than that, the plaza is rarely used for fights except during Ronda's May festival. ☎ *95/287–4132.* 🎫 *400 ptas.* ⏲ *Daily 10–6 (10–8 in summer).*

Beyond the bullring, you can relax in the shady **Alameda del Tajo** gardens, one of the loveliest spots in Ronda. At gardens' end, a balcony protrudes from the face of the cliff, offering a vertigo-inducing view of the valley below. Stroll along the clifftop walk to the Old World Reina Victoria hotel (☞ Dining and Lodging, *below*), built by British settlers from Gibraltar at the turn of the century as a fashionable rest stop on their Algeciras–Bobadilla railroad line.

About 20 km (12 mi) west of Ronda is the prehistoric **Cueva de la Pileta** (Pileta Cave). To see it, head west out of Ronda, toward Seville, and exit left for the village of **Benaoján**—from here the caves are well signposted. The caretaker will show you around; if the place looks deserted, wait at the entrance to the cave and he'll eventually emerge with the previous group of visitors. Armed with lamps, you'll set off on a roughly 90-minute walk that reveals prehistoric wall paintings of bison, deer, and horses outlined in black, red, and ocher. One highlight is the Cámara del Pescado (Chamber of the Fish), whose drawing of a huge fish is thought to be 15,000 years old. 🎫 *800 ptas.* ⏲ *Daily 10–1 and 4–5.*

Another excursion takes you to Ronda la Vieja, the site of the old Roman settlement of **Acinipo,** 20 km (12 mi) west of Ronda. (Take the A473 toward Algodonales; the turnoff for the ruins is 9 km/5 mi from Ronda.) This was a thriving town in the 1st century AD, but it was subsequently abandoned for reasons that continue to baffle historians. Today Acinipo is a windswept hillside with piles of stones, the foundations of a few Roman houses, and what remains of a theater. 🎫 *Free.* ⏲ *Tues.–Sat. 11–5 (11–7 in summer), Sun. 11–3.*

Clinging to the mountainsides of the vast landscape around Ronda are villages of white houses with honey-color tile roofs. These are the remote ***pueblos blancos*** of the province of Cádiz, on the onetime frontier between the Moors and the Christians. All are within a day's drive of Ronda; if you only have time for one, make it Grazalema (☞ *below*).

Dining and Lodging

$$$ ★ ✕ **Tragabuches.** This stylish restaurant around the corner from Ronda's parador and the tourist office has taken the Spanish culinary scene by storm. The clever, urbane decor combines traditional and modern materials in two dining rooms (one with a picture window), and the food has earned the Ronda-born cook, Sergio López, a national award as Best Young Chef in Spain. The *menú de degustación,* a taster's menu of five courses and two desserts, is proof enough: imaginative treatment of classic ingredients. Where else would you find *rabo de toro* (oxtail stew) accompanied by a sweet chestnut puree, or thyme ice cream for dessert? ✉ *José Aparicio 1,* ☎ *95/219–0291. AE, DC, MC, V. Closed Mon. No dinner Sun.*

$$ ✕ **Pedro Romero.** Named after the father of modern bullfighting, this restaurant opposite the bullring is packed with colorful taurine decor. Sad-eyed bulls peer down at you as you tuck into the *sopa del mesón* (house soup), *rabo de toro, orperdiz a la cazuela* (stewed partridge), and, for dessert, *tocinillo del cielo al coco* (a sweet caramel custard flavored with coconut). ✉ *Virgen de la Paz 18,* ☎ *95/287–1110. AE, DC, MC, V.*

$ ✕ **Mesón Santiago.** Eating at this tavern is like dining in with your extended Spanish family. Always packed, it feels more like a home than a restaurant; the several dining rooms are decorated with Sevillian tiles and ceramic plates. In summer, you can lunch outdoors on the patio. The cuisine is simple Spanish fare, including tongue, partridge, quail, and the rib-sticking *cocido de la casa,* a savory stew of chard, potatoes, and chickpeas. ✉ *Marina 3,* ☎ *95/287–1559. MC, V. No dinner.*

$$$ ✕🏨 **El Molino del Santo.** Housed in a converted mill ("The Saint's Mill") next to a rushing stream near Benaoján, 10 km (7 mi) from Ronda, this British-run establishment was one of Andalusia's first country hotels and has served as a model for the rest. Guest rooms are arranged around a pleasant patio and come in various sizes, some with terrace. This is a good base for walks in the mountains, and the hotel rents mountain bikes as well. The restaurant is justifiably popular. ✉ *Estación de Benaoján, 29370 Benaoján,* ☎ *95/216–7151,* FAX *95/216–7327. 15 rooms. Restaurant, pool. AE, DC, MC, V.*

$$$ ✕🏨 **Parador de Ronda.** This relatively new parador is an architectural feat. The exterior is the old town hall, perched at the very edge of the Tajo gorge, but only the shell of the building remains—inside, the design is daringly modern. The combination of old and new is spectacular from the moment you step into the glass-enclosed courtyard. Common areas are bright and airy; the staff is professional; and the large guest rooms, in modern cream tones, are comfortable, with enormous bathrooms. The restaurant is famous in its own right: try the gazpacho based on green peppers (the chef's own invention), followed by a regional dish such as *cabrito asado* (roast kid) or *conejo a la rondeña* (Ronda-style rabbit). ✉ *Plaza de España, 29400,* ☎ *95/287–7500,* FAX *95/287–8188. 62 rooms, 8 suites. Restaurant, pool, meeting room. AE, DC, MC, V.*

$$$ 🏨 **Reina Victoria.** This classic Spanish hotel was built in 1906 by the Gibraltar British as a weekend stop for passengers on the new rail line between Algeciras and Bobadilla. It rose to fame in 1912, when the ailing German poet Rainer Maria Rilke came here to convalesce. (His room has been preserved as a museum.) Today the Reina Victoria maintains a mood of faded decadence and has a somewhat neglected, tumbledown air. It's no longer the only—or even the second-best—place to stay in Ronda, but the views from its garden are still unbeatable. ✉ *Jerez 25, 29400,* ☎ *95/287–1240,* FAX *95/287–1075. 89 rooms. Restaurant, pool. AE, DC, MC, V.*

$$ 🏨 **Polo.** Cozy, old-fashioned, homey, and centrally located, the Polo offers comfortably furnished rooms and a good, reasonably priced restaurant. The common areas are spacious, with black and white tiles and huge white settees. Guest rooms have blue carpets and brand-new beds dressed in white. ✉ *Mariano Souvirón 8, 29400,* ☎ *95/287–2447,* FAX *95/287–2449. 33 rooms. Restaurant. AE, DC, MC, V.*

Olvera

18 *59 km (37 mi) north of Ronda (via Agodonales), 68 km (42 mi) west of Antequera.*

Two imposing silhouettes dominate the crest of Olvera's hill: the 11th-century castle **Vallehermoso,** a legacy of the Moors, and the neoclassical church of **La Encarnación,** reconstructed in the 19th century on the foundations of the old Arab mosque.

Setenil de las Bodegas

19 *13 km (8 mi) southeast of Olvera.*

Setenil de las Bodegas lies south of the N342, just southeast of Olvera on a small mountain road. The village nestles in a cleft in the rock cut by the River Guadalporcín, and seems to have been sculpted out of the rock itself: the streets resemble long, narrow caves, and on many houses the roof is formed by a projecting ledge of heavy rock.

Zahara de la Sierra

20 *35 km (22 mi) northwest of Ronda, 32 km (20 mi) southwest of Olvera.*

West of the C339, a little south of Algodonales, a solitary **watchtower** dominates a crag above the village of Zahara de la Sierra, its outline visible for miles around. The tower is all that remains of a Moorish castle where Alfonso X once fought the emir of Morocco. It remained an important Moorish stronghold until it fell to the Christians in 1470. Along the streets of Zahara you can see door knockers fashioned like the hand of Fatima: the fingers represent the five laws of the Koran and serve to ward off evil.

En Route The winding mountain road between Zahara and Grazalema, via the Puerto de las Palomas (4,300 ft), is for adventurous drivers only. The views from its heights are breathtaking, but unless you have nerves of steel and a head for heights, take the more conventional approach, turning off the A473 midway between Ronda and Algodonales.

Sierra de Grazalema

21 *The village of Grazalema is 28 km (17 mi) northwest of Ronda, 23 km (14 mi) northeast of Ubrique.*

Protected as a nature park, the 323-square-km (200-square-mi) Sierra de Grazalema straddles the provinces of Málaga and Cádiz. These mountains trap the rain clouds that roll in from the Atlantic and thus have the distinction of being the wettest place in Spain, with an average annual rainfall of 88 inches. Thanks to the park's altitude and prevailing humidity, it's one of the last habitats for the rare fir tree *abies pinsapo* and is home to ibex, vultures, and numerous birds of prey. Parts of the park are restricted, accessible only on foot and accompanied by an official guide.

Standing dramatically at the entrance to the park, the village of **Grazalema** is the prettiest of the *pueblos blancos.* Its cobbled streets of houses with pink-and-ocher roofs wind up the hillside; red geraniums splash white walls; and black, wrought-iron lanterns and grilles cling to the house fronts.

From Grazalema, the winding C3331 takes you to **Ubrique,** spread on the slopes of the Saltadero Mountains and known for its leather tanning and embossing industry. Look for the **Convento de los Capuchinos** (Capuchin Convent) and the churches of **San Pedro** and **Nuestra Señora de la O.**

Another excursion from Grazalema takes you through the heart of the nature park: follow the A344 west through dramatic mountain scenery, past the village of Benamahoma, to **El Bosque,** home of the main park-information center and a trout stream.

Lodging

$–$$ **Villa Turística de Grazalema.** Across the valley from the village of Grazalema, this complex consists of a hotel proper and a village of 38 semidetached apartments sleeping two to six. Most have splendid views of the village and the mountains beyond. It's popular with families, so the noise level can rise during school holidays; at other times, it offers excellent value and a fine base for exploring the Grazalema park. ✉ *El Olivar (exit just before village), 11610 Grazalema,* ☎ *956/132136,* FAX *956/132213. 24 rooms, 38 apartments. Restaurant, pool. MC, V.*

ESTEPONA TO GIBRALTAR

You can still see Estepona's fishing village and Moorish old quarter amid its booming coastal development. Just inland, Casares piles whitewashed houses over the bright-blue Mediterranean below. Sotogrande, with its golf courses and long beach, and old San Roque are the last stops before the British colony at Gibraltar, a bizarre anomaly of Moorish, Spanish, and British influences. Finally, the windy town of Tarifa marks the southernmost tip of mainland Europe.

Estepona

22 *17 km (11 mi) west of San Pedro de Alcántara.*

Estepona used to mark the tail end of the Costa del Sol's urban sprawl, but today—thanks largely to the increasing importance of Gibraltar's airport—it's fast becoming the biggest boomtown on the coast. Still, the old fishing village hangs on. The beach, more than 1 km (½ mi) long, is lined with fishing boats, and the promenade passes well-kept, aromatic flower gardens. Back from the main Avenida de España, the old Moorish village is surprisingly unspoiled.

Dining and Lodging

$$–$$$ ✕ **Alcaría de Ramos.** José Ramos, a winner of Spain's National Gastronomy Prize, opened this restaurant in the El Paraíso complex, between Estepona and San Pedro de Alcántara, and has watched it garner a large and enthusiastic following. Try the *ensalada de lentejas con salmón ahumado* (lentil salad with smoked salmon), followed by *cordero asado* (roast lamb) and Ramos's deservedly famous fried ice cream. ✉ *Urbanización El Paraíso, Carretera N340, Km 167,* ☎ *95/288–6178. MC, V. Closed Sun. No lunch.*

$$$$ 🏨 **Kempinski.** From the outside, this brand-new, ocher luxury resort between the coastal highway and the beach looks like a cross between a Moroccan Casbah and the hanging gardens of Babylon. Tropical gardens with a succession of large swimming pools spread down to the beach. Dressed in cream colors, the rooms are spacious, modern, and luxurious, with faux–North African decor and balconies overlooking the Mediterranean. ✉ *Playa El Padrón, Carretera N340, Km 159, 29680,* ☎ *95/280–9500,* FAX *95/280–9550. 133 rooms, 16 suites. Restaurant, 1 indoor and 3 outdoor pools, beauty salon, exercise room, shops. AE, DC, MC, V.*

$$$$ 🏨 **Las Dunas.** This spectacular new hotel rises like a multicolor apparition next to the beach, halfway between Estepona and Marbella. The setting is palatial, with trickling fountains and copious exotic plants; the large rooms are bright and airy, with large easy chairs, hemp carpets, and light-green furniture. The restaurant serves first-class international food, and the health center offers a range of alternative therapies. ✉ *La Boladilla Baja, Carretera de Cádiz, Km 163, 29689,* ☎ *95/279–4345,* FAX *95/279–4825. 34 rooms, 39 suites, 33 apartments. 2 restaurants, pool, massage, sauna, health club. AE, DC, MC, V.*

$$$ 🏨 **Atalaya Park.** Closer to San Pedro de Alcántara than to Estepona, this comfortable resort hotel is set in subtropical gardens beside the sea and has extensive sports facilities. Rooms overlook either the Mediterranean or the mountains; some have nice touches like exposed brick, dark carpets, and picture windows. ✉ *Carretera N340, Km 163, 29680,* ☎ *95/288–9000,* FAX *95/288–9022. 438 rooms, 33 suites, 10 bungalows. 3 restaurants, 2 bars, 1 indoor and 4 outdoor pools, beauty salon, massage, sauna, 2 18-hole golf courses, 9 tennis courts. AE, DC, MC, V.*

Casares

23 *20 km (12 mi) northwest of Estepona.*

The mountain village of Casares lies high above Estepona in the Sierra Bermeja. Streets of ancient white houses piled one on top of the other perch on the slopes beneath a ruined but impressive Moorish castle. The heights afford stunning views over orchards, olive groves, and cork woods to the Mediterranean, sparkling in the distance.

San Roque

24 *92 km (57 mi) southwest of Ronda, 64 km (40 mi) west of Marbella.*

The town of San Roque was founded within sight of Gibraltar by Spaniards who fled the Rock when the British captured it in 1704. Almost 300 years of British occupation have done little to diminish the chauvinism of San Roque's inhabitants, who still see themselves as the only genuine Gibraltarians.

Fourteen kilometers (10 mi) east of San Roque is the luxury **Sotogrande** complex, a gated community with sprawling millionaires' villas, a yacht marina, and four golf courses, including the legendary Valderrama, host of the Ryder Cup in 1997.

Dining and Lodging

$$$$ ✕ **Los Remos.** The dining room in this gracious colonial villa has peach-colored walls with quasi-Baroque adornments: gilt rococo mirrors, swirling cherubs, friezes of grapes, and crystal lamps. It overlooks a formal, leafy garden full of palms, cedars, and trailing ivy. Entrées include *urta del estrecho en salsa de erizos marinos* (perch from the Straits of Gibraltar in sea-urchin sauce). All seafood comes from the Bay of Algeciras area—the restaurant's name means "The Oars"—and the wine cellar boasts some 20,000 bottles. ✉ *Villa Victoria, Campo de Gibraltar (between San Roque and Campamento),* ☎ *956/698412. AE, DC, MC, V. Closed Sun.*

$$$$ **Almenara.** Six kilometers (4 mi) from the coast in the Sotogrande development, this deluxe resort is a complex of ocher, semi-detached, Andalusian-style houses clustered around a main building on the edge of an 18-hole golf course. Accessed via golf cart, each house is surrounded by gardens and has a private terrace or patio. The best views—over the golf course with the Mediterranean in the distance—are from rooms in the 600s. An additional nine-hole course will open in early 2001. ✉ *Avda. Almenara, 11310 Sotogrande,* ☎ *956/582000,* FAX *956/582001. 140 rooms, 10 suites. Restaurant, bar, snack bar, in-room data ports, outdoor pool, 18-hole and 9-hole golf course, exercise room. AE, DC, MC, V.*

$$$–$$$$ **The Suites.** This sumptuous, Moorish-Andalusian–style *pueblo* sits next to the San Roque golf course, halfway between the village and Sotogrande. The ocher main building houses the reception area, golf clubhouse, and two restaurants, one specializing in Japanese food. The rooms and suites are in white houses scattered around a luxuriant garden with fountains and exotic plants; each room has a little garden patio, and each suite has an enclosed courtyard as well. The houses are connected by paved paths, on which the cleaning staff tool around on golf carts. ✉ *San Roque Club, Carretera N340, Km 126.5, 11360 San Roque,* ☎ *956/613030,* FAX *956/613013. 50 rooms, 50 suites. 2 restaurants, pool, 18-hole golf course, 4 tennis courts, horseback riding. AE, DC, MC, V.*

Nightlife

The brand-new **Casino de San Roque** (✉ Carretera N340 Km 127, ☎ 965/780 100) has a gaming room with roulette and blackjack tables, and a less formal slot-machine area. The casino is open 8 PM–5 AM; passport, jacket, and tie are required.

Gibraltar

25 *20 km (12 mi) east of Algeciras, 77 km (48 mi) west of Marbella.*

The tiny British colony of Gibraltar—nicknamed Gib, or simply "the Rock"—whose impressive silhouette dominates the strait between Spain and Morocco, is actually a rock 6 km (4 mi) long, 1 km (½ mi) wide, and 1,369 ft high. In ancient times it was one of the two Pillars of Hercules, marking the western limits of the known world. (The other was the mountain Djebel Musa, between the Moroccan cities of Ceuta and Tangier.) Gibraltar's ace position, commanding the narrow entrance to the Mediterranean, inspired the Moors to seize it in 711 as a preliminary to the conquest of Spain. They held it longer than either the Spaniards or the British ever have—a fact to which tribute is paid whenever anyone says its name, for Gibraltar is a corruption of Djebel Tariq (Tariq's Rock), Tariq being the Moorish commander who built the first fort here.

After the Moors had ruled for 750 years, the Spaniards recaptured Tariq's Rock in 1462, on the feast day of St. Bernard (now the colony's copatron saint along with Our Lady of Europe, whose shrine stands at the Rock's southernmost tip). The English, heading an Anglo-Dutch fleet in the War of the Spanish Succession, seized the Rock in 1704 after three days of fighting; and following several years of local skirmishes, Gibraltar was finally ceded to Great Britain in 1713 by the Treaty of Utrecht. Spain has been trying to get it back ever since. In 1779 a combined French and Spanish force laid siege to the Rock for three years, to no avail. In the Napoléonic Wars, Gibraltar served as Admiral Nelson's base for the decisive naval Battle of Trafalgar, and during the two World Wars, it served the Allies well as a naval and air base. In 1967, Franco closed the land border with Spain to strengthen his claims over the colony, and it remained closed until 1985.

Today, much of Gibraltar looks rather like a faded garrison town. The number of British troops stationed here has been cut back, and millions of dollars are being invested in developing the Rock's tourist potential. The Costa del Sol's 100,000-plus expatriate Britons have given the economy of this tiny colony another boost: many take advantage of Gibraltar's status as an offshore financial center.

There must be few places in the world that you enter by walking or driving across an airport runway, but that's what happens in Gibraltar. First, show your passport; then make your way out onto the narrow strip of land linking Spain's La Linea with Britain's Rock. Unless you have a good reason to take your car—like loading up on cheap gas or duty-free goodies—you're best off leaving it in a guarded parking area in La Linea, the Spanish border town, and relying on buses and taxis in Gibraltar, whose streets are narrow and congested. The Official Rock Tour—conducted either by minibus or, at a greater cost, taxi—takes about 90 minutes and includes all the major sights, allowing you to choose which places to come back and linger at later.

Although the British pound is Gibraltar's official currency, Spanish pesetas are universally accepted. Note that when dialing Gibraltar from Spain, the area code is 9567; when dialing from other countries, the code is 350.

Numbers in the margin correspond to points of interest on the Gibraltar map.

Begin on the Rock's eastern side: turn left down Devil's Tower Road
26 as you enter Gibraltar. Here, on the eastern shores, is **Catalan Bay,** a fishing village founded by Genoese settlers, now a picturesque resort. You'll see the massive water catchments that once supplied the colony's

drinking water. The road beyond here is closed, so head back west through the town of Gibraltar (which you'll explore later) and out to the Rock's 27 southern tip, **Punta Grande de Europa** (Europa Point). Stop here for the view across the straits to Morocco, 23 km (14 mi) away. You are now standing on one of the two ancient Pillars of Hercules. In front of you, the Europa Point lighthouse has dominated the meeting place of the Atlantic and the Mediterranean since 1841; sailors can see its light from a distance of 27 km (17 mi). Near the lighthouse, on **Europa Flats,** is 28 an ancient Moorish cistern known as the **Nun's Well,** and the **Shrine of Our Lady of Europe,** venerated by seafarers since 1462.

From Europa Flats, follow Europa Road back along the Rock's west- 29 ern slopes, high above **Rosia Bay,** to which Nelson's flagship, HMS *Victory,* was towed after the Battle of Trafalgar in 1805. On board were the dead, who were buried in Trafalgar Cemetery on the southern edge of town—except, of course, for Admiral Nelson, whose body went home to England preserved in a barrel of rum.

From Rosia Bay, continue on Europa Road as far as the Casino, above the Alameda Gardens. Make a sharp right here up Engineer Road to 30 **Jews' Gate,** an unbeatable lookout point over the docks and Bay of Gibraltar to Algeciras. Here you can access the **Upper Nature Preserve,** which includes St. Michael's Cave, the Apes' Den, the Great Siege Tunnel, and the Moorish Castle. *£5 (includes all attractions), plus £2 per vehicle.* *Daily 9:30–sunset.*

31 Queens Road leads to **St. Michael's Cave,** the largest of Gibraltar's 150 caves. A series of underground chambers hung with stalactites and stalagmites, it provides an incredible setting for concerts, ballet, and drama. Sound-and-light shows are held here most days at 11 and 4. The skull of a Neanderthal woman (now in the British Museum) was found at nearby Forbes Quarry eight years *before* the world-famous discovery in Germany's Neander Valley in 1856; nobody paid much attention to it at the time, which is why we call this prehistoric race Neanderthals rather than *homo calpensis* (literally, "Gibraltar Man"—after the Romans' name for the Rock, *Calpe*).

32 Drive down Old Queens Road from St. Michael's Cave to the **Apes' Den,** near the Wall of Charles V. The famous Barbary Apes are a breed of cinnamon-color, tailless monkeys native to Morocco's Atlas Mountains. Legend holds that as long as the apes remain, the British will keep the Rock; Winston Churchill went so far as to issue an order for their preservation when the apes' numbers began to dwindle during World War II. Today they are publicly fed twice daily, at 8 and 4. Among their mischievous talents are purse and camera snatching.

33 At the northern end of the Rock, the **Great Siege Tunnel,** formerly known as the Upper Galleries, was carved out during the Great Siege of 1779–82. Governor Lord Napier of Magdala entertained former U.S. president Ulysses S. Grant here in 1878, with a banquet in St. George's Hall. The Holyland Tunnel leads to a vantage point on the east side of the Rock, high above Catalan Bay.

34 The **Moorish Castle,** on Willis Road, was originally built by the descendants of Tariq, who conquered the Rock in 711. The present Tower of Homage dates from 1333, and its walls bear the scars of sieges in which stones from medieval catapults (and, later, cannonballs) were hurled against it. Admiral Rooke hoisted the British flag from its summit when he captured the Rock in 1704, and it has flown here ever since.

35 Willis Road leads steeply down to the colorful, congested town of **Gibraltar,** where the dignified Regency architecture of Great Britain blends

Gibraltar

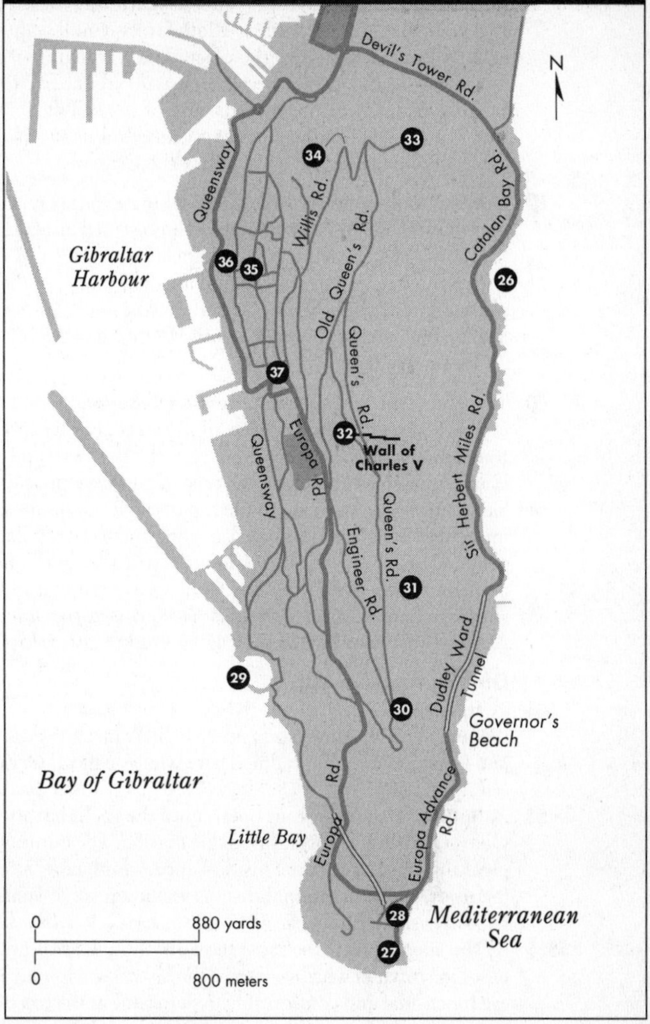

Apes' Den **32**

Catalan Bay **26**

Europa Flats **28**

Gibraltar Museum **36**

Great Siege Tunnel **33**

Jews' Gate **30**

Moorish Castle **34**

Nefusot Yehudada Synagogue . **37**

Punta Grande de Europa . . **27**

Rosia Bay. . . **29**

St. Michael's Cave **31**

Town of Gibraltar . . . **35**

well with the shutters, balconies, and patios of southern Spain. The tourist office is on Cathedral Square. Apart from the shops, restaurants, and pubs that beckon on busy Main Street, you'll want to see the **Governor's Residence,** where the ceremonial Changing of the Guard and Ceremony of the Keys take place, usually about five times a year; the **Law Courts,** where the famous case of the sailing ship *Mary Celeste* was heard in 1872; the Anglican **Cathedral of the Holy Trinity;** and the Catholic **Cathedral of St. Mary the Crowned.**

36 Don't miss the **Gibraltar Museum,** whose exhibits recall the history of the Rock throughout the ages. Its well-presented displays include a beautiful 14th-century Moorish bathhouse, evocations of the Great Siege and of the Battle of Trafalgar, and an 1865 model of the Rock. There's also a reproduction of the "Gibraltar Woman," the Neanderthal skull discovered here in 1848. ✉ *Bomb House La.,* ☎ *9567/74289.* *£2.* *Weekdays 10–6, Sat. 10–2.*

37 The 18th-century **Nefusot Yehudada Synagogue,** on Line Wall Road, is worth a look for its inspired architecture. For weapons aficionados, **Koehler Gun,** in Casemates Square at the northern end of Main Street, is an impressive example of the type of gun developed during the Great ★ Siege. Finally, take a ride to the top of the Rock on the **cable car.** Reminiscent of a ski gondola, the car does not go particularly high off the ground, but the views of Spain and Africa from the Rock's pinnacle are superb. It leaves every day from a station on Grand Parade, at the southern end of Main Street. *£4.90 round-trip (includes cable car, Michael's Cave, and Apes' Den).* *Daily 9:30–5:15*

Dining and Lodging

$$$ ✕ **La Bayuca.** One of the Rock's oldest restaurants, La Bayuca is renowned for its onion soup and Mediterranean dishes. Prince Charles and Prince Andrew both dined here while on naval service. ✉ *21 Turnbull's La.,* ☎ *9567/75119. AE, DC, MC, V. Closed Tues. No lunch Sun.*

$$ ✕ **Raffles.** This restaurant opens onto the yacht harbor at Queensway Quay, Gibraltar's most fashionable marina. The outdoor terrace is very pleasant; the dining room inside is more cramped. The extensive menu incorporates international dishes, including some Spanish specialties. ✉ *Queensway Quay,* ☎ *9567/40362. MC, V. Closed Mon.*

$$$$ **The Eliott.** This is the most modern of the Rock's hotels, in the center of the town in what used to be the Gibraltar Holiday Inn. The rooms are functional and comfortable. Ask for one at the top of the hotel with a view over the Bay of Gibraltar. ✉ *2 Governor's Parade,* ☎ *9567/70500,* FAX *9567/70243. 114 rooms, 2 suites. Pool, sauna. AE, DC, MC, V.*

$$$ ★ **The Rock.** Overlooking Gibraltar, this Rock first opened in 1932. Furnishings in the rooms and restaurant can compete with those in good international hotels anywhere, yet they manage to preserve something of the English colonial style, with bamboo, ceiling fans, and a fine terrace bar. ✉ *3 Europa Rd.,* ☎ *9567/73000,* FAX *9567/73513. 112 rooms, 8 suites. Restaurant, bar, pool, beauty salon. AE, DC, MC, V.*

$$ **Bristol.** This colonial-style hotel is in the heart of town, with splendid views of the bay and the cathedral. Rooms are spacious but basic. The tropical garden is a real haven, and the wood-panel lounge has two pool tables. ✉ *10 Cathedral Sq.,* ☎ *9567/76800,* FAX *9567/77613. 60 rooms. Bar, breakfast room, pool, free parking. AE, DC, MC, V.*

Nightlife

The **Stakis International Casino** (✉ 7 Europa Rd., ☎ 9567/76666) is open from 7:30 PM (cocktail bar) and 9 (gaming room) until 4 AM; dress in the gaming room is smart casual.

Tarifa

38 *35 km (21 mi) west of San Roque.*

Standing on the Straits of Gibraltar at the southernmost tip of mainland Europe—where the Mediterranean and the Atlantic meet and the Rif Mountains of Africa seem so close you can almost touch them—Tarifa was one of the earliest Moorish settlements in Spain. Its 10th-century **castle** is famous for its siege of 1292, when the defender Guzmán el Bueno refused to surrender even though the attacking Moors threatened to kill his captive son. In defiance, he flung his own dagger down to them, shouting "Here, use this"—or something to that effect. The Spanish military turned the castle over to the town in the mid-1990s, and it now contains a **museum** devoted to Guzmán and the sacrifice of his son. *200 ptas. Tues.–Sun. 10–2 and 4–6.*

Strong prevailing winds kept Tarifa off the tourist maps for years, but they have ultimately proven a source of wealth. Aeolic power is generated on the vast wind farm occupying the surrounding hills, and the wide, white-sand beaches stretching north of the town have become Europe's biggest windsurfing center.

Ten kilometers (6 mi) north of Tarifa on the Atlantic coast are the Roman ruins of **Baelo Claudia.** This settlement was a thriving production center of *garum,* a salty fish paste appreciated in Rome. *956/688530. 250 ptas. Tues.–Sat. 10–6 (mid-Sept.–June, 10–5), Sun. 10–2.*

Lodging

$$$ **Hurricane Hotel.** This laid-back, palm-kissed hotel next to the beach is a favorite hangout of the windsurfing set. The atmosphere is fun and informal, the rooms simple but adequate. The staff can organize horseback-riding trips along the beach or inland. *Carretera Cádiz–Málaga, Km 77, 11380, 956/684919, FAX 956/684329. 28 rooms, 5 suites. Restaurant, pool, horseback riding. AE, MC, V.*

THE COSTA DEL SOL A TO Z

Arriving and Departing

By Bus

Long-distance buses serve Málaga from Madrid, Cartagena, Almería, Granada, Ubeda, Córdoba, Seville, and Badajoz. Málaga's main bus station is on Paseo de los Tilos (95/235–0061). Marbella and Algeciras can be reached directly from Madrid or Seville; other connections are between Fuengirola and Seville, and Cádiz and Algeciras. Marbella's bus station is at Avenida Trapiche (95/276–4400).

By Car

Málaga is 580 km (360 mi) from Madrid by way of the N IV to Córdoba, then N331 to Antequera and N321; 182 km (114 mi) from Córdoba via Antequera; 214 km (134 mi) from Seville; and 129 km (81 mi) from Granada by the shortest route of N342 to Loja, then N321 to Málaga.

By Plane

If you're coming from Great Britain and heading for the coast west of Marbella, consider **Gibraltar Airport** (9567/73026). It's right next to the frontier, and once you've crossed into Spain you can catch buses in La Linea for all coastal resorts.

Málaga Airport (95/204–8804) lies 10 km (6 mi) west of Málaga. From the United States, you'll have to connect in Madrid. Iberia and GB Airways (an affiliate of British Airways) fly several times daily from

London; numerous British charter companies also link London with Málaga. Most major European cities have direct flights to Málaga on either Iberia or their own national airlines. Iberia and its subsidiary, Aviaco, have up to eight flights a day from Madrid (flying time one hour), three flights a day from Barcelona (1½ hours), and regular flights from other Spanish cities.

Iberia has offices in Málaga (✉ Molina Lario 13, ☎ 95/213–6147) and at the airport (☎ 95/213–6166). Inquiries: ☎ 902/400500.

BETWEEN THE AIRPORT AND DOWNTOWN

From Málaga Airport, trains run regularly to nearby cities (☞ Getting Around, *below*), and an Iberia bus leaves every 20 minutes for downtown Málaga (6:30 AM–midnight) at a fare of 150 ptas. Taxis are plentiful, and official fares to Málaga, Torremolinos, and other resorts are posted inside the terminal. The trip from the airport to Torremolinos costs about 2,000 ptas.

By Train

Málaga is the main rail terminus, with eight trains a day from Madrid and one from Barcelona and Valencia. Most Málaga trains leave from Madrid's Atocha station, though some leave from Chamartín. Travel time varies between 4½ and 10 hours; the best and fastest are the daytime *Talgo 200* trains from Atocha. There is also an overnight train, the *Estrella* (9½ hours). All Madrid–Málaga trains stop at Córdoba; there are also direct local trains from Córdoba to Málaga. From both Seville (four hours) and Granada (3–3½ hours), you have to change at Bobadilla for Málaga, making buses a more efficient mode of travel from those cities. In fact, other than the direct Madrid–Córdoba–Málaga line, trains in Andalusia can be slow due to the terrain. You may generally find buses quicker and more convenient.

Málaga Station (✉ Explanada de la Estación, ☎ 95/236–0202) is 15 minutes' walk from the city center, across the river. For schedules and fares, call **RENFE** (☎ 902/240202).

Getting Around

By Bus

Buses are the best way to get around the Costa del Sol (as well to as reach it from Seville or Granada). Málaga's bus station is on the Paseo de los Tilos (☎ 95/235–0061). The **Portillo** bus company, with offices at the Málaga station (☎ 95/236–0191), serves most of the Costa del Sol. Another company with offices in Málaga, **Alsina Gräells** (☎ 95/231–8295), has service to Granada, Córdoba, Seville, and Nerja. Málaga's tourist office has details on other bus lines.

By Car

A car allows you to explore some of Andalusia's rightly famous mountain villages. Mountain driving can be an adventure—hair-raising curves, precipices, and mediocre road services are often the norm—but it's getting more manageable as highways throughout the region are resurfaced and widened and, in some cases, completely new roadbeds built. To take a car into Gibraltar, drivers need—in theory—an international driver's license, an insurance certificate, and a logbook; in practice, all you need to show is your passport. Be prepared for parking problems—space is scarce—but beware of phony offers of help from "parking-insurance agents" on the frontier approach.

By Train

A useful suburban train service connects Málaga, Torremolinos, and Fuengirola, calling at the airport and all resorts along the way. It leaves

Málaga every half hour between 6 AM and 10:30 PM and Fuengirola every half hour from 6:35 AM to 11:35 PM. Its terminus in Málaga is the **Guadalmedina** station, near the Corte Inglés department store; it also calls at Málaga's RENFE station. The Fuengirola terminus is just across from the bus station, where you can catch buses for Mijas, Marbella, Estepona, and Algeciras.

Two trains a day run between Málaga and Ronda through the dramatic Chorro gorge, with a change at Bobadilla. Travel time is around three hours. Three trains a day make the direct two-hour trip between Ronda and Algeciras on a spectacular mountain track.

Contacts and Resources

Consulates

Canada (☒ Plaza de la Malagueta 3, Málaga, ☎ 95/222–3346). **United Kingdom** (☒ Mauricio Moro 2,, Malaga, ☎ 95/235–2300). **United States** (☒ Centro Comercial Las Rampas, Fuengirola, ☎ 95/247–4891).

Guided Tours

Numerous one- and two-day excursions from Costa del Sol resorts are run by the national company **Pullmantur** (☒ Avda. Imperial, Torremolinos, ☎ 95/238–4400) and various smaller firms. Most hotels have their leaflets on hand and can book you a tour, as can any travel agent. Excursions leave from Málaga, Torremolinos, Fuengirola, Marbella, and Estepona. Prices vary slightly according to your departure point; in most cases you can be picked up at your hotel.

Hotels and local travel agents can arrange the following local tours, most of which last half a day: Málaga, Cuevas de Nerja, Mijas, Marbella, and Puerto Banús; burro safari in Coín; countryside tour of Alhaurín de la Torre, Alhaurín el Grande, Coín, Ojén, and Ronda. Night tours include a barbecue evening, a bullfighting evening with dinner, and a night at the Casino Torrequebrada.

Travel Agencies

The main international agencies are **American Express** (☒ Avda. Duque de Ahumada, Marbella, ☎ 95/282–1494) and **Wagons-Lits Viajes** (☒ Strachan 10, Málaga, ☎ 95/221–7695).

Visitor Information

The **regional tourist office** for the Costa del Sol is in Málaga (☒ Pasaje de Chinitas 4, ☎ 95/221–3445). Local tourist offices: **Algeciras** (☒ Juan de la Cierva, ☎ 956/572636). **Antequera** (☒ Palacio de Najera, Coso Viejo, ☎ 95/270–2505). **Benalmádena Costa** (☒ Avda. Antonio Machado 14, ☎ 95/244–2494). **Estepona** (☒ Paseo Marítimo, ☎ 95/280–0913). **Fuengirola** (☒ Avda. Jesús Santos Rein 6, ☎ 95/246–7457). **Gibraltar** (☒ 6 Kent House, Cathedral Sq., ☎ 9567/74950). **Málaga** (☒ Avda. Cervantes 1, Paseo del Parque, ☎ 95/260–4410. **Marbella** (☒ Glorieta de la Fontanilla, ☎ 95/282–2818). **Nerja** (☒ Puerta del Mar 2, ☎ 95/252–1531). **Ronda** (☒ Plaza de España 1, ☎ 95/287–1272). **Torremolinos** (☒ Ayuntamiento, C. Rafael Quintana Rosado, ☎ 95/237–9511).

11 GRANADA, CÓRDOBA, AND EASTERN ANDALUSIA

Ruled by the Moors for centuries, these resonant lands encompass smart cities with a deep sense of history; rolling plains sown with ordered ranks of olive trees; airy alpine vistas; and whitewashed villages clinging to parched hillsides. Here are two of Spain's most famous monuments, Granada's legendary Alhambra palace and Córdoba's great mosque, as well as the snowy Sierra Nevada and the source of the mighty Guadalquivir River.

Updated by Mark Little

FROM THE DARK MOUNTAINS of the Sierra Morena down to the mighty, snowcapped peaks of the Sierra Nevada, Andalusia (Andalucía) rings with echoes of the Moors. These North African Muslims dwelled here for almost 800 years, from their first conquest of Spanish soil (Gibraltar) from the Visigoths in AD 711 to their final expulsion from Granada in 1492. The name Andalucía comes from the Moors' own name for their new acquisition: Al-Andalus. Two of Spain's most famous monuments, Córdoba's mosque and Granada's Alhambra palace, were the inspired creations of Moorish architects and craftsmen. Typical Andalusian architecture—brilliant-white villages with narrow, shady streets; thick-walled houses clustered around cool, private patios; whitewashed facades with modest, grilled windows—comes from centuries of Moorish occupation. The Guadalquivir, the Moors' "Great River," runs through the entire region; town names like Úbeda and Jaén are derivations of old Arabic names; ruined *alcazares* (fortresses) dot the landscape; and *azahar* (orange blossom) perfumes the patios. It's hard to find a church in Andalusia that wasn't built on the site of a former mosque. And high on the southern slopes of the Sierra Nevada, the villages of the Alpujarras, with their cubic houses, flat roofs, and chimney stacks, could just as easily be North African.

In the 13th century, King Ferdinand III, one of the champions of the Christian Reconquest, captured Baeza, Úbeda, Córdoba, and Jaén. The Moors fled south to Granada, where they tarried for another 250 years. The next two centuries (14th and 15th) were filled with constant battles and skirmishes between Moors and Christians, until Ferdinand of Aragón and Isabella of Castile, known jointly as the Catholic Monarchs, scored the ultimate victory of the Reconquest in 1492: they entered Granada and accepted the Moors' final surrender. In honor of this victory, Ferdinand and Isabella chose to be buried in Granada.

The Moors left their mark here, but so did the Christian conquerors and their descendants. Andalusia today has Gothic chapels, Renaissance cathedrals, and Baroque monasteries and churches, and the sturdy, golden-stone mansions of Úbeda and Baeza contrast intriguingly with the humble, whitewashed villages elsewhere in the province.

The landscape, too, is varied and powerful. Granada's fertile plain (known as *la vega*), covered with lush orchards and tobacco and poplar groves, stretches up to the mountains of the majestic Sierra Nevada. Snowclad for half the year, this range boasts the highest peaks on mainland Spain, the 11,407-ft Mulhacén and the 11,215-ft Veleta. Farther north, the Guadalquivir flows west toward Córdoba from the heights of the Sierra de Cazorla, bounded by the rugged, shrub-covered Sierra Morena to the north and by the rolling olive groves of Jaén to the south. Fruit and almond trees line the river's banks in Córdoba's orchards. Vineyards cover the Córdoban *campiña* (fertile plain south of the Guadalquivir), and white villages cling to hillsides beneath ruined castles.

Pleasures and Pastimes

Dining

Córdoba has a fair number of gourmet restaurants, whereas in Granada the selection is more limited. Córdoba's specialties are *salmorejo* (a thick version of gazpacho) and *rabo de toro* (bull's-tail or oxtail stew), and many Córdoban restaurants are now inventing creative new dishes based on old Arab recipes. Here, *fino de Montilla,* a dry, sherrylike wine from the local Montilla-Moriles district, makes a good aperitif or bar drink. In Granada, taverns serve the earthy *vino de la costa,* from the Alpujarras region. Granada's typical dishes are *tortilla al Sacromonte* (an omelet traditionally made of calf's brains, sweetbreads, diced ham, potatoes, and peas), *habas con jamón* (ham stewed with broad beans), *sopa sevillana* (tasty fish and seafood soup made with mayonnaise), and *choto al ajillo* (braised kid with garlic).

Lunch is the main meal here. Restaurants start serving around 2, but most tables don't fill up until at least 3, and most people are still at the table at 5. After such a long, late lunch, few Andalusians dine out in the evening; instead, they make the rounds of the bars, dipping into tapas and plates of ham or cheese. (Hams from the Pedroches valley, in Córdoba province, and from the Alpujarran village of Trevélez are famous throughout Spain.) If you go for lunch around 2, you won't need a reservation; wait until 3 and you may have trouble finding a table. Similarly, in the evening, you shouldn't have a problem if you dine early—at, say, 9 or 10.

CATEGORY	COST*
$$$$	over 6,500 ptas.
$$$	4,000 ptas.–6,500 ptas.
$$	2,500 ptas.–4,000 ptas.
$	under 2,500 ptas.

**per person for a three-course meal, excluding drinks, tax and service*

Fiestas

Granada celebrates **La Toma** (the Capture), the 1492 surrender to the Catholic Monarchs, on January 2. On January 5, the eve of the **Día de los Reyes** (Feast of the Three Kings), every city and village holds processions of the three Wise Men. On February 1, Granada organizes a **romería** (pilgrimage) to the Monastery of San Cecilio, on Sacromonte. Both Granada and Córdoba party hard during **Carnival,** on the days leading up to Ash Wednesday (February 28 in 2001); and both celebrate **Semana Santa** (Holy Week) with dramatic religious processions. The shrine of the **Virgen de la Cabeza,** near Andújar in the province of Jaén, is the scene of one of Spain's biggest romerías, or pilgrimages, on the last weekend in April. May brings to Córdoba **Las Cruces de Mayo** (May Days of the Cross), the Fiesta de los Patios (Patio Festival), and the **Feria de Nuestra Señora de la Salud** (Feast of Our Lady of Health). In Granada **Día de la Cruz** (Day of the Cross) is celebrated the first Sunday in May, **San Isidro** on May 15, and **Mariana Pineda** (a 19th-century political heroine) on May 26. In June, Granada celebrates **Corpus Christi** (June 14 in 2001) and **San Pedro** (June 29); the **International Festival of Music and Dance,** with some events in the Alhambra, begins in late June and runs into July. The **International Guitar Festival** brings major artists to Córdoba in early July. Córdoba celebrates **Nuestra Señora de Fuensanta,** and Granada honors **Nuestra Señora de las Angustias** (Our Lady of Distress), on the last Sunday in September and the **Romería de San Miguel** (Procession of St. Michael) on September 29.

Hiking and Walking

Thanks to a number of well-run outdoor clubs and a general interest in preserving the wilderness, Andalusia is well endowed with parks for both recreation and camping. The village of Cazorla, in the province of Jaén, leads to the pine-clad slopes of the Cazorla Nature Park. South of Granada, the Sierra Nevada and the Alpujarras have some of the most impressive vistas in all of Spain, terrific skiing in winter, and a gamut of outdoor activities in summer.

Lodging

Andalusia has accommodations for all budgets, from simple bed-and-breakfasts to luxurious paradors. At the high end, the Parador de San

Francisco, nestled beside Granada's Alhambra, is a magnificent way to enjoy both Granada and the storied past of southern Spain. Bed-and-breakfast lodgings, available in many villages, give you better access to the countryside and its rich folk traditions. Córdoba has some pleasant hotels set in houses in the old quarter, close to the mosque.

It's normally quite easy to find a room in Córdoba, even if you haven't reserved; just watch out for Holy Week and the May Patio Festival. Granada, on the other hand, can be very difficult: the Alhambra is the most popular monument in Spain. The city has plenty of hotels, but the high season runs long, from Easter to late October. Hotels on the Alhambra hill must be reserved long in advance, and those in the city center, around the Puerta Real and Acera del Darro, are unbelievably noisy—ask for rooms at the back. Beware Holy Week and the International Festival of Music and Dance (mid-June–mid-July). If you're traveling by car, inquire with hotels in both cities about parking, especially in Córdoba.

CATEGORY	COST*
$$$$	over 20,000 ptas.
$$$	12,000 ptas.–20,000 ptas.
$$	8,000 ptas.–12,000 ptas.
$	under 8,000 ptas.

**All prices are for a standard double room, excluding tax.*

Exploring Eastern Andalusia

Numbers in the text correspond to numbers in the margin and on the Andalusia: Granada to Córdoba; Granada; and Córdoba maps.

Great Itineraries

These suggested trips cover three of Andalusia's eight provinces: Granada, Jaén, and Córdoba. If you have a full week in eastern Andalusia, begin your tour in Córdoba and move on to Úbeda and Baeza, the cave towns of Guadix and Purullena, and Granada. End your odyssey in the Alpujarras.

IF YOU HAVE 3 DAYS

Begin in **Granada** ①–⑰. On day one, visit the Alhambra (having perhaps reserved tickets in advance) and wander the Albaicín, Granada's ancient Moorish quarter. Have lunch and tea along the Calderería. Spend the afternoon in the alleyways of the Alcaicería, visiting the cathedral and the Capilla Real; then take an evening tour of the Alhambra. The morning of the second day, leave Granada for the village of Baena, in the **Subbética** ㊼ region. Take in the scenery before heading to **Córdoba** ㉙–㊻ for the night. Spend the morning of the third day touring Córdoba's magical Mezquita and wandering the old Jewish Quarter, the Judería. Walk out to the River Guadalquivir and cross the Puente Romano to the Torre de la Calahorra, which houses a fine museum of the region's history.

IF YOU HAVE 5 DAYS

Córdoba ㉙–㊻ makes a good starting point for this medium-size Andalusian tour. Explore the city on day one, giving the Mezquita and the Judería a good, long look. Stay the night, then move the next morning toward Granada, stopping in the wine-growing town of **Montilla** ㊽ and the villages of the **Subbética** ㊾ region on the way. Spend the night in **Granada** ①–⑰, and devote day three to the Alhambra, the Albaicín, and the alleys of the Alcaicería. After a second night in Granada, rise early to hit the mountain roads toward the **Sierra Nevada** ㉑. Spend your fourth night in the **Alpujarras** ㉒, then take a morning walk and return to Granada.

Andalusía: Granada to Córdoba

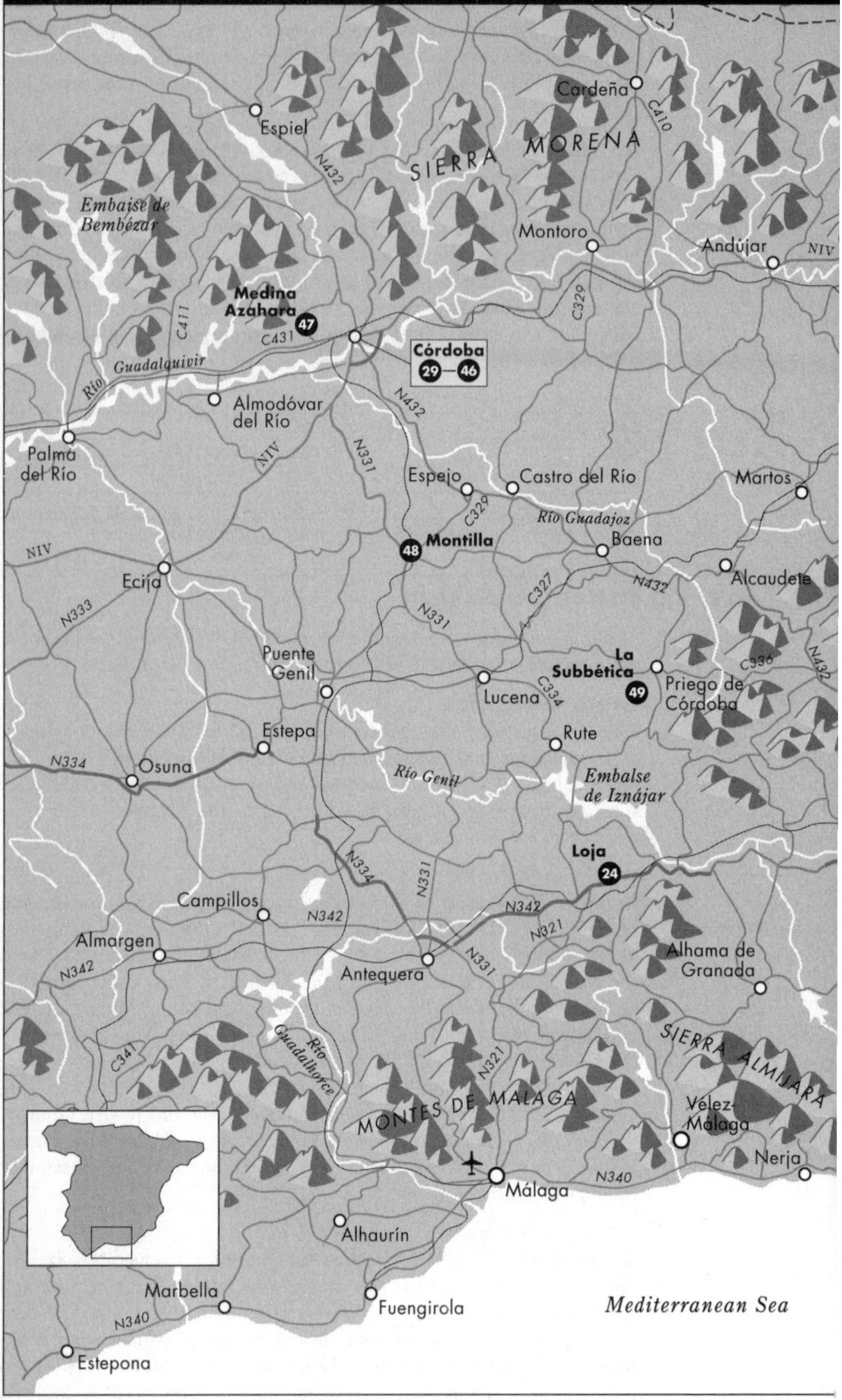

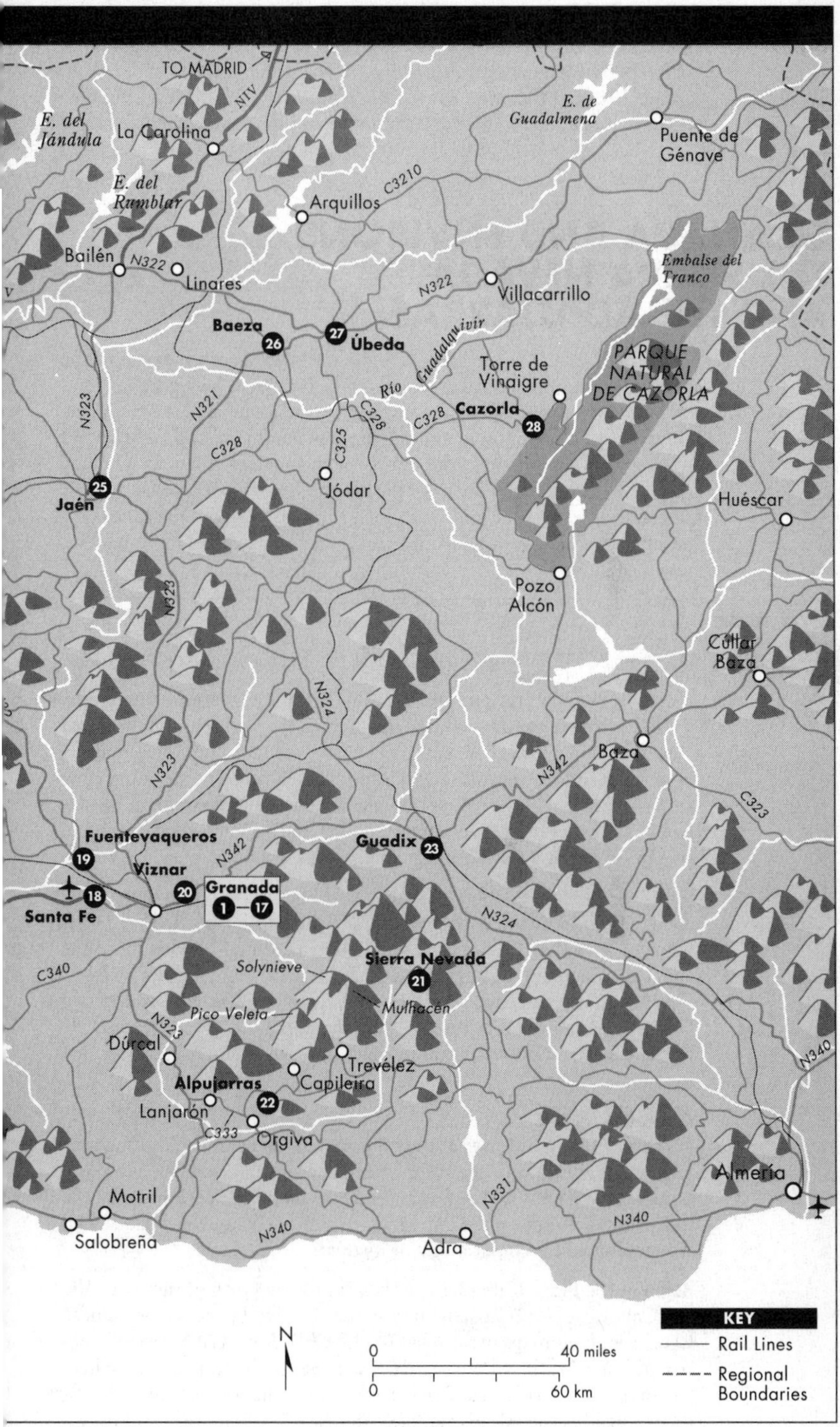
TO MADRID
NIV
E. del Jándula
La Carolina
E. del Rumblar
Arquillos
C3210
E. de Guadalmena
Puente de Génave
Bailén
N322
Linares
Villacarrillo
Embalse del Tranco
Baeza 26
27 Úbeda
Río Guadalquivir
Torre de Vinaigre
PARQUE NATURAL DE CAZORLA
Cazorla 28
N321
C328
C325
N323
25 Jaén
Jódar
Huéscar
Pozo Alcón
Cúllar Baza
N324
Baza
N342
C323
Fuentevaqueros 19
Víznar
20
Granada 1–17
18 Santa Fe
Guadix 23
C340
Solynieve
Sierra Nevada 21
Mulhacén
Pico Veleta
Dúrcal
Trevélez
Capileira
Alpujarras 22
Lanjarón
C333
Orgiva
N340
Motril
Salobreña
N331
Adra
Almería
KEY
Rail Lines
Regional Boundaries
N
0 40 miles
0 60 km

When to Tour Andalusia

Spring and autumn are the best times to come here. Summer can be stiflingly hot, especially in Córdoba; in winter, temperatures can drop to the 30s, and the wind off the Guadalquivir in Córdoba can be as stiff as any in New England. Note that most monuments close for the lunch hour, anywhere between 1:30 and 4, and most museums are closed on Monday.

GRANADA AND ENVIRONS, THE SIERRA NEVADA, AND THE ALPUJARRAS

The city of Granada, the last stronghold of the Moors, is home to the splendid hilltop Alhambra, replete with fountains, lush gardens, and once-luxurious baths. Next door, you can relax in the gardens of the Generalife; down in town, visit the tomb of Ferdinand and Isabella and weave your way through the streets of the ancient Albaicín. Outside the city rise the craggy peaks of the Sierra Nevada, seventh heaven for skiers; the picturesque and crafts-rich Alpujarra region; the cave communities of Guadix and Purullena; and the fantasy hotel La Bobadilla, near Loja.

Granada

★ ❶ *430 km (265 mi) south of Madrid, 261 km (162 mi) east of Córdoba.*

Granada rises lightly and majestically from a plain onto three hills, dwarfed—on a clear day—by the mighty snowcapped peaks of the Sierra Nevada. Atop one of these hills perches the pink-gold Alhambra palace, at once splendidly imposing and infinitely delicate. The stunning view from its mount takes in the sprawling ancient Moorish quarter, the Albaicín; the caves of the Sacromonte; and, in the distance, the fertile *vega,* rich in orchards, tobacco fields, and poplar groves.

Split by internal squabbles, Granada's Moorish Nasrid dynasty presented Ferdinand of Aragón with the chance he needed in 1491. Spurred by Isabella's religious fanaticism, Ferdinand laid siege to the city for seven months, and on January 2, 1492, Boabdil, the "Rey Chico" (Boy King), was forced to surrender the keys of the city to the triumphant Catholic Monarchs. As Boabdil fled the Alhambra by the Puerta de los Siete Suelos (Gate of the Seven Sighs), he asked that the gate be sealed forever.

A Good Walk

It's best to save a full day for the **Alhambra** ② and the neighboring sites on the Alhambra hill: the Alcazaba, Generalife, Alhambra Museum, **Casa-Museo de Manuel de Falla** ③, and **Carmen de los Mártires** ④. The following walk covers the *other* major spots in Granada's nucleus, and we recommend giving it a day of its own.

Begin at the Plaza Isabel La Católica (at the junction of the Gran Vía and Calle Reyes Católicos), with its statue of Columbus presenting Queen Isabella with his maps of the New World. Walk down Calle Reyes Católicos and turn left into the **Corral del Carbón** ⑤. The tourist office here has maps and brochures. Cross back over Calle Reyes Católicos: directly ahead is the **Alcaicería,** once the Arabs' silk market and now a maze of alleys packed with souvenir shops and restaurants. Turn left from the Alcaicería to reach the relaxed **Plaza Bib-Rambla,** with its flower stalls and the colorful Gran Café Bib-Rambla, the perfect place to grab an ice cream. From the northeast corner of the square, Calle Oficios

Granada

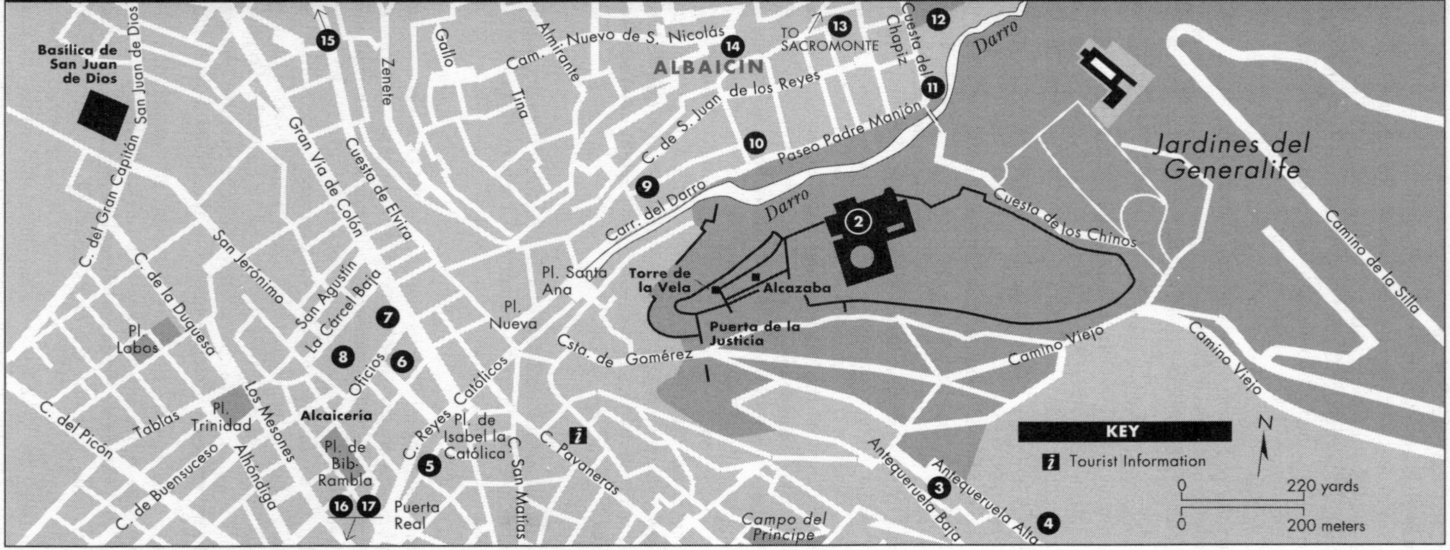

Albaicín **14**	Casa-Museo Federico García Lorca **17**	Monasterio de la Cartuja **15**
Alhambra **2**	Casa-Museo de Manuel de Falla **3**	Palacio de los Córdoba **11**
Capilla Real **7**	Cathedral **8**	Palacio Madraza . . . **6**
Carmen de los Mártires **4**	Corral del Carbón **5**	Parque de las Ciencias **16**
Casa de Castril . . . **10**	El Bañuelo **9**	Sacromonte **13**
Casa del Chapíz **12**		

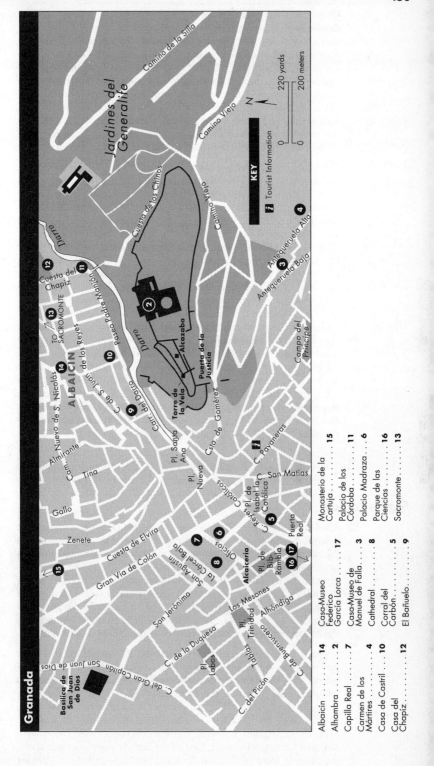

takes you to the **Palacio Madraza** ⑥, the old Arab University, and the **Capilla Real** ⑦, next to which is the **cathedral** ⑧. Just outside the cathedral's west front is the 16th-century **Escuela de las Niñas Nobles,** with a plateresque facade. Next to the cathedral, along the Plaza de Alonzo Cano, are the impressive **Curia Eclesiástica,** used as an Imperial College until 1769; the **Palacio del Arzobispo**; and the 18th-century Iglesia de Sagrario, with Corinthian columns. Behind the cathedral is the Gran Vía de Colón, named after Columbus, one of Granada's main thoroughfares. This artery was built in the late 19th century in an effort to modernize cross-town transportation; unfortunately, several wonderful old palaces were destroyed in the process.

Cross the Gran Vía and head right, back to the Plaza de Isabel la Católica; turn left to reach the Plaza Nueva, overlooked by the 16th-century **Real Cancillería** (Royal Chancery), which now houses the Tribunal Superior de Justicia (High Court). Artisans have set up shops in the surrounding area. At the north end of the plaza is the adjacent Plaza Santa Ana, where you'll find the church of **Santa Ana,** designed by Diego de Siloé. Walk north through the Plaza Santa Ana onto Carrera del Darro and you'll reach the 11th-century Arab bathhouse, **El Bañuelo** ⑨. Just up Carrera del Darro is the 16th-century **Casa de Castril** ⑩, which houses Granada's Archaeological Museum. Follow the river along the Paseo del Padre Manjón—also known as the Paseo de los Tristes—to the end, and have a look at the **Palacio de los Córdoba** ⑪. Head north up the Cuesta del Chapíz to the Morisco **Casa del Chapíz** ⑫. East of here are the caves of the **Sacromonte** ⑬, which require a special expedition by minibus. For now, turn west and plunge into the narrow streets of the ancient Moorish quarter, the **Albaicín** ⑭. Granada's other major sights are just outside town and best reached by car or taxi: 2 km (1 mi) north of the city center, off Calle Real de Cartuja, is the 16th-century Baroque **Monasterio de La Cartuja** ⑮. To the south are the **Parque de las Ciencias** ⑯, an interactive science museum, and **Casa-Museo Federico García Lorca** ⑰.

TIMING

This walk takes the better part of a day. Again, it does not include the Alhambra hill, for which we recommend a separate day.

Sights to See

⓮ **Albaicín.** Covering a hill of its own, across the Darro ravine from the Alhambra, this ancient Moorish neighborhood is a fascinating mix of dilapidated white houses and immaculate *carmenes* (private villas in gardens enclosed by high walls). It was founded in 1228 by Moors expelled from Baeza after that city was captured by the Saint King Ferdinand. Full of intriguing cobbled alleyways and secret corners, the Albaicín guards its old Moorish atmosphere jealously, though its 30 mosques were long since converted to Baroque churches. A stretch of the Moors' original city wall runs beside the Cuesta de la Alhacaba.

If you're walking—the best way to explore this neighborhood—you can enter the Albaicín from either the Cuesta de Elvira or the Plaza Nueva. (On Cuesta de Elvira and the adjoining Calderería, be sure to try one of the delightful tea shops; thanks to its Moorish heritage, Granada serves some of the best mint tea in all of Spain.) Alternately, on foot or by car (take a taxi, as parking is impossible), begin in the Plaza Santa Ana and follow the Carrera del Darro, Paseo Padre Manjón, and Cuesta del Chapiz. One of the highest points in the quarter, the plaza in front of the church of San Nicolás—called the **Mirador de San Nicolás**—has one of the finest views in all of Granada: on the hill opposite, the turrets and towers of the ocher Alhambra form a dramatic silhouette against the snowy peaks of the Sierra Nevada. The sight is most magical at dawn, dusk, and on nights when the Alhambra is floodlit.

★ ❷ **Alhambra.** Walking *to* the Alhambra can be as inspiring as walking *around* it. If you're up to a long, scenic approach, start in the Plaza Nueva and climb the Cuesta de Gomerez—through the slopes of green elms planted by the Duke of Wellington—to reach the **Puerta de las Granadas** (Pomegranate Gate), a Renaissance gateway built by Charles V and topped by three pomegranates, symbols of Granada. Just past the gate, take the path branching off to the left to the **Puerta de la Justicia** (Gate of Justice), one of the Alhambra's entrances. Yusuf I built the gate in 1348; on its two arches are carved a key and a hand, with the five fingers representing the five laws of the Koran.

Unless you've already bought a ticket (☞ *below*), continue up the hill along the Alhambra's's outer walls to the parking lot and the adjacent ticket office. If you're driving, you'll approach the Alhambra from the opposite direction; just be warned that parking here is expensive, and the lot has virtually no shade. It's more convenient to take a taxi, or the minibus that runs from the Plaza Nueva every 15 minutes.

The Alhambra was begun in the 1240s by Ibn el-Ahmar, or Alhamar, the first king of the Nasrids. The great citadel once comprised an entire complex of houses, schools, baths, barracks, and gardens surrounded by defense towers and seemingly impregnable walls. Today, only the Alcazaba fortress and the Nasrid Royal Palace, built chiefly by Yusuf I (1334–54) and his son Mohammed V (1354–91), remain. The palace is an endless, intricate fantasy of patios, arches, and cupolas fashioned from wood, plaster, and tile; lavishly colored and adorned with marquetry and ceramics in geometric patterns; and surmounted by delicate, frothy profusions of lacelike stucco and *mocárabes* (ornamental stalactites). Built of perishable materials, it was never intended to last, but to be forever replaced and replenished by succeeding generations.

By the early 17th century, ruin and decay had set in, and the Alhambra was abandoned by all but tramps and stray dogs. Napoléon's troops commandeered it in 1812, but their attempts to blow it up were, happily, foiled. In 1814, the Alhambra's fortunes rose with the arrival of the Duke of Wellington, who came here to escape the pressures of the Peninsular War. Soon afterward, in 1829, Washington Irving arrived to live on the premises and helped revive interest in the crumbling palace, in part through his 1832 book *Tales of the Alhambra*. In 1862, Granada finally launched a complete restoration program that has been carried on ever since.

Across from the main entrance is the original fortress, the **Alcazaba.** Its ruins are dominated by the **Torre de la Vela** (Watchtower), whose summit offers superlative views of the city—to the north, the Albaicín; to the northeast, the Sacromonte; and to the west, the cathedral. The tower's great bell was once used, by both the Moors and the Christians, to announce the opening and closing of the irrigation system on Granada's great plain.

The Renaissance **Palacio de Carlos V** (Palace of Charles V), with a perfectly square exterior but a circular interior courtyard, stands imposing but totally incongruous on the site where the sultans' private apartments once stood. Designed by Pedro Machuca—a pupil of Michelangelo—and begun in 1526, the palace was once used for bullfights and mock tournaments. Today, its perfect acoustics make it a fine setting for summer symphony concerts during Granada's International

The Alhambra

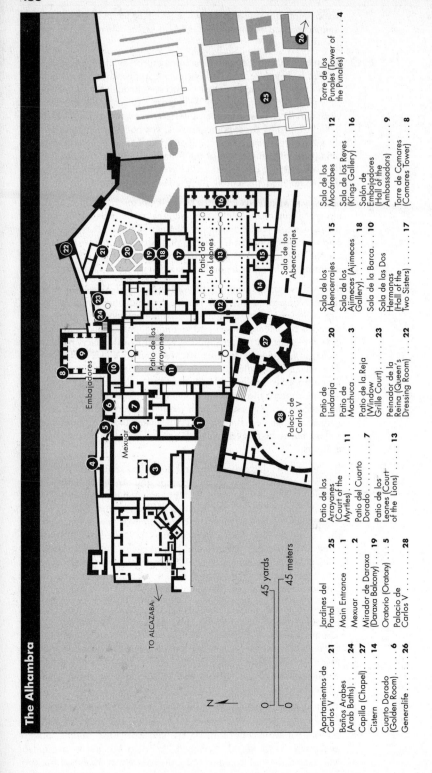

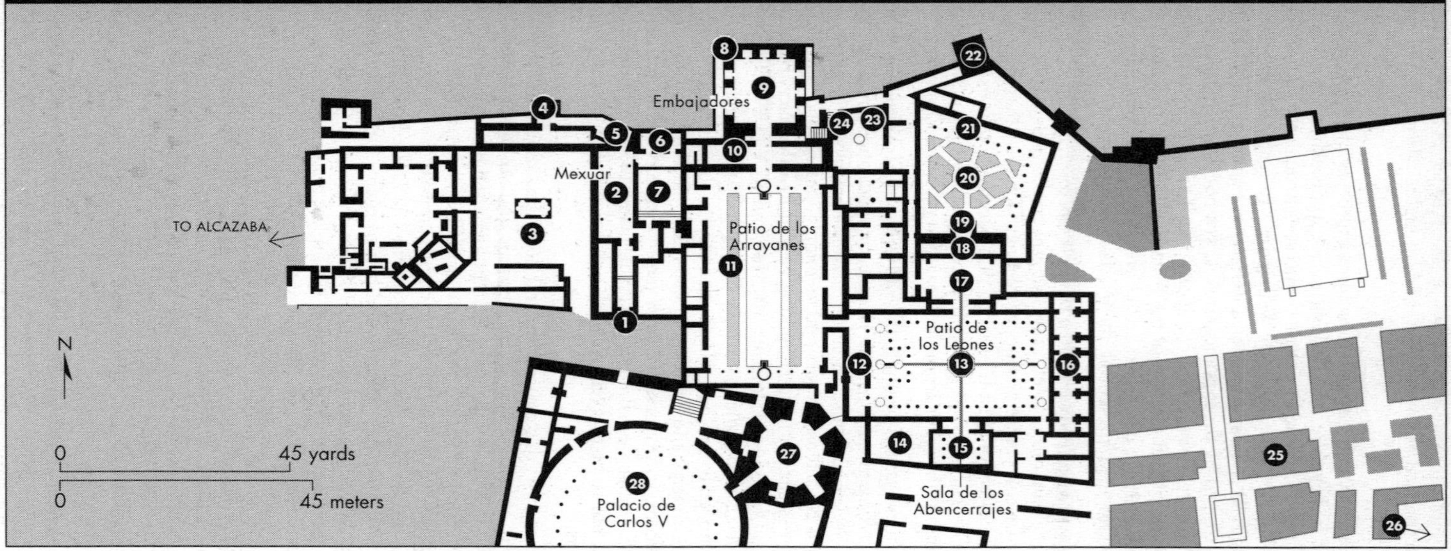

Place	Key
Apartamientos de Carlos V	21
Baños Arabes (Arab Baths)	24
Capilla (Chapel)	27
Cistern	14
Cuarto Dorado (Golden Room)	6
Generalife	26
Jardines del Partal	25
Main Entrance	1
Mexuar	2
Mirador de Daraxa (Daraxa Balcony)	19
Oratorio (Oratory)	5
Palacio de Carlos V	28
Patio de los Arrayanes (Court of the Myrtles)	11
Patio del Cuarto Dorado	7
Patio de los Leones (Court of the Lions)	13
Patio de Lindaraja	20
Patio de Machuca	3
Patio de la Reja (Window Grille Court)	23
Peinador de la Reina (Queen's Dressing Room)	22
Sala de los Abencerrajes	15
Sala de los Ajimeces (Ajimeces Gallery)	18
Sala de la Barca	10
Sala de las Dos Hermanas (Hall of the Two Sisters)	17
Sala de los Mocárabes	12
Sala de los Reyes (Kings Gallery)	16
Salón de Embajadores (Hall of the Ambassadors)	9
Torre de Comares (Comares Tower)	8
Torre de los Punales (Tower of the Punales)	4

Festival of Music and Dance. Part of the building houses the **Museo de la Alhambra,** devoted to Islamic art; it's open Tuesday through Saturday 9–2:30. Upstairs is the more modest **Museo de Bellas Artes** (Museum of Fine Arts), open Wednesday through Saturday 9–6, Sunday 9–2:30, and Tuesday 2:30–6. You can visit the Palace of Charles V and the museums independent of the Alhambra, and admission is free.

A wisteria-covered walkway leads to the heart of the Alhambra, the **Palacios Nazaries** (Nasrid Royal Palace), sometimes also called the Casa Real (Royal Palace). Here, delicate apartments, lazy fountains, and tranquil pools contrast vividly with the hulking fortifications outside, and the interior walls are decorated with elaborately carved inscriptions from the Koran. The Royal Palace is divided into three sections. The first is the *mexuar,* where business, government, and palace administration were headquartered. These chambers include the Oratory and the Cuarto Dorado (Golden Room); don't miss the views of the Albaicín and Sacromonte from their windows.

The *serrallo* is a series of state rooms where the sultans held court and entertained their ambassadors. In the heart of the *serrallo* is the **Patio de los Arrayanes** (Court of the Myrtles), with a long goldfish pool surrounded by shrubs. At its northern end, in the **Salón de Embajadores** (Hall of the Ambassadors)—which has a magnificent cedar door—Boabdil signed the terms of surrender and Queen Isabella received Christopher Columbus.

The final section is the **harem,** which in its time was entered only by the sultan, his family, and their most trusted servants, most of them eunuchs. To reach it, you'll pass through the **Sala de los Mocárabes** (Hall of the Mocárabes, or ornamental stalactites): note the splendid, though damaged, ceiling, followed by your first glimpse of stalactite stonework in the arches above. The postcard-perfect **Patio de los Leones** (Court of the Lions) is the heart of the harem. From the fountain in the center, 12 lions, which may represent the months or signs of the zodiac, leer out at today's tourists. Four streams flow symbolically to the four corners of the earth and more literally to the surrounding state apartments.

The **Sala de los Abencerrajes** (Hall of the Moors), on the south side of the palace, may be the Alhambra's most beautiful gallery, with a stalactite ceiling and a star-shaped cupola reflected in the pool below. Here Boabdil's father is alleged to have massacred 16 members of the Abencerrajes family—whose chief was the lover of his own favorite, Zoraya—and piled their bloodstained heads in this font.

The **Sala de los Reyes** (Kings' Hall) lies on the patio's east side, decorated with ceiling frescoes that may have been painted by Christians in the last days of the Moors' tenure. To the north, the **Sala de las Dos Hermanas** (Hall of the Two Sisters) was the abode of the king's favorite. Its name comes from the two white-marble slabs in its floor, and its ceiling is resplendent with some of the Alhambra's most superb stucco work, an intricate pattern of honeycomb cells. Note the symmetrically placed pomegranates on the walls.

The **Baños Arabes,** the Alhambra's semi-subterranean bathhouse, is where the sultan's favorites luxuriated in baths of brightly tiled mosaic and performed their ablutions lit by star-shaped pinpoints of light from the ceiling above. The baths are currently closed to the public, but you can catch a glimpse of them through the door.

The **Generalife** was the ancient summer palace of the Nasrid kings. It stands on the Cerro del Sol (Hill of the Sun), and its name comes from the Arabic Gennat Alarif—Garden of the Architect. The terraces and promenades here grant incomparable views of the city, stretching away to the distant *vega.* During summer's International Festival of Music and Dance, these stately cypresses are the backdrop for evening ballets in the Generalife amphitheater. Between the Generalife and the Alhambra is the 16th-century convent of San Francisco, now one of the most luxurious paradors in Spain (☞ Dining and Lodging, *below*).

With nearly 2 million visitors a year, the Alhambra is Spain's most popular attraction. In an effort to contain the crowds, the monument restricts admission to the Nasrid Royal Palace to 350 people every half hour and sometimes closes rooms or sections for restoration. You can buy tickets when you arrive if they're available, but you're better off reserving them in advance through the Banco Bilbao Vizcaya (BBV) for a 125-pta. surcharge. Same-day tickets are sold at the BBV branch on Plaza Isabel Católica 1, or you can reserve by phone or at any BBV branch up to a year in advance. (By phone, you pay by Visa or MasterCard, then pick up your tickets at any BBV branch when you arrive in Spain.) Your ticket will show the half-hour time slot for your entry; once inside, you can stay as long as you like. On busy days, you may have several hours to spare before your visit to the interior palaces, in which case you can spend the interim visiting the Generalife, the Alcazaba, the Alhambra Museum, and the Fine Arts Museum. There might even be enough time to walk to the charming Casa-Museo de Manuel de Falla and the Carmen de los Mártires, and to have lunch at one of the restaurants on the Alhambra hill.

For an entirely different (and calmer) perspective, come back for a floodlit tour of the Alhambra at night. ✉ *Cuesta de Gomérez,* ☎ *958/220584 or 958/220912. Advance ticket sales (BBV):* ☎ *902/224460 within Spain,* ☎ *91/374–5420 from outside Spain.* *Alhambra and Generalife 1,000 ptas.* ⏲ *Mar.–Oct., Mon.–Sat. 9–8, Sun. 9–7; floodlit visits Tues., Thurs., and Sat. 10 PM–midnight. Nov.–Feb., daily 8:30–6; floodlit visits Fri. and Sat. 8 PM–9:30 PM. Ticket office opens 30 min before opening time and closes 1 hr before closing time.*

★ ❼ **Capilla Real (Royal Chapel).** The Royal Chapel is a shrine of local history second only to the Alhambra, as it is the burial place of the momentous Catholic Monarchs, Isabella of Castile and Ferdinand of Aragón. The couple originally planned to be buried in Toledo's San Juan de los Reyes, but Isabella changed her mind when the pair conquered Granada in 1492. When she died, in 1504, her body was first laid to rest in the Convent of San Francisco (now the parador), on the Alhambra hill. The architect Enrique Egas began work on the Royal Chapel in 1506 and completed it 15 years later; it is a masterpiece of the ornate Gothic style now known in Spain as Isabelline. In 1521 Isabella's body was brought to a simple lead coffin in the Royal Chapel crypt, where it was joined by that of her husband, Ferdinand, and later her unfortunate daughter, Juana la Loca (Joan the Mad), and son-in-law, Felipe el Hermoso (Philip the Handsome). Felipe died young, and Juana had his casket borne about the peninsula with her for years, opening the lid each night to kiss her embalmed spouse good night. A small coffin to the right contains the remains of Prince Felipe of Asturias, a grandson of the Catholic Monarchs and nephew of Juana la Loca who died in his infancy. (Had he lived longer, he would have inherited the throne.) The underground crypt containing the five lead coffins is quite simple, but above it are the elaborate marble tombs showing Ferdinand and Isabella lying side-by-side; these were commissioned by their grandson Charles V and fashioned by the sculptor Domenico Fancelli. The altarpiece, by Felipe Vigarini (1522), consists of 34 carved panels depicting religious and historical scenes. The bottom row shows Boabdil surrendering the keys of the city to its conquerors and the forced baptism of the defeated Moors. In the sacristy are Ferdinand's sword, Isabella's crown and scepter, and a fine collection of Flemish paintings once owned by Isabella. ✉ *Oficios,* ☎ *958/229239.* 🎟 *300 ptas.* ⏲ *Mar.–Sept., daily 10:30–1 and 4–7; Oct.–Feb., Mon.–Sat. 10:30–1 and 3:30–6:30, Sun. 11–1 and 3:30–6:30.*

4 **Carmen de los Mártires.** Located just up the hill from the Hotel Alhambra Palace, this elegant turn-of-the-century Granada *carmen* (villa) and its gardens are like a Generalife in miniature. ✉ *Paseo de los Mártires,* ☎ *958/227953.* 🎟 *Free.* ⏲ *Mon.–Sat. 10–2 and 5–7 (4–6 Mar.–Sept.), Sun. 2–6.*

10 **Casa de Castril.** A richly decorated 16th-century palace, this *casa* once belonged to Bernardo Zafra, secretary to Queen Isabella. Before you enter, notice the exquisite portal, and the facade carved with scallop shells and a phoenix. Inside is the **Museo Arqueológico** (Archaeological Museum), where you'll find a beautiful Moorish room with original furnishings; Phoenician burial urns from Almuñécar, on Granada's coast; and artifacts from provincial caves. ✉ *Carrera del Darro 41,* ☎ *958/225640.* 🎟 *250 ptas.; EU citizens free.* ⏲ *Wed.–Sat. 9–8, Sun. 9–2:30; Tues. tour groups only.*

NEED A BREAK? The park at **Paseo Padre Manjón,** along the Darro River—also known as the Paseo de los Tristes (Promenade of the Sad)—is a terrific place for a coffee break. Dappled with fountains and stone walkways, the park has a stunning view of the Alhambra's northern side.

12 **Casa del Chapíz.** This fine 16th-century Morisco house has a delightful garden. It houses the School of Arabic Studies and is not generally open to the public, but if you knock, the caretaker might show you around. ✉ *Cuesta del Chapiz at Camino del Sacromonte.*

3 **Casa-Museo de Manuel de Falla.** The composer Manuel de Falla lived and worked for many years in this rustic house, which is tucked into a charming little hillside lane with stunning views of the Alpujarra mountains. The house is now a small museum. In 1986 Granada finally paid homage to Spain's classical champion by naming its new concert hall the Auditorio Manuel de Falla. ✉ *C. Antequeruela Alta 11,* ☎ *958/229421.* 🎟 *250 ptas.* ⏲ *Tues.–Sat. 10–3.*

17 **Casa-Museo Federico García Lorca.** Granada's most famous native son, the poet Federico García Lorca, gets his due here, in the middle of a new park on the southern fringe of the city. The poet's onetime summer home, **La Huerta de San Vicente,** is now a museum—run by the poet's nice, Laura García Lorca—with such artifacts as the poet's beloved piano and temporary exhibits on specific aspects of Lorca's life. ✉ *Parque García Lorca, C. Arabial,* ☎ *958/258466.* 🎟 *300 ptas.; free Wed.* ⏲ *Oct.–Apr., Tues.–Sun. 10–1 and 4–7; May–Sept., Tues.–Sun. 10–1 and 5–8. Guided tours every half-hour until 30 mins before closing.*

8 **Cathedral.** Granada's cathedral was commissioned in 1521 by Charles V, who considered the Royal Chapel "too small for so much glory" and determined to house his illustrious late grandparents someplace more worthy. Charles undoubtedly had great designs, as the cathedral was created by some of the finest architects of its time: Enrique Egas, Diego de Siloé, Alonso Cano, and sculptor Juan de Mena. But his ambitions came to little, for the cathedral is a grandiose and gloomy monument, not completed until 1714 and never used as the crypt of

his parents *or* grandparents. You enter through a small door at the back, off the Gran Vía. ✉ *Gran Vía s/n,* ☎ *958/222959.* 🎫 *300 ptas.* ⏲ *Mar.–Sept., Mon.–Sat. 10:30–1 and 4–7, Sun. 4–7; Oct.–Feb., Mon.–Sat. 10:30–1:30 and 3:30–6:30, Sun. 3:30–6.*

5 **Corral del Carbón** (Coal House). This building was used to store coal in the 19th century, but it's actually one of the oldest Moorish buildings in the city. Dating from the 14th century, when Moorish merchants used it as a lodging house and stored their goods on the upper floor, it's the only Arab inn of its kind in Spain. It was later used by Christians as a theater, but it has been expertly restored and now houses the regional tourist office. Grapevines climb the walls. ✉ *C. Mariana Pineda,* ☎ *958/225990.* 🎫 *Free.* ⏲ *Mon.–Sat. 9–8, Sun. 10–2.*

9 **El Bañuelo** (Little Bath House). These 11th-century Arab steam baths may be a little dark and dank now, but try to imagine them filled, some 900 years ago, with Moorish beauties, backed by bright ceramic tiles, tapestries, and rugs on the dull brick walls. Light comes in through star-shaped vents in the ceiling, à la the bathhouse in the Alhambra. ✉ *Carrera del Darro 31,* ☎ *958/222339.* 🎫 *Free.* ⏲ *Tues.–Sat. 10–2.*

15 **Monasterio de La Cartuja.** This Carthusian monastery in northern Granada (2 km/1 mi from the center) was begun in 1506 and moved to its present site in 1516, though construction continued for the next 300 years. In time, it became one of the most outstanding Baroque buildings in Andalusia. The exterior is somewhat sober and monolithic, but when you enter the church and see its twisted, multicolor marble columns; profusion of gold, silver, tortoiseshell, and ivory; intricate stucco; and extravagant Churrigueresque sacristy, you'll see why Cartuja has been called the Christian answer to the Alhambra. ✉ *Camino de Alfacar,* ☎ *958/161932.* 🎫 *300 ptas.* ⏲ *May–Sept., Mon.–Sat. 10–1 and 4–7, Sun. 10–noon; Oct.–Apr., Mon.–Sat. 10–1 and 3:30–6, Sun. 10–noon.*

11 **Palacio de los Córdoba.** This palace, at the end of the Paseo Padre Manjón, was a noble house of the 17th century. Today it houses Granada's municipal archives and is used for municipal functions and art exhibits. You're free to wander the large garden.

6 **Palacio Madraza.** This building conceals the old Moorish university, built in 1349 by Yusuf I. The Baroque facade is dark and intriguing; inside, across from the entrance, an octagonal room is crowned by a Moorish dome. The building is now an exhibition and cultural center, open only for special exhibits. ✉ *Oficiose,* ☎ *958/223447.* 🎫 *Free.*

16 **Parque de las Ciencias** (Science Park). Across from Granada's convention center, this hands-on museum features interactive exhibits, scientific experiments, and a planetarium. ✉ *Avda. del Mediterráneo,* ☎ *958/131900.* 🎫 *400 ptas.; planetarium, 250 ptas.* ⏲ *Tues.–Sat. 10–7, Sun. 10–3.*

13 **Sacromonte.** The third of Granada's three hills, the Sacromonte rises behind the Albaicín, dotted with prickly pear cacti and riddled with caverns. These caves may have sheltered early Christians; 15th-century treasure hunters found a collection of bones inside and assumed they belonged to San Cecilio, the city's patron saint. Thus the hill was sanctified—*sacro monte* (holy mountain)—and an abbey built on its summit. The **Abadía de Sacromonte** (✉ Camino del Sacromonte, 958/221445) is open Tuesday through Saturday 11–1 and 4–6, Sunday noon–1 and 4–6 (closed Mon.); guided tours are every half hour; admission is 300 ptas.

The Sacromonte is the domain of Granada's Roma (Gypsies). Though fewer and fewer Roma actually live on the hill, a good number still earn a healthy living there fleecing tourists. The flamenco shows they stage are generally abysmal, the drinks watered down, and the prices vastly inflated for performances that are not so very *auténtico*. The shows are certainly colorful, and they do provide a chance to venture inside the famous *cuevas* (caves). Richly colored rugs and gleaming copper utensils adorn the interiors—as do such modern conveniences as refrigerators and dishwashers. On summer evenings, enterprising Granadinos run minibus tours to the Gypsy caves; your hotel can often put you in touch. Though not cheap, a tour may be the safest way to visit the Sacromonte, and it usually includes a drink in the Albaicín first.

Dining and Lodging

$$$ ✕ **Cunini.** Around the corner from the cathedral is Granada's best fish house. Fresh seafood is heaped on the long tapas bar, and the menu gathers fish dishes from all over Spain, including some Basque specialties. Both the *pescaditos fritos* (fried) and the *parrillada* (grilled) fish are good choices, and if it's chilly you can warm up with *zarzuela* (fish stew). There are tables outdoors in warm weather. ✉ *Pescadería 14,* ☎ *958/250777. AE, DC, MC, V. Closed Mon.*

$$$ ★ ✕ **Ruta del Veleta.** Just over 5 km (3 mi) out of town, in Cenes de la Vega, this traditionally decorated restaurant serves some of Granada's best cuisine. The many house specialties include *carnes a la brasa* (succulent grilled meats) and fish dishes from Cantabria and the Levante cooked in rock salt, as well as regional dishes like *jabalí estilo mozárabe* (wild boar cooked with apples). Dessert might be pudding *de manzanas en salsa de moras* (apple pudding in blackberry sauce). ✉ *Carretera Sierra Nevada, Km 5.4,* ☎ *958/486134. AE, DC, MC, V. No dinner Sun.*

$$ ✕ **La Mimbre.** Location, location, location: this small, slightly cramped lunch spot is tucked right under the walls of the Alhambra, next to the Generalife. Inside, you sit on chairs upholstered with typical Alpujarran fabric; outside, the spacious patio is shady, romantic, and delightful in warm weather. The food is classically Granadino: *habas con jamón* (broad beans and ham) and *choto al ajillo* (braised kid with garlic). ✉ *Avda. del Generalife,* ☎ *958/222276. AE, MC, V. Closed Sat. No dinner.*

$$ ✕ **Los Manueles.** This ancient tavern is usually packed. The food is not remarkable—*tortilla al Sacromonte,* and other local fare—but the decor, atmosphere, and friendly waiters make this inn off Reyes Católicos popular with both Granadinos and travelers. Alpujarran rugs, ceramic plates, and other knickknacks cover the walls, and a ceramic plaque commemorates a visit from Spain's royal family in 1982. Gigantic hams adorn the bar. ✉ *Zaragoza 2,* ☎ *958/223413. AE, DC, MC, V.*

$$ ★ ✕ **Sevilla.** This colorful, central, two-story restaurant has been going strong since 1930 and has fed the likes of de Falla and García Lorca over the years. There's a small but superb tapas bar and four picturesque dining rooms; you can also dine on an outdoor terrace overlooking the Royal Chapel. The menu features such Granadino favorites as *sopa sevillana* and *tortilla al Sacromonte* (omelet with kid's brains, ham, and vegetables). ✉ *Oficios 12,* ☎ *958/221223. AE, DC, MC, V. Closed Mon. No dinner Sun.*

$$ ✕ **Velázquez.** On a side street one block west of the Puerta de Elvira and Plaza del Triunfo, this cozy, very Spanish restaurant has long been popular with locals. At street level is a brick-wall bar hung with hams; the intimate, wood-beam dining room is upstairs. Specialities include *zancarrón cordero a la miel* (lamb with honey) and *lomitos de rape* (braised monkfish medallions). ✉ *Emilio Orozco 1,* ☎ *958/289109. MC, V. Closed Sun.*

$$$ ✕🏨 **Triunfo.** This comfortable hotel is at the far end of the Gran Vía de Colón. The public rooms have gleaming marble floors, deep sofas, and copious paintings; guest rooms are traditional, with dark wood and pink or light-green curtains and bedspreads. The handsome Puerta

Elvira Restaurant serves typical Andalusian dishes. ✉ *Plaza Triunfo 19, 18010,* ☎ *958/207444,* FAX *958/279017. 37 rooms. Restaurant, cafeteria, parking (fee). AE, DC, MC, V.*

$$ **Reina Cristina.** Occupying the former Rosales residence, where the poet Lorca was arrested after taking refuge here when the Spanish Civil War broke out, the Reina Cristina is near the lively and central Plaza de la Trinidad. Plants trail from the windowsills of the reception area, a covered patio where a small marble fountain splashes beneath a Moorish lamp; and a marble stairway leads to the bedrooms, which are simply but cheerfully furnished with red fabrics on a white background. The restaurant, El Rincón de Lorca, is one of the best in Granada, serving tasty renditions of classic local dishes in a setting reminiscent of an elegant old home. ✉ *Tablas 4, 18002,* ☎ *958/253211,* FAX *958/255728. 43 rooms. Restaurant, bar, cafeteria. AE, DC, MC, V.*

$$$$ ★ **Alhambra Palace.** A flamboyant, ocher-red, neo-Moorish pile, this 1910 hotel commands a superb position on leafy grounds at the back of the Alhambra hill. The interior is exotic, very Arabian Nights, with orange and brown overtones, multicolor tiles, and Moorish arches and pillars. Even the bar is incongruously decorated as a mosque. The rooms overlooking the town have incredible views, as does the terrace, a perfect place to watch the sun set on the city of Granada and its fertile *vega.* ✉ *Peña Partida 2, 18009,* ☎ *958/221468,* FAX *958/226404. 122 rooms, 13 suites. Restaurant, 2 bars. AE, DC, MC, V.*

$$$$ ★ **Parador de San Francisco.** Magnificently set within the Alhambra precincts, Spain's most popular parador occupies an old Franciscan convent built by the Catholic Monarchs after they captured Granada. The rooms in the old section are furnished with antiques, woven curtains, and bedspreads; those in the new wing are simpler. Reserve four to six months in advance. ✉ *Alhambra, 18009,* ☎ *958/221440,* FAX *958/222264. 36 rooms. Restaurant, bar. AE, DC, MC, V.*

$$$–$$$$ **Palacio de Santa Inés.** The chief attraction of this small lodging is its special location in the heart of the Albaicín. The setting is a converted 16th-century palace centered on a frescoed courtyard. The rooms occupy the two upper floors, and each is uniquely decorated with tasteful antiques and low-key modern art. Some of the suites have balconies with Alhambra views. The same managers have a similar, even smaller hotel nearby, Carmen de Santa Inés. ✉ *Cuesta de Santa Inés 9, 18010,* ☎ *958/222362,* FAX *958/222465. 7 rooms, 6 suites. AE, DC, MC, V.*

$$$ **Inglaterra.** Just two blocks east of the Gran Vía de Colón, in the heart of town, this hotel combines the best of three worlds: a central location, a 19th-century house with an old-world facade, and a modern, comfortable interior. The lounges have polished wood floors; guest rooms are carpeted and painted a pleasing salmon color, with contemporary blond-wood furniture. ✉ *Cetti Meriem 4, 18010,* ☎ *958/221558,* FAX *958/227100. 36 rooms. Restaurant, meeting rooms, parking (fee). AE, DC, MC, V.*

$$$ **Tryp Albayzin.** Located on the tree-lined Carrera del Genil, the Tryp is next to El Corte Inglés department store and well placed for general downtown shopping. Decor in the common areas and the large, air-conditioned guest rooms is a tasteful modern-Moorish, light and airy. The inner patio comes complete with an Alhambra-style trickling fountain. ✉ *Carrera del Genil 48, 18005,* ☎ *958/220002,* FAX *958/220181. 108 rooms. Restaurant, sauna, parking (fee). AE, DC, MC, V.*

$$ **Alixares.** Large and modern but not unattractive, the Alixares has a prime location between the Alhambra and the Generalife. The cream-color rooms are modern and functional; those on the fourth and fifth floors have the best views. The staff is friendly and professional. In summer, the rooftop barbecue is an added dining option. ✉ *Avda. Alixares del Generalife, 18009,* ☎ *958/225575,* FAX *958/224102. 176 rooms. Restaurant, cafeteria, pool, meeting rooms. AE, DC, MC, V.*

$$ **América.** This simple but charming hotel within the Alhambra precincts is very popular, albeit more for the unbeatable location than for the service. Reserve months in advance. The place feels like a private home, with simple bedrooms, a sitting room decorated with local handicrafts, and a shaded patio where home-cooked meals are served in summer. ✉ *Real de la Alhambra 53, 18009,* ☎ *958/227471,* FAX *958/227470. 13 rooms. Restaurant. MC, V. Closed Dec.–Feb.*

$ **Suecia.** This modest, laid-back hostelry occupies a villa tucked into a quiet residential alley, not far from the Campo de Príncipe and some of Granada's most popular taverns. The atmosphere is friendly and informal. Rooms vary in size, so you may want to look at several if offered a choice. ✉ *Huerta de los Angeles 8 (off C. Molinos), 18009,* ☎ *958/227781,* ☎ FAX *958/225044. 12 rooms, 8 with bath. MC, V.*

Nightlife and the Arts

Granada's large student population makes for a lively bar scene. Some of the trendiest bars are in converted houses in the Albaicín, on the Paseo de los Tristes (next to the Darro River, between the Plaza Nueva and the Albaicín), and in the modern part of town, on Pedro Antonio de Alarcon and Martinez de la Rosa. Another gathering place is the Campo del Príncipe, a large plaza surrounded by typical Andalusian taverns. The **Granada 10** (✉ Carcel Baja 10, ☎ 958/224001), in the Albaicín, is a former theater converted into a discotheque.

Get the latest on arts events, including diversions for young people, at the **Area de Bienestar Social Cultura y Juventud** (City Department of Social Welfare, Culture, and Youth), in the Palacio de los Condes de Gabia (✉ Plaza de los Girones 1, ☎ 958/247383). Plays are performed at the **Teatro Alhambra** (✉ Molinos 56, ☎ 958/220447). Granada's orchestra performs often in the **Centro Cultural Manuel de Falla** (✉ Paseo de los Mártires, ☎ 958/222188).

Granada's **International Theater Festival,** organized by Granada's *ayuntamiento* (town hall; ✉ Plaza del Carmen, ☎ 958/229344), fills 10 days each May. The **International Festival of Music and Dance** (☎ 958/276200; tickets ☎ 958/221844) is held annually from mid-June to mid-July; tickets are available at the Corral del Carbón on Mariana Pineda, one block from Reyes Católicos. Contact the tourist office for information on the **November Jazz Festival.**

The flamenco show at **Jardines Neptuno** (✉ C. Arabial, ☎ 958/522533 or 958/251112), though tourist-oriented, can be colorful and often includes a mixture of ballet and folk music. There's a similar show nightly in the somewhat smaller **Reina Mora** (✉ Mirador de San Cristóbal, ☎ 958/401265). Many hotels have tickets. Flamenco is also performed at **El Corral del Príncipe** (✉ Campo del Príncipe, ☎ 958/228088). Never come here before 11 PM; things peak around 1 AM. For *zambra* (song and dance) performances by Gypsies in the Sacromonte caves, join a tour through a travel agent or your hotel. If you want to go on your own, try **El Museo de María la Canastera** (✉ Camino del Sacromonte 89, ☎ 958/121183) or **Cueva los Tarantos** (✉ Camino del Sacromonte 9, ☎ 958/224525). Call ahead for performance times, and be prepared to part with lots of money.

Shopping

Granada's handicrafts are very much a legacy of the Moors, whose aesthetic influence shows up in brass and copperware, ceramics, marquetry, and woven textiles. The main shopping streets, centering on the Puerta Real, are **Reyes Católicos, Zacatín, Ángel Ganivet,** and the **Gran Vía de Colón.** Most of the antiques stores are on **Cuesta de Elvira.**

Tapas Bars

For the most colorful bars, look around the Albaicín, Campo del Príncipe, the Plaza del Carmen–Calle Navas, and Pedro de Alarcón-Martínez de la Rosa. **Bar El Ladrillo** (✉ Plaza de Fátima) is a tiny but popular tapas bar in the Albaicín with outdoor tables in summer. For a splendid array of regional wines with your nibbles, try **La Puerta del Vino** (✉ Paseo Padre Manjón 5, ☎ 958/210026), a 10-table bar hung with old paintings. **Chikito** (✉ Plaza del Campillo 9, ☎ 958/223364) is best known for its tasty sit-down meals, but the bar is an excellent spot to nosh tapas. The place is usually packed, even in summer, when additional tables are set up in the plaza. The popular **Bodegas Castañeda** (✉ Elvira 6, ☎ 958/226362) draws a local crowd. On the Plaza Nueva, **La Gran Taberna** (✉ Plaza Nueva 12, ☎ 958/228846), a bi-level bar with wooden gallery upstairs, is famous for its *montaditos,* little open-face sandwiches made with the ingredients of your choice. Favored by intellectuals, **Casa Enrique** (✉ Acera del Darro 8), known to locals as "El Elefante," is a dark little hole-in-the-wall founded in 1870 and specializing in ham and fine wine.

Santa Fe

18 *8 km (5 mi) west of Granada just south of N342.*

The village of Santa Fe was founded in winter 1491 as a campground for Ferdinand and Isabella's 150,000 troops as they prepared for the Siege of Granada. It was in Santa Fe, in April 1492, that Isabella and Columbus signed the agreements that financed his historic voyage, and thus the town has been called the Cradle of America. Santa Fe was originally laid out in the shape of a cross, with a gate at each of its four ends, inscribed with Ferdinand and Isabella's initials. The town has long since transcended those boundaries, but the four gates still stand—to see them all at the same time, stand in the square next to the church at the center of the old town.

Fuentevaqueros

19 *10 km (6 mi) northwest of Santa Fe.*

Federico García Lorca was born in this village on June 5, 1898, and lived here until the age of six. The **Casa Museo Federico García Lorca,** the poet's childhood home, opened as a museum in 1986, when Spain commemorated the 50th anniversary of Lorca's assassination and celebrated his reinstatement as a national figure after 40 years of nonrecognition during the Franco regime. The house has been restored with original furnishings, while the former granary, barn, and stables have been converted into exhibition spaces, with temporary art shows and a permanent display of photographs, clippings, and other memorabilia. A two-minute video shows the only existing footage of Lorca on film. ✉ *Poeta García Lorca 4,* ☎ *958/516453.* 🎫 *200 ptas.* ⏲ *July–Sept., Tues.–Sun. 10–1 and 6–8; Oct.–Mar., Tues.–Sun. 10–1 and 4–6; Apr.–June, 10–1 and 5–7; guided tours hourly.*

The village of **Valderrubio,** not far from Fuentevaqueros, inspired Lorca's *Libro de Poemas* and one of his best-loved plays, *La Casa de Bernarda Alba.*

Viznar

20 *9 km (5½ mi) northeast of Granada (head northeast on N342, then turn left, then left again when you see signs for Viznar).*

If you're a Lorca devotee, make the short trip to Viznar. The **Federico García Lorca Memorial Park,** 3 km (2 mi) from Viznar up a narrow winding road, marks the spot where Lorca was shot without trial by Nationalists at the beginning of the civil war in August 1936 and where he is probably buried. Lorca, who is now venerated by most Spaniards, was hated by Fascists for his liberal ideas and his homosexuality.

The Sierra Nevada

21 *The drive southeast from Granada to Pradollano along C420, by way of Cenes de la Vega, takes about 45 minutes. It's wise to carry snow chains even as late as April or May.*

Even if you don't have a car, the mountains of the Sierra Nevada make for an easy and worthwhile excursion. The Sierra Nevada ski resort—with two stations, Pradollano and the higher Borreguiles—draws crowds from December to May, but the same slope is quiet in summer. Year-round **buses** to Pradollano leave Granada daily at 8, returning at 6 (✉ Autocar Bonal, ☎ 958/273100); they depart from the Bar El Ventorillo (where you also buy tickets, for 800 ptas. round-trip), next to the Palacio de Congresos. In July and August you can drive right up to the summit of the Veleta on Europe's highest road. It's cold up here, so bring a warm jacket and scarf with your sunglasses, even if the weather in Granada is sizzling-hot. The **Pico de Veleta,** Spain's third-highest mountain, stands at 11,125 ft, and the view from its summit across the Alpujarra range to the sea, at distant Motril, is stunning; on a very clear day you can even see the coast of North Africa. Away to your left, the mighty **Mulhacén,** the highest peak in mainland Spain, soars to 11,407 ft.

Skiing

The Sierra Nevada **Estación de Esquí** is one of Europe's best-equipped, having hosted the World Alpine Skiing Championships in 1996. There are 21 lifts, 45 runs, and about 60 km (37 mi) of marked trails, not to mention a snowboarding circuit and two floodlit slopes for night skiing on weekends. A **children's ski school** and rental shop round out the facilities. Contact the **Sierra Nevada Information Center** (✉ Plaza de Andalucía 4, ☎ 958/249111); you can also dial for **snow, weather, and road conditions** (☎ 958/249119).

The Alpujarras

22 *The village of Lanjarón is 46 km (29 mi) south of Granada.*

A trip to the Alpujarras, on the southern slopes of the Sierra Nevada, will take you to one of Andalusia's highest, most remote, and most picturesque areas. Here, attractive villages hide handsome crafts shops where you can buy handwoven textiles and handmade basketware, pottery, and other goods. If you're driving, the road as far as Lanjarón and Orgiva is smooth sailing; after that come steep, twisting mountain roads with few gas stations. Buses run from Granada to Orgiva seven to nine times a day, from Granada to Capileira three times a day.

The Alpujarras region was originally populated by Moors fleeing the Christian Reconquest (from Seville after its fall in 1248, then from Granada after 1492). It was also the last fiefdom of the unfortunate Boabdil, conceded to him by the Catholic Monarchs after he surrendered Granada. In 1568, rebellious Moors made their final stand against the Christian overlords, a revolt ruthlessly suppressed by Philip II and followed by the forced conversion of all Moors to Christianity and their resettlement farther inland and up Spain's eastern coast.

The villages of the Alpujarras were then repopulated with Christian soldiers from Galicia, who were granted land in return for their service against the Moors. To this day, the Galicians' descendants continue the Moorish custom of weaving rugs and blankets in the traditional Alpujarran colors of red, green, black, and white, and they sell their crafts in many of the villages. Houses here are squat and square; they spill down the southern slopes of the Sierra Nevada one on top of another, bearing a strong resemblance to the Berber homes in the Rif Mountains, just across the sea in Morocco.

En Route A few miles south of Granada on N323, the road reaches a spot known as the **Suspiro del Moro** (Moor's Sigh). Pause here a moment and look back at the city, just as Granada's departing "Boy King," Boabdil, did 500 years ago. As he wept over the city he'd surrendered to the Catholic Monarchs, his scornful mother pronounced her now famous rebuke: "You weep like a boy for the city you could not defend as a man."

Marking the entrance to the Alpujarras, **Lanjarón,** some 46 km (29 mi) from Granada, is a spa town famous for its mineral water, gathered from the melting snows of the Sierra Nevada and drunk throughout Spain. Lanjarón is also known for its wicker baskets and furniture. There are numerous *hostales,* but during the spa season (May–November) these cater mainly to people seeking cures for a variety of ailments, so the atmosphere can be somewhat grim. Press on to **Orgiva,** the main town in the western Alpujarras, where you can leave the C333 and follow signs for Pampaneira and Capileira, in the Alpujarra Alta (High Alpujarra).

The villages of the **Barranco del Poqueira** (Poqueira Ravine)—Pampaneira, Bubión, and Capileira—are the best known in the Alpujarras. The looms in **Pampaneira**'s workshops produce many of the textiles sold nearby. **Capileira,** at the end of the road, is one of the prettiest villages, and its Museo Alpujarreño, in the Plaza Mayor, has a colorful display of local crafts (☎ 958/763051). It's open Tuesday–Sunday 11:30–2. From Capileira, a winding track leads over the mountain peaks to join the road to the Veleta summit; it's passable only in July or August, and then only in a four-wheel-drive vehicle.

Continue along C332, passing a succession of picturesque villages: Pitres, Pórtugos, and Busquístar. If you make it as far as **Trevélez,** which lies on the slopes of the Mulhacén at 4,840 ft above sea level, you will have driven one of the highest roads in Europe. Reward yourself with a plate of the locally produced *jamón serrano.* Trevélez has three levels, the Barrio Alto, Barrio Medio, and Barrio Bajo; the butchers are concentrated in the lowest section (Bajo). The higher levels are far more rewarding, with narrow cobblestone streets, whitewashed houses, and fewer shops. From Trevélez you can return to Granada the way you came; alternately, if you continue eastward on C332, you will eventually reach Almería (☞ Chapter 8).

Dining and Lodging

$$–$$$ ✕🏨 **Villa Turística de Bubión.** Here you're set up in a whitewashed semidetached apartment with its own sitting room, bathroom, and bedrooms for two, four, or six people. Nestled beneath the Veleta, the buildings overlook splendid mountain scenery. The restaurant was instrumental in reviving classic Alpujarran recipes. Try the *revoltillo de espárragos trigueros* (cumin-seasoned scrambled eggs with wild asparagus) or *migas* (savory fried bread crumbs), and finish with locally picked walnuts with whipped cream. ✉ *Barrio Alto, 18412 Bubión,* ☎ *958/763111,* FAX *958/763136. 43 apartments. Restaurant, bar. AE, DC, MC, V.*

$$ ✕🏨 **Taray.** Less than a decade old, this delightful hotel on its own farm is still spanking-new and very friendly. The main hotel is a low, whitewashed building. A stone building was added in 1997, but the rooms with the best views (Nos. 1–15) are in the older wing. The sunny guest rooms are decorated with Alpujarran bedspreads and curtains; two have rooftop terraces. There's a pleasant common terrace, and most of the food served in the restaurant comes from the estate, including fresh trout and lamb. In season, you can pick your own raspberries for breakfast. ✉ *Carretera Tablate–Albuñol, Km 18, 18400 Órgiva,* ☎ *958/784525,* FAX *958/784531. 28 rooms. Restaurant, pool. AE, DC, MC, V.*

$ ✕🏨 **La Fragua.** Spotless rooms with bath (and some with balcony), fresh air by the lungful, and views over the rooftops of Trevélez are the rewards of this small, friendly hostelry in a typical village house behind the town hall. The restaurant is in a separate house up the street, serving regional dishes like *arroz liberal* (hunter's rice), *lomo a los aromas de la sierra* (herb-scented pork loin), and *conejo al ajillo* (rabbit in garlic sauce). ✉ *San Antonio 4, Barrio Medio, 18417 Trevélez,* ☎ *958/858626,* FAX *958/858614. 12 rooms. Restaurant. MC, V.*

Guadix

23 *47 km (30 mi) east of Granada on A92.*

Guadix was an important mining town as far back as 2,000 years ago, and it has its fair share of monuments, including a cathedral (built between 1594 and 1706) and a 9th-century Moorish *alcazaba.* But Guadix and the neighboring village of **Purullena** are best known for their cave communities. Around 2,000 caves were carved out of the soft, sandstone mountains at various times, and most are still inhabited. Far from being troglodytic holes in the wall, they are well furnished and comfortable, with a pleasant year-round temperature; there's even a cave hotel (☞ *below*). Follow signs to the **Cueva Museo,** a small cave museum, in the heart of Guadix's cave district. Closer to the town center, another cave-museum, the **Cueva la Alcazaba,** houses a ceramics workshop. A number of private caves have signs welcoming visitors to inspect the premises; a tip is expected if you do. Purullena, 6 km (4 mi) from Guadix, is also known for ceramics.

Dining and Lodging

$ ✕🏨 **Comercio.** This 1905 building in the center of Guadix is the town's most charming establishment, an enchanting little family-run hotel. Rooms have thick bedspreads in rich red; marble floors; and brand-new bathrooms. The public areas include an art gallery, a concert room, and the best restaurant in Guadix, serving such local specialties as roast lamb with raisins and pine nuts. ✉ *C. Mira de Amezcua 3, 18500,* ☎ *958/660500,* FAX *958/665072. 24 rooms. AE, DC, MC, V.*

$$ 🏨 **Cuevas Pedro Antonio de Alarcón.** There's not much of a view, but what can you expect from a cave? Located not in Guadix's main cave district but in a cave "suburb" outside town, this unique lodging is installed in 19 different but adjoining caves. Each of the 20 suites (which sleep two to five) has a kitchenette, and the honeymoon cave has a whirlpool bath. The whitewashed walls are decorated with charming Granadino crafts; colorful rugs cover the clay-tile floors; and handwoven Alpujarran tapestries serve as doors between the rooms. The restaurant, also subterranean, serves regional dishes. ✉ *Barriada San Torcuato, 18500,* ☎ *958/664986,* FAX *958/661721. 20 suites. Restaurant. AE, MC, V.*

Loja

24 *55 km (34 mi) west of Granada, 40 km (25 mi) northeast of Málaga.*

Standing guard at the entrance to Granada's *vega,* halfway between Granada and Málaga on the A92, Loja is a traditional pit stop for travelers, who like to munch on the famous *roscos de Loja,* a hard, doughnut-shape, sugar-coated pastry. The town's name comes from the "Lascivis" of Roman times, meaning "place of water and delight," and the town still has numerous fountains, including the 25-spout Fuente de los Veinticinco Caños.

Eight kilometers (5 mi) west of Loja on A92 is the hamlet of **Riofrío,** next to a rushing trout stream. Trout and sturgeon raised at Riofrío's fish farm are enjoyed throughout Andalusia. Eight restaurants, all inexpensive, serve fresh trout in a variety of ways: *a la plancha* (grilled), *a la romana* (batter-fried), *a la navarra* (with ham), and *ahumado* (smoked).

Dining and Lodging

$$$$ ★ **La Bobadilla.** This luxurious complex 14 km (9 mi) west of Loja stands on its own 860-acre estate amid olive and holm-oak trees, a sumptuous island in the Andalusian hinterland. With its white walls, tile roofs, patios, fountains, and artificial lake, it resembles a Moorish village, or a rambling Andalusian *cortijo* (ranch). The guest buildings center on a 16th-century-style chapel, whose 1,595-pipe organ is used for occasional concerts and weddings. Each room is individually designed and decorated and has its own terrace or garden. The elegant restaurant La Finca serves highly creative international cuisine, while a second restaurant, El Cortijo, serves more down-to-earth regional fare. Prices are princely, but special deals are frequent, so it's worth inquiring. ✉ *Finca La Bobadilla (north of A92 between Salinas and Rute; exit north onto 334, toward Iznajar), 18300,* ☎ *958/321861,* FAX *958/321810. 52 rooms, 8 suites. 2 restaurants, indoor and outdoor pools, hot tub, sauna, 2 tennis courts, exercise room, horseback riding, convention center. AE, DC, MC, V.*

JAÉN, BAEZA, ÚBEDA, AND CAZORLA

Jaén, north of Granada, has a rich Moorish legacy—Arab baths and a former alcázar—and an ornately decorated cathedral. From Jaén, head northeast along the N321 to the olive-producing towns of Baeza and Úbeda. The typical Andalusian town of Cazorla is the gateway to the Cazorla Nature Park, where you might spot wild boar.

Jaén

25 *93 km (58 mi) north of Granada.*

The city of Jaén nestles in the foothills of the Sierra de Jabalcuz, surrounded by towering peaks and rolling, olive-clad hills. The Arabs called it Geen (Route of the Caravans) because it formed a crossroad between Castile and Andalusia. Captured from the Moors by the Saint King Ferdinand in 1246, Jaén became a frontier province, the site of many a skirmish and battle over the next 200 years between the Moors of Granada and Christians from the north and west. Today the province has lead and silver mines and endless olive groves.

★ The **Castillo de Santa Catalina,** perched on a rocky crag 5 km (3 mi) from the center of Jaén, is the city's star monument. The castle may have originated as a tower erected by Hannibal; the site was fortified continuously over the centuries. The Nasrid king Alhamar, builder of Granada's Alhambra, constructed an alcázar here, but King Ferdinand III captured it from him in 1246 on the feast day of Santa Catalina (St. Catherine). Catalina consequently became Jaén's patron saint, so when the Christians built a new castle and chapel here, they dedicated both to her. The castle ruins make a dramatic setting for the parador in their midst (☞ below). ✉ *Castillo de Santa Catalina.* 🎫 *Free.* ⏲ *Summer, Thurs.–Tues. 10:30–1:30; winter, Thurs.–Tues. 10–2.*

Jaén's **cathedral** is an imposing hulk that looms above the modest buildings around it. Begun in 1500 on the site of a former mosque, it was not finished until the end of the 18th century. Its chief architect was the brilliant Andrés de Vandelvira (1509–75), many more of whose buildings can be seen in Úbeda and Baeza. The ornate facade was sculpted by Pedro Roldán, and the figures on top of the columns include San Fernando (King Ferdinand III) surrounded by the four evangelists. The cathedral's most treasured relic is the Santo Rostro (Holy Face), the cloth with which, according to tradition, St. Veronica cleansed Christ's face on the way to Calvary, leaving his image imprinted on the fabric. The *rostro* is displayed every Friday. In the underground **museum,** look for the *Immaculate Conception,* by Alonso Cano; *San Lorenzo,* by Martínez Montañés; and a Calvary scene by Jácobo Florentino. ✉ *Plaza Santa María.* 🎫 *Cathedral free, museum 200 ptas.* ⏲ *Cathedral daily 8:30–1 and 4:30–7; museum weekdays 9–1 and 4–7, Sat. 11–1, Sun. 11–1 and 4–7.*

Explore the narrow alleys of old Jaén as you walk from the cathedral to the **Baños Árabes** (Arab Baths), which once belonged to Ali, a Moorish king of Jaén, and probably date from the 11th century. Four hundred years later, a viceroy of Peru built himself a mansion, the **Palacio de Villardompardo,** right over the baths; it took years of painstaking excavation to restore them to their original form. The palace contains a small museum of folk crafts and a larger museum devoted to naive art. ✉ *Palacio de Villardompardo, Plaza Luisa de Marillac,* ☎ *953/236292.* 🎫 *Free.* ⏲ *Tues.–Fri. 9–8, weekends 9:30–2:30.*

Jaén's delightful little **Museo Provincial** has one of the best collections of Iberian (pre-Roman) artifacts in Spain. A brand-new wing displays an outstanding collection of 20 life-size Iberian sculptures discovered by chance near the village of Porcuna in 1975. The museum proper, housed in a 1547 mansion, centers on a patio containing the facade of the erstwhile Church of San Miguel, another work of Andrés de Vandelvira. A highlight of the fine-arts section is the roomful of Goya lithographs. ✉ *Paseo de la Estación 29,* ☎ *953/250600.* 🎫 *Free.* ⏲ *Tues. 3–8, Wed.–Sat. 8–8, Sun. 9–3. Closed summer afternoons.*

Dining and Lodging

$–$$ ✕ **Casa Vicente.** This popular, family-run restaurant around the corner from the cathedral square is usually packed with locals. You can have drinks and tapas in the colorful tavern, then move on to the cozy dining room. The traditional Jaén dishes—such as game casseroles, Jaén-style spinach, and *cordero Mozárabe* (Mozarab-style roast lamb with a sweet-and-sour sauce)—are especially good. ✉ *Francisco Martín Mora 1,* ☎ *953/232222. AE, MC, V. Closed Sun.*

$$$ ★ 🏨 **Parador de Santa Catalina.** Built on a mountain amid the towers of a medieval Moorish castle, Jaén's parador is one of the showpieces of the parador chain and a reason in itself to visit Jaén. Lofty ceilings, tapestries, baronial shields, and suits of armor add to the castle atmosphere. The comfortable bedrooms, with canopied beds, have balconies overlooking the mountains. ✉ *Castillo de Santa Catalina, 23001,* ☎ *953/230000,* FAX *953/230930. 45 rooms. Restaurant, pool. AE, DC, MC, V.*

Shopping

The province of Jaén is known for its **pottery and ceramics** as well as wares woven from **esparto grass**—baskets, mats, and ornaments.

Baeza

★ 26 *48 km (30 mi) northeast of Jaén on the N321.*

The historic town of Baeza snuggles between rolling hills and olive groves. Founded by the Romans, it later housed the Visigoths and became the capital of a *taifa* (kingdom) under the Moors. The Saint King Ferdinand captured Baeza in 1227, and for the next 200 years it stood on the frontier of the Moorish kingdom of Granada. In the 16th and 17th centuries, Baeza's nobles gave the city a wealth of splendid Renaissance palaces.

The **Casa del Pópulo,** in the central *paseo*—where the Plaza del Pópulo (or Plaza de los Leones) and Plaza del Mercado Viejo merge to form a delightful cobbled square—is a beautiful plateresque structure from around 1530. The first mass of the Reconquest was reputedly celebrated on its curved balcony. It now houses the town's tourist office. In the center of the town square is an ancient Iberian-Roman statue thought to depict Imilce, wife of Hannibal; at the foot of her column is the **Fuente de los Leones** (Fountain of the Lions).

You can find Baeza's **university** by following a series of steps on the plaza's south side. The college opened in 1542, closed in 1824, and later became a high school, where the poet Antonio Machado taught French from 1912 to 1919. The building still functions as a school, but you can visit Machado's classroom and the patio. ⏲ *Tues.–Sun. 10–1 and 4–6.*

The golden-stone **Palacio de Jabalquinto,** on the Cuesta (Slope) de San Felipe, was built by Juan Alonso Benavides, second cousin of Ferdinand of Aragón. Its facade is a masterpiece of the late-15th-century Isabelline Gothic. At press time the interior was closed for restoration.

Baeza's **cathedral** was originally begun by Ferdinand III on the site of a former mosque, but it has undergone many a transformation since his day. The structure was largely rebuilt by Andrés de Vandelvira, architect of Jaén's cathedral, between 1570 and 1593, though the west front has architectural features from an earlier period. A fine 14th-century rose window crowns the 13th-century Puerta de la Luna (Moon Door). Don't miss the Baroque silver monstrance, which is carried in Baeza's Corpus Christi processions; it's kept in a concealed niche behind a painting. To see the piece in all its flamboyant splendor, you put a coin in a slot to reveal its hiding place and light it up (money well spent). Next to the monstrance is the entrance to the clock tower, where a donation of 100 ptas. and a narrow spiral staircase take you to one of the best views of Baeza. The remains of the original mosque are in the cathedral's Gothic cloisters. ⏲ *Daily 10:30–1 and 4–6 (5–7 in summer).*

The seminary of **San Felipe Neri,** built in 1660, is opposite Baeza's cathedral at the end of Cuesta de San Felipe. The ancient student custom of inscribing names and graduation dates in bull's blood (as in Salamanca) is still evident on the walls.

The ***ayuntamiento*** (town hall), on the Plaza Cardenal Benavides, just north of the Plaza del Pópulo, has an ornate plateresque facade. The building was designed by Andrés de Vandelvira. Look up at the facade between the balconies and you'll see the coats of arms of Felipe II, the city of Baeza, and the magistrate Juan de Borja.

Dining and Lodging

$$ ✕🏨 **Hacienda La Laguna.** Installed in a 17th-century country manor on a 500-acre estate, this rural complex takes its name from the La-

guna Grande, a nearby lagoon with a variety of resident aquatic birds. The restaurant has long been popular for its fine regional cooking; the hotel opened in 1997. The latest addition is a full-fledged museum devoted to the olive, sponsored by the regional government. Guest rooms, set around an interior patio, have marble floors and olive-wood furniture. The on-site catering school serves weekday lunches in its own, more upmarket restaurant. ✉ *Puente del Obispo (8 km/5 mi outside Baeza off N321 to Jaén), 23529,* ☎ *953/127172,* FAX *953/127174. 17 rooms. Restaurant, pool, horseback riding. AE, MC, V.*

$–$$ ✕🏨 **Juanito.** On the edge of town (next to a gas station) on the way to Úbeda, this small, unpretentious hotel has simple, clean, comfortable rooms. The real drawing card is the well-known restaurant: the proprietor is a champion of the Jaén region's excellent olive oil, and the cuisine reflects his dedication to promoting Andalusian dishes. The chef has done much to revive regional specialties, such as *alcochafas Luisa* (braised artichokes), *ensalada de perdiz* (partridge salad), and *cordero con habas* (lamb and broad beans); desserts are based on old Moorish recipes. ✉ *Paseo Arca del Agua, 23440,* ☎ *953/740040,* FAX *953/742324. 36 rooms, 1 suite. Restaurant. MC, V.*

$ 🏨 **Fuentenueva Hospedería.** This small, charming, informal hotel was once a women's prison and later the residence of the town judge. The service is helpful and cheerful, and the comfortable rooms are attractively decorated in pastels. Most rooms face out onto the road. ✉ *Paseo Arca del Agua, 23440,* ☎ *953/743100,* FAX *953/743200. 12 rooms. Restaurant, cafeteria, pool. AE, MC, V.*

Úbeda

★ 27 *9 km (5½ mi) northeast of Baeza on the N321.*

Úbeda stands in the heart of Jaén's olive groves, and olive oil is indeed the main concern here. Although this modern town of 30,000 is relatively dull, the **Casco Antiguo** (Old Town) is a superbly pure example of a Renaissance town and one of the most outstanding enclaves of 16th-century architecture in Spain. Follow the signs to the **Zona Monumental,** where you'll pass countless Renaissance palaces and stately mansions, each with its own distinctive features—an unusual balcony, or a fine sculptured facade. Most of these homes are closed to the public, but you can wander into many of Úbeda's churches.

The **Plaza del Ayuntamiento,** in the Old Town, is crowned by the **Palacio de Vela de los Cobos**—built by architect Andrés de Vandelvira in the mid-16th century for Úbeda's magistrate, Francisco de Vela de los Cobos. Its special feature is the corner balcony, with a central white-marble column, which you can see echoed in the gallery above.

Another Vandelvira work, the Palacio Juan Vázquez de Molina, is better known by its nickname, the **Palacio de las Cadenas** (House of Chains), because decorative iron chains were once affixed to the columns of its main doorway. It currently houses the city government.

The Plaza Vázquez de Molina, in the heart of the Old Town, is home ★ to the **Sacra Capilla del Salvador,** the most elaborate and ornate of Úbeda's churches. Not surprisingly, this building is photographed so often that it has become the city's unofficial symbol. The Sacra Capilla was built by Vandelvira, but he based his design on some 1536 plans by Diego de Siloé, architect of Granada's cathedral. It was sacked in the frenzy of church burnings at the outbreak of the civil war but retains its ornate west front and its altarpiece, which holds a rare Berruguete sculpture. Next door is the Renaissance palace that now serves as Úbeda's parador (☞ below).

The Plaza Primero de Mayo, by way of the Calle Horno Cantador, leads you to the **Ayuntamiento Antiguo** (Old Town Hall), begun in the early 16th century but restored as a beautiful arcaded Baroque palace in 1680. It's now a conservatory of music. From the hall's upper balcony, the town council watched celebrations and *autos-da-fé* ("acts of faith," or executions of heretics sentenced by the Inquisition) in the square below. On the north side is the 13th-century church of San Pablo, with an Isabelline south portal.

The **Hospital de Santiago,** on Avenida Cristo Rey in the modern section, is a short walk from the bus depot and the main drag, Ramón y Cajal. Often jokingly called the Escorial of Andalusia, this huge, angular building is Vandelvira's masterpiece. Its generally plain facade is decorated with ceramic medallions, and over the main entrance is a relief of St. James as a warrior on horseback. Inside are a fine arcaded patio and a grand staircase, as well as the local tourist office.

Dining and Lodging

$$$–$$$$ ★ ✕ 🏨 **Parador Condestable Dávalos.** This splendid parador occupies a 16th-century ducal palace on the Plaza Vázquez de Molina, right next to the Capilla del Salvador. A grand stairway, decked with tapestries and suits of armor, leads up to the guest rooms, which have tile floors, lofty wood ceilings, dark, Castilian-style furniture, and deliciously large bathtubs. The dining room—complete with waitstaff in traditional dress—serves perhaps the best food in Úbeda, specializing in regional dishes; try one of the *perdiz* (partridge) entrées. Desserts have intriguing names like *suspiros de monja* (nun's sighs). There's an atmospheric bar in the vaulted basement. ✉ *Plaza Vázquez de Molina 1, 23400,* ☎ *953/750345,* FAX *953/751259. 36 rooms. Restaurant, bar. AE, DC, MC, V.*

$$$ 🏨 **Palacio de la Rambla.** This wonderful 16th-century mansion in old Úbeda has been in the same family since it was built, and part of it still hosts the Marquesa de la Rambla when she's in town. Eight of the rooms are open to guests. Each is different, but all are large and furnished with original antiques, tapestries, and works of art, and some have chandeliers. The palace is arranged on two levels around a cool, ivy-covered patio. ✉ *Plaza del Marqués 1, 23400,* ☎ *953/750196,* FAX *953/750267. 8 rooms. Breakfast room. AE, MC, V.*

$ 🏨 **La Paz.** This homey hostel on a busy street in modern Úbeda is a good budget alternative. The rooms are simply furnished but well maintained, with plain white walls and traditional dark-wood furniture. ✉ *Andalucía 1, 23400,* ☎ *953/750848,* FAX *953/752140. 44 rooms. Breakfast room. AE, MC, V.*

Shopping

Calle Valencia, which runs from the bottom of town to northwest of the old quarter (follow signs to Calle Valencia or Barrio de Alfareros) is Úbeda's crafts center. **Antonio Almazara** (✉ Valencia 34, ☎ 953/751200) is a small ceramics shop specializing in Úbeda's green-glazed pottery. **Paco Tito** (✉ Valencia 22, ☎ 953/751496) is a large pottery workshop run by two generations of the same family; there's a showroom above the studio area. All kinds of ceramics are sold at **Alfarería Góngora** (✉ Cuesta de la Merced 32, ☎ 953/754605). For handmade *esparto* grassware, such as rugs, mats, and baskets, hit the sprawling **Ana Ubalde Plaza** (✉ Real 47, ☎ 953/750456), supplied by its own local factory.

Cazorla

28 *48 km (35 mi) southeast of Úbeda.*

The remote and unspoiled Andalusian village of Cazorla, at the east end of the province of Jaén, is a treat for both young and old. The pine-clad slopes and towering peaks of the Cazorla and Segura sierras rise above the village, and below it stretch endless miles of olive groves. In spring, purple Judas trees blossom in picturesque plazas.

For a break from man-made sights, drink in the scenery or watch for wildlife in the **Parque Natural de Cazorla** (Cazorla Nature Park), administered by the environmental agency Agencia de Medio Ambiente (AMA). For information on hiking, camping, canoeing, horseback riding, or guided Jeep excursions, contact the AMA's offices in Cazorla (✉ Tejares Altos, ☎ 953/720125) or Jaén (✉ Avda. de Andalucía 79, ☎ 953/215000) or the park visitor center (☞ *below*). For hunting or fishing permits, apply to the Jaén office well in advance. Deer, wild boar, and mountain goats roam the slopes of this carefully protected patch of mountain wilderness 80 km (50 mi) long and 30 km (19 mi) wide, and hawks, eagles, and vultures soar over the 6,000-ft peaks. Within the park, at Cañada de las Fuentes (Fountains' Ravine), is the source of Andalusia's great river, the Guadalquivir. The road through the park follows the river to the shores of **Lago Tranco de Beas.** Alpine meadows, pine forests, springs, waterfalls, and gorges make Cazorla a perfect place to hike.

At the **visitor center,** at Torre de Vinagre, a short film introduces you to the park's main sights; displays explain the park's plants and geology; and the staff can advise you on camping, fishing, and hiking trails. There's also a hunting museum, with such attractions as the interlocked antlers of bucks who clashed during the autumn rutting season, became helplessly trapped, and died of starvation. Nearby are a **botanical garden** and a **game reserve.** The park has seven well-equipped campsites (open June–October).

Dining and Lodging

$$ ✕🏨 **Parador El Adelantado.** This modern, whitewashed parador with a red-tile roof stands isolated in a valley at the edge of Cazorla Nature Park, 26 km (16 mi) above Cazorla village. It's a quiet place, popular with hunters and fishers. The restaurant specializes in regional cooking, such as *ajo blanco* (almond soup with garlic) and, in season, game dishes. ✉ *Sierra de Cazorla, 23470,* ☎ *953/727075,* FAX *953/727077. 33 rooms. Restaurant, pool. AE, DC, MC, V.*

$ ✕🏨 **La Hortizuela.** Deep in the heart of Cazorla Nature Park in what was once a game warden's house, this small hotel makes the perfect base for exploring the wilderness. Guest rooms are in the back, beyond the central courtyard, and most have unhindered views of the forest-clad mountainside (a few look onto the patio). Wild boar and fresh trout are usually on offer in the restaurant. ✉ *Carretera del Tranco, Km 50.5 (2 km/1 mi east of visitor center up a dirt track), 23478 Coto Ríos,* ☎ FAX *953/713150. 23 rooms. Restaurant, pool. MC, V.*

$ 🏨 **Sierra de Cazorla.** This low, white hotel nestles in a bend of the road leading up into the mountains 2 km (1 mi) above Cazorla village, at La Iruela. Rooms in the two-story modern section are functional but comfortable, and larger than those in the older building. Most rooms in both sections have nice views of the olive groves in the valley below and of the ruins of La Iruela castle, teetering on its rocky outcrop. ✉ *Carretera Sierra de Cazorla, Km 2, 23476 La Iruela,* ☎ *953/720015,* FAX *953/720017. 53 rooms, 2 suites. Restaurant, pool. AE, DC, MC, V.*

CÓRDOBA AND ENVIRONS

The city of Córdoba holds one of Spain's most spectacular monuments, the Moorish Mezquita (mosque), which dates from the 8th through 10th centuries. The city's old quarters, and particularly the old Jewish Quarter, lend themselves to quiet exploration: you wander through narrow, whitewashed alleys past tiled private patios and effusions of jewel-tone flowers, and visit the only synagogue in Andalusia to survive the expulsion of the Jews in 1492. If you have time to move beyond Córdoba, go west to the ruins of Medina Azahara, site of a once-magnificent palace complex, or south to the wine country around Montilla and the Subbética region, a cluster of small towns virtually unknown to travelers.

Córdoba

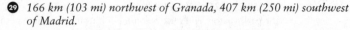

29 *166 km (103 mi) northwest of Granada, 407 km (250 mi) southwest of Madrid.*

Perched on the south bank of the Guadalquivir, Córdoba is chilly and small, but it's absolutely integral to the cultural history of the Iberian Peninsula. Córdoba was both the Roman and Moorish capital of Spain, and its old quarter, clustered around its famous mosque (Mezquita), remains one of the country's grandest and yet most intimate examples of its Moorish heritage. The Moorish emirs and caliphs of the West held court here from the 8th to the 11th centuries, and Córdoba's magnificence and opulence became legendary. Under the Moors Córdoba became one of the greatest centers of art, culture, and learning in the Western world; one of its libraries had more than 400,000 volumes, a staggering number at the time. Moors, Christians, and Jews lived together in harmony within its walls. Chroniclers of the day put the city's population at around a million, making it the largest city in Europe, though historians believe the real figure was closer to half a million (there are 285,000 today).

Córdoba remained in Moorish hands until it was conquered by the Saint King Ferdinand in 1236, after which the Catholic Monarchs used the city as a base from which to plan the conquest of Granada. In Columbus's time, the Guadalquivir was navigable as far upstream as Córdoba, and great galleons sailed its waters. Today, the river's muddy water and marshy banks evoke little of Córdoba's glorious past, but the city's impressive bridge—of Roman origin, though much restored by the Arabs and successive generations—and old Arab waterwheel are vestiges of a far grander era.

A Good Walk

Allow a full day for this walk through Córdoba's historic center. Begin on Cardenal Herrero, at the awesome **Mezquita** (30). Facing the western side of the mosque, in the sacristy of a former hospital on Calle Torrijos, is the regional tourist office, where you can examine a scale model of the mosque. Walk up Calle Velázquez Bosco to a tiny alleyway known as **Calleja de las Flores** (31), famous for its plethora of ebullient, hanging flower baskets. Come back to Cardenal Herrero and enter the **Judería** (32), Córdoba's old Jewish Quarter. Go up Calle Judería and continue along Calle Albucasis past the **Plaza Juda Levi,** where the municipal tourist office is located. Just around the corner, in the Plaza Maimónides, is the **Museo Taurino** (33). Leading northwest from here, Calle Judíos takes you past the tiny Plaza Tiberiades and the **statue of Maimónides,** the famous 12th-century Jewish philosopher. Continue along Calle Judíos to the **Zoco** (34), on the right, and go through the arch to the courtyard, where a former Arab *souk* (market) hosts working artisans by day and flamenco on summer evenings. A bit farther up Calle Judíos, on the left, is Córdoba's **synagogue** (35), the only one in Andalusia to survive the inquisition and expulsion of the Jews in 1492. The **Puerta de Almodóvar** (36) marks the western limit of the Judería. From here, you may want to detour north to the Mudéjar church of **San Nicolás de Villa** (37).

Córdoba

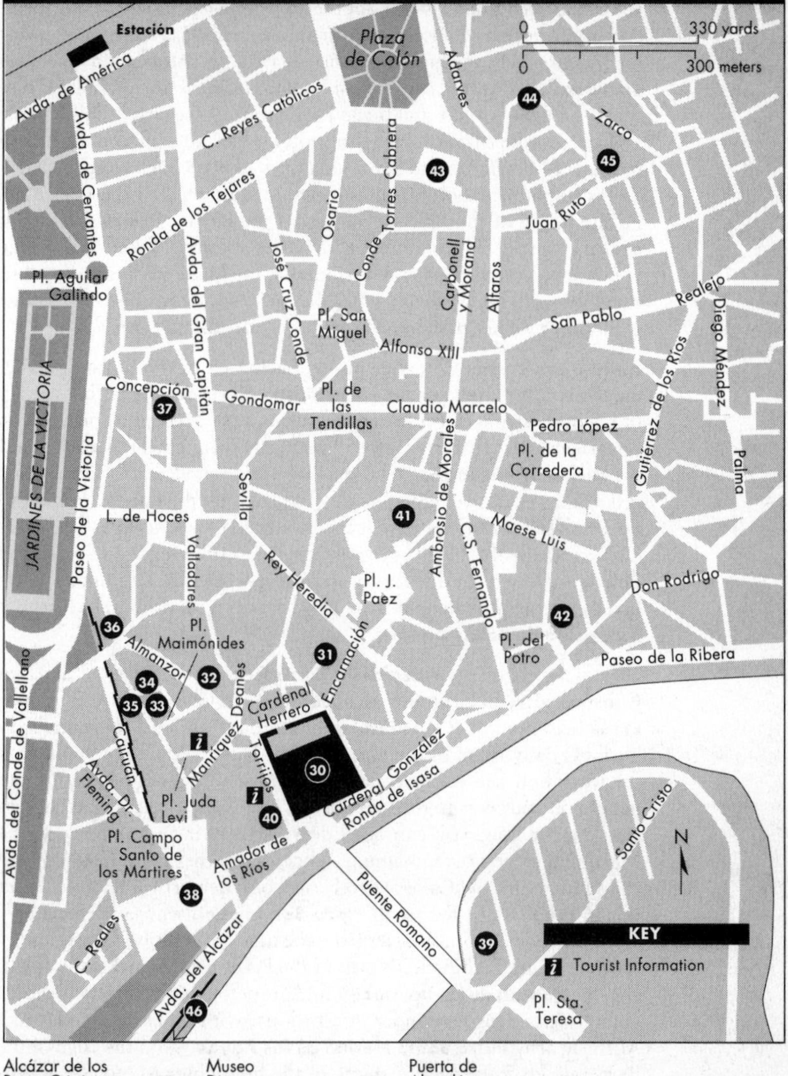

Alcázar de los Reyes Cristianos . . . **38**
Calleja de las Flores **31**
Jardín Botánico. . . . **46**
Judería **32**
Mezquita **30**
Museo Arqueológico **41**
Museo de Bellas Artes **42**
Museo Diocesano **40**
Museo Taurino **33**
Palacio de los Marqueses de Viana **45**
Plaza de los Dolores **43**
Plaza Santa Marina de las Aguas **44**
Puerta de Almodóvar **36**
San Nicolás de Villa **37**
Synagogue **35**
Torre de la Calahorra **39**
Zoco **34**

Travel down Cairuán, along a restored section of Córdoba's Moorish walls and past the statue of another prominent Córdoban, the 12th-century Moorish philosopher Averröes, to the Plaza Campo Santo de los Mártires. On the far side of the square is the **Alcázar de los Reyes Cristianos** (38). From Plaza Campo Santo, you have three choices: hire a *coche caballo* (horse and buggy) for a tour of the city, at 4,000 ptas. an hour; wander back to the shops on Deanes and Cardenal Herrero by way of Manríquez and Plaza Juda Levi; *or* walk back along Amador de los Ríos to the bottom of Torrijos, turn down past the Puerta del Puente (Gate of the Bridge), and cross the **Puente Romano** (Roman Bridge), whose 16 arches span the Guadalquivir. From the bridge you'll have a good view of **La Albolafia,** the huge wheel once used to carry water to the gardens of the Alcázar. On the far side of the bridge is the **Torre de la Calahorra** (39), now a historical museum.

From whichever option you choose, backtrack to the Mezquita. Facing the south of the mosque is the **Museo Diocesano** (40), with a variety of religious artifacts. From here, go around the Mezquita and head up Encarnación to Plaza Jerónimo Paez; pass through the plaza to find the **Museo Arqueológico** (41), on the Plaza Jerónimo Paez. Off to the east is the Plaza del Potro (Colt Square), named after the Fuente (Fountain) del Potro, in its center, which is mentioned in *Don Quixote.* Cervantes himself reputedly stayed at the plaza's beautifully restored **Posada del Potro,** now used for displays of local craftwork and painting. The relaxed cafés around the plaza are good places for a drink. Here, too, is the **Museo de Bellas Artes** (42).

Go northwest to the **Plaza de la Corredera** (some maps call it Plaza Constitución), an intriguing arcaded square built around 1690. A market is held here on Thursdays and Saturdays, though some stalls do business daily. West of the plaza, along Claudio Marcelo, you'll pass the town hall and the towering columns of what was once a **Roman temple** on your way to the Plaza de las Tendillas. If you've had enough walking for now, you can head down Jesús María and back to the Mezquita, saving the remaining sights for another time. If you're still raring to go, follow Calle Diego León from the north side of the Plaza de las Tendillas to the small **Plaza San Miguel,** whose 13th-century Gothic-Mudéjar church dates from the time of Córdoba's conquest by the Saint King Ferdinand. North of the Plaza San Miguel is the small, charming **Plaza de los Dolores** (43), and around the corner from Dolores is the Casa de los Fernández de Córdoba, with a plateresque facade. At the nearby **Plaza Santa Marina de las Aguas** (44), on the edge of the Barrio de los Toreros, is a statue of the bullfighter Manolete. Southeast of here stands the **Palacio de los Marqueses de Viana** (45), an outstanding example of 17th-century residential architecture. Córdoba's interesting **Jardín Botánico** (Botanical Garden) (46), across from the zoo by the river south of the city center, is best visited by car (there's plenty of parking) or taxi.

Sights to See

(38) **Alcázar de los Reyes Cristianos** (Fortress of the Catholic Monarchs). Built by Alfonso XI in 1328, the Alcázar is a Mudéjar-style palace with splendid gardens. (The original Moorish Alcázar stood beside the Mezquita, on the site of the present Bishop's Palace.) This is where, in the 14th century, the Catholic Monarchs held court and launched their conquest of Granada. Boabdil was imprisoned here for a time in 1483, and for nearly 300 years the Alcázar served as a base for the Inquisition. ✉ *Plaza Campo Santo de los Mártires,* ☎ *957/421015.* 🎫 *425 ptas.; free Fri.* ⏲ *Apr.–Sept., Tues.–Sat. 10–2 and 6–8, Sun. 9:30–3; Oct.–Mar., Tues.–Sat. 10–2 and 4:30–6:30, Sun. 9:30–2:30.*

31 **Calleja de las Flores.** You'd be hard pressed to find prettier patios than the ones along this tiny street, with their ceramics, lush foliage, and wrought-iron grilles. Patios are very much the key to Córdoba's architecture, at least in the old quarter, where life is lived behind sturdy, outer walls—a legacy of the Moors, who honored both the sanctity of the home and the need to shut out the fierce summer sun. In early May, Córdoba throws a **Patio Festival,** for which private patios are filled with flowers, opened to the public, and judged in a municipal competition.

Córdoba Tourist Office. The municipal tourist office has maps and historical information to make your rambles more enlightening. Particularly useful is the *Ruta de Tabernas de Córdoba,* a map pointing out more than 50 tapas bars. In May, ask for the map guiding you to the patios taking part in the annual patio competition. ✉ *Plaza de Juda Levi s/n,* ☎ *957/200522.* ⏲ *Daily 9–2 and 4–8.*

46 **Jardín Botánico.** Across from Córdoba's modest zoo is its modern botanical garden, with both outdoor spaces—including a section devoted to aromatic herbs—and greenhouses full of interesting plants from South America and the Canary Islands. The Ethno-Botanical Museum explores humans' relationships with the plant world. ✉ *Avda. del Zoológico,* ☎ *957/200018.* 🎟 *300 ptas.* ⏲ *Tues.–Sun. 10:30–2:30 and 4:30–6:30 (5:30–7:30 in summer).*

32 **Judería.** Córdoba's medieval Jewish Quarter is its most photogenic warren, a fascinating labyrinth of narrow streets and alleyways lined with ancient white houses. The quarter is packed with buildings and monuments that best illustrate Córdoba's storied past. Alas, the streets around the Mezquita leading up to the Judería have a few too many tourist shops selling the same souvenirs.

NEED A BREAK? The lively, tree-lined **Plaza de Juda Levi** is great for a snack, particularly an ice cream from the Helados Juda Levi.

★ 30 **Mezquita** (Mosque). Built between the 8th and 10th centuries, Córdoba's mosque is one of the earliest and most transportingly beautiful examples of Spanish Muslim architecture. The plain, crenulated walls of the outside do little to prepare you for the sublime beauty of the interior. As you enter through the **Puerta de las Palmas** (Door of the Palms), some 850 columns rise before you in a forest of jasper, marble, granite, and onyx. The pillars are topped by ornate capitals taken from the Visigothic church that was razed to make way for the mosque. Crowning these, an endless array of red-and-white-striped arches curves away into the dimness (horseshoe arches in alternating colors are characteristic of Moorish architecture). The ceiling is carved of delicately tinted cedar. The indirect lighting is meant to reproduce the Moors' own illumination of the mosque, though at their time the building's side arches would have been open to the outdoors, making the interior much brighter than it is now.

The Mezquita has served as a cathedral since 1236, but its origins as a mosque are clear. Built in four stages, it was founded in 785 by Abd ar-Rahman I (756–788) on a site he bought from the Visigoth Christians. He pulled down their church and replaced it with a mosque, one-third the size of the present one, into which he incorporated marble pillars from earlier Roman and Visigothic shrines. Under Abd ar-Rahman II (822–852), the Mezquita boasted an original copy of the Koran and a bone from the arm of the prophet Mohammed, and became a Muslim pilgrimage site second only to Mecca in importance.

Al Hakam II (961–976) built the beautiful **Mihrab,** the Mezquita's greatest jewel. Make your way over to the **Qiblah,** the south-facing wall in which this sacred prayer niche was hollowed out. (Muslim law decrees that a Mihrab face east, toward Mecca, and that worshipers do likewise when they pray. Here, because of an error in calculation, the Mihrab faces more south than east. Al Hakam II spent hours agonizing over a means of correcting such a serious mistake, but he was persuaded by wise architects to let it be.) In front of the Mihrab is the **Maksoureh,** a kind of anteroom for the caliph and his court; its exquisite mosaics and plasterwork make it a masterpiece of Islamic art. The last addition to the mosque as such was completed around 987 by Al Mansur, who more than doubled its size.

After the Reconquest, the Christians left the Mezquita largely undisturbed; they simply dedicated it to the Virgin Mary and set about using it as a place of Christian worship. The clerics did erect a wall closing off the mosque from its courtyard, which helped dim the interior and thus separate the house of worship from the world outside. In the 13th century, Christians had the **Villaviciosa Chapel** built by Moorish craftsmen, its Mudéjar architecture blending harmoniously with the lines of the mosque. Not so the heavy, incongruous Baroque structure of the **cathedral,** sanctioned in the very heart of the mosque by Charles V in the 1520s. To the emperor's credit, he was supposedly horrified when he came to inspect the new construction, exclaiming to the architects, "To build something ordinary, you have destroyed something that was unique in the world" (not that this sentiment stopped him from tampering with the Alhambra, to build the Palacio Carlos V, or with Seville's Alcázar).

The **Patio de los Naranjos** (Orange Court), perfumed in springtime by orange blossoms, is a good place to rest and reflect. The **Puerta del Perdón** (Gate of Forgiveness), on the north wall, serves as the formal entrance to the mosque. The **Virgen de los Faroles** (Virgin of the Lanterns), a small statue in a niche along the north wall of the mosque, on Cardenal Herrero, stands behind a lantern-hung grille, rather like a lady awaiting a serenade. The painting of the Virgin is by Julio Romero de Torres, an early 20th-century Córdoban artist. The **Torre del Alminar,** the minaret once used to summon the faithful to prayer, has a Baroque belfry. ✉ *Torrijos and Cardenal Herrero,* ☎ *957/470512.* 🎫 *800 ptas.* ⏲ *Mon.–Sat. 10–5 (10–7 in summer), Sun. for morning mass and 2–5 (2–7 in summer).*

41 **Museo Arqueológico** (Museum of Archaeology). In the heart of the old quarter (to the north and east of the mosque), this museum displays finds from Córdoba's varied cultural past, including Mudéjar and Renaissance objects. Warning: avoid exploring this area in the deserted siesta hours, as the narrow streets are prime territory for muggers. Otherwise, the alleys and steps along Altos de Santa Ana make for great wandering. ✉ *Plaza Jerónimo Paez,* ☎ *957/471076.* 🎫 *250 ptas.; EU citizens free.* ⏲ *Tues. 3–8, Wed.–Sat. 9–8, Sun. 9–3.*

42 **Museo de Bellas Artes** (Museum of Fine Arts). Faced in deep pink, in a courtyard just off the Plaza del Potro, this museum belongs to a former Hospital de la Caridad (Charity Hospice). It was founded by Ferdinand and Isabella, who twice received Columbus here. The collection includes paintings by Murillo, Valdés Leal, Zurbarán, Goya, and Sorolla. Across the courtyard from the entrance is a museum devoted to the early 20th-century Córdoban artist **Julio Romero de Torres,** who specialized in portraits of demure Andalusian temptresses and is regarded locally as something of a hero. ✉ *Off Plaza del Potro,* ☎ *957/473345.* 🎫 *250 ptas.; EU citizens free.* ⏲ *Tues. 3–8; Wed.–Sat. 9–8, Sun. 9–3.*

40 **Museo Diocesano.** Housed in the former Bishop's Palace, facing the mosque, the Diocesan Museum is devoted to religious art, with illustrated prayer books, tapestries, paintings (including some of Julio Romero de Torres's tamer works), and sculpture. The medieval wood sculptures are especially interesting. ✉ *Torrijos 12,* ☎ *957/479375.* 🎫 *150 ptas.* ⏲ *Winter, weekdays 9:30–1:30 and 3:30–5:30, Sat. 9:30–1:30; summer, weekdays 9:30–3 and Sat. 9:30–1:30.*

NEED A BREAK? Wander over to the **Plaza de las Tendillas,** the nexus of modern Córdoba. The outdoor terraces of the **Café Boston** and **Café Siena** are good places to relax with a coffee in warm weather.

33 **Museo Taurino** (Museum of Bullfighting). This impressive museum on the Plaza Maimónides (or Plaza de las Bulas) is housed in two adjoining mansions. Whatever your thoughts on bullfighting, the museum is worth a visit, as much for the chance to see a restored mansion as for the well-presented posters, Art Nouveau paintings, and memorabilia of famous bullfighters who were native sons of Córdoba. ✉ *Plaza Maimónides,* ☎ *957/201056.* 🎫 *450 ptas.; free Fri.* ⏲ *Tues.–Sat. 10–2 and 4:30–6:30 (6–8 in summer), Sun. 9:30–2:30.*

45 **Palacio de los Marqueses de Viana.** This 17th-century palace is one of Córdoba's most splendid aristocratic homes. It is known as the Museum of Patios for its 12 patios, each one different. Inside are a carriage museum, a library, embossed leather wall hangings, filigree silver, and grand galleries and staircases. The patios and gardens are planted with cypresses, orange trees, and myrtles. ✉ *Plaza Don Gomé,* ☎ *957/480134.* 🎫 *500 ptas.* ⏲ *June–Sept., Thurs.–Tues. 9–2; Oct.–May, weekdays 10–1 and 4–6, Sat. 10–1.*

43 **Plaza de los Dolores.** This small square north of Plaza San Miguel is surrounded by the 17th-century Convento de Capuchinos. It's a secret place, one where you can feel most deeply the city's languid pace. In its center, a statue of **Cristo de los Faroles** (Christ of the Lanterns) stands amid eight lanterns hanging from twisted, wrought-iron brackets.

44 **Plaza Santa Marina de las Aguas.** At the edge of the **Barrio de los Toreros,** a quarter where many of Córdoba's famous bullfighters were born and lived, stands a statue of the famous bullfighter Manolete. Not far from here, on the Plaza de la Lagunilla, is a bust of Manolete.

36 **Puerta de Almodóvar.** Outside this old Moorish gate is a **statue of Seneca,** the Córdoban-born philosopher who rose to prominence in Nero's court in Rome and who committed suicide on his emperor's command.

37 **San Nicolás de Villa.** This classically dark Spanish church, featuring the Mudéjar style of Islamic decoration and art forms, lies at the top of the narrow and colorful Calle San Felipe. Córdoba's well-kept city park, the **Jardínes de la Victoria,** with tiled benches and manicured bushes, is just a block west of here.

35 **Synagogue.** Córdoba's synagogue is the only Jewish temple in Andalusia to survive the expulsion and inquisition of the Jews in 1492 and one of only three ancient synagogues left in all of Spain (the other two are in Toledo). Though it's no longer in use as a place of worship, it has become a treasured symbol for Spain's modern Jewish communities. The outside is plain, but inside you'll find some exquisite Mudéjar stucco tracery—look for the fine plant motifs and the Hebrew inscription stating that the synagogue was built in 1315. The women's gallery still stands, and in the east wall you can see the arch where the sacred scrolls of the law were kept. ✉ *C. Judíos,* ☎ *957/202928.* 🎫 *Free.* ⏲ *Tues.–Sat. 10–2 and 3:30–5:30, Sun. 10–1:30.*

39 **Torre de la Calahorra.** The tower on the far side of the Puente Romano (Roman Bridge) was built in 1369 to guard the entrance to Córdoba. It now houses the **Museo Vivo de Al-Andalus** (Museum of Al-Andalus), where films and audiovisual guides (in English) help you learn more about Córdoba's history, particularly its tricultural period, the time of the Moorish caliphate. Climb the narrow staircase to the top of the tower for the view of the Roman bridge and city on the other side of the Guadalquivir. ✉ *Avda. de la Confederación,* ☎ *957/293929.* *500 ptas; 650 ptas. with audiovisual show.* ⊙ *May–Sept., daily 10–2 and 4:30–8:30; Oct.–Apr., daily 10–6. Last tour one hour before closing.*

34 **Zoco.** *Zoco* is the Spanish word for the Arab *souk* (market), the one-time function of this courtyard near the synagogue. It now hosts a daily crafts market, where you can see artisans at work, and evening flamenco in summer.

Dining

$$$ ✕ **El Blasón.** Owned by El Caballo Rojo (☞ *below*), this restaurant has earned itself a name for fine food and unbeatable ambience. It's tucked away in an old inn one block west of Avenida Gran Capitán; a Moorish-style entrance bar leads onto a patio enclosed by ivy-covered walls. Upstairs are two elegant dining rooms where blue walls, aquamarine silk curtains, and candelabras evoke early 19th-century luxury. The innovative menu includes *salmón con naranjas de la mezquita* (salmon in oranges from the mosque) and *musclo de oca al vino afrutado* (leg of goose in fruited wine). ✉ *José Zorrilla 11,* ☎ *957/480625. AE, DC, MC, V.*

$$$ ✕ **El Caballo Rojo.** The "Red Horse," on the north side of the mosque, is both a Córdoba institution and a winner of the National Gastronomy Prize. The interior resembles a cool, leafy Andalusian patio, and the menu mixes traditional specialties, such as *rabo de toro* (oxtail stew) and *salmorejo* (cold, tomato-based soup), with exotic dishes inspired by Córdoba's Moorish and Jewish heritage, such as *alboronia* (a cold salad of stewed vegetables flavored with honey, saffron, and aniseed) and the popular *cordero a la miel* (lamb roasted with honey). ✉ *Cardenal Herrero 28,* ☎ *957/478001. AE, DC, MC, V.*

$$$ ✕ **La Almudaina.** This attractive restaurant is in a 15th-century house across the square from the Alcázar gardens, at the entrance to the Judería. The cellar hides both an Andalusian patio topped with a stained-glass cupola and a *mesón bodega* (wine cellar). The menu focuses on fresh market produce and innovative entrées; you might try *calabacín con salsa de carabineros* (squash with prawn sauce), *lubina al hinojo* (sea bass in fennel), or *lomo de venado en salsa de setas* (venison in wild-mushroom sauce). ✉ *Campo Santo de los Mártires 1,* ☎ *957/474342. AE, DC, MC, V. Closed Sun. in summer. No dinner Sun.*

$$–$$$ ★ ✕ **El Churrasco.** The name suggests grilled meat, but this outstanding restaurant, located in the heart of the Judería just two minutes' walk from the mosque, serves much more than that. The colorful bar is an ideal place for tapas. The steak is the best in town, and the grilled fish is superfresh; add to that a picturesque environment, including alfresco dining in the inner patio, and a staff that functions with pinpoint precision. In a separate house, two doors down the street, is the restaurant's formidable wine cellar, which is also a small museum. Ask your waiter to take you there before or after your meal. ✉ *Romero 16,* ☎ *957/290819. AE, DC, MC, V. Closed Aug.*

$$ ★ ✕ **Bodegas Campos.** One block from the Plaza del Potro, this maze-like restaurant in a converted wine cellar offers the complete Andalusian experience in a warren of barrel-heavy dining rooms and leafy courtyards. Regional dishes prepared with flair include *ensalada de bacalao y naranja* (salad of salt cod and orange with olive oil) and *man-*

itas de cerdo relleno com jamón iberico (pork knuckles with Iberian ham), and the menu also has dishes from elsewhere in Spain, such as the Basque specialty *cogote de merluza* (hake's neck with prawns). ✉ *Los Lineros 32,* ☎ *957/497643. AE, MC, V. No dinner Sun.*

$$ ✕ **Casa Pepe de la Judería.** This three-floor labyrinth of neat rooms is just around the corner from the mosque, toward the Judería. There is live Spanish guitar music most nights, and in summer the rooftop opens for barbecues, serving a full selection of tapas and house specialties such as *rabo de toro* (oxtail stew). ✉ *Romero 1, off Deanes,* ☎ *957/200744. AE, DC, MC, V.*

$ ✕ **Federación de Peñas Cordobesas.** You'll find this popular budget restaurant on one of the main thoroughfares of the old quarter, halfway between the mosque and the Plaza Tendillas. You can eat inside or at one of several tables around the fountain in the spacious courtyard, surrounded by horseshoe arches. The food is traditional Spanish fare, and there are several fixed menus at attractive prices. ✉ *Conde y Luque 8,* ☎ *957/475427. MC, V.*

Lodging

$$$–$$$$ **Conquistador.** Located right next to the mosque, this contemporary hotel is decorated in Andalusian-Moorish style, making good use of ceramic tiles and inlaid marquetry in the bar and public rooms. The reception area overlooks a colonnaded patio, fountain, and small enclosed garden. Rooms are comfortable, elegant, and classically Andalusian; those at the front have small balconies overlooking the walls of the mosque, which are floodlit at night. ✉ *Magistral González Francés 17, 14003,* ☎ *957/481102 or 957/481411,* FAX *957/474677. 99 rooms, 3 suites. Breakfast room, bar, sauna, parking (fee). AE, DC, MC, V.*

$$$ **Al Mihrab.** Outside town, past the parador (☞ *below*), this three-story, dark-ocher building is set among trees in the tranquil foothills of the Sierra de Córdoba. Rooms are large, with white marble floors and colorful, patterned bedspreads and curtains. Most have good mountain or city views, and the view of Córdoba from the greenhouse restaurant (open to guests only) is spectacular. ✉ *Avda. del Brillante, Km 5, 14012,* ☎ FAX *957/272198. 29 rooms. Restaurant, pool, sauna, outdoor hot tub. MC, V.*

$$$ ★ **Amistad Córdoba.** This stylish hotel is built around two former 18th-century mansions that look out upon the Plaza de Maimónides in the heart of the Judería. (You can also enter through the old Moorish walls on Calle Cairuan.) It features a Mudéjar courtyard, carved-wood ceilings, and a plush lounge area. The rooms are large and comfortable. The newer wing has a more modern look, with blues and grays and Norwegian wood. ✉ *Plaza de Maimónides 3, 14004,* ☎ *957/420335,* FAX *957/420365. 84 rooms. Restaurant, bar, parking (fee). AE, DC, MC, V.*

$$$ **Parador La Arruzafa.** Five kilometers (3 mi) north of town, this modern parador is set in a peaceful, leafy garden on the slopes of the Sierra de Córdoba. Rooms are sunny, with wood or wicker furnishings, and many have balconies overlooking the garden or looking toward Córdoba. ✉ *Avda. de la Arruzafa, 14012,* ☎ *957/275900,* FAX *957/280409. 89 rooms, 5 suites. Pool, tennis courts. AE, DC, MC, V.*

$$ **Albucasis.** Tucked away in the heart of the old quarter is the friendly, family-run Albucasis. The air-conditioned rooms are spotless, with marble-tile floors and green-tile bathrooms. Doubles overlook the pretty patio and have a limited view of the Torre del Alminar. Breakfast and drinks are served in the attractive reception area. ✉ *Buen Pastor 11, 14003,* ☎ FAX *957/478625. 15 rooms. Bar. MC, V.*

$$ **Omeyas.** Just one block north of the mosque, this new, comfortable, small hotel has rooms on two floors around an arcaded central patio. The lobby is neo-Moorish, complete with horseshoe arches

echoing those in the mosque. Rooms are comfortably appointed and, despite the central location, quiet. ✉ *Encarnación 17, 14003,* ☎ *957/492267,* FAX *957/491659. 29 rooms. Cafeteria. AE, DC, MC, V.*

$–$$ **Mezquita.** Brand-new and ideally located next to the mosque, this hotel occupies a restored 16th-century home. Dappled with bronze sculptures on Andalusian themes, the public areas reflect the owner's penchant for collecting antiques. The best rooms face the interior patio; their decor is on the plain side. The only real drawback is the lack of parking. ✉ *Plaza Santa Catalina 1, 41003,* ☎ *957/475585.* FAX *957/476219. 21 rooms. Restaurant. MC, V.*

$ **Maestre.** This small hotel around the corner from the Plaza del Potro has some of the best-value lodgings in Córdoba. Room decor is simple but modern, and there is a pleasant patio. The management also runs an even cheaper lodging, the Hostal Maestre, and self-catered apartments down the street. ✉ *Romero Barros 4–6, 14003,* ☎ *957/472410,* FAX *957/475395. 26 rooms. Parking (fee). AE, MC, V.*

Nightlife and the Arts

Concerts, ballets, and plays are performed in the **Gran Teatro** (✉ Avda. del Gran Capitán 3, ☎ 957/480237). The International Guitar Festival attracts top Spanish and international **guitarists** for more than two weeks of great music in July, and **orchestras** perform in the Alcázar's garden on Sundays throughout the summer. **Flamenco** is performed (mainly for tourists) in the Zoco, off Calle Judíos, on summer evenings. Two of Córdoba's most popular flamenco clubs are **Tablao Cardenal** (✉ Torrijos 10, facing the Mezquita, ☎ 957/483112), open year-round, and **Mesón la Bulería** (✉ Pedro López 3, ☎ 957/483839), open Easter through September.

Shopping

Córdoba's main shopping district is around Avenida Gran Capitán, Ronda de los Tejares, and Plaza de Colón. **Artesanía Andaluza** (✉ Tomás Conde 3), near the Museum of Bullfighting, sells a wide range of Cordoban handicrafts, including fine embossed leather (a legacy of the Moors) and jewelry made of filigree silver from the mines of the Sierra Morena. The **Association of Córdoban Artisans** (✉ C. Judíos, opposite synagogue) sells crafts in the Zoco; note that many stalls are open May–September only. **Meryam** (✉ Calleja de las Flores 2) is one of Córdoba's best workshops for embossed leather.

Medina Azahara

47 *8 km (5 mi) west of Córdoba on the C431.*

The ruins and partial reconstruction of the fabulous Muslim palace Medina Azahara (sometimes spelled Madinat Al-Zahra) are well worth a detour. Begun in 936, Medina Azahara was built by Abd ar-Rahman III for his favorite concubine, az-Zahra. According to contemporary chroniclers, it took 10,000 men, 2,600 mules, and 400 camels 25 years to erect this fantasy of 4,300 columns in dazzling pink, green, and white marble and jasper brought from Carthage. Here, on three terraces, stood a palace, a mosque, luxurious baths, fragrant gardens, fishponds, even an aviary and a zoo. In 1013 the place was sacked and destroyed by Berber mercenaries. In 1944 the Royal Apartments were rediscovered, and the Throne Room was carefully reconstructed. The outline of the mosque has also been excavated. The only covered part of the site is the Salon de Abd Al Rahman III; the rest is a sprawl of foundations, defense walls, and arches that hint at the splendor of the original city-palace. ✉ *Off C431; follow signs en route to Almodóvar del Río,* ☎ *957/329130. 250 ptas.; EU citizens free.* ⏲ *May–Sept., Tues.–Sat. 10–2 and 6–8:30, Sun. 10–2; Oct.–Apr., Tues.–Sat. 10–2 and 4–6:30, Sun. 10–2.*

OFF THE BEATEN PATH **ALMODÓVAR DEL RÍO** – If you're driving, continue to Almodóvar del Río, 18 km (11 mi) farther along C431, where just beyond the town a restored castle towers dramatically over the countryside.

Montilla

48 *46 km (28 mi) south of Córdoba.*

Heading south from Córdoba to Málaga through rolling hills, ablaze with sunflowers in early summer, you reach the Montilla-Morilés vineyards of the Córdoban *campiña* (countryside; lower farmlands). Every fall, 47,000 acres' worth of Pedro Ximénez grapes are crushed here to produce the region's rich Montilla wines, not unlike sherry except that, because the local grapes contain so much sugar (transformed into alcohol during fermentation), they are not fortified with the addition of extra alcohol. For this reason—or so the locals claim—Montilla wines do not give you a hangover. The oldest of the wineries, in the town of Montilla itself, is **Alvear,** founded in 1729 (✉ Avda. María Auxiliadora 1, ☎ 957/664014). You can also visit **Bodegas Gracia Hermanos** (☎ 957/650162) or **Bodegas Robles** (☎ 957/650063), all by appointment. On the outskirts of Montilla, coopers' shops produce barrels of various sizes, some small enough to serve as creative souvenirs.

Dining and Lodging

$$ ✕ **Las Camachas.** The best-known restaurant in southern Córdoba province, Las Camachas occupies an Andalusian-style hacienda outside Montilla near the main Málaga–Córdoba road. Start with tapas in the attractive, tiled bar; then make yourself comfortable in one of the four dining rooms. Regional dishes include *alcachofas al Montilla* (artichokes braised in Montilla wine), *salmorejo, perdiz campiña* (country-style partridge), and *cordero a la miel de Jara* (lamb with Jara honey). You can also buy local wines here. ✉ *Antigua Carretera Córdoba–Málaga,* ☎ *957/650004. AE, DC, MC, V.*

$$ 🏨 **Don Gonzalo.** Just 2 km (1 mi) south of Montilla, the Don Gonzalo is one of Andalusia's better roadside hostelries. The wood-beamed common areas sport an eclectic mixture of decorative elements (note the elephant tusks flanking the TV in the lounge). The clay-tiled rooms are large and comfortable; some look onto the road, others onto the garden and pool. Be sure to visit the wine cellar. ✉ *Carretera Córdoba–Málaga, Km 47, 14550,* ☎ *957/650658,* FAX *957/650666. 29 rooms. Restaurant, pool, tennis. AE, MC, V.*

La Subbética

49 *Priego de Córdoba is 103 km (64 mi) southeast of Córdoba.*

In the southeastern corner of Córdoba's province lies a largely undiscovered cluster of villages and small towns known to locals as the Subbética and protected as a nature park. For general information or hiking advice, contact the Mancomunidad de la Subbética (✉ C. Pilarejo, Carcabuey, ☎ 957/704106) or Iniciativas Subbéticas (☎ 957/694545). You'll need a car to explore this area, and in some places you'll find the roads bumpy and rather rough.

At the southern tip of the province, southeast of Lucena, C334 crosses the **Embalse de Iznájar** (Iznájar Reservoir) amid spectacular scenery. On C334 halfway between Lucena and the reservoir, in **Rute,** you can sample the potent *anís* liqueur for which this small, whitewashed town is famous. In **Lucena** you can see the Torre del Moral, where Boabdil was imprisoned in 1483 after launching an unsuccessful attack on the Christians. Today the town makes furniture and brass and copper pots.

The jewel of this area is **Priego de Córdoba,** a town of 14,000 lying at the foot of Mt. Tinosa (from Lucena, head north 9 km/5½ mi on C327 to Cabra, where you'll turn right, or east, on C336; after 32 km/20 mi, you'll reach Priego). Wander down Calle del Río opposite the ayuntamiento to see fine 18th-century mansions, once the homes of silk merchants. At the end of the street is the Fuente del Rey (King's Fountain), with some 130 water jets, built in 1803. Don't miss the lavish Baroque churches of La Asunción and La Aurora or the Barrio de la Villa, an old Moorish quarter.

Baena, surrounded by chalk fields producing top-quality olive oil, is an old town of narrow streets, whitewashed houses, ancient mansions, and churches clustered beneath Moorish battlements. **Zuheros,** at the northern edge of the Subbética, is a jewel of a mountain village. Within the rocky mountain face that towers over the town is the **Cueva de los Murciélagos** (Cave of the Bats), which you can explore by appointment (☎ 957/69545).

Lodging

$$ 🏨 **Santo Domingo.** This dignified, stone-faced, 17th-century convent in Lucena was only recently converted to a hotel. The lobby opens onto a large interior courtyard with a fountain. Rooms are stylishly dressed in blue or in white, brown, and red; the best of the lot face the patio from the top floor. Exterior rooms can be noisy. ✉ *El Agua 12, 14900 Lucena,* ☎ *957/511100,* FAX *957/516295. 28 rooms, 2 suites. Restaurant, parking (fee). AE, DC, MC, V.*

$$ 🏨 **Villa Turística de Priego.** Near the hamlet of Zagrilla, 6 km (4 mi) from Priego de Córdoba, this gleaming-white complex is in the heart of the Subbética nature park. Each self-catered unit has a kitchenette. ✉ *Aldea de Zagrilla, 14816,* ☎ *957/703503,* FAX *957/703573. 52 units. Restaurant, kitchenettes, pool. AE, DC, MC, V.*

$ 🏨 **Zuhayra.** This simple but comfortable hotel on a narrow street in picturesque Zuheros makes a good base of exploration. The large rooms have splendid views over the village rooftops to the valley below. ✉ *C. Mirador 10, 14870 Zuheros,* ☎ *957/694693,* FAX *957/694702. 18 rooms. Restaurant. AE, DC, MC, V.*

EASTERN ANDALUSIA A TO Z

Arriving and Departing

By Bus

If you're not driving, buses are the best method of transportation in this region. They run to most of the outlying towns and villages, and their connections between major cities are generally faster and more frequent than those of the trains (☞ By Train, *below*). If you're taking public transportation to the villages of the Alpujarras, check bus schedules and accommodations carefully with Granada's tourist office and the Alsina Gräells bus company before you set off.

Buses connect **Córdoba** with several Spanish cities. For bus information, go to the **bus station,** next to the AVE (high-speed train) station (✉ Glorieta de las Tres Culturas, ☎ 957/404040) and inquire with the following bus companies: **Alsina Gräells** (✉ Glorieta de las Tres Culturas, Córdoba, ☎ 957/278100) for service to Badajoz, Cádiz, Granada, Seville, and Málaga; **Ureña** (✉ Glorieta de las Tres Culturas, Córdoba, ☎ 957/404558) for Seville and Jaén; **Priego** (✉ Paseo de la Victoria 29, Córdoba, ☎ 957/290158) for Madrid (via N IV), Barcelona, and Valencia; **Secorbus** (✉ Camino de los Sastres 1, Avda. de la República Argentina, across from Hotel Meliá, Córdoba, ☎ 902/229292) for

Madrid and Andújar; and **López** (✉ Glorieta de las Tres Culturas, Córdoba, ☎ 957/767077) for Ciudad Real and Madrid (via Ciudad Real). **Ramírez** (✉ Avda. de la República Argentina 26, Córdoba, ☎ 957/422106) serves small towns near Córdoba.

Granada's bus station is on the highway to Jaén. The main company, **Alsina Gräells** (☎ 958/185480), serves Madrid, Algeciras, Málaga, Córdoba, Seville, Jaén, Motril, and Almería.

By Car

Be prepared for parking problems in the cities of Granada and Córdoba, and for the ever-present threat of break-ins, particularly in Granada. Most of Córdoba's hotels are in a labyrinth of narrow streets that can be a nightmare to negotiate, even with a small car. In Córdoba, all sights are within walking distance of one another; in Granada, it's simpler to take a taxi up to the Alhambra or the Albaicín than to tackle the extremely complicated one-way system and narrow Moorish streets in a rental car.

The route from Granada to Jaén, Baeza, Úbeda, and Cazorla is one of Andalusia's least tourist-clogged, though you'll probably encounter the odd tour bus between Granada and Jaén. The roads are smooth, and driving through this region is one of the most pleasant ways to see the countryside.

By Plane

Granada Airport (☎ 958/245200) is 18 km (11 mi) west of the city. Aviaco has daily flights to and from Madrid and Barcelona and three flights a week to Valencia.

BETWEEN THE AIRPORT AND DOWNTOWN

J. González buses (☎ 958/131309) run between the airport and the city center, leaving the Plaza Isabel la Católica about 1¼ hours before flight departures. Times are listed at the bus stop; service is reduced in winter.

By Train

The wonderful, high-speed AVE connects Madrid with Córdoba in less than two hours. Train service from Córdoba to Granada and Jaén, however, is poor, and there is no service at all between Granada and Jaén. Both Córdoba and Jaén have trains to Linares-Baeza, but from there you must take a bus into Baeza or Úbeda. For information, call **RENFE** at ☎ 902/240202.

Contacts and Resources

Car Rental

Hertz, Avis, and **Europcar** have branches at Granada's airport. **Autos Fortuna** (✉ Camino de Purchil 2, at Camino Ronda, Granada, ☎ 958/260254).

Emergencies

Police: ☎ 092, ☎ 091.

Guided Tours

Pullmantur and **Juliá Tours** (☞ Bus Travel *in* Smart Travel Tips) run numerous tours to this region, which you can book through most travel agents, many hotels, or through the companies' Madrid and Costa del Sol offices. **Córdoba Vision** offers both daytime and nighttime tours, among them trips to Medina Azahara (✉ Rafael Márquez Manzzantini 5, ☎ 957/231734, FAX 957/237394).

SPECIAL-INTEREST TOURS

Horseback-riding tours—some with English guides—are offered in the villages of the Alpujarras and the Sierra Nevada and sometimes elsewhere. Contact tourist offices for information. One agency in the Alpujarras is **Cabalgar Rutas Alternativas** (✉ Bubión, Granada, ☎ 958/763135, FAX 958/763136).

In the **Cazorla Nature Park,** Jeep or horseback excursions and more specific nature tours, such as bird-watching, can be arranged through Quercus (☎ 953/720115).

WALKING TOURS

In Córdoba, you can hire English-speaking guides for the mosque and synagogue through the **Asociación Profesional de Informadores Turísticos** (✉ Museo Diocesano, Torrijos 12, Córdoba, ☎ 957/486997). In Granada, contact a multilingual guide through the **Asociación Provincial de Guías** (✉ Puerta del Vino, La Alhambra, Granada, ☎ 958/229936). Guided tours of Úbeda and Jaén are offered by **Artificis** (✉ Juan Ruiz Gonzalez 19, next to parador in Úbeda, ☎ 953/758150).

Visitor Information

Municipal tourist offices: **Baeza** (✉ Plaza del Pópulo, ☎ 953/740444. **Córdoba** (✉ Plaza de Juda Levi, ☎ 957/200522, FAX 957/200277). **Granada** (✉ Plaza Mariana Pineda 10, ☎ 958/223528). **Úbeda** (✉ Hospital de Santiago, Avenida Cristo Rey 2, ☎ 953/750897). Granada and Córdoba also have **regional tourist offices** for Andalusia, at the Corral del Carbón (✉ C. Mariana Pineda, Granada, ☎ 958/225990) and the Palacio de Exposiciones, next to the mosque (✉ Torrijos 10, Córdoba, ☎ 957/471235).

12 SEVILLE AND WESTERN ANDALUSIA

The flat expanse of fertile pastures, muddy marshlands, chalky vineyards, and sandy beaches in western Moorish Spain contrasts vividly with the mountainous terrain to the east. In their midst, Seville exudes history, romance, and tapas; seaside Cádiz is a charming mix of Moorish and 18th-century quarters; Carmona and Itálica present Roman ruins; and Arcos exemplifies the white Andalusian village.

By Hilary Bunce

Updated by Mark Little

WITHIN THE TRIANGLE formed by the cities of Huelva, Seville, and Cádiz lies the estuary of Andalusia's great river, the Guadalquivir. The riverbanks are lined with cotton and rice fields, orange groves, stud farms, and bull ranches.

This is a land with a proud seafaring heritage. History buffs can follow the footsteps of Christopher Columbus from the monastery at La Rábida, whose friars pleaded his cause with Queen Isabella, to Palos, where he set sail on his epic voyage of 1492, and finally to Seville, where Columbus is believed to be buried. The province's shores and rivers echo with the names of other maritime adventurers as well: Ferdinand Magellan, Juan Sebastián de Elcano, Sir Francis Drake, and Pierre de Villeneuve, to name just a few. Spain's trade with the New World centered on Seville for more than 200 years, and treasures from the Americas flowed into her coffers. Later, when this maritime and trading role passed to Cádiz, New World riches funded that city's most impressive buildings.

Many towns in this region are named "de la frontera," including Arcos, Jerez, and Palos, because for 250 years they stood on the frontier between Christian Spain and Muslim Granada.

Pleasures and Pastimes

Bullfighting

Seville is home to one of Spain's most celebrated bullrings, the Maestranza. Few *toreros* (bullfighters) gain nationwide recognition until they have fought in this "cathedral of bullfighting." The season runs from Easter until late October, but it peaks early on, when Seville's April Fair draws Spain's leading *toreros* for a string of daily fights.

Dining

Western Andalusia is known throughout Spain as a gourmand's paradise. Spaniards drive for miles to sample the giant shrimp and succulent seafood of Puerto de Santa María and Sanlúcar de Barrameda, and to enjoy *fino* (a dry and light sherry from Jerez) and *manzanilla* (a dry and delicate Sanlúcar sherry with a hint of saltiness). Others come just to feast on tapas in Seville. The village of Jabugo, in Huelva, is famous for its cured ham from the free-ranging Ibérico pig.

Note that many restaurants are closed on Sunday evenings, and several close for a month's vacation in August.

CATEGORY	COST*
$$$$	over 6,500 ptas.
$$$	4,000 ptas.–6,500 ptas.
$$	2,500 ptas.–4,000 ptas.
$	under 2,500 ptas.

**per person for a three-course meal, excluding drinks, tax, and service*

Fiestas

Western Andalusia's festivals are known well beyond the borders of Spain. People come from far and away to witness the pageant of Seville's Holy Week processions and join in the fun of its April Fair. The Carnival in Cádiz is one of the best in the land. Folks also flock to the revelries of Jerez's May Horse Fair and September Harvest Festival. If you prefer to travel crowd-free, take care to avoid these events.

Cádiz celebrates the weeklong Carnival in February, just before Lent begins. Seville's dramatic **Semana Santa** (Holy Week) processions (April 8–15 in 2001) are the most famous in Spain. Jerez and Cádiz also have

Semana Santa processions. The **Feria de Abril** (April Fair), Seville's annual city fair, is celebrated with top bullfights; horse parades; flamenco costumes; and singing, dancing, and fireworks nightly in the fairground across the river. In May, Jerez de la Frontera shows off its Andalusian horses in the **Feria del Caballo** (Horse Fair). In June, worshipers make a popular Whitsuntide pilgrimage to the shrine of the **Virgen del Rocío** (Virgin of the Dew) in the village of El Rocío (Huelva). **Corpus Christi** (the second Thursday after Whitsun; June 14 in 2001) is celebrated with processions in Cádiz, Jerez, and Seville. The Assumption of the Virgin Mary is celebrated throughout Spain on August 15, but especially in Seville, where it's the day of the city's patron, **Nuestra Señora de los Reyes** (Our Lady of the Kings). In September, all wine-producing towns in the province of Cádiz celebrate the **Fiesta de la Vendimia** (Grape Harvest Festival). Jerez's **Fiesta de Otoño** (Autumn Festival) is particularly spectacular. Cádiz commemorates its patron, the **Virgen del Rosario** (Virgin of the Rosary) in October.

Flamenco

Seville and Jerez are widely acknowledged as Spain's flamenco headquarters, and Jerez now has an institute dedicated to the history of this quintessentially Andalusian art form. Particularly in Seville, you can experience the energy and emotion of this music and dance at some of the finest clubs in Spain.

Horses

Jerez's purebred Carthusian horses are shown off in the annual Feria del Caballo, in May, and these handsome animals perform every Thursday throughout the year at Jerez's Royal Andalusian School of Equestrian Art. Horse races are held on the beach in Sanlúcar de Barrameda on two weekends in August (the dates depend on the tides), a tradition dating back to 1845.

Lodging

Fine hotels are in abundance here. Western Andalusia has four paradors, including converted palaces at Carmona and Arcos de la Frontera; both of these have great views and are worth a special visit. The parador at Mazagón and the parador Hotel Atlántico, in Cádiz, are comfortable modern hotels. You can also stay at a converted monastery, in Puerto de Santa María, or on a private luxury ranch, near Arcos de la Frontera. Seville has grand old hotels like the Alfonso XIII and the Colón and a number of former palaces recently converted into sumptuous hostelries.

If you want to catch a glimpse of a fabulous festival, such as Seville's Holy Week or April Fair or Jerez's Horse Fair or Harvest Festival, you *must* book early—four to eight months in advance in Seville. To see Cádiz during Carnival, try to reserve at least a month in advance. All hotel prices in Seville rise steeply—by at least half—during Holy Week and the April Fair; the same applies in Jerez during the May and September *ferias*.

It *is* possible to sleep cheaply in Seville, but your room will be tiny, and you'll have to scour areas far from the city center. Prices fluctuate dramatically with the seasons—much more so than in most other parts of Spain—so it's best to inquire in advance.

CATEGORY	COST*
$$$$	over 20,000 ptas.
$$$	12,000 ptas.–20,000 ptas.
$$	8,000 ptas.–12,000 ptas.
$	under 8,000 ptas.

**All prices are for a standard double room, excluding tax.*

Exploring Seville and Western Andalusia

This chapter covers the provinces of Seville and Cádiz and part of Huelva. You'll probably want to start your perambulations, or at least make transport connections, in the legendary city of Seville.

Numbers in the text correspond to numbers in the margin and on the Andalusia: Seville and the Guadalquivir Delta and Seville maps.

Great Itineraries

A week in this region gives you time to sample the various landscapes. If time is short, however, a few days will be enough time for sunny Seville to make a lasting impression. From there, you can go west to wander with wildlife at Doñana National Park and visit the villages that played important roles in the voyage of Christopher Columbus; or head south to sip sherry at the source in Jerez de la Frontera, relax in the whitewashed village of Arcos de la Frontera, and feast on seafood in ancient Cádiz. Your mode of transport may help determine your itinerary—the major cities and towns are accessible by train and bus, but driving gives you the freedom to explore some smaller, often charming *pueblos.*

IF YOU HAVE 3 DAYS

Base yourself in **Seville** (1)–(30). On your first day, visit the cathedral, the Giralda, and the nearby Moorish-style Alcázar, followed after lunch by an amble through the orange-scented lanes of the Barrio de Santa Cruz. On the second day, enjoy the Parque de María Luisa and the colorful Plaza de América. Before leaving the city, stop at the monumental Plaza de España, and head over to the Torre de Oro before dipping into the tapas bars of the lively Calle Betis. Devote the next day to Spain's Roman heritage: explore the ancient town of **Carmona** (31), with its Roman necropolis, and then the Roman ruins at **Itálica** (32) before returning to Seville.

IF YOU HAVE 5 DAYS

Start with **Seville** (1)–(30)—see the cathedral and Giralda, and spend some time in the Alcázar. After lunch, relax with a walk through the narrow lanes of the Barrio de Santa Cruz. The next day, take in the Museo de Bellas Artes (Museum of Fine Arts); then head toward the river and walk the Paseo de Colón, where you can see the Maestranza Bullring and visit the Torre de Oro. On your third day, wander the Parque de María Luisa, stopping at the Plaza de América and monumental Plaza de España. On your way back to the city center, look for the University of Seville, the former tobacco factory of *Carmen* fame. On day four, leave Seville for **Jerez de la Frontera** (41). Tour a local *bodega* and taste the world's finest sherry; and if you happen to be here on a Thursday, watch the spectacular horse show at the Royal Andalusian School of Equestrian Art. Spend your last night in the small port town of **Puerto de Santa María** (44). On your last day, visit the ancient town of **Cádiz** (45) before returning to Seville.

When to Tour Seville and Western Andalusia

If you want to experience the pomp and crackle of a Spanish fiesta, this is the place to come—just reserve a room far in advance (and read the Seville chapter of James Michener's classic *Iberia*). Aside from the big fiestas, spring and late fall are particularly nice, when the weather is warm but not unpleasantly hot. Winters are mild and uncrowded. If you plan to visit Jerez de la Frontera, try to get there on a Thursday so you can catch the horse show at the Royal Andalusian School of Equestrian Art. Keep in mind that many museums and monuments are closed on Monday.

Andalusia: Seville and the Guadalquivir Delta

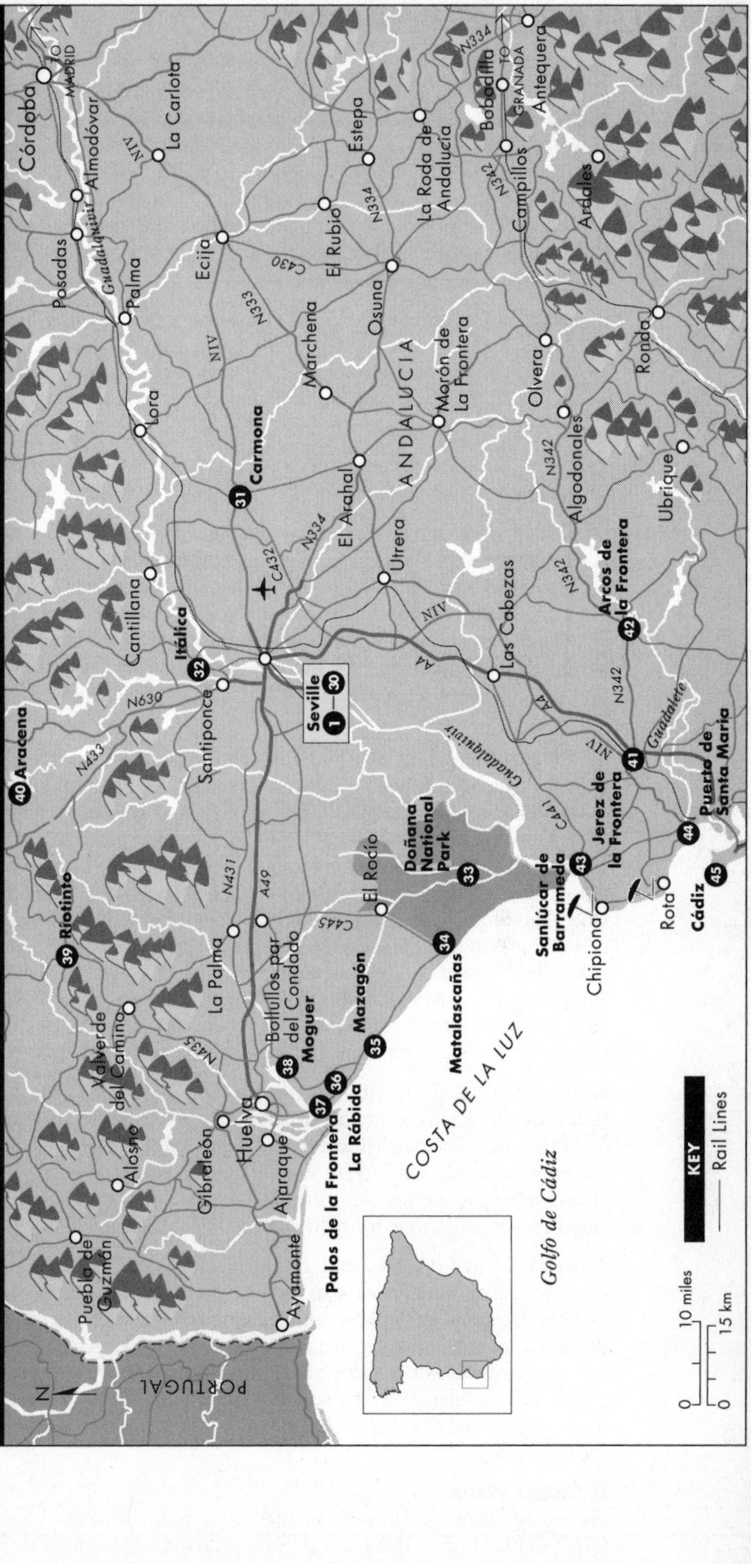

SEVILLE AND ENVIRONS

Seville's whitewashed houses bright with bougainvillea, its ocher-color palaces, and its Baroque facades have long enchanted both Sevillanos and travelers. Lying on the banks of the Guadalquivir, Seville is Spain's fourth-largest city and the capital of Andalusia. Of course, this bustling city of almost 800,000 also has a downside: traffic-choked streets, high unemployment, a notorious petty-crime rate, and at times the kind of impersonal treatment you won't find in smaller cities like Granada and Córdoba. But Seville's artistic heritage and its citizens' zest for life more than compensate for its disadvantages.

If you want to venture out of Seville on a very quick day trip, head to Carmona, with its stunning Roman necropolis and terrific hotels (the parador is perfect for a leisurely lunch), or the ancient town of Itálica.

Seville

❶ *550 km (340 mi) southwest of Madrid, 220 km (140 mi) northwest of Málaga.*

Seville has a long and noble history. Conquered by the Romans in 205 BC, it gave the world two great emperors, Trajan and Hadrian (you can see Hadrian's birthplace at nearby Itálica). The Moors held Seville for more than 500 years and left it one of their greatest works of architecture, the much-loved Giralda tower. Saint King Ferdinand (Ferdinand III) lies enshrined in the glorious cathedral; and his rather less saintly descendant, Pedro the Cruel, builder of the splendid Alcázar, is buried here as well.

Seville is justly proud of its literary and artistic associations. The painters Diego Rodríguez de Silva Velázquez (1599–1660) and Bartolomé Estéban Murillo (1617–82) were sons of Seville, as were the poets Gustavo Adolfo Bécquer (1836–70), Antonio Machado (1875–1939), and Nobel prize winner Vicente Aleixandre (1898–1984). The tale of the ingenious knight of La Mancha was begun in a Seville jail—Don Quixote's creator, Miguel de Cervantes, twice languished in a debtors' prison here. Tirso de Molina's Don Juan wooed and seduced in Seville's mansions, later scheming as Don Giovanni in the Barrio de Santa Cruz; the Barrio was also the setting for the nuptials of Rossini's barber, Figaro. Nearby, at the old tobacco factory (now the University of Seville), Bizet's sultry Carmen first met Don José.

Seville's color and vivacity are most intense during Semana Santa (Holy Week), when lacerated Christs and bejeweled, weeping Virgins from the city's 24 parishes are paraded through the streets on floats borne by penitents, who often walk barefoot. Some carry crosses or chains, having made a promise during a serious illness that if they were cured they would atone for their sins.

A week later, and this time in flamenco costume, the Sevillanos throw their April Fair, the greatest party of the year. This celebration began as a horse-trading fair in 1847 and still honors its equine origins: midday horse parades feature men in broad-brimmed hats and Andalusian riding gear astride prancing steeds, with their women in long, ruffled dresses riding sidesaddle behind them. Bullfights, fireworks, and all-night singing and dancing in the fairground's *casetas* (tents) complete the spectacle.

A Good Walk

Our main Seville stroll takes in the major sights in central Seville. Other sights north of this area call for special outings (☞ *below*). Start with the **cathedral** ②, in the Plaza Virgen de los Reyes. Then climb the Giralda, the minaret of the former Moorish mosque—from the top you have a tremendous view over the city. Walk down Avenida de la Constitución and visit the **Archivo de Indias** ③, which holds the surviving documents related to the discovery of the New World. Behind the archive is the **Alcázar** ④, a palace surrounded, Moorish-style, by high walls. Backtrack to the Giralda and the Plaza Virgen de los Reyes and plunge into the **Barrio de Santa Cruz** ⑤, home of Seville's Jews in the Middle Ages—its shady lanes hide whitewashed buildings, courtyards, and plenty of flowers. While you're in the neighborhood, don't miss the **Hospital de los Venerables** ⑥. On Calle Santa Teresa is the **Casa de Murillo** ⑦, named for one of Seville's best-known painters; from there you can stroll through the **Jardines de Murillo** ⑧, complete with a statue of Christopher Columbus. At the far end of the gardens is the **University of Seville** ⑨, once the tobacco factory where the mythical Carmen worked as a cigar roller. Across the Glorieta de San Diego is the **Parque de María Luisa** ⑩, which encompasses the **Plaza de España** ⑪ at its east end as well as the **Plaza de América** ⑫ at its south end. In the Plaza de América you'll find the **Museo Arqueológico** ⑬, with marble statues and mosaics from the Roman era. Opposite is the **Museo de Artes y Costumbres Populares** ⑭.

Head back north along the Paseo de las Delicias toward the city center. Near downtown Seville, on Avenida de Roma, stands the Baroque **Palacio de San Telmo** ⑮, home of the Andalusian regional government. Behind the Palacio is the Mudéjar-style **Hotel Alfonso XIII** ⑯. On the north side of Puerta de Jerez is **Palacio de Yanduri** ⑰, birthplace of the Nobel prize winner Vicente Aleixandre.

Walking toward the Guadalquivir River along Calle Almirante Lobo, you'll come to the riverside **Torre de Oro** ⑱, which stands opposite the **Teatro de la Maestranza** ⑲. Behind the theater is the **Hospital de la Caridad** ⑳, with a collection of works by Seville's leading painters. Continuing north along the river, you'll reach the **Plaza de Toros Real Maestranza** ㉑, arguably the most beautiful bullring in Spain. Finally, head away from the river toward the Plaza Nueva, in the heart of Seville, and have a look at the ***ayuntamiento*** ㉑.

If you have energy and about 90 minutes left, extend your tour a bit by walking north from the town hall to the Plaza del Salvador and the **Iglesia del Salvador** ㉔, a former mosque. Walk up Alcaiceria to Plaza de la Alfalfa and along Sales Ferre toward Plaza Cristo del Burgos—in a small alley off the square is the **Casa Natal de Velázquez** ㉕, where the painter Velázquez was born in 1599. From Plaza Cristo de Burgos follow the narrow streets Descalzos and Caballerizas to the **Casa de Pilatos** ㉖, believed to be modeled on Pilate's house in Jerusalem.

A number of other sights are scattered throughout northern Seville and require separate trips. If you're an art lover, set aside half a day for the **Museo de Bellas Artes** ㉓, as it has a fine collection of paintings by Zurbarán and El Greco, among others. From here, head down to the river and across the Pasarela de la Cartuja bridge to the 14th-century **Monasterio de Santa María de las Cuevas** ㉚, which now houses the Andalusian Center of Contemporary Art.

To visit the **Basílica de la Macarena** ㉗, home of Seville's most revered image, the Virgen de la Macarena, it's best to take a taxi from the city center. Other religious sites in the Macarena area are the Gothic **Convento de Santa Paula** ㉘ and the church of **San Lorenzo y Jesús del Gran Poder** ㉙, where colorful floats used in Seville's Holy Week processions are on display.

TIMING

Allow a full day for the grand Seville tour. A trip to the Museo de Bellas Artes and the monastery at La Cartuja will take half a day, and a trip to La Macarena will take two to three hours. Be warned that hours for the city's monuments and other institutions have a habit of changing almost monthly.

Sights to See

★ 4 **Alcázar** (Reales Alcázares). The Plaza Triunfo forms the entrance to the Mudéjar palace built by Pedro I (1350–69) on the site of Seville's former Moorish *alcázar* (fortress). Don't mistake the Alcázar for a genuine Moorish palace, like Granada's Alhambra—it may look like one, and it was indeed designed and built by Moorish workers brought in from Granada, but it was commissioned and paid for by a Christian king more than 100 years after the reconquest of Seville. In its construction, Pedro the Cruel incorporated stones and capitals he pillaged from Valencia, from Córdoba's Medina Azahara, and from Seville itself. The Alcázar is the finest example of Mudéjar architecture in Spain today, though its purity of style has been much diluted by the alterations and additions of successive Spanish rulers. The palace serves as the official Seville residence of the king and queen of Spain.

You enter the Alcázar through the Puerta del León (Lion's Gate) and the high, fortified walls. These are of genuine Moorish origin, but they belie the exquisite delicacy of the interior. You'll first find yourself in a garden courtyard, the **Patio del León.** Off to the left are the oldest parts of the building, the 14th-century **Sala de Justicia** (Hall of Justice) and, next to it, the intimate **Patio del Yeso** (Courtyard of Plaster), part of the original 12th-century Almohad Alcázar. Cross the **Patio de la Montería** to Pedro's Mudéjar palace, arranged around the beautiful **Patio de las Doncellas** (Court of the Damsels), resplendent with delicately carved stucco. Its name probably refers to the annual gift of 100 virgins to the Moorish sultans. Although its Granadan craftsmanship instantly recalls the Alhambra, the upper galleries were added by Carlos V. Opening off this patio, the **Salón de Embajadores** (Hall of the Ambassadors), with its cedar cupola of green, red, and gold, is the most sumptuous hall in the palace. It was here that Carlos V married Isabel of Portugal in 1526, for which occasion he added the wooden balconies.

Other royal rooms include Felipe II's dining hall and the three baths of Pedro's wily mistress, María de Padilla. María's hold over her royal lover—and apparently over his courtiers, too—was so great that they supposedly lined up to drink her bathwater. The **Patio de las Muñecas** (Court of the Dolls) takes its name from two tiny faces carved on the inside of one of its arches, no doubt as a joke on the part of its Moorish creators. Here Pedro reputedly had his half brother, Don Fadrique, slain in 1358, and here, too, he murdered guest Abu Said of Granada for his jewels. Pedro presented one of these, a huge, uncut ruby, to the Black Prince (Edward, Prince of Wales [1330–76], eldest son of England's Edward III) in 1367. It now sits among other priceless gems in the Crown of England.

You come next to the Renaissance **Palacio de Carlos V,** built by the emperor at the time of his marriage and endowed with a rich collection of Flemish tapestries depicting Carlos's victories at Tunis. Look for the map of Spain: it shows the Iberian Peninsula upside-down, as was the custom in Arab mapmaking. There are more goodies—rare clocks, antique furniture, paintings, and more tapestries—on the Alcázar's upper floor, in the **Estancias Reales** (Royal Chambers). These are the apartments used by King Juan Carlos I and his family when in town. The required guided tour leads you through the dining room,

Seville

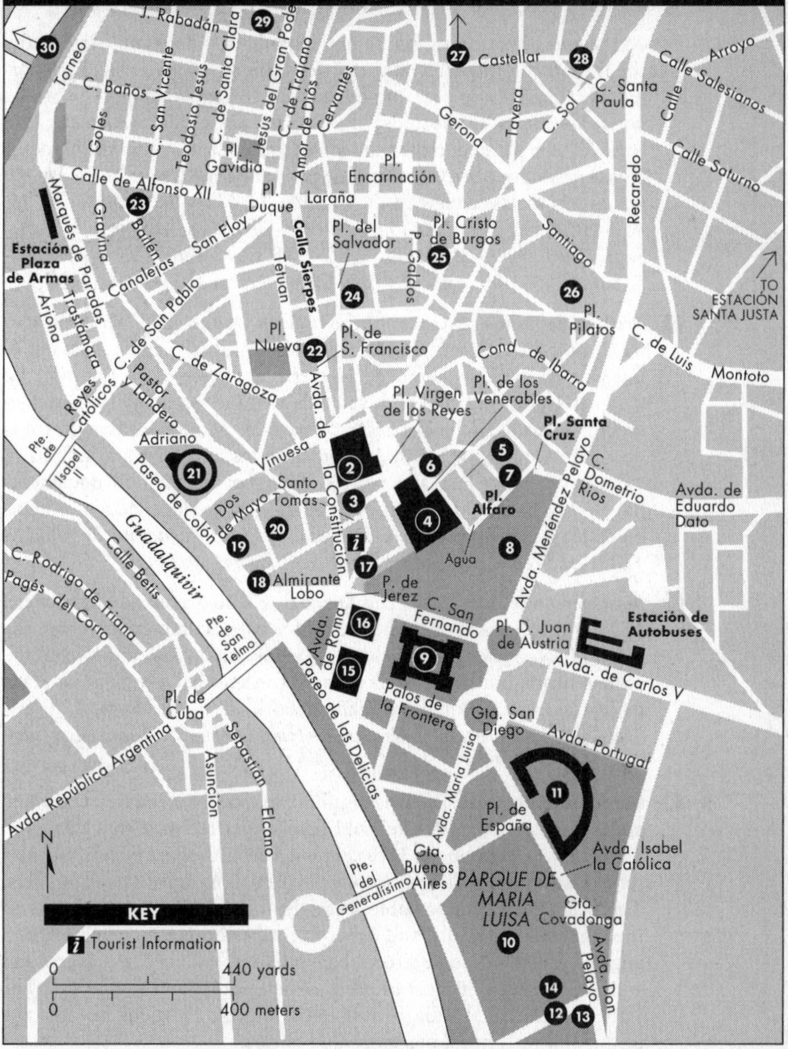
J. Rabadán
Torneo
C. Baños
Goles
C. San Vicente
Teodosio
Jesús
C. de Santa Clara
Jesús del Gran Poder
C. de Trajano
Amor de Diós
Cervantes
Pl. Gavidia
Pl. Encarnación
Castellar
C. Santa Paula
Calle Arroyo
Calle Salesianos
Calle Saturno
Gerona
Tavera
C. Sol
Recaredo
Calle de Alfonso XII
Pl. Duque
Laraña
Marqués de Paradas
Gravina
Bailén
San Eloy
Canalejas
Estación Plaza de Armas
Pl. del Salvador
Calle Sierpes
Tetuán
P. Galdós
Pl. Cristo de Burgos
Santiago
TO ESTACIÓN SANTA JUSTA
Arjona
Trastámara
C. de San Pablo
Pl. Nueva
Pl. de S. Francisco
Pl. Pilatos
C. de Luis Montoto
Cond de Ibarra
Reyes Católicos
Pastor y Landero
C. de Zaragoza
Avda. de la Constitución
Pl. Virgen de los Reyes
Pl. de los Venerables
Pl. Santa Cruz
Pte. de Isabel II
Adriano
Vinuesa
Santo Tomás
C. Dometrio Ríos
Avda. de Eduardo Dato
Paseo de Colón
Dos de Mayo
Pl. Alfaro
Agua
Avda. Menéndez Pelayo
Guadalquivir
Calle Betis
C. Rodrigo de Triana
Pagés del Corro
Almirante Lobo
P. de Jerez
C. San Fernando
Pl. D. Juan de Austria
Estación de Autobuses
Pte. de San Telmo
Avda. de Roma
Avda. de Carlos V
Paseo de las Delicias
Palos de la Frontera
Gta. San Diego
Avda. Portugal
Pl. de Cuba
Avda. República Argentina
Asunción
Sebastián
Elcano
Avda. María Luisa
Pl. de España
Avda. Isabel la Católica
N
Pte. del Generalísimo
Gta. Buenos Aires
PARQUE DE MARIA LUISA
Gta. Covadonga
Avda. Don Pelayo
KEY
Tourist Information
0
440 yards
0
400 meters

other protocol rooms, and the king's office. Tours depart in the morning only, every half hour in summer and every hour in winter.

At the end of your visit, pause in the **gardens,** where you can breathe the fragrance of jasmine and myrtle, wander lovely terraces and ornamental baths, and peer into the well-stocked goldfish pond, covered with water lilies. In the midst of this green oasis is an orange tree said to have been planted in the time of Pedro the Cruel. From the gardens, a passageway leads to the **Patio de las Banderas** (Court of the Flags), which has a classic view of the Giralda. ✉ *Plaza del Triunfo,* ☎ *95/450–2324.* 🎟 *700 ptas.; tour of Royal Chambers 400 ptas.* ⏲ *Apr.–Sept., Tues.–Sat. 9:30–7, Sun. 9:30–1:30; Oct.–Mar., Tues.–Sat. 9:30–5, Sun. 9:30–1:30; tour of Royal Chambers weekdays 10–1.*

❸ **Archivo de Indias** (Archives of the Indies). Opened in 1785 in the former Lonja (Merchants' Exchange), this dignified Renaissance building was designed by Juan de Herrera, architect of El Escorial (☞ Chapter 1), in 1572. The archive holds an impressive collection of documents relating to the discovery of the New World—drawings, trade documents, plans of South American towns, even the autographs of Columbus, Magellan, and Cortés. Many of the 38,000 documents have yet to be sorted and properly cataloged, so the selection of items on display changes regularly. ✉ *Avda. de la Constitución,* ☎ *95/421–1234.* 🎟 *Free.* ⏲ *Weekdays 10–1 (8–3 for researchers).*

㉒ **Ayuntamiento** (City Hall). This Diego de Riaño original, built between 1527 and 1564, stands in the heart of Seville's commercial center, the Plaza Nueva. The facade, which overlooks the plaza, dates from the 19th century, but if you walk around to the other side, on the Plaza de San Francisco, you'll see Riaño's work. ✉ *Plaza Nueva 1,* ☎ *95/459–0101.* 🎟 *Free.* ⏲ *Tours Tues.–Thurs. 5:30–7. Closed mid-July–mid-Sept.*

★ ❺ **Barrio de Santa Cruz.** The twisting alleyways, cobbled squares, and white and ocher houses of Seville's old Jewish quarter were much favored by the city's nobles in the 17th century. The houses are beautifully preserved, and some still rank among Seville's most expensive properties. The atmosphere is unbeatable: wrought-iron lanterns cast shadows on the whitewashed walls, and ocher-framed windows hide behind rectangular grilles. On some streets, bars alternate with antiques stores and souvenir shops, but most of the quarter is quiet and residential. The Callejón del Agua, beside the wall of the Alcázar's gardens, boasts some of the quarter's finest mansions and patios.

Pause to enjoy the antiques shops and outdoor café on the **Plaza Alianza.** A starkly simple crucifix hangs on the dazzling-white wall shrouded in bougainvillea, and blue and white tiles bear the square's name. In the **Plaza de Doña Elvira,** with its fountain and *azulejo* benches, young Sevillanos gather to play guitars. Here you'll see one side of the **Hospital de los Venerables** (☞ *below*). Just around the corner from the hospital, at Callejón del Agua and Jope de Rueda, Rossini's Figaro serenaded Rosina on her **Plaza Alfaro** balcony. Adjoining the Plaza Alfaro, in the **Plaza Santa Cruz,** a 17th-century filigree iron cross marks the site of the erstwhile church of Santa Cruz, destroyed by Napoléon's General Soult. The painter Murillo was buried here in 1682, though his current resting place is unknown.

㉗ **Basílica de la Macarena.** This church holds Seville's most revered image, the Virgin of Hope—more familiarly known as La Macarena because her church adjoins the Puerta de la Macarena, a remnant of the old Roman wall. Bedecked with candles and carnations, her cheeks streaming with glass tears, the Macarena is the focus of the procession on Holy Thursday, the highlight of Seville's Holy Week pageant. She is the patron of Gypsies and the protector of the matador: few matadors would dream of entering the ring without saying a prayer to her. So great are her charms that the Sevillian bullfighter Joselito spent half his personal fortune buying her four emeralds. When he was killed in the ring at the tender age of 25, in 1920, the Macarena was dressed in widow's weeds for a month. ✉ *Puerta de la Macarena,* ☎ *95/437–0195.* 🎫 *Basilica free, treasury 400 ptas.* ⏲ *Basilica daily 9–1 and 5–9, treasury daily 9:30–1 and 5–8.*

Calle Sierpes. This is Seville's main shopping street. Near the southern end, at number 85, a plaque marks the spot where the Cárcel Real (Royal Prison) once stood. Miguel de Cervantes began writing *Don Quixote* in one of its cells. The site is now occupied by a bank.

7 **Casa de Murillo.** Calle Santa Teresa 8, in the Barrio de Santa Cruz, houses the Andalusian Department of Culture, a library, and an exhibition hall hosting changing displays of all kinds, with a focus on contemporary art. Ask the tourist office about current exhibits. The house is named for the painter Bartolomé Esteban Murillo (1617–82), who lived here for a time; the street is named for Santa Teresa de Ávila (1515–82), who once stayed here and was so enchanted by Seville that she decreed that anyone who stayed free from sin in this city was indeed on the path to God. ✉ *C. Santa Teresa.* 🎫 *Free* ⏲ *Exhibits Tues.–Sun. 10:30–1:30 and 5–9.*

26 **Casa de Pilatos.** This palace was built in the first half of the 16th century by the dukes of Tarifa, ancestors of the present owner, the Duke of Medinaceli. It's known as Pilate's House because of a popular belief that Don Fadrique, first marquis of Tarifa, modeled it on Pontius Pilate's house in Jerusalem, where he had gone on a pilgrimage in 1518. With its fine patio and superb *azulejo* decorations, the palace is a beautiful blend of Spanish Mudéjar and Renaissance architecture. The upstairs apartments, which you can see on a guided tour, contain frescoes, paintings, and antique furniture. ✉ *Plaza Pilatos,* ☎ *95/422–5298.* 🎫 *1,000 ptas.* ⏲ *Oct.–June, daily 9–6; July–Sept., daily 9–8; apartments 10–1 and 4–6 year-round.*

25 **Casa Natal de Velázquez.** One of Spain's greatest painters, Diego de Velázquez was born in this *casa de vecinos* (town house shared by several families) in 1599. The house—whose modest ocher facade belies its size—fell into ruin, but was bought in the 1970s by the well-known fashion designers Victorio y Lucchino, who carefully restored it for use as their studio. Unfortunately for art lovers, the required tour concentrates more on haute couture than on Velázquez. ✉ *Padre Luis María Llop.* 🎫 *800 ptas.* ⏲ *Daily 10–2 and 4–6; last guided tour half hour before closing.*

★ 2 **Cathedral.** The best place to start exploring Seville is the Plaza Virgen de los Reyes: from next to the central fountain you can gaze up at the magnificent Giralda, symbol of Seville, and the east facade of the great Gothic cathedral. After Ferdinand III captured Seville from the Moors in 1248, the great mosque begun by Yusuf II in 1171 was reconsecrated to the Virgin Mary and used as a Christian cathedral, much as the mosque at Córdoba was. But in 1401 the people of Seville decided to erect a new and glorious cathedral, one that would equal the status of their great city. They promptly pulled down the old mosque, leaving only its minaret and outer court, and set about their task with a zeal and enthusiasm unparalleled elsewhere. The mighty building before you was completed in just over a century—a remarkable feat for the time. The clergy renounced their incomes for the cause, and a member of the chapter is said to have proclaimed, "Let us build a church so large that we shall be held to be insane." This they proceeded to do, for today Seville's cathedral can be described only in superlatives: it is the largest and highest cathedral in Spain, the largest Gothic building in the world, and the world's third-largest church, after St. Peter's in Rome and St. Paul's in London.

You enter the cathedral grounds via the **Patio de los Naranjos** (Courtyard of Orange Trees), part of the original mosque. The old fountain in the center was used for ritual ablutions before entering the mosque. Near the Puerta del Lagarto (Lizard's Gate), in the corner near the Giralda, see if you can find the wooden alligator—thought to have been a gift from the emir of Egypt in 1260 as he sought the hand of the daughter of Alfonso the Wise—and the elephant tusk, found in the ruins of Itálica.

The cathedral's exterior, with its rose windows and magnificent flying buttresses, is a monument to pure Gothic beauty. Aside from the well-lit high altar, the dimly illuminated interior can be disappointing, its five naves and numerous side chapels shrouded in gloom; Gothic purity has been largely submerged in ornate Baroque decoration. Still, there is a great deal worth seeing here, even if you have to strain your eyes.

Enter the cathedral itself through the Puerta de la Granada or the Puerta Colorada. Before you, in the central nave, rise the **Capilla Mayor** (Main Chapel) and its intricately carved altarpiece, begun by a Flemish carver in 1482. This magnificent *retablo* (altarpiece) is the largest in Christendom (65 ft by 43 ft). It depicts some 36 scenes from the life of Christ; its pillars are carved with more than 200 figures; and the whole work is lavishly adorned with immeasurable quantities of gold leaf.

Make your way to the opposite (southern) side of the cathedral, where you can't miss the flamboyant **monument to Christopher Columbus.** The great explorer knew both triumph and disgrace, but found no repose—he died, bitterly disillusioned, in Valladolid in 1506 and is purported to be buried here. Columbus's coffin is borne aloft by the four kings representing the medieval kingdoms of Spain: Castile, León, Aragón, and Navarre. Columbus's son, Hernando Colón (1488–1539), is also interred here; his tombstone, inscribed with the words A CASTILLA Y A LEÓN, MUNDO NUEVO DIO COLÓN (TO CASTILE AND LEÓN, COLUMBUS GAVE A NEW WORLD), lies between the great west door, the Puerta Mayor, and the central choir.

Between the elder Columbus's tomb and the Capilla Real, at the eastern end of the central nave, the cathedral's treasuries display a wealth of gold and silver (much of it from the New World), relics, and other works of art. In the **Sacristía de los Cálices** (Sacristy of the Chalices) look for Martínez Montañés's wood carving, *Crucifixion, Merciful Christ*; Valdés Leal's *St. Peter Freed by an Angel*; Zurbarán's *Virgin and Child*; and Goya's *St. Justa and St. Rufina.* The **Sacristía Mayor** (Main Sacristy) holds the keys to the city, which Seville's Moors and Jews presented to their conqueror, Ferdinand III. Finally, in the dome of the **Sala Capitular** (Chapter House), in the cathedral's southeastern corner, is Murillo's *Immaculate Conception,* painted in 1668.

One of the cathedral's highlights, the **Capilla Real** (Royal Chapel), is reserved for prayer and concealed behind a ponderous curtain, but you can duck in if you're quick, quiet, and properly dressed. To do so, explore the rest of the cathedral and the Giralda (☞ *below*) and enter again from a separate door, the Puerta de los Palos, on Plaza Virgen de los Reyes (signposted ENTRADA PARA CULTO—entrance for worship). Along the sides of the chapel are the tombs of the wife of Ferdinand III, Beatrix of Swabia, and his son, Alfonso X, called The Wise (died

1284); in a silver urn before the high altar rest the precious relics of Ferdinand III himself, Seville's liberator (canonized 1671), who was said to have died from excessive fasting. In the (rarely open) vault below lie the tombs of Ferdinand's descendant Pedro the Cruel and Ferdinand's mistress, María de Padilla. Above the entrance grille, you can see a Jerónino Roldán sculpture of Ferdinand III receiving the keys to Seville.

Before you duck into the Capilla Real, climb to the top of the **Giralda,** the undisputed symbol of Seville, which dominates the skyline and can be glimpsed from almost every corner of the city. Once the minaret of Seville's great mosque, from which the faithful were summoned to prayer, it was built between 1184 and 1196, just 50 years before the reconquest of Seville. The Christians could not bring themselves to destroy this tower when they tore down the mosque, so they incorporated it into their new cathedral. In 1565–68 they added a lantern and belfry to the old minaret and installed 24 bells, one for each of Seville's 24 parishes and the 24 Christian knights who fought with Ferdinand III in the Reconquest. They also added the bronze statue of Faith, which turned as a weather vane—*el giraldillo,* or "something that turns," thus the name Giralda. To give it a rest after 400 years of wear and tear, the original statue was replaced with a copy in 1997.

With its Baroque additions, the slender Giralda rises 322 ft. Inside, instead of steps, 35 sloping ramps—wide enough for two horsemen to pass abreast—climb to a viewing platform 230 ft up. It is said that Ferdinand III rode his horse to the top to admire the city he had conquered. If you follow in his (horse's) footsteps, you'll be rewarded with a glorious view of tile roofs and the Guadalquivir shimmering beneath palm-lined banks. ✉ *Plaza Virgen de los Reyes,* ☎ *95/456–3321.* 🎫 *700 ptas.; free Sun.* ⏲ *Cathedral Mon.–Sat. 11–5, Sun. 2–6, and for mass.*

28 **Convento de Santa Paula.** This 15th-century Gothic convent has a fine facade and portico, with ceramic decoration by Nicolaso Pisano. The chapel has some beautiful *azulejos* and sculptures by Martínez Montañés. ✉ *C. Santa Paula,* ☎ *95/453–6330.* 🎫 *Free.* ⏲ *Tues.–Sun. 10:30–1 and 4:30–6.*

20 **Hospital de la Caridad.** Behind the Maestranza Theater is this almshouse for the sick and elderly, where six paintings by Murillo (1617–82) and two gruesome works by Valdés Leal (1622–90) depicting the Triumph of Death are displayed. The Baroque hospital was founded in 1674 by Seville's original Don Juan, Miguel de Mañara (1626–79). A nobleman of licentious character, Mañara was returning one night from a riotous orgy when he had a vision of a funeral procession in which the partly decomposed corpse in the coffin was his own. Accepting the apparition as a sign from God, Mañara renounced his worldly goods and joined the Brotherhood of Charity, whose unsavory task it was to collect the bodies of executed criminals and bury them. He devoted his fortune to building this hospital and is buried before the high altar in the chapel. Artist Murillo was a personal friend of Mañara's, thus La Caridad's chief attractions. ✉ *C. Temprado 3,* ☎ *95/422–3232.* 🎫 *400 ptas.* ⏲ *Mon.–Sat. 9–1:30 and 3:30–6:30, Sun. 9–1.*

6 **Hospital de los Venerables.** Once a retirement home for priests, this Baroque building in the heart of the Barrio de Santa Cruz has a splendid *azulejo* patio and a small museum of floats from the Cruces de Mayo (May Crosses) processions. All visits are guided. ✉ *Plaza de los Venerables,* ☎ *95/456–2696.* 🎫 *600 ptas.* ⏲ *Daily 10–2 and 4–8.*

16 **Hotel Alfonso XIII.** Seville's most emblematic hotel, this grand, Mudéjar-style building next to the university was built—and named—for the king's visit to the 1929 fair. You don't have to stay here to admire the

inner courtyard or sip a cool martini in the bar and enjoy the ornate Moorish decor (☞ Lodging, *below*).

24 **Iglesia del Salvador.** Built between 1671 and 1712, the Church of the Savior stands on the site of Seville's first great mosque. Inside, look especially for the image of *Jesús de la Pasión,* carved by Martínez Montañés: this statue is borne through the streets on Holy Thursday in one of Holy Week's most moving processions. ✉ *Plaza San Salvador,* ☎ *95/421–1679.* *Free.* *Mon.–Sat. 9–1 and 6:30–8:30.*

8 **Jardines de Murillo** (Murillo Gardens). From the Plaza Santa Cruz you can embark on a stroll through these shady gardens, where you'll find a statue of Christopher Columbus.

La Cartuja. Named after its 14th-century Carthusian monastery (☞ Monasterio de Santa María de las Cuevas, *below*), the island of La Cartuja, across the river from northern Seville, was the site of the decennial Universal Exposition in 1992. Five new bridges were built across the river for this event. The eastern shore of the island holds the largest theme park in Andalusia, **Isla Mágica,** with 14 different attractions including the hair-raising Jaguar roller coaster. ☎ *95/448–7000.* *3,400 ptas.* *Mar.–Oct., daily 11 AM–midnight.*

30 **Monasterio de Santa María de las Cuevas.** Commonly known as the Monasterio de La Cartuja, this former Carthusian monastery dates from the 14th century. Christopher Columbus, a regular visitor, was buried here for a few years. From 1841 to 1980 the building housed a ceramics factory, where Seville's famous Cartuja china was made. The monastery was fully restored for use as the Royal Pavilion during the 1992 Exposition (☞ La Cartuja, *above*) and is now open to the public; part of the building houses the Centro Andaluz de Arte Contemporáneo, which has permanent and temporary art exhibits. ☎ *95/448–0611,* *300 ptas.; free Tues.* *Open Tues.–Sat. 10–8, Sun. 10–3.*

13 **Museo Arqueológico.** Housed in a fine Renaissance-style building, Seville's Museum of Archaeology holds artifacts from Phoenician, Tartessian, Greek, Carthaginian, Iberian, Roman, and medieval times. Some of the best displays are marble statues and mosaics from the Roman excavations at Itálica and a faithful replica of the fabulous Carambolo treasure found on a hillside outside Seville in 1958: twenty-one pieces of jewelry, all of 24-karat gold, dating from the 7th and 6th centuries BC. ✉ *Plaza de América,* ☎ *95/423–2401.* *250 ptas.; EU citizens free.* *Tues. 3–8, Wed.–Sat. 9–8, Sun. 9–2.*

14 **Museo de Artes y Costumbres Populares** (Museum of Folklore). The Mudéjar pavilion opposite the Museum of Archaeology houses this museum of mainly 19th- and 20th-century Spanish folklore. The first floor has re-creations of a forge, a bakery, a wine press, a tanner's shop, and a pottery studio. Upstairs, exhibits include 18th- and 19th-century court dress, regional folk costumes, carriages, and musical instruments. ✉ *Plaza de América,* ☎ *95/423–2576.* *250 ptas.; EU citizens free.* *Wed.–Sat. 9–8, Sun. 9–2.*

★ 23 **Museo de Bellas Artes**(Museum of Fine Arts). Along with, perhaps, its counterpart in Bilbao, this museum is second only to Madrid's Prado in Spanish art. Opened in 1841, it occupies the former convent of La Merced Calzada, most of which dates from the 17th century. The excellent collection, presented in chronological order on two floors, features Murillo, Zurbarán, Valdés Leal, and El Greco. (Disappointingly, there is only one work by Seville's greatest artist, Velázquez, and not a particularly interesting one at that; most of Seville's Velázquez paintings were purloined by the French during the Peninsular War, and what remained was picked over by the British in the 19th century.) The museum's first few rooms have outstanding examples of Seville Gothic art, including sculpture and a church *retablo.* There are also fine examples of Baroque religious sculpture in wood, a quintessentially Andalusian art form. Upstairs, in the rooms dedicated to Sevillian art of the 19th and 20th centuries, look for Gonzalo Bilbao's *Las Cigarreras,* a group portrait of Seville's famous cigar makers. ✉ *Plaza del Museo,* ☎ *95/422–0790.* 🎫 *250 ptas.; EU citizens free.* ⊙ *Tues. 3–8, Wed.–Sat. 9–8, Sun. 9–3.*

15 **Palacio de San Telmo.** This splendid Baroque palace is largely the work of architect Leonardo de Figueroa. Built between 1682 and 1796, it is now the seat of the Presidencia de Junta de Andalucía, the regional government's chief executive. Look for the exotic main portal, vintage 1734, a superb example of the fanciful Churrigueresque style. ✉ *Avenida de Roma.*

17 **Palacio de Yanduri.** Nobel prize–winning poet Vicente Aleixandre was born here. ✉ *North side of Puerta de Jerez.*

10 **Parque de María Luisa.** To see one of the loveliest parks in Spain, make time for this one. You'll see a **statue of El Cid** by Rodrigo Díaz de Vivar (1043–1099), who fought both for and against the Muslim rulers during the Reconquest, and the old **Casino** building from the 1929 Hispanic-American Exhibition, now the Teatro Lope de Vega. The park itself, formerly the garden of the Palacio de San Telmo, is a blend of formal design and wild vegetation. In the burst of development that gripped Seville in the 1920s, it was redesigned for the 1929 Exhibition, and the impressive villas you see now are the fair's remaining pavilions, many of them now consulates or schools. ✉ *Main entrance: Glorieta San Diego.*

12 **Plaza de América.** Walk to the south end of the Parque de María Luisa, past the Isla de los Patos (Island of Ducks), to find this plaza, designed by Aníbal González. It's a blaze of color, with deep-orange sand, flowers, shrubs, ornamental stairways, and fountains tiled in yellow, blue, and ocher. The three impressive buildings surrounding the square—in neo-Mudéjar, Gothic, and Renaissance styles—were built by González for the 1929 fair. Two of them now house Seville's museums of archaeology and folklore (☞ *above*).

11 **Plaza de España.** This monumental attraction is on the eastern edge of the Parque de María Luisa. Designed by architect Aníbal González, the grandiose half-moon was Spain's centerpiece pavilion at the 1929 Exhibition. The brightly colored *azulejo* pictures in its arches represent the 50 provinces of Spain, and the four bridges over its ornamental lake symbolize the medieval kingdoms of the Iberian Peninsula.

21 **Plaza de Toros Real Maestranza.** (Royal Maestranza Bullring). Sevillanos have spent many a thrilling Sunday afternoon in this bullring, built between 1760 and 1763. Painted a deep ocher, the stadium is the one of the oldest and loveliest *plazas de toros* in Spain. The adjoining museum has posters, prints, and photos. ✉ *Paseo de Colón 12,* ☎ *95/422–4577.* 🎫 *Plaza and bullfighting museum 400 ptas.* ⊙ *Daily 9:30–2 and 3–7 (9:30–2 only on bullfight days).*

29 **San Lorenzo y Jesús del Gran Poder.** This church has many fine works by such artists as Montañés and Pacheco, but its outstanding piece is Juan de Mesa's *Jesús del Gran Poder* (*Christ Omnipotent*). The *paso* (float), used in the Good Friday morning procession of El Gran Poder, is the work of Ruíz Gijón (1690). ✉ *C. Jesús del Gran Poder,* ☎ *95/438–4558.* 🎫 *Free.* ⊙ *Daily 8–1:30 and 6–9.*

19 **Teatro de la Maestranza** (Maestranza Theater). Opposite the Torre de Oro is Seville's opera house, opened in 1991. Now one of Europe's leading halls, the Maestranza presents opera, classical music, *zarzuela* (Spanish light opera), and jazz. ✉ *Paseo de Colón,* ☎ *95/422–6573 or 95/422–3344.*

18 **Torre de Oro.** One of Seville's great landmarks, the Tower of Gold stands on the banks of the Guadalquivir near the Puerta de Jerez. A 12-sided tower built by the Moors in 1220 to complete the city's ramparts, it served to close off the harbor when a chain was stretched across the river from its base to another tower on the opposite bank. In 1248 Admiral Ramón de Bonifaz succeeded in breaking through this barrier, and thus did Ferdinand III capture Seville. The tower now houses a small but well-presented Naval Museum. ☎ *95/422–2419.* *100 ptas.; free Tues.* *Tues.–Fri. 10–2, weekends 11–2.*

9 **University of Seville.** At the far end of the Jardines de Murillo, opposite Calle San Fernando, stands what used to be the **Real Fábrica de Tabacos** (Royal Tobacco Factory). Built between 1750 and 1766, the factory employed some 3,000 *cigarreras* (female cigar makers) less than a century later, including, of course, the heroine of Bizet's opera *Carmen,* who rolled her cigars on her thigh. The enormous building has only been the university's home since the 1950s; today's factory is across the river. ✉ *C. San Fernando,* ☎ *95/455–1000.* *Free.* *Weekdays 9–8:30.*

Dining

$$$–$$$$ ★ ✕ **Egaña-Oriza.** One of Seville's most acclaimed restaurants, the Egaña-Oriza is beautifully situated on the edge of the Murillo Gardens. The decor is modern, with walls of deep peach. José Mari Egaña, the owner, is Basque, but his cuisine has metamorphosed over the years, and he is now considered one of the fathers of modern Andalusian cooking. The menu changes with the seasons, but might include favorites like *lomos de lubina con salsa de erizos de mar* (sea bass with sea-urchin sauce) or *solomillo con foie natural y salsa de ciruelas* (fillet steak with foie gras and plum sauce). The adjoining Bar España is a good place for refined tapas. ✉ *San Fernando 41,* ☎ *95/422–7211. AE, DC, MC, V. Closed Sun. and Aug. No lunch Sat.*

$$$–$$$$ ✕ **La Albahaca.** One of Seville's prettiest restaurants is ensconced in one of its prettiest neighborhoods, the Barrio de Santa Cruz. This typical Andalusian house was built by the celebrated architect Juan Talavera as a home for his own family; inside, three dining rooms are colorfully decorated with ceramic tiles and leafy potted plants. Service is friendly and professional. Entrées include *lubina al horno con sofrito de ciruelas y almendras* (baked sea bass with plum and almond sauce). ✉ *Plaza Santa Cruz 12,* ☎ *95/422–0714. AE, DC, MC, V. Closed Sun.*

$$$–$$$$ ✕ **La Isla.** Fresh fish is hauled daily from the Cádiz and Huelva coasts to supply the many bars and restaurants here in the Arenal district, between the cathedral and the bullring. La Isla is one of the best, and *parrillada de mariscos y pescados,* a fish and seafood grill for two people, is one of its best meals. *Zarzuela,* the Catalan seafood stew, is another; and simple meat dishes are also served. The two attractive dining rooms feature blue-and-white tile designs and cream-colored stucco walls. ✉ *Arfe 25,* ☎ *95/421–5376. AE, DC, MC, V.*

$$$ ✕ **Becerrita.** Around the corner from the Hotel Giralda, this restaurant is favored by Sevillanos and found by few tourists. It's a small establishment—cozy verging on cramped—with diligent service and tasty modern treatments of classic Spanish dishes, such as *estofado de jarrete de ternera* (veal stew). *Pescado de roca a la espalda* (rockfish split and grilled) is a specialty, but inquire about the fresh dish of the day as well. ✉ *Recaredo 9,* ☎ *95/441–2057. AE, MC, V. No dinner Sun.*

$$$ ★ ✕ **Casa Robles.** One block north of the cathedral is one of Seville's classic restaurants, established in 1954. The busy bar downstairs does a roaring trade in tapas. There is a small dining room downstairs and a larger one upstairs, where the yellow tablecloths match the walls. The food is classically Andalusian: try the *ensalada de pimientos asados* (roast-pepper salad with tuna), followed by the herb-flavored *cordero asado* (roast lamb). Service is efficient and discreet, though the wine list is limited. ✉ *Alvarez Quintero 58,* ☎ *95/456–3272. AE, DC, MC, V.*

$$$ ✕ **Enrique Becerra.** This cozy restaurant is a short walk from the cathedral in a whitewashed house with wrought-iron window grilles. The lively, crowded bar, decorated with ceramic tiles, is a meeting place for locals, who appreciate the excellent selection of tapas. The menu focuses on traditional, home-cooked Andalusian dishes, such as *pez espada al amontillado* (swordfish cooked in dark sherry), *rape al azafrán* (monkfish in saffron sauce), and *cordero a la miel* (honey-glazed lamb). ✉ *Gamazo 2,* ☎ *95/421–3049. AE, DC, MC, V. Closed Sun.*

$$$ ✕ **San Marco.** Set in an old neoclassical house in the shopping district, this Italian restaurant has a leafy patio and is furnished with antiques. The menu is a happy combination of Italian, French, and Andalusian cuisines. Count on good pasta dishes, such as ravioli stuffed with shrimp and pesto sauce. The restaurant now has four satellites, but this one, the original, is the most charming. ✉ *Cuna 6,* ☎ *95/421–2440. Reservations essential. AE, DC, MC, V.*

$$$ ✕ **Taberna del Alabardero.** Installed in a 19th-century mansion near the Plaza Nueva, this restaurant is also a small hotel, with seven guest rooms furnished with antiques. Preceded by a courtyard and a bar, the dining area is decorated in Sevillian tiles. The modern Spanish cuisine includes *milhojas de pulpo con patatas y pimientos asados* (octopus in pastry with potatoes and roast peppers) and the Basque-inspired *bacalao con kokotxas al pil-pil* (cod and hake cheeks in sizzling olive oil). ✉ *Zaragoza 20,* ☎ *95/456–0637. AE, DC, MC, V.*

$$–$$$ ✕ **La Judería.** This bright, modern restaurant gained fast recognition for the quality of its Spanish and international cuisine. Fish dishes from northern Spain and meats from Ávila are specialties. Try *cordero lechal* (roast lamb) or *urta a la roteña* (a fish dish from Rota, on the coast of Cádiz). ✉ *Cano y Cueto 13,* ☎ *95/441–2052. Reservations essential. AE, DC, MC, V. Closed Mon. and Aug.*

$$ ✕ **Mesón Don Raimundo.** Tucked into an alleyway off Calle Argote de Molina (which leads up from the cathedral's Plaza Virgen de los Reyes), Don Raimundo is decorated with an odd collection of blue and white tiles, marble columns, stained-glass windows, iron sculptures, farm implements, a deer's head, and assorted other bric-a-brac. The house specialties are meat dishes, such as Mozarab-style wild duck (braised in sherry) and *solomillo a la castellana* (Castilian-style steak), but you'll find fish, too. Open with the crunchy *tortillitas de camarones* (batter-fried shrimp pancakes) or stuffed peppers. Portions are generous. ✉ *Argote de Molina 26,* ☎ *95/422–3355. AE, DC, MC, V.*

$–$$ ✕ **Hostería del Laurel.** This restaurant—also a small hotel—is geared toward tourists, capitalizing on its location in the Barrio de Santa Cruz. In summer you can dine outdoors on the plaza, surrounded by beautiful white and ocher houses. The indoor dining rooms are decorated in traditional Castilian style, with wood paneling, white walls, and heavy wooden tables and chairs. The menu, available in English, has a wide selection of traditional Spanish fare. ✉ *Plaza de los Venerables 5,* ☎ *95/422–0295. AE, DC, MC, V.*

$–$$ ✕ **Modesto.** This restaurant on the edge of the Barrio de Santa Cruz is popular with Sevillanos, who come for the excellent value. Downstairs is a lively, crowded tapas bar; upstairs is the dining room, whose stucco walls are decorated with blue and white tiles. You can dine outside on the terrace in warm weather. The house specialty is a crisp *fritura Modesto* (a selection of small fish fried in top-quality olive oil); another excellent choice is the *cazuela al Tío Diego* (Uncle Jim's casserole—ham, mushrooms, and shrimp). ✉ *Cano y Cueto 5,* ☎ *95/441–6811. AE, DC, MC, V.*

Lodging

$$$$ ★ ✕🏨 **Alfonso XIII.** Inaugurated by King Alfonso XIII on April 28, 1929, this grand hotel is a splendid, historical Mudéjar Revival palace, built around a huge central patio surrounded by ornate brick arches and filled with potted plants and a fountain. The public rooms are resplendent with marble floors, wood-paneled ceilings, heavy Moorish lamps, stained glass, and ceramic-tile decor in the typical Sevillian colors. The imposing main restaurant, with a painted and wood-paneled ceiling, heavy drapes, a huge central table, and an ornate wrought-iron gate, serves high-class international fare; there is also a Japanese restaurant. ✉ *San Fernando 2, 41004,* ☎ *95/422–2850,* FAX *95/421–6033. 127 rooms, 19 suites. 2 restaurants, bar, pool, beauty salon, meeting rooms. AE, DC, MC, V.*

$$$$ ✕🏨 **Hacienda Benazuza.** Live the life of a true Andalusian *señorito,* or country squire, at this rambling country palace on the edge of the village of Sanlúcar la Mayor, 15 km (10 mi) outside Seville off the main road to Huelva. Surrounded by olive and orange trees and centered on a courtyard with towering palm trees, the building incorporates an 18th-century church and stands on the site of a 10th-century Moorish farmhouse. The interior, with clay-tile floors and ocher walls, is tastefully furnished with antiques. The restaurant, Alquería, is a favorite with Sevillian foodies. ✉ *Virgen de las Nieves, 41800 Sanlúcar la Mayor,* ☎ *95/570–3344,* FAX *95/570–3410. 41 rooms, 3 suites. Restaurant, pool, tennis court, putting green, paddle tennis. AE, DC, MC, V.*

$$$$ ★ 🏨 **Los Seises.** This stylish hotel occupies a section of Seville's 16th-century Palacio Episcopal (Bishop's Palace). The combination of modern and Renaissance architecture is striking: segments of the original structure appear intriguingly in hallways and even in the guest rooms. Room 219, for instance, is divided by a 16th-century brick archway, and breakfast is served in the old chapel. Each room is a different shape, and most are split-level. A pit in the center of the subterranean restaurant reveals the building's foundations and some archaeological finds, including a Roman mosaic. The rooftop pool and summer restaurant are in full view of the Giralda. ✉ *Segovias 6, 41004,* ☎ *95/422–9495,* FAX *95/422–4334. 40 rooms, 2 suites. Restaurant, pool, parking (fee). AE, DC, MC, V.*

$$$$ ✕🏨 **Tryp Colón.** The grand old Colón was built for the 1929 Exhibition. A white-marble staircase leads up to the central lobby, which has a magnificent stained-glass dome and crystal candelabra. The reception area, La Fuente restaurant, and Bar Majestic open off this circular space. Downstairs is the renowned El Burladero restaurant, with a bullfight theme, and La Tasca tavern. The old-fashioned rooms are elegantly furnished with silk drapes and bedspreads and wood fittings. ✉ *Canalejas 1, 41001,* ☎ *95/422–2900,* FAX *95/422–0938. 204 rooms, 14 suites. 2 restaurants, 2 bars, beauty salon, meeting rooms. AE, DC, MC, V.*

$$$$ 🏨 **Casa Imperial.** Adjoining the Casa de Pilatos, and at one time connected to it via underground tunnel, this restored 16th-century palace was once the residence of the Marquis of Tarifa's majordomo. Public areas surround four different courtyards. The 24 suites are approached by a stairway adorned with trompe l'oeil tiles. Each suite is different—one has a private courtyard complete with trickling fountain—but all have kitchenettes. The bathroom fixtures are stylishly old-fashioned, and the curvy bathtubs are made of masonry. Some rooms have king-

size beds. ✉ *Imperial 29, 41003,* ☎ *95/450–0300,* FAX *95/450–0330. 14 suites, 10 junior suites. AE, DC, MC, V.*

$$$–$$$$ **Doña María.** This is one of Seville's most charming hotels, and it's not far from the cathedral. Some rooms are small and plain; others are tastefully furnished with antiques. Room 310 has a four-poster double bed, and 305 has two single four-posters; both have spacious bathrooms. There's also a rooftop pool with a good view of the Giralda, just a stone's throw away. ✉ *Don Remondo 19, 41004,* ☎ *95/422–4990,* FAX *95/421–9546. 67 rooms. Pool. AE, DC, MC, V.*

$$$–$$$$ **Meliá Sevilla.** This vast, modern hotel behind the Plaza de España resembles the best American business hotels. Ask for a room at the front, facing the pool and the Plaza de España, which is illuminated on weekends; those in the back have poor views. The best rooms and suites are on the ninth floor. Travelers with disabilities are well accommodated here. ✉ *Dr. Pedro de Castro 1, 41004,* ☎ *95/442–2611,* FAX *95/442–1608. 364 rooms, 5 suites. Restaurant, bar, coffee shop, pool, beauty salon, meeting rooms, parking (fee). AE, DC, MC, V.*

$$$ **Bécquer.** Well maintained and well located near the main shopping district, the Bécquer is one of Seville's best mid-range lodgings. Marble floors, dark wood, and leather furniture dominate the public areas, which include a small sitting room dedicated to the poet Gustavo Adolfo Bécquer. The guest rooms are traditionally Spanish, with peach-color walls, floral prints, matching woven bedspreads, and carved-wood headboards. ✉ *Reyes Católicos 4, 41001,* ☎ *95/422–8900,* FAX *95/421–4400. 137 rooms, 2 suites. Bar, breakfast room, cafeteria, parking (fee). AE, DC, MC, V.*

$$$ **Inglaterra.** This classic hotel on the central Plaza Nueva has long been known for excellent service. Next door to the British Consulate, it's something of a historic British outpost in Spain, and the room decor might be said to reflect this—furnishings are understated, a bit faded, and sometimes anachronistically floral. Rooms on the fifth floor have large balconies. these have spacious balconies. The second-floor dining room overlooks orange trees and the busy Plaza Nueva. The spacious lobby lounge is comfortable and civilized, and the on-site Irish pub lends a twist. ✉ *Plaza Nueva 7, 41001,* ☎ *95/422–4970,* FAX *95/456–1336. 113 rooms, 1 suite. Restaurant, bar, lobby lounge, pub. AE, DC, MC, V.*

$$$ **Las Casas de la Judería.** Tucked into a passageway just off the Plaza Santa María, in the heart of the Barrio de Santa Cruz, this labyrinthine hotel occupies three of the barrio's old palaces, each arranged around inner courtyards. Ocher predominates in the suitably palatial common areas; the spacious guest rooms are dressed in tasteful pastels and decorated with prints of Seville. ✉ *Callejón de Dos Hermanas, 41004,* ☎ *95/441–5150,* FAX *95/442–2170. 41 rooms, 16 suites. AE, DC, MC, V.*

$$$ **Pasarela.** Also behind the Plaza de España, the Pasarela is cozier than its giant neighbor, the Meliá Sevilla (☞ *above*). Several ground-floor sitting rooms, some with oil paintings and table lamps, give the place a homey atmosphere. Guest rooms are large and fully carpeted, with predominantly brown-and-beige modern decor and white bedspreads. ✉ *Avda. de la Borbolla 11, 41004,* ☎ *95/441–5511,* FAX *95/442–0727. 77 rooms, 5 suites. Bar, breakfast room, sauna, exercise room, meeting rooms. AE, DC, MC, V.*

$$ **Giralda.** This modern hotel in a cul-de-sac off Recaredo caters largely to the tour-bus crowd, but service is friendly and professional, and rates are reasonable. The rooms, comfortable, spacious, and light, are dressed in relaxing, contemporary beige tones. ✉ *Sierra Nevada 3, 41003,* ☎ *95/441–6661,* FAX *95/441–9352. 101 rooms. Restaurant, bar, meeting rooms. AE, DC, MC, V.*

$$ **La Rábida.** Convenient to both sights and shops, this hotel occupies a converted Andalusian house in the Arenal district and retains an Old World atmosphere with its large, covered central patio. Many rooms overlook a second, leafy patio with oblique views of the Giralda. Decor in the guest rooms is dreary, but the mattresses are firm and the price is right. ✉ *Castelar 24, 41001,* ☎ *95/422–0960,* FAX *95/422–4375. 103 rooms. Restaurant, bar. AE, DC, MC, V.*

$ **Internacional.** If you want cheap lodging and can live without the comforts of home, this old Andalusian house near the Casa de Pilatos is for you. Friendly and family-run, the hotel announces itself with a wrought-iron gate that opens into the central patio–reception area. A white-marble staircase leads to the bedrooms, which have twin beds and are very simply furnished. ✉ *Águilas 17, 41003,* ☎ FAX *95/421–3207. 24 rooms. DC, MC, V.*

$ **Simón.** Housed in a rambling 19th-century town house, the Simón is a good choice for inexpensive, basic accommodation thanks to its location near the cathedral. You're greeted by a spacious, airy courtyard. ✉ *García de Vinuesa 19, 41001,* ☎ *95/422–6660,* FAX *95/456–2241. 29 rooms. AE, DC, MC, V.*

Nightlife and the Arts

To find out what's on, look in the local newspapers or in *ABC Sevilla, Correo de Andalucía, Sudoeste,* or *Nueva Andalucía.* The free monthly arts leaflet *El Giraldillo* also lists classical concerts, jazz, films (for films in English, look for "v. o."), plays, art exhibits, and dance performances in Seville and all major Andalusian cities. The tourist office has a quarterly leaflet of events at municipal theaters ("Programación Teatros Municipales").

BARS AND CAFÉS

Because most locals eat their main meal at lunchtime, Seville's bars are packed in the evenings with people making a supper of tapas. Founded in 1670, **El Rinconcillo** (✉ C. Gerona 40, near the Casa de Pilatos, ☎ 95/422–3183) claims to be the oldest tavern in Seville. Popular **La Alicantina** (✉ Plaza del Salvador 2, ☎ 95/422–6122) has a tapas bar with pastoral scenes of wine- and beer-making on its *azulejo* walls. Open since 1934, **Casa Román** (✉ Plaza de los Venerables, ☎ 95/421–6408) is a classic tapas bar, with wood-paneled walls and ceilings and hanging hams. The **Cervecería Giralda** (✉ Mateos Gago 9, ☎ 95/422–7435) is a lovely corner bar, set with Moorish-style marble columns and *azulejo* walls and is usually thronged with a hip, young crowd. At **El Bacalao** (✉ Plaza Ponce de León 15, ☎ 95/421–6670) the specialty is, of course, *bacalao* (salt cod), prepared virtually 101 different ways.

FLAMENCO

Seville has three regular flamenco clubs, patronized more by tourists than by locals. Tickets are sold in most hotels; otherwise, make your own reservations (essential for groups, advisable for everyone in high season) by calling the club in the evening.

El Arenal is in the back room of the picturesque Mesón Dos de Mayo. Here you get your own table, rather than having to sit in rows. ✉ *Rodo 7,* ☎ *95/421–6492.* *4,100 ptas., excluding dinner.* ⌚ *Daily 9:30 and 11:30 (9:30 and 11 Oct.–Mar.).*

El Patio Sevillano caters mainly to tour groups. The show is a mixture of regional Spanish dances (often performed to taped music) and pure flamenco by some outstanding guitarists, singers, and dancers. ✉ *Paseo de Colón 11,* ☎ *95/421–4120.* *3,800 ptas.* ⌚ *Daily 7:30 and 10.*

Los Gallos is an intimate club in the heart of the Barrio de Santa Cruz. Performances are good and reasonably pure. ✉ *Plaza Santa Cruz 11,* ☎ *95/421–6981.* *3,500 ptas.* ⌚ *Daily 9 and 11:30.*

MUSIC

Long prominent in the opera world, Seville is particularly proud of its opera house, the **Teatro de la Maestranza** (✉ Paseo de Colón, ☎ 95/422–3344). Be sure to check out what's on here—it's usually the best show in town. Classical music and ballet are performed at the **Teatro Lope de Vega** (✉ Avda. María Luisa, ☎ 95/459–0853). You can also catch classical concerts at the **Conservatorio Superior de Música** (✉ Jesús del Gran Poder), in the cathedral, and in the church of **San Salvador.** The **Teatro Alameda** (✉ Crédito, ☎ 95/438–8312) stages a variety of productions in Spanish, including some children's plays.

Outdoor Activities and Sports

BOATING

The Guadalquivir is prime territory for boating enthusiasts. Paddleboats, canoes, and river cruises are great ways to see Seville and the surrounding countryside from the water. Among the many options are paddleboats and canoes; inquire at the tourist office or on the riverbank near the Torre del Oro. **Cruceros Turísticos Torre del Oro** (✉ Paseo Alcalde Marqués de Contadero beside Torre del Oro, ☎ 95/421–1396) runs hourly river cruises for 1,500 ptas. per person.

BULLFIGHTING

Fights take place at the **Maestranza Bullring,** on the Paseo de Colón 12 (☎ 95/422–4577). The season runs from Easter until late October, with most *corridas* held on Sundays except during special fiestas. The season highlight is the April Fair, when daily fights feature Spain's leading *toreros.* Tickets for these fights are expensive, and you should buy them in advance from the official *despacho de entradas* (ticket office) on Calle Adriano, alongside the bullring. Other legitimate *despachos* sell tickets on Calle Sierpes, but these are unofficial and charge a 20% commission.

Shopping

Seville is the region's main shopping center and ground zero for archetypal Andalusian souvenirs. Most souvenirs are sold in the Barrio de Santa Cruz and on the streets around the cathedral and Giralda, especially Calle Alemanes.

The main shopping area for Sevillanos themselves is Calle Sierpes, along with its neighboring streets Tetuan, Velázquez, Plaza Magdalena, and Plaza Duque. Fashionable boutiques abound here. Near the Puente del Cachorro bridge, the old Estación de Córdoba train station has been converted to a stylish shopping center, the **Centro Comercial Plaza de Armas** (✉ Enter on Plaza de la Legión), with swish boutiques, bars, fast-food joints, a microbrewery, and a cinema complex. **El Corte Inglés** (✉ Plaza Duque 7, ☎ 95/422–0931; ✉ Marqués por Luis Montoto, 122–128, ☎ 95/457–1440) is a well-run department store that stays open throughout the day.

ANTIQUES

For antiques, look along Mateos Gago, opposite the Giralda, and in the Barrio de Santa Cruz on Jamerdana and on Rodrigo Caro, between Plazas Alianza and Doña Elvira.

BOOKS

A large assortment of books in English, Spanish, French, and Italian is sold at the American-owned **Librería Vértice** (✉ San Fernando 33–35, ☎ 95/421–1654), near the gates of the university.

CERAMICS

Martian Ceramics (✉ Sierpes 74, ☎ 95/421–3413) has a good range of high-quality plates and dishes, especially the flowers-on-white patterns native to Seville. It's a bit touristy, but fairly priced. In the Barrio de Santa Cruz, try along Mateos Gago; Romero Murube, between Plaza Triunfo and Plaza Alianza, on the edge of the Barrio; and between Plaza Doña Elvira and Plaza de los Venerables.

FANS

Casa Rubio (✉ Sierpes 56, ☎ 95/422–6872) is Seville's premier fan store—no mean distinction. It has everything from traditional to entirely contemporary fans.

FLAMENCO DRESSES

Beware: these are prohibitively expensive. You'll find the cheapest ones in **El Corte Inglés,** or, surprisingly, in the souvenir shops on Calle Alemanes. For those interested in serious, and seriously expensive, flamenco dresses and other costumery, **Pardales** (✉ Cuna 23, ☎ 95/421–3709) is the place to go. Proprietor Esperenza Pardales Acosta makes most items to order, but she also sells some off-the-rack pieces.

GUITARS

Cayuela (✉ Zaragoza 4, ☎ 95/422–4557) is run by the second generation of a family of guitar makers from Andújar, near Jaén. They carry unique, hand-crafted guitars and quality factory-made instruments.

PASTRIES

Andalusia's convents are known for their homemade pastries. A wide selection from a number of convents is sold at **El Torno** (✉ Plaza El Cabildo, ☎ 95/421–9190), a tiny shop on a quiet square near the cathedral.

PORCELAIN

La Cartuja china, originally crafted at La Cartuja Monastery but now made outside Seville, is sold at **La Alacena** (✉ Alfonso XII 25, ☎ 95/422–8021). **El Corte Inglés** (☞ *above*) is a good second choice.

STREET MARKETS

The **Plaza del Duque** has a crafts market on Friday and Saturday. The flea market **El Jueves** is held on Calle Feria on Thursday morning. Sunday morning brings the **Alameda de Hercules** crafts market and, in the **Plaza del Cabildo,** a coin and stamp market.

TEXTILES

You'll find all kinds of blankets, shawls, and embroidered tablecloths woven by local artisans at **Artesanía Textil** (✉ García de Vinuesa 33, ☎ 95/456–2840), a modern store on a busy shopping street.

Carmona

31 *32 km (20 mi) east of Seville off N-IV.*

Claiming to be one of the oldest inhabited places in Spain (the Phoenicians and Carthaginians had settlements here), Carmona later became an important town under both the Romans and the Moors. Its incredible Roman necropolis contains about 900 tombs dating from the 2nd century BC. Today Carmona is a quiet Andalusian town with a dramatic position on a steep, fortified hill. As you wander its ancient, narrow streets, you'll see a wealth of Mudéjar and Renaissance churches, medieval gateways, and simple whitewashed houses of clear Moorish influence, punctuated here and there by a Baroque palace.

Park your car near the Puerta de Sevilla in the imposing **Alcázar de Abajo** (Lower Fortress), a Moorish fortification built on Roman foundations at the edge of the old town. In the tower beside the gate is the tourist office, where you can grab a map.

On the edge of the "new town," across the road from the Alcázar de Abajo, stands the church of **San Pedro,** begun in 1466. Its extraordinary interior is an unbroken mass of sculptures and gilded surfaces, and its Baroque tower, erected in 1704, is an unabashed imitation of Seville's Giralda. Make your way up Calle Prim to the **Plaza San Fernando,** in heart of the old town, whose 17th-century houses have Moorish overtones. Continuing from the square up Calle Martín, you'll reach the Gothic church of **Santa María,** built between 1424 and 1518 on the site of Carmona's former Great Mosque. Santa María is a contemporary of Seville's cathedral, and it, too, retains its Moorish courtyard, once used for ritual ablutions. Behind the church is the 18th-century **Palacio del Marqués de las Torres,** which has been restored to house a small museum on the history of Carmona. (October through May, the museum is open Wednesday through Monday 11–7, Tuesday 11–2; June through September, it's open Wednesday through Monday 10–2 and 6:30–9:30, Tuesday 10–2. Admission is free.)

Stroll down to the **Puerta de Córdoba** (Córdoba Gate) on the eastern edge of town. This old gateway was first built by the Romans around AD 175, then altered by Moorish and Renaissance additions. End your walk in the Moorish **Alcázar de Arriba** (Upper Fortress), built on Roman foundations and later converted by King Pedro the Cruel into a fine Mudéjar palace. Pedro's summer residence was destroyed in 1504 by an earthquake, but the parador (☞ Lodging, *below*) that now stands amid its ruins commands a breathtaking view.

At the western end of town lies Carmona's most outstanding monument, the splendid **Roman necropolis.** Here, in huge underground chambers, some 900 family tombs were chiseled out of the rock between the 2nd and 4th centuries BC. The walls, decorated with leaf and bird motifs, are punctuated with niches for burial urns. The most spectacular tombs are the **Elephant Vault** and the **Servilia Tomb,** which resembles a complete Roman villa with its colonnaded arches and vaulted side galleries. Its lone occupant, a young woman, was embalmed, unlike the rest of the dead in the necropolis, who were cremated. ✉ *C. Enmedio,* ☎ *95/414–0811.* 🎫 *250 ptas.; EU citizens free.* ⏲ *Mid-Sept.–mid-June, Tues.–Fri. 9–5, weekends 10–2; mid-June–mid-Sept., Tues.–Sat. 9–2, Sun. 10–2.*

If you have time and a car, venture to the historic neighboring towns of Ecija and Osuna, within easy driving distance of Carmona. **Ecija,** 48 km (30 mi) from Carmona on the N-IV to Córdoba, is particularly well endowed with Baroque church towers: it has 11. (It is also known as "the frying pan of Andalusia," as midsummer temperatures often reach 100°F/37°C here.) From Ecija, take C430 south to **Osuna.** In the 16th century, the Dukes of Osuna were among the wealthiest people in Spain, which accounts for the now-sleepy town's impressive Renaissance palaces, Colegiata de Santa María church, and old university. From Osuna, take the A92 (N334) back to Seville (64 km/40 mi).

Dining and Lodging

$$$$ ✕ **San Fernando.** You enter from a side street, but this second-floor restaurant looks out onto the Plaza de San Fernando. The beige dining room is pleasant in its simplicity, with nothing to distract from the view of daily life below. The kitchen presents straightforward modern versions of Spanish dishes with a bit of flair—as in thin, fried potato slivers shaped as a bird's nest. Kid and partridge are perennial favorites, and there's a fine range of desserts. ✉ *Sacramento 3,* ☎ *95/414–3556. AE, DC, MC, V. Closed Mon. and Aug. No dinner Sun.*

$$$$ 🏨 **Casa de Carmona.** Set in the historic Palacio Lasso de la Vega, the Casa de Carmona is one of the most elegant hotels in Spain. The public rooms are decorated with antiques, rich fabrics, and museum-quality rugs, and the guest rooms are large and luxuriously furnished. Between jaunts you can relax in the Arabian-style garden, with orange trees and fountain, or swim in the pool. The Casa's drawbacks are notoriously indifferent service and uneven maintenance, both of which can lessen the thrill of the palatial setting. ✉ *Plaza de Lasso, 41410,* ☎ *95/414–3300,* FAX *95/419–0189. 30 rooms, 3 suites. Restaurant, bar, pool, sauna, health club, library, laundry service, concierge. AE, DC, MC, V.*

$$$ **Alcázar de la Reina.** Stylish and contemporary, this new hotel is a welcome addition to Carmona's lodging scene. The public areas, which include a large, mainly Italian restaurant, are bright and airy, with marble floors and pastel walls. Guest rooms are spacious and comfortable. ✉ *Plaza de Lasso 2, 41410,* ☎ *95/419–6200,* FAX *95/414–0113. 66 rooms, 2 suites. Restaurant, bar, pool, meeting rooms. AE, DC, MC, V.*

$$$ ★ **Parador Alcázar del Rey Don Pedro.** This delightful parador has superb views from its hilltop position among the ruins of Pedro the Cruel's summer palace. The public rooms open off a central, Moorish-style patio, and the vaulted dining hall and adjacent bar open onto an outdoor terrace that overlooks the sloping garden, where even the pool is tiled in Moorish patterns. The spacious rooms have traditional decor, with rugs and dark furniture. All but six, which face onto the front courtyard, face south over the valley; the best rooms are on the top floor. ✉ *Alcázar, 41410,* ☎ *95/414–1010,* FAX *95/414–1712. 63 rooms. Restaurant, bar, pool. AE, DC, MC, V.*

Itálica

32 *12 km (7 mi) north of Seville, 1 km (½ mi) beyond Santiponce.*

This ancient city was founded by Scipio Africanus in 206 BC as a home for veteran soldiers. By the 2nd century AD, it had grown into one of Roman Iberia's most important cities and given the Roman world two great emperors, Trajan (52–117) and Hadrian (76–138). Ten thousand people once lived here, in 1,000 dwellings. About 25% of the site has been excavated, and work is still in progress.

The most important monument is the huge, elliptical **amphitheater,** which held 40,000 spectators. You'll also find traces of city streets, cisterns, and the floor plans of several villas, some with mosaic floors, though all the best mosaics and statues have been removed to Seville's Museum of Archaeology.

Itálica was abandoned and plundered as a quarry by the Visigoths, who preferred Seville. It fell into decay around AD 700. Some of its other remains, including a **Roman theater** and **Roman baths,** are visible in the small town that has grown up next door, Santiponce. ☎ *95/599–7376.* *250 ptas.; EU citizens free.* ⏲ *Oct.–Mar., Tues.–Sat. 9–5:30, Sun. 10–4; Apr.–Sept., Tues.–Sat. 9–8, Sun. 9–3.*

PROVINCE OF HUELVA

Doñana National Park, Matalascañas, Mazagón, La Rábida, Palos de la Frontera, Moguer, Riotinto, and Aracena

Whenever you're ready to bid farewell to Seville's urban bustle, nature awaits in the province of Huelva. The Parque Nacional de Doñana, one of the largest and richest wildlife refuges in Europe, and pristine beaches on the Costa de la Luz are all about an hour's drive from Seville. This is also a land rich in history: Columbus's voyage to the New World was sparked here, at the monastery of La Rábida and in Palos de la Frontera. From Seville, turn off the Seville–Huelva highway, drive through Almonte and El Rocío—scene of the Whitsuntide pilgrimage to the Virgin of the Dew—and you'll come to the visitor center at La Rocina.

Doñana National Park

33 *100 km (62 mi) southwest of Seville.*

One of Europe's last swaths of wilderness, these wetlands beside the Guadalquivir estuary form one of Spain's largest national parks. The site was named for Doña Ana, wife of a 16th-century duke: prone to bouts of depression, she crossed the river and wandered into the wetlands one day, never to be seen alive again. Doñana covers 188,000 acres (an area 64 km by 15 km/40 mi by 9 mi) and is a paradise for nature lovers, especially bird-watchers: the park sits on the migratory route from Africa to Europe and is the winter home and breeding ground for as many as 150 species of rare birds. The park's habitats range from beaches and shifting sand dunes to marshes, dense brushwood, and sandy hillsides of pine and cork oak. Two of Europe's most endangered species, the imperial eagle and the lynx, make their homes here, and kestrels, kites, buzzards, egrets, storks, and spoonbills breed among the cork oaks.

At the visitor center at **La Rocina** (☎ 959/442340), less than 2 km (1 mi) from El Rocío, you can peer at the many species of birds from a 3½-km (2-mi) footpath. It's open daily 9–2 and 3–sundown. Five kilometers (3 mi) away, an exhibit at the **Palacio de Acebrón** explains the park's ecosystems; it's open daily 8–3 and 4–sundown (last entrance one hour before closing). Two kilometers (1 mi) before Matalascañas, you'll find **Acebuche,** the park's main reception and interpretation center (☎ 959/448711), open daily 9–7. Jeep tours, which you must reserve in advance (☎ 959/430432), start from here; tours last four hours, cost 2,750 ptas., and cover a 70-km (43-mi) route across beaches, sand dunes, marshes, and scrub. Off-season, from November to February, you can usually book a tour with just a day's notice; at other times, book as far in advance as possible (☞ Guided Tours *in* Seville and Western Andalusia A to Z, *below*).

Lodging

$$ **Cortijo Los Mimbrales.** This one-story Andalusian farm-hacienda on the Rocío–Matalascañas road is the perfect base for exploring Doñana: it's perched on the park's edge, a mere 1 km (½ mi) from the visitor center at La Rocina. The atmosphere is convivial, and the large common lounge with comfy chairs and fireplace makes for relaxed evening chit-chat with fellow nature lovers. Accommodations are in colorfully decorated rooms or in bungalows sleeping two to four, with kitchenettes and small private gardens. Some rooms and bungalows have fireplaces. There are stables on the premises, and the hotel can arrange horseback rides on the fringes of the park. ✉ *Carretera del Rocío (A483), Km 30,* ☎ *959/442237,* FAX *959/442443. 14 rooms, 6 bungalows. Restaurant, pool, horseback riding.* AE, DC, MC, V.

Matalascañas

34 *3 km (2 mi) south of Acebuche; 85 km (53 mi) southwest of Seville.*

Close proximity to Acebuche, the main reception center at Doñana, makes this town a convenient lodging base for park visitors. Otherwise, it's a rather incongruous and ugly sprawl of hotels and vacation homes, very crowded at Easter and in summer and eerily deserted the rest of the year (most hotels are closed from November to March). There are some nice beaches for those who just want to relax, and the local ocean waters draw windsurfers and other water athletes.

Lodging

$$ **Tierra Mar.** Check into this large beachfront hotel if you want to combine Doñana with the seashore. ✉ *Matalascañas Parc, 120 Sector M, 21760,* ☎ *959/440300,* FAX *959/440720. 254 rooms. Restaurant, café, pool, sauna. AE, DC, MC, V. Closed Dec.–Jan.*

Mazagón

35 *22 km (14 mi) northwest of Matalascañas.*

True, there isn't much to see or do in this coastal town, but its parador makes a nice base for touring La Rábida, Palos de la Frontera, and Moguer. Mazagón's beautiful beach is among the nicest in the region.

Dining and Lodging

$$$ ✕ **Parador Cristóbal Colón.** This peaceful modern parador stands on a cliff surrounded by pine groves, overlooking a sandy beach 3 km (2 mi) southeast of Mazagón. Most rooms have balconies overlooking the garden. The restaurant serves traditional Andalusian dishes and local seafood specialties, like *sopa viña AB* (a fish soup flavored with sherry and thickened with mayonnaise), stuffed baby squid, and hake medallions. ✉ *Carretera Huelva–Matalascañas, Km 24, 21130,* ☎ *959/536300,* FAX *959/536228. 43 rooms. Restaurant, bar, pool, 2 tennis courts, meeting rooms. AE, DC, MC, V.*

La Rábida

★ 36 *30 km (19 mi) northwest of Doñana, 8 km (5 mi) northwest of Mazagón.*

You may want to extend your Doñana tour to see the monastery of **Santa María de La Rábida,** "the birthplace of America." In 1485 Columbus came from Portugal with his son Diego to stay in this Mudéjar-style Franciscan monastery. Here he discussed his theories with friars Antonio de Marchena and Juan Pérez, who interceded on his behalf with Queen Isabella. The early 15th-century church holds a much-venerated 14th-century statue of the **Virgen de los Milagros** (Virgin of Miracles). The **frescoes** in the gatehouse were painted by Daniel Vázquez Díaz in 1930. Next to the monastery is a small, basic, inexpensive hostelry, the **Hostería de la Rábida** (☎ 959/350312). ☎ *959/350411.* *Donation suggested.* ⏲ *Tues.–Sun. 10–1 and 4–6:15 (4–7 Mar.–Oct.).*

Two kilometers (1 mi) from the monastery, on the seashore, is the **Muelle de las Carabelas** (Caravels' Wharf), a reproduction of a 15th-century port. The star exhibits here are the full-size replicas of Columbus's flotilla, the *Niña, Pinta,* and *Santa María,* which were built using the same techniques as in Columbus's day. You can climb aboard each one and learn more (or refresh your memory) about discovery of the New World in the adjoining museum. ✉ *Paraje de le Rábida,* ☎ *959/530597.* *500 ptas.* ⏲ *Oct.–Mar., Tues.–Sun. 10–7; Apr.–Sept., Tues.–Fri. 10–2 and 5–9, weekends 11–8.*

Palos de la Frontera

37 *4 km (2½ mi) northeast of La Rábida, 12 km (7 mi) northeast of Mazagón.*

Did you learn *this* detail in school? On August 2, 1492, Columbus's three famous caravels, the *Niña,* the *Pinta,* and the *Santa María,* set sail from Palos de la Frontera. Most of the crew were men from Palos and neighboring Moguer. At the door of the church of **San Jorge** (1473), the royal letter ordering the levy of the ships' crew and equipment was read aloud, and the voyagers took their water supplies from the Fontanilla (fountain) at the town's entrance.

Moguer

38 *12 km (7 mi) northeast of Palos de la Frontera.*

The inhabitants of this old port town now spend more time growing strawberries than they do seafaring, as you'll see from the surrounding fields. The **Convento de Santa Clara** dates from 1337. *300 ptas. Tues.–Sat. 11–1 and 4:30–6:30.*

While in Moguer, see the **Casa-Museo Juan Ramón Jiménez,** former home of the Nobel prize–winning poet who penned the much-loved *Platero y Yo.* ✉ *C. Juan Ramón Jiménez,* ☎ *959/372148. 300 ptas. Mon.–Sat. 10–2 and 5–8, Sun. 10–2.*

Riotinto

39 *74 km (46 mi) north of Huelva.*

Heading north from Palos and Huelva on the N435, you'll reach the turnoff to Minas de Riotinto, the mining town near the source of the Riotinto (literally, "Red River"). The river's waters are the color of blood due to the minerals leeched from the surrounding mountains: this area contains some of the richest copper deposits in the world, as well as gold and silver. It has been mined since antiquity, as the many Iberian, Tartessian, and Roman artifacts found here attest. In 1873 the mines were taken over by the British Rio Tinto Company Ltd., which started to dig a massive open-pit mine and build a 64-km (40-mi) railway to the port of Huelva to transport mineral ore. The British left in 1954, but mining activity continues today, albeit on a smaller scale.

The multicolor landscape, scarred by centuries of intensive mining, makes for an unusual and well-organized tour conducted by the Fundación Riotinto. The tour's first stop, the **Museo Minero** (Museum of Mining), has archaeological finds, exhibits on the area's mining history, and a collection of historical steam engines and rail coaches. Next comes the **Corta Atalaya,** one of the largest open-pit mines in the world (4,000 ft across and 1,100 ft deep), and **Bellavista,** the elegant English quarter where the British mine managers lived. The tour ends with an optional ride on the **Tren Minero** (Miners' Train), which follows the course of the Riotinto along more than 24 restored km (15 mi) of the old mining railway. *Fundación Riotinto,* ☎ *959/590025. Full tour 1,900 ptas. Oct.–June, daily 10–7; July–Sept., daily 10–4. Miners' Train departs July–Sept., Tues.–Sun. 1 PM; Oct.–mid-Apr., weekends 4 PM; mid-Apr.–May, weekends 5 PM; June, weekends 1 PM.*

Aracena

40 *105 km (65 mi) north of Huelva, 100 km (62 mi) northwest of Seville.*

Stretching north of the Riotinto mines is the 460,000-acre Sierra de Aracena nature park, an expanse of rolling hills cloaked in cork and holm oak. This region is known for its cured hams, which come from the prized free-ranging Iberian pigs that gorge on acorns in the autumn months prior to slaughter; the hams are buried in salt and then hung in cellars to dry-cure for at least two years. The best hams come from the village of **Jabugo.** The capital of the region is Aracena, whose main attraction is the spectacular cave known as the **Gruta de las Maravillas** (Cave of Marvels). The 12 caverns hide long corridors, stalactites and stalagmites arranged in wonderful patterns, and stunning underground lakes. ✉ *Plaza Pozo de Nieves, Pozo de Nieves,* ☎ *959/128355.* *1,000 ptas.* ⊙ *Guided tours of caverns daily at 10:30, 11:30, 12:30, 1:30, 3, 4, 5, and 6.*

Dining and Lodging

$$ ✕ **José Vicente.** Diners come all the way from Seville and beyond for the food at this small restaurant near the Seville exit from Aracena. The menu is short but tempting. This is an ideal place to try dishes made with fresh pork (as opposed to the more commonly available cured ham) from the free-ranging Iberian pig. Appetizers always include a few vegetable dishes and soups. If the main dining room is full, and it often is, you can dine at one of four tables in the adjoining Despensa de José Vicente, which doubles as a bar and a shop selling local produce. ✉ *Avda. de Andalucía 51, Aracena,* ☎ *959/128455. AE, MC, V. Closed Fri.*

$ **Galaroza Sierra.** This whitewashed hotel is on the outskirts of the village of Galaroza, 3 km (2 mi) from Jabugo. Decor in the common areas and rooms is modern rustic, with light wood and woven blankets. Rooms have small balconies and views of the mountains, while the four bungalows face the swimming pool. Noise from the nearby road can be a problem. The restaurant specializes in preparations of fresh Ibérico pork. ✉ *Carretera Sevilla–Lisboa, Km 69.5, 21291 Galaroza,* ☎ *959/123237,* FAX *959/123236. 22 rooms, 4 bungalows. Restaurant, pool. DC, MC, V.*

$ **Los Castãnos.** This hotel offers basic but comfortable accommodations in small, simple rooms. Some face the street, others an interior patio; upstairs rooms have balconies. ✉ *Avenida de Huelva 5, 21200 Aracena,* ☎ *959/126300,* FAX *959/126287. 33 rooms. Restaurant. AE, DC, MC, V.*

PROVINCE OF CÁDIZ

Jerez de la Frontera, Arcos de la Frontera, Sanlúcar de Barrameda, Puerto de Santa María, and Cádiz

A trip through Cádiz is a trip back in time. Winding roads take you through scenes ranging from flat and barren plains to seemingly endless vineyards, and the rolling countryside is carpeted with blindingly white soil known as *albariza*—unique to this area, and the secret to the grapes used in sherry. Throughout the province, *los pueblos blancos* (the white villages) provide striking contrasts with the terrain, especially at Arcos de la Frontera, where the village sits dramatically on a crag overlooking the gorge of the Guadalete River. In Jerez, you can savor the town's internationally known sherry or delight in the skills and forms of purebred Carthusian horses. Finally, in the city of Cádiz, absorb about 3,000 years of history: this may be the oldest continuously inhabited city in the Western world.

Jerez de la Frontera

41 *97 km (60 mi) south of Seville.*

Jerez, world headquarters for sherry, is surrounded by immense vineyards of chalky soil, whose Palomino grapes have funded a host of churches and noble mansions. An hour's stroll around the center is all you need to get a feel for this small city. May and September are the most exciting times to visit Jerez, as their spectacular fiestas transform the town. For the Feria del Caballo (Horse Fair), in early May, carriages and riders fill the streets, and purebreds from the School of Equestrian Art compete in races and dressage displays. September brings the Fiesta de Otoño (Autumn Festival), when the first of the grape harvest is blessed on the steps of the cathedral.

The 12th-century **Alcázar** was once the residence of the caliph of Seville. Its small, octagonal **mosque,** with an outstanding cupola, and **baths** were built for the Moorish governor's private use. The baths are among the best-preserved in Spain and have three sections: the *sala fria* (cold room), the larger *sala templada* (warm room), and the *sala caliente* (hot room), for steam baths. In the midst of it all is the 17th-century **Palacio de Villavicencio,** built on the site of the original Moorish palace. A *camera obscura,* a lens-and-mirrors device that projects the outdoors onto a large indoor screen, offers a 360-degree view of Jerez and its principal monuments from the palace's highest tower—a perfect introduction to the town. ✉ *Alameda Vieja,* ☎ *956/319798.* 🎟 *200 ptas.; camera obscura 500 ptas.* ⏲ *Daily 10–6 (10–8 in summer).*

The **cathedral** has an octagonal cupola and a separate bell tower. ✉ *Plaza del Arroyo.* ⏲ *Weekdays 6 AM–8 PM, Sun. 11–2.*

On the **Plaza de la Asunción,** one of Jerez's most intimate squares, you'll find the Mudéjar church of **San Dionisio** and the ornate **cabildo municipal** (city hall), whose lovely plateresque facade dates from 1575.

The unusual and interesting **Museo de los Relojes** is a museum devoted entirely to clocks. For the full effect, time your visit for noon, when all of the clocks chime at once. ✉ *C. Cervantes 3,* ☎ *956/182100.* 🎟 *400 ptas.* ⏲ *Mon.–Sat. 10–2.*

Names such as González Byass, Domecq, Harvey, and Sandeman are inextricably linked with Jerez. The word *sherry,* first used in Great Britain in 1608, is actually an English corruption of the town's old Moorish name, Xeres. Both sherry and horses are very much the domain of Jerez's Anglo-Spanish aristocracy, whose Catholic ancestors came here from England two or three centuries ago.

★ At any given time, more than half a million barrels of sherry are maturing in Jerez's vast aboveground wine cellars. If you visit a **bodega** (winery), your guide will explain the *solera* method of blending old wine with new, and the importance of the *flor* (a sort of yeast that forms on the surface of the wine as it ages) in determining the kind of sherry. Most bodegas welcome visitors, but it's always advisable to phone ahead for an appointment, if only to make sure you join a group that speaks your language. Cellars usually charge a token admission fee, rarely more than 500 ptas., and most close for the month of August. Tours last between 40 minutes and an hour and usually start with an audiovisual program or short film about sherry and the history of that particular winery. You'll then tour the aging cellars, with their endless rows of casks. (You won't see the actual fermenting and bottling, which take place in more modern, less romantic plants outside town.) Finally, you'll be invited to sample generous amounts of pale, dry *fino*; nutty *amontillado*; or rich, deep *oloroso,* and, of course, to purchase a few bottles at interesting prices in the winery shop.

Domecq is Jerez's oldest bodega, founded in 1730, and aside from sherry produces the world's best-selling brandy, Fundador (☎ 956/151500). Other wineries worth visiting include **Sandeman** (☎ 956/301100), **Harvey** (☎ 956/346004), and **Wisdom and Warter** (☎ 956/184306). But if you only have time for one, tour the prestigious **González Byass** (☎ 956/357000), home of the famous Tío Pepe; this tour is well organized and includes La Concha, an open-air aging cellar designed by Eiffel.

★ The **Real Escuela Andaluza del Arte Ecuestre** (Royal Andalusian School of Equestrian Art) operates on the grounds of the Recreo de las Cadenas, a splendid 19th-century palace. This prestigious school was masterminded by Alvaro Domecq in the 1970s. Every Thursday the Cartujana horses—a breed created from a cross between the native Andalusian workhorse and the Arabian—and skilled riders in 18th-century riding costume demonstrate intricate dressage techniques and jumping in the spectacular show "Cómo Bailan los Caballos Andaluces" (roughly, "The Dancing Horses of Andalusia"). Reservations are essential. ✉ *Avda. Duque de Abrantes,* ☎ *956/319635.* *Numbered seats 2,500 ptas., unnumbered seats 1,500 ptas.* ⏲ *Nov.–Feb., Thurs. at noon; Mar.–Oct., Tues. and Thurs. at noon.*

The rest of the week, you can visit the stables and tack room, watch the horses being schooled, and witness **rehearsals** for the show. *500 ptas.* ⏲ *Mon., Wed., and Fri. 11–1.*

Bullfighting

Jerez's bullring is on Calle Circo, northeast of the city center. Tickets are sold at the official ticket office on Calle Porvera, though only about five bullfights are held each year, in May and October.

Dining and Lodging

$$$ ✕ **Gaitán.** Within walking distance of the riding school, this restaurant has white walls and brick arches decorated with colorful ceramic plates and photos of famous guests. It's crowded with businesspeople at lunchtime. The menu is Andalusian, with a few Basque dishes thrown in. *Setas* (wild mushrooms) make a delicious starter in season. ✉ *Gaitán 3,* ☎ *956/345859. AE, DC, MC, V. No dinner Sun.*

$$$ ★ ✕ **La Mesa Redonda.** Chef-owner José Antonio Valdespino has spent years researching the classic recipes once served in aristocratic Jerez homes, and he presents them in this small, friendly restaurant off Avenida Alvaro Domecq, around the corner from the Hotel Avenida Jerez. It feels like a family dining room: the eight tables are surrounded by shelves lined with cookbooks. (The round table at one end of the room gives the restaurant its name.) The menu changes constantly; your best bet is to take the advice of the chef's wife, Margarita, who also has an encyclopedic knowledge of Spanish wines. ✉ *Manuel de la Quintana 3,* ☎ *956/340069. AE, DC, MC, V. Closed Sun. and late July–late Aug.*

$$–$$$ ✕ **Venta Antonio.** Crowds come to this roadside inn from far and wide to dine on superb, fresh seafood cooked in top-quality olive oil. You enter through the busy bar, where fresh fish bask and lobsters await their demise in a tank. Try the specialties of the Bay of Cádiz, such as *sopa de mariscos* (shellfish soup) followed by *bogavantes de Sanlúcar* (succulent local lobster). ✉ *Carretera de Jerez–Sanlúcar, Km 5,* ☎ *956/140535. AE, DC, MC, V.*

$$ ✕ **La Posada.** This place is strange in that its two small dining rooms, both enlivened by bullfight-red tablecloths, are on opposite sides of the street, with staff dashing back and forth to attend to their customers. The menu strikes another unusual note: it offers only grilled meat and grilled fish, according to what's best at the market, plus salad. Each course can be ordered in a full or half portion. ✉ *Arboledilla 1 and 3,* ☎ *956/337474. AE, MC, V. Closed Sun. and Aug. No dinner Sat.*

$$ ✕ **Tendido 6.** This restaurant is near the bullring, opposite Gate 6—hence its name. The tables are set in an enclosed patio decorated with bullfight posters and draped with bright-red tablecloths. The menu has all the Spanish standbys: *jamón serrano* (cured ham), *gambas al ajillo* (garlic shrimp), and *tarta de almendra* (almond tart). ✉ *Circo 10,* ☎ *956/344835. AE, DC, MC, V. Closed Sun.*

$$$$ **Montecastillo Hotel and Golf Resort.** Situated outside Jerez near the race track, the sprawling, modern Montecastillo adjoins a golf course designed by Jack Nicklaus. The spacious common areas have marble floors. Rooms are cheerfully decorated, with off-white walls, bright floral bedspreads, and rustic clay tiles. Ask for a room with a terrace overlooking the golf course. ✉ *Carretera de Arcos, Km 9, 11406, ☎ 956/151200, FAX 956/151209. 116 rooms, 5 suites. Restaurant, pool, sauna, 18-hole golf course. AE, DC, MC, V.*

$$$ **Avenida Jerez.** Opposite the Royal Sherry Park (☞ *below*), this modern hotel has bright, sunny rooms with hardwood floors and beige and blue decor. All rooms have VCRs. Ask for one at the back; rooms in front are close to the road and can be noisy, despite double glazing. ✉ *Avda. Alvaro Domecq 10, 11405, ☎ 956/347411, FAX 956/337296. 95 rooms. Restaurant, bar, coffee shop, in-room VCRs. AE, DC, MC, V.*

$$$ **Jerez.** This luxury hotel occupies a low, white, three-story building in the residential neighborhood north of town. The bar and the elegant restaurant, El Cartujano, overlook the sun terrace, large pool, and big, leafy garden. Public rooms get lots of natural light through picture windows. The best guest rooms overlook the pool and garden; those in back face the tennis courts and parking lot. ✉ *Avda. Alvaro Domecq 35, 11405, ☎ 956/300600, FAX 956/305001. 116 rooms, 4 suites. Restaurant, bar, pool, 2 tennis courts, free parking. AE, DC, MC, V.*

$$$ ★ **Royal Sherry Park.** Gleaming and modern, the Royal Sherry Park is set back from the road in an unusually large, tree-filled garden. It's designed around several patios filled with exotic foliage, and the sunny hallways are hung with contemporary paintings. The rooms are bright and airy, and most have balconies overlooking the garden. ✉ *Avda. Alvaro Domecq 11, 11405, ☎ 956/303011, FAX 956/311300. 173 rooms. Restaurant, bar, coffee shop, pool, meeting rooms. AE, DC, MC, V.*

$–$$ **Ávila.** This friendly hostelry in a side street off Calle Arcos offers affordable central lodgings. A TV lounge and a small bar and breakfast room adjoin the lobby. The rooms have basic furnishings and tile floors; beds are European twin-size. ✉ *Ávila 3, 11401, ☎ 956/334808, FAX 956/336807. 32 rooms. Bar, breakfast room. AE, DC, MC, V.*

Racing

Formula One Grand Prix races—including the Spanish motorcycle Gran Prix on the first weekend in May—are held at Jerez's race track, the **Circuito Permanente de Velocidad.** Call the track (☎ 956/151100) or check with the tourist office for more information.

Shopping

Duarte (✉ Lancería 15, ☎ 956/342751) is the best-known saddle shop in this horse town, sending beautifully wrought leather all over the world, including to the British royal family. It's worth a visit; you can choose from all kinds of smaller but beautifully worked leather items. You can also browse for wicker and ceramic items along **Calle Corredera** and **Calle Bodegas.**

Arcos de la Frontera

★ 42 *31 km (19 mi) east of Jerez.*

With its narrow and steep cobblestone streets, whitewashed houses, and finely crafted wrought-iron window grilles, Arcos is the quintessence of the Andalusian *pueblo blanco*. Make your way to the main square, the Plaza de España, the highest point in the village: one side of the square is open, and a balcony at the edge of the cliff offers views of the Guadalete valley. On the opposite end is the church of **Santa María,** a fascinating blend of architectural styles: Romanesque, Gothic, and

Mudéjar, with a plateresque doorway, a Renaissance *retablo* (altarpiece), and a 17th-century Baroque choir. The *ayuntamiento* stands at the foot of the old castle walls on the northern side of the square; across from here is the Casa del Corregidor, onetime residence of the governor and now a parador (☞ *below*).

Dining and Lodging

$$$ ★ ✕🏨 **Parador Casa del Corregidor.** The terrace has a spectacular view—this parador clings to the cliffside overlooking the rolling valley of the Guadalete River. Public rooms include a bar decorated with tiles and bullfight pictures; a panoramic restaurant that opens onto the terrace; and an enclosed patio. Rooms are furnished in traditional parador style, with dark Castilian furniture, *esparto* rugs, and abundant tiles; and most are so big that it would be hard to watch TV from the bed. The best rooms are Nos. 15–18, which overlook the valley. The restaurant's local dishes include *berenjenas arcenses* (spicy eggplant with ham and chorizo); or you can ask for the *menu gastronómico,* featuring 10 different regional specialities. ✉ *Plaza del Cabildo, 11630,* ☏ *956/700500,* FAX *956/701116. 24 rooms. Restaurant, bar. AE, DC, MC, V.*

$$–$$$ 🏨 **Cortijo Faín.** This resort hotel occupies a 17th-century farmhouse on a ranch 3 km (2 mi) southeast of Arcos. The old *cortijo* (farm estate) is surrounded by olive groves and enclosed in high, white walls covered in bougainvillea. The atmosphere is personal and intimate. Aim for one of the two suites that have their own fireplaces. Reservations are essential. ✉ *Carretera de Algar, Km 3, 11630,* ☏ FAX *956/231396. 3 rooms, 5 suites. Restaurant, pool, horseback riding, library, meeting rooms. AE, DC, MC, V.*

$$ 🏨 **El Convento.** An inexpensive alternative, this tiny hotel is in part of an old convent. Perched on top of the cliff right behind the parador, it shares the same amazing view, though the rooms are much smaller, more simply furnished, and cheaper (half the price, in fact). ✉ *Maldonado 2, 11630,* ☏ *956/702333,* FAX *957/704128. 11 rooms. Cafeteria. AE, DC, MC, V.*

$$ 🏨 **Marqués de Torresoto.** This hotel is set in a restored 17th-century palace with a large courtyard and an ornate Baroque chapel of its own. Each guest room is different, but most are spacious. Those on the uppermost of the three floors are the nicest, and some look over the village rooftops; but you'll have to walk up, as there is no elevator, and rooms that face the street can be noisy. ✉ *Marqués de Torresoto, 11630,* ☏ *956/700717,* FAX *956/704205. 15 rooms. Bar. AE, DC, MC, V.*

Sanlúcar de Barrameda

43 *24 km (15 mi) west of Jerez.*

Columbus sailed from here on his third voyage to the Americas, in 1498. Twenty years later, Magellan steered his ships out of the same harbor to begin his circumnavigation of the planet. Today this unspoiled fishing town is known primarily for its *langostinos* (giant shrimp) and *manzanilla,* an exceptionally dry sherry. The most popular restaurants are in the **Bajo de Guía** neighborhood, on the banks of the Guadalquivir. Here, too, is the Fábrica de Hielo, which serves as a visitor center for Doñana National Park. Boat trips can take you up the river, stopping at various points in the park; the ***Real Fernando*** (✉ Bajo de Guí, Sanlúcar de Barrameda, ☏ 956/363813) makes a four-hour cruise up the Guadalquivir to the Coto de Doñana twice daily from May through September, morning only in fall and winter.

From the *puerto pesquero* (fishing port) of **Bonanza,** 4 km (2½ mi) upriver from Sanlúcar, there's a fine view of fishing boats and the pine trees of Doñana on the opposite bank. Sandy beaches extend along Sanlúcar's southern promontory to Chipiona, where the Roman general Scipio Africanus built a beacon tower.

Dining and Lodging

$$$ ✕ **Bigote.** The Bajo de Guía beach is renowned for its seafood, and this colorful, informal fish restaurant sits right on it. The kitchen is known for its fried *acedias* (a type of small sole) and *langostinos* (large shrimp), which come from these very waters—if you want them any fresher, you'll have to catch them yourself. The seafood paella is also good. Reservations are essential in summer. ✉ *Bajo de Guía,* ☎ *956/362696. AE, DC, MC, V. Closed Sun.*

$$$ ✕ **Mirador de Doñana.** Another Bajo de Guía landmark, the Mirador de Doñana serves superfresh sole, shrimp, and *puntillas* (baby squid). The dining area overlooks the large bar, which is always busy. ✉ *Bajo de Guía,* ☎ *956/364205. MC, V.*

$–$$ 🏨 **Posada de Palacio.** Across the street from the luxuriant gardens of the Palacio de los Infantes de Orleans—now the Sanlúcar town hall—this restored 18th-century palace houses a friendly and affordable family-run hotel, with rooms grouped around a cool patio adorned with potted plants. ✉ *Caballeros 11, 11540,* ☎ FAX *956/365060. 13 rooms. Restaurant. AE, DC, MC, V.*

Puerto de Santa María

★ ❹❹ *12 km (7 mi) southwest of Jerez, 17 km (11 mi) north of Cádiz.*

This attractive, if somewhat dilapidated, little fishing port on the northern shores of the Bay of Cádiz sports an array of white houses with peeling facades and floor-length green grilles covering the doors and windows. The town is dominated by the Terry and Osborne sherry and brandy *bodegas.* Columbus once lived in a house on the square that bears his name (Cristóbal Colón), and Washington Irving spent the autumn of 1828 at Calle Palacios 57. The town's chief monuments are its castle, the **Castillo San Marcos,** built in the 13th century by King Alfonso X, and the **bullring,** one of the most attractive in Spain. The castle is open Saturday 11–1, with free admission; the bullring, also free, is open Tuesday–Sunday 11–2 and 5:30–7, except on bullfight days. You can arrange a guided tour of the town through the tourist office on Calle Guadalete 1.

The *marisco* (seafood) bars along the Ribera del Marisco (Seafood Way) are Puerto Santa María's current claim to fame. **Romerijo, Casa Paco,** and neighboring **Bar Salva** are among the most popular.

Dining and Lodging

$$$ ✕ **El Faro de El Puerto.** Set in a villa just outside town, the "Lighthouse in the Port" is run by the same family that established the classic El Faro in Cádiz (☞ *below*). Like its predecessor, it serves excellent fish dishes, but you can also browse the meat department for such delicacies as veal rolls filled with foie gras in a sweet sherry sauce. ✉ *Carretera del Puerto-Rota, Km 0,* ☎ *956/858003 or 956/870952. AE, DC, MC, V. No dinner Sun.*

$$ ✕ **Casa Flores.** A bit more upmarket than most other Ribera del Marisco haunts, Flores serves the same fresh seafood. You approach the two dining rooms, decorated with tiles and wood paneling, through a long bar hung with hams. Specialties include *filete de urta al camarón* (fillet of bream in shrimp sauce) and *fritos de la bahía* (assorted fried fish from the Bay of Cádiz). ✉ *Ribera del Marisco 9,* ☎ *956/543512. AE, MC, V.*

$$ ✕ **Los Portales.** A Ribera del Marisco favorite, this comfortable dining room is decorated with a marine motif. At the large, very popular bar, you can sample such unusual sea creatures as *ortiguillas* (fried sea anemones, a local favorite) plus the more standard fish and shellfish, grilled or fried. ✉ *Ribera del Río 13,* ☎ *956/542116. AE, DC, MC, V.*

$$$ ★ **Monasterio de San Miguel.** Dating from 1733, this monastery is in the heart of town, a few blocks from the harbor. There's nothing spartan about the former cells; they're now air-conditioned rooms with all the trappings, though you might need a map just to locate yours along the long corridors. The restaurant is in a large, vaulted hall; the Baroque church is now a concert hall; and the cloister's gardens provide a peaceful refuge. Beamed ceilings, polished marble floors, and huge brass lamps only enhance the 18th-century atmosphere. ✉ *Larga 27, 11500,* ☎ *956/540440,* FAX *956/542604. 139 rooms, 11 suites. Restaurant, bar, pool, squash, parking (fee). AE, DC, MC, V.*

Nightlife

The **Casino Bahía de Cádiz,** on the road between Jerez and Puerto de Santa María, is the only casino in this part of Andalusia. You can play the usual range of games, and there's a restaurant and a disco. You must present your passport to enter. ✉ *N-IV, Km 649,* ☎ *956/871042.* *550 ptas.* ⏲ *Weekdays 7 PM–4 AM, weekends 7 PM–6 AM.*

Sailing

Most towns on and around the Bay of Cádiz have yacht clubs and marinas, and together they host about 50 regattas each year for all kinds of boats. Inquire at the tourist office about crewed charters and boat rentals. The newest bay marina is **Puerto Sherry** (☎ 956/870203), near Puerto de Santa María.

Cádiz

★ 45 *32 km (20 mi) southwest of Jerez, 149 km (93 mi) southwest of Seville.*

Spaniards flock here in February to revel in Cádiz's famous Carnival celebrations, but few foreigners have yet discovered the real charm of this city. Surrounded by the Atlantic Ocean on three sides, Cádiz was founded as Gadir by Phoenician traders in 1100 BC and claims to be the oldest continuously inhabited city in the Western world. Hannibal lived here for a time, and here Julius Caesar first held public office.

After centuries of decline during the Middle Ages and under Moorish rule, Cádiz regained its commercial importance after the discovery of the Americas. Columbus set out from here on his second voyage, and Cádiz later became the home base of the Spanish fleet. Its merchants competed fiercely with those of Seville, and when the Guadalquivir silted up in the 18th century, Cádiz monopolized New World trade and became the wealthiest port in Western Europe. Most of its buildings date from this period, including the cathedral, which was built in part with gold and silver from the New World.

The old city is African in appearance and immensely intriguing—a cluster of narrow streets opening onto charming small squares. The golden cupola of the cathedral looms above low white houses, and the whole place has a slightly dilapidated air. In a few hours' walk around the headlands, you'll see the entire old town and pass through some enchanting parks with fine views of the bay.

You might begin your explorations in the Plaza de Mina, a large, leafy square with palm trees and plenty of benches. On the square's western flank, the ornamental facade of the **Colegio de Arquitectos** (College of Architects) is especially beautiful. In the northwestern corner of the square is the tourist office. On the east side, you'll find the **Museo de Cádiz** (Provincial Museum), well worth visiting for its works by

Murillo and Alonso Cano, and the *Four Evangelists* and set of saints by Zurbarán, which have much in common with his masterpieces at Guadalupe, in Extremadura (☞ Chapter 13). The archaeological section contains Phoenician sarcophagi from the time of this ancient city's birth. ✉ *Plaza de Mina,* ☎ *956/212281.* *250 ptas.; EU citizens free.* ⏲ *Tues. 2:30–8, Wed.–Sat. 9–8, Sun. 9:30–2:30.*

A few blocks east of the Plaza de Mina, next door to the Iglesia del Rosario, is the **Oratorio de la Santa Cueva,** an oval-shape 18th-century chapel with three frescoes by Goya. The Oratorio was closed for restoration in 2000. ✉ *C. Rosario,* ☎ *956/287676.* *100 ptas.* ⏲ *Weekdays 10–1.*

Don't forget to look up while walking the streets around here—the facades are quite splendid. Heading up Calle San José from the Plaza de la Mina, you'll see the **Oratorio de San Felipe Neri.** Spain's first liberal constitution was declared at this church in 1812, and here the Cortes (Parliament) of Cádiz met when the rest of Spain was subjected to the rule of Napoléon's brother, Joseph Bonaparte (more popularly known as Pepe Botella, for his love of the bottle). On the main altar is an *Immaculate Conception* by Murillo, the great Sevillian artist who in 1682 fell to his death from a scaffold while working on his *Mystic Marriage of St. Catherine* in Cádiz's Chapel of Santa Catalina. ✉ *Santa Inés,* ☎ *956/211612.* *150 ptas.* ⏲ *Mon.–Sat. 10–1.*

Next door to the Oratorio de San Felipe Neri, the small but pleasant **Museo Histórico Municipal** has a 19th-century mural depicting the establishment of the Constitution of 1812. Its real showpiece, however, is a fascinating 1779 ivory and mahogany model of Cádiz, which depicts all of the city's streets and buildings in minute detail, looking much as they do now. ✉ *Santa Inés,* ☎ *956/221788.* *Free.* ⏲ *Tues.–Fri. 9–1 and 4–7 (5–8 June–Sept.), weekends 9–1.*

Four blocks west of Santa Inés is the Plaza Manuel de Falla, overlooked by an amazing neo-Mudéjar redbrick building, the **Gran Teatro Manuel de Falla.** The classic interior is impressive as well; try to attend a performance (☞ Nightlife and the Arts, *below*).

Back-tracking along Calle Sacramento toward the city center, you'll come to **Torre Tavira.** At 150 ft, this tower, attached to a 18th-century palace that is now a conservatory of music, is the highest point in the old city. More than a hundred such watchtowers were used by Cádiz ship owners to spot their arriving fleets. A *camera obscura* (a device that projects the outdoor scene onto a screen in a darkened room) gives a good overview of the city and its monuments. ✉ *Marqués del Real Tesoro, 10,* ☎ *956/212910.* *500 ptas.* ⏲ *Mid-June–mid-Sept., daily 10–8; mid-Sept.–mid-June, daily 10–6.*

Five blocks southeast of the Torre Tavira are the gold dome and Baroque facade of Cádiz's **cathedral,** begun in 1722, when the city was at the height of its power. The Cádiz-born composer Manuel de Falla, who died in 1946 at the age of 70, is buried in the **crypt.** The cathedral **museum,** on Calle Acero, overflows with gold, silver, and precious jewels from the New World; one of its priceless possessions is Enrique de Arfe's processional cross, which is carried in the annual Corpus Christi parades. The cathedral is known as the New Cathedral because it supplanted the original 13th-century structure next door, which was destroyed by the British in 1592, rebuilt, and renamed the church of **Santa Cruz** when the New Cathedral came along. The cathedral is currently being restored, but you can visit the crypt, museum, and church of Santa Cruz. ✉ *Plaza Catedral,* ☎ *956/286154 for museum.* *Museum 500 ptas.* ⏲ *Mass Sun. noon; museum Tues.–Sat. 10–1.*

Next door to the church of Santa Cruz are the remains of a 1st-century BC **Roman theater**, discovered by chance in 1982. ✉ *Campo del Sur.* *Free.* ⏲ *Tues.–Sun. 11–1:30.*

The impressive ***ayuntamiento*** (city hall) overlooks the Plaza San Juan de Diós, one of Cádiz's liveliest hubs. Built in two parts, in 1799 and 1861, the building is attractively illuminated at night.

The **Plaza San Francisco,** near the *ayuntamiento,* is a pretty square surrounded by white and yellow houses and filled with orange trees and elegant street lamps. It's especially lively during the evening *paseo.*

Dining and Lodging

$$$ ★ ✕ **El Faro.** Gonzalo Córdoba's fishing-quarter restaurant deserves its fame as the best restaurant in the province. Outside, it's one of many low white houses decorated with bright-blue flowerpots; inside, the decor is warm and inviting, with half-tile walls, glass lanterns, oil paintings, and photos of old Cádiz. Fish and seafood dominate the menu, but there are plenty of alternatives, such as *cebón al queso de cabrales* (venison in blue-cheese sauce). ✉ *San Felix 15,* ☎ *956/211068. AE, DC, MC, V.*

$$$ ✕ **El Ventorrillo del Chato.** Standing on its own on the sandy isthmus connecting Cádiz to the mainland, this former inn was founded in 1780 by a man ironically nicknamed "El Chato" (pug-nosed) for his prominent proboscis. Run by a scion of El Faro's Gonzalo Córdoba (☞ *above*), the restaurant serves tasty regional specialties in a charming Andalusian setting. Seafood is a specialty, but meat is well represented on the menu, and the wine list is very good. ✉ *Vía Augusta Julia,* ☎ *956/250025. AE, MC, V. Closed Sun.*

$ ✕ **Achuri.** Founded in 1947, this old-fashioned, green-tiled eatery offers excellent value for money with a menu that combines Andalusian and Basque flavors. Try the Basque specialities, such as *cocochas* (delicate hake morsels) or the Biscay-style hake. ✉ *Plocia 15,* ☎ *956/253613. MC, V. No dinner Sun.–Wed.*

$$$ **Parador Atlántico.** Cádiz's modern parador commands a privileged position on the headland overlooking the bay, and is the only hotel in its class in the old part of Cádiz. The spacious indoor public rooms have gleaming marble floors, and tables and chairs surround a fountain on the small patio. The cheerful, bright-green bar, decorated with ceramic tiles and bullfighting posters, is a popular meeting place for Cádiz society. Most rooms have small balconies facing the sea. ✉ *Duque de Nájera 9, 11002,* ☎ *956/226905,* FAX *956/214582. 143 rooms, 6 suites. Restaurant, bar, pool. AE, DC, MC, V.*

$$ **Francia y Paris.** The advantage here is the central location, on a pretty pedestrian square in the heart of the old town. The rather dull modern interior includes a vast lobby, a large sitting room, and a small bar and breakfast room. Guest rooms are simple; some have small balconies facing the square. ✉ *Plaza San Francisco 2, 11004,* ☎ *956/222348,* FAX *956/222431. 57 rooms. Bar, breakfast room. AE, DC, MC, V.*

Nightlife and the Arts

Ground zero for cultural events in Cádiz is the **Gran Teatro Manuel de Falla** (✉ Plaza de Falla, ☎ 956/220828). The tourist office has performance schedules.

Shopping

You'll find all the traditional Andalusian handicrafts here, especially ceramics and wicker. Just off the Plaza de la Mina, **Belle Epoque** (✉ Antonio Lopez 2, ☎ 956/226810) is one of Cádiz's better—and more reasonably priced—antiques stores, specializing in furniture.

SEVILLE AND WESTERN ANDALUSIA A TO Z

Arriving and Departing

By Bus

Long-distance buses connect Seville with Madrid; with Cáceres, Mérida, and Badajoz in Extremadura; and with Córdoba, Granada, Málaga, Ronda, and Huelva in Andalusia. Regional buses take the coastal route from Granada, Málaga, and Marbella to Cádiz. Buses from Ronda run to Arcos, Jerez, and Cádiz. Buses throughout Andalusia, and between Extremadura and Seville, tend to be more frequent and convenient than trains.

By Car

The main road from Madrid is the N-IV through Córdoba. This has recently been made into a four-lane *autovía,* but it's one of Spain's busiest roads, and trucks can cause delays. From Granada or Málaga, head for Antequera; then take N334 by way of Osuna to Seville. Road trips from Seville to Córdoba, Granada, and the Costa del Sol (by way of Ronda) are reasonably quick and pleasant. From the Costa del Sol, the coastal N340 highway is rarely very busy west of Algeciras.

By Plane

The region's main airport is Seville's **San Pablo** (☏ 95/444–9000), 12 km (7½ mi) east of the city on the N-IV to Córdoba. International flights arrive from Amsterdam, Brussels, Frankfurt, London, and Paris, domestic flights from Madrid, Barcelona, Valencia, and other major cities. Seville's **Iberia** office is on Almirante Lobo 2 (☏ 95/422–8901 or 902/400500). There is a bus from the airport to the center of Seville every half hour on weekdays (between 6:30 AM and 8 PM), less often on weekends.

The region's other airport is Jerez de la Frontera's **Aeropuerto de la Parra** (☏ 956/150000), 7 km (4 mi) from Jerez on the road to Seville. **Iberia** (☏ 956/150010) flies from here to Madrid, Barcelona, Valencia–Palma de Mallorca, and Zaragoza.

By Train

Seville, Jerez, and Cádiz all lie on the main rail line from Madrid to southwestern Spain. From Madrid, roughly six trains run to Seville daily, via Córdoba; three of these continue on to Jerez and Cádiz. RENFE also operates the high-speed AVE train between Madrid and Seville; it costs more than regular trains, but it makes the journey in 2½ hours and has become the most popular mode of travel between the two cities. From Granada, Málaga, Ronda, and Algeciras, trains go to Seville by way of Bobadilla, where, more often than not, you have to change.

Crime

WARNING: With chronic high unemployment, Seville and Cádiz have built up something of a record in petty crime, such as purse snatchings and thefts from parked cars, even the occasional robbery. Drive with your car doors locked; lock all your luggage out of sight in the trunk; *never* leave *anything* in a parked car; and keep a wary eye on scooter riders, who have been known to snatch purses or even smash the windows of moving cars. Take only a small amount of cash and one credit card out with you. Leave your passport, traveler's checks, and other credit cards in the hotel safe, if possible, and avoid carrying purses and expensive cameras or wearing valuable jewelry.

Getting Around

By Bus

Buses connect all of the towns and villages in this region. **Cádiz** has two bus depots: **Comes** (✉ Plaza Hispanidad, Cádiz, ☎ 956/224271), which serves most destinations in Andalusia, and **Los Amarillos** (✉ Diego Fernández Herreras 34, Cádiz, ☎ 956/285852), which serves Jerez, Seville, Córdoba, Puerto de Santa María, Sanlúcar de Barrameda, and Chipiona. The bus station in **Jerez,** on the Plaza Madre de Dios, is served by two companies: **La Valenciana** (☎ 956/341063) and **Los Amarillos** (☎ 956/329347). **Seville** now has two bus stations. The older one is the **Estación del Prado de San Sebastián** (✉ Prado de San Sebastián, ☎ 95/441–7111), just off the Plaza de San Sebastián between Manuel Vázquez Sagastizabal and José María Osborne; buses from here serve points west and northwest. The second, a glittering modern terminal on the banks of the Guadalquivir River downtown, is the **Estación Plaza de Armas** (✉ Cristo de la Expiración, next to east end of Cachorro Bridge, ☎ 95/490–8040), which serves central and eastern Spain. The tourist office can confirm which station you need.

By Car

Driving in Western Andalusia is easy—the terrain is mostly flat land or gently rolling hills, and the roads are straight. From Seville to Jerez and Cádiz, you can choose between the N-IV and the slightly faster A4 toll road. The only way to access Doñana National Park by road is to take the A49 Seville–Huelva highway, exit for Almonte/Bollullos par del Condado, then follow the signs for El Rocío and Matalascañas. Getting into and out of Seville is not unduly difficult thanks to the SE30 ring road, but getting around the city by car is still trying. Try to avoid the 7:15–8:30 rush hour in Seville and Cádiz, and be wary of the lunchtime rush hour, around 2–3 PM. Don't try to bring a car to Cádiz at Carnival time (pre-Lent) or to Seville during Holy Week or the April Fair—processions close most of the streets to traffic. *See* Crime, *above,* if you're considering driving and parking in Seville.

By Train

A dozen or more local trains each day connect Cádiz with Puerto de Santa María, Jerez, and Seville. Journey time from Cádiz to Seville is 1½ to 2 hours. There are no trains to Doñana National Park, Sanlúcar de Barrameda, or Arcos de la Frontera or between Cádiz and the Costa del Sol.

Cádiz's station is on Plaza de Sevilla near the docks. **Jerez**'s station is on Plaza de la Estación, off Diego Fernández Herrera, in the eastern part of town. For general train information, call the national **RENFE** information line (☎ 902/240202). In **Seville,** the sprawling **Santa Justa** station is on Avenida Kansas City; contact the downtown **RENFE** office (✉ Zaragoza 29, ☎ 95/454–0202) for information and reservations.

Contacts and Resources

Consulates

United States (✉ Paseo de las Delicias 7, Seville, ☎ 95/423–1883). **United Kingdom** (✉ Plaza Nueva 8, Seville, ☎ 95/422–8874 or 95/422–8875).

Emergencies

Police: ☎ 091 **Ambulance:** ☎ 061.

Guided Tours

In Seville, any of the following organizations can put you in touch with qualified English-speaking guides: **Asociación Provincial de Infor-**

madores Turísticos (✉ Glorieta de Palacio de Congresos, Seville, ☎ 95/425–5957). **Guidetour** (✉ Lope de Rueda 13, ☎ 95/422–2374 or 95/422–2375). **ITA** (✉ Santa Teresa 1, ☎ 95/422–4641). City tours in open buses, with stops at the Torre del Oro and Plaza de España, are offered by Servirama and Hispalense de Tranvias. For English-speaking local guides in Cádiz or Jerez, contact the local tourist office.

DOÑANA NATIONAL PARK

Jeep tours of the reserve depart twice daily (Tuesday–Sunday 8:30 and 3) from the park's reception center, 2 km (1 mi) from Matalascañas. Tours are limited to 125 people and should be booked well in advance. Passengers can often be collected from hotels in Matalascañas. Write or call the **Parque Nacional de Doñana** (✉ Cooperativa Marisma del Rocío, Centro de Recepción, 21760 Matalascañas, Huelva, ☎ 959/430432).

LUXURY TRAIN

Al Andalus is a vintage 1920s luxury train that makes a weekly six-day trip in season from Seville to Córdoba, Granada, and Antequera, with side trips to Carmona and Jerez. For details, *see* Train Travel *in* Smart Travel Tips.

SHERRY BODEGAS

Tours can be arranged from Seville and Cádiz. In Jerez, most *bodegas* are open to visitors weekdays except during August. Tours, which include a tasting of brandy and sherry, should be reserved in advance; English-speaking guides are usually available. Call the *bodega* and ask for Public Relations. **Domecq** (☎ 956/151500) charges 375 ptas. weekdays, 500 ptas. weekends; **González Byass** (☎ 956/357000) charges 500 ptas.; **Harvey** (☎ 956/346004) charges 325 ptas. weekdays, 500 ptas. weekends; **Sandeman** (☎ 956/301100) charges 400 ptas; and **Wisdom** (☎ 956/184306) charges 300 ptas. For schedules, call the winery or check with the Jerez tourist office.

To visit *bodegas* in Puerto de Santa María, contact **Osborne** (✉ Fernán Caballero 3, ☎ 956/855211) or **Terry** (✉ Santa Trinidad, ☎ 956/857700). In Sanlúcar de Barrameda contact **Barbadillo** (✉ Calle Luis de Eguilaz, ☎ 956/360894). If possible, reserve a tour one day in advance; otherwise, call before noon.

Visitor Information

The **regional tourist office** for western Andalusia is in Seville (✉ Avda. de la Constitución 21, ☎ 95/422–1404 or 95/421–8157, FAX 95/422–9753). Local tourist offices: **Arcos de la Frontera** (✉ Cuesta de Belén, ☎ 956/702264). **Cádiz** (✉ Calderón de la Barca 1, ☎ 956/211313). **Jerez de la Frontera** (✉ Larga 39, ☎ 956/331150 or 956/331162). **Puerto de Santa María** (✉ Guadalete 1, ☎ 956/542413). **Sanlúcar de Barrameda** (✉ Calzada del Ejército, ☎ 956/366110). **Seville** (✉ Costurero de la Reina, Paseo de las Delicias 9, ☎ 95/423–4465).

13 EXTREMADURA

Extremadura is Spain's Wild West, one of the least explored regions in the country. A deep-blue sky stretches over forests, lakes, rivers, gorges, and stark plains, whispering of leisurely walks and some of the best bird-watching in Spain. In lively Cáceres and quiet Trujillo, medieval quarters and conquistadors' palaces stand perfectly preserved; in Mérida, myriad Roman ruins bake in the sun.

By Michael Jacobs

Updated by Mark Little

THE VERY NAME *EXTREMADURA*—the "land beyond the Duero"—suggests the wild, remote, and isolated character of this haunting region. With its poor soil and minimal industry, Extremadura has experienced extreme poverty; only in recent decades has a series of dams brightened the region's agricultural outlook. The film director Luis Buñuel established his reputation in the late 1920s with a powerful documentary, *Tierra sin Pan* (*Land Without Bread*), about the mountainous northern Extremaduran district of Las Hurdes—then virtually unchanged since the Middle Ages, desperately poor, and accessible only on foot or donkey. The Nobel prize–winning novelist Camilo José Cela made his own debut with *La Familia de Pascual Duarte* (*The Family of Pascual Duarte*), a bleakly realistic study set in a southern Extremaduran village "crouched over a road as long and as flat as a day without bread."

The great artist Francisco de Zurbarán was born in 1601 in Fuente de Cantos, between Andalusia and Extremadura, and a visit to the region of his birth is essential to an understanding of his art. The simplified forms, untrammeled colors, and powerful austerity of Zurbarán's works are mirrored in the treeless, undulating ocher expanses that surround his birthplace; it's one of the most abstract landscapes imaginable. After a long period of neglect, Zurbarán's art was hailed in the 19th century as representing all that was profound in the Spanish temperament. Similarly, Extremadura is recognized today as the pure, unsullied essence of Spain—a place that has resisted the onslaught of modernity, a place where travel is still an adventure.

Despite its strongly provincial character, Extremadura has long been influenced by its diverse neighbors. Officially, Extremadura comprises two provinces: Badajoz to the south, Cáceres to the north. The dazzlingly white villages and sunbaked landscapes of Badajoz have much in common with neighboring Andalusia; Cáceres, with its wooded mountain valleys and half-timbered, gray-stone houses, recalls both Castile and northern Spain. And Portugal, which borders both Badajoz and Cáceres, lends its accent as well.

Extremadura has not always been so isolated and impoverished. No other place in Spain has so many Roman monuments as Mérida, the capital of the vast Roman province of Lusitania (the Iberian Peninsula); the town guarded the Vía de la Plata, the major Roman highway that crossed Extremadura from north to south, connecting León with the port of Seville. Economic and artistic decline set in after the Romans left, but the region revived in the 16th century, when the surviving explorers and conquerors of the New World—from Francisco Pizarro and Hernán Cortés to Nuñez de Balboa and Francisco de Orellana, first navigator of the Amazon—returned to their birthplace. These men built the magnificent palaces that now glorify towns such as Cáceres and Trujillo, and they turned the remote monastery of Guadalupe—whose miraculous Virgin had inspired their exploits overseas—into one of the great artistic repositories of Spain.

Pleasures and Pastimes

Boating

Extremadura hosts all kinds of water sports in its many artificial lakes, most notably Borbollón and Gabriel y Galán, in northern Cáceres, and Cíjara and García Sola, in northeastern Badajoz.

Dining

Extremaduran food reflects the austerity of the landscape. It is true peasant cuisine, conditioned by poverty but with a strong character and a reliance on fresh produce. Its base is the pig, of which no part is spared, including the *criadillas* (testicles)—not to be confused with the *criadillas de la tierra* (earth testicles), which are truffles. The dressed meats are outstanding, most notably the sweetish cured hams from Montánchez; chorizo (spiced sausage); and *morcilla* (blood pudding), which is often made here with potatoes.

The lamb stew *caldereta* is particularly tasty, as is the beef from the *retinto,* a local breed of long-horned cattle. Game is also common, with *perdiz al modo de Alcántara* (partridge cooked with truffles) a favorite specialty. Local lake tench and river trout, prepared a variety of ways, are also worth trying. Some Extremaduran dishes appall foreigners, as well as other Spaniards—such as those involving *ranas* (frogs)—although the local favorite *lagarto* (lizard) is no longer available, as the main ingredient is now a protected species. Andalusian specialties show up in the south, such as gazpacho and *ajo blanco,* a cold almond-and-garlic soup; and Extremadurans make a gazpacho of their own based on cucumbers, green peppers, and broth rather than tomatoes and water. A common accompaniment is *migas,* bread crumbs soaked in water and fried in olive oil with garlic and pieces of sausage. The excellent local cheeses generally have a crumbly texture and strong flavors. If you have a chance, savor *tortas,* the round, semisoft cheeses of Cáceres; those from Casar and La Serena are especially prized. Favorite *extremeño* desserts include the *técula mécula* (an almond-flavored marzipan tart), which combines the flavors of Spain and next-door neighbor Portugal. Marketed under the generic appellation "Ribera del Guadiana," Extremadura's little-known, light and fruity red wines are good values; try Lar de Lares. Wine production is centered in Almendralejo, capital of the Tierra de Barros. Typical digestifs include liqueurs made from cherries or acorns.

Dining out is not much of a tradition in Extremadura; some of the best food is served in modest bars. Reservations are usually unnecessary.

CATEGORY	COST*
$$$$	over 6,500 ptas.
$$$	4,000–6,500 ptas.
$$	2,500–4,000 ptas.
$	under 2,500 ptas.

**per person for a three-course meal, excluding drinks, service, and tax*

Fiestas

Extremadura is not the liveliest region for fiestas, hardly the place to come if you're looking for running bulls and wild carryings-on. The province of Cáceres, however, has its share of colorful festivals commemorating past saints and sinners. If you're here on January 20, the **Fiesta de San Estéban** (Feast of St. Stephen), you'll witness interesting folklore in several small towns. In Acehúche (near Garovillas), *carantoñas* ("ugly mugs," men costumed in animal skins and frightening masks) bow before the statue of St. Stephen during his procession through town. In Piornal (near Plasencia), a *jaramplas* (a grotesquely costumed, masked jester) is pursued through the town and pelted with turnips. February 3 is the day to toast **San Blas** (St. Blaise), believed to heal sore throats, with hot cakes bearing his name and various feasts. On Shrove Tuesday, during February's **Carnival,** you can see the **Pero Palo,** a large rag-doll figure with a deadpan expression, carried throughout the town of Villanueva de la Vera (near Jarandilla). **Semana Santa** (Holy

Week) is celebrated with various rituals, the most dramatic of which is the **Empalaos** ("impaled ones"), on Holy Thursday in Valverde de la Vera, when young men's outstretched arms are tightly bound with rope to heavy logs across their backs for a procession recalling Christ's crucifixion. (Each man essentially carries the horizontal part of a large cross.) More savory is November's **Celebración del Cerdo y Vino** (Pig and Wine Celebration), in Cáceres, during which the area's innumerable sausages and other pork products are prepared the old-fashioned way. If observing the process doesn't ruin your appetite, you can sample free wine and pork after the presentations. Perhaps most impressive of all is December's medieval festival **La Encamisá,** in Torrejoncillo (off the highway between Plasencia and Cáceres), in which white-robed riders brandish torches and thunder through the narrow streets on horseback.

Badajoz says *adios* to winter with the fiestas of **La Primavera** and **Los Mayos** (Spring Festival and Maydays, respectively), usually at the end of April and beginning of May. The most important date in Badajoz is May 3, **El Día de la Santa Cruz** (the Exaltation of the Holy Cross), celebrated in the villages of Corte de Peleas and Feria. A local family is selected a month in advance to prepare a processional cross in its own home, and some of these crosses become magnificent works of art and patience, lovingly created and tended to the point of depleting hard-earned savings. The crowd sings as a stone cross and a statue of the Virgin Mary are paraded through various neighborhoods.

Fishing

Trout fishing is popular in the Vera and Jerte districts, while tench, carp, royal carp, barbel, and pike abound in the Tajo (Tagus) and Guadiana rivers.

Lodging

Extremadura has the most remarkable group of paradors in Spain. Serving all the main tourist areas, they occupy buildings of great historical and architectural interest. Make reservations well in advance for weekend stays. Most of the region's other high-end hotels are in modern buildings with little character. If you prefer charm to amenities, try one of the region's modest *fondas* (inns). In recent years, a number of charming bed-and-breakfast country inns and guest houses have sprouted in rural areas, particularly the Valle del Jerte; but their space is limited, so reservations are a must. If you want to establish a base for a series of day trips, consider Cáceres—from there it's a hop, skip, and a jump to Trujillo, Mérida, and Plasencia.

CATEGORY	COST*
$$$$	over 20,000 ptas.
$$$	12,000–20,000 ptas.
$$	8,000–12,000 ptas.
$	under 8,000 ptas.

**All prices are for a standard double room, excluding tax and service.*

Wildlife

Outdoor enthusiasts will find plenty to keep them here: trails in the Gredos and Tormantos ranges; forests of oak, poplar, and cherry; massive gorges; and the winding waterways of the Jerte River valley. Extremadura is especially attractive to bird-watchers. All five species of eagles that exist in Spain (including the golden and imperial eagle), peregrine falcons, kites, black vultures, and other raptors can be spotted in Monfragüe Nature Park; some of Europe's last colonies of great and lesser bustards survive in the dry steppes between Cáceres and Trujillo; and thousands of European cranes spend the winter in the rolling country around La Serena, in eastern Badajoz. From February to August, white storks nest on every available church tower, battlement, and electricity pylon.

Exploring Extremadura

Extremadura is one of the most beautiful and least celebrated of Spain's interior regions. The Toledo Mountains divide it into upper Extremadura (Cáceres) and lower Extremadura (Badajoz). The best way to see this part of Spain is by car, as bus and train connections are not ideally suited to roaming such sparsely populated terrain.

Numbers in the text correspond to numbers in the margin and on the Extremadura map.

Great Itineraries

If you're after landscapes and the great outdoors, plan to see the Valle del Jerte and La Vera (the area around the Monasterio de Yuste), both of which will also appeal to anyone interested in the life of the Holy Roman Emperor Carlos V. If Roman ruins call you, go straight to Mérida. Cáceres and Trujillo are essential if you enjoy good food and are intrigued by medieval surroundings or the parched palaces and trappings of the conquistadors. Guadalupe is worth a trip of its own: it combines a spectacular setting, an appealing village, and one of the most richly endowed and historically important monasteries in Spain.

IF YOU HAVE 1 DAY

You can get a lightning impression of Extremadura in a day's drive from Madrid. Take the N-V to **Trujillo** ⑦, follow the N521 to **Cáceres** ⑥, and then head south to **Mérida** ⑨, ancient Roman capital of the Iberian Peninsula and home of the best-preserved Roman ruins in Spain. From here you can return to Madrid on the N-V *or* continue south from Mérida to Seville: this indirect drive from Madrid to Andalusia is more scenic than the usual route through the monotonous plains of La Mancha.

Another one-day outing is a drive from Madrid to the monastery of **Guadalupe** ⑧, one of the most revered sites in Spain, nestled in the heart of conquistador country and symbolizing the link between Spain and Spanish America. Christopher Columbus had his two Native American servants baptized in the fountain at the monastery's main entrance. The sacristy here contains eight paintings by the Spanish master Zurburán. You can return to Madrid the same afternoon or spend the night here, surrounded by mountains.

IF YOU HAVE 3 DAYS

From Madrid, take the slow and winding but highly scenic C501 to **Plasencia** ③ and wander through the *casco viejo* (old town). Drive next to the ⊠ **Monasterio de Yuste** ④, and spend the night nearby. The next day, head south to the provincial capital of **Cáceres** ⑥ and continue on to 🏨 **Mérida** ⑨, with its evocative Roman ruins. On day three, travel back north by way of **Trujillo** ⑦ and **Guadalupe** ⑧. Spend the night there *or* return to Madrid that evening on the N-V.

IF YOU HAVE 5 DAYS

From Madrid, drive over the Tornavacas Pass on the N110 through the lovely **Valle del Jerte** ① to **Plasencia** ③. Time permitting, make a slight detour and wander through the ancient Judería (Jewish Quarter) of **Hervás** ②. Visit the the town of 🏨 **Jarandilla de la Vera** and spend the night in its parador—the fortified palace where Carlos V lived—before visiting his final home, the nearby **Monasterio de Yuste** ④. On day two, go south on the C524 to the **Parque Natural del Mon-**

Extremadura

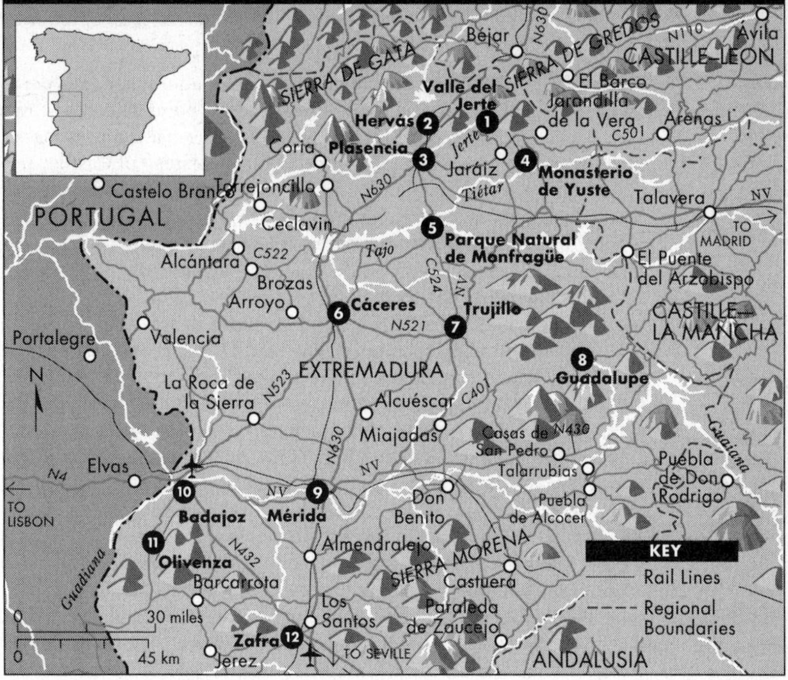

fragüe ⑤, a top national wildlife preserve. Spend the night in **Trujillo** ⑦ and explore the town the next morning. Continue to picturesque **Cáceres** ⑥ for lunch and afternoon sightseeing. Spend night three in **Mérida** ⑨ and take in its Roman monuments on day four. Head west to the provincial capital, **Badajoz** ⑩, with a side trip to the Spanish-Portuguese town of **Olivenza** ⑪. From here you can move on to Andalusia, stopping to see the castle-parador at **Zafra** ⑫ *or* drive back north on the N-V and turn off to admire breathtaking scenery and the monastery of **Guadalupe** ⑧.

When to Tour Extremadura

Summer is a good time to come if you want to hike in nature parks or spend time in the mountains; just note that southern Extremadura can get brutally hot. Spring and fall may be ideal, since winter can be cold and rainy. The spectacle of the cherry-blossom season in the Jerte Valley and La Vera erupts over two weeks around mid-March. Bird-watchers should time a visit for late February, after the migrating storks have arrived to nest and before the European cranes have returned to northern Europe.

UPPER EXTREMADURA

Extremadura stretches from Portugal to Ciudad Real and from Salamanca to Seville. Crossed from east to west by two important rivers, the Tajo (Tagus) and the Guadiana, its rugged and fertile landscape has exported food to much of Europe for centuries, including wheat, lamb, and pork. The Serena reservoir (fed by the Zújar River, which is fed by the Guadiana River) is one of the largest in Europe.

Valle del Jerte

1 *34 km (21 mi) northeast of Plasencia, 260 km (160 mi) west of Madrid. For a scenic route, follow N110 from Ávila.*

There is no more striking introduction to Extremadura than the **Puerto de Tornavacas** (Tornavacas Pass)—literally, the "point where the cows turn back." Part of the N110 northeast of Plasencia, the pass marks the border between Extremadura and the stark plateau of Castile; and at 4,183 ft above sea level, it has a breathtaking view of the valley formed by the fast-flowing Jerte River. In 1556 the ailing Holy Roman Emperor Carlos V was carried over Tornavacas on a stretcher en route to Jarandilla and the Monasterio de Yuste (☞ *below*), where he would spend his last years. Rather than take the more comfortable but longer route via Plasencia, the royal entourage wended its way over the Sierra de Tormantos through the dramatically named Garganta de los Infiernos (Gorge of Hell); today their route is marked and is popular with hikers. The valley's lower slopes are covered with a dense mantle of ash, chestnut, and cherry trees, whose richness contrasts with the granite cliffs of the Sierra de Gredos. Cherries are the principal crop, and for two weeks in March the valley turns white and pale pink with flowering trees. (The fruit is harvested May–July.) Camping is popular in this region, and even the most experienced hikers can find some challenging trails. Full of half-timbered stone houses, **Cabezuela del Valle** is one of the best preserved of the valley's many attractive villages. Like other local settlements, it once had a significant Jewish population. From the Jerte Valley, you can either follow the N110 along the river to Plasencia or, if you have a taste for mountain scenery, detour from the village of Jerte to Hervás (☞ *below*), traveling a narrow road that winds 15 km (10 mi) through forests of low-growing oak trees and over the Honduras Pass, Extremadura's highest road (at 4,700 ft).

Dining and Lodging

$$ ✕🏨 **Valle del Jerte.** A small, busy bar welcomes you in this family-run restaurant and inn just off the highway in the village of Jerte. Service is cheerful, the food is straightforward and flavorful, and the family's son very knowledgeable about Spanish wines (ask to see the wine cellar). Specialties include Extremaduran-style gazpacho, *cabrito* (kid), and superfresh local trout. If your Spanish is up to snuff, ignore the posted menu and opt for one of the verbally delivered suggestions of the day. Upstairs, five large guest rooms decorated with chestnut wood furniture, cotton bedspreads, and beamed ceilings make a comfortable base of exploration. ✉ *Gargantilla 16, Jerte 10612,* ☎ *927/470052,* FAX *927/470307. 5 rooms. MC, V.*

$ 🏨 **La Casería.** One of the first rural guest houses to open in Extremadura, this rambling home is on a 120-acre working farm where the owners also raise sheep and grow plums and cherries. Run by a British-Spanish couple, it's more a home than a hotel, with a charming country ambience that compensates for the lack of amenities. You do have to love animals, as the household includes plenty of dogs and cats. Aside from the six rooms, there are three cottages sleeping two each. It's wise to reserve in advance, and keep your eyes peeled as you approach: the sign is easy to miss. ✉ *N110, Km 378.6, Navaconcejo 10613,* ☎ FAX *927/173141. 6 rooms, 3 cottages. Pool. MC, V.*

Hervás

2 *63 km (39 mi) northeast of Plasencia, 142 km (88 mi) northeast of Cáceres, 25 km (16 mi) west of Cabezuela del Valle.*

Surrounded by pine and chestnut groves, this picturesque village makes an interesting detour from either the Valle del Jerte or Plasencia. Hervás is believed to have become a predominantly Jewish settlement during the Middle Ages, populated by Jews escaping Christian and Muslim persecution in the larger cities. In 1492, when the Jews were expelled from Spain altogether, their neighborhood was left intact (rather than spruced up and expanded) but their possessions were ceded to the local nobility. Stripped of its wealth, the village lost its commercial reputation and faded into the background. Now fully restored, the **Judería** (Jewish Quarter) is among the best-preserved in Spain.

Plasencia

3 *270 km (169 mi) west of Madrid, 79 km (49 mi) north of Cáceres, 126 km (78 mi) northwest of Trujillo.*

Rising dramatically from the banks of the narrow Jerte River, backed by the peaks of the Sierra de Gredos, Plasencia is the most important town in far-northern Extremadura. Surrounded by brown fields and dominated by an earth-tone cathedral, this dusty community was founded by Alfonso VIII in 1180, just after he captured the whole area from the Moors. The town's motto, *placeat Deo et hominibus* ("It pleases both God and men"), might well have been a ploy on Alfonso's part to attract settlers to this wild and isolated place on the southern border of the former kingdom of León. Badly damaged during the Peninsular War of 1808, Plasencia retains far less of its medieval quarter than do other Extremaduran towns; but it still has extensive fragments of its medieval walls and a smattering of fine old buildings, and it makes a good base for side trips to Hervás and the Jerte Valley (☞ *above*), the Monasterio de Yuste and Monfragüe park (☞ *below*) or, farther northwest, the wild Las Hurdes and Sierra de Gata.

Plasencia's **cathedral** was founded in 1189 and rebuilt after 1320 in an austere Gothic style that looks a bit incongruous looming over the town's red-tile roofs. In 1498, the great architect Enrique Egas designed a new structure, intending to complement or even overshadow the original; but despite the later participation of other notable architects of the time, such as Juan de Alava and Francisco de Colonia, Egas's plans were never fully realized. The entrance to this incomplete, curious, and not wholly satisfactory complex is through the portal on the new cathedral's ornate but somber north facade. The dark interior of the new cathedral is notable for the beauty of its pilasters, which sprout like trees into the ribs of the vaulting. You enter the old cathedral through the Gothic cloister, off which stands the building's oldest surviving section, the 13th-century chapter house (now the chapel of San Pablo)—a late-Romanesque structure with an idiosyncratic, Moorish-inspired dome. The **museum** in the truncated nave of the old cathedral has a motley collection of ecclesiastical and archaeological objects. ☎ *927/414852.* 🎫 *Old cathedral 150 ptas.* ⏲ *Mon.–Sat. 9–12:30 and 4–6 (5–6 in summer), Sun. 9–1.*

Surrounding Plasencia's old and new cathedrals are several soberly elegant Renaissance structures, most notably the **Palacio Episcopal** (Bishop's Palace), whose cloister is open weekdays from 9 to 2; the **Casa del Deán** (Dean's House), now a courthouse; and the **Hospital de Santa María,** now a cultural center.

At the back of the Hospital is the **Museo Etnográfico-Textil,** with displays of colorful regional costume. ✉ *Enter on C. Plaza Marqués de la Puebla,* ☎ *927/421843.* 🎫 *Free.* ⏲ *Sept.–June, Wed.–Sat. 11–2 and 5–8, Sun. 11–2; July–Aug., Mon.–Sat. 9:30–2:30.*

At the northwest end of the old quarter is the narrow **Plaza de San Vicente.** At one end is the 15th-century church of San Vicente Ferrer, whose adjoining convent has just been converted into a parador. Lined with orange trees, the carefully preserved square is dominated on its north side by the Renaissance **Palacio de Mirabel** (Palace of the Marquis of Mirabel); go through the arch in its middle and you'll come to an alley with a back view of the palace. ☎ *927/410701.* *Tip caretaker.* *Usually daily 10–2 and 4–6.*

East of the Plaza de San Vicente, at the other end of the Rúa Zapatería, is the **Plaza Mayor,** a cheerful, arcaded square where a market has been held every Tuesday morning since the 12th century. The mechanical figure clinging to the town hall clock tower on the east side of the square depicts the clockmaker himself, and is called the **Mayorga** in honor of the craftsman's Castilian hometown. Farther east is a large section of the town's medieval wall, on the other side of which is a heavily restored Roman aqueduct.

Dining and Lodging

$$–$$$ **Alfonso VIII.** The sturdy, gray facade of this central hotel hides a lobby that attempts a French-rococo elegance, with gilt plaster and red upholstery. Grand but slightly past its prime, with undistinguished modern rooms, this curious Franco-era relic is strangely agreeable. The restaurant has long been regionally renowned for its food, which has a strong Extremaduran accent; the menu changes seasonally, but the typical *caldereta de cordero* (lamb stew) is usually offered. Parking is available in a garage around the corner. ✉ *Alfonso VIII 32–34, 10600,* ☎ *927/410250,* FAX *927/418042. 55 rooms, 2 suites. Restaurant, parking (fee). AE, DC, MC, V.*

$ **Rincón Extremeño.** It's basic, but it's well maintained and well situated in the heart of the old quarter, just off the Plaza Mayor. The ground floor contains a popular bar and restaurant, the latter serving regional dishes. Some rooms face the narrow street, which is more attractive but noisier than the alternative. ✉ *Vidrieras 6, 10600,* ☎ *927/411150,* FAX *927/420627. 12 rooms. Restaurant, bar. MC, V.*

Shopping

If you happen to be in Plasencia on a Tuesday morning, head for the **Plaza Mayor** and do what Extremeños have been doing since the 12th century: scout bargains in the weekly market. The **Casa del Jamón** (✉ C. Sol 18, east of Plaza Mayor, ☎ 927/414271) is a good place to stock up on sausages, cheeses, and cherry liqueur from the Jerte Valley.

Monasterio de Yuste and La Vera

4 *17 km (11 mi) southeast of Jarandilla de la Vera, 45 km (28 mi) from Plasencia. Turn left off C501 at Cuacos and follow signs for the monastery (1 km [½ mi]).*

The **Monasterio de Yuste** (Yuste Monastery) was founded by Hieronymite monks in the early 15th century. It was badly damaged in the Peninsular War and left to decay after the suppression of Spain's monasteries in 1835, but it has since been restored and taken over once more by the Hieronymites. The approach ramp, originally meant to be climbed on horseback, leads to a terrace overlooking a fishpond. Carlos V spent his last years in the Royal Chambers—the bedroom where he died has a view into the church, which enabled the emperor to hear mass from his bed. The required guided tour also includes the church, the crypt where Carlos V was buried before being moved to El Escorial (near Madrid), and a glimpse of the monastery's two cloisters. At press time the floor above the Gothic cloister was being renovated into a small hostelry. ☎ *927/172130.* *100 ptas.* *Oct.–May, daily 9:30–12:30 and 3–6; June–Sept., daily 9:30–12:30 and 3:30–6:30.*

The monastery is in the heart of **La Vera,** the region occupying the southern slopes of the Sierra de Tormantos, a place of steep ravines (*gargantas*), rushing rivers, and villages with curious customs such as the Holy Thursday Empalaos in Valverde de la Vera, and the Pero Palo festival in Villanueva de la Vera (☞ Fiestas, *above*). Following the road that climbs from the monastery into the mountains for 6 km (4 mi), you'll come to the village of **Garganta La Olla**—as you approach, the road winds through cherry orchards and eventually dips into the village's narrow, twisting streets. In town is the **Casa de la Muñeca** (Doll's House; also called the Casa de Putas), once a brothel used by soldiers of Carlos V's army. It's still painted the traditional "brothel" blue, and the bas-relief figure on the doorway hints at its former purpose. The building recently held a butcher shop, but the proprietor finally tired of all the jokes, sold up, and moved to Plasencia. There are no hotels here, but if you're enchanted with the mountainous isolation and want to relax in the company of the villagers, El Abuelo Marciano (Grandpa Marciano; Cruce Jaraiz s/n, ☎ 927/460426) can arrange rustic **room and board** in the countryside.

Dining and Lodging

$$$ ✕🏨 **Parador Nacional Carlos V.** Nestled in the town of Jarandilla de la Vera, this important parador was built in the early 16th century as a fortified palace, and has an arcaded patio with flattened arches. Adding to its historical significance, the emperor Carlos V stayed here for an entire year while he waited for his quarters at Yuste to be completed. The halls are filled with stylish quasimedieval furnishings, and its regal dining room is the perfect place to indulge royal fantasies. Start with the *sopa de gañan* (hearty chicken and vegetable soup); then savor one of the house specialties, *cuchifrito extremeño* (roast suckling pig). ✉ *García Prieto 1 (62 km/40 mi east of Plasencia, 17 km/11 mi west of Monasterio de Yuste), 10450,* ☎ *927/560117,* FAX *927/560088. 53 rooms. Restaurant, bar, pool, tennis court, playground. AE, DC, MC, V.*

$ 🏨 **Antigua Casa del Heno.** This 150-year-old stone farmhouse (*finca*) was lovingly restored in 1991 as an eight-room rural guest house, providing a lovely get-away-from-it-all refuge near a natural spring. With wood floors and colorful bedspreads, the rooms are comfortable and cheerful; some have balconies, others have skylights, and all have unhindered views of the countryside. The inn is a favorite with stressed-out executives from Madrid, so reservations are essential. The restaurant, open to guests only, serves Spanish dishes and Argentinian-style grilled meat. ✉ *Finca Valdepimienta, Losar de la Vera (follow signs from village), 10460,* ☎ FAX *927/198077. 8 rooms. Restaurant. MC, V.*

Shopping

If you like to cook, pick up a tin or two of *pimentón de la Vera* (paprika), made from the region's famed red peppers. You'll find it in Jarandilla and other towns around La Vera.

Parque Natural de Monfragüe

5 *20 km (12 mi) south of Plasencia, off C524.*

At the junction of the rivers Tiétar and Tajo is the Monfragüe Nature Park, a rocky-mountain wilderness known for its wide range of plant and animal life, including lynx, boar, deer, fox, black storks, imperial eagles, and the world's largest colony of black vultures. Bring binoculars to better enjoy these graceful birds. The visitor center is in the hamlet of Villareal de San Carlos, on the C524 road between Plasencia and Trujillo. ☎ *927/199134.* ⏲ *Daily 9–2:30 and 5–7 (4–6 in winter); audiovisual show 5 times a day.*

Lodging

$$–$$$ **Hospedería Parque de Monfragüe.** On the main road just south of the park, this striking hotel is housed in a striking trio of stark modern buildings faced in gray slate. The interior is furnished entirely with contemporary designer pieces, and in fact this hotel has been featured in numerous Spanish interior-design magazines. Neutral grays and browns are backed in the guest rooms by salmon-color walls. Rooms in the wing farthest from the road have the best mountain views. Opened in 1999, this is the first in a chain of Extremadura *hospederías,* a regional version of the national paradors. ✉ *Carretera Plasencia–Trujillo Km. 39.1, Torrejón el Rubio 10694,* ☏ *927/455245,* FAX *927/455016. 48 rooms, 12 suites. Restaurant, pool, meeting rooms. AE, DC, MC, V.*

Cáceres

★ 6 *307 km (190 mi) west of Madrid.*

An oasis of monuments in rustic Extremadura, Cáceres is a provincial capital and prosperous agricultural town whose vibrant nightlife draws villagers from the surrounding *pueblos* every weekend. Originally a Roman colony, and later heavily disputed between the Moors and Christians, Cáceres also draws tourists who want to escape into the fairy-tale labyrinth of the Ciudad Monumental, the town's startlingly well preserved old quarter. The bus and train stations are next to each other on the uninspiring Avenida de España, a good half-hour walk from the old quarter. Once you reach Calle San Antón, the look of the town improves considerably, particularly as you reach the intimate Plaza de San Juan, home of one of Extremadura's greatest restaurants, El Figón de Eustaquio (☞ Dining and Lodging, *below*). Beyond this square is the long, inclined, arcaded **Plaza Mayor,** where you'll see several pleasant outdoor cafés, the tourist office, and—on breezy summer nights—nearly everyone in town, strolling or sitting on the long steps leading up to the Ciudad Monumental. In the middle of the arcade opposite the old quarter is the entrance to the lively Calle General Ezponda, lined with tapas bars, student hangouts, and discos that keep the neighborhood awake and moving until dawn.

On high ground on the eastern side of the Plaza Mayor is the beckoning portal through the town's intact (though heavily restored) wall, which surrounds one of the best-preserved old quarters in Spain. Literally packed with treasures, Cáceres's **casco antiguo** (old town; also called the Ciudad Monumental) is a marvel: small, but without a single modern building to distract from its aura. Setting foot in this surreal place is like walking into a time warp, and is one of the high points of a trip to Extremadura. With very few shops, restaurants, or bars, the old town is virtually deserted in winter; crammed with somber, gray medieval and Renaissance palaces, at night it looks like a stage set for a tragedy, while the warm glow of the sun makes it look like the mythical city of gold that so moved the conquistadors. Several movies have shot scenes here, including *1492,* Ridley Scott's 1992 saga of Christopher Columbus.

Wear comfortable walking shoes to explore the cobbled streets of the old quarter. From the Plaza Mayor, where you can pick up a map at the tourist office, enter the quarter through the gate next to the Torre de la Hierba. Once inside, turn right onto Adarve Estrella, continue along Calle Adarve de Santa Ana, and you'll soon pass the **Palacio de los Golfines de Arriba** on your left, dominated by a soaring tower dating from 1515. The ground floor is a restaurant.

Skirt the town walls until you reach **Plaza de Santa Clara,** on the southern side of the old town, recognizable by its palm trees. Leading north from here to the center of the old town is Calle Ancha, at the beginning of which is the **Casa de Sanchez de Paredes,** a 16th-century palace that now serves as a parador (☞ Dining and Lodging, *below*).

On the Plaza San Mateo, at the northern end of Calle Ancha, stands **San Mateo,** one of the most important churches in Cáceres. Built mainly in the 14th century, but with a 16th-century choir, it has an austere interior, the main decorative notes being the Baroque high altar and some heraldic crests. On the square facing the eastern side of San Mateo is the battlemented tower of **Palacio de Las Cigüeñas** (Palace of the Storks), so called because of the storks' nests that adorned it before its restoration.

Farther down, on the adjoining Plaza de los Veletas, is the **Casa de las Veletas** (House of the Weather Vanes), a magnificent, 12th-century Moorish mansion. The Casa now houses the **Museo de Cáceres.** With an emphasis on local archaeological finds, some dating as far back as the Neolithic era, this collection is an excellent way to acquaint yourself with the many peoples who have inhabited this area. One highlight is the eerie but superb Moorish cistern—the *aljibe*—with arches supported by moldy stone pillars. ☎ *927/247234.* 🎫 *200 ptas.; EU citizens free.* ⏲ *Tues.–Sat. 9:30–2:30, Sun. 10:15–2:30.*

Cuesta de la Companía, the narrow street that descends between the San Mateo church and Las Cigüeñas to the town's other main church, Santa María, passes first the Jesuit church of **San Francisco Xavier,** then the **Palacio de los Golfines de Abajo.** The latter has the finest exterior of any palace in Cáceres; its stony severity is relieved by Mudéjar and Renaissance decorative motifs.

The Gothic church of **Santa María,** built mainly in the 16th century, is now Cáceres's cathedral. You can visit during Mass; the elegantly carved high altar, from 1551, is just about visible in the gloom. Nearby, on the Plaza de Santa María, is the **Palacio de Carvajal,** the only old palace you can tour apart from the Casa de las Veletas. 🎫 *Free.* ⏲ *Mon.–Sat. 9–2 and 4–8, Sun. 9–2.*

From Santa María, a 110-yard walk down Calle Tiendas takes you to the town's northern wall. Don't miss the 16th-century **Palacio de los Moctezuma-Toledo** (now a public-record office), built by Juan Cano de Saavedra with his wife's dowry—his wife being the princess daughter of the Aztec ruler Montezuma.

The chief building of interest outside the town wall is the church of **Santiago de los Caballeros** (go through the Socorro Gate; then continue north along Calle de Villalobos). It was rebuilt in the 16th century by Rodrigo Gil de Hontañón, Spain's last great Gothic architect.

Just up the hill behind the Ciudad Monumental is **El Santuario Virgen de la Montaña** (Sanctuary of the Virgin of the Mountain), which has a golden Baroque altar. The statue of the patroness virgin is paraded through the town in May. The picturesque view from outside is worth the drive up here. 🎫 *Donation suggested.* ⏲ *Daily 8:30–2 and 4–8.*

OFF THE BEATEN PATH

GAROVILLAS – A possible excursion from Cáceres is Garovillas, 10 km (6 mi) off the main road between Cáceres and Plasencia (turn left/northwest onto the C522, 25 km/15 mi north of Cáceres). Now partially deserted, it's a perfectly preserved village from the late 15th century. The walls and pillars appear to be tilting at dangerously uneven angles, but they were built this way to offset the slope of the land.

Dining and Lodging

$$$ ✕ **Atrio.** Slickly elegant, on a side street off the southern end of Cáceres's leafy main boulevard, this restaurant offers ultrarefined yet adventurous modern cooking in a modern setting. Truffles appear in many dishes, including the tastefully presented *perdiz al modo de Alcántara* (partridge cooked with truffles), a traditional Extremaduran delicacy. ✉ *Signo 18 (off Avenida de América),* ☎ *927/242928. DC, MC, V. No dinner Sun.*

$$–$$$ ★ ✕ **El Figón de Eustaquio.** A fixture on the quiet and pleasant Plaza San Juan, the justly famed Eustaquio is always busy, especially at lunchtime. Its jumble of small, old-fashioned dining rooms serves mainly regional delicacies, including excellent cured ham from Montánchez, *perdiz al modo de Alcántara,* and tench or trout from the Jerte Valley, prepared a number of ways. There's also a wide selection of fine Spanish wines. ✉ *Plaza San Juan 12,* ☎ *927/244362 or 927/248194. Reservations essential. AE, MC, V.*

$$$$ ✕🏨 **Parador Nacional de Cáceres.** This parador occupies a 16th-century palace right in the heart of the old town. Soft cream tones and wooden beams warm up the plain decor, and the rooms are cozy and comfortable. Enjoy fine food on the terrace or in the noble dining room: tasty local game specialties such as *lomo de venado al queso del Casar* (venison with Casar cheese sauce) or *el cabrito asado al romero* (roast kid with rosemary). You can also sample wines in the parador's wine cellar, Enoteca Torregaz, Thursday through Sunday. ✉ *Ancha 6, 10003,* ☎ *927/211759,* FAX *927/211729. 30 rooms, 1 suite. Restaurant, minibars, meeting rooms. AE, DC, MC, V.*

$$$$ ★ 🏨 **Meliá Cáceres.** Just as historic and somewhat more comfortable than the parador, the Meliá Cáceres has its own 16th-century palace, just outside the walls of the old town on the Plaza San Juan. It gracefully blends exposed stone, indirect spotlighting, and designer furnishings. Rooms have huge double beds, wall-to-wall carpeting, and ample baths. La Cava del Emperador, a street-level bar with a vaulted brick ceiling and charming wine-bottle lighting, is a popular meeting place for the town's well-heeled. ✉ *Plaza San Juan 11–13, 10003,* ☎ *927/215800,* FAX *927/214070. 84 rooms, 2 junior suites. Restaurant, bar, room service, laundry service, meeting rooms. AE, DC, MC, V.*

Nightlife and the Arts

Bars in Cáceres are lively until the wee hours and easy to find, as the crowds spill into the streets. Nightlife centers on the **Plaza Mayor,** which fills after dinner with families out for a *paseo* as well as students swigging *cuchimollo,* a combination of, believe it or not, red wine and Coca-Cola. To escape the college crowd, or to hang in more modern surroundings, try the **Calle de Pizarro,** on the west side of town. With the best (and priciest) discos, the new town starts hopping when the old one starts dying. Crowds make for **Acuario,** a multilevel dance club (✉ Avda. de España, 6, ☎ 927/220614), at around 3 AM.

Trujillo

★ ❼ *48 km (30 mi) east of Cáceres, 250 km (155 mi) southwest of Madrid; at the junction of N521 and N-V.*

No one who comes to the province of Cáceres should miss Trujillo. It's an extreme example of the Extremaduran look: a lonely, nearly deserted place, built of cold and imposing stone, that is nonetheless thrilling to behold. The stork nests that top several towers in and around the center of the old town—and have become something of a symbol of Trujillo—only add to this strange effect. Unlike Cáceres, Trujillo has none of the bustle of the new Spain; it seems almost stuck in the past. Dating back at least to Roman times, when its castle was first constructed, Trujillo was captured from the Moors in 1232 and colonized by a number of leading military families. It was only after Spain's discovery of the Americas in 1492, however, that the town's renown spread. Known today as the Cradle of the Conquistadors, Trujillo spawned some of the leading explorers and conquerors of the New World—men who returned, in the 16th and 17th centuries, to build a splendid series of palaces, radically changing what had been a poverty-stricken provincial town into a showcase of conspicuous consumption. The most famous of these action heroes was Francisco Pizarro, conqueror of Peru, born in Trujillo in 1475. Francisco's educated half brother Hernando, also an adventurer in Peru, built what is arguably the most magnificent palace in Trujillo.

Trujillo's economic boom during Spain's golden age led the town to expand well beyond its medieval walls. Then, from the mid-17th century on, building ceased almost entirely, and the town entered a long decline. Today you can wander randomly around its maze of streets and still uncover poignant memorials of the illustrious past at every turn. Note that it is only practical to see Trujillo on foot, as the streets are mostly cobbled or crudely paved with stone, and are rarely flat. The two main roads through Trujillo leave you at the unattractive bottom of town. Things get progressively older the farther you climb, but even on the lower slopes—where most of the shops are concentrated—you need walk only a few yards to step into what seems like the Middle Ages.

Trujillo's large **Plaza Mayor,** one of the finest in Spain, is a superb Renaissance creation with very few contemporary embellishments, among them—what else?—the tourist office. At the foot of the stepped platform on the plaza's north side stands a large, bronze equestrian statue of Francisco Pizarro.

The church behind Pizarro, **San Martín,** is a Gothic structure from the early 16th century, with some fine Renaissance tombs and an old organ. If you visit at dusk, you may be lucky enough to hear the men's choir rehearsing, adding a magical note to eventide.

Next to the church in the northeastern corner of the Plaza Mayor is the **Palacio de los Duques de San Carlos** (Palace of the Dukes of San Carlos), whose majestically decorated facade dates from around 1600. The building is now a convent of Hieronymite nuns, who can occasionally be glimpsed on the balconies in full habit, hanging laundry or watering their flowers. To visit, pull the chain in the foyer to ring a bell and summon one of the nuns. The convent also produces and sells typical pastries, including *perrunillas* (small lard cakes) and *tocinillos del cielo* (custardlike egg-yolk sweets). ☎ *927/320058.* 🎫 *Minimum donation 100 ptas.* ⊙ *Mon.–Sat. 9:30–1 and 4:30–6:30, Sun. 10–12:30.*

NEED A BREAK? If the summer sun has you parched, pop into the sparkling-clean **Bar Pillete Cafeteria** (✉ Plaza Mayor 28, ☎ 927/321449). The menu has an endless variety of fresh-squeezed juices, shakes, and other exotic fruit concoctions—a rarity in these parts.

The most interesting part of Trujillo extends west of the Plaza Mayor. Begin your tour near the plaza's southwestern corner, outside the **Palacio de la Conquista** (Palace of the Conquest), the most dramatic building on the square. Built by Francisco Pizarro's half brother Hernando, the stone palace is immediately recognizable by its rich covering of exquisite Renaissance ornamentation. Flanking its corner balcony, around which most of the decoration is clustered, are lively, imaginative busts of the Pizarro family. Representations of chained Native Americans are prominent in the coat of arms just above, an interesting reflection of the spirit of the conquests.

Adjacent to Trujillo's Palacio de la Conquista is the arcaded former town hall, now a court of law. The alley that runs through this building's central arch takes you to the **Palacio de Orellana-Pizarro,** now a school with the most elegant Renaissance courtyard in town. Cervantes spent a great deal of time writing here. *Donation suggested. Weekdays 10–1 and 4–6 (4:30–7 in summer), weekends 11–2 and 4–6.*

The oldest part of Trujillo, known as **La Villa,** is entirely surrounded by its original (if much restored) walls. Follow the wall along Calle Almenas, which runs west from the Palacio de Orellana-Pizarro, beneath the **Alcázar de Los Chaves,** a castle-fortress that was turned into a guest lodge in the 15th century and hosted visiting dignitaries, including Ferdinand and Isabella. The building has seen better days and is now a college. Passing the Alcázar, continue west along the wall to the **Puerta de San Andrés,** one of La Villa's four surviving gates (there were originally seven). Inside, you enter a world inhabited by storks, who, in spring and early summer, hunker down in the many crumbling chimneys and towers of Trujillo's palaces and churches.

The cobbled Calle Palomas leads up to the Plaza de Santa María, where you'll see Trujillo's major artistic monument, the church of **Santa María.** Attached to a Romanesque bell tower, this Gothic structure is occasionally used for masses, but its interior has been virtually untouched since the 16th century. The upper choir has an exquisitely carved balustrade; the coats of arms at each end indicate the seats Ferdinand and Isabella occupied when they attended Mass here. The church's main attraction is its high altar, circa 1480, adorned with great 15th-century Spanish paintings. To see the altar properly illuminated, place a 100-pta. coin in the box next to the church entrance. *100 ptas. Daily 11–2 and 4:30–7 (5–8 in summer).*

Climbing north from Santa María, you'll come almost immediately to the Pizarro family home. This small house has been restored and turned into a museum, the **Casa Museo de Pizarro,** dedicated to the links between Spain and Latin America. *250 ptas. Daily 11–2 and 4:30–6 (until 8 in summer).*

The same theme is addressed in the **Museo de la Coria,** installed nearby in a restored section of the former convent of San Francisco el Real, at the northern edge of the old town. *927/321898. Free. Weekends 11:30–2.*

Standing in isolation beyond the Casa Museo de Pizarro is the fortress of Trujillo's large **castle,** built by the Moors on Roman foundations. Climb to the top for spectacular views of the town and its surroundings. From here you can compare modern with medieval: to the south are grain silos, warehouses, and residential neighborhoods. To the north are only green fields and flowers, partitioned by a maze of nearly leveled Roman stone walls. *Free. Daily 9 AM–dusk.*

Dining and Lodging

$$ ★ ✕ **Pizarro.** This celebrated restaurant is in a small but quietly elegant upstairs room with a warm, friendly atmosphere and a menu of traditional Extremaduran home cooking. A house specialty is *gallina trufada,* an elaborately prepared chicken pâté with truffles. This was once a common Christmas dish, but today few people know how to make it. ✉ *Plaza Mayor 13, 927/320255. MC, V.*

$ ✕ **Mesón La Troya.** While the food here is not up to the standard of the neighboring Pizarro, there are few more entertaining places to eat a meal. Don't be daunted by the gamblers playing the slots in the front room; once you pass the bar, littered with dirty napkins from the tapas crowd, you'll enter a pleasant dining room, a vaulted chamber within a beautiful old building. The elderly woman who runs the place is a known eccentric who scolds you if you fail to finish the enormous helpings. At the beginning of the meal you're served a *tortilla de patatas* (potato omelet) whether you want it or not. ✉ *Plaza Mayor 10,* ☎ *927/321364. MC, V.*

$$$ ★ ✕🏨 **Parador Nacional de Trujillo.** This parador was originally the Convent of St. Clare, and its guest rooms surround a harmonious Renaissance courtyard. As in most paradors, the decor aims for mock-medieval chic, but the atmosphere here is endearingly homey. One entire wall of the dining room is lined with shelves displaying typical regional plates and copperware; depending on the season, you can sup on such local dishes as *criadillas de la tierra en caldereta* (meat stew with white truffles), *prueba de matanza* ("slaughter sampler," or assorted cuts of pork), *caldereta,* and *chuleta de novillo retinto con patatas* (braised fillet of young bull with potatoes). ✉ *Plaza Beatriz de Silva 1, 10200,* ☎ *927/321350,* FAX *927/321366. 45 rooms, 1 suite. Restaurant, bar, meeting rooms. AE, DC, MC, V.*

$ ✕🏨 **Mesón La Cadena.** In a rambling 16th-century palace on the Plaza Mayor, this restaurant-bar has simple but very comfortable guest rooms upstairs, with great views. Old-fashioned woven bedspreads brighten the basic decor. Savor the gazpacho *de fiesta extremeña* (with brilliant, yellow-orange tomatoes). ✉ *Plaza Mayor 8, 10200,* ☎ *927/321463,* FAX *927/323116. 7 rooms. Restaurant, bar. AE, MC, V.*

$$ 🏨 **Finca Santa Marta.** Surrounded by 60 acres of olive, cherry, and almond trees, this ancient olive-oil and wine farm is now owned by a retired couple and functions as an oh-so-comfortable country refuge. Located 14 km (9 mi) outside Trujillo on the road to Guadalupe, it's a relaxing alternative to staying in town. The restored living quarters have stone floors (rugs keep your feet warm), wood-beam ceilings, and fresh flowers everywhere. Meals are available if requested in advance. Reservations are essential. ✉ *Pago de San Clemente, 10600,* ☎ FAX *927/319202; for reservations,* ✉ *Juan Ramón Giménez 12, 8A, 28036 Madrid,* ☎ FAX *91/350–2217. 13 rooms, 1 suite. Bar, pool, meeting room. MC, V.*

Shopping

Trujillo sells a wider range of folk arts and crafts than almost any other place in Extremadura, among the most attractive of which are multicolor rugs, blankets, and embroideries. Several shops on the **Plaza Mayor** have enticing selections; the one right next door to the tourist office displays a centuries-old loom along with the work of local craftswoman Maribel Vallar, though opening times are erratic. **Eduardo Pablos Mateos** (✉ Plazuela de San Judas 12, ☎ 927/321066), just 100 yards from the parador, specializes in locally produced wood carvings, basketwork, and furniture.

Guadalupe

★ ❽ *200 km (125 mi) southwest of Madrid, 143 km (88 mi) east of Cáceres, 96 km (60 mi) east of Trujillo, 200 km (125 mi) northeast of Mérida.*

The **Monasterio de Nuestra Señora de Guadalupe** (Monastery of Our Lady of Guadalupe) is one of the most inspiring sights in Extremadura. The approach alone is worth the trip. Whether you come from Madrid, Trujillo, or Cáceres, the last stage of the trip takes you through wild, astonishingly beautiful mountain scenery. The monastery itself clings to the slopes, forming a magical profile that echoes the gaunt wall of mountains behind it. Pilgrims have been coming here since the 14th century, but only in recent years have they been joined by a growing number of tourists; even so, the monastery's very isolation—it's a good two-hour drive from the nearest town—has saved it from touristic excess.

The story of Guadalupe goes back to around 1300, when a local shepherd uncovered a miraculous statue of the Virgin, supposedly carved by St. Luke. Its fame might have remained local had it not come to the attention of King Alfonso XI, who often hunted here. Alfonso had a church built to house the statue and later vowed to found a monastery should he defeat the Moors at the battle of Salado in 1340. After his victory, he kept his promise. The greatest period in the monastery's history was between the 15th and 18th centuries, when, under the rule of the Hieronymites, it was turned into a pilgrimage center rivaling Santiago de Compostela in importance. Documents authorizing Columbus's first voyage to the New World were signed here, and the first Native Americans converted to Christianity were brought here to be baptized. The Virgin of Guadalupe became the patroness of Latin America, honored by the dedication of thousands of churches and towns in the New World. The monastery's decline coincided with Spain's loss of overseas territories in the 19th century. Abandoned for 70 years and left to decay, it was adopted after the civil war by Franciscan brothers, who slowly restored it.

On sale everywhere in Guadalupe is the copperware that has been made here since the 16th century. In the middle of the tiny, irregularly shaped Plaza Mayor (also known as the Plaza de Santa María de Guadalupe, and transformed during festivals into a bullring) is a 15th-century **fountain,** where Columbus's two Native American servants were baptized in 1496. Looming in the background is the late-Gothic south facade of the **monastery church,** covered in swirling decorative motifs and flanked by battlemented towers.

The entrance to the monastery is to the left of the church. From the large Mudéjar cloister, the required guided tour progresses to the **chapter house,** which has a collection of hymnals, vestments, and paintings, including a series of small panels by Zurbarán. The ornate 17th-century **sacristy** contains the monastery's most important works of art—a series of eight Zurbarán paintings of 1638–47. These powerfully austere representations of monks of the Hieronymite order and scenes from the life of St. Jerome are the artist's only significant paintings still in the setting for which they were intended. The monastery's outstanding collection of illuminated manuscripts, numbering nearly 100, is on display in the **museum,** off one corner of the cloister. The tour concludes with the garish, late-Baroque **Camarín,** the chapel where the miraculous Virgin is housed. The focal point is the Virgin of Guadalupe, a dark and mysterious wooden figure hiding under a great veil and mantle. Outside, the monastery's gardens have been re-landscaped in their original, geometric Moorish style. ☎ *927/367000.* *300 ptas.* *Daily 9:30–1 and 3:30–6:30.*

Dining and Lodging

$ ✕ **Isabel.** Across the square from the monastery, this cozy, family-run bar and restaurant serves fairly priced, home-cooked regional food in a small dining room decorated with copper and ceramic crafts. The *migas* and *cuchifrito* (roast suckling pig) are good bets. ✉ *Plaza Santa María de Guadalupe, 13,* ☎ *927/367126.*

$$$ ★ ✕ **Parador Nacional Zurbarán.** The first autopsy in Spain was performed in this building, a former hospital and pilgrim's hostel from the 15th century. Thanks to its Mudéjar architecture, Moorish-style rooms, and exotic vegetation, the parador has an unusually luxuriant feel. The best rooms are in the newer wing, as these look out on the monastery. In keeping with the spirit of the region, the restaurant serves simple local dishes, such as *bacalao monacal* (cod with spinach and potatoes) and *migas.* ✉ *Marqués de la Romana 12, 10140,* ☎ *927/367075,* FAX *927/367076. 41 rooms. Restaurant, bar, pool, tennis court, meeting rooms. AE, DC, MC, V.*

$ ✕ **Hospedería del Real Monasterio.** An excellent alternative if the parador is full, this inn was built around the 16th-century Gothic cloister of the monastery itself. The simple, traditional rooms with wood-beam ceilings are exceptionally quiet. The dining room is a haven of unpretentious charm, specializing in modest local dishes, such as *sopa de tomate* (tomato soup). ✉ *Plaza Juan Carlos I s/n, 10140,* ☎ *927/367000,* FAX *927/367177. 46 rooms, 1 suite. Restaurant, bar. MC, V. Closed Jan. 15–Feb. 15.*

Shopping

Guadalupe is the place to go for copper and tinware, as the local metalwork industry is 400 years old.

LOWER EXTREMADURA

The flavors of Extremadura's southern half are sometimes more Andalusian or even Portuguese than classically Spanish. Long stretches of dusty farmland and a dialect tinged with Portuguese make it feel light-years away from Castile. Mérida was established in 25 BC as a settlement for Roman soldiers; it soon became the capital of the Roman province of Lusitania, and its many ruins bear witness to its former splendor. Badajoz has also been a settlement since prehistoric times; Paleolithic remains have been found nearby. Minutes from the Portuguese border, it has long served as a gateway to Portugal and is home to many Portuguese as well as Portuguese descendants. Extremadura's links with Portugal come alive in Olivenza, while Zafra, near the southern end of the province, is more reminiscent of an Andalusian town.

Mérida

★ 9 *70 km (43 mi) south of Cáceres, 66 km (40 mi) east of Badajoz, 250 km (155 mi) north of Seville.*

Strategically situated at the junction of major Roman roads from León to Seville and Toledo to Lisbon, Mérida was founded by the Romans in 25 BC on the banks of the River Guadiana. Then named Augusta Emerita, it became the capital of the vast Roman province of Lusitania (the Iberian Peninsula) soon after its founding. A bishopric in Visigothic times, Mérida never regained the importance that it had under the Romans; and as the administrative capital of Extremadura, it is now a rather plain large town—with the exception of its dramatic Roman complex. Mérida boasts the finest series of Roman monuments in Spain (as well as an outstanding Museum of Roman Art), and they pop up all over town, surrounded by thoroughly modern buildings; so in a sense the ancient facilities appear in context, rather than in an isolated clump.

The new, glass-and-steel bus station is in a modern district on the other side of the river from the town center. It commands a good view of the exceptionally long **Roman bridge,** which spans two forks of this sluggish river. On the farther bank is the Alcazaba fortress. If you're driving, follow signs to the MUSEO DE ARTE ROMANO to reach Mérida's best-preserved **Roman monuments,** the **teatro** (theater) and the **anfiteatro Romano** (amphitheater), arranged in a verdant park. Parking is usually easy here. Next to the entrance to the Roman ruins is the main tourist office, where you can pick up maps and brochures. You can buy a ticket to see only the Roman ruins or, for a slightly higher fee, an *entrada conjunta* (joint admission), which also grants access to the Basílica de Santa Eulalia and the Alcazaba.

The Roman theater, dating from around 24 BC, is notable for the elegant colonnade on its stage. Spectacularly lighted plays are performed here in summer. While the theater has been sensitively restored, the amphitheater was, and remains, a much cruder construction; at one time 14,000 spectators gathered on the mammoth stone bleachers for morbidly fascinating duels between gladiators and wild beasts. In a different part of the site, on the other side of the parking lot and accessible through a separate gate, is the **Casa del Anfiteatro**, the remains of a Roman villa with interesting mosaics. ☎ *924/312530.* 🎫 *Theater and amphitheater 600 ptas.; combined admission to Roman sites, basilica, and Alcazaba 800 ptas.* ⏲ *Daily 9–1:45 and 4–6:15 (5–7:15 in summer).*

Across the street from the entrance to the Roman sites, and connected ★ by an underground passageway, is Mérida's superb, modern **Museo Nacional de Arte Romano** (National Museum of Roman Art), housed in a monumental building in light-colored brick, designed by the award-winning Spanish architect Rafael Moneo and worth a visit in its own right. Seldom does a museum building complement and enhance the exhibits as skillfully as this one does (and unlike the nearby Roman sites, it's entirely wheelchair-accessible). You walk through a series of passageways to the luminous, cathedral-like main exhibition hall, supported by arches the same proportion and size (50 ft) as the Roman arch in the center of Mérida, the Arco de Trajano (Trajan's Arch). The exhibits, arranged on three open-ended levels to one side of the nave, include outstanding mosaics, frescoes, jewelry, statues, pottery (surprisingly similar to that produced in Extremadura today), household utensils, and other Roman works. Interestingly, there are no weapons. One space contains the reconstruction of a room in a Roman villa. Before leaving, be sure to visit the **cripta** (crypt) beneath the museum—it houses the remains of several homes and a necropolis that were uncovered while the museum was built, in 1981, and were incorporated into the project as part of the exhibits. ✉ *José Ramón Mélida 2,* ☎ *924/311690.* 🎫 *400 ptas.; free Sat. afternoon and Sun.* ⏲ *Tues.–Sat. 10–2 and 4–6 (5–7 in summer), Sun. 10–2.*

From the museum, make your way west down Suarez Somontes toward the river and the city center. Turn right at Calle Baños and you'll see the towering columns of the **Templo de Diana**, the oldest of Mérida's Roman buildings. If you continue toward the river along Sagasta and Romera, you'll come to the sturdy, square **Alcazaba** (fortress), built by the Romans and later strengthened by the Visigoths and Moors. To go inside, follow the fortress walls around to the side farthest from the river. Climb up to the battlements for sweeping river views. ☎ *924/317309.* 🎫 *800 ptas. (includes Roman theater and amphitheater).* ⏲ *Daily 9–1:45 and 4–6:15 (5–7:15 in summer).*

Mérida's main square, the **Plaza de España,** adjoins the northwestern corner of the fortress and is highly animated both day and night. Its oldest building is the 16th-century palace, which houses the Hotel Emperatriz (☞ Dining and Lodging, *below*). Behind this hotel stretches Mérida's best-preserved and most charming area, its Andalusian-style white houses shaded by palms, and in their midst the **Arco de Trajano,** which used to be part of one of the Roman city gates.

Off the tiny Plaza de Santa Clara, just north of the Plaza de España in the heart of the *casco viejo,* is an abandoned 18th-century church containing a dusty, old-fashioned **Museo Visigótico,** filled with fragments of Visigothic stonework. ☎ *924/300106.* *Free.* *Tues.–Sat. 10–2 and 4–6 (5–7 July–Sept.), Sun. 10–2.*

From the Plaza de España, take Calle Santa Eulalia, a lively pedestrian shopping street, and continue along the Rambla Mártir Santa Eulalia to the **Basílica de Santa Eulalia.** This originally Visigothic structure marks both the site of a Roman temple and the supposed place where the child martyr Eulalia was roasted alive in AD 304 for spitting in the face of a Roman magistrate. The church is now famous for a somewhat different reason: in 1990, excavations surrounding the tomb of the famous saint revealed layer upon layer of Paleolithic, Visigothic, Byzantine, and Roman settlements. ☎ *924/303407.* *Mon.–Sat. 10–2 and 4–6.*

Some other Roman sites are some distance from the center of town and require a drive. Across the train tracks in a modern neighborhood is the **circo** (circus), where chariot races were held. Little remains of the grandstands, which seated 30,000, but the outline of the circus is clearly visible and impressive for its size: 1,312 ft long and 377 ft wide. Of the various remains of aqueducts, the most impressive is the **Acueducto de los Milagros** (Aqueduct of Miracles), north of the train station. It carried water from the Roman dam of Proserpina, which still stands, 5 km (3 mi) away.

OFF THE BEATEN PATH

EXTREMADURAN SIBERIA – For a taste of truly elemental Spain, drive to the "Extremaduran Siberia," which lies between Mérida and the Castilian town of Ciudad Real (leave N430, which links the two towns, by following signs for Casas de Don Pedro, and continue south toward Talarrubias). This poor area of wild, rolling scrubland owes its nickname to the 12th duke of Osuna, who in the late 1800s came here after 10 years as the Spanish ambassador to Russia and was reminded of the Siberian steppes. Of the handful of villages, the oldest is Puebla de Alcocer, which has an arcaded square. In nearby Peloche, to the north of Talarrubias, women still embroider in the streets. Many people come to this region to enjoy water sports, such as fishing and windsurfing, on its three reservoirs: Cíjara, García de Sola, and Orellana.

Dining and Lodging

$$$ ✕ **Nicolás.** Mérida's best-known restaurant, around the corner from the parador, has a tavern serving tapas downstairs and a dining room, decorated in dark wood, upstairs. The regionally inspired food includes various lamb dishes, *perdiz en escabeche* (marinated partridge), brains, and frogs' legs. Dessert could be the traditional *técula mécula,* or creamy cheese from La Serena. The wine list is extensive, and the service professional. ✉ *Felix Valverde Lillo 13,* ☎ *924/319610. AE, DC, MC, V. No dinner Sun.*

$$$ ★ ✕ **Parador Nacional Vía de la Plata.** Built over the remains of what was first a Roman temple, then a Baroque convent, and then a prison, this spacious, whitewashed building exudes an Andalusian cheerfulness, tinged with hints of its Roman and Mudéjar past. Guest rooms are bright, with traditional dark-wood furniture. Some overlook the parador's gardens, others the rooftops of Mérida. The brilliant-white interior of the convent's former church has been turned into a particularly restful lounge. In the dining room, be brave and try the *revuelto de criadillas* (scrambled eggs with pigs' testicles) or *ranas con aroma de pimentón* (frogs' legs in paprika sauce). Other traditional offerings include *cabrito al ajillo* (fried kid with garlic). ✉ *Plaza Constitución 3, 06800,* ☎ *924/313800,* FAX *924/319208. 80 rooms, 2 suites. Restaurant, bar, pool, sauna, exercise room. AE, DC, MC, V.*

$$ ✕🅿 **Emperatriz.** Installed in the 16th-century palace overlooking Mérida's main square, this three-story hotel with mock-medieval rugs, wood furniture, and suits of armor is a sort of poor man's parador (the lack of elevator is a major drawback). It centers on a large, enclosed inner courtyard, with tables for dining year-round. The simple guest rooms are on the two upper floors, each identified with a ceramic plaque inscribed with snippets of history or information on illustrious personalities. The best rooms are on the middle floor, overlooking the square. The restaurant's *menú del di'a* is a good value, and there's a bar in the vaulted basement. ✉ *Plaza de España 19, 06800,* ☎ *924/313111,* FAX *924/313305. 40 rooms, 2 suites. Restaurant. AE, DC, MC, V.*

Nightlife and the Arts

Surrounding the Plaza España are numerous cafés, tapas bars, and restaurants filled with boisterous crowds late into the evening. Locals pack **Rafael II** on Calle Santa Eulalia 13 for platters of ham, cheese, and sausages; there's also a small, cork-lined dining room in the back. As you walk south on Santa Eulalia, the bars get cheaper and the music gets louder. Calle John Lennon, off the northwest corner of the plaza, is your best bet for late-night dance action, especially in summer.

The highlight of the cultural calendar is the annual **theater festival,** held in the Roman theater from late June to early August. Contact the tourist office for information and tickets.

Shopping

Antonio Zambrano (✉ José Ramón Mélida 40, ☎ 924/312818) has a large selection of southern Extremaduran pottery, which is reddish-brown with delicate engravings (incised into the wet clay with a stone).

Badajoz

10 *66 km (40 mi) west of Mérida, 90 km (59 mi) southwest of Cáceres.*

A sprawling mass of concrete and glass in the midst of desolate terrain, Badajoz looks like an urban oasis on approach. Hardly an aesthetic haven, however, Badajoz has little to offer the tourist aside from the bustling excitement of a college town. Modern and urban relative to the surrounding towns, it tries (not quite successfully) to make up for its lack of architectural interest with nighttime energy and the intellectual punch of its university. A mere 7 km (4 mi) from Portugal, this "border town" is known mainly as a suitable resting point on the way though Extremadura.

The newish **Museo Extremeño e Iberoamericano de Arte Contemporáneo,** however, is an added incentive to spend a few hours here. Dedicated to contemporary Spanish and Latin American painting and sculpture, the museum is south of the city center in a striking circular building that was once the Badajoz prison. ✉ *Nuestra Señora de Guadalupe s/n,* ☎ *924/260384.* 🎫 *Free.* ⏲ *Tues.–Sat. 10:30–1:30 and 5–8 (6–9 in summer), Sun. 10:30–1:30.*

Make your way to the older section of town and wander down to the edge of the Guadiana River to admire the **Puerta de Palmas,** the 16th-century gateway to the city and the symbol of Badajoz. It consists of two circular, crenellated towers surrounded by decorative guardposts with different motifs on each facade. Badajoz's other noteworthy sight is the **Torre Espantaperros** (literally, Dog-Scarers' Tower—effectively a Christian-scarers' tower), the watchtower of the city's Alcazaba (fortress). The practice of building such towers eventually inspired Seville's Giralda. Within the Alcazaba is the city's Museo Arqueológico (☎ 924/222314), free, open Tuesday through Sunday 10–2.

Dining and Lodging

$$$ ✕🏨 **Gran Hotel Zurbarán.** This large, modern building has a beautiful position near the River Guadiana, overlooking the Parque de Castelar. The decor is brash and slightly dated, but service is impeccable, and few hotels in Extremadura have such a range of amenities. The elegant restaurant, Los Monjes, is one of the best in town. ✉ *Paseo Castelar s/n, 06001,* ☎ *924/223741,* FAX *924/220142. 210 rooms, 4 suites. Pool, dance club, meeting rooms. AE, DC, MC, V.*

$ 🏨 **Condedu.** Here's a comfortable budget option in the old town, halfway between the Plaza Mayor and the Puerta de Palmas. The rooms, white with white-tile floors, are basic but clean, and a few have balconies. ✉ *Muñoz Torero 27, 06001,* ☎ *924/224641,* FAX *924/220003. 34 rooms. Cafeteria. AE, DC, MC, V.*

Nightlife and the Arts

The Plaza España and its side streets to the south are filled nightly with the local college crowd. More upscale after dark is Avenida República Argentina, with plenty of bars and restaurants.

Olivenza

⓫ *22 km (14 mi) south of Badajoz.*

An easy jaunt from Badajoz, Olivenza is worth seeing for its curious double personality. Looking at the airy, elongated main square, with its patterned cobblestones and various facades in the Portuguese Manueline style, you might think you've inadvertently crossed the border into Portugal. In fact, this originally Spanish town was occupied by Portugal in 1297, recaptured by the Spanish Duke of San Germán in 1657, recovered by Portugal in 1668, and definitively reclaimed for Spain again in 1801. Up until a generation or two ago, locals conversed equally well in both languages. The Portuguese influence is most evident in the twisted Manueline columns and tilework in the **Iglesia de la Magdalena** (Church of Mary Magdalene). As befits a disputed border town, Olivenza has numerous fortifications, the largest of which is the castle, with its 15th-century **Torre del Homenaje** (Tower of Homage). Adjoining the tower is the **Museo Etnográfico González Santana** (✉ Plaza de Santa María, ☎ 924/490222), surprisingly ambitious for a town this size. It's open Tuesday through Sunday 11–2 and 4–6 (5–8 June–Sept.), and admission is free. One room is devoted to archaeological finds (including a stone stele from the 8th century BC), but the main thrust is recent history: exhibits cover traditional trades and crafts along with collections of musical instruments, toys, and other paraphernalia of daily rural life in the first half of the 20th century.

Zafra

⓬ *62 km (38 mi) south of Mérida, 85 km (53 mi) southeast of Badajoz, 135 km (84 mi) north of Seville.*

Worth a stop on your way to or from Seville, Zafra is unusual for its **Plaza Mayor,** which is actually two contiguous squares, the Plaza Chica (once a marketplace) and the 18th-century Plaza Grande (ringed by mansions flaunting their coats of arms), connected by a graceful archway. Both plazas make for enjoyable tapas crawls.

There are several churches here, the finest being **Nuestra Señora de Candelaria,** near the parador; its *retablo* has nine extraordinary panels by Zurburán. The main reason travelers stop in Zafra, however, is the 15th-century **Alcázar de los Duques de Feria,** now a parador.

Dining and Lodging

$$$ ★ ✕🏨 **Parador Nacional Hernán Cortés.** The dominant building in this attractive and lively town is the parador, which occupies the 15th-century castle where Cortés stayed before his voyage to Mexico. The military exterior conceals an elegant, 16th-century courtyard attributed to Juan de Herrera. The rooms are white and cheerful, some with wood-beam ceilings, others with windows overlooking the marble courtyard. The suite has a superbly elaborate *artesonado* (coffered) ceiling and a hot tub, and the magnificent chapel now serves as a conference room. The dining-room staff will make you feel like an honored explorer just home from a valorous journey, and will probably suggest you restore yourself with *caldereta de cordero* (lamb stew). For dessert, try the poached figs with vanilla ice cream or *leche frita* (fried milk custard). ✉ *Plaza María Cristina 7, 06300,* ☎ *924/554540,* FAX *924/551018. 44 rooms, 1 suite. Restaurant, pool. AE, DC, MC, V.*

$$–$$$ ✕🏨 **Huerta Honda.** Across a small square from the castle-parador, this gleaming-white Andalusian-style hotel is a comfortable alternative at a similar price, though rates vary widely between high and low season. Rooms are painted in pastel pink or blue tones, and some have views of the parador. Adjoining the hotel is the upmarket Barbacana restaurant, where you can savor *gazpacho a la extremeña,* tasty *retinto* beef, and other local specialties. The lively cafeteria serves more modest fare, and there's also an English-style pub. ✉ *Lopez Asme 30, 06300,* ☎ *924/554100,* FAX *924/552504. 34 rooms, 1 suite. Restaurant, cafeteria, pub. AE, DC, MC, V.*

EXTREMADURA A TO Z

Arriving and Departing

By Bus

Bus links between Extremadura and the other Spanish provinces are far more plentiful and reliable than train or plane service. Regular buses, some of them express, serve Extremadura's main cities from Madrid, Seville, Lisbon, Valladolid, Salamanca, and Barcelona. The main company involved is **Auto Res** (✉ Plaza Conde de Casal 6, Madrid, ☎ 91/551–7200; Estación de Autobuses, Avenida de la Libertad, Mérida, ☎ 924/371955).

By Car

It's best to reserve a car outside Extremadura, either in Madrid or Seville, or before you leave for Spain. Traffic moves quickly on the four-lane N-V, the main highway from Madrid to Extremadura. The N630, or Vía de la Plata, which crosses Extremadura from north to south, is also effective. The fastest approach from Portugal is the N-IV from Lisbon to Badajoz.

By Plane

There are no airports in Extremadura. The nearest international airports are in Madrid and Seville.

By Train

Trains from Madrid and Seville stop at Plasencia, Cáceres, Mérida, and Zafra. The journey from Madrid to Plasencia takes three hours; from Seville to Zafra, 3½ hours. There is also a direct train from Lisbon to Badajoz, which takes five hours. Unfortunately, the trains run infrequently, making them a potentially inconvenient mode of travel. Call the **RENFE** information line for details (☎ 902/240202).

Getting Around

By Bus

Buses serve nearly every village in Extremadura. Note, however, that on lesser routes, buses tend to set off extremely early in the morning; plan carefully to avoid getting stranded.

By Car

If you're in any kind of hurry, driving is the most feasible way to get around Extremadura. The main roads are well surfaced and not too congested. Side roads—particularly those that cross the wilder mountainous districts, such as the Sierra de Guadalupe—can be poorly paved and badly marked.

By Train

Only the main towns are accessible by train, and service is infrequent. The line connecting Plasencia, Cáceres, Mérida, and Zafra, for instance, has just two trains a day, one of which runs at night. Train stations also tend to be some distance from the town centers.

Contacts and Resources

Emergencies

Police: ☎ 091.

Fishing Permits

You can obtain a fishing permit from **Agencia de Medio Ambiente** (✉ Enrique X Canedo, Mérida, ☎ 924/382967 or 924/382600).

Visitor Information

Local tourist offices: **Badajoz** (✉ Plaza de la Libertad 3, ☎ 924/222763), **Cáceres** (✉ Plaza Mayor 33, ☎ 927/246347), **Mérida,** (✉ Avda. José Álvarez Saez de Buruaga s/n, at entrance to Roman theater, ☎ 924/315353). **Plasencia** (✉ C. del Rey 8, ☎ 927/422159), **Trujillo** (✉ Plaza Mayor s/n, ☎ 927/322677), and **Zafra** (✉ Plaza de España 30, ☎ 924/551036).

14 THE CANARY ISLANDS

Closer to North Africa than to Spain, this rugged volcanic archipelago mixes seaside resorts with parched sand dunes. Long Europe's favorite retreat for infusions of coastal sunshine, the Canaries are just as compelling inland. Each isle is different—between them you can tramp through caves once inhabited by ancient tribes, hike to snow-covered peaks, and savor a meal grilled over the heat from a volcanic crater.

By Deborah Luhrman

Updated by Michael de Zayas

A **VOLCANIC CONSTELLATION** 1,280 km (800 mi) southwest of mainland Spain and 112 km (70 mi) off the coast of southern Morocco, the Canary Islands lie at about the same latitude as central Florida. Each of the seven islands has its own character: La Gomera and El Hierro, as well as parts of La Palma and Gran Canaria, are fertile and overgrown with exotic tropical vegetation, while Lanzarote, Fuerteventura, and stretches of Tenerife are as dry as a bone, with lava caves and desert sand dunes. Yet Spain's highest peak, Mt. Teide, on Tenerife, is capped with snow several months of each year.

The Canaries are geographically African, culturally European, and spiritually Latin American. Many islanders have closer blood ties to Cuba and Venezuela than to mainland Spain. The language spoken here is, in both diction and pronunciation, a South American variety of Spanish. Salsa music, exotic to peninsular Spain, is the exclusive genre of the Canaries' wild Carnival fiestas.

The best thing about the Canaries is their climate, warm in winter and tempered by cool Atlantic breezes in summer. You can swim year-round. This is no secret to vacationing Europeans: the islands' first modern-day tourists arrived from England at the turn of the 20th century to spend the winter at Puerto de la Cruz, in Tenerife. Today, huge charter flights from Düsseldorf, Stockholm, Zürich, Manchester, and dozens of other northern European cities unload 6 million sun-starved visitors a year. Only a handful of tourists on these islands at any given time are from the United States, in contrast with mainland Spain.

The presence of northern visitors helps create a strange duality of natural beauty and heavy tourism. On Gran Canaria and Tenerife in particular, you'll hear more German than Spanish, and the resort towns' endless international eateries, car-rental agencies, water parks, travel agents, and miniature-golf parks suggest a sort of foreign annexation. Most people congregate, however, on a few unexceptional beaches, leaving the Canaries' purer aspects intact. An excellent system of natural parks and protected zones preserves one-of-a-kind opportunities for hikers, bikers, and beachcombers.

Before the Spanish arrived, the Canaries were populated by cave-dwelling people called Guanches. In the late 15th century the islands fell one at a time to Spanish conquistadors, then lay on the edge of navigators' maps for centuries. Columbus resupplied his ships here in 1492 before heading west to the New World; having gone on to help establish the archipelago as an important trading port, he is sometimes called the Canaries' first tour operator.

The Guanches were decimated by slave traders by the end of the 16th century. Their most significant remains are the Cenobio de Valerón ruins on Gran Canaria.

Pleasures and Pastimes

Beaches

Most visitors to the Canaries come for the sun, and each island has different kinds of beaches on which to soak it up. The longest and most pristine beaches are the white-sand strands of Fuerteventura. Lanzarote and Gran Canaria offer golden-sand beaches with plenty of amenities, such as lounge chairs and parasailing. Tenerife, despite its fame as a resort, has few natural beaches; the crowded ones that do exist are man-made with imported yellow sand.

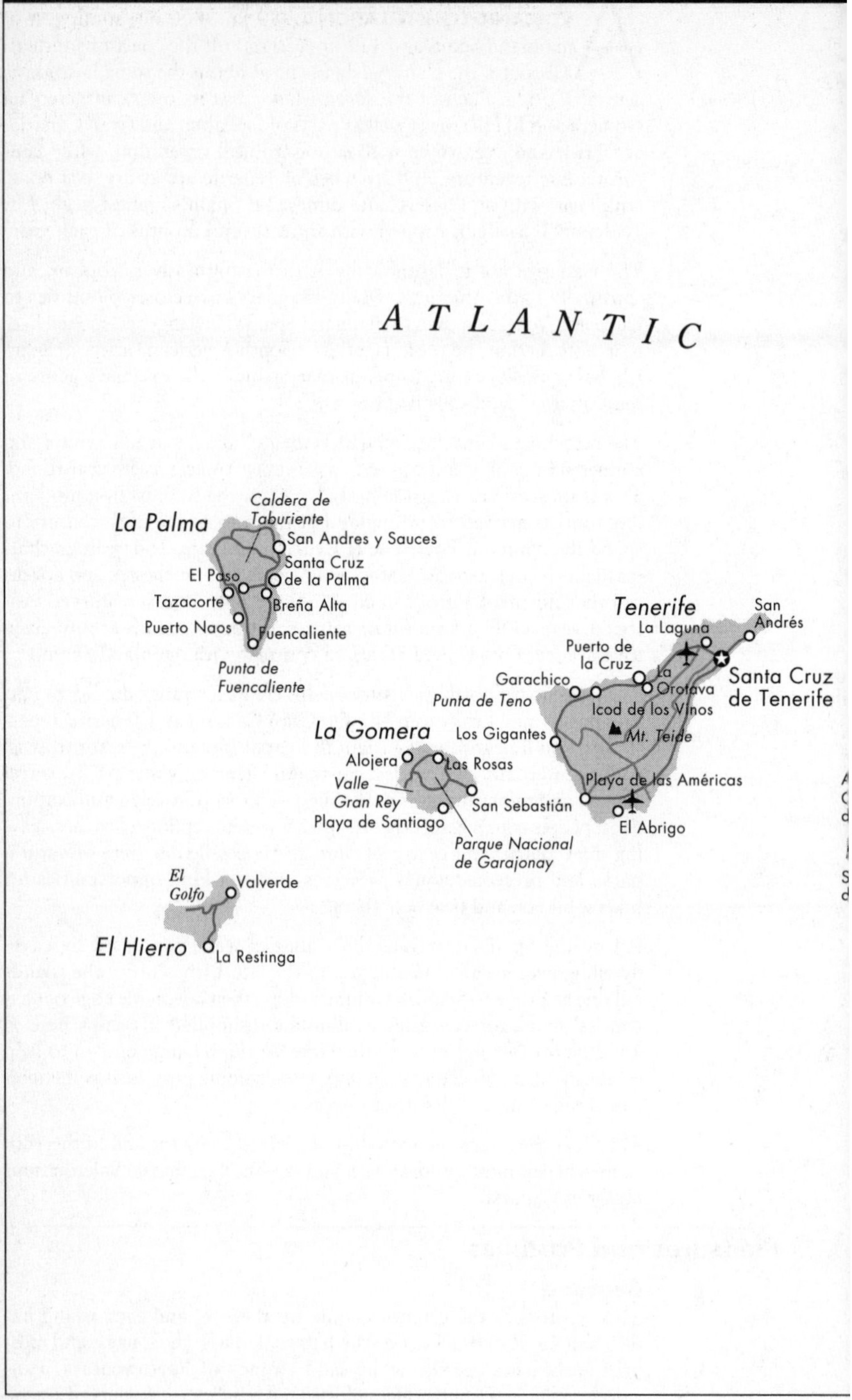
ATLANTIC
La Palma
Caldera de Taburiente
San Andres y Sauces
Santa Cruz de la Palma
El Paso
Tazacorte
Breña Alta
Puerto Naos
Fuencaliente
Punta de Fuencaliente
Tenerife
San Andrés
La Laguna
Puerto de la Cruz
Garachico
La Orotava
Santa Cruz de Tenerife
Punta de Teno
Icod de los Vinos
Los Gigantes
Mt. Teide
Playa de las Américas
El Abrigo
La Gomera
Alojera
Las Rosas
Valle Gran Rey
San Sebastián
Playa de Santiago
Parque Nacional de Garajonay
El Golfo
Valverde
El Hierro
La Restinga

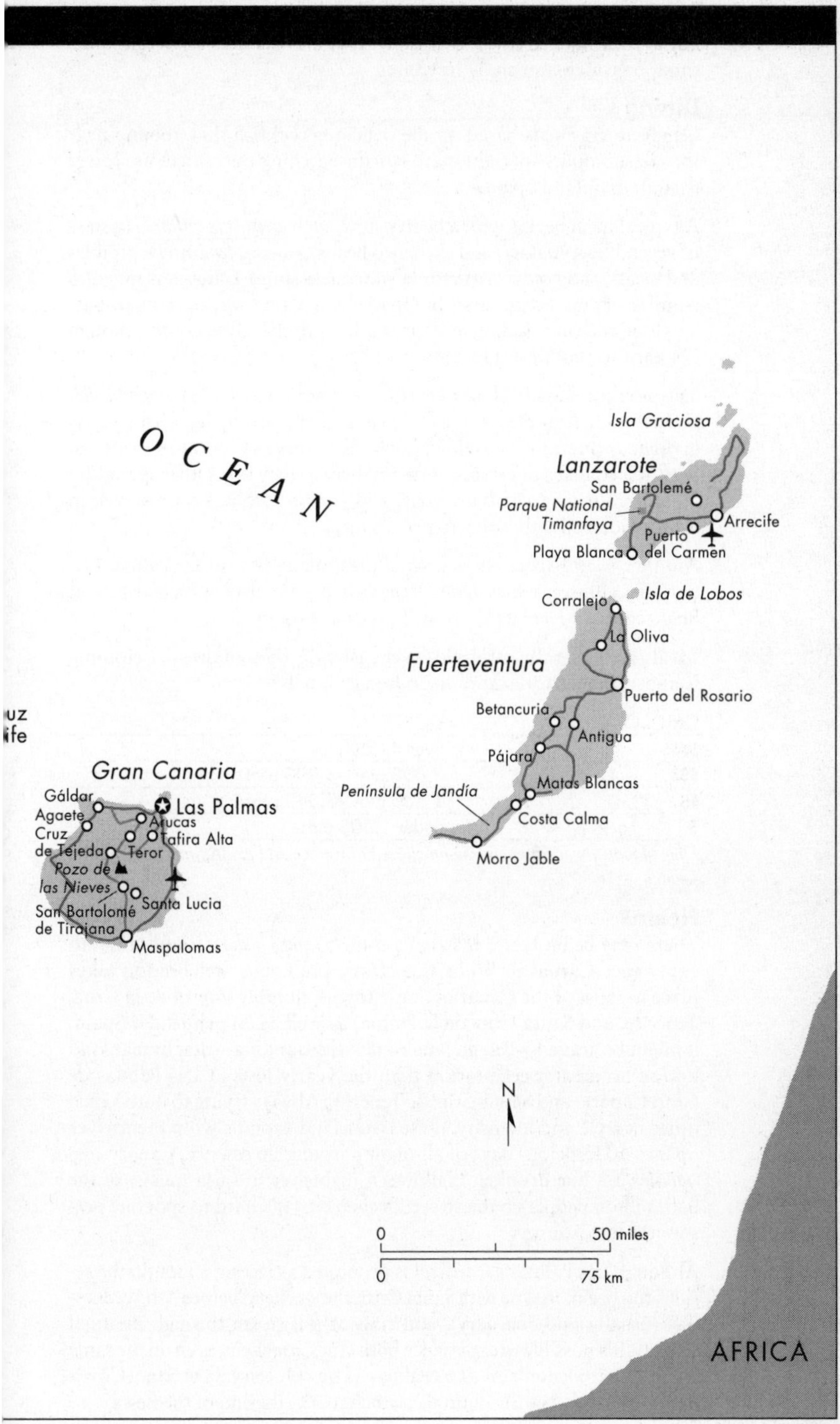
OCEAN
Isla Graciosa
Lanzarote
San Bartolemé
Parque National
Timanfaya
Arrecife
Puerto
del Carmen
Playa Blanca
Isla de Lobos
Corralejo
La Oliva
Fuerteventura
Puerto del Rosario
Betancuria
Antigua
Pájara
Matas Blancas
Península de Jandía
Costa Calma
Morro Jable
uz
ife
Gran Canaria
Gáldar
Las Palmas
Agaete
Arucas
Cruz
de Tejeda
Tafira Alta
Teror
Pozo de
las Nieves
Santa Lucia
San Bartolomé
de Tirajana
Maspalomas
N
0
50 miles
0
75 km
AFRICA

La Palma, La Gomera, and El Hierro have black-sand beaches, usually in rock-flanked coves. Remember that the Atlantic Ocean can sometimes be rough and chilly in winter.

Dining

Canarian cuisine is based on the delicious rockfish that abound near the coast, and its specialties are worth searching out. Prices are lower than in mainland Spain.

A typical meal begins with a hearty stew, such as *potaje canario* (a stew of vegetables, potatoes, and garbanzo beans), *rancho canario* (vegetables and meat), and *potaje de berros* (a watercress soup). Canarians eat *gofio* (similar to mashed potatoes but made by toasting wheat, corn, or barley flour and then adding milk or broth) with their first course, though it's hard to find in restaurants.

The next course is fresh native fish, the best of which are *vieja, cherne,* and *sama,* all firm-flesh white rockfish. Accompanying the fish are *papas arrugadas* (literally, "wrinkled potatoes"), tiny new potatoes boiled in seawater so that salt crystals form on them as they dry. Other specialties include *cabrito* (roast baby goat) and *conejo* (rabbit), both served in *salmorejo,* a slightly spicy paprika sauce.

Another island specialty is goat cheese, made best in La Palma. Canarian malmsey wines from Lanzarote, a favorite with Falstaff in Shakespeare's *Henry IV,* are still produced today.

Meals are generally informal on the islands, though dressier clothing is appropriate for restaurants in luxury hotels.

CATEGORY	COST*
$$$$	over 4,000 ptas.
$$$	3,000 ptas.–4,000 ptas.
$$	1,500 ptas.–3,000 ptas.
$	under 1,500 ptas.

**per person for a three-course meal, including tax and excluding drinks and service*

Fiestas

There may be no better reason to come to the Canary Islands than to experience **Carnaval.** While this classic pre-Lenten celebration takes place in most of the Canaries' large towns, notably Puerto de la Cruz, Tenerife, and Santa Cruz de la Palma, as well as on peninsular Spain, it might be argued—Rio de Janeiro notwithstanding—that humankind knows no greater celebration than the yearly fests at Las Palmas de Gran Canaria and Santa Cruz de Tenerife. Always trying to outdo each other in style and intensity, these two island capitals whip themselves up into 10 ferocious days of all-night partying. In essence, Canary *carnavales* are like drunken Halloween nights set to salsa music: of the half million people on the streets in each city, it's hard to spot one person not in costume.

Although Las Palmas's Carnival is promoted as lasting a month, the serious fun begins in sync with Santa Cruz, the weekend before Ash Wednesday (usually mid-February), and runs at full steam through the final Sunday. It's possible to experience both cities' mayhem, even on the same night, by jetfoil; don't miss Las Palmas's Drag Queen gala or Santa Cruz's hilarious mock "sardine burial," which marks the end of the fiesta.

Lodging

There are hundreds of hotels on the Canary Islands, but they tend to fray rapidly under heavy use. With a few exceptions, noted in the individual reviews, it's best to stay in the newest facilities.

Through package tours, most vacationers pay reasonable prices for hotel rooms, but rates for independent travelers are often exorbitant and do not reflect the quality of accommodation. Budget-minded independent travelers should look into newly constructed apartment complexes: though simply furnished, these have reception desks, swimming pools, and often restaurants, and each unit has a kitchenette. Note that arriving in the Canary Islands without either a package or independent reservations can create real hassles. A good percentage of the islands' lodgings are booked solid by package travelers most of the year, and some hotels do no business whatsoever with indie travelers. Finding a last-minute room can be extremely difficult.

Tenerife's Gran Melia Bahía del Duque has consistently been voted Spain's best vacation hotel and is worth a trip in itself. The Canaries also boast two of the most romantic paradors in the national chain, the colonial Parador Conde de La Gomera, and the seafront Parador Nacional El Hierro, both unbeatable retreats.

CATEGORY	COST*
$$$$	over 19,000 ptas.
$$$	12,000 ptas.–19,000 ptas.
$$	6,500 ptas.–12,000 ptas.
$	under 6,500 ptas.

**All prices are for a standard double room, including tax.*

Shopping

The Canary Islands are free ports, meaning that no value-added tax is charged on luxury goods such as jewelry, alcohol, and cigarettes. The streets are packed with shops, but the prices on these items do not represent significant savings for Americans. The islands are also known for lacy, hand-embroidered tablecloths and place mats.

Water Sports

The Canaries' steady winds and perfect waves attract sailboarders and surfers from all over the world. International windsurfing competitions are held each year on Tenerife. Surfers claim that the best waves in Europe break on the west coast of Lanzarote.

Exploring the Canary Islands

Tenerife has suffered most at the hands of developers, but it also has the most attractions. Here you can ride a cable car up the slopes of Mt. Teide, swim in a huge artificial lake, wander botanical gardens, or dance at glittering discos. The beaches are small, with black sand. The verdant (read: rainy) north coast retains unspoiled villages, while the southern Playa de las Américas is becoming unsightly, with a growing skyline of high-rise hotels.

Gran Canaria was the hot spot of the '60s and is seen as rather passé, but its Maspalomas beach is one of the islands' most beautiful, and some sand dunes behind the beach are being turned into a nature reserve. The capital, Las Palmas, is crawling with sailors, soldiers, and tourists. Though the city is a bit seedy, it does have a sparkling stretch of beach right downtown, with a lantern-lit boardwalk lined with restaurants and bars.

Lanzarote is a desert isle kept beautiful through thoughtful development. It has golden beaches, white villages, caves, and a volcanic national park where heat from an eruption in 1730 is still rising through vents in the earth. Vegetation is scarce, but the grapes grown by farmers in volcanic ash produce a distinctive Canarian wine.

Fuerteventura was ignored until recently, but construction is now racing to keep up with the demands of tourists, who come to windsurf and enjoy the endless white beaches. Luxury hotels now dot the coast, though the barren interior remains largely the domain of goatherds.

La Palma, called "the Garden Isle," has only recently been "discovered." It has lush foliage, tropical storms, rainbows, and black crescents of beach. The capital, Santa Cruz, is a beautifully preserved example of Spanish colonial architecture, and its people are some of the most genuine and hospitable in all of Spain.

La Gomera is a paradise for backpackers. Ruggedly mountainous, it offers good hiking, and UNESCO protects its forests. Most of the black-sand beaches are fringed by banana plantations.

El Hierro is the smallest and least-visited Canary, ideal for those who really want to be alone. It has a few black-sand beaches and a cool, highland pine forest for walking and picnicking.

Many places on these islands have the same or similar names. Be careful not to confuse the island of La Palma with the city of Las Palmas, which is the capital of Gran Canaria. Equally confusing, the capitals of La Palma and Tenerife are both called Santa Cruz. When writing to an address on one of the islands, note that they comprise two provinces: the province of Santa Cruz de Tenerife, which includes Tenerife, La Palma, La Gomera, and El Hierro, and the province of Las Palmas, which includes Gran Canaria, Lanzarote, and Fuerteventura.

Numbers in the margin correspond to points of interest on the Tenerife and Gran Canaria maps.

Great Itineraries

The main reasons to go to the Canary Islands are rest and relaxation, but it's worth digging a bit deeper once you're there. Try to combine a visit to the more congested islands (Tenerife, Gran Canaria, or Lanzarote) with side trips to the quieter ones (Fuerteventura, La Palma, La Gomera, or El Hierro).

IF YOU HAVE 3 DAYS

A long weekend in the Canary Islands is a pricey but effective antidote to the stress of city life or fast-paced sightseeing. If you're flying in from mainland Spain, pick one resort, go directly there, and unwind. Tenerife is a good option for first-time visitors—Playa de las Américas in the winter, **Puerto de la Cruz** ② in the summer. On your second day, rent a car and drive up to **Mt. Teide** ⑤, stopping at the historic town of Orotava and the Casa de Vino near Los Rodeos Airport. Spend the third day working on your tan.

An indulgent alternative is to fly into Reina Sofía Airport and go to **Los Cristianos** ⑥, where a 35-minute hydrofoil ride can whisk you to tiny La Gomera for three days of swimming and hiking.

IF YOU HAVE 7 DAYS

One week on the Canary Islands is enough time for a combination trip to two islands. Those who fancy touring should visit Tenerife and Lanzarote, both with interesting mixtures of lush green and volcanic desert landscapes. Begin your stay in Tenerife with an afternoon at the beach or pool. The next day, rent a car to explore the center of the island, visiting **Mt. Teide** ⑤ and the town of Orotava. On day three, spend the morning in **Santa Cruz** ① and perhaps the nearby town of La Laguna. Stop for lunch or wine-tasting at the Casa de Vino, and in the afternoon explore the north-coast villages of **Icod de los Vinos** ③ and **Garachico** ④. A 30-minute flight brings you to Lanzarote, where you can spend the next two days exploring the northern part of this island, with stops at the Jameos del Agua, Cuevas Verdes, Fundación César Manrique, and Mirador del Río lookout. On your sixth day, hit Timanfaya National Park for a tour of the volcanic zone. In the afternoon, detour to **Playa Blanca** and Playa Papagayo, at the island's southern tip. Save your last day for sunning and swimming.

IF YOU HAVE 14 DAYS

Most European visitors spend two weeks here. A fortnight allows you to complete the above itinerary with a few extra days to relax and to see a third island. From Tenerife, La Gomera is a one-hour ferry ride; from Lanzarote it's a 45-minute ride to Fuerteventura. Either option allows you to keep the same rental car and take advantage of weekly rates. If you choose La Gomera, make an excursion to the **Parque Nacional de Garajonay** and the island's northern coast. You'll need a second day to explore the southern coast with a drive out to **Valle Gran Rey.** Fuerteventura is a better choice for beachcombers or windsurfers; one day here should be sufficient for exploring the island, leaving the rest of the time for loafing or sports.

When to Tour the Canary Islands

As the tourist office loves to point out, the Canary Islands enjoy warm weather in the winter and cool breezes in summer. Winter, especially Christmas, and Easter are peak periods for northern Europeans, while Spaniards and Italians tend to come in the summer, particularly during the August holidays. Reservations are extremely difficult at those times. Spring—when a profusion of wildflowers colors the islands—is the low season, and the most beautiful time to be here.

Since the Canaries are a year-round destination, prices tend to be roughly the same no matter when you come. You may have some luck negotiating discounts during the slowest months, May and November.

TENERIFE

Tenerife is the largest of the Canary Islands. Roughly triangular in shape, it is towered over by the volcanic peak of Mt. Teide, which at 12,198 ft is Spain's highest mountain. The slopes leading up to Teide are forested with pines in the north and covered with barren lava fields in the south.

Tenerife's capital, Santa Cruz de Tenerife, is a giant urban center. Forget whitewashed villas and sleepy streets, and imagine the traffic, activity, and crowds of an important shipping port, as well as the site of Spain's most raucous fiesta—no mean honor—the pre-Lenten Carnival. (Hotels hand out awards to the fiesta's regulars, some of whom have spent 30 consecutive winters here.) In the rainy north, mixed among the tourist attractions, are banana plantations and vineyards.

In the dry south, the resort Playa de las Américas has sprung up at the edge of the desert over the last 15 years. It's especially popular with young couples and singles, who appreciate the world-class hotels and swinging nightlife.

Santa Cruz

❶ *10 km (6 mi) southwest of Los Rodeos Airport, 75 km (45 mi) northeast of Playa de las Américas.*

The heart of Santa Cruz de Tenerife is the **Plaza de España.** The cross is a monument to those who died in the Spanish Civil War, which was actually launched from Tenerife by General Franco during his exile here.

Tenerife

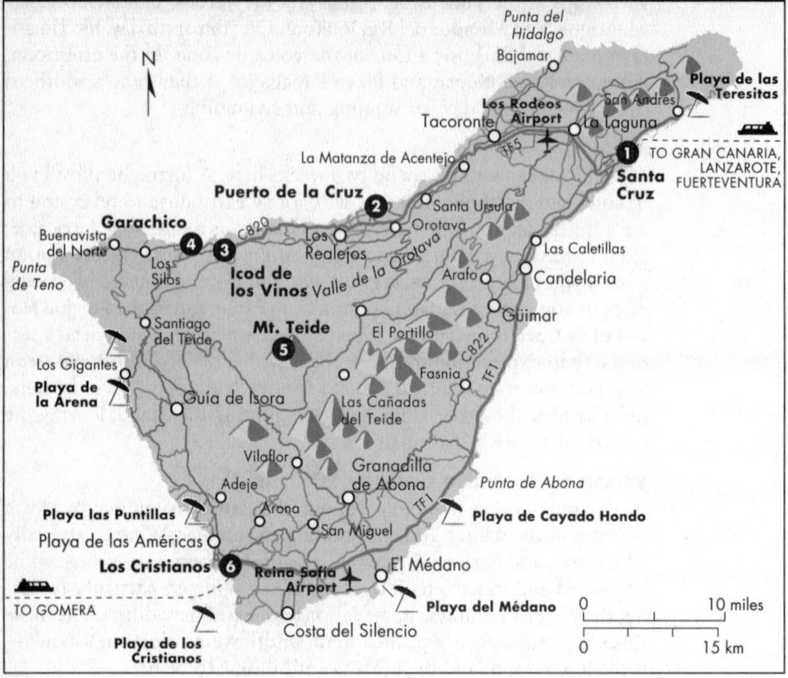

For two weeks before Lent each year, during Carnival, Santa Cruz throbs to a Latin beat emanating from this plaza.

Primitive ceramics and mummies are on display at the **Museo de la Naturaleza y el Hombre** (Museum of Nature and Man). The ancient Guanches mummified their dead by rubbing the bodies with pine resin and salt and leaving them in the sun to dry for two weeks. ✉ *Fuentes Morales s/n,* ☎ *922/209320.* 🎫 *400 ptas.; free Sun.* ⏲ *Tues.–Sun. 10–8.*

The **Iglesia de la Concepción,** or Church of the Conception (✉ Plaza de la Iglesia), noted for its six-story Moorish bell tower, was closed for restoration at press time but should be open by 2001. It's part of a massive urban-renewal project that has already razed blocks of slums in this area.

The colorful city market **Mercado de Nuestra Señora de Africa,** or Market of Our Lady of Africa (✉ Avda. de San Sebastián), is part bazaar and part food emporium. Stalls outside sell household goods; inside, stands selling everything from flowers to canaries are arranged around a sunny patio. Downstairs, a stroll through the seafood section will acquaint you with the local fish. A flea market with antiques and secondhand goods is held here on Sunday. The market is open daily from 6 AM to 2 PM.

Old masters and modern works are housed in the two-story **Museo de Bellas Artes** (Museum of Fine Arts), including canvases by Breughel and Rivera. Many works depict local events. The museum is on the Plaza Príncipe de Asturias. ✉ *José Murphy 12,* ☎ *922/244358.* 🎫 *Free.* ⏲ *Weekdays 10–8.*

A plaza on the northern outskirts of town preserves 18th-century cannons on the site of what was the **Paso Alto Fortress.** In 1794 these weapons held off an attack led by Britain's Admiral Nelson; the cannon on the right fired the shot that cost Nelson his right arm.

Santa Cruz's beach, **Las Teresitas,** is about 7 km (4½ mi) northeast of the city, near the town of San Andrés, and is especially popular with local families. It was created using white sand imported from the Sahara and planted with palms.

OFF THE BEATEN PATH

LA LAGUNA—The university town of La Laguna was the first capital of Tenerife and retains many colonial buildings along Calle San Agustín. One of these buildings, the 400-year-old colonial home of a former slave trader, was reopened as the **Tenerife Museo de Historia** (Tenerife History Museum). Here you can see antique navigational maps and learn the evolution of the island's economy. It's just 5 km (3 mi) northwest of Santa Cruz. Afterward, soak up the sun and the academic ambience at the coffee shops and bars frequented by local students. ✉ *C. San Agustín 22,* ☏ *922/825949.* *400 ptas.; free Sun.* ⏲ *Tues.–Sun. 10–8.*

Dining and Lodging

After dinner, you may want to kick back in the **Condal & Peñamil House** (✉ Callejón del Combate, ☏ 92/224–4976). Waitresses dress like the city's early 19th-century *pureras* (cigar rollers) in this civilized tea-and-cigar café on a pleasant pedestrian alley: in garb the color of *café con leche,* they deliver inexpensive liqueurs and toasted baguettes with jam. An interesting menu option called "Copa, Café y Puro" combines brandy, whiskey, or rum, a specialty coffee, and a select cigar.

$$$$ ★ ✕ **El Coto de Antonio.** One of the best restaurants in the Canaries, this place puts a gourmet spin on local dishes and combines elegant dining with the coziness of a tavern. Dip into a succulent earthenware pot of seafood stew, enhanced with potatoes, yams, blanched *gofio,* and cheese; or order the house specialty, *pejines* (similar to sardines), dried in the sun, soaked in liquor, and served flambé at your table. ✉ *C. de General Goded 13,* ☏ *922/272105. AE, DC, MC, V. Closed Sun.*

$$ ✕ **Los Troncos.** In a middle-class neighborhood near the bullring is one of the few restaurants in Santa Cruz serving Canarian cuisine. You're greeted by a white Andalusian entryway; inside, steak and spare ribs are grilled to perfection. ✉ *C. de General Goded 17,* ☏ *922/284152. AE, DC, MC, V.*

$$$$ **Mencey.** "Mencey" was the ancient Guanches' name for their kings, and you may well feel like one at this grandiose, beige stucco-and-marble hotel. Crystal chandeliers and gold-leaf columns ornament the lobby, behind which is a placid interior courtyard with a fountain. The rooms are furnished à la Louis XIV. ✉ *Dr. José Naveiras 38, 38004,* ☏ *922/276700,* FAX *922/280017. 298 rooms. Restaurant, bar, pool, tennis court, casino. AE, DC, MC, V.*

$$ **Taburiente.** Across the street from the city park, this hotel is favored by those with early morning flights at Los Rodeos Airport. The white-marble lobby is luxurious, and the rooms are large and comfortable. Try to get one with a balcony facing the park. ✉ *Dr. José Naveiras 24A, 38001,* ☏ *922/276000,* FAX *922/270562. 116 rooms. Restaurant, pool, sauna. AE, MC, V.*

Nightlife and the Arts

Avenida Anaga, facing the port, is the core of Santa Cruz nightlife. For about seven blocks beginning at Plaza España, Anaga crawls with upscale disco-bars, perfect for cocktails and movement. The most prominent venues are BB+, Mastil, Nooctua, and The Camel Bar; a five-minute stroll will tell you all you need to know.

Outdoor Activities and Sports

DIVING

Call **Club Nautico** (☎ 922/273700) for information on diving and underwater fishing.

GOLF

Club de Golf El Peñon (☎ 922/636487) is open to nonmembers on weekdays from 8 to 1 only. Reservations are essential. The club is near the northern airport, between La Laguna and Tacorante at Guamasa.

HORSEBACK RIDING

The **Club Hípica La Atalaya** (✉ La Luna 88, La Laguna, ☎ 922/253997), on the outskirts of Santa Cruz, can help arrange horseback excursions.

Puerto de la Cruz

❷ *36 km (22 mi) west of Santa Cruz.*

Puerto de la Cruz is the oldest resort in the Canaries. Despite mass tourism, it has retained some of its Spanish charm and island character. The old sections of town have colonial plazas and *paseos* for evening strolls.

Because Puerto de la Cruz has uninviting black beaches, the town commissioned Lanzarote artist César Manrique in 1965 to build **Lago Martianez,** a forerunner of today's water parks. It's an immense, immensely fun public pool on the waterfront, complete with landscaped islands, bridges, and a volcano-like fountain that sprays sky-high. The complex also includes a restaurant-nightclub and several smaller pools.

Stroll from Lago Martianez along the coastal walkway until you reach the **Plaza de la Iglesia,** beautifully landscaped with flowering plants. Here you can stop at the **tourist office** for a copy of a walking tour that details all of Puerto's architecturally important buildings.

Loro Parque is a subtropical garden with 1,300 parrots, many of which are trained to ride bicycles and perform other tricks. Within the garden is one of Europe's largest aquariums, with an underwater tunnel and a dolphin show, as well as a replica of a village in Thailand. ✉ *Puerto de la Cruz,* ☎ *922/373841.* *2,600 ptas.* *Daily 8:30–5.*

Filled with thousands of varieties of tropical trees and plants—not to mention sonorous birds—the **Jardin de Aclimatación de La Orotava** (Orotava Botanical Garden) was founded in 1788, on the orders of King Carlos III, to propagate warm-climate species brought back to Spain from the Americas. The grounds are perfectly maintained, and each species is meticulously labeled. ✉ *Calle Retama 2,* ☎ *922/383572.* *100 ptas.* *Oct.–Mar., daily 9–6; Apr.–Sept., daily 9–7.*

Wine lovers should make a point of visiting the **Casa de Vino La Baranda,** located about halfway between Puerto de la Cruz and Los Rodeos Airport, at the El Sauzal exit on the main highway. Opened by the Canary Islands' government in 1996 to promote local vintners, it includes a wine museum, shop, and tasting room, where for a small fee you can sample and learn about some of Tenerife's best wines. The complex also houses a tapas bar and a gourmet restaurant specializing in nouvelle Canarian cuisine. ✉ *Autopista General del Norte, Km 21,* ☎ *922/572535.* *Tues.–Sat. 11–10, Sun. 11–6.*

Dining and Lodging

$$$ ✕ **La Magnolia.** Named for its proximity to the botanical garden, La Magnolia offers dining in a garden or a simply decorated dining room. The open kitchen, specializing in Catalan and international cuisine, serves

huge platters of seafood in garlicky sauces. ✉ *Avda. Marqués de Villanueva del Prado s/n,* ☎ *922/385614. AE, DC, MC, V.*

$$$ ✕ **Mi Vaca y Yo.** The name, "My Cow and I," hints at the outdoor summer feast you can put together at this laid-back, plant-filled farmhouse. Few places in the city combine such great food with such a friendly atmosphere. With something for everyone (including finicky kids), the menu presents tasty barbecued beef and a huge variety of fried and grilled fish as well as spaghetti, pizza, chocolate cake, and Canarian meringue cookies. It's popular with local families. ✉ *Cruz Verde 3,* ☎ *922/385247. AE, DC, MC, V.*

$$ ✕ **Casa de Miranda.** Just off the central square, this restored house can trace its history back to 1730. On the ground floor is an inviting tapas bar, strung with hams, gourds, and garlands of red peppers; farther inside is a plant-filled patio. Upstairs, the high-ceilinged dining room serves such favorites as filet mignon in pepper sauce and turbot in shrimp sauce. ✉ *Santo Domingo 13,* ☎ *922/373871. AE, DC, MC, V. Closed June.*

$$ ✕ **El Pescador.** This restaurant claims to be located in the oldest house in town, and you'll believe it when you feel the wood floor shake as the waiters walk by. Slatted green shutters, high ceilings, and salsa music create a tropical air. The specialties include avocado stuffed with shrimp. Ask for *papas arrugadas* (wrinkled potatoes) or you'll get French fries. ✉ *Puerto Viejo 8,* ☎ *922/384088. AE, DC, MC, V.*

$$$$ ✕🏨 **Botánico.** The extensive, soothing subtropical garden at this luxury hilltop hotel is famous in its own right. The hotel's plain exterior belies its elegant furnishings, marble baths, and flowery terraces. Owner Wolfgang Kiessling, an honorary consul of Thailand, opened Tenerife's first Thai restaurant, **The Oriental,** on the ground floor. A fine spiral staircase leads to the second-floor restaurant, **La Parilla,** specializing in Spanish cuisine and seafood. The adjacent piano bar has live music nightly. ✉ *Avda. Richard J. Yeoward 1, 38400 Urb. Botánico,* ☎ *922/381400,* FAX *922/381504. 250 rooms. 3 restaurants, bar, minibars, 2 pools, beauty salon, sauna, miniature golf, putting green, 2 tennis courts, health club. AE, DC, MC, V.*

$$$–$$$$ 🏨 **San Felipe.** Eighteen stories tall, the San Felipe has the best location in Puerto de la Cruz—steps from the beach, with million-dollar views of the coast and Mt. Teide. The large rooms have balconies and spacious bathrooms. Rates include an excellent breakfast buffet, served with champagne twice a week. ✉ *Avda. de Colón 22, 38400,* ☎ *922/383311,* FAX *922/373718. 260 rooms. Restaurant, 2 bars, pool, sauna, 2 tennis courts. AE, DC, MC, V.*

$$ 🏨 **Monopol.** You're welcomed here by hibiscus scattered across the front steps. The Monopol has had over a century to perfect its brand of hospitality: built as a private home in 1742, the property opened as a hotel in 1888, and has been run by the same family for more than 70 years. The small, neatly furnished rooms are arranged on four stories with wooden balconies around a verdant central courtyard. Most overlook the sea or one of the town's main squares, Plaza de la Iglesia. ✉ *Quintana 15, 38400,* ☎ *922/384611,* FAX *922/370310. 100 rooms. Restaurant, 2 bars, pool, hot tub. AE, DC, MC, V.*

Nightlife and the Arts

The **Casino Taoro** (✉ Parque Taoro 22, ☎ 922/380550) makes room for gambling in a stately former hotel.

Almost all hotels have live music at night. For dancing, try **Victoria,** at the Hotel Tenerife Playa (✉ Avda. de Colón s/n), a favorite with all age groups, or **Cotton Club** (✉ Avda. Litoral 24), usually jammed with a fast-moving young crowd. The side streets of Avenida Colón are packed with bars and underground clubs; catering mostly to tourists, many offer imported beer, German food, or Irish music. For a more authentic experience, try **Dos Besos** (✉ C. Genovés 12), where you can sip a fruity island drink or sangría to Latin and African rhythms.

Shopping

The largest selection of hand-embroidered tablecloths and place mats is at **Casa Iriarte** (✉ San Juan 17), tucked into the patio of a ramshackle Canarian house.

Icod de los Vinos

❸ *26 km (16 mi) west of Puerto de la Cruz.*

In the quiet town of Icod de los Vinos, attractive plazas rimmed by unspoiled colonial architecture and Canarian pine balconies form the heart of Tenerife's most historic wine district.

A 3,000-year-old **dragon tree** towers 57 ft above the coastal highway, C820. The Guanches worshiped these trees as symbols of fertility and knowledge; the sap, which turns red upon contact with air, was used in healing rituals.

The **Casa Museo del Vino** (✉ Plaza de la Pila 4) is a tasting room where you can sample the sweet local malmsey and other Canary Island wines and cheeses.

Garachico

❹ *5 km (3 mi) west of Icod de los Vinos.*

Garachico is one of the most idyllic and best-preserved towns on the islands. It was the main port of Tenerife until May 5, 1706, when Mt. Teide blew its top, sending twin rivers of lava downhill. One filled Garachico's harbor, and the other destroyed most of the town. Legend has it that the eruption was unleashed by an evil monk.

One of the buildings that withstood the eruption was the **Castillo San Miguel,** a tiny 16th-century fortress on the waterfront. Island crafts, such as embroidery and basketmaking, are demonstrated inside. From the roof you can see the two rivers of lava, now solidified on the mountainside. You can also visit the **Convento de San Francisco,** also unscathed, and the 18th-century parish church of **Santa Ana.**

Mt. Teide

❺ *60 km (36 mi) southwest of Puerto de la Cruz, 63 km (39 mi) north of Playa de las Américas.*

Four roads lead to Mt. Teide from various parts of Tenerife, each getting you to the park in about an hour, but the most beautiful approach is the road from Orotava. As you head out of town into the higher altitudes, banana plantations give way to fruit and almond orchards that bloom in early in the year. Higher up is a fragrant pine forest.

Just a mile uphill from Puerto de la Cruz, Orotava flaunts a row of stately mansions on Calle San Francisco, just north of the Baroque church Nuestra Señora de la Concepción. At the **Casa de los Balcones** (✉ C. San Francisco 3, Orotava), and just across the street at the **Casa del Turista** (✉ C. San Francisco 4), you can see a variety of island craftspeople at work: basketmakers, cigar rollers, and sand painters. 🎫 *Free.* ⏲ *Daily 8:30–6:30.*

You enter the **Parque Nacional del Teide** (Teide National Park) at El Portillo. Exhibits at the visitor center explain the region's natural history; a garden outside labels the flora found within the park. The center also offers trail maps, video presentations, guided hikes, and bus tours. ☎ *922/290129.* ⏲ *Daily 9:15–4.*

The park includes the volcano itself and the **Cañadas del Teide,** a violent jumble of volcanic leftovers from El Teide and the neighboring **Pico Viejo.** These stark landscapes suggest another planet. Within the park one can find blue hills—the result of a process called hydrothermal alteration—spiky, knobby protusions of rock, and different textures and colors of lava.

The bizarre, photogenic rock formations known as the **Roques de García** are especially memorable. A two-hour trail around these rocks that have eroded into fantastic shapes—one of 21 well-marked hikes inside the park—is recommended. A second park information center, near Los Roques de García and next to the Parador Nacional Cañadas del Teide, can provide complete details and trail maps.

A **cable car** carries you close to the top of Mt. Teide. The difficult final 534 ft take about 40 minutes to climb. On the way up, you'll notice sulfur steam vents. The station has a bar and restaurant. ☎ FAX *922/383711.* 🎫 *2,000 ptas.* ⏲ *Daily 9–5; last trip up at 4.*

The trail to the rim of the volcano is closed when it's snowy, usually about four months of the year. You can still get a good view of southern Tenerife and Gran Canaria from the top of the cable-car line, but you'll be confined to the tiny terrace of the bar.

Dining and Lodging

$$ ✕🏨 **Parador Cañadas del Teide.** The rooms in this classic mountain retreat overlook the intriguing rock formations of the Las Cañadas plateau, at the foot of Mt. Teide. It's a privileged position: the only accommodation inside this huge park. The large, inviting rooms have wood floors. A friendly waitstaff in folk costume serves tasty Canarian cuisine in the mountain-view restaurant, **Teide.** ✉ *38300 La Orotava,* ☎ *922/386415,* FAX *922/382352. 37 rooms. Restaurant, bar, cafeteria, pool, sauna, exercise room, chapel. AE, DC, MC, V.*

Shopping

Browse for contemporary island crafts and traditional musical instruments at the government-sponsored shop **Casa Torrehermosa** (✉ Tomás Zerolo 27) in Orotava.

Los Cristianos

❻ *74 km (44 mi) southwest of Santa Cruz, 10 km (6 mi) west of Reina Sofía Airport.*

This is the newest, largest, and sunniest tourist area on Tenerife, with high-rise hotels built chockablock above the beaches. Sun, beaches, and nightlife constitute the attractions here. Playa de Las Américas and Los Cristianos are on the southwestern shore, about 1 km (½ mi) from each other.

The town of **Los Cristianos** has two small crescents of gray sand surrounded by apartment houses. **Playa de las Américas,** around the corner, is a series of man-made yellow-sand beaches protected by an artificial reef.

Los Gigantes, about 12 km (7 mi) north of Playa de las Américas, is a smallish, gray-sand cove surrounded by rocks and towering cliffs.

Aquapark, a huge water park, has tall slides, meandering streams for inner tubes, and swimming pools. ✉ *Avda. Austria 15, San Eugenio Alto,* ☎ *922/715266.* 🎫 *2,100 ptas.* ⏲ *Daily 10–6.*

Dining and Lodging

$$$$ ✕ **El Patio.** This seaside eatery has a spectacular location on the grounds of the Jardín Tropical hotel (☞ *below*). It ranks as the top restaurant on the south coast, serving such treats as cold mussel-cream soup with saffron and duck-liver terrine with pear in Málaga wine. ✉ *Gran Bretaña s/n, San Eugenio, Adeje,* ☎ *922/746061. AE, DC, MC, V. No lunch.*

$$ ★ ✕ **Masía del Mar.** There's no menu here; you simply point to what you want from the vast display of fresh fish and shellfish. Add a salad and a bottle of white wine to the order, and find a seat on the wide terrace. ✉ *Caleta de Adeje, 5 km (3 mi) west of Playa de las Américas,* ☎ *922/710895. AE, DC, MC, V.*

$$$$ ★ 🏨 **Gran Melia Bahía del Duque.** A cross between a Canarian village and an Italian hill town, this sprawling hotel is a striking jumble of pastel houses and palaces, all presided over by a clock tower copied from the Torre de la Concepción in Santa Cruz. The five-story lobby is a marvel in itself, with tropical birds, palm-filled bars, and two glass elevators, and the staff wears traditional Canarian costume. Guest rooms have oversize beds and summery wicker and pine furnishings. The newest of the five restaurants serves Mexican food, something of a rarity in these parts. The hotel can arrange sailing and diving expeditions, and runs boat trips to see the whales that cavort just off the coast. ✉ *Playa del Duque, 38670 Adeje,* ☎ *922/713000,* FAX *922/712616. 362 rooms. 5 restaurants, 4 bars, 4 pools, beauty salon, sauna, miniature golf, tennis court, exercise room, squash, dive shop, boating. AE, DC, MC, V.*

$$$$ 🏨 **Jardín Tropical.** Spread on many levels over several hills, the Jardín Tropical has white turrets and archways, Moorish tile floors, and cascading profusions of bright, flowering plants. The rooms are furnished with carved-pine and wicker furniture and pastel paisley prints; all have balconies. Baths are decorated with colorful Spanish tile. ✉ *Gran Bretaña s/n, San Eugenio, 38670 Adeje,* ☎ *922/746000,* FAX *922/746060. 433 rooms. 5 restaurants, bar, 2 pools, beauty salon, sauna, exercise room. AE, DC, MC, V.*

$$$$ 🏨 **Marco Antonio Palace.** This hotel, one of five in the Mare Nostum Resort complex, occupies the best site on Playa de Los Cristianos. Massive columns and reproduction Greek statues line the entrance and the vast pool, while the six-story lobby is a high-tech synthesis of marble, neon, and chrome. Glass elevators glide up to the rooms, which are filled with black leather and brass. The beds are oversize, the baths are black marble, and every room has a balcony. ✉ *Avda. de las Américas s/n, 38660 Arona,* ☎ *922/757509,* FAX *922/757510. 116 rooms. 2 restaurants (12 within complex), piano bar, pool, beauty salon, sauna, tennis court, exercise room, squash. AE, DC, MC, V.*

$$ 🏨 **Atlantic Playa.** This beachfront hotel near Reina Sofía Airport is a favorite with windsurfers. The lobby is arranged around a rock fountain in an interior atrium; the rooms have separate sleeping and sitting areas, black modern furniture, and terraces. A breakfast buffet is included, and children under 12 stay at half price. ✉ *Avda. Europa 2, 38612 El Médano,* ☎ *922/176234,* FAX *922/176114. 152 rooms. Restaurant, pool, hot tub, sauna, exercise room, squash, windsurfing, recreation room. AE, DC, MC, V.*

Nightlife and the Arts

For gambling on the south island, hit **Casino Playa de las Américas** (✉ Avda. Marítima s/n, ☎ 922/793758), in the Hotel Gran Tenerife.

Most bars in Playa de las Américas are in a three-building complex called Veronica's. Here, places like the Kangaroo Pub, Busby's, and Sgt. Pepper's draw young, rowdy, mostly foreign crowds. The **Banana Garden** (☎ 922/790365) attracts an older but no less lively crowd with live salsa music, and the disco **Prismas** (in the Hotel Tenerife Sol) has become a perennial favorite.

Outdoor Activities and Sports

DIVING

The PADI-licensed school at **Las Palmeras Hotel** (✉ Avda. Marítima, ☎ 922/752948), in Playa de las Américas, has information on diving and underwater fishing.

GOLF

Near Reina Sofía Airport, **Campo Golf de Sur** (☎ 922/738170) has 27 holes, and not far away there are two 18-hole links at the **Amarilla Golf Club** (☎ 922/730319), in San Miguel.

WINDSURFING

Windsurfing rentals and lessons can be arranged at the **SunWind Windsurf School** (☎ 922/176174), in Playa del Médano.

GRAN CANARIA

The circular island of Gran Canaria has three distinct identities. Its capital, Las Palmas, population 370,000, is a thriving business center and shipping port, while the white-sand beaches of the south coast are tourist magnets. The interior is rural.

Las Palmas, the largest city in the Canary Islands, is a multicultural whirlwind, overrun by sailors, tourists, traffic jams, diesel-spewing buses, and hordes of shoppers. One side of the city is lined with docks for huge container ships, while the other harbors the 7-km (4½-mi) Canteras beach.

The south coast, a boxy 1960s development along wide avenues, is a family resort. At the southern tip of the island, the popular Playa del Inglés gives way to the empty dunes of Maspalomas.

The isle's interior is a steep highland that reaches 6,435 ft at Pozo de las Nieves. Although it's green in winter, Gran Canaria does not have the luxurious tropical foliage of the archipelago's western islands.

Las Palmas

❼ *35 km (21 mi) north of Gran Canaria Airport, 60 km (36 mi) north of Maspalomas.*

Las Palmas is strung out for 10 km (6 mi) along two waterfronts of a peninsula. Though most of the action centers on the peninsula's northern end, the sights are clustered around the city's southern edge. Begin in the old quarter, La Vegueta, at the **Plaza Santa Ana,** with its bronze dog statues. You may be surprised to learn that the Canary Islands were named not for the yellow songbirds but for a breed of dog (*canum* in Latin) found here by ancient explorers. The birds were later named after the islands.

The smog-stained **Catedral Santa Ana** (St. Anne's Cathedral) faces the Plaza Santa Ana. The cathedral took four centuries to complete, so the 19th-century exterior with its neoclassical Roman columns contrasts sharply with the Gothic ceiling vaulting of the interior. Baroque statues in the Andalusian style are displayed in the cathedral's **Museo de Arte Sacro** (Museum of Religious Art), which is arranged around a peaceful cloister. Ask the curator to open the *sala capitular* (chapter house) so you can see the 16th-century Valencian tile floor. The treasury is closed to the public. ✉ *Espíritu Santo 20,* ☎ *928/314989.* 💴 *300 ptas.* ⏲ *Weekdays 10–2 and 2:45–4:30, Sat. 9–1:30.*

The **Casa Museo Colón** (Columbus Museum) is housed in a palace where Christopher Columbus may have stayed when he stopped to repair the

Gran Canaria

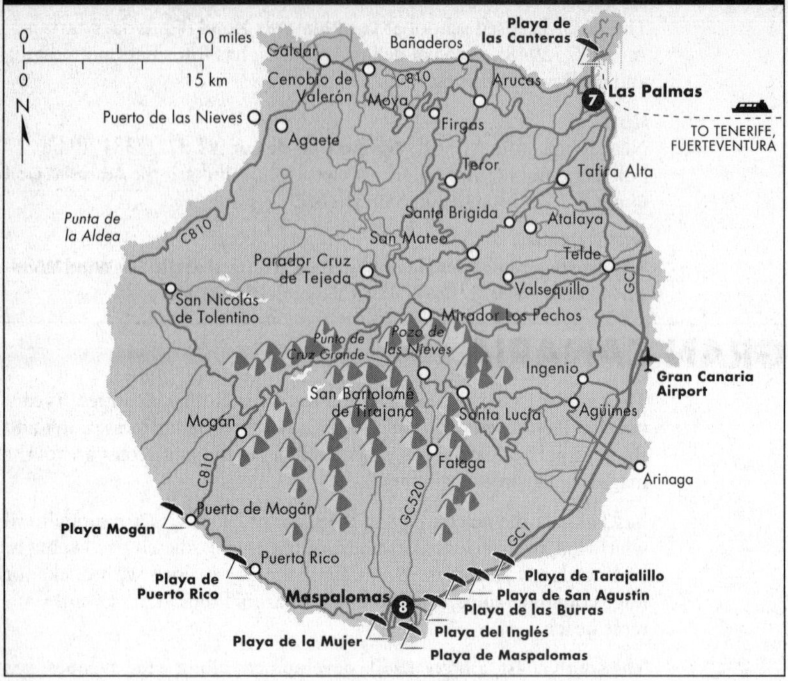

Pinta's rudder. Nautical instruments, copies of early navigational maps, and models of Columbus's three ships are on display. Two rooms hold pre-Columbian artifacts. ✉ *C. Colón 1,* ☎ *928/311255.* 🎫 *Free.* 🕐 *Sept.–July, weekdays 9–6, weekends 9–3. Closed Aug.*

It's only been open since 1991, but the **Centro Atlántico de Arte Moderno** (Atlantic Center for Modern Art) has already earned a name for curating some of the best avant-garde shows in Spain. ✉ *Los Balcones 11,* ☎ *928/311824.* 🎫 *Free.* 🕐 *Tues.–Sat. 10–9, Sun. 10–2.*

It's quite a walk to the other end of town, so you may want to hop one of the many canary-yellow buses, named *guaguas* (pronounced "wawas") in honor of the Guanches. Ride to Parque Santa Catalina or get off at the **Parque Doramas** (stops are listed on big yellow signs; the 2, 3, and the 30 generally cover the entire city) to peek at the elegant Santa Catalina Hotel and Casino. Inside the park is the **Pueblo Canario,** a model village with typical Canarian architecture. Regional folk dances are performed here on Thursday (5–7) and Sunday (11:30–1).

NEED A BREAK?

Whether you're sunning or shopping, Las Palmas can be exhausting. Escape to the tranquil, air-conditioned quiet of the **Casa Suecia Salon de Té** (Swiss Tea House; ✉ Luis Morote 41, near Playa de las Canteras, ☎ 928/271626), with comfortable booths, foreign newspapers, picture windows, delicious pastries and sandwiches, and perhaps the only free coffee refills on the islands.

On a hill north of Parque Santa Catalina, looming over the rather tough port district, is the **Castillo de la Luz,** a fortress built in 1494 (currently closed to the public). Due west of Parque Santa Catalina are the sparkling white sands of **Las Canteras,** a perfect spot for a stroll along the *paseo*.

Beaches

The beaches along Gran Canaria's eastern and southern coasts are the island's major attraction. **Las Canteras,** in Las Palmas, is made safe for swimming by an artificial reef. It can be extremely crowded in summer, but the sand is swept clean every night.

Dining and Lodging

$$$ ✕ **Casa Montesdeoca.** In the heart of the historic quarter, this romantic restaurant is housed in a 14th-century mansion built by a Jewish businessman named Montesdeoca. The hallways are stone labyrinths—during the Inquisition, the Montesdeoca family escaped from their pursuers through hidden doors and secret tunnels. The beautiful outdoor patio is draped with bougainvillea; the wine list features the best bottles from each island; and fresh fish is prepared on an outdoor grill just steps from your table. ✉ *Montesdeoca 10,* ☎ FAX *922/333466. AE, DC, MC, V. Closed Sun.*

$$$ ✕ **Julio.** In this small dining room, decorated with ropes, portholes, and polished wood, you can tuck into 12 different types of shellfish or local fish, such as *cherne* (sea bass) served in a white-wine clam sauce. A different Canarian soup or stew is prepared each day. ✉ *La Naval 132,* ☎ *928/460139. AE, DC, MC, V. Closed Sun.*

$ ✕ **Tapadel.** It's easy to fill up at this classic Spanish tapas bar, with every kind of diversion from paella to calamari to mussels with garlic. To the delight of hungry night owls, it's open until 2 AM. ✉ *Plaza de España 5,* ☎ *928/271640. No credit cards.*

$$$$ 🏨 **Meliá Las Palmas.** Aimed at business and upscale leisure travelers, the Meliá has a superb location at the narrowest point of the isthmus, and offers large, bright rooms. The terrace pool overlooks the sea. ✉ *Gomera 6, 35008,* ☎ *928/267600,* FAX *928/268411. 316 rooms. Restaurant, coffee shop, piano bar, pool, dance club. AE, DC, MC, V.*

$$$ 🏨 **Imperial Playa.** This business-oriented hotel sits on the far end of Las Canteras beach. The bright rooms have Scandinavian furniture and marble baths, and their small terraces have nice beach views. ✉ *Ferreras 1, 35008,* ☎ *928/468854,* FAX *928/469442. 142 rooms. Restaurant, snack bar, minibars, beach. AE, DC, MC, V.*

$$ 🏨 **Apartments Brisamar Canteras.** The best maintained of all the local beach apartments, Brisamar is popular with travelers from Finland. The rooms are merely functional, but they're freshly painted and cheerful. ✉ *Paseo de las Canteras 49, 35010,* ☎ *928/269400,* FAX *928/269404. 52 studio apartments. AE, DC, MC, V.*

Nightlife and the Arts

The **Orquesta Filarmonica de Gran Canaria** (✉ Bravo Murillo 2123, ☎ 928/320513), one of Spain's oldest orchestras, offers an ample program between October and May. Its January festival draws leading musicians from around the world. Ticket information is available at the box office at Teatro Pérez Galdós (✉ Plaza Mercado, ☎ 928/361509).

Gamblers choose the **Gran Casino de Las Palmas** in the Santa Catalina Hotel (✉ León y Castillo 227, Parque Doramas, ☎ 928/291103). The elegant and expensive Restaurant Doramas (☎ 928/233908), inside the casino, will make you feel like a high roller.

Las Palmas has a lively, if sometimes scruffy, nightlife, with most of the bars and discos clustered between Playa de las Canteras and Parque Santa Catalina. **Calle Tómas Miller** is lined with restaurants featuring foods from every corner of the world, and dance music emanates from **Wilson** (✉ C. Franchy Roca) as well as the nearby **Pacha** (✉ C. Simón Bolivar 3), which draws beautiful people with cash to burn on the pricey cover and drinks. The discotheque **Coto,** in the Meliá Las

Palmas (✉ C. Gomera 6, ☎ 928/268050), is alive with a middle-aged international crowd.

Outdoor Activities and Sports

GOLF

Founded in 1891, the **Royal Golf Club** (☎ 928/350104), on the rim of the Bandama crater roughly 15 minutes outside Las Palmas, is Spain's oldest golf course. Redesigned and relocated in 1956, it now has 18 holes, two putting greens, a sports shop, two tennis courts, a restaurant, and a bar.

HORSEBACK RIDING

To rent horses, contact the **Royal Golf Club** (☎ 928/350104), with 48 stables and five riding rings.

Shopping

Gran Canaria has the best duty-free shops in the islands, and a department store, **El Corte Inglés,** on Avenida Mesa y Lopez in central Las Palmas. For more unusual gift items, try **Antigüedades Linares** or **La Fataga,** in the Pueblo Canario, with a good selection of crafts from all over Spain. The glittering form at the southern edge of the beach is Las Palmas's new glass-and-chrome shopping mall, **Las Arenas** (✉ C. Pavia 18, ☎ 928/277008), packed with boutiques, restaurants, and cinemas.

Maspalomas

8 *60 km (36 mi) southwest of Las Palmas, 25 km (15 mi) southwest of Gran Canaria Airport.*

Maspalomas is a built-up beach resort with all the trappings, incongruously backed by empty sand dunes that resemble the Sahara. Despite beachfront overdevelopment in the town, it retains appealing stretches of isolated beach on the outskirts, as well as a bird sanctuary. In recent years, German tour operators, who bring masses of visitors, have helped place a new emphasis on protecting the environment.

Holiday World amusement park has bumper cars and other carnival rides, including a Ferris wheel that kids will see from miles away. ✉ *Carretera General, Campo Internacional Lote 18, Maspalomas,* ☎ *928/767176,* FAX *928/766355.* *1,950 ptas.; children 1,250 ptas.* *Daily 6 PM–midnight.*

AquaSur is the largest water park in the Canary Islands. It has wave pools, slides, and everything else splash-related. ✉ *Carretera Palomitas Park,* ☎ *92/814–0525,* *1,800 ptas.; children 1,150 ptas.* *Daily 10–5.*

Ocean Park is next to Holiday World, closer to town than AquaSur but not as extensive. There's a branch of this park, called **Aqua Park,** in the south-coast resort town of Puerto Rico. ✉ *Av. Touroperator Tui,* ☎ *928/764361,* FAX *928/765331.* *1,600 ptas.; children 900 ptas.* *Daily 10–5.*

Palmitos Park is part botanical garden and part zoo, with tropical birds and a butterfly house. Trained parrots perform. ✉ *Carretera Palmitos, 6 km (4 mi) inland from Maspalomas,* ☎ *928/143050.* *2,175 ptas.; children 1,225 ptas.* *Daily 9–6.*

Beaches

Playa de Tarajalillo, with alternating areas of black sand and gravel, is the first beach of the southern resort area and a popular choice with local families. **Playa de San Agustín** is a 1-km (½-mi) strip of black sand fringed with a palm garden; it has rental areas for sailboards, pedal boats, and lounge chairs. **Playa de las Burras** is a gray-sand beach surrounding a crescent-shaped harbor sometimes used by local fishermen.

★ **Playa del Inglés** is Gran Canaria's most famous beach. Its white sands, more than 3 km (2 mi) long, swarm with beach-chair rentals, ice cream vendors, and fast-food restaurants. West of here are sand dunes and a signposted nude beach.

The **Maspalomas** beach, a 1-km (½-mi) stretch of golden sand, is bordered by endless dunes that provide a sense of isolation and refuge from the chaos of other Canarian resorts. Dozens of varieties of native birds and plants also take refuge in a lagoon alongside the dunes. The western edge of Maspalomas is marked by a lighthouse. **Playa de la Mujer,** a rocky beach around the point from Maspalomas, is a good place to watch the sunset.

All these beaches abut one another, and you can walk them in sequence (hindered only by a pair of rocky dividers) along the shore. A boardwalk links Playa de Tarajillo to the rest of the beaches until the dunes separate it from the Maspalomas beach and Playa de la Mujer.

Dining and Lodging

$$ ✕ **Loopy's Tavern.** An island tradition that few travelers can resist, Loopy's is styled as an American steak house, with friendly waiters, imaginative cocktails, a western motif, and great meat. Try the shish kebabs, which are served dangling from a hook. ✉ *Las Retamas 7, San Agustín,* ☎ *928/762892. MC, V.*

$$ ★ ✕ **Tenderete II.** Canarian cuisine is cherished at Tenderete, one of the islands' better places to order fresh *gofio,* made here with roasted-corn flour and fish broth. The first course consists of typical soups and stews, and the main course is always fish, grilled or baked in rock salt. Pick it out from the display hooks inside. Wines from Lanzarote, El Hierro, and Tenerife are available. ✉ *Avda. de Tirajana 5, Edificio Aloe,* ☎ *928/761460. AE, DC, MC, V.*

$$$$ 🏨 **Don Gregory.** This modern, eight-story, brown-brick hotel sits on the crescent-shaped Las Burras beach, and the atmosphere is appropriately relaxed. The large, carpeted rooms have blond-wood furniture, marble baths, and large terraces; all overlook the beach. ✉ *Las Dalias 11, 35100,* ☎ *928/773877,* FAX *928/769996. 244 rooms. Restaurant, bar, pool, tennis court, beach. AE, DC, MC, V.*

$$$$ ★ 🏨 **Palm Beach.** The most sophisticated and luxurious hotel in the Canary Islands, the Palm Beach is a stone's throw from the edge of Maspalomas beach. Its backyard is a thousand-year-old palm oasis, arranged around the pool. The pleasant chirping of birds wafts from the sanctuary and nearby pond. The tastefully decorated rooms have huge closets and large marble baths; terraces overlook the sea or the palms. ✉ *Avda. del Oasis s/n, 35106,* ☎ *928/140806,* FAX *928/141808. 358 rooms. Restaurant, bar, pool, beauty salon, hot tub, sauna, tennis court, exercise room, beach. AE, DC, MC, V.*

$$$ 🏨 **Buenaventura.** A veritable wonderland of color, music, pool parties, and dancing, this resort may be the happiest place on the Playa del Inglés. The rooms are a bright (and appropriate) canary yellow, with flowers and big sliding-glass doors opening onto pool-view balconies. With a thatched-roof poolside bar that energizes sunbathers with thumping music from noon 'til late, Buenaventura is popular with young couples, singles, and anyone who doesn't mind late-night laughter in the halls. ✉ *Plaza Ansite, C. Ganigo 6, 35100,* ☎ *928/763450,* FAX *928/768348. 724 rooms. 4 restaurants, bar, 2 pools, sauna, 4 tennis courts, table tennis, beauty salon, billiards, dance club, playground. AE, DC, MC, V.*

Nightlife

Gamblers go to the **Casino Gran Canaria** (✉ La Retama 3, Playa de San Agustín, ☎ 928/762724) in the Hotel Tamarindos, in San Agustín.

Hot nightspots on the south coast include **Spider** (✉ Avda. Italia s/n, Playa del Inglés), which plays Euro-techno to an international college crowd, and the slightly more sedate **San Agustín Beach Club** (✉ Playa Cocoteros s/n), with less-frenetic dancing to the sounds of Euro-pop. **La Bamba** (✉ Avda. Tirajana s/n, Playa del Inglés) is your best bet for salsa, meringue, and a general Latino ambience.

Outdoor Activities and Sports

GOLF

The 18-hole **Maspalomas Campo de Golf** (☎ 928/762581) is near the dunes.

HORSEBACK RIDING

To rent horses, contact the **Palmitos Park** (✉ Carretera Palmitos, about 6 km [4 mi] inland from Maspalomas, ☎ 928/760458).

SAILING

The famous **Escuela de Vela de Puerto Rico** sailing school (☎ 928/560772), where Spain's 1984 Olympic gold medalists trained and teach, is at Puerto Rico, about 13 km (8 mi) west of Maspalomas.

WINDSURFING

You can rent windsurfing equipment from the **Club Mistral** at the Hotel Bahía Feliz (✉ Carretera del Sur, Km 44, Playa del Tarajalillo, 35479, ☎ 928/764600, FAX 928/764612).

Central Highlands

From Maspalomas, take Route GC520 toward Fataga for a good drive through the center of the island. This is sagebrush country, with interesting rock formations and cacti. A *mirador* (lookout) about 7 km (4½ mi) uphill offers views of the coast and mountains.

San Bartolomé de Tirajana

23 km (14 mi) north of Maspalomas, 20 km (12 mi) east of Cruz de San Antonio.

The administrative center of the south coast, San Bartolomé de Tirajana is an attractive town planted with pink geraniums. Its Sunday-morning market, in front of the church, is popular with travelers, who can pick up tropical produce and island crafts. Just to the east, the village of **Santa Lucía** is filled with crafts shops and has a small museum devoted to Guanche artifacts.

En Route Drive up to the Cruz Grande summit on GC520. To the left are several of the island's reservoirs, known as the lakes of Gran Canaria; they're stocked with trout, and you can fish in them with a permit from the forest service, ICONA (☎ 928/248735).

Drive along GC520 in the direction of Tejeda, past rural mountain villages. On the right is the spike-shape Roque Nublo, an eroded volcanic chimney worshiped by the Guanches.

Tejeda

About 7 km (4 ½ mi) southwest of Las Palmas de Gran Canaria.

At the village of Tejeda, the road begins to ascend through a pine forest dotted with picnic spots to the **Parador Cruz de Tejeda,** currently awaiting renovation. From the parador, continue uphill about 21 km (13 mi) to the **Mirador Pico de las Nieves,** the highest lookout on Gran

Canaria. Here, too, is the **Pozo de la Nieve,** a well built by clergymen in 1699 to store snow.

OFF THE BEATEN PATH

ARTENARA – From the road leading to the parador, follow signs west to the village of Artenara (about 13 km [8 mi]) for nonstop great views of the rocky valley and its salient chimney-like formations. You can see both Roque Nublo and Roque Ventaiga, sitting like a temple on a long ridge in the valley. Artenara itself is unremarkable except for its many houses built cave-style into the mountainside. The entrance to the restaurant **Mirador de la Silla** (☎ 928/666108) takes you through a long tunnel, on the far side of which you can sit in the sun and enjoy a spectacular view—more than worth the trip to Artenara. Canarian specialties are served at bargain prices.

Lodging

$$ **El Refugio.** Ideal for excursions into Roque Nublo National Park, the Refuge does quite nicely while the illustrious parador across the street is out of commission. Decorated in American country style, it's small, homey, and rents bikes to guests. The restaurant serves traditional local cuisine, including *potaje canario,* a vegetable soup. ✉ *Cruz de Tejeda s/n,* ☎ *928/666513,* FAX *928/666520. 10 rooms. Restaurant, pool, sauna, miniature golf, bicycles. AE, DC, MC, V.*

San Mateo

15 km (9 mi) northeast of Parador Cruz de Tejeda.

From Tejeda, the road winds down to San Mateo, home to the **Casa Cho Zacarias** museum of rural life and a winery. The museum is open Monday–Saturday 9–1. Pass **Santa Brigida** and turn right toward the golf club on the rim of the Bandama crater. Continue to the village of **Atalaya,** with cave houses and pottery workshops.

Tafira Alta

7 km (4½ mi) west of Las Palmas.

Along the main road leading into Las Palmas from San Mateo is Tafira Alta, an exclusive enclave of the city's wealthy families. Here are the botanical gardens of the **Jardín Canario Viero y Clavijo,** with a respected collection of plants from all the Atlantic islands grouped in their natural habitats. ⏲ *Daily 9–6.*

The North Coast

Leaving Las Palmas by the northern road, you pass grim shantytowns before reaching the banana plantations of the coastal route. This is the greenest part of the island and is worth the trip for a seaside lunch in the pleasant village of Agaete.

Arucas

13 km (8 mi) west of Las Palmas.

An agricultural center, Arucas is the island's third-largest town. Its great, gray-stone Gothic church looks wildly out of place among the small white houses.

Teror

10 km (6 mi) south of Arucas.

Amid the most verdant vegetation on Gran Canaria is the village of Teror, an obligatory stop on all island tours. In the 18th-century church of **Nuestra Señora del Pino** (Our Lady of the Pine Tree), Gran Canaria's patron saint is seated on a silver throne above the altar. The statue, said to have been found in a pine tree in the 15th century, is now taken out for special fiestas.

As you head west, you'll see increasingly tropical foliage in the hillside villages of **Firgas** and **Moya.**

SHOPPING

Parfumes Oceano, near the church parking lot in the village of Teror, sells perfumes made locally from tropical flowers.

Agaete

8 km (5 mi) southwest of Galdar.

The quiet, leafy town of Agaete is famous for the annual fiesta of the *rama* (branch), on August 4, in which pine branches from the island's upper slopes are carried to the town by dancing crowds. The ritual is a variation on a pre-Christian rain dance that was used by the Guanches in times of drought.

Just beyond Agaete is **Puerto de las Nieves** (Port of the Snows), where painted boats bob in the tiny harbor and larger ferries depart for Tenerife. The short Avenida de las Poetas leads to an old windmill on the point. Look for the rocky point called the **Dedo de Dios** (Finger of God), just off the tall cliffs.

LANZAROTE

With mostly solidified lava and dark, disconcerting dunes, Lanzarote's interior is right out of a science-fiction film. There are no springs or lakes, and it rarely rains, so all fresh water comes from desalination plants. Despite its surreal and sometimes intimidating volcanic landscape, Lanzarote—the fourth-largest Canary—has turned itself into an inviting resort through good planning, an emphasis on outdoor adventure, and conservation of its natural beauty. No buildings over four stories are allowed, leaving views of the spectacular geology unobstructed.

Lanzarote was named for the Italian explorer Lancelotto Alocello, who arrived in the 14th century. The founder of modern-day Lanzarote, however, was artist and architect César Manrique, the unofficial artistic guru of the Canary Islands. Manrique's aesthetic hand is evident throughout Lanzarote; he designed most of the tourist attractions and convinced authorities to require all new buildings to be painted white with green trim to suggest coolness and fertility. He also led the fight against overdevelopment.

Arrecife

6 km (4 mi) east of the airport.

The island's cinderblock capital, Arrecife (named for its many reefs), is the most unattractive part of Lanzarote. The well-organized **tourist office,** in the municipal park, can guide you toward the highlights.

The **Castillo San Gabriel** is a double-walled fortress once used to keep pirates at bay. It now houses an archaeology museum, where you can see copies of some of the Guanche cave drawings found on Lanzarote. 🎫 *250 ptas.* ⏲ *Weekdays 9–1 and 5–8.*

The old, waterfront fortress **Castillo San José** was turned into the stunning **Museo de Arte Contemporáneo** (Museum of Contemporary Art) by Manrique, one of whose paintings is on display along with other modern Spanish works. Go down the space-tunnel staircase for a look at the glass-walled, harbor-view restaurant. ✉ *Avda. de Naos s/n,* ☎ *928/812321.* 🎫 *Free.* ⏲ *Museum daily 11–9.*

Dining

$$$ ✕ **Castillo San José.** Black-and-white furniture, glass walls, and modern art give this remodeled fortress an elegant feel. In the equally sophisticated restaurant, try the cold avocado soup with caviar or the salmon steak wrapped in cured ham. ✉ *C. Puerta de Naos s/n,* ☎ *928/812321. AE, MC, V.*

Costa Teguise

7 km (4½ mi) northeast of Arrecife.

Costa Teguise is a tasteful green-and-white complex of apartments and a few large hotels. Each of the chimneys on the bungalows has a different decorative shape. King Juan Carlos owns a villa here, near the Meliá Salinas hotel. Costa Teguise has several small beaches; the best is Las Cucharas.

The **Jardín de Cactus** (Cactus Garden), just north of Costa Teguise between Guatiza and Mala, was Manrique's last creation for Lanzarote. The giant metal cactus that marks the entrance comes perilously close to tacky, but the gardens artfully display nearly 10,000 cacti. A restored windmill grinds and sells *gofio.* ☎ *928/529397.* 🎟 *500 ptas.* ⏲ *Daily 10–5:45.*

Playa de la Garita, not far from the Jardín de Cactus, is a wide bay of crystal water favored by surfers in winter and snorkelers in summer.

★ **Los Jameos del Agua** (water caverns), 15 km (9 mi) north of the Costa Teguise, is a natural wonder created when molten lava streamed through an underground tunnel and hissed into the sea. Eerie music creates a mysterious aura as you explore, and at 11 PM on Tuesday, Friday, and Saturday, musicians appear for live Canarian folk tunes in this incomparable acoustic environment. Look for the tiny white crabs on the rocks in the underground lake—this species, a blind albino crab, is found nowhere else in the world. The Casa de los Volcanes is a good museum of volcanic science. ☎ *928/835010.* 🎟 *Days 1,000 ptas., nights 1,100 ptas.* ⏲ *Sun., Mon., Wed., and Thurs. 9:30–6:45; Tues., Fri., and Sat. 9:30–6:45 and 7 PM–3 AM.*

★ ☺ Across the highway from the Jameos del Agua, the **Cuevas Verdes** (Green Caves) are for more adventurous cave explorers. Guided walks take you through a 1-km (½-mi) section of underground volcanic passageway. Due to the nature of volcanic rock, no stalactites have formed, but this gentle spelunk is one of the best tours on the island. ☎ *928/848484.* 🎟 *1,000 ptas.* ⏲ *Daily 10–6; last tour at 5.*

The little fishing village of **Orzola** is 9 km (5½ mi) north of Jameo del Agua. Small boat excursions leave here each day for the neighboring islet of **La Graciosa,** with only 500 residents and plenty of quiet beaches. A look at La Graciosa from the wonderful **Mirador del Río** may convince you to make the trip; three smaller protected isles—Montaña Clara, Legranza (the Canary closest to Europe), and Roque del Este—are also visible from this Manrique-designed lookout. A glassed-in café allows protected perusal. 🎟 *400 ptas.* ⏲ *Daily 10–5:45.*

☺ **Guinate Tropical Park,** in the northern part of the island, has 1,300 species of exotic birds and animals and great views of La Graciosa. ☎ *928/835500.* ⏲ *Daily 10–5.*

Dining and Lodging

$$$ ✕ **La Jordana.** This unpretentious venue with a beamed ceiling and white walls is one of Lanzarote's most popular dining spots. The fare is international, with French touches. Try the homemade pâté, veal with

apples, or locally caught cherne in orange sauce. ✉ *Centro Comercial Lanzarote Bay, Los Geranios 10–11,* ☎ *928/590328. AE, MC, V. Closed Sun. and Sept.*

$$ ✕ **El Pescador.** You can't miss this place; local cats will lead you here as they prowl neighboring alleys for tasty scraps. With the sights, sounds, and smells of the marina so close by, you know upon entering that you're getting the freshest of fish. Carved wooden ceilings, fishnets on the walls, and simple benches at long plank tables make El Pescador an authentic haunt for local fishermen. ✉ *Centro Comercial Pueblo Marino,* ☎ *no phone. No credit cards. Closed Mon.*

$$ ✕ **Grill Casa Blanca.** Inside a tiny octagonal house, this restaurant has the atmosphere of an English country cottage, with stained-wood floors and wreaths of dried flowers. You can watch the chef in the open kitchen of the main dining room. Try the avocado-and-shrimp salad, steak with green peppercorns, or local fish dishes. ✉ *Las Olas 4,* ☎ *928/590155. MC, V. No lunch.*

$$$$ ★ ✕🏨 **Gran Meliá Salinas.** A stunning hotel built around an interior tropical garden with hanging vines, palms, waterfalls, and songbirds, the Meliá Salinas offers a chance to rub elbows with vacationing European political leaders. The rooms have louvered closets and doors and large, flower-filled, sea-view terraces. The hotel's gourmet restaurant, La Graciosa, is Lanzarote's swankiest dining spot; savor giant prawns, duck breast in plum sauce, or halibut wrapped in chard. The private garden villas pamper utterly, with 24-hour butler service and individual pools. ✉ *Urb. Costa Teguise 35509,* ☎ *928/590040,* FAX *928/590390. 310 rooms, 10 villas. 3 restaurants, 2 bars, pool, beauty salon, sauna, putting green, golf privileges, tennis court, archery, basketball, exercise room, beach. AE, DC, MC, V.*

$$$–$$$$ 🏨 **Teguise Playa.** Don't be put off by this hotel's cold, glass exterior; the six-story lobby is filled with plants, and the staff is friendly. The rooms have white-tile floors and bamboo furniture, and each has a geranium-filled terrace with a sea view over the beach. ✉ *Avda. del Jabillo s/n, Urb. Costa Teguise 35509,* ☎ *928/590654,* FAX *928/590979. 314 rooms. Restaurant, 2 bars, 2 pools, beauty salon, hot tub, sauna, tennis court, exercise room, squash, beach. AE, DC, MC, V.*

Outdoor Activities and Sports

DIVING

The island's only official diving center is at Las Cucharas. **Diving Lanzarote** (☎ 928/590407) is run by a German who speaks perfect English; he rents equipment, leads dives, and offers a certification course.

GOLF

Lanzarote's 18-hole **Campo de Golf Costa Teguise** (☎ 928/590512) is just outside the Costa Teguise development and features unusual sand traps filled with black-lava cinders.

SURFING

Some of the best surfing in the world is found on Lanzarote's west coast. Ride the waves at **La Santa Surf** (☎ 928/840279).

WINDSURFING

You can arrange windsurfing lessons and rent equipment from the **Lanzarote Surf Company** (☎ 928/591974) at Las Cucharas beach.

Shopping

For a good selection of island crafts, drop by the open market in the village of **Teguise** on Sunday between 10 and 2. Some vendors set up stalls in the plaza; others simply lay out a blanket in the street and sell embroidered tablecloths, leather goods, costume jewelry, African masks, and thousands of other items.

Puerto del Carmen

11 km (7 mi) southwest of Arrecife.

Most beach-bound travelers to Lanzarote head to the sandy strands of the Puerto del Carmen area. **Playa Grande,** the main beach, is a long strip of yellow sand where you can rent sailboards, Jet Skis, skates, and lounge chairs. It's backed by a 3-km (2-mi) stretch of souvenir shops and restaurants of every national persuasion. **Playa de los Pocillos** is slightly north of Puerto del Carmen and the site of most of the area's development; hotels and apartments are restricted, however, to the other side of the highway, leaving the 2-km (1-mi) yellow-sand beach surprisingly pristine. **Playa Matagorda,** the northern extension of Playa de los Pocillos, has alternating sections of gravel and gray sand; it's favored by surf fishermen.

Dining and Lodging

$$$ ✕ **La Casa Roja.** A harborside terrace makes this place a favorite; there's also a cozy upstairs dining room decorated with old black-and-white photos of Puerto del Carmen. The authentically Canarian cuisine centers on fresh fish and seafood. ✉ *Varadero s/n,* ☏ *928/596114. AE, DC, MC, V.*

$$ ✕ **El Varadero.** This converted fishermen's warehouse on the tiny harbor has an informal marine atmosphere. The food is typically Canarian, with fresh fish and *papas arrugadas* in ready supply. The tapas bar at the entrance is littered with toothpicks and napkins dropped by a lively crowd enjoying bite-size portions of marinated *calamares* and *pulpo en tinto* (octopus in its own ink). ✉ *Varadero 26,* ☏ *928/513162. MC, V.*

$$$$ ★ 🏨 **Los Jameos Playa.** The huge lobby atrium here is typically Canarian, with brown wooden balconies overlooking tall palms and a wide wooden staircase leading outside. The central outdoor area—featuring fun pools, lots of shady bars, and white villas with light-blue trim—is pure Lanzarote. Most of the stylish new rooms have terraces overlooking the garden, pool, or beach. There's a nude zone on the grounds. ✉ *Playa de los Pocillos, 35510 Puerto del Carmen,* ☏ *928/511717,* FAX *928/514219. 530 rooms. Restaurant, piano bar, pool, beauty salon, sauna, tennis court, exercise room, playground. AE, DC, MC, V.*

$$ 🏨 **Los Fariones.** The granddaddy of Lanzarote's resorts has retained an exclusive, elegant atmosphere as its tropical gardens designed by César Manrique have matured. Rooms are smallish, with rattan furniture and linoleum flooring, but each has a terrace with views of the gardens and sea. Guests may use the sports center a block away, which has five tennis courts, a heated pool, a gym, and a sauna. ✉ *Roque del Oeste 1, 35510 Puerto del Carmen,* ☏ *928/510175,* FAX *928/510202. 248 rooms. Restaurant, bar, pool, beauty salon, hot tub, massage, squash, miniature golf, tennis court, exercise room, billiards. AE, DC, MC, V.*

Nightlife and the Arts

Most nightlife in Lanzarote centers on the hotel bars, all of which feature live music. For dancing, try **Tiffany's** (✉ Avda. de Suiza 2, Playa de los Pocillos, ☏ 928/511344), an upscale club for all ages, or the **Big Apple** (✉ Avda. de las Playas, ☏ no phone) in the Centro Comercial Atlántico, with a good mix of young Spaniards and foreigners. The **Casino** (✉ Avda. de las Playas, ☏ no phone) is a classic spot.

Outdoor Activities and Sports

Mountain biking has become very popular here in the last few years and is actually a very practical way to tour the island, as Lanzarote is not particularly hilly. You can rent bikes at **Fire Mountain Biking** (☏ 928/512267), in Puerto del Carmen.

Tahíche

5 km (3 mi) south of Teguise.

In Tahíche, the unusual former home of artist Manrique has been opened to visitors as the **Fundación César Manrique.** On display are a collection of Manrique's paintings and sculptures, as well as works by other 20th-century artists. But the real attraction is the house itself, designed by Manrique to blend with the volcanic landscape. Built into a series of lower-level caves, with palm trees ascending into the upper floor, are a series of unusual, whitewashed living rooms. The maze of spaces invites you to walk from room to room through indoor tunnels and outdoor courtyards. ✉ *Carretera Tahíche–San Bartolomé, 2 km (1 mi) west of Tahíche,* ☏ *928/843138.* 🎫 *1,000 ptas.* ⏲ *Mon.–Sat. 10–6, Sun. 10–3.*

Yaiza

13 km (8 mi) west of Puerto del Carmen.

Yaiza is a quiet, whitewashed village with good restaurants. Largely destroyed by a river of lava in the 1700s, it's best known as the gateway to the volcanic national park.

★ The **Parque Nacional Timanfaya** (Timanfaya National Park), popularly known as "the Fire Mountains," takes up much of southern Lanzarote. As you enter the park from Yaiza, the first thing you'll see is the staging area for the Canaries' best-known **camel rides.** A bumpy camel trek lasts about 20 minutes.

The volcanic landscape inside Timanfaya is a violent jumble of exploded craters, cinder cones, lava formations, and heat fissures. The park is strictly protected; and you can visit only on a bus tour. A taped commentary in English explains how the parish priest of Yaiza took notes during the 1730 eruption that buried two villages. ☏ *928/840057.* 🎫 *1,000 ptas.* ⏲ *Daily 9–6; last trip at 5.*

Dining

$$ ✕ **El Diablo.** This must be one of the world's most unusual restaurants. Here, in the middle of Timanfaya National Park, chicken, steaks, and spicy sausages are cooked over a volcanic crater using the earth's natural heat. ✉ *Timanfaya National Park,* ☏ *928/840057. AE, MC, V.*

$$ ✕ **La Era.** One of only three buildings to survive the 1730 eruption of Yaiza's volcano, this farmhouse restaurant has simple dining rooms with blue-and-white checked tablecloths on tables arranged around a center patio. It's a great place to try regional dishes such as goat stew, cherne in cilantro sauce, and Canarian cheeses. ✉ *Barranco 3, Yaiza,* ☏ *928/830016. AE, DC, MC, V.*

Playa Blanca

15 km (9 mi) south of Yaiza.

Playa Blanca is Lanzarote's newest resort. The ferry for Fuerteventura leaves from here, but there's not much more to the town. Tourists come for the exquisite white beaches, reached via hard-packed dirt roads on **Punta de Papagayo.** The most popular beach is **Playa Papagayo.** Bring your own picnic; there's just one bar.

Just north of Playa Blanca is Lanzarote's agricultural belt. In **La Geria,** grapes are grown in cinder pits surrounded by a ring of volcanic rock.

The rocks provide protection from the wind, and the cinders allow dew to drip down to the roots.

Lodging

$$$$ ★ **Timanfaya Palace.** At the far end of Playa Blanca rises the graceful sight of whitewashed Arabic towers, backed by the sea and Fuerteventura. Enhanced by the cool Moorish fountain in the lobby, this vision is almost a tourist attraction in itself. It's on the water, and a two-minute walk from Playa Flamingo, but Timanfaya Palace has no beach; it compensates with a small, sandy, palm-lined ledge overlooking the sea. The spacious rooms have terraces or balconies, and the high prices include breakfast and dinner. Twenty rooms are specially equipped for travelers with disabilities, and Internet access is a perk for all. ✉ *Playa Blanca, 35570 Yaiza,* ☎ *928/517108,* FAX *928/517011. 307 rooms. 2 restaurants, 2 bars, piano bar, 2 pools, hot tub, miniature golf, tennis court, archery, recreation room, convention center. AE, DC, MC, V.*

$$$ **Lanzarote Princess.** Near the virgin beaches of Lanzarote's south shore, the Lanzarote Princess is a modern, white four-story building with an airy, plant-filled lobby. The rooms are a bit small and have linoleum floors; bright floral bedspreads compensate a bit for the somewhat sterile effect. The grounds, on the other hand, are vast and encompass good sports facilities and a huge pool with a bar in the middle. ✉ *Playa Blanca, 35570 Yaiza,* ☎ *928/517108,* FAX *928/517011. 410 rooms. Restaurant, 3 bars, beauty salon, miniature golf, tennis court, squash, dance club, playground, recreation room. AE, DC, MC, V.*

Outdoor Activities and Sports

Rent mountain bikes at **Zafari Cycle** (☎ 928/517691).

FUERTEVENTURA

Some of Fuerteventura's towering sand dunes have blown across the sea from the Sahara Desert, just 96 km (60 mi) away, and indeed it's not hard to imagine Fuerteventura as a detached piece of Africa.

Despite being the second-largest Canary Island, Fuerteventura is the least populous, and tourism is relatively new to its 20,000 inhabitants. The two main resort areas are at the island's far north and south ends. Corralejo, across from Lanzarote, is known for its acres of sand dunes, many miles of which are protected and pristine. The Jandia peninsula, with dozens of beaches—including one that's 26 km (16 mi) long—is in the midst of an uncontrolled building craze, but there are still miles of virgin coastline left.

Puerto del Rosario

5 km (3 mi) north of the airport.

Fuerteventura's capital, Puerto del Rosario, has long suffered from an image problem. It used to be called Puerto de Cabra (Goat Port), but the new and improved name has not changed the fact that this is a poor city with little of interest to travelers.

Corralejo

38 km (23 mi) north of Puerto Rosario.

This small port town has one street of tourist restaurants and some pedestrian plazas with good seafood.

South 19 km (11 mi) on the inland road is the **Casa de los Coroneles,** the island's main historic building. Military governors built the immense house in the 1700s and ruled the island from it until the turn of the century. It is not open to the public.

Beaches

Playa de Corralejo, about 2 km (1 mi) south of the town, is fringed by mountainous sand dunes and faces Los Lobos Island, across the channel. Nude sunbathing is common at the more remote spots.

Playa del Aljibe de la Cueva, on the northwest side of the island, has a castle once used to repel pirates. It's popular with locals.

Lodging

$$$$ **Tres Islas.** Sitting right on the empty white beach near the Corralejo dunes, this luxury resort is built around a swimming-pool complex with green-and-white-stripe tents. The bedrooms are more formal, with soft green carpeting, dark-wood furniture, and floral prints. All have terraces. ✉ *Avda. Grandes Playas, 35660 Corralejo,* ☎ *928/535700,* FAX *928/535858. 365 rooms. Restaurant, piano bar, 4 pools, beauty salon, sauna, 4 tennis courts, exercise room, beach, playground. AE, DC, MC, V.*

$$ **Oliva Beach.** The rooms in this boxy, eight-story hotel are fairly small, with linoleum floors and orange drapes, but each has a furnished terrace with views of the endless beach. The hotel needs a paint job, but it's Tres Islas' only neighbor on this side of the dunes—which is to say it has a perfect location. There is an Olympic-size swimming pool, and the friendly staff runs a miniclub to keep youngsters busy all day. ✉ *Avda. Grandes Playas, 35660,* ☎ *928/535334,* FAX *928/866154. 410 rooms. Restaurant, bar, pool, beauty salon, tennis court, children's programs, playground. AE, DC, MC, V.*

Outdoor Activities and Sports

DIVING

The channel between Corralejo and the tiny Isla de Lobos is rich in undersea life and favored by divers as well as sportfishermen.

WINDSURFING

One of Fuerteventura's biggest attractions is **windsurfing.** You can rent boards at most hotels; one of the main schools is **Ventura Surf** (☎ 928/866040).

Betancuria

25 km (15 mi) southwest of Puerto Rosario.

Betancuria was once the capital of Fuerteventura but is now almost a ghost town, with only 150 residents.

The weather-worn colonial church of **Santa María de Betancuria** was meant to be the cathedral of the Canary Islands. The **Museo de la Iglesia** (Church Museum) contains a replica of the banner carried by the Norman conqueror Juan de Bethancourt when he seized Fuerteventura in the 15th century. Most of the artwork was salvaged from the nearby convent, now in ruins. The museum is open weekdays 9:30–5 and Saturday 9:30–2; admission is 100 ptas.

The **Museo Arqueológico** (Museum of Archaeology) and a crafts workshop are on the other side of the ravine that cuts through the tiny hamlet.

In **Antigua,** 8 km (5 mi) east, you can visit a restored, white Don Quixote–style windmill that was once used for grinding *gofio.* The modern metal windmills you see throughout the island were imported from the United States and are used to pump water.

Pájara

16 km (10 mi) south of Betancuria.

Pájara is the administrative center of the booming southern peninsula of Jandia and sports a two-block strip of boulevard, pretty wrought-iron street lamps, and a brand-new city hall.

Fuerteventura was once divided into two kingdoms, and a wall was built across the Jandia peninsula to mark the border. Remnants of that wall are still visible today inland from **Matas Blancas** (White Groves), 42 km (26 mi) south of Pájara on Highway GC640.

Costa Calma

7 km (4½ mi) south of Matas Blancas.

As you continue south along the coast from Matas Blancas, the beaches get longer, the sand gets whiter, and the water gets bluer. The famous **Playas de Sotavento** begin near the Costa Calma developments and extend gloriously for 26 km (16 mi). Nude sunning is favored here, except directly in front of hotels.

Dining and Lodging

$ ✕ **Don Quijote.** One of Costa Calma's few independent restaurants, Don Quijote does its best to bring Old Castile to the beach. Shields bearing coats of arms hang amid wooden beams, near a a suit of armor that would have been too fancy for Don Quixote himself. Though the food is mainly Castilian, you mustn't leave without a taste of the island's famous *majorero* cheese. ✉ *Jandia Beach Center 39,* ☎ *no phone. V.*

$$$$ 🏨 **Costa Calma Beach.** The building may resemble a convention center, and the lobby may be excessively colorful, but at least you can book a room here—Costa Calma is one of few hotels on the coast that will deal with individuals as well as tour groups. Besides regular rooms, private apartments with kitchens are available. Prices at this entirely modern hotel include breakfast and dinner; all-inclusive packages are also available. ✉ *Av. de las Palmeras, 35627,* ☎ *928/875204,* FAX *928/875202. 322 rooms, 75 apartments. 2 restaurants, bar, 2 pools, beauty salon, hot tub, sauna, 2 tennis courts, exercise room, playground, dance club. MC, V.*

$$$$ ★ 🏨 **Jandia Princess.** If tour groups haven't booked all the rooms, your stay at the Princess will be memorable for its gorgeous pools with island bars, complete amenities, and the best design on Fuerteventura—a graceful white Moorish look. Every room has a balcony facing the sea or the gardens. ✉ *Urb. Esquinzo, 35626,* ☎ *928/544089,* FAX *928/544097. 528 rooms. Restaurant, 6 bars, 6 pools, beauty salon, 6 tennis courts, sauna, hot tub, laundry service. AE, DC, MC, V.*

$$$$ 🏨 **Robinson Club Playa Jandia.** People come here to really let go. No cash changes hands; all meals are included; and drinks are paid for with brightly colored chips that make it easy to forget how much you're spending at the flower-strung terrace bar, cozy tavern bar, and romantic cocktail lounge. With nude beaches to the north and south, a thumping nightclub, and lots of tanned European yuppies on holiday, this is Fuerteventura's answer to Club Med. ✉ *Playa Jandia, 35625,* ☎ *928/541348,* FAX *928/541100. 362 rooms. Restaurant, 3 bars, 2 pools, beauty salon, 10 tennis courts, volleyball, windsurfing, dance club. AE, DC, MC, V.*

$$$ 🏨 **Fuerteventura Playa.** This sophisticated, low-slung hotel, built around a large, kidney-shape pool and thatched-roof bar, is at the north end of the Sotovento Beaches. Rooms have slate-blue carpets and modern white furnishings, including oversize beds, and a few have sea

views. ✉ *Urb. Cañada del Río Poligono C1, 35627,* ☎ *928/547344,* FAX *928/547097. 300 rooms. Restaurant, bar, pool, beauty salon, sauna, tennis court, exercise room, windsurfing. AE, DC, MC, V.*

Outdoor Activities and Sports

For windsurfing lessons and board rentals, try **Fun Center** (☎ 928/535999) on Sotavento Beach.

Morro Jable

At the southernmost tip of the island.

At the very southern tip of Fuerteventura is the old fishing port of Morro Jable. Many more miles of virgin coast stretch beyond here—down a dirt road that eventually leads to the lighthouse—and beaches along the entire windward side of the peninsula remain untouched.

Beaches

Beyond the town of Morro Jable, a dirt road leads to the isolated beaches of Juan Gomez and **Playa de las Pillas.** Following the dirt tracks across the narrow strip of land, you can enjoy the equally empty **Playa de Cofete** and **Playa de Barlovento de Jandia.**

Outdoor Activities and Sports

For **scuba diving** and **snorkeling,** head for the rocky outcrops on the windward side of Jandia.

LA PALMA

La Palma is a green and prosperous island that managed quite successfully in the past without tourism. But now that it has been "discovered," La Palma is handling its guests with good taste by emphasizing the island's natural beauty, traditional crafts, and cuisine. The residents, called Palmeros, are especially friendly.

Santa Cruz de la Palma

★ *6 km (4 mi) north of the airport.*

Santa Cruz is the capital of La Palma and was an important port and bustling shipbuilding center in the 16th century. Then, in 1533, a band of buccaneers led by French pirate François le Clerc raided the city and burned it to the ground. La Palma was rebuilt with money from the Spanish king, which is why it now has such a unified colonial appearance.

Walk up the cobblestone main street, Calle O'Daly, which everyone calls Calle Real. Take a peek inside the elegant patio of the **Palacio Salazar,** which contains the tourist office.

The triangular **Plaza de España,** in front of the church of El Salvador, is the focus of La Palma's social life and fills with people in the early evening. The church is the only building that survived the pirate fire; it has a handsome carved Moorish ceiling. Bring a flashlight if you want to see the religious art on the walls. Note the stone shields on the city hall, across the plaza. One is the coat of arms of Spain's Habsburg kings, and the other is the emblem of La Palma. Walk uphill one block to the corner of Calle de la Puente; then look back at one of the most charming streets in the Canaries.

In the restored 16th- and 18th-century cloisters of the church of San Francisco, the **Museo Insular** (Island Museum) traces the navigational and trading history of La Palma and displays Guanche remains. The Museo de Bellas Artes (Museum of Fine Arts) upstairs has a good collection of 19th-century Spanish paintings. ✉ *Plaza de San Francisco*

3, ☎ 922/420558. 💵 300 ptas. ⏲ Oct.–June, weekdays 9:30–1:50 and 4–6:30; July–Sept., weekdays 9–2.

You can't miss the life-size cement replica of Columbus's ship the *Santa María,* at the end of the Plaza de la Alameda. There's a tiny **naval museum** inside; climb up to the deck for a look at a collection of old maps. *☎ 922/416550. 💵 150 ptas. ⏲ Oct.–June, Mon.–Thurs. 9:30–2 and 4–7, Fri. 9:30–2; July–Sept., Mon.–Thurs. 9:30–2, Fri. 9:30–2.*

The star-shape **Castillo Real** (Royal Castle), on Calle Mendez Cabezola, is a 16th-century fortress. Nearby, along **Avenida Marítima,** is a much-photographed row of colorful Canarian houses with typical double balconies, complete with shielded posts looking out to the sea. The balconies are actually on the backs of the houses; they front Calle Pérez de Brito, which is a continuation of O'Daly. Stop in at **Tabacos Vargas** (✉ Avda. Marítima 55) to buy some famous *palmero* cigars, or just watch them being hand-rolled at the **factory** (✉ Balthasar Martin 83) a few blocks uphill. The cigar industry is a result of constant migration between the Canary Islands and Cuba. Many with a taste for fine cigars claim that hand-rolled *palmeros* are better than today's Cubans.

The hilltop village of **Las Nieves** (The Snows), 3 km (2 mi) northwest of Santa Cruz, has a beautifully preserved colonial plaza and the opulent church of **Nuestra Señora de las Nieves**, which houses La Palma's patron saint, the Virgin of the Snows. The Virgin, credited with saving many a ship from disaster, sits on a silver altar wearing vestments studded with pearls and emeralds.

Dining and Lodging

$$ ✕ **Antica Trattoria.** La Palma's best Italian restaurant is housed in one of its best-known houses. The red-on-yellow balconies stand out even among the colors of Avenida Marítima's old seaside row. Seating choices include a two-table room overlooking the sea and an open-air cobblestone patio. Among the fresh pastas, the *gnocchi alla Sorrentina* stands out. *✉ Avda. Maritima 42, ☎ 922/417116. MC, V.*

$$ ✕ **Mesón del Mar.** If you venture to the north part of the island, follow the road down from San Andrés to the tiny fishing harbor at Puerto Pesquero Espindola, and you'll end up at this popular seafood house. Fish couldn't be any fresher. *✉ Puerto Pesquero Espindola, ☎ 922/450305. AE, MC, V.*

$–$$ ✕ **Restaurant Tamanca.** A sign marks the entrance to this restaurant-in-a-cave, 16 km (10 mi) north of Fuencaliente. The menu centers on traditional meat and fish dishes with an island flair. *✉ Carretera General s/n, Montaña Tamanca, Las Manchas, ☎ 922/462155. AE, DC, MC, V.*

$ ★ ✕ **Chipi Chipi.** This unlikely restaurant is tucked away behind dense tropical gardens—complete with chirping parrots—in the hills above Santa Cruz, 3 km (2 mi) beyond the church in Las Nieves. Each party is seated in a private stone hut. The food is strictly local, and portions are huge. You can start with salad or garbanzo-bean soup, followed by grilled meats washed down with local red wine. *✉ Carretera de las Nieves 42, ☎ 922/411024. AE, MC, V. Closed Wed. and Sun.*

$ ✕ **Los Braseros.** From Santa Cruz, follow the signs to the OBSERVATORIO high above the city. The restaurant's outdoor terrace has wonderful views, and the friendly and funny staff serves grilled steaks, pork, and hearty Canarian soups. *✉ Candelaria Mirca, Carretera del Roque 54, Los Alamos, ☎ 922/414360. DC, MC, V. Closed Tues.*

$$$ ★ 🏨 **Parador de Santa Cruz de la Palma.** The site of the Canaries' parador, 8 km (5 mi) inland from Santa Cruz, was chosen for its sweeping views of both the capital and the sea. Guest rooms have parquet floors and traditional wooden balconies. The parador's wonderful reading room sports a high wooden ceiling, and tranquil interior patios and outdoor terraces pull you in all directions. ✉ *Carretera de Zumacal s/n, 38712,* ☎ *922/435828,* FAX *922/435999. 78 rooms. 2 restaurants, bar, minibars, pool, sauna, exercise room, recreation room, meeting room. AE, DC, MC, V.*

$$ **Castillete Aparthotel.** Right on the ocean but down the street from the heavy traffic, Castillete is the best choice if you want to stay in the city proper. Most of the units are studios with separate sleeping and sitting areas and small kitchens. White wood and natural-pine furniture give the rooms a clean, modern look. ✉ *Avda. Marítima 75, 38700,* ☎ *922/420054,* FAX *922/420067. 42 apartments. Restaurant, pool. AE, DC, MC, V.*

Shopping

La Palma's best crafts and foods are sold at **La Graja Centro de Artesanía,** near the Mirador de la Concepción outside Santa Cruz, where you'll find embroidery, baskets, pottery, cookbooks, bottled *mojo* sauce, cigars, and more.

Playa de los Cancajos

5 km (3 mi) south of Santa Cruz de la Palma.

La Palma is not known for its beaches, but these black-sand coves are popular with swimmers in the summer. Los Cancajos, 5 km (3 mi) south of the capital, is a small town with a crescent-shaped beach and crystalline water.

Dining and Lodging

$$ ✕ **Las Tres Chimineas.** An outgoing Palmero and his English wife run this attractive black-stone restaurant in Breña Alta, 6 km (4 mi) west of Santa Cruz. The building is named for its three decorative chimneys; inside, the sunny aesthetic is heightened by fresh flowers. Local fish are the specialty—*vieja* is the best. ✉ *Carretera de Los Llanos de Aridane, Km 8,* ☎ *922/429470. MC, V. Closed Tues.*

$$$–$$$$ **Taburiente Playa.** Opened in 1996, this crescent-shaped resort has fantastic sea views from nearly every room. It's designed so that the guest need never leave the premises, with two swimming pools, a gym, activities for kids, and nighttime entertainment. ✉ *Playa de los Cancajos, 38712,* ☎ *922/181277,* FAX *922/181285. 293 rooms. Restaurant, 2 pools, wading pool, sauna, exercise room, nightclub, children's programs, playground. AE, MC, V.*

$$ ★ **Hacienda San Jorge.** Built to resemble a Canarian village, the San Jorge groups apartments in pastel bungalows. The apartments have summer-house furniture and separate bedrooms, living rooms, kitchenettes, baths, and terraces. The complex is built on several different levels surrounding a lake-size swimming pool just steps from the black-sand beach. ✉ *Playa de los Cancajos 22, Breña Baja 38712,* ☎ *922/181066,* FAX *922/434528. 155 apartments. Restaurant, bar, kitchenettes, pool, hot tub, sauna, exercise room, beach. AE, DC, MC, V.*

Fuencaliente

28 km (17 mi) south of Santa Cruz de la Palma.

Near Fuencaliente, the scenery grows dry as you reach La Palma's volcanic southern tip. Visit the **San Antonio volcano** and the **Teneguía volcano,** the site of the Canaries' most recent eruption. In 1971, Teneguía burst open, sending rivers of lava toward the sea and extending the length of the island by 3 km (2 mi). There are good beaches in the cinders below the volcano, reached via unpaved roads.

Fuencaliente is the heart of La Palma's wine region. While there, visit the modern **Llanovid winery,** makers of the islands' best-known label, *Teneguía.* ✉ *C. Los Canarios 8,* ☎ *922/444078.*

Tazacorte

28 km (17 mi) northwest of Fuencaliente.

Drive down through the banana plantations to Tazacorte, the old Guanche capital, or explore **Puerto Naos,** 5 km (3 mi) south, where a sunny, black-sand bay created by a 1947 volcanic eruption is now a beach resort.

Beaches

The black-sand bay of **Puerto Naos** is the island's biggest beach and the most popular on the west coast.

Dining and Lodging

$$ ★ ✕ **Restaurant Playa Mont.** Looking like an upscale beach shack, open on one side to the ocean breezes, the Playa Mont serves some of the best seafood in the islands. The secret is in the sauces: traditional *mojos* and a delicious lemon-butter. ✉ *Puerto de Tazacorte,* ☎ *922/480443. MC, V. Closed Thurs.*

$$ ✕🏨 **Sol La Palma.** Perched at the end of La Palma's best beach, the Sol hotel was the island's first real resort and is still the place to be on the west coast. The rooms are huge, with understated beige furnishings, gray-tile floors, sun terraces, and enormous baths. The bountiful restaurant buffet features expensive treats (such as fresh shrimp and papaya) not normally found at moderately priced hotels. ✉ *Puerto Naos, 38760,* ☎ *922/408000,* FAX *922/408014. 307 rooms, 163 apartments. Restaurant, 3 bars, 2 pools, tennis court, exercise room. AE, DC, MC, V.*

Parque Nacional de La Caldera de Taburiente

10 km (6 mi) east of Tazacorte.

The striking Taburiente Crater National Park fills most of the center of La Palma. The visitor center is 3 km (2 mi) east of El Paso. The park is inside what looks like a huge crater; modern geologists think that the crater was formed by a series of small eruptions that pulled the center of the mountain apart.

A narrow paved road leads through pine forests to the **Mirador Cumbrecita,** a lookout at 6,014 ft, on the crater's rim. It's often raining or snowing up here, and bright rainbows span the canyon. The white dome and tower on the opposite side are the **Observatorio Roque de los Muchachos** (Boys' Castle Observatory), home of Europe's largest telescope. Astronomers say the Canary Island peaks have some of the cleanest air and darkest skies in the world.

Canarian pine trees are especially adapted to fire and volcanic eruptions, taking only four years to regenerate themselves. The park has lots of interesting hiking trails, and you can camp on the valley floor with a permit, obtainable at the visitor center.

LA GOMERA

One of the least developed of the Canary Islands, tiny La Gomera attracts scores of denim-clad backpackers on shoestring budgets, as well as other travelers who care little for the disco beat of the more touristy islands. The mossy, fern-filled central peaks make up the **Garajonay National Park** and include a rare forest of fragrant laurel trees. The forest, a UNESCO World Heritage Site, preserves Tertiary flora that the Ice Age wiped out everywhere else in the world.

The park's mountains fan out into six steep-sided valleys called *barrancos*. Villages in the *barrancos* are dedicated mainly to small-scale banana growing, and you'll see three or four stalks of bananas outside each house in the morning awaiting pickup. The serpentine roads leading in and out of the valleys are so filled with switchbacks that traveling is slow, and villages remain isolated.

Allow plenty of time—two days if possible—for a drive around La Gomera. The distances are short, but they take a long time to cover, and the roads are not for those afraid of heights.

San Sebastián

La Gomera's scraggly capital makes the most of its historical links with Christopher Columbus—he made his last stop on charted territory at San Sebastián before setting out for the edge of the earth in 1492. The sights east of the capital are all in close proximity.

The **Torre del Conde** (Tower of the Count) was built by the Spanish in 1450 for protection from Guanche tribes. It came in particularly handy in 1487, when the count's wife, Beatriz de Bobadillo, took refuge in the tower after island chieftains killed her husband. The beautiful, black-haired widow is better known for her love affair with Columbus.

The explorer used the **Pozo de la Aguada** (Water Well) at the head of Calle del Medio to resupply his ships with water, which he also used to baptize the New World. 🎫 *Free.* ⏲ *Mon.–Sat. 9–1:30 and 3:30–6, Sun. 9–1:30.*

The church of **Nuestra Señora de la Asunción** (Our Lady of the Assumption) was just a tiny chapel when Columbus prayed there. Since then it has been enlarged in a variety of styles. Farther up the street you can visit the **Casa Colón,** the simple Canarian house where the explorer supposedly stayed during his time with Beatriz. It's now devoted to exhibits by local artists. ✉ *C. Real 56,* ☎ *no phone.* 🎫 *Free.* ⏲ *Tues.–Thurs. 4–6.*

The **Degollada de Peraza,** 15 km (9 mi) south of San Sebastián over a winding road, has a lookout with great views. Guanche chiefs pushed Beatriz's cruel husband, Fernan Peraza, to his death from this cliff.

Beaches

A strong current makes La Gomera's northern beaches dangerous for swimming. If you want sun, head for the volcanic sands of the southern shores. **San Sebastián**'s black-sand beach near the ferry dock is clean and popular with local families.

Dining and Lodging

$$ ✗ **Marqués de Oristano.** This is really two restaurants in one. The Canarian patio in the entryway is a tapas bar; in the back, reserved for special occasions, is an informal, open-air grill where you can select your fresh fish or a cut of beef or lamb from a butcher's case. The dining room upstairs serves more-sophisticated cuisine at higher prices, such as pork tenderloin in palm honey, or bass fillet in champagne with saffron and pine nuts. ✉ *C. del Medio 24,* ☎ *922/141457. AE, V. Closed Sun.*

$$$ ★ ✗🏨 **Parador Conde de La Gomera.** Built in 1970 in the style of an old island manor, the parador has breezeways decorated with Spanish antiques. The large rooms combine bare-wood floors with French provincial furniture and have louvered shutters that open onto interior patios. The pool and yard, perched above the city, have sea views. The dining room has a barnlike Canarian ceiling, and the kitchen specializes in such local dishes as rabbit in *salmorejo* with *papas arrugadas.* ✉

38800 San Sebastián, ☎ 922/871100, FAX 922/871116. 58 rooms. Restaurant, bar, pool. AE, DC, MC, V.

Shopping

La Gomera has a refreshing lack of shops. If you're looking for typical souvenirs, buy a bottle of palm syrup or a bag of macaroons from the little market on the Plaza de América in San Sebastián. Typical ceramics, made without a potter's wheel, are still made and sold by village women in El Cercado.

Playa de Santiago

34 km (20 mi) southwest of San Sebastián.

Playa de Santiago, complete with fishing port and banana plantations, is at the bottom of a steep canyon. Until very recently, the people who lived on the almost vertical slopes of the island's canyons used a mysterious whistling language called Silbo to communicate across the gorges. Although the language is dying out, most of the older generation in the rural areas still understand it, and the gardeners at the parador in San Sebastián sometimes give demonstrations.

Boat excursions leave several times a week from Playa de Santiago to view **Los Organos,** a cliff made up of hundreds of tall basalt columns that resemble organ pipes.

Beaches

Playa de Santiago is a rocky black-sand beach surrounding a small fishing bay. It has the sunniest weather on the island and is destined to become La Gomera's major resort area.

Dining and Lodging

$$ ✕ **Tagoror.** From the outside, Tagaror looks like a small, rather ramshackle pit stop, but through the white archway is a lovely stone patio that smells of burning coals and sizzling island food. In addition to Canarian grilled meats and fish, the menu offers several paellas and a wonderful seafood pizza of sorts. ✉ *Tecina 93, Playa de Santiago, 38800, ☎ 922/895425, FAX 922/895234. AE, MC, V.*

$$$ ★ 🏨 **Jardines Tecina.** La Gomera's only real resort, the Tecina sprawls luxuriously over a series of terraces high above the sea and provides an elevator down to the beach. The rooms, grouped in hillside bungalows, all have summery-green pine furniture and decor, with big wooden terraces for sunbathing. Bathrooms are decorated with Spanish tile. Internet access is available. ✉ *Playa de Santiago, 38811, ☎ 922/145850, FAX 922/145851. 434 rooms. 4 restaurants, 5 pools, 4 bars, piano bar, sauna, miniature golf, 5 tennis courts, exercise room, 2 squash courts, dance club. AE, MC, V.*

$ 🏨 **Apartamentos Tapahuga.** This attractive building sits right on the fishing harbor, and the apartments' Canarian, carved-pine balconies overlook it. Kitchens and country-style Spanish decor make the apartments homey, and there's a swimming pool on the roof. ✉ *Avda. Marítima, 38800, ☎ 922/895159, FAX 922/895127. 29 apartments. Kitchenettes, pool. MC, V.*

Parque Nacional de Garajonay

20 km (12 mi) west of San Sebastián.

You drive past fantastic geological formations as you enter Garajonay National Park from the central highway. The road heads into dense forest; much of the year this area is in the clouds thanks to the natural mountain barrier that diverts the tradewinds, and the mossy trees drip with mist. La Gomera's humidity, mild temperatures, and geographic isolation have proved just the right mixture for the survival of the various evergreens here. The highest point on the island, the peak of Garajonay (4,832 ft), is to your right.

To learn more about the park, take the turnoff at Las Rosas for the **Juego de Bolas** visitor center. Exhibits and an excellent 20-minute video, with English translation, explain the laurel forest; and a garden outside labels vegetation from the 150 species exclusive to this park. In nearby crafts shops, you can watch artisans at work (☞ Shopping, *below*). *Visitor center,* ☎ *922/800993.* 🎫 *Free.* ⏲ *Tues.–Sun. 9:30–4:30.*

Outdoor Activities and Sports

Garajonay National Park has miles of interesting hikes. Pick up a trail map at the visitor center or the San Sebastián tourist office.

Shopping

Look before you buy at **Artisans Cooperación Los Organos** (✉ Carretera Las Rosas, Centro de Visitantes del Parque N. Garajonay, ☎ 922/800993), where you'll find local artists making and selling everything from rag rugs and baskets to local white wines and Gomeran drums. It's right next to the visitor center in Garajonay National Park.

Valle Gran Rey

72 km (43 mi) west of San Sebastián.

The terraced farms of Valle Gran Rey, planted with bananas and palms, look like something out of a Gauguin painting. The valley boasts two black-sand beaches and is home to a number of German families who have followed the artist's example.

OFF THE BEATEN PATH

CASA EFIGENIA – Take your taste buds on a trip to the inexpensive Casa Efigenia, in the hamlet of Las Hayas, about 30 minutes uphill from Valle Gran Rey. The restaurant's plain, whitewashed walls are decorated with a few cobs of dried corn and a dusty case of citations—many handwritten—that Doña Efigenia has received for her efforts in preserving traditional Gomeran cookery. It's simple food, prepared and served by Doña Efigenia herself—not gourmet, but truly authentic. The main course is a vegetable stew; dessert is a heavy, cheese-filled cake that you smother in palm-tree syrup. The Casa is open 9–7 daily for breakfast and lunch.

Beaches

In Valle Gran Rey, **Playa del Inglés** is a sandy black crescent of a beach favored by young people in search of a cheap hideaway, while **Las Vueltas** beach is popular with residents.

Dining and Lodging

$$ ✕ **Mirador de César Manrique** Take in a powerful view of the entire Gran Rey valley through the angled glass walls of this government-run restaurant school. Service, ambience, and food are on par with the island's best, yet prices are low. The terrace lookout—indeed the entire complex, which merges with its natural surroundings—was built by Lanzarote architect César Manrique. ✉ *Carretera de Arure,* ☎ *922/805868. AE, DC, V, MC. Closed Mon.*

$ ✕ **Charco del Conde.** This attractive, modern beachfront restaurant exudes an effortless style. Sample good fish, steaks, and chicken with *papas arrugadas* and *mojo* sauce from a great backyard patio or a people-watching front porch. Across from Playa del Charco, the restaurant is named for the beach inlet that creates a naturally occurring pool (*charco*), refilled at high tide. This is also where the Guanche chiefs hatched their plot to toss the *conde* (count) of La Gomera off the cliff.

Prices are precipitously low. ✉ *Carretera Puntilla Vueltas,* ☎ *922/805403. AE, DC, V. Closed Sun.*

$$ 🏨 **Hotel Gran Rey.** The largest hotel in the area is right on the black-sand beach. The best thing about the tidy three-story complex is the rooftop pool, which overlooks the sea and the valley town. ✉ *La Puntilla s/n, 38870,* ☎ *922/805859,* FAX *922/805651. 99 rooms. Restaurant, pool, tennis court, meeting room. MC, V.*

$ 🏨 **Apartamentos Charco del Conde.** These low-rise, flower-clad apartments across from Las Vueltas Beach have simple pine furnishings, a kitchen, and a private terrace. ✉ *Avda. Marítima s/n, 38870,* ☎ *922/805597,* FAX *922/805502. 50 apartments, 50 studios. Kitchenettes, pool. MC, V.*

Alojera

43 km (26 mi) northwest of San Sebastián.

With its beautiful little black-sand beach, Alojera, like other northern Gomeran villages, is becoming a center of bed-and-breakfast tourism. Contact the tourist office in San Sebastián for color brochures of the small homes available.

This area is known for its palm syrup (*miel de palma*). At night, the syrup trees, which have metal collars around them, produce up to 3 gallons of sap each, which is boiled down into syrup over wood fires the following day.

EL HIERRO

The smallest Canary Island, El Hierro is strictly for those who enjoy nature and solitude. Most residents live in mountain villages that have little in common with the other islands' tropical beach towns. The few travelers who do find their way to El Hierro come for the hiking, scuba diving, or relaxing.

Valverde

10 km (6 mi) west of the airport.

El Hierro's capital, Valverde, sits on a hillside at 2,000 ft. The town was built inland, in the clouds, to protect it from pirate raids, and its cobblestone streets always seem to be wet with mist. The church, with a balconied bell tower, was once a lookout for pirates.

Driving around El Hierro, you'll pass terraced farms still plowed with mules. The **Mirador de la Peña,** 8 km (5 mi) west of Valverde, stands at 2,200 ft and offers a spectacular view of El Golfo (☞ *below*), on the island's northeastern corner.

El Golfo (the Bay) is formed by what looks like a half-submerged volcanic crater. The part above water is a fertile, steep-sided valley. At the far end is a health spa with salty medicinal waters, called **Pozo de la Salud**; those who prefer tastier medicine can visit the island's **winery** in the big, beige building near Frontera. The rocky coast along El Golfo is safe for swimming only in summer.

The **Hoya del Morcillo** picnic area is in the fragrant pine forest that covers the center of El Hierro. It has barbecue pits, rest rooms, and a playground. Camping is permitted, and this makes a good starting point for forest hikes.

Dining and Lodging

$$ ✕ **Mirador de la Peña.** One of César Manrique's final works, the Mirador is surely El Hierro's most elegant dining spot. Glass walls gra a panoramic view of the bay below. ✉ *Carretera General de Guarazoca 40,* ☎ *922/550300. AE, DC, MC, V.*

$$$ ✕🏨 **Parador Nacional El Hierro.** The road to the parador takes you around a point jutting into the sea and deposits you at the bottom of a 3,500-ft cliff. Guest rooms are large, with Castilian furniture and heavy folk-art bedspreads. In the dining room, delicious tidbits of island specialties are laid out as appetizers, but the rest of the menu goes beyond the chef's abilities; it's best to stick to grilled fish and steak. ✉ *Las Playas 26, 38915,* ☎ *922/558036,* FAX *922/558086. 47 rooms. Restaurant, bar, pool. AE, DC, MC, V.*

$$ 🏨 **Boomerang.** Owned by a local islander who once worked in Australia, the Boomerang is right in the middle of town. Rooms are clean and comfortable, with country pine furniture and tile baths. ✉ *Dr. Gost 1, 38900,* ☎ *922/550200,* FAX *922/550253. 17 rooms. Restaurant, bar. AE, DC, V.*

La Restinga

54 km (33 mi) south of Valverde.

At the southern tip of El Hierro, La Restinga is a small, rather ugly fishing port surrounded by lava fields. The few who come here tend to be scuba fanatics; some say the diving is the best in the Canaries.

Dining and Lodging

$ ✕ **Casa Juan.** These two plain dining rooms have large tables to accommodate families, who come from all over the island for the delicious seafood soup. The *mojo* sauces, served with *papas arrugadas,* are also outstanding. ✉ *Juan Gutierrez Monteverde 23,* ☎ *922/557102. MC, V.*

$$ ✕🏨 **Punta Grande.** Built on an old dock that extends into the sea, the four-room Punta Grande was cited in the *Guinness Book of Records* as the world's smallest hotel. The place has personality: rooms have exposed rock walls and nautical decor, with erstwhile porthole windows as nightstands. An old diving suit and ships' lanterns hang in the dining room, which serves piping-hot shellfish soups and stews with homestyle hunks of bread and goat cheese. Call at least a month ahead; this little lodging is really a must. ✉ *Las Puntas, Frontera 38911,* ☎ FAX *922/559081. 4 rooms. Restaurant, bar. No credit cards.*

$ 🏨 **Apartamentos La Marina.** These tourist apartments occupy a brand-new, three-story building on the harbor. The furnishings are basic but clean, and all units have kitchens and, better still, balconies with unbeatable sunset views. ✉ *Avda. Marítima 10, 38915,* ☎ *922/559016. 8 apartments. Kitchenettes. No credit cards.*

Outdoor Activities and Sports

Club El Submarino (✉ Frontera 38915, ☎ FAX 922/5597068) organizes diving, hiking, spelunking, hang-gliding, windsurfing, mountain biking, and deep-sea fishing in La Restinga and El Golfo.

THE CANARY ISLANDS A TO Z

Arriving and Departing

By Boat

Trasmediterránea (✉ Alcalá 6, Madrid, ☎ 91/423–8832, FAX 91/423–8565) operates a slow, comfortable ferry service between Cádiz and the Canary Islands (Tenerife, 42 hrs; Gran Canaria, 48 hrs). The boat is equipped with cabins, a tiny pool, restaurants, a recreation room, and a dance club, but it's not a luxury cruise.

By Plane

There are no nonstop flights to the Canary Islands from the United States; Americans can transfer in Madrid, in England, or elsewhere in Europe. **Iberia** and its sister carrier **Aviaco** have several direct flights daily to Tenerife, Gran Canaria, La Palma, and Lanzarote from most cities in mainland Spain (2½ hrs from Madrid). **Air Europa** and **Spanair** have flights from Madrid and Barcelona at slightly lower prices. The other three islands are accessible by connecting flights.

Package information is available from **Spanish Heritage Tours** (✉ 116–47 Queens Blvd., Forest Hills, NY 11375, ☎ 718/544–2752 or 800/221–2580). You can sometimes buy a seat without the hotel package if space is available.

Getting Around

By Boat

Fred Olsen and Trasmediterránea operate inexpensive ferries between all seven islands. Fred Olsen's fleet is newer, and Olsen is the only company to provide helpful brochures with timetables and prices. Most trips from island to island take one to four hours; the few boats departing near midnight are equipped with sleeping cabins.

From Tenerife you can reach any of the other six islands. Ferries to La Palma, El Hierro, and La Gomera depart Los Cristianos; from Santa Cruz you can sail to both of Gran Canaria's main ports, Agaete in the west and Las Palmas in the north.

From **Gran Canaria** you can ferry to Lanzarote and Fuerteventura, which are mutually connected.

Fred Olsen (☎ 922/628200) has branch offices on Tenerife (✉ Muelle Ribera, Santa Cruz, ☎ 922/290011; ✉ Muelle Los Cristianos, Los Cristianos, ☎ 922/790556), Gran Canaria (✉ C. Luis Morote 4, Las Palmas, ☎ 928/495040; ✉ Puerto de las Nieves, Agaete, ☎ 928/554005), La Palma (✉ Muelle Santa Cruz, Santa Cruz de la Palma, ☎ 922/417495), La Gomera (✉ Estación Marítima del Puerto, San Sebastián, ☎ 928/850877), and El Hierro (✉ Puerto de la Estaca).

Trasmediterránea (☎ 902/454645 toll-free) has branches on Tenerife (✉ Marítima Muelle Rivera, Santa Cruz, ☎ 922/842246), Gran Canaria (✉ Muelles de León y Castillo, Las Palmas, ☎ 928/474439), Lanzarote (✉ José Antonio 90, Arrecife, ☎ 928/811188), La Palma (✉ Avda. Perez de Brito 2, Santa Cruz de la Palma, ☎ 922/411121), La Gomera (✉ Estación Marítima del Puerto, San Sebastián, ☎ 922/871324), Fuerteventura (✉ León y Castillo 58, ☎ 928/850877), and El Hierro (✉ Puerto de la Estaca, ☎ 922/550129).

Trasmediterránea also runs passenger-only **jetfoil** service three times a day between Las Palmas and Tenerife (80 mins). The ultra-sleek Fred Olsen jetfoil, which accommodates vehicles, takes only 55 minutes from Gran Canaria (Agaete) to Santa Cruz de Tenerife. Free bus service is provided between Agaete and Las Palmas in both directions.

One Trasmediterránea hydrofoil daily links Morro Jable, in southern Fuerteventura, with Las Palmas (90 mins) and Tenerife (3½ hrs). At press time Fred Olsen was beginning daily service between Las Palmas, Arrecife (Lanzarote), and Puerto Rosario (Fuerteventura).

La Gomera can be reached by ferry (55 mins) from Los Cristianos, in southern Tenerife. Fred Olsen runs a jetfoil that takes less time from Los Cristianos to La Gomera.

The **Ferry Gomera** takes cars and people between Tenerife (✉ Muelle Los Cristianos, ☎ 922/628231) and La Gomera (✉ Avda. Fred Olsen, San Sebastián, ☎ 922/871007) three times daily. At night, the same ferry plies between La Gomera and La Palma.

Southern Lanzarote and northern Fuerteventura are linked by two companies. **Fred Olsen** (✉ Avda. de Llegada s/n, Playa Blanca, ☎ 928/517266, FAX 928/517214) makes four round-trips a day from Lanzarote. It offers free bus service between Puerto del Carmen and Playa Blanca one hour prior to two of these daily departures. The Fuerteventura office is in Corralejo (☎ 928/535090). **Naviera Armas** (✉ Main Pier, Playa Blanca, ☎ 928/517912, FAX 928/517912) covers the same one-hour route. Armas is also the least expensive way to reach Lanzarote or Fuerteventura from Santa Cruz, Tenerife (☎ 922/534052) or Las Palmas, Gran Canaria (☎ 928/267700).

By Bus

In Tenerife, buses meet all arriving Iberia flights at Reina Sofía Airport and transfer passengers to the bus terminal on the outskirts of Santa Cruz. From there, you can take a taxi or another bus to the northern side of the island. Buses also meet the Gomera hydrofoil and ferry to take passengers on to Santa Cruz.

Each island has its own bus service geared toward residents. Buses generally leave the villages early in the morning for shopping in the capital and depart from its main plaza in the early afternoon. Tourist offices have details.

By Car

Most travelers rent a car or a four-wheel-drive vehicle for at least part of their stay on the Canaries; this is by far the best way to explore the countryside. The roads are generally not good for those with vertigo, as they often curve over high mountain cliffs with nothing but the sea below. Car-rental companies abound on every island, sometimes doubling as bars. You can find good prices with a little shopping around.

Reservations for rentals are necessary only during the Christmas and Easter holidays. **Hertz** and **Avis** have representatives on all the islands, though rates are better at the Spanish company **Cicar** (☎ 922/372856), which has branches in all the airports and major towns.

By Plane

All of the Canary Islands are served by air except La Gomera. Tenerife has two airports: **Reina Sofía** (TFS), near Playa de las Américas in the south, and **Los Rodeos** (TFN), in the north near Puerto de la Cruz. As a general rule, long-distance flights arrive at the southern terminal while interisland flights use the northern one, but there are exceptions. Try to book a flight that gets you to the part of the island where you'll be staying, and be sure to allow plenty of time to travel between airports for connecting flights. Driving time from one airport to the other is about 1½ hours; taxis charge up to 7,500 ptas., or you can rent a car for about 4,000 ptas.

Airport information: Tenerife (Reina Sofía/TFS, ☎ 922/759200; Los Rodeos/TFN, ☎ 922/635998). Gran Canaria (Gando/LPA, ☎ 928/579094). Lanzarote (Arrecife/ACE, ☎ 928/823450). Fuerteventura (Puerto Rosario/FVE, ☎ 928/860600). La Palma (Santa Cruz/SPC, ☎ 922/426100). El Hierro (VDE, ☎ 922/553700). La Gomera (QGZ, ☎ 922/873003).

Interisland flights are handled by **Iberia** and its regional subsidiary, **Binter** (928/579561), using small turboprop planes that offer great low-altitude views of the islands. Binter has a new fixed-rate coupon that allows you to hop from island to island. Reserve in **Tenerife** (✉ Aeropuerto de los Rodeos, ☎ 922/234346), **Gran Canaria** (✉ Alcalde Ramirez de Bethancourt 8, Las Palmas, ☎ 928/370877), **Lanzarote** (✉ Avda. Rafael Gonzalez 2, Arrecife, ☎ 928/810358), **Fuerteventura** (✉ 23 de Mayo 11, Puerto de Rosario, ☎ 928/852310), **La Palma** (✉ Apurón 1, ☎ 922/411345), or **El Hierro** (✉ Dr. Quintero 6, ☎ 922/550854).

Contacts and Resources

Guided Tours

One-day tours of Tenerife, and excursions to other islands with English-speaking guides, can be arranged through **Viajes Insular** (✉ Avda. Generalísimo 15, Puerto de la Cruz, ☎ 922/380262), which has branches on every island except La Gomera and El Hierro. Tours generally last all day and include lunch and/or a folklore presentation.

Visitor Information

Tourist offices: Tenerife (✉ Plaza de España 1, Santa Cruz, ☎ 922/239592; ✉ Plaza de la Iglesia, Puerto de la Cruz, ☎ 922/386000). **Gran Canaria** (✉ Parque de Santa Catalina, Las Palmas, ☎ 928/264623). **Lanzarote** (✉ Parque Municipal, Arrecife, ☎ 928/801517). **Fuerteventura** (✉ 1 de Mayo 33, Puerto de Rosario, ☎ 928/851024). **La Palma** (✉ O'Daly 22, Santa Cruz de la Palma, ☎ 922/412106). **La Gomera** (✉ C. del Medio 20, San Sebastián, ☎ 922/140147). **El Hierro** (✉ Licinardo Bueno 1, Valverde, ☎ 922/550302).

15 MOROCCO

The ferry ride from Spain to Morocco—just 15 km (9 mi) across the Straits of Gibraltar—may be the longest short trip on the globe. A two-hour ride from Algeciras to Tangier replaces 21st-century Europe with timeless and tumultuous North Africa. Islam is the state religion, and Arabic the official language, but Morocco's cosmopolitan history means you'll also hear French, Berber, Spanish, and English in the streets.

By George Semler

MOROCCO'S GEOGRAPHICAL and social diversity are unrivaled this close to Western Europe. Between the Atlantic Ocean's paradigmatic freshness and the Sahara—the world's largest desert, extending all the way to the Red Sea—are the snowcapped mountains of the High Atlas, with their highest peak, Djebel Toubka, soaring to 13,751 ft. The road from the Merzouga dunes to Fez goes through the Azrou cedar forest, an alpine enclave with fauna ranging from Barbary apes to brook trout. While storytellers still entertain rapt and illiterate Berbers at Djemâa el Fna square in Marrakesh, the Kairaouine University in Fez has been educating the intellectual elite of both the Islamic and non-Islamic worlds for more than a thousand years, predating Oxford by three centuries. The consummate luxury of Marrakesh's Mamounia Hotel is only minutes from the humblest of suburbs and less than an hour from the stark adobe villages of the High Atlas.

Morocco's striking clarity, brilliant colors, and romantic allure have been irresistible to painters: Eugène Delacroix, Henri Matisse, Mariano Fortuny, contemporary Spain's Claudio Bravo, and countless others have succumbed to its spell. Writers and musicians have also fallen hard; the late composer and novelist Paul Bowles lived in Tangier for more than 50 years. Tennessee Williams, William Burroughs, Allen Ginsberg, Jack Kerouac, Federico García Lorca, and Edith Wharton also had passionate relationships with Morocco. Berber Gnaoua music is one of the origins of blues, and the trance music of the *Joujouka* drums has been compared to the modern jazz of John Coltrane.

Morocco's history has been turbulent. The Berbers, Caucasian North African peoples of uncertain origin, were Morocco's first inhabitants and still form the majority of its population of 26 million. Romans and Vandals invaded and colonized the region until the Arabs (and Islam) arrived in the late 7th century. Incessant conflict between Arabs and Berbers fragmented the area until 788, when Morocco became an independent state under the dynasty of Idriss I.

In the early 10th century, the country disintegrated once more into small tribal states until the Almoravids, a dynasty of Muslim Berbers, overran both Morocco and Moorish Spain in 1062. The Almohad and Merinid dynasties succeeded in partially uniting the country through the middle of the 16th century, when the Saadian (or first Sherifian) dynasty took over. From the 17th to the 19th century, Morocco, like the other so-called Barbary States (Tunisia, Tripolitania, and Algeria), was a base for Mediterranean pirates.

In the 19th century, Morocco's strategic importance aroused the interest of the European powers. Imperial rivalries were resolved in 1912 with the establishment of a French protectorate. French Morocco included nine-tenths of the country; Spanish Morocco was based at Tetouan and controlled the Spanish Sahara; and Tangier was declared an international zone.

In 1956, under pressure from the Moroccan national movement (led by the Istiqlal party), France finally relinquished all rights to Morocco. The highly respected Sultan Sidi Muhammed—father of independence, the "Moroccan Gandhi"—became King Muhammed V and was succeeded in 1961 by his son Hassan II, who ruled until his death in July 1999. Considered Commander of the Faithful by Moroccans—both secular and religious leader of the nation, endowed with *baraka* (divine protection)—Hassan II initially exercised full executive and legislative control, yielding some power only after an abortive 1971 coup d'état convinced him to embrace a policy of increased democratization. Deftly juggling pressures from religious fundamentalists, leftists, nationalists, and militarists, Hassan was a shrewd manager of Morocco's fortunes. The new king, Mohammed VI, 33 years old, has promised to modernize the country, stressing territorial integrity, educational reform (80% of Morocco's rural poor are illiterate), and increased public freedom, including women's rights. His abrupt sacking of former Interior Minister Driss Basri in late 1999 was the new king's first bold move toward national renewal and reconciliation; time will tell whether sufficient baraka was passed to this latest incarnation of the Alaouite dynasty, which has ruled Morocco since 1672.

Pleasures and Pastimes

Beaches

With coasts on both the Mediterranean and the Atlantic, Morocco has hundreds of miles of sandy beaches, many of them lonely strands with little or no development. The best-known resorts are at Tangier, Asilah, Essaouira, and Agadir, the best of which is by far Essaouira, a lovely fortified town with a fishing port. Agadir could just as easily be on the Riviera or the Costa del Sol, and Tangier is too plagued by hustlers. Asilah is a picturesque fortified village with an important arts festival in late July. Plage des Nations, just north of Rabat, is an excellent beach for swimming and surfing, though beware: this part of the Atlantic coast is known for undertow and dangerous currents.

Dining

Like Morocco itself, Moroccan cuisine mixes tastes and ingredients in surprising ways. Sweet-and-salty combinations such as *pastilla de pigeon* (pigeon in a flaky phyllo pastry—a sort of pigeon potpie) and lemon and olives with *tagine de poulet* (stewed chicken) are common. Dishes are based on a wide range of spices and vegetables and tends away from thick sauces. For simple street fare, you can grab a bowl of *harira* (chickpea, lentil, and meat soup) for about 50¢ in any *souk* (market). *Brochettes* and beef or lamb kebabs may cost as much as 10 dirhams, just over a U.S. dollar. Restaurant fare varies widely. The standard Moroccan menu is nearly always composed of hors d'oeuvres followed by *pastilla, tagine, couscous,* and, for dessert, another flaky *pastilla* with sweet cream. After sampling the traditional menu, order à la carte to try new dishes. *Mechoui,* roast lamb, must be ordered before you arrive at the restaurant. The best wines are the red Medaillon, Cuvée du Président, Ksar, and the white Coquillage, all from around Meknes. Mint tea (known affectionately as Moroccan whiskey, though it's nonalcoholic) is the standard hot beverage.

CATEGORY	COST*
$$$$	over 450DH
$$$	300–450DH
$$	150–300DH
$	under 150DH

**per person for a three-course meal, excluding drinks, service, and tax*

Fiestas and Moussems

Check with local tourist offices for the exact dates of annual fiestas and *moussems* (celebrations of *marabouts,* or saints). These are exciting events, including Moroccan music, dance, food, and the famous *fantasias,* mock cavalry charges complete with equestrian acrobatics and musket barrages. Moussem Moulay Abdallah (in El Jadida) and Moussem Moulay Idriss (near Meknes), both in August, are two big attractions. Other festivals include the Rose Festival (Kelaa M'Goun, in the Dadès Valley), in May; Symphonies in the Desert (Ouarzazate), in June; Asilah's arts festival, in August; and the famous Marriage Moussem (Imilchil), in September, when Berber brides are brought to meet and marry their husbands in mass ceremonies.

Lodging

Hotels range from some of the best and most expensive in the world to inexpensive and decent to dirt-cheap and dodgy. Generally speaking, we suggest splurging on first-class lodging whenever possible, though there are some excellent mid-range choices as well. In the Moroccan maelstrom, or what can feel like one, it's comforting to have your car safely off the street. When calling or faxing from overseas, note that the country code for Morocco is 212.

CATEGORY	COST*
$$$$	over 2,000DH
$$$	1,000–2,000DH
$$	500–1,000DH
$	under 500DH

**per person for a three-course meal, excluding drinks, service, and tax*

Outdoor Activities

In a single trip to Morocco, weather permitting, you can sail, swim, and surf in the Atlantic; ski and hike in the High Atlas; and ride a camel out into the desert. For a breather, you can play golf on a course designed by Robert Trent Jones or fly fish in the Azrou cedar forest.

Shopping

Moroccan crafts are irresistible even to the inveterate nonconsumer. The souks (markets) are filled with handmade ceramics, handwoven *kilims,* knotted rugs, marquetry, leather goods, and jewelry. Dyes have an extraordinarily bright, pure, and natural quality. Spice markets are a great chance to take Morocco's smells and tastes home with you. Bargaining for any of these wares can be arduous: decide how much you're willing to pay for an item and quote a third of that price to start. Better still, resolve to buy nothing and refuse to quote a price; prices will drop very quickly.

Exploring Morocco

Between uneven surfaces, donkey carts, wandering camels, and drifting sand, driving in Morocco is an adventure. Moreover, the spectacular scenery presents constant surprises, so the main difficulty is keeping your eyes on the road. The light is so sharp and clear that it's crucial to avoid driving into it; travel early when headed west and in late afternoon when headed east. Early evening is prime driving time, as Moroccan sunsets are stunning. Women traveling alone or without men will have occasional difficulty; the only solution—which does keep trouble at bay—is to wear conservative clothing, walk fast (as if you know exactly where you are going), and avoid eye contact completely. Just whiz on by. Women and men alike can hire licensed guides through any municipal tourist office; they cost $15–$20 for half a day, are invariably excellent, and help fend off hustlers.

Great Itineraries

IF YOU HAVE 3 DAYS

Find a way to see Marrakesh and Fez, spending a day and a half in each, arriving either by plane (to save time) or by train (to save money). Flying from Spain to Marrakesh saves time and hassle; otherwise, take the boat to **Tangier** ①, visit the medina and the American Legation Museum, dine at the Hotel Minzah, and take the overnight train to **Marrakesh** ⑧. On day two, explore that city's souks and monuments, especially the Djemâa el Fna square around sunset. Early the next morning, fly to **Fez** ⑬ and have a guide take you through the medina, Fez el Bali—the world's largest still-functioning medieval city.

IF YOU HAVE 5 DAYS

Fly to **Marrakesh** ⑧ and spend two days. On day three, rent a car and drive over the High Atlas to **Ouarzazate** ⑨ for lunch at Chez Dimitri before driving the Route of the Kasbahs (fortified houses and granaries) through the Dadès Valley to **Erfoud** ⑪ and the Auberge Derkaouah. Get up in time for the sunrise over the desert rim at the **Merzouga** ⑫ dunes before driving north through the Azrou cedar forest en route to **Fez** ⑬. On day five, spend at least a full morning exploring the medina, Fez el Bali, with a guide.

IF YOU HAVE 10 DAYS

With 10 days, you can just about do it all: Atlantic beaches, the major cities, Atlas mountains, and the Sahara. Take the Trasmediterránea ferry from Algeciras to **Tangier** ① and spend the first night in the Hotel Minzah. After seeing the souk, the medina, and the American Legation Museum, head for Rabat, with an optional lunch stop on the beach at **Asilah** ② or Plage des Nations. In **Rabat** ③, explore the Medina, Oudaïa Kasbah, and Hassan Mosque, and in Salé, just across the estuary, visit the *medersa* (medieval student residence) before driving the slower but more panoramic beach road to **Casablanca** ④. On day three, visit Casablanca's spice market and, on the way out of town, the colossal Hassan II Mosque. Continue through El Jadida to **Essaouira** ⑤, a good five hours down the coast from Casablanca, and stay overnight at the Villa Maroc, one of Morocco's most charming little inns. On day four, drive south past **Agadir** ⑥ and inland to **Taroudant** ⑦, known as the pocket Marrakesh, and stay at La Gazelle d'Or. On day five, drive over the Tizi n'Test through Ouirgane to **Marrakesh** ⑧, a good four- to five-hour drive. Spend a day or two in Marrakesh exploring the main souks and sights. In the late afternoon of the sixth day, drive over the High Atlas to **Ouarzazate** ⑨ and establish a base camp at the Hotel Riad Salam. From here, explore the Drâa Valley south to **Zagora** ⑩ and M'hamid, taking time to see some of the kasbahs along the way. Drive back to **Ouarzazate** ⑨ in late afternoon. On day eight, drive east along the Route of the Thousand Kasbahs through the panoramic Dadès Valley to **Erfoud** ⑪ and check into the Auberge Derkaouah. On day nine, get up at 5 AM to see the sun rise over the rim of the desert at the **Merzouga** ⑫ dunes before driving back north through the Azrou cedar forest to **Fez** ⑬. In Fez, explore the medina, Fez el Bali, on the 10th day. From Fez, fly or drive to Rabat or Casablanca for connections elsewhere. If you have more time, make the short drive to **Meknes** ⑭ for the night, and the next day see the city's walls, souk, and *medersa* (Koranic school); the sacred town of **Moulay Idriss**; and the Roman ruins at **Volubilis** ⑮ (marked as Oualili, Arabic for Volubilis) before making for either **Rabat** ③ or **Casablanca** ④ for flights out. Alternately, if you're headed back to Spain, drive to **Asilah** ② for a last night and a morning on the beach before you catch the sunset boat from Tangier.

When to Tour Morocco

Spring (late March–late May) is the high season in Morocco and generally the best time to come. Early April might allow sunning and swimming in the south, skiing in the Atlas Mountains, and peeking at the desert without extreme temperatures. It's very hot from mid-June to mid-September, though temperatures are fine on the coast and in the High Atlas. Winter can be cold, especially in the desert, and the less expensive hotels may not be heated. Remember the Muslim holiday Ramadan when planning a trip to Morocco: this monthlong fast requires abstention from food, drink, tobacco, and sex during daylight hours. Toward the end of the month tempers can get short; that said, nocturnal festivities are wilder than ever. Foreigners are not required to observe the fast, but public consumption of food, drink, or tobacco is considered rude and will sometimes result in a rebuke. Ramadan begins late November in 2000, early November in 2001.

Tangier

❶ *15 km (9 mi) from Algeciras across the Straits of Gibraltar, 350 km (220 mi) northeast of Casablanca.*

Just right of the exit from the port area, walk up Rue Portugal, skirting the medina. Continue up the hill through a small gate in the medina wall to the **Fondouk Market,** where you'll be surrounded by the very color and vitality—men and women dressed in bright *djellabas* (full-length robes with pointed hoods), bringing produce in from the mountains—that inspired painters Delacroix, Regnault, Matisse, Fortuny, and so many others to make Morocco a leitmotif. A left on Rue de la Liberté leads up to Place de France and the sumptuous French consulate. Another left on Boulevard Pasteur takes you down past a belvedere to the tourist office.

Walk down through the **Grand Socco** (Great Market) through the pointed archway to the **Petit Socco** (Small Market) and into the heart of Tangier's old quarter and artisan district. Uphill to the left is the **Place de la Kasbah,** where another belvedere has views over the port.

Don't miss the **American Legation Museum** on your way up Rue Portugal. Fifty yards before the first intersection, you'll see a plaque announcing the Legation; steps lead up to the right through a yellow arch into an oasis of peace and quiet (two things you may welcome on your first day in Morocco). An 1821 gift of the Sultan of Morocco to the young American Republic, this museum has a unique history. It was the first property acquired abroad by the United States and served as the consular and diplomatic mission of the United States in Morocco for 140 years. It also is the only U.S. National Historic Landmark on foreign soil. The Legation's two libraries are an important resource for scholars of North Africa—the rooms and the collections of paintings and memorabilia include a letter from George Washington to the Sultan of Morocco, a Kokoschka painting, and a room of Paul Bowles artifacts: letters, documents, leather traveling cases, and photographs.

Dining and Lodging

$$$–$$$$ ★ ✕🏨 **El Minzah.** Ask anyone in Tangier for the finest hotel *or* restaurant in town, and the immediate answer will be El Minzah. Studded wooden doors, a staff in Ottoman costume, beautiful gardens, an elegant patio, the constant sound of falling water (a music much cherished by Moroccans), and fine views over the Straits of Gibraltar to Spain prove them right. ✉ *85 rue de la Liberté,* ☎ *9/935885,* FAX *9/934546. 142 rooms. 3 restaurants, piano bar, pool. AE, DC, MC, V.*

$$ 🏨 **Hotel Continental.** Overlooking the port from the edge of the medina, this wonderful Old World palace, vintage 1888, is the best buy in town for aesthetes and romantics—and who else goes to Morocco? Bertolucci stayed in Room 108 while shooting *The Sheltering Sky.* Monsieur Abdessalam is a gracious host. ✉ *36 rue Dar el Baroud,* ☎ *9/931024,* FAX *9/931143. 15 rooms with bath, 30 rooms share 10 baths. Bar. AE, DC, MC, V.*

$ 🏨 **Hotel Muniria.** William Burroughs wrote *Naked Lunch* in Room 9—now the home of Madame Rabia, the lovely owner. The Tangerinn, underneath, is *the* late-night haunt of the expatriate set, once the stomping ground of Kerouacs and Ginsbergs. Room 8 overlooks the Bay of Tangier. Rue Magellan can be tricky to find; approach from above at night, i.e., from Boulevard Pasteur. ✉ *2 rue Magellan,* ☎ *9/935337. 6 rooms with bath, 2 rooms share bath. Bar. No credit cards.*

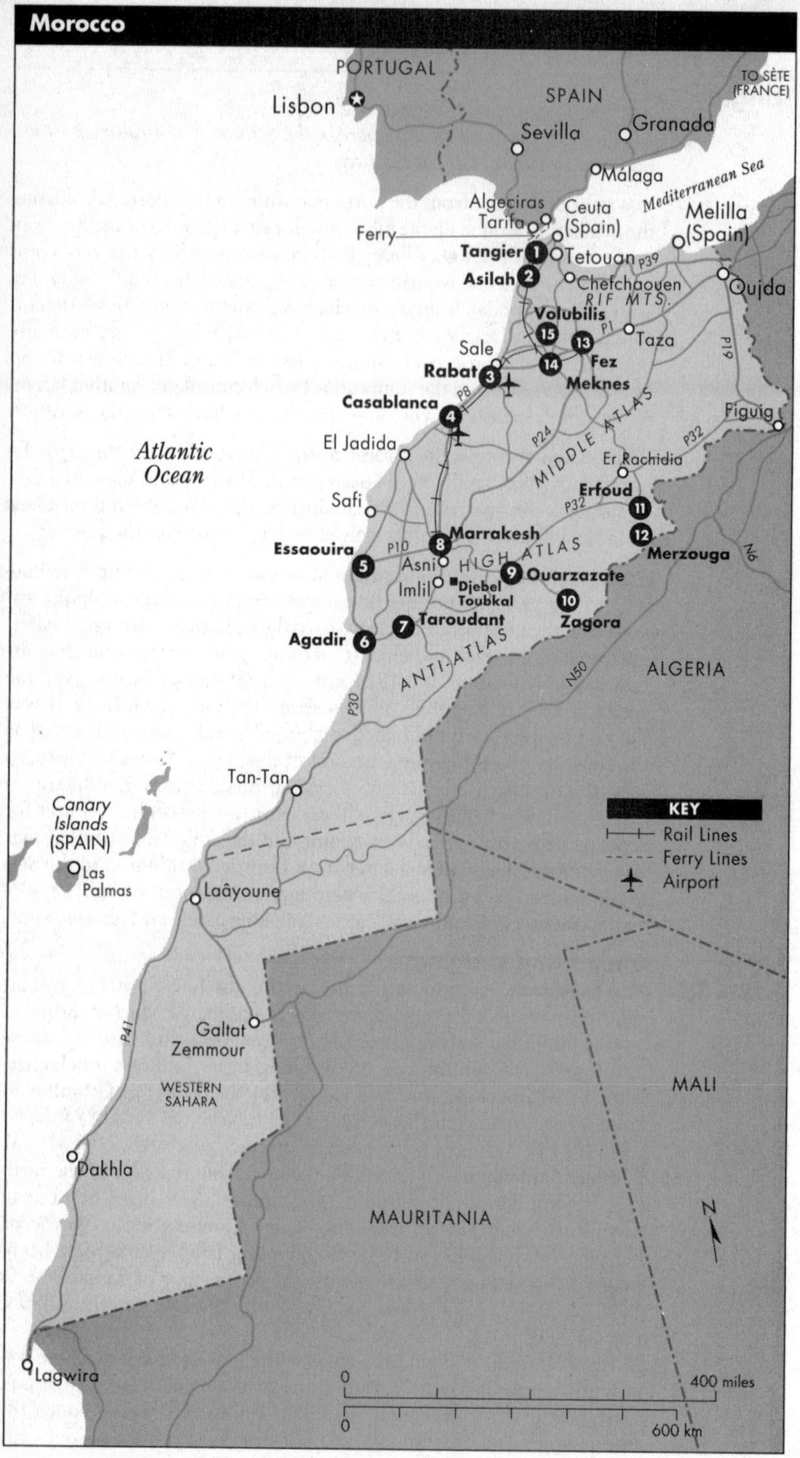
Morocco
PORTUGAL
Lisbon
SPAIN
TO SÈTE (FRANCE)
Sevilla
Granada
Málaga
Mediterranean Sea
Algeciras
Tarifa
Ceuta (Spain)
Melilla (Spain)
Ferry
Tangier 1
Tetouan
P39
Asilah 2
Chefchaouen
RIF MTS.
Oujda
Volubilis
15
13
P1
Taza
P19
Sale
Rabat 3
14
Fez
Meknes
P8
Casablanca 4
MIDDLE ATLAS
Figuig
P24
P32
Atlantic Ocean
El Jadida
Er Rachidia
Erfoud
P32
Safi
11
12
Marrakesh 8
Merzouga
N6
Essaouira 5
P10
Asni
HIGH ATLAS
9 Ouarzazate
Imlil
Djebel Toubkal
10
Zagora
7 Taroudant
Agadir 6
ANTI-ATLAS
N50
ALGERIA
P30
Tan-Tan
Canary Islands (SPAIN)
Las Palmas
Laâyoune
KEY
Rail Lines
Ferry Lines
Airport
Galtat Zemmour
P41
WESTERN SAHARA
MALI
Dakhla
MAURITANIA
N
Lagwira
0
400 miles
0
600 km

Asilah

❷ *46 km (30 mi) southwest of Tangier, 272 km (164 mi) northeast of Rabat.*

Asilah is a lovely fortified beach town less than an hour from Tangier. Known for its summer arts festival (held in late July) and its Sunday flea market, Asilah also has an excellent beach and an interesting medina. The Palais Raisuli, recently restored, was built in 1909 by Er Raisuli, a famous bandit who gained power through a skillful combination of cattle rustling and kidnapping. The best places for lunch are El Espigón, on the beach at the east end of the waterfront, and La Alcazaba, overlooking the Bab (Gate) el Kasaba into the medina.

Dining and Lodging

$ ✕ **El Espigón.** A great combination of seafood and simple beach atmosphere, this place serves the freshest fish and finest green salads in town. Lines form in summer. ✉ *Rue Yacob el Mansour,* ☎ *9/917157. AE, DC, MC, V.*

$ 🏨 **Al Khaima.** Al Khaima is the best hotel in Asilah, and would be altogether ideal were it not for a merciless combination of mosquitoes and a dance club that thumps from around midnight to 3 or 4 AM. Bring bug juice and earplugs. The roar of the surf is constant, and from pillow level you can see the lights of fishing boats working the Atlantic. ✉ *BP 101/Rte. de Tanger, Km 1, Asilah,* ☎ *9/917428,* FAX *9/917566. 90 rooms, 20 apartments. Restaurant, bar, pool, billiards, dance club, playground. AE, DC, MC, V.*

Rabat

❸ *318 km (191 mi) from Tangier, 91 km (55 mi) from Casablanca.*

Despite being the nation's capital, Rabat seems only mildly Moroccan. Functionaries rush to work at 8:45 AM looking for all the world like European bureaucrats, and the streets are wide and orderly. **Salé,** across the estuary of the Oued (River) Bou Regreg, is more interesting, with its stunning Medersa Bou Inan and its Grande Mosque. Key Rabat monuments include the tower of the Hassan Mosque, the Chellah Necropolis, and the Mohammed V Mausoleum. Bab er Rouah (Gate of the Wind), designed to be the most inspiring approach to the imperial city, is one of the most beautiful gates in Morocco.

Dining and Lodging

$$ ✕ **Koutoubia.** One of Rabat's best traditional Moroccan restaurants, this small one serves classics: *pastilla de pigeon* (pigeon in phyllo pastry), *harira* (chickpea, lentil, and meat soup), *tagine* (meat or fish stewed in almonds, plums, and/or vegetables), *mechoui* (roast lamb), and couscous. ✉ *10 rue Pierre Pavent,* ☎ *7/760125. AE, DC, MC, V.*

$$$$ ★ ✕🏨 **Rabat Hyatt Regency.** This complex near the Dar es Salam golf course is a world of its own, with four on-site restaurants, one of which is Moroccan. You get complete comfort in an atmosphere that's only remotely—if at all—related to the host country. ✉ *Aviation Souissi, BP 450,* ☎ *7/671234,* FAX *7/672492. 218 rooms. 4 restaurants, piano bar, sauna, Turkish bath, 4 tennis courts, exercise room, meeting rooms. AE, DC, MC, V.*

Casablanca

❹ *289 km (180 mi) southwest of Fez, 238 km (148 mi) north of Marrakesh.*

A booming metropolis of 3½ million, Casablanca is bound to disappoint cineasts and romantics expecting to bump into Ingrid Bergman and

Humphrey Bogart at the counterfeit Rick's Bar, in the Hyatt Regency (where waiters take orders in trench coats and fedoras). The **Grande Mosquée Hassan II,** however, will not disappoint. Opened in 1994, it accommodates 25,000 worshipers inside—where the glass floor reveals the ocean below—and 80,000 in the courtyard. The 656-ft minaret is Morocco's tallest structure, and the mosque is the third-largest in the world after those in Mecca and Medina. The **Corniche** is a pleasant promenade, and the medina's **spice market** is a rich jumble of sights and smells. **Place Mohammed V** is surrounded by elegant buildings: the Palace of Justice, Bank of Morocco, French Consulate, and post office.

Dining and Lodging

$$ ✕ **Al-Mounia.** The best restaurant in Casablanca for authenticity and value, Al-Mounia serves classic Moroccan fare as well as à la carte selections covering a wide range of both seafood and upland dishes. ✉ *95 rue du Prince Moulay Abdallah,* ☎ *2/222669. AE, DC, MC, V. Closed Sun.*

$$$$ ★ ✕🏨 **Royal Mansour.** One of Morocco's finest hotels, the Royal Mansour comes with lots of perks: fabulous food served in a lush garden courtyard, live Cole Porter tunes, and a rooftop *hammam* (Turkish bath). The rooms are luxurious, if not especially memorable. ✉ *27 av. des F.A.R.,* ☎ *2/313011,* FAX *2/312583. 159 rooms, 23 suites. 3 restaurants, piano bar, sauna, Turkish bath, meeting rooms. AE, DC, MC, V.*

$$ 🏨 **Hotel Al Moussafir.** It's new, impeccably clean, well located (near the Casa-Voyageurs train station), and a fraction of the price of the Royal Mansour. ✉ *Blvd. Bahmad,* ☎ *2/401984,* FAX *2/400799. 88 rooms, 9 suites. Restaurant, bar. AE, DC, MC, V.*

Essaouira

5 *351 km (211 mi) southeast of Casablanca, 172 km (103 mi) north of Agadir, 171 km (102 mi) west of Marrakesh.*

Essaouira's blue-and-white medina is one of Morocco's sweetest retreats, a refuge if you've just come from Casablanca, Tangier, or Marrakesh. An 18th-century fortified port built by French architect Theodore Cornut, who had been captured by Sultan Sidi Mohammed Ben Abdallah, the town is a blend of the Moroccan medina and the French grid plan. Orson Welles found it so compelling that he filmed his version of *Othello* here in 1949. Famous for fresh fish grilled in the port, for woodworkers in cedar and thuya wood, and for the spice markets in its medina, Essaouira is a difficult place to leave. Walk through the Skala de la Ville (the woodworkers' souk) to the North Bastion for marvelous views of the town and the rocky shoreline, or walk around the beach to the village of Diabat, a Jimi Hendrix hangout in the '60s.

Dining and Lodging

$$ ✕ **Chez Sam.** Neatly placed at the farthest edge of the dock, Chez Sam is an institution in Essaouira, the first-choice restaurant and watering hole for foreign travelers, local artists, surfers, and honeymooners alike. The fresh fish and a good Coquillage white wine are more than welcome after the drive down from Casablanca or over from Marrakesh. ✉ *Port, Essaouira,* ☎ *4/476513. AE, DC, MC, V.*

$$ ✕🏨 **Villa Maroc.** You know you're in the right hotel when you dread checking out. Villa Maroc's charm lies in its simplicity, its good taste, and the easygoing manners of owners Abderrahim Ezzaher and Cornelia Hendry. Each room is different; the nestlike tower room has sea views and continuous surf sounds from pillow level. Dinner, which must be ordered in advance, is excellent Moroccan *cuisine du terroir* (home cooking). ✉ *10 rue Abdellah Ben Yassine, Essaouira,* ☎ *4/476147,* FAX *4/476758. 22 rooms. Restaurant. AE, DC, MC, V.*

Agadir

6 *173 km (104 mi) south of Essaouira, 303 km (187 mi) southwest of Marrakesh, 85 km (51 mi) west of Taroudant.*

Agadir's best feature is its airport, from which you can easily get to Essaouira, Taroudant, or Marrakesh. Unless you feel the need to leave Morocco and join the world of package tours, you can skip it as a cultural destination. Built in 1505, Agadir became an important port under Mohamed Echeikh el Medhi, founder of the Saadian dynasty, exporting dates, spices, oils, and gold. It was destroyed by an earthquake in 1960 and rebuilt with paradise in mind, but the modern architecture is dull. The beaches, bazaars, and terraces are enjoyable, however, and athletes can indulge in tennis, golf, sailing, or scuba diving.

$$ ✕ **Agadir Beach Club.** If you want to regroup before plunging into the real Morocco, this modern, cosmopolitan hotel in the center of Agadir's long beach will cater to your every need. ✉ *Rte. de l'Oued Souss, Box 310, Agadir,* ☎ *8/844344,* FAX *8/840863. 438 rooms. 4 restaurants, bar, grill, sauna, meeting rooms. AE, DC, MC, V.*

Taroudant

7 *85 km (51 mi) east of Agadir, 223 km (134 mi) southwest of Marrakesh.*

The ocher walls of Taroudant against a hazy background of snow-capped Atlas mountains are one of Morocco's great sights. This Berber market town of some 30,000 seems largely undiscovered—hence its charm. The ramparts and the souks are the main attractions; the Souk Arab Artisanal specializes in rugs, leather, and jewelry, and the Marché Berbère sells spices, vegetables, clothing, and ceramics. The ramparts were built in the 16th century by the Saadian dynasty, who made Taroudant their capital. The town is a prime base camp for both trekking the High Atlas and driving the dramatic Tizi n'Test pass to Marrakesh.

Dining and Lodging

$$$$ ✕ **Hôtel Gazelle d'Or.** Long one of Morocco's best hotels, the Gazelle d'Or gained fame in 1992 when the Duchess of York, then married, turned up here sans the Duke. The restaurant is equally renowned and requires jacket and tie. Originally a hunting lodge built in the 1920s by a French baron, the hotel consists of bungalows surrounding a lush garden. ✉ *Agadir road, Km 2,* ☎ *8/852039,* FAX *8/852537. 30 rooms. Restaurant, pub, 2 tennis courts, horseback riding, Turkish bath. AE, DC, MC, V. Closed Aug.*

$$ ✕ **Salam.** For less wallet strain yet just as grand, if somewhat threadbare, surroundings, head straight for the Salam. Housed in a former palace that's built right into the city walls, the hotel has a central patio with luxuriant banana palms. ✉ *Kasbah,* ☎ *8/852312,* FAX *8/852654. 75 rooms, 30 suites. 2 restaurants, bar, pool. AE, DC, MC, V.*

Marrakesh

8 *238 km (148 mi) south of Casablanca, 483 km (300 mi) southwest of Fez.*

The tumultuous and panoramic square **Djemâa el Fna** (translated alternately as "Assembly of the Dead" and "Mosque of the Void") is a sensorial feast and the highlight of a visit to Marrakesh, if not all of Morocco. Here clouds of aromatic smoke from outdoor kitchens combine with Berber music, snake charmers' flutes, water vendors' bells, the muezzin's call to prayer, scribes and their clients tucked under umbrellas, and tooth pullers surrounded by even rows of molars. Beyond it all, the snowcapped Atlas peaks rise behind the 800-year-old Kotoubia minaret. In the evening, the warmth of the fires meets the cool breeze from the mountains while fire-lit faces raptly follow the tales of Berber storytellers.

Essential sights in Marrakesh include the great minaret of the **Koutoubia Mosque,** the **Saadian Tombs,** the **Badi Palace,** the **Bahia Palace,** and, of course, the **souks.** Equidistant from the Atlantic and the High Atlas, Marrakesh was originally a man-made oasis served by underground aqueducts leading in from the mountains. As a result, it's a paradise of gardens, among the finest of which are the **Jardin Agdal,** the **Jardin Majorelle,** and the **Jardin Menara.**

Dining and Lodging

$$$$ ✕ **Le Yacout.** This graceful space, designed by renowned interior designer Billy Willis, is generally considered the most elegant restaurant in Marrakesh. You're greeted with a drink on the roof or, in colder weather, in front of a fireplace. The cuisine is excellent, the service flawless, and reservations essential. ✉ *79 Sidi Ahmed Soussi,* ☎ *4/382929,* FAX *4/382538. AE, DC, MC, V.*

$$$ ★ ✕ **Dar Marjana.** You'll feel like you've walked into a Delacroix painting. Daj Marjana serves excellent cuisine in beautiful surroundings, accented by folk music, belly dancers, and Nubian waiters dressed in rich greens. Reserve in advance and be punctual or you might lose your table. ✉ *15 Derb Sidi Ali Tair, Bab Doukkala,* ☎ *4/445773. Reservations essential. MC, V. Closed Tues. No lunch.*

$$$ ✕ **Stylia.** Not far from Djemâa el Fna, Stylia is housed in an elegant building originally built by a Jewish refugee from Spain in 1492. (The dining room is in the former concubinage.) Specializing in Moroccan standards, the menu also spotlights *tangía,* a special *marrakshi* lamb stew. ✉ *34 rue Ksour,* ☎ *4/445837. AE, DC, MC, V.*

$$$$ ★ ✕▣ **La Mamounia.** Everyone from Winston Churchill to Bryan Ferry has loved this unique oasis-within-an-oasis. One of the most famous hotels in the world despite its queasy mixture of Art Deco and Moroccan design, La Mamounia is worth every one of the many nickels it costs. The grounds, facilities, and service are all sensational; the staff in particular is impeccably courtly and friendly. You're walking distance from Djemâa el Fna. ✉ *Av. Bab Jdid,* ☎ *4/448981,* FAX *4/444940. 171 rooms, 57 suites, 3 villas. 5 restaurants, 5 bars, pool, beauty salon, massage, sauna, Turkish bath, tennis courts, squash, billiards, meeting rooms. AE, DC, MC, V.*

$$$$ ✕▣ **Palmeraie Golf Palace.** This enclave near the Robert Trent Jones golf course has balconies overlooking gardens and—count 'em—eight restaurants, each with a different atmosphere and cuisine. Dining options include Moroccan, Italian, and French. Rooms are simple and faultless, if unremarkable. ✉ *Les Jardins de la Palmeraie,* ☎ *4/301010,* FAX *4/305050. 280 rooms, 34 suites. 8 restaurants, 4 bars, 5 pools, 18-hole golf course, 3 tennis courts, bowling. AE, DC, MC, V.*

$$$ ✕▣ **Imperial Borj.** In the heart of town, very close to the city walls, the Imperial offers rooms with marbled bathrooms and balconies overlooking exotic gardens. The Moroccan restaurant, La Rose de Sables, makes excellent *harira* and couscous. ✉ *Av. Echouhada,* ☎ *4/447322,* FAX *4/446206. 187 rooms, 20 suites. 3 restaurants, cafeteria, piano bar, 3 pools, beauty salon, meeting rooms. AE, DC, MC, V.*

Ouarzazate

❾ *204 km (122 mi) from Marrakesh, 170 km (102 mi) from Zagora, 260 km (156 mi) from M'Hamid, 300 km (180 mi) from Erfoud.*

After the oasis of Marrakesh, a late-afternoon drive to Ouarzazate over the Tizi n'Tichka pass seems as dark, remote, and starkly beautiful as the far side of the moon. The palm trees and gardens of Marrakesh quickly give way to the rocky soil of the Atlas and the sweeping buffs and browns of these rolling hills. Treeless mountains are sporadically punctuated by adobe villages that seem left over from a remote and primitive past. Boys selling split quartz rush your car (don't be alarmed; they're not dangerous, and it's probably a good buy); bands of colorfully clad children wave as you drive by; Berber women stagger under enormous bundles of firewood. The luxury and chaos of Marrakesh seem a distant memory, the Atlantic freshness of Essaouira pure fantasy. The turn for the **Alcazaba de Teluet** (Teluet Fortress) cuts east just after the pass; if you have enough daylight left (and a vehicle with good clearance, preferably a four-wheel-drive), take it. The road eventually comes around to Ouarzazate, a good base for ventures into the desert.

Dining and Lodging

$$ ★ ✕ **Chez Dimitri.** Founded in 1928 as the first store, gas pump, post office, telephone booth, dance hall, and restaurant in town, Chez Dimitri may look unimpressive, but the food is excellent, the owners are friendly and helpful, and you may find yourself surrounded by movie stars on location. If Ouarzazate is a crossroads of the desert and the southern oasis routes, Chez Dimitri is the heart of it. ✉ *22 av. Mohammed V,* ☏ *4/882653. MC, V.*

$$ ✕▣ **Riad Salam.** This is the place to stay in Ouarzazate: it's simple, friendly, and unpretentious, and the staff tries hard. Berber musicians perform until midnight, often in front of a roaring fire. The manager, Monsieur Benjeddin, is happy to advise you on excursions. ✉ *Av. Mohammed V,* ☏ *4/883335,* FAX *4/882766. 62 rooms. Restaurant, bar, pool. AE, DC, MC, V.*

Zagora

❿ *170 km (102 mi) southeast of Ouarzazate.*

The trip to Zagora through the **Drâa Valley** is a lovely panoramic drive, leading to the boundary between the Sahara and what some writers have called "reality." After Zagora, time and distance are measured in camel days: a sign at the end of Zagora's main street reads "TIMBUKTU 52 DAYS"—as in "52 Days by Camel." The town of M'hamid, 98 km (65 mi) ahead, marks the end of the paved road and the beginning of the Sahara, but beware: even the paved road may be drifted over with sand. En route to M'hamid are the town of Tamegroute and the Tinfou Dunes (marked simply "Dunes" on some maps).

Dining and Lodging

$$ ✕▣ **Ksar Tinsouline.** Zagora's Old World hotel is making a definite comeback. The pool, bar, and lobby are all graceful, with a somewhat colonial look. The rooms are anticlimactic by comparison but perfectly adequate. ✉ *Av. Hassan II,* ☏ *4/847252,* FAX *4/847042. 14 rooms. Restaurant. AE, DC, MC, V.*

$ ▣ **Auberge Repos du Sable.** For a taste of the desert, spend a night at this charming inn, 29 km (18 mi) south of Tamegroute on Route 6958, and walk out to the dunes at daybreak. Be warned: the plumbing is primitive, but the aesthetics of the place more than compensate. Hassan and Fatima El Farouj are painters and have exhibited all over Europe. The medieval wooden door-lock system was reinvented (restored) by Hassan's father. ✉ *Chez El Farouj, Tinfou Dunes,* ☏ FAX *4/848566. 18 rooms, none with bath. Restaurant, pool, Turkish bath. MC, V.*

En Route There are now two ways to reach Erfoud from Zagora. Branching east 29 km (18 mi) south of Agdz, Route 6956 through Tazzarine (where it becomes 3454) and Alnif is a spectacular 233-km (140-mi) drive to Rissani. This road is one of the best paved, least crowded, and most scenic in the country. Beware of the official map of Morocco in this area; some roads are poorly drawn or erroneously placed, and others have not been updated. Trust only the Michelin 959 for accurate detail.

The drive from Ouarzazate through the **Dadès Valley** is one of the great Moroccan adventures, with enough scenery to distract you for a week. Known as the Route of the Thousand Kasbahs, this river valley is lined with fortified village houses and granaries with crenellated battlements. The **Skoura Oasis,** the **Vallée des Roses** (Asif M'Goun), the town of Boumalne and the **Dadès Gorges,** and the town of Tinerhir and the **Todra Gorges** are all huge and dramatic. The Dadès Gorges are navigable by the average automobile, but the Todra gorges should be explored either on foot or in a four-wheel-drive vehicle. From Tinejdad, Route 3451 branches right and is paved all the way to Erfoud.

Erfoud

⓫ *300 km (180 mi) from Ouarzazate, 446 km (268 mi) from Fez.*

Erfoud is little more than a jumping-off point for the Merzouga dunes. Its best architectural feature is the main door into the medina, designed in the typical Almohad style. Surrounded by one of Morocco's most important oases and more than a million date palms, Erfoud holds a date festival every October.

Dining and Lodging

$$–$$$ ✕🏨 **Kasbah Derkaouah.** This extraordinary lodging is at the edge of the desert, 30 minutes' drive from the Merzouga dunes. Michel Auzat and his daughter Bouchra and son Saïd serve excellent Moroccan and French cuisine and offer cozy, well-designed accommodations of various kinds: there are nine doubles, two duplexes, two bungalows, one apartment, and two tents. Michel's 20 Arabian purebreds are ideal for horseback (*much* more comfortable than camelback) treks to desert oases. ✉ *24 km (14 mi) southeast of Erfoud (☞ En Route, below). Write c/o Michel Auzat,* ✉ *Erfoud,* ☎ *5/577140,* FAX *5/577140. 14 rooms. Restaurant. AE, DC, MC, V. Closed June–Aug.*

En Route To find Kasbah Derkaouah from Erfoud, cross the market square (Place des Far) and follow signs for Dunes Sables d'Or straight out into the desert. Don't be surprised when you find yourself driving across the Oued (River) Ziz—this is not a mirage but a dam and bridge over which, in early spring, the river flows at a depth of an inch or two. Once the pavement ends, follow the green-and-white markers that Michel has provided to guide you in.

Merzouga

⓬ *53 km (32 mi) southeast of Erfoud.*

A sunrise trip to the **Sahara dunes** (Erg Chebbi) at Merzouga has become a classic Moroccan adventure. A series of café-restaurant-hotels overlooks the dunes, and the Café du Sud runs camels (specifically, one-humped dromedaries) out to the top of the dunes, a 45-minute walk on foot. The Auberge Dunes d'Or, distinguished by a small wooden airplane used in the filming of Saint-Exupéry's *Le Petit Prince,* has simple rooms and running water. Kasbah Derkaouah (☞ *above*) is 11 km (7 mi) from the dunes, 25 km (15 mi) from the town of Merzouga; follow the telephone poles to be sure you're on the right track. The nearby seasonal salt lake is a surprising sight, filled in early spring with pink flamingos. The town has little to recommend it other than a few not-too-compelling hotels; if you get as far south as Merzouga, complete the loop through Rissani and the Tafilalt oasis before heading north to Er Rachidia, Midelt, Azrou, and Fez.

En Route The drive from Merzouga to Fez is another astonishing tour: from the desert through the date-palm oases of Tafilalt and the Ziz Valley; then, after the town of Er Rachidia, to the Ziz Gorges, the brown-then-green expanses of the High and Middle Atlas, and finally the Azrou cedar forest, often described as alpine and likely to be filled with snow and foraging Barbary apes in winter. Ifrane, a ski resort in winter, is only 63 km (38 mi) south of Fez.

Fez

13 *483 km (290 mi) northeast of Marrakesh, 60 km (36 mi) east of Meknes, 303 km (182 mi) southeast of Tangier.*

Morocco's Arabic (as opposed to Berber) intellectual and spiritual capital, Fez can at first seem almost too civilized after Marrakesh or the desert. Fez is more refined, more Mediterranean, more Islamic. The city has three sections—the French-built Ville Nouvelle; Fez el Djedid (New Fez, founded in 1276); and the 9th-century medina, **Fez el Bali** (Old Fez, founded in 808)—the oldest of which is a fascinating labyrinth of mosques (no fewer than 360), *medersas* (medieval residential colleges), shops, and artisans' workshops. Craftsmen and vendors of all ages carve wood on hand- and foot-powered lathes, chisel copper, carve wood, dye skins, bake bread, and peddle spices, ceramics, cloth, antiques, jewelry, and food products of all kinds. The largest functioning and self-sufficient medieval city in the world, the medina limits its traffic to donkeys and pedestrians, with only an occasional motorbike; and none of it is staged for tourists. Large numbers of travelers pass through here, but the life of the medina absorbs them easily. Nowhere else in Morocco is a good guide more indispensable.

Fez's architectural highlights include the **Bou Inania Waterclock,** the **Bou Inania Medersa,** the **Nejjarine Fondouk and Woodworking Museum,** the **Kairaouine Mosque,** and the **Kairaouine University,** which, having been founded in the 9th century, predates Bologna by 200 years and Oxford by 300. Don't miss the foul-smelling **tannery**; the **henna market,** with its plaque commemorating the world's first psychiatric hospital (1286); the 14th-century **Tsetouanien Fondouk**; or the wood furnaces for heating *hammams,* the Moroccan version of Turkish baths.

Dining and Lodging

$$$ ✕ **Al Firdaous.** Going far beyond tagines, pastillas, and couscous, Al Firdaous offers Moroccan art, belly dancing, and Berber Gnaoua music along with typical Moroccan cuisine and excellent service. This is an excellent choice for a complete evening. ✉ *10 rue Zenjfour,* ☏ *5/634343,* FAX *5/634343. AE, DC, MC, V.*

$$$ ✕ **Dar Saada.** This mid-medina 16th-century palace is one of Fez's traditional treats and retreats. The kitchen is known for the quality and quantity of everything from beef tagines to pastilla de pigeon to mechoui, which must be ordered a day in advance. High ceilings, carved stucco, and elaborate woodwork all add to the sensorial rush of the place. ✉ *21, Souk Attarine,* ☏ *05/637370. Reservations essential. AE, DC, MC, V.*

$–$$ ✕ **Palais Tijani.** Near the Tijani Mosque in Fez el Bali, this simple but commendable restaurant serves real Moroccan food to both locals and foreigners. Warmth and authenticity are the strong suits: *briouates au kefta* (ground-beef dumplings), *tagine d'agneau aux pruneaux* (lamb stewed in prunes), and mechoui are staples. Wine is not served here, but management will not object if you discreetly bring your own. ✉ *51–53, Derb ben Chekroune–La Blida,* ☏ *05/633335. MC, V.*

$$$$ ✕🏨 **Merinides.** Strategically placed to overlook Fez, the Merinides is deservedly popular, so reserve well in advance. The views of Fez el Bali from the pool—nicely raised above the fray—are the best in town. ✉ *Borj Nord,* ☎ *5/646040,* FAX *5/645225. 79 rooms, 11 suites. 2 restaurants, 2 bars, pool. AE, DC, MC, V.*

$$$$ ✕🏨 **Palais Jamai.** With an unbeatable combination of proximity to the medina, comfort, and elegance, the Palais Jamai is *the* place to stay in Fez. Built 120 years ago, this elegant former residence of the Vizir Jamai (prime minister under Sultan Moulay Hassan in the late 19th century) was lavishly renovated in 1999. The rooms, decorated in typical Moroccan cedar painted with bright geometrical motifs, overlook the gardens and the medina. The two restaurants serve fine Moroccan and international cuisine. ✉ *Bab Guissa,* ☎ *5/634331,* FAX *5/635096. 123 rooms, 14 suites. 3 restaurants, pool, Turkish bath, tennis court. AE, DC, MC, V.*

$$$–$$$$ ★ ✕🏨 **La Maison Bleue.** The Abbadi family has renovated the house of a famous Moroccan astrologer into a sumptuous setting for dining, lodging, and music. High ceilings and intricately carved stucco and cedar walls surround a central patio and fountain, and owner Mehdi Abaddi will graciously show you the eminent scientist and philosopher's rooms, the library, and rooftop terrace. The food is carefully prepared—try the *chwa'k dar,* a Fassi (from Fez) beef tagine—and the Andalusian-style guest rooms are equally mouthwatering. ✉ *2 place de l'Istiqlal Batha,* ☎ *5/741843,* FAX *5/741843. Reservations essential. 6 suites. Hammam. AE, DC, MC, V.*

Meknes

⑭ *60 km (37 mi) west of Fez, 138 km (85 mi) east of Rabat.*

Meknes is known for the 40 km (24 mi) of walls surrounding its medina, its Imperial City (a stronghold within the medina), and, within that, its Royal Palace. The city became Morocco's capital in 1673 under the tyrannical but ambitious Sultan Moulay Ismail (1672–1727). An obsessive builder—he was said to have owned 60,000 slaves, 12,000 horses, and 500 concubines—Moulay Ismail united Morocco and built palaces and mosques that earned Meknes comparisons to Versailles.

The mammoth, horseshoe-arched **Bab al-Mansour** is one of the most beautiful doors in North Africa. It forms a grand entrance to **Moulay Ismail's mausoleum,** one of four mosques in Morocco open to non-Muslims (the others are Casablanca's Hassan II, Rabat's Mohammed V Mausoleum, and Rissani's Moulay Ali Mausoleum). The **Heri as-Souani** (granary), one of the most important sights in the Imperial City, once stored barley for the royal cavalry. For an architectural treat, visit the **Bou Inania Medersa,** one of the best in Morocco. The **Dar Jamai** houses the Museum of Moroccan Art, which has superb collections of carpets, jewelry, and needlework. The building itself is exquisite, especially the carved cedar ceilings on the second floor. The souks in Meknes, just behind the Dar Jamai, are known for high-quality workmanship and comparatively low-key salesmanship.

Dining and Lodging

$$$–$$$$ ✕ **Le Dauphin.** Respected for the quality of its French and international cuisine, Le Dauphin has a refined yet boisterous bistrolike ambience and excellent service. Fish, duck, and foie gras are standards on the menu, as are wines from beyond North Africa. ✉ *5 av. Mohamed V,* ☎ *05/523423. AE, DC, MC, V.*

$$ ✕ **Riad.** Hidden inside the ramparts of the Royal Palace, this garden is owned and managed by Raouf Alaoui Ismail, a direct descendant of Moulay Ismail. Raouf speaks excellent English and serves fine Moroccan cuisine in an elegant setting. Wine is not served in the medina. ✉ 79 *Ksar Chaacha–Dar Lakbira,* ☎ *5/530542. AE, DC, MC, V.*

$$ ✕ **Hotel Transatlantique.** Overlooking Meknes from across the river, the Transatlantique offers poolside comfort, a good Moroccan restaurant, and all the necessary amenities. The rooms themselves are not luxurious, but those with balconies over the pool and orange trees have an Old World charm. ✉ *El-Merinyine,* ☎ *5/525053,* FAX *5/520057. 118 rooms. 2 restaurants, bar, 2 pools, tennis court. AE, DC, MC, V.*

Volubilis and Moulay Idriss

30 km (18 mi) north of Meknes.

Moulay Idriss is Morocco's sacred town—the site of the tomb of the nation's religious and secular founder, for whom it is named. It is said that five pilgrimages to Moulay Idriss are the spiritual equivalent of one to Mecca, hence its nickname, "the poor man's Mecca." A bird's-eye view of the town is interesting, but Moulay Idriss is unremarkable compared to Meknes or Volubilis. Non-Muslims are not allowed inside the tomb.

15 Just 4 km (2½ mi) from Moulay Idriss is **Volubilis,** a virtual cross section of a Roman city and one of Morocco's highlights. These rich mosaic floors, baths, brothel, and even bathrooms bring Rome's remotest 1st- to 3rd-century outpost vividly to life. You can engage a guide at the entrance for 100 dirhams ($15); see if you can get El Hadi, No. 171, who speaks excellent English. His explanations of the different mosaics, the House of Orpheus, the Labors of Hercules, Bacchus discovering Ariadna sleeping, and other historical points are bound to fascinate. ✉ *Follow signs from Meknes, then from Moulay Idriss.* *30DH.* *Daily sunrise–sunset.*

MOROCCO A TO Z

You do not need a visa to enter Morocco. Although the water is potable, it's always advisable to stick to bottled spring water. The time is one hour behind Spain, and the telephone country code is 212.

Arriving and Departing

By Boat

Trasmediterránea offers one fast ferry (1 hr) and 12 slower boats (2½ hrs) daily in winter and departures nearly every hour from March through September. Call 902/454645 for central reservations. There are branch offices in Algeciras (✉ Recinto del Puerto s/n, ☎ 956/663850, FAX 956/665216), Madrid (✉ C. Pedro Muñoz Seca 2, ☎ 902/454645), and Tangier (✉ 3 rue Ibn Roch, ☎ 9/933173).

Having your passport stamped, filling out an entry card, and changing money on the boat can save time in Tangier. Tangier's port can be confusing; rest assured that things tend to work out fine in the end. Upon arrival, it's best to tip someone 5 dirhams to get you a taxi, preferably a *petit taxi* (make sure the meter is turned on), and get quickly out of the port to your hotel or, if you don't have a reservation, to the tourist office at 29 Boulevard Pasteur. When departing, do not believe hustlers who try to convince you that you're missing your boat.

By Plane

Royal Air Maroc (☎ 91/547–7907 in Madrid; 93/301–8474 in Barcelona; 800/344–6726 in the U.S.) and **Iberia** (☎ 800/772–4642 or 902/400500 in the U.S.) fly to Casablanca from Madrid in 90 minutes. Royal Air Maroc's flight, departing Madrid daily at 9:10 PM, is the most dependable and regular. Connections serve Barcelona and Málaga twice weekly. Royal Air Maroc also flies direct from Paris to Marrakesh, as does Air France, though not daily. Royal Air Maroc flies direct from New York to Casablanca on Tuesday, Thursday, Saturday, and Sunday. International connections occasionally serve Tangier, Rabat, Fez, Marrakesh, Ouarzazate, and Agadir.

Getting Around

By Bus

Buses connect the major cities with Agadir, Asilah, Erfoud, Essaouira, Ouarzazate, Rabat, Taroudant, and Zagora. For general information, contact **CTM** (Compagnie Transporte Marocaine; ✉ 23 rue Léon l'Africain, Casablanca, ☎ 4/448127, FAX 4/317406). Major bus stations include the following: **Casablanca** (✉ 23 rue Léon l'Africain, ☎ 2/268061). **Fez** (✉ Av. Mohammed V, ☎ 5/622041). **Marrakesh** (✉ Bab Doukkala, ☎ 4/433993). **Tangier** (✉ Av. des F.A.R., ☎ 9/932415).

By Car

Only by car can you fully appreciate Morocco's great panoramas. Surfaces can be spotty, and freeways are nearly unknown (there's only one, between Tangier and Casablanca), but you'll be fine if you drive slowly and defensively. Some roads in the south seem designed for only one-and-a-half cars; one or both approaching vehicles need to give way. Rent with a reputable agency, as repair shops and spare parts are few and far between; and rent a four-wheel-drive vehicle if you can, as they're safer and they gain you access to some of the most interesting parts of Morocco.

Rental agencies in Casablanca: **Budget** (✉ Torres de los Habous, Av. des F.A.R., ☎ 2/313945) and **Hertz** (✉ 25 rue Foucauld, ☎ 2/484710); Fez: **Avis** (✉ 50 blvd. Chefchaouen, ☎ 5/626746), **Budget** (✉ Bureau Grand Hotel, Av. Chefchaouen, Fez, ☎ 5/620919), and **Hertz** (✉ Hotel de Fez, Av. des F.A.R., ☎ 5/622812); Marrakesh: **Budget** (✉ 157 av. Mohammed V, ☎ 4/434604) and **Hertz** (✉ 154 av. Mohammed V, ☎ 4/434680); Tangier: **Budget** (✉ 79 av. du Prince Moulay Abdallah, ☎ 9/937994) and **Hertz** (✉ 36 av. Mohammed V, ☎ 9/933322).

By Plane

Royal Air Maroc (☞ Arriving and Departing, *above*) has comprehensive domestic service; cities served include Agadir, Casablanca, Fez, Marrakesh, Ouarzazate, Rabat, Tangier, and Tetouan.

By Train

For general information, contact **ONCF** (☎ 7/774747, FAX 7/774480). The overnight train from Madrid to Algeciras leaves Chamartín Station at 10 PM and arrives at 8:30 AM; you can then buy a boat ticket and change money at the train station before walking to the ferry terminal. The train from Tangier to Casablanca leaves at 4 PM and arrives at 10 PM, and the overnight train from Tangier to Marrakesh leaves at 10:15 PM and arrives at 8:20 AM. There are two stations in Casablanca, the **Gare du Port** (also called Casa-Port, ☎ 2/223011) and the **Gare des Voyageurs** (also called Casa-Voyageurs, ☎ 2/243818). The latter serves Marrakesh and the south. There are also **ONCF** stations in Asilah (☎ 9/917327), Fez (☎ 5/625001), Marrakesh (☎ 4/447768), Meknes (☎ 5/521060), Rabat (☎ 7/767353), and Tangier (☎ 9/931201). ONCF runs buses from Marrakesh to Essaouira, Agadir, and points farther south.

Contacts and Resources

Embassies

United States (✉ Av. de Marrakesh 2, Rabat, ☎ 7/762265). **United Kingdom** (✉ Av. de la Tour Hassan 17, Rabat, ☎ 7/731403). **Canada** (✉ Rue Jaafar Assadik 13, Rabat, ☎ 7/672880).

Emergencies

Police (☎ 19). **Fire brigade** (☎ 15). **Highway SOS** (☎ 177). **Information** (☎ 16). **International Directory Assistance** (☎ 12).

Golf

Morocco is a boon for traveling golfers, with 14 courses in action and 16 more slated to open by 2001. Greens fees vary from 150 to 600 dirhams ($17–$70). There's even a nine-hole "golf garden" inside the Imperial City of Meknes, illuminated at night. For general information, contact the **Royal Moroccan Golf Federation** (✉ Royal Golf Dar-Es-Salam, Rabat, ☎ 7/755960, FAX 7/751026).

Major courses include **Royal Golf of Anfa** (✉ BP 12, Anfa Racetrack, Casablanca, ☎ 2/365355), 9 holes; **Royal Golf of Fez** (✉ Rte. D'Imouzzer, Fez, ☎ 7/763849), 9 holes; **Royal Golf of Marrakech** (✉ BP 634, Ancienne Rte. de Ouarzazate, Marrakesh, ☎ 4/444341), 18 holes; **Golf de la Palmeraie** (✉ Jardins de la Palmeraie, BP 1488, ☎ 4/301010), 18 holes; and **Royal Golf of Tangier** (✉ BP 41, Tangier, ☎ 9/944484), 18 holes.

Horseback Riding

Horseback riding is a superb way to experience the countryside. For details, contact the **Royal Moroccan Federation of Equestrian Sports** (✉ Dar Es-Salam, BP 742, Rabat, ☎ 7/754424, FAX 7/754738).

Guided Tours

Most Moroccan cities have a swarm of unofficial but very insistent "guides." The best way to get rid of these volunteers—who may falsely tell you that all hotels are full and take you to shops where they get commissions on purchases—is to ignore them and look like you know exactly where you're going. If you do want a guide, hire a cheaper and better one at the local tourist office.

An American tour operator specializing in Morocco is **G.W.T. Inc.** (✉ 190 Moore St., Suite 470, Hackensack, NJ 07601, ☎ 201/343–3929 or 800/868–7498, FAX 201/343–7591). **Globus** (✉ 5301 S. Federal Circle, Littleton, CO 80123, ☎ 303/797–6000 or 800/221–0090, FAX 303/795–0962) has packages that include both Spain and Morocco. The excellent Canadian outfit **Butterfield & Robinson** (✉ 70 Bond St., Toronto, Canada MSB 1X3, ☎ 416/864–1354 or 800/678–1147, FAX 416/864–0541)—"Biking and Walking Since 1966"—runs treks and bike trips.

If you decide to join a group once you're in Spain, try **A Taste of Morocco** (✉ Apdo. 349, 29680 Estepona, Málaga, ☎ 95/288–6590), which runs tours in autumn and winter, or **Ambassador Tours** (☎ 93/482–7100 in Barcelona; 91/780–1300 in Madrid; 96/351–6200 in Valencia), which is high-end.

Hiking and Trekking

With more than a dozen peaks over 13,200 ft and no fewer than 400 over 9,900 ft, Morocco is a stage set for superb hiking and climbing. A network of mountain huts maintained by the **Club Alpin Français** (✉ BP 6178, Casablanca 01, ☎ 2/270090, FAX 2/297292) helps with expeditions from mule-skiing in the High Atlas to hiking through the Azrou cedar forest in the Middle Atlas.

Sailing

For details on sailing, yachting, and chartering boats, contact the **Royal Moroccan Sailing Federation** (☎ 7/670956) or the **Royal Moroccan Yacht Club** (☎ 7/720264), both in Rabat. The ocean resort **Mohammedia** (☎ 3/322331), near Casablanca, is a sort of Moroccan Newport.

Surfing and Windsurfing

Atlantic winds and waves make Morocco a favorite of both surfers and windsurfers. Essaouira and Dar Bouazza, near Casablanca, are on the international competition circuits. Contact the **Royal Moroccan Surf Federation** (☎ 2/259530, FAX 2/236385).

Visitor Information

Tourist offices: **United States** (✉ 20 E. 46th St., Suite 1201, New York, NY 10017, ☎ 212/557–2520). **United Kingdom** (✉ 205 Regent St., London DEW 1R7, U.K., ☎ 44171/437–0073). **Madrid** (✉ C. Ventura Rodríguez 24, Madrid 28008, ☎ 91/542–7431). **Agadir** (✉ Pl. du Prince Héritier Sidi Mohammed, Agadir, ☎ 8/846377). **Casablanca** (✉ 55 rue Omar Slaoui, Casablanca, ☎ 2/271177). **Er Rachidia** (✉ Blvd. Moulay Ali Cherif, Er Rachidia, ☎ 5/570944). **Essaouira** (✉ Blvd. La Princesse Lala Amina 54, Essaouira, ☎ 4/474247). **Fez** (✉ Place de la Résistance, Fez, ☎ 5/623460). **Marrakesh** (✉ 176 blvd. Mohammed V, Marrakesh, ☎ 4/432097; ✉ Place Abdel-Moumen Ben Ali, Marrakesh, ☎ 4/436239). **Meknes** (✉ Place Administrative, Meknes, ☎ 5/524426). **Ouarzazate** (✉ Av. Mohammed V, BP 297, Ouarzazate, ☎ 4/882485). **Rabat** (✉ 22 av. d'Alger, Rabat, ☎ 7/730562). **Tangier** (✉ 29 blvd. Pasteur, Tangier, ☎ 9/948661).

16 BACKGROUND AND ESSENTIALS

SPAIN'S SECOND GOLDEN AGE

The sense of excitement in Spain today is contagious. The first thing that's bound to strike the traveler is this palpable exhilaration, a feeling that seems to electrify Spain from remote mountain villages to the poshest avenues of Madrid and Barcelona. Naturally, there are dark spots in the picture—beggars in the streets, Basque terrorism, huge economic adjustments required by the country's 1986 entry into the European Union—yet it's difficult not to be infected by the overall optimism. You can see it in the general sprucing up of recent years. You can feel it, especially in the bars and restaurants. Life is loved and celebrated here; few peoples seem to have such a capacity for enjoyment. In many ways, the Spanish have always been like this—Richard Wright, visiting in the 1950s, called it "pagan Spain"—but for 36 years of the 20th century, they lived and labored under a repressive, ultraconservative regime that ended only with the death of Francisco Franco in 1975. The renaissance that followed has been not just political but also creative and economic.

In imagining the Spanish landscape, you may picture the scorched, orange plains of La Mancha, where Don Quixote tilted, or the softly rolling hills of Andalusia, or even the overdeveloped beaches of the Costa del Sol. But after Switzerland, Spain is the most mountainous country in Europe, and also one of the most geographically diverse, ranging from the soggy northwest (wetter than Ireland) to the haunting plains of the central *meseta,* from the cascading trout streams of the Pyrenees to the marshes and dunes of Doñana National Park, on the Costa de la Luz. There are deep caves, lonely coves, rock canyons, mountain meadows, coastal rice paddies, volcanic island peaks . . . and, of course, the great, snowy wall of the Pyrenees, which has always isolated Spain from France and northern Europe as well as separated the different Pyrenean peoples and cultures.

More than almost any other country its size—it's the second largest in Europe, after France—Spain is characterized by the distinctness of its many parts and peoples. The Galicians of the northwest are descended from the same Celtic tribes that colonized the British Isles. Bagpipes are a local instrument, and kilts not unknown; and the local language, Gallego, is a mixture of Spanish and Portuguese. The Basque country, whose eastern end abuts the French border, also has its own language, Euskera, a tongue so mysterious that linguists have never agreed where it began. Local pride is fierce here; the Basque language and culture are purposefully celebrated, and independentist sentiment is strong. Outright separatism is embodied in the terrorist group ETA (Euskadi Ta Askatasuna), which has killed almost 900 Spaniards over the past three decades. (The violence is extremely unlikely to affect travelers.) The Catalans, who populate northeastern Spain around Barcelona, speak the country's most substantial regional language, Catalan, which is closer to Provençal French than to Castilian (Spanish); residents of the province of Valencia and the Balearic islands speak and study in their own local versions of Catalan. All of these areas suffered systematic cultural and linguistic repression under the totalitarian centralist pressure of the Franco regime.

The Iberian Peninsula's early peoples included Basques, Celts, Iberians, Greeks, Romans, and Visigoths. But Christians in the centuries after Christ widely intermarried with Jewish and Moorish minorities. Most Spaniards today see themselves as purely Catholic, but almost all have Jewish and/or Muslim ancestors.

Most of Spain transformed itself from an agrarian and largely feudal economy to a modern, capitalist one in remarkably little time, over the first half of the 20th century. Now, a lively economy and optimistic outlook are giving modern Spain an anything-is-possible air, despite a high unemployment rate and the continuing scourge of terrorism. The 1992 Olympic Games, the Guggenheim Museum Bilbao, new freeways, high-speed trains, and state-of-the-art technology have replaced a country that was often described 25 years ago as borderline third-world.

Modernity has come at a price. For generations, Spain was the travel destination of choice for the penniless artist, the adventurer willing to forego comfort for rugged romance. All that has changed. After years of inflation, and a value-added tax imposed as a condition of entry into the European Union, Spain's cost of living compares to that of partners like France. The festivities of 1992—the Summer Olympics in Barcelona, and the Universal Exposition in Seville—further inflated hotel and restaurant prices in those cities. The rate of price increases slowed in the late 1990s, however, and Americans in particular can now enjoy the benefits of a relatively strong dollar.

Spain has an extraordinary heritage of history, art, and architecture. It begins with the ancient caves at Altamira, in which people wearing skins for warmth painted delicate animals on a rock ceiling. During the Age of Exploration, robust adventurers left hardscrabble Extremadura, Spain's poorest province, to probe the New World, and some returned to build great stone palaces on Extremadura's stark, scrubby landscape. Stretched across northern Spain are the Romanesque churches of the Camino de Santiago (Way of St. James), which was Europe's most famous Christian pilgrimage in the Middle Ages; the journey culminated at the soaring cathedral of Santiago de Compostela. Cave churches of the Visigoths (early Christians) are scattered across the north as a sort of graphic counterpoint. Seville, the pastel-color city of Don Juan, still spreads elegantly along the banks of the Guadalquivir. More than ten thousand castles are sprinkled across the Iberian Peninsula, some merely ruins, others in extraordinarily good shape. Villages of whitewashed buildings, harbors stuffed with brightly painted fishing boats, and majestic towns welded to craggy mountaintops are easy to find. Still washed by that subtle light that inspired Velázquez, the Spanish countryside remains mercifully unchanged.

The story of this land, a romance-tinged tale of counts, caliphs, crusaders, and kings, begins long before written history. The Basques were among the first here, huddling in the cold mountain valleys of the north. The Iberians came next, apparently crossing the Mediterranean from North Africa around 3,000 BC. The Celts arrived from the north about a thousand years later. The seafaring Phoenicians founded Gadir (now Cádiz) and several coastal cities in the south. The parade continued with the Greeks, who settled parts of the east coast, and then the Carthaginians, who founded Cartagena around 225 BC—and who dubbed the then-wild, forested country Spania.

Modern civilization really began with the Romans, who expelled the Carthaginians and turned the peninsula into three imperial provinces. It took the Romans 200 years to subdue the fiercely resisting Celts, Iberians, and Basques—ending shortly before the birth of Christ—but their influence was lasting. Evidence of the Roman epoch is left today in the great ruins at Mérida, Segovia, Tarragona, and other cities; in the peninsula's legal system; and in the Latin base of its three Romance languages. In the early 5th century, various invading barbarians crossed the Pyrenees to attack the weakening Roman empire. The Visigoths became the dominant force in northern Spain by 419, establishing their kingdom at Toledo and eventually adopting Christianity.

But they, too, were to fall before a wave of invaders, this time that of the Moors, a Berber-led Arab force that crossed the Strait of Gibraltar from North Africa in 711. The Moors swept through Spain in an astonishingly short time, meeting only token resistance and launching almost eight centuries of Muslim rule—a period that in many respects was the pinnacle of Spanish civilization. Unlike the semibarbaric Visigoths, the Moors were extremely cultured. Arabs, Jews, and Christians lived together in peace during their reign, although many Christians did convert to Islam. The Moors also brought with them citrus fruits, rice, cotton, sugar, palm trees, glassmaking, and the complex irrigation system still used around Valencia. Their influence is evident in modern Spanish, where most words beginning with "al" are Arabic in origin, such as *albóndig* (meatball), *alcalde* (mayor), *almohada* (pillow), and *alcázar* (fortress). To the traveler, Moorish culture is most spectacularly evident in modern-day Andalusia, the kingdom the Moors called al-Andalus. The grand, fairytale Alhambra palace, which still crowns the beautiful city of Granada, embodies both the ambition and the delicacy of the Moorish aesthetic.

The Moors never managed to subdue northwestern Galicia and Asturias, and it was in the latter that a minor Christian king, Pelayo, began the long crusade that came to be known as the *Reconquista* (Reconquest). By 1085, Alfonso VI of Castile had captured Toledo, giving the Christians a firm grip on the north. In the 13th century, Valencia, Seville, and finally Córdoba—the capital of the Muslim caliphate in Spain—fell to Christian forces, leaving only Granada in Moorish hands. Two hundred years later, two Catholic monarchs, Ferdinand of Aragón and Isabella of Castile, were joined in a marriage that would change the world.

The year 1492 is a watershed in Spanish history, the beginning of the nation's political golden age and the moment of some of its worst excesses of intolerance. That year, the 23rd of Ferdinand and Isabella's marriage, Christian forces conquered Granada and unified all of current-day Spain as a single kingdom. Jews and Muslims who did not convert to Christianity were expelled from the country en masse. Christopher Columbus, under the sponsorship of Isabella, landed in the Americas, initiating the Age of Exploration; but the departure of educated Muslims and Jews was a blow to the nation's economy from which it would never recover. The Inquisition, which had been established in 1478, further persecuted those who chose to stay. The colonies of the New World greatly enriched Spain at first, but massive shipments of Peruvian and Mexican gold later produced terrible inflation. The so-called Catholic Monarchs and their centralizing successors maintained Spain's unity, but they sacrificed the spirit of international free trade that was beginning to bring capitalist prosperity to other parts of Europe.

Ferdinand and Isabella were succeeded by their grandson Carlos, who became the first Spanish Habsburg and one of the most powerful rulers in history. Cortés reached Mexico and Pizarro conquered Peru under his rule. Carlos also inherited Austria and the Netherlands and in 1519, three years into his reign, was elected Holy Roman Emperor (as Charles V), wasting little time in annexing Naples and Milan. He championed the Counter-Reformation and saw the Jesuit order created to help defend Catholicism against European Protestantism. But Charles cost the nation with his penchant for waging war, particularly against the Ottomans and German Lutherans. His son, Philip II, followed in the same, expensive path, ultimately defeating the Turks and ordering the construction of the somber Escorial monastery, outside Madrid. It was here that Philip died, 10 years after losing the Spanish Armada in an attack on Protestant England.

The War of the Spanish Succession was ignited by the death, without issue, in 1700 of Charles II, the last Spanish Habsburg. Philip of Anjou was crowned Philip V and inaugurated the Bourbon line in Spain (a representative of which sits on the throne today). The Bourbons of that era, a Frenchified lot, copied many of the attitudes and fashions of their northern neighbors, but the infatuation ended with Napoleon's 1808 installation of his brother, José Bonaparte. Mocked bitterly as "Pepe Botella" for his fondness for drink (*botella* means "bottle"), Bonaparte was widely despised, and an 1808 uprising against him in Madrid—chronicled harrowingly by the great painter Francisco de Goya y Lucientes (1746–1828)—began the War of Independence, known to foreigners as the Peninsular War. Britain, siding with Spain, sent the Duke of Wellington to the rescue. With the aid of Spanish guerillas, the French were finally expelled, but not before they had looted Spain's major churches and cathedrals. Most of Spain's American colonies took advantage of the war to claim their independence.

The rest of the century was not a happy one for Spain, as conservative regimes grappled with civil wars and revolts inspired by the currents of European republicanism. The final blow came with the loss of Cuba, Puerto Rico, and the Philippines in 1898, a military disaster that ironically sparked a remarkable literary renaissance—the so-called Generation of '98, whose members included writers Miguel de Unamuno and Pío Baroja and poet Antonio Machado. In 1902 Alfonso XIII came to the throne, but rising civil strife got the better of him and ended in his self-imposed exile in 1931. A fledgling republic followed, to the delight of most Spaniards, but the 1936 election of a left-wing Popular Front government ignited bitter opposition from the right. In the end, a young general named Francisco Franco used the assassination of a monarchist leader as an excuse for a military revolt.

The Spanish Civil War (1936–39) was the single most tragic episode in Spanish history. More than half a million people died in the conflict. Intellectuals and leftists the world over sympathized with the elected government, and the International Brigades, with many American, British, and Canadian volunteers, took part in some of the worst fighting, including the storied defense of Madrid. But Franco, backed by the Catholic Church, got far more help from Nazi Germany, whose Condor legions destroyed the Basque town of Guerníca (in a horror made infamous by Picasso's monumental painting), and from Fascist Italy. For three years, European governments stood quietly by as Franco's armies vanquished Barcelona, Madrid, and the last capital of the Republic, Valencia.

Officially neutral during World War II but sympathetic to the Axis powers, Spain was largely shunned by the world until, in a 1953 agreement, the United States provided aid in exchange for the building of NATO bases. Gradually, the shattered economy began to pick up, especially with the surge of tourism that gathered steam in the late 1960s. But when Franco announced in 1969 that his successor would be Juan Carlos, the grandson of Alfonso XIII and a prince whose militaristic education had been strictly overseen by the aging general, the hopes of a nation longing for freedom sagged. Imagine the Spaniards' surprise when, six years later, Franco died and the young monarch revealed himself to be a closet democrat. Under his nurturing, a new constitution restoring civil liberties and freedom of expression was adopted in 1978. On February 23, 1981, the king proved his mettle once and for all, when a nostalgic Civil Guard colonel with visions of a return to Franco's authoritarian regime, along with a unit of would-be rebels, held the Spanish parliament—then center-right—captive for some 24 hours. Only the heroism of King Juan Carlos, who personally called military commanders across the country to ensure their loyalty to the elected government, quelled the coup attempt. The Socialists ruled Spain from 1982 until early 1996, when conservative José María Aznar was elected prime minister.

In the arts, Spain seems to have picked up where it left off when the civil war and the ensuing 40-year cultural silence of the Franco regime intervened. Whereas the first third of the century produced such towering figures as poet Federico García Lorca, filmmaker Luis Buñuel, and painters Pablo Picasso, Joan Miró, and Salvador Dalí, the final quarter (since Franco's death in 1975) will be known for novelist Camilo José Cela's 1989 Nobel Prize (for *The Family of Pascual Duarte*), filmmaker Pedro Almodóvar's postmodern Spanish films, Basque sculptor Eduardo Chillida's blocky forms, and the conceptually challenging works of Catalan painter Antoni Tapiès.

When you get here, take the country as the Spanish do, piece by piece. Spain at the turn of the 21st century is a patchwork of cultures and nationalities: Andalusia and Catalonia are as different as France and England, maybe more so. The miracle is that a common language and a central government have managed to bring these "Autonomous Communities" as close together as they are. Castilians, Basques, Galicians, Asturians, Catalans, and Andalusians all contribute separately and equally to a Spain that begins the new millennium as one of the most vibrant nations in Europe.

A TALE OF TWO CITIES

The eternal rivalry between Barcelona, medieval capital of an opulent Mediterranean empire, and Madrid, once the nerve center of one of the greatest global empires ever assembled, may be a driving force behind Spain's current vitality. The two cities debate every national issue from politics to sports to the economy, even as three domestic airlines shuttle thousands of businesspeople daily between the two.

How to get a Catalan to speak Spanish? Misunderstand the price by a peseta. Madrid bureaucrats don't work after lunch? No, that's in the morning; after lunch they don't even show up.

Catalan avarice, Madrid sloth: old standbys in the arsenal of barbs that citizens of Spain's two largest cities routinely toss at each other.

Beneath the humor lies a well-aged and historically rooted bitterness combining elements of the world's great internecine tensions—Québec and the rest of Canada, Milan and Rome, even the United States' North–South divide more than a century after the American Civil War.

Though largely undetectable to a visitor, traces of this rivalry crop up everywhere. Cars with Madrid license plates may encounter extra discourtesies in Catalonia. Madrileños are not known for their patience with the Catalan language and are apt to insist upon being addressed in Castilian Spanish; Catalans, in turn, seem to "forget" their Castilian, or deliberately lapse into bizarre grammatical distortions. A foolproof way to ruin a social gathering in Madrid is to proselytize the Catalan point of view vis à vis Catalonian history and culture. Meanwhile, in Barcelona, the "language of Cervantes" can be a surefire soporific at dinner parties that would crackle with humor and innuendo in Catalan.

This mutual antipathy has been centuries in the making and will not go away anytime soon, even if feelings have cooled considerably since the 1714 siege and conquest of Barcelona by Spain's first Bourbon monarch, Felipe V. Armed conflict between the two is no longer a threat. Catalans are a pragmatic people who have always managed to prosper no matter whose army was manning the cannon over Barcelona; and the cities are now so intertwined and interdependent that a Catalan, Narcis Serra, was Spanish Minister of Defense not long ago, while the present Socialist candidate for president is Catalan José Borrell. And Spain's present conservative government, elected in 1997, is able to govern only with the support of Catalonian president Jordi Pujol's Catalan nationalist party.

The dramatic changes of the last 25 years—the end of Franco, the establishment of the constitutional monarch—have actually reversed some of the qualities that have traditionally characterized the two cities. Thus, whereas Barcelona was always considered Spain's most European city up to 1975, Catalonia's zealous restoration of its long-suppressed language and culture has made it somewhat self-absorbed and cost it a few points in cosmopolitanism. Madrid, on the other hand, has burst back onto the world stage with a vigor and energy unimaginable when it was the seat of Franco's reactionary and repressive regime. The capital's legendary bureaucratic indolence has been replaced by a frenzy of activity in the arts and business and a powerful international orientation and appeal.

But some things don't change. Madrid remains open; Barcelona, despite its seaport, is less so. Even the topography reinforces this fact: Madrid stands on a promontory at the center of Spain's central steppe, while Barcelona nestles in a crease between the hills and the sea. Barcelona is moist, pungent, even fetid, slippery. Madrid is high, arid, brittle. Madrid's streets are broader and seem to embrace the sky, while Barcelona's are predominantly darker and narrower, leafier and more intimate, older: tunnels to the city's medieval past. Barcelona is, after all, 2,000 years old, to Madrid's mere millennium.

Even—maybe especially—the air is different. Barcelona's steamy and passionate Mediterranean breath is a far cry from Madrid's legendary highland air, with its sharp and icy lightness.

Catalans are more private and self-contained, feline, Gallic. Madrileños are a little of everything, coming as they do from all corners of the peninsula and the world, but they are known for a more gregarious, accessible, open, generous spirit. In Madrid they *give* you things—tapas, hot broth, the time of day. In Barcelona, trade is absolutely fundamental to every nuance of social contact.

Catalonia's *fets diferencials,* or "differentiating facts," are based on linguistic and historical realities often dismissed as fantasy by non-Catalans educated during the unity-oriented Franco regime. Barcelona is geographically closer to Marseilles than to Madrid, and medieval Catalonia included much of what is today southern France. The Roussillon, or French Catalonia, stretched as far north as Avignon and Nîmes, where the Catalan language is still spoken. Grammatically closer to Provençal French than to Castilian Spanish, Catalan lacks the fricative phonemes and nearly all of the Arabic-rooted vocabulary that modern Spanish inherited from 700 years of Moorish occupation. Sacked but never colonized by the Moors, Catalonia was the border zone for Charlemagne's Frankish empire, finally gaining independence from the Carolingians in 988, only a few years after Madrid was made a military outpost by the Moorish command defending regional headquarters at Toledo. When Catalonia became, through royal marriage, part of the House of Aragón in 1137, Barcelona's commercial and maritime power made it the kingdom's business center and royal court. But in 1469, when Isabella of Castile married Ferdinand of Aragón, Barcelona found itself left dangling on the eastern edge of an Iberian power about to turn its attention west, across the Atlantic.

The "discovery" of the New World and the great enterprise of exploiting its riches definitively sealed Catalonia's fate as a declining power within the new, unified Spain. Legally excluded from participation in Castile's colonization and plunder of the Americas, Catalonia did manage to retain a measure of home rule and cultural identity until 1714, when, as a reprisal for having supported Archduke Carlos of Austria in the War of the Spanish Succession, Felipe V stripped Catalonia of all of its institutions and privileges.

Deprived of the loot pouring in from the colonies, Barcelona developed an industrial power base that led to a resurgence of Catalan nationalism—*la Renaixença*—in the latter half of the 19th century. Limited home rule returned from 1914 to 1924 and, later, during the Second Republic, from

1931 to 1936; but after the Spanish Civil War, 1936–1939, the Franco regime's "National Movement" endeavored to eradicate all traces of the Catalan language and culture, along with any political parties that might threaten the national fabric of church, state, oligarchy, and the army. Officially suppressed but never abandoned, Catalan language and culture have returned more powerfully than ever since Franco's death in 1975.

Madrid's history, shorter but less checkered, took the city from military observation post to provincial town to world capital in just over 500 years. When the previously itinerant royal court was permanently established there in 1561, riches were already pouring in from the Spanish empire's far-flung colonies. Soon Madrid was a teeming boom town, with a burgeoning population and government subsidies promoting architecture, theater, and, especially, painting. Rubens and Velázquez shared a studio; Cervantes and Lope de Vega (the "Spanish Shakespeare") exchanged acerbic sonnets; and the city's literary quarter was a crush of poets, actors, composers, and playwrights. The lavish cultural spending of Spain's golden age left a legacy of artistic masterpieces that today fill the Prado and other museums, as well as convents, churches, foundations, and more than 100 art galleries.

From the twisting streets of its early Moorish and Jewish quarter through the stately and austere Habsburg architecture of the 16th and 17th centuries and the broad avenues of the 18th- and 19th-century Bourbon monarchy, Madrid has grown into a sprawling industrial and cultural giant with (like Barcelona) more than 4 million people.

Comparing the pros and cons and respective assets of these two cities—an endless exchange of proposals and rebuttals—may be valuable only as a means of better characterizing and defining each of the two. They seem perfectly organized for debate: Madrid's landlocked, highland monochrome contrasts with Barcelona's vivid and varied palette, a rich mixture of the Pyrenees, the Mediterranean, and metropolitan hues. Madrid offers convenient access to all of the Iberian Peninsula, whereas Barcelona is nearly equidistant from Rome and London, as close to Geneva as it is to Madrid. Madrid is most appealing in winter, when the hearty Castilian cuisine of roasts and thick stews makes the most sense, where Barcelona's sweetest season is springtime, between the lovers' fiesta of Sant Jordi, in late April, and the all-night bonfires of Sant Joan, on Midsummer's Eve. Madrid's treasury of paintings is countered by Barcelona's relentless innovation in art, architecture, and design and by the legacies of Picasso, Miró, Dalí, and Gaudí. Barcelona has delicious markets such as the central Boqueria; Madrid has its Sunday flea market, the Rastro, and bookstall for browsing through along the Cuesta de Moyanes. Madrid's superb day trips—Toledo, Segovia, El Escorial—are balanced by Barcelona's excellent beaches on the Costa Brava, to the north, and the Delta del Ebro, to the south. Madrid is centered on its peerless and peaceful Plaza Mayor, whereas Barcelona has the meandering Rambla. Madrid has a midtown forest in the stately Retiro, while Gaudí's Parc Güell hovers on a hill above Barcelona. Madrid's oldest quarters mix Mudéjar brick buildings with a jumble of red, clay-tiled rooftops, while Barcelona's are of Roman and Gothic stone.

Ultimately, Barcelona's Mediterranean vitality draws heavily on its rich triangle of mountains, sea, and city life, whereas modern Madrid, brisk and lively, is broader and more universal, the melting pot of the many Spains. Today, both cities are riding a wave of excitement that even terrorism and political scandals can't seem to discourage. Barcelona continues to generate energy in the afterglow of the 1992 Olympic Games, Catalonia's greatest domestic and international triumph since the glory days of its medieval Mediterranean prominence. Madrid, meanwhile, has reassumed an energy and outlook comparable only to that of its own 16th-century pinnacle.

–George Semler

SPANISH FOOD AND WINE

Spain's post-Franco cultural Renaissance has encouraged richness and variety in everything from arts and letters to gastronomy. As with all things Iberian, food and wine take a great many forms. This is a country where each valley and village takes pride in its unique way of preparing the simplest dishes, where a Pyrenean valley serves dishes whose very names are linguistically incomprehensible to fellow Catalans from the next valley.

Each of modern Spain's 17 Autonomous Communities, from the equatorial Canary Islands to the snow-capped Pyrenees, has its own cuisine. The only Spanish dishes that might be called universal are the *tortilla española de patatas* (potato and onion omelette), gazpacho (a cold Andalusian soup of ground vegetables, garlic, and bread in a tomato base), and paella (a Valencian feast of saffron-spiked rice and seafood). Generally speaking, central Spain is known for roasts and stews, eastern Spain for rice and seafood dishes, northern Spain for meat and fish, and southern Spain for deep-fried seafood. Fresh vegetables, onions, and garlic are consumed in abundance throughout.

Blessed with a geological diversity unusual for a country its size, Spain has been known since ancient times for rich wheat fields, vineyards, olive groves, and pig and sheep farming. The upper slopes of Andalusia's snow-capped Sierra Nevada, for example, have Alpine gentian, while the lower ones yield tropical produce unique to southern Europe, such as olives.

Nearly surrounded by a combination of the Atlantic and the Mediterranean, Spain is in large part a maritime nation. A statistic surprising to all but the Spanish themselves is that Spain ranks third in the world in per-capita fish and seafood consumption, closely behind Japan and Iceland. Moreover, those two islands have no population more than 200 km (120 mi) from the coast, whereas Spanish villagers in tiny Aranda de Duero, 500 km (300 mi) inland, were cooking fish back in the 14th century. Madrid, at the dead center of the Iberian Peninsula, has long been considered a first "port" for the freshest fish in Spain. And, of course, the Mediterranean diet—high in fresh vegetables, fruit, virgin olive oil, fish, fowl, rabbit, garlic, onions, and wine; low in red meat, dairy products, and carbohydrates—is one of the healthiest of all regimes.

The 781-year Moorish presence on the Iberian Peninsula was a major influence on Spanish cuisine. The Moors brought exotic ingredients such as saffron, almonds, and peppers; introduced sweets and pastries; and created refreshing dishes such as cold almond- and vegetable-based soups still popular today. One of the world's culinary pioneers was Ziryab, a 10th-century Moorish chef who worked in Córdoba: he's credited with bringing to Europe the Arab fashion for eating a standard sequence of dishes, beginning with soup and ending with dessert.

Another legacy of the Moorish taste for small and varied delicacies is Spain's best-known culinary innovation, the *tapa* (hors d'oeuvre; derived from the verb *tapar,* meaning to cover). Early tapas are said to have been pieces of ham or cheese laid across glasses of wine, both to keep flies out and to keep stagecoach drivers sober. It is said that as far back as the 13th century, ailing Spanish king Alfonso X El Sabio ("The Learned") took small morsels with wine by medical prescription and so enjoyed the cure that he made it a regular practice in his court. Even Cervantes refers to tapas as *llamativos* (attention getters), for their stimulating properties, in *Don Quixote.* Often miniature versions of classic Spanish dishes, tapas originated in Andalusia, where a combination of heat and poverty made nomadic grazing preferable to the formal meal. Today tapas are generally taken as appetizers before lunch or dinner, but in the south they are still often regarded as a meal in themselves. Eating tapas allows you to sample a wide variety of food and wine with minimal alcohol poisoning, especially on a *tapeo*—the Spanish version of a pub crawl but lower in alcohol and higher in protein. You basically walk off your wine and tapas as you move around.

In some of the more old-fashioned bars in Madrid and points south, you may be automatically served a tapa of the barman's choice upon ordering a drink—olives, a piece of cheese, sausages, or even a cup of hot broth. A few standard tapas to watch for: *calamares fritos* (fried squid or cuttlefish, often mistaken for onion rings), *pulpo feira* (octupus on slices of potato), *chopitos* (baby octopi), *angulas* (baby eels), *chistorra* (fried spicy sausage), *chorizo* (hard pork sausage), *champiñones* (mushrooms), *gambas al ajillo* (shrimp cooked in parsley, oil, and garlic), *langostinos* (jumbo shrimp or prawns), *patatas bravas* (potatoes in spicy sauce), *pimientos de Padrón* (peppers, some very hot, from the Galician town of Padrón), *sardinas* (fresh sardines cooked in garlic and parsley), *chancletes* (whitebait cooked in oil and parsley), and *salmonetes* (small red mullet).

Just to complicate things, the generic term *tapas* covers various forms of small-scale nibbling. *Tentempiés* are, literally, small snacks to designed to "keep you on your feet."*Pinchos* are bite-size offerings impaled on toothpicks; *banderillas* are similar, so called because the toothpick is wrapped in colorful paper resembling the barbed batons used in bullfights. *Montaditos* are canapés, innovative combinations of delicacies "mounted" on toast; *raciones* (rations, or servings) are hot tapas served in small earthenware casseroles. The preference for small quantities of different dishes also shows up in restaurants, where you can often order a series of small dishes *para picar* (to pick at). A selection of *raciones* or *entretenimientos* (a platter of delicacies that might range from olives to nuts to cheese, ham or sausage) makes a popular starter for those dining in a group. The modern gourmet *menú de degustación* (taster's menu) is little more than a succession of complex tapas.

A standard Spanish soup, especially in and around Madrid, is *sopa de ajo* (garlic soup), made with water, oil, garlic, paprika, bread, and cured ham. *Sopa de pescado* (fish soup) appears on many menus, prepared in many different ways. The classic *gazpacho* is a cold blend of tomatoes, water, garlic, bread, and vegetables. Though most gazpacho today is made in a blender, it tastes best when prepared by hand in an earthenware mortar. There are several variations on gazpacho, including *salmorejo,* which comes from Córdoba and has a denser texture, and *ajo blanco,* based on almonds rather than tomatoes and served with peeled muscatel grapes or slices of honeydew melon—another example of Moorish influence, combining sweet and spicy flavors.

Far more substantial are the heavy soups and bean stews of the central Castilian *meseta* (plain) and northern coast. *Cocido madrileño* is a hearty highland stew or thick soup of garbanzos, black sausage, cabbage, potatoes, carrots, pork, and chicken served in three courses, called *vuelcos* ("overturnings" of the pot): the broth, the vegetables and legumes, and finally the meat. *Escudella* is the Catalan version of *cocido,* using ground pork and no garbanzos. *Fabada asturiana* is the best-known Asturian dish, a powerful stew of white kidney beans, fatback, ham, black sausage, and hard pork sausage. *Judias estofadas,* made of white kidney beans with chorizo, black sausage, onion, tomato, and bacon, is a close cousin found across the north of Spain. *Pisto manchego,* from La Mancha, is a stew of sausage and ham with onions, peppers, tomatoes, and squash. *Migas de pastor* (shepherd's crumbs) is a legendary Aragonese and Castilian specialty consisting of bread crumbs and bacon sautéed in garlic and olive oil. Don't miss a chance to try *marmitako,* a hearty tuna and potato stew, during one of the Basque country's frequent Atlantic storms.

Spain is kind to carnivores, who can choose from thick and tender *txuletas de buey* or *solomillos* (beef steaks) in the Basque country and fragrant roasts in Castile. In Segovia, Burgos, and Madrid, the *cochinillo al horno* (roast suckling pig) and *cordero asado* (roast lamb) are cooked in wood ovens until at once crisp and tender enough to portion out with the edge of a blunt plate.

Fish and seafood are prepared countless ways in Spain, but the Basques and the Andalusians are particular masters of the art. The Basque country is known for *txangurro* (stuffed king crab) and, especially, *bacalao al pil-pil*—cod cooked in oil and garlic at a low temperature, generating a sauce of juice from the fish itself. (The dish is named for the popping sound that the oil makes as the fish cooks.) *Besugo* (sea bream), either *al horno* (roasted) or *a la brasa* (over coals), is another Basque fish classic. *Rape* (angler fish) in sauce; *merluza* (hake) in tomato, pepper, or green (olive oil, garlic, and parsley) sauce; and *dorada* (gilthead bream) *a la sal* (baked in salt) are also popular. Common all over Spain is *trucha a la Navarra,* trout wrapped in, or stuffed with, pieces of bacon or ham. In Andalusia most fish is deep-fried in batter, a practice requiring very fresh fish and the right kind of oil to achieve the proper counterpoint of crispness and succulence. *Chancletes* (whitebait) and *sardinas* (sardines) are especially good in Málaga, while the *salmonetes* (red mullet) and *acedías* (miniature sole) of the Cádiz coast are legendary. *Adobo,* also delicious, is fried fish marinated in wine.

Spanish ham and sausage products are renowned, particularly those derived from the *cerdo ibérico,* a remarkable breed of free-range pig that produces *jamón serrano*—roughly translatable as "ham from the sierra or mountains." This term covers three levels of quality: *bellota* (the finest, from pigs fed exclusively acorns), *de recebo* (from pigs fed acorns but finished off with corn over the last three months), and simply *serrano* (from pigs fattened on feed pellets). Extremadura and the provinces of Salamanca and Huelva produce Spain's best cured hams; look for those of Hijuelo, Lasa, and Jabugo. The *chorizo* (hard pork sausage) and *morcilla* (blood sausage) of Pamplona, Granada, and Burgos are known beyond Spain. *Sobrasada* is a delicious pork-and-pepper paste from Majorca. *Fuet* (literally, "whip," named for its slender shape) is Catalonia's best sausage, although the *botifarra* is Catalonia's most emblematic and universal spicy sausage, usually consumed with *secas* or *mongetes* (white beans), a popular Catalan dish.

The country's most sophisticated and elaborate poultry dishes are prepared in the Catalan province of Girona. These include *pollastre amb llangosta* (chicken with lobster), *gall dindi amb panses, pinyones, i botifarra* (turkey stuffed with raisins, pine nuts, and sausage), and *oca (anec) amb naps* (goose, or duck, with turnips). *Pollo al ajillo,* fried chunks of chicken smothered in chips of garlic, is beloved all over Spain. Rabbit is another standard light meat, prepared either *al ajillo* (in garlic), *a la brasa* (roasted over coals), or in stews and ragouts with peppers and assorted vegetables.

Fish, meat, and seafood meet exuberantly in paella, a saffron-flavored rice dish widely considered the most emblematic of Spanish dishes. The dish is actually comparatively new, having originated in Valencia and the Levante, Spain's rice-growing eastern coastal plain, in the early 19th century. Paella is cooked in a wide, flat, round pan and has many versions, including *marinera* (seafood), *conejo* (rabbit), *pollo* (chicken), and *mixta* (mixed). Chosen from a *menú del día,* paella will always be disappointing, little more than rice with some saffron and a few ingredients mixed in. Prepared on the spot and in the pan for anywhere from two to two hundred, with a caramelized crust around its edges, paella is invariably delicious. The archetypal version is *paella a la marinera,* a seafood anthology including shrimp, crayfish, monkfish, and mussels on a bed of saffron rice cooked in a seafood broth with peppers and tomatoes. Related dishes include *arroz abanda,* a paella with the seafood pre-shelled; *fideuà,* paella based on pasta rather than rice; and *arroz negro* (black rice), paella that takes its color and flavor from cuttlefish ink instead of saffron.

Spanish cheeses are many and varied. The cheeses of La Mancha can be consumed *tierno* (soft and creamy, cured under three months), *semi-seco* (half-cured, for three to six months), or *seco* (dry, cured for more than six months). A mature *manchego seco* is nearly the equal of an Italian Parmesan. *Cabrales,* a powerful sheep's cheese from Asturias, makes a Roquefort seem innocent. Other prominent northern cheeses include the soft and creamy breast-shaped *tetilla gallega* and the sharper Asturian *pitu al' fuego.* The Basque country's smoky *idiazábal* is like a cedar-flavored sharp cheddar.

Spanish wines are rapidly emerging from the long shadow cast by their neighbors to the north. La Rioja is justly considered Spain's finest winegrowing region. The deep, woody flavor of its celebrated reds comes from up to eight years of aging in casks of American oak, usually preferred over French oak for its superior porosity and faster oxidating properties. This aging technique was introduced by French vintners from Bordeaux and Burgundy who moved to the Rioja in the 19th century to escape a phylloxera epidemic that was destroying the vines in their own country. Among the better Rioja labels are Rioja Alta, Viña Ardanza, Imperial, Muga, Marqués de Murrieta, Pomal, Ramón Bilbao, Marqués de Riscal, and Viña Tondonia.

Southwest of Valladolid, the Rueda winegrowing district produces some of Spain's most distinguished white wines, and Huesca's Somontano wines, especially the Enate and Señorío de Lazán labels, are rapidly gaining respect. The Valdepeñas wine country, 200 km (120 mi) south of Madrid, remains Spain's prime producer of simple table wines in unabashedly greater quantity than quality. That said, a pitcher of Valdepeñas with a meal or a round of tapas in and around Castile is never disappointing.

Catalonia's Penedès region specializes in *cava* (sparkling white wine). The most famous cavas are Codorniu and Freixenet, but many smaller outfits, such as Juvé i Camps, Augustí Torelló, Mascaró, and Gramona, actually produce better bubbly. Along with the Torres reds and whites and the Raventós cavas and whites, the Penedès produces Spain's greatest variety of wines overall. New artisanal wines, however, are steadily emerging from such unlikely places as the rugged hills of the Priorat area, west of Tarragona; the Costers de Siurana labels Clos de l'Obac and Miserere are standouts. The Raimat wines from Costers del Segre are excellent, as are the Gran Caus, the Castillo Perelada, and the exciting new Oliver Conti wines from northern Catalonia's Ampurdán region.

Many Spanish oenophiles favor wines from La Ribera del Duero, north of Madrid. This increasingly prestigious region produces excellent bottles of both young wine and wine that will improve with age. Vega Sicilia is the most famous winery in La Ribera del Duero; Pesquera, Protos, and Viña Pedrosa are other reputable labels.

Galicia's Ribeiro and Rías Baixas wines, especially the young green Albariños, are increasingly served in top restaurants throughout Spain with appetizers and fish courses. The Basque country's *txakolí,* an even greener young white with a slight effervescence, has always been popular locally but is now gaining a real following as Basque restaurants and tapas bars flourish all over Spain.

Sherry has always been popular abroad, especially with the British, who have dominated the sherry trade in Jerez de la Frontera since the 16th century. Indeed, many of the most famous labels are foreign—Domecq, Harvey, Sandeman. The classic dry sherry is the *fino. Amontillado* is deeper in color and flavor, and *oloroso* is really a sweet dessert wine, as are the even-sweeter creams. Another fortified Andalusian wine, often difficult for the inexperienced palate to distinguish from sherry, is *manzanilla,* from the coastal town of Sanlúcar de

Barrameda. Manzanilla has a tangy, saline savor that comes from the cool Atlantic breezes at the mouth of the Guadalquívir River. With its faint taste of the sea, this wine does not travel well; there are even those who believe it tastes better in the lower part of Sanlúcar than in the upper town. Sherry and manzanilla are generally thought of as aperitif wines and are ideal with tapas. A Sanlúcar prawn with a glass of manzanilla is many a Spanish epicurean's idea of paradise. In England, sherry still has the genteel associations of an Oxbridge college, but Spain has a more robust attitude toward the beverage, especially during Sevilla's Feria de Abril, where more sherry and manzanilla are reputedly drunk in a week than in the whole of Spain the rest of the year.

Some of Spain's finest brandies, such as Osborne, Terry, Duque de Alba, and Carlos III, also come from Jerez. Málaga makes a sweet dessert wine that enjoyed a vogue with the English in the 19th century; look for the label Scholtz. *Aguardientes* (aquavits) are manufactured throughout Spain, with the most famous brands coming from Chinchón, near Madrid. A sweet and popular Jerez brandy, Ponche Caballero, is easy to identify by its silver-coated bottle, which looks like an amateur explosive. *Sangría,* a tourist potion imported from Mexico, is generally composed of cheap liquors and bad wine and should be avoided at all costs by those in search of Spanish delicacies.

Spain's gourmet restaurants offer a selection of postprandial cheeses, but most meals end with dessert. Standard enticements are fresh fruit, such as strawberries with orange juice or vanilla ice cream, and *flan,* a caramel cream that comes close to being Spain's national dessert. In Catalonia, look for the ubiquitous *crema catalana,* a sort of crème brûlée, or the honey-and-fresh-cheese combination known as *mel i mató.*

The main problem with food and wine in Spain—perhaps an ironic one, in light of Spain's not-so-distant past—may be their very abundance. Dining heartily twice a day and taking full advantage of the tapas hour requires some management. The Spanish, looking forward to a substantial midday meal after having finished dinner late the previous night, breakfast on little more than coffee and a roll. Lunch, served between 2 and 4 in the afternoon—preceded by an *aperitivo*—is generally considered the main meal of the day. The workday lasts until at least 8, after which it's time for the itinerant *tapeo.* Finally, often after 10, comes dinner, which is often festive and can last until the wee hours. The traveler's key to surviving this delicious but demanding regimen is to partake zestily of tapas in the early evening—roam freely and you'll soon fill up on cleverly arrayed items from all four food groups. Above and after all, Spain is the ultimate moveable feast.

— George Semler and Michael Jacobs

WHAT TO READ & WATCH BEFORE YOU GO

A star contributor to this guide, George Semler has authored two guides of his own, *Barcelonawalks* and *Madridwalks,* each of which takes readers on five walking tours full of historic and literary detail. Jan Morris discusses Spanish history and culture via monuments and landscapes in a series of essays called *Spain,* while James A. Michener relates sightseeing anecdotes at length in *Iberia: Spanish Travels and Reflections.* Based on a long drive around mostly rural Spain, Cees Nooteboom's *Roads to Santiago* is a richly intellectual yet deeply personal meditation on Spain's history and resonance. The first English-language guidebook on Spain, Richard Ford's 1845 *Handbook for Travellers in Spain,* is still worth a peek.

Ernest Hemingway is the English-language writer most responsible for promulgating the classic image of Spain. Read *The Sun Also Rises* (published as *Fiesta* in Britain) for a vicarious visit to Pamplona's running of the bulls. *For Whom the Bell Tolls* depicts the physical and psychological horrors of the Spanish Civil War, and *Death in the Afternoon* masterfully explores the technical, artistic, and philosophical aspects of bullfighting. Larry Collins and Dominique LaPierre's *Or I'll Dress You in Mourning* tells the saga of El Cordobés, one of Spain's most famous matadors.

V. S. Pritchett (*The Spanish Temper*), H. V. Morton (*A Stranger in Spain*), George Orwell (*Homage to Catalonia*), and Washington Irving (*Tales of the Alhambra*) have all paid their respects to Spain. Gerald Brenan's works portray Spain during the Franco years: *The Face of Spain, The Spanish Labyrinth,* and *South from Granada. Moorish Spain,* by Richard Fletcher, details the cultural and intellectual riches of the Islamic era; *Farewell España,* by James Gerber, covers the Sephardim, the Spanish Jews who were forced to flee during the Inquisition. Ronald Frasier's *Blood of Spain* is an oral history of the Spanish Civil War, woven from hundreds of interviews with survivors. Journalist John Hooper examines the post-Franco era in *The New Spaniards.*

Among Spanish texts, the story of the errant knight *Don Quixote,* by Miguel de Cervantes, will always be Spain's towering classic. For more modern fare, try translations of the realism-drenched novels of Galician Camilo José Cela, the 1989 recipient of the Nobel Prize for Literature: his best-known works are *The Beehive* and *The Family of Pascual Duarte.* One of Spain's great 20th-century novels is Mercé Rodoreda's *The Time of the Doves,* the story of a woman buffeted by the misfortunes of the Civil War. Federico García Lorca's play *Blood Wedding* is a disturbing drama of Spain's repressed yet powerful women of the early 20th century. Novelist Javier Marías has been hugely successful in several countries; among his best works in translation are *A Heart So White* and *Tomorrow in the Battle Think on Me.* Arturo Pérez-Reverte has written several popular and acclaimed mysteries, including *The Flanders Panel, The Club Dumas,* and *The Fencing Master.*

The tragic bullfighting novel *Blood and Sand,* by Vicente Blasco Ibáñez, has three Hollywood adaptations: the first starring Rudolph Valentino; the second, Tyrone Power, the third, Sharon Stone. The last version shows quite a bit of Andalusia.

Carlos Saura has directed several beautifully crafted classics consisting mostly of dance—*Carmen, Bodas de Sangre* (*Blood Wedding*) and *El Amor Brujo* (Love, the Magician). Luis

Buñuel's *Un Chien Andalou* is still a hallmark of surrealism, and *Belle de Jour, Tristana,* and *That Obscure Object of Desire* contain fascinating psychological studies. The last has lovely photography of Seville.

Set in 1931, *Belle Epoque* is a 1992 male-fantasy film about a man desired by four beautiful sisters. Set in 1930s Galicia, José Luis Cuerda's gorgeous *Butterfly* (released in the U.K. as *The Butterfly's Tongue*) shows how the Civil War divided communities before the first shots were fired. Whit Stillman, an American married to a Catalan, directed *Barcelona,* a contemporary romantic comedy about three American men and three Barcelona women.

The current bad-boy darling of Spanish cinema is Pedro Almodóvar, whose *Women on the Verge of a Nervous Breakdown* (with some nice shots of Madrid), *Tie Me Up! Tie Me Down!,* and *All About My Mother* were greeted enthusiastically on both sides of the Atlantic. *All About My Mother* won the 2000 Academy Award for Best Foreign Film.

ESSENTIAL INFORMATION

AIR TRAVEL

Regular nonstop flights serve Spain from the eastern United States; flying from other North American cities usually involves a stop.

Flights from the United Kingdom to Spain are more frequent, cover small cities as well as large ones, and are priced very competitively. If you're coming from North America and would like to land in a city other than Madrid or Barcelona, consider flying a British or other European carrier; just know that you may have to stay overnight in London or another European city on your way home. There are no nonstop flights to Spain from Australia or New Zealand.

There are numerous daily flights within Spain.

BOOKING

When you book, **look for nonstop flights** and **remember that "direct" flights stop at least once.** Try to avoid connecting flights, which require a change of plane.

CARRIERS

From North America, American, Continental, US Airways, Air Europa, Spanair, and TWA fly to Madrid; Delta and Iberia fly to Madrid and Barcelona. For flights to the Canary Islands, *see* Chapter 14.

Within Spain, Iberia is the main domestic airline; two independent airlines, Air Europa and Spanair, fly a number of domestic routes at lower prices.

The Spanish predilection for cigarettes notwithstanding, most airlines serving Spain, including Iberia, do not allow smoking on either international or domestic flights.

➤ FROM NORTH AMERICA: **Air Europa** (☎ 888/238–7672). **American** (☎ 800/433–7300). **Continental** (☎ 800/231–0856). **Delta** (☎ 800/221–1212). **Iberia** (☎ 800/772–4642). **Spanair** (☎ 888/545–5757). **TWA** (☎ 800/892–4141). **US Airways**(☎ 800/622–1015).

➤ FROM THE U.K.: **British Airways** (☎ 0345/222–111). **Iberia** (☎ 0207/830–0011).

➤ WITHIN SPAIN: **Iberia** (902/400500). **Air Europa** (☎ 902/401501). **Spanair** (☎ 902/131415).

CUTTING COSTS

The cheapest airfares to Spain must usually be purchased in advance and are non-refundable. Call a number of airlines, and **when you're quoted a good price, book it on the spot**—the same fare may not be available the next day. Always **check different routings** or look into using different airports. Travel agents, especially low-fare specialists (☞ Discounts & Deals, *below*), can be helpful.

Consolidators are another good source: they buy tickets for scheduled international flights at reduced rates from the airlines, then sell them at prices that beat the best fare available directly from the airlines, usually without restrictions. Sometimes you can even get your money back if you need to return the ticket. Carefully read the fine print detailing penalties for changes and cancellations, and **confirm your consolidator reservation with the airline.**

➤ CONSOLIDATORS: **Cheap Tickets** (☎ 800/377–1000). **Discount Airline Ticket Service** (☎ 800/576–1600). **Unitravel**(☎ 800/325–2222). **Up & Away Travel** (☎ 212/889–2345). **World Travel Network** (☎ 800/409–6753).

➤ DISCOUNT PASSES: If you buy a round-trip transatlantic ticket on **Iberia** (☞ *above*), you might want to purchase a Visit Spain pass, good for four domestic flights during your trip. The pass must be purchased before you arrive in Spain, all flights must be booked in advance, and the cost is $260 ($350 if you want to include flights to the Canary Islands). Prices are $20–$50 less if you travel between October 1 and June 14.

On certain days of the week, Iberia also offers *minitarifas* (minifares), which can save you 40% on domestic flights. Tickets must be purchased in advance, and you must stay over Saturday night (☞ Discounts and Deals, *below*).

FLYING TIMES

Flying time from New York is seven hours; from London, just over two hours.

HOW TO COMPLAIN

If your baggage goes astray or your flight goes awry, complain right away. Most carriers require that you **file a claim immediately.**

AIRPORTS

Most flights from the United States and Canada land in, or pass through, Madrid's Barajas (MAD). The other major gateway is Barcelona's El Prat de Llobregat (BCN). From the U.K. and elsewhere in Europe, regular flights also land in Málaga (AGP), Alicante (ALC), Palma de Mallorca (PMI), and on Gran Canaria (LPA) and Tenerife (TFN).

➤ AIRPORT INFORMATION: Madrid: **Barajas** (☎ 91/305–8343). Barcelona: **El Prat de Llobregat** (☎ 93/298–3838).

BIKE TRAVEL

Long distances, an abundance of hilly terrain, and climate (hot summers, rainy winters) make touring Spain by bike less than ideal for all but the fittest bikers. That said, Spain's numerous nature preserves are perfect for mountain biking, especially in spring and fall, and many have specially marked bike paths. It's usually better to rent a bike locally than deal with the logistics of bringing your own bike with you. Bikes are not usually allowed on trains, for instance; they must be packed and checked as luggage. At most nature preserves, at least one agency rents mountain bikes and, in many cases, leads guided bike tours. Check with the park's visitor center for details. In addition, rural hotels often make bikes available to guests, sometimes free of charge.

BIKES IN FLIGHT

Most airlines accommodate bikes as luggage, provided they're dismantled and boxed. You'll pay about $5 for a bike box (often free at bike shops), and at least $100 for a bike bag. International travelers can sometimes substitute a bike for a piece of checked luggage at no charge; otherwise, the cost is about $100. Domestic and Canadian airlines charge $25–$50.

BOAT & FERRY TRAVEL

Regular car ferries connect the U.K. with northern Spain. Brittany Ferries sails from Portsmouth to Santander; P&O European Ferries sails from Plymouth to Bilbao. Spain's major car-ferry line, Trasmediterránea, connects mainland Spain to the Balearic and Canary Islands. If you want to drive from Spain to Morocco, you can take a car ferry from Málaga, Algeciras, or Tarifa, run by Trasmediterránea or Buquebus; both lines also offer a catamaran service that takes half the time of the standard ferry.

➤ FROM THE U.K.: **Brittany Ferries** (☎ 0752/221321 or 0990/360360). **P&O European Ferries** (☎ 0990/980555).

➤ IN SPAIN: **Buquebus** (☎ 902/414242).**Trasmediterránea**(☎ 902/454645).

BUS TRAVEL

Within Spain, an array of private companies provide bus service that ranges from knee-crunchingly basic to luxurious. Fares are lower than the corresponding train fares, and service is more extensive: if you want to reach a town not served by train, you can be sure a bus will go there. Smaller towns don't usually have a central bus depot, so ask the tourist office where to wait for the bus to your destination. Spain's major national long-haul bus line is **Enatcar;** see the appropriate chapters for companies serving specific regions. Note that service is less frequent on weekends.

For a longer haul, you can travel to Spain by bus from London or Paris. It's a long journey, but the buses are modern, and the fares are a fraction of what you'd pay to fly.

FARES & SCHEDULES

➤ FROM THE U.K.: **Eurolines/ National Express** (☎ 01582/404511 or 0990/143219).

➤ WITHIN SPAIN: **Enatcar**(✉ Calle Mendazábal, Madrid, ☎ 91/527–9927).

➤ BUS TOURS: **Marsans** (✉ Gran Vía 59, Madrid,☎ 902/306090). **Pullmantur** (✉ Plaza de Oriente 8, Madrid, ☎ 91/541–1805).

BUSINESS HOURS

BANKS & OFFICES

Banks are generally open weekdays from 9 to 2 and Saturday from 8:30 or 9 to 1. In the summer, most banks close at 1 PM on weekdays and stay closed on Saturday. Currency exchanges at airports and train stations stay open later; you can also cash traveler's checks at El Corte Inglés department stores until 9 PM. Most government offices are open weekdays from 9 to 2 only.

MUSEUMS & SIGHTS

Most museums are open from 9:30 to 2 and 4 to 7 six days a week, usually every day but Monday. Opening hours vary, of course, and change with the high and low seasons, so confirm them before you make plans. A few large museums, such as Madrid's Prado and Reina Sofía and Barcelona's Picasso Museum, stay open all day.

PHARMACIES

Pharmacies keep normal business hours (9–1:30 and 5–8), but every town (or city neighborhood) has a duty pharmacy that stays open 24 hours.

SHOPS

When planning a shopping trip, remember that **almost all shops in Spain close at midday** for at least three hours. The only exceptions are large supermarkets and the department-store chain El Corte Inglés. Stores are generally open from 9–10 to 1:30 and from 5 to 8. Most shops are closed on Sunday, and in Madrid and several other places they're also closed Saturday afternoon. That said, larger shops in tourist areas may stay open Sunday in summer and during the Christmas holiday.

CAMERAS & PHOTOGRAPHY

Spain's multifarious landscapes lend themselves to memorable photographs. Short of leaving the lens cap on, it's hard to take bad pictures here. Note that many museums and monuments ban photography; others prohibit the use of flash or a tripod. You are not allowed to take photographs of military installations, nor should you take pictures of police.

You'll probably get the best outdoor pictures in the early morning and evening, as harsh midday sun can make contrasts excessive. On the beach, bear in mind that reflected glare can confuse your light meter.

FILM & DEVELOPING

All major brands of film are readily available in Spain, and at reasonable prices. Try to buy film in large stores or photography shops; film sold in smaller outlets may be out of date or stored in poor conditions.

To have film developed, **look for shops displaying the Kodak Q-Lab sign,** a guarantee of quality. If you're in a real hurry and happen to be in a large town or resort, you will, of course, find shops that will process film in a few hours. Always **keep your film out of the sun.** X-ray machines in Spanish airports are said to be film-safe.

VIDEOS

Video systems in Spain are on the PAL system (used in Britain and much of continental Europe, though not France). Tapes for other systems are hard to come by, so take a good supply with you. In airports, keep videotapes away from metal detectors.

CAR RENTAL

Avis, Hertz, Budget, and National (partnered in Spain with the Spanish agency Atesa) all have branches at major Spanish airports and in large cities. Smaller, regional companies offer lower rates. All agencies have a wide range of models, but virtually all cars in Spain have a manual transmission—**if you don't want a stick shift, reserve weeks in advance and specify automatic transmission,** then call to reconfirm your automatic car before you leave for Spain. Rates in Madrid begin at the equivalents of U.S.$55 a day and $240 a week for an economy car with air-conditioning, manual transmission, and unlimited mileage. Add to this a 16% tax on car rentals.

➤ INTERNATIONAL AGENCIES: **Alamo** (☎ 800/522–9696; 0208/759–6200 in the U.K.). **Avis** (☎ 800/331–1084; 800/879–2847 in Canada; 02/9353–9000 in Australia; 09/525–1982 in New Zealand). **Budget** (☎ 800/527–0700; 0144/227–6266 in the U.K.). **Dollar** (☎ 800/800–6000; 0208/897–0811 in the U.K., where it is known as Eurodollar; 02/9223–1444 in Australia). **Hertz** (☎ 800/654–3001; 800/263–0600 in Canada; 0208/897–2072 in the U.K.; 02/9669–2444 in Australia; 03/358–6777 in New Zealand). **National** (☎ 800/227–3876; 0208/750–2800 or 1293/567790 in the U.K.).

➤ LOCAL AGENCIES: **National/Atesa** (☎ 902/100101).

INSURANCE

When driving a rental car, you are generally responsible for any damage to or loss of the vehicle. The collision policies sold with European rentals usually do not cover theft; before you buy insurance from the rental agency, see what coverage your personal auto-insurance policy and credit cards provide.

REQUIREMENTS & RESTRICTIONS

Your own driver's license is valid in Spain, but you may want to get an International Driver's Permit for extra assurance. Permits are available from the American or Canadian automobile association, or, in the United Kingdom, from the Automobile Association or Royal Automobile Club. Note that while anyone over 18 with a valid license can drive in Spain, some rental agencies will not rent cars to drivers under 21.

SURCHARGES

Before you pick up a car in one city and leave it in another, **ask about drop-off charges or one-way service fees,** which can be substantial. Note, too, that some rental agencies charge extra if you return the car *before* the time specified in your contract. To avoid a hefty refueling fee, **fill the tank just before you return the car,** remembering that gas stations near the rental outlet are likely to overcharge.

CHILDREN IN SPAIN

Children are greatly indulged in Spain. You'll see kids accompanying their parents everywhere, including bars and restaurants, so bringing yours along should not be a problem. Shopkeepers will shower your child with *caramelos* (sweets), and even the coldest waiters tend to be friendlier when you have a youngster with you. And although you won't be shunted into a remote corner when you bring kids into a Spanish restaurant, **you won't find high chairs or special children's menus.** Children are expected to eat what their parents do, so it's perfectly acceptable to ask for an extra plate and share your food. Be prepared for late bedtimes, especially in summer—it's common to see toddlers playing cheerfully outdoors until midnight. Because children are expected to be with their parents at all times, few hotels provide baby-sitting services; but those that don't can often refer you to an independent baby-sitter (*canguro*).

If you decide to rent a car, **arrange for a car seat when you reserve.**

FOOD

Visiting children may turn up their noses at some of Spain's regional specialties. Although kids seldom get their own menus, most restaurants are happy to provide simple dishes, such as plain grilled chicken, steak, or fried potatoes, for the little ones. *Pescadito frito* (batter-fried fish) is one Spanish dish that most kids do seem to enjoy. If all else fails, familiar fast-food chains such as McDonald's, Burger King, and Pizza Hut are well represented in the major cities and popular resorts.

LODGING

Most hotels in Spain allow children under a certain age to stay in their parents' room at no extra charge, but others charge them as extra adults. **Find out the cutoff age for children's discounts.**

SIGHTS & ATTRACTIONS

Museum admissions and bus and metro rides are generally free for children up to age five. We indicate places that children might especially enjoy with a rubber duck (🐥) in the margin.

SUPPLIES & EQUIPMENT

Disposable diapers (*pañales*), formula (*papillas*), and bottled baby foods are readily available at supermarkets and pharmacies.

COMPUTERS ON THE ROAD

A few of Spain's newer hotels, mainly in the major cities, provide data ports for Internet access in guest rooms. If you need to bring your computer, *see* Electricity, *below*.

Virtually every town with more than two traffic lights has at least one cybercafé, most with hourly rates under 500 ptas.

CONSUMER PROTECTION

Whenever shopping or buying travel services in Spain, **pay with a major credit card** so you can cancel payment or get reimbursed if there's a problem. If you're doing business with a particular company for the first time, **contact your local Better Business Bureau and the attorney general's offices** in your own state and the company's home state. Have any complaints been filed? Finally, if you're buying a package or tour, always **consider travel insurance** that includes default coverage (☞ Insurance, *below*).

➤ BBBs: **Council of Better Business Bureaus**(✉ 4200 Wilson Blvd., Suite 800, Arlington, VA 22203, ☎ 703/276–0100, FAX 703/525–8277, www.bbb.org).

CRUISE TRAVEL

Barcelona is the cruise capital of Spain, and the point of departure for many Mediterranean cruises. Other popular ports of call are Gibraltar, Málaga, Alicante, and Palma de Mallorca. Among the many that call at Spain are Royal Caribbean, Holland America Line, Renaissance Cruises, the Norwegian Cruise Line, and Princess Cruises.

CUSTOMS & DUTIES

Keep receipts for all purchases. Upon reentering your home country, **be ready to show customs officials what you've bought.** If you feel a duty is incorrect, or you object to the way your clearance was handled, note the inspector's badge number and ask to see a supervisor. If the problem isn't resolved, write to the appropriate authorities, beginning with the port director at your point of entry.

European Union residents who have traveled only within the EU need not pass through customs upon returning to their home country. If you plan to come home with large quantities of alcohol or tobacco, check EU limits beforehand.

From countries that are not part of the European Union, visitors age 15 and over may *enter* Spain duty-free with up to 200 cigarettes or 50 cigars, up to one liter of alcohol over 22 proof, and up to two liters of wine. Dogs and cats are admitted as long as they have up-to-date vaccination records from their home country.

➤ INFORMATION: **Australian Customs Service** (Regional Director, ✉ Box 8, Sydney, NSW 2001, ☎ 02/9213–2000, FAX 02/9213–4000). **Revenue Canada** (✉ 2265 St. Laurent Blvd. S, Ottawa, Ontario K1G 4K3,☎ 613/993–0534; 800/461–9999 in Canada, FAX 613/957–8911, www.ccra-adrc.gc.ca). **New Zealand Customs** (Custom House, ✉ 50 Anzac Ave., Box 29, Auckland, New Zealand, ☎ 09/359–6655, FAX 09/359–6732). **HM Customs and Excise** (✉ Dorset House, Stamford St., Bromley, Kent BR1 1XX, ☎ 0207/202–4227). **U.S. Customs Service** (✉ 1300 Pennsylvania Ave. NW, Washington, DC 20229, www.customs.gov; inquiries ☎ 202/354–1000; complaints ✉ Office of Regulations and Rulings; registration of equipment ✉ Resource Management, ☎ 202/927–0540).

DINING

Spaniards love to eat out, and restaurants in Spain have evolved dramatically thanks to a favorable economic climate and burgeoning tourism. A new generation of Spanish chefs—some with international reputations—has transformed classic dishes to suit contemporary tastes, drawing on some of the freshest ingredients in Europe. For more on Spanish cuisine, *see* "Spanish Food and Wine" *in* Chapter 16.

The restaurants featured in this book are the cream of the crop in each price range. Restaurants are identified by a crossed knife-and-fork icon ✕; establishments with a ✕🏨 symbol are hotels with restaurants that stand out for their cuisine and are open to non-guests.

MEALS

Most restaurants in Spain do not serve breakfast (*desayuno*); for coffee and carbohydrates, head to a bar or *cafetería*. Outside major hotels, which serve buffet breakfasts, breakfast in Spain is usually limited to coffee and toast or a roll. Lunch (*comida* or *almuerzo*) traditionally consists of an appetizer, a main course, and dessert, followed by coffee and perhaps a liqueur. Between lunch and dinner the best way to snack is to sample some *tapas* (appetizers) at a bar; normally you can choose from quite a variety. Dinner (*cena*) is somewhat lighter, with perhaps only one course.

In addition to an à la carte menu, most restaurants offer a daily fixed-price menu (*menú del día*) consisting of two courses, coffee, and dessert at a very attractive price. If the server does not suggest the menú del día when you're seated (perhaps on the assumption that foreigners will order à la carte), feel free to ask for it—"Hay menú del día, por favor?"

MEALTIMES

Mealtimes in Spain are later than elsewhere in Europe, and later still in Madrid. Lunch starts around 2 or 2:30 (closer to 3 in Madrid), dinner between 8 and 10 (9 and 11 in Madrid). In areas with heavy tourist traffic, some restaurants open a bit earlier. Unless otherwise noted, restaurants listed in this book are open for lunch and dinner.

PAYING

Credit cards are widely accepted in Spanish restaurants. If you pay by-credit card, leave the tip in cash (☞ Tipping, *below*).

RESERVATIONS & DRESS

Reservations are always a good idea. We mention them only when they're essential or not accepted. For top restaurants, book as far in advance as you can, and confirm when you arrive in Spain. We mention dress only when men are required to wear a jacket or a jacket and tie.

SPECIALTIES

Spain does not have a single cuisine, but rather various cuisines representing its distinct regional cultures. Spain's most famous dish, paella, originated in Valencia and is not actually prevalent throughout the country. Basque and Catalan cooking are considered the finest in Spain—Basque cuisine centers on fresh fish and meat dishes, while Catalan cooking revolves around vegetables and interesting sauces. Galician cuisine is a bit simpler, but centers on equally fresh fish and shellfish. The roasts of central Castile are renowned, as are the fried fish and the cold soups—gazpacho and the almond-based *ajo blanco*—of Andalusia. The classic dish in Madrid and many other parts of Spain is the *cocido,* a hearty stew eaten in two parts: the soup, then the solids.

WINE, BEER & SPIRITS

Apart from its famous wines (☞ Spanish Food and Wine *in* Chapter 16), Spain produces many brands of lager, the most popular of which are San Miguel, Cruzcampo, Aguila, and Mahou. Jerez de la Frontera is Europe's largest producer of brandy, and Catalonia the world's major source of *cava* (sparkling wine). Spanish law prohibits the sale of alcohol to persons under 16.

DISABILITIES & ACCESSIBILITY

Unfortunately, Spain has done little to make traveling easy for visitors with disabilities. Only the Prado and some newer museums, such as Madrid's Reina Sofía and Thyssen-Bornemisza, have wheelchair-accessible entrances or elevators. Most of the churches, castles, and monasteries on a sightseer's itinerary involve quite a bit of walking, often on uneven terrain.

RESERVATIONS

When discussing accessibility with an operator or reservations agent, **ask hard questions.** Are there any stairs, inside *or* out? Are there grab bars next to the toilet *and* in the shower/tub? How wide is the doorway to the room? To the bathroom? For the most extensive facilities, **opt for newer accommodations.**

TRAVEL AGENCIES

In the United States, the Americans with Disabilities Act requires that travel firms serve the needs of all travelers. Some agencies specialize in working with people with disabilities.

➤ TRAVELERS WITH MOBILITY PROBLEMS: **Access Adventures**(✉ 206 Chestnut Ridge Rd., Rochester,NY 14624, ☎ 716/889–9096,dltravel@prodigy.net), run by a formerphysical-rehabilitation counselor. **CareVacations** (✉ 5-5110 50th Ave., Leduc, Alberta T9E 6V4, ☎ 780/986–6404 or 877/478–7827, FAX 780/986–8332, www.carevacations.com), for group tours and cruise vacations. **Flying Wheels Travel** (✉ 143 W. Bridge St., Box 382, Owatonna, MN55060, ☎ 507/451–5005 or 800/535–6790, FAX 507/451–1685, thq@ll.net, www.flyingwheels.com).

DISCOUNTS & DEALS

Be a smart shopper and **compare all your options** before making decisions. A plane ticket bought with a promotional coupon from a travel club, coupon book, or direct-mail offer may not be cheaper than the least expensive fare from a discount-ticket agency. Always keep in mind that what you get is as important as what you save.

DISCOUNT RESERVATIONS

Look into discount-reservation services, which use their buying power to get better prices on hotels, airline tickets, even car rentals. When reserving a hotel room, ask about special packages or corporate rates.

When shopping for the best deals on hotel rooms and car rentals, **look for guaranteed exchange rates,** which protect you against a falling dollar. With the rate locked in, you won't pay more even if the price goes up in the local currency.

➤ AIRLINE TICKETS: ☎ **800/FLY–4–LESS.** ☎ **800/FLY–ASAP.**

➤ HOTEL ROOMS: **International Marketing & Travel Concepts** (☎ 800/790–4682, imtc@mindspring.com). **Steigenberger Reservation Service** (☎ 800/223–5652, www.srs-worldhotels.com). **Travel Interlink** (☎ 800/888–5898, www.travelinterlink.com).

PACKAGE DEALS

Don't confuse package vacations with guided tours. When you buy a package, you travel on your own, just as though you had planned the trip yourself. Fly/drive packages, which combine airfare and car rental, are often a good deal. If you buy a rail/drive pass, you may save on train tickets and car rentals. All Eurail- and Europass holders get a discount on Eurostar fares through the Channel Tunnel.

DRIVING

Driving is the best way to see Spain's rural areas and get off the beaten track. The main cities are connected by a network of excellent four-lane *autovías* (freeways) and *autopistas* (toll freeways; "toll" is *peaje*), which are designated with the letter A and have speed limits of up to 120 km/h (74 mph). The letter N indicates a *carretera nacional* (basic national route), which may have four or two lanes. Smaller towns and villages are connected by a network of secondary roads maintained by regional, provincial, and local governments.

Spain's major routes bear heavy traffic, especially during holiday periods. Drive with care: the roads are shared by a potentially perilous mixture of local drivers, Moroccan immigrants traveling between North Africa and northern Europe, and non-Spanish vacationers, some of whom are accustomed to driving on the left side of the road. Be prepared, too, for heavy truck traffic on national routes, which, in the case of two-lane roads, can have you creeping along for hours.

AUTO CLUBS

➤ IN AUSTRALIA: **Australian Automobile Association** (☎ 02/6247–7311).

➤ IN CANADA: **Canadian Automobile Association** (CAA, ☎ 613/247–0117).

➤ IN NEW ZEALAND: **New Zealand Automobile Association** (☎ 09/377–4660).

➤ IN THE U.K.: **Automobile Association** (AA, ☎ 0990/500–600). **Royal Automobile Club** (RAC, ☎ 0990/722–722 for membership; 0345/121–345 for insurance).

➤ IN THE U.S.: **American Automobile Association** (AAA, ☎ 800/564–6222).

➤ IN SPAIN: **RACE** (✉ José Abascal 10, Madrid,☎ 900/200093).

EMERGENCY SERVICES

The rental agencies Hertz and Avis have 24-hour breakdown service. If you belong to an auto club (AAA, CAA, or AA), you can get emergency assistance from their Spanish counterpart, RACE (☎ 900/112222).

FUEL

Gas stations are plentiful, and some of those on major routes are open 24 hours. Most stations are self-service, though prices are the same as those at full-service stations. You punch in the amount of gas you want (in pesetas, not in liters), unhook the nozzle, pump the gas, and then pay. At night, however, you must pay before you fill up. Most pumps offer a choice of gas, including leaded, unleaded, and diesel, so **be careful to pick the right one** for your car. All newer cars in Spain use *gasolina sin plomo* (unleaded gas), which is available in two grades, 95 and 98 octane. *Super,* regular 97-octane leaded gas, is gradually being phased out. Although prices were decontrolled in 1993, they vary little between stations, and were at press time 148 ptas. a liter for super, 138 ptas. a liter for *sin plomo* (unleaded; 95 octane), and 152 ptas. a liter for unleaded, 98 octane. Credit cards are widely accepted.

ROAD CONDITIONS

Spain's highway system now includes some 6,000 km (3,600 mi) of beautifully maintained superhighways. Still, you'll find some stretches of major national highways that are only two lanes wide, where traffic often backs up behind slow, heavy trucks. *Autopista* tolls are steep.

Most Spanish cities have notoriously long morning and evening rush hours. Traffic jams are especially bad in and around Barcelona and Madrid. If possible, **avoid the morning rush hour, which can last until noon, and the evening rush hour, which lasts from 7 to 9.**

ROAD MAPS

Detailed road maps are readily available at bookstores and gasstations.

RULES OF THE ROAD

Spaniards drive on the right. Horns are banned in cities, but that doesn't keep people from blasting away. Children under 10 may not ride in the front seat, and seat belts are compulsory everywhere. Speed limits are 50 kph (31 mph) in cities, 100 kph (62 mph) on N roads, 120 kph (74 mph) on the *autopista* or *autovía,* and, unless otherwise signposted, 90 kph (56 mph) on other roads.

Spanish highway police are particularly vigilant about speeding and illegal passing. Fines start at 15,000 ptas., and police are empowered to demand payment from non-Spanish drivers on the spot. Although local drivers, especially in cities like Madrid, will park their cars just about anywhere, you should **park only in legal spots.** Parking fines are steep, and your car might well be towed, resulting in fines, hassle, and wasted time.

ELECTRICITY

To use electric equipment from the United States, **bring a converter and adapter.** Spain's electrical current is 220 volts, 50 cycles alternating current (AC); wall outlets take Continental-type plugs, with two round prongs.

If your appliances are dual-voltage you'll need only an adapter. Don't use 110-volt outlets, marked FOR SHAVERS ONLY, for high-wattage appliances such as hair dryers. Most laptop computers operate equally well on 110 and 220 volts, so they require only an adapter.

EMBASSIES

➤ IN MADRID: **Australia** (Plaza Descubridor Diegos de Ordas 3, ☎ 91/441–9300). **Canada** (Calle Nuñez de

Balboa 35, ☎ 91/423–3250). **New Zealand** (Plaza Lealtad 2, ☎ 91/523–0226). **United Kingdom** (C. Fernando el Santo 16, ☎ 91/319–0200). **United States** (C. Serrano 75, ☎ 91/587–2200).

EMERGENCIES

The pan-European **emergency phone number 112** is operative in some parts of Spain, but not all. If it doesn't work, dial the emergency numbers below for national police, local police, fire department or medical services. On the road, there are emergency phones marked SOS at regular intervals on *autovías* (freeways) and *autopistas* (toll highways).

If your documents are stolen, contact both the local police and your embassy (☞ *above*). If you lose a credit card, phone the issuer immediately (☞ Money, *below*).

➤ CONTACTS: **National police** (☎ 091). **Local police** (☎ 092).**Fire department** (☎ 080).**Medical service** (☎ 061).

ENGLISH-LANGUAGE MEDIA

In cities and major resorts, you'll have no trouble finding newspapers and magazines in English. U.K. newspapers are available on the day of publication. From the U.S., you'll see major news magazines, such as *Time,* along with the *International Herald Tribune* and *USA Today.*

BOOKS

Major airports sell books in English, including the latest paperback best-sellers. Bookshops in Madrid, Barcelona, Costa del Sol towns, Alicante, and the Canary Islands also sell English-language books.

NEWSPAPERS & MAGAZINES

Several major cities and resorts in Spain have local English-language publications, including Madrid (the monthly *Broadsheet*); Barcelona (the monthly *Barcelona Metropolitan*); Alicante (the weekly *Costa Blanca News, Post,* and *Entertainer*); Málaga (the weekly *Sur, Entertainer,* and *Costa del Sol News*, and the monthly magazines *Lookout, Essential,* and *Absolute Marbella*); Majorca (the *Majorca Daily Bulletin*), and the Canary Islands (the biweekly *Island Connections, Island Sun, Paper,* and *Tenerife News*).

RADIO & TELEVISION

Spain is served by two state-owned national channels, two private networks, regional channels in some parts of Spain, and local channels serving individual towns. Many hotels have satellite service, which usually includes at least one news channel in English (CNN, BBC World, or Sky News).

ETIQUETTE & BEHAVIOR

The Spanish are very tolerant of foreigners and their strange ways, but you should always behave with courtesy. Be respectful when visiting churches: casual dress is fine if it's not gaudy or unkempt. Spaniards do object to men going bare-chested anywhere other than the beach or poolside, and generally do not look kindly on public displays of drunkenness.

When addressing Spaniards with whom you are not well acquainted, use the formal *usted* rather than the familiar *tu.* For more on language, *see* Language, *below.*

BUSINESS ETIQUETTE

Spanish office hours can be confusing to the uninitiated. Some offices stay open more or less continuously from 9 to 3, with a very short lunch break. Others open in the morning, break up the day with a long lunch break of 2–3 hours, then reopen at 4 or 5 until 7 or 8. Spaniards enjoy a certain amount of notoriety for their lack of punctuality, but this has changed dramatically in recent years: you are expected to show up for meetings on time. Smart dress is the norm. Spaniards in international fields tend to conduct business with foreigners in English. If you speak Spanish, address new colleagues with the formal usted and the corresponding verb conjugations, then follow the lead in switching to the familiar tu once a working relationship has been established.

GAY & LESBIAN TRAVEL

Since the end of Franco's dictatorship, the situation for gays and lesbians in Spain has improved dramatically: the paragraph in the Spanish civil code that made homosexuality a crime was repealed in 1978. Violence against gays does occur, but it's generally restricted to the rougher areas of very large cities.

In summer, the beaches of the Balearics (especially Ibiza), the Costa del Sol (Torremolinos and Benidorm), and the Costa Brava (Sitges and Lloret del Mar) are gay and lesbian hot spots. Playa del Inglés and Maspalomas, in the Canary Islands, are popular in winter.

➤ Local Resources: **GaiInform** (✉ Fuencarral 37, 28004 Madrid, ☎ 91/523–0070). **Teléfono Rosa** (✉ C. Finlandia 45, Barcelona, ☎ 900/601601).

HEALTH

Sunburn and sunstroke are real risks in summertime Spain. On the hottest sunny days, even those who are not normally bothered by strong sun should cover themselves up; carry sunblock lotion; drink plenty of fluids; and limit sun time for the first few days.

If you require medical attention, ask your hotel's front desk for assistance or go to the nearest public **Centro de Salud** (day hospital); in serious cases, you'll be referred to the regional hospital. Medical care is good in Spain, but nursing is perfunctory, as relatives are expected to stop by and look after inpatients' needs. In some popular destinations, such as the Costa del Sol, there are volunteer English interpreters on hand.

Spain was recently documented as having the highest number of AIDS cases in Europe. Those applying for work permits will be asked for proof of HIV-negative status.

OVER-THE-COUNTER REMEDIES

Over-the-counter remedies are available at any *farmacia* (pharmacy). Some will look familiar, such as *aspirina* (aspirin), while other medications are sold under various brand names. If you regularly take a nonprescription medicine, take a sample box or bottle with you, and the Spanish pharmacist will provide you with its local equivalent.

HOLIDAYS

In 2001, Spain's national holidays include: January 1, January 6 (Epiphany), April 13 (Good Friday), May 1 (May Day), August 15 (Assumption), October 12 (National Day), November 1 (All Saints), December 6 (Constitution), December 8 (Immaculate Conception), and December 25.

In addition, each region, city, and town has its own holidays honoring political events and patron saints. Madrid holidays include May 2 (Madrid Day), May 15 (St. Isidro), and November 9 (Almudena). Barcelona celebrates April 23 (St. George), September 11 (Catalonia Day), and September 24 (Mercy).

If a public holiday falls on a Tuesday or Thursday, remember that **many businesses also close on the nearest Monday or Friday** for a long weekend called a *puente* (bridge). If a major holiday falls on a Sunday, businesses close on Monday.

INSURANCE

The most useful travel-insurance plan is a comprehensive policy that includes coverage for trip cancellation and interruption, default, trip delay, and medical expenses (with a waiver for preexisting conditions).

Without insurance you will lose all or most of your money if you cancel your trip, regardless of the reason. Default insurance covers you if your tour operator, airline, or cruise line goes out of business. Trip-delay covers expenses that arise because of bad weather or mechanical delays. Study the fine print when comparing policies.

On international trips, a key component of travel insurance is coverage for medical bills incurred if you get sick on the road. Such expenses are not generally covered by Medicare or private policies. U.K. residents can buy a travel-insurance policy valid for most vacations taken that year, but check the rules concerning preexisting conditions. British and Australian citizens need extra medical coverage when traveling overseas.

Always **buy a travel policy directly from the insurance company.** If you buy it from a cruiseline, airline, or tour operator that goes out of business, you will probably not be covered for the agency or operator's default, a major risk. Before making any purchase, **review your existing health and homeowner's policies** to find what they cover away from home.

➤ TRAVEL INSURERS: In the U.S.: **Access America** (✉ 6600 W. Broad St., Richmond, VA 23230, ☎ 804/285–3300 or 800/284–8300, FAX 804/673–1583, www.previewtravel.com), **Travel GuardInternational** (✉ 1145 Clark St., Stevens Point, WI 54481, ☎ 715/345–0505 or 800/826–1300, FAX 800/955–8785, www.noelgroup.com). In Canada: **Voyager Insurance** (✉ 44 Peel Center Dr., Brampton, Ontario L6T 4M8,☎ 905/791–8700; 800/668–4342 in Canada).

➤ INSURANCE INFORMATION: In the U.K.: **Association of British Insurers** (✉ 51–55 Gresham St., London EC2V 7HQ, ☎ 0207/600–3333, FAX 0207/696–8999, info@abi.org.uk, www.abi.org.uk). In Australia: **Insurance Council of Australia** (☎ 03/9614–1077, FAX 03/9614–7924).

LANGUAGE

Although Spaniards exported their language to all Central and South America, you may be surprised to find that Spanish is not the principal language in all of Spain. The Basques speak Euskera; in Catalonia, you'll hear Catalan; in Galicia, Gallego; and in Valencia, Valenciano. While almost everyone in these regions also speaks and understands Spanish, local radio and television stations may broadcast in these languages, and road signs may be printed (or spray-painted over) with the preferred regional language. Spanish is referred to as Castellano, or Castilian.

Fortunately, **Spanish is fairly easy to pick up, and your efforts to speak it will be graciously received.** Learn at least the following basic phrases: *buenos días* (hello—until 2 PM), *buenas tardes* (good afternoon—until 8 PM), *buenas noches* (hello—after dark), *por favor* (please), *gracias* (thank you), *adiós* (good-bye), *sí* (yes), *no* (no), *los servicios* (the toilets), *la cuenta* (bill/check), *habla inglés?* (do you speak English?), *no comprendo* (I don't understand). For more helpful expressions, *see* the Spanish Vocabulary following Smart Travel Tips, or, better yet, pick up a copy of *Fodor's Spanish for Travelers.*

If your Spanish breaks down, you should have no trouble finding people who speak English in major cities and coastal resorts, but you won't necessarily be able to count on the bus driver or the passerby on the street. Those who do speak English may speak the British variety, so don't be surprised if you're told to queue (line up) or take the lift (elevator) to the loo (toilet). Many guided tours offered at museums and historic sites are in Spanish; ask about the language that will be spoken before you sign up.

➤ PHRASE BOOK & LANGUAGE TAPES: ***Fodor's Spanish for Travelers*** (☎ 800/733–3000 in the U.S.; 800/668–4247 in Canada; $7 for phrasebook, $16.95 for audio set).

LANGUAGE PROGRAMS

A number of private schools in Spain offer Spanish-language courses of various durations for foreigners. **Don Quijote** is one network with schools in several locations around Spain. The international network **Inlingua** has 30 schools in Spain. Some Spanish universities, including Salamanca and Málaga, have longer-term Spanish programs, usually covering two months or more.

Back home, the state-run **Instituto Cervantes,** devoted to promoting Spanish language and culture, teaches both in their offices worldwide, and can advise you on other courses in Spain.

➤ LANGUAGE PROGRAMS: **Instituto Cervantes** (✉ 122 E. 42nd St., Suite 807, New York, NY 10168, ☎ 212/689–4232). **Don Quijote** (✉ C. Placentinos 2, Salamanca, 37998, ☎ 923/268860). **Inlingua International** (✉ Belpstrasse 11, Berne, CH-3007, Switzerland, ☎ 4131/388–7777).

LODGING

The Spanish government has spent decades buying up old castles and historic buildings and converting them into outstanding lodgings called **paradors.** In contrast, most of Spain's private hotels are modern high-rises, though more and more innkeepers are restoring historic properties. By law, hotel prices must be posted at the reception desk and should indicate whether or not the value-added tax (IVA; 7%) is included. Breakfast is normally *not* included. Note that high-season rates prevail not only in summer but also during Holy Week and local fiestas.

The lodgings we review are the cream of the crop in each price category. We always list the facilities available, but we don't specify whether they cost extra; so when pricing accommodations, always ask what's included and what's not.

APARTMENT & VILLA RENTALS

If you want a home base that's roomy enough for a family and comes with cooking facilities, **consider a furnished rental.** These can save you money, especially if you're traveling with a group. Home-exchange directories sometimes list rentals as well as exchanges.

➤ INTERNATIONAL AGENTS: **Europa-Let/Tropical Inn-Let** (✉ 92 N. Main St., Ashland, OR 97520, ☎ 541/482-5806 or 800/462-4486, FAX 541/482-0660). **Hideaways International** (✉ 767 Islington St., Portsmouth, NH 03801, ☎ 603/430-4433 or 800/843-4433, FAX 603/430-4444 info@hideaways.com, www.hideaways.com; membership $99). **Hometours International** (✉ Box 11503, Knoxville, TN 37939, ☎ 865/690-8484 or 800/367-4668, hometours@aol.com). **Interhome** (✉ 1990 N.E. 163rd St., Suite 110, N. Miami Beach, FL 33162, ☎ 305/940-2299 or 800/882-6864, FAX 305/940-2911, interhomeu@aol.com, www.interhome.com). **Vacation Home Rentals Worldwide** (✉ 235 Kensington Ave., Norwood, NJ 07648, ☎ 201/767-9393 or 800/633-3284, FAX 201/767-5510, vhrww@juno.com). **Villas and Apartments Abroad** (✉ 1270 Avenue of the Americas, 15th floor, New York, NY 10020, ☎ 212/897-5045 or 800/433-3020, FAX 212/897-5039, vaa@altour.com,www.vaanyc.com). **Villas International** (✉ 950 Northgate Dr., Suite 206, San Rafael, CA 94903, ☎ 415/499-9490 or 800/221-2260, FAX 415/499-9491, villas@best.com, www.villasintl.com).

CAMPING

Camping in Spain is not a wilderness experience. The country has more than 500 campgrounds, and many have excellent facilities, including hot showers, restaurants, swimming pools, tennis courts, and even nightclubs. But in summer, especially in August, be aware that **the best campgrounds fill with Spanish families, who move in with their entire households:** pets, grandparents, even the kitchen sink and stove. You can pick up an official list of all Spanish campgrounds at the tourist office.

It can be hard to find a site for independent camping outside established campgrounds. For safety reasons, you cannot camp next to roads, on riverbanks, or on the beach, nor can you set up house in urban areas, nature parks (outside designated camping areas), or within one kilometer of any established campsite. To camp on a private farm, seek the owner's permission.

HOME EXCHANGES

If you'd like to exchange your home for someone else's temporarily, **join a home-exchange organization,** which will send you its listings of available exchanges and include your own home in at least one of them. You make the arrangements yourself.

➤ EXCHANGE CLUBS: **HomeLinkInternational** (✉ Box 650, Key West, FL 33041, ☎ 305/294-7766 or 800/638-3841, FAX 305/294-1448, usa@homelink.org, www.homelink.org; $98 per year). **IntervacU.S.** (✉ Box 590504, San Francisco, CA 94159, ☎ 800/756-4663, FAX 415/435-7440, www.intervac.com; $89 per year includes two catalogs).

HOSTELS

No matter what your age, you can **cut lodging costs by staying in hostels.** In some 5,000 locations in more than 70 countries, Hostelling International (HI), the umbrella group for a number of national youth-hostel associations, offers single-sex, dorm-style beds and, in many hostels, rooms for couples and family accommodations.

Membership in any HI national hostel association, open to travelers of all ages, allows you to stay in HI-affiliated hostels at member rates; one-year membership is about U.S.$25 for adults (C$26.75 in Canada, £9.30 in the U.K., $30 in Australia, and $30 in New Zealand). Members have priority if the hostel is full; they're also eligible for discounts around the world, even on rail and bus travel in some countries.

➤ ORGANIZATIONS: **Hostelling International—American Youth Hostels** (✉ 733 15th St. NW, Suite 840, Washington, DC 20005, ☎ 202/783–6161, FAX 202/783–6171, www.hiayh.org). **HostellingInternational—Canada** (✉ 400–205 Catherine St., Ottawa, Ontario K2P1C3, ☎ 613/237–7884, FAX 613/237–7868, www.hostellingintl.ca). **Youth Hostel Association of England and Wales** (✉ Trevelyan House, 8 St. Stephen's Hill, St. Albans, Hertfordshire AL1 2DY, ☎ 01727/855215 or 01727/845047, FAX 01727/844126, www.yha.uk). **Australian Youth Hostel Association** (✉ 10 Mallett St., Camperdown, NSW 2050, ☎ 02/9565–1699, FAX 02/9565–1325, www.yha.com.au). **Youth Hostels Association of New Zealand** (✉ Box 436, Christchurch, New Zealand, ☎ 03/379–9970, FAX 03/365–4476, www.yha.org.nz).

HOTELS

The Spanish government classifies hotels with one to five stars. While quality is a factor, **the rating is technically only an indication of how many facilities the hotel offers.** For example, a three-star hotel may be just as comfortable as a four-star hotel but lack a swimming pool. Similarly, Fodor's price categories (**$–$$$$**) indicate room rates only, so you might find a well-kept **$$$** inn more charming than the famous **$$$$** property down the street.

All hotel entrances are marked with a blue plaque bearing the letter H and the number of stars. The letter R (standing for *residencia*) after the letter H indicates an establishment with no meal service. The designations *fonda* (F), *pensión* (P), *hostal* (Hs), and *casa de huéspedes* (CH) indicate budget accommodations. In most cases, especially in smaller villages, rooms in such buildings will be basic but clean; in large cities, they can be downright dreary.

Spain's major private hotel groups include the Sol Meliá, Tryp, and Hotusa. The NH chain, which is concentrated in major cities, appeals to business travelers. Dozens of reasonably priced beachside high-rises along the various coasts cater to package tours.

There is a growing trend in Spain toward small country hotels. Estancias de España is an association of more than 40 independently owned hotels in restored palaces, monasteries, mills, and post houses, generally in rural Spain; contact them for a free directory. Similar associations serve individual regions.

Although a single room (*habitación sencilla*) is usually available, singles are often on the small side. Solo travelers might prefer to pay a bit extra for single occupancy of a double room (*habitación doble uso individual*). All hotels we review have private bathrooms unless otherwise noted.

➤ MAJOR SPANISH HOTEL CHAINS: **Hotusa** (✉ ☎ 93/319–9062). **NH Hoteles**(✉ ☎ 902/115116, www.nh-hoteles.es). **Sol Meliá** (☎ 902/144444, www.solmelia.es). **Tryp** (✉ ☎ 901/116199).

➤ SMALL HOTELS: **AHRA**(Andalusian Association of Rural Hotels; ✉ C. Cristo Rey 2, 23400 Úbeda, Jaén, ☎ 953/755867, FAX 953/756099). **Estancias de España** (✉ Menéndez Pidal 31-bajo izq., 28036 Madrid, ☎ 91/345–4141, FAX 91/345–5174). **Hosterías y Hospederías Reales** (hotels in Castile–La Mancha; ✉ Frailes 1, 13320 Villanueva de los Infantes (Ciudad Real), ☎ 902/202010, FAX 926/361788).

PARADORS

Spain runs more than 80 paradors. Some are in castles on a hill with sweeping views; others are in historic monasteries or convents filled with artistic treasures; still others are in modern buildings on choice beachfront, alpine, or pastoral property. Rates are reasonable, considering that most paradors are four- and five-star hotels; and the premises are invariably immaculate and tastefully furnished, often with antiques or reproductions. All paradors have restaurants that serve regional specialties, and you can stop in for a meal or a drink without spending the night. Breakfast, however, is an expensive buffet; if you just want coffee and a roll, you'll do better to walk down the street to a local café.

Because paradors are extremely popular with foreigners and Spaniards alike, **make reservations well in advance.**

➤ INFORMATION: In Spain: **Paradores de España** (✉ Central de Reservas, Requena 3, 28013 Madrid, ☎ 91/516–6666, FAX 91/516–6657 www.parador.es). In the United States: **Marketing Ahead** (✉ 433 5th Ave., New York, NY 10016, ☎ 212/686–9213 or 800/223–1356). In the United Kingdom: **Keytel International** (✉ 402 Edgeware Rd., London W2 1ED, ☎ 0207/402–8182).

RURAL LODGINGS

A growing number of *casas rurales* (country houses similar toB&Bs) offer a pastoral lodging experience either in guest rooms or in self-catering cottages. Comfort and conveniences vary widely; it's best to book this type of accommodation through one of the appropriate regional associations. Ask the local tourist office about casas rurales in your chosen area.

MAIL & SHIPPING

Spain's postal system, the *correos,* does work, but delivery times can vary widely. An airmail letter to the United States may take anywhere from four days to two weeks; delivery to other destinations is equally unpredictable. Sending your letters by priority mail ("*urgente*") ensures speedier arrival.

OVERNIGHT SERVICES

When time is of the essence, or when you're sending valuable items or documents overseas, you can use a courier (*mensajero*). The major international agencies, such as Federal Express and UPS, have representatives in Spain; the biggest Spanish courier service is Seur.

➤ MAJOR SERVICES: **DHL**(☎ 902/122424). **Federal Express** (☎ 900/100871). **MRW** (☎ 900/300400). **Seur** (☎ 902/101010). **UPS** (☎ 900/102410).

POSTAL RATES

Airmail letters to the United States and Canada cost 115 ptas. up to 20 grams. Letters to the United Kingdom and other EU countries cost 70 ptas. up to 20 grams. Letters within Spain are 35 ptas. Postcards are charged the same rates as letters. You can buy stamps at post offices and at licensed tobacco shops.

RECEIVING MAIL

Because mail delivery in Spain can often be slow and unreliable, it's best to have your mail sent to American Express. Mail can also be held at a Spanish post office; have it addressed to **Lista de Correos** (the equivalent of Poste Restante) in a town you'll be visiting. Postal addresses should include the name of the province in parentheses, e.g., Marbella (Málaga).

➤ INFORMATION: In the U.S., call **American Express** (☎ 800/528–4800) for a list of offices overseas.

MONEY

Spain is no longer a budget destination, but prices still compare slightly favorably to those elsewhere in Europe. Coffee in a bar generally costs 125 ptas. (standing) or 150 ptas. (seated). Beer in a bar: 125 ptas. standing, 150 ptas. seated. Small glass of wine in a bar: 100 ptas. Soft drink: 150–200 ptas. a bottle. Ham-and-cheese sandwich: 300–450 ptas. Two-kilometer (1-mile) taxi ride: 400 ptas., but the meter keeps ticking in traffic jams. Local bus or subway ride: 135–150 ptas. Movie ticket: 500–800 ptas. Foreign newspaper: 300 ptas. In this book we quote prices for adults only, but note that **children, students, and senior citizens almost always pay reduced fees.** For information on taxes in Spain, *see* Taxes, *below.*

CREDIT CARDS

Throughout this book, the following abbreviations are used: **AE**, American Express; **DC**, Diner's Club; **MC**, MasterCard; and **V**, Visa.

➤ REPORTING LOST CARDS: **American Express** (☎ 900/941413). **Diners Club** (☎ 901/101011). **MasterCard** (☎ 900/974445). **Visa** (☎ 900/971231).

CURRENCY

As of January 1, 1999, Spain's official currency is the European monetary unit, the Euro. Prices in Spain are often quoted in both pesetas and Euros—convenient for Americans, as the Euro is close in value to the U.S. dollar—but until 2002 the Euro will be used only on the level of trade and banking, so **the peseta continues to be legal tender.** You can, however, purchase traveler's checks in Euros, which is convenient if you'll be traveling to more than one Euro-denominated country (Austria, Belgium, Finland, France, Germany, Ireland, Italy, Luxembourg, the Netherlands, Portugal, and Spain). Spanish bills are worth 10,000, 5,000, 2,000, and 1,000 ptas.; coins are 500, 200, 100, 50, 25, 10, 5, and 1 pta. Be careful not to confuse the 100- and 500-pta. coins—they're the same color and almost the same size. At press time **exchange rates** were extremely favorable for English-speaking travelers: 184 ptas. to the U.S. dollar, 124 ptas. to the Canadian dollar, 276 ptas. to the pound sterling, 160 ptas. to the Australian dollar, and 88 ptas. to the New Zealand dollar. One Euro was worth U.S. 90¢.

CURRENCY EXCHANGE

For the most favorable exchange rates, **change money in banks.** Although ATM transaction fees may be higher abroad than at home, ATM rates are excellent because they're based on wholesale rates offered only by major banks. You won't do as well at exchange booths in airports or train and bus stations, in hotels, in restaurants, or in stores. To avoid standing in line at an airport exchange booth, **get a bit of Spanish currency before you leave home.**

➤ EXCHANGE SERVICES: **International Currency Express** (☎ 888/278–6628 for orders, www.foreignmoney.com). **Thomas Cook Currency Services** (☎ 800/287–7362 for phone orders and retail locations, www.us.thomascook.com).

TRAVELER'S CHECKS

Traveler's checks are widely accepted in cities. If you'll be staying in small towns or rural areas, bring extra cash. Lost or stolen checks can usually be replaced within 24 hours. To ensure a speedy refund, buy your own traveler's checks—don't let someone else pay for them—and make the call yourself if you need to request a refund. Irregularities can cause delays.

OUTDOOR ACTIVITIES

Spain's fair weather is ideally suited to outdoor sports virtually year-round, though in summer you should restrict physical activity to early morning or late afternoon. Spain has more golf courses than any other country in Europe, and is also kind to hikers, water-sports enthusiasts, and, believe it or not, skiers. The country's sports federations have the best information; local tourist offices (☞ Visitor Information, *below*) can also be helpful.

GOLF

Spain's best golf courses are on the Mediterranean coast, especially the Costa del Sol. Greens fees can be on the high side (they're cheaper in summer), but many hotels linked to golf courses offer all-inclusive deals.

➤ INFORMATION: **Real Federación Española de Golf** (✉ Capitán Haya 9, 28020 Madrid, ☎ 91/555–2682).

HIKING

Spain's national parks and regional nature preserves are perfect for hiking and rock climbing. The parks' visitor centers and local outing clubs usually have plenty of information.

➤ INFORMATION: **Federación Española de Montañismo** (✉ Alberto Aguilera 3, 28015 Madrid, ☎ 91/445–1382).

SKIING

Not everyone thinks of sunny Spain as a skier's destination, but it's the second most mountainous country in Europe (after Switzerland) and has an impressive 28 ski centers. The best slopes are in the Pyrenees; there's also good skiing in the Sierra Nevada, near Granada.

➤ INFORMATION: **FederaciónEspañola de Deportes de Invierno** (Winter Sports Federation; ✉ Arroyo Fresno 3A, 28035 Madrid, ☎ 91/376–9930). **Recorded ski report** in Spanish (☎ 91/350–2020).

WATER SPORTS

With 1,200 miles of coastline, Spain has no shortage of water sports. Yacht harbors dot the Mediterranean coast. The coast near Tarifa, on Spain's southernmost tip, constitutes the windsurfing capital of mainland Europe, and surfing is good on the northern coast and, especially, the shores of the Canary Islands. Spain's best dive sites are Granada province and the Cabo de Gata (near Almería); regional tourist offices can direct you to the local diving clubs.

➤ INFORMATION: **Federación Española de Vela** (Spanish Sailing Federation; ✉ Luís de Salazar 12, 28002 Madrid, ☎ 91/519–5008). **Federación de Actividades Subacuáticas** (Underwater Activities Federation; ✉ Santaló 15, 08021 Barcelona, ☎ 93/200–6769).

PACKING

Pack light. Although baggage carts are free and plentiful in most Spanish airports, they're rare in train and bus stations.

On the whole, Spaniards dress up more than Americans or the British. Summer is hot nearly everywhere; visits in winter, fall, and spring call for warm clothing and, in winter, boots.

It makes sense to wear casual, comfortable clothing and shoes for sightseeing, but you'll want to **dress up a bit in large cities, especially for fine restaurants and nightclubs.** American tourists are easily spotted for their sneakers—if you want to blend in, wear leather shoes.

On the beach, anything goes; it's common to see females of all ages wearing only bikini bottoms, and many of the more remote beaches allow nude sunbathing. Regardless of your style, **bring a cover-up** to wear over your bathing suit when you leave the beach.

In your carry-on luggage, **pack an extra pair of eyeglasses or contact lenses** and **enough of any medication you take** to last the entire trip. You can also ask your doctor to write a spare prescription using the drug's generic name, since brand names may vary from country to country. **Never pack prescription drugs or valuables** in luggage to be checked. To avoid delays in customs, carry medications in their original packaging. Finally, don't forget to carry the addresses of offices that handle refunds of lost traveler's checks.

CHECKING LUGGAGE

Your airline decides how many bags (or how much weight) you can carry onto the plane. Most, but not all, allow two bags, so make sure that everything you carry aboard will fit under your seat or in the overhead bin, and line up for boarding early for the best dibs on bin space. Note that if you have a seat at the back of the plane, you'll probably board first, while the overhead bins are still empty.

Label each of your bags with your name, address, and phone number (if you use your home address, cover it so potential thieves can't see it readily). **Pack a copy of your itinerary** inside each piece of luggage. When you check in, **make sure that each bag is correctly tagged** with the destination airport's three-letter code. If your bags arrive damaged or fail to arrive at all, file a written report with the airline *before* leaving the airport.

PASSPORTS & VISAS

Make two photocopies of your passport's data page—one for someone at home and another for you, carried separately from your passport. If you lose your passport, promptly call the nearest embassy or consulate *and* the local police.

ENTERING SPAIN

Visitors from the U.S., Australia, Canada, New Zealand, and the U.K. need a valid passport to enter Spain. Australians who wish to stay longer than a month also need a visa, available from the Spanish Embassy in Canberra.

PASSPORT OFFICES

The best time to apply for a passport, or to renew your old one, is in fall or winter. Before any trip, check your passport's expiration date, and, if necessary, renew it as soon as possible.

➤ Australian Citizens: **Passport Office** (☏ 131–232, www.dfat.gov.au/passports).

➤ Canadian Citizens: **Passport Office Information Service** (☏ 819/994–3500 or 800/567–6868, www.dfait-maeci.gc.ca/passport).

➤ New Zealand Citizens: **Passport Office** (☏ 04/494–0700, www.passports.govt.nz).

➤ U.K. Citizens: **Passport Agency** (☏ 0990/210410, www.ukpa.gov.uk/ukpass.htm).

➤ U.S. Citizens: **National Passport Information Center** (☏ 900/225–5674; 35¢ per minute for automated service, $1.05 per minute for operator service; http://travel.state.gov/passport_services.html).

REST ROOMS

Spain has some public rest rooms, including, in larger cities, small coin-operated booths. Your best option, however, is to use the facilities in a bar or cafeteria, remembering that it's customary to order a drink in such cases. Gas stations have rest rooms, but you usually have to request the key to use them.

SAFETY

Petty crime is a huge problem in Spain's most popular tourist destinations. The most frequent offenses are pickpocketing (particularly in Madrid) and theft from cars (all over the country). We cannot overemphasize the fact that you should **never, ever leave anything valuable in a parked car,** no matter how friendly the area feels, how quickly you'll return, or how invisible the item seems once you lock it in the trunk. Thieves can spot rental cars a mile away, and they work very efficiently. In airports, laptop computers are choice prey.

WOMEN IN SPAIN

The traditional Spanish custom of the *piropo* (a shouted "compliment" to women walking down the street) is fast disappearing, though women traveling alone may still encounter it on occasion. The piropo is harmless, if annoying, and should simply be ignored.

SENIOR-CITIZEN TRAVEL

While there are few early-bird specials or movie discounts in Spain, senior citizens generally enjoy discounts at museums. Spanish social life encompasses all ages—it's very common to see seniors next to young couples or families in late-night cafés.

To qualify for age-related discounts, **mention your senior status up front** when making hotel reservations (not when checking out) and before you're seated in restaurants (not when paying the bill). Ask about discounts when renting a car as well.

➤ Educational Programs: **Elderhostel** (✉ 75 Federal St., 3rd floor, Boston, MA 02110, ☏ 877/426–8056, FAX 877/426–2166, www.elderhostel.org). **Interhostel** (✉ University of New Hampshire, 6 Garrison Ave., Durham, NH 03824, ☏ 603/862–1147 or 800/733–9753, FAX 603/862–1113, www.learn.unh.edu).

SHOPPING

Spain has plenty to tempt the shopper, from simple souvenirs to high-quality regional crafts. Clothing is highly fashionable, if expensive. Shoes and leather accessories are as chic as you'll find. Many of the best buys are food items; just check customs restrictions in your home country before purchasing edibles (☞ Customs & Duties, *above*). Spanish wines make lovely souvenirs.

Spain's major department store is **El Corte Inglés,**with branches in all major cities and towns.

STUDENTS IN SPAIN

Students can often get discounts on admission to museums and other sights.

➤ I.D.s & Services: In the U.S.: **Council Travel** (CIEE; ✉ 205 E. 42nd St., 14th floor, New York, NY 10017, ☏ 212/822–2700 or 888/268–6245, FAX 212/822–2699, info@councilexchanges.org, www.councilexchanges.org). In Canada: **Travel Cuts** (✉ 187 College St., Toronto, Ontario M5T 1P7, ☏ 416/979–2406 or 800/667–2887, www.travelcuts.com).

TAXES

VALUE-ADDED TAX

Value-added tax, similar to sales tax, is called IVA in Spain (pronounced "*ee*-vah"; for *impuesto sobre el valor añadido*). It is levied on both products and services such as hotel rooms and restaurant meals. When in doubt about whether tax is included, ask, "*Está incluido el IVA*"?

The IVA rate for hotels and restaurants is 7%, regardless of their number of stars or forks. A special tax law for the Canary Islands allows hotels and restaurants there to charge 4% IVA. Menus will generally say at the bottom whether tax is included (*IVA incluido*) or not (*más 7% IVA*).

While food, pharmaceuticals, and household items are taxed at the lowest rate, most consumer goods are taxed at 16%. A number of shops, particularly large stores and boutiques in holiday resorts, participate in Global Refund (formerly Europe Tax-Free Shopping), a V.A.T. refund service that makes getting your money back relatively hassle-free. On purchases of more than 15,000 ptas., you're entitled to a refund of the 16% tax. **Ask for the Global Refund form** (called a Shopping Cheque) in participating stores. You show your passport and fill out the form; the vendor then mails you the refund, or—often more convenient—you **present your original receipt to the VAT office at the airport** when you leave Spain. (In both Madrid and Barcelona, the office is near the duty-free shops. Save time for this process, as lines can be long.) Customs signs the original and refunds your money on the spot in cash (pesetas), or sends it to their central office to process a credit-card refund. Credit-card refunds take a few weeks.

TELEPHONES

Spain's phone system, Telefónica, is perfectly efficient. Direct dialing is the norm. Note that only cell phones conforming to the European GSM standard will work in Spain.

AREA & COUNTRY CODES

The country code for Spain is 34. Phoning home: country codes are 1 for the United States and Canada, 44 for the United Kingdom, 61 for Australia, and 64 for New Zealand.

DIRECTORY & OPERATOR ASSISTANCE

For general information in Spain, dial 1003. International operators, who generally speak English, are at 025.

INTERNATIONAL CALLS

International calls are awkward from coin-operated pay phones because of the enormous number of coins needed; and they can be expensive from hotels, as the hotel often adds a hefty surcharge. The best way to phone home is to use a public phone that accepts phone cards (☞ Phone Cards, *below*) or go to the local telephone office, the *locutorio:* every town has one, and major cities have several. You converse in a quiet, private booth, and you're charged according to the meter. If the call ends up costing 500 ptas. or more, you can pay with Visa or MasterCard.

To make an international call yourself, dial 00, then the country code, then the area code and number.

Madrid's main telephone office is at Gran Vía 28. There's another at the main post office, and a third at Paseo Recoletos 43, just off Plaza Colón. In Barcelona you can phone overseas from the office at Carrer de Fontanella 4, off Plaça de Catalunya.

Before you leave home, **find out your long-distance company's access code in Spain.**

LOCAL CALLS

All area codes begin with a 9. To call within Spain—even locally—dial the area code first. Numbers preceded by a 900 code are toll-free; those starting with a 6 are going to a cellular phone. Note that calls to cell phones are significantly more expensive than calls to regular phones.

LONG-DISTANCE SERVICES

AT&T, MCI, and Sprint access codes make calling long distance relatively convenient, but you may find the local access number blocked in many hotel rooms. First ask the hotel operator to connect you. If the hotel operator can't comply, ask for an international operator, or dial the international operator yourself. One way to improve your odds of getting connected to your long-distance carrier is to travel with more than one company's calling card (a hotel may block Sprint, for example, but not MCI). If all else fails, call from a pay phone.

➤ ACCESS CODES: **AT&T USADirect** (☎ 800/874–4000). **MCI WorldCom** (☎ 800/444–4444). **Sprint Express** (☎ 800/793–1153).

➤ ACCESS CODES IN SPAIN: **AT&T** (☎ 900/990011). **MCI** (☎ 900/990014). **Sprint** (☎ 900/990013).

PHONE CARDS

To use a newer pay phone you need a special phone card (*tarjeta telefónica*), which you can buy at any tobacco shop or newsstand, in denominations of 1,000 or 2,000 ptas. Some such phones also accept credit cards, but phone cards are more reliable.

PUBLIC PHONES

You'll find pay phones in individual booths, in special telephone offices (*locutorios*), and in many bars and restaurants. Most have a digital readout so you can see your money ticking away. If you're calling with coins, you need at least 25 ptas. to call locally, 75 ptas. to call another province. Simply insert the coins and wait for a dial tone. (With older models, you line coins up in a groove on top of the dial and they drop down as needed.)

TIME

Spain is on Central European Time, one hour ahead of Greenwich Mean Time, six hours ahead of Eastern Standard Time. Like the rest of the European Union, Spain switches to daylight saving time on the last weekend in March, and switches back on the last weekend in October.

TIPPING

Waiters and other service staff expect to be tipped, and you can be sure that your contribution will be appreciated. On the other hand, if you experience bad or surly service, don't feel obligated to leave a tip.

Restaurant checks almost always include service, which is not the same as a voluntary tip. **Do not tip more than 10% of the bill,** and leave less if you eat tapas or sandwiches at a bar—just enough to round out the bill to the nearest 100. Tip cocktail servers 50–75 ptas. a drink, depending on the bar.

Tip taxi drivers about 10% of the total fare; add more for long rides or extra help with luggage. Note that rides from airports carry an official surcharge plus a small handling fee for each piece of luggage.

Tip hotel porters 100 ptas. a bag, and the bearer of room service 100 ptas. A doorman who calls a taxi for you gets 100 ptas. If you stay in a hotel for more than two nights, tip the maid about 100 ptas. per night. The concierge should receive a tip for any additional help he or she provides.

Tour guides should be tipped about 300 ptas., ushers in theaters or at bullfights 25–50 ptas., barbers 100 ptas., and women's hairdressers at least 200 ptas. for a wash and style. Rest-room attendants are tipped 25 ptas.

TOURS

Because everything is prearranged on a guided tour, you'll spend less time planning—and often get it all for a reasonable price.

BOOKING WITH AN AGENT

Travel agents are excellent resources. Do collect brochures from several agencies, however, as some agents' suggestions may be influenced by relationships with tour and package firms that reward them for volume sales. If you have a special interest, **find an agent with expertise in that area**; ASTA (☞ Travel Agencies, *below*) has a database of specialists worldwide.

Make sure your travel agent is familiar with the rooms and other services in any hotel he or she recommends. Ask about the hotel's location, room size, beds, and whether the hotel has any specific amenities you need. Has your agent been there in person or sent others whom you can contact?

Do some homework on your own, too: local tourism boards can provide information about lesser-known and small-niche operators, some of which may sell only directly.

BUYER BEWARE

Every year consumers are stranded or lose their money when tour operators—even large ones with excellent reputations—go out of business. **Check out the operator.** Ask several travel agents about its reputation, and try to **go with a company that has a consumer-protection program.** (Look for information in the company's brochure.) In the United States, members of the National Tour Association and the United States Tour Operators Association are required to set aside funds to cover your payments and travel arrangements in the event that the company defaults. It's also a good idea to choose a company that participates in the American Society of Travel Agents' Tour Operator Program (TOP); ASTA will act as mediator in any disputes between you and your tour operator.

Remember that the more your package or tour includes, the better you can predict the ultimate cost of your vacation. Make sure you know exactly what is covered, and **beware of hidden costs.** Are taxes, tips, and transfers included? Entertainment and excursions? These can add up.

➤ TOUR-OPERATOR RECOMMENDATIONS: **American Society of Travel Agents** (☞ Travel Agencies, *below*). **National Tour Association** (NTA; ✉ 546 E. Main St., Lexington, KY 40508, ☎ 606/226–4444 or 800/682–8886, www.ntaonline.com). **United States Tour Operators Association** (USTOA; ✉ 342 Madison Ave., Suite 1522, New York, NY 10173, ☎ 212/599–6599 or 800/468–7862, FAX 212/599–6744, ustoa@aol.com, www.ustoa.com).

TRAIN TRAVEL

International overnight trains run from Madrid to Lisbon and from Barcelona to Paris (both 11½ hours). A daytime train runs from Barcelona to Grenoble and Geneva (10 hours).

If you purchase a same-day round-trip ticket while in Spain, you'll get a 20% discount; if you purchase a different-day round-trip ticket, a 10% discount applies.

Spain's wonderful high-speed train, the 180-mph AVE, travels between Madrid and Seville (with a stop in Córdoba) in less than three hours at prices starting around 10,000 ptas. each way. The fast Talgo service is also efficient. However, the rest of the state-run rail system—known as RENFE—remains below par by European standards. Local train travel can be tediously slow, and most long-distance trips run at night. While overnight trains have comfortable sleeper cars, first-class fares that include a sleeping compartment are comparable to airfares.

For routes with convenient schedules, trains are the most economical way to go. First- and second-class seats are reasonably priced, and you can get a bunk in a compartment with five other people for a supplement of about U.S.$25.

Most Spaniards buy train tickets in advance by standing in long lines at the station. The overworked clerks rarely speak English, however, so if you don't speak Spanish, you're better off going to a travel agency that displays the blue-and-yellow RENFE sign. The price is the same. Note that if your itinerary is set in stone and has little room for error, you can buy RENFE tickets through Rail Europe (☞ *below*) before you leave home.

Commuter trains and most long-distance trains forbid smoking, though some long-distance trains have smoking cars.

CUTTING COSTS

If you're coming from the United States or Canada and planning extensive train travel, **look into rail passes.** If Spain is your only destination, consider a **Spain Flexipass.** Prices begin at U.S.$150 for three days of second-class travel within a two-month period and $190 for first class. Other passes cover more days and longer periods.

Spain is one of 17 European countries in which you can use the **Eurailpass,** which buys you unlimited first-class rail travel in all participating countries for the duration of the pass. If you plan to rack up the miles, get a standard pass. These are available for 15 days ($544), 21 days ($718), one month ($890), two months ($1,260), and three months ($1,558). If your needs are more limited, look into a **Europass,** which costs less than a Eurailpass and buys you a limited number of travel days, in a limited number of countries (France, Germany, Italy, Spain, and Switzerland), during a specified time period.

In addition to the Eurailpass and Europass, Rail Europe sells the Eurail Youthpass (for those under age 26), the Eurail Saverpass (which gives a discount for two or more people traveling together), a Eurail Flexipass (which allows a certain number of travel days within a set period), the Euraildrive Pass, and the Europass Drive (which combines travel by train and rental car). Whichever you choose, remember that you must **buy your pass before you leave** for Europe.

Many travelers assume that rail passes guarantee them seats on the trains they wish to ride: not so. You need to **reserve seats in advance** even if you're using a rail pass. Seat reservations are required on some trains, particularly high-speed trains, and are wise on any train that might be crowded. You'll also need a reservation if you want a sleeping berth.

➤ General Information: **RENFE** (☎ 902/240202, www.renfe.es).

➤ Rail Passes: **Rail Europe** (✉ 226–230 Westchester Ave., White Plains, NY 10604, ☎ 914/682–5172 or 800/438–7245;✉ 2087 Dundas E, Suite 105, Mississauga, Ontario, Canada L4X1M2, ☎ 416/602–4195; www.raileurope.com). **DER Tours** (✉ Box 1606, Des Plaines, IL 60017, ☎ 800/782–2424, FAX 800/282–7474). **CIT Tours Corp.** (✉ 342 Madison Ave., Suite 207, New York, NY 10173, ☎ 212/697–2100; 800/248–8687; 800/248–7245 in western U.S.).

FROM THE U.K.

Train services to Spain from the United Kingdom are not as frequent, fast, or affordable as flights, and you have to change trains (and stations) in Paris. Allow two hours for the changing process, then 13 hours for the trip from Paris to Madrid. It's worth paying extra for a Talgo express or the Puerta del Sol express to avoid having to change trains again at the Spanish border. If you're under 26 years old, Eurotrain has excellent deals.

➤ Information: **British Rail Travel Centers** (☎ 0207/834–2345). **Eurotrain** (✉ 52 Grosvenor Gardens, London SW1W OAG, U.K., ☎ 0207/730–3402). **Transalpino** (✉ 71–75 Buckingham Palace Rd., London SW1W ORE, U.K., ☎ 0207/834–9656).

LUXURY TOURING TRAINS

The luxurious turn-of-the-20th-century *Al Andalus Express* makes five-day trips in Andalusia with sightseeing in Córdoba, Granada, and Seville. The cost is about U.S. $2,600 per person. A similar train, the *Transcantábrico,* travels on its own track along Spain's northern coast, from San Sebastián to Santiago de Compostela via the Basque Country, Cantabria, Asturias, and eastern Galicia. The cost is about U.S.$1,800 per person.

➤ Reservations: **Marketing Ahead** (✉ 433 5th Ave., New York, NY 10016, ☎ 212/686–9213 or 800/223–1356). **DER Tours** (✉ Box 1606, Des Plaines, IL 60017, ☎ 800/782–2424, FAX 800/282–7474).

➤ In Spain: **Iberrail** (✉ Capitán Haya 55, 28020 Madrid, ☎ 91/571–6692).

TRANSPORTATION WITHIN SPAIN

After France, Spain is the largest country in Western Europe, so seeing any more than a fraction of the country involves considerable domestic travel. If you want the freedom of straying from your fixed itinerary to follow whims as they come, driving is the best choice. The roads are generally fine, although traffic can be heavy on major routes, trucks can clog minor routes, and parking is a problem in cities (☞ Driving, *above*).

Spain is well served by domestic flights, though of course these cost more than ground options. Train service between the largest cities is fast, efficient, and punctual, but trains on secondary regional routes can be slow and involve frequent changes of train (☞ Train Travel, *above*). In such cases, buses are far more convenient (☞ Bus Travel, *above*).

TRAVEL AGENCIES

A good travel agent puts your needs first. Look for an agency that has been in business at least five years, emphasizes customer service, and has someone on staff who specializes in your destination. In addition, **make sure the agency belongs to a professional trade organization.** The American Society of Travel Agents (ASTA), with 27,000 agents in some 170 countries, is the largest and most influential in the field. Operating under the motto "Integrity in Travel," it maintains and enforces a strict code of ethics and will step in to help mediate any agent-client disputes if necessary. ASTA also maintains a Web site that includes a directory of member agents. (If a travel agency is also acting as your tour operator, *see* Buyer Beware *in* Tours & Packages, *above.*)

➤ LOCAL AGENT REFERRALS: **American Society of Travel Agents** (ASTA; ☎ 800/965–2782 24-hr hot line, FAX 703/684–8319, www.astanet.com). **Association of British Travel Agents** (✉ 68–71 Newman St., London W1P 4AH, ☎ 0207/637–2444, FAX 0207/637–0713, abta.co.uk, www.abtanet.com). **Association of Canadian Travel Agents** (✉ 1729 Bank St., Suite 201, Ottawa, Ontario K1V 7Z5, ☎ 613/521–0474, FAX 613/521–0805, acta.ntl@sympatico.ca). **Australian Federation of Travel Agents** (✉ Level 3, 309 Pitt St., Sydney 2000, ☎ 02/9264–3299, FAX 02/9264–1085, www.afta.com.au). **Travel Agents' Association of New Zealand** (✉ Box 1888, Wellington 10033, ☎ 04/499–0104, FAX 04/499–0827, taanz@tiasnet.co.nz).

VISITOR INFORMATION

➤ TOURIST OFFICE OF SPAIN: **Chicago** (✉ 845 N. Michigan Ave., Chicago, IL 60611, ☎ 312/642–1992, FAX 312/642–9817). **Los Angeles** (✉ 8383 Wilshire Blvd., Suite 960, Beverly Hills, CA 90211, ☎ 213/658–7188, FAX 213/658–1061). **Miami** (✉ 1221 Brickell Ave., Suite 1850, Miami, FL 33131, ☎ 305/358–1992, FAX 305/358–8223). **New York** (✉ 666 5th Ave., 35th floor, New York, NY 10103, ☎ 212/265–8822, FAX 212/265–8864). **Canada** (✉ 2 Bloor St. W, 34th floor, Toronto, Ontario M4W 3E2, Canada, ☎ 416/961–3131, FAX 416/961–1992). **United Kingdom** (✉ 22–23 Manchester Sq., London W1M 5AP, U.K., ☎ 0207/486–8977, FAX 0207/486–8034).

➤ U.S. TRAVEL ADVISORIES: **U.S. Department of State** (✉ Overseas Citizens Services Office, Room 4811 N.S., 2201 C St. NW, Washington, DC 20520, ☎ 202/647–5225 for interactive hotline, 301/946–4400 for computer bulletin board, FAX 202/647–3000 for interactive hotline). If you write, enclose a self-addressed, stamped, business-size envelope.

WEB SITES

Check out the World Wide Web when you're planning. You'll find everything from current weather forecasts to virtual tours of major cities. Fodor's Web site, www.fodors.com, is a great place to start your on-line travels. When you see a in this book, go to www.fodors.com/urls for an up-to-date link to that destination's site. For more information on Spain, visit www.okspain.org, www.tourspain.es, ww.cyberspain.com, and www.red2000.com/spain. For a virtual brochure on Spain's paradors, go to www.parador.es.

WHEN TO GO

May and October are the optimal times to come to Spain, as the weather is generally warm and dry. May gives you more hours of daylight, while October offers a chance to enjoy the harvest season, which is especially colorful in the wine regions.

In April you can see some of Spain's most spectacular fiestas, particularly Semana Santa (Holy Week); and by then the weather in southern Spain is warm enough to make sightseeing comfortable.

Spain is the number-one destination for European travelers, so **if you want to avoid crowds, come before June or after September.** Crowds and prices increase in the summer, especially along the coasts, as the Mediterranean is usually too cold for swimming the rest of the year, and beach season on the Atlantic coast is shorter still. Spaniards vacation in August, and their migration to the beach causes huge traffic jams on August 1 and 31. Major cities are relaxed and empty for the duration; small shops and some restaurants shut down for the entire month, but museums remain open.

CLIMATE

Summers in Spain are hot: temperatures frequently hit 100°F(38°C), and air-conditioning is not widespread. Try to **limit summer sightseeing to the morning hours.** That said, warm summer nights are among Spain's quiet pleasures.

Winters in Spain are mild and rainy along the coasts, especially in Galicia. Elsewhere, winter blows bitterly cold. Snow is infrequent except in the mountains, where you can ski from December to March in the Pyrenees and other resorts near Granada, Madrid, and Burgos.

➤ FORECASTS: **Weather Channel Connection** (☎ 900/932–8437 in the U.S.), 95¢ per minute.

The following are average daily maximum and minimum temperatures for some major Spanish cities.

MADRID

Jan.	48F	9C	May	70F	21C	Sept.	77F	25C
	36	2		50	10		57	14
Feb.	52F	11C	June	81F	27C	Oct.	66F	19C
	36	2		59	15		50	10
Mar.	59F	15C	July	88F	31C	Nov.	55F	13C
	41	5		63	17		41	5
Apr.	64F	18C	Aug.	86F	30C	Dec.	48F	9C
	45	7		63	17		36	2

BARCELONA

Jan.	55F	13C	May	70F	21C	Sept.	77F	25C
	43	6		57	14		66	19
Feb.	57F	14C	June	77F	25C	Oct.	70F	21C
	45	7		64	18		59	15
Mar.	61F	16C	July	82F	28C	Nov.	61F	16C
	48	9		70	21		52	11
Apr.	64F	18C	Aug.	82F	28C	Dec.	55F	13C
	52	11		70	21		46	8

SEVILLE

Jan.	59F	15C	May	81F	27C	Sept.	90F	32C
	43	6		55	13		64	18
Feb.	63F	17C	June	90F	32C	Oct.	79F	26C
	45	7		63	17		57	14
Mar.	68F	20C	July	97F	36C	Nov.	68F	20C
	48	9		68	20		50	10
Apr.	75F	24C	Aug.	97F	36C	Dec.	61F	16C
	52	11		68	20		45	7

GRANADA

Jan.	54F	12C	May	73F	23C	Sept.	84F	29C
	36	2		50	10		59	15
Feb.	57F	14C	June	86F	30C	Oct.	73F	23C
	37	3		59	15		50	10
Mar.	63F	17C	July	93F	34C	Nov.	63F	17C
	41	5		63	17		43	6
Apr.	68F	20C	Aug.	91F	33C	Dec.	54F	12C
	45	7		63	17		37	3

FESTIVALS AND SEASONAL EVENTS

Reserve rooms far in advance for Spain's biggest fiestas—Pamplona's San Fermín, Seville's Holy Week, Valencia's Las Fallas, and Carnival.

➤ DECEMBER: **New Year's Eve** ticks away at Madrid's Puerta del Sol, where crowds gather to eat one grape on each stroke of midnight.

➤ JANUARY: **Ephiphany** (Jan. 6) is a Spanish child's Christmas: youngsters leave their shoes on the doorstep to be filled with gifts from the Three Kings. In many towns the Wise Men arrive the night of January 5 by boat, camel, or car and are featured in parades.

➤ FEBRUARY: **Carnival** dances through Spain just before Lent, most flamboyantly in Cádiz, Sitges, and Santa Cruz de Tenerife.

➤ MARCH: In Valencia, giant papier-mâché figures are torched for **Las Fallas.**

➤ APRIL: Horseback parades and traditional dress make Seville's **Feria de Abril** photogenic. **Semana Santa** (Holy Week) is the most spectacular feast of all, with Seville staging the most elaborate processions.

➤ MAY: The **Jerez Horse Fair** is a pageant of equestrian events. Barcelona is fragrant on **Sant Ponç** (May 11), when farmers come into the city to sell their products. In Madrid, **San Isídro** (May 15) kicks off two weeks of the best bullfighting in Spain.

➤ JUNE: From mid-June to mid-July, Granada's **International Festival of Music and Dance** brings orchestras, opera companies, and ballet corps from around the world to the grounds of the Alhambra. **Corpus Christi** (June 14) is celebrated with processions, most famously in Toledo. The **Wine War** in Haro (La Rioja, June 29) wastes thousands of gallons of Rioja wine.

➤ JULY: The **Fiesta de San Fermín** and the accompanying **running of the bulls** (July 6–13) through the streets of Pamplona unleash wine, bravado, and merriment. Late in the month, Valencia's **Moros y Cristianos** finds locals reenacting ancient feuds in medieval Moorish and Christian costume. The summer-long **Classical Theater Festival** presents Greek and Roman dramas in Mérida's 2,000-year-old Roman theater.

➤ AUGUST: The **International Music and Ballet Festival** enlivens the resort town of Santander. **El Místeri** (Aug. 11–15), in Elche, near Alicante, is Europe's oldest Christian mystery play. A **Tomato Battle** reddens the town of Buñol, near Valencia, on the last Wednesday of the month. Consuegra, near Toledo, turns another color for the **Saffron Rose Festival.**

➤ SEPTEMBER: Jerez celebrates harvest time with **Fiestas de Otoño** (Autumn Festivals). On September 24, Barcelona celebrates **La Mercè** with concerts, fireworks, and parades in which people wear giant papier-mâché heads.

➤ OCTOBER: **El Pilar** (Oct. 12) gives the children of Zaragoza a chance to dress up in regional costume and cut loose in *jota*-dancing contests.

Spain

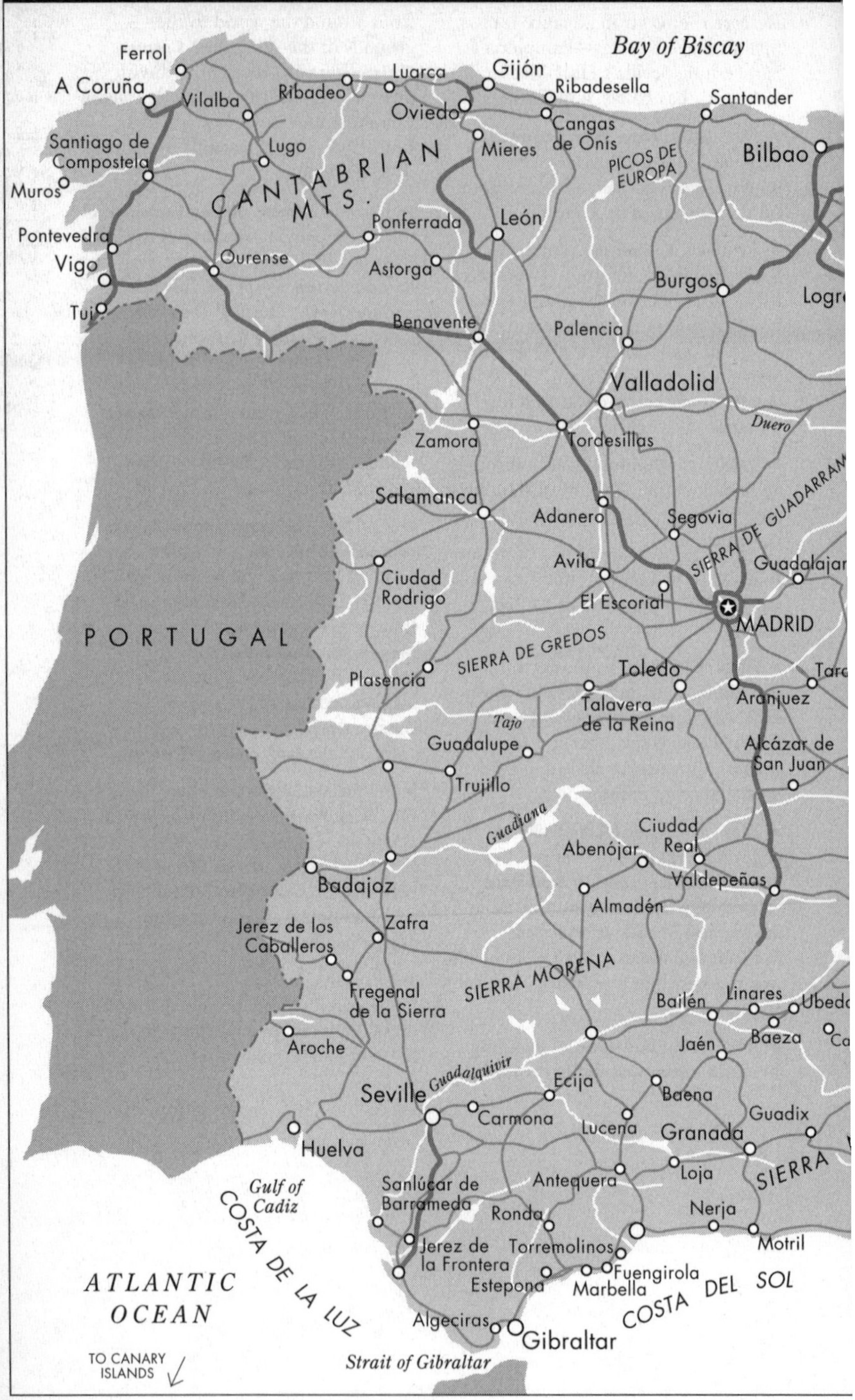
Bay of Biscay
Ferrol
A Coruña
Vilalba
Ribadeo
Luarca
Gijón
Ribadesella
Santander
Oviedo
Cangas de Onís
Santiago de Compostela
Lugo
Mieres
PICOS DE EUROPA
Bilbao
Muros
CANTABRIAN MTS.
Pontevedra
Ponferrada
León
Vigo
Ourense
Astorga
Burgos
Tui
Benavente
Palencia
Valladolid
Duero
Zamora
Tordesillas
Salamanca
Adanero
Segovia
SIERRA DE
Ávila
Ciudad Rodrigo
El Escorial
MADRID
PORTUGAL
SIERRA DE GREDOS
Plasencia
Toledo
Aranjuez
Talavera de la Reina
Tajo
Guadalupe
Alcázar de San Juan
Trujillo
Guadiana
Ciudad Real
Abenójar
Badajoz
Valdepeñas
Almadén
Jerez de los Caballeros
Zafra
Fregenal de la Sierra
SIERRA MORENA
Bailén
Linares
Baeza
Jaén
Aroche
Guadalquivir
Seville
Écija
Baena
Carmona
Lucena
Granada
Guadix
Huelva
Gulf of Cadiz
Sanlúcar de Barrameda
Antequera
Loja
SIERRA
COSTA DE LA LUZ
Ronda
Nerja
Jerez de la Frontera
Torremolinos
Motril
Estepona
Marbella
Fuengirola
ATLANTIC OCEAN
Algeciras
Gibraltar
COSTA DEL SOL
TO CANARY ISLANDS
Strait of Gibraltar

FRANCE
San Sebastián
Hondarribia
Roncesvalles
Vitoria
Pamplona
ANDORRA
Jaca
PYRENEES
La Seu d´Urgell
Figueres
Huesca
Gerona
Tudela
Barbastro
Vic
Ebro
Soria
Manresa
Zaragoza
Lleida
Montserrat
COSTA BRAVA
Barcelona
Calatayud
Medinaceli
Daroca
Alcañiz
Tarragona
Caminreal
COSTA DORADA
Tortosa
Monreal del Campo
Tajo
La Jana
Vinaròs
Teruel
TO MINORCA
Balearic Sea
Cuenca
Castellón de la Plana
COSTA DEL AZAHAR
Palma
Sagunto
Majorca
Requena
Valencia
Ibiza
Jucar
BALEARIC ISLANDS
Albacete
Eivissa
Formentera
Alcaraz
Hellín
Alicante
Minorca
Ciutadella
Mahón
Segura
Elche
COSTA BLANCA
Orihuela
Cazorla
Murcia
Lorca
Manga del Mar Menor
Cartagena
Mediterranean Sea
NEVADA
Almería
COSTA DE ALMERIA
ALGERIA
N
0
100 miles
0
150 km

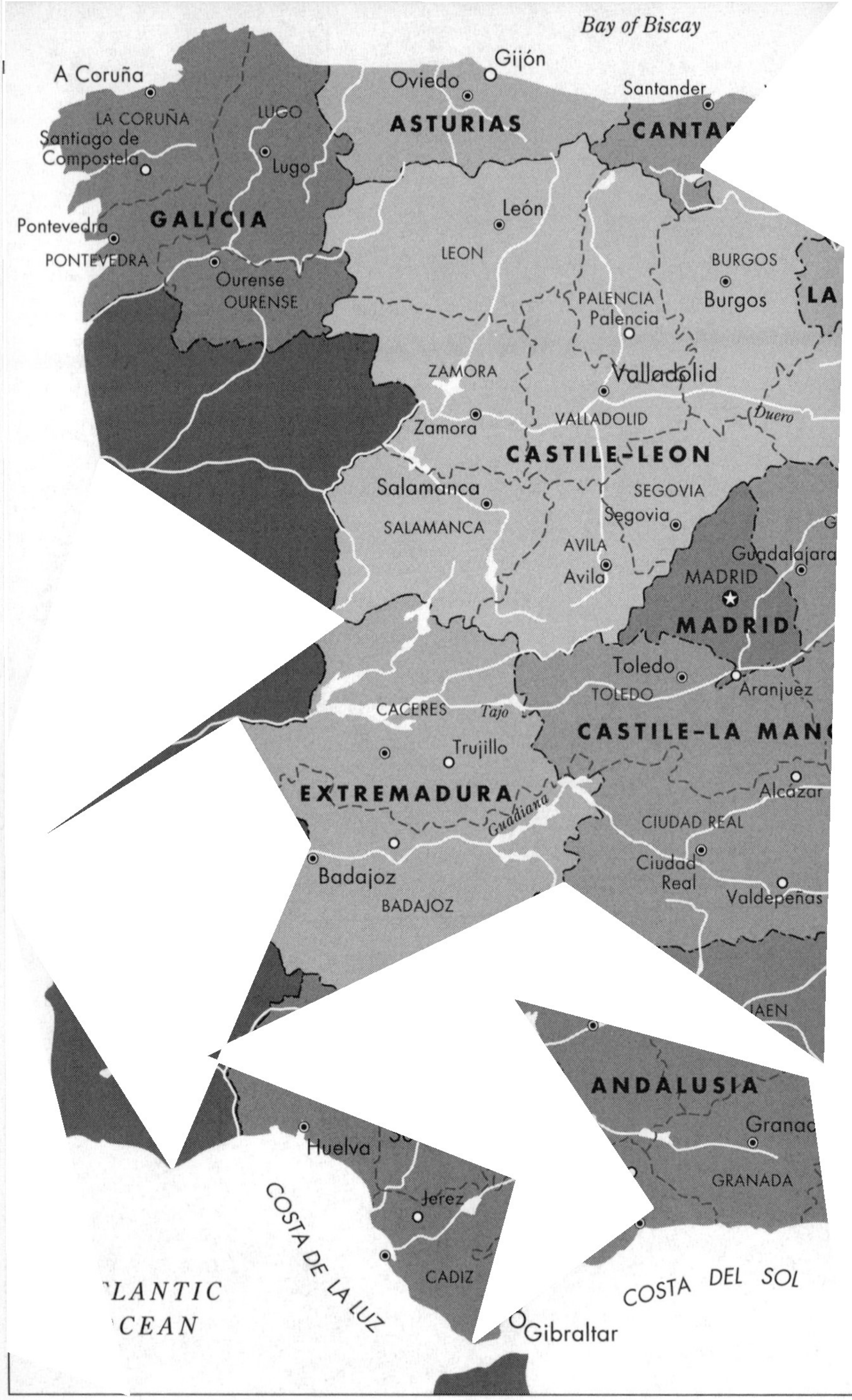
Bay of Biscay
A Coruña
Gijón
Oviedo
Santander
LA CORUÑA
LUGO
ASTURIAS
Santiago de Compostela
Lugo
León
GALICIA
Pontevedra
PONTEVEDRA
LEON
BURGOS
Ourense
OURENSE
PALENCIA
Palencia
Burgos
ZAMORA
Valladolid
Zamora
VALLADOLID
Duero
CASTILE-LEON
Salamanca
SEGOVIA
SALAMANCA
Segovia
AVILA
Guadalajara
Avila
MADRID
MADRID
Toledo
TOLEDO
Aranjuez
CACERES
Tajo
Trujillo
EXTREMADURA
Guadiana
Alcázar
CIUDAD REAL
Badajoz
Ciudad Real
BADAJOZ
Valdepeñas
ANDALUSIA
Huelva
Jerez
GRANADA
CADIZ
COSTA DE LA LUZ
COSTA DEL SOL
Gibraltar

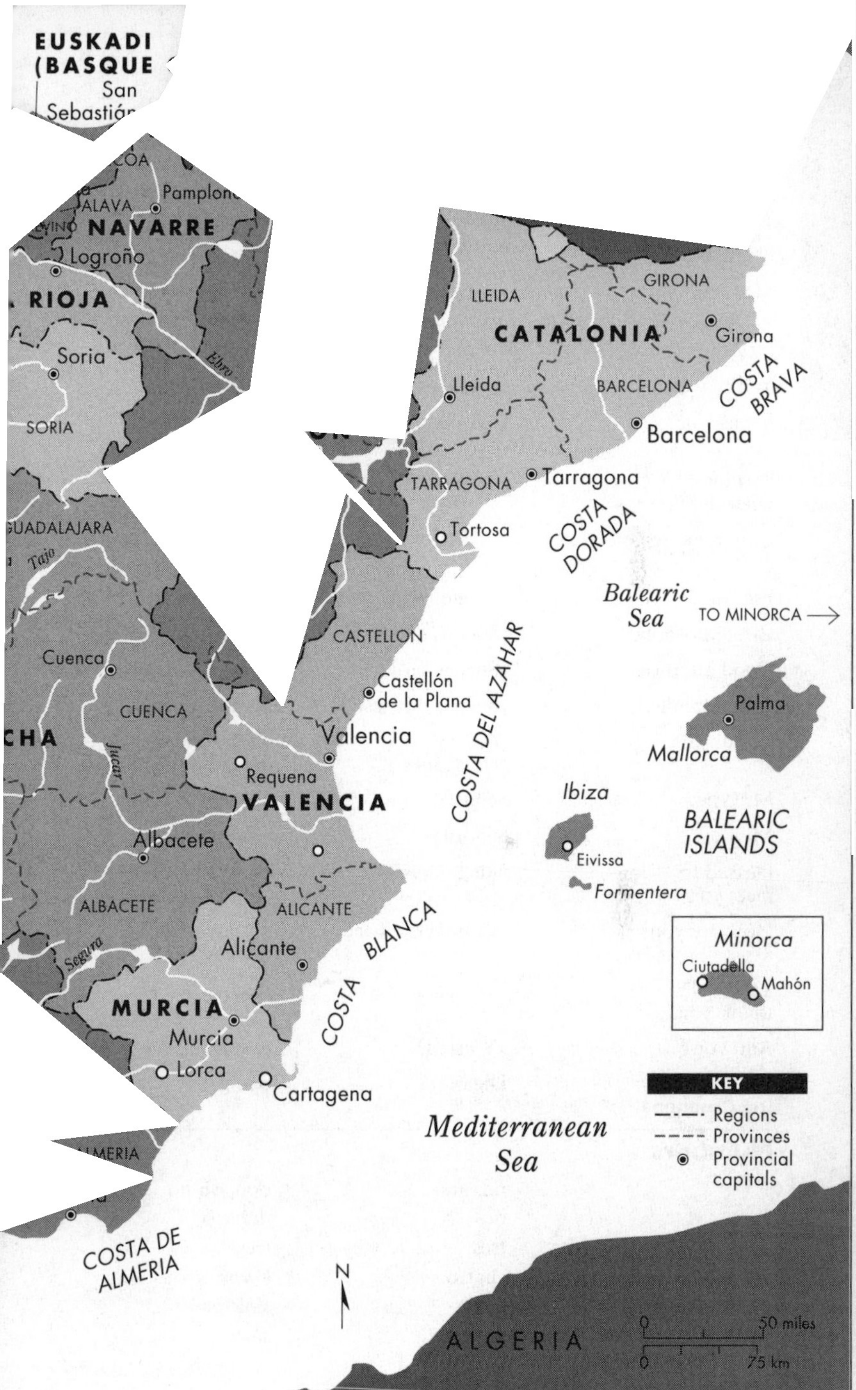
EUSKADI
(BASQUE
San
Sebastián
Pamplona
ALAVA
NAVARRE
Logroño
RIOJA
Soria
SORIA
Ebro
GUADALAJARA
Tajo
Cuenca
CUENCA
Júcar
LLEIDA
CATALONIA
GIRONA
Girona
Lleida
BARCELONA
Barcelona
COSTA BRAVA
TARRAGONA
Tarragona
Tortosa
COSTA DORADA
Balearic Sea
TO MINORCA
CASTELLON
Castellón de la Plana
COSTA DEL AZAHAR
Valencia
Requena
VALENCIA
Palma
Mallorca
Ibiza
Eivissa
Formentera
BALEARIC ISLANDS
Albacete
ALBACETE
ALICANTE
Alicante
COSTA BLANCA
Segura
MURCIA
Murcia
Lorca
Cartagena
Minorca
Ciutadella
Mahón
KEY
Regions
Provinces
Provincial capitals
Mediterranean Sea
COSTA DE ALMERIA
N
ALGERIA
0
50 miles
0
75 km

WORDS AND PHRASES

English	Spanish	Pronunciation
Basics		
Yes/no	Sí/no	see/no
Please	Por favor	pohr fah-**vohr**
May I?	¿Me permite?	meh pehr-**mee**-teh
Thank you (very much)	(Muchas) gracias	(**moo**-chas) **grah**-see-as
You're welcome	De nada	deh **nah**-dah
Excuse me	Con permiso/perdón	con pehr-**mee**-so/ pehr-**dohn**
Pardon me/ what did you say?	¿Perdón?/Mande?	pehr-**dohn/mahn**-deh
Could you tell me . . . ?	¿Podría decirme . . . ?	po-**dree**-ah deh-**seer**-meh
I'm sorry	Lo siento	lo see-**en**-to
Good morning!	¡Buenos días!	**bway**-nohs **dee**-ahs
Good afternoon!	¡Buenas tardes!	**bway**-nahs **tar**-dess
Good evening!	¡Buenas noches!	**bway**-nahs **no**-chess
Goodbye!	¡Adiós!/ ¡Hasta luego!	ah-dee-**ohss/ ah**-stah-**lwe**-go
Mr./Mrs.	Señor/Señora	sen-**yor**/sen-**yohr**-ah
Miss	Señorita	sen-yo-**ree**-tah
Pleased to meet you	Mucho gusto	**moo**-cho **goose**-to
How are you?	¿Cómo está usted?	**ko**-mo es-**tah** oo-**sted**
Very well, thank you.	Muy bien, gracias.	**moo**-ee bee-**en, grah**-see-as
And you?	¿Y usted?	ee oos-**ted**
Hello (on the phone)	Diga	**dee**-gah
Numbers		
1	un, uno	oon, **oo**-no
2	dos	dohs
3	tres	tress
4	cuatro	**kwah**-tro
5	cinco	**sink**-oh
6	seis	saice
7	siete	see-**et**-eh
8	ocho	**o**-cho
9	nueve	new-**eh**-veh
10	diez	dee-**es**
11	once	**ohn**-seh
12	doce	**doh**-seh

13	trece	**treh**-seh
14	catorce	ka-**tohr**-seh
15	quince	**keen**-seh
16	dieciséis	dee-**es**-ee-**saice**
17	diecisiete	dee-**es**-ee-see-**et**-eh
18	dieciocho	dee-**es**-ee-**o**-cho
19	diecinueve	dee-**es**-ee-new-**ev**-eh
20	veinte	**vain**-teh
21	veinte y uno/ veintiuno	**vain**-te-oo-noh
30	treinta	**train**-tah
32	treinta y dos	train-tay-**dohs**
40	cuarenta	kwah-**ren**-tah
50	cincuenta	seen-**kwen**-tah
60	sesenta	sess-**en**-tah
70	setenta	set-**en**-tah
80	ochenta	oh-**chen**-tah
90	noventa	no-**ven**-tah
100	cien	see-**en**
200	doscientos	doh-see-**en**-tohss
500	quinientos	keen-**yen**-tohss
1,000	mil	meel
2,000	dos mil	dohs meel

Days of the Week

Sunday	domingo	doh-**meen**-goh
Monday	lunes	**loo**-ness
Tuesday	martes	**mahr**-tess
Wednesday	miércoles	me-**air**-koh-less
Thursday	jueves	hoo-**ev**-ess
Friday	viernes	vee-**air**-ness
Saturday	sábado	**sah**-bah-doh

Useful Phrases

Do you speak English?	¿Habla usted inglés?	**ah**-blah oos-**ted** in-**glehs**
I don't speak Spanish	No hablo español	no **ah**-bloh es-pahn-**yol**
I don't understand (you)	No entiendo	no en-tee-**en**-doh
I understand (you)	Entiendo	en-tee-**en**-doh
I don't know	No sé	no seh
I am American/ British	Soy americano (americana)/ inglés(a)	soy ah-meh-ree-**kah**-no (ah-meh-ree-**kah**-nah)/in-**glehs**(ah)
My name is . . .	Me llamo . . .	meh **yah**-moh
Yes, please/ No, thank you	Sí, por favor/ No, gracias	**see** pohr fah-**vor**/ no **grah**-see-ahs
Yesterday/today/ tomorrow	Ayer/hoy/mañana	ah-**yehr**/oy/mahn-**yah**-nah
This morning/ afternoon	Esta mañana/tarde	**es**-tah mahn-**yah**-nah/**tar**-deh
Tonight	Esta noche	**es**-tah **no**-cheh

This/Next week	Esta semana/ la semana que entra	**es**-tah seh-**mah**-nah/lah seh-**mah**-nah keh **en**-trah
This/Next month	Este mes/el próximo mes	**es**-teh mehs/el **prok**-see-moh mehs
How?	¿Cómo?	**koh**-mo
When?	¿Cuándo?	**kwahn**-doh
What?	¿Qué?	keh
What is this?	¿Qué es esto?	keh es **es**-toh
Why?	¿Por qué?	por **keh**
Who?	¿Quién?	kee-**yen**
Where is . . . ?	¿Dónde está . . . ?	**dohn**-deh es-**tah**
the train station?	la estación del tren?	la es-tah-see-**on** del **train**
the subway station?	la estación del metro?	la es-ta-see-**on** del **meh**-tro
the bus stop?	la parada del autobus?	la pah-**rah**-dah del oh-toh-**boos**
the bank?	el banco?	el **bahn**-koh
the hotel?	el hotel?	el oh-**tel**
the post office?	la oficina de correos?	la oh-fee-**see**-nah deh-koh-**reh**-os
the museum?	el museo?	el moo-**seh**-oh
the hospital?	el hospital?	el ohss-pee-**tal**
the bathroom?	el baño?	el **bahn**-yoh
Here/there	Aquí/allá	ah-**key**/ah-**yah**
Open/closed	Abierto/cerrado	ah-bee-**er**-toh/ ser-**ah**-doh
Left/right	Izquierda/derecha	iss-key-**er**-dah/ dare-**eh**-chah
Straight ahead	Todo recto	**toh**-doh-**rec**-toh
Is it near/far?	¿Está cerca/lejos?	es-**tah sehr**-kah/ **leh**-hoss
I'd like . . .	Quisiera . . .	kee-see-**ehr**-ah
a room	una habitación	**oo**-nah ah-bee-tah-see-**on**
the key	la llave	lah **yah**-veh
a newspaper	un periódico	oon pehr-ee-**oh**-dee-koh
a stamp	un sello	**say**-oh
How much is this?	¿Cuánto cuesta?	**kwahn**-toh **kwes**-tah
A little/a lot	Un poquito/ mucho	oon poh-**kee**-toh/ **moo**-choh
More/less	Más/menos	mahss/**men**-ohss
I am ill	Estoy enfermo(a)	es-**toy** en-**fehr**-moh(mah)
Please call a doctor	Por favor llame un medico	pohr fah-**vor ya**-meh oon **med**-ee-koh
Help!	¡Ayuda!	ah-**yoo**-dah

On the Road

Avenue	Avenida	ah-ven-**ee**-dah
Broad, tree-lined boulevard	Paseo	pah-**seh**-oh
Highway	Carretera	car-reh-**ter**-ah
Port; mountain pass	Puerto	poo-**ehr**-toh
Street	Calle	**cah**-yeh
Waterfront promenade	Paseo marítimo	pah-**seh**-oh mahr-**ee**-tee-moh

In Town

Cathedral	Catedral	cah-teh-**dral**
Church	Iglesia	**tem**-plo/ee-**glehs**-see-ah
City hall, town hall	Ayuntamiento	ah-yoon-tah-me-**yen**-toh
Door, gate	Puerta	poo-**ehr**-tah
Main square	Plaza Mayor	plah-thah mah-**yohr**
Market	Mercado	mer-**kah**-doh
Neighborhood	Barrio	**bahr**-ree-o
Tavern, rustic restaurant	Mesón	meh-**sohn**
Traffic circle, roundabout	Glorieta	glor-ee-**eh**-tah
Wine cellar, wine bar, wine shop	Bodega	boh-**deh**-gah

Dining Out

A bottle of . . .	Una bottella de . . .	**oo**-nah bo-**teh**-yah deh
A glass of . . .	Un vaso de . . .	oon **vah**-so deh
Bill/check	La cuenta	lah **kwen**-tah
Breakfast	El desayuno	el deh-sah-**yoon**-oh
Dinner	La cena	lah **seh**-nah
Menu of the day	Menú del día	meh-**noo** del **dee**-ah
Fork	El tenedor	ehl ten-eh-**dor**
Is the tip included?	¿Está incluida la propina?	es-**tah** in-cloo-**ee**-dah lah pro-**pee**-nah
Knife	El cuchillo	el koo-**chee**-yo
Large portion of tapas	Ración	rah-see-**ohn**
Lunch	La comida	lah koh-**mee**-dah
Menu	La carta, el menú	lah **cart**-ah, el meh-**noo**
Napkin	La servilleta	lah sehr-vee-**yet**-ah
Please give me . . .	Por favor déme . . .	pohr fah-**vor** **deh**-meh
Spoon	Una cuchara	**oo**-nah koo-**chah**-rah

INDEX

Icons and Symbols

★ Our special recommendations
✕ Restaurant
▦ Lodging establishment
✕▦ Lodging establishment whose restaurant warrants a special trip
Good for kids (rubber duck)
☞ Sends you to another section of the guide for more information
✉ Address
☎ Telephone number
Opening and closing times
Admission prices
Sends you to www.fodors.com/urls for up-to-date links to the property's Web site

Numbers in white and black circles ③ ❸ that appear on the maps, in the margins, and within the tours correspond to one another.

A

B

C

M

R

S

T

NOTES

FODOR'S SPAIN 2001

EDITOR: Christine Cipriani

Editorial Contributors: Michael de Zayas, Mark Little, Edward Owen, George Semler, Katherine Semler

Editorial Production: Rebecca Zeiler Wintle

Maps: David Lindroth, *cartographer*; Rebecca Baer and Bob Blake, *map editors*

Design: Fabrizio La Rocca, *creative director*; Guido Caroti, *art director*; Jolie Novak, *photo editor*; Melanie Marin, *photo researcher*

Cover Design: Pentagram

Production/Manufacturing: Robert B. Shields

COPYRIGHT

ISBN 0–679–00569–2

ISSN 0071–6545

SPECIAL SALES

Fodor's Travel Publications are available at special discounts for bulk purchases for sales promotions or premiums. Special editions, including personalized covers, excerpts of existing guides, and corporate imprints, can be created in large quantities for special needs. For more information contact your local bookseller or write to Special Markets, Fodor's Travel Publications, 280 Park Avenue, New York, NY 10017. Inquiries from Canada should be directed to your local Canadian bookseller or sent to Random House of Canada, Ltd., Marketing Department, 2775 Matheson Boulevard East, Mississauga, Ontario L4W 4P7. Inquiries from the United Kingdom should be sent to Fodor's Travel Publications, 20 Vauxhall Bridge Road, London, England SW1V 2SA.

PRINTED IN THE UNITED STATES OF AMERICA

10 9 8 7 6 5 4 3 2 1

IMPORTANT TIP

Although all prices, opening times, and other details in this book are based on information supplied to us at press time, changes occur all the time in the travel world, and Fodors cannot accept responsibility for facts that become outdated or for inadvertent errors or omissions. So always confirm information when it matters, especially if you're making a detour to visit a specific place.

PHOTOGRAPHY

Magnum Photos: Harry Gruyaert, *cover (statue of Pizzaro, Trujillo).*

CalTour: *Robert Holmes, 29D.*

Capilla Real de Granada: *Martinez Cardeña, 2 (top left). Morales Henares, 2 (bottom right). Valdivieso, 3 (top left).*

Christine Cipriani, *13B*

Corbis, *2 (top right and bottom center), 3 (bottom left and bottom right), 27B, 28C.*

Owen Franken, *1, 12C, 14A, 17B, 23B.*

Gala-Salvador Dali Foundation: *Torner, 2 (bottom left).*

The Image Bank: *Lucas Abreu, 30J. Steve Allen, 24A. P. & G. Bowater, 8B. Luis Castañeda, 6B. Andy Caulfield, 14B. Flip Chalfant, 6A. Kay Chernush, 8 bottom. T. Chinami, 22A Gary Cralle, 30G. Vergani Egidio, 18A. Larry Dale Gordon, 18D. David W. Hamilton, 7F. Don Klumpp, 6C. Romilly Lockyer, 7D, 19A, 22 (center left). Mahaux Photography, 26A. Francisco Ontañon, 4-5, 8A, 9C, 9D, 10A, 11B, 12A, 13A, 15C, 15D, 16A, 16B, 16 bottom left, 17A, 17C, 20B, 21F, 22C, 23A, 24B, 24C, 30A, 30B, 30E, 30F, 30I, 32. Andrea Pistolesi, 9E, 19B, 20C. John R. Ramey, 21D, 30C. Anne Rippy, 11D, 15E. Marc Romanelli, 21E. Guido Alberto Rossi, 7E, 11C, 25B, 25C, 30H. Stefano Scatà, 18C. Terry Williams, 22B. Hans Wolf, 19C, 30D.*

Real Academia de Bellas Artes de San Fernando, *3 (top right).*

Nik Wheeler, *12B, 18B, 20A, 25A.*

ABOUT OUR WRITERS

To direct you to the places that are truly worth your time and money, we've rallied the team of endearingly picky know-it-alls we're pleased to call our writers. Having seen all corners of the regions they cover for us, they're real experts. If you knew them, you'd poll them for tips yourself.

Born in Miami, **Michael de Zayas** can trace his roots via Cuba to the island of Gran Canaria. After attending graduate school in New York, Michael lived in Barcelona and Madrid before journeying around Spain in search of the mythical perfect party for a book on Spanish fiestas. In addition to *Fodor's Spain 2001,* Michael has contributed to the *New York Post* and the *Miami Herald,* and most recently wrote a whopping four chapters of Fodor's forthcoming *upCLOSE Spain.*

Mark Little was born in New York but has lived in southern Spain since age 10. For 15 years he was the editor of *Lookout* magazine, an English-language glossy aimed at Spain's large expatriate community. He is now a freelance writer specializing in Spanish travel, food, and wine. Mark lives in Mijas (near Málaga) with his Spanish wife and their three children.

Raised in Cornwall, England, journalist **Edward Owen** has worked in London, Toronto, and Sydney, and, since 1980, Madrid. Long a foreign correspondent for London's *Times, Sunday Times,* and *Daily Express,* he now specializes in travel, wine, and gastronomy. Ed extols the Spanish climate and the Spaniards' vim and vigor, and makes the most of the country's tremendous variety.

Born and educated in Connecticut, writer and journalist **George Semler** has lived in Spain for the last 30 years. During that time he has written on Spain, France, Morocco, and the Mediterranean region for *Forbes, Saveur,* the *International Herald Tribune,* and the *Los Angeles Times,* and published walking guides to Madrid and Barcelona. When not hiking, fly-fishing, or sampling Catalonia's hottest new restaurants, he finds time to work on a magnum opus about the Pyrenees.

Raised in Madrid, San Sebastián, and Barcelona, **Katherine Semler** attended preschool in Euskera (the Basque language), kindergarten in Spanish, elementary school in French, and secondary school in the United States in English. She went on to earn a B.A. in French and Russian literature at Vassar and an M.A. in French and Catalan literature at Dartmouth. (We are not making this up.) Married to singer-songwriter Sam Lardner, she now lives in Barcelona.

Immersed in *Fodor's Spain* for three years now, New York–based editor **Christine Cipriani** has traveled to Spain four times, written a chapter on Galicia for Fodor's forthcoming *upCLOSE Spain,* hosted two travelers' forums on fodors.com, and successfully roused herself from many a workday meditation on the precise color of Spanish winter sunshine.

For their kind assistance with travel arrangements, we'd also like to thank Pilar Vico of the Tourist Office of Spain, New York, and Antonio Alonso of Marketing Ahead (a quick human link to Spain's paradors and finer hotels).

Don't Forget to Write

Keeping a travel guide fresh and up-to-date is a big job. So we love your feedback—positive and negative—and follow up on all suggestions. Contact the Spain editor at editors@fodors.com or c/o Fodor's, 280 Park Avenue, New York, New York 10017. And have a wonderful trip!

Karen Cure
Editorial Director